PLAY DIAGNOSIS AND ASSESSMENT

SECOND EDITION

PLAY DIAGNOSIS AND ASSESSMENT

SECOND EDITION

Edited by

Karen Gitlin-Weiner
Alice Sandgrund
Charles Schaefer

John Wiley & Sons, Inc.

New York • Chichester • Weinheim • Brisbane • Singapore • Toronto

ISBN 0-471-25457-6

Printed in the United States of America.

10 9 8 7 6 5 4 3 2 1

Karen Gitlin-Weiner, Psy.D.

To Joseph and Henrietta—my inspirational wellspring of playful wisdom.

To Richard—whose perpetual love has sustained me through endless hours of work and play.

To Ronna, Dana, Debbie, Vivian, Nathan, Esther, and Mac—ever supportive of my professional pursuits and playful adventures.

In loving memory of Gertie and Mary

Alice Sandgrund, Ph.D.

To David, Amy, and Jeffrey whose playful spirits have enriched and inspired me.

Charles E. Schaefer, Ph.D.

To Anne, Karine, and Eric—my partners in play.

Contents

Contributors

Anat Barlev
Doctoral Student
Department of Psychology
Michigan State University
East Lansing, Michigan

Kelly W. Beck, Ph.D.
Private Practice
Nashville, Tennessee

Karen L. Bierman, Ph.D.
Psychology Department
The Pennsylvania State University
University Park, Pennsylvania

Phyllis B. Booth, M.A.
The Therapy Institute
Wilmette, Illinois

Lisa Boyce, Ph.D.
Department of Family and Human
  Development
Utah State University
Logan, Utah

Rochelle Caplan, M.D.
Division of Child and Adolescent
  Psychiatry
Neuropsychiatric Institute and Hospital
University of California, Los Angeles
Los Angeles, California

Candace L. Chambers, Psy.D.
Private Practice
Chicago, Illinois

Robert J. Coplan, Ph.D.
Department of Psychology
Carleton University
Ottawa, Ontario, Canada

Cindy Day, MS, OTR
Cerebral Palsy Center of Bergen County
Fair Lawn, New Jersey

Jean E. Dumas, Ph.D.
Department of Psychological Sciences
Purdue University
West Lafayette, Indiana

John W. Fantuzzo, Ph.D.
Graduate School of Education
Psychology in Education Division
University of Pennsylvania
Philadelphia, Pennsylvania

Thomas M. Gehring, Ph.D., Psy.D.
Department of Social and Preventative
Medicine
University of Zurich
Zurich, Switzerland

Karen Gitlin-Weiner, Psy.D.
Private Practice
Hicksville, New York

Virginia R. Hampton, M.A.
Graduate School of Education
Psychology in Education Division
University of Pennsylvania
Philadelphia, Pennsylvania

Steve Harvey, Ph.D.
U.S. Army Health Clinic
Vicenza, Italy

Eleanor C. Irwin, Ph.D.
Department of Psychiatry
School of Medicine
University of Pittsburgh
Pittsburgh, Pennsylvania

Timothy J. Iverson, Ph.D.
Private Practice
Coconut Creek, Florida

Ioanna D. Kalogiros
Doctoral Student
Department of Psychology
Michigan State University
East Lansing, Michigan

Astrida S. Kaugars, M.A.
Psychology Department
Case Western Reserve University
Cleveland, Ohio

Susan M. Knell, Ph.D.
Hillcrest Behavioral Medicine
Cleveland Clinic Health System
Cleveland, Ohio

Peter J. LaFreniere, Ph.D.
Department of Psychology
University of Maine
Orono, Maine

Karin Lifter, Ph.D.
Department of Counseling Psychology,
    Rehabilitation, and Special Education
Northeastern University
Boston, Massachusetts

Sandra L. Lindaman, M.A., M.S.W.
The Therapy Institute
Wilmette, Illinois

Toni Linder, Ed.D.
College of Education
University of Denver
Denver, Colorado

Adam P. Matheny, Jr., Ph.D.
Department of Pediatrics
School of Medicine
University of Louisville
Louisville, Kentucky

Marilee Menarchek-Fetkovich, MS,
    OTR/L
West Moreland County Immediate
    Unite #7
Greenburg, Pennsylvania

Kay Mogford-Bevan, Ph.D.
Department of Speech
University of Newcastle upon Tyne
Newcastle upon Tyne, United Kingdom

Jeanne Montie, Ph.D.
Nova University
Fort Lauderdale, Florida

Kristin Moore Taylor, Ph.D.
Lakeside Family and Children's Services
Brooklyn Heights, New York

Ned Mueller, Ph.D.
Clinical Psychology Service
Beaumont House
Herne Bay, Kent, United Kingdom

Lisa Newland, M.S.
Department of Family and Human
    Development
Utah State University
Logan, Utah

Larissa N. Niec, Ph.D.
Department of Psychology
Central Michigan University
Mount Pleasant, Michigan

Julie Page, M.A.
Department of Social and Preventative
  Medicine
University of Zurich
Zurich, Switzerland

Alice W. Pope, Ph.D.
Department of Psychiatry
New York University Medical Center
New York, New York

Thomas J. Power, Ph.D.
Department of Pediatric Psychology
University of Pennsylvania School of
  Medicine
Philadelphia, Pennsylvania

Jerilynn Radcliffe, Ph.D.
Department of Pediatric Psychology
University of Pennsylvania School of
  Medicine
Philadelphia, Pennsylvania

Lori A. Roggman, Ph.D.
Department of Family and Human
  Development
Utah State University
Logan, Utah

Patricia Ross, Ph.D.
Ross Psychological Services
Cincinnatic, Ohio

Sandra W. Russ, Ph.D.
Psychology Department
Case Western University
Cleveland, Ohio

Alice Sandgrund, Ph.D.
Department of Child and Adolescent
  Psychiatry
Kings County Hospital
Brooklyn, New York

Charles E. Schaefer, Ph.D.
Department of Psychology
Farleigh Dickinson University
Hackensack, New Jersey

Marilyn Segal, Ph.D.
Nova University
Fort Lauderdale, Florida

Tracy Sherman, Ph.D.
Research Consultant
Bethesda, Maryland

David T. Smith, Ph.D.
Department of Psychology
Children's Hospital Medical Center
University of Cincinnati
Cincinnati, Ohio

Gavin Smith, Ph.D.
Sanctuary Psychological Services
Abington, Pennsylvania

Gary E. Stollak, Ph.D.
Department of Psychology
Michigan State University
East Lansing, Michigan

Janet A. Welsh, Ph.D.
Psychology Department
Pennsylvania State University
University Park, Pennsylvania

Carol Westby, Ph.D.
Department of Communicative Disorders
  and Sciences
Wichita State University
Witchita, Kansas

Sue White, Ph.D.
Child Psychiatry
MetroHealth Medical Center
Cleveland, Ohio

Preface —————————————————————————————————————

In 1991, the first edition of *Play Diagnosis and Assessment* was published. Drawing from clinical as well as research literature, it presented a large assortment of scales and practical procedures for the assessment and diagnosis of children through play. At the time, this was a fairly new and budding area that was being explored and developed in a variety of settings as well as professional fields that addressed children's developmental as well as therapeutic needs. Many of the techniques were in the initial stages of creation and were found in a scattering of journal articles. This was the first volume of its kind to provide a comprehensive overview of play assessment and diagnosis. It was hoped that the information presented would not only be useful in broadening traditional assessment protocols but would also stimulate professional interest in expanding and enhancing the available methods.

This, in fact, has occurred during the past several years. Numerous changes within the field of play diagnosis and assessment have recently been documented in journal articles and book chapters as well as addressed at professional conferences. Increasing access to and use of the Internet as a means of communication has geometrically expanded the opportunities for obtaining and sharing information within the field at a moments notice. This ready source of information has hastened the development of techniques and research in ways that were previously impossible. Utilizing many of these technological advances, several of the authors contributing to this volume have established web sites for the purpose of disseminating updated information about their specific instruments.

In addition to increased information availability, changes in the delivery of health care services have encouraged the development of improved techniques. An even greater demand for short but reliable and valid assessment procedures has been propelled by the managed care mandates for time-limited treatment. Furthermore, increasing economic constraints have necessitated the use of inexpensive instruments that require only limited training or are self-explanatory. Finally, the recent emphasis on the assessment of younger and younger children through the expansion of the early intervention movement has resulted in the establishment of procedures that are better able to address the unique needs of this population. Consequent to these influences, many new scales and instruments have recently been developed within the context of the many different ways of thinking about and measuring children's functioning which are based in a variety of theoretical orientations.

The revised edition of *Play Diagnosis and Assessment* has attempted to address and reflect these on-going changes within the field. Primary attention has been focused on the needs of the clinician since it has been this group of professionals who most welcomed the first edition. However, the importance of integrating formal research with clinical methods in support of their value and accuracy has been maintained. Some of the chapters that have been retained from the first edition have been revised and updated with regard to their clinical use as well as their psychometric properties. A few chapters have been reprinted in their original form because of their continuing clinical relevance. New contributions have been selected on the basis of their ability to demonstrate an improvement in the field, either by addressing a new area, by introducing a more focused procedure or by presenting an instrument with a higher level of reliability and validity than has previously been established. With these changes, it is hoped that the revised edition will be a welcomed and useful contribution that will further promote the assessment and diagnosis of children through play techniques.

The book is divided into six sections: "Developmental Play Assessments," "Diagnostic Play Assessments," "Parent-Child Interaction Play Assessments", "Family Play Assessments", "Peer Interaction Play Assessments," and "Projective Play Assessments". These categories are not intended to be mutually exclusive. A chapter's inclusion in a specific section is based on the primary area of emphasis for the assessment instrument being described. Because overlap between developmental issues, diagnostic impressions, interrelational behaviors, and intrapsychic functioning is inevitable, readers who are interested in a specific type of evaluation are encouraged to peruse the entire book for related applicable procedures.

The procedures described in each part of the book target a variety of ages and populations, some being more specific than others. Certainly, many of the techniques may prove to be amenable to a greater number of applications than those specified in this book. This broad ranging selection is not intended to be an all-inclusive collection of methods currently in use. However, they represent some of the most valuable, informative, and sensitive contributions to the field. Additionally, it is hoped that they will bring a sense of enjoyment to the evaluator and the client during what, otherwise, can become a cumbersome and overwhelming process of finding out what the problems are and how best to intervene. Certainly, it is hoped that these techniques will spark as much fascination and interest in the reader as they have for the editors.

It is with great pleasure that the editors of this book acknowledge the diligent efforts of all contributors in their pursuit of advancing this field. It is hoped that their enthusiasm will be contagious to the reader. New discoveries as well as modifications of already established techniques are looked forward to with great anticipation.

In preparing the first volume as well as the revised edition, the editors were often reminded of Plato's observation, "You can learn more about a person in an hour of play than in a year of conversation." It is with these words that the readers are wished many productive hours of play in their efforts to help children and families understand and overcome the difficulties facing them.

Karen Gitlin-Weiner, Psy.D.
Hicksville, New York

Alice Sandgrund, Ph.D.
Brooklyn, New York

Charles E. Schaefer, Ph.D.
Hackensack, New Jersey

INTRODUCTION

EMERGENCE AND EVOLUTION OF
CHILDREN'S PLAY AS A FOCUS OF STUDY

"Now, it is perfectly clear that children have played since the beginning of time and archaeological diggings show us that every civilization has provided toys for their use.... The loving care expended upon these toys in all human groups shows that grown-up human beings since the beginning of historical times have understood that the way to make contact with a child and to understand his way of thought is to play with him" (Lowenfeld, 1939, p. 66).

Without a doubt, children have played through the ages. Museums attest to the presence of miniature doll-like figures given to children from earlier cultures on. However, from a psychological perspective, it was not until the late 1800s that play was seen as an important and relevant activity for children. Prior to this, play had only been perceived as an expression of surplus energy (Spencer, as cited in Garvey, 1977) or as a way of passing on religious and cultural rituals (Reilly, 1974).

At the turn of the century, views toward play started to change, and it came to be considered a meaningful activity. For some (Groos, 1899), play was seen as the expression of an instinct to train for future roles that were required for survival. Others (Hall, 1896) viewed play as a recapitulation of the progress of the race as well as an important medium for revealing the inner life of the child. Hall (1896) stated, "Perhaps nothing so fully opens up the juvenile soul to the student of childhood as well-developed doll play" (p. 192).

Certainly, Freud's writings on psychosexual development caused the scientific community to focus on early childhood development and child behavior as a way of understanding the development of the adult personality. Through his analysis of his early cases, such as Little Hans (originally reported in 1909), Freud (1950) broadened the understanding of children's overt behaviors as reflecting unconscious concerns and conflicts. Later, he (Freud, 1961) was able to expand upon these ideas by describing play as a specific means of mastery and abreaction. He stated, "We see that children repeat in their play everything that has made a great impression on them in actual life" (p. 147).

In this way, Freud recognized the importance of children's play, even though his own therapeutic efforts were geared solely toward an adult population. For instance, in his analysis of Little Hans, Freud did not consider using play as a direct treatment modality. Instead, the parent was employed to implement an intervention and communicate about the progress of the identified patient (i.e., Little Hans).

It was not until the work of Melanie Klein (1955, 1960) and Anna Freud (1946, 1966) that play was actually incorporated into the therapeutic process. Using the theoretical background of psychoanalytic concepts, they legitimized and popularized the use of play materials in effective treatment with children.

In an attempt to formalize a structure for play therapy, Margaret Lowenfeld (1939, 1969) devised what she called the "Miniature World Technique." This was one of the first organized systems that incorporated a formal presentation of toys and miniature objects for use in play therapy. She defined the concept of play even more broadly than did previous analytic therapists: "Play in childhood is a function of childhood.... Toys to children are like culinary implements to the kitchen, every kitchen has them and has also the elements of food. It is what the cook does with these implements and elements that determines the dish" (1939, p. 66). Her technique expanded the focus of the therapist from interpretation to more structured and methodical observation of children's use of toys in the therapeutic process. Lowenfeld did not, however, advocate for this technique to be used as a diagnostic tool. This did not occur until several years later when her ideas were incorporated into standardized assessment tools and procedures.

Following in the tradition of these play therapists, Erikson (1950, 1951, 1958, 1968) began to formulate and publish his work on youth and child analysis. Using his theory of psychosocial development as a foundation, he explained play as an expression of a combination of forces, including individual development, family dynamics, and cultural expectations. "To evaluate play, the observer must, of course, have an idea of what all the children of a given age in a given community are apt to play. Only thus can he decide whether or not the unique meaning transcends the common meaning. To understand the unique meaning itself requires careful observation not only of the play's content and form, but also of accompanying words and visible affects" (Erikson, 1950, p. 219). Indeed, Erikson likened play to Freud's notion of dreams. For him, play became the royal road to the unconscious in children. It was believed that only during play were children's censors relaxed, allowing free-flowing fantasy to blossom in a manner similar to that attributed by Freud to the concept of dreams.

Erikson was also one of the first to highlight the concept of play disruption. He noted that in play, children so closely approached the feelings experienced during anxiety-laden events in their lives that the resulting discomfort often led to a need to cease playing. It was noted that, at the time of the disruption, there was a disintegration of effective defenses, as well as a breaking down of the ability to organize and express the aroused feelings or ideas. Thus, play disruption became a diagnostic marker of those issues central to children's emotional needs and level of functioning.

By this time (1940s to 1950s), the play therapy movement was in full swing. It was enriched by contributions from individuals representing diverse aspects of psychology. Most notable was the work of Piaget (1952), whose theory of cognitive development detailed, among other things, the impact of symbolic thinking on fantasy and make-believe play. Using extensive observations of his own children as a basis, Piaget (1952) formulated a complex system of classifying play and games along developmental lines. He suggested that changes in play reflected intellectual development, as well as increased competence in general. Play also provided the opportunity for children to practice what they had already learned. Modified versions of Piaget's writings have continued to be used today as a theoretical foundation for research and testing of children. In supporting the use of play as an important way in which professionals can get to know children intimately, Piaget (1952) indicated that conversations with children were much more fruitful (a) when they were related to activities involving concrete materials and (b) when children, instead of trying to communicate abstractly, were talking about play actions just performed.

With the publishing of *Dibs: In Search of Self,* Virginia Axline's (1964) highly accessible case study of play therapy, there resulted a greater public awareness of the potential and the importance of play in the treatment of children. Axline (1969) incorporated the nondirective client-centered approach of Carl Rogers, previously applied only to adult therapy. In advocating play as an important medium in the therapeutic process, Axline stated, "There is a frankness, and honesty, and a vividness in the way children state themselves in a play situation. Their feelings, attitudes, and thoughts emerge, unfold themselves, twist and turn and lose their sharp edges. The child learns to understand himself and others a little better. … He learns that in this playroom with this unusual adult he can let in and out the tide of his feelings and impulses. He can create his own world with these simple toys that lend themselves so well to projected identities…. He can select and discard. He can create and destroy" (preface of *Play Therapy,* 1969).

The works of these psychologists and many others gave impetus to a period of rich interest in play, particularly with regard to child treatment and intervention. Among those contributing to the diverse literature of the time were such well-known professionals as Despert (1976), Ginott (1964), Moustakas (1973), and Peller (1964). Children's play was scrutinized with growing attention as psychologists and psychiatrists became increasingly sophisticated in their application of play and in their understanding of its role in children's development.

While play therapy and its analytic underpinnings continued to be popular among a segment of the professional world, this approach was soon rivaled by a growing interest in methods of treatment that challenged the analytic movement. The medical model of treatment prevailed. By the 1960s, for many, the observation and use of children's play faded into the background as professionals moved toward forms of treatment that were behavioral, time-limited, cognitive, and family oriented. Analytic play therapy became only one of a variety of ways of viewing and treating children who were emotionally troubled.

Throughout the years, from the 1930s until well into the 1960s, play was primarily viewed by clinicians as a treatment rather than as an assessment technique. Meanwhile, a body of literature was being amassed by developmentalists who attempted to describe and classify children's play within a normative framework. Their work eventually became the precursor to the idea of using play within a diagnostic format. Most of this material, however, did not become fully integrated into the clinical literature until much later.

One of the few notable exceptions of the time was the work of Parton (1932), who attempted to devise a structured assessment strategy for studying normal social development in play. The resulting scale was divided into six categories: (1) unoccupied behavior, (2) solitary independent play, (3) onlooker behavior, (4) parallel activity, (5) associative play, and (6) cooperative play. Currently, the Parton scale, after undergoing a few revisions with regard to the definition of terms as well as the names of categories, continues to be used in many research projects. As a clinical instrument, its use remains limited.

While many others in the field also attempted to utilize observations of play in arriving at diagnostic statements and treatment plans, their approaches tended to be highly subjective and unsystematic. However, as was previously mentioned, in London, Lowenfeld

(1939, 1969) originated one of the more structured and focused psychodynamic approaches to play therapy, which was later modified for use in the assessment process. Using the "Miniature World Technique," Lowenfeld instructed children to build a series of worlds with a sand tray and a large assortment of small objects representing all aspects of past and present environments. Created over several sessions, the miniature world productions were analyzed in terms of a variety of characteristics, such as content, form, themes, sequential changes, process of completion, space used, number of categories, and types of categories. The resulting information was systematically interpreted to determine functioning levels in a variety of areas such as speech, motor, intellectual, social, intrapsychic, and affective development (Kamp & Kessler, 1970; Lowenfeld, 1939). Lowenfeld believed this to be an "objective, recordable and interpretable" technique. She said, "(It is) an apparatus ... which will give a child power to express his ideas and feelings, (it is) independent of knowledge or skill, (it is) capable of the representation of thought simultaneously in several planes at once, (it) allows representation of movement and yet (is) sufficiently circumscribed to make a complete, whole, ... (it) combines elements of touch and sensation, as well as of sight, and (it is) entirely free from a necessary relation to reality" (1939, p. 67).

Lowenfeld's (1939) world technique led to the development of two other diagnostic tools that were notable exceptions to the earlier tendency toward subjective observations. In Germany, Buhler (1951a, b) and her colleagues devised the "World Test." At approximately the same time, in Sweden, during the 1930s and 1940s, Hanna Bratt and Gosta Harding developed the "Erica Method," a three-dimensional, comprehensive projective technique (cited in Sjolund, 1982) that can be likened to the Thematic Apperception Test (TAT). Both the World Test and the Erica Method have standardized procedures and equipment, as well as a systematic process for diagnostic interpretation. Based on work with so-called normal and handicapped populations of various ages, Buhler (1951a, b), along with other British and American therapists (Buhler & Carrol, 1951; Lumbry, 1951), developed norms and described specific signs indicative of emotional difficulties for the World Test. Over the years, the Erica Method (Sjolund, 1993) was modified to include refined administrative, recording, and scoring processes. Continuous research with this method in the Scandinavian countries has yielded much information regarding clinical interpretation, as well as performance norms for different age groups. Unfortunately, although these approaches gained great popularity in Europe, they have been greatly overlooked in the United States.

In the 1970s and 1980s, play reemerged as central to the understanding and treatment of children. Many of the aforementioned diverse therapeutic approaches began to include a focus on play as an integral as well as adjunctive approach to the therapeutic process. Clinicians became more familiar with the growing body of developmental literature on normal play, with its provision for more objective standards for observing and comparing play behaviors. This resulted in the proliferation of a variety of play diagnostic instruments based on normative data that could be used with greater reliability in the clinical setting. Rather than seeing play only as a broad window into the inner life of children, theorists and researchers began to agree that the observation of play had the potential for resulting in more specific information.

Currently, it is believed that play behaviors and patterns reflect a wide variety of aspects of a child's inner life, developmental level of functioning, and competence abilities (Fenson, 1986; O'Connor & Ammen, 1997; O'Connor, 1991). Among those characteristics noted as being observable in play are ego development, cognitive style, adaptability, language functioning, emotional and behavioral responsiveness, social level, moral development, intellectual capacity, coping styles, problem-solving techniques, and approaches to perceiving and interpreting the surrounding world.

In an attempt to examine how certain characteristics of play reflect the aforementioned areas of functioning, there has been an increasing effort to describe and define play behaviors objectively (Fenson, 1986). This allows for a more reliable manner of observing and interpreting the play of children. McCune, Nicolich, and Fenson (1984) suggest certain properties, apart from the social context, which differentiate play from other behaviors. In general, it is defined by them as a disposition occurring in "describable and reproducible contexts" that has observable behaviors. It is considered to be different from other behaviors, in that it is (a) pursued for its own sake; (b) focused on means rather than ends; (c) directed toward exploring objects in order to do something with the objects; (d) not considered a serious endeavor because no realistic result is expected (i.e., there is no external purpose with a required outcome); (e) not governed by external rules; and (f) characterized by active engagement of the player. Others (Garvey, 1977; Piaget, 1962) suggest that play can be additionally defined as being (a) pleasurable (having a positive value to those involved); (b) spontaneous, voluntary, intrinsically motivated; (c) flexible; and (d) a natural product of physical and cognitive growth.

In addition to attempts to refine the definition of play, researchers have turned their attention to such process variables as: (a) the types and numbers of toys used; (b) the context of play; (c) the participants involved; (d) the sequences of play themes; (e) the space used; (f) the style with which the play activities are performed; and (g) the degree of effort invested in the play. One model (Knox, 1974), using an Eriksonian orientation, indicates four dimensions of the play process as important; (a) space management; (b) material management; (c) imitation, and (d) participation.

This concern with the process and definition of play has been part and parcel of the development of play as an assessment tool. As the play therapy movement has moved toward subdividing into classifications based on the various theoretical orientations (O'Connor & Schaefer, 1994; Schaefer & Carey, 1994; Moustakas, 1997), each requiring their own form of assessment, there has developed an even greater need for available and adaptable play evaluation techniques. Indeed, each chapter of this book reflects the growing sophistication of research and theory about play as it is applied increasingly to techniques that guide the observation of children at play.

ASSESSMENT: A BRIEF LOOK AT CURRENT ISSUES

Breadth of Variables to be Assessed

Assessment can be seen as a problem-solving approach that fosters an appreciation for the whole child. It must provide a comprehensive image of the youngster that is informative and accurate, with a primary aim of identifying and putting into perspective the child's strengths and weaknesses. In order to do this, clinicians need to acquire information about a wide range of factors that will lead to a full understanding of the biopsychosocial aspects of the individual's life. This breadth of understanding requires a complete evaluation of the child that encompasses such aspects as temperament, cognitive level, motivational traits, ego development, expression of moods, personality characteristics, behavioral responses, and physiological factors.

Additionally, clinicians must become aware of the social realm within which the child functions. In order to accomplish this, information about the following needs to be gathered and analyzed: cultural factors, family dynamics (including parent-child dyads), peer groups, school settings, and the many other environments surrounding the child. Specific problems detected in any of the individual and/or environmental factors may necessitate specific techniques for remediation.

Goals as a Factor in Selection of Assessment Techniques and Formats

Any assessment requires specification of the aims and goals of the evaluation process. Such specification permits appropriate selection of the critical factors to be studied. Evaluations have a variety of clinical purposes: diagnosis, selection of appropriate treatment, evaluation of treatment progress, selection of placement settings, and prediction of future behaviors. As a tool for research, assessments serve multiple functions too numerous to identify for the purposes of this book. In any case, a well-defined goal that is suited to the individual situation enhances accuracy in choosing the most appropriate assessment procedures that will yield valuable and functional information.

The format of assessment techniques for potential use in most evaluative situations includes many possibilities such as formal testing (e.g., IQ, achievement, and projective tests), observational play scales, structured and nonstructured interviews, self-reports, and checklists. Multiple factors must be scrutinized before a selection is made. Each case involves coping with the major questions related to interpretation and quantitative measurement. Thus, whether recording data observed through a one-way mirror or scoring a formal test battery, the questions of objectivity, reliability, and validity must be kept in mind (Suen, 1988). Issues of standardization, normative data, behavioral stability, interobserver agreement, and measurement error all affect the significance and usefulness of the data gleaned from an assessment. Without an awareness of these factors as they relate to the material collected, the evaluator cannot present meaningful and worthwhile conclusions about and recommendations for the subject.

Once the format (or combination of formats) of the assessment procedure is selected, all of the alternatives within that format must then be considered. A tremendous variety of formal tests, structured interviews, questionnaires, and checklists are available. The pros and cons for each must be carefully weighed.

Similarly, the advantages and disadvantages need to be considered when devising an appropriate play observation system (Cohen, Stern, & Balaban, 1983; Karp, Herzog, & Weinberg, 1985; Repp, Nieminen, Olinger, & Brusca, 1988). Depending on the observational situation and goals, several questions must be answered such as: (a) How long should the observation be?; (b) When does the actual recording take place (during or after the observation), and at what time intervals does it occur (recording every 10 seconds for 30-minute periods seems to be most common)? (c) What types of data will be collected (absence/presence of behavior, frequency, duration, intensity, etc.)?; (d) Are the behavioral definitions clear, concrete, specific, and discrete enough to yield accurate information?; (e) How global or specific should the behavioral categories be?; (f) What kind of training is necessary to minimize rater bias and errors?; (g) Will the chosen behaviors and the assessment format reveal the most relevant information for the goals of the assessment?; (h) Is the recording system set up so that the raters do not become overloaded or overwhelmed?; and (i) What is the most effective and the most efficient (in terms of both time and money) system to use for the particular situation? Other factors to be considered and controlled (as much as possible) include the effects of social desirability, observer drift, and observer expectations.

Molar versus Molecular Units of Assessment

When general, summarizing information is desired as a result of the formal play observation, data collection should involve molar units. These are broad classes of behaviors such as responsivity, sensitivity level, directedness, aggressiveness, or impulsivity. Molar units supply categories that highlight the essential meaning of complex behaviors that occur over time. Although molar units do not yield much information about specific behaviors and interaction patterns, they do eliminate important sources of bias, such as the influence of peculiarities in the environment or idiosyncratic behaviors.

On the other hand, when more details about specific play behaviors are needed, molecular units may be used. These units are more narrowly defined and may include such observable behaviors as smiles, hugs, vocalizations, slaps, or eye blinks. Because the information that is yielded from molecular assessment is often highly fragmented, these units are more popular with researchers than with clinicians who are assessing the whole child.

In some cases, both types of assessment may be used to enhance the meaning of the obtained information. The specifics of the microscopic analysis may lead to a macroscopic case formulation. For instance, the understanding of the minute details of verbal and nonverbal patterns of communication may lead to conclusions about the general dysfunctional state of a family in crisis (Ariel, 1992).

Objectivity, Reliability, and Validity of Assessments

In play assessment, achieving high standards of objectivity, reliability, and validity can be difficult. In this book, the term "play assessment" means the process by which trained professionals scrutinize play behaviors to understand an individual's or a group of individual's psychosocial functioning. This process lends itself to intuitive and clinical observations that result in the generation and the confirmation or disconfirmation of hypotheses about the child's functioning. The accuracy of these conclusions reflects the level of dependability of the instruments used in the evaluation.

In many ways, play assessment and its analysis face the same problems as the understanding of data obtained from projective diagnostic tools. Therefore, the need for careful recording and structuring as well as for thoughtful and systematic examination of the data is paramount. Furthermore, whenever possible, play data should be approached through the use of valid and reliable scales. As Palmer (1983) notes, "When no rating scale is provided for the novitiate, she/he tends either to become lost or to over-estimate and over-generalize from the scraps of behavior she/he is trying to analyze" (p. 170). However, not only novices are subject to such errors. The use of rating scales contributes to the operationalization of the behavior to be assessed. While this may limit the observation to a specific behavior, it also serves to clarify and increase the reliability of the observation.

It is only recently that clinicians have started developing standardized play assessment techniques. Those play instruments that are designed to elicit a specific symptom or that point to a particular diagnosis are even newer. Much more research is needed to confirm the few existing studies that are optimistic about the value, reliability, and validity of play assessment instruments.

Another area of concern in the assessment of children's play is that of the environment. As noted, children exist within a social and cultural setting that contributes to and molds their behaviors. The influence of the environment is most clearly appreciated when play observations take place in children's natural and, therefore, familiar settings. This type of observation adds a unique depth and insight into the issues at hand. It allows for the acquisition of first-hand knowledge of various potential cause-effect factors related to the presenting problem (environmental precipitants, relationships with others, nature of attachments, level of organization, etc). For some purposes, naturalistic observations are preferred in order to obtain specific types of data—particularly when issues of parent-child interactions or abuse and neglect are the focus of the assessment. The evaluator of naturalistic observations is, however, faced with substantial problems in terms of the reliability of such data.

With regard to reliability, the variables affecting naturalistic observations tend to be formidably complex to stabilize and quantify. It is well known that as the flexibility and informality of the observation increases, the reliability decreases. This effect can be counteracted somewhat by carefully choosing appropriate time-sampling, event sampling, or checklist procedures for each individual situation.

In contrast to naturalistic observation assessments are evaluations conducted in a structured play setting such as a clinic or laboratory playroom. While limiting the nature of the data available, this type of setting can increase the likelihood of developing normative comparisons. These observations tend to be more orderly, less fast-paced, less uncertain (i.e., more predictable), less complex, and more reliable. The environmental stimuli can be prearranged in order to elicit specific types of information needed to answer the evaluation questions. Laboratory observations also tend to be less time consuming than naturalistic observations (Lytton, 1973). Obviously, a combination of techniques would provide complementary checks and balances of the advantages and disadvantages of each kind of assessment.

Despite the difficulties inherent in the use of play assessment techniques, they present much that cannot be acquired from the formal testing techniques previously mentioned. Although play assessment can be used by itself, more typically it is used to support, complement, contradict, or elaborate the information obtained through other means and sources. In general, the greater the consistency of information from multiple sources, the greater the confidence in the conclusions drawn from the data. Multiple sources of information safeguard against overstatements or overexclusions in deductions drawn from a limited sample of behavior as observed in the laboratory play assessment.

Advantages of Play Assessment

Certainly, in the assessment of young children, play constitutes a major area of behavioral expression. For preschoolers, play is central and is therefore a particularly powerful evaluation tool. It provides a familiar and less stressful arena in which children can demonstrate their strengths and weaknesses. Play reveals, as noted earlier, children's emotional concerns that may be overwhelming or frightening them, their cognitive style of understanding their experiences, their ability to imitate and interact in the social environment, and much more. Because of limitations in language and conceptual development, the ability of young children to verbally express what they feel and know is inadequate and often unreliable. Play assessment offsets this difficulty.

Children's use of play is their most comprehensive form of expression. Like adults' dreams, children's play has been found to offer a unique access to the unconscious (Klein, 1955). The information that play observations yield cannot be equaled in its richness and depth. Therefore, this data must be studied in order to directly learn enough about specific problems so that accurate and completely informed diagnoses can be made.

For children with special disabilities, play also provides a wealth of otherwise unobtainable material. Such populations include those with general cognitive delays for which formal testing is limited in value, as well as children with specific disabilities, including sensory and language limitations for which there is but a restricted array of assessment techniques. Further, play provides access to children who—because of specific behavior problems (i.e., selective mutism, autistic spectrum disorders, conduct disorders, etc.)—are not amenable to classic test batteries. It allows children to gain a safe distance from sensitive, threatening, distasteful, or taboo issues, thereby reducing their anxiety and freeing them to express and recall what may otherwise be denied or unidentified in a verbal interview. For these populations, without the use of play assessment, most evaluative information is obtained from reports by significant others, which is known to be fraught with the problems of inaccurate informants (Edelbrock et al., 1985; Kashani et al., 1985).

The assessment of play can function as an important adjunct to more formalized testing and interviewing in any population of children. It can be used as an aid to verbal communication or as a substitute for it. When viewed as a reflection of cognitive and emotional levels, play assessment serves to validate and expand the information acquired from more specific instruments such as IQ tests or the Children's Apperception Test (CAT). It also assists in resolving conflicts arising from information obtained through the use of different tests in a test battery or from contradictions and discrepancies between parent and teacher reports or between such reports and clinical observations.

Especially helpful when working with test-anxious or excessively inhibited children, the play format allows these children to fully express themselves and demonstrate their skill in a familiar and nonfrightening atmosphere. Additionally, play provides a setting within which interactions can be observed on a behavioral level between children and their families, caregivers, teachers, and peers. That is, it deals with real-life samples of the interactions rather than reported behaviors.

Another advantage of play assessment is the availability of information from sequential observations. Because play allows for endless variations on a theme, observations can be repeated over a period of time without the interference of boredom or test knowledge effects. The materials themselves are intrinsically interesting and invite the participation of children by their very nature. This creates a situation in which evaluators are more likely to obtain the cooperation and involvement of their clients, thus increasing the validity of the observations. Due to the highly variable nature of young children's behaviors, repeated sessions minimize the potential for misreading behaviors in a single evaluation. Evaluators are also able to obtain a stronger sense of the level of internalization, stability, pliability, and reactivity of the target symptoms.

Play assessments offer information not only about the children but also about the ways in which environmental factors reinforce and change their behavior over time and vice versa. They provide a window on the multicultural aspects of the children's natural worlds and their families. In this way, play offers a flexible and sensitive means of assessing individuals from a variety of backgrounds and cultures throughout the world.

Available to the clinician is a variety of formats for play assessments, ranging from naturalistic free-play observations through highly structured laboratory play interviews. In each case, the evaluator must set the stage by structuring the assessment protocol in some way in order to obtain the relevant information that may be needed to answer the referral questions. Fortunately, play assessment is easily adaptable to children of different ages. For younger children, only specific toy materials may be made available for the play interview in order to direct their focus of attention. Because older children are more likely to engage in structured reality-based games, the clinician may choose a storytelling technique. This would allow older children to comfortably enter into the world of "pretend," in which communication can be safely achieved through the use of the characters in the story.

After the play observation is completed, the clinician's attention becomes focused on analyzing and interpreting the data that have been collected. Similar to formal testing procedures, the accuracy of the final conclusions drawn from the play evaluation depends greatly on the skills of the evaluator. Of greatest importance is the clinician's ability to integrate and compare the information gleaned from the play with: (a) a broad-based knowledge of normal age-appropriate developmental issues; (b) the acquired details about the client's current life situations as well as past histories; and (c) the data regarding the children's functioning that were collected from other sources. As long as the information is used judiciously and cautiously, it will add a newer and deeper dimension to the understanding of the strengths and weaknesses presented by the children being assessed.

REFERENCES

Ariel, S. (1992). *Strategic family play therapy*. New York: Wiley.

Axline, V. (1964). *Dibs: In search of self*. New York: Ballantine Books.

Axline, V. (1969). *Play therapy*. New York: Ballantine Books.

Buhler, C. (1951a). Manual for the World Test. *Journal of Child Psychiatry, 2*(1), 69–81.

Buhler, C. (1951b). The World Test: A projective technique. *Journal of Child Psychiatry, 2*(1), 4–23.

Buhler, C., & Carrol, H. (1951). A comparison of the results of the World Test with the teacher's judgment concerning children's adjustment. *Journal of Child Psychiatry, 2*(1), 36–65.

Cohen, D., Stern, V., & Balaban, N. (1983). *Observing and recording the behavior of young children*. New York: Teachers College Press.

Despert, J. L. (1976). Play therapy. In C. Schaefer (Ed.), *Therapeutic use of child's play* (pp. 463–474). New York: Jason Aronson.

Edelbrock, C. et al. (1985). Parent-child agreement on child psychiatric symptoms assessed via structured interview. *Journal of Child Psychology and Psychiatry, 27,* 181–190.

Erikson, E. (1950). *Childhood and society*. New York: Norton.

Erikson, E. (1951). Sex differences in the play configurations of preadolescents. *American Journal of Ortho-Psychiatry, 21,* 667–692.

Erikson, E. (1958). The psychosocial development of children. In World Health Organization, *Discussions in child development* (Vol. 3). New York: International Universities Press.

Erikson, E. (1968). *Identity, youth and crisis.* New York: Norton.

Fenson, L. (1986). The developmental progression of play. In A. Gottfried & C. Brown (Eds.), *Play interactions: The contribution of play materials and parental involvement to children's development.* MA: Heath.

Freud, A. (1946). *The psychoanalytic treatment of children.* London: Imago.

Freud, A. (1966). *The ego and the mechanisms of defense.* New York: International Universities Press.

Freud, S. (1950). Selected papers. In J. Strachey (Ed.), *The standard edition of the complete psychological works of Sigmund Freud* (Vol. 3). London: Hogarth Press.

Freud, S. (1961). *Beyond the pleasure principle.* New York: Norton.

Garvey, C. (1977). *Play.* Cambridge, MA: Harvard University Press.

Ginott, H. (1964). The theory and practice of therapeutic intervention in child treatment. In M. Haworth (Ed.), *Child psychotherapy: Practice and theory* (pp. 148–158). New York: Basic Books.

Groos, K. (1899). *Play of man.* New York: Appleton.

Hall, G. S. (1896). A study of dolls. *Pedagogical Seminary, 4,* 129–175.

Kamp, L., & Kessler, E. (1970). The World Test: Developmental aspects of a play technique. *Journal of Child Psychology and Psychiatry, 11,* 81–108.

Karp, N., Herzog, E., & Weinberg, A. (1985). The diagnostic nursery: A new approach to evaluating preschoolers. *Journal of Clinical Child Psychology, 14*(3), 202–208.

Kashani, J. et al. (1985). Informant variance: The issue of parent-child disagreement. *Journal of the American Academy of Child Psychiatry, 24* (4), 437–441.

Klein, M. (1955). The psychoanalytic play technique. In Travistock (Ed.), *New directions in psychoanalysis.* London: Hogarth Press.

Klein, M. (1960). *The psychoanalysis of children.* New York: Grove Press.

Knox, S. (1974). A play scale. In M. Reilly (Ed.), *Play as exploratory behavior.* Beverly Hills, CA; Sage Publications.

Lowenfeld, M. (1939). The world pictures of children: A method of recording and studying them. *British Journal of Medical Psychology, 18,* 65–101.

Lowenfeld, M. (1969). *Play in childhood.* London: Cedric Chivers.

Lumbry, G. (1951). A study of World Test characteristics as a basis for discrimination between various clinical categories. *Journal of Child Psychiatry, 2*(1), 24–35.

Lytton, H. (1973). Three approaches to the study of parent-child interaction: Ethological, interview and experimental. *Journal of Child Psychology and Psychiatry, 14,* 177.

McCune, Nicolich, L., & Fenson, L. (1984). Methodological issues in studying early pretend play. In T. Yawkey & A. Pellegrini (Eds.), *Child's play: Developmental and applied* (pp. 81–104). Hillsdale, NJ: Erlbaum.

Moustakas, C. (1973). *Children in play therapy.* New York: Jason Aronson.

Moustakas, C. (1997). *Relationship play therapy.* Northvale, NJ: Jason Aronson.

O'Connor, K. (1991). *The play therapy primer: An integration of theories and techniques.* New York: Wiley.

O'Connor, K., & Ammen, S. (1997). *Play therapy treatment planning and interventions: The ecosystemic model and workbook.* San Diego, CA: Academic Press.

O'Connor, K., & Schaefer, C. (1994). *Handbook of play therapy, volume two: Advances and innovations.* New York: Wiley.

Palmer, J. (1983). *The psychological assessment of children.* New York: Wiley.

Parton, M. (1932). Social participation among preschool children. *Journal of Abnormal and Social Psychology, 27,* 243–269.

Peller, L. (1964). Libidinal development as reflected in play. In M. Haworth (Ed.), *Child psychotherapy: Practice and theory* (pp. 176–184). New York: Basic Books.

Piaget, J. (1952). *The origins of intelligence in children.* New York: International Universities Press.

Piaget, J. (1962). *Play, dreams and imitation in childhood.* London: Routledge.

Reilly, M. (1974). *Play as exploratory behavior.* Beverly Hills, CA: Sage Publications.

Repp, A., Nieminen, G., Olinger, E., & Brusca, R. (1988). Direct observation: Factors affecting the accuracy of observers. *Exceptional Children, 55*(1), 29–36.

Schaefer, C., & Carey, L. (1994). *Family play therapy.* Northvale, NJ: Jason Aronson.

Sjolund, M. (1982). *The Erica Method: An introduction and short manual.* Unpublished manuscript.

Sjolund, M. (1993). *The Erica Method: A technique for play therapy and diagnosis: A training guide.* CO: Carron.

Suen, H. (1988). Agreement, reliability, accuracy, and validity: Toward clarification. *Behavioral Assessment, 10,* 343–366.

PART I

DEVELOPMENTAL PLAY ASSESSMENTS

In studying infants and young children, it is always important to focus on the normal developmental process. Assessment based on standardized age-related criteria stands as a backbone to all attempts at diagnosis and evaluation of pathology. Part I of this book contains a number of instruments designed to trace typical growth progress as well as to detect deviations and delays in functioning through the use of play. In some cases, the developmental changes in children's play are the focus of the assessment. In others, play behaviors are assessed as a reflection of specific characteristics and skills representative of different ages and developmental stages.

A number of the chapters in Part I primarily focus on infant assessment. It is clear that play-based techniques serve to provide clinicians with a unique understanding of this population. That is, play offers a ready, attractive, and natural method for acquiring a wide range of information directly from infants who are unable to respond to language-based tests. The collected data additionally function as a concrete validation of such secondary sources as parent interviews and observer rating procedures.

In her updated chapter, Carol Westby presents a detailed discussion of the issues relating to the development of symbol comprehension and expression in play, noting its relation to language development. In particular, she presents a design for play assessment that considers the various cultural and environmental factors affecting the nature and themes of play. This evaluation is specific in terms of setting, organization, and adult role, making it easily replicable. Recognizing the fundamental use of symbolic play as a means of clarifying and differentiating the developmental patterns of normal-versus-handicapped children, Westby provides case material from a variety of age groups including toddlers, preschoolers, and school-aged children.

Thomas Power and Jerilynn Radcliff, as in the first edition of *Play Diagnosis and Assessment,* provide a useful and welcome general introduction and exploration of the Lowe and Costello Symbolic Play Test (SPT). The SPT is an easily administered assessment technique that gives an account of functional play skills of children who are exhibiting behaviors typical of developmental levels normally occurring between the ages of 12 and 36 months. The SPT is a promising means of differentiating certain diagnostic categories through the focus on symbolic play and its relation to cognitive ability. The authors have provided new information concerning the psychometric properties of the test as well as new case material. While continuing to be a valuable instrument in the play assessment field, the SPT is in need of more attention from those interested in the study of reliability and validity of evaluation instruments. Such research would strengthen the scale, increasing its attractiveness to clinicians and researchers.

Adam Matheny's chapter presents a well-researched play assessment method for the measurement of infant temperament. This scale covers a series of ages from 3 to 30 months and describes an instrument that is applicable to both cross-sectional and longitudinal study. In the original volume, Matheny noted that the complexities of the scale and its procedures rendered it mostly applicable to research. However, in the updated version, an adaptation for clinical assessment has been added.

Moving from the annotated bibliography of the first edition to a full fledged chapter, Kristin Moore Taylor, Marilee Menarchek-Fetkovich, and Cindy Behnke-Day offer a complete discussion and presentation of the Play History Interview. Frequently lacking when parents are questioned about their children's play behaviors is a specific, well-organized, and standardized interview procedure. This chapter presents a manual as well as a developmentally based questionnaire to guide the examiner in acquiring information about key elements of children's present and past play experiences in order to detect any gaps, deviations, delays, or precocities in development.

The final chapter in this section presents Toni Linder's Transdisciplinary Play-Based Assessment (TBPA). This unique and new method of play evaluation greatly assists in any endeavors to coordinate a multidisciplinary team in the process of evaluating development from infancy through the preschool period. It specifically addresses the need for a way of integrating the information gleaned from such efforts. This method is particularly geared toward the current popularity of early intervention programs throughout the country. Clinicians will find this an exceptionally useful and exciting new tool.

Clearly the chapters in this section present a sampling of scales indicating the extensive interest and research that has been focused on play in infancy and early childhood from a developmental perspective. The range of tools runs from parent interviews to arena-style assessments. In the future, it would be interesting to be able to extend this kind of attention to development during the rest of the life cycle. Latency-aged and adolescent play activities are definitely reflective of differences in cognitive, social, and emotional development and, therefore, are worthy of study. Furthermore, considering the increasing numbers of older individuals as well as the increasing focus on their leisurely activities, a broadened developmental approach to the play patterns throughout adulthood and old age would certainly prove to be a functional endeavor.

Chapter 1

A SCALE FOR ASSESSING DEVELOPMENT OF CHILDREN'S PLAY

Carol Westby

Man is an incurable player. He is not only programmed for culture, but also programmed to acquire and maintain this cultural nature through play.

(Vandenberg L. Kielhofner, 1982)

INTRODUCTION

Play serves both as a means of *expression* and a means of *interpretation* (Lifter & Bloom, 1998). As a means of expression, play provides a way for children to embody their mental representations of the world. As a means of interpretation, play provides a way for children to learn about objects, events, and relations in the world by interpreting the results of their own actions and revising what they know about the world. Play as expression provides a window on what children know, which allows for the use of play for assessment. Observation of play behaviors and communication in play reveals a child's view of the world. Cosaro and Tomlinson (1980) maintain that "spontaneous play can be viewed as the continual practice of reality production" (p. 105). In play, children demonstrate their knowledge of the complex spatial-temporal-causal interrelationships among objects, environments, persons, actions, and motives that make up the world of human action, and they experiment with these interrelationships.

Play as interpretation provides a rationale for using play in intervention programs as a way for children to acquire knowledge. Current research links play to the development of cognitive, social, emotional, language, and literacy abilities. But play has a purpose and value beyond developing children's skills (Sawyer, 1997; Vandenberg, 1986). Play can be symbolic, and through symbolic play, we humans create imagined worlds and the stories of our lives. Through symbolic systems, we share in human culture.

To be truly competent in the world, children must be able to do more than repeat a string of facts, and they must understand more than the laws governing the physical world. To exist successfully within the world also requires an understanding of people—how they think and feel, what motivates them, their roles, the relationships among people, and how they maintain these relationships through communication. The laws that govern the physical world are the same throughout the world, but the social and psychological rules that govern people vary from culture to culture. A number of investigators have suggested that a different type of intelligence is required for understanding the behavior of people compared to understanding physical events in the world (Bruner, 1986; Gardner, 1983; Wellman, Hickling, & Schult, 1997). Understanding people requires a developing *theory of mind,* which involves the recognition of mental states in oneself and others (Baron-Cohen, 1995). Pretend play represents an early manifestation of a child's theory of mind. The act of pretending requires that children acknowledge real versus unreal and that they recognize that others will make this same distinction.

In addition to theory of mind and related knowledge of the social world, play requires a special type of communication. For play to be shared with others, children must communicate their intentions and orient themselves and others to their intended meaning, and they must negotiate roles, settings, and action sequences (Garvey & Kramer, 1989; Sawyer, 1997; Sutton-Smith, 1980). Play can occur only if the participants are capable of some degree of metacommunication—that is, exchanging signals that convey the message "this is play" (Bateson, 1955). Observation of children's play provides insight into the social knowledge and communicative competence they possess and how they use this knowledge. Children's performance on standardized cognitive and language tests provides knowledge of discrete pieces of information that a child possesses, but it does not tell how a child integrates and uses this information in realistic situations.

HISTORY OF PLAY EVALUATIONS

Evaluation of Typically Developing Children

Modern theories of play view children's play as a means for mastering traumatic experiences; for practicing and consolidating learned skills; for promoting abstract thought, problem solving, and flexibility in thinking; and for promoting the ability to comprehend multiple levels of meaning (Ellis, 1973). Researchers have explored (1) the development of children's social interaction with other children in play, (2) the types of play (functional use of objects, constructional building, and symbolic pretend), (3) the types of play themes, (4) the negotiation of play themes, and (5) the ability to take the perspective of others in pretend play.

Several taxonomies have been proposed to document aspects of children's developing play. Piaget suggested broad play stages: sensorimotor play for infants and toddlers, symbolic pretend for preschool children, and games with rules for older children (Piaget, 1962). Parten (1932) focused on children's developing socialization within play activities, suggesting that children move from solitary play to parallel play with children playing alongside each other without interacting, to associative play in which children join in play on the same theme and exchange toys and activities within the play but in which each child carries out her or his own activities independent of the activities of other children, and finally to cooperative play in which children work together to develop and carry out the themes of the play. More recent research suggests that toddlers are capable of some playful interactive exchanges and that solitary play does not disappear but continues to occur in children who show associative and cooperative play. In fact, solitary play may reflect personality and play orientation as much as developmental level (Rubin, 1982; Smith, 1978).

Within recent years, particular attention has been given to exploring the relationships between symbolic play and creativity, cognition, social skills (negotiating and role-taking), impulse control, language, and literacy (Bates, Benigni, Bretherton, Camaioni, & Volterra, 1979; Lifter & Bloom, 1998; McCune, 1995; Nicolich, 1977; Pellegrini, 1985; Pellegrini & Galda, 1993; Pepler & Ross, 1981; Rubin, 1980; Saltz & Johnson, 1974). Such studies have required more specific analysis of the components of pretend play. A few detailed analyses documenting development of cognitive aspects of symbolic play development are available. Fischer and Corrigan (1980) and Wolf, Rygh, and Altshuler (1984) presented developmental sequences of social roles in pretend play; Nicolich (1977) identified the development of combinations of actions in pretend play of children under 3 years; and Westby (1980, 1991) presented a scale that documented aspects of symbolic play and development of several dimensions of pretend play in children between 18 months and 5 years of age.

Pretend play is embedded within sociocultural contexts. The majority of studies on children's developing pretend have used mainstream American children and have focused on use of objects as opposed to interaction with people (Haight & Miller, 1993). In mainstream contexts, mothers (or other adults) typically negotiate play particularly with children under 3 years of age. After age 3, the role of mothers as play partners continues but decreases and pretend play shifts to peers. These interactive play patterns may differ in other cultures. Farver (1993) reported that in a study of Mexican families, older siblings provided early play scaffolding for toddlers rather than mothers. In some cultures, such as the !Kung San (Konner, 1975) and the Maya (Gaskins & Goncu, 1992), relatively little pretend play is manifested. Numerous studies have compared the play of children from middle and from lower socioeconomic levels (Griffing, 1980; McLoyd, 1982; Saltz & Johnson, 1974; Smilansky, 1968; Smith & Dodsworth, 1978). Many of these studies suggested that the play of children from lower socioeconomic backgrounds is less developed and less imaginative, but other studies have criticized these interpretations, suggesting that researchers have overlooked expressions of imaginative play that differ from the play of mainstream children (Schwartzman, 1984). Blake (1994) noted that African-American mothers engaged children more in affective social play than in object play.

Evaluation of Children with Disabilities

The study of play in infants and children with disabilities has become an increasingly popular area of investigation, especially as play relates to later competence in social and academic skills (Bretherton, 1984; Christie, 1991; Galda & Pellegrini, 1985; Garwood, 1982; Pellegrini & Galda, 1993; Yawkey & Pellegrini, 1984). For example, the amount of relational play (in which objects are simply combined by stacking) at 22 months, contrasted with symbolic play, is negatively related to language abilities at the same age and negatively associated with general intelligence at 5 years of age (Sigman & Sena, 1993). A number of investigators have explored the emergence of symbolic play and language in children with disabilities and the nature of play behavior and interaction in children with disabilities (Casby & Ruder, 1983; Hill & McCune-Nicolich, 1981; Sigman & Sena, 1993; Terrell, Schwartz, Prelock, & Messick, 1984; Wing, Gould, Yeates, & Brierly, 1977). A few studies have been done with groups of children having specific diagnoses such as mental retardation, autism, Down syndrome, or language impairment, but the majority of such studies have had heterogeneous populations of children. One study that compared the play of children ages $3^1/_2$ to 6 years with mild mental retardation, behavior disorders, and learning disabilities found that these three groups of children with disabilities did not differ significantly from each other on any formal measure, but they did differ significantly from typically developing children on several play measures. The children with disabilities did not play with the same kinds of materials as typically developing children, and they engaged in more nonplay activities and fewer group interactions and had less cognitively sophisticated play than typically developing children (Mindes, 1982).

Regardless of the populations studied, the investigations of play of children with disabilities generally reveal similar findings. The data indicate that children with disabilities exhibit the same developmental play sequences as typically developing children, but with some qualitative and quantitative differences (Field, Roseman, De Stefano, & Koewler, 1982). Less combinatorial play has been observed in some children with mental retardation than would be expected based on their other abilities (Hill & McCune-Nicolich, 1981; Quinn & Rubin, 1984) and autosymbolic or self-directed pretend play appeared later than symbolic play actions on dolls. Atypically developing children are less likely to initiate play (Brooks-Gunn & Lewis, 1982); they more frequently engage in isolated and toy-directed behaviors and less in social interactive play (Field et al., 1982; Johnson & Ershler, 1985); they are more dependent on concrete toys for play, yet they play with a small variety of toys (Johnson & Ershler, 1985); and they exhibit a greater heterochronous development, i.e., skills that usually emerge together do so less frequently in children with disabilities, and there is greater variability in the skills present at any developmental level (Hill & McCune-Nicolich, 1981; Motti, Cicchetti, & Sroufe, 1983). These qualitative differences cannot be completely explained by the children's general cognitive levels. Perez and Schuler (unpublished manuscript) reported that 4-year-old high-risk premature children, whose performance on the Stanford-Binet was in the average to high-average range, differed significantly from nonpremature 4-year-olds in the completeness and organization of their block play structures and the degree of fantasy they used in describing their structures. The premature children relied on descriptions of the physical appearance of their structures, and the nonpremature children transcended the visual and created imaginary settings and character goals.

Pretend play and language development are closely related in most children, both typically and atypically developing. There are some instances in which this is not the case, however. In several studies, the symbolic play of 2- through 4-year-old children with language delays was behind that of children the same age with normal language development (Rescorla & Goossens, 1992; Terrell, Schwartz, Prelock, & Messick, 1984; Thal & Bates, 1988). When children with language delays are compared to younger children with similar levels of language development, however, the findings are mixed. The level of symbolic play of 2- through 4-year-olds with language delays is equal to or exceeds that of younger language matched children (Terrell, et al., 1984; Thal & Bates, 1988). In contrast, 5- to 7-

year-olds with language impairments had lower levels of symbolic play than language matches (Roth & Clark, 1987). It also appears that specific dimensions of pretend play may be affected differently among children with language impairments. Thal and Bates (1988) found that 2-year-olds who were using very few words engaged in fewer different pretend actions than language matches, but they engaged in more sequential actions following adult models than younger, language matched children.

The pretend play of deaf children is closely related to their language development. In general, among deaf children slower language development is associated with slower symbolic play development whether they are acquiring spoken or signed language (Blum, Fields, Scharfman, & Silber, 1994; Spencer, 1996). Spencer (1996) found that deaf children of deaf parents who used sign language with their children were as likely to have advanced play and language development as hearing children of hearing parents. In contrast, deaf children of hearing parents tended to be functioning at somewhat lower levels of language and symbolic play.

Children with Down syndrome spend more time in visual exploration of toys and less time in manual exploration than control subjects matched for chronological age or mental age (Sigman & Sena, 1993). In contrast to exploratory competence, children with Down syndrome demonstrate symbolic competence at a level commensurate with their general cognitive level. They do, however, tend to exhibit less variety in their play, repeating the same schemes more than children without mental disabilities.

Children with autism spectrum disorders exhibit a different pattern of pretend play development. The pretend play of autistic children is delayed compared to their other cognitive abilities (Baron-Cohen, 1987; Wing, et al., 1977). Autistic children who do engage in pretend play show qualitative differences such as less-frequent self-directed pretend (McCune, 1986) and stereotyped unvarying play routines (Wing, et al., 1977). In addition to impairments in symbolic play development, abnormal development of social relationships, affect, and communication are distinguishing characteristics of autism. Deficiencies in symbolic play are seen as one manifestation of the difficulty autistic individuals exhibit with theory of mind and understanding and representing subjective aspects of experience.

In recent years, attention has shifted from a focus on children's IQ to a focus on their confidence and competence (Westby, Stevens-Dominguez, & Oetter, 1996). Facilitating play skills has been found to increase children's social competence and language skills (McHale & Olley, 1982; Saltz & Saltz, 1986). To use play therapy most effectively with children with disabilities, educators and therapists must understand a child's current play abilities and design therapeutic and educational programs to facilitate play systematically. In a play assessment, evaluators can actively interact with the children. They can explore what supports or enables a child to perform optimally and what compromises a child's performance. This chapter presents a developmental play scale, guidelines for assessing children's play and language levels using the play scale, and considerations in the interpretation of the children's performance on the play evaluation.

PLAY SCALE

There is a plethora of formal cognitive and language assessment measures for children. The majority of these measures focus on a narrow range of discrete cognitive skills, removed from context. In some instances, children's physical, language, and cognitive abilities are evaluated as they engage in play activities (Linder, 1993). The playscale presented in this chapter provides a means of evaluating play development per se and the way language is used to instantiate and negotiate the play. Evaluation of children's play skills permits assessment not only of the knowledge children have, but also of how they use this knowledge in a real-world context.

The original version of this scale (Westby, 1980) was based on observations of typically developing infants, toddlers, and preschool children in child care centers and children with disabilities enrolled in preschool and elementary school special education programs. Original age levels were based on 80% of middle-class preschoolers performing the play and language behaviors at each level. Because of this criterion, it is common for many middle-class children to exhibit the behaviors identified on the scale at somewhat younger ages, particularly in the earlier stages. The scale was divided into two dimensions—play and language. As the original scale was used in the assessment of infants, toddlers, preschool, and young elementary school children, it became clear that children with disabilities (autistic, speech-language impaired, attention deficit hyperactivity disordered, and cognitively impaired) often exhibited qualitative as well as quantitative differences in their play and language compared to typically developing children. On the original two-dimension scale, typically developing children might exhibit play and language abilities at two adjacent levels on the scale, with most of the items in these levels being observed or reported. Scattering of isolated play behaviors across more than two adjacent levels was rarely observed. Thus, for typically developing children, it was possible to assign an overall play level. Children with disabilities, however, often exhibited some, but not all, of the behaviors in a particular stage, the behaviors were exhibited less frequently, their play often did not appear playful, they seldom indicated "this is play," and they were more dependent on adults to initiate the activities. In addition, children with disabilities above 3 years of age often exhibited a wide scattering of skills across several stages and less complete skills at each stage.

Much of the variability or decalage demonstrated by children with disabilities in play can be understood by considering development within dimensions of each stage. For the presymbolic levels, these dimensions include object permanence, means–ends problem solving, and object use. Within the symbolic levels, play varies along the dimensions of decontextualization, thematic content, integration or organization of play themes, and self–other relationships. At the presymbolic levels, "language" is considered in terms of its communicative intentions. In the symbolic levels, language is considered in terms of its functions and its form and content. The following sections present the play and communicative characteristics of children from 8 months to 5 years. The scale begins at the point at which infants can attend to both objects and people. It is important to determine whether children are truly engaging in symbolic pretend or are simply exploring and demonstrating the functional use of objects. For this reason, it is necessary to be aware of the nature of children's play before the emergence of symbolic pretend play. Table 1.1 presents the play scale, organized according to the various dimensions of play and communication/language. In the table, there are blank spaces in categories at many of the age levels; a blank category indicates that there has been no change in this dimension from the previous levels.

Table 1-1. Developmental playscale

Phase 1: Presymbolic

Object Permanence	PLAY		COMMUNICATION
	Means–End/ Problem Solving	Object Use	
Presymbolic Level I: 8 to 12 Months			
__Aware that objects exist when not seen; finds toy hidden under cloth, box, etc., associates object with location	__Attains toy by pulling cloth on which toy is resting __Attains toy by pulling string __Touches adult to continue activity	__Explores moveable parts of toy __Does not mouth all toys. Uses several different schemes (patting, banging, turning, throwing, etc.); uses some differential schemas on familiar objects	__Joint attention on toy and person __No true language; may have performative words that are associated with action or the total situation __Shows and gives objects Exhibits the following communicative intents: __Request (instrumental) __Command (regulatory)
Presymbolic Level II: 13 to 17 months			
__Aware that objects exist separate from location; finds objects hidden first in one place and then in a second or third location	__Understands "in-ness"; dumps objects out of bottle __Hands toy to adult if unable to operate __Hands toy to adult to get attention __Uses index finger to point to desired object	__Recognizes operating parts of toys (attends to knobs, levers, buttons) __Discovers operations of toys through trial and error __Construction of toy relationships (e.g., puts one toy in another such as figure in car; nests boxes) __Uses familiar objects appropriately	__Context-dependent single words, e.g., child may use the word "car" when riding in a car, but not when he sees a car; words tend to come and go in child's vocabulary Exhibits the following communicative functions: __Request ___Protest __Command ___Label __Interactional ___Response __Personal ___Greeting

(Continues)

21

Table 1-1. (continued)

Phase 2: Symbolic

PLAY			LANGUAGE	
Decontextualization: What props are used in pretend play?	Thematic Content: What schemas/scripts does the child represent?	Organization: How coherent and logical are the child's schemas/scripts?	Self Other Relations: What roles does the child take and give to toys and other people?	Function
Symbolic Level I: 17 to 19 months				
Child exhibits internal mental representation	___Familiar, everyday activities (eating, sleeping) in which child has been an active participant	___Short isolated schemas (single pretend actions)	___Self as agent (auto-symbolic or self-representational play, i.e., child pretends to go to sleep, to eat from a spoon, or to drink from an empty cup)	Directing ___Requesting ___Commanding ___Interactional Self-Maintaining ___Protesting ___Protecting self and self-interests Commenting ___Labeling (objects and activity) ___Indicating personal feelings
___Tool-use (uses stick to reach toy)				
___Finds toy invisibly hidden (when placed in a box and box emptied under scarf)				
___Pretends using life-like props				
___Does not stack solid ring				

Form and Content

Beginning of true verbal communication. Words have following functional and semantic relations:

___Recurrence
___Existence
___Nonexistence
___Rejection
___Denial
___Agent
___Object
___Action or state
___Object or person associated with object or person

22

Symbolic Level II:
19 to 22 months

___Activities of familiar others (cooking, reading, cleaning, shaving)

___Short, isolated schema combinations (child combines two actions or toys in pretend, e.g., rocking doll and putting it to bed; pouring from pitcher into cup, or feeding doll from plate with spoon)

___Child acts on doll (doll is passive recipient of action); brushes doll's hair, covers doll with blanket

___Child performs pretend actions on more than one object or person, e.g., feeds self, a doll, mother, or another child

___Refers to objects and persons not present

___Requests information

Beginning of word combinations with following semantic relations:
___Agent-action
___Action-object
___Attributive
___Dative
___Action-locative
___Possessive

Symbolic Level III:
2 years

___Elaborated single schemas (represents daily experiences with details, e.g., puts lid on pan, puts pan on stove; collects items associated with cooking/eating such as dishes, pans, silverware, glasses, highchair)

___Reverses roles— "I'll play you and you play me."

___Comments on activity of self (get apple)
___Comments on doll (baby sleep)

___Uses phrases and short sentences

Appearance of morphological markers:
___Present progressive (ing) on verbs
___Plurals
___Possessives

(Continues)

23

Table 1-1. *(continued)*

Phase 2: Symbolic

PLAY				LANGUAGE	
Decontextualization: What props are used in pretend play?	Thematic Content: What schemas/scripts does the child represent?	Organization: How coherent and logical are the child's schemas/scripts?	Self Other Relations: What roles does the child take and give to toys and other people?	Function	Form and Content
Symbolic Level IV: 2 ½ Years	Represents less frequently personally experienced events, particularly those that are memorable because they are pleasurable or traumatic: ___ Store shopping ___ Doctor–nurse–sick child		___ Talks to doll ___ Reverses dyadic/ complementary roles ("I'll play x and you play y"), e.g., doctor/patient; shopper/ cashier		Responds appropriately to the following *wh* questions in context: ___ What ___ Who ___ Whose ___ Where ___ What … do ___ Asks *wh* question (generally puts *wh* at beginning of sentence) ___ Responses to why questions inappropriate except for well-known routines ___ Asks why, but often inappropriate and does not attend to answer

Symbolic Level V:
3 years

—Compensatory play: reenacts experienced events, but modifies original outcomes	—Evolving episode sequences, e.g., child mixes cake, bakes it, washes dishes; or doctor checks patient, calls ambulance, takes patient to hospital (sequence not planned)	—Transforms self into role —Engages in associative play, i.e., children do similar activities, may share same role, but no organized goal	—Reporting —Predicting —Emerging narrating or story-telling	—Uses past tense, such as, "I ate the cake," "I walked" —Uses future aspect (particularly "gonna") forms, such as "I'm gonna wash dishes."

Symbolic Level VI:
3 to 3 ½ years

—Carries out pretend activities with replica toys (Fisher Price/Playmobil dollhouse, barn, garage, village, airport) —Uses one object to represent another (stick can be a comb, chair can be a car) —Uses blocks and sandbox for imaginative play. Blocks used as enclosures (fences, houses) for animals and dolls	—Represents observed events, i.e., events in which child was not an active participant (policemen, firemen, war, cowboys, schemas/scripts from TV shows—Batman, Ninja Turtles, Power Rangers)	—Child assigns roles to other children; negotiates play —Multiple reversible roles ("I'll be a and b and you be x"), e.g., child is ticket seller, pilot, and airline steward, but coplayer is always passenger Uses doll or puppet as participant in play: —Child talks for doll —Reciprocal role taking—child talks for doll and as parent of doll	—Projecting: gives desires, thoughts, feelings, to doll or puppet —Uses indirect requests, e.g., "mommy lets me have cookies for breakfast." —Changes speech depending on listener —Reasoning (integrates reporting, predicting, projecting information) —Metacommunicative strategies	Descriptive vocabulary expands as child becomes more aware of perceptual attributes; uses terms for following concepts (not always correctly): —shapes —sizes —colors —textures —spatial relations —Uses metalinguistic and metacognitive language, e.g., "He said ...; I know...."

(Continues)

Table 1-1. *(continued)*

Phase 2: Symbolic

PLAY				LANGUAGE	
Decontextualization: What props are used in pretend play?	Thematic Content: What schemas/scripts does the child represent?	Organization: How coherent and logical are the child's schemas/scripts?	Self Other Relations: What roles does the child take and give to toys and other people?	Function	Form and Content
Symbolic Level VII: 3½ to 4 years __Uses language to invent props and set scene __Builds 3-dimensional structures with blocks	__Improvisations and variations on themes	__Schemas/scripts are planned __Hypothesizes "what would happen if"	__Uses dolls and puppets to act out schemas/scripts __Child or doll has multiple roles (e.g., mother and wife; fireman, husband, father)	__Uses language to take roles of character in the play, stage manager for the props, or as author of the play story	__Uses modals (can, could, may, might, would) __Uses conjunctions (and, but, so, because, if) *Note:* Full competence for modals and conjunctions does not develop until 10–12 years of age. __Some appropriate responses to why and how questions requiring reasoning
Symbolic Level VIII: 5 years __Can use language to set the scene, actions, and roles in play	__Highly imaginative activities that integrate parts of known schemas/scripts for events child has never participated in or observed (e.g., astronaut builds ship, flies to strange planet, explores, eats unusual food, talks with creatures on planet)	__Plans several sequences of pretend events. Organizes what is needed—both objects and other children. Coordinates several scripts occurring simultaneously	__Engages in collaborative play, i.e., play roles are coordinated and themes are goal-directed		__Uses relational terms (then, when, first, last, next, while, before, after) *Note:* Full competence does not develop until 10–12 years of age.

Presymbolic Levels

It is difficult to know at just what point to call a behavior "play." Certainly infants have playful interactions with their parents during their first few months of life. They recognize faces, and they take turns in vocal exchanges. Between 4 and 8 months of age, infants begin to explore the outside world—batting at mobiles, reaching for objects, and mouthing objects. Around 8 to 9 months of age, infants are able to establish joint reference—the ability to look at an object that someone else is interested in, with the awareness that they are looking at the same object. This shared attention mechanism is essential if an infant is to communicate about a shared reality (Baron-Cohen, 1995). With shared attention, infants begin to integrate their object and social understanding so as to use objects when they play with people. Infants also begin to differentiate the functions of objects (e.g., they discover that not everything can be mouthed). They also become aware that people can do things for them. Although infants at this age do not have linguistic systems, they purposively attract adult attention, and they intentionally communicate. The ability to attend to objects that others are interested in and to share that interest forms both the basis for play activities with people and objects and the basis for communication because people talk with other people about objects.

Evaluation of infants' and toddlers' play behavior should not be limited to their success or lack of success with a task. The manner in which children respond to tasks is as important as or more important than the completion of the task. Yarrow (1981) has reported four qualitative aspects of behavior, termed *mastery motivation,* that are predictive of later competence:

- *Latency to task involvement.* The amount of time that elapses between the presentation of the item and the child's efforts to seek a solution; a fairly rapid involvement reflects the child's eagerness to become involved with the task.
- *Persistence.* The length of time spent in task-directed behavior, which is an indicator of the child's ability to focus on the task and maintain attention to it.
- *Positive affect.* Shown by the child while engaged in or after completing a task.
- *Task completion.* The number of times the child completes the task successfully.

The focus of the play evaluations with presymbolic children involves observing children's communicative intents, their performance on object permanence tasks, their means–ends behaviors, and their exploration and use of objects. Attention should also be given to the affect children display as they engage in play with people and objects.

Presymbolic Level I: 8 to 12 Months

Eight- to 12-month-old children can coordinate attention to both an object and a person by showing or giving an object. The 8- to 12-month-old child is developing object permanence and is aware that a person or object continues to exist when out of view. If a child sees a toy being covered with a scarf or box, the infant will remove the scarf or box in search of the toy. The child, however, associates the object with the location and will often appear not to recognize an object in an unfamiliar setting. The child displays means–ends behavior by pulling a cloth on which the desired toy is resting or by pulling a string to obtain the toy at the end of the string. The child is developing different schemas for different toys and no longer immediately mouths or bangs all toys, but uses some appropriate action schemas. When presented with a toy, the child is likely to attend to the toy's moveable parts—twirling wheels;

batting at springs; pushing, pulling, or twisting switches, knobs, and dials. For example, a child may mouth smooth, hard objects, but stroke furry, soft objects.

At this age, children generally attend to only one toy at a time, and their actions with the toys are often unpredictable (i.e., not yet related to the function of the object). Play actions consist of *separating* actions in which objects are moved apart or taken apart, for example, such as taking hold of an object, then exploring it and dropping it or taking pegs out of pegboards or toy figures out of toy cars (Lifter & Bloom, 1998). Some children use vocalizations or gestures at this stage as they show or give objects or to request objects or command actions (Halliday, 1975). These vocalizations are not true words but are part of the total activity and are uttered only as the activity is performed. For example, "momma" may not refer to mother or even a specific person, but to the activity of being held, fed, or comforted.

Presymbolic Level II: 13 to 17 Months

At this age children no longer associate objects exclusively with a location, and they are able to find an object that is hidden first in one location and then in a second or third location, unlike younger children, who will return to the first location, even when they have watched where the toy is hidden. The 13- to 17-month-old child explores toys more systematically, quickly locating the part of the toy that is responsible for its operation (e.g., levers, strings, buttons) and attempting a variety of motor schemas on it (pushing, pulling, turning, pounding, shaking). They recognize familiar objects and spontaneously use them appropriately (e.g., drinking from a cup, combing hair, wiping faces with a cloth, talking on the telephone).

Children become active problem-solvers, engaging in a wide range of means–ends behaviors. Children this age begin to *construct* relationships between toys that they have seen or that are based on simple physical properties (for containment and support), for example, putting a figure into a car or putting one nesting cup into another. Children develop the concept of "in-ness" and engage in problem-solving, means–ends behaviors to get objects that are inside other objects (e.g., they will turn bottles upside down to dump out the contents, rather than trying to obtain the contents by reaching their hands into the bottle). If a desired toy is beyond reach, they will look toward an adult and use their index finger to point to the object. If they are unable to operate a toy, they frequently hand it to an adult and wait for the adult to operate the toy. This handing a toy to an adult for operation is termed a *protoimperative* and indicates that the child understands that adults are agents who can act on objects. Children will also engage in *protodeclaratives,* in which they bring a toy to an adult simply to seek attention (Bates, 1976). Some children use single words at this stage, but these words are extremely context dependent and unstable and are often used only in the context in which they were learned (for example, the word puppy may refer only to their dog in the yard and to no other dog) (Bloom, 1973). Children increase the variety of their purposeful communication functions and use gestures and vocalizations to request, command, call attention to themselves, establish interaction, convey feelings, greet, protest, and label (Dore, 1975; Halliday, 1975). At this age, there appears to be some tradeoffs between spoken language and high affect, perhaps related to limitations of working memory, which allows one to do more than one thing at a time. Spoken language is most likely to occur when affect is neutral rather than high in either positive or negative directions.

Symbolic Levels

The transition to symbolic thought involves not just the addition of a skill, but the reorganization of thought. Typically developing children make this transition quickly. Children with profound or severe retardation may never enter the symbolic stage. Other children with disabilities often plateau at the presymbolic levels for many months, or in some cases for years, before developing some symbolic abilities. Symbolic abilities involve the ability to allow one object to stand for another object and to transform and transcend immediate reality. Symbolic abilities develop in a variety of areas: play, art, language, mathematics, music. Within each of these areas, specific dimensions can be studied. Language can be studied in terms of its form (syntax), function (use), and content (semantics, vocabulary). Play can be considered along four dimensions:

- *Decontextualization and object substitution.* This trend allows play to occur with decreasing environmental support or changing reliance on props (from realistic, to abstract, to invented) and increasing use of language.
- *Thematic content.* Play themes develop from themes in which the children have been frequent active participants, to themes in which they have participated less frequently, to themes they have only observed, and finally to themes they have invented.
- *Organization of themes.* Sequential combinations or integrations of actions lead to sequentially and later hierarchically organized play with greater coherence and complexity of action representations (Bretherton, 1984; Rubin, Fein, & Vandenberg, 1983).
- *Self–other relationships or decentration.* This dimension frees symbolic actions from children's own bodies, allowing them to adopt the roles of others in pretend activities and include others in their pretend. Development of theory of mind is critical for development in this dimension.

Symbolic Level I: 17 to 19 Months

At this stage, the children exhibit the beginning of representational and symbolic pretend play. Internal mental representational abilities underlie the beginning of decontextualization. Children are able to find a toy that has been hidden invisibly (as when it is placed in a box and the box is emptied under a scarf) and they exhibit tool-use ability (e.g., moving a chair to climb on it to get something out of reach, or attaining a toy using a stick). They use toys and objects not only functionally, but also in pretend. Now they are willing to pretend to drink when there is nothing in the cup. Because of their internal representational abilities, they also recognize that a solid ring cannot be stacked, and they will put it aside without attempting to place it on a ring stand.

Peer interactions at this level are limited and not sustained. The majority of approaches are not reciprocated, and those that are reciprocated generally last for only one exchange (Fein & Schwartz, 1986). Children require life-size, realistic props in order to engage in pretend play. They represent in pretend actions only those highly familiar events, such as washing, eating, or sleeping, in which they have personally participated on a daily basis. Their pretend schemas or scripts consist of single behaviors or isolated schemas, and the children move quickly from one pretend action to another. For example, children may pretend to sleep, then abruptly pretend to eat, with no links between these events. They engage in autosymbolic or self-representational pretend play—that is, practicing their own activities on themselves outside of their usual context. The children do not extend these pretend activities beyond themselves to other animate or inanimate objects in their environment.

The emergence of tool use and symbolic play abilities have been closely linked to the emergence of true language (Bates et al., 1979; Lifter & Bloom, 1998). There is rapid development of single words that code a variety of semantic relationships. Frequency of symbolic play has been linked to the diversity of semantic relationships used (Tamis-LeMonda & Bornstein, 1993). Children not only label objects, people, and actions, but they also use language (1) to acknowledge ("see," "look"); (2) to indicate that something does not exist or has disappeared ("allgone"), or that either something has appeared again or they want it to recur ("more," "'gain," "too"); (3) to reject and deny ("no"); or (4) to indicate that an object or person is associated with another person or object ("daddy chair"). Language serves a variety of communicative functions focusing on imminent actions related to children's needs and desires. Much of the language that accompanies play from 17 months to the 2 $^1/_2$- to 3-year level, involves (1) directing of others in the play environment (commanding: "put the baby in the high chair"; seeking attention: "look"), (2) maintaining self-rights (protesting: "I don't wanna"; "gimme, that's mine, you can't have it"), and (3) labeling or commenting on ongoing action ("Baby's sleeping. I put baby bed." "Change diaper.").

Symbolic Level II: 19 to 22 Months

In this stage, children continue to be dependent on realistic props to initiate and maintain pretend play, and they continue to represent in play only those events that they themselves have directly experienced. The pretend representations, however, include not only reenactments of their own activities, but also reenactments of activities of familiar others in their environment, such as cooking like mom, shaving like dad, or reading a book like big brother. Their pretend scripts continue to be brief and isolated from other scripts, but their constructions increase; children begin to combine two actions on a doll or two toys for use in the scripts (e.g., rocking the doll and then putting it to bed, pouring from a pitcher into a cup, feeding a doll from a plate using a spoon, or putting a lid on a pan). Children extend the pretend scripts beyond themselves to others in the environment and to dolls. They pretend to feed a parent or another child. A doll functions as a passive recipient of the children's actions. Children comb a doll's hair, feed it a bottle, or put it to bed. This beginning elaboration of scripts or schemas results from the child's developing awareness of interrelationships among objects and people. With the emergence of action and object combinations in play appears the emergence in language of true word combinations having a variety of semantic relationships, such as the following:

Agent-action: daddy come
Action-object: throw ball
Agent-object: daddy (throw) ball
Attribution: big dog
Dative: give (to) mommy
Action-location: run home
Object-location: cookie table
Possessive: daddy chair

It should be noted that not all children are word-by-word language learners; some children are gestalt or "chunk" language learners (Peters, 1983). They learn whole phrases as single words (e.g., "get out," "what's that," "let's go to McDonalds"). These words appear only as part of specific phrases and are not combined in novel ways as in true two-word combinations. At this stage, earlier language functions continue, but now children also use language for heuristic purposes—to request information and to learn about the world. Their sensorimotor knowledge is consolidated, and they possess internalized action schemas that make it possible for them to refer to nonpresent people and objects.

Symbolic Level III: 2 Years

The themes at this level are still highly familiar participatory ones. Children will engage in reversed roles with adults (particularly the mother)—"I'll play you and you play me"—but are not likely to engage in this type of interactive play with their peers (First, 1994). Between ages 2 and 3 years, children vary considerably in pursuit of collaborative play ventures, with the majority still uninterested in negotiating shared activities. For most children, play themes focus on common household activities such as cooking, eating, sleeping, cleaning, and so on. This is true even for boys. If children have other common experiences in their everyday lives, they will reenact these. For example, the father of a 2-year-old boy worked on several cars that sat in the family's yard. The son spent a lot of time with his father "fixing" cars, and so in play pretended to fix cars.

The primary change in pretend play at age 2 years is seen in the organization dimension. The pretend scripts are still isolated—that is, children do not represent a sequence of events—but the individual events or scripts can become highly elaborated because children know the kinds of objects that generally appear together in the world. When children pretend to cook and eat or put a doll to bed, they know the many materials that are associated with these activities and will search for and ask for them. Children will set a table, making certain that each person or doll receives a plate, a glass, and a spoon. The baby doll must sit in a high chair and wear a bib; bigger children sit in standard chairs. Some children are fascinated with organizing the toys—lining up boxes, putting pans in one place, dishes in another, and utensils in another. In their language, children comment on the doll's behavior ("baby sleeping") or their ongoing activities ("I get apples"), using short sentences that may include *ing,* plural, and possessive markers.

Symbolic Level IV: 2 1/2 Years

The major change at this stage is in the thematic content of the play. Children begin to represent events they have personally experienced less frequently. These events have been particularly memorable, because they are either pleasurable or traumatic. With normally developing children, common scripts that emerge are shopping or doctor play. As these scripts emerge, children begin to engage in reversibility of roles beyond "I'll play you and you play me." Now the game is expanded to include other dyadic or complementary roles, "I'll play x and you play y" (doctor/patient, cooker/eater, cashier/shopper). They will talk to the doll ("baby go sleep"; "drink your milk"). They do not, however, project feelings or desires onto the doll. At this time, play scripts have only the organization that appeared at age 2 years. The child may fill a grocery cart with food, put the doll in the seat, and walk up and down the hall pushing the cart; or the child will use each of the items in a doctor kit on another child or a doll. Although these scripts appear early, they will require many years before they are complete. By late elementary school, children will understand the exchange of money for goods, that one receives change if one gives more than the cost of the item, as well as what causes some illnesses and how illnesses are treated.

As children at this stage attend to and remember greater detail in their experiences, they also begin to use language selectively to analyze their perceptions. This analysis enables children to give appropriate syntactic and semantic responses to *who, what, whose, where, what ... do* questions. Children could, of course, answer these questions as early as 17 to 19 months, but at that time the child was totally dependent on contextual cues to know what was expected. The child responded only when the referent was specifically pointed out (e.g., if the object or action was the focus of attention). At age 2 $^1/_2$ years, the child can remember the question, look around the environment, and match the question to the activity. For example, at 19 months, children may correctly respond to the question, "Who has the ball?" when their attention is directed to the person. At age 2 $^1/_2$ years, children hear the question, can themselves look around the group of children, locate the child, and then answer. They are now asking questions by placing the *wh* word at the beginning of a sentence, such as, "Where the duck is?" They are likely to ask *why* questions, particularly in response to negative statements made by an adult ("don't touch that" or "you can't have a cookie"), but they do not necessarily listen to the response, nor do they comprehend it if they do listen. With the exception of well-known routines (e.g., "Why is the doctor here?" ... "baby's sick"), children's answers to *why* questions are inappropriate or limited to "cause." Although they seldom answer a *why* question appropriately, they recognize that *why* is different from other *wh* questions.

Symbolic Level V: 3 Years

Three-year-olds continue the pretend themes of the earlier stages; however, they begin to combine isolated scripts into multischeme sequential episodes (e.g., setting the table, cooking, serving and eating a meal, clearing the table, and then washing the dishes; or checking the baby, deciding it's sick, dressing it, taking it to the doctor, and then giving it medicine). With competent older children or adult players, they may engage in multiple reversible roles in a play episode, being a doctor, a nurse, a mother, while the co-player is always the patient ("I'll be a and b, while you be x") (First, 1994). The sequence of events evolves—one activity leading to the next—rather than being planned ahead. With peers, children engage in associative rather than full cooperative play. They play alongside each other, using similar materials and representing similar themes (e.g., everyone playing in the household area cooking and eating food), but they do not coordinate their activities with each other, and they have no organized goal or direction for the play.

Children now also modify scripts of their own personal experiences so that the outcomes are more favorable. For example, Nancy had recently been to the hospital for a tonsillectomy. Her mother had not been permitted to stay with her after her admission. In reconstructing the event with a doll, Nancy took the role of the doctor, and the speech therapist took the role of the mother. In her doctor role, Nancy told the mother that she would have to leave. The mother made several requests to stay. The child turned away, whispered to an imaginary nurse, then announced, "We decided it would be a very good thing for moms to stay with their little girls in the hospital." The emergence of evolving sequential scripts signals a cognitive basis for the use of language for reporting (referring to past or earlier events) and for predicting (language referring to possible future events) and the associated appearance of use of past tense and future aspect markers, such as "will" and "gonna." This ability to talk about the past and future sets the stage for narrative language. Narrative language involves an extended monologue sustained by the speaker, rather than a series of short utterances and interactive language between two parties, as occurs in dialogue. This is the beginning of storytelling and the emergence of decontextualized language that is associated with literate language skills and later success in reading and writing.

Symbolic Level VI: 3 to 3 1/2 Years

Very quickly after typically developing children engage in sequences of scripts or schemas, they exhibit growth in decontextualization abilities, thematic content, and knowledge of self–other relationships. Marked changes occur in development of explicit and implicit metacommunicative skills—the ability to use language to talk about communication:

> Explicit metacommunication: "Let's play ninja turtles."
> Implicit metacommunication: "I'm Donnatello!"

With metacommunication skills, children are better able to adopt a shared pretend focus, mark their interactions as pretend, as well as relate to other's intentions in a pretend activity (Goncu, 1993). They now begin to attempt to negotiate play with peers.

Children become less dependent on realistic, life-size props. They can use miniature props and replica toys, such as doll houses and Fisher-Price and Playmobil play sets. Fisher-Price figures, which have heads on cylinders, are less realistic than dolls that have arms and legs. One 4-year-old boy with language impairment did not recognize these replicas and rejected playing with the Fisher-Price farm people when his mother suggested that the man was driving the tractor by saying, "no man, no arms, no legs, no man." Children at this stage can engage in object transformations, proclaiming that a chair is a car or that a block is an airplane, a book, or a meat loaf. They can use blocks to build structures—fences, houses, barns—whereas earlier, they simply stacked blocks to knock them down. If small replica toys are included in the block area, children will incorporate them in the play situation.

Domestic play continues, but its frequency diminishes, especially for boys. In addition to representations of events in which they have been personally involved, children now add scripts for events that they may have observed in the community or on television, but in which they were not active participants, for example, police officer and firefighter scripts, or slightly later, scripts for Hercules, Batman, Zena, Power Rangers, or other popular movie or television figures. Children proclaim their roles and assign roles to others ("I'm Batman, and you're the Joker"; I'm the good guy, and you're the bad guy"). This is also the stage at which children's play becomes more aggressive. Carlsson-Paige and Levin (1987) suggest that war play represents a necessary developmental stage of seeking independence. Play characters attack, shoot, and kill one another. Even if parents and preschools prohibit toy guns and swords, children will use sticks, brooms, and fingers to shoot each other. The ability to represent these observed scripts through the use of replica toys in play requires that children project a role onto the replicas. The dolls, figures, and puppets become active agents or participants in the play. Children talk for dolls and puppets. Shortly after children begin to talk for replica toys, they also engage in reciprocal role taking, first talking as a child for the doll, and then talking as a mother to the doll. For example, 3 1/2-year-old Jerem first asked a puppet, "Do you want some orange juice?" and then responded "no" for the puppet in a high squeaky voice.

Role taking requires the ability to project into the thoughts and feelings of others and to convey this knowledge through language. Integration of knowledge of past, present, and future events, and other peoples' actions, thoughts, and feelings permits reasoning regarding the interrelationships among these components of the physical and social worlds. In using language for projective purposes, children give dialogue and personality to dolls and puppets. This ability to project into the thoughts and actions of others requires perspective taking, reflective of increasing growth in development of a "theory of mind" (Bretherton, McNew, & Beeghly-Smith, 1981).

With this ability to project arises metalinguistic language such as "He said," "I think," "I forgot," "I know," "I remember" (Wellman, 1985). Metacognitive language is associated with the ability to plan ahead, to self-monitor, to self-question, and to self-correct. Awareness of the internal mental states of others and the ability to plan and monitor behavior enable children to modify their speech for politeness purposes and for the needs and status of different listeners, simplifying their speech for a younger child and adding politeness and deference features for adults. Children begin to negotiate play with each other. They will initiate complementary role play in which differentiated roles are assigned, but the roles are played independently.

A marked growth in descriptive vocabulary language occurs as children attend to attributes of objects and characteristics of people in constructing their representations and in substituting or transforming objects for the purposes of the play. These transformations require that children recognize similarities and differences in the real and pretend objects and in the critical attributes of objects in order to substitute one for another.

Symbolic Level VII: 3 1/2 to 4 Years

Changes in this level involve increasing decontextualization and elaboration of the thematic content, organization, and self–other relationships that emerged between ages 3 and 3 1/2 years. By 3 1/2 years, children are able to use gestures and language to set the play scene. For example, one 3 1/2-year-old waiting in a doctor's office put her stuffed dog on a chair near her, climbed on another chair, reached forward as though to turn a key, and then pretended to drive a car. She stopped driving, then commented to her brother, "Tony, we're watching a movie. It's a movie about a kitty." Her autistic older brother looked at the stuffed dog and replied, "That's a doggie," to which his sister responded, "I know Tony. I know it's a doggie, but pretend it's a kitty."

The sequence of pretend events in this level does not simply evolve, but rather it is planned, and the planning may take as long or longer than the actual pretend play. With this planning comes improvisation of the play themes. Children are able to hypothesize about future events and to solve problems through actions that they have not experienced or observed. For example, a group of 4-year-olds decided to build a church. Some children systematically searched through the blocks to find archlike pieces of wood that could be used as windows, while others looked for narrow pieces of wood that could be used as pews. In another instance, several children planned a pretend birthday party. They assigned roles to different children (mother, father, baby, boy who was having the birthday, teacher, friend), wrote invitations to the party, decorated the room, planned what gifts to buy, and then proceeded to play through the preparations and the party itself. In still another instance, a girl announced that she was having a sale at her store. She then organized many of the items around the room into categories and "displayed them" before announcing that her store was open for business.

The self–other relationship becomes more elaborated in this stage. Children exhibit both a landscape of action (what the play characters do) and a landscape of consciousness (what characters think and feel) in their play (Bruner, 1986). Children begin to recognize that any individual may function in more than one role. For example, a woman may be a wife, a mother, and a business executive; a man may be a husband, a father, a doctor, and an uncle. Each of these roles requires different language and interaction patterns used in different contexts. Dolls and replica figures become more than partners in children's play. They now come to life. Children use dolls and replica figures to act out entire scripts. The ability to use both landscape of action and landscape of consciousness in play involves the use of multiple voices. Children are able to be the voices of several characters, having the characters interact with each other (and not with the child who is managing them), and to assume multiple roles for each character (Wolf & Hicks, 1989). Four-year-old Jenny, playing with a set of Fisher-Price squirrels—a mother, a father, and a little boy—spontaneously took the roles of both the mother and the wife. In the role of the mother, she spoke to the little boy squirrel: "Take your bath and put on your blue pajamas. Then you can watch TV and have some cookies. Okay, you've watched enough TV. Time to go to bed. I'll kiss you goodnight." She put the boy squirrel in the house, then turned to the father squirrel and in a different tone of voice said, "We really should think about having another baby. Maybe we should talk to the doctor about it."

By this age, children use multiple voices not only as they play multiple characters, but also as they organize the play. They can smoothly switch their own roles during play, ranging from outside the play frame to within it. They can take the role of a character ("I'm cooking macaroni and cheese for dinner."), act as a stage manager for the props ("There's not enough fire hose. Can you get some string?"), and speak as the author of the play story ("Now the mother squirrel decided to have a birthday party for her little boy."). Consider the following example of Matthew acting out the story of *Stellaluna,* a fruit bat that is raised by birds. In one voice, Matthew described the action in the play, in a second voice he gave dialogue to the characters, and in a third voice he commented on the play activity itself.

Narrative	Dialogue	Stage-Managing
Matthew has a large and small fruit bat puppet and some plastic foods on the floor. He wraps the small bat in the wings of the large bat and has it fly.		
Momma bat went flying with Stellaluna. She dropped Stellaluna.		
He has the mother bat drop the baby bat.		
	Ohhh nooo! I'm falling.	
		I need something for a bird nest. You gotta box?
(Teacher gives Matthew a small box. He takes a doll blanket and puts it in the box).		
Stellaluna fell in a bird nest. The baby birds were surprised. They never saw a bird like her.		

> Momma's gonna feed us
> some good grasshoppers.
>
> You got any bugs?

(Teacher gives Matthew a box of plastic bugs.) Holding Stellaluna, Matthew says:

> These are yucky. I want
> some pears.

Children who can plan such events will generally verbalize their intentions about future events and their predictions, and they will hypothesize by using modals, such as *can, may, might, would, could, will,* and conjunctions such as *and, but, so, because, if ... then.* This is in accord with reports that children begin to reason about perception and use hypothetical statements at 4 years of age (Blank, Rose, & Berlin, 1978). For example, a group of children were playing doctor, and several of them decided that the patient had died. The child playing doctor objected, saying he had cured the patient. The play "mother" of the patient insisted that the patient had died because the ambulance took too long to come and because the doctor did not know what he was doing. The child playing the doctor responded, "Well, if he died, then you gotta cry, call the priest, and bury him." This is only the beginning use of modals and conjunctions and does not indicate that the child has full competence of these linguistic forms. Children will be nearly 12 years of age before they have full mastery of these terms (Beilin, 1975).

Symbolic Level VIII: 5 Years

By age 5 years, play can be completely decontextualized. Children can use language alone to define scenes, roles, actions, and invented objects in the play. Changes also occur at this level in the thematic content and organization dimensions. The themes expand to include events in which the children themselves have neither participated nor observed. Children are able to integrate information from their own experiences and observations in novel ways with knowledge of the physical and social world to develop elaborate themes about astronauts, pirates, scientists, or friendly monsters. For example, 6-year-old Daryl arranged a set of Playmobil cowboys and Indians around a wagon and campfire. On the periphery of this arrangement, he placed the Star Wars robots, R2D2 and C3PO. He then flew in Luke Skywalker's X-wing fighter ship and announced, "Boy, will those cowboys and Indians be surprised when they meet C3PO and R2D2," and he proceeded to act out a conflict of cultures. Although he had seen numerous cowboy movies and had seen Star Wars several times, he had never seen what might happen if cowboys encountered Star Wars characters.

By age 5 years, children not only can plan out their own behavior in play, but they also can plan and monitor the roles and behaviors of others. This is most frequently seen in the more competent children in kindergarten classes, who announce the play theme, everyone's role in the play, and precisely what each child is to say, how they are to say it, and when and where they are to say and do it. They now engage in full cooperative play. The role structures of the play are integrated—the activities of each player are tied to the activities of others, and in their roles, they express reciprocity among players. Children's use of both implicit and explicit metacommunication increases.

Children who are able to decontextualize their play completely use a literate-style language characterized by use of temporal and causal conjunctions and noun phrases elaborated by adjectives and prepositional phrases. In order to coordinate the complex scenarios of this stage, children must have command of a variety of complex semantic and syntactic structures that enable them to coordinate and subordinate events. They must be able to indicate which events are to occur simultaneously by using the conjunction *and;* they must be able to indicate temporal relationships among events by using relationship terms, such as *then, when, first, next, while, before, after;* they must be able to indicate clearly who is to perform the activities and how they are to be performed by using explicit descriptions requiring elaborated noun phrases or relative clauses, such as "the big black dog that bit the little boy" (Beilin, 1975; Pelligrini, 1985). As with the modals and conjunctions of Level VII, children will be almost 12 before they develop full competence with these linguistic elements.

PLAY ASSESSMENT PROCEDURES

The play scale presents developmental levels from ages 8 months through 5 years, but the scale has been used with students with learning disabilities through the middle school grades (sixth through eighth grade). In conducting a play assessment, several issues should be considered: (1) the child's past experiences; (2) the environment for the play evaluation, and (3) the adult's role in the evaluation process.

Cultural Considerations

Children's environmental and cultural backgrounds affect the manner in which they play and the materials and themes they use in their play (Roopnarine, Lasker, Sacks, & Stores, 1998). The interrelationships between children and families and nature of family values and beliefs vary and these differences affect the roles children assume in play. Certain principles of the physical world hold for all children—fragile glass breaks when dropped on a hard surface; dry wood burns when placed in a fire; objects fall down not up; and so on. Some aspects of the physical world vary across different groups of children. Rural children see tractors, cows, pigs, and chickens; city children see firetrucks, police cars, pigeons, and squirrels. Children on the northeast coast see oceans, snow, ice, and sailboats. Children in the southwest inland regions see desert, cactus, rattlesnakes, and dry arroyos (gulches).

Some themes are similar in all cultures. People all over the world eat, sleep, work, get sick, help others, and hurt others. The details of these themes can, however, vary. Some people eat grubs, some eat cows, and some eat only vegetables; some people work in offices, others on ranches. Some fix cars; others fix computers. Some themes are culture specific.

Sutton-Smith (1972) suggested that the nature of play is different in Western technological cultures and traditional cultures. Traditional cultures tend to be ascriptive cultures; children in these cultures engage in play that is primarily imitative and that relies on realistic toy representations. Children in Western achievement-oriented cultures engage in considerable make-believe transformations. In addition, there is evidence showing that adult attitudes about pretend play greatly influence the likelihood of children's pretend play. Cross-cultural research has shown that pretend play is virtually absent in some societies and rich and diversified in others. Consequently, care must be taken when using play assessment with children from other than Western mainstream cultures or with children whose parents or other key caregiving adults discourage some or all uses of pretend play.

Much of children's play is done with other children, with little involvement from adults. In dominant Western culture homes and preschools, however, adults often structure the environment and encourage or modify the nature of children's play. They may suggest themes or variations in themes, and they may actually take a role within the play. Adult guidance of play is especially common for children with disabilities, who may come to view adult guidance as an essential part of a play experience. In other cultures, adults neither structure nor are involved in children's play. In fact, adult intrusion into the play activities may quickly result in their cessation.

Before beginning any play assessment, the evaluator should gather information regarding the child's experiences: Where does the child live? What kinds of activities go on in the homes and in the neighborhood? In what kinds of activities do children in the home and community participate? Are there differences for boys and girls? If one's work is limited to a particular part of a community, this may not be necessary for every child. When one is responsible for evaluating children from a variety of environmental, cultural, and socioeconomic backgrounds, however, this information is critical if one is to interpret children's play correctly.

Structuring the Play Assessment Environment

Available Toys

A comprehensive play assessment requires a well-provisioned playroom. Children require environmental support to facilitate retrieval of play schemas. There should be a variety of toys representing differing cognitive developmental levels, sexual preferences, and themes. Children under 18 months of age require a variety of manipulative toys and cause–effect toys: toys that can be mouthed, squeezed, pushed, pulled; toys with different textures—soft, silky, rough; toys that can be opened and closed; toys that can be taken apart and put together; toys that make music or move; toys such as rattles, busy boxes, windup toys, jack-in-the-boxes, string-pull toys, and pull toys; and talking toys. Children in the early stages of symbolic play require high-realism toys to bolster their newly emerging representational skills. High-realism toys help children portray more exact detailed actions and contribute to their feeling that they are behaving like adults, but they may limit creativity. Low realism toys can be more conducive to creative fantasy, but only if the children are at the level where they can use such toys. Low-realism toys can set a broader context for pretend by suggesting thematic scenarios that call for role and situational transformations.

For children functioning in the symbolic levels, play materials should include familiar and unfamiliar play materials and materials at varying levels of representation (i.e., materials that are realistic and materials that are not realistic). Toys should be available that allow for play centered on familiar and unfamiliar themes. Small representational toys should be available that may reflect things the children have witnessed in their environments—these can include firefighters and police officers; action sets for villages, airports, farms; and activity sets that are highly imaginative, such as space ships and castles.

Organization of Materials

A formal playroom is best for play evaluations because it facilitates the child's initiation of play activities. Toys should be grouped according to their developmental level. Children should be able to move easily between areas in the room, but the areas should be separate enough so that the child is not distracted by materials in other areas. The room should have the following sections:

- *Presymbolic area.* For children functioning under 17 months who are not yet engaging in pretend play, toys should include rattles, windup toys, talking toys (Mattel See 'n Say, talking animals, talking telephones), busy boxes, musical toys, push toys, soft stuffed animals. The toys should require the use of a variety of motoric schemas and should involve a variety of causes and effects.

- *Familiar, high-realism toy area.* For children between 18 months and 3 years, this area should provide children with highly realistic props to represent themes they have personally experienced. At a minimum this area should include:

  - A home area containing dolls, doll bed, high chair, doll carriage, kitchenette with sink, stove, refrigerator, cooking utensils, cooking appliances (mixer, blender, toaster), pretend foods, cleaning tools, dress-up clothes, small table and chairs, and telephone.

  - A store area containing a cash register, play money, shopping cart, miniature food, telephone (preferably intercom connected to house area).

  - A doctor's kit (if the playroom is large enough, a separate area near the home and store area can be designated as the doctor's office, but this is not essential).

  - Area with small representational toys and low-realism toys on familiar and unfamiliar themes. This area includes a large dollhouse; large blocks; a sandbox; Lego block sets; Mattel, Fisher-Price, and Playmobil play sets (e.g., airport, farm, village, service station, mine, space station); X-Men, Batman, Power Rangers, and other figures; and puppets. Blocks and construction sets should be placed with small representational toys because children will often build structures and then use the small figures and vehicles around the structures.

If space is available, the room can have additional areas:

- *A gross motor area.* This might include a slide, steps, a walking board, a tunnel, riding toys, scooter boards, and a net swing. This can allow for evaluation of motor skills during the play evaluation and can be used to trigger more imaginative play in the older children (e.g., suggesting that the steps are a mountain, the slide is a ski run, or the swing is an airplane).

- *An area with realistic props devoted to specific thematic play.* These themes might center on a doctor's office/hospital, a bakery, a shoe store, airport, or a restaurant. These areas are particularly useful for exploring the thematic knowledge of older children with disabilities.

Although a playroom setting is best for the evaluation, if one is not available, it is possible to obtain a good estimate of a child's play by presenting a child with selected toys. In doing a play assessment in this way, however, evaluators must be careful that they do not overly direct the children's play.

Conducting the Evaluation

In preparing for a play assessment, the evaluator should:

- Determine the specific purpose for the evaluation. Why was the child referred for evaluation? What questions do parents or teachers hope to have answered by the assessment?

- Gather information about the child's typical functioning, activities, and preferences. Interview those who know the child.
- Based on the information obtained, determine the play materials to be used in assessment, who should conduct the assessment, and the appropriate format and sequence of the assessment.

Estimating Developmental Level

The diagnostic evaluation can be expedited by having an estimate of the child's developmental level before beginning the play evaluation. If the evaluator has no idea of the child's level, time is lost because the child tends to explore a wide variety of toys. This may not be a problem if there is unlimited time to conduct the evaluation, or if the child is in therapy and will be seen for numerous sessions. For most diagnostic evaluations, however, there is a limited amount of time in which to complete the assessment. If evaluators do not place some structure on the assessment and make some selection of the play materials, they will not discover the full range of the child's play skills. Even children capable of playing at high symbolic levels will usually be attracted to appealing cause–effect manipulative toys intended for toddlers. Once children become enthralled with a set of toys, it can be difficult to move them onto other, more age-appropriate toys. For this reason, it is best initially to present children with toys at their estimated developmental play level.

Estimates of children's developmental levels can be obtained through formal and informal interviews with family members and through standardized tests. Ethnographic interviewing techniques can be used to discover the types of activities in which the children engage at home and how they compare to other children. Formal cognitive standardized tests such as the Bayley Scales of Infant Development, the Mullens, or the McCarthy Scales are useful for infants and preschool children. Performance on these tests cannot be used to predict children's play abilities, but it can provide guidelines of the possible range of play abilities. For example, a 3-year-old child whose performance on the Bayley scales is at a 15-month level is unlikely to be able to engage in symbolic play. A 5-year-old performing in the 4-year age range on the McCarthy Scales should be able to engage in play with small representational toys; consequently, one need not begin the evaluation with cause–effect toys.

The Adult's Role in the Evaluation

After estimating the child's play level, the evaluator should present the child with toys appropriate to this estimated level. If a playroom is being used, take the child to the area appropriate for his or her developmental level. For children functioning below 3 years of age, it is usually best not to overwhelm the child with many toys at once. Because even very young children have preferences, however, a variety of toys should still be presented.

If the child comes from an environment in which adults seldom engage in pretend play with children, it is usually best to have at least one additional child in the playroom, preferably a sibling or a friend. Initially, let the child or children play on their own. Position yourself so that the child(ren) can include you in the play. The amount of time given to child-initiated activities varies, depending on what the child does. Try to become aware of the children's goals and to facilitate their intentions without taking over the play. For assessment purposes, the evaluator wants to determine the full extent of the child's play skills. If, after several minutes, the child has only looked at the toys and manipulated them, suggest an activity:

"The baby's hungry. Would you fix her some food?"
"My car's broken. Can you fix it?"

If the child does not respond, take a more active part in the play, and model the pretend activities, inviting the child to join you as a participant. For example, put a figure in a small car and have her or him drive to a gas pump and ask for gas; or pretend that a small figure has been hurt, call the doctor, and have the doctor check the person. If the child does not follow your lead, it may be that the theme is unfamiliar, the child is uncomfortable with the theme, or that the level of play is too advanced for the child. Ask the parent whether the child has had any experience with the themes you have introduced or whether, for any reason, the child would be hesitant to play a particular theme. Try a variety of toys and themes at that particular level. If the child still does not respond, drop to a lower level in the scale by using more realistic toys and/or using a more familiar play theme. For example, pretend to cook food on the stove, smell it, taste it, and offer it to the child. For children under age 3 years, use replicas of food—small boxes and cans and plastic foods. If the child responds to your suggestions, allow him or her to control the play as much as possible. Follow the child's lead. If the child is pretending to cook, then you pretend to be hungry and eat the food that is prepared.

Consider each play dimension as you carry out the assessment by asking yourself the questions for each of the play dimensions: How dependent is the child on realistic props? What themes does the child exhibit in play? How organized is the play? What self–other relationships does the child exhibit? If the child has been relying on realistic props, introduce less-realistic props (decontextualization). If the child has engaged in only home-centered activities, suggest going to the store or someone getting sick to bring in a doctor (thematic content). If the child has engaged in an evolving sequence, introduce planning by talking aloud to yourself as you plan a play theme (organization). If the child has acted on passive dolls or animals, talk for a doll (self–other relationships). Use the play scale as a guide for the concepts to be assessed. Children's play following a model will be higher than their spontaneously initiated play, but they will not follow a model if they do not comprehend the activities.

For play activities that the child spontaneously initiates, place an "S" (spontaneous) before the item on the scale. If you, a parent, or another child initiates the activity and the child follows and easily joins in, place a "J" (joins) before the item. If you model an activity and the child follows your lead but does not vary your presentation, place an "I" for imitation before the item. For young and low-functioning children, much of the play scale can be coded during the actual observation, but it is helpful to take notes describing the play and language used by the child during the session. Noting the child's verbalizations within the context in which they occurred is usually necessary to obtain an accurate assessment of the children's language. For older, more verbal children, the session should also be tape-recorded and the language sample analyzed.

INTERPRETING PLAY-LANGUAGE PERFORMANCE

Determining Play-Language Levels

For preschool children who exhibit an even pattern of development across play and language dimensions, a play and language level or range can be stated. An overall play level is often difficult to determine, however, when children exhibit different levels of performance in each of the play and language dimensions. If the child is of preschool age, the evaluator can give the age level for each play and language dimension. For school-age children, it is confusing and inappropriate to give age levels for play. The play scale is assessing behaviors not typically assessed, and saying that an 8-year-old child whose performance on formal testing is in the 6 $1/2$- to 7-year range is performing like a 2-year-old in organization skills (no sequential episodes) is not readily understood and accepted. Consequently, for older children, it is best simply to describe the child's play and language in each dimension. Parents and teachers will usually readily agree with a description that characterizes the child's language and behavior and explains some of the patterns they have seen. The remainder of this section describes the types of play and language patterns observed and their significance.

Patterns of Cognitive Test-Play Relationships

One function of the play evaluation is to relate children's performance on the play scale with their performance on formal or standardized cognitive tests. Children's play abilities may be commensurate with their performance on standardized testing or above or below their performance on standardized testing.

Commensurate levels on formal cognitive tests and play are the most common pattern and are usually seen in typically developing children from middle-class backgrounds. Such children have good social skills, have been encouraged to engage in symbolic play, and are familiar with the formal adult-child question-answer patterns of standardized testing—they know how to play the testing game. They have had practice in answering questions for which adults have the answers—the types of questions on tests.

The pattern of play abilities above cognitive testing levels is most frequently seen in typically developing children who are unfamiliar with the decontextualized test concepts and testing discourse patterns. They come from families in which the parents' role is primarily that of caregiver, and the primary role of peers is socialization. These children tend to lack experiences with the concepts and interaction patterns required by standardized testing. They do, however, have a good understanding of how the world works. Their play levels may be higher when playing with other children, rather than an adult.

Play levels below cognitive testing levels are very common in children who exhibit developmental delays due to medical, physical, or genetic influences. This may include premature infants, children with Down syndrome, specific language impairment, autism, or learning disabilities. Many items on formal standardized tests do not require the symbolic skills required in play. The language items on many of these tests require only single words or short phrases for responses that can be trained. Children can master many of the visual-perceptual tasks on formal tests through trial and error, and relatively high performance on these perceptual tasks raises their overall score. Many children who are referred for speech/language delays, and who exhibit average performance on formal tests, exhibit this pattern. Their speech/language delays are secondary to generalized cognitive deficits in the symbolic areas.

Play-Language Relationships

The play evaluation can provide particular insight into the child's understanding and use of language. The following relationships may exist between the child's play and language abilities:

1. Play = language form, function, and content
2. Language form, function, content > play
3. Play > language form, function, and content
4. Play > language form, but = language function and content
5. Language form > play and language content and function

The first pattern is characteristic of the majority of typically developing children and in a number of children with generalized developmental delays. In this pattern, all aspects of the children's language skills are commensurate with their play skills.

In the second pattern, all aspects of language slightly lead play. This pattern is most frequently observed in typically developing children from highly verbal environments. With such children, adults may use the children's language to guide them into more elaborate pretend play. Children with this pattern are very talkative, but may not have a complete understanding of everything they say.

In the third pattern, play leads all language skills. For some children, this is just a development style. For other children, it occurs because language requires all of the cognitive skills of play plus additional linguistic skills. For many young children with hearing impairment or with generalized developmental delays, their play skills are somewhat better than their language skills. This is most true when children's play skills are below the $3\frac{1}{2}$-year level or when children are second-language learners. Cognitive abilities are necessary but not sufficient for language. It is possible for children to carry out a simple sequence of events with little or no verbal communication. Language is so intertwined with play above the $3\frac{1}{2}$-year level, however, that it is less common to find children with disabilities with play skills at a 4- to 5-year level without commensurate language. High play levels with limited language are, however, seen with second-language learners. For example, one Vietnamese child who knew little English and who did not respond well to formal testing through an interpreter conducted highly elaborate play. He had a helicopter and the Star Wars X-wing fighter spaceship fly over the Mattel village. His actions suggested shooting, with people running and falling down. He had people from the Playmobil emergency set carry people away, and he pretended to bury the people.

The fourth pattern, in which the functions and content of the children's communication are commensurate with the play, while language form or syntactic structure is below these levels, appears to represent a very specific linguistic deficit. These children often have a history of unclear articulation. Such children may carry out sophisticated play themes, such as having a snow monster attack a spaceship they have built, but their language patterns are immature (e.g., "Me stop him. Him no hurt her. Monster break door now. Her run."). These children tend to be quite responsive to speech-language therapy, but they are at risk for learning problems in school.

The fifth pattern, in which the language form is above the children's play and the function and content of their language, is the least common. It is seen most frequently in children with autism or hydrocephalus. In severe cases, these children do not engage in any true symbolic play, but instead simply manipulate objects. They may be quite talkative, but their talk is often unrelated to what they are doing, or it consists of a limited number of scripts that are frequently repeated. The children are able to remember complex syntactic strings without comprehending their meaning.

Variation in Play Dimensions

From birth, infants show preferences. By the end of the first year, some children show clear preferences for interactions with objects or interactions with people. Object-oriented children spend much of their time exploring objects, and early words are requests or labels for the objects. They figure out how to use objects to solve problems. People-oriented or socially oriented children spend more of their time making contact with people, and their early words are often commands to make things happen (e.g., "up," "out") (Nelson, 1981). They figure out how to use people to solve problems. These object- versus social-oriented patterns can be lifelong characteristics. Children acquire some degree of skill both in dealing with people and in dealing with objects, but they may show a preference for one over the other. Children with disabilities occasionally show marked discrepancies between the two areas. Autistic children are often characterized as being object-oriented. They may have exceptionally strong skills in figuring out how objects work, but minimal understanding of how to relate to people. Children with Down syndrome have at times been characterized as more socially oriented. They are able to relate in socially appropriate ways to people but have less skill in determining how to use objects themselves.

At the symbolic level, children's play differs not only in terms of an object orientation or a social orientation, but also in terms of decontextualization, thematic content, organization, and self–other relationships. Each aspect of play is linked to different cognitive, social, and language abilities. Children above age $3^1/_2$ years with learning problems may exhibit wide variations in performance across the play dimensions. For example, a 5-year-old child may engage in age-appropriate themes, but without a clear sequence of events and with heavy dependence on highly realistic props.

Decontextualization

The ability to engage in decontextualized play has been linked to the use of decontextualized language—the style of language required for literacy success in school. Like the higher levels of symbolic play, reading and writing require the ability to comprehend and use language without the benefit of contextual support from the environment. Pellegrini (1984, 1985) reported that children's play was a powerful predictor of writing achievement in kindergarten and that children who exhibited greater decontextualization in their play also used more explicit language involving (1) endophoric reference (i.e., linguistic coding of referents rather than pointing and gesturing), (2) elaborated noun phrases,

(3) temporal and causal conjunctions, and (4) past tense and future aspect and metacognitive verbs.

Inability to use decontextualized language has been associated with lack of academic success (Michaels & Collins, 1984; Scott, 1994). Students with learning disabilities often exhibit deficits in the ability to decontextualize. This deficit was reflected in a middle-school (grades 6–8) language-learning disabilities classroom where students were playing with Lego blocks and Playmobil and Star Wars characters. Among themselves, the students had agreed to role-play a Santa Fe prison riot (a violent event that had recently occurred and that had commanded considerable media attention). One student began to worry because they had no way to escape. Another student suggested that he would build a car out of Legos and they could use this to escape to the forest. Another student rejected the idea saying, "It won't work—It won't look like a car."

Thematic Content

In play, children both display and further their scriptal knowledge. Having scripts or schemes for situations provides a sense of security. Scriptal knowledge provides knowledge of what is coming, how to behave, and what to say. Without this knowledge, the world is a frightening, unpredictable place. For years, child psychiatrists and psychologists have been using pretend play as a way to facilitate emotionally disturbed children's ability to understand and cope with their world (Schaefer & O'Connor, 1983). Children with disabilities often exhibit behavior problems in addition to learning problems. For some of these children, the behavior difficulties are related to their fear of the unknown and/or the limited options they have for coping. Children with autism spectrum disorders who do engage in play are likely to have few scripts or themes that they repeat in highly stereotypical ways. For example, 4-year-old Davin played in the kitchen area each day pretending to make macaroni and cheese. He thwarted all attempts to have him pretend to cook or bake any other foods.

The relationship between limited schema knowledge and emotional coping is exemplified by the following example:

Anthony, an 8-year-old language-disordered child, was enrolled in a program that provided frequent structured pretend play experiences. As part of a health unit, a pediatrician visited the program and allowed the children to explore all the tools in her black bag. She talked about how and why each tool was used. The teacher read the children books about doctors, such as *Your Turn, Doctor* (Robinson & Perez, 1982), a story in which the child performs the examination on the doctor. For several weeks, the children played doctor. They pretended to get sick, to have an accident, or to need a check-up for camp; they got ready to go to the doctor, drove in a car, or rode on a bus; they waited in the waiting room, acted as nurse, receptionist, doctor, parent, or patient; they examined patients or were examined themselves.

When Anthony's grandmother came for conference day, the teacher asked what significant changes she had noticed in Anthony. She responded that she was particularly pleased about changes in Anthony's behavior when she took him places, and most specifically when she had taken him to the doctor recently. She reported that in the past, she has always had to carry a screaming, kicking Anthony into the doctor's office. On this visit, Anthony walked into the doctor's office himself, sat down, tolerated the examination, and then announced, "It's your turn, Doctor."

Organization

The development of increasing organization or integration in play appears to reflect not only increasing understanding of the spatial, temporal, and cause–effect relationships within the physical and social world, but also increasing metacognitive skills that enable children to monitor their own behavior. Deficits in the organizational dimension of play may represent lack of understanding of the interrelationships within the physical and social world or deficits in the child's metacognitive abilities. Language is critical for the development of metacognitive self-control and self-monitoring behaviors, for it is largely through language that individuals plan their behavior (Luria, 1982). The ability to organize or plan play at advancing levels would appear to be highly dependent on a child's ability to use language to reflect on past experiences, to predict future experiences, and to reason about the relationships between past and future events.

Children with learning disabilities or attention deficit hyperactivity disorder (ADHD) characteristically exhibit deficits in organization abilities (Barkley, 1997; Miller, 1985; Wong, 1985). These organizational deficits have often been attributed to poor attention, but more recently, they have been viewed as reflections of more basic deficits in knowledge and metacognition. Patterson (1981) compared the play of three 7-year-old boys matched for intelligence: a normal 7-year-old boy and two boys with ADHD, one on medication and one not on medication. The boys with ADHD spent much of their time in the playroom looking around and manipulating toys, but not engaging in pretend play. The child with ADHD on medication spent more time with each toy than did the child not on medication, but he did not organize his play any better than the child not on medication. The boys with ADHD were less likely than the typically developing child to initiate a pretend theme. They readily joined the child without ADHD in pretend, but they often did not appear to be able to follow his suggestions for elaboration in sequencing of events and would, instead, replay the same aspect of an event over and over. For example, a fire truck would be rushed to a house, but they did not pursue the theme of putting out the fire, rescuing people from the burning house, and calling an ambulance (activities suggested by the boy without ADHD). Attentional issues alone could not explain all the differences between the boy without ADHD and the boys with ADHD. The boy with ADHD on medication stayed with the tasks and attended to the play, but he, like the boy with ADHD not on medication, did not initiate play themes, nor was he able to continue themes initiated by the child without ADHD.

Self–Other Relations

The distinction between self and others is critical to the development of emotional experience and to the understanding that emotional experience underlies all behavior of animate beings. This distinction is the basis for all social cognition. The theory of mind mechanism is especially critical for development of self–other relations. Awareness of one's own emotionality and the emotionality of others underlies communicative competence. Dore (1986) proposed that "the subsystems of communicative competence include FEELINGS between participants that motivate utterance FORMS used to effect various intentional and sequential FUNCTIONS relative to the contextual FRAMES in which they occur (Dore, 1986, p. 7).

Children with autism spectrum disorders exhibit long-term deficits in this aspect of play. They may manipulate toys through familiar scripts, but they are unlikely to attribute feelings and desires to dolls and animals.

Because written narratives are reports of character behaviors, it is imperative that readers recognize the feelings, intentions, and plans of characters (Bruce, 1980). Consequently, although many high-functioning autistic children learn to read words, they frequently fail to comprehend narratives that they read. Many poor readers may exhibit a deficit in ability to take the roles of characters in stories. Westby, Van Dongen, and Maggart (1986) explored oral and literate language skills in high-average and low-average fourth-grade readers. In one of the assessment tasks, students played together in dyads. The high-average readers were more likely to pretend that people were driving the battery-powered vehicles, and they imputed goals to the characters, such as taking over a mine, winning a race, or capturing space invaders. The low-average readers were more likely to line up the vehicles, turn them on, and watch to see which was the first to reach the other end of the room. The low-average readers exhibited significantly less mature play behavior, focusing on actions rather than role behaviors—a characteristic of younger children (Forbes & Yablick, 1984).

The distinction between self and others is seen in children's abilities to carry on multiple discourse roles in play (e.g., the roles of characters, stage manager, and narrator). Wolf and Hicks (1989) noted that these three types of discourse are encountered in reading a story: One reads the words uttered by the characters, description of the thought and actions in the story, and perhaps the narrator's reflection about the story.

CASE EXAMPLES

In this section, the play and language performances of two typically developing children and three children with disabilities are described and analyzed in terms of the play scale dimensions. The cases are presented as the sessions evolved, in an effort to convey both quantitative and qualitative differences among the children.

Play in Typically Developing Children

As Sember, a 26-month-old girl, plays in the kitchen area of the playroom, she sets the table, putting a plate and spoon in front of each chair. She pulls a high chair up to the corner of the table, puts a doll in the chair, and puts a bowl in front of the doll. She searches for a spoon, and when she does not find one, she looks toward her brother, points to the table, and says, "spoon." Her brother finds a spoon for her, and Sember then feeds the doll from the bowl using a spoon. She pretends to turn a faucet in the sink and fill a teapot with water. She puts the teapot on a stove burner, then turns the knobs of the stove, and says, "hot."

Sember finds the toy telephone, brings it over to the table where her mother is sitting, and hands her mother the receiver. The mother takes the phone, pretends to listen, then hands the phone back to Sember saying, "It's daddy. He wants to talk to you." Sember puts the receiver to her ear, listens, shakes her head "yes," and says, "uh huh, uh huh."

She finds a shopping cart, places her doll in the seat of the cart, walks down the hall looking back and forth between the walls (as though to check shelves), and places food items in her cart. Later during the play session, Sember makes a face from Play Doh, shows it to her brother, saying "monster, scare" and then, laughing, she chases her brother with the Play Doh face saying, "Here he come." Her brother gives a playful scream and runs. In this brief episode, Sember has conveyed considerable knowledge of the arrangement of objects and organization of events around her. Sember has exhibited age-appropriate play behavior. She engaged in pretend play but required realistic props. She combined toys in play and reproduced in play activities that she has participated in daily (cooking-eating) and less frequently (shopping). She was aware of some of the sequence of a cooking schema—filling a pot, putting it on a stove, turning the stove on; she was aware that plates and spoons go together and that generally a plate is put in front of each chair; she was aware that babies sit in high chairs, not in chairs around the table, and that they eat from bowls and not from plates. This pretend play reflects Sember's own experience at home, where she is the baby who sits in the high chair and eats from a bowl. She also showed awareness of emotional and behavioral reactions—that is, that monsters are scary, and people run from them. Sember carried out activities with a doll but did not treat the doll as an active participant in her play. During the session, the majority of Sember's communication was limited to two- and three-word utterances without morphological markers—a language level (19–22 months) below what would be expected considering her play levels. Sember has, however, had a history of frequent otitis media and had an ear infection during this particular session. The research literature documents that frequent otitis media does result in delayed speech/language development (Kavanagh, 1986).

Jerem, Sember's 3 1/2-year-old brother, exhibits even greater knowledge of the world, and he also experiments with this knowledge. Jerem finds a fire hat, puts it on his head, gets on the tricycle, announces he is a fireman, and speaks through the megaphone saying, "Where's the fire? Come on you guys. We hafta get to the fire!" He rides the tricycle to the dollhouse, gets off the tricycle, pulls up the Fisher-Price firetruck, raises the ladder, has firefighters climb up the ladder and carry dolls down the ladder, and puts the dolls in the Playmobil ambulance to take them to the hospital.

When Jerem joins Sember in pretending to eat a meal, he stops her and his mother when they begin to eat by reminding them, "We hafta pray." He cautions them, "Don't take too much," and "We'll save some for later," as he puts some of the food into the play refrigerator. He pretends to scoop food out of the containers. He asks a puppet, "Do you want some orange juice?" and then answers "no" for the puppet in a high squeaky voice. When Sember knocks some food on the floor, Jerem quickly finds the toy vacuum cleaner and sweeps up the pretend mess. Jerem clearly exhibits his sensitivity to social constraints around the dinner table. In this context, Jerem also uses compensatory play to develop the world as he would like it to be. His parents never have soda in the house, and snacks are generally limited to "health foods." When Jerem offers to serve drinks, he takes Pepsi cans from the refrigerator, gives himself two cans and his mother and sister each one can. He intentionally calls an empty cottage cheese carton ice cream and makes certain that he gets a double serving, saying, "two scoops for me and one for you."

Jerem is able to engage in pretend play without any props. Sember insists on having a plastic spoon when she pretends to eat, whereas Jerem pretends he is holding forks, spoons, or knives as he pretends to eat. At one point while eating, he comments, "It's raining outside" (in reality, it was not raining). He looks through an opening in a partition and calls to his imaginary friend, Boy, to come in out of the rain. He opens an imaginary door and offers Boy a seat at the table. When the evaluator asks where Boy had been, Jerem responds, "He was bad today, so he couldn't come with us in the car. He's late 'cause he had to run here."

Jerem's parents reported that Boy was Jerem's frequent companion and ally. They reported that one night when they went to their room, they found Jerem in their bed. They reminded him that he had his own bed and that he did not sleep in their bed. To this he responded, "Boy's sick in my bed. He's got the flu. You don't want me to sleep with someone who's sick, do you?" In this situation, Jerem has combined his pretend abilities with his knowledge of social rules and behavior to achieve his own ends. He realized that he must give a reason if he wanted to sleep in his parents' bed, and that reasons that focused on his own intent would generally not be sufficient. He can project into the thoughts and feelings of his parents to give an explanation they will accept.

Jerem spontaneously exhibited most of the play and language behaviors expected for a 3 $\frac{1}{2}$-year-old child. He played with less-realistic toys, and in fact, could use language to set the scene, as exhibited by his imaginary friend; he pretended themes that he had observed on television but had not actually been a participant in; he exhibited an evolving sequence in his play—both with the fire theme and with eating at the table; he engaged in reciprocal interaction with the puppet—both talking to it and talking for it; and he used language to report on earlier events, to predict what was coming next, to reason, and to report on what someone said. It is possible that Jerem may have been capable of more advanced play if the evaluator had suggested or modeled higher levels.

Play of a Toddler with Microcephaly

Sember's and Jerem's play is quantitatively and qualitatively different from what is often seen in children with disabilities. Rita was also 26 months old—the same age as Sember. She was referred for a developmental evaluation because her pediatrician was concerned about Rita's small head size—below the second percentile. On the Bayley Scales of Infant Development, Rita achieved an overall developmental quotient within the average range, although she exhibited a range of scores—passing puzzles and block-building tasks at a level of 30+ months, while failing to name the objects at the 18-month level and exhibiting difficulty on the tool-use (attaining a toy with a stick) and object-permanence tasks at the 17- to 19-month levels.

When Rita enters the playroom, she opens the doors beneath the sink and begins removing one kitchen item at a time, holding it up and showing it to her mother. She does not attempt to use any of the items appropriately, nor does she spontaneously attempt to interact with the doll. Rita's mother gives her the doll and a bowl and suggests that she feed the baby. Rita shakes the bottle, then goes to the play sink and attempts to reach the faucet. When she is unable to reach the faucet, she stands with her back to the sink and begins to whine. Her mother responds to her whining by moving a chair close to the sink and helping Rita climb onto it. When Rita can get no water from the faucet, she begins to scream, and does not calm until the evaluator brings her a pitcher of real water. Rita then pours the water back and forth between pitchers and bowls. When her mother reminds her that the baby is hungry, tells her to feed the baby, and gives her the bottle, Rita picks the doll up by the leg, lays it on the table, and mechanically puts the bowl to the baby's mouth. Because it appears that Rita does not understand pretend play, the evaluator presents some cause–effect toys. Rita spontaneously operates the busy box, the See 'n Say, and the jack-in-the box—toys that her mother says she has at home. When an unfamiliar activity set is presented, she pats at some of the knobs and levers but returns to the busy box. The evaluator places a windup truck (that is already wound) on the floor. Rita watches it move and then picks it up. she rolls it back and forth a few times but does not explore the toy carefully and does not discover the way to wind it. She gives the truck to her mother, watches her mother wind it, and after several demonstrations she begins to wind it. When the evaluator gives her a large plastic bottle with blocks in it, she quickly dumps the blocks out, then puts them in a pan, and empties them from the pan. Throughout the play session, the only words heard were "up" when she attempted to remove the basin from the sink, "off" when she turned the knobs on the sink, "spoon" as she gave her mother a spoon after her mother had requested it, and "bye" as she left the playroom. These words functioned more as comments on the setting than as requests or commands.

How different Rita's play is from Sember's. Sember spontaneously initiated the play activities, and her mother simply acted as a participant or extended what Sember had begun. Without the active involvement of her mother or the evaluator, Rita spontaneously engaged only in manipulation of objects. While Sember exhibited a clear understanding of the familiar situation around eating, Rita did not show awareness either of the functional uses of many of these objects or of which ones were to be used together. She also did not solve the problems that arose for her during the course of the play. For example, she did not spontaneously move a nearby chair to the sink when she wanted to reach the knobs (a common strategy for children, which demonstrates tool-use behavior). Although she fed the doll a bottle, it was never clear that she would have recognized the doll–bottle relationship herself, nor did she appear to be engaging in true pretend play. Instead, her actions on the doll seemed no more than a functional use behavior in response to an adult's demands. She had learned through imitation to operate familiar toys, but she did not exhibit the persistent exploratory behavior necessary to discover the operation of toys herself. When unsuccessful, she occasionally handed the toy to her mother, but more frequently she simply whined and did not actively seek her mother's assistance.

In many respects, Rita's behavior in the play session did not have the quality of true play. Rita's play did not appear to be intrinsically motivated, spontaneous, voluntary, or fun (Bronfenbrenner, 1979). Rita was dependent on adults to guide the play themes; otherwise, she resorted to repetitive manipulation of the toys. Her play also appeared to be serious business for her, like coping with real life. At no time did she indicate, either verbally or nonverbally, that "this is play," nor did she give any clue that she was enjoying the activity. Rita had been refused admission to a special preschool program because her developmental quotient was within an average range, and she was considered "simply language delayed." The play evaluation revealed that Rita's language delay was a reflection of broad-based cognitive deficits in symbolic thought and in her understanding of physical and social relationships in the world—knowledge that is not well tapped by traditional testing. Some of her interactions with the toys and her mother-suggested play behaviors were in the 13- to 17-month range, but she did not exhibit the quality and quantity of play behaviors expected within that age range. Communicative skills were characteristic of the 8- to 12-month period but without the quantity and quality expected at that level.

Play of a Preschool Child with Specific Language Impairment

Miguel, a 4-year-old Hispanic boy, was diagnosed with a specific language impairment. He was enrolled in a preschool program that served both typically developing children and children with disabilities. At the time of the play evaluation, Miguel had been enrolled in the program for 8 months. He reportedly had made marked gains in language skills during the year and tested at the 3 $\frac{1}{2}$-year level on the *Preschool Language Scale.* With the teacher and speech-language pathologist, Miguel could give brief picture descriptions, request what he wanted or needed, and follow common classroom instructions. The teacher and speech-language pathologist felt that Miguel was the highest functioning of the children with disabilities in the classroom and they had few concerns about his development. Miguel's mother was pleased with the language progress Miguel had made during the year, but expressed concern because "he doesn't play with his brothers and sisters."

Two typically developing boys, Andrew and Jose, are playing in the household area. One of the boys announces there is a fire, grabs a fire hose made from a toilet paper roll and crepe paper, and makes water noises as he pretends to spray water on the fire. Miguel stands off to the side and watches. Andrew and Jose then sit at the table and Andrew announces, "time for breakfast." He looks toward Miguel and says, "bring me some cereal." Miguel watches. Valerie, the speech-therapist intervenes and repeats, "Miguel, bring Andrew some cereal." Miguel complies, putting a small box of cereal on the table. "Milk, where's the milk?" asks Jose. Miguel stands by the table. Valerie says, "Miguel, go to the refrigerator." Miguel does so. "Get the milk." Miguel picks up a plastic milk bottle and brings it to the table. He continues to stand off to the side and makes no attempt to join the boys at the table. Andrew and Jose request utensils and other food items. Miguel dutifully brings each requested item, saying nothing as he does so. Valerie asks for eggs. She tells Miguel to put them in a pan and cook them. He does so, then puts the eggs on a plate, brings the plate to Valerie and says, "Here's your eggs."

Andrew and Jose leave for the store area. Miguel watches. Valerie suggests that Miguel go to the store. He follows Andrew and Jose to the store, puts on an apron, stands by the cash register, and punches the keys. As Andrew and Jose take items out of a shopping cart and put them on the counter, Miguel names them. Valerie models weighing and running items over the scanner. Miguel imitates her behavior. Valerie suggests that Miguel get a bag and put the items in it. Miguel does so. Valerie suggests that they drive back to the house. Miguel looks puzzled. Valerie puts Miguel in a chair, announces that it is a car, and pushes Miguel to the household area. Once back in the household area, Andrew and Jose tell Miguel the items they want for lunch. He brings each item as requested. After pretending to eat a variety of plastic food, Jose announces, "Time to clean up." Miguel takes the plates off the table, puts them in the sink, pretends to turn on the water, gets an empty soap dispenser from under the sink, pretends to squirt soap into the water, and then wipes the dishes and says, "all done."

Later in the day, Valerie introduces a new toy, an airport set with a terminal, two large toy planes that can hold several play people, a helicopter, luggage, and trucks to haul luggage. Andrew and Jose quickly begin exploring all the pieces. They put people in one of the planes, fuel the plane, load luggage, and have the plane fly off. Miguel hesitantly approaches the toys and reaches out to pick up an airplane. Without looking at him, Jose pushes Miguel's hand away from the toy. Miguel says nothing. He picks up the helicopter, which is separated from the other pieces, moves to the end of the mat, and sits by himself exploring how to operate the toy. He is not observed to engage in pretend with the helicopter.

Miguel exhibits broad-based symbolic deficits. With intervention, he has acquired a vocabulary and syntactic patterns that appear to be only slightly below age level. He is able to use these language skills in contexts in which they have been trained, but he does not readily transfer these skills to other contexts, suggesting that he does not fully comprehend the relationships represented by the words. His play is below his language performance on structured activities with adults. In the play evaluation, however, Miguel's play and language are both significantly below his chronological age; and, in fact, his language is below his play level. Miguel appears to have few play scripts. He followed instructions to cook some food and he spontaneously carried out a dish-washing sequence. He appeared unfamiliar with the shopping script, and he did not use small toys in pretend. He never really engaged in reciprocal role-taking; instead he simply reproduced a few highly familiar scripts. Miguel is dependent upon adult guidance in play, much like a 2- to 2 $^1/_2$-year-old; he appeared to have no strategies for negotiating play that are expected to be present in 3- to 3 $^1/_2$-year-olds.

Play of an Older Child with Learning Disabilities

The children described so far exhibited fairly even patterns of development. Play skills in each dimension were at a similar age level. As learning-disabled children get older, however, it is common to see more variability in their play performance. Andy, an 8-year-old boy who exhibited difficulty with reading comprehension, exemplifies this variable performance. The school reported that Andy is within the average range on cognitive testing and the speech-language pathologist reported that Andy performed within the low-average range on the Test of Language Development (Newcomer & Hammill, 1982).

In the playroom, Andy goes to the store area and explores the cash register. He puts money in the slots, presses keys, and opens and closes the drawer. Because of Andy's age and performance on standardized cognitive measures, the evaluator directs his attention to the small representational toys by sitting near the large dollhouse and suggesting that it is on fire.

Andy comes over to the house and begins to manipulate the firetruck and ambulance, fitting the small figures into them. The evaluator suggests that she needs help putting out the fire. Andy follows the evaluator's instructions to have firefighters climb the ladder and carry people out and put them in the ambulance, but he gives the evaluator a blank look when she suggests driving the people to the hospital. At this point, Andy becomes interested in the toy vehicles, particularly the battery-operated cars, and he suggests that they race them to the end of the room. He and the evaluator line up the cars and turn them on. As the cars rush across the room, one of the cars turns over. The evaluator comments, "Oh, I think the man in the car is hurt." Andy responds, "Men can't fit in that car." Andy then discovers the Star Wars spaceships. He takes one in each hand and flies them around the room, pressing the buttons to fire the guns. He makes explosion sounds and has the ships crash. They break apart; he puts them back together and repeats the activity. After one crash, the evaluator speaks for Luke Skywalker, "I'm hurt, I'm hurt. Get the doctor." She gives Andy the doctor kit and tells him to check Luke. Andy uses the stethoscope appropriately on Luke, gives him a shot, and says, "He's okay now."

Andy shows an interest in themes he has not personally participated in, but has witnessed on television. He can use the small representational props, but he does not use language to set the scene, as suggested by his ignoring the examiner's suggestions for any imaginary places (hospital) or characters (people driving cars). Andy exhibits interest in the themes played by children ages 3 $^1/_2$ through 4 years, but he does not organize his play or display the self–other interaction expected of children at that age level. Although he will follow through on someone else's suggested sequences of activities, he does not spontaneously initiate a sequential play episode. His play organization is more similar to that of the 2- to 2 $^1/_2$-year-old, who assembles items having similar functions. Andy acts on the toy figures, but he never engages in reciprocal interactions with them. He never credits the characters with intentions or feelings, and he does not talk for them. Because Andy did not spontaneously show age-level play behaviors, it was necessary for the evaluator to become more actively involved in the play session.

CONCLUSION

Play affects all of development and facilitates healthy development of emotions, convergent and divergent thought, language, literacy, impulse control, perspective taking, and socialization. If the effects of play are to be maximized for children with disabilities, teachers and therapists must know more than the children's IQ or mental age level on standardized tests. They must also understand children's present developmental levels in the multiple play and language dimensions if they are to plan the most appropriate intervention programs. Therapists' and educators' goals should be to help children to develop in each of the play and language dimensions:

- To facilitate children's ability to deal with decontextualization so that they can learn from text;
- To enable children to understand the temporal, cause–effect, and social relationships that exist in situations in the world (home, doctor's office, restaurant, stores, etc.);
- To promote children's ability to organize and monitor their own behavior so that they can become independent self-motivated learners;
- To nurture children's ability to interpret the needs, desires, and roles of others, and to recognize how to relate appropriately to these needs, desires, and roles so that they can play and work effectively with others; and
- To stimulate children's language so that they can reason, plan, and create.

With these skills, children can be both competent and confident.

REFERENCES

Barkley, R. A. (1997). *ADHD and the nature of self control.* New York: Guilford.

Baron-Cohen, S. (1987). Autism and symbolic play. *British Journal of Developmental Psychology, 5,* 139–148.

Baron-Cohen, S. (1995). *Mindblindness: An essay on autism and theory of mind.* Cambridge, MA: MIT Press.

Bates, E. (1976). *Language and context: The acquisition of pragmatics.* New York: Academic Press.

Bates, E., Benigni, L., Bretherton, I., Camaioni, L., & Volterra, V. (1979). *The emergence of symbols: Cognition and communication in seinfancy.* New York: Academic Press.

Bateson, G. (1955). A theory of play and fantasy. *Psychiatric Research Reports, 2,* 39–51.

Beilin, H. (1975). *Studies in the cognitive basis of language development.* New York: Academic Press.

Blake, I. (1994). Language development and socialization in African-American children. In P. Greenfield & R. Cocking (Eds.), *Cross-cultural roots of minority child development* (pp. 167–195). Hillsdale, NJ: Erlbaum.

Blank, M., Rose, S. A., & Berlin L. (1978). *The language of learning: The preschool years.* New York: Grune & Stratton.

Bloom, L. (1973). *One word at a time.* The Hague: Mouton.

Blum, E. J., Fields, B. C., Scharfman, H., & Silber, D. M. (1994). Development of symbolic play of deaf children, aged 1 to 3. In A. Slade & D. P. Wolf (Eds.), *Children at play* (pp. 238–260). New York: Oxford University Press.

Bretherton, I. (Ed.). (1984). *Symbolic play: The development of social understanding.* New York: Academic Press.

Bretherton, I., McNew, S., & Beeghly-Smith, M. (1981). Early person knowledge as expressed in gestural and verbal communication: When do infants acquire a "theory of mind"? In M. E. Lamb & L. R. Sherrod (Eds.), *Infant social cognition.* Hillsdale, NJ: Erlbaum.

Bronfenbrenner, U. (1979). *The ecology of human development: Experiments by nature & design.* Cambridge, MA: Harvard University Press.

Brooks-Gunn, J., & Lewis, M. (1982). Development of play behavior in normal and handicapped infants. *Topics in Early Childhood Special Education, 2* (3), 1–27

Bruce, B. C. (1980). Plans and social action. In R. J. Spiro, B. C. Bruce, & W. F. Brewer (Eds.), *Theoretical issues in reading and comprehension.* Hillsdale, NJ: Erlbaum.

Bruner, J. (1986). *Actual minds, possible worlds.* Cambridge, MA: Harvard University Press.

Carlsson-Paige, N., & Levin, D. E. (1987). *The war play dilemma: Balancing needs and values in the early childhood classroom.* New York: Teachers College Press.

Casby, M., & Ruder, K. (1983). Symbolic play and early language development in normal and mentally retarded children. *Journal of Speech and Hearing Research, 26,* 40–411.

Cosaro, W. A., & Tomlinson, C. (1980). Spontaneous play and social learning in the nursery school. In H. B. Schwartzman (Ed.), *Play and culture.* West Point: Leisure Press.

Christie, J. F. (1991). *Play and early literacy development.* Albany, NY: SUNY Press.

Dore, J. (1975). Holophrases, speech acts, and language universals. *Journal of Child Language, 2,* 21–40.

Dore, J. (1986). The development of conversational competence. In R. L. Schiefelbusch (Ed.), *Language competence: Assessment and intervention.* San Diego, CA: College Hill Press.

Ellis, M. J. (1973). *Why people play.* Englewood Cliffs, NJ: Prentice-Hall.

Farver, J. (1993). Cultural differences in scaffolding pretend play: A comparison of American and Mexican mother-child and sibling-child pairs. In K. MacDonald (Ed.), *Parent-child play: Descriptions & Implications* (pp. 349–366). Albany, NY: SUNY Press.

Fein, G., & Schwartz, S. (1986). The social coordination of pretense in preschool children. In G. Fein & M. Rivkin (Eds.), *The young child at play.* Washington, DC: National Association for Education of Young Children.

Field, T., Roseman, S., De Stefano, L., & Koewler, J. (1982). The play of handicapped and non-handicapped children in integrated and nonintegrated situations. *Topics in Early Childhood Special Education, 2*(3), 28–38.

First, E. (1994). The leaving game, or I'll play you and you play me: The emergence of dramatic role play in 2 year olds. In A. Slade & D. P. Wolf (Eds.), *Children at play: Clinical and developmental approach to meaning representation* (pp. 111–132). New York: Oxford University Press.

Fischer, K. W., & Corrigan, R. (1980). A skill approach to language development. In A. P. Rielly (Ed.), *The communication game.* Skillman, NJ: Johnson & Johnson.

Forbes, D., & Yablick, G. (1984). The organization of dramatic content in children's fantasy play. In F. Kessel & A. Goncu (Eds.), *Analyzing children's play dialogues.* San Francisco: Jossey-Bass.

Galda, L., & Pellegrini, A. (Eds.) (1985). *Play, language, and stories.* Norwood, NJ: Ablex.

Gardner, H. (1983). *Frames of mind.* New York: Basic Books.

Garvey, C., & Kramer, T. L. (1989). The language of social pretend play. *Developmental Review, 9,* 364–382.

Garwood, S. G. (Ed.). (1982). Play and development. *Topics in Early Childhood Special Education, 2*(3).

Gaskins, S., & Goncu, A. (1992). Cultural variation in play: A challenge to Piaget and Vygotsky. *The Quarterly Newsletter of the Laboratory of Comparative Human Cognition, 14,* 31–35.

Goncu, A. (1993). Development of intersubjectivity in social pretend play. *Human Development, 36,* 185–198.

Griffing, P. (1980). The relationship between socioeconomic status and sociodramatic play among black kindergarten children. *Genetic Psychology Monographs, 101,* 3–34.

Halliday, M. A. K. (1975). *Learning how to mean: Explorations in the development of language.* London: Edward Arnold.

Haight, W. L., & Miller, P. J. (1993). *Pretending at home: Early development in a sociocultural context.* Albany, NY: SUNY Press.

Hill, P. M., & McCune-Nicolich, L. (1981). Pretend play and patterns of cognition in Down's syndrome children. *Child development, 52,* 611–617.

Johnson, J. E., & Ershler, J. L. (1985). Social and cognitive play forms and toy use by handicapped and nonhandicapped preschoolers. *Topics in Early Childhood Special Education, 5*(3), 69–82.

Kavanagh, J. F. (Ed.). (1986). *News media and child development.* Parkton, MD: York Press.

Konner, M. (1975). Relations among infants and juveniles in comparative perspective. In M. Lewis & L. A. Rosenblum (Eds.), *Friendship and peer relations* (pp. 99–129). New York: Wiley.

Lifter, K., & Bloom, L. (1998). Intentionality and the role of play in the transition to language. In A. M. Wetherby, S. F. Warren, & J. Reichle (Eds.), *Transitions in prelinguistic communication* (pp. 161–195). Baltimore: Paul Brookes.

Linder, T. W. (1993). *Transdisciplinary play-based assessment: A functional approach to working with young children* (Rev. ed.). Baltimore: Paul Brookes.

Luria, A. (1982). *Language and cognition.* Washington, D.C.: Wiley.

McCune, L. (1986). Symbolic development in normal and atypical infants. In G. Fein & M. Rifkin (Eds.), *Reviews of research: The young at play* (pp. 45–61). Washington, D.C.: National Association for the Education of Young Children.

McCune, L. (1995). A normative study of representational play at the transition to language. *Developmental Psychology, 31*(2), 198–206.

McHale, S., & Olley, J. (1982). Using play to facilitate social development of handicapped children. *Topics in Early Childhood Special Education, 2* (3), 76–86.

McLoyd, V. C. (1982). Social class differences in sociodrmatic play: A critical review. *Developmental Review, 2*(1), 1–30.

Michaels, S., & Collins, J. (1984). Oral discourse styles: Classroom interaction and acquisition of literacy, In D Tannen (Ed.), *Coherence in spoken and written discourse.* Norwood. NJ: Ablex.

Miller, P. H. (1985). Metacognition and attention. In D. L. Forrest-Pressley, G. E. MacKinnon, & T. G. Waller (Eds.), *Metacognition, cognition, and human performance* (Vol. 2, pp. 181–221). New York: Academic Press.

Mindes, G. (1982). Social and cognitive aspects of play in young handicapped children. *Topics in Early Childhood Education, 2*(3), 39–52.

Motti, F., Cicchetti, D., & Sroufe, L. A. (1983). From infant affect expression to symbolic play: The coherence of development in Down syndrome children. *Child Development, 54,* 1168–1175.

Nelson, K. (1981). Individual differences in language development Implications for development and language. *Developmental Psychology, 17,* 287.

Newcomer, P. L., & Hammill, D. D. (1982). *Test of Language Development.* Austin, TX: Pro Ed.

Nicolich, L. (1977). Beyond sensorimotor intelligence: Assessment of symbolic maturity through analysis of pretend play. *Merrill-Palmer Quarterly, 23*(2), 89–99.

Parten, M. B. (1932). Social participation among preschool children. *Journal of Abnormal and Social Psychology, 27,* 243–269.

Patterson, J. (1981). Characteristics of play activities in two hyperactive children. Unpublished manuscript, University of New Mexico, Albuquerque.

Pellegrini, A. D. (1984). Symbolic functioning and children's early writing: The relationship between kindergartners' play and isolated word-writing fluency. In R. Beach & L. Bridwell (Eds.), *New directions in composition research* (pp. 274–284). New York: Guilford.

Pellegrini, A. D., (1985). Relations between preschool children's symbolic play and literate behavior. In L. Galda & A. D. Pellegrini (Eds.), *Play, language, and stories* (pp. 79–97). Norwood, NJ: Ablex.

Pellegrini, A. D., & Galda, L. (1993). Ten years after: A reexamination of symbolic play and literacy research. *Reading Research Quarterly, 28,* 163–175.

Pepler, D. J., & Ross, H. S. (1981). The effects of play on convergent and divergent problem-solving. *Child Development, 52,* 1202–1210.

Perez L.,& Schuler, A. An evaluation of play behaviors as an index of cognitive differences in premature preschool children of very low birthweight. Unpublished manuscript.

Peters, A. (1983). *The units of language acquisition.* Cambridge,UK: Cambridge University Press.

Piaget, J. (1962). *Play, dreams, and imitation in childhood.* New York: Norton.

Quinn, J., & Rubin, K. (1984). The play of handicapped children. In T. A. Yawkey & A. Pellegrini (Eds.), *Child's play: Developmental and applied* (pp. 63–81). Hillsdale, NJ: Erlbaum.

Rescorla, L., & Goossens, M. (1992). Symbolic play development in toddlers with expressive specific language impairment. *Journal of Speech and Hearing Research, 48,* 347–359.

Robinson, D., & Perez C. (1982). *Your turn, doctor.* New York: Scholastic.

Roopnarine, J. L., Lasker, J., Sacks, M., & Stores, M. (1998). The cultural contexts of children's play. In O. N. Saracho & B. Spodek (Eds.), *Multiple perspectives on play in early childhood education.* Albany, NY: SUNY Press.

Roth, F., & Clark, D. M. (1987). Symbolic play and social participation abilities of language impaired and normally developing children. *Journal of Speech and Hearing Research, 52:1,* 17–29.

Rubin, K. H. (1980). Fantasy play: Its role in the development of social skills and social cognition. *New directions in child development: Child's play, 9,* 69–84.

Rubin, K. H. (1982). Nonsocial play in preschoolers: Necessary evil? *Child Development, 53,* 651–657.

Rubin, K. H., Fein, G. G., & Vandenberg, B. (1983). In P. H. Mussen (Ed.), *Handbook of child psychology* (Vol. 4) (pp. 693–774). New York: Wiley.

Saltz, E., & Johnson, J. (1974). Training for thematic fantasy play in culturally disadvantaged children: Preliminary results. *Journal of Educational Psychology, 66,* 623–630.

Saltz, R., & Saltz E. (1986). Pretend play training and its outcomes. In G. Fein & M. Rivkin (Eds.), *The young child at play.* Washington, DC: National Association for the Education of Young Children.

Sawyer, R. K. (1997). *Pretend play as improvisation: Conversation in the preschool classroom.* Mahwah, NJ: Erlbaum.

Schaefer, C., & O'Connor, K. (1983). *Handbook of play therapy.* New York: Wiley.

Schwartzman, H. B. (1984). Imaginative play: Deficit or difference. In T. D. Yawkey & A. D. Pellegrini (Eds.), *Child's play: Developmental and applied* (pp. 49–62). Hillsdale, NJ: Erlbaum.

Scott, C. (1994). A discourse continuum for school-age students. In G. P. Wallach & K. G. Butler (Eds.), *Language learning disabilities in school-age children and adolescents* (pp. 217–252). New York: Merrill.

Sigman, M., & Sena, R. (1993). Pretend play in high-risk and developmentally delayed children. *New Directions in Child Development, 59,* 29–42.

Smilansky, S. (1968). *The effects of sociodramatic play on disadvantaged preschool children.* New York: Academic Press.

Smith, P. K. (1978). A longitudinal study of social participation in preschool children. Solitary and parallel play re-examined. *Developmental Psychology, 14,* 517–523.

Smith, P., & Dodsworth, C. (1978). Social class differences in the fantasy play of preschool children. *Journal of Genetic Psychology, 133,* 183–190.

Spencer, P. E. (1996). The association between language and symbolic play at two years: Evidence from deaf toddlers. *Child Development, 67,* 867–876.

Sutton-Smith, B. (1972). *The folkgames of children.* Austin: University of Texas Press.

Sutton-Smith, B. (1980). Children's play: Some sources of play theorizing. *New Directions in Child Development, 9,* 1–16.

Tamis-LeMonda, C. S., & Bornstein, M. H. (1993). Play and its relations to other mental functions in the child. *New Directions in Child Development, 59,* 17–27.

Terrell B., Schwartz R., Prelock, P., & Messick, C. (1984). Symbolic play in normal and hearing impaired children. *Journal of Speech and Hearing Research, 27,* 424–429.

Thal, D., & Bates, E. (1988). Language and gesture in late talkers. *Journal of Speech and Hearing Research, 31,* 115–123.

Vandenberg, B. (1986). Play theory. In G. Fein & M. Rivkin (Eds.), *The young child at play: Reviews of research.* Washington, DC: National Association for the Education of Young Children.

Vandenberg, B., & Kielhofner, G. (1982). Play in evolution, culture, and individual adaptation: Implications for therapy. *American Journal of Occupational Therapy, 36,* 20–28.

Wellman, H. (1985). The origins of metacognition. In D. L. Forrest-Pressley, C. E. Mackinnon, & T. G. Waller (Eds.), *Metacognition, cognition, and human performance* (Vol. 2). New York: Academic Press.

Wellman, H. M., Hickling, A. K., & Schult, C. A. (1997). Young children's psychological, physical, and biological explanations. *New Directions in Child Development, 75,* 7–25.

Westby, C. E. (1980). Assessment of cognitive and language abilities through play. *Language, Speech, and Hearing Services in Schools, 11,* 154–168.

Westby, C. E. (1991). A scale for assessing children's pretend play. In C. E. Schaefer, K. Gitlin, & A. Sandgrund (Eds.), *Play diagnosis and assessment* (pp. 131–161). New York: Wiley.

Westby, C. E., Van Dongen, R., & Maggart, Z. (1986). The concept of trickery: Its development and role in culture and reading. Paper presented at the meeting of the International Reading Association, Philadelphia PA, May 1986.

Westby, C. E., Stevens-Dominguez, M., & Oetter, p. (1996). A performance/competence model of observational assessment. *Language, Speech, and Hearing Services in Schools, 27,* 144–156.

Wing, L, Gould, J., Yeates, S. R., & Brierly, L. M. (1977). Symbolic play in severely mentally retarded and autistic children. *Journal of Child Psychology and Psychiatry, 18,* 167–178.

Wolf, D., & Hicks, D. (1989). The voices within narratives: The development of intertextuality in young children's stories. *Discourse Processes, 12,* 329–351.

Wolf, D., Rygh, J., & Altshuler, J. (1984). Agency and experience: Actions and states in play narratives. In I. Bretherton (Ed.), *Symbolic play: The development of social understanding.* New York: Academic Press.

Wong, B. (1985). Metacognition and learning disabilities. In D. L. Forrest-Pressley, G. E. MacKinnon, & T. G. Waller (Eds.), *Metacognition, cognition, and human performance.* New York: Academic Press.

Yarrow, L. (1981). Beyond cognition: The development of mastery motivation. *Bulletin of the National Center for Clinical Infant Programs, 1*(3), 1–5.

Yawkey, T. D., & Pellegrini, A. (Eds.). (1984). *Child's play: Developmental and applied.* Hillsdale, NJ: Erlbaum.

Chapter 2 ───────────────────────────────

ASSESSING THE COGNITIVE ABILITY OF INFANTS AND TODDLERS THROUGH PLAY: THE SYMBOLIC PLAY TEST

Thomas J. Power and Jerilynn Radcliffe

The assessment of cognitive ability in toddlers and preschool children is a challenging task for clinicians and educators. Young children typically are referred for developmental evaluation because of delays in language or visual-motor skills. However, most conventional measures used in developmental evaluation assess the cognitive ability of young children through the administration of language and visual-motor tasks. Thus, these tests may fail to provide an accurate assessment of cognitive ability in children with deficient language or motor skills. In addition, most tests of cognitive ability for toddlers and preschoolers impose a set of demands that can be very uncomfortable for young children to cope with, particularly referred youngsters who may have language delays, attention deficits, or impulse control problems.

In contrast to conventional methods of evaluating cognitive ability, measures of play provide an assessment of cognitive ability that is relatively independent of linguistic skill and do so in a manner that is comfortable and often enjoyable to preschoolers. This chapter describes (1) the association between play and cognitive development, (2) the importance of including an assessment of play in the developmental evaluation of toddlers and preschoolers, and (3) the advantages and limitations of including the Symbolic Play Test (Lowe & Costello, 1988) as an adjunctive measure in the cognitive assessment of young children.

PLAY AND COGNITIVE DEVELOPMENT

The Relationship between Play and Cognitive Ability

The manner in which children play is clearly related to their cognitive ability. Piaget (1967) asserted that language and play are both manifestations of a child's ability to think symbolically; developments in language and play occur simultaneously with or are successive to advances in children's ability to mentally represent and manipulate the objects of their experience. Developmental psychologists have repeatedly demonstrated that developments in play proceed in a predictable, sequential pattern (Lowe, 1975), and that advances in play are closely linked with developments in language (Largo & Howard, 1979; Ungerer, Zelazo, Kearsley, & O'Leary, 1981). For instance, the emergence of doll-related play typically occurs after a short period of self-related play and often appears at a time when young children begin to use language to signify objects and to communicate what they want (i.e., at about 18 to 20 months).

The relationship between play development and advances in cognitive ability is also revealed in research examining the correlation between children's functioning on measures of play and conventional tests of cognitive ability. Correlations between measures of play and cognitive ability are generally significant, but their magnitude varies greatly. For instance, Clune, Paolella, and Foley (1979) found a correlation of approximately .30 between performance on the Stanford-Binet (Form L-M) and clinician ratings of play for a group of normal preschool-age children. In contrast, Riquet, Taylor, Benaroyay, and Klein (1981) found a much higher correlation (approximately .70) between the Peabody Picture Vocabulary Test and clinician ratings of play for normal preschool children. Variations in the correlation between play measures and conventional tests of ability for normal preschoolers appear to be related to the manner in which play is assessed, sample size, and restriction in the age range of children evaluated in some studies. The relationship between measures of play and cognitive ability also appears to vary among children with different types of developmental disabilities. For instance, Power and Radcliffe (1989) reported that correlations of the Bayley Scales of Infant Development (Bayley, 1969) and Stanford-Binet (Form L-M; Terman & Merrill, 1972) with the Symbolic Play Test were in the low-to-moderate range (.31–.33) for children with mild retardation but essentially zero (.01–.11) for children with autistic characteristics.

The Play of Children with Language Impairments

A hypothesis emanating from Piaget's conception of the relationship between play and language development is that delays in language, particularly language comprehension, are related to a more fundamental deficit in the ability to think symbolically. A corollary is that children with language impairments should demonstrate deficits in symbolic play that are similar in magnitude to their language problems. Research over the past 20 years generally does not support this hypothesis (for a review, see Casby, 1997). For instance, Terrell, Schwartz, Prelock, and Messick (1984) compared a group of language impaired children (2–11 years of age) with a normal language group matched for level of language ability (1–7 years old). These researchers found that the complexity of spontaneous symbolic play was more advanced in the language-impaired group than the younger group with normal language ability. Lombardino, Stein, Kricos, and Wolf (1986) replicated these findings: Although children with impaired language had a much lower mean length of verbal utterance than the normal language group, these groups were essentially the same with regard to the mean length of their play sequences. Children with language impairments have been found to demonstrate symbolic play behaviors less frequently than a normal-developing control group matched for language ability (Rescorla & Goosens, 1992), but there appear to be essentially no differences between the groups in the quality of their symbolic play (Casby, 1997).

Although children with language impairments typically demonstrate symbolic play at a level similar to normal children matched for language ability, there is still evidence of a mediating role of language in symbolic play development. For instance, research has shown that the symbolic play of deaf children is facilitated by their level of language ability and their access to a fluently functioning linguistic system (Spencer, 1996).

The Play of Autistic Children

Research regarding the symbolic play of autistic children has been characterized by many methodological problems, most notably the lack of an adequate control group, that is, a group of children matched for level of language ability (Jarrold, Boucher, & Smith, 1993). However, research including an acceptable control group consistently points to the conclusion that the symbolic play of autistic children is impaired (Gould, 1986; Lewis & Boucher, 1988; Whyte & Owens, 1989). Further, the symbolic play deficit of autistic children is most apparent in spontaneous, free-play situations. That is, there is evidence that the play of autistic children is enhanced in structured settings (Lewis & Boucher, 1988; Whyte & Owens, 1989). (For a review of the symbolic play abilities of autistic children, please refer to Jarrold et al., 1993.)

IMPORTANCE OF ASSESSING PLAY

Adjunctive Index of Cognitive Ability

Given the relationship between play skills and cognitive ability (see above), assessing children's play provides an index of their ability to think symbolically and to use objects adaptively. Most existing measures of cognitive ability for infants and preschoolers do not include a component that assesses play ability; adding an instrument that evaluates play ability separately is often a useful adjunct to a cognitive assessment battery.

Method of Assessing Cognitive Ability in Language-Impaired Children

Conventional methods of assessing cognitive ability, such as the Bayley Scales of Infant Development: Second edition (Bayley, 1993) and Stanford-Binet: Fourth Edition (Thorndike, Hagen, & Sattler, 1986), assess cognitive ability through the administration of language and visual-motor tasks. Children with language impairments often score poorly on these instruments because they include so many items requiring receptive and expressive language skills. As described above, the language ability of children with linguistic impairments is often not an accurate estimate of their ability to think symbolically and to adapt socially. Among children with language impairments, measures of play may often yield a more accurate and useful index of their cognitive ability and be a better prognosticator of later cognitive outcomes.

Diagnostic Indicator of Pervasive Developmental Disorder

The symbolic play of children with autism or some form of pervasive developmental disorder (PDD) is typically deficient, even in relation to their assessed level of linguistic ability (Jarrold et al., 1993). Comparing a child's level of play with his or her overall level of cognitive ability and language skills can be useful in making diagnostic decisions about PDD (Power & Radcliffe, 1989). In addition, Lovaas (1987) has suggested that in autistic children, the level of play development in the early preschool years may be a useful predictor of developmental outcome and response to educational intervention.

Acceptability to Toddlers and Preschoolers

Cognitive testing may place demands on young children that are uncomfortable and unpleasant. Toddlers and preschoolers often resist the constraints imposed by clinicians during formal testing. Children with language impairments, particularly those with PDD, as well as those with attention deficits or impulse control problems may become particularly unsettled during formal testing. In contrast, play is usually an enjoyable and rewarding experience for young children. Further, the format of the Symbolic Play Test (SPT)—simply presenting sets of toys to the child and observing play—is one that is nearly universally well-received by young children.

TEST DESCRIPTION

The SPT (Lowe & Costello, 1988) evaluates the development of functional play skills among children from 12 through 36 months of age. Four sets of toys are presented in a prescribed manner, and the child's behavior is observed in various modes of play, including tactile exploration, functional self-oriented usage, and functional doll-oriented usage. For example, children may orient a spoon to a cup (tactile exploration), attempt to feed themselves using a toy cup and spoon (self-oriented usage), or attempt to feed a doll using a fork and spoon (doll-oriented usage).

A diagram of the toys used in the SPT and the specified manner of presentation is illustrated in Figure 2.1. A listing of the play behaviors associated with each activity and the scoring criteria for each behavior is provided in Appendix A. The child is credited for each of the play behaviors demonstrated, and the behaviors are recorded as they occur on the score sheet included with the test materials (see Appendix B for a sample score sheet). Also, the clinician is encouraged to record the child's play behaviors on the score sheet. A child is permitted to play with a set of toys until it becomes clear that the child is no longer interested or has exhausted the possibility of generating new combinations. At this point, a new set of toys is introduced. Total administration time is 15 to 20 minutes. The recorded play behaviors are summed to yield a total raw score, which can be converted to an estimated developmental age by referring to the test manual. In addition, the clinician can convert the raw score to an estimated standard score using Table 2.1.

PSYCHOMETRIC PROPERTIES

Standardization

Data in the standardization sample were collected over 20 years ago. The SPT was standardized on 137 children in the age range from 12 to 36 months. Almost one-half of the

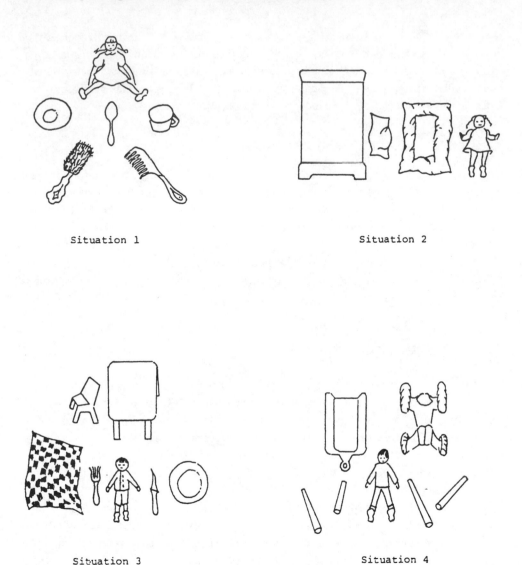

Figure 2-1.   **Materials for each of the SPT play situations.**

children in the normative sample were tested repeatedly, sometimes as often as five times. Altogether, 241 testings comprise the standardization sample (Lowe & Costello, 1988).

Normative data were collected in London, England. The sample comprised children from welfare centers and day nursery schools. The ratio of testings from welfare centers as compared to nursery schools was approximately 4:1. Lowe and Costello (1988) reported that the difference in performance between children from welfare centers and those in nursery schools was not significant. Families from lower socioeconomic status (SES) groups were overrepresented in the normative sample. Of the families for whom information about SES was available (82% of cases), only 15% belonged to the highest two of five levels of SES.

Children in the standardization sample were tested at 12, 15, 18, 21, 24, 30, and 36 months of age. Included in the sample were test results for 123 boys and 118 girls. The

Table 2-1. Standard scores corresponding to SPT raw scores

SPT Raw Score	Chronological Age (in months)

SPT Raw Score	12	13	14	15	16	17	18	19	20	21	22	23	24	25	26	27	28	29	30	31	32	33	34	35	36
1																									
2																									
3	73	68	51	44		41			53	50	46	58	55	52	50	47									
4	80	75	60	54	46	49	43	—	58	54	51	61	58	56	53	51									
5	88	83	70	63	56	57	50	45	63	59	55	65	62	59	57	54	42								
6	95	90	79	73	65	65	58	53	68	64	60	68	66	63	60	58	47	44	40						
7	102	97	89	82	75	73	66	61	72	69	65	72	69	67	64	61	51	48	44	41					
8	109	104	98	92	84	81	74	69	77	74	70	75	73	70	67	65	55	52	49	46	42	40			
9	117	112	108	101	93	89	82	77	82	79	75	79	76	74	71	68	59	56	53	50	47	44			
10	124	119	117	110	103	97	90	85	87	84	80	83	80	77	74	72	63	60	57	54	51	48			
11	131	126	126	120	112	105	98	93	92	88	84	86	83	81	78	75	68	65	61	58	55	52			
12	139	133	136	129	122	113	106	101	97	93	89	90	87	84	82	79	72	69	65	63	59	56			
13	146	141	145	139	131	121	114	109	101	98	94	93	90	88	85	83	76	73	70	67	63	60			
14	153	148	155	148	140	129	122	117	106	103	99	97	94	91	89	86	80	77	74	71	68	65			
15	160	155		157	150	137	130	125	111	108	104	100	98	95	92	90	84	81	78	75	72	69			
16					160	145	138	133	116	113	109	104	101	99	96	93	89	86	82	79	76	73			
17						153	146	141	121	117	114	107	105	102	99	97	93	90	87	84	80	77	42		
18							154	149	126	122	118	111	108	106	103	100	97	94	91	88	84	81	51	45	
19								157	131	127	123	115	112	109	106	104	101	98	95	92	89	86	60	54	46
20									135	132	128	118	115	113	110	107	105	103	99	96	93	90	70	63	56
21									140	137	133	122	119	116	114	111	110	107	103	100	97	94	79	73	65
22									145	142	138	125	122	120	117	115	114	111	108	105	101	98	89	82	75
23									150	147	143	129	126	123	121	118	118	115	112	109	105	103	98	92	84
24									155	151	148	132	130	127	124	122	122	119	116	113	110	107	108	101	93
25										156	152	136	133	131	128	125	127	124	120	117	114	111	117	110	101
26											157	140	137	134	131	129	131	128	124	121	118	115	126	120	112

Note: Mean is 100, and standard deviation is 16.

number of boys and girls tested at each age was virtually equal. The number of children tested at each age level ranged from 27 to 42, with a mean of 34.4. Children with physical or mental handicaps were not included in the normative sample.

Reliability

Split-half reliability coefficients, corrected by the Spearman-Brown formula, ranged from .52 to .92. Reliability coefficients were low at the 15- and 18-month age levels (.57 and .52 respectively), borderline acceptable at the 12-, 21-, and 36-month levels (range of .74 to .79), and acceptably high at the 24- and 30-month levels (greater than .90). Test-retest reliability was .72 at 3 months. The standard error of measurement was computed at each age level, given that the internal consistency of the scale varied considerably for each age group. The standard error of measurement in raw score units (standard scores in parentheses) was 1.16 (8.5) at 12 months, 1.09 (10.4) at 15 months, 1.40 (11.2) at 18 months, 1.53 (7.2) at 21 months, 1.34 (4.6) at 24 months, 1.10 (4.7) at 30 months, and 1.80 (17.1) at 36 months.

Validity

Age Effects

Raw scores on the SPT have been shown to increase steadily over the age span of the scale; a linear model fits the data quite well. At the extreme ends of the test, the distributions are markedly skewed, representing considerable floor and ceiling effects. For instance, approximately 5% of children tested at 12 months failed to earn a raw score of even 1, and about 20% of children tested at 30 and 36 months achieved a perfect score.

When using the scale clinically, a conversion from raw score to standard score units is useful. The test manual provides standard scores associated with raw scores for each of the age groups tested, but it is desirable to perform this conversion at each month in the age range of the test. Given that normative data are provided only for seven age levels and that the data fit a linear model reasonably well, a regression equation was used to interpolate mean scores for each month. The standard deviation for each month was assumed to be the same as that for the closest age group, as reported in the manual. For example, the standard deviation for 16 months was assumed to be 1.7, which is the standard deviation reported in the manual for children at 15 months. The mean standard score was set at 100 with a standard deviation of 16. The norms table is presented in Table 2.1.

Because standard deviations vary considerably across the seven age levels included in the standardization sample, there are some irregularities in the standardization sample. For example, at 19 months of age a raw score of 5 converts to a standard score of 45, but at 20 months the same raw score converts to a standard score of 63. This aberration is corrected to some extent, however, by the fact that the standard error of measurement at 19 months is 11.2 standard score points, whereas the standard error of measurement at 20 months is 7.2.

Only for children in the age range from 13 to 25 months could SPT raw scores be converted to standard score units in a range reflecting two standard deviations above and below the mean (i.e., 68–132). At 12 months the lowest standard score that a child can attain is a 73, and at 30 and 36 months the highest attainable standard scores are 124 and 112 respectively. Thus, the SPT can be used to assess a relatively wide range of functioning only for children in the 13- to 25-month age range.

Because of floor effects, the SPT should be administered with infants who are 12 months of age only when there is evidence of average or above cognitive ability. Due to ceiling effects, the SPT should be administered to toddlers who are older than 25 months only when there is evidence of developmental functioning that is average or below. Further, given the negatively skewed distribution of scores in the upper age levels, standard scores derived from the SPT in this age range should be cautiously interpreted. Standard scores may be expected to underestimate level of play functioning when the child's score is below average.

Gender Differences

Normative data are not provided separately for boys and girls. In the manual, Lowe and Costello (1988) reported that "sex differences in mean score at each age level are small and inconsistent." However, in an earlier paper, Lowe (1975) indicated boys and girls above the age of 21 months demonstrate differences in how they play. Girls demonstrate functional doll-related play at a younger age than boys, and boys display interest in and competence with truck-related play at an earlier age than girls. Because no data are presented in the manual with regard to how boys and girls manipulate the toys in each of the play situations of the SPT, it is not possible to evaluate the significance of gender differences.

Relation to Measures of Cognitive Ability

Power & Radcliffe (1989) evaluated the relationship between the SPT and two commonly used measures of cognitive ability, the Bayley Scales of Infant Development (Bayley, 1969) and the Stanford-Binet Intelligence Scale: Form L-M. (Terman & Merrill, 1972). Participants were children referred to a child development program in a tertiary-care children's hospital because of concerns about developmental problems. Although children enrolled in the study ranged in age from 16 to 62 months, all of the children had mental ages on the Bayley and Stanford-Binet that were well within the age range of the SPT. The correlation between raw scores on the SPT and raw scores on the Bayley was .30 ($p < .001$, $n = 154$). The correlation between raw scores on the SPT and raw scores on the Stanford-Binet was .25 ($p < .05$, $n = 93$). The findings demonstrated a significant relationship between performance on the SPT and functioning on these measures of cognitive ability, but the magnitude of the correlations was somewhat low. The relatively low reliability of the SPT may have contributed to the low correlations. Further, a restriction in the range of Bayley and Binet scores, due to limitations in the instruments used, may have served to reduce the correlations. Correlations between the SPT and Bayley were examined only with children who had mental ages in the 15- to 25-month range; the association between the SPT and Binet was investigated only among children who had mental ages in the 24- to 32-month range. The impact of range restriction is further suggested by the research of Cunningham, Glenn, Wilkinson, and Sloper (1985), who found a correlation of .59 when scores on the SPT were correlated with mental age scores derived from either the Bayley or Binet in a sample of children with a broad range of developmental levels who had Down's syndrome.

The relationship between the SPT and measures of cognitive ability has been shown to vary greatly as a function of the child's disability. Power and Radcliffe (1989) found that children with borderline, mild, and moderate levels of mental retardation, as well as those with developmental language disorders, demonstrated a low-to-moderate correlation (range from .19 to .51) between functioning on the SPT and Bayley or Binet. In contrast, with children meeting criteria for Pervasive Developmental Disorder (PDD), using the third edition of the *Diagnostic and Statistical Manual of Mental Disorders* (American Psychiatric Association, 1980), there was essentially no association between the SPT and these measures of cognitive ability (correlations ranged from .01 to .11).

To further evaluate the relationship between the SPT and measures of cognitive ability, Power and Radcliffe (1989) conducted mean comparisons between SPT mental ages and Bayley/Binet mental ages in relation to the standard deviation of the SPT. Mean differences between the SPT and the Bayley or Binet were negligible to small for children with borderline, mild, or moderate mental retardation. This finding confirms that delays in the performance of children with mental retardation tend to be global in nature, and suggests that the SPT provides a rough estimate of overall cognitive functioning in children with varying levels of mental retardation. In contrast, differences between the SPT and Bayley/Binet mental ages were moderately high (about one-half of a standard deviation) for children in the groups with developmental language disorder and PDD.

Children with PDD demonstrated mean mental ages that were almost four months lower on the SPT than on the Bayley or Binet (Power & Radcliffe, 1989). This finding confirms the results of other studies (Gould, 1986; Riquet et al., 1981; Whyte & Owens, 1989) demonstrating that the play of children with PDD is inferior to that of children matched for mental age or developmental language age. The implication of this research is that for children with PDD, the SPT yields information that is unique from that provided by measures of cognitive ability. However, although children with PDD typically perform more poorly on the SPT than they do on the Bayley or Binet, low functioning on the SPT in relation to these measures of cognitive ability is not highly predictive of a diagnosis of PDD. Thus, clinicians need to be careful about using a marked difference between the SPT and Bayley or Binet to make diagnostic decisions (Power & Radcliffe, 1989).

For children with developmental language disorders, the direction of the difference between mental ages on the SPT and measures of cognitive ability varied according to whether the Bayley or Binet was administered. Children assessed with the Bayley achieved SPT mental ages that were on average 3 months lower than Bayley mental ages. In contrast, those assessed with the Binet achieved SPT mental ages that were on average 2 months higher than their Binet mental ages (Power & Radcliffe, 1989). The results suggest that the SPT yields useful and unique information when used in combination with the Bayley or Binet. The difference in the direction of the difference when using the Bayley versus the Binet may have reflected variations in what these cognitive ability tests measure. The Bayley includes many items assessing visual-motor skill and spatial processing; children with language disorders generally are relatively strong with these kinds of materials. However, children with language disorders by definition are weaker on language activities (Casby, 1997). The L-M form of the Binet contains mostly items that tap verbal ability at these levels, which may have contributed to the suppression of the Binet IQ in relation to the SPT score.

Interpreting Differences between the SPT and Bayley

In the evaluation of young children with developmental problems, it is useful to know whether the difference between functioning on the SPT and a measure of cognitive ability is significant. A significant difference may signal relatively strong nonverbal play skills or a deficit in independent, functional play. Comparison between the SPT and Bayley Scales is feasible because the Bayley is appropriate for administration in the age range that can be satisfactorily assessed using the SPT (i.e., 13–25 months). For children from 26 to 30 months, comparisons between the SPT and Bayley are appropriate only for children in the lower IQ levels (e.g., less than 85). A comparison between the SPT and Binet is problematic because of the ceiling effects on the SPT at the age range in which the Binet and SPT overlap (i.e., 24–36 months).

To determine the magnitude of the difference between SPT and Bayley (1993) scores needed for significance, difference scores were evaluated in relation to the standard error of the difference (Anastasi, 1988) between these two measures. Table 2.2 presents the magnitude of the difference between the SPT and Bayley scores needed for significance at the .05 level. Given the skewed distribution of SPT scores at the upper levels of the scale, it is recommended that the difference between SPT and Bayley scores be at least 17 points in order to interpret the discrepancy as significant.

Relationship to Measures of Language Functioning

Two primary purposes for designing the SPT were to assess symbolic functioning independent of language and to predict language proficiency in the future. Lowe and Costello (1988) evaluated the concurrent and predictive validity of the SPT in relation to the Reynell Developmental Language Scales (Reynell, 1969) and a measure of sentence length. Correlations between the SPT and the Reynell administered concurrently varied greatly depending on the age of the children. Children who were 21 and 24 months of age demonstrated a moderate correlation between the SPT and Reynell, but children older and younger than these levels demonstrated a low-to-negligible relationship between these measures. Further, the concurrent relationship between the SPT and the measure of sentence length was generally low. These findings support the hypothesis that the SPT assesses functions that are largely independent of language ability.

The predictive validity of the SPT was evaluated by correlating scores on the SPT with performance on the Reynell and a measure of sentence length administered several months later. Correlations between the SPT and later administrations of the Reynell generally were in the moderate range. The relationship between the SPT and Reynell was highest when the interval between these measures was the longest (i.e., 12 months). The association between the SPT and later assessment of sentence length was in the moderate-to-high range (i.e.,

Table 2-2. Bayley-SPT differences needed for significance (.05 level)

Age (months)	Difference Needed[a]
12–13	16
14–16	21
17–19	14
20–22	12
23–27	10
28–30	13[b]

[a] The difference needed for significance is given in standard score units.
[b] Given the skewed distribution of SPT scores at this age level, a difference of 17 points is actually recommended.

.57–.75). These results support the conclusion that the SPT has a reasonable degree of predictive validity and can be useful in predicting language competence 6 to 12 months after its administration. However, a replication of this study with more recently developed and comprehensive measures of language functioning is needed to confirm this hypothesis.

CASE STUDIES

The following case studies describe how the SPT was used to evaluate cognitive functioning and plan strategies of remediation. In each case, follow-up data are reported to describe outcome and illustrate issues involved in using the SPT to make predictions.

The Case of Peter

Peter, age 30 months, was referred for psychological evaluation by a pediatric neurologist who had diagnosed him with Pervasive Developmental Disorder, Not Otherwise Specified (PDD-NOS). The neurologist, along with the parents, requested that his skills be evaluated and that recommendations for educational programming be provided. Peter's medical history was uncomplicated. He was the second child of college-educated parents with no history of learning or developmental problems in their families. Pregnancy, labor, delivery, and neonatal course were uncomplicated. Peter, described as a very quiet, placid infant, achieved motor milestones within normal limits, walking unassisted at age 12 months. However, he exhibited delays in language milestones; he uttered a nonspecific "mama" and "dada" by age 18 months, and used only a few single words by age 2 years. He had a history of acquiring words, using them briefly, then not using them again. He had no history of illnesses and only a few ear infections.

During the testing session, Peter presented as very quiet and passive. Although he sat obediently at the testing table, his involvement with the assessment tasks was variable. He was most responsive to manipulative tasks, such as form boards or pegboards, and least responsive to language tasks, such as naming pictures shown to him or pointing to pictures. With language tasks, he would refuse to point or to name, and typically sought to leave the table.

Peter showed very limited eye contact and engagement with others, despite very skillful efforts on the parts of both parents to engage him in interactions with themselves or others. Although he would turn to his mother to escape testing tasks he disliked, Peter did not otherwise become engaged with her as he played with toys. His parents confirmed that at home he preferred to play alone, instead of with his parents or four-year-old brother. The parents shared videotapes of his behavior at home, which showed a striking degree of disengagement from others. For example, he was observed walking by people without acknowledging or responding to them in any way.

On the Bayley Scales of Infant Development, Second Edition, Peter obtained a Mental Development Index of 62. His functioning was like that of a 23-month-old child. Peter passed such tasks as completing a three-hole form board, reversed, and a nine-hole board within time limits, but did not name pictures, produce three-word utterances, or use pronouns. Surprisingly, Peter obtained an age level score of 31 months on the SPT (see Appendix B). His standard score of 95 on the SPT was in the average range and significantly higher than his score on the Bayley. His play with the toys was remarkably well developed. He engaged in short sequences of pretend play with the objects, such as pretending to put a doll to bed, or filling a tractor with logs and having a toy man "drive" the tractor. On the Vineland Adaptive Behaviour Scales, Peter obtained these scores: Adaptive Behaviour Composite 65; Communication 55; Daily Living Skills 60; Socialization 50; Motor Skills 80. His score on the Childhood Autism Rating Scale was 32, falling in the Mild to Moderate range of Autism.

The impression given was PDD-NOS with Mild range Developmental Delay. Recommendations included (1) a specialized early intervention program with a strong emphasis on developing language skills; (2) behavior consultation to the parents on strategies to promote more appropriate social interaction skills; (3) speech and language therapy; and (4) encouraging more symbolic play at home by scheduling daily play periods with the parents and providing toys (e.g., cooking toys, woodworking tools; doctor set) that could promote the development of social, pretend play.

Follow-Up

Peter returned for a follow-up assessment 1 year later, at age $3^1/_2$ years. The parents had followed the recommendations proposed the year before, and all the therapists who worked with Peter were pleased with his responsiveness to their work with him. During the assessment, he presented as markedly more engaged with both people and materials. Eye contact was significantly increased with the parents as well as the examiner. Peter spoke, using two- and three-word utterances, to communicate his wants. Full sentences were not used, and he omitted articles such as "the" and "a," but his vocabulary was extensive and his articulation was fairly clear. On the Bayley Scales, Revised, Peter earned a Mental Development Index of 85. He again did well with the nonverbal tasks, such as completing a simple form board within 30 seconds, but he also passed a number of the language tasks, such as using prepositions correctly, identifying the picture that was the same as the one shown to him earlier, and pointing to the picture that was not like the others in a set of four. On the SPT, he achieved a score at the ceiling of 36 months, passing all the tasks of the test. He continued to use the objects appropriately, but his play sequences were much more extended. From reports of his parents, Peter achieved an Adaptive Behavior Composite of 90 on the Vineland, with these Domain scores: Communication 80; Daily Living Skills 95; Socialization 86; Motor Skills 90. His score on the Childhood Autism Rating Scale was 25, in the Nonautistic range.

The impression given was Developmental Language Disorder, Combined Type, and no longer PDD. The clinician who saw the child expressed surprise that the PDD-NOS diagnosis no longer applied to Peter, and attributed this to the intensive intervention he had received, as well as the relatively mild degree of PDD he exhibited at the time of earlier assessment. Although a number of factors undoubtedly contributed to this remarkable change in functioning, his relatively strong play skills at age $2^1/_2$ years proved to be a prognosticator of this very favorable outcome.

The Case of Jennifer

Jennifer was referred at age 26 months for evaluation of delayed speech by her pediatrician. At that time, she used fewer than 10 single words. She was the only child of two working parents, and she had been in a group child care program since age 12 months.

There was a positive family history of speech delay, in that her father and uncle did not begin speaking until age $2^1/_2$ years. The medical history revealed an uncomplicated pregnancy, labor, delivery, and neonatal period. Motor milestones were achieved normally; she walked unassisted at 12 months. However, there were delays in the acquisition of speech milestones, with first words occurring at age 2, and reportedly fewer than 10 words at the time of assessment. Apart from this, the medical history was unremarkable except for periods of upper respiratory congestion.

Jennifer presented as a small, pretty child. She was for the most part quiet and still during the evaluation. She could be engaged in social interaction, and participated with a smile in simple games with a ball, as well as "tug-of-war" with pop-off beads. However, she more typically engaged in somewhat self-absorbed and solitary activity. Even when presented with the structured activities of testing, at times she would lapse into nonproductive behavior, which interfered with adaptive use of the materials. For example, when presented with a pegboard, she began to turn each peg after it was inserted into the hole, which prevented her from accomplishing the task within the time period needed for a maximum score. Similarly, she was competent with form boards but would spin the round blocks in their recesses after she had placed them.

On the Bayley Scales, Revised, Jennifer performed overall at a 21-month level and achieved borderline developmental status (MDI = 76). This summary score is quite deceptive, for it masks quite wide-ranging discrepancies in her abilities. In her work with concrete materials, such as blocks, form boards, and pegs, Jennifer performed generally at age level despite her interest in turning the materials in their recesses. However, language abilities were quite deficient. The examiner heard only some softly offered jargoning, and this only occasionally. Once, though, when playing with the doll, Jennifer handed it to the examiner and said, "Good-bye, baby," waving bye-bye. Of greater concern was Jennifer's poor comprehension of language. On the language comprehension items of the Bayley, Jennifer performed well below age level. She did not correctly follow directions with a doll or point to body parts on a doll. Her expressive and receptive language skills were estimated at around the 16-month level. Jennifer's play was also quite delayed, as was observed directly and by her performance on the SPT. She occasionally used play materials in a functional or symbolic way, but quickly regressed into more immature uses, such as randomly piling up the materials while seeming to disregard their typical functional use. She achieved an age-equivalent score on the SPT of only 12 months and a standard score of 53. Performance on the SPT was significantly below that on the Bayley.

In summary, Jennifer was seen as a child presenting with delays not only in expressive language, but also in language understanding and play maturity. Her ability to manipulate concrete objects was close to her age level, but often, if she were not directed and structured, she lapsed into idiosyncratic, nonproductive uses of materials. The significantly lower score on the SPT was suggestive of Jennifer's difficulty organizing her efforts on independent tasks. She was diagnosed with mild range developmental delay. Recommendations included (1) hearing evaluation; (2) consideration of a change in child care setting to a specialized early intervention program; (3) parent counseling to enhance Jennifer's language development, social responsiveness, and play skills; and (4) follow-up evaluation.

Follow-Up

Jennifer was seen for follow-up evaluation at age 48 months. She had received early intervention services, and transitioned to a specialized preschool program. An audiological evaluation had shown normal hearing. The parents did not pursue the counseling suggested at the original evaluation. At the time of the follow-up evaluation, the parents expressed concern about her progress in language development.

Jennifer presented again as a quiet child, most likely to engage in self-contained play with rather restricted content. Typically, she lined up objects or moved them from one place to another. When demonstrations of more elaborate play schemes were given, Jennifer watched carefully but did not readily incorporate these into her own play. At the outset of the assessment, Jennifer vocalized sparingly and this was typically in a whisper. However, as time passed, she became louder and her body movements were lively and more spontaneous. She showed marked articulation difficulties, and tended to rely on gesture to augment her communication. At one point, frustrated in her attempts to open one of the doors of the Lock Box (Goodman & Field, 1991), she said, "ope ... de ... door...," which the examiner translated as "can't open the door." This was, for Jennifer, a meaningful, rather long sentence, which stood in contrast to her more typical one- to two-word utterances.

On the Wechsler Preschool Scale, Revised, Jennifer obtained these indices: Performance Score 61, Verbal Score 55, and Full Scale Score 54. These scores fall in the Mentally Deficient range and were considerably lower than those obtained on the Bayley at earlier testing. Although the decline could be attributed in part to differences in the test instruments used, it also seemed to indicate that Jennifer had not progressed to the degree expected, given her earlier performance. The other tests administered confirmed her level of functioning. On the SPT, she achieved an age-equivalence score of 26 months (See Appendix C). Here, she showed inconsistently appropriate play and immature uses of the toys. Thus, although she appropriately brushed and fed a doll, she also piled up the materials as if they were blocks, showing little recognition of their functional properties. On the Vineland Adaptive Behavior Scale, Jennifer obtained an Adaptive Behavior Composite of 60. She achieved these area scores: Communication 58; Daily Living Skills 55; Socialization 57; Motor Skills 72.

Jennifer was seen as a child whose functioning fell within the mildly mentally retarded range. Recommendations included (1) further speech and language therapy; (2) follow-up hearing evaluation; (3) increased parental involvement and play with Jennifer, guided by parent counseling; and (4) a specialized preschool program. In this case, the significant discrepancy between the Bayley and the SPT on initial testing highlighted Jennifer's important cognitive deficits. On follow-up testing, there was no discrepancy between cognitive ability testing, adaptive functioning, and play. In retrospect, the Bayley score obtained on the initial visit was not as strong a predictor of later functioning as was the SPT, perhaps a reflection of the relative importance of play in overall cognitive development as compared with the ability to manipulate objects.

EVALUATION OF THE SYMBOLIC PLAY TEST

Limitations of the SPT

Measure of Functional, Not Necessarily Symbolic Play

Hallmarks of symbolic play are (1) decentration, that is, the use of an object as an agent in pretense, and (2) decontextualization, that is, the use of an object in pretence in a manner that goes beyond its typical or conventional way of being used (Piaget, 1967; Watson

& Fischer, 1977). Researchers have contrasted symbolic play (using objects of play in unconventional and imaginative ways) with functional play (the appropriate or conventional use of play objects). Although functional play, such as the orientation of a doll to bed, may emanate from representational thinking, it may also be presymbolic in nature, reflecting an understanding of how two or more objects are conventionally related to each other (Baron-Cohen, 1989). Several researchers have noted that the SPT assesses primarily functional play as opposed to symbolic play (Casby, 1997; Jarrold et al., 1993). Although the development of functional play is important and appears to proceed in a predictable, sequential developmental course during the first three years of life, this type of play is not necessarily symbolic in nature. Thus, the name of this test may be misleading.

Inadequate Normative Data

Normative data were obtained on only 137 children. A relatively high percentage of the data was collected from the repeated testing of the same children, for a total of 247 testings. Normative data are provided for seven age ranges, so the sample size within each age range is quite small. Further, normative data were collected in Great Britain and appear to underrepresent children from upper socioeconomic status categories. The generalizability of the normative data to children living in other countries from varying ethnic and socioeconomic backgrounds needs to be demonstrated.

Questionable Reliability

The reliability of this scale, particularly at the lower age ranges assessed, is borderline acceptable. Including more items and perhaps one or two more play situations in this scale would improve its reliability. Further, an item analysis would be useful to determine the extent to which each item contributes to overall test reliability.

Appropriate for a Restricted Age Range

Although the SPT has been standardized with children from 12 to 36 months of age, ceiling and floor effects on this measure limit its usefulness with certain populations at the extreme ends of the age range. For instance, the SPT is not appropriate for children of 12 or 13 months who have borderline or lower levels of cognitive ability. Similarly, the SPT has limited utility for children 30 months or older who are developmentally advanced.

Restricted Scoring System

The scoring system of the SPT requires a determination as to whether the child can use discrete play objects adaptively (e.g., feeding a doll, pulling a tractor). The current system does not reflect the complexity of a child's play, including the duration of play, the sequence of schemes, and the relatedness of schemes in a sequence. Obtaining information about the complexity of play is very important when assessing young children. For instance, Gould (1986) has shown that autistic children frequently are able to use objects in a functionally appropriate manner. Their deficit is often most apparent in the way they play. That is, play schemes typically are very brief and unrelated to each other. Thus, with children who have PDD, scores on the SPT may be an overestimation of their ability to play in an adaptive manner.

Small Size of Play Objects

A further limitation of the SPT is the small size of the play materials. Children with motor difficulties often find it difficult to make some of the scorable play maneuvers, such as putting the doll in a chair, and orienting eating utensils to the doll. Further, children with visual impairments may have difficulty identifying the fine details of the play objects.

Utility of the SPT

Assessing the play of infants and toddlers with developmental delays is very important because conventional measures of cognitive ability sometimes do not yield an accurate index of developmental functioning. Children with language impairments, in particular, may perform poorly on conventional measures because so many items on these tests require relatively strong verbal proficiency. Visual-manipulative tasks, which are usually included in traditional cognitive tests, assess some aspects of nonverbal functioning but may not assess a child's ability to adapt and solve problems in a relatively independent, self-directed setting. The measurement of play skills can indicate a child's ability to function adaptively independent of language skill and the presence of a supervising adult. The SPT is a useful method of assessing children's play skills for several reasons.

Easy to Use

The SPT can be administered in a brief period of time. Play situations have been standardized and are easy to administer. Children from a broad range of cultural groups find the play situations interesting and fun. The scoring criteria are generally clear and can be used consistently across test situations and examiners.

Norm-Referenced Measure

Because the SPT is norm-referenced, it allows the clinician to determine how a child is functioning in relation to peers of the same age.

Predictive of Language Competence

Although performance on the SPT is relatively independent of language proficiency, functioning on the SPT appears to be moderately correlated with language competence 6 to 12 months later. Thus, assessing play ability using the SPT may be useful to clinicians in predicting a child's risk for language problems in the future.

Useful Adjunct to Cognitive Ability Measures

Research indicates that it is useful to make comparisons in functioning between the SPT and measures of cognitive ability, in particular the Bayley Scales. Large differences between the Bayley and SPT often signal the presence of developmental irregularities. For instance, the performance of children with PDD on the SPT is generally weak in relation to their performance on cognitive ability measures. Further, there is evidence that the performance of language-disordered children on the SPT is quite different from their functioning on traditional, cognitive tests.

In conclusion, the SPT is a norm-referenced play measure that allows the clinician to determine a child's ability to use objects in a functionally appropriate manner in relation to developmental expectations. Problems with standardization, reliability, validity, and scoring warrant a revision of the scale. However, in its current form, the SPT serves as a valuable adjunctive measure in a preschool assessment battery for children in the developmental age range from 13 to 25 months. The SPT appears to be particularly useful in the assessment of children with known or suspected developmental language disorders and pervasive developmental disorders.

REFERENCES

American Psychiatric Association. (1980). *Diagnostic and statistical manual of mental disorders* (3rd ed.). Washington, DC.

Anastasi, A. (1988). *Psychological testing.* New York: Macmillan.

Baron-Cohen, S. (1989). The autistic child's theory of mind: A case of specific developmental delay. *Journal of Child Psychology and Psychiatry, 30,* 285–297.

Bayley, N. (1969). *Bayley Scales of Infant Development.* San Antonio, TX: Psychological Corporation.

Bayley, N. (1993). *Bayley Scales of Infant Development* (2nd ed.). San Antonio, TX: Psychological Corporation.

Casby, M. W. (1997). Symbolic play of children with language impairment: A critical review. *Journal of Speech, Language, and Hearing Research, 40,* 480–492.

Clune, C., Paolella, J. M., & Foley, J. M. (1979). Free-play behavior of atypical children: An approach to assessment. *Journal of Autism and Developmental Disorders, 9,* 61–72.

Cunningham, C. C., Glenn, S. M., Wilkinson, P., & Sloper, P. (1985). Mental ability, symbolic play, and receptive and expressive language of young children with Down's syndrome. *Journal of Child Psychology and Psychiatry, 26,* 255–265.

Goodman, J. F., & Field, M. (1991). Assessing attentional problems in preschoolers with the Goodman Lock Box. In C. E. Schaeffer, K. Gitlin, & A. Sandgrund (Eds.), *Play diagnosis and assessment.* New York: Wiley.

Gould, J. (1986). The Lowe and Costello Symbolic Play Test in socially impaired children. *Journal of Autism and Developmental Disorders, 16,* 199–213.

Jarrold, C., Boucher, J., & Smith, P. (1993). Symbolic play in autism: A review. *Journal of Autism and Developmental Disorders, 23,* 281–307.

Largo, R. H., & Howard, J. A. (1979). Developmental progression in play behavior of children between nine and thirty months: I. Spontaneous play and imitation. *Developmental Medicine and Child Neurology, 21,* 299–310.

Lewis, V., & Boucher, J. (1988). Spontaneous, instructed and elicited play in relatively able autistic children. *British Journal of Developmental Psychology, 6,* 325–339.

Lombardino, L., Stein, J., Kricos, P., & Wolf, M. (1986). Play diversity and structural relationships in the play and language of language-impaired and language-normal preschoolers: Preliminary data. *Journal of Communication Disorders, 19,* 475–489.

Lovaas, O. I. (1987). Behavioral functioning and normal educational and intellectual functioning in young autistic children. *Journal of Consulting and Clinical Psychology, 55,* 3–9.

Lowe, M. (1975). Trends in the development of representational play in infants from one to three years: An observation study. *Journal of Child Psychology and Psychiatry, 16,* 33–47.

Lowe, M., & Costello, A. J. (1988). *Symbolic Play Test* (2nd ed.). Windsor, Berkshire, England: NFER-Nelson.

Piaget, J. (1967). *Play, dreams, and imitation in childhood.* London: Routledge & Kegan Paul.

Power, T. J., & Radcliffe, J. (1989). The relationship of play behavior to cognitive ability in developmentally disabled preschoolers. *Journal of Autism and Developmental Disorders, 19,* 97–107.

Rescorla, L., & Goosens, M. (1992). Symbolic play development in toddlers with expressive specific language impairment (SLI-E). *Journal of Speech and Hearing Research, 35,* 1290–1302.

Reynell, J. (1969). *Reynell Developmental Language Scales manual.* Windsor, Berkshire, England: NFER-Nelson.

Riquet, B. C., Taylor, N. D., Benaroyay, S., & Klein, L. S. (1981). Symbolic play in autistic, Down's, and normal children with equivalent mental age. *Journal of Autism and Developmental Disorders, 11,* 439–448.

Spencer, P. E. (1996). The association between language and symbolic play at two years: Evidence from deaf toddlers. *Child Development, 67,* 867–876.

Terman, L., & Merrill, M. (1972). *Stanford-Binet Intelligence Scale: Manual for the third edition (Form L-M).* Boston: Houghton-Mifflin.

Terrell, B., Schwartz, R., Prelock, P., & Messick, C. (1984). Symbolic play in normal and language-impaired children. *Journal of Speech and Hearing Research, 27,* 424–429.

Thorndike, R. L., Hagen, E. P., & Sattler, J. M. (1986). *Guide for administering and scoring the Stanford-Binet Intelligence Scale* (4th ed.). Chicago: Riverside.

Ungerer, J. A., Zelazo, P. R., Kearsley, R. B., & O'Leary, K. (1981). Developmental changes in the representation of objects in symbolic play from 18 to 34 months of age. *Child Development, 52,* 186–195.

Watson, M. W., & Fischer, K. W. (1977). A developmental sequence of agent use in late infancy. *Child Development, 48,* 828–836.

Whyte, J. & Owens, A. (1989). Language and symbolic play: Some findings from a study of autistic children. *Irish Journal of Psychology, 10,* 317–332.

Appendix A

SITUATION I:

1. *Discriminate handling of the doll:* any indication that child is aware of specific characteristics of the doll, such as standing it up, feeding it, hugging it, brushing its hair; scoring is liberal

2. *Relates spoon to cup or saucer:* places spoon in cup or on saucer, pretends to stir with spoon in cup

3. *Feeds, combs, or brushes self or other person:* as stated; also credited if brush is clearly used as a toothbrush; scored retrospectively if the child feeds, combs, or brushes the doll in Situation I or feeds him or herself in Situation III

4. *Feeds, combs, or brushes doll:* as stated, including bringing the brush or comb to the doll's hair without actually combing it; if child scores this item, credit also given for Item 3

5. *Places cup on saucer:* as stated; not scored if saucer is placed on cup or if cup or saucer is upside down

SITUATION II:

6. *Discriminate handling of doll:* as stated under Item 1; also scored if child handles doll appropriately in Situation III

7. *Relates doll to bed:* child lays or seats doll on bed (head can be at foot of bed); not scored if doll is stood on bed or if doll is placed casually across bed, unless there is additional indication of intention, such as use of pillow or blanket

8. *Relates blanket or pillow to doll:* as stated, including wiping doll's face with blanket

9. *Puts doll to bed:* as stated

10. *Uses pillow correctly:* as stated, including placing pillow at either end of the bed

SITUATION III:

11. *Relates knife or fork to plate:* as stated

12. *Relates fork, knife, or plate to table:* places either of these objects on the table; liberal scoring

13. *Relates tablecloth to other object:* as stated, including (a) wiping cutlery, table, or doll's face with tablecloth; (b) using cloth as blanket for doll; or (c) using the cloth as either a carpet or a tablecloth

14. *Places doll on chair:* as stated; not scored if doll is laid across chair or faces the back of chair

15. *Relates fork, knife, or plate to doll:* as stated

16. *Relates chair to table:* as stated; not scored if chair is placed on table or if chair has its back against table

17. *Relates doll to table:* as stated, including doll sitting on chair that is placed at table or standing at table; not scored if doll is stood or laid down on table, if doll is placed underneath table, or if table is upside down

18. *Places tablecloth on table:* as stated, including indication that the tablecloth is being used specifically (e.g., plate or cutlery placed on tablecloth or chair is placed at the table)

SITUATION IV:

19. *Moves tractor or trailer along:* as stated; liberal scoring, but not scored if vehicle is upside down

20. *Relates log(s) to tractor, trailer, or man:* as stated, including (a) placing log(s) in tractor or trailer, (b) using logs as rails, (c) adding them to vehicles to make a train, (d) placing a log in the man's hand or mouth ("cigarette"), (e) seating the man on the logs, (f) using the log as a tool to "mend" wheel; not scored if log placed in child's mouth, if child "writes" with log, or if child pokes with log into the tractor or trailer

21. *Places man in tractor or trailer:* as stated; liberal scoring

22. *Places man in driver's seat:* as stated; child's intent in placing the man must be clear, although examiner may offer some help in placing the doll; however, position of man must be correct

23. *Lines up tractor and trailer:* as stated; relative position need not be correct; not scored if one vehicle is stacked on top of the other

24. *Attaches tractor to trailer:* as stated; relative position of the two vehicles must be correct; again, child must show clear intention, but examiner may offer some help in attaching vehicles; if child connects vehicles but in wrong position, credit is given for Item 23, but not for Item 24

Reprinted by permission of The NFER-Nelson Publishing Co., Ltd., Windsor, England.

Appendix B

Peter at 30 Months

PROTOCOL

SYMBOLIC PLAY TEST

SITUATION I:

    1. Discriminates doll _+_
    2. Relates spoon to cup or saucer _+_
    3. Feeds, combs or brushes self or other person _+_
    4. Feeds, combs or brushes doll _+_
    5. Places cup on saucer _-_

SITUATION II:

    6. Discriminates doll _+_
    7. Relates doll to bed _+_
    8. Relates blanket or pillow to doll _+_
    9. Puts doll to bed _+_
   10. Uses pillow correctly _+_

SITUATION III:

   11. Relates knife or fork to plate _+_   *did these activities*
   12. Relates fork, knife or plate to table _+_   *separately —*
   13. Relates tablecloth to other object _-_   *related fork to plate*
   14. Places doll on chair _+_   *plate to table*
   15. Relates fork, knife or plate to doll _+_
   16. Relates chair to table _+_   *chair to table*
   17. Relates doll to table _+_   *doll on chair to table*
   18. Places tablecloth on table _-_

SITUATION IV:

   19. Moves tractor or trailer along _+_   *pushed tractor*
   20. Relates log(s) to tractor, trailer or man _+_ *logs into wagon*
   21. Places man in tractor or trailer _+_   *man into wagon*
   22. Places man in driver's seat _-_
   23. Lines up tractor and trailer _+_   *lined up briefly*
   24. Attaches tractor to trailer _-_

TOTAL RAW SCORE: _19_   AGE EQUIVALENT SCORE: _31 months_

Score	Age (mos.)	Score	Age (mos.)
0-4	below 12	14	24.5
5	12.7	15	25.8
6	14	16	27.1
7	15.3	17	28.5
8	16.6	18	29.8
9	18	19	31.1
10	19.3	20	32.4
11	20.6	21	33.7
12	21.9	22	35
13	23.2	23-24	36 or more

Adapted score sheet for the Symbolic Play Test. Reprinted by permission of
NFER-Nelson Publishing Company, Ltd., Windsor UK

Appendix C

PROTOCOL

SYMBOLIC PLAY TEST

SITUATION I:

   1. Discriminates doll __+__
   2. Relates spoon to cup or saucer __+__
   3. Feeds, combs or brushes self or other person __+__
   4. Feeds, combs or brushes doll __+__
   5. Places cup on saucer __−__

SITUATION II:

   6. Discriminates doll __+__
   7. Relates doll to bed __+__
   8. Relates blanket or pillow to doll __+__
   9. Puts doll to bed __+__
  10. Uses pillow correctly __−__

SITUATION III:

  11. Relates knife or fork to plate __+__
  12. Relates fork, knife or plate to table __+__
  13. Relates tablecloth to other object __−__
  14. Places doll on chair __−__
  15. Relates fork, knife or plate to doll __+__
  16. Relates chair to table __−__
  17. Relates doll to table __−__
  18. Places tablecloth on table __−__

SITUATION IV:

  19. Moves tractor or trailer along __+__
  20. Relates log(s) to tractor, trailer or man __+__
  21. Places man in tractor or trailer __+__
  22. Places man in driver's seat __+__
  23. Lines up tractor and trailer __−__
  24. Attaches tractor to trailer __−__

TOTAL RAW SCORE: __15__   AGE EQUIVALENT SCORE: __26 mos.__

Score	Age (mos.)	Score	Age (mos.)
0-4	below 12	14	24.5
5	12.7	(15)	25.8
6	14	16	27.1
7	15.3	17	28.5
8	16.6	18	29.8
9	18	19	31.1
10	19.3	20	32.4
11	20.6	21	33.7
12	21.9	22	35
13	23.2	23-24	36 or more

Adapted score sheet for the Symbolic Play Test. Reprinted by permission of
NFER-Nelson Publishing Company, Ltd., Windsor UK

Chapter 3 —————————————————————————————

STANDARDIZED PLAY ASSESSMENT OF INFANT AND TODDLER TEMPERAMENT

Adam P. Matheny, Jr.

INTRODUCTION

To understand the invariant trends of play during child development and to consider important deflections from these trends from a clinical vantage, developmental theories of play have helped us to structure our view of the essentials of children's play. To a great extent these theories have concentrated on the normative expressions, during play, of cognitive, interpersonal, and affective behaviors. Children playing with other children or adults may be described in normative terms for problem-solving skills, social conflict, communication, positive or negative affective displays, role-playing, and so on. In this fashion, play becomes another means to calibrate the child's developmental trajectory toward adulthood, as formulated by Gesell, Freud, Piaget, or Erikson, among others. Each of these formulations has its own particular perspective as depicted by a wide, but not necessarily independent, variety of research interests. A glimpse of the variety has been provided by Erikson (1972), who gave an example of recorded observations of one boy playing with blocks, toy vehicles, and figures of animals and human dolls. Erikson noted that the play may be read one way to portray cognitive characteristics, another way to portray psychoanalytic themes, another way to identify sex differences, and so on. Quite obviously, there is not a perspective that is paramount to all others.

Supported in part by the Courier-Journal and Louisville Times Foundation, the John D. and Catherine T. MacArthur Foundation, the National Science Foundation (BNS-17315), the National Institute of Child Health and Human Development (HD03217; HD21395; HD22637), the National Institute of Mental Health (MH23884; MH39772), and the Office of Child Development (90-C-933).

The professional assistance of A. B. Dolan, S. Nuss, D. Batres, J. Krantz, R. Arbegust, P. Gefert, C. Hurst, J. Lechleiter, B. Moss, D. O'Hara, M. Slaton, L. Teets, and A. Thoben, and the cooperation of families of twins are gratefully appreciated.

When one watches children playing either alone or with others, one is often struck by the individual differences of expressive and emotive behaviors peripheral to the modal features of the play itself. For example, if the modal feature of a game is for two children to toss a ball back and forth, both children may pursue the game with equal diligence and competence but one child may be more sober in mien while the other smiles broadly, one may have more extraneous movements (more active) than the other, one may be more vocal than the other, or one may be more critical of self or other's performance. These differences in actions and reactions are not necessarily intrinsic to the play, yet they are readily apparent even in early infancy. No matter how constrained the child's play may be, these attendant features often mark children's individuality.

Although individual differences of children's expressive and emotive behaviors have not been ignored, it was not until the 1950s that there was a shift toward examining these characteristics in their own right. This shift was heralded by a view that the newborn is an active rather than a passive organism, a recognition that a source of developmental differences may include biological as well as environmental influences, and a heightened awareness that within highly organized environments children differ. By and large this shift in focus has taken place within a broad constituency of research studies that make use of a loosely defined set of concepts under the rubric of temperament.

TEMPERAMENT

Temperament refers to individual differences for dimensions of overt behaviors that appear during infancy, are relatively stable over time, seem to be based on a biological foundation, and make up at least part of the precursors of later personality. By tradition, temperament is considered to be the *stylistic*—individually typical or preponderant—manner of behavior, rather than the "what" (content or abilities) or "why" (causes) of behavior.

The contemporary conceptualizations of temperament recognize that aspects of temperament may be correlated with cognitive or motivational characteristics, but one behavioral domain need not map directly onto the other. Temperament is considered as a behavioral admixture that interacts with or modifies the more direct relation between cognitive and motivational characteristics and some behavioral outcome. Although characteristically sociable, active, and emotionally positive infants tend to perform at a higher level on infant mental tests, these temperament attributes are not concurrently or predictively equivalent to performance on infant mental tests. Temperament characteristics do not substitute for such concepts as achievement motivation, the "need to know," or similar motivational concepts. Neither does temperament translate directly into concepts of emotion or affect, although the overlap between theories of temperament and theories of emotion-affect has been noted in several publications (e.g., Derryberry & Rothbart, 1984; Campos, Barrett, Lamb, Goldsmith, & Stenberg, 1983). The lines of demarcation between these domains have not been drawn, but there are certainly distinctions of emphasis if nothing else. Temperament theories call attention more to individual differences with an emphasis on traits while theories of emotion and affect are more likely to focus on central tendencies with an emphasis on states. An infant's predisposition to become easily upset in a variety of contexts would not be considered an expression of temperament if that same degree of upset was found for most or all infants in the same contexts. In essence, theories of emotion or affect need not consider individual differences, but theories of temperament must.

Temperament Dimensions

Within the general conceptual aspects of temperament traced above, the behavioral domains of temperament have varied somewhat as to the number of temperament characteristics typically listed; these range from three independent dimensions (Buss & Plomin, 1975) to nine, not necessarily independent, characteristics issuing from the New York Longitudinal Study (NYLS). (See Thomas & Chess, 1980, for a review.)

The psychometric approach to creating temperament dimensions typified by Buss and Plomin (1975) consists of constructing a temperament theory from the essential attributes of historical definitions of temperament, creating pools of items to reflect the theoretical dimensions, and then refining the item pool so that eventually the independent dimensions can be identified. For example, in the theory by Buss and Plomin (1975), three dimensions—Emotionality, Activity, and Sociability—represent the core of temperament that should be identified at any age. In effect, this approach stipulates, *a priori*, dimensions of temperament that adhere to a theoretical stance (for review, see Goldsmith & Rothbart, 1991).

The clinical approach typified by the tradition of the NYLS has been to examine, through interviews and observations, preponderant behavioral differences among infants and older children manifest in a number of situations; then by inductive analysis of content, the number of behaviors are reduced to a smaller set of stylistic characteristics. For the NYLS data, this approach yielded nine characteristics. Although this approach has been criticized for failure to establish that the nine characteristics of temperament were independent dimensions, the NYLS investigators recognized that some of the nine characteristics were correlated (Thomas, Chess, & Birch, 1968), but retained all nine because of their clinical utility.

To date, the NYLS approach and its refinements represent the most extensive application of temperament as measured by questionnaires provided in clinical and research settings. Moreover, the refinements of the NYLS approach were the only ones that led to clinical assessments of temperament by questionnaires throughout childhood (Carey & McDevitt, 1978; Fullard, McDevitt, & Carey, 1984; Hegvik, McDevitt, & Carey, 1982) and with a life-span perspective (Lerner, Palermo, Spiro, & Nesselroade, 1982).

Direct Assessments of Temperament

The assessment of temperament by questionnaire or interviews has not proceeded uncontested, largely because the typical informants have been parents. Parents' perceptions of their children's temperament may be influenced or biased by attributes of the parents, and the error attached to temperament questionnaires may be considerable (Hubert, Wachs, Peters-Martin, & Gandour, 1982). On the other hand, the correlations between parental reports of temperament and measures obtained from other sources indicate some moderate degree of overlap (Bates & Bayles, 1984). Nevertheless, systematic procedures for the direct observation of temperament have been considered the optimal approach for temperament assessment.

The development of systematic procedures has typically concentrated on home observations. Although this source is practical and certainly yields information about temperament in a naturalistic setting, there remain sources of error and possibly bias by observing temperament within settings and attended by sequences of events in settings that are not controlled by the investigators. Thus, direct observations of temperament in the home environment may confound features of temperament with features of the home. In this respect, standardized play procedures of temperament became particularly important (Wilson & Matheny, 1980). An overview of standardized methods has been provided by Goldsmith and Rothbart (1991).

Standardized Play Procedures

Our approach to the use of the laboratory to assess temperament initially capitalized on observations of children's activities during free-play sessions. Twin children playing together or singly were simply observed and rated in a playroom prior to and after more structured events such as Bayley testing. These free-play sessions provided some interesting findings regarding the stability and consistency of temperament characteristics (Matheny & Dolan, 1975), but the sequence of events was not replicated from one child to the next. By the definition of free play, a child was allowed considerable latitude to play with anything available in any manner. While these conditions provided for large individual differences, there was no assurance that the opportunities were equivalent for all children. If one were to compare free-play temperament observations with temperament observations made during Bayley testing, one can easily see that the structured Bayley examination provides more equivalent procedures for all infants. By contrast, a free-play Bayley examination might consist of permitting the infant to have access to all test materials and play with them according to the infant's inclination.

Because of our experience with Bayley testing (Wilson, 1978) and the concomitant assessment of temperament during Bayley testing (Matheny, 1980, 1983; Matheny, Dolan, & Wilson, 1976) we devised a variety of structured play activities (vignettes) provided in a fixed sequence to permit observations of temperament (Matheny & Wilson, 1981; Wilson, 1982). Once the systematic procedures were established, the previous sources of data from Bayley testing were not discontinued. Nevertheless, through a series of pilot studies, the nature of the laboratory procedures evolved to encompass the main behavioral trends that would unfold during infancy and, at the same time, elicit individual differences around a common reference for children observed at several ages: 3, 6, 9, 12, 18, 24, and 30 months. From these efforts issued the standardized procedures described below.

DEVELOPMENTAL TASKS AND RATING SCALES FOR THE LABORATORY ASSESSMENTS OF INFANT TEMPERAMENT

I. Organization of Temperament Visits

A typical temperament visit to the laboratory occupies about 3 hours. During this period, a total of 60 minutes is videotaped according to a prescribed schedule. The episodes of the visits are chronologically listed below, and the episodes and manner of observations are noted.

Episode	Persons and Situations	Manner of Recording Observations	Duration of Videotaping
Orientation	Twins and parents in playroom, with Examiner-Interactionists 1 and 2	Videotape	6 minutes
Duo: Twins A & B together	Twins A & B, Examiner-Interactionists 1 and 2 in playroom (parent to interview)	Videotape	12 minutes
Reunion:	Parent returns from interview room and rejoins twins	Videotape	2 minutes
Separation and Solo: Twin A	Twin A and Examiner-Interactionist 3 in playroom (Parent and Twin B in testing)	Videotape (Bayley Mental Testing—Infant Behavior Record)	18 minutes
Reunion: Twin A	Parent and co-twin return to playroom	Videotape	1 minute
Separation and Solo: Twin B	Twin B and Examiner-Interactionist 4 in playroom (Parent and Twin A in testing)	Videotape (Bayley Mental Testing—Infant Behavior Record)	18 minutes
Reunion: Twin B	Parent and co-twin return to playroom	Videotape	1 minute
Physical Measurements	Each twin taken individually along with parent to physical measurement room	Behavioral ratings made in situ	
Conclusion	Both twins and parent together in playroom prior to departure	Videotape	2 minutes
Total Videotape Time			60 minutes

The playroom in which the videotapes are made is carpeted, and equipped with age-appropriate toys and materials. The rooms for interviewing, infant testing, and physical measurements are adjacent to the playroom.

II. General Description of Less-Structured Episodes

The episodes listed above represent different combinations of twins, parents, and staff members participating in different events. The episodes with events that are least structured will be described briefly in this section. These episodes are the following: Orientation, Reunions, Physical Measurements, and Conclusion. The remaining episodes are more highly structured and will be described in more detail in the next section.

Orientation

When the twins and parent arrive at the laboratory, housekeeping activities such as removing their outerwear are carried out in the lobby. At this point, if the twins have not been dressed in contrasting outfits, some feature of clothing is rearranged on one of the twins to provide a visible contrast between the twins.

After these preparations, twins, parent, and assigned examiner-interactionists go to the playroom. As soon as they enter the playroom, the videotape is started and allowed to run continuously for 6 minutes. The examiner-interactionists function as supportive, interested persons responsive to, rather than directing, the infants and the parent. The examiner-interactionists may offer to hold the twins, but their interaction is directed by the parent or infants. It is apparent that this episode is relatively unchallenging, and for the older infants, there is an opportunity for play to be dictated by the infants themselves.

Reunion (Duo Episode)

This 2-minute episode commences after the interview when the parent rejoins the twins in the playroom. During the interview, the parent has been told that, upon returning to the twins, the parent can play with the twins or do whatever is customary. As the parent enters the playroom, each examiner-interactionist assures that their assigned twin is aware that the parent has returned. The examiner-interactionists cease their previous activities with the twins; however, if the twins continue the activity, the examiner-interactionists resume participation.

Reunion: Twin A (Solo Episode)

When the parent and Twin B return to the playroom after Twin B completes Bayley testing, a brief period of 1 minute is videotaped. There is no established routine for the parent and Twin B to follow upon the return—the primary interest is in obtaining Twin A's responses to the return of the parent and co-twin.

Reunion: Twin B (Solo Episode)

A repetition of the reunion episode described above. In this instance, the parent and Twin A return from Bayley testing to rejoin Twin B in the playroom.

Physical Measurements

Another set of observations is made during the episode when each infant is measured for head circumference, weight, and reclining length. These measures are made in a room to which the parent takes the infant. Because of practical limits imposed by the equipment within the room and the indeterminant period for obtaining a complete set of measures, videotaping is not carried out. Instead, behaviors are rated in situ.

A set of ratings is made immediately after each of four separate activities during the physical measurements: (1) undressing the infant, (2) measuring head circumference, (3) obtaining weight by placing the infant on an infant scale, and (4) obtaining reclining length by requiring the infant to be stretched out in a supine position and held stationary while a footboard is brought into contact with the infant's heels.

Pilot studies of the infant's reactions to physical measurements indicated that measuring head circumference was the most benign procedure and measuring reclining length was the most upsetting; therefore, the sequence was arranged so that the reclining length was measured last. Thereby, the behaviors related to the measurement of reclining length did not override the rest of the activities.

Conclusion

After all of the procedures of the visit have been completed, there is a short period during which the twins and parent have a chance to "unwind" in the playroom. When the twins and parent are situated in the playroom, the first 2 minutes of the episode are videotaped. By and large, the comments pertaining to the Orientation episode apply to this episode as well.

III. General Description of Structured Episodes

During the earlier years of the research program of the Louisville Twin Study, when the primary purpose for the twins' visit to the laboratory had been to obtain an optimal assessment of mental development, play with the twins was directed toward maximizing rapport and minimizing upset, particularly during periods in which one twin was separated from the parent. Staff members typically employed toys and activities to hold the infants' attention and keep them engaged in play so that the periods of separation would be more enjoyable. As one might expect, not all toys and activities were equally successful for placating all infants at all ages, but after tailoring the activities for many infants, staff members developed "free-play" prototypes to fit a variety of styles seen for many infants.

When formal assessments of temperament were planned, the previous experiences with each infant's "free-play" provided the foundation for developing more extended activities; however, pilot studies suggested the necessity for developing those activities into a set of structured, age-specific tasks so that common points of reference could be established. These structured, age-specific tasks for reference—called vignettes—were created to be commonplace so that several comparisons with other occasions (e.g., home or testing) would be practical, yet the tasks had to be somewhat interesting or unusual for infants in a laboratory setting. Moreover, because developmental considerations set the limits for the tasks, the nature of the vignettes varied according to the ages of the infants. Finally, in order to make it possible to show developmental continuity across successive ages, some of the vignettes introduced at one age were repeated during subsequent ages.

The vignettes are described below according to the age at which they are introduced. Throughout the descriptions, *E* refers to the Examiner-Interactionist: the staff member engaged in activities with an assigned infant.

Standard Play Vignettes—03 Months

Toy/Activity	Episode	Time Allotted
CUDDLING	Duo	2 minutes

The infant is picked up by *E* and held by one of *E*'s arms in an upright position with the infant's head resting on *E*'s shoulder. *E*'s other arm provides support for the infant's back. After the infant is placed in this position, *E* comments on the infant's postural adjustment. (The comments pertain to the degree to which the infant's body stiffens, pushes away, or yields to *E*'s cuddling.) As *E* holds the infant, *E* also turns around slowly so that the infant's posture can be videotaped from several angles. The routine is carried out with the infant held in *E*'s left arm and then *E*'s right arm.

MOTION	Duo	2 minutes

The infant is held with *E*'s hands around the infant's body under the infant's arms, and then, with *E* seated in a chair, the infant is placed on *E*'s knees so that the infant faces *E*. The infant is bounced gently, then after a pause, rocked from side to side. After another pause, the entire procedure is repeated. *E* smiles and talks to the infant during the activities.

SMILE – LAUGH – PLAY	Duo	2 minutes

E attempts peek-a-boo, tickle, or vocalizes a noise so as to elicit a smile or laugh (i.e., frolic play) from the infant who is seated on *E*'s knees. Because this activity occurs during an episode in which both infants are together with two staff members, each *E* attempts the activity for about one minute and then infants are exchanged and the activity is repeated.

5-minutes pause in videotaping

MOBILE	Duo	6 minutes

During this vignette, each infant is lying supine on a mat on the floor. A combination of a mobile and music box, actuated by a wind-up mechanism, is mounted on an upright and placed near each infant so that the mobile is directly over the infant's head at a distance of about 12 inches. The vignette consists of three phases: (a) the mobile is removed from the apparatus and only the music box is played, (b) the mobile is replaced and rotated without the music box playing, and (c) the music box plays and the mobile rotates in combination.

Transition from Duo to Solo episodes

VERBAL ACTIVITY	Solo	2 minutes

The infant is placed in a supine position in a crib and *E* talks to the infant as *E* smiles and leans over the infant's face.

CHEWEY, RATTLE	Solo	2 minutes

The infant is lying supine in a crib and the chewey is waved or shaken in front of the infant's face and then placed in one of the infant's hands. When about 30 seconds have elapsed or when the infant releases the chewey, the object is placed in the infant's other hand. The same sequence is then carried out for a rattle.

6-minutes pause in videotaping

CRADLE GYM	Solo	2 minutes

The infant is lying in a supine position on a mat on the floor. A cradle gym, suspended between two uprights, is positioned over the infant and at a height that allows the infant to touch red rings dangling from the apparatus. If the infant does not attend to the cradle gym, the entire apparatus is jiggled intermittently until the infant shows some regard.

PRONE	Solo	2 minutes

The infant is placed in a prone position on a mat on the floor and allowed to remain there. If the infant turns over, then the infant is repositioned in the prone position.

6-minutes pause in videotaping

FEEDING, INTERRUPTION	Solo	10 minutes

The general purpose of this vignette is to obtain a view of the infant's response to the interruption of feeding and to consider how easily the infant can be soothed after feeding is interrupted.

During the preceding pause, the infant's bottle (supplied by the parent) is made ready for the feeding and *E* is seated with the infant cradled in a feeding position. When the videotape is started, the vignette is followed according to the following sequence:

1. *Feeding*: The infant's head is supported by *E*'s arm in such a way that the neck is not hyperextended. The bottle is held so that the nipple is full at all times. When the bottle is presented, the outer corner of the infant's mouth is stroked to elicit the rooting reflex, and then the nipple is placed in the infant's mouth. After feeding starts, the infant is allowed to continue feeding for 1 minute before the bottle is removed.

2. *Bottle removal*: The bottle is removed and placed to one side out of the infant's line of sight. If the infant does not become upset at the interruption of feeding within 30 seconds after the bottle is removed, the bottle is returned. If the infant becomes upset within the 30-second period, then soothing procedures are initiated.

3. *Soothing I: Talking*: The object of the soothing procedure is to placate the infant simply by verbal intervention. The infant is turned (in one smooth motion) so that *E* can face the infant directly. Then *E* talks to the infant in a soothing, crooning tone and uses the infant's name frequently. If the infant fully quiets within a 30-second interval, then the bottle is returned. If the infant continues to fuss at the end of the 30-second interval, then the soothing procedures are augmented.

4. *Soothing II: Stroking*: As in Soothing I, talking to the infant continues, but mild stroking of the infant's head, arms, trunk, legs, back, and face is added. During a 30-second interval, if the infant is soothed, the bottle is returned, but if the infant is not soothed, the next level of intervention is applied.

5. *Soothing III: Prone*: The infant is placed in a prone position across *E*'s lap and the procedures in Soothing II are continued. If necessary, the infant's face is supported with one hand while stroking the infant's back with the other. If this procedure soothes the infant within 30 seconds, the bottle is returned. If not, a final procedure is applied.

6. *Soothing IV: Shoulder*: The infant is lifted from the lap and placed in a cuddling position with the infant's face against *E*'s shoulder. The talking and stroking of the infant continues. If the infant soothes before a 30-second interval elapses, the bottle is returned, and if the infant is not soothed by the end of the 30-second interval, the bottle is returned.

7. *Continuation of feeding*: The infant is fed until the bottle is completed, even if the videotaped portion of the feeding has finished. Remarks: During this sequence, *E* comments on the nature of the infant's sucking (strength and frequency of sucking) and the infant's respiration. In some instances, *E* may offer comments about the infant's eyes being open or closed. All comments offered by *E* are incorporated within *E*'s soothing, crooning vocalizations.

Standard Play Vignettes—06 Months

The toys/activities and time allotted for all vignettes at 06 months are as described for the vignettes at 03 months. In some rare instances the vignette involving the interruption of feeding, soothing, and completion of feeding would not last until the end of the 10-minute videotaped interval. For these instances, the infant remains seated in *E*'s lap and is allowed to play with a rattle or some other small toy.

Standard Play Vignettes—09 Months

Toy/Activity	Episode	Time Allotted
BUSY BOX	Duo	6 minutes

The infant is seated on the floor near a busy box mounted to an upright. *E* gains the infant's attention by activating one of the noisemakers incorporated in the apparatus (e.g., a sliding bar that makes a ratchet noise). While the infant is watching, *E* demonstrates all of the features of the apparatus, and encourages the infant to participate.

PRONE	Duo	2 minutes

The infant is placed in a prone position on the floor. If the infant turns over or sits, *E* makes no immediate efforts to return the infant to a prone position unless assistance is necessary.

5-minutes pause in videotaping

RASPBERRY	Duo	2 minutes

E, sitting in a chair, holds the infant so that the infant sits on *E*'s knees and faces *E*. *E* looks at and talks to the infant and then, with animation, makes a raspberry or some other unusual vocalization. Contingent upon the infant's response, *E* may repeat the raspberry so as to set up a "game." The raspberry or unusual vocalization can also be made with *E*'s holding a toy animal as a prop. The procedure attempts to elicit imitative vocalizations from the infant as well as anticipatory reactions.

MOTION	Duo	2 minutes

E remains seated as in the previous vignette and carries out a repetitive bouncing or swinging motion with the infant seated on *E*'s knees. *E* then stops to allow the infant to act in such a manner to promote *E*'s moving again. If the contingency is established, *E* may vary the sequence or the type of motions, so that the infant's anticipatory response is not always followed by exactly the same motion by *E*.

CUDDLING	Duo	2 minutes

The vignette is carried out in exactly the same manner as the one described at 03 months.

Transition from Duo to Solo episodes

CLUTCH BALL	Solo	2 minutes

The infant is seated on the floor. A clutch ball is presented to the infant and the infant is encouraged to hold it and give it back to *E*. If the infant does not show interest in the ball, *E* may juggle the ball or lightly toss it into the air. If the infant can be encouraged to take the ball from and give it back to *E*, the sequence can be expanded to include rolling the ball back and forth between *E* and the infant. The main purpose of the sequence is to engage the infant in a participatory game.

PAT-A-CAKE or		
IMITATIVE GAME	Solo	2 minutes

E instigates a game (pat-a-cake, waving bye-bye, peek-a-boo) combining gestures with animated expressions and vocalizations. The cadences of the activities are repeated so that the infant can anticipate, imitate, or promote the ongoing sequences. After the infant participates, *E*'s own gestural sequence is stopped so as to permit the infant to show encouragement for the game to continue. *E* also can continue the sequence by giving a spoken request unaccompanied by gestures.

ACTION BALL	Solo	2 minutes

The infant, seated on the floor, is given a transparent plastic ball that has an hour-glass inside. The hour-glass contains brightly colored plastic granules that pass through the vortex of the hour-glass. *E* rolls the ball, shakes it to show the granules falling through the hour-glass and encourages the infant to play with the ball. This vignette need not engage the infant in a participatory game between the infant and *E*.

SOUEEZE TOY	Solo	2 minutes

A squeeze toy (animal or some recognizable object), that makes a whistling sound along with a puff of air, is demonstrated to the infant. By squeezing or hitting the toy, *E* makes the toy whistle and then gives the toy to the infant. *E* may repeat the demonstration as often as necessary to keep the infant engaged with the toy.

DRUM	Solo	2 minutes

A plastic drum and drumstick are set before the infant, and *E* bangs upon the drum with the drumstick. The drumstick is given to the infant and *E* encourages the infant to bang. *E* may tap with a hand upon the drum head to promote banging. *E* may repeat the demonstration.

6-minutes pause in videotaping

HIDDEN OBJECT	Solo	2 minutes

The infant is seated in a feeding table that has a large tray in front of the infant. The infant is shown an attractive small toy. If the infant reaches for the toy, *E* places the toy upon the tray and quickly covers the toy with a white washcloth. If the infant does not attempt to lift the washcloth, loses interest or is unsuccessful, the procedure is demonstrated again. If the infant does not participate, another demonstration may be given with a different toy. If the infant shows no success, the procedure is repeated once with the toy only partially covered.

If the infant successfully obtains the toy during any of the demonstrations involving the toy being completely covered, *E* places two washcloths several inches apart from each other. A toy is placed under the first washcloth, then removed in full view of the infant and placed under the second washcloth. The sequence may be demonstrated twice, and the order of the sequence is reversed.

VISIBLE BARRIER	Solo	2 minutes

This vignette is based on a test item from the Cattell Infant Intelligence Scale (1947). The infant remains seated at the feeding table. The infant is given an attractive small toy.

When the infant holds the toy and proceeds to play with it, the toy is taken from the infant and moved away from, but within reach of, the infant. As the infant reaches for the toy, a transparent plexiglass screen is placed upright between the infant and the toy. If the infant does not attempt to obtain the toy, the screen is removed and the same or another toy is given to the infant. If the toy evokes interest, the procedure is repeated.

6-minutes pause in videotaping

MIRROR   Solo   4 minutes

This vignette is adapted from a sequence outlined by Bertenthal and Fischer (1978). The infant is placed on the floor in front of a large upright mirror so that the infant faces the mirror. *E* points to the mirror and asks "Who is that?" After the infant shows attention to the mirror, approximately 1 minute is allotted for the infant to vocalize, move toward, and touch the reflected image, or lose interest in the mirror. If the infant's behaviors suggest that there is a coordination between the reflected image and the infant's movements, *E* holds an attractive toy above and behind the infant's head so that the toy is out of the infant's direct line of sight but visible from the mirror's reflection. After 1 minute is allotted to this part of the procedure, an additional 2 minutes are allotted if the infant continues to participate.

If the infant does not participate in the latter part of the vignette, *E* may try to engage the infant in some activity that can take place in front of the mirror.

Standard Play Vignettes—12 Months

Toy/Activity	Episode	Time Allotted
BUSY BOX	Duo	6 minutes

The vignette is a repetition of the one described for the Duo episode at 09 months.

ACTION BALL   Duo   2 minutes

This vignette is a repetition of the one described for the Solo episode at 09 months. The present vignette is modified to take account of the twins being together; therefore, *E* tries to engage the assigned infant in participatory play with *E,* but each *E*'s infant is permitted to look on or participate with the activities of the other infant and the other *E*.

5-minutes pause in videotaping

BABY BLOCKS   Duo   4 minutes

The infant, seated on the floor, is given a soft plastic gallon bucket containing about a dozen plastic blocks. *E* dumps the blocks from the bucket, then *E* encourages the infant to fill the bucket, and, at the same time, demonstrates putting blocks in the bucket. The filling and dumping play is encouraged throughout the vignette; however, if the infant proceeds to play only with the blocks or only with the bucket, such play is also allowed to continue. In effect, any play that exploits some or all of the materials is permitted.

CUDDLE   Duo   2 minutes

This vignette is the same as that outlined at 03 and 06 months.

Transition from Duo to Solo episodes

CLUTCH BALL Solo 2 minutes

The procedures are the same as those described for the vignette at 09 months. *E* places more emphasis on the interaction possible by the infant's rolling (and throwing) the ball to *E*.

DRUM Solo 2 minutes

As described in the vignette at 09 months, the procedure for banging the drum is demonstrated by *E*. In addition, on the opposite side of the drum is a drop box into which brightly colored balls may be dropped. (The balls are retrieved through a slot in the side of the drum.) The vignette permits use of all of the features of the drum-drop box, drum stick, and balls.

PAT-A-CAKE or
IMITATIVE GAME Solo 2 minutes

This vignette is the same as the one described for 09 months except that *E* places more emphasis on continuing the game by spoken requests.

BLOCKS Solo 2 minutes

The infant, seated on the floor, is given two soft plastic gallon buckets containing about a dozen plastic blocks (see 12 months, BABY BLOCKS, Duo episode). *E* pours the blocks from one bucket into the other and encourages the infant to do the same. Whatever use the infant makes of the blocks and buckets is allowed to continue; however, only the pouring of blocks is demonstrated.

CUDDLE DOLL Solo 2 minutes

A small plastic baby doll that has moveable limbs is given to the infant seated on the floor. By demonstration and vocal request, *E* tries to engage the infant in kissing, cuddling, and rocking the doll. A blanket and small bottle are supplied with the doll and these may be included in the sequence of play. *E* tries to keep the number of demonstrations to a minimum so that the infant can exploit the toys without sustained demonstrations.

6-minutes pause in videotaping

VISIBLE BARRIER Solo 2 minutes

This vignette is the same as that given at 09 months. For some infants who resist sitting in the feeding table, the vignette may be staged so that the infants are seated at a low table or standing in front of a waist-high table or tray.

VERBAL ACTIVITY Solo 2 minutes

This vignette is primarily staged so that *E* can engage the infant in any verbal activity including echoing melodies, words, or any vocalizations that *E* makes. *E* may also echo the infant's vocalizations so as to promote a vocalizing "game."

6-minutes pause in videotaping

MIRROR Solo 4 minutes

This vignette is staged like the vignette at 09 months. Before seating the infant in front of the mirror, *E* applies a colored adhesive dot to the tip of the infant's nose. (The dot is applied during some distracting play carried out in a preceding pause.) When the infant is seated facing the mirror, *E* follows the procedure outlined for the vignette at 09 months.

Standard Play Vignettes—18 Months

Toy/Activity	Episode	Time Allotted
DRUM (BALL DROP)	Duo	2 minutes

The toy is the one described in the vignette at 09 and 12 months. In this vignette, concentrated emphasis is placed on the infant's dropping the balls into the drum's end that contains a drop-hole. The balls are retrieved through the side of the drum, but it is not easy to retrieve the balls by reaching through the drop-hole. As an additional feature of this vignette, *E* shows the infant that the ball can be made to spin around the lip on the perimeter of the drum before dropping into the hole. If the infant does not become involved in these features of the activity and plays with the drum or balls in some other fashion, *E* permits the infant's activities to continue.

COBBLER BENCH	Duo	2 minutes

The infant, seated on the floor, is shown a small wooden bench with 6 pegs inserted through round holes in the bench. *E* demonstrates hitting a peg with the hammer so that most of the peg is driven through the bench. *E* gives the hammer to the infant who is then encouraged to carry out the same activity. *E* may also show the infant that the bench can be turned over so that the pegs can be driven in the opposite direction.

TYKE BIKE	Duo	2 minutes

E provides the infant with a low four-wheeled "bike," and, if the infant does not get on the vehicle spontaneously, *E* sits the infant on the bike. *E* encourages the infant to propel the bike; however, any play with the bike is permitted to continue. This vignette involves two infants being provided with two bikes at the same time; therefore, the potential for a range of play exists.

5-minutes pause in videotaping

BLACKBOARD-WATER	Duo	2 minutes

During this vignette, a container of water and a standard 1- to 2-inch paintbrush are used. *E* shows the infant how water may be "painted" on a large blackboard mounted on the wall by "painting" a vertical line and a few dots on one end of the board. Then the infant is given the brush and encouraged to try. Again, both infants are given the opportunity to become engaged in the shared activity at the same time.

BLACKBOARD-CHALK	Duo	2 minutes

This vignette immediately follows the previous one. After removing the container of water and paintbrush used in the previous vignette, *E* takes white chalk, draws a vertical line and scribbles on the blackboard. The infant is given the chalk and encouraged to draw some lines. If the infant does, then *E* takes a damp cloth and shows the infant how the marks can be erased. The infant is provided the opportunity to use the chalk and the damp cloth without further participation by *E*.

SUPER-BRIX	Duo	2 minutes

Large, lightweight, cardboard blocks of different sizes are placed in front of both infants and then the infants are encouraged and helped to build a tall structure. (This vignette especially focuses on a common task for both infants. Each *E* continues to assist the assigned infant, but both *E*'s shape the activity toward the single goal.) Once the structure is built, the *E*'s first suggest or encourage their assigned infants to shove or knock down the structure. Large balls, conveniently at hand, can be given to the infants and the infants can be encouraged to knock down the structure by throwing the balls. Both *E*'s provide a lot of encouragement and excitement during this vignette, particularly when the structure is to be torn down.

Transition from Duo to Solo episodes

SLINKY	Solo	2 minutes

The coiled spring toy called Slinky is shown to the infant and the changeable properties of the toy are demonstrated. The infant is given the toy and no further assistance is provided by *E* unless the infant solicits participation by *E*.

BABY DOLL	Solo	2 minutes

This vignette and the one immediately following are based on a developmental sequence of pretend play (Watson & Fischer, 1977). A baby doll set—doll, doll bed, blanket, and baby bottle—is placed on the floor before the infant. *E* cuddles, rocks the doll, and puts the doll to bed. Then the infant is given the doll and encouraged to do the same. *E* may expand any of these activities to elicit "role-playing" behavior from the infant.

UNCOMMON EVENT	Solo	2 minutes

This vignette is an immediate extension of the preceding vignette. *E* removes the doll and substitutes a plain wooden block for all of the activities previously centered around the doll (i.e., *E* cuddles the block, rocks it, and so on). Again, the infant is encouraged to do the same.

PUPPET	Solo	2 minutes

Behind *E*'s back, *E* puts on a hand puppet, and, after gaining the infant's attention, reveals the puppet. *E* describes the puppet, then initiates interaction between the infant and puppet: *E* may have the puppet "talk" and ask for a kiss and so on, or *E* may try to get the infant engaged in a conversation with the puppet. If the infant is willing, *E* encourages the infant to work the puppet.

MECHANICAL TOY	Solo	2 minutes

A battery-powered dog that barks and moves is placed in front of the infant. The controlling mechanism, connected to the dog by a long wire, is held by *E,* who activates the dog, and, at the same time, shows the infant how the toy works. The infant is offered the control and encouraged to make the dog bark and move. If the infant does not take the control, it is placed on the floor within reach of the infant. *E* encourages the infant to get the control, but if the infant does not make an attempt within about 10 seconds, *E* regains the control and repeats the procedure.

6-minutes pause in videotaping

BOOK   Solo   2 minutes

E takes a colorful picture book to the infant who is seated at a low table. *E* places the book in front of the infant, slowly turns the pages, and talks (naming, describing) about the pictures. *E* tries to engage the infant in conversation by asking questions (e.g., "What is that?" "What is the ____ doing now?").

HIDDEN OBJECT   Solo   2 minutes

The infant is seated at a low table on which two screens are arranged side by side. *E* introduces and demonstrates a small mechanical toy, offers it to the infant, and helps the infant to make the toy work. *E* then takes the toy and places it under one of the screens and asks the infant to find it. The procedure is repeated for the other screen. If the infant has not been successful on either trial, the sequence is repeated. If the infant is successful, *E* places the toy under the first screen, removes it and places it under the second screen. The infant is asked to find it, then the sequence is repeated in the opposite order of screens. If the infant is successful, a third screen may be introduced and the procedures are repeated.

At this age (and at the ages of 24 and 30 months), some infants may "solve" the problem readily. In these instances, the screens are removed and two specially constructed boxes are placed side by side on the table. (The two boxes are constructed to be identical in size and external appearance. Each box has a lid at the top and a door at the side. One "ordinary" box is completely empty inside. The other box—"trick box"—has a mirror inside that makes the box's interior appear empty when, in fact, only a part of the interior is visible and the remaining part is a hidden compartment reached by the lid at the top. *E* opens the side doors of both boxes and shows the infant that the boxes are empty. Then *E* takes an attractive toy, opens the top lid of the "ordinary" box and points out to the infant, who can see through the side door of the box, that the toy is inside the box. *E* asks the infant to remove the toy. Then *E* closes the side doors of both boxes, opens the top lid of the "ordinary" box and places the toy inside. *E* asks the infant to find the toy. If the infant finds or retrieves the toy from the "ordinary" box, *E* applauds the infant's performance and closes the door of the "ordinary" box. Then *E* opens the top lid of the "trick box" and places the toy in the hidden compartment. Again, the infant is asked to find the toy. The procedure may be repeated if time permits.

6-minutes pause in videotaping

MIRROR   Solo   4 minutes

The staging of this vignette is outlined at 09 months. Prior to placing the infant in front of the mirror, *E* surreptitiously applies a colored adhesive dot to the tip of the infant's nose. After the infant is in position, *E* initiates the interactions involving the infant's recognition of self and coordination between reflected and actual events. At this age, *E* places more emphasis upon the interpersonal play involving the reflections (*E* and infant waving or talking to each other by means of the reflection). Any other game during which the infant exploits the mirror and *E*'s participation is permitted to continue.

Toward the latter part of this vignette, during a moment when the infant is not facing the mirror or has moved away from or behind the mirror, *E* allows a curtain (attached to the top of the mirror frame) to fall down and cover the mirror. If the infant does not notice the change, *E* points out that something has happened to "(child's name) picture." *E* may also ask "Where is (child's name) now?"

Standard Play Vignettes—24 and 30 Months

The toys/activities and times allotted for the vignettes at 24 and 30 months are as described for the vignettes at 18 months. Although the structure of the vignettes remains the same, the latitude for verbal exchanges widens because of the increased competence of the infant's language. Therefore, *E* tries to evoke and encourage verbal exchanges within the limits of the structure of each vignette.

IV. Behavioral Rating Scales and Checklist

The rating scales and checklist were derived from the experience with the scales of Bayley's Infant Behavior Record (IBR). Extensive pretesting then brought about refinements, such as the creation of descriptors for every rating point of some of the IBR scales. The number of points for the scales and the previously provided IBR descriptors for each of those points were retained as much as possible, however. In addition, certain features of behavior, such as state of arousal, were noted on a checklist during each rating period.

Playroom Rating Scales

Emotional Tone
The range and descriptors correspond to a similarly named scale on the IBR. Ratings are not based solely on overt facial expressions and take into account other features of an infant's behaviors that give clues to emotionality (e.g., motor excitement, vocalizations).

1. Extremely upset: wailing, protest
2. Upset, but not overwrought
3. Momentary upset: puckering up to cry, short verbal protest, initiation of escape movement
4. Slight indication of disturbance: uneasiness, wariness, guarded or avoidant stance
5. Indifferent; bland; undifferentiated emotionality
6. Slight recognition of change: perfunctory smile, wave, salutation, but can be bland awareness
7. Momentary: sustained smile—approachful and reactive
8. Excited
9. Highly excited: gleeful, expressive, animated

Activity

This scale, like the identical scale from the IBR, refers to body motion with or without locomotion. An infant is not likely to receive a rating of 1, but this rating should be considered for sleep or feeding periods. The rating is to be used for self-initiated overt movements of part or whole body, except mouth movements. In addition to whole body, the descriptors below refer to part-body movements as well:

1. Stays quietly in one place, with practically no self-initiated movement.
2. Between 1 and 3
3. Usually quiet and inactive, but responds appropriately in situations calling for some activity
4. Between 3 and 5
5. Moderate activity
6. Between 5 and 7
7. In action during much of the period of observation
8. Between 7 and 9
9. Hyperactive; cannot be quieted for sedentary tests

Social Orientation (to Staff, to Twin, and to Parent)

The ratings for these three scales refer to the positive and negative aspects of social orientation of the twin in relation to others, and a single rating dimension is used. (In those instances when several staff members or both parents are present, the infant's social orientation is rated as if the staff or parents were one person.) It may be helpful to consider this continuum apart from emotional tone (negative–positive) and place emphasis on avoidance–approach behaviors. An infant can be quite upset and still approach or show a gesture of wanting to be picked up, held, or the like.

— For ratings 1–4, assure that the ratings apply to the negative reactions of the infant to the person rather than to the apparent activity in which the person is engaging. For example, the infant may be negative to having some maintenance (nose-wipe, diaper change) but not negative to the provider of the maintenance.

1. Actively negativistic, struggling, aggressive, strongly avoiding, fleeing, or withdrawn
2. Fussing, frowning, grimacing, whining
3. Wary, hesitant, passively resistant, avoidant
4. Sobered, turning away, stilling, perfunctory negative acts
5. Indifferent or ignoring
6. Acceptant in a passive sense; can be bland in facial expression but compliant in interaction; spectator
7. Positive (friendly, eager, smiling) participation; approachful, reactive
8. Excited, eager, responsive participation
9. Very strongly oriented, demanding; possessive of interaction (can be negative in emotional tone)

Attentiveness

This scale corresponds to the scale Attention Span on the IBR. It refers to the degree to which the infant alerts to and maintains attention on objects or events (including vocalizations of the caretaker or others). Although the infant may be a spectator or a participant, the infant's active participation is a more obvious indication of attention than being a spectator.

1. Unoccupied, nonfocused (e.g., vacant staring)
2. Between 1 and 3
3. Minimal or fleeting attention (distractibility)
4. Between 3 and 5
5. Moderate attention—generally attentive but may shift at times because of other's direction, demonstration, or command
6. Between 5 and 7
7. Focused and sustained attention
8. Between 7 and 9
9. Continued and persistent attention to the point of "being glued" or "fixed" to the event

Vocalizing

This category is to be employed in the same manner as the category provided by the IBR. Vocalizations refer to noncrying utterances or to recognizable utterances embedded in crying. Crying, per se, no matter how varied, does not qualify.

1. Definitely quiet, no vocalizations
2. Between 1 and 3
3. Few vocalizations and of short duration
4. Between 3 and 5
5. Vocalizations occur as part of activities but too intermittently to constitute vocal excitement, chatter, or the like
6. Between 5 and 7
7. Vocalizations constitute an obvious part of the infant's activity: infant vocalizes for the sake of vocalizing
8. Between 7 and 9
9. Excessive vocalizations; high vocal excitement

Initial Reaction

At specific times during the sequence of observations, the parent separates from or rejoins the infant(s). This scale refers to the behavior of the infant during a 10-second interval after the parent's exit or entry. It should be noted that this rating scale is equivalent to *Emotional Tone.*

1. Extremely upset; wailing, protest
2. Upset, but not overwrought
3. Momentary upset: puckering up to cry, short verbal protest, initiation of escape movement

4. Slight indication of disturbance: uneasiness

5. Indifferent; bland; undifferentiated emotionality

6. Slight recognition of change: perfunctory smile, wave, salutation, but can be bland awareness with a momentary sustained smile; approachful and reactive

8. Excited

9. Highly excited: gleeful, expressive, animated

Number of Activities (Toys/Play)

This category represents a count, and the intent is to indicate whether the infant is involved with a few or many activities other than those represented by vignettes. (If the infant is engaged in a vignette, a specific code represents the toy/play activity.) The following constraints apply to the coding:

— If a toy is employed by the infant, with interruption, more than once in a sequence of play, it is counted only once.

— Two of the same toy, used in combination, count as two toys (e.g., two cards). When two toys are brought together in demonstration and both toys are necessary to reproduce the demonstrated activity, they count as one toy/activity (e.g., drum and drumstick).

— If the infant initiates activity independently (no demonstration) with two separate toys, count as two toys unless activity is inherent property of toys.

— If the infant is a participant in play, but waiting a turn, then the infant is involved in the activity. This qualifier includes social interactive games, taking turns, and spectator activities.

1. No involvement with toys or play

2. (1 = count)

3. (2 = count)

4. (3 = count)

5. (4 = count)

6. (5 = count)

7. (6 = count)

8. (7 = count)

9. Involved with many toys; goes from toy to toy almost continually—frenetic play.

Locomotion

The extent of general body movements in space, such as would be noted for the infant rolling over, crawling, walking, climbing, or propelling a vehicle. The ratings should reflect the infant's self-determined movements to change location or position in any direction. It should be obvious that the younger infant will receive lower ratings for this category.

1. No change in position; lies or sits in place

2. Between 1 and 3

3. Few changes in position; sporadic or short-lived movement in space; brief repositioning to obtain or exploit objects as part of an activity

4. Between 3 and 5

5. Changes in position are frequent but are not an apparent end

6. Between 5 and 7

7. Changes in position are frequent enough to keep the interactionist "on the go"; locomotion is an interest in itself

8. Between 7 and 9

9. Change in position extremely pronounced—can be reflected by staff having to restrain the infant or reposition the infant

Mouthing

This rating category refers to all mouthing or sucking behaviors except when the infant takes food from a bottle. If it is apparent that a bottle's nipple is used as a pacifier, and the infant is not feeding, then mouthing the nipple is included in this category. Sucking thumbs, fingers, and tongue are particularly noteworthy. For purposes of comparisons, this category refers to a combination of three scales from the *IBR:* Mouthing—thumb or fingers (22), Mouthing—pacifier (23), Mouthing—toys (24).

1. None

2. Between 1 and 3

3. Mouthing occurs briefly as part of an ongoing program

4. Between 3 and 5

5. Mouthing occurs for a short period but could be (or was) interrupted by other events

6. Between 5 and 7

7. Mouthing occurred enough to constitute a major part of the infant's activity or was an end in itself

8. Much or excessive: mouthing is essentially the only activity seen

Playroom Checklist: State

The following features of state-related behaviors during each rating period may qualify or supplement features of the preceding Playroom Rating Scales. Other checklists may be found in Matheny and Wilson (1981). State refers to general level of arousal of an infant. Some of the checkpoints reflect qualitative differences during sleep as well.

1. Quiet or regular sleep (regular respiration, no eye movements, little or no body movements, rhythmic mouth movements can occur)

2. Transitional sleep (between quiet and active; *E* will usually give more verbal comments about infant's activities)

3. Active sleep (irregular or shallow respiration, many eye movements, movements of limbs, face, mouth, body)

4. Drowsy (going into or coming out of sleep, between awake and sleep, infant still, eyes open and close)

5. Sleepy, fatigued, tired (gestural—yawning, rubbing eyes, vocalizing, pulling on ears; infant is still active and awake; cranky, giving clues that he/she could be put to sleep; possible negative affect)

6. Awake

Physical Measurements Rating Scales

Five sets of ratings are made during the physical measurement episode. The first four are for the different aspects of the activities during the episode: undressing the infant, measuring head circumference, weighing the infant, and obtaining reclining length. The same three 9-point rating scales are used for each of these activities. The three are identified and described as follows:

1. *Emotional tone*: The same rating scale as was described for the playroom observations.

2. *Activity*: The same rating scale as was described for the playroom observations.

3. *Cooperation*: The degree to which the infant resists, acquiesces, or helps in the activities of physical measurement; the range of this scale and its relevance is comparable to that of the like-named scale on the *IBR*.

    1. Actively resistant, tries to disengage
    2. Between 1 and 3
    3. Somewhat resistant but "gives in"
    4. Between 3 and 5
    5. Neither resistant nor cooperative—acquiescent
    6. Between 5 and 7
    7. Generally cooperative
    8. Between 7 and 9
    9. Very readily accedes to demands (even attempts to help)

The fourth and fifth set of ratings are made after the physical measurements are completed. These consist of two 9-point rating scales rated on the basis of the total physical measurement episode. The two scales are identified and described as follows:

4. *Caretaker orientation*: The same rating scale as that described for the scale *Social Orientation* (To Staff), employed in the playroom.

5. *Vocalizing (Non-crying)*: The same rating scale as that described for the like-named scale employed in the playroom.

Scoring Laboratory Visits

Videotapes

After the visit is completed for a pair of twins, raters work independently from the videotapes and make their ratings for each successive 2-minute period of the visit. No rater scores the episodes for which the rater served as an examiner-interactionist with the twin during the visit.

Among the 11 rating scales, there are 5 scales that represent the broadest expanse of activities videotaped throughout a visit. Each of these rating scales—Emotional Tone, Activity, Social Orientation: Staff, Attentiveness, Vocalizing—provides a maximum of 22 ratings from twenty 2-minute periods (Orientation, Duo, Reunion, Solo, and Conclusion) and two 1-minute reunions (Reunion-A and Reunion-B). The other rating scales, such as Social Orientation (Parent) or Number of Activities, are applicable to fewer episodes; as a consequence, these rating scales represent a narrower expanse of the videotaped activities and have not been exploited by analyses.

A series of pilot analyses assessed the internal consistency of each of the rating scales by determining the extent to which each of the 2-minute (or 1-minute) ratings correlated with the total of 22 ratings. The rating periods that provided the highest correlations with the total were retained as the best representation for each rating scale. On the strength of these analyses, the six 2-minute ratings for the DUO episode, the nine 2-minute ratings for the SOLO episode, and the one 2-minute rating for the Reunion episode after DUO were retained. Thus, there were 16 ratings for each of the 5 rating scales. The internal consistency coefficients for the 5 rating scales were .70 or higher at ages 9, 12, 18, 24, and 30 months. At ages 3 and 6 months, coefficients for the rating scales Vocalizing and Social Orientation (Staff) were between .50 and .70. Vocalizing was deleted from further analyses. Social Orientation (Staff) was retained, however, because it was one of the central features of children's play at 9 months and older. Moreover, this is the one rating scale most similar to the temperament characteristic, sociability, identified by Buss and Plomin (1975).

The large number of ratings for each rating scale was reduced further by creating composite scores representing the average of the 16 ratings for each of the five scales. In addition to the evidence that aggregate measures are more reliable (Epstein, 1980; Paunonen, 1984), the condensation of ratings across time and for different events typifies the notion of temperament as stylistic or manneristic behaviors across time or situations. Thus, at each age, there were five indices of temperament for each child when the child was confronted with an organized succession of activities and persons, some of which were more evocative than others.

Physical Measurements

There were fewer ratings made during physical measurements and these were made in situ because of practical limitations. A pilot study of ratings possible from this situation indicated that ratings of Emotional Tone, Cooperation, and Activity were useful for four activities: (1) undressing the child, (2) and measuring head circumference, (3) weight, and finally (4) length. The average of the four ratings for each of the three rating scales, along with single global ratings of Social Orientation and Vocalizing, represented temperament during physical measurements.

Inter-rater reliabilities for each of the condensed scores from the rating scales have been continually checked for about every fifth set of observations. The reliabilities vary somewhat by age and rating scale; in general, however, coefficients for the scores obtained from videotapes have ranged from .70 to .95, with ratings of Attentiveness at younger ages providing the lower coefficients, and ratings of Emotional Tone providing the higher coefficients. Coefficients for the ratings made during physical measurements were in the range from .50 to .85, with the lower coefficients represented by the global ratings. As a consequence, the global ratings have been ignored in subsequent studies. Furthermore, the scores for Emotional Tone and Cooperation were highly correlated (from .70 to .90) with each other and both were negatively correlated with Activity which, in this situation, represented struggling. Therefore, a derived composite score labeled Reaction to Restraint was generated. This composite score reflected the characteristic demeanor from negative resistance (lower score) to positive cooperation (higher score) seen during the entire procedures of physical measurements.

RESEARCH FINDINGS

Descriptive Statistics of the Laboratory Observations

Table 3.1 provides the means and standard deviations for the composite scores representing six temperament characteristics. Measures from the 3-month visit were eventually removed from further analyses because some of the young infants were sleepy during the vignettes and it was difficult to standardize the entire set of procedures around sleep–wake cycles.

Several longitudinal trends are apparent among the means. As might be expected, the children's Activity scores increased with age as did Attentiveness, and positive Social Orientation (to staff). The scores for Emotional Tone remained at about the same level for all ages except 18 months—the visit during which the children are most likely to be negative, difficult, or upset. The decrease in positive emotionality is also seen for the lower mean score for Reaction to Restraint, the composite measure representing behavior during physical measures.

Table 3-1. Means and standard deviations for laboratory temperament rating scales

Rating Scales	Age (months)					
	6	9	12	18	24	30
1. Emotional Tone						
$\overline{X}$	4.65	4.75	4.61	4.31	4.38	5.07
SD	.72	.89	.99	1.30	1.43	1.32
2. Activity						
$\overline{X}$	4.51	4.53	4.68	4.69	4.92	5.01
SD	.85	.75	.75	.73	.67	.72
3. Attentiveness						
$\overline{X}$	4.04	4.32	4.35	4.35	4.58	4.65
SD	.64	.82	.80	.97	1.04	1.03
4. Social Orientation: Staff						
$\overline{X}$	4.01	5.88	5.86	6.01	5.85	6.22
SD	.62	.68	.81	.89	1.04	.96
5. Vocalization						
$\overline{X}$	1.07	1.92	2.09	2.11	2.78	3.60
SD	.92	1.41	1.31	.84	1.22	1.35
6. Reaction to Restraint						
$\overline{X}$	5.86	5.06	4.06	3.61	4.62	5.70
SD	1.26	1.33	3.07	3.21	2.19	1.76

Sample N at each age $\geq$ 65.

Inter-scorer reliabilities for the composite scores, all ages combined, were generally high (above .70), with Emotional Tone representing the more reliable measure for all ages (above .80).

Relations Among Ratings

Although some investigators (e.g., Buss & Plomin, 1975; Lerner, et al., 1982; Rothbart, 1981) have attempted to develop independent scales for ratings of temperament, the overlap among temperament characteristics can be extensive from ratings obtained for play situations. For example, one might expect that children who are highly attentive to play objects and activities would be rated as more positive for emotional tone; negative emotions are almost by definition disruptive. Moreover, the developmental organization and reorganization of children's behavior might produce relatively independent temperament characteristics at one age and considerable redundancy at another. Therefore the correlations among the temperament scores were computed for each age. Table 3.2 provides the patterns of the correlations for 9, 12, 18, and 30 months. The correlations for 6 and 24 months were deleted because the 6-month pattern was quite similar to that of 9 months and the 24-month pattern was quite similar to that of 30 months.

Table 3-2. Correlations among rating scales for laboratory observations of temperament

A: 9 and 12 Months					
	1	2	3	4	5
Rating Scale	Emot Tone	Activity	Att.	Soc. Orient	React. Res.
1. Emotional Tone	—	.46*	.68*	.38*	.29*
2. Activity	.68*	—	.29*	.27*	−.11
3. Attentiveness	.79*	.57*	—	.22*	.28*
4. Social Orientation: Staff	.53*	.25*	.37*	—	.08
5. Reaction to Restraint	.28*	.05	.19	.14	—

Note. 9-months correlations above diagonal; 12-months correlations below. Sample size: 9-months, N = 139; 12-months, N = 100. Significant r at $p \le .05$, indicated by *.

B: 18 and 30 Months					
	1	2	3	4	5
Rating Scale	Emot Tone	Activity	Att.	Soc. Orient	React. Res.
1. Emotional Tone	—	.40*	.81*	.49*	.56*
2. Activity	.42*	—	.32*	−.10	.12
3. Attentiveness	.82*	.26*	—	.30*	.47*
4. Social Orientation: Staff	.70*	.12	.63*	—	.39*
5. Reaction to Restraint	.43*	.26*	.47*	.37*	—

18-months correlations above diagonal; 30-months correlations below. Sample size: 18-months, N = 121; 30-months, N = 104. Significant r at $p \le .05$, indicated by *.

Examination of the patterns evolving over age shows that Emotional Tone seems to be the key temperament vector around which the other scales become organized. For example, in Table 3.2B Emotional Tone for 18 and 30 months has a moderate to high correlation with almost every feature of the children's behavior. Children with positive emotional tone were more likely to be active (busy playing), attentive, socially participating with the staff members during play, and more positive and cooperative during physical measurements. By contrast, the child exhibiting higher upset and distress over the course of the observations participated less in play, was avoidant or withdrawn from the staff, was less attentive during the scheduled activities, and was resistant during physical measurements.

Factor Analysis

In view of the relations among the rating scales, factor analyses were performed on the laboratory ratings. The first unrotated factors issuing from these analyses at each age are outlined in Table 3.3. From 9 months on, it is clear that the first factor tended to be loaded heavily with ratings of Emotional Tone, Attentiveness, Social Orientation, and Reaction to Restraint. This factor at each age became the dimensional representation of the main temperament cluster apparent in the correlations shown in Table 3.2. Most research issuing from the Louisville Twin Study has concentrated on this factor, which has been labeled "Tractability" (Matheny, Wilson, & Nuss, 1984). A similar set of characteristics identified for infant behavior has been identified as "Manageability" (e.g., Hagekull & Bohlin, 1986). The negative aspects of the dimension appear related to temperament descriptors attached to the concept of "difficult" temperament (e.g., Bates, 1980).

Studies of the age-to-age stability of the laboratory-based temperament factor have shown that it is moderately stable for 6-month intervals. Stability coefficients for these 6-month intervals have ranged from .48 to .59 for the ages from 12 to 30 months (see Table 3.4). Prior to 12 months, the Tractability factor has provided low-order correlations ($r \leq$ .25) with later ages.

Table 3.4 also provides age-to-age stability for Bayley Mental Development Index (MDI) scores for comparison with the age-to-age stability of the temperament factors. It is apparent that for the 6-month intervals from 12 to 24 months, the 6-month stability of the temperament dimension compares favorably with the stability of mental test scores (Wilson, 1978).

Table 3-3. Primary temperament factor at 6, 9, 12, 18, 24, and 30 months

Behaviors	6 months	9 months	12 months	18 months	24 months	30 months
			Factor Loading			
Emotional Tone	—	.86	.86	.92	.94	.95
Activity	—	.73	—	—	—	—
Attentiveness	.87	.74	.84	.87	.92	.90
Social Orientation	—	—	.65	.64	.84	.89
Reaction to Restraint	.72	.52	.59	.71	.55	.58

Behaviors with loadings ≥ .50 are shown. Tabular material adapted in part from Matheny (1984); Matheny, Wilson, & Nuss (1984); Wilson (1982); Wilson & Matheny (1983, 1986).

Table 3-4.   Age-to-age stability of tractability factor from laboratory observations

Age—months	Age (mos.)		
	18	24	30
12	.48	.30	.26
	(.53)	(.42)	(.49)
18		.59	.49
		(.63)	(.60)
24			.54
			(.74)
30			

For comparison, stability correlations for Bayley MDI scores are provided in parenthesis. All correlations are significant, $p \leq$ .05; $N = 130$.

Correlative Measures

Thomas and Chess (1977) have stressed the potential relations to be expected between temperament and other developmental characteristics including cognition. Moreover, the overlap between emotional and cognitive development has received considerable attention (Izard, Kagan, & Zajonc, 1984). Therefore, tracing the networks to be found among temperament and other measures has been a subject of several studies for the laboratory measures. These studies are traced here next.

Cognitive Measures

The relations between laboratory Tractability and the Bayley Scales (1969) have been examined for concurrent associations because Bayley testing is part of the sequence of episodes described for the laboratory visits at each age. While one twin is engaged in Solo play, the other twin, accompanied by a parent, is given the Bayley test in an adjacent room. The MDI scores or mental test scores from the Bayley scales were correlated with the factor scores for Tractability at each age. These analyses have been reported elsewhere (Matheny, 1989b) and are summarized in Table 3.5. As depicted, the correlations are low-order.

Table 3-5.   Concurrent correlates of tractability factor from laboratory observations

Tractability Age (mos.)	Bayley MDI Score	Temperament Questionnaire Approach	Bayley IBR	
			Emotional Tone	Fearfulness
12	.14	.37*	.33*	−.55*
18	.23*	.42*	.36*	−.64*
24	.16	.36*	.39*	−.63*
30	.24*	.33*	.39*	−.55*

*, Correlation is significant, $p \leq$ .05. N's vary from 65 to 150.

Other Temperament Measures

The association between the factor scores representing Tractability at each age and other temperament measures obtained at the same ages are shown in Table 3.5.

The temperament characteristic Approach was obtained from the Toddler Temperament Questionnaire completed by parents. Approach is the temperament characteristic that provides the most consistent bridge with the laboratory-based ratings, as reflected by the recurrent correlations in the moderate range. Other relations between the laboratory measures and temperament measures from questionnaires can be found in several reports (Matheny, 1989a; Matheny, Wilson & Nuss, 1984; Wilson & Matheny, 1983; Wilson & Matheny, 1986).

Temperament measures can be obtained from the Infant Behavior Record (IBR), a component of the Bayley scales that is completed after Bayley testing is completed. Previous analyses of the IBR have been reported elsewhere (Matheny, 1980, 1983). More recent analyses indicate that the association between the laboratory observations and the IBR can be found for the IBR ratings of Emotional Tone and Fearfulness. Emotional Tone as rated in the IBR is equivalent to Emotional Tone rated in the laboratory. Therefore, the link between the two scales, completed during the same laboratory visit, is not unexpected. More interesting are the stronger links between Tractability and the IBR ratings of Fearfulness. These concurrent correlations depict the tractable child during the laboratory episodes as being less fearful during Bayley testing. A study (Matheny, 1989a) of these relations, supplemented by measures of Approach from temperament questionnaires, suggests that the common link among laboratory, Bayley testing, and questionnaire is the inhibited–uninhibited dimension identified by Kagan and his colleagues (Garcia-Coll, Kagan, & Reznick, 1984; Kagan, Reznick, & Snidman, 1986). Thus, the laboratory temperament measures add to or help support an increasing body of research that depicts some children as wary or avoidant in the face of the unfamiliar in contrast with children who move toward or seek out the unfamiliar.

Neonatal Measures

As part of the longitudinal assessment of twin infants, a detailed neonatal assessment has been developed (Riese, 1983), that takes account of neonatal behaviors observed during a 3-hour appraisal taking place during an entire metabolic cycle. Neonatal assessment scores pertaining to neonatal irritability, resistance to soothing, reactivity, responsivity to manipulation, and activity have been examined for their relations to the playroom observations at later ages.

In a series of reports (Matheny, Riese, & Wilson, 1985; Riese, 1987; Riese, Wilson, & Matheny, 1985), it has been demonstrated that, by 9 months of age, infant temperament, rated in the playroom, is associated with characteristics of the neonate. At 9 months and later at 24 months, ratings of Emotional Tone, Social Orientation, and Attentiveness were predicted from newborn characteristics such as irritability and responsivity to manipulation. In general, more irritable newborns who negatively react to the neonatal assessment procedures tended to have more negative emotional tone and to be more avoidant of the staff members at 9 or 24 months (*r*'s between −.23 and −.38). Playroom observations at 6 months did not provide such predictive relations. A report by Riese (1987), however, indicated that prematurity may obscure the longitudinal stability of temperament. At 6 months, the residual effects of prematurity and perinatal events would be expected to mask or distort temperament features.

Attachment

Attachment theory (Bowlby, 1969), arising from clinical observations and associated with clinical outcome, has largely been grounded by a procedure that classifies infants and toddlers as being securely or insecurely attached to a parent as a consequence of children's behavior after a brief separation—the Strange Situation (Ainsworth, Blehar, Waters, & Wall, 1978). The rudimentary classification consists of categories: Type A, insecurely attached–avoidant, representing children who avoid contact; Type B, securely attached, representing children who warmly greet the parent, enjoy the parent's presence, and recover quickly from separation; and Type C, insecurely attached–resistant, representing children who are ambivalent toward the parent as reflected by anger and resistance while, at the same time, clinging to the parent. Results from numerous studies have shown that when the trichotomous classification is used, approximately two-thirds of infants have been classified as Type B, approximately one-fifth of infants have been classified as Type A, and the remainder of infants have been classified as Type C. Longitudinal studies have generally shown that clinical outcomes, such as antisocial behavior, have been reliably associated with the two classifications of insecure attachment (e.g., Bretherton, 1985). Given the relatively brief period and simplicity of the Strange Situation procedure and the clinically informative links with later-appearing psychosocial behaviors, the merits of attachment classification of infants and toddlers are obvious.

The standardized play procedures described in this chapter also provide an instance when the individual infant or toddler has a reunion with the parent. After the Solo episode during which the individual child is separated from the parent, the parent returns and the reunion, lasting one minute, is videotaped. Because of the similarity of this reunion to the Strange Situation procedure, a study was conducted to determine the concordance between classifications of attachment made from videotaped reunions and the Strange Situation procedure carried out a few months later. The study (Finkel, Wille, & Matheny, 1998) indicated that 78% of a sample of toddlers had the same classification of attachment when classified by both procedures. In addition, the proportion of types A, B, and C attachment from the standardized play procedure described in this chapter did not differ from the proportions typically described by the literature for comparable samples of children. Therefore, our standardized play assessment potentially offers a derivative that could serve as a surrogate for the clinically informative Strange Situation.

Adrenocortical Activity

Recent efforts to link physiological and psychological processes during normal development have focused on the adrenocortical system, known to be involved in stress reactivity and regulation of stress. This link is discussed by Gunnar, Mangelsdorf, Larson, & Hertsgaard (1989), who examined the change in cortisol, assayed from saliva obtained from infants, as a function of infant temperament. Gunnar et al. employed the playroom assessment described in this chapter to measure emotional tone and determine the relation between ratings of emotionality and measures of cortisol. A composite score of emotional tone rated during the 9-month vignettes of the Solo episode period was correlated ($r = -.37$) with changes in cortisol concentrations. That is, stress-induced activity of the adrenocortical system was higher for infants with more negative emotional temperaments. It is of further interest that ratings of emotional tone obtained from the 9-month vignettes were correlated (r's between .26 and .54) with emotional tone measured during Strange Situation testing (Ainsworth, et al., 1978) at

13 months. In effect, there were convergent correlations between emotionality in the play-room and stress reactivity at 9 months and predictive correlations between the same 9-months playroom measures and attachment behaviors at 13 months.

Childhood Injuries

As part of a longitudinal study examining the psychosocial aspects of unintentional injuries of children, children's temperament was examined for its contribution to injury liability. The temperament factor Tractability (see Tables 3.3–3.5) was found to be negatively correlated ($r = -.27$) with injury liability (Matheny, 1986). In terms of the behaviors contributing to the factor, the correlation indicated that young children who were positive in mood, attentive, approachful, and generally adaptable in the playroom setting were less likely to sustain serious injuries from ages 1 to 3 years.

Adaptation for Clinical Assessment

Our procedures, when applied as a whole for a standardized assessment of temperament of twin pairs, are not directly practical for routine clinical assessments. The procedures are complex; they require at least two hours for completion; they require special training for staff; and obviously they are designed for assessing two siblings within the same family. A shorter version of the standardized play assessment has been developed for singletons, however, and this version may become useful for clinical assessments.

The shorter version essentially consists of the activities listed for the two Episodes: Separation and Solo for Twin A, and Reunion for Twin A (see Organization of Temperament Visits, p. 84). The only modification for these two Episodes is that when the parent leaves the infant or toddler for solo play, the parent is taken to another location for a purpose other than Bayley testing of Twin B. (When we assess singletons, we use the Episode involving solo play for an interview with the parent, for example.) These two Episodes span approximately half an hour of which 19 minutes (18 minutes for Separation and Solo, and 1 minute for the Reunion) are videotaped.

Pilot results obtained from a sample of about 30 infant and toddler singletons have shown that the means and standard deviations for the laboratory temperament scales are quite similar to those found for twins assessed by the entire laboratory procedure (Table 3.2). In addition, the correlation matrices generated from the ratings of singletons are comparable to those obtained from ratings of twins (Table 3.3). Given the small sample of singletons, however, further analyses have not been made. Therefore, it remains to be seen if larger samples of singletons will provide results that mimic completely all of the results for twins as shown by Tables 3.3 to 3.5. Nevertheless, the pilot sample does provide results that suggest that the standardized procedures can be partially adapted for clinical assessments of singletons.

SUMMARY AND CONCLUSIONS

Rutter (1982) has pointed out that the problem that "bedevils the study of temperament concerns the question of how to measure temperament..." (p. 5). Most efforts to assess infant temperament have concentrated on questionnaires that capture parents' or perhaps nurses' views of infant behavior in a variety of situations. The attractive aspects of this approach are that it is relatively inexpensive and provides quick appraisals of a wide range of temperament characteristics.

The utility and limitations of temperament questionnaires have been reviewed elsewhere (Goldsmith & Rothbart, 1991; Hubert, et al., 1982). In general, the limitations are those that pertain to any questionnaires or checklists that report others' views of children's behaviors. The problem with parental reports of temperament (or any other features of children's behaviors) is that a parent's view may be distorted by the parent's own personality or the parent-child relationship. It is this problem that is addressed by a laborious research assessment of temperament.

The development of laboratory-based assessments of temperament rated from children's play is not likely to lead to direct applications within clinical settings because, to put it simply, these assessments are expensive. For the most part, a laboratory methodology helps to certify the validity of temperament constructs, identify which of the constructs are assessed by questionnaires, and sharpen our developmental appraisals so that temperament characteristics with clinical import may be isolated. In effect, the more laborious assessment methodologies based on objective observations should buttress putatively flimsier methods depending on parental interviews and questionnaires. Thus, the standardized longitudinal procedures described in this chapter, as well as others' home-based or laboratory procedures developed or being developed offer research to substantiate the importance of temperament (e.g., Bornstein, Gaughran, & Homel, 1986; Feiring & Lewis, 1980; Garcia-Coll, et al., 1984; Goldsmith & Campos, 1986; Hagekull & Bohlin, 1986; Plomin & Rowe, 1979; Rothbart, 1986).

The more practical implication of the research approach described herein is that specific temperament characteristics from questionnaires may be linked to and confirmed by temperament assessed in playroom settings. Specifically, the NYLS characteristics Approach/Withdrawal, Mood, and Adaptability (Thomas, et al., 1968) or Emotionality and Sociability (Buss & Plomin, 1975), assessed by questionnaires, seem to be validated for playroom settings and could serve as markers for behavior in playroom settings and behavioral changes as a consequence of play therapy. In addition, the results from our adaptation of the standardized play assessments for a briefer assessment of the temperament of singletons suggest that a standardized play assessment could become a more practical clinical tool in its own right.

Children's behavior assessed during play is, at best, a perspective on behavior in other "real-life" contexts, such as the family. Our research indicates that temperament may serve as a moderator variable for interactive processes between children and parents within the contexts of the home environment (e.g., Matheny, Wilson, & Thoben, 1987), and hazards within home environments (Matheny, 1986). In accord with Thomas and Chess (1980), child temperament may contribute to the interactive "fit" between child and parent within home environments. Whether or not the psychological adjustment between children and parents can be assessed by playroom observations remains to be established. The converging evidence to date, however, indicates that infant temperament as a salient feature of infant play informs us of infant behavior in other settings.

REFERENCES

Ainsworth, M. D. S., Blehar, M., Waters, E., & Wall, S. (1978). *Patterns of attachment: Observations in a stranger situation at home.* Hillsdale, NJ: Erlbaum.

Bates, J. E. (1980). The concept of difficult temperament. *Merrill-Palmer Quarterly, 26,* 299–319.

Bates, J. E., & Bayles, K. (1984). Objective and subjective components in mother's perceptions of their children from age 6 months to 3 years. *Merrill-Palmer Quarterly, 30,* 111–130.

Bayley, N. (1969). *Bayley scales of infant development.* New York: Psychological Corporation.

Bertenthal, B. I., & Fischer, K. W. (1978). Development of self-recognition in the infant. *Developmental Psychology, 14,* 44–50.

Bornstein, M. H., Gaughran, J. M., & Homel, P. (1986). Infant temperament: theory, tradition, critique and new assessments. In C. E. Izard & P. B. Read (Eds.), *Measuring emotions in infants and children* (Vol. 2, pp. 172–199). New York: Cambridge Univ. Press.

Bowlby, J. (1969). *Attachment and loss: Vol. 1. Attachment.* New York: Basic Books.

Bretherton, I. (1985). Attachment theory: Retrospect and prospect. In I. Bretherton & E. Waters (Eds.), Growing points of attachment theory and research, *Monographs of the Society for Research in Child Development* (pp. 3–35), *50* (1–2, Serial No. 209).

Buss, A. H., & Plomin, R. (1975). *A temperament theory of personality development.* New York: Wiley-Interscience.

Campos, J. J., Barrett, K., Lamb, M. E., Goldsmith, H. H., & Stenberg, C. (1983). Socioemotional development. In M. M. Haith, & J. J. Campos (Eds.), Infancy and developmental psychobiology, Vol. 2 of P. H. Mussen (Ed.), *Handbook of Child Psychology* (4th ed., pp. 783–915). New York: Wiley.

Carey, W. B., & McDevitt, S. C. (1978). Revision of the infant temperament questionnaire. *Pediatrics, 61,* 735–739.

Cattell, P. (1947). *Cattell infant intelligence scale.* New York: Psychological Corporation.

Derryberry, D., & Rothbart, M. K. (1984). Emotion, attention, and temperament. In C. E. Izard, J. Kagan, & R. B. Zajonc (Eds.), *Emotions, condition, and behavior.* New York: Cambridge University Press.

Epstein, S. (1980). The stability of behavior, II: Implications for psychological research. *American Psychologist, 35,* 790–806.

Erikson, E. H. (1972). Play and actuality. In M. W. Piers (Ed.), *Play and development* (pp. 127–167). New York: Norton.

Escalona, S. K. (1968). *Roots of Individuality.* Chicago: Aldine.

Feiring, C., & Lewis, M. (1980). Temperament: Sex differences and stability in vigor, activity and persistence in the first three years of life. *Journal of Genetic Psychology, 136,* 65–75.

Finkel, D., Wille, D. E., & Matheny, A. P., Jr. (1998). Preliminary results from a twin study of infant-caregiver attachment. *Behavior Genetics, 28,* 1–8.

Fullard, W., McDevitt, S. C., & Carey, W. B. (1984). Assessing temperament in one- to three-year-old children. *Journal of Pediatric Psychology, 9,* 205–217.

Garcia-Coll, C., Kagan, J., & Reznick, J. S. (1984). Behavioral inhibition in young children. *Child Development, 55,* 1005–1019.

Goldsmith, H. H., & Campos, J. J. (1986). Fundamental issues in the study of early temperament: The Denver Twin Temperament Study. In M. E. Lamb, A. Brown, & B. Rogoff (Eds.), *Advances in developmental psychology.* Hillsdale, NJ: Erlbaum (pp. 231–283).

Goldsmith, H. H., & Rothbart, M. K. (1991). Contemporary instruments for assessing early temperament by questionnaire and in the laboratory. In J. Strelau & A. Angleitner (Eds.), *Explorations in temperament* (pp. 249–272). New York: Plenum Press.

Gunnar, M. R., Mangelsdorf, S., Larson, M., & Hertsgaard, L. (1989). Attachment, temperament, and adrenocortical activity in infancy: A study of psychoendocrine regulation. *Developmental Psychology, 25,* 355–363.

Hagekull, B., & Bohlin, G. (1986). Mother-infant interaction and perceived infant temperament. *International Journal of Behavioral Development, 9,* 297–313.

Hegvik, R. L., McDevitt, S. C., & Carey, W. B. (1982). The middle childhood temperament questionnaire. *Developmental and Behavioral Pediatrics, 3,* 197–200.

Hubert, N. C., Wachs, T. D., Peters-Martin, P., & Gandour, M. J. (1982). The study of early temperament: Measurement and conceptual issues. *Child Development, 54,* 571–600.

Izard, C. E., Kagan, J., & Zajonc, R. B. (1984). (Eds.) *Emotions, cognition, and behavior.* New York: Cambridge University Press.

Kagan, J., Reznick, J. S., & Snidman, N. (1986). Temperamental inhibition in early childhood. In R. Plomin & J. Dunn (Eds.), *The study of temperament: Changes, continuities and challenges.* Hillsdale, NJ: Erlbaum.

Lerner, R. M., Palermo, M., Spiro, A. III, & Nesselroade, J. R. (1982). Assessing the dimensions of temperamental individuality (DOTS). *Child Development, 53,* 149–159.

Matheny, A. P., Jr. (1980). Bayley's Infant Behavior Record: Behavioral components and twin analyses. *Child Development, 51,* 1157–1167.

Matheny, A. P., Jr. (1981). Assessment of temperament in twin children: A reconciliation between structured and naturalistic observations. In L. Gedda, P. Parisi, & W. Nance (Eds.), *Twin research 3: Intelligence, personality, and development.* New York: Alan Liss.

Matheny, A. P., Jr. (1983). A longitudinal study of stability of components from Bayley's Infant Behavior Record. *Child Development, 54,* 356–360.

Matheny, A. P., Jr. (1984). Twin similarity in the developmental transformation of temperament as measured in a multi-method longitudinal study. *Acta Geneticae Medicae et Gemellologiae, 33,* 181–190.

Matheny, A. P., Jr. (1986). Injuries among toddlers: Contributions from child, mother, and family. *Journal of Pediatric Psychology, 11,* 163–175.

Matheny, A. P., Jr. (1989a). Children's behavioral inhibition over age and across situations: Genetic similarity for a trait during change. *Journal of Personality, 57.*

Matheny, A. P., Jr. (1989b). Temperament and cognition: Relations between temperament and mental test scores. In G. A. Kohnstamm, J. F. Bates, & M. K. Rothbart (Eds.), *Temperament in childhood* (pp. 263–282). New York: Wiley.

Matheny, A. P., Jr. (1991). Play assessment of infant temperament. In C. E. Schaefer, K. Gitlin, & A. Sandgrund (Eds.), *Play diagnosis and assessment.* New York: Wiley.

Matheny, A. P., Jr. & Dolan, A. B. (1975). Persons, situations, and time: A genetic view of behavioral change. *Journal of Personality and Social Psychology, 32,* 1106–1110.

Matheny, A. P., Jr., Dolan, A. B., & Wilson, R. S. (1976). Twins: Within-pair similarity on Bayley's Infant Behavior Record. *Journal of Genetic Psychology, 128,* 263–270.

Matheny, A. P., Jr., Riese, M. L., & Wilson, R. S. (1985). Rudiments of infant temperament: Newborn to 9 months. *Developmental Psychology, 21,* 486–494.

Matheny, A. P., Jr. & Wilson, R. S. (1981). Developmental tasks and rating scales for the laboratory assessment of infant temperament. *JSAS Catalog of Selected Documents in Psychology, 11,* 81 (Ms. No. 2367).

Matheny, A. P., Jr., Wilson, R. S., & Nuss, S. M. (1984). Toddler temperament: Stability across settings and over ages. *Child Development, 55,* 1200–1211.

Matheny, A. P., Jr., Wilson, R. S., & Thoben, A. (1987). Home and mother: Relations with infant temperament. *Developmental Psychology, 23,* 323–331.

Paunonen, S. V. (1984). Optimizing the validity of personality assessments: The importance of aggregation and item content. *Journal of Research in Personality, 18,* 411–431.

Plomin, R., & Rowe, D. C. (1979). Genetic and environmental etiology of social behavior in infancy. *Developmental Psychology, 15,* 62–72.

Reiss, A. J. (1961). *Occupations and social status.* New York: Free Press of Glencoe.

Riese, M. L. (1983). Assessment of behavioral patterns in neonates. *Infant Behavior and Development, 6,* 241–246.

Riese, M. L. (1987). Longitudinal assessment of temperament from birth to 2 years: A comparison of full-term and preterm infants. *Infant Behavior and Development, 10,* 347–363.

Riese, M. L., Wilson, R. S., & Matheny, A. P., Jr. (1985). Multimethod assessment of temperament in twins: Birth to six months. *Acta Geneticae Medicae et Gemellologiae, 34,* 15–31.

Rothbart, M. K. (1981). Measurement of temperament in infancy. *Child Development, 52,* 569–578.

Rothbart, M. K. (1986). Longitudinal observation of infant temperament. *Developmental Psychology, 22,* 356–365.

Rutter, M. (1982). Temperament: Concepts, issues, and problems. In R. Porter & G. M. Collins (Eds.), *Temperamental differences in infants and young children.* Ciba Symposium 89. London: Pitman (pp. 1–16).

Schaefer, C. E., Gitlin, K., & Sandgrund, A. (Eds.). (1991). *Play diagnosis and assessment.* New York: Wiley.

Thomas, A., & Chess, S. (1977). *Temperament and development.* New York: Bruner/Mazel.

Thomas, A., & Chess, S. (1980). *The dynamics of psychological development.* New York: Bruner/Mazel.

Thomas, A., Chess, S., & Birch, H. G. (1968). *Temperament and behavior disorders in children.* New York: New York University.

Thomas, A., Chess, S., Birch, H. G., Hertaig, M. E., & Korn, S. (1963). *Behavioral Individuality in Early Childhood.* New York: New York University Press.

Watson, M. W. & Fischer, K. W. (1977). A developmental sequence of agent use in late infancy. *Child Development, 48,* 828–836.

Wilson, R. S. (1978). Synchronies in mental development: An epigenetic perspective. *Science, 202,* 939–948.

Wilson, R. S. (1982). Intrinsic determinants of temperament. In R. Porter & G. M. Collins (Eds.), *Temperamental differences in infants and young children.* Ciba Foundation Symposium 89. London: Pitman.

Wilson, R. S., & Matheny, A. P. (1980). Temperament research: Presentations. *JSAS, Catalog of Selected Documents in Psychology, 10,* 10 (20 pages).

Wilson, R. S., & Matheny, A. P., Jr. (1983). Assessment of temperament in infant twins. *Developmental Psychology, 19,* 172–183.

Wilson, R. S., & Matheny, A. P., Jr. (1986). Behavior-genetics research in infant temperament: The Louisville Twin Study. In R. Plomin & J. Dunn (Eds.), *The study of temperament: Changes, continuities, and changes* (pp. 81–97). Hillsdale, NJ: Erlbaum.

Chapter 4 ————————————————————————

THE PLAY HISTORY INTERVIEW

*Kristin Moore Taylor, Marilee Menarchek-Fetkovich,
and Cindy Day*

INTRODUCTION

Play is an important element in the development of many life skills, such as rule learning
and problem solving. Children who acquire skills through play can build them into habits
and roles. It assists in the development of interests, values, and motivation. Through play,
children are better able to master control over their environment (Munoz, 1986). Although
it continues in one form or another throughout life, the play of children is different from
that of adults in that it is recognized as a major mechanism facilitating the first activities
of exploring and learning about the world (Kielhofner & Burke, 1980). Children's ability
to play, to explore the environment, and to exercise motor skills forms the foundation
which they are later able to use to effectively negotiate demands of the adult world
(Kielhofner, 1980).

Play emerges in a methodical developmental sequence and expands in conjunction with
children's growing cognitions. Numerous studies have found this to be true. For example,
Goodson and Greenfield (1975) found that as children gain mastery of language, play
increases in complexity. Piaget (1962) wrote that there are three developmental stages of
play that coincide with cognitive stages of development, including practice play (sensorimotor), symbolic make-believe play (preoperational), and rule games (concrete opera-
tions). It has been noted that active play encourages verbalization and promotes manual
strength (Murphy & O'Driscoll, 1989). Because it is universal (Takata, 1971) and follows
developmental trends, play observations can be employed to assess the competence of children (Bond, Creasey, & Adams, 1990).

The Play History Interview (Rogers & Takata, 1975; Behnke, 1982) is one tool that has
been created to assess children's strengths as well as to identify problem areas. Based on
the premise that play follows a specific sequential developmental pattern, it assumes that
a historical account of play behaviors leads to a better understanding of current play patterns. The Play History is a semistructured qualitative questionnaire aimed at identifying
play experiences, interactions, environments, and opportunities. It was originally designed
for use with children who were diagnosed with a variety of disabling conditions.

The Play History was developed with the notion that intervention into play dysfunction is vital to the healthy development of children (Behnke, 1982). To determine how children's play behaviors are progressing, it is necessary to be able to systematically evaluate their play patterns. Depending on a variety of factors, the exhibited play behaviors may be within the expected range of functioning or may be precocious, delayed, or deviant in nature. For example, mentally challenged children who are otherwise unimpaired tend to exhibit play behaviors which are a year or more delayed but generally follow the standard sequence of acquisition. Children with "normal" physical and mental endowment and with adequate opportunities for "normal" experiences exhibit age-appropriate play skills. Children who exhibit limited cognitive and physical abilities and who have restricted opportunities for exploring the environment generally do not profit from experience in a typical manner (Behnke, 1982) and, therefore, may evidence deviant play development. Given the significant contribution of play to children's general level of functioning, the complexity of factors that influence play development, and the wide range of possible outcomes resulting from any type of interference in the process, it becomes clear that play evaluation is a critical mechanism by which the treatment of children can be enhanced. The Play History is one important assessment tool that contributes to the diagnostic process as well as to treatment planning and implementation.

PLAY AND THE SPECIAL NEEDS CHILD

Although play is generally assumed to occur as a natural process, there are factors that inhibit its development. According to Takata (1967, 1969), a child's inability to play may be the result of sensory-motor deficits, emotional or social maladjustment, or the lack of suitable opportunities. Such deficits may result in delays in play development, as seen in mentally retarded children, or deviations in play, as seen in autistic children.

The play of mentally retarded children typically follows the same basic sequence as that of nondisabled children (Bond, Creasey, & Adams, 1990), but given the cognitive limitations, the play tends not to be as sophisticated or well developed. For these children, play is related to mental age rather than chronological age. That is, the development of play seems to be based on underlying developmental competencies rather than discrete age-related experiences (Bond, Creasey, & Adams, 1990).

According to Antia and Kreimeyer (1992), children with hearing impairments do not have the same opportunities as their hearing peers to engage in reciprocal interactions. They do not interact or play with each other as frequently as same-age hearing peers. As a result, they often fail to acquire the social competence necessary to interact appropriately with their peers. One research study found that solitary-constructive activities were the preferred mode of play among a group of hearing-impaired preschoolers, while their hearing peers were more likely to engage in cooperative-dramatic play (Higginbotham & Baker, 1981, as cited in Antia & Kreimeyer, 1992). It was suggested that these hearing-impaired children preferred solitary play because they lacked the verbal skills to engage in dramatic play. Furthermore, they tended to isolate themselves during play, thus restricting the opportunities to develop play skills (Higginbotham & Baker, 1981, as cited in Antia & Kreimeyer, 1992).

The play of visually impaired children also is often restricted. Many young children with visual impairments spend a large portion of their playtime in perseverative, self-stimulatory behaviors (Skellenger, Hill, & Hill, 1992). Those who attempt to engage in group play are at a disadvantage because they do not benefit from the important visual cues used to communicate nonverbally with each other. For instance, they are unable to receive visual permission to enter a group, an important factor in the play of sighted children. These limitations may prevent them from being accepted by their peers. In addition to negatively impacting the development of their social competence, restricted play experiences of the visually impaired may interfere with other benefits of play such as cognitive growth and language development (Skellenger, Hill, & Hill, 1992).

Children with developmental disabilities tend to have difficulty with group play. The research of Gurlanick and Groom (as cited in Beckman & Leiber, 1992) suggests that these children often lack entry skills that permit joining an ongoing playgroup. Additionally, they may not have sufficiently established the skills required to participate in more sophisticated group play. Developmentally disabled children are less likely to organize as well as direct play activities and tend not to generate social interactions with their nondisabled peers. Partly because nondisabled children prefer to play with similarly unimpaired peers, the disabled children may lack the exposure and opportunity to learn from and model the play of their typically developing peers. Thus, these children do not have the experiences necessary to gain the same sense of mastery.

Children with behavioral disorders often have difficulty playing in groups, sharing, and relating well with other children. Many conduct-disordered children do not know how to play cooperatively. They may have difficulty using certain play materials because of their tendency to be destructive. Special play materials may be required, such as cushions and pillows, so that they can express their aggressive behaviors in a nondestructive manner (Kernberg & Chazen, 1991). Hyperactive children may have difficulty following the rules of a game and waiting their turn. They may disturb their peers by interrupting and intruding, resulting in rejection and isolation from appropriate playmates.

The play of neglected and abused children may also differ from their peers. These children are often reticent to involve themselves in play activities and may appear withdrawn or impassive. The quality of their play tends to be constricted and poorly organized. Strong emotions such as rage may be demonstrated through play themes that are violent, chaotic, and illogically sequenced (Richman & Dawe, 1988). In addition, the environmental concomitants of neglect, in particular, often lead to inadequate exposure to appropriate play materials and activities.

Because the literature suggests that children with disabling conditions lack the skills and/or the opportunity for successful play experiences, it is crucial that inadequate play behaviors be detected early so that intervention can be initiated. In an effort to assist in the process of identifying those children who are in need of treatment in this area, the Play History Interview was designed. For this instrument to be most effectively implemented, clinicians should have an in-depth understanding of the play styles of disabled as well as nondisabled children.

THE PLAY HISTORY INTERVIEW

The Play History Interview is designed to elicit information from the parent about the child's past and present play development. Information may also be obtained from the child if he or she is old enough. This instrument provides a five-part guide to gathering information about and interpreting play experiences. These elements include general information, previous play experiences, examination of current play behaviors, play description, and play prescription. The information pertaining to the child's previous play experiences is designed to follow the sequential progression of play development. It informs the examiner of any deviations or gaps that may have occurred in the past. The data from the play examination are intended to identify the child's play style as it parallels development. It helps to determine if play behaviors, experiences, and opportunities are age appropriate and adequate. The play description is based on the synthesis and interpretation of obtained play evidence and assists in the process of diagnosis. Finally, the play prescription provides a treatment plan for intervention in order to address the identified areas of concern resulting from the Play History Interview.

Development of the Play History Interview

Originally developed by Takata in 1969, the Play History was transformed into an assessment tool by Rogers and Takata in 1975. Further revision of the scale by Behnke and Menarchek-Fetkovich (1984) resulted from their study of its reliability and validity. They added an ordinal scale to quantify information and developed the Play History Interview Guide as a specific protocol for obtaining play history information. Some interview questions were modified, as well. The description of the instrument described herein is based on the work of Behnke and Menarchek-Fetkovich (1984), also known as the Revised Play History.

Analysis and Interpretation of the Play History

Once the interview is completed, the compiled information is analyzed and interpreted within a specific developmental framework that includes five play epochs (originally described by Takata in 1969): (1) sensorimotor (0–2 years); (2) symbolic and simple constructive (2–4 years);(3) dramatic, complex constructive and pregame (4–7 years); (4) games (7–12 years); and (5) recreational (12–16 years). Instead of being mutually exclusive, each epoch is continuous and flows into the next. That is, the achievements of previous stages are integrated into and then built upon to create the achievements of the following stages.

Within each epoch there are four main elements of play (Takata, 1974): materials, action, people, and setting. The *materials* element answers the question, "With what does the child play?" The identification of playthings (i.e., toys, materials, objects) is important because it reveals information about accessibility and appropriateness of play items to which the child is exposed. The *action* element answers the question, "How does the child play?" Once materials are identified, then a description of *how* the child manages them follows. The way in which the child interacts with toys is indicative of the quality of the play skills in several domains, such as gross motor, fine motor, social imitation, and participation. The *people* element answers the question, "How does the child play with others?" The nature of the child's play with others, such as peers and family members, requires detailed description in order to gain a true representation of the child's play style. Such related characteristics as spontaneity and self-initiative need to be considered during solitary as well as interactive play. The *setting* element answers the question, "Where and when does the child play?" Ascertaining whether the play space is confining, limited, or expansive provides information that may become a qualifying factor in the understanding of specific play patterns.

After the data are collected, they are recorded on the Play History chart. The chart contains the epochs of play as well as the elements of materials, action, people, and setting and serves as a guide for analyzing and interpreting the play data. In order to use the interview information to its fullest potential, a thorough knowledge of the elements that form Takata's epoch theory is required. In the following discussion, the first three epochs, which subsume the early childhood years, are summarized in detail according to the four major categories of play. A complete description of the final two epochs is beyond the scope of this chapter because games and recreational activities are a qualitatively different form of play than is found in the first three epochs. Therefore, they will be only briefly discussed.

Play Epochs

Sensorimotor Epoch (0–2 Years)

This epoch emphasizes independent play and sensory experiences as expressed in trial-and-error behaviors. Six stages of sensorimotor development as described by Piaget (1962) and others are embedded within this period of development. The sequence of the stages is believed to be the same for all children. The first stage (0–1 month) is characterized by a level of pure reflexes. There is no functional assimilation and nothing identifiable as either play or imitation. The second stage (1–4 months) is marked by the general integration of one scheme with another. At first, the infant performs only individual sensorimotor schemes. With practice, the schemes become more refined. Stage three (4–8 months) is characterized by an increased interest in the outside world. The child becomes an object explorer. As coordination between vision and prehension is developed, the child uses his or her hands more actively. Imitation is present but is limited by mobility. The child imitates movements that are in his or her field of vision or that he or she has previously performed. Distinguishing features of stage four (8–12 months) include actions which are purposeful and goal-directed. The child performs an act to achieve a certain result. Paying little attention to the means he or she is going to employ, a different coordination of means and ends are invented with each new situation. The child in stage five (12–18 months) spends much of his or her time in active experimentation. Socially, the child is receiving lots of attention from family and thus repeatedly imitates their actions. The last stage (18–24 months) marks the beginning of symbolic play. Additionally, as fine and gross motor skills rapidly improve, the child is interested in activities that require application of these skills.

1. *Materials:* In the earlier stages of the Sensorimotor Epoch, the child plays with objects which intensify sensory experiences such as rattles, teething rings, blankets, mobiles, and busy boxes. As the infant becomes more adept with his or her hands, he or she becomes more interested in materials which can be manipulated, such as balls, blocks, dolls, cars, and musical instruments. Materials such as kitchen equipment and puppets may be used in the later stages as symbolic play emerges.

2. *Action:* As eye-hand coordination improves, the infant's actions become more advanced. In the early stages of the Sensorimotor Epoch, the infant will not grasp an object unless it is placed in his or her hand. Later, objects within sight are

grabbed and manually manipulated. Actions in the later stages will include push-ing toys, opening and closing the door, throwing a ball, climbing, banging toys, and imitating adult actions.

3. *People:* At first, the infant is highly attached to his or her mother and will fixate pri-marily on her. He or she later will start responding to her with a smile. As the infant matures, imitation of other family members occurs and is incorporated into play activities. Affectivity is centered primarily on the family (Piaget, 1962).

4. *Setting:* The setting for play changes as the child's mobility increases. Initially, the infant will play in the crib or bouncy seat. As the child begins to crawl, and later walk, the immediate environment is his or hers to explore.

The Sensorimotor Epoch thus begins with an infant who is a near-helpless being. By the end of the epoch, the child has acquired the basic foundations upon which to build skills physically, mentally, and emotionally. The child is ready to explore the real world and the roles in it through the world of make-believe. This transition leads into the next epoch.

Symbolic and Simple Constructive Epoch (2–4 years)

The major emphasis of this epoch is the focus on simple constructive work that is charac-teristic of parallel play and present in symbolic games. The child slowly progresses from purely gross motor play to symbolic play (Piaget, 1962) and from predominantly solitary to parallel play (Gesell, 1940). Pretend and make-believe play develop as the child plays out representations of objects and situations which he or she encounters. The child also begins to share.

1. *Materials:* The play materials of the 2-year-old include such items as balls, blocks, dolls, sandbox, playdough, crayons, and small figures. Accessories for cars and dolls, such as a garage or house, are greatly enjoyed as symbolic play progresses. As the child ages, he or she continues to play with these toys but a longer attention span also allows for exploration of raw materials such as paints, clay, and water.

2. *Action:* The younger child directs his or her energy toward motor activities, such as jumping, chasing others, building with blocks, stringing beads, buttoning, scrib-bling, and imitating housework. Fine motor skills are better defined at age three and he or she may enjoy drawing, hitting a ball with a bat, and building taller tow-ers with blocks. The older child may also enjoy playing house.

3. *People:* For the younger child, the parent-child relationship is often acted out with dolls. There may be imitation of domestic actions such as dusting the furniture. As the child ages, he or she still enjoys solitary and parallel types of play but may engage in make-believe conversations with toys. As this child begins to take com-mand of words, interest in playing with others increases and he or she learns to share toys as well as bargain for what is wanted.

4. *Setting:* The child begins to play in the neighborhood and at the playground, giv-ing more opportunities for exploration and experience. A trip to the park is greatly enjoyed because the child can play on the slides and swings. The child may play at a friend's house. Although still under constant supervision, the child is able to play alone in the backyard if responsible adults are watching.

The Symbolic and Simple Constructive Epoch begins with a child who is more interested in solitary and gross motor play. As the child matures and speech becomes more refined, parallel play emerges. Improved coordination results in a greater emphasis on fine motor activities.

Dramatic, Complex Constructive and Pre-Game Epoch (4–7 years)

A milestone in this epoch is the expansion of social participation in play (Erikson, 1950; Mead, 1934; Piaget, 1962). Increased fine motor ability also expands the child's interest in tools. Furthermore, school now becomes the venue at which the child can learn basic skills essential to participate in culture and society. Imaginative play also expands at this time. Symbolic play provides the avenue for mastery of external reality (Takata, 1974). The child may play out social roles which helps him or her to differentiate between his or her role and the role(s) of others.

During the beginning of this epoch, the child plays without regard for rules, allowing everyone to win at once. As the child becomes conscious of rules, he or she begins to practice them. To the latency-aged child, rules are regarded as sacred, emanating from adults and lasting forever.

1. *Materials:* The 4-year old is learning to use paints, playdough, and crayons in a more creative way. The 5-year-old is interested in raw materials but also uses paste and scissors. He or she uses blocks to make houses, roads, and bridges. Dressing up dolls is especially important to girls in this stage. The materials of the 6-year-old may include simple board games, cards, books, music, water, and clay. The child is learning to read and write and thus enjoys markers and pencils.

2. *Action:* The 4-year-old is beginning to take more risks requiring fine motor coordination. This child can skip but may not yet hop. Often activities are short-lived and there is much movement from one toy to the next. The 5-year-old is increasingly involved in the development of gross motor skills. He or she skips, dances, rides a bike with training wheels, jumps rope, and role-plays community situations such as grocery store or hospital. This child can put away toys in an orderly way. In contrast, the 6-year-old exhibits much more interest in pretend play. The child is able to use raw materials to make his or her own books or boxes. Tool manipulation is practiced by taking things apart and putting them back together again. Activities that require a lot of action such as tag and hide-and-seek are frequently performed.

3. *People:* The 4-year-old may associate with two or three children. Imaginary friends are also common. The play of the 5-year-old may continue to be parallel even though being with other children is enjoyable. The child may play well with younger or older siblings, but may prefer to play with someone his or her age. The 5-year-old will share toys. The 6-year-old prefers to play with friends, rather than to play with siblings or alone. This child plays better with children his or her own age or older and does not show a preference for gender. Winning is important to the 6-year-old, who will even tattle on friends if they are believed to have cheated. At this stage, there may be play in unorganized groups.

4. *Setting:* Children in this stage enjoy the outdoors where they can practice gross motor skills. They also enjoy spectator events, such as the circus or a puppet show.

They may be permitted to go to a neighbor's house alone if they do not have to cross busy streets.

During the Dramatic, Complex Constructive and Pre-Game Epoch, play becomes increasingly social. The child begins to incorporate social roles into his or her play. As the child progresses through this epoch, pretend play increases. There is a growing awareness of rules, which sets the stage for the next epoch.

Game Epoch and Recreation Epoch

The final two epochs, the Game Epoch and the Recreation Epoch, reveal more organization within play. During the Game Epoch, the emphasis is on the enhancement of constructional and sports skills as expressed through rule-bound behavior (Takata, 1974). A child 7 to 12 years is involved in more games with rules, and may be involved in informal clubs and organized group activities. During the Recreation Epoch, there is an emphasis on team participation and an interest in groups (Takata, 1974). A child older than twelve is often involved in organized team activities or social interest groups as his or her main avenue for play.

Conducting the Interview

The interview follows the format of Materials, Action, People, and Setting. The clinician begins by eliciting information about what kinds of toys the child enjoys playing with (materials), and proceeds to asking questions regarding the child's skill in play activities (action), the child's play companions (people), and the child's play area (setting). Each content area consists of 6 to 19 questions. Interviews take about 45–75 minutes to conduct. As with any parent report measure, it is important to develop good rapport with the informant to obtain the most accurate responses. It may be helpful to provide the parent with a general list of what kinds of questions will be asked before the actual interview to help improve the quality of their answers. The interview questions are listed in Appendix A.

Questions are included or omitted depending on the child's chronological age. For example, it is not necessary to ask the parent of an infant if the child participates in make-believe play. The interviewer first asks questions relating to the child's present play preferences, then explores the child's past play behaviors. For example, when asking about a child's play materials, the interviewer first asks what the child's favorite toys are now. This is followed by questions concerning what they were in the past (i.e., What did he or she play with at 6 months, 1 year, 2 years? etc). Each content area ends with a question asking the informant to recall the child's past play. This enables the clinician to look at play sequentially and to understand how the child's play has developed.

The Revised Play History (Behnke & Menarchek-Fetkovich, 1984) contains a Time Schedule that asks the parent to describe the child's daily routine. This allows the clinician to get an idea of how often a child plays, when he or she plays, and what he or she is doing when not engaged in leisure activities.

Behnke and Menarchek-Fetkovich (1984) further revised the original interview by developing the Play History Interviewer's Guide, which can be found in Appendix B. The Interviewer's Guide consists of probe questions that should be used during the actual interview as a supplement to the Play History questions. The guide provides the clinician with supplemental information and facilitates the interview process by providing examples that help to clarify the answers to specific questions for both the clinician and the informant. The guide also provides useful information for the scoring of the Play History Interview because it specifies what type of information each question elicits, or yields. For example, the question, "What type of fine motor activity has he/she mastered over the past year?" yields, in part, information about patterns of failure that may be emerging. If a 2-year-old child has not mastered any fine motor activities over the past year, this may be indicative of a significant problem, such as dyspraxia. Thus, the Interviewer's Guide helps to streamline the play diagnosis.

Scoring the Interview

The Play History Interview was designed as a qualitative measure. That is, the interview information can be used as the basis for scoring, interpretation, and treatment planning. The qualitative information reveals patterns of achievement and failure. Identifying clusters of failure assists in the process of diagnosis. The detailed description of the child's play provides valuable information for detecting play dysfunctions as well as determining the type of intervention(s) required. For example, if all questions relating to fine motor activity show a pattern of avoidance, this may indicate a motor planning disorder, and therefore, an occupational therapist may need to be consulted.

In their efforts to improve the statistical properties of the Play History Interview, Behnke and Menarchek-Fetkovich (1984) created a quantitative scoring system for use with the Revised Play History. This system should be used with caution as it was created for research purposes only. Scores cannot be interpreted clinically. Norms have not yet been developed. However, the scoring system may be useful in following a child over time in order to assess progress. At this time, scores are most effectively applied to research projects.

The categories (materials, action, people, and setting) are individually rated for each epoch from the first epoch to the child's current age epoch. For example, a 5-year-old would be rated for the first three epochs. Each epoch has an individual chart for scoring, which lists the four elements, a description of the play, and an ordinal scale. For example, on the Sensorimotor Epoch scoring chart, under the "Materials" heading, there is a list of toys that a child under two would be expected to play with (i.e., objects for sensory experiences). The column headed "Description" asks whether there is evidence/no evidence of these materials and whether their use is encouraged or discouraged. Each element is listed and the description is made. Next, each element is scored using the following scale: 0— play behavior not yet evident; 1—inadequate play, progressive therapy indicated; 2—borderline play, definite need for play intervention and enrichment; 3—adequate play experiences, opportunity, and action but lacking in some inner area; and 4—excellent play experiences, opportunity, and action. Scores for each epoch are determined by adding the four categories in that epoch. A maximum score of 16 is possible for each epoch.

The next step is to determine the total play score by totaling all of the epochs' scores. An overall score can be given by looking at the mean score for the epochs scored. These scores are recorded on the Play History Scoring Chart and Scoring Chart Summary (Behnke, 1982), which can be found in Appendix C and D, respectively. By using a quantitative scoring system, the clinician can more easily compare scores over time and compare the scores of groups of children.

Reliability and Validity

In a 1984 study by Behnke and Menarchek-Fetkovich, the parents of 15 disabled and 15 nondisabled children were interviewed about their children's play behaviors using the Revised Play History Interview. Information was obtained by interviewing the parents about their children's play behaviors from birth to present age. The 30 children were divided into two equal groups. Each researcher conducted 15 interviews, audiotaped them, and later listened to the others' tapes to determine interrater reliability (r). An r of .90 was found, indicating a good level of interrater reliability for the Revised Play History.

Ten parents were reinterviewed within three weeks to determine test-retest reliability. Once again, reliabilities were strong, all reaching statistically significant levels.

Finally, the scores from the Play History were correlated with scores from the Minnesota Child Development Inventory (MCDI) to examine the concurrent validity of the Play History (Menarchek-Fetkovich, 1982). Positive and significant correlations with the MCDI scores were found, demonstrating that the Revised Play History is a valid instrument.

Behnke and Menarchek-Fetkovich (1984) found that the mean score on the Play History was 22 points for the disabled population and 32 points for the nondisabled children. Although the two groups were only three months apart chronologically, their scores were significantly different on the Play History. A difference of 10 points in Play History mean scores places the two groups almost an epoch apart in play development. The disabled children spent more time in passive activities, such as watching television or watching other children play. They tended to avoid fine motor activities and gross motor activities that involved balance or swinging.

The Revised Play History was used in another study to compare the play behaviors of visually impaired children with their sighted peers (Berliner, 1994). The results of the study found that children with visual impairment tended to have lower play scores than their same-age sighted peers. Berliner found statistically significant differences between the two groups on the total play scores as well as on the action category scores (how they played, moved, and manipulated objects) on the Revised Play History Interview.

Clinical Considerations

Therapists from varying disciplines can administer the Revised Play History Interview. Practitioners need to consider the following suggestions before using the instrument. It is important that the clinician have good interviewing skills so that the informant feels at ease. A thorough understanding of the theoretical basis for assessment, the process of play development as it occurs in each epoch, normal development in general, and the characteristics associated with the play styles of disabled children is essential. Caution must be used to avoid emphasizing quantitative data obtained from the Revised Play History Interview as their applicability requires further study. The qualitative information yields the best description of the child's current play status. To obtain the most accurate information from the interview, the Revised Play History Interview as well as the Play History Interview Guide need to be employed together.

It is highly recommended that the Revised Play History Interview be used in conjunction with actual play observations to check the parents' reports and to help elaborate the information through direct observation. The Revised Play History Interview is a useful tool for individual practitioners and for those working in a multidisciplinary team approach. By looking at which play behaviors are evident/not evident and which behaviors are encouraged/discouraged, the clinician can formulate a specific play prescription. For instance, it may focus on teaching the child new play skills, enhancing his or her current skills, or some combination of the two. The prescription may also include treatment from a variety of other professionals such as occupational therapists, physical therapists, and speech/language pathologists.

SUMMARY

The Revised Play History Interview is a semistructured qualitative questionnaire aimed at identifying play experiences, interactions, environments, and opportunities. It is one of the few tools that looks at a child's past as well as current play behaviors, allowing the clinician to assess how the child's play has developed. By using a historical approach, the therapist obtains a complete portrait of the child, not just a snapshot. The information from the interview yields a total play description, providing therapists with valuable information. The Revised Play History Interview is a useful tool for evaluating children with possible developmental delays and other disorders. The interview should not be the sole instrument for making a diagnosis. Because it is a qualitative measure and responses can be subjective, it is best to use it in conjunction with other measures and direct observation. The Revised Play History Interview is a reliable tool that is useful in planning treatment for children with play deficits.

REFERENCES

Antias, S., & Kreimeyer, K. (1992). Social competence intervention for young children with hearing impairments. In S. Odom, S. McConnell, & M. McEvoy (Eds.), *Social competence of Young children with disabilities* (pp. 135–164). Baltimore: Paul Brookes.

Beckman & Leiber (1992). Parent-child social relationships and peer social competence of preschool children with disabilities. In S. Odom, S. McConnell, & M. McEvoy (Eds.), *Social competence of young children with disabilities* (pp. 65–92). Baltimore: Paul Brookes.

Behnke, C. (1982). *Examining the reliability of the play history.* Unpublished master's thesis, Virginia Commonwealth University, Richmond, VA.

Behnke, C., & Menarchek-Fetkovich, M. (1984). Examining the reliability and validity of the play history. *American Journal of Occupational Therapy, 38,* 94–100.

Berliner, K. (1994). *The play behaviors of children with visual impairment compared to sighted peers.* Unpublished master's thesis, University of Illinois.

Bond, L., Creasey, G., & Adams, C. (1990). Play assessment: Reflecting and promoting cognitive competence. In E. Gibbs & D. Teti (Eds.), *Interdisciplinary assessment of infants: A guide for early intervention professionals* (pp. 113–128). Baltimore: Paul Brookes.

Erikson, E. (1950). *Childhood and society.* New York: Norton.

Gesell, A. (1940). *The first five years of life.* New York: Harper & Row.

Goodson, B., & Greenfield, P. (1975). The search for structural principles in children's manipulative play: A parallel with linguistic development. *Child Development, 46,* 734–746.

Higginbotham, D., & Baker, B. (1981). Social participation and cognitive play differences in hearing-impaired and normally hearing preschoolers. *Volta Review, 83,* 135–149.

Kernberg, P., & Chazen, S. (1991). *Children with conduct disorders.* New York: Basic Books.

Kielhofner, G. (1980). A model of human occupation, part 2: Ontogenesis from the perspective of temporal adaptation. *American Journal of Occupational Therapy, 34,* 657–663.

Kielhofner, G., & Burke, J. (1980). A model of human occupation, part 1: Conceptual framework and content. *American Journal of Occupational Therapy, 34,* 572–581.

Mead, M. (1934). *Mind, self, and society.* Chicago: University of Chicago Press.

Menarchek-Fetkovich, M. (1982). *Examining the validity of the play history.* Unpublished master's thesis, Virginia Commonwealth University, Richmond, VA.

Munoz, J. (1986). The significance of fostering play development in handicapped children. In American Occupational Therapy Association, *Play: A skill for life* (pp. 1–12). Maryland: American Occupational Therapy Association.

Murphy, F., & O'Driscoll, M. (1989). Observations on the motor development of visually impaired children. *Physiotherapy, 75,* 505–508.

Piaget, J. (1962). *Play, dreams, and imitation in childhood.* New York: W. Norton.

Richman, N., & Dawe, N. (1988). *Play problems of preschool children.* New York: Wiley.

Rogers, J., & Takata, N. (1975). *The play history as assessment tool.* Unpublished manuscript, University of North Carolina at Chapel Hill.

Skellenger, A., Hill, M., & Hill, E. (1992). The social functioning of children with visual impairments. In S. Odom, S. McConnell, & M. McEvoy (Eds.), *The social competence of young children with disabilities* (pp. 165–188). Baltimore: Paul Brookes.

Takata, N. (1967). *Development of a conceptual scheme for analysis of play milieu.* Unpublished thesis, University of Southern California.

Takata, N. (1969). The play history. *American Journal of Occupational Therapy, 23,* 314–318.

Takata, N. (1971). The play milieu: A preliminary appraisal. *American Journal of Occupational Therapy, 25,* 281–284.

Takata, N. (1974). Play as prescription. In M. Reilly (Ed.), *Play as exploratory learning* (pp. 209–246). Beverly Hills: Sage.

Appendix A

THE REVISED PLAY HISTORY INTERVIEW

The interviewer begins by telling the informant, "The first set of questions pertains to the kind of toys your child enjoys playing with."

MATERIALS

What are your child's favorite playthings?

What does he do with his toys; for instance, is he most apt to use the toy as intended by the toymaker or not?

As you think back on your child's development, what have been some other favorite toys? For example, what did he enjoy playing with as a baby? As a one-year-old? and so on...

Is your child responsible for keeping his toys in order?

How long does your child usually play with one toy?

How much time per day does your child spend watching television? What is his favorite program?

If your child is given a choice, what would he choose to do?

Does your child have a favorite game? If yes, what is it? Does he play the game according to the rules?

What kind of play activities does your child least enjoy or avoid?

What does your child do when a toy isn't working properly or he can't manage it in the way he would like?

Does your child collect any objects? If yes, what are they?

Does your child show a preference for any kind of arts and crafts activity? If yes, what kind?

To what extent does your child enjoy book reading or storytelling?

What kind of outdoor play equipment is available?

As you look back on your child's choice of playthings from infancy to the present, what seems to stand out most in your mind?

ACTION

"This series of questions is directed at your child's skill in play activities."

How would you characterize your child's gross motor skills? Have they shown improvement over the past year? Give me an example.

Does your child enjoy rough-housing?

What body position does he prefer when playing alone?

Does your child frequently sit and watch other children play?

Does your child have a preference for active physical play rather than quiet, sedentary activities? What factors contribute to this judgment?

How would you describe his fine motor skills such as painting or using tools in eating?

What fine motor activity has he mastered over the past year?

What new fine motor activity has he attempted over the past year?

Does he seem to prefer gross motor or fine motor activities?

Does he enjoy any spectator activities such as watching a live sports activity or a puppet show?

At what age did your child begin to play make-believe? Did you encourage this?

Does your child still participate in make-believe play? What does he pretend to be?

What were some of his favorite themes? Were costumes important?

Does your child make up stories? What are his favorite themes?

As your recall the focus of your child's play behavior from infancy to the present, what seems to stand out the most? Do you see any kind of pattern or sequence?

PEOPLE

"The following questions concern your child's play companions."

During the after-school hours, how many children does your child usually play with?

Who would you say is your child's favorite playmate?

When other children are available, does your child prefer to play by himself or with others?

Would you say that he plays well with others or are there frequent fights?

Would you describe him as a leader or a follower in his play group?

Can you give me an example of how he plays with other children? For example, does he share toys?

What does he do when he is unable to manage the game selected by the group?

What does he do when he wants to play with a toy that another child is already using?

Does he easily lose interest when he plays by himself?

Does he (did he) have an imaginary friend?

Does he include other children in his pretend play?

Does he belong to an organized group such as scouts?

Does he belong to any informal group such as a club?

Does your child prefer to do things with adults rather than with children?

What kinds of things do you play with your child? Your spouse?

Does your child have a pet? Is he totally responsible for taking care of it?

If you were trying to make your child laugh or smile, what would you do?

As you look back, how would you describe his interaction with his play companions over the years?

SETTING

"The last set of questions refers to your child's play area."

Does you child prefer to play indoors or outdoors?

When he is indoors, what is his favorite play area?

When he plays outdoors, what is his favorite play area?

How far from home do you permit him to go by himself to play?

Does your child have an outdoor play area available—a yard or public playground?

Have you lived at the same location since your child was born? If not, please describe prior play areas available to your child.

Appendix B

PLAY HISTORY INTERVIEWER'S GUIDE

Directions: Probe questions should be used during the actual interview as a supplement to the play history questions. Yield information should be used to aid in scoring the play history.

MATERIALS

1. *What are your child's favorite playthings?*

    Yield:

    (1) availability of materials

    (2) appropriateness of materials

    (3) variety of materials

    (4) reflects familial attitudes and values about play

2. *What does he do with these toys? For instance, is he most apt to use the toy as the toymaker intended or not?*

    Yield: Look for patterns of nonpurposeful actions. Mode of dealing with objects should change with age. Is creative and realistic play apparent?

    Example: Parent said her 3-year-old banged his toys all the time with no real purpose.

    Comment: Constantly banging toys and playing with them in a perseverative manner is symptomatic of autism.

3. *As you think back on your child's development, what have been some of his favorite toys?*

    (*Probe:* What did he do with these toys?)

    Yield: Form and content of play should change with increasing age. Do toys promote gross motor or sedentary activities? Availability of toys.

    Example: As a baby, child showed little interest in objects or people. He explored little.

    Comment: Lack of change in form and content of play may indicate cognitive delay.

4. *How long does your child usually play with one toy?*

    (*Probe:* Does he focus his attention on the toy? How quickly does he move from one toy to another?)

    Yield: Attention span should vary with the activity.

    Comment: Rapid shifts in activity are symptomatic of Attention Deficit Hyperactivity Disorder.

5. *Is your child responsible for keeping his toys in order?*

(*Probe:* Is there a designated place for toys?)

Yield: Are toys easily accessible to child? Is parent putting excessive responsibility on child or not enough?

6. *If your child were given a choice, what would he choose to do?*

   (*Probe:* This implies any activity—not just play.)
   Comment: A child who chooses not to play may lack play skills or opportunities.

7. *What kind of play activities does your child least enjoy or avoid?*

   Yield: Look for patterns emerging and being reinforced by the environment.
   Comment: A child who avoids gross motor activity may have poor muscle tone.

8. *What does your child do when a toy isn't working properly?*

   Yield: Indicates ability to problem solve and tolerance for frustration.
   Comment: Child who destroys toy may have underlying emotional problems.

9. *Does your child collect any objects?*

   Yield: Quality versus quantity. Hobbies emerging?

10. *Does your child show any preference for any kind of arts and crafts activities?*

    Yield: Indicates specific skill learning and opportunities for tool use.
    Comment: Does child resist touching certain materials, such as clay or glue? Note tactile defensiveness.

11. *Does your child have a favorite game? If yes, what is it? Does he play the game according to the rules?*

    (*Probe:* Examples—Peek-a-boo, chase, board games, group games).
    Yield: Indicates stage of rule learning. Indicates stage of social participation (i.e., solitary, parallel, etc.).

12. *To what extent does your child enjoy book reading or storytelling?*

    (*Probe:* Is there a special time set aside for this activity?)
    Yield: Indicates child's interests (i.e., fantasy or realistic themes). Gives information about parental/environmental attitude toward learning.

13. *How much time per day does your child spend watching television?*

    Yield: Indicates time spent in passive activity.
    Comment: Children who prefer passive activity may have physical or cognitive delay.

14. *What is his favorite program?*

    Yield: Does the program promote active participation? What role models are available?

15. *What kind of outdoor play equipment is available?*

Yield: Availability of materials to promote skill learning.

16. *As you look back on your child's choice of playthings from infancy to the present, what seems to stand out most in your mind?*

    Yield: Gives a clue to unhealthy patterns emerging (i.e., is there a lack of change in types of materials as age increases?)

ACTION

1. *How would you characterize your child's gross motor skills?*

   Yield: Provides a general time schedule of skills learned or not yet developed.

2. *Does your child enjoy rough-housing?*

   (*Probe:* Whom does he usually do this with?)

   Yield: Indicates degree of risk taking and trust in human environment.

3. *Does your child have a preference for active physical play rather than quiet sedentary activities? What factors contribute to this judgment?*

   (*Probe:* Would you say that there is a balance between the two?)

   Yield: Note unusually strong preferences. Is this preference being reinforced by the environment?

   Example: Child participates in quiet activities due to poor muscle control.

   Comment: Hyperactive children are more likely to engage in constant gross motor activity. Children with low muscle tone may avoid gross motor activities.

4. *What body position does he prefer when playing alone?*

   Yield: Body position should vary with activity. Evidence of a predominant posture should be explored further.

   Comment: Children with low or high muscle tone may prefer one position.

5. *Does your child frequently sit and watch other children play?*

   (*Probe:* Does he relate to the other children or simply watch them?)

   Yield: Do physical restrictions encourage this behavior? Indicates quality of social participation.

   Comment: Children who are anxious or depressed may avoid playing with others. Children with developmental delays may lack the entry skills to engage in play.

6. *How would you describe you child's fine motor skills?*

   Yield: Indicates opportunities for specific skill learning leading to habit formation. Is child experiencing competency? Note fine motor patterns.

   Comment: Children with dyspraxias and children with tactile dysfunctions often display delayed fine motor skills.

7. *What fine motor activity has the child mastered over the past year?*

   Yield: Signals patterns of failures emerging.

8. *What new fine motor activity has he attempted over the past year?*

   Yield: Do abilities match opportunities? Indicates child's tolerance for novelty.

9. *Does he seem to prefer gross motor or fine motor activities?*

   (*Probe:* Does there seem to be a balance?)
   Yield: A strong preference of one activity over the other signals imbalanced growth.
   Comment: Does the child avoid one type of activity because he is unable to perform?

10. *Does he enjoy spectator activities such as watching a live sports activity or a puppet show?*

    Yield: Opportunity.

11. *At what age did your child begin to play make believe?*

    Yield: Designates at what age the milestone occurred between sensorimotor and symbolic play. Indicative of a change in cognitive development.
    Comment: Lack of make-believe play could indicate cognitive delay.

12. *Did you encourage it or not?*

    Yield: Play attitudes in family.

13. *Does your child still participate in make-believe play?*

    Yield: Ascertain the distinction between imitation and pretend.

14. *Who does he pretend to be?*

    Yield: Source of role models.

15. *What are some of his favorite themes?*

    (*Probe:* i.e., school, house, hospital, store…)
    Yield: Tells about situations encountered and those the child has attempted to master.
    Comment: Abused children often display violent play themes.

16. *Are costumes important?*

    Yield: Degree of complexity of play.

17. *Does your child make up stories?*

    Yield: Realism versus fantasy.

18. *As you recall the focus of your child's play behavior from infancy to the present, what seems to stand out most?*

Yield: Indicates whether play form has changed with age.

Example: Child has always had plenty of toys but not much interaction with them.

Comment: A child who does not interact with his toys may have cognitive delays or a disorder such as autism.

PEOPLE

1. *During after-school hours, whom does your child play with?*

   Yield: Identification of availability of others for play. Note balance in ages and sex of playmates.

2. *Who would you say is your child's favorite playmate?*

   Yield: Changes in social aspects of play may indicate movement from one phase to another (i.e., parent, sibling, to friend).

3. *When other children are available, does your child prefer to play by himself or with others?*

   Yield: Indicates level of social play (i.e., solitary, parallel, associative, etc.)
   Comment: Anxious or depressed children may avoid playing with others.

4. *Would you say he plays well with other children or are there frequent fights?*

   Yield: Is the child developing acceptable social skills and tolerance for adherence to rules?
   Comment: Conduct-disordered children have difficulty getting along with peers.

5. *Would you describe him as a leader or follower in his play group?*

   (*Probe:* Does this vary depending on the ages of the children in the play group?)
   Yield: Indicates child's initiative and ability to take on a role.

6. *Is he willing to share toys?*

   Yield: Indicates transition to associative/cooperative play. Does child have adequate social skills?

7. *What does he do when he is unable to manage the game selected by his peers?*

   Yield: Child's tolerance for novelty and complexity.
   Comment: Hyperactive children often have difficulty following rules.

8. *What does he usually do when he wants a toy that another child is already using?*

   Yield: Indicates stage of development (i.e., bargaining, trading, etc.)

9. *Does he lose interest when he plays by himself?*

   Yield: Degree of spontaneity and initiative.
   Comment: Is child afraid to be alone?

10. *Does he have an imaginary friend?*

   Yield: Evidence of imaginary play. Reenactment of experiences to practice and master them.

11. *Does he include other children in his pretend play?*

   Yield: Complexity and themes of pretend play.

12. *Does he belong to an organized group such as scouts?*

   Yield: Extent of involvement in community.

13. *Does he belong to an informal group, such as a club?*

   Yield: Is there a neighborhood peer group available?

14. *What kinds of things do you play with your child? Your spouse?*

   Yield: What type of play does the family engage in together? Indicates familial attitudes about play.

15. *Given a choice, does your child prefer to do things with adults rather than with children?*

   Yield: Is there an adequate amount of interaction with both peers and adults? *Comment:* Child may prefer adults because he is unable to make friends.

16. *Does your child have a pet? Is he totally responsible for taking care of him?*

   Yield: Child's ability to practice a nurturing role. Does the child relate better to animals than to people?

17. *If you were trying to make your child laugh or smile, what would you do?*

   Yield: Information about the nature of the parent/child interactions. Child's playful attitude (i.e., does he ever smile?)

18. *As you look back, how would you describe his interaction with his play companions over the years?*

   Yield: Are there any distinct patterns emerging? *Comment:* Lack of interaction with others is symptomatic of autism. Conduct-disordered children often lack peers.

SETTING

1. *Does your child prefer to play indoors or outdoors?*

   (*Probe:* Or is there a balance?)
   Yield: Does environment allow independent, nonthreatening exploration? Does environment reinforce one over the other?
   Example: Child likes outdoors but cannot go outside alone.

2. *Does your child have an outdoor play area available?*

> *Yield:* Is there adequate play space? Note availability of extended surroundings (i.e., parks, playgrounds).

3. *How far from home do you permit him to go by himself to play?*

> *Yield:* Do parents impose too many restrictions on the child or fail to provide adequate limits and boundaries?
>
> *Example:* Child must be with someone at all times. Parent cannot trust child to be alone for even a short time.

4. *When he plays indoors, what is his favorite play area?*

> (*Probe:* Is this where most of his toys are?)
>
> *Yield:* Does the child prefer to play where others are?

Appendix C

PLAY HISTORY CHART

SENSORIMOTOR EPOCH (0–2 years)

Elements	Description		Scale
Materials Toys, objects for sensory experiences—(see, mouth, touch, hear, smell) rattles, ball, nesting blocks, straddle toys, chimes, simple pictures, color cones, large blocks.	*Evidence* *No Evidence*	*Encouraged* *Discouraged*	0 1 2 3 4
Action Gross—stand/fall, walk, pull, sit on, climb, open/close. Fine—touch, mouth, hold, throw/pick up, bang, shake, carry, motoric imitation of domestic actions.	*Evidence* *No Evidence*	*Encouraged* *Discouraged*	0 1 2 3 4
People Parents and immediate family.	*Evidence* *No Evidence*	*Encouraged* *Discouraged*	0 1 2 3 4
Setting Home—crib, playpen, floor, yard, immediate surroundings.	*Evidence* *No Evidence*	*Encouraged* *Discouraged*	0 1 2 3 4
Emphasis: independent play with exploration habits expressed in trial and error.	Nonevident Inadequate Borderline Adequate Excellent		0 1 2 3 4

TOTAL_____

PLAY HISTORY CHART

SYMBOLIC AND SIMPLE CONSTRUCTIVE (2–4 years)

Elements	Description		Scale
Materials Toys, objects, raw materials (water, sand, clay, paints, crayons) for fine motor manipulation and simple combining and taking apart; wheeled vehicles and adventure toys to practice gross motor actions.	*Evidence* *No Evidence*	*Encouraged* *Discouraged*	0 1 2 3 4
Action Gross—climb, run, jump, balance, drag, dump, throw. Fine—empty/fill; scribble/draw; squeeze/pull; combine/take apart; arrange in spatial dimensions. Imagination with story telling, fantasy; objects represent events/things.	*Evidence* *No Evidence*	*Encouraged* *Discouraged*	0 1 2 3 4
People Parents, peers, other adults.	*Evidence* *No Evidence*	*Encouraged* *Discouraged*	0 1 2 3 4
Setting Outdoors—playground; play equipment immediate neighborhood. Indoors—home, "nursery."	*Evidence* *No Evidence*	*Encouraged* *Discouraged*	0 1 2 3 4

Emphasis: parallel and beginning to share; symbolic play expressed in simple pretense and simple 2 constructional use of materials.		Nonevident	0
		Inadequate	1
		Borderline	2
		Adequate	3
		Excellent	4

TOTAL_____

PLAY HISTORY CHART

DRAMATIC, COMPLEX CONSTRUCTIVE AND PRE-GAME (4–7 years)

Elements	Description		Scale
Materials Objects, toys, raw materials for fine motor actions and role-playing; large adventure toys for refining gross actions for speed and coordination; pets; nonselective collections.	*Evidence* *No Evidence*	*Encouraged* *Discouraged*	0 1 2 3 4
Action Gross—"daredevil" fcats of hopping, skipping, turning somer-saults; dance. Fine—combining materials and making products to do well, to use tools, to copy reality. Dramatic role-playing—imitating reality in part/whole costumes, storytelling.	*Evidence* *No Evidence*	*Encouraged* *Discouraged*	0 1 2 3 4
People Peer group (2–5 members) "imaginary friends." Parents, immediate family, other adults.	*Evidence* *No Evidence*	*Encouraged* *Discouraged*	0 1 2 3 4
Setting School, neighborhood and extended surroundings (excursions); upper space and off the ground.	*Evidence* *No Evidence*	*Encouraged* *Discouraged*	0 1 2 3 4
Emphasis: cooperative play with purposeful use of materials for constructions, dramatization of reality and building habits of skill and tool use.	Nonevident Inadequate Borderline Adequate Excellent	0 1 2 3 4	

TOTAL_____

Appendix D

PLAY HISTORY SCORING CHART SUMMARY

Child's Name _____   Interview Date _____

Age _____   Male _____   Female _____   Birth Date _____

Describe any health problem or disability

Scores:

Epochs (Highest score in each epoch is 16)   *Categories*

Sensorimotor (0–2)   _____   Materials _____

Symbolic/Simple   _____   Action _____
Constructive (2–4)

Dramatic/Complex   _____   People _____
Constructive
   Pregame (4–7)

Game (7–12)   _____   Setting _____

Recreation (12–16)   _____

TOTAL PLAY SCORE   _____

Scale: (Most meaningful in age appropriate epoch)

4 – Excellent play experiences, opportunity, and action

3 – Adequate play experiences, opportunity, and action but lacking in some minor area

2 – Borderline play; definite need for play intervention and enrichment

1 – Inadequate play; progressive therapy indicated

0 – Nonevident

Comments:

Chapter 5

TRANSDISCIPLINARY PLAY-BASED ASSESSMENT

Toni Linder

INTRODUCTION

"Wake up! Wake up! One, two, three, wake up!" Caleb shakes his father who is lying on the floor pretending to be asleep. Caleb and his dad have been racing around the room with towels tucked into the necks of their T-shirts like a cape. Caleb has been squealing with joy as his father swoops him up and "flies" him through the air. They take turns chasing each other until his father falls to the floor and pretends to be asleep. This animated, spontaneous play is quite a contrast to the play that was observed with his mother, the play facilitator, and a peer.

With his mother, Caleb quietly put together a shape puzzle without prompting when she placed it before him. He drew a picture of a face after his mother drew a circle on the paper and requested that he draw specific features. "Now he needs a mouth.... Good. Where's your mouth, Caleb?" Caleb pointed to his mouth. He continued answering her questions with single-word, monotone responses, naming a shape, a body part, or a color. "Good, Caleb. Now look at me. What color is this crayon?" "Red," Caleb answered, looking quickly back at his paper, his face revealing little affect.

With the play facilitator, a psychologist, Caleb was even more quiet, looking at toys around him, rocking back and forth, and playing with cars by ritualistically lining them up. "I'm going to drive my car under the bridge," commented the facilitator, as she drove a car under a block bridge. Caleb continued to line up his cars in a row. When the facilitator turned to get more blocks, Caleb drove a car under her bridge and then back into his line.

With a peer, Caleb stood watching the peer playing with a tape recorder. When Jarrod abandoned the tape recorder, Caleb sat down and began to experiment with the buttons. He smiled as he pushed the buttons and made noises into the microphone. His glance did not follow Jarrod who was loudly "tooting" as he pushed a train across the floor.

The Transdisciplinary Play-Based Assessment of Caleb, who had been diagnosed with Pervasive Developmental Disorder (PDD), reveals the importance of observation of a child interacting with various people, including parents and peers, as well as with the examiner. Caleb responded differently to each of the above people and situations. Yet each of the above scenarios reveals something about Caleb that is important for both diagnosis and treatment.

With the peer, Caleb was interested in the toy with which the child was playing, but not in playing with the toy and the peer at the same time. We observed that he was motivated by a toy that had buttons that allowed him to cause something auditory and captivating to occur. Although he observed the peer, he was more interested in relating to the toy than engaging with the peer. He initiated no verbal or nonverbal interactions.

With the play facilitator, who was a stranger to Caleb, he engaged in parallel play, but did not verbally communicate. He was interested in what she was doing, but was careful not to let her see his imitation of her actions. He demonstrated no eye contact with the facilitator, instead choosing to watch her actions with the toys. Some self-stimulating vestibular movement was observed during his play with the stranger.

With his mother, Caleb was verbally responsive, but did not initiate conversation. He needed to be prompted to give eye contact and cued for a response. His answers were accurate, demonstrating understanding of several basic concepts. The toys presented to Caleb by his mother were toys used in structured teaching both at home and at school, so Caleb was familiar with the stimuli, the cues, and the sequences presented. He did not spontaneously comment on the materials presented. Although responsive to the structured presentations, he did not appear to enjoy the interactions.

With his father, Caleb was a different little boy. Running, chasing, "flying" elicited excited affect. He understood dramatic play sequences related to the actions performed and initiated appropriate dialogue. Caleb demonstrated rote counting to three and remembered and applied appropriately the use of counting as a preliminary phrase to elicit an action.

Over the period of approximately one hour, observations of Caleb across people, toys, and situations allowed the observing assessment team to ascertain Caleb's cognitive, communicative, motor, and social skills, how his interactions varied across people and interaction styles, the types of toys, materials, and interactions that motivated Caleb, and the type of interactions that elicited more spontaneous language, higher levels of play, and a broader range of affect. This information could then be used in collaboration with the parents to develop an intervention plan for Caleb for both home and school. The videotape made during the TPBA was useful, as well, as the team could illustrate various aspects of Caleb's progress, his learning style, and interaction patterns that seemed to be effective in promoting higher levels of behavior.

Caleb's parents left the assessment session with information about the developmental level at which Caleb was functioning in each developmental domain and information about behaviors that were observed that contributed to the diagnosis of PDD. In addition, they received suggestions and helped to generate practical ideas for: (1) increasing his spontaneous communication through active play, where Caleb could be the leader; (2) producing higher levels of language and thinking through playful games involving turn-taking, where the adults or peers could model the appropriate use of concepts and action sequences in a meaningful context; (3) using highly motivating cause-and-effect toys to encourage problem-solving and interaction, again using turn-taking as a means of producing more spontaneous social interchange; (4) generalizing skills learned through structured teaching to more spontaneous, practical applications throughout Caleb's day; and (5) providing Caleb with vestibular, auditory, and other types of sensory input using movement toys and sound toys that Caleb can activate and control in order to provide higher levels of sensory input to his body and encourage increased affective response.

A DEVELOPMENTAL, PLAY-BASED MODEL

The past decade has seen the development of a proliferation of instruments for assessing the development of young children suspected of having, or being at risk for, disabilities. Transdisciplinary Play-Based Assessment (TPBA) (Linder, 1990, 1993) was developed in response to the need for a more functional, holistic approach to determining a child's level of development, skills, learning style, and interaction patterns. Designed for use with infants through age 5, TPBA builds upon the work of numerous developmental theorists, including Bronfenbrenner (1979), Piaget (1970), Vygotsky (1967), Erikson (1963), and Fischer (1987) and previous work on play by Ainsworth, Blehar, Waters, and Wall (1978), Belsky and Most (1981), Calhoun and Newson (1984), Fewell (1984), McCune-Nicholich (1980), Nicholich (1977), Parten (1932), Rogers (1986), and Westby (1980). The process is transdisciplinary, with a cross-disciplinary team of professionals observing the child's play. Using the guidelines from *Transdisciplinary Play-Based Assessment* (Linder, 1990, 1993), it determines the child's highest or qualitatively strongest skills and processes, the level of functioning, and the types of skills or processes for which the child is ready across four domains, including cognitive, language and communication, social-emotional, and sensorimotor development. The child is observed playing alone, with a play facilitator, a peer, and his or her parents. The play facilitator follows the child's lead, encourages, motivates, and when necessary provides scaffolding for eliciting higher-level behaviors. The assessment process is intended to be child-centered and family inclusive, with the parents serving an active role on the assessment team before, during, and after the assessment. The process is, preferably, videotaped for both professional and parent reference. Age tables are provided within the manual to assist professionals in ascertaining the developmental level of behaviors observed during the assessment. Team discussion after the assessment allows professionals and parents to discuss their observations, compare interpretations, determine the interrelationships among developmental issues, determine program eligibility, and plan for home and/or school intervention.

Transdisciplinary Play-Based Assessment has numerous advantages over more traditional approaches to assessing young children. Because the assessment employs a play environment utilizing a variety of motivating toys and materials appropriate to the child's level of functioning, *observers have an opportunity to see the child interact in a more typical way with toys and materials than is usually the case with standardized test materials.* The assessment can also be conducted in a more natural environment such as a playroom, preschool classroom, or home. The use of the more natural environment and the inclusion of the parents as part of the assessment process allows the examiner, or facilitator, to develop rapport more easily than is usually the case in more structured interactions between the examiner and child using traditional tests.

The ability to modify the setting, toys, and materials, rather than using a standardized set of materials, allows flexibility in meeting the individual needs of each child. The facilitator can, thus: (1) alter the level or type of language used with the child; (2) incorporate toys or materials relevant to a specific culture; (3) follow the child's preferred sequence of activities; (4) adapt toys or materials to enable the child with disabilities to demonstrate higher levels of performance; (5) incorporate parents or peers as much or as little as is beneficial to the child's performance; (6) observe the child's differential response depending on setting, people, and materials included; and (7) modify the method of presentation and level of scaffolding provided to determine what methods best promote learning and interaction.

The flexibility of the TPBA process also enables the persons evaluating the child to gain a more holistic view of the child. One of the fundamental premises of the TPBA model is that children's development and learning is a result of complex interrelations among developmental domains, and that in order to more fully understand a child, it is necessary to examine the interactive aspects of observed behaviors. In other words, it is important that interactive effects of cognition, communication, sensorimotor and social-emotional development be examined. Unlike traditional methods of assessment, which typically have specific disciplines that conduct compartmentalized assessments for each developmental area (e.g., the speech therapist conducts language assessments, the psychologist conducts cognitive and emotional assessments, the occupational or physical therapist conducts sensorimotor evaluations), the TPBA process encourages the use of a team of professionals looking at the child in concert and discussing the meaning and implications of their observations in an integrated fashion. The holistic approach is less fragmented and more interrelated, giving team members a more cohesive view of the issues and the treatment implications. The concept of *transdisciplinary* implies that each member of the assessment team is going beyond his or her specific discipline to incorporate information and meaning from all developmental areas.

Involvement of the child's parents in the assessment process is also a somewhat revolutionary concept. One of the cornerstones of TPBA is that children are to be viewed within the context of their family (McGonigel, Woodruff, & Roszmann-Millican, 1994), and therefore, the family's concerns, priorities, and values are important to the assessment process (Bruder & Bologna, 1993; Howard, 1982). Traditionally, parents have been used to provide developmental history and background information to the professionals, who then conduct their assessments. Frequently the parents are left outside of the assessment room and are only reunited with their child after the assessment is completed. *The parents are considered integral to the TPBA process. They are viewed as part of the assessment team and play various roles before, during, and after the assessment. They are information providers, observers, interpreters, and facilitators.*

Before the assessment, the parents provide information, not only about the child's background and history, but also about the child's favorite playthings, their typical behaviors at home, and interaction patterns that seem to be most successful. They also provide direction to the assessment, by indicating what questions they would like to have answered or what information they would like to obtain as a result of the assessment process.

During the assessment the parents observe the play along with the professionals and provide information about how the behaviors that are being seen compare with the child's typical behaviors at home or in other settings. This allows the team to determine the validity of the assessment. Parents are also asked to play or interact with their child as part of the assessment, if they feel comfortable doing so. This allows comparisons of the child's interactions with a familiar person versus the play facilitator. Many times children use more language or higher levels of play with their parents than with a stranger. The parents can be (1) involved throughout the assessment, if necessary due to the age, disability, or disposition of the child, (2) seated close to the child, to enable the child to physically or visually check in with the parents, or (3) if the child's behavior is negatively affected by the presence of the parents, the parents can be seated so that they can see the child, but the child is unaware of the parents' presence. Parents are also asked to leave the room for a few minutes at some point in the assessment, so that separation and reunion behaviors can be observed. In addition, any changes in behavior that may result from the parents' absence may be seen at this time.

Parents also serve as interpreters during the assessment session. Children with language delays or disorders may not be readily understandable. The parents can "translate" the child's idiosyncratic patterns for the team. Children with severe disabilities or emotional problems may also demonstrate cues, or behaviors, that are "read" by parents as having a certain meaning. For example, one parent commented, "When he makes that face, I know I'd better back off or a tantrum will follow." Without the assistance of the parent in reading the child's cues, the team might inappropriately respond to the cue or might misinterpret the behavior. Parents also frequently share important insights about their child as they observe the play session. Many times these insights would not have otherwise reached the team, as a direct question relating to the insight was not asked on a preassessment questionnaire.

Both the family-centered approach and the focus and cross-disciplinary input are consistent with Part H of IDEA (the federal law mandating services to young children with disabilities) and with recommended "best practices" (Bruder & Bologna, 1993; Foley, 1990; Linder, 1990; McGonigel & Garland, 1988; McCollum & Thorp, 1988; McGonigel, Kauffman, & Johnson, 1991; Shonkoff & Mersels, 1990). *The involvement of parents in the transdisciplinary play-based assessment has the ancillary benefit of building the parents' trust in the outcome of the assessment process.* In a study by Meyers, McBride, and Peterson (1996), parents gave higher ratings to play-based assessment over traditional assessments, particularly in relation to a feeling of comfort about seeking information from team members and in feeling that important goals were identified by the assessment. The greater the confidence the parents have in the assessment results and recommendations, the greater the likelihood they will follow through on implementing recommendations.

Another advantage of the TPBA process is that specific *qualitative* questions are built into the assessment observation guidelines that require the team to analyze how the child seems to process information. In addition to looking at skill levels across domains, the TPBA will address the child's learning style, temperament characteristics, mastery motivation, and interaction patterns. The assessment also examines underlying developmental processes (such as problem-solving approach or muscle tone) that relate to how a child acquires a skill or what may be inhibiting the development or expression of an ability.

Unlike many standardized tests, which result in the label of "untestable," the TPBA can be used with all young children, regardless of disability. Even if the child is unable to interact with toys or people, the transdisciplinary guidelines enable the team to look at the child's characteristics, response patterns, and basic motor patterns necessary for further development. Combined with the information obtained from the parents before and during the assessment, the team can gain a picture of overall functioning, learning processes, and interaction patterns.

Using all of the information, from the parents and the TPBA, *the results of the assessment provide a direct link to intervention.* Traditional forms of assessment may provide results in terms of percentiles, stanines, standard deviations, age equivalents, and so on. The scores may be used to determine a diagnosis and, perhaps, appropriate placement or therapy needs. Little information, however, may be gained with regard to intervention suggestions for home and school. Rather than using one number to portray the child's ability level, the TPBA process will result in information on the child's developmental range of functioning, including the lowest, the highest, and the *most typical range* of functioning. Terms relating to "deficits" are avoided, as these tend to promote a negative view of the child. Results are shared in terms of "strengths" (current abilities) and "Things I'm Ready For" (present needs). In addition, because results are obtained based on functional observations, TPBA is intended to be used to develop specific recommendations relating to: (1) functional skills for which the child is ready, (2) the need for expansion of breadth and depth of skills to enable generalization, (3) the most successful ways to scaffold the child's learning, and (4) interaction patterns that tend to promote language and positive social expression.

One study comparing play-based assessment and traditional assessment (Meyers, McBride, & Peterson, 1996) found that staff members rated play-based assessment as providing significantly more information than standardized tests on communication, social skills, and motor skills. They also found that reports resulting from play-based assessments took fewer hours of staff time to complete and reports were completed significantly sooner than reports resulting from traditional assessments.

THE TEAM

Composition

The composition of the TPBA team may vary from child to child, depending on the needs of the child, but team composition always begins with the parents or guardians of the child. To this basic element various professionals are added. The observational guidelines of the TPBA include cognitive, language and communication, social-emotional, and sensorimotor development. These domains may be observed by professionals with corresponding competence, such as a psychologist or developmental specialist, a speech pathologist, an occupational and/or physical therapist. Alternatively, team composition may be determined by availability of staff, with each staff member or professional being assigned to observe one or more domains. The guidelines have been written in such a way that professionals from many diverse backgrounds can understand and utilize them to guide observations. In some cases, if a child is observed to need further observation by an expert in a given domain, an additional evaluation can be scheduled at a later time. For children with specific low-incidence disabilities, such as deafness, vision impairment, or severe cerebral palsy, the addition of specialists to the initial TPBA team may be warranted.

Roles

Although the composition of the assessment team may vary, the roles played by the team members remain the same. A *play facilitator* is desired who will play with the child during the session. Rather than have each professional interact with the child in turn, having one person to whom the child relates is less disruptive to the child and provides continuity to the session. Not having to adjust to a sequence of strange adults may also result in enhanced performance on the part of the child (Benner, 1992; Haynes, 1976; Linder, 1990;

McGonigel, Woodruff, & Roszmann-Millican, 1994; Woodruff, 1980). The play facilitator needs to be able to relate well to young children, to be able to be animated and *fun,* and to be able to follow the lead of the child, rather than be directive. The play facilitator must be able to engage the child and play *with* the child. At the same time, the facilitator needs to note what is happening in the child's play, determine the level and significance of the behaviors and communication that are taking place, and be able to "bump-up" or scaffold the child's play to elicit higher levels of behavior or learning. Being a *good* facilitator can be accomplished with practice and feedback. Being a *great* play facilitator is truly an art.

A *parent facilitator* is needed to sit with the parents and obtain information about how what they are seeing compares to what they typically see at home, to elicit interpretive comments, and to gather important insights the parents may share about their child. The parent facilitator also provides information about what is happening in the play session and what the play facilitator is trying to derive through the play. Opportunities may also arise for the parent facilitator to share with the parent comments about strategies the play facilitator is using that may be particularly effective. The interaction between the parents and the parent facilitator should be informal and interactive. When needed, the parent facilitator may want to provide information from the parents to the play facilitator to enhance the play opportunities.

When the child being assessed is an infant, it is advisable to have a parent as a co-child facilitator rather than sitting with the parent facilitator. In this way the parent can provide necessary emotional support to the child. As the child becomes more comfortable, the parent can move away to sit with the parent facilitator if desired. Likewise, a child who is severely motorically impaired may benefit from having a parent as a co-child facilitator. Many times parents of children with multiple involvements have learned specific ways to handle or relate to the child or methods of reading the subtle, idiosyncratic communicative cues the child gives. By co-facilitating the parent can provide valuable modeling for the professionals and, thus, expedite the play session. In situations where the play facilitator is co-facilitating with a parent, the play facilitator also plays the role of the parent facilitator in obtaining and providing information as the play session proceeds.

One team member is also assigned the role of *videographer.* This is not as easy as it may seem, as it is important for this person to be able to: (1) move with the child (without moving the camera excessively), (2) get closeups, when appropriate, of oral motor or fine motor movements, (3) get shots of the child's interactions with adults and peers, and (4) get full-body shots of the child's gross motor movements. The videotape is a valuable resource for many purposes. First, the tape will allow the team to go back and analyze specific elements about which there are questions. Second, the tape will be useful for illustrating various aspects of the child's characteristics and intervention approaches when meeting with the family. Third, the tape can be used (with permission) for consultation purposes with professionals who were not involved in the play session, but whose input would provide needed expertise. Fourth, the tape can serve as a documentation of the child's progress over time, with additional tapings being added on in future assessment or intervention sessions. Fifth, the tape is an invaluable method of connecting with families. Many families do not have their own video cameras at home, and the tape of the play session can be copied and given to the family to keep, a gift many view as a treasure.

All members of the team are *observers,* regardless of the other roles they may be assuming. Each team member is responsible for observing and responding to the questions put forward in the guidelines for at least one domain. It is possible for one person to conduct a play assessment alone, but this requires a great deal of transdisciplinary knowledge and practice with the model. A team approach is preferred and results in more comprehensive discussions and suggestions.

THE TPBA PROCESS

Preassessment Questionnaires

The TPBA process begins with the parents. Although not included in the manual, which includes only the guidelines for observing the child, it is recommended that information be obtained about the child before the actual assessment is completed. The person who is to be the parent facilitator can be responsible for this task, as the initial contact with the family enables the establishment of early rapport with the parents. Parent-administered developmental checklists and/or informal interviews with the parents can be incorporated. Child Development Resources, in Norge, Virginia (P. O. Box 280, Norge, VA 23127, 757-566-3300) has developed several useful instruments to aid professionals in gaining information from the parents as well as a checklist for professionals to use when providing information to the parents about what the TPBA process entails.

Parents can also be advised to bring: (1) some of the child's favorite toys and books (for purposes of making the child comfortable and providing a comparison between how the child responds to familiar versus unfamiliar toys and materials), (2) a snack and the child's eating and drinking utensils (so that oral motor and self-help skills may be observed while the child is eating and drinking a snack), and (3) comfortable clothing and shorts or a bathing suit (so the child can move freely and comfortably and so that the child's skeletal and muscular systems may be better observed).

Preassessment Planning

After information is obtained from the parents, the professionals who will be involved in the assessment need to meet to determine how the information provided by the parents can be utilized in the TPBA. During this brief session, the team discusses what was learned about the child that can help in planning the assessment. Information such as: (1) the parents' priorities for the type of information they would find most useful from the assessment; (2) the type, number, and level of toys to which the child responds best; (3) arrangement of toys and materials to entice the child to play; (4) temperament or disability information that may help determine which team member would be best to facilitate the child's play; (5) information regarding a preferred sequence for different types of activities (e.g., don't begin with motor activities for a child suspected of hyperactivity); (6) assignment of roles to the various professionals (play facilitator, parent facilitator, camera operator); and (7) assignment of observational areas (which team member will be primarily responsible for observing each of the four domains). This preassessment planning meeting allows the team to coordinate their efforts in order to maximize the usefulness of their observations during the TPBA.

The Transdisciplinary Play-Based Assessment

The Setting

The play session can be done in almost any setting, as long as the environment is not too chaotic or overstimulating, where appropriate, motivating toys and materials are available to the child (some within the child's immediate vision), and the room feels inviting and nonthreatening. A home environment, classroom, or playroom can be used. If conducted in a home, the team will want to use the furniture, toys, and materials available within the home, as well as bring additional interesting objects with which the child is not familiar. When conducted in a school or clinical setting, the team will want to use a variety of materials, but also incorporate some of the child's favorite things brought from home.

The playroom ideally will be of sufficient size to enable the child to move around comfortably and the team to observe without being intrusive. Several distinct areas, or centers, may be set up so that toys and materials are grouped in meaningful ways. Such areas might include a house or dramatic play area, a block and box area with cars and trucks, a sensory exploration area, an art area, a gross motor area, a manipulatives or games area at a table, a floor play area, a science or woodworking area, a computer area, and so on. The room needs to be adaptable so that the amount and type of materials can be shifted to meet the needs of individual children. In small playrooms, toys and materials can be housed in cupboards and several different types of objects can be presented at a time, so that the child is still able to make choices. For infants, a floor play area is usually sufficient; though some children with disabilities will need to use adaptive seating to maintain stability and be able to play.

Types of Materials

The above areas will house a variety of toys, materials, and equipment. One key to a successful play session is the presence of the "right stuff." Professionals need to be able to select from objects that are likely to appeal to the child, are able to be used by the child, and will reveal important information about the child's functioning. The following ten types of materials for infants and an additional ten types of items for preschoolers are recommended:

For Infants:

1. Sensory toys or materials, including bright objects or objects with high contrast; objects that make noise; materials that provide varying tactile sensations, such as bubbles, water, soap (also things that are rough, sticky, gooey, smooth, grainy, warm, cold); objects that enable the child to experience vestibular sensation or movement (swinging, bouncing, riding).

2. Cause-and-effect toys requiring use of mouth, finger, hand, or foot activation (or for motorically involved children, eye or head movement). This can include, but is not limited to, a computer.

3. Early representational toys or functional items, such as phones, dolls, or stuffed animals with bottles, blankets, combs, or other household items.

4. Both large and small toys that can be combined in numerous ways (banged, inserted, placed on top of, pulled apart, etc.).

5. Balls or other objects that can be tossed, kicked, dropped, or exchanged.

6. Objects that require problem-solving, such as objects with lids, handles, knobs, switches, or levers that require pushing, pulling, turning, poking, twisting, and so on.

7. Early books with pictures of familiar people, animals, and objects.

8. Tools for marking on paper or making marks in a substance (sand, playdough, paint, etc.).

9. Items to stimulate vocalization, such as mirrors, music, microphones, bubbles, or computer games.

10. Liquid and solid (if appropriate) snack.

For Preschool Age:

All of the above, at the appropriate developmental level, are needed. In addition:

1. Simple familiar and unfamiliar predictable books and storybooks.

2. Climbing apparatus and equipment requiring complex movement patterns.

3. Building or art materials for combining, painting, coloring, cutting, pasting, tearing, stapling, sawing, taping, and so on.

4. More complex construction materials, such as large blocks, Legos, Tinker Toys, Rube Goldberg–type constructions with balls, tubes, ramps, wheels, and so on.

5. Puppets, costumes, and props for dramatic play with various characters.

6. Miniature scenarios, such as a house and family members, a farm with people, equipment, and animals, a zoo with wild animals, an airport, and so on.

7. Materials for sorting and classifying by various characteristics, such as color, shape, size. These may be included in the above categories.

8. Musical instruments, tape recorder, or record player.

9. Simple games, such as card games or board games, requiring turn-taking.

10. A computer with simple games, if available.

Beginning the Play

After the team has had an opportunity to plan and set up the play environment, the TPBA can proceed. Depending on the age of the child being assessed and any disabilities the child may have, the beginning of the play session will need to be adapted. For the child who is mobile and separates easily from the parents, the facilitator will allow the child to explore the environment and choose toys with which to play. The facilitator will then follow the child's lead and, beginning with parallel play, will move toward associative or cooperative play. The facilitator will use techniques employed by language therapists and play therapists within the interactions with the child. The goal is to elicit spontaneous, meaningful, interactive play that expresses the child's full range of skills and feelings. Mirroring, or imitating the child; using reflective remarks; using parallel talk (elucidating the child's actions) or self-talk (describing the facilitator's own actions); interpreting the child's actions; commenting on the play; expanding or modeling language and actions are techniques employed by the play facilitator. The play facilitator will begin each play interaction by observing what the child does spontaneously with the toys or materials selected.

Then, as needed, the facilitator can structure, prompt, suggest, or expand the play in a variety of ways to be able to determine the child's skills, problem-solving approaches, feelings, learning style, and so on. As much as possible, the use of directives or "testing" questions is minimized. Establishing a meaningful relationship with the child is essential to being able to see "typical" behaviors.

As the child warms up to the play facilitator and the setting, the facilitator may begin to entice the child to play with the various materials in the centers. The child frequently will move from one area to another without prompting, but the facilitator may transition the child as needed, so that the full range of play skills may be observed. The play facilitator may take a motivating toy to another area and begin to incorporate the toy in that area, or, many times, just calling the child's attention to a new and interesting object or material is enough to motivate the child to want to move to a new toy or play area. With each transition, the play facilitator again allows the child to play in whatever way is natural before modeling any new behaviors. The play facilitator is responsible for ensuring that all of the team members can see the behaviors they need to see in order to have a complete picture of the child's abilities. The play facilitator not only entices the child to play with the various toys, materials, and equipment, but also extracts cognitive abilities, receptive and expressive language and communication, gross and fine motor skills, and social and emotional responses. As this is a major task, team members may cue the play facilitator to elicit certain skills or interactions in each play area, as needed.

Not all children will readily enter the play area. Many children will want to stay near their parents until they are more comfortable. In this instance, the play facilitator will want to incorporate one of the parents into triadic play. As the child becomes more interactive with the play facilitator, the parent can either remain a part of the play, or may choose to move to the role of observer with the parent facilitator off to the side.

As mentioned previously, for infants or more severely disabled children, a parent is usually involved in the play at the beginning, and sometimes throughout the play session. The goal is for the child to be spontaneous, so whatever arrangement results in the child playing contentedly should be utilized.

Structure of the Session

The structure of the TPBA session is meant to be fluid and responsive to the needs and desires of the child. During the play session, which typically lasts 45 minutes to an hour, the child will engage in play with many of the materials listed above across a variety of centers. The child will also interact with the play facilitator, the parents, siblings, if present, and a peer, if possible. The child's language, play, and interactions across these people are observed to see if differences are evident. The parents are asked to play, read to, or interact with their child in whatever way they do at home. In addition, the parents may be asked to do a more structured task with the child, to see how the child responds to this "teaching" situation.

With children who are approximately a year or older, it is useful to observe the child without the presence of the parent. The child's behavior when the parent leaves, after the parent is gone, and when the parent returns may give indications of the child's level of trust, autonomy, and resilience. At some point during the session, when the parents feel the child is comfortable, the parents are asked to tell the child they need to leave the room for a few minutes, but they will be back. If the parents indicate that separation is traumatic for the child, this element will be postponed until the end of the session. If the child does deteriorate emotionally when the parents leave, the subsequent reunion can provide information about how the child self-comforts or what efforts are needed on the part of the parents to restore equanimity.

Siblings and/or peers (observation of both is beneficial) may be included in the play at any time that seems appropriate. Some children will feel more comfortable beginning play with a sibling or peer, while others may have a peer join the play later in the session for an activity requiring social problem-solving or joint effort. Peers who are slightly higher functioning than the child being assessed assume the role of facilitator through modeling higher levels of language and play. It is also beneficial to have a familiar, same-sex peer, if possible, as mutual play will typically begin sooner. The sibling or peer may remain a part of the play as long as is necessary to enable the team to observe typical peer interactions. Some children may actually withdraw when a peer enters the play. The play facilitator may then serve as a mediator to the play and may engage both children in a game or interaction.

Ending the Session

A successful play session is not easy to terminate, as all involved have been having a good time. Ending the play session with a snack provides a means of removing the child from the toys and playthings and allows the team to observe oral-motor skills, self-help skills, and social interaction. The parents and/or the peer may also be included in the snack time. It is recommended that the parents be asked to bring something for the child to eat and drink, as well as the child's typical utensils. In this way, the team may see what constitutes a typical snack, and they can also avoid the problem of allergic reactions to something they might serve. Using the child's utensils enables the team to see if adaptive utensils are used at home, or in some instances, whether the utensils are developmentally appropriate for the child.

Before the parents and child leave, the team should determine whether there is anything else they would like to observe. In addition, it is a good idea to ask the parents several questions before terminating the session. First, was what they observed typical of how their child usually plays, talks, moves, and interacts? If not, the team may want to follow up with further observations or assessments to ensure a valid evaluation. Second, is there anything the parents would like the team to see or know about what the child does that has not been observed during the session? If so, the parents may be asked to try to elicit the behavior or to discuss the circumstances under which the behavior occurs. Third, is there anything they saw during the play session that surprised them? If the answer is "yes," the behavior and the circumstances under which the behavior occurred should be noted. Frequently parents are surprised by a skill they did not know their child had or a behavior the child did or did not display. For example, "I can't believe he played with you for a whole hour and never had a tantrum!" In this case, the team needs to note the importance and expected frequency of tantrums as well as analyze what about the interactions resulted in more positive behavior. The fourth question relates to the parents' expectations of the assessment process. What questions do the parents have, and what information can the team provide that would be most useful to the parents? This is an essential question, that, though asked at the beginning of the assessment process, deserves to be reiterated. If the team provides a great deal of information, but none related to the parents' questions and concerns, then the parents will be dissatisfied with the results of the assessment and will probably not adhere to the recommendations.

Recording the Observations

During the play session, all team members who are not occupied as a facilitator or videographer will be taking notes on their observations. Those who were actively involved in the play session may take notes after the session, while reviewing the videotape. Worksheets are available in the same format as the guidelines within the text to remind observers of subcategories of each domain and to assist them in organizing their observations. The guidelines ask questions related to each of the four domains: cognitive, language and communication, social-emotional, and sensorimotor development. Questions relate to not only what skill or behavior was observed, but also *how* the child performed a specific behavior and under what circumstances. The content of the guidelines for each of the four domains is outlined below. Within each of these subcategories, additional questions are addressed.

I. Cognitive development

 A. Categories of play—the types of play observed during the session

 B. Attention span—to what types of activities the child attended for the longest and shortest times.

 C. Early object use—the types and sequences of actions used by the child on objects

 D. Symbolic and representational play—cognitive level of dramatic play

 E. Imitation—ability to imitate familiar and unfamiliar actions and sequences

 F. Problem-solving approaches—interest in and means of accomplishing goals

 G. Classification/discrimination—knowledge of concept classification

 H. One-to-one correspondence—understanding of number and relational concepts

 I. Sequencing ability—ordering of concepts, stories, time

 J. Drawing ability—level of drawing skill

II. Social-emotional development

 A. Temperament—activity level, adaptability, and reactivity

 B. Mastery Motivation—purposeful goal-oriented activity

 C. Social interactions with the parents—reaction of the child, characteristics of the interaction

 D. Social interaction with the facilitator—reaction of the child, characteristics of the interaction

 E. Characteristics of dramatic play—structure, content, and awareness of self and others

 F. Humor and social conventions—developmental level of humor, use of adaptive or maladaptive behaviors

 G. Social interaction with peers—in a dyad and/or in a group

III. Communication and language development

 A. Modalities of communication—methods of communication used by the child

 B. Pragmatics—level, meaning, and functions of communication, discourse skills

C. Phonology—sound production patterns, errors, and intelligibility

E. Semantic and syntactic understanding—word usage, structure, and morphological markers

E. Comprehension of language—forms of language understood

F. Oral motor development—lip, tongue, and jaw control in eating and drinking

G. Other—hearing, voice quality, and relation to developmental pre- or corequisites

IV. *Sensorimotor development*

A. General appearance of movement—physical appearance of child and child's movement

B. Muscle tone, strength, and endurance—the degree of tension in the child's muscles when at rest, the power of the muscles, and the stamina of the child

C. Reactivity to sensory input—reaction to touch, movement, visual, and auditory input

D. Stationary positions used for play—child's behavior in various static positions

E. Mobility in play—child's behavior when transitioning from one position to another

F. Developmental achievements—jumping, climbing, and ball skills

G. Prehension and manipulation—use of fingers and hands in isolation and together

H. Motor planning—child's awareness of body in space and ability to sequence movements

Summarizing Raw Data

The raw data, or notes on the child, can be quite extensive. Summarizing and prioritizing the information thus become important. Summary forms are available that allow team members to describe, for each domain and subcategory listed above, the child's strengths (highest or best performance), to rate each subcategory (as age-appropriate or qualitatively strong), to justify the rating (with descriptions or age levels), and to note "Things I'm Ready For" (skills, processes, or types of activities the child needs to enhance development). The summary forms are best completed immediately after the TPBA session, with segments of the videotape being reviewed as needed. An important phase of the process involves a discussion among team members (preferably involving the parents) of the information on the summary sheets. The discussion allows team members to compare their observations and interpretations, to integrate findings, and to draw conclusions about appropriate next steps. Based on this discussion, team members make modifications to their summary forms.

The information from the summary forms is then available to be incorporated into a report and/or to be discussed with parents for planning program and intervention alternatives. If parents are unable to be involved in the transdisciplinary discussion of findings immediately following the TPBA, a subsequent meeting with the parents can be held to review the videotape and consider the implications of the findings.

RESEARCH ON TPBA

Validity

Validity generally refers to the degree to which a test measures what it purports to measure (Borg & Gall, 1989). Three forms of validity, including content validity, criterion-related validity, and social validity have been studied. Borg and Gall (1989) describe content validity as the degree to which the sample of test items represents the content that the test is designed to measure. In two studies of content validity, Friedli (1994) and Linder, Green, and Coates (1996) found that the TPBA guidelines were supported by early childhood professionals most likely to use the process, such as psychologists, educators, speech-language pathologists, and motor specialists. In the first study, professionals who used TPBA and those who did not use TPBA, and in the second study, experts from around the country rated the content of the developmental domains and subcategories for relevance, clarity, and comprehensiveness using a Likert scale ranging from 1 to 7. All of the subcategories of the TPBA were judged favorably (higher than 4) in both studies, with the means of most ratings between 6 or 7.

Social validity, as described by Meyers, McBride, and Peterson (1996) typically involves asking program participants or consumers to rate the acceptability of various procedures. Myers, McBride, and Peterson (1996) examined parent's perceptions of the evaluation and the written report for both standardized and play-based assessments. Through questionnaires with 17 statements describing various aspects of the assessment and report process, parents were asked to rate their degree of agreement or disagreement with each of the statements using a 5-point Likert scale. Findings revealed that the means for 13 of the 17 items, along with the overall total for play-based assessments, were significantly higher than those for standardized assessments. A nonparametric sign test showed these to be significantly different (p < .05).

The same study also examined the staff perceptions of the amount of information obtained from each of the assessments, as well as the usefulness of the information. Following each evaluation, each staff member rated the amount of information obtained from the primary developmental domains using a Likert scale from 1 (none) to 5 (great). They found that significantly more information was obtained through the use of the play-based assessments in the domains of communication, social, and motor skills. Speech pathologists also rated play-based assessments as significantly more useful in identifying a child's strengths and weaknesses and for developing program planning.

Functional utility, which refers to the clarity, completeness, and usefulness of information was also studied by Meyers, McBride, and Peterson (1996). The functional utility of play-based assessment reports was also rated higher in their study, including: (1) ease of obtaining an overview of the child's abilities, (2) ease of determining which developmental areas were of concern, (3) the number of developmental areas discussed in the report, (4) the report being written in jargon-free language, (5) the integration of discipline-specific information, and (6) the objectives being clearly based on the child's strengths and weaknesses.

Criterion-related or concurrent validity is determined by relating the test scores of a group of subjects to a criterion measure administered at the same point in time or within a short interval of time (Borg & Gall, 1989). The concurrent validity of TPBA was measured by comparing the outcomes of play-based assessment to traditional standardized and norm-referenced testing for children with and without disabilities. In one study, Friedli (1994) found that the TPBA was as accurate as standardized measures for determining whether a child was eligible for services as compared to the results of the Batelle Developmental Inventory. The two assessments also produced similar profiles regarding strengths and needs. In addition, Friedli determined that TPBA was actually more accurate in identifying one child with social-emotional problems.

Meyers, McBride, and Peterson (1996) also compared the outcomes of TPBA to other standardized tests, including the Bayley Scales of Infant Development-II and the Receptive-Expressive Emergent Language Scale-3. They found that 19 (95%) of the children receiving play-based assessments and 18 (90%) of the children receiving standardized assessments qualified for early intervention services based upon a state-specified criterion of a 25% or more delay in at least one area of development. In addition, greater agreement was found between parents and professionals on individual profile items, along with greater congruence in judgment-based rating between team members.

Reliability

Borg & Gall (1989) define reliability as the level of internal consistency or stability of the measuring device over time. Reliability of TPBA across time and raters has been studied (Friedli, 1994; Linder, Green, & Friedli, 1996). TPBA was well supported for both test-retest reliability and interrater reliability.

Interrater reliability refers to the degree of agreement between two or more raters on the point value of responses to specific test items (Newbord, Stock, Wrek, Guidubaldi, & Svinicki, 1984). Meyers, McBride, and Peterson (1996) studied interrater reliability through an analysis of the ratings of each of the 15 developmental profile items by each of the team members and parents. For the play-based assessments, they found that 11 of the 15 developmental domains had higher percentages of exact agreement than standardized measures on every developmental profile item. Significantly higher percentages of agreement within one point were found on 12 domains.

The interrater reliability was also examined by Friedli (1994) using videotapes of TPBA sessions, with independent raters assessing each child. The reliability for the language, motor, and overall combined domains met acceptable criteria, the same as standardized tests, used to make eligibility decisions. Friedli also found that professionals from various disciplines were as accurate in rating young children's developmental competence in other domains as they were in their domains of expertise when they were given specific guidelines for observation. This finding substantiates the transdisciplinary nature of the TPBA process and is an indicator of the ability of professionals to be holistic in their approach to observing children.

SUMMARY

Transdisciplinary Play-Based Assessment is both a useful observation tool and a dynamic process that can be used to assess a child's various levels of development, determine strengths and weaknesses, identify areas needing intervention, and distinguish learning styles and interaction patterns. The process can assist educators and therapists in ascertaining appropriate targets for intervention and in discovering strategies that are likely to enhance developmental progress. The guidelines may also serve as an observational tool for the purpose of ongoing evaluation of developmental progress and behavioral change. As a result of the direct involvement of parents as part of the assessment team and the team discussions that allow comparison of perceptions, the probability of obtaining valid and reliable results is increased.

REFERENCES

Ainsworth, M., Waters, E., & Wall, S. (1978). *Patterns of attachments: A psychological study of the stranger situation.* Hillsdale, NJ: Lawrence Erlbaum Associates.

Belsky, J., & Most, R. K. (1981). *Developmental psychology, 17*(5), 630–639.

Benner, S. M. (1992). *Assessing Young Children with Special Needs: An Ecological Perspective.* New York: Longman.

Borg, W. R., & Gall, M. D. (1989). *Educational research: An introduction.* (5th ed.) New York: Longman.

Bricker (Ed.), *Intervention with at-risk and handicapped infants: From research to application.* Baltimore: University Park Press.

Bronfenbrenner, U. (1979). Toward an experimental ecology of human development. *American Psychologist, 32,* 513–531.

Bronfenbrenner, U. (1989). Ecological systems theory. *Annals of Child Development, 6,* 187–249.

Bruder, M. B., & Bologna, T. (1993). Collaboration and service coordination for effective early intervention. In W. Brown, S. K. Thurman, & L. F. Pearl (Eds.), *Family-centered early intervention with infants and toddlers: Innovative cross-disciplinary approaches* (pp. 103–127). Baltimore: Paul H. Brookes Publishing Co.

Calhoun, M. L., & Newson, E. (1984). Parents as experts: An assessment approach for hard-to-test children. *Diagnostique, 9*(4), 239–244.

Campos, J. J., & Berthenthal, B. I. (1989). Locomotion and psychological development. In F. Morrison, K. Lord, & D. Keating (eds.), Applied developmental psychology (vol. 3, pp. 229–258). New York: Wiley.

Campos, J. J., Caplovitz, K. B., Lamb, M. E., Goldsmith, H. H., Sternberg, C. (1983). Socioemotional development. In M. M. Harth & J. J. Campos (eds.), Handbook of child psychology: vol. 3. Infancy and developmental psychology (pp. 783–915). New York: Wiley.

Campos, J. J., Svejda, M. J., Campos, R. G., & Berthenthal, B. (1982). The emergence of self-produced locomotion: Its importance for psychological development in infancy.

Erikson, E. H. (1963). *Childhood and Society,* (2nd ed.). New York: Norton.

Fewell, R. R. (1984). *Play assessment scale* (4th ed.). Unpublished document. Seattle: University of Washington.

Fischer, K. W. (1987). Commentary–Relations between brain and cognitive development. *Child Development,* 581, 623–632.

Fischer, K. W., & Pipp, S. L. (1984). Processes of cognitive development: Optimal level and skill acquisition. In R. J. Sternberg (Ed.), Mechanisms of cognitive development, (pp. 45–80). New York: Freeman.

Foley, G. M. (1990). Portrait of an arena evaluation: Assessment in the transdisciplinary approach. In E. D. Gibbs & D. M. Teti (Eds.), *Transdisciplinary assessment of infants: A guide for early intervention professionals* (pp. 271–286).

Friedli, C. (1984). Transdisciplinary play-based assessment: A study of reliability and validity. Unpublished doctoral dissertation, University of Colorado at Boulder.

Haynes, U. (1976). *Staff development handbook: A resource for the transdisciplinary process.* New York: United Cerebral Palsy Association, Inc.

Howard, J. (1982). The role of the pediatrician with young exceptional children and their families. *Exceptional Children, 48,* 316–322.

LaMontagne, J. B. Jordan, J. J. Gallagher, P. L. Hutinger, & M. B. Karnes, (eds.). *Meeting early intervention challenges: Issues from birth to three* (2nd ed., pp. 95–132). Baltimore: Paul H. Brookes Publishing Co.

Linder, T. W. (1990). *Transdisciplinary play-based assessment: A functional approach to working with young children.* Baltimore: Paul H. Brookes Publishing Co.

Linder, T. W. (1993). *Transdisciplinary play-based assessment: A functional approach to working with young children* (Revised ed.). Baltimore: Paul H. Brookes Publishing Co.

Linder, T. W., Green, K., & Friedli, C. (1996). Validity of Transdisciplinary play-based assessment. Unpublished manuscript.

McCollum, J. A., & Thorp, E. K. (1988). Training of infant specialists: A look to the future. *Infants and Young Children, 1*(2), 55–65.

McCune-Nicolich, L. (1980). *A manual for analyzing free play.* New Brunswick: Douglas College, Rutgers University.

McGonigel, M. J., & Garland, C. W. (1988). The individualized family service plan and the early intervention team: Team and family issues and recommended practices. *Infants and Young Children, 1*(1), 10–21.

McGonigel, M. J., Kauffman, R. K., & Johnson, B. H. (1991). *Guidelines and recommended practices for the individualized service plan* (2nd ed.). Bethesda, MD: Association for the Care of Children's Health.

McGonigel, M. J., Woodruff, G., & Roszmann-Millican (1994). The transdisciplinary team: A model for family-centered early intervention. In L. J. Johnson, R. J. Gallagher, M. J.

Meyers, C. L., McBride, S. L., & Peterson, C. A. (1996). Transdisciplinary play-based assessment in early childhood special education: An examination of social validity. *Topics in Early Childhood, 16,* 102–126.

Newborg, J., Stock, J. R., Wnek, L., Guidubaldi, J., & Svinicki, J. (1984) *Battelle Developmental Inventory.* Allen, TX: DLM Teaching Resources.

Nicholich,, L. (1977). Beyond sensorimotor intelligence: Assessment of symbolic maturity through analysis of pretend play. *Merrill-Palmer Quarterly, 16,* 136–141.

Parten, M. (1932). Social participation among preschool children. *Journal of abnormal and Social Psychology, 27,* 243–269.

Piaget, J. (1970). Piaget's theory. In P. H. Mussen (ed.). Carmichael's manual of child psychology (vol. 1, 3rd ed.) (pp. 703–732). New York: Wiley.

Piaget, J. (1971). *Biology & Knowledge.* Chicago: University of Chicago Press.

Rogers, S. J. (1986). *Play observation scale.* Unpublished document. Denver, CO: University of Colorado Health Sciences Center.

Shonkoff, V. P., & Mersels, S. J. (1990). Early childhood intervention: The evolution of a concept. In S. J. Mersels & J. P. Shonkoff (eds.), pp. 630–635. *Handbook of early childhood intervention.* Cambridge: Cambridge University Press.

Vygotsky, L. (1967). Play and its role in the mental development of the child. *Soviet Psychology, 12,* 62–76.

Westby, C. E. (1980). Assessment of cognitive and language abilities through play. *Language, Speech, and Hearing Services in the Schools, 11,* 154–168.

Woodruff, G. (1980, June). Transdisciplinary approach for preschool children and parents. *The Exceptional Parent,* pp. 13–15.

Name of child: _____ Date of birth: _____ Age: _____

Name of observer: _____ Discipline or job title: _____ Date of assessment: _____

On the following pages, note specific behaviors that document the child's abilities in the social-emotional categories. Qualitative comments should also be made. The format provided here follows that of the Observation Guidelines for Social-Emotional Development in **Transdisciplinary Play-Based Assessment.** *It may be helpful to refer to the guidelines while completing this form.*

I.   Temperament

    A. Activity level

        1. Motor activity:

        2. Specific times that are particularly active
            a. Beginning, middle, or end:

            b. During specific activities:

    B. Adaptability

        1. Initial response to stimuli
            a. Persons:

            b. Situations:

            c. Toys:

        2. Demonstration of interest or withdrawal *(circle one)*:
            a. Smiling, verbalizing, touching
            b. Crying, ignoring or moving away, seeking security

        3. Adjustment time:

        4. Adjustment time after initially shy or fearful response *(circle one)*:
            a. Self-initiation   b. Adult as base of security   c. Resists; stays uninvolved

    C. Reactivity

        1. Intensity of stimuli for discernible response:

        2. Type of stimulation needed to interest child *(circle those that apply)*:
            a. Visual, vocal, tactile, combination
            b. Object, social

         3. Level of affect and energy:

        4. Common response mode:

        5. Response to frustration:

From *Transdisciplinary Play-Based Assessment: A Functional Approach to Working with Young Children* (revised edition), by Toni W. Linder. Copyright © 1993 by Paul H. Brookes Publishing Co., Inc.

TPBA ⹀Play-Based⹀ TPBI

II. Mastery Motivation

A. Purposeful activity
1. Behavioral demonstration:

2. Exploration of complex objects:

B. Goal-directed behaviors
1. Behaviors observed:

2. Response to challenging objects or situations *(circle those that apply)*:
   a. Looking   c. Appropriate use
   b. Exploring   d. Persistence, task directedness
3. Repetition of completed, challenging task? *(yes or no)*
4. Persistence in goal-directed behavior
   a. With cause-and-effect toys:

   b. With combinatorial tasks:

   c. With means–end behavior:

5. Selection of easy or challenging task:
6. Demonstration of self-initiation in problem-solving
   a. Frequency of requests for assistance:

   b. Problem-solving organization:

III. Social Interactions with Parent

A. Characteristics of child
1. Level of affect:

2. Reaction to the parent's emotions:

From *Transdisciplinary Play-Based Assessment: A Functional Approach to Working with Young Children* (revised edition), by Toni W. Linder. Copyright © 1993 by Paul H. Brookes Publishing Co., Inc.

TPBA ≡ *Play-Based* ≡ TPBI

Name of child: _____   Date of birth: _____   Age: _____

Name of observer: _____   Discipline or job title: _____   Date of assessment: _____

---

   3. Response to parent's vocal, tactile, or kinesthetic stimulation:

   4. Type and ease of interpretation of cues given by child:

   5. Active versus inactive time:

   6. Frequency of initiation of interchange:

   7. Number of interactive behaviors child maintains:

   8. Reaction to parent's requests, limit-setting, or control:

B. Characteristics of parent–child interaction
   1. Level of mutual involvement
     a. Continuity of content:

     b. Synchrony of timing:

     c. Similarity in level of intensity:

     d. Equality in turn-taking:

   2. Sequence of behaviors demonstrated:

     a. Themes repeated with variation or expansion:

     b. Anticipation of others' actions:

     c. Parent modification of sequences to match child's capabilities:

From *Transdisciplinary Play-Based Assessment: A Functional Approach to Working with Young Children* (revised edition), by Toni W. Linder. Copyright © 1993 by Paul H. Brookes Publishing Co., Inc.

TPBA ≡Play-Based≡ TPBI

3. Indication of enjoyment:

C. Characteristics of child in relation to parent while not in direct interaction
   1. Type and amount of sensory cues child gives to maintain emotional contact:

   2. Seeking of proximity to parent:

   3. Change in child's reactions to parent:

   4. Reaction to parental separation or absence:

   5. Mechanisms used to cope with parent's absence:

   6. Reaction to parent's return:

   7. Awareness of self and others (circle those that apply):
      a. Identification of self and others
      b. Identification of emotions in self and others
      c. Use of pronouns
      d. Identification of gender
      e. Use of adjectives to label concrete or abstract

IV. Social Interactions with Facilitator

A. Characteristics of child
   1. Level of affect:

   2. Reaction to the facilitator's emotions:

   3. Response to facilitator's vocal, tactile, or kinesthetic stimulation:

   4. Type and ease of interpretation of cues given by child:

   5. Active versus inactive time:

From *Transdisciplinary Play-Based Assessment: A Functional Approach to Working with Young Children* (revised edition), by Toni W. Linder. Copyright © 1993 by Paul H. Brookes Publishing Co., Inc.

TPBA ⊒Play-Based⊒ TPBI

Name of child: _____   Date of birth: _____   Age: _____

Name of observer: _____   Discipline or job title: _____   Date of assessment: _____

6. Initiation of interchange:

7. Number of interactive behaviors child maintains:

8. Reaction to facilitator's requests, limit-setting, or control:

B. Characteristics of facilitator–child interaction
   1. How child relates to facilitator:

   2. Effect of facilitation techniques of matching child's content, timing, and intensity on:
      a. Initiation:

      b. Turn-taking:

      c. Affect:

   3. Affect of repetition and expansion of themes on:
      a. Sequence length:

      b. Quality and degree of communication:

      c. Child's initiation of interaction:

      d. Affect:

V. Characteristics of Dramatic Play in Relation to Emotional Development

A. Structure of play
   1. Continuity and logical sequence versus fragmented thought:

   2. Recognition of past, present, and future:

From *Transdisciplinary Play-Based Assessment: A Functional Approach to Working with Young Children* (revised edition), by Toni W. Linder. Copyright © 1993 by Paul H. Brookes Publishing Co., Inc.

TPBA ≡Play-Based≡ TPBI

3. Rigid or inflexible thought patterns:

B. Content of play
   1. Dominant themes *(circle those that apply)*:
      a. Dependency   d. Fear/anxiety
      b. Loss   e. Self-image
      c. Power/control
   Examples:

   2. Recognition of boundaries between reality and fantasy:

C. Awareness of self and others in dramatic play
   1. Joint referencing:

   2. Seeing another's point of view:

   3. Incorporation of adult into play with shared goals:

   4. Making judgments about consequences:

   5. Recognizing and labeling emotions:

   6. Expressing and modulating emotions:

   7. Demonstrating impulse control:

VI. Humor and Social Conventions

A. Smiling and laughter directed at appropriate events?
   1. Physical events involving self and others? *(yes or no)*
   2. Physical events involving objects? *(yes or no)*
   3. Physical events involving others? *(yes or no)*
   4. Verbal jokes from self, parent, adult, child *(circle those that apply)*:
      a. Labeling ambiguities
      b. Conceptual ambiguities
   Examples:

TPBA ≡*Play-Based*≡ *TPBI*

Name of child: _____   Date of birth: _____   Age: _____

Name of observer: _____   Discipline or job title: _____   Date of assessment: _____

B. Awareness of socially acceptable behaviors in specific contexts
    1. Greetings? *(yes or no)*
    2. Sharing, helping? *(yes or no)*
    3. Behaviors around eating, toileting? *(yes or no)*
    4. Respect for adult authority? *(yes or no)*
    Examples:

C. Maladaptive or socially inappropriate behaviors
    1. Self-stimulating or self-abusive behaviors? *(yes or no)*
    2. Eccentric habits or rituals? *(yes or no)*
    3. Unacceptable behaviors directed toward others? *(yes or no)*
    Examples:

VII. Social Interactions with Peers

A. In dyad
    1. Acknowledgment of peer *(circle those that apply)*:
        a. Ignoring, withdrawing, unaware
        b. Looking at, watching
        c. Touching, gesturing
        d. Vocalizing toward, talking with peer
        Examples:

    2. Level of play *(circle those that apply)*:
        a. Unoccupied   e. Associative play
        b. Isolated play   f. Cooperative play
        c. Onlooker play   g. Games with rules
        d. Parallel play
        Examples:

    3. Role of child in dyad *(circle those that apply)*:
        a. No role   b. Follows other child's lead   c. Initiates and directs
        Examples:

    4. Prosocial behaviors *(circle those that apply)*:
        a. Takes turns   c. Helps other child accomplish goal
        b. Shares   d. Responds to other child's feelings
        Examples:

    5. Handling of conflict *(circle those that apply)*:
        a. Assertiveness versus acquiescence
        b. Physical means
        c. Verbal means
        Examples:

TPBA ⊒Play-Based⊒ TPBI

6. Differences between play with peers and play with adults
    a. Qualitative:
    b. Quantitative:
    Examples:

B. Interactions with peers in group
    1. Awareness of being in group experience *(circle those that apply)*:
        a. Oblivious
        b. Watches others
        c. Imitates others
        d. Initiates activities
        Examples:

    2. Adult support needed to maintain group involvement *(circle one)*:
        a. Demands attention
        b. Occasional reinforcement and encouragement
        c. Waits for turn without adult support
        d. Operates independently without group awareness
        Examples:

    3. Response of others to child:

    4. Social interaction and engagement of others:

    5. Type of activities with most social interaction *(circle those that apply)*:
        a. Exploratory
        b. Manipulative or constructive
        c. Representational or dramatic
        d. Motor
        e. Tactile/social
        Examples:

    6. With whom does child exhibit most social interaction?

Additional Comments

From *Transdisciplinary Play-Based Assessment: A Functional Approach to Working with Young Children* (revised edition), by Toni W. Linder. Copyright © 1993 by Paul H. Brookes Publishing Co., Inc.

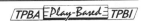

Summary Sheet for Social-Emotional Guidelines

Name of child: _____ Date of birth: _____ Age: _____

Name of observer: _____ Discipline or job title: _____ Date: _____

Observation categories	Areas of strength	Rating	Justification	Things I'm ready for
I. Temperament				
II. Mastery Motivation				
III. Social Interactions with Parent				
IV. Social Interactions with Facilitator				

From *Transdisciplinary Play-Based Assessment: A Functional Approach to Working with Young Children* (revised edition), by Toni W. Linder. Copyright © 1993 by Paul H. Brookes Publishing Co., Inc.

TPBA | Play-Based | TPBI

Summary Sheet for Social-Emotional Guidelines

Name of child: _____ Date of birth: _____ Age: _____

Name of observer: _____ Discipline or job title: _____ Date: _____

Observation categories	Areas of strength	Rating	Justification	Things I'm ready for
V. Characteristics of Dramatic Play				
VI. Humor and Social Conventions				
VII. Social Interactions with Peers				

From *Transdisciplinary Play-Based Assessment: A Functional Approach to Working with Young Children* (revised edition), by Toni W. Linder. Copyright © 1993 by Paul H. Brookes Publishing Co., Inc.

TPBA □Play-Based□ TPBI

PART II

DIAGNOSTIC PLAY ASSESSMENTS

The differential diagnosis of children is always a difficult and challenging process that requires the gathering of information from many sources and often includes formal testing of the identified client. Although most latency-age and older children are able to engage in the tasks required for standard diagnostic testing, young children are often incapable of dealing with the language and cognitive demands of such procedures. At best, the clinician obtains from such youngsters only minimal responses, which are frequently difficult to interpret. For lower-functioning, severely impaired, and/or language-disordered latency-age or older children, many commonly used standardized tests have limited value.

Prior to the development of play evaluations, clinicians needed to rely on a variety of indirect sources of information for the assessment of "untestable" children, including parent and teacher checklists and rating sheets. However, it was well known that these were often prey to bias and halo effects, causing serious questions regarding their validity. Thus, clinicians began using play observations with these populations in an attempt to clarify and expand upon diagnostic impressions. As noted in the introductory chapter, these early attempts to gather information directly from the identified children were fraught with difficulties because they were not based on standardized procedures.

This section of the book offers a broad array of articles that highlight specific key diagnostic questions. The assessment techniques focus on such significant issues as child abuse, childhood psychosis, and autistic-spectrum disorders, as well as speech and language disorders. Certainly, these are among some of the important diagnostic questions facing today's clinicians.

Recognizing the need for a developmental approach to the diagnosis of thought disorders, Rochelle Caplan and Tracy Sherman researched and formalized a storytelling technique and rating scale that is appropriate for use with a latency-aged population. Their reprinted chapter from the first edition of *Play Diagnosis and Assessment* presents an overview of the historical, theoretical, and diagnostic issues surrounding the concept of schizophrenia in childhood. It sheds much light on this often confusing and murky diagnostic category. The Kiddie Formal Thought Disorder Rating Scale and Story Game assist in operationalizing diagnostic criteria and constitute a welcome instrument that has been found to be valid and reliable. This technique involves videotaping and is of great use, especially in inpatient settings, where the difficult issues related to diagnosing this disorder are frequently raised.

Sue White, known for her considerable writing and thought in the area of child sexual abuse, provides an important and well-organized discussion about the use of anatomically detailed dolls. Essentially a clinically descriptive article, it also includes an outline of some specific structured approaches for the doll interview. This chapter, reprinted from the 1991 volume, was one of the first presentations of this type of assessment. It was also prescient in its broaching of the questions concerning the use of evaluative techniques in diagnosing sexual abuse, which continues to perplex and trouble the clinical as well as legal communities.

Using a developmental foundation, Karin Lifter's Developmental Play Assessment scale demonstrates how play behaviors can be employed as the basis for diagnostic statements leading to specific interventions. Lifter's technique and scale are particularly geared toward the assessment of children who are classified within the autistic-spectrum disorders. Most promising about this technique is its presentation of a play-based intervention for these typically difficult-to-treat youngsters. In tying therapeutic interventions to her developmental diagnostic scheme, Lifter provides the reader with a most useful new instrument.

Finally, from England, Kay Mogford-Bevan presents the POKIT. This delightful technique for young children combines an attractive play scenario with tightly banded developmental/diagnostic observational checklists. Examining such behaviors as attention, persistence, and problem solving, Mogford-Bevan's assessment enables the clinician to differentiate children with varying disabilities who might otherwise be lumped together. The clinician is thus able to plan interventions especially geared to play-revealed diagnostic problems.

Despite the inclusion of four valuable chapters in this section, play assessment in the area of childhood diagnosis remains relatively underdeveloped. The future for this area needs to move in the direction of the development of specific play diagnostic assessment procedures that are tied to the DSM IV categories. Certainly, there is a great demand for materials focused on important issues such as childhood depression, phobic disorders, and habit disorders including obsessive-compulsive disorder. It is hoped that this volume will stimulate others to develop play assessment methods for these and other childhood difficulties.

Chapter 6

KIDDIE FORMAL THOUGHT DISORDER RATING SCALE AND STORY GAME

Rochelle Caplan and Tracy Sherman

INTRODUCTION

Formal thought disorder refers to the clinical evaluation of the form or manner in which patients present their thoughts to the clinician. Numerous clinical signs have been used to describe these communicative characteristics, such as illogical thinking, incoherence, loose associations, digressive speech, circumstantiality, tangentiality, vagueness, overelaboration, clanging, neologisms, poverty of speech, poverty of content of speech, echolalic speech, and others (Andreasen, 1979a). The *Diagnostic and Statistical Manual* (3rd ed.—*DSM-III;* American Psychiatric Association, 1980, pp. 188–189) included the following four formal thought disorder signs: illogical thinking, loose associations, incoherence, and poverty of content of speech. The *Diagnostic and Statistical Manual* (3rd ed., rev.—*DSM-III-R;* American Psychiatric Association, 1987, p. 342), however, requires the presence of loose associations or incoherence to diagnose formal thought disorder.

The instruments described in this chapter, the Kiddie Formal Thought Disorder Rating Scale (K–FTDS) and the Kiddie Formal Thought Disorder Story Game, have used a developmental approach to measure formal thought disorder in middle childhood. The K–FTDS has operationalized the four *DSM-III* signs of formal thought disorder for use in middle childhood. The story game is an interview technique for eliciting children's speech examples that are adequate for measuring formal thought disorder. In the first section of the chapter, we describe the background and rationale for the development of the K–FTDS. In the second section of the chapter, we present the background and rationale for the development of the story game, as well as a detailed description of the story game. This is followed by a synopsis of the K–FTDS. The chapter's third section focuses on case material with K–FTDS ratings from the story game of a schizophrenic and of a normal child. In the

The research described in this chapter was supported by NIMH grants MH000538 to Rochelle Caplan and MH30897 to the UCLA Child Psychiatry Clinical Research Center, and by the UCLA Women's Hospital Auxiliary.

169

fourth section of the chapter, we describe the studies that were conducted to examine the effectiveness of the story game and the reliability and validity of the K–FTDS.

BACKGROUND FOR THE DEVELOPMENT OF THE KIDDIE FORMAL THOUGHT DISORDER RATING SCALE (K–FTDS)

Formal thought disorder has been considered a primary symptom of schizophrenia since the earliest descriptions of this disorder. Kraepelin (1896) emphasized the disturbed logical train of thought of the schizophrenic, and Bleuler (1950) hypothesized that impaired thought association processes in schizophrenics are due to a split between affect and thinking. The clinical importance of thought disorder in adult schizophrenia is reflected in the large number of clinical studies (Andreasen, 1979a; Harrow & Quinlan, 1977; Johnston & Holzman, 1979), linguistic studies (Chaika, 1974; Rochester & Martin, 1979), and information processing studies (Asarnow & MacCrimmon, 1981; Neuchterlein, Edell, Norris, & Dawson, 1986; Sacuzzo & Braff, 1986), as well as in the diverse approaches used to study this phenomenon.

In contrast to the wealth of studies on formal thought disorder in adults, there has been little research on formal thought disorder in early and middle childhood. There are two possible reasons for this paucity of studies. The first is the controversy of the use of the term *childhood schizophrenia* since the 1940s. The second is the multiple difficulties involved in the clinical assessment of formal thought disorder in children in the absence of developmental data.

To understand the background for the development of the K–FTDS, we first briefly review the historical changes in the approach to the diagnosis of childhood schizophrenia. We also address how these diagnostic dilemmas affected the diagnosis of formal thought disorder in children.

Historical Approaches to the Diagnosis of Childhood Schizophrenia

Prior to the introduction of the *DSM-III,* there were two major schools of thought regarding the childhood psychoses. The first school of thought maintained that the childhood psychoses were etiologically related to adult schizophrenia but had varying clinical expressions at different ages (Bender, 1942, 1947; Bradley & Bowen, 1941; Fish, 1957; Goldfarb, 1961; Mahler, 1952; Potter, 1933). The second school of thought contended that infantile autism and childhood schizophrenia were separate nosological entities (Eisenberg & Kanner, 1956; Kanner, 1943; Kolvin, Ounstead, Humphrey, & McNay, 1971; Rutter & Lockeyer, 1967; Rutter, Greenfield, & Lockeyer, 1967). According to this school of thought, childhood schizophrenia does not occur before late childhood or prepubescence (Kolvin et al., 1971).

Bender's findings in her follow-up study of 100 cases of childhood psychosis supported the hypothesis that children with an early or late onset of psychosis were schizophrenic. Fifty children in this sample were autistic, with an early onset of psychosis. The remaining 50 became psychotic during middle and late childhood. At follow-up 18 years later, Bender found that 34% of the autistic subgroup had organic defects, deteriorated functioning, and schizophrenic symptomatology. She reported that 48% of the remaining 50 children with a later onset of the disorder had schizophrenia at follow-up. Several additional follow-up studies have reported schizophrenia in patients with a prior history of infantile autism (Brown, 1963; Dahl, 1976; Havelkova, 1968; Reiser & Brown, 1964). The diagnostic criteria for schizophrenia, however, were not clearly spelled out in these studies.

In contrast to Bender's findings, Rutter's 15-year follow-up study of autistic children demonstrated that children with this diagnosis did not become schizophrenic (Rutter et al., 1967). In a cross–sectional comparison of the clinical characteristics of children with early and late onset psychosis, Kolvin demonstrated formal thought disorder, delusions, and hallucinations only in the children with late onset psychosis (Kolvin et al., 1971). The age range of the children in these two diagnostic groups differed. The children with early onset psychosis were between 5 and 11 years of age. The children with late onset psychosis, however, were 13 years old or more.

The findings of these studies led to the conclusion that there was no etiological continuity between childhood schizophrenia and infantile autism. In addition, they also suggested that schizophrenia does not occur in early and middle childhood. This latter conclusion, however, is inconclusive and needs to be further explored for two reasons. First, a careful review of Kolvin's data shows that although the children with late onset psychosis were only studied during late childhood and early adolescence, 42% of this sample had an onset of illness during middle childhood. Second, Kolvin did not match the early and late onset groups of psychotic children by age, IQ, and verbal fluency. Given the importance of the child's verbal skills in eliciting the *DSM-III* inclusionary criteria for hallucinations, delusions, and formal thought disorder, the lack of verbal matches limits the generalizability of Kolvin's data.

Kolvin's findings were the basis for the *DSM-III* approach to the diagnosis of schizophrenia in childhood. On the assumption that schizophrenia does not occur prior to late childhood, the *DSM-III* saw no need for a developmental approach to the diagnosis of schizophrenia in the child. Childhood–onset schizophrenics are, therefore, required to meet the same diagnostic criteria as adults and adolescents.

During the past 10 years, two studies tried to replicate Kolvin's findings and to examine whether schizophrenic children fulfill the *DSM-III* diagnostic requirements (Green et al., 1984; Russell, Bott, & Sammons, 1989). Using medical chart notes, Green compared 24 schizophrenic children, aged 6.7–11.1 years to 25 autistic children, between the ages of 5.2 and 12.1 years. As in Kolvin's study, these groups were not matched on full scale and verbal IQ scores. Green demonstrated that the schizophrenic children, but not the autistic children, met the *DSM-III* criteria for schizophrenia. In addition, auditory hallucinations, visual hallucinations, and delusions occurred in 79.2%, 45.8%, and 54.2%, respectively, of the schizophrenic sample. Formal thought disorder was noted in the medical charts of all the schizophrenic children included in this study.

Russell and his colleagues conducted structured psychiatric interviews using the Interview for Childhood Disorders and Schizophrenia (ICDS) on 35 schizophrenic children, aged 4.9–13.3 years (Russell et al., 1989). They found auditory hallucinations (80%), visual hallucinations (37%), delusions (63%), and formal thought disorder (40%) in their sample. Their findings, therefore, suggest that the *DSM-III* criteria for schizophrenia can be reliably applied in middle and late childhood, using a structured psychiatric interview.

Both studies also examined the age of onset of schizophrenia in children. Green reported that half the schizophrenic children had psychotic symptoms during middle childhood (i.e., between ages 5 and 9 years) and the remaining half during late childhood (i.e., between ages 9 and 13 years) (Green et al., 1984). Russell also reported that the age of onset of psychotic symptoms occurred between ages 8 and 11 years for most of the schizophrenic children in his sample (Russell et al., 1989). These studies' findings suggest that childhood onset schizophrenia occurs during middle childhood.

Several additional studies have reexamined whether autism is, in fact, a developmental precursor of schizophrenia in childhood. Cantor described a sample of 19 children with a mean onset of *DSM-III* signs of schizophrenia at age 4.82 years and 11 adolescents with a mean onset at age 8.5 years (Cantor, Evans, Pearce, & Pezzot-Pearce, 1982). The mean IQ scores of both subgroups were similar. The children had a full scale IQ of 84.15 and the adolescents of 83.11. All these subjects met the *DSM-III* criteria for schizophrenia except for deterioration from a previous level of functioning. The children with the early onset disorder also appeared to have a history of autistic-like symptoms—in particular, withdrawal, speech delay, perseveration, and echolalia. A similar history of withdrawal, speech delay, and perseveration was also found in the adolescent group. These findings led Cantor to conclude that while schizophrenia does occur in children of all ages, those with early onset schizophrenia have more autistic-like symptoms.

Petty and Ornitz presented a case study of three children who had been followed from their diagnosis of infantile autism in early childhood through late childhood, when they developed schizophrenia (Petty, Ornitz, Michelman, & Zimmerman, 1984). Unlike most autistic children, the verbal IQ scores of these children were higher than their performance scores. In addition, their full-scale IQ scores were borderline or normal, not at the retarded level, as found in the majority of autistic children. Petty and Ornitz speculated that the verbal and cognitive skills of these children allowed them to express their psychotic symptomatology. In their opinion, the lack of high-functioning autistic children in follow-up studies of autistic children could have led to a mutually exclusive dichotomy between infantile autism and childhood schizophrenia.

Watkins examined the symptom development of 18 schizophrenic children in a carefully designed retroactive study (Watkins, Asarnow, & Tanguay, 1988). The developmental symptoms of 39% of the children in this sample fulfilled criteria for infantile autism. He also found that the clinical signs of psychosis differed in the children with and without a prior history of autistic signs. Children with a history of autistic-like symptoms primarily presented with disorganization of thought. The children without such a history, however, had hallucinations and delusions when examined.

The findings of these three studies suggest that a subgroup of autistic children may, in fact, present as schizophrenic during adolescence. In addition, children with an early onset of schizophrenia have some autistic-like symptoms.

In *summary,* this historical review demonstrates that two very different approaches have been used to diagnose schizophrenia in children. Proponents of the first approach regarded psychotic behavior in children of different ages as developmental variants of schizophrenia. Proponents of the second approach, however, emphasized the clinical similarity between late childhood onset schizophrenia and adult schizophrenia. Extensive research on infantile autism failed to demonstrate etiological continuity with childhood onset schizophrenia. The findings of studies conducted since the early 1970s indicate that schizophrenic children meet *DSM-III* criteria for this diagnosis. The onset of the disorder, however, appears to be primarily during middle childhood. Finally, it is possible that a subgroup of children with infantile autism develop schizophrenic symptoms during late childhood and adolescence. This finding, however, needs to be reassessed using longitudinal studies.

Review of the Literature on Formal Thought Disorder in Childhood

In reviewing the literature on formal thought disorder in children, one is struck by the small number of studies that have been conducted in this area. This paucity of studies could be related to the relative infrequency of schizophrenia in childhood (Tanguay & Asarnow, 1985). In addition, it could also reflect the difficulties involved in assessing formal thought disorder in children.

From the historical perspective, the different diagnostic approaches to the childhood psychoses have influenced the conceptualization of formal thought disorder in childhood. On the one hand, the proponents of the theory that the childhood psychoses are different developmental expressions of childhood schizophrenia have suggested that the communication deficits of these children could be developmental precursors of formal thought disorder (Fish & Ritvo, 1979; Shapiro & Huebner, 1976). As these children acquire more speech, the illogicality, looseness of associations, incoherence, distorted grammar and fragmented speech become more noticeable (Fish & Ritvo, 1979; Shapiro & Huebner, 1976).

In contrast, the proponents of the theory that late childhood onset schizophrenia has clinical characteristics similar to the adult form of the disease have demonstrated the presence of formal thought disorder in these children (Kolvin et al., 1971). Neither approach, however, described how adult criteria of formal thought disorder were operationalized for use with children.

Seven studies have been conducted on formal thought disorder in schizophrenic and schizotypal children (Arboleda & Holzman, 1985; Cantor et al., 1982; Caplan, Guthrie, Fish, Tanguay, & David-Lando, 1989; Green et al., 1984; Kolvin et al., 1971; Russell et al., 1989), and one such study has been done with children at risk for schizophrenia (Arboleda & Holzman, 1985). Only two of these childhood studies, however, have used reliable and valid instruments for the measurement of formal thought disorder (Arboleda & Holzman, 1985; Caplan et al., 1989).

In terms of studies conducted on schizophrenic children, Kolvin found that children with late onset psychosis have formal thought disorder, unlike children with infantile psychosis (Kolvin et al., 1971). More specifically, he reported that 60% of the children with late onset psychosis had disorder of association, 45% had derailment of thought, and 51% had "talking past the point," as described by F.J. Fish (Fish, 1962; Kolvin et al., 1971). The criteria for assessing formal thought disorder, however, were not based on an objective and reliable instrument.

Cantor identified formal thought disorder signs, such as loose associations, neologisms, illogicality, clanging, poverty of speech, and poverty of content of speech, in both the early onset (mean age of 4.82 years) and adolescent onset (mean age of 8.5 years) groups of children with schizophrenia (Cantor et al., 1982). Like Kolvin, Cantor did not use an objective instrument for assessing formal thought disorder in these children. In addition, she did not clarify how she operationalized these formal thought disorder signs for the younger group.

Green, Campbell, and their colleagues also reported that all the schizophrenic children in their sample fulfilled the *DSM-III* schizophrenic inclusionary criterion for formal thought disorder signs, such as incoherence, marked loosening of associations, illogical thinking, or poverty of content of speech associated with at least one of the following: blunted, flat, or inappropriate affect; delusions or hallucinations; or catatonic or other grossly disorganized behavior (Green et al., 1984). Because the clinical characteristics of the schizophrenic children in this study were retrospectively obtained from medical charts, it is, however, not clear how the *DSM-III* formal thought disorder signs were operationalized in this 6.7 to 11.11-year-old sample.

Russell and his colleagues made reliable global clinical ratings of the *DSM-III* criteria of formal thought disorder from the ICDS (Russell et al., 1989). This interview was compiled and developed from the *Diagnostic Interview for Children and Adolescents* (DICA; Herjanic & Campbell, 1977) and the Schedule for Affective Disorders and Schizophrenia for School-Age Children (Kiddie-SADS—Puig-Antich & Chambers, 1978). It includes questions that ensure an adequate assessment of schizophrenia and schizotypal personality disorder. Russell reported that 40% of his schizophrenic sample exhibited incoherence or marked loosening of associations, illogical thinking, or poverty of content of speech accompanied by affect disturbance, delusions, hallucinations, or disorganized behavior (Russell et al., 1989).

Arboleda and Holzman used the Thought Disorder Index (TDI) (Johnston & Holzman, 1979) to code thought disorder in children. This instrument has demonstrated reliability and validity in schizophrenic, manic, and depressed adults and in their first degree relatives (i.e., siblings, parents, and offspring) (Holzman, Shenton, & Solovay, 1986; Johnston & Holzman, 1979). It codes 22 categories of verbal responses to the standardized percepts on the Rorschach cards as associative, combinatory, disorganized, and unconventional verbalizations (Holzman et al., 1986; Johnston & Holzman, 1979). The TDI, therefore, examines a broader range of thought disturbance categories than the four *DSM-III* formal thought disorder signs.

Through the TDI, Arboleda and Holzman compared four groups of children: (1) eighteen 6-to 16-year-old hospitalized children with *DSM-III*–based psychotic-spectrum disorders, such as schizophrenia, major affective disorder, and pervasive developmental disorder; (2) twelve 13.6-to 15.1-year-old hospitalized nonpsychotic children with nonpsychotic psychiatric conditions; (3) thirteen 5-to 16-year-old children of mothers with schizophrenia, bipolar manic–depressive disorder, and unipolar major affective disorder; and (4) seventy-nine 5-to 16-year-old normal children. They found that children with psychosis, psychotic-spectrum disorders, and children at risk for schizophrenia and affective disorder had more severe TDI levels than normal children and children with nonpsychotic psychiatric diagnoses.

Arboleda and Holzman also demonstrated the importance of controlling for cognitive development when studying thought disorder in children under age 10 years (Arboleda & Holzman, 1985). The level of severity of the TDI scores of the normal children indicated only mild "thought slippage" (p. 1008). The younger normal children, aged 5–10 years, however, had moderately higher TDI scores than the 11- to 16-year-old normal children.

They found no age effects in the children with psychotic-spectrum disorder, nonpsychotic psychiatric diagnoses, and children at risk for schizophrenia and major affective disorder.

Unlike the earlier studies (Cantor et al., 1982; Green et al., 1984; Kolvin et al., 1971; Russell et al., 1989) reviewed in the preceding paragraphs, Arboleda and Holzman's work used a reliable and valid instrument, both normal and psychiatric contrast groups, and a developmental approach to studying thought disorder in children. The diagnostic heterogeneity of the psychotic- and nonpsychotic-spectrum groups in their study, their relatively small sample size, and their use of chart diagnoses, however, suggest a need to further examine the applicability of the *DSM-III* signs of formal thought disorder to childhood schizophrenia.

In summary, this review of the literature on the measurement of formal thought disorder in children has demonstrated two things: First, there have been few studies on this topic. Second, the studies that do exist have used adult criteria for formal thought disorder with young children, without specifying how these criteria were operationalized for use with children.

Rationale for the Development of the K-FTDS

The rationale for the development of the K-FTDS was based on the need for developmental norms for assessing formal thought disorder in children. The age of onset of schizophrenia in studies by Kolvin (Kolvin et al., 1971), Green (Green et al., 1984), and Russell (Russell et al., 1989) suggests that schizophrenia can begin in middle childhood and in late childhood. Children learn to present the listener with their thoughts in a logical and coherent fashion from the toddler period through adolescence (Maratsos, 1976; Piaget, 1959; Shatz, 1982). Because formal thought disorder is a clinical measure of the way the patient presents his or her thoughts to the listener, it is, therefore, important to ascertain whether formal thought disorder, as defined by the *DSM-III* and *DSM-III-R,* are applicable to children of different ages.

In addition, existing studies presented no developmental norms for evaluating formal thought disorder in children. Therefore, clinicians who evaluate children need to rely on their own sense of the norms of children's speech to identify formal thought disorder in children and to distinguish it from the speech of normal young children. This lack of developmental guidelines poses a significant problem to clinicians because young normal children are often unaware of an adult listener's needs and assume that the adult makes logical (Piaget, 1959) and linguistic (Maratsos, 1976) connections for them. Children, however, become more skilled at presenting their thoughts to the listener in a logical and cohesive way during the later part of middle childhood (Olson & Nickerson, 1978; Romaine, 1984). In the absence of norms for rating formal thought disorder in middle childhood, clinicians could either overdiagnose or underdiagnose children's immature conversation skills as illogical thinking and loose associations. It is, therefore, necessary to determine the norms for rating formal thought disorder in children of different ages.

Because Andreasen's Thought, Language, and Communication Scale was the basis for the definitions of the *DSM-III* formal thought disorder signs (Andreasen, 1979a), we originally operationalized all the items of this scale for use with schizophrenic children. Our preliminary findings, however, demonstrated that most of the Thought, Language, and

Communication Scale signs were infrequently coded in the children studied. This low base rate, most probably a reflection of the nondiscursive nature of children's speech, could have resulted in the poor interrater reliability of early versions of the scale (Shrout, Spitzer, & Fleiss, 1987).

We therefore modified the final version of the K-FTDS to include only those formal thought disorder signs that were found in the *DSM-III*. These included the following four signs: illogical thinking, loose associations, incoherence, and poverty of content of speech. By operationalizing these formal thought disorder signs for use with children, we were able to confirm whether, as suggested by the *DSM-III,* adult criteria for formal thought disorder were applicable to children with schizophrenia.

THE PLAY PROCEDURE

Background for the Development of the Kiddie Formal Thought Disorder Story Game

Storytelling is a universal play form for children, which represents a window into the thinking of the child. It has been extensively studied by linguists and developmental psychologists because children use both linguistic and cognitive skills to present their thoughts to the listener via the story. This play form has also been used clinically because it provides the therapist with a tool to gain access to the child's fantasy life and emotional problems. We first briefly review pertinent linguistic, cognitive, and clinical findings on storytelling and then present the rationale for choosing this play form to obtain speech samples for the measurement of formal thought disorder in middle childhood.

Storytelling: Linguistic and Cognitive Perspectives

Piaget introduced the concept of *egocentricity* to describe the thinking of young children (Piaget, 1959). He felt that young children were poor communicators because they were egocentric and could not take the listener's needs into account. Shatz demonstrated that this is not the case and that children's ability to monitor their communication to the listener begins to develop during the toddler period and undergoes marked acceleration during middle childhood and adolescence (Shatz, 1982).

In storytelling, the narrator presents the listener with a verbal report of events that are decontextualized and autonomous from the external environment. The linguistic and cognitive skills involved in the process of narrating and comprehending stories are complex and are acquired during childhood (Frederiksen, 1985; Mandler & Johnson, 1977; Pellegrini & Galda, 1982; Stein, 1982; Weaver & Dickinson, 1982).

In terms of the development of narration skills, Nelson has demonstrated that preschool children are relatively good communicators when engaged in general event representations or scripts (Nelson & Gruendel, 1981). In settings that elicit interaction around scripts, children demonstrate more advanced syntactic, semantic, and pragmatic skills than in non-script-based interactions (French, Lucariello, Seidman, & Nelson, 1985). Piaget maintained that preoperational children were not sensitive to the logical constraints that govern temporal relationships (Piaget, 1971). French and Nelson, however, reported that the sequential descriptions of events in preschoolers' scripts indicate that they are able to form and maintain mental representations of temporal relationships (French & Nelson, 1981). These findings suggest that when preschoolers use a precursor of narrative—scripts—the linguistic characteristics and cognitive context are superior to those of non-script-based forms.

In a longitudinal study on children aged 1–7 years, Wolf found that by age 5 years, children have gained an understanding for the role of a narrator (Wolf & Pusch, 1985). They can plan the long-term course of their narrative independent of contextually available information.

In a study on the narrative style of black children, aged 7–8 years, 10–11 years, and 13–14 years, Kernan found important age-related differences (Kernan, 1977). The latency-aged group focused on the narrative section proper, but these children provided little information to the listener on the setting of the story. When they presented background information, these children gave dates, places, and names without elaborating on the motivation, character, and circumstance of the narrative. The older children, however, spent more time orienting the listener to the development of the events in the story. Kernan concluded that latency-aged children seem to assume that by communicating the events to the listener, the listener will have the same understanding of the story as the child. Older children realize that the listener's understanding of the narrative depends on knowledge that orients the listener to events that are external to the narrative proper.

From the perspective of the child's ability to comprehend narratives, several researchers have proposed that prior knowledge helps children to determine the main events of the story and to recall them (Mandler & Johnson, 1977). Others have suggested that story comprehension is related to the child's ability to produce narratives and that both these functions represent linguistic-discourse and cognitive skills (Frederiksen, 1985; Guttman & Frederiksen, 1985).

In summary, children's narrative skills develop in early childhood as scripts of familiar series of events. During middle childhood, the child assumes the role of the narrator and presents decontextualized information. The narrative, however, focuses mainly on the events of the story. By the end of latency, children become adept at providing the listener with the background information and setting of the story, as well as the relationships among characters, motives, and events. Children's comprehension and memory for stories appear to be related to the story's structure and the child's discourse skills.

Storytelling: A Clinical Tool

Despite the preponderance of storytelling as a play form from early childhood, it has not been regularly used as a clinical tool. Gardner introduced the Mutual Storytelling Technique as a therapeutic tool for children (Gardner, 1971). He proposed that this technique allows the therapist to obtain information on the child's conflicts and fantasies and then to interpret them through mutual storytelling. Although the therapist includes the same characters and setting the child presented, the therapist introduces healthier adaptations and resolutions of the conflicts expressed in the child's story. Gardner has used this technique for children with Oedipal problems (Gardner, 1968), posttraumatic neurosis (Gardner, 1970), anger inhibition (Gardner, 1972), and emotional problems secondary to attention deficit disorder (Gardner, 1974).

Brooks reported that a similar technique, Creative Characters, is appropriate to treat latency-aged children and children with learning disabilities (Brooks, 1981, 1987). In this technique, the therapist develops characters and involves them in situations that reflect the emotional issues underlying the child's need for therapy. Brooks reported that this technique is indicated in latency-aged children because of the difficulties these children have formulating and expressing their needs. Because this technique also binds anxiety and allows displacement of problems onto the involved character, Brooks feels it is an effective therapeutic tool, in particular for passive children.

Storytelling has also been used successfully to treat children who undergo painful medical interventions and children with chronic medical illness (Kuttner, 1988; Robertson & Barford, 1970). Kuttner found that the "favorite story" technique can be used as the hypnotic induction method and the framework for the substance of the trance in leukemic children who expressed difficulty coping with recurrent bone marrow aspirations and lumbar punctures (Kuttner, 1988). Kuttner reported that the hypnotic procedure alleviated the child's pain, stress, and anxiety significantly more than behavior distraction and standard medical practice methods.

She also found that by tailoring the child's favorite bedtime story as a metaphor for competence and courage, the child's anxiety and pain were reduced during these painful procedures. This method also evoked a sense of security because of its association with the child's familiar bedtime comforts.

Robertson also reported that the storytelling method was particularly useful in chronically ill and immobilized children who are unable to act out their emotional problems (Robertson & Barford, 1970). Mutual storytelling by the child and therapist serves as a medium for the child to express his or her inner world and to deal with the problems related to the chronic illness.

In summary, these reports suggest that mutual storytelling appears to be a useful clinical tool, particularly during middle childhood, for encouraging children to talk and express their feelings in the therapeutic situation without enhancing their anxiety. With the exception of Kuttner's study (Kuttner, 1988), the reports reviewed in this section were case studies and did not include control groups. Therefore, we cannot reach any conclusions on the efficacy of storytelling compared to other therapeutic interventions.

Rationale Underlying the Development of the Story Game

In adults, formal thought disorder is measured from speech samples obtained through non-structured and structured interview procedures (Andreasen, 1979b). During the former procedure, patients are asked to speak about recent experiences, current events, interests, and personal relationships. The structured procedure involves questions about psychiatric symptomatology and has been done with interviews, such as the Schedule for Affective Disorders and Schizophrenia (SADS) (Andreasen, 1979b).

Use of both structured and unstructured interviews in middle childhood could pose the following problems: First, there is a relative paucity of spontaneous or expansive speech in middle childhood. Whereas adults talk spontaneously in paragraphs—thus providing the listener with speech samples long enough for rating formal thought disorder—young children use only one to two utterances to express themselves. This limits the use of the first technique because children need prodding by means of questions or statements to encourage them to continue to speak about a topic.

Second, children under the age of 9 years may resist answering interview questions, particularly those that probe for psychotic symptomatology. As a result, their answers tend to be brief and unelaborated, often limited to a simple "Yes," "No," or "I don't know." In contrast to the more elaborate speech samples of adult patients, the speech samples elicited in psychiatric interviews of children may therefore be inadequate for determining the presence of formal thought disorder.

Third, the child usually does not know the adult who interviews her or him during a first diagnostic interview or an experimental situation. To maintain fluent conversation with a latency-aged child, the interviewer, therefore, needs to decrease the child's anxiety and apprehensions and to use maneuvers that engage the child in the conversation.

These three potential problems led us to hypothesize that structured psychiatric interviews would not provide us with adequate speech samples for rating formal thought disorder in middle childhood. We chose a storytelling technique, Gardner's Mutual Storytelling (Gardner, 1971), on the assumption that the latency-aged child would find it enjoyable and interesting. The child would, therefore, engage willingly in the task, and this would alleviate the initial anxiety related to the interviewer and to the testing situation.

In summary, the speech of latency-aged children is nondiscursive, particularly in response to a request to talk about general topics or to answer questions in a structured psychiatric interview. We based the Story Game on Gardner's Mutual Storytelling technique because we assumed that, if children enjoy this play form, they would be less anxious and would, therefore, be more willing to talk and would provide us with speech samples of adequate length.

Description of the Story Game

For its research application to the study of formal thought disorder, we standardized the storytelling technique so that it could be used in the same way with all children. The Story Game, presented in the following section, includes three parts. In the first and third parts, the child hears a recorded story, retells the tale, and is then asked a series of standard, open-ended questions about the story. In the second part, the child is asked to make up a story on one of four topics. The Story Game, therefore, utilizes three techniques for eliciting speech from the child: the child's verbal recall of each recorded story, his or her responses to the standardized questions that follow both of these stories, and the child's own story.

We included these three techniques to examine whether they would each be associated with different formal thought disorder ratings. More specifically, we predicted that a structured and demanding task, such as the series of standardized questions, would be associated with higher formal thought disorder scores, compared to the child's own story and recall of the tales. Unlike during the standardized question section, the interviewer remains quiet during the child's story and the child's recall. The demands for the child to respond are therefore not as immediate as in the standardized question section. Our prediction was based on Asarnow and Sherman's findings that the momentary processing capacity deficits of schizophrenic children becomes evident under conditions of processing overload (Asarnow & Sherman, 1984; Sherman & Asarnow, 1985).

The topics of the stories in the Story Game are a friendly ghost, the Incredible Hulk, a witch, a good or a bad child, an unhappy child, and an ostracized little boy. We chose these topics because of their potential for eliciting pathological thought content in children. It was hoped that while actively engaged in thinking about pathological thought content, the nonthreatening and indirect interview technique used in the Story Game would allow the psychotic child to be more expansive and to reveal more formal thought disorder through speech.

To ensure standardization, the stories and the instructions to the child are audiotaped. The standard questions that follow the stories, however, are not prerecorded. This enables the interviewer to elicit additional speech from the child by means of open-ended questions.

The 20- to 25-minute Story Game is administered by a clinician using techniques that encourage children to talk about a topic. Videotapes of the Story Game are then rated for formal thought disorder, using the K-FTDS.

The Storytelling Session[1]

After explaining to the child what the task involves, the interviewer switches on a tape recorder, and the child hears the following story:

> Hi kids, this is the story hour, and I'm going to tell you one of my best stories for kids. After that, I am going to make sure that you have a chance to tell me one of your very best stories. After you're done with your story, it will be my chance again. And I'm going to tell you another story, maybe even one better than the story you are going to tell me. Now, be sure to listen real carefully because once I'm done with the story, you're going to have a chance to answer some real fun questions about them.
>
> One night, Peter was asleep, and he had a dream. He dreamt about a ghost called Mannekin who lived in a faraway land. Mannekin liked to play with children and tried to make their wishes come true. So he would go to earth and visit children while they were asleep at night. One night, he came to Peter's house. Peter was fast asleep in bed. Mannekin hopped through the window to Peter's room and said, "I am Mannekin, the good ghost. I visit children and play with them and make their wishes come true. I have come to make your wishes come true." Peter shouted, "Please don't do anything to me, I am a good kid, please go away from my house." And Mannekin said, "But I want to play with you and help you." And then, do you know what happened? Peter woke up and realized that he had just had a dream.

After hearing the story, the interviewer asks the child to retell to the interviewer the story just told. The interviewer then asks the child the following questions:

1. "Did you like that story?"
2. "What did you like about this story?"
3. "What did you dislike about this story?"
4. "Is this a true story?"
5. "How do you know?"

---

[1] Caplan et. al., 1989. The Kiddie Formal Thought Disorder Scale (K-FTDS): Clinical assessment, reliability, and validity. *Journal of American Academy of Child Psychiatry, 28,* 408–416.

6. "Are there really such things as ghosts? ... How do you know? ... Do you believe in ghosts? ... Do you know anyone who believes in ghosts?"

7. "If Peter dreamt about Mannekin, can it be a true story? ... Can a boy have a dream about a ghost?"

8. "How did Peter know it was a dream?"

9. "Are you scared of ghosts? ... What do you think they can do to scare you?"

10. "Were you scared of ghosts when you were little?"

11. "How come? ... Tell me about it"

12. "How do you think the child in the story felt?"

13. "How would you have felt?"

14. "How did he feel when he woke up?"

15. "Why?"

16. "Peter's dream wasn't scary, but some children have scary dreams. Do you have scary dreams? ... Can you tell me one of your scary dreams?"

17. "Do you ever have daydreams? ... What do you like to daydream about? ... Good things, funny things, sad things, or bad things?"

After the questions, the interviewer switches on the audiotape again, and the child hears the following instructions.

> And now that you have answered the questions, I am going to let you tell a story of your own, one of your best stories. You can tell the story about four different things. You can pick one of these four topics: The first topic is the "Incredible Hulk." If you didn't like that topic, maybe you'll like the second topic, a story about a witch. If you don't like either of those topics, you can tell a story about a good or bad child. That's the third topic. If you don't like any of those topics, how about this fourth topic, a story about an unhappy child. Remember now, these are the four different topics that you can pick to tell the story about: the Incredible Hulk, a witch, a good or bad child, or an unhappy child.

During the child's story, the interviewer remains silent. After the child finishes her or his story, the interviewer thanks the child for the story and then switches on the tape recorder for the child to hear the second story.

> This is my second story and I am going to see if I can tell a really good one. This is a story about Tim. Tim is 6 years old and is in the first grade. Every day, when he gets to school, he says, "Hi" to the kids in his class, and they don't answer him. When he wants to play with them, they don't let him. In class, Tim sees kids talking and laughing, and he thinks they are laughing and talking about him. One day, Tim was walking home after school. It suddenly started to rain. Tim had no raincoat or umbrella so he started to run as fast as possible. Tim was running so fast that he didn't see a big puddle of water on the ground. All of a sudden, Tim slipped and fell into the water. All the kids started to laugh.

As after the first story, the interviewer asks the child to retell the tale and then asks the child the following questions:

1. "Did you like that story?"
2. "What did you like about that story?"
3. "What did you dislike about this story?"
4. "How does Tim feel at school? ... Why?"
5. "How did Tim feel when he fell?"
6. "And when all the children started to laugh at him?"
7. "How would you have felt? ... What would you have done?"
8. "Why do you think the other children don't like Tim?"
9. "Why is that a reason not to like him?"
10. "What would you do if the children at school didn't like you?"
11. "When Tim saw the children talking and laughing and thought they were talking and laughing at him, do you also think the children were talking and laughing about him? ... Why? ... What do you think they were saying? ... Could it have been Tim's imagination?"
12. "Did you ever have friends who act sneaky like the children in the story? ... What did they do to you? ... Do you ever do sneaky things to other kids?"
13. "Can this be a true story?"
14. "Why?"

Synopsis of the Kiddie Formal Thought Disorder Scale (K-FTDS)

The K-FTDS has operationalized the definitions of the Research Diagnostic Criteria (RDC) (Spitzer, Endicott, & Robbins, 1975) and Andreasen's Thought, Language, and Communication Scale (Andreasen, 1979a) so that incoherence can be rated with one utterance while illogical thinking, loose associations, and poverty of content of speech are rated with a minimum of two utterances. Each of the four K-FTDS signs are mutually exclusive. The operationalization guidelines for the K-FTDS were derived from studies on the development of children's conversation skills (McTear, 1985; Ochs & Schieffelin, 1979; Romaine, 1984) and from the senior author's clinical experience with schizophrenic and other psychotic children and have been included in the Appendix to this chapter.

Incomplete utterances (e.g., word fillers and false starts) and signs of immature discourse (e.g., inappropriate use of the definite article, the indefinite article, demonstrative, and pronouns) are distinguished from formal thought disorder. They are coded separately and have been studied in a project on the pragmatic–discourse skills of schizophrenic children (Caplan, Guthrie, & Foy, 1990).

Illogical Thinking

To rate *illogical thinking,* the rater needs to determine whether, in adult terms, the facts, causes, and conclusions of the child's utterances are logically sound. Illogical thinking is evaluated in three conditions. In the first condition, the child's ability to use causal linguistic constructs appropriately is assessed when the child uses utterances introduced by "because," "so that," or "if" (Emerson & Gekonski, 1980; Olson & Nickerson, 1978). For example, "God saves all good people because they're bad." In this utterance, the reasoning the child gives for God saving the people is the antithesis of the usual moral ethics. It is, therefore, rated as illogical thinking.

The second condition is one in which the child presents the listener with an explanation or reasoning that is clearly unfounded. For example, a child was asked by the interviewer if he thought the story he heard in the Story Game is true. The child responded, "Well, it could if you just let it bother people, it could happen." This response is also rated as illogical thinking because the truth of a story is not determined by its emotional effect on people. If the content of the story is feasible, it could happen.

In the third condition, the child contradicts him- or herself within one to two utterances by simultaneously making and refuting statements without informing the listener of the apparent contradiction. For example, when asked by the interviewer, "Do you really think there's a devil in hell?" a child replied; "No. And the devil said to them `Get down to hell.'" The contradiction in this example is self-explanatory. If there is no devil, the devil cannot speak.

Loose Associations

A *loose association* is rated when the child makes an utterance that is off the topic without having previously prepared the listener for the topic change. The K-FTDS provides the rater with guidelines for how to determine whether the child's speech is on or off the topic for the three sections of the Story Game. During the "Question and Answer" sections of the Story Game, the interviewer introduces the topic of conversation with each standardized question. Because of the open-ended structure of these questions, the K-FTDS instructs the rater how to track the topic changes during the ensuing conversation. Thus, a rating of loose associations is given if there is no clear connection between the child's response and the interviewer's question. For example, when the interviewer asked a child what kind of bad dreams he had, the boy replied, "I think in a movie like when they maked cars and stuff, that's how it happens." In this example, the child changed the conversation topic (i.e., bad dreams) to an unrelated topic (i.e., movies) without preparing the listener for this topic change. Loose association is also rated again if, in the subsequent conversation on the new topic of conversation, the child again digresses to an unrelated topic without having prepared the interviewer for this second transition.

For the other sections of the Story Game—the child's recall of the recorded stories and his/her own narrative—the initial topic of the story is considered to be the ongoing topic of conversation. For example, if, while telling a story about a witch, the child digresses and tells a story about magic ponies, this would be rated as loose association.

Incoherence

An utterance is rated to be *incoherence* if the rater cannot comprehend the contents of the utterance because of scrambled syntax. In the following example, the interviewer asked a child to tell her one of his scary dreams. The child responded, "Well ... yeah ... I went ... I visit what bad days and on the nighttimes." This statement, "I visit what bad days and on the nighttimes," is incomprehensible.

Poverty of Content of Speech

The *DSM-III* definition of *poverty of content of speech* stipulates that despite an adequate length of speech, the patient provides the listener with insufficient information. Based on our pilot work, adequate length was defined as two or more utterances in response to a given question. If the child elaborated and developed the topic of conversation, this was not rated as poverty of content of speech. If, however, the child merely rephrased the question or his or her own first statement, without providing the listener with a new aspect, this was rated as poverty of content of speech. For example, the interviewer asked the child to tell her what magic does. The child replied: "Things that can be done by magic can really be done." The two utterances included in this response, "Things can really be done," and, "that can be done by magic," merely repeat that magic does things, but it does not elaborate what magic does. During the child's own story, if she or he does not elaborate the topic in two or more utterances, this would be rated as poverty of content of speech. For example, while telling a story about an unhappy child, the child says, "Every morning Sam would get up early. When he woke up, it was early in the morning so he would get up. And then he went to eat his breakfast." The child made five utterances. In the third and fourth utterances "it was early in the morning so he would get up" he merely rephrases his earlier statement. This is rated as one instance of poverty of content of speech.

Coding the K-FTDS

Two trained raters, who have no knowledge of the child's diagnosis, score the frequency with which each K-FTDS sign occurred during the Story Game, to obtain the illogical thinking, loose associations, incoherence, and poverty of content of speech scores (see the Appendix for coding form). The sum of these scores is the total FTD (i.e., formal thought disorder) score for each subject. To control for the variable amount of speech elicited from each child, the K-FTDS score per utterance is computed by dividing the illogical thinking, loose associations, incoherence, poverty of content of speech, and total FTD scores by the number of utterances made by each child. Because the K-FTDS categories are mutually exclusive, one utterance cannot be scored for more than one FTD category.

CASE ILLUSTRATION

In this section, we present samples of K-FTDS ratings from the Story Game of a schizophrenic girl, a schizotypal boy, and a normal child. We recommend that the reader refer back to the text of the Story Game (p. 180–182) while reading this section.

The K-FTDS Ratings of a Schizophrenic Girl

This case illustration is taken from a Story Game used with an 8.4-year-old schizophrenic girl who had demonstrated auditory hallucinations since age 5 years. During her early history, she had demonstrated several autistic-like features. At the time of testing, this child had not been on neuroleptics for at least 4 weeks.

After hearing the story about a ghost, she was asked to retell the story. Her response, "One time I had a bear cub," was rated as a loose association because she unpredictably changed the topic of conversation. When asked if the story was a true story, the patient answered, "No." She was then asked how she knew this was not a true story. She answered, "'Cause I already know. And I do a lot of things, so I already know." The causal utterances beginning with "cause" and "so" were rated as illogical thinking because they do not provide the listener with a logical explanation for why the story was not true.

In response to the question, "Are you scared of ghosts?" this child answered, "When I am across from a cat I won't be scared at all." This response was also rated as loose association, because the child unpredictably changed the topic of conversation from fear of ghosts to fear of cats. The interviewer then tried to clarify, "When won't you be scared?" The child responded, "I just talk to ghosts." Here the child changed the topic of conversation back to ghosts without preparing the listener for the topic change. She was then asked by the interviewer, "How come you're not scared?" She replied, "Because I'm brave, because I got my hat in Carrie's office." The second causal utterance was rated as illogical thinking; the reasoning used was inadequate.

During her own story, this child demonstrated no formal thought disorder. After hearing the story about the ostracized boy, the child was asked if this story could happen to a child. She responded, "Yes, because the ghost be nice to him." This answer was rated as illogical thinking because the reasoning for saying it was a true story was inappropriate. In her response, the patient also unpredictably introduced information from the earlier story about a ghost. This utterance was not also rated as loose association, however, because the K-FTDS items are mutually exclusive. By definition, illogical thinking and not loose association is rated if the logic of a causal utterance is inappropriate.

The K-FTDS Ratings of a Schizotypal Boy

This 7.6-year-old boy was referred for psychiatric evaluation because of learning difficulties. His developmental and psychiatric history were not known because he had been in foster care since age 5 years. He had never been treated with psychoactive medication prior to his participation in the Story Game.

After the first story, the child was asked if there really are such things as ghosts. He replied that there were not. When asked how he knew that there were no ghosts, he replied, "Because ghostbusters have ghosts." This was rated as illogical thinking because the fact that ghostbusters have ghosts does not explain why there are no ghosts.

The child told the interviewer about a scary dream. The interviewer asked the child how the dream ended. He responded, "After I put a period." This utterance was rated as loose association because the child unpredictably changed the topic of conversation to the punctuation of the story, the period.

After the story about the ostracized boy, this child was asked what he thought the children in the story were saying about the ostracized boy. He replied, "They were saying he is a faggot. And called a different finger at her and then she ragged and tell the teacher. Now do you see my tears coming out?" "And called a different finger at her" was rated as incoherence because the phrase "call a different finger" is incomprehensible. The child's next utterance about the tears coming out was rated as loose association because he unpredictably changed the topic of conversation to an unrelated topic.

The K-FTDS Ratings of a Normal Child

This was an 11.3-year-old normal boy. After hearing the story about the ghost, he was asked if he liked the story. He responded, "I've always liked to talk about a dream, and you can never talk about a dream 'cause a dream is never this simple. Dreams are always funny; that's why they are dreams." The last utterance was rated as illogical because the dreams are not dreams because they are funny.

When asked if the story was true, he began to talk about "fake" things like magic. He then continued to say, "It's not magic. That's what magic really is." This was rated as illogical because the child contradicted himself (see definition). He then continued, "And it's something very powerful; it's the only type of magic; it's what magic really is—being able to control something. Things that can really be done by magic can be done, so that's really magic itself." The two utterances included in the first part of this response, "Things can really be done," and "that can be done by magic," merely repeat that magic does things, but it does not elaborate what magic does. This was, therefore, rated as poverty of content of speech. The last utterance, a causal utterance, was rated as illogical thinking because the fact that things are done by magic is not the reason why they are, in fact, magic.

RESEARCH FINDINGS

The studies that were conducted to evaluate the Story Game and the K-FTDS had four main goals. The first goal was to examine whether the Story Game elicits speech samples that are adequate for the measurement of formal thought disorder in children. The second goal was to determine the interrater reliability of the K-FTDS. The third goal was to determine whether the K-FTDS is a valid instrument.

Prior to reviewing the individual studies conducted to achieve these goals, we first describe the subjects included in these studies. These studies were conducted on subsamples of 31 schizophrenic, 11 schizotypal, and 54 normal subjects, aged 5–12.5 years (Caplan et al., 1989; Caplan, Perdue, Tanguay, & Fish, in press). The patient sample was recruited from the UCLA Neuropsychiatric Institute's Inpatient and Outpatient Child Services, as well as from two Los Angeles schools for the emotionally disturbed. The children were diagnosed by the Diagnostic Unit of UCLA's Childhood Psychoses Clinical Research Center with the ICDS, independent of the research team (Russell et al., 1989). To be included in the subsamples of schizophrenics or schizotypal subjects in the study, the children had to meet *DSM-III* criteria for schizophrenia or schizotypal personality disorder.

Normal subjects were recruited from four Los Angeles schools and from the community. Most of the patients (83%) and the normal (81%) children were from middle-class families. Unlike the patient sample, 41% of the normal children were Anglos, 33% were bilingual Asian, and 25% bilingual Hispanic. The majority of the schizophrenic (67%) and schizotypal (73%) subjects were Anglos.

The Story Game was administered to all the children, and two trained raters with no knowledge of the child's diagnosis coded the Story Game with the K-FTDS, as previously described. A psychometrist, who knew the child's diagnosis, administered the Wechsler Intelligence Scale for Children—Revised (WISC-R) to all children. Clinical information, including use of neuroleptic medication, psychiatric hospitalization, age at diagnosis, and length of illness was obtained retrospectively from the patients' files in the Clinical Research Center. The date of the first diagnosis, given either by a mental health professional in the community or by the Clinical Research Center's Diagnostic Unit, was recorded. The length of illness was calculated from the parent's reports in the chart on the onset of hallucinations, delusions, or bizarre disorganized behavior.

Study on the Effectiveness of the Story Game

Methods

In this study, we compared the speech samples obtained by the Story Game with those elicited by an open-ended clinical interview, the Children's Schizophrenia Inventory (CSI), which focused specifically on psychotic symptomatology (Caplan et al., 1989). The CSI, developed by Barbara Fish and the senior author of this chapter, is an open-ended, structured interview on psychotic symptomatology. It was used for this study as a source of speech samples assumed to be similar to and, therefore, representative of typical speech samples obtained from children by traditional psychiatric interviews. We compared the speech elicited from the first 20 minutes of the 45- to 60-minute videotaped CSI to that elicited by the entire Story Game. The average talking time of the patient and normal subjects during the Story Game was 15.3 minutes.

This study was conducted on a subsample of 14 schizophrenic and 3 schizotypal children, aged 7–12.5 years, and 8 younger and 7 older normal children, aged 5–8.1 years and 11–13 years, respectively. We saw children participating in this study on two occasions. At the first meeting, the children participated in the Story Game, a play session, and other cognitive testing. At the second meeting, held no later than I week after the Story Game, the same interviewer administered the CSI.

Two trained raters, with no knowledge of the child's diagnosis, coded the number of utterances, the quality of speech, and the child's compliance to evaluate the speech yield from the Story Game and the CSI. They obtained the number of utterances from a 5-minute segment that followed the first 2 minutes of the Story Game and the CSI. They judged the child's utterances as either good or poor, based on a global rating of how well the child elaborated the topics of conversation. If there were numerous "Yes," "No," "I don't know," "When will we be done?" or similar responses, the speech sample was rated as poor. The raters also gave a global rating of the child's compliance during the Story Game and the CSI as either good or poor.

Results

We found no difference in the number of utterances elicited from each child between the Story Game and the CSI, either by diagnostic group or across all subjects. The Story Game, however, produced significantly better speech quality and compliance than the CSI for the combined patient and normal groups. Two additional related findings provided further evidence for the effectiveness of the Story Game in eliciting adequate speech samples from children for rating formal thought disorder. First, the K-FTDS scores we obtained from the Story Game were significantly higher than those obtained from the CSI. Second, the kappa values for the illogical thinking and loose association scores of the CSI speech samples were significantly lower than those obtained with the Story Game speech samples. This finding probably reflected the low base rate of formal thought disorder scores in the CSI speech samples (Shrout et al., 1987).

Finally, a comparison of the K-FTDS scores of the three sections of the Story Game demonstrated considerably less formal thought disorder during the child's story and the recall sections of the Story Game than during the open-ended standardized questions.

Discussion

These findings confirmed our initial hypothesis that a play technique such as the Story Game would be an effective technique for obtaining speech samples that are adequate for the rating of formal thought disorder. It is important to emphasize that the CSI was administered to the patients up to 1 week after the interviewer had previously conducted the Story Game, a play session, and cognitive testing. When seen 1 week later for the CSI, the children were familiar with the interviewer and might have felt less anxiety than during the Story Game. Despite the fact that the Story Game was administered at the child's first meeting with the interviewer, it nonetheless elicited superior speech samples.

These results are better understood if viewed in terms of the different techniques used in the Story Game and the CSI. Both techniques focused on pathological thought content. The CSI, however, approached symptoms with direct questions, whereas the Story Game used an indirect method of questioning by focusing on the characters in the stories. The results of this study indicate that the indirect, projective approach, as used in the TDI (Johnston & Holzman, 1979), appears to be far superior than direct questioning for eliciting speech suitable for evaluating formal thought disorder in children.

Our findings also confirmed our hypothesis that the highly structured question and answer section of the Story Game could have taxed the cognitive skills of the children with schizophrenia-spectrum disorder so that they revealed formal thought disorder. To be more conclusive, however, these findings need to be replicated using a research design that controls for a possible order effect of the different sections of the Story Game.

Studies on K-FTDS Reliability and Validity

We examined interrater reliability on a subsample of 17 schizophrenic, 4 schizotypal, and 7 normal children, aged 5–12.5 years. Illogical thinking and loose associations were reliably rated, with kappa values of .78 and .71, respectively. The overall K-FTDS kappa for both illogical thinking and loose associations was .77. Due to a low base rate, the kappa values for incoherence and poverty of content of speech were not statistically meaningful. Incoherence and poverty of content of speech were each rated in only one child.

We conducted three validity studies to determine whether the K-FTDS is a valid instrument that differentiates schizophrenic and schizotypal children from normal children and schizophrenic from schizotypal children irrespective of the child's age and intellectual functioning. In the first study, we compared the K-FTDS scores of 16 schizophrenic and 4 schizotypal children, aged 4.9–12.5 years, with those of two groups of normal children. The patients were yoked with the first group by sex and chronological age and with the second group by sex and mental age (Caplan et al., 1989). In the second study, we extended and replicated the findings of our earlier study and compared the K-FTDS scores of 29 schizophrenic children, aged 7.4 to 12.5 years, with a group of yoked sex and mental age normal matches, as well as a group of yoked sex and chronological age normal matches (Caplan et al., in press). In the third study, we compared the K-FTDS scores of 10 schizotypal children, aged 7.2 years to 12.5 years, both to normal and to schizophrenic children (Caplan et al., in press). The schizotypal children were yoked with both the normal and schizophrenic children by sex and mental age, as well as by sex and chronological age.

Diagnostic Validity

We found that the schizophrenic children had significantly higher illogical thinking scores than their normal chronological age and mental age matches (Caplan et al., 1989, in press). Loose associations, however, occurred almost exclusively in the schizophrenic children.

The schizotypal children also had significantly higher illogical thinking and loose association scores than their yoked normal mental age and chronological age matches (Caplan et al., in press). The K-FTDS scores of the schizotypal children were, however, similar to those of the schizophrenic children. We found no relationship between the Axis I diagnosis of these children and the severity of their K-FTDS scores. This suggests that schizotypy and not the Axis I diagnoses accounted for the high formal thought disorder scores found in these children.

These studies also demonstrated that the K-FTDS scores of total FTD, illogical thinking, and loose associations were sensitive and specific measures of formal thought disorder in schizophrenic and schizotypal children, irrespective of age (Caplan et al., 1989, in press). The diagnostic validity of the total FTD score was clearly superior to that of its two components, illogical thinking and loose associations. We found a sensitivity and specificity of 85% for total FTD scores. A loose associations score above 0 correctly classified 97% of the normal children and 71% of the schizophrenic and schizotypal children. Illogical thinking had a sensitivity of 82% and a specificity of 66% for the normal children.

Effects of Age and IQ on the K-FTDS Validity

The younger schizophrenic, schizotypal, and normal children had significantly higher illogical thinking and loose associations scores than the older children in their respective groups (Caplan et al., 1989, in press). The age cut off for the developmental changes was 7 years in the normal children. Despite the age-related decrease in the K-FTDS scores, we demonstrated significant diagnostic differences between the patient groups and their mental-age and chronological-age matches across the three age groups studied: 4.9–6.9 years, 7–9.6 years, and 9.7–12.5 years (Caplan et al., 1989, in press).

The age at which the schizophrenic children were diagnosed, but not the length of time that they had been ill, was significantly related to the severity of their loose associations and illogical thinking (Caplan et al., in press). Because the older schizophrenic children who had been diagnosed at an earlier age had also been sick for longer, we examined the relationship between severity of formal thought disorder scores and age of diagnosis separately for the patients older than 9.6 years. Those older children with an early age at diagnosis had higher K-FTDS scores than the children with diagnosis at a later age (Caplan et al., in press).

To identify the effects of the child's intellectual functioning on the diagnostic validity of the K-FTDS, we also compared the K-FTDS scores of the schizophrenic and schizotypal children to those of children with whom they were yoked by IQ, age, and sex (Caplan et al., in press). We demonstrated that the schizophrenic and schizotypal children had significantly higher illogical thinking and loose associations scores, even after matching on both age and IQ. We also found that the score for loose associations, but not illogical thinking, was related to the full scale, verbal, and performance IQ scores (WISC-R) of the schizophrenic and schizotypal children (Caplan et al., in press).

Discussion

From the diagnostic perspective, the K-FTDS is a reliable, valid, sensitive, and specific instrument for differentiating children with middle–childhood schizophrenia and schizotypal personality disorder from normal children matched by chronological age, mental age, and IQ. We next discuss the clinical and research implications of four main findings of the reliability and validity studies: (1) the infrequency of incoherence and poverty of content of speech in children with schizophrenia-spectrum disorder, (2) the diagnostic significance of loose associations in children, (3) the similarity of the K-FTDS scores of schizophrenic and schizotypal children, and (4) the role of developmental and cognitive factors on the K-FTDS validity.

Infrequency of Incoherence and of Poverty of Content of Speech.   In terms of the low base rate of incoherence, this formal thought disorder sign also occurs infrequently in adult schizophrenics (Andreasen, 1979a). We therefore had not anticipated a high base rate of incoherence in schizophrenic children. We were surprised, however, that we coded this sign in only two children for the following reason: This formal thought disorder sign involves scrambling of syntax. Given the continued development of children's syntactic skills through early and middle childhood (Romaine, 1984), we predicted that this formal thought disorder sign would occur in schizophrenic children with a history of delayed or impaired language development. This was not the case. A history of delayed or deviant language development was obtained from the medical charts of 50% of the patients in the reliability study. These children, however, had no associated incoherence ratings.

Because incoherence occurs in severely ill adult schizophrenics (Andreasen, 1979a), the most likely explanation for the low base rate of incoherence in our sample is that these children were not severely ill.

We suggest that the infrequency of poverty of content of speech could reflect the nondiscursive nature of children's speech in middle childhood. This explanation for the infrequency of poverty of content of speech is supported by the observation that the only child in this study with poverty of content of speech was a very bright 12.9-year-old normal boy with excellent verbal skills and with a tendency to be very expansive in his speech.

Two additional factors could have affected the base rate of poverty of content of speech in this study. The first involves the stipulation that the four K-FTDS signs are mutually exclusive. It is possible that poverty of content of speech was under-rated because this definition could not be applied to utterances that met criteria for illogical thinking, loose associations, or incoherence. Unlike Andreasen's Thought Language and Communication Scale (1979a; 1979b), the K-FTDS restricted the definition of poverty of content of speech to instances where the child does not elaborate on the topic of conversation within at least two utterances. This excluded global impressions of poor content secondary to other formal thought disorder signs, such as loose associations, illogical thinking, and incoherence.

The second possible factor is the reported relationship between chronic schizophrenia and negative symptoms, such as poverty of content of speech (Andreasen & Olson, 1982). The average duration of illness in the children, however, was 3.3 years, so it is unlikely that the infrequency of poverty of content of speech resulted from a pre-ponderance of children with acute schizophrenia in the sample.

Diagnostic Significance of Loose Associations. From the diagnostic perspective, we were struck by the specificity of loose associations in our validity studies (Caplan et al., 1989, in press). According to the K-FTDS definition, the child with loose associations unpredictably changes the topic of conversation to an unrelated topic. This unpredictable change makes it difficult for the listener to follow the conversation.

Rochester hypothesized that adult schizophrenic patients with formal thought disorder do not take the listener's needs into consideration. She reported that schizophrenic adults with and without formal thought disorder had different discourse patterns (Rochester & Martin, 1979). We hypothesized that schizophrenic and schizotypal children with and without loose associations could represent two different subgroups (Caplan et al., in press). We are currently examining this hypothesis by assessing the discourse skills of schizophrenic and schizotypal children (Caplan, Guthrie, & Foy, 1990).

Although ratings of loose associations were highly specific (97%), this formal thought disorder sign had relatively lower sensitivity (71%). This finding could have been confounded by the medication status of the patient sample. The schizophrenic (50%) and schizotypal (33%) subjects on neuroleptic medication tended to have lower K-FTDS scores, and in particular lower loose association scores, than the nonmedicated subjects. Reports on adult schizophrenics suggest that neuroleptics mitigate mild and moderate thought disorder involving signs such as loose associations (Hurt, Holzman, & Davis, 1983; Spohn et al., 1986). If our data reflected a medication effect, the sensitivity of loose associations could have been biased downward. This possible medication effect underscores the importance of conducting a well-controlled study on the effects of neuroleptics on formal thought disorder in childhood onset schizophrenia and schizotypal personality disorder.

Similarity of K-FTDS Scores in Schizophrenic and Schizotypal Children. Regarding the diagnosis of formal thought disorder in children with schizotypal personality disorder, we originally predicted that the K-FTDS scores of schizotypal children would fall between those of the schizophrenic and normal children. We hypothesized that a sensitive and specific instrument, such as the K-FTDS, could detect formal thought disorder not otherwise identified by structured psychiatric interviews in children. Our hypothesis was based on evidence for formal thought disorder in schizotypal children (Russell, Bott, & Sammons, 1987) and in children at risk for schizophrenia (Arboleda & Holzman, 1985; Griffith, Mednick, Schulsinger, & Diderichsen, 1980; Oltmanns, Weintraub, Stone, & Neale, 1978; Parnas, Schulsinger, Schulsinger, Mednick, & Teasedale, 1982).

Evidence for formal thought disorder in children at risk for schizophrenia is pertinent to the findings of this study because of the observed relationship between parental schizophrenia and schizotypal personality disorder in their offspring (Kendler, Gruenberg, & Strauss, 1981).

Our findings suggest that the K-FTDS could be used as a clinical marker of formal thought disorder in children at risk for schizophrenia. Thus, K-FTDS ratings might be associated with the schizophrenic trait, as found for other clinical markers (Arboleda & Holzman, 1985; R. Asarnow, Steffy, MacCrimmon, & Cleghorn, 1978; Cornblatt & Erlenmeyer-Kimling, 1985; Holzman, Solomon, Levin, & Waternaux, 1984; Neuchterlein, 1983). This potential use of the K-FTDS as a clinical marker should, however, be evaluated by further study on a larger sample of schizotypal children.

Role of Developmental Factors.   From a developmental perspective, our results confirmed our initial predictions that formal thought disorder in childhood has two components: a diagnostic component and a developmental component (Caplan et al., 1989; in press). Because these findings were related to the child's age at diagnosis, but not to the duration of illness, this suggests that an early onset of the disorder could reflect a greater morbidity. Several other clinical studies have indicated that an early onset of schizophrenia is associated with more severe chronicity, severity, and developmental impairments (Bender & Faretra, 1970; Bettes & Walker, 1987; Fish, 1977; Fish & Ritvo, 1979; Watkins et al., 1988).

As previously defined, the clinical signs of formal thought disorder are measures of the form or manner in which the child presents his or her thoughts to the listener. Beginning from the toddler period, normal children acquire the ability to present their thoughts to the listener in a coherent manner and to monitor the listener's needs (Shatz, 1982). If Rochester's theory is applicable to childhood schizophrenia, it is possible that the more severe formal thought disorder in the younger schizophrenic child could have reflected the disease's effect on the normal acquisition of listener-sensitive skills.

Role of Cognitive Factors.   Finally, our cognitive findings demonstrated that the K-FTDS is a valid diagnostic instrument independent of IQ (Caplan et al., in press). Our findings that the score for loose associations, but not for illogical thinking, is associated with IQ measures suggested that these two formal thought disorder signs have different cognitive correlates. This led us to study the relations among illogical thinking, loose associations, and cognitive measures, such as the WISC-R distractibility factor score (Caplan, Foy, Asarnow, & Sherman, 1990a), the span of apprehension (Caplan et al., 1990a), and conservation (Caplan, Foy, & Sigman, 1990b).

Summary

In summary, the research findings presented in this section have demonstrated that the Story Game and the K-FTDS are effective, reliable and valid instruments for the assessment of formal thought disorder in middle-childhood schizophrenia-spectrum disorder. The use of a play form, the Story Game, has allowed us to effectively collect the speech data needed to study formal thought disorder in children. Our studies using these instruments have led us to begin to tease out the cognitive and discourse correlates of formal thought disorder in children with schizophrenia-spectrum syndrome.

SUMMARY AND CONCLUSIONS

In this chapter, we described the historical evolution of the term *childhood schizophrenia* and how this affected the diagnostic approaches to the psychiatric evaluation of formal thought disorder in children. In reviewing the few studies that have been conducted on formal thought disorder in the child, we emphasized the lack of a developmental approach in most of these studies. Our rationale for the development of the K-FTDS was based on the need for a developmental approach to the study of formal thought disorder in middle childhood.

We then described the clinical, linguistic, and cognitive background for the use of a play form, the Story Game, to obtain speech samples for rating formal thought disorder in children. We selected this play form because of the nondiscursive nature of speech during middle childhood. Storytelling presents the listener with a window into the thinking and the fantasy of the latency-aged child without inducing anxiety.

The Story Game was used to obtain speech samples that were rated with the K-FTDS. In this instrument, we operationalized the four *DSM-III* signs of formal thought disorder to examine whether they could be reliably and validly assessed in middle-childhood schizophrenia-spectrum disorder.

Our research findings indicate that the use of the Story Game enabled us to obtain speech samples that were superior to those elicited by the structured psychiatric interview. In addition, two of the four *DSM-III* signs of formal thought disorder—illogical thinking and loose associations—are reliable, valid, sensitive, and specific measures of formal thought disorder in schizophrenic and schizotypal children, independent of the effects of sex, age, and IQ. Incoherence and poverty of content of speech, however, were infrequent in the samples tested.

From the diagnostic perspective, loose association was coded in children with schizophrenia-spectrum disorder, but not in normal children above age 7 years. There were no significant differences in the illogical thinking and the loose association scores of the schizotypal and the schizophrenic children. From the developmental perspective, the youngest schizophrenic, schizotypal, and normal children had the highest illogical thinking and loose association scores. Finally, illogical thinking and loose associations could have different cognitive and discourse correlates.

In conclusion, the use of play has allowed us to develop research techniques for the assessment of formal thought disorder in middle childhood. We are currently adapting our research techniques for use in clinical practice.

REFERENCES

American Psychiatric Association. (1980). *Diagnostic and statistical manual of mental disorders* (3rd ed.). Washington, DC: Author.

American Psychiatric Association. (1987). *Diagnostic and statistical manual of mental disorders* (3rd ed. rev.). Washington, DC: Author.

Andreasen, N. C. (1979a). Thought, language, and communication disorders: I. Clinical assessment, definition of terms, and evaluation of their reliability. *Archives of General Psychiatry, 36,* 1315–1323.

Andreasen, N. C. (1979b). Thought, language, and communication disorders: II. Diagnostic significance. *Archives of General Psychiatry, 36,* 1325–1330.

Andreasen, N. C., & Olsen, S. (1982). Negative vs. positive schizophrenia: Definition and validation. *Archives of General Psychiatry, 39,* 789–794.

Arboleda, C., & Holzman, P. S. (1985). Thought disorder in children at risk for psychosis. *Archives of General Psychiatry, 42,* 1004–1013.

Asarnow, R. F., & MacCrimmon, D. J. (1981). Span of apprehension deficits during postpsychotic stages of schizophrenia: A replication and extension. *Archives of General Psychiatry, 38,* 1001–1006.

Asarnow, R. F., & Sherman, T. (1984). Studies of visual information processing in schizophrenic children. *Child Development, 55,* 249–261.

Asarnow, R. F., Steffy, R. A., MacCrimmon, D. J., & Cleghorn, J. M. (1978). An attentional assessment of foster children at risk for schizophrenia. In L. C. Wynne, R. L. Cromwell, & S. Matthysse (Eds.), *The nature of schizophrenia: New approaches to research and treatment* (pp. 339–358). New York: Wiley.

Bender, L. (1942). Schizophrenia in childhood. *The Nervous Child, 1,* 138–140.

Bender, L. (1947). Childhood schizophrenia: Clinical study of one hundred schizophrenic children. *American Journal of Orthopsychiatry, 17,* 40–55.

Bender, L., & Faretra, G. (1970). The relationship between childhood schizophrenia and adult schizophrenia. In A. R. Kaplan (Ed.), *Genetic factors in schizophrenia* (pp. 28–64). Springfield, IL: Charles C. Thomas Publisher.

Bettes, B. A., & Walker, E. (1987). Positive and negative symptoms in psychotic and other psychiatrically disturbed children. *Journal of Child Psychology and Psychiatry, 28,* 555–568.

Bleuler, E. (1950). *Dementia praecox or the group of schizophrenias.* New York: International Universities Press.

Bradley, C., & Bowen, M. (1941). Behavior characteristics of schizophrenic children. *Psychiatric Quarterly, 15,* 298–315.

Brooks, R. (1981). Creative characters: A technique in child therapy. *Psychotherapy, Research and Practice, 18,* 131–138.

Brooks, R. (1987). Storytelling and the therapeutic process for children with learning disabilities. *Journal of Learning Disabilities, 20,* 546–550.

Brown, J. L. (1963). Follow-up of children with atypical development (infantile psychosis). *American Journal of Orthopsychiatry, 33,* 885–891.

Cantor, S., Evans, J., Pearce, J., & Pezzot-Pearce, T. (1982). Childhood schizophrenia: Present but not accounted for. *American Journal of Psychiatry, 139,* 758–763.

Caplan, R., Foy, J. G., Asarnow, R. F., & Sherman, T. L. (1990a). Information processing deficits of schizophrenic children with formal thought disorder. *Psychiatry Research, 31,* 169–177.

Caplan, R., Foy, J. G., & Sigman, M. (in 1990b). Conservation and formal thought disorder in schizophrenic children. *Development and Psychopathology, 2,* 183–192.

Caplan, R., Guthrie, D., Fish, B., Tanguay, P. E., & David-Lando, G. (1989). The Kiddie Formal Thought Disorder Scale (K-FTDS): Clinical assessment, reliability, and validity. *Journal of American Academy of Child Psychiatry, 28,* 408–416.

Caplan, R., & Foy, J. G. (1990). The discourse deficits of schizophrenic children. Manuscript submitted for publication.

Caplan, R., Perdue, S., Tanguay, P. E., & Fish, B. (in press). Formal thought disorder in childhood onset schizophrenia and schizotypal personality disorder. *Journal of Child Psychology and Psychiatry.*

Chaika, E. O. (1974). A linguist looks at "schizophrenic" language. *Brain and Language, 1,* 257–276.

Comblatt, B., & Erlenmeyer-Kimling, L. (1985). Global attentional deviance in children at risk for schizophrenia. Specificity and predictive validity. *Journal of Abnormal Psychology, 11,* 397–408.

Dahl, V. (1976). A follow-up study of a child psychiatric clientele with special regard to the diagnosis of psychosis. *Acta Psychiatrica Scandinavia, 54,* 106–112.

Eisenberg, L., & Kanner, L. (1956). Childhood schizophrenia. *American Journal of Orthopsychiatry, 26,* 556–564.

Emerson, H. F., & Gekonski, W. L. (1980). Development and comprehension of sentences with "because" or "if." *Journal of Experimental Child Psychology, 29,* 202–224.

Fish, B. (1957). The detection of schizophrenia in infancy. *Journal of Nervous and Mental Diseases, 125,* 1–24.

Fish, B. (1977). Neurobiological antecedents of schizophrenia in children. *Archives of General Psychiatry, 34,* 1297–1977.

Fish, B., & Ritvo, E. R. (1979). Psychoses of childhood. In J. D. Noshpitz (Ed.), *Basic handbook of child psychiatry* (Vol. 2, pp. 249–304). New York: Basic Books.

Fish, F. J. (1962). *Schizophrenia.* London: Wright.

Fleiss, J. (1973). *Statistical methods for rates and proportions.* New York: Wiley.

Frederiksen, C. H. (1985). Cognitive models and discourse analysis. In C. Cooper & S. Greenbaum (Eds.), W*ritten communication annual: An international survey of research and theory: Vol. 1. Linguistic approaches to the study of written discourse* (pp. 227–268). Beverly Hills, CA: Sage.

French, L.A., Lucariello, J., Seidman, S., & Nelson, K. (1985). The influence of discourse content and context on preschooler's use of language. In L. Galda & A. D. Pellegrini (Eds.), *Play, language, and stories: The development of children's literate behavior* (pp. 1–28). Norwood, NJ: Ablex.

French, L. A., & Nelson, K. (1981). Temporal knowledge expressed in preschooler's description of familiar activities. *Papers and Reports on Child Language Development, 20,* 61–69.

Gardner, R. A. (1968). The mutual storytelling technique: Use in alleviating childhood oedipal problems. *Contemporary Psychoanalysis, 4,* 161–177.

Gardner, R. A. (1970). The mutual storytelling technique: Use in the treatment of a child with a post-traumatic neurosis. *American Journal of Psychotherapy, 24,* 419–439.

Gardner, R. A. (1971). *Therapeutic communication with children: The mutual storytelling technique.* New York: Jason Aronson.

Gardner, R. A. (1972). The mutual storytelling technique in the treatment of anger inhibition problems. *International Journal of Child Psychotherapy, 1,* 34–64.

Gardner, R. A. (1974). The mutual storytelling technique in the treatment of psychogenic problems secondary to minimal brain dysfunction. *Journal of Learning Disabilities, 7,* 135–143.

Gardner, R. A. (1975). *Psychotherapeutic Approaches to the Resistant Child.* New York: Jason Aronson.

Goldfarb, W. (1961). *Childhood schizophrenia.* Cambridge: Harvard University Press.

Green, W. H., Campbell, M., Hardesty, A. S., Grega, D. M., Padron-Gayol, M., Shell, J., & Erlenmeyer-Kimling, L. (1984). A comparison of schizophrenic and autistic children. *Journal of American Academy of Child Psychiatry, 4,* 399–409.

Griffith, J. J., Mednick, S. A., Schulsinger, F., & Diderichsen, B. (1980). Verbal associative disturbances in children at high risk for schizophrenia. *Journal of Abnormal Psychology, 89,* 125–131.

Guttman, M., & Frederiksen, C. H. (1985). Preschool children's narratives: Linking story comprehension, production, and play discourse. In L. Galda & A. D. Pellegrini (Eds.), *Play, language, and stories: The development of children's literate behavior* (pp. 99–128). Norwood, NJ: Ablex.

Harrow, M., & Quinlan, D. (1977). Is disordered thinking unique to schizophrenia. *Archives of General Psychiatry, 34,* 15–21.

Havelkova, M. (1968). Follow-up study of 71 children diagnosed as psychotic in preschool age. *American Journal of Orthopsychiatry, 38,* 846–857.

Herjanic, B., & Campbell, W. (1977). Differentiating psychiatrically disturbed children on the basis of a structured interview. *Journal of Abnormal Child Psychology, 5,* 127–134.

Holzman, P. S., Shenton, M. E., & Solovay, M. R. (1986). Quality of thought disorder in differential diagnosis. *Schizophrenia Bulletin, 12,* 360–372.

Holzman, P. S., Solomon, C. M., Levin, S., & Waternaux, C. S. (1984). Pursuit eye movement dysfunctions in schizophrenia: Family evidence for specificity. *Archives of General Psychiatry, 41,* 136–139.

Hurt, S. W., Holzman, P. S., & Davis, J. M. (1983). Thought disorder: The measurement of its changes. *Archives of General Psychiatry, 40,* 1281–1285.

Johnston, M. H., & Holzman, P. S. (1979). *Assessing schizophrenic thinking: A clinical and research instrument for measuring thought disorder.* San Francisco: Jossey-Bass Publishers.

Kanner, L. (1943). Autistic disturbances of affective contact. *Nervous Child, 2,* 217–250.

Kaufman, A. S. (1979). *Intelligence testing with the WISC-R.* New York: Wiley.

Kendler, K. S., Gruenberg, A. M., & Strauss, J. S. (1981). An independent analysis of the Copenhagen sample of the Danish adoption study: II. The relationship between schizotypal personality disorder and schizophrenia. *Archives of General Psychiatry, 38,* 982–984.

Kernan, K. T. (1977). Semantic and expressive elaboration in children's narratives. In S. Ervin-Tripp & C. Mitchell-Kernan (Eds.), *Child discourse* (pp. 91–102). New York: Academic Press.

Kolvin, I., Ounstead, C., Humphrey, M., & McNay, A. (1971). Studies in the childhood psychoses: I. The phenomenology of childhood psychoses. *British Journal of Psychiatry, 118,* 385–395.

Kraepelin, E. (1896). *Psychiatrie: Ein Lehrbich fur studierende and Arzte.* Leipzig: Barth.

Kuttner, L. (1988). Favorite stories: A hypnotic painreduction technique for children in acute pain. *American Journal of Clinical Hypnosis, 30,* 289–295.

Mahler, M. (1952). On child psychosis in schizophrenia: Autistic and symbiotic infantile psychosis. *Psychoanalytical Study of the Child, 7,* 265–305. New York: International Universities Press.

Mandler, J. M., & Johnson, N. S. (1977). Remembrance of things parsed: Story structures and recall. *Cognitive Psychology, 9,* 111–151.

Maratsos, M. P. (1976). *The use of definite and indefinite reference in young children.* Cambridge: Cambridge University Press.

McTear, M. F. (1985). *Children's conversation.* Oxford: Basil Blackwell Publisher.

Nagler, S., Marcus, J., Sohlberg, S. C., Lifshitz, M., & Silberman, E. K. (1985). Clinical observations of high risk children. *Schizophrenia Bulletin, 11,* 107–111.

Nelson, K., & Gruendel, J. (1981). Generalized event representations: Basic building blocks of cognitive development. In M. Lamb & A. L. Brown (Eds.), *Advances in developmental psychology* (pp. 131–158). Hillsdale, NJ: Erlbaum.

Neuchterlein, K. H. (1983). Signal detection in vigilance tasks and behavioral attributes among offspring of schizophrenic mothers and among hyperactive children. *Journal of Abnormal Psychology, 92,* 4–28.

Neuchterlein, K. H., Edell, W. S., Norris, M., & Dawson, M. E. (1986). Attentional vulnerability indicators, thought disorder, and negative symptoms. *Schizophrenia Bulletin, 12,* 408–426.

Ochs, E., & Schieffelin, B. B. (1979). *Developmental pragmatics.* New York: Academic Press.

Olson, D. R., & Nickerson, N. (1978). Language development through the school years: Learning to confine interpretation to the information in the text. In K. E. Nelson (Ed.), *Children's language* (Vol. 1, pp. 117–170). New York: Gardner Press.

Oltmanns, T. F., Weintraub, S., Stone, A. A., & Neale, J. M. (1978). Cognitive slippage in children vulnerable to schizophrenia. *Journal of Abnormal Psychology, 6,* 237–245.

Parnas, J., Schulsinger, F., Schulsinger, H., Mednick, F. A., & Teasedale, T. W. (1982). Behavioral precursors of schizophrenia spectrum. *Archives of General Psychiatry, 39,* 658–664.

Pellegrini, A. D., & Galda, L. (1982). The effects of thematic-fantasy play on the development of children's story comprehension. *American Educational Research Journal, 19,* 443–452.

Petty, L. K., Ornitz, E. M., Michelman, J. D., & Zimmerman, E. G. (1984). Autistic children who become schizophrenic. *Archives of General Psychiatry, 41,* 129–135.

Piaget, J. (1959). *The language and thought of the child.* New York: Humanities Press.

Piaget, J. (1971). *The child's conception of time.* New York: Ballantine Books.

Potter, H. W. (1933). Schizophrenia in children. *American Journal of Psychiatry, 12,* 1253–1270.

Puig-Antich, J., & Chambers, W. (1978). *The schedule for affective disorders and schizophrenia for school-age children (Kiddie-SADS).* New York: New York State Psychiatric Institute.

Reiser, D. E., & Brown, J. L. (1964). Patterns of later development in children with infantile psychosis. *Journal of American Academy of Child Psychiatry, 3,* 650–667.

Robertson, M., & Barford, F. (1970). Story-making in psychotherapy with a chronically ill child. *Psychotherapy, Research and Practice, 7,* 104–107.

Rochester, S. R., & Martin, J. R. (1979). *Crazy talk: A study of the discourse of schizophrenia speakers.* New York: Plenum Press.

Romaine, S. (1984). *The language of children and adolescents.* New York: Basil Blackwell.

Russell, A., Bott, L., & Sammons, C. (1987, October). *The phenomenology of schizotypal disorder of childhood: A schizophrenia spectrum disorder?* Paper presented at the 34th annual meeting of the American Academy of Child Psychiatry, Washington, DC.

Russell, A. T., Bott, L., & Sammons, C. (1989). The phenomenology of schizophrenia occurring in childhood. *Journal of American Academy of Psychiatry, 28,* 399–407.

Rutter, M., Greenfield, D., & Lockeyer, L. (1967). Five to fifteen years follow-up study of infantile psychosis: II. Social behavioral outcome. *British Journal of Psychiatry, 113,* 1183–1199.

Rutter, M., & Lockeyer, L. (1967). A five to fifteen year follow-up study of infantile psychosis: I. Description of sample. *British Journal of Psychiatry, 113,* 1169–1182.

Sacuzzo, D. P., & Braff, D. L. (1986). Information-processing abnormalities: Trait- and state-dependent components. *Schizophrenia Bulletin, 12,* 448–459.

Shapiro, T., & Huebner, H. F. (1976). Speech patterns of five psychotic children. *Journal of American Academy of Child Psychiatry, 15,* 278–293.

Shatz, M. (1982). Communication. In P. Musson (Ed.), *Carmichael's manual of child psychology* (pp. 841–889). New York: Wiley.

Sherman, T., & Asarnow, R. F. (1985). The cognitive disabilities of the schizophrenic child. In M. Sigman (Ed.), *Children with emotional disorders and developmental disabilities: Assessment and treatment* (pp. 153–170). Orlando, FL: Grune & Stratton.

Shrout, P. E., Spitzer, R. L., & Fleiss, J. L. (1987). Quantification of agreement in psychiatric diagnosis revisited. *Archives of General Psychiatry, 44,* 172–177.

Singer, M. T. (1978). Attentional processes in verbal behavior, in L. C. Wynne, R. L. Cromwell, S. Matthysse (Eds.), *The nature of schizophrenia: New approaches to research and treatment* (pp. 329–336). New York. Wiley.

Spitzer, R. L., Endicott, J., & Robbins, E. (1975). *Research diagnostic criteria (RDC) for a selected group of functional disorders* (2nd ed.). New York: Biometric Research, New York State Psychiatric Institute.

Spohn, H. E., Lolafaye, C., Larson, J. Mittleman, F., Spray, J., & Hayes, K. (1986). Episodic and residual thought pathology in chronic schizophrenics: Effect of neuroleptics. *Schizophrenia Bulletin, 12,* 394–407.

Stein, N. L. (1982). What's in a story: Interpreting the interpretations of story grammars. *Discourse Processes, 5,* 319–335.

Tanguay, P. E., & Asarnow, R. F. (1985). Schizophrenia in children. In R. Michaels & J. O. Cavenar (Eds.), *Psychiatry* (pp. 1–9). New York: J. B. Lippincott.

Watkins, J. M., Asarnow, R. F., & Tanguay, P. E. (1988). Symptom development in childhood onset schizophrenia. *Journal of Child Psychology and Psychiatry, 29,* 865–878.

Weaver, P. A., & Dickinson, D. K. (1982). Scratching below the surface. Exploring the usefulness of story grammars. *Discourse Processes, 5,* 225–243.

Wolf, D. P., & Pusch, J. (1985). The origins of autonomous texts in play boundaries. In L. Galda & A. D. Pellegrini (Eds.), *Play, language, and stories: The development of children's literate behavior* (pp. 63–78). Norwood, NJ: Ablex.

Appendix

KIDDIE FORMAL THOUGHT DISORDER RATING SCALE (K-FTDS)[1]

GUIDELINES FOR THE RATERS

1. A Complete Utterance

This is defined as a group of words—usually followed by a pause—that has at least one subject, with a finite verb or verb phrase (Rochester & Martin, 1979). According to this definition, a clause is also considered a complete utterance.

Examples:[2]

a. I will go.

b. When my mother comes home, I will go to the store.

c. I: How does the devil make you do bad things?

  S: I don't know how but he makes me be bad, bad.

d. I: Do you think that was a good story?

  S: Yes. (It was a good story)

e. I: What would you do if the children at school didn't like you?

  S: Nothing. (I would not do anything)

Example a includes only one utterance. Examples b and the child's response in c, however, each include two utterances. When occurring alone, the single word answers in Examples d and e imply more to the listener than the single word. For instance, "Yes" in Example d implies that it was a good story. Similarly, "nothing" in Example e implies that the child would not do anything if the children at school did not like him. In both these examples, the single-word response would be coded as a complete utterance.

2. Incomplete Utterances

If an utterance does not fulfill the criteria of a complete utterance, it is considered to be incomplete. An incomplete utterance may take the form of a false start or a word filler.

Examples:

a. I: Did you like that story?

  S: Well … I … you know … sometimes … it was … that wasn't a good story.

b. I: How do you know there are such things as ghosts?

  S: Like … Like if you … Like my grandmother says there are spirits.

In Example a, "Well," "I," and "sometimes" are false starts that are incomplete utterances. In Example b, "Like" is a word filler.

---

[1] Caplan et al., The Kiddie Formal Thought Disorder Rating Scale (K-FTDS). (1989). Clinical Assessment, reliability, and validity. *Journal of American Academy of Child Psychiatry, 28,* 408–416.

[2] I = Interviewer, S = Subject.

The K-FTDS criteria are used only with complete utterances. Thus, only those false starts that fulfill the criteria of a complete utterance will be coded for formal thought disorder (FTD). It has been suggested that incomplete utterances are indices of the disturbed attention involved in thought disorder (Singer, 1978). They are, therefore, coded and analyzed separately (guidelines obtainable from senior author).

3. The Statement

The statement refers to the contents of the utterance. The rater needs to be able to define the statement of every utterance in the speech sample.

Examples:

a. I: What do you like about that story?

   S: I liked about the ghost.

b. I: Do you think this is a true story?

   S: No, there are no such things as ghosts.

In Example a, the statement is that the child liked the part of the story about the ghost. In example b, there are two statements. The first is that the child does not think the story is true and the second is that the child does not think there are such things as ghosts.

4. Conversation Units

The rater uses the conversation unit to determine the ongoing topic of conversation needed to rate loose associations. The conversation unit is defined for the three sections of the Story Game as follows:

a. *Recall of the stories*—The conversation unit begins after the interviewer asks the child to retell the story. It ends when the child finishes retelling his or her account of the story. The end of the child's story is determined by the child's response to the interviewer's question "Do you remember anything else that happened in the story?" or "How did the story end?" The topic of conversation is the story about the ghost or the story about Tim.

b. *Questions following the stories*—here the conversation unit begins at the end of the interviewer's question and continues until the end of the child's response. The topic of conversation is introduced by the interviewer with each standardized question.

c. *The child's story*—In this section, the conversation unit begins as the child starts to tell her or his story. It ends when the interviewer has determined that the child's story is completed by asking, "And is that the end of your story?" The topic, chosen by the child for his or her narrative, is the topic of conversation.

5. Linguistic Immaturity

Signs of linguistic immaturity, such as grammatical errors, inappropriate and incorrect use of pronouns, or the indefinite and definite articles, and of demonstratives are not rated as FTD. They are, however, coded separately under reference for a project on pragmatics/discourse (guidelines obtainable from the senior author).

Examples:

a. I dream about somebody I never know. And he run and stab me.

b. And Peter woke up and he think it was a dream.

c. I think he does … he makes … he just draws something on the different girl's window curtains.

d. And … and … and so when Halloween came, her Dad made a hat, and then her mother made a witch costume, and so we went trick or treating.

In Examples a and b the tenses are incorrectly used. In Example c, there is reference to "the different girl," whereas in the text, no prior reference had been made to any girl. The listener, therefore, does not know who this person is. Similarly, in Example d, the child is telling a story about a witch, and it is not at all clear to the listener who "we" are.

6. Nonverbal Communication

Only clear nonverbal communication, such as head nods for "Yes," headshakes for "No," and shoulder shrugging for "I don't know," are regarded as part of the subject's speech. Any other nonverbal communication that demands interpretation by the rater is not rated as part of the subject's speech.

Example:

While describing how guardian angels protect him in the day, a child gets a quizzical look on his face and says "Day is when they come down, night they go up. *Day is no day, night is no night.*"

The two italicized utterances in this example would be rated as illogical thinking. It is possible, however, to claim that this is not an example of illogical thinking for the following reason. The child's quizzical look suggests that he is expressing the fact that because of these angels, he does not understand what happens in the day and what happens in the night, and might not have been rated. By not including the wide range of facial expressions, we have tried to limit the amount of subjective interpretations during the rating process.

THE K-FTDS SIGNS

1. Illogical Thinking (ILL)

To rate illogical thinking, the rater needs to determine whether the facts, causes, and conclusions of the child's utterances are logically sound in adult terms. This sign is evaluated in the three conditions described in the following listings—a, b, and c.

a. *Use of Causal Utterances* ("because", "so that", and "if").

Whenever the child uses a causal utterance, the rater should ascertain whether the contents of the utterance explain the causality appropriately (Emerson & Gekenski, 1980).

Examples:

(i)   I have nightmares when I eat a lot because I start to laugh.

(ii)   God saves all good people because they're bad.

(iii) I went to fetch my hat because her name is Mary.

(iv)   I: Did you ever have friends who did sneaky things to you?

       S: So he found a big guy and beat those heck of them up … 'cause one of them is Heckler and one Jeckler.

(v) I: Do you think this was a true story?

S: Yes it is.

I: How do you know?

S: 'Cause I already know, and I do a lot of things, so I always know.

(vi) I: Why do you like this story?

S: Because I do.

(vii) I: Why do you think this is a good story?

S: Because it is.

In Examples (i)–(v), the children have used illogical reasoning in causal utterances. Thus, the child's explanation for having nightmares in Example (i) is contradictory to the very experience of nightmares. Laughing is a pleasant experience, whereas a nightmare is an unpleasant experience. One does not have a nightmare because of laughing. Similarly, in Example (ii), if it's culturally accepted that God saves people who are good, the reason for their salvation cannot be that they are not good—that is, bad. In Example (iii), the name Mary is an illogical reason for the child to want to fetch her hat. In Example (iv), the reason presented by the child for the beating is the names of the people, and this is illogical. This reasoning is an example of a clang association in which the term "beating the heck of them up" leads to the clang association with Heckler which, in turn rhymed with Jeckler. This example, however, was rated as ILL because of the presence of the causal utterance. Finally, the child's assertion in Example (v)—that she does a lot of things—is not a logical explanation for the verity of the story.

Examples (iv)–(vi) demonstrate that the children are using causal utterances appropriately after "Why?" questions. The content of these causal utterances, however, is inadequate because the children used the causal construct to simply reaffirm the interviewer's question.

b. *Use of Noncausal Utterances*

In this condition, the child gives unfounded and inappropriate explanations for things he or she says.

Examples:

(i) I: Do you ever have these kinds of dreams during the daytime even when you're not asleep?

S: No ... A dream means you're ... you're ... you're turning into—er—something that's bad and has a nightmare.

(ii) I: Did you think this could be a true story?

S: Well, it could if you just let it bother people it could happen.

(iii) S: Sometime's I'll go to bed and when I'm done laughing and I start wheezing and I ... and I ... and that's when I relax and that's when I start thinking about that.

In each of these examples, the child's reasoning is illogical. A dream does not indicate that one is bad or turning into something that is bad, as in Example (i). The truth of a story is not determined by whether it bothers people, as in Example (ii). Finally, the child's statement that he relaxes when he stops laughing and starts wheezing is also illogical.

c. *Contradictions*

The child simultaneously makes and refutes a statement within a minimum of two utterances. To rate this as ILL, the contradictory statement has to occur within the same conversation unit. If it occurs at a later point of the Story Game, it cannot be rated as ILL unless the child repeats both original statements.

Examples:

(i)   I didn't like that story, but I liked it as a story.

(ii)   They're nice, they're mean guys.

(iii) People don't talk to adults. They talk to ... they be nice to adults.

(iv) I: Do you really think there's a devil in hell?

       S: No. And the devil said to them, "Get down to hell."

The contradictions in these examples are self-explanatory. In this category, it is important not to over-rate ILL when, in fact, the child is repairing her or his utterances. For example, in (ii) if the child would have said "They're nice ... I mean they're mean guys," this would be considered an example in which the child changed his or her mind and decided to say that the guys are mean. Similarly, children are often eager to please the interviewer. They, therefore, often refute their statements if they sense that the interviewer thinks otherwise or is interested in another answer. For example, if a child answers "Yes" to a question and after the interviewer asks "Yes?" she or he then says "No," this would not be scored as a contradiction. To be coded as ILL due to a contradiction, the child needs to clearly make and refute a statement or include two incompatible statements within two utterances.

2. Incoherence (INC)

In INC, the rater is unable to formulate the statement expressed in an utterance because of scrambled syntax. In some cases, one is tempted to interpret what the subject meant to say. This is not acceptable, and the rater should be able to define the content of the utterance without additional interpretations. However, if the rater cannot determine the statement of an utterance because of unclear reference, this is not incoherence.

Examples:

a. I: Can you tell me one of your scary dreams that you have on bad days?

    S: Well ... yeah ... I went ... I visit what bad days and on the nighttimes.

b. I: What happened next in your story?

    S: The day witches no day goes.

In both a and b the rater cannot define what the child is saying without additional interpretations.

3. Loose Associations (LA)

LA is rated when the child changes the topic of conversation to an unrelated topic without preparing the listener for this topic change. ILL is differentiated from LA, in that in ILL, the child's utterances are on the topic, but the child's explanations and reasoning are unfounded.

"On" and "Off" Topic. The following guidelines are provided to aid the rater in determining "on" and "off" topic during the three parts of the Story Game.

To rate an utterance as LA, the rater must first ascertain what the topic of conversation is, within the framework of the conversation units. After identifying the topic of conversation, the rater must determine whether the child's utterances are on or off the topic. At any point, both the child and the interviewer can change the topic of conversation. If, as in the following example, the listener is informed of the topic change, and of its connection with the previous topic of conversation, this is not regarded as LA.

Example:

I: How is your mood—happy, sad, or in between?

S: Happy, I guess. I'm very good at sports. Today we had a good game, and I scored three goals.

In this example, the child starts to talk about sports while the topic of conversation is his mood. The congruency between the child's mood and his success in sport is indicative of the connection between the two topics in this example.

Off topic is defined for each of the Story Game sections as follows:

a. *Recall of stories*—If, while retelling the audiotaped narratives, the child tells some other story, this is regarded as off the topic. LA would be rated each time he or she goes off the topic. If, however, the child confabulates and adds additional details while retelling the audiotaped story, this would not be rated as LA.

b. *The child's own story*—If, while telling a story about a witch, the child talks about her or his plans for the summer or tells a story about Smurfs, this would be rated as LA. LA would be rated each time the topic of the story is changed. If, however, the child continued to tell the new story to which he or she has digressed, this becomes the ongoing topic of conversation. In the latter situation there would be no additional ratings of LA.

c. *Questions and answers*—As previously described, the topic of the interviewer's question is the ongoing topic of conversation in this section of the Story Game. The child can change the topic of conversation in several ways. If the child informs the listener of the topic change or uses linguistic cues that guide the listener as to a change in topic (see Example (i)), this would not be rated as LA. If, however, the child begins to talk about an unrelated topic and does not prepare the listener for the topic change, this would be rated as LA. The following examples demonstrate how LA is rated in the Question and Answer sections.

Examples:

(i)   I: How would you have felt if you fell in a puddle of water?

      S: Bad. Do you know what I like to do when it rains?

      I: What?

      S: Watch the rain from my room.

(ii) I: What can ghosts do to scare you?

      S: They can kill me. But I have a friend Mike who I play with at school and stuff like that and he and I make scary faces and play the stereo and listen to a lot of music and stuff like that.

(iii) I: Why did you like this story?

      S: I liked ... I don't know why ... The devil isn't going to catch me.

(iv)   I: Why do you think that's a reason not to like Tim?

S: And I call my mom Sweety.

(v)   I: Do you believe in ghosts? (A noise was heard from the outside.)

S: What was that noise? Are the kids going to the pool?

(vi)   S: (The child is describing a dream.) He fell down a big hole. Like the big guy told him that. He took the big hammer. He had never come back to see that place. That was pretty scary.

(vii)   I: What kind of bad dreams do you have?

S: I think in a movie like when they maked cars and stuff, that's how it happen.

The rater needs to distinguish between LA and distractiblity. If the child changes topic because of an external or internal stimulus, as in the preceding Example (v), this is an example of distractibility and not of LA.

In Example (vi), it is difficult to follow the topic of conversation because of inappropriate use of demonstratives and the definite article. This is not rated as LA. If, as in Example (vii), it is not clear whether the utterance is off the topic because of linguistic immaturity, LA, or both, it should not be rated as LA.

Once the child is off the topic, the rater needs to consider the following. As long as the child and/or interviewer continue to speak about the new topic, this should not be rated as a recurrence of LA. If the interviewer tries to return to the original topic, and the subject again goes off-topic, it should be rated as an additional occurrence of LA. If the child unpredictably returns to the original topic of conversation, this, too, would be rated as LA. Finally, if the subject's speech went off-topic, the interviewer joined her or him in the new topic, and the topic again changed unpredictably, this would be rated as two instances of LA.

Guidelines for Ambiguous Instances of Unpredicted Topic Change. In the preceding examples, the child's digression from the ongoing topic of conversation is readily apparent. During the conversation with the subject, there are frequent occasions when this relationship is ambiguous, as demonstrated by the following Examples (i)–(v).

Examples:

(i)   I: How is your mood—happy, sad, or in-between?

S: Happy, I guess, I'm a pro. But when John comes home from school there will be lots of trouble.

In this example, the child says that he is a pro, and this might appear to be off-topic. The child, however, is talking about being happy and the fact that he is a pro is quite congruent with his being happy. He then goes on to talk about possible trouble when his brother comes home. The use of "but" informs the listener that John's homecoming is related to the topic. It implies that his mood might change because of his brother's homecoming.

(ii)   I: Are there really such things as ghosts?

S: I have special shields that protect me. So if the flat faced one comes after me, he can't do a thing.

I: Is that a flat faced ghost?

S: Yes.

In example (ii), because the child has special shields to protect him against what most probably is a ghost, his answer to the question is on-topic.

(iii)   I: Do you ever daydream?

      S: I put my head down. My teacher goes on talking and talking. I just close my eyes and go to sleep.

Here the child has understood the question literally and is describing how he falls asleep in class. This would, therefore, be rated as on-topic.

(iv)   I: Do you really think there are such things as ghosts?

      S: If this guy went to this house, he wouldn't come back. In *Poltergeist,* they show haunted houses and that's what happens to you.

In example (iv), the story about *Poltergeist* and haunted houses indicates that the child believes in ghosts and is on-topic.

(v)   I: Do you believe in ghosts?

      S: At Universal Studio, they have moving pictures. They only have them on movies.

In this last example, the child refers to moving pictures at Universal Studios in conjunction with the fact that ghosts only are found on movies. The child therefore has not drifted from the topic of conversation.

In these ambiguous examples, the rater should be guided by the contiguity of the topic of conversation. If there is clearly no relationship between what is being said and the ongoing topic of conversation, then LA should be rated. If, however, there is some relationship between the topics, this should not be rated as LA.

4. Poverty of Content of Speech (POC)

This definition stipulates that in the presence of adequate length of speech, there is a lack of information or insufficient content. The child's speech is of adequate length if he or she has made at least two utterances. The rater's decision on the adequacy of the information in the child's conversation is based on the following. First, the rater must be able to state that the child has elaborated on the topic of conversation and is not merely reiterating what she or he has said before. Second, the rater must be able to clearly establish what the subject is conveying in these utterances. If this cannot be done, the utterances should be rated as POC. If the lack of content is associated with ILL, INC, or LA, it is not rated as POC. *Perseveration* (i.e., the repetition of words, phrases, and sentences) is not rated as POC. Thus, if the child simply repeats what he has said, this is not rated as POC.

Examples:

a. I: Why do you think you have trouble making friends?

      S: I'm always having a problem with friends. I might have some problems. I think a lot about making friends. The problem is simple: I have trouble making friends.

b. S: I suppose … What's that? Maybe … Well yes, I see. I suppose that's all.

c. I: Why is that magic?

      S: It's not magic. It's the only type of magic there is. And it's something very powerful. It is the only type of magic. And it's what magic really is being able to control something.

d. I: What does magic do? S: Things that can be done by magic can really be done. So that's really magic itself.

In Example a, the child has made five utterances. The content of these utterances was merely a repetition of the interviewer's question, and it should, therefore, be rated as POC. In Example b, each utterance is coherent and does not demonstrate LA or ILL. Because it is difficult to clearly formulate what the subject is saying in these five utterances, this would be rated as POC.

In Example c, the child contradicts himself by saying that something is not magic and yet is the only type of magic. This would be rated as ILL. In the following three utterances, the child restates what magic is but does not provide the listener with additional information on what magic really is. This is, therefore, rated as POC. In Example d, the first two utterances fulfill the criteria as POC because there is no elaboration of the topic. The child merely rephrases the question and says that things can be done by magic. The last utterance is a causal utterance and would be rated as ILL because there is no logical explanation for why things can be done by magic.

Formal Thought Disorder Rating Form   ID # _____

Date of Testing _____

Date of Rating _____

Name of Rater _____

	Illogical Thinking	Incoherence	Loose Associations	Poverty of Content	Total
Story #1					
Memory	_____	_____	_____	_____	_____
	_____	_____	_____	_____	_____
Questions					
1.	_____	_____	_____	_____	_____
2.	_____	_____	_____	_____	_____
3.	_____	_____	_____	_____	_____
4.	_____	_____	_____	_____	_____
5.	_____	_____	_____	_____	_____
6.	_____	_____	_____	_____	_____
7.	_____	_____	_____	_____	_____
8.	_____	_____	_____	_____	_____
9.	_____	_____	_____	_____	_____
10.	_____	_____	_____	_____	_____
11.	_____	_____	_____	_____	_____
12.	_____	_____	_____	_____	_____
13.	_____	_____	_____	_____	_____
14.	_____	_____	_____	_____	_____
15.	_____	_____	_____	_____	_____
16.	_____	_____	_____	_____	_____
17.	_____	_____	_____	_____	_____
Story #2	_____	_____	_____	_____	_____
	_____	_____	_____	_____	_____
	_____	_____	_____	_____	_____

	Illogical Thinking	Incoherence	Loose Associations	Poverty of Content	Total
Story #3					
Memory	_____	_____	_____	_____	_____
	_____	_____	_____	_____	_____
Questions					
1.	_____	_____	_____	_____	_____
2.	_____	_____	_____	_____	_____
3.	_____	_____	_____	_____	_____
4.	_____	_____	_____	_____	_____
5.	_____	_____	_____	_____	_____
6.	_____	_____	_____	_____	_____
7.	_____	_____	_____	_____	_____
8.	_____	_____	_____	_____	_____
9.	_____	_____	_____	_____	_____
10.	_____	_____	_____	_____	_____
11.	_____	_____	_____	_____	_____
12.	_____	_____	_____	_____	_____
13.	_____	_____	_____	_____	_____
14.	_____	_____	_____	_____	_____

Total

Chapter 7

USING ANATOMICALLY DETAILED DOLLS IN INTERVIEWING PRESCHOOLERS

Sue White

The exact date of the appearance of anatomically detailed dolls in the field of clinical interviewing is unknown. The best guess is that the first dolls that were manufactured with genital representations appeared in the mid-1970s although there may have been some clinicians who were using dolls that had been individually modified prior to that time. In the late 1970s and early 1980s, however, the use of anatomically detailed dolls became widespread in the evaluation of alleged sexual abuse victims (Boat & Everson, 1988). Just how these dolls were selected as tools in sexual abuse evaluations cannot be documented extensively. Two historically separate experiences, however, illustrate how these dolls have come to be used. The first occurred in Eugene, Oregon in the mid-1970s when Virginia Friedemann, a police detective, and Marcia Morgan, director of a rape victim assistance program recognized the need "to establish more clear communication between interviewers and children" (Friedemann & Morgan, 1985, p. iv) in cases of alleged sexual abuse. As a result, they developed the anatomical "Natural Dolls" and subsequently formed a company to produce these dolls on a large scale. Since that time, dolls have been professionally produced by companies that were specifically aimed at making dolls or by companies that added dolls to their already child-oriented therapy products.

The second historical line of doll development was more serendipitous. In the late 1970s and early 1980s, Cleveland (Ohio) Metropolitan General Hospital (CMGH) was unofficially designated as the county's receiving hospital for the majority of sexual abuse cases. Although other hospitals accepted older rape victims, the young, frequently nonverbal children were brought to CMGH. As one of the mental health workers at CMGH, I found myself at a loss as to what to do because there had been no graduate school or postdoctoral training in evaluating such patients. As I was struggling with this problem, I came upon some dolls being handmade for another clinic in the hospital. This clinic served multi-handicapped children and adolescents, and the sexualized dolls were used in teaching these individuals about the impending medical procedures (e.g., catheterizations) and instructing in sexual education. Out of desperation, I began using these dolls in interviewing young victims of alleged sexual abuse. Although the exact date of my first interview with these dolls is unknown, it is likely that it occurred in late 1981 or early 1982.

By 1983, the dolls were a regular part of my abuse evaluations with young children, and data from my assessments were being presented in juvenile court as being diagnostic of sexual abuse. I became concerned, however, that there was no basis on which to make such conclusions as my clinical sample was small and there were no normative data on nonabused children. All my judgments, right or wrong, were based on clinical data. With this concern, the study that eventually became the first research doll paper ever published was initiated (White, Strom, Santilli, & Halpin, 1986) and out of which grew a structured protocol that is still in use today in a modified form.

There are undoubtedly many more stories of how dolls became a part of interviewing abuse victims. In this chapter, however, the focus is on topics that directly relate to this first study and the structured interview protocol: (a) research findings; (b) procedures for interviewing with dolls; and (c) present legal ramifications of doll usage.

To date, only seven articles have appeared in peer-reviewed journals as of mid-1989. One paper is psychoanalytically oriented (Gabriel, 1985). Two contain data comparing allegedly abused children with children who had not been referred for an abuse evaluation (Jampole & Weber, 1987; White et al., 1986). The fourth one presents data on nonabused children (Sivan, Schor, Koeppl, & Noble, 1988). The fifth one reviews a survey that was conducted in 1985 with professionals who were evaluating abuse victims (Boat & Everson, 1988). The last two were invited debates on the efficacy of doll usage (Yates & Terr, 1988a; 1988b). Thus, when comparing the field of anatomical dolls with one of the other play assessment techniques, it is very young and sparsely studied. We truly know very little. This is problematic because dolls are used daily in investigations that result in judicial decisions concerning the lives of alleged victims and the alleged perpetrators.

RESEARCH FINDINGS

Nonreferred Children's Responses to the Dolls

The only published study that has provided data on how nonreferred children respond to anatomical dolls is that of Sivan et al. (1988). Although there were some problems of sampling (upper middle class, university town) and data analysis (equipment failed in some recording sessions), the results of the Sivan study should be viewed as a tentative description of what nonreferred children do with anatomical dolls under certain conditions. By observing 3- to 8-year- olds children in three experimental conditions (with adult present; without adult present and with dolls undressed), Sivan et al. found that these children played with dressed dolls about 20% of the time and with undressed dolls about 26% of the time. The older children played with the dressed dolls more than the younger ones, although age was not a factor when the dolls were undressed. As expected, girls (26%) played with the dolls by choice about twice as much as the boys (11–12%). When alone with undressed dolls, the girls' doll play increased to 41%, the primary activity being dressing the dolls. Sivan et al. did not find that the dolls elicited sexual behaviors and/or aggressive play in their sample.

In a yet-unpublished study of nonreferred children's responses to anatomical dolls versus nonanatomical dolls, Goodman and Aman (1987) presented a small group of 3- and 5-year-olds with a real-life event and subsequently questioned them under three possible conditions: with anatomical dolls; with identical dolls which have no anatomical parts; without any dolls. After interrogating the children with leading questions, they found that the 5-year- olds were correct more often with the aid of any dolls, with or without anatomical parts, whereas the 3-year-olds did better without any type of doll present. Interestingly, the presence or absence of dolls had no significant effect when the children responded to questions containing more abuse-type content, such as, "Did he touch your peepee?" Although Goodman and Aman demonstrated that 3-year-olds were more suggestible than 5-year-olds, both age groups' correct response rate dramatically increased when the researchers attempted to ask them questions with incorrect content. The presence or absence of the dolls again made no difference.

Comparison of Referred and Nonreferred Children's Responses

Only two studies that compare referred and/or sexually abused children's responses with those of nonreferred children have reached the peer-reviewed literature. Results have consistently supported the conclusion that nonreferred children display fewer responses thought to reflect sexual abuse experiences. In the first such published study (White et al., 1986), we administered a structured doll protocol to 25 2- to 6-year-olds children referred for an abuse evaluation and 25 nonreferred children of the same age range. The children's responses to the dolls were coded based on a 5-point scale of indicators ranging from "no suspicion" to "very high suspicion." Results demonstrated that the responses from the nonreferred children resulted in a significantly lowered rating of suspected abuse.

In the second published study (Jampole & Weber, 1987), 10 abused and 10 nonreferred children between 3 and 8 years of age were interviewed briefly with the dolls and then left in a free-play situation. Like the results in White et al.'s study, the abused children demonstrated more sexual behaviors than did the nonreferred children.

PRACTICAL ASPECTS OF DOLL USAGE

In spite of not having the answers to the many factors that underlie the use of dolls in assessment and treatment of child sexual abuse, clinicians and others in the field of child sexual abuse are regularly using them. Because techniques of doll usage are presently not taught in graduate programs, those clinicians who choose to use dolls must either develop their own interview-specific procedures, incorporate the dolls into other interview techniques, and/or seek specific training. The following section provides some guidelines and suggestions for doll usage. Care must be taken not to assume that there is only one way to use dolls in abuse evaluations.

It must be realized that in contrast to many child-interviewing techniques described in this book, the clinician should assume that the information from doll interviews may be forwarded to the judicial system, even though in the majority of cases this does not happen. One does not know, however, before entering a case whether "this one will go." Thus, it is imperative that the data be collected objectively and in as unbiased a fashion as possible.

General Attitudes

Independence

The first and foremost attitude that a clinician must assume when introducing dolls into either a diagnostic or a therapeutic session is that of independence (Benedek & Schetky, 1987; Goodwin, Sahd, & Rada, 1982; Jones & McQuiston, 1985; White & Quinn, 1988; White, Santilli, & Quinn, 1988). *Independence* involves the concept of not assuming that the interviewer knows which doll the child may wish to investigate, how the child wishes (if at all) to identify the doll(s), and/or what the child plans to do with the dolls. Such independence dictates that the interviewer *not* provide any direction as to who, what, when, or how. The interviewer must be careful not to introduce leading material—that is, not introduce any concept or content that has not already been brought to the session by the child (White & Quinn, 1988). Questions that are posed in an open-ended style are most useful in eliciting more spontaneous information. Other helpful queries include "Tell me more" and "Did anything else happen?"

Consistent Presentation

The issue of presentation method of anatomical dolls continues to be debated (Boat & Everson, 1986; Friedemann & Morgan, 1985; MacFarlane & Krebs, 1986; White, 1988; Yates & Terr, 1988). Friedemann and Morgan (1985) suggest that the dolls be used only after the child has made a disclosure. They contend that the dolls may be presented dressed or undressed as do MacFarlane and Krebs. Boat and Everson (1986) and White, Strom, Santilli, and Quinn (1987) present the dolls in a structured interview, and the dolls are always presented dressed. MacFarlane and Krebs indicate that a "humorous approach to undressing the anatomical dolls" (p. 73) may help to reduce the child's anxiety. While debating the pros and cons of doll usage, neither Yates nor Terr present formal guidelines for their use. It is my opinion that the clinician should develop a consistent plan of presentation of the dolls, especially in evaluation sessions. As clinicians may find themselves in judicial situations in which they must explain what occurred in the session, more credibility within the judicial system will be gained if the same basic approach is taken with each child. Because there is a dearth of comparative data, clinicians will be forced to use their own data experiences to evaluate the data from the child in question. By using one basic method, interviewers will be better able to make comparisons.

While it is important that the clinician develop a consistent approach, it is not necessary that one particular procedure be used. Presently, them are three nationally known protocols that suggest how to interview suspected victims of sexual abuse (Boat & Everson, 1986; Friedemann & Morgan, 1985; White et al., 1987). No one method has been proven to be superior to the others. Each has qualities that clinicians may want to incorporate into their own techniques. In addition, other writers have made recommendations concerning doll usage (Jones & McQuiston, 1985; MacFarlane & Krebs, 1986; Schetky, 1988; Yates & Terr, 1988). Regardless of the choice of technique, each clinician should have specific reasons that can be recited concerning why the specific technique is being used.

Not a Test

Contrary to the opinions of a number of individuals (these primarily being within the judicial community), the anatomically detailed dolls *are not a diagnostic test for child sexual abuse.* They are only a tool to obtain information from the child, just as are drawings, nonverbal behaviors, physical gestures, and general play. They just happen to have some specific characteristics that may make it easier for a child to relate sexual experiences through them as props. In spite of recent court rulings in California *(In re Amber B. v. Ron B.,* 1987), efforts are underway in the major professional organizations to make sure that dolls are not declared to be a test.

Part of a Complete Psychosocial Assessment

The doll/abuse interview should be a part of a complete psychosocial assessment. This evaluation should include a detailed psychosocial history, family patterns of privacy, parent history interviews, and a medical examination of the child (see White et al., 1988, for a detailed description).

When to Use Anatomical Dolls

Anatomical dolls may be utilized in any situation in which it is felt that the individual bring assessed would benefit from having these props available, most usually when there is a suspicion of sexual abuse. In spite of Goodman and Aman's (1987) data, which indicated that anatomical dolls were not necessarily useful in eliciting more correct information regarding a nonabusive experience, certain children suspected of being abuse victims may find that dolls are helpful for relating their experiences. These individuals include very young children (2–3 years old), children with language difficulties, and children, youth, or adults with mental retardation that interferes with normal communication as well as adults with developmental problems or medical indications that interfere with verbal communication (e.g., mutism, aphasia after a stroke). Dolls may also be considered when the person to be interviewed has normal communication abilities but is unable to employ those skills due to anxiety and/or fear. In our clinic, dolls are kept available in all sexual abuse evaluations even though the child or adolescent may elect not to use them.

Who May Make Use of Them?

Those who use anatomical dolls in interviewing of abuse victims do not have to be mental health professionals. With the proper training, we have seen police detectives, victim advocates, and protective service workers become quite adept in interviewing even very young victims. The key is in making sure the interviewer (a) is well-trained in general child interviewing techniques (including management of difficult and/or upset children); (b) is knowledgeable in child development, sexual abuse, and witness issues; (c) is generally comfortable being around children; and (d) is not embarrassed to discuss sexual topics.

As each of these interviews is potentially critical to the planning of the child's life (e.g., being removed from his or her parents), *each* interview must be done in an optimal fashion. Interviewers must make it their responsibility to maintain the highest standards of interviewing and following the established protocol for their agency. Periodic review by interviewing a training subject while being videotaped, as well as regular review of each actual abuse interview, should be done by the interviewer, as well as by a colleague who can provide constructive feedback.

Selection of Dolls

Ten years ago, those using anatomical dolls had very few choices. By the mid-1980s, about half of those using dolls had adapted other dolls to serve as anatomical doll props (Boat & Everson, 1988). These included Barbies, Raggedy Anns, and Cabbage Patch dolls with adapted genitalia. In 1985, there were about 4 professional manufacturers; today the number is at least 15. When selecting dolls, a number of issues must be considered–issues that have no experimentally based answers. These issues include number of dolls to use, size of the dolls, presumed race, details of fingers, cavity openings (oral, vaginal. anal), types of clothing, and size of genitalia.

Most doll sets are sold with four dolls (mother, father, son, daughter), although some manufacturers are now offering infants and grandparents for an extra fee. Sets of four range from $200 to $400. In the early days, we recommended a family of four, but we now consistently have eight dolls available to the child. We found that the typical family constellation in our clinic setting was not the average middle-class family of four, but was rather extended. Thus we now have available four adult and four child dolls, often mixing the races.

Historically, adults are notorious for assuming that they know what children perceive. In this field, the result of such thinking is the manufacture of dolls in three basic races: Caucasian, Hispanic, and African-American. No one has taken the time, however, to see whether the children perceive these dolls as representative of the designated races. Even more fundamental, however, is whether it really matters when the child uses these dolls as props when a mismatch in race is made.

A second question is whether the designated race of the dolls should be matched with that of the child. By doing so, one is either assuming that the alleged perpetrator is of the same race as the victim or that it does not matter. It probably is wise to have a mix of dolls available to the interview subject.

The clinician must decide whether the dolls have webbed or individual fingers; and what the types of cavity openings are to be. Although there are no data to support one particular style, it seems logical that the dolls have oral, genital, and anal openings to allow children to fully express their experiences. These openings should be big enough to allow the child to poke a finger inside. Clothes should be well-made because of the frequent rough treatment they receive. It is most helpful to have velcro closures.

Regular examination of the condition of the dolls and clothes is important so that they are always in good repair. Having a traumatized child find something amiss is not helpful in maintaining rapport. In one instance of which I am aware, the child was demonstrating how his penis had been pulled when the penis on the doll came off due to poor stitching.

Arrangement of Interview Room

Dolls have been used in just about every setting imaginable: regular interview room, police station interrogation room, hallways, hospitals, children's homes, back seats of police cars, and desks in a busy police station or protective service agency. While some investigators give little heed to where they interview a child, it is strongly recommended that the location have several characteristics. First, it should be private so that there will be no interruptions and/or inappropriate individuals observing the interview. Second, ambient noise (telephone ringing, overhead paging systems) should be minimized, as these intrusions become very distracting for an already anxious child. Third, if others are observing the interview and/or videotaping is being done, the environment should be established so that no intrusions disrupt the interview. Although children of consent age (somewhere between 6 and 8 years of age) need to know that they are being videotaped and/or observed, the taping equipment and observers should be behind a one-way mirror or otherwise out of sight of the child.

The room itself should be furnished to fit the age of the individual being interviewed. In any case, it should be fairly sparsely furnished so that the interviewer can more easily maintain the child's attention. For preschoolers, several toys should be available. These may include crayons/markers and paper, doll house, trucks and cars, telephones, and blocks. Too many toys become distracting and often makes the task of maintaining the child's attention much more difficult. The chosen toys should be centrally located (usually the floor) within easy access of the child, and the anatomical dolls should be placed in the background.

Who Should be Present

The presence of a parent or other supportive adult during the doll interview continues to be debated. On one side of the issue is the argument for the psychological comfort of the child. On the other is other is the potential contaminating influence on the child's responses. In arguing for the child's always being seen alone, White and Quinn (1988) contend that the parent's presence in the interview room may, even inadvertently, influence the child's disclosures. As Jones and McQuiston (1985) point out, the parent may have "become an expert at nonverbally, reminding the child to keep the secret while 'telling the truth... (p. 17). Others argue that adults should be present if the child is unable to separate from the adult or asks for support (Boat & Everson, 1986; Friedemann & Morgan, 1985; Sgroi, Porter, & Blick, 1982). We have found that the following is very useful in helping parents to understand their need to remain in the waiting room: Explain to the parents or other adults that it is important in advocating for the child's best interests that they not be in the room while the child is being interviewed in order to avoid biasing the child's responses for later legal use. This even helps them become active partners in getting the child to separate rather than encouraging the child to cling to them.

The parent or other adult also needs to know that unless there is concern for the child's immediate safety, no information will be discussed with the parent until the evaluation is completed. This again is to decrease the potential of contamination (White et al., 1987).

Recommending that the alleged perpetrator be present for part of the evaluation is done rarely (Green, 1986) and is usually done so only very cautiously, as when sexual abuse allegations arise during custody disputes (American Academy of Child and Adolescent Psychiatry Committee on Rights and Legal Matters, 1988). In such instances, behaviors of both the child and the alleged perpetrator may provide important information to the courts relative to their general relationship. Contrary to what Green suggests, various reactions of a child to an alleged perpetrator should not be used as the primary diagnostic criteria in sexual abuse allegations. A child's reactions may arise from multiple sources.

Introduction of the Child to the Interview

The issue of the doll interview should be presented to the parent or other adult within the context of the entire plan of the evaluation. Prior to the child's being brought to the interview, the parent or other individual responsible for the child should be informed that the child will be having an interview that will probably include the use of anatomical dolls. The explanation should center on how a child's play is usually indicative of his or her life experiences. Emphasis should be made concerning how these dolls are specially designed to provide the child with the opportunity to demonstrate an experience that he or she may find difficult to discuss verbally.

Caregiving adults should be instructed to tell children that they are going to talk with a person who talks to children about various concerns they may have. Children should be told that they will be talking to this individual alone, that "mom has to wait outside." Adults should be warned not to discuss particulars about the suspected abuse with the child.

Upon arriving at the interview, the child should be greeted in the waiting room, and a few minutes should be spent talking about general things to help both the adult and the child relax somewhat. The interviewer should then inform the child that "We're going back to my playroom to talk. Mom is going to wait for us here. Tell her bye," and then walk away with the child. If given in a positive and firm voice, the child will usually accompany the interviewer. If the child demonstrates extreme reluctance to separate, the interviewer may offer a compromise, such as, "We can have Mom come see the room where we'll be, then she'll have to come back here. Come on, Mom." At the door of the room, the interviewer should firmly and positively state, "Thanks for coming this far, Mom. Now Josie and I are going to see what's in the room. Tell Mom 'bye.'" Once the child sees the toys in the room, he or she usually becomes much more willing to separate.

If the child starts crying, the interviewer is advised to bring the child into the room and to begin playing with one of the toys. The interviewer should sit comfortably, preferably on the floor, while drawing or playing with another toy. Occasionally, asking the child some simple question regarding the play, such as "What color is this?" can be successful in gaining the child's cooperation. If the distress continues, reflect that the child is sad, but that "We will be staying here for a while. Then we'll go see your mom." Continue to play with a toy, and eventually the child should join in. Care must be taken not to reinforce the child for the crying behavior.

If the child is totally unable to quit crying by the implementation of appropriate behavioral techniques, the interviewer may decide to allow an adult to join the child for free play, but not for the doll/abuse interview. The child (and adult) is to be told, "Today we'll let Mom come in, but the next time you come, we'll have to let her wait for us out front." Caution should be given to the parent that the allegation should not be addressed. As the child and interviewer become more comfortable with each other, the parent should be urged to "fade" into the, background. At a suitable point, the interviewer should attempt to have the parent leave, bidding the child goodbye. It is becoming increasingly important relative to legal involvement that the child *not* be interviewed in the presence of the parent.

The interviewer must remember that the primary reason for the interview is to gather *independent* information from the child, not from the adult. The fear of contamination of the child's information must always be kept in mind (Jones & McQuiston, 1985; White & Quinn, 1988).

The Interview

Types of Evidence

The doll/abuse interview of White et al. (1987) has two basic parts: (1) free play and (2) doll evaluation. Information may be gathered in each which supports an allegation of abuse. In the minds of most mental health practitioners, each piece of information should be viewed with equal weight by the legal system, but this may not be true. Some courts are more likely to admit evidence gathered during the free-play session, as it is considered as totally spontaneously emitted from the child. This may be considered nonassertive behavior. On the other hand, behaviors (verbal and/or physical gestures) that are in response to specific questioning or to a particular situation (such as a structured doll interview) may be considered unspontaneous and may be ruled to be assertive in legal terms (see Myers, 1986). Because of the interpretation of the child abuse hearsay exception statutes of a number of states, however, frequently both types of information may be admitted in your particular locale. Each interviewer should be familiar with the legal standards to which evidence from these interviews will be subjected.

Free Play

The free-play part of the doll interview has several purposes. First is the establishment of rapport and defining of the relationship between the interviewer and child. The child needs to know that the interviewer will keep the child safe while not subjecting him or her to any medical procedures or harsh psychological treatment. The child needs to learn that the interviewer will maintain control of the session but will do so in a positive manner.

The second purpose of the free play is to have the interviewer informally assess the child's developmental levels in language usage, speech skills, cognitive abilities, and interactional skills. By gaining an understanding of the child's developmental status, the interviewer can then adjust the interview techniques (e.g., level of vocabulary in the questions) and set expectation levels for the child's responses. For instance, when the child demonstrates an articulation disorder, the interviewer should use the free-play situation to learn to "hear" the child's errors without making the child feel self-conscious about his or her problem.

The free-play period should be as long or as short as necessary to establish rapport and to gauge the child's abilities. This may be 5 minutes or 35. Meeting the goals of the free-play period is more important than counting the time. During the free-play situation, the dolls are in the background, and the child may elect to play with them. If so, the interviewer should allow the child freedom to explore and should record the child's behaviors and vocalizations. In some jurisdictions, the responses will be viewed as more credible and less likely subject to hearsay (Myers, 1986).

Doll Interview

Once rapport has been developed and the interviewer has gained an assessment of the child's developmental levels, the non-doll toys are placed out of reach of the child in order to minimize the child's desire to return to them during the doll interview. This is usually accomplished quite easily by saying, "We'll put these toys over here because now we are going to look at the dolls." If resistance is met, the interviewer should calmly but firmly put the toys out of the child's reach and direct the child to get one of the dolls. As it is the interviewer's difficult task to keep the child's attention on the dolls and given the anxiety the child may have concerning discussing his or her experiences, the environment must be arranged to optimize the doll interview. The environment includes the interviewer's ability to control the basic events of the interview.

After the non-doll toys are put aside, the interviewer introduces the anatomical dolls by directing the child's attention to them and saying, "These are special dolls that have parts like people." The child is then directed (not asked) to bring one of the dolls from the collection. Only one doll at a time should be examined. Once the child selects a doll, the child should be seated near the examiner, preferably on the floor, while the interviewer holds the doll. According to the Cleveland protocol, the following phases are then introduced:

Doll Identification. Three specific questions are asked about the doll presented and will be repeated whenever future dolls are examined:

1. "Is this a girl or boy doll?" Even if the child has selected an adult doll, we continue to use "boy" and "girl," as most preschoolers understand these sexual identity terms better than "man" and "woman" or "lady." The idea is to determine whether the child can put a sexual identity on the doll, not whether the child knows the words "man," "woman," or "lady."
2. "How do you know it is a ... doll?" This question is designed to help the interviewer understand further the classification system of sexual identification that the child uses.
3. "Who is this? Does this doll have a name?" This question is used to search for any particular identity the child may wish to impose on the doll. The interviewer must be very careful not to impose his or her own set of identities on the doll. For instance, the interviewer should never refer to a male doll as "daddy-doll" unless the child has previously done so.

Body Parts Identification and Function. Important in assessment of an allegation of sexual abuse is determining just what a child knows about body parts and his or her names for the parts and functions designated for each. Thus, with the doll still dressed, the interviewer begins evaluation of the child's knowledge by asking these questions of each major body part:

1. "What is this part?", "What do you call this part?", or "What's the name for this part?"
2. "What do we do with this "part?" or "What's this part for?"

The interviewer must accept and subsequently use the name given to each part. If a child refuses or resists naming of a body part or function, the interviewer should proceed with the next item without any negative comment or reaction. Insisting that a child answer is coercive. Care must be taken not to translate the child's labeling. For instance, the penis may be labeled the "weewee." The interviewer should never call it "penis" until a time the child does.

Neutral parts (hair, eyes, nose, mouth, ears, arms, hands, and fingers) are evaluated just as the sexual parts are for several reasons. First, there should be no apparent difference in the manner in which nonsexual and sexual body parts are presented, so as not to sensitize the child that the sexual parts are more exciting than the others. Second, by not immediately interviewing the child with respect to sexual parts, the child may become more comfortable with these dolls prior to being shown the more sensitive areas. Third, the interviewer should be able to assess further the child's developmental skills and willingness to respond to specific questions as these parts are identified. As a result, adjustments may be necessary in the manner of presentation of questioning. Fourth, experience has shown that it is not unusual that young children who have been sexually abused are often asked by the perpetrator to use one of the "neutral" parts in the sexual act.

After these neutral parts have been examined, the interviewer then states (not asks), "This doll's clothes come off. Let's take the doll's clothes off" as he or she begins to take off the shirt or blouse/dress. The child should be asked to help if he or she does not volunteer. It has been my experience that children are accustomed to undressing the dolls and do not resist this procedure. The interviewer should still maintain control of the doll and of the presentation of the body parts. After the shirt/blouse/dress is off, the interviewer points to the following parts and continues to seek the same information (identification, function): nipples, breasts, chest hair (male adult doll), bellybutton.

After these parts have been examined, the remaining clothing is removed. Once the underpants have been removed, the other body parts are examined: penis, clitoris, vagina, testicles, anus, legs, knees, feet. If the child happens to note some body part or demonstrates a function not on the check list or demonstrates a function, the interviewer should follow the child's lead as long as knowledge of the required parts is evaluated at a later time.

With successive dolls, the body part identification process can be abbreviated to avoid tedium. Attempts should be made, however, that each doll be identified by sex and, if possible, by social position in the child's scheme. It is important, however, to identify at least two nonsexual parts prior to the sexual parts and at least one nonsexual part after. All sexual parts should be asked on all dolls examined.

If a child becomes upset when being exposed to sexually relevant parts of the interview, the interviewer must decide what is the underlying cause: separation, fear of the interviewer, fear of others, reaction to the abuse memory, or some other factor. If a child wishes to leave the room, the interviewer should try to convince the child to stay for a little while more. In order to inhibit the child from learning that he or she can escape by crying, the interviewer should insist, "You can leave when you have quit crying." Under no circumstances should the child be told, "You can leave when you've told me who hurt you."

A minimum of three dolls should be examined: 1 adult male, 1 adult female, 1 child doll of the child's own gender. If, after the third selection, this requirement has not been met, the interviewer must insist on continuing. The interviewer can direct the child to pick a doll based on its general location (e.g., "Let's look at a doll in the back"), but should take care *not* to designate a particular doll or role or gender. After the requirement of the three designated dolls is met, the other dolls may be evaluated if the child seems to want to do so or as it seems appropriate based on the information provided by the child. Surprising as it may seem, many children demand to evaluate all eight dolls!

Once the evaluation of each doll is completed, the interviewer should place the *undressed* doll to the side and direct the child to get another doll of his or her choice. The dolls are to remain undressed until the end of the interview. If the child wishes to redress them at the end of the interview, the interviewer should cooperate in this activity.

Abuse Evaluation: General Body Contact Questions. Once body part function and identity have been completed, the next step is (a) to address general issues of the child's having been touched or hurt on his or her body or having done so to someone else's body, and (b) to have these concepts addressed relative to the child's specific body parts. Both nonsexual and sexual body parts are evaluated. Following are some specific questions that may be used but do not have to be considered a required, all-inclusive list. The interviewer should feel free to ask his or her own questions or to rephrase these, as long as they fulfill the aforementioned requirements of independence (White & Quinn, 1988). The dolls might be used as props to assist children in demonstrating their verbal responses regarding general body contact experiences.

1. Have you ever been touched on any part of your body?
2. Have you ever touched a part on anybody else's body?
3. Have you ever been hurt on any part of your body?
4. Have you hurt a part on anybody else's body?
5. Has anyone done something you didn't like to your body?
6. Have you ever been asked to do something you didn't like to someone else's body?
7. Has anyone put anything on or in any part of your body?
8. Have you ever been without your clothes?
9. Has anyone else asked you to take off your clothes?
10. Have you seen anyone else without clothes?
11. Has anyone asked you not to tell something about your body?
12. Has anyone said that something bad might happen to you or to someone else if you told some secret about your body?
13. Has anyone ever kissed you?
14. Has anyone ever kissed you when you didn't want them to?
15. Has anyone taken your picture?
16. Has anyone ever taken your picture without your clothes on?

It is expected that some of the responses to these questions will receive a positive response. *All of the positive responses should be fully evaluated for the specifics supporting the answer.* Care must be taken not to use leading and/or coercive techniques to obtain the details (White & Quinn, 1988). It is also very important that special care be taken to delineate the differences between hygienic touching and abuse contact.

Abuse Evaluation: Specific Body Part Questions. The interviewer should then ask whether the child has been *touched, hurt, or had anything put in or on* a number of his or her body parts, both nonsexual and sexual. Assessment of positive responses should be performed as described previously.

Closing the Interview

After the interviewer feels that he or she has obtained as much information as possible or that the child has reached his or her limit of questioning for the day, the interviewer must decide whether to encourage free play, which would relax the child prior to ending the interview. Most children, however, want to end it without further play. The child should then be told whether they will be meeting again, followed by the suggestion, "Let's find...." The child is returned to the responsible adult who brought him or her, and, if necessary, the next appointment is confirmed. No information concerning the content of the interview is conveyed to the adult, but comments such as, "Julie worked very hard today," are appropriate.

Number of Interviews

White et al. (1987) recommend a minimum of two interviews in order to assess consistency of the child's information and to allow for the child to feel comfortable enough to reveal as much information as he or she wishes. If the child balks at the second or third interview because "I've already done this" or "I've told you already." the interviewer should calmly state, "But I need to hear again what you said." This is usually sufficient to gain the child's cooperation. Consistency of the complaint is assessed based on the child's responses over the two to three interviews. At each interview, the interviewer should follow the child's answers and not introduce other materials. Only when information seems inconsistent should the interviewer introduce material from a previous interview, such as "Last time you told me that X touched you. This time you said Y. I'm confused. Tell me again what X did and what Y did."

General Concepts Regarding the Doll Interview

Responsiveness of the Child

In general child interviewing, the clinician who receives little or no response from the child when questions are posed will ask the question in other ways until an answer is given. In this protocol, if the child does not respond to the interviewer's directions or questions or says that he or she does not know, it is recommended that the interviewer continue to the next item without making any negative response. Perhaps early in the interview, the examiner may wish to "push" the child minimally, as the child may be nervous or shy, but this should be done sparingly. The child may be given the option of "If you remember later, let me know." The child should never be coerced into answering, even in a gentle fashion. The interviewer should recognize that too much pressure on the child may result in one of several negative consequences:

1. The already anxious child may cease to make *any* response.
2. The manipulative child may realize that he or she is able to irritate the interviewer and may increase the rate of his or her refusals in an effort to have the session terminated.
3. Once the data are presented to the judicial system, it may be argued that the child was answering under duress or coercion.

   All answers should be accepted from the child, and no answers should be supplied (White & Quinn, 1988).

Clarification of Language

The interviewer should consistently repeat responses of the child. This is especially important if the session is being videotaped or observed, as the children's voices are sometimes
difficult to record or the very young child may have such immature language that he or she
is difficult to understand. In repeating the child's responses, the interviewer should be
especially careful not to suggest answers. Attempts are to be made to imitate the same
sound as the child. This technique is very useful in allowing the child the opportunity to
correct the interviewer if a misinterpretation has been made. Many children very easily
correct the interviewer with, "No, I said…"

Teaching Aspects

The doll/abuse interview is not designed to teach body parts and/or function nor is it to be
used as prevention education. The interviewer must remember that it is a *data-gathering*
process.

Behaviors of the Interviewer

The interviewer must acknowledge that regardless of what he or she does, the act of interviewing the child has the potential of changing the child's memory for the information
being sought. Every effort needs to be made for the interviewer not to introduce information and/or behave in ways that would unnecessarily influence the child's data (see Quinn,
White, & Santilli, 1989, for a fuller discussion).

Data Recording

Data from a doll/abuse interview need to be preserved in as close a state to the original as
possible. Videotaping is the optimal form of data recording. While these videotapes may
not be useful as actual evidence in court due to the lack of guarantees according to the U.S.
Constitution (Chaney, 1985; Colby & Colby, 1987; Harrison, 1987; Krause. 1984; Mac-
Farlane, 1985), they may be useful in keeping the child from being interviewed by multiple individuals. They also preserve the disclosure and allow others to evaluate the actual
interview methods to determine contamination issues, if any.

   If videotaping is not feasible, audiotaping is the next best thing. With audiotaping, however, the interviewer must keep notes of behavioral responses to make the record complete
as possible.

   If neither of these recording methods is possible, then having a trained observer watching through a one-way mirror and taking detailed notes should be considered. In the
absence of either videotaping availability or one-way mirror observations, the investigators must rely on their own ability to record (in writing) the information as the interview
unfolds or to have someone in the background doing so. Simultaneous notes are critical,
especially if the case reaches the judicial system. Recording the events after the interview
is not an acceptable method of data recording in these cases. Too much memory is lost
even in a span of 30 minutes.

Diagnosis of Child Sexual Abuse

The diagnosis of child sexual abuse by those using doll interviews continues to be debated.
The basic issue is whether the interviewer has the right and/or responsibility to make such

a diagnosis in the interview report and/or on the witness stand (Bersoff, 1986; Duquette, 1981; Melton, Petrila, Polythress, & Slobogin, 1987; Weithorn, 1987). Most legally oriented leaders in this field suggest that it is the judge or jury who must make this diagnostic decision. The witness is only assisting by providing them with uncontaminated data. Included in this uncontaminated data should be a complete accounting of what was done and how the child responded. If such data were gathered with minimal contamination, then they may be useful in court proceedings.

In actuality, the interviewer who testifies may not have a choice, as the court may force (through threat of contempt) the interviewer to render an opinion regarding a diagnosis of child sexual abuse. If such a diagnosis is made, the interviewer using data from a doll interview must be exceptionally careful that a complete evaluation has been done so that more than just doll information is offered as a basis for the diagnosis.

LEGAL RAMIFICATIONS

Like it or not, some results of doll interviews will end up in judicial proceedings. They have consistently been judged to be appropriate tools in preparation of a witness *(State v. Eggert,* 1984), in the legal consideration of the dolls as being anatomically "correct" *(Commonwealth* v. *Reid,* 1987; *Cleaveland v. State,* 1986), and as props during a victim's court testimony *(Kehinde v. Commonwealth,* 1986; *People v. Rich,* 1987). Depending on the jurisdiction, they have variously been accepted or rejected as a "psychological technique" *(In re Amber B. v. Ron B.,* 1987; *Rinesmith v. Williams,* 1985). As part of a more complete evaluation, the way in which they have been used (e.g., repeated questioning, coercive techniques) (In re J. H., 1987; In *the matter of X v. Syme,* 1986) has been questioned. Dolls have been used in court proceedings that involved the following types of people: nondisabled individuals between 2.5 and 15 years of age; a 5-year-old deaf boy *(In re J. H.,* 1987); a 31 -year-old mute woman *(People v. Spencer,* 1983); a 73year-old aphasic man *(People v. Herring,* 1987); mentally retarded children and adults *(People v. Rich,* 1987; *State v. DeLeonardo,* 1986); children and adult Down's syndrome victims *(Matter of Welfare of S.* J., 1985; *State v. Brown,* 1986).

The rules of evidence governing doll interviews frequently falls to that of hearsay. Because of the multiple criteria for hearsay and the many ways in which the criteria are interpreted, evidence from doll interviews have been both accepted and rejected as part of hearsay statements fulfilling the criteria of excited utterances, medical diagnosis, the residual hearsay exception, and the tender years' exception. Each practitioner should be aware of the appellate decisions in his or her state.

RESEARCH NEEDS AND AN ADVISORY NOTE

As noted in the recent review of clinical and research findings on anatomical dolls (White & Santilli, 1988), many aspects of dolls should be studied, such as the following: (a) characteristics of the children being interviewed (socioeconomic status, race, type of abuse, culture, emotional status, intellectual abilities); (b) characteristics of the dolls (racial attributions, detail of physical characteristics, number present in the interviewing room); (c) presentation method (structured protocol, free play, dolls alone or presented with other toys); (d) characteristics of the interviewer (matching victim's gender with interviewer, or interviewer's level of training); (e) characteristics of the interview (individuals present, location); (f) types of questions (nonleading versus leading). It will be many years before information on these issues will be presented in a manner useful to clinicians.

In the meantime, those using dolls must be vitally aware that the results of their interview may well result in legal action against an individual. In contrast to many of the other interviewing techniques described in this book, the doll/abuse interview is designed specifically to provide data to the judicial system–data that are as unbiased as possible and that can serve as evidentiary material in all types of court settings. Until the research data are available that will help the interviewer to make a more studied decision about the data the child is presenting, it is imperative that doll data be collected in the most objective fashion if the courts are to accept them as reliable and as sufficiently trustworthy to make them acceptable in judicial settings.

REFERENCES

American Academy of Child and Adolescent Psychiatry Committee on Rights and Legal Matters. (1988). Guidelines for the clinical evaluation of child sexual abuse. *Journal of the American Academy of Child and Adolescent Psychiatry, 27,* 655–657.

Benedek, E. P., & Schetky, D. (1987). Problems in validating allegations of sexual abuse: Part 2. Clinical evaluation. *Journal of the American Academy of Child and Adolescent Psychiatry, 26,* 916–921

Bersoff, D. N. (1986). Psychologists and the judicial system: Broader perspectives. *Law and Human Behavior, 10,* 151– 165.

Boat, B., & Everson, M. (1986). *Using anatomical dolls: Guidelines for interviewing young children in sexual abuse investigations.* Chapel Hill, NC: University of North Carolina.

Boat, B., & Everson, M. (1988). Use of anatomical dolls among professionals in sexual abuse evaluations. *Child Abuse and Neglect, 12,* 171–179.

Chaney, S. (1985). Videotaped interviews with child abuse victims: The search for truth under a Texas procedure. In J. Bulkley (Ed.), *National policy conference an legal reforms in child sexual abuse cases,* pp. 209–217. Washington, DC: American Bar Association National Legal Resource Center for Child Advocacy and protection.

Cleaveland v. State, 490 N.E. 2d 1140 (1986).

Colby. 1. C., & Colby, D. N. (1987). Videotaped interviews in child abuse cam: The Texas example. *Child Welfare,* 66,25–34.

Commonwealth v. Reid, 511 N.E. 2d 331 (1987).

Duquette, D. (1981). The expert witness in child abuse and neglect. An interdisciplinary process. *Child Abuse and Neglect,* 5.325–334.

Friedemann, V., & Morgan, M. (1985). *Interviewing sexual abuse victim using anatomical dolls: The professional's guidebook.* Eugene, OR: Shamrock Press.

Gabriel R. M. (1995). Anatomically correct dolls in the diagnosis of sexual abuse of children. *Journal of the Melanie Klein Society,* 3, 40–5 1.

Goodman, G., & Aman, C., (1987, April). Children's use of anatomically correct dolls to report an event. In M. Steward (Chair), *Evaluation of suspected child abuse: Developmental, clinical, and legal perspectives on the use of anatomically correct dolls.* Symposium conducted at the meeting of the Society for Research in Child Development, Baltimore, MD.

Goodwin. J., Sahd, D., & Rada, R. T. (1982). False accusations and false denials of incest: Clinical myths and clinical realities. In J. Goodwin (Ed.). *Sexual abase: Incest victim and their families (pp.* 17–26). Boston: John Wright.

Green, A. (1986). True and false allegations of sexual abuse in child custody disputes. *Journal of the American Academy of Child Psychiatry,* 25, 449–456.

Harrison, D. M. (1987). Guidelines for the use of videotape in the validation of child sexual abuse. *American Journal of Forensic Psychology,* 5, 18–20.

In the matter of X v. Syme, 714 p. 2d 13 (1986).

In re Amber B. v. Ron B., 236 Cal. Rptr. 623 (1987).

In re J. H., 505 N.E. 2d 1360 (1987).

Jampole, L., & Weber, M. (1987). An assessment of the behavior of sexually abused and nonsexually abused children with anatomically correct dolls. *Child Abuse and Neglect, 11,* 197–192.

Jones, D. P. H., & McQuiston, M. (1985). *Interviewing the sexually abused child.* Denver: Kempe Center.

Kehinde v. Commonwealth, 338 S.E. 2d 356 (1986).

Krause, R. (1994). Videotape: CCTV help child abuse victims tell their story but legal problems remain. *Law Enforcement Technology, Nov.,* 16–18.

MacFarlane, K. (1985). Diagnostic evaluations and the use of videotapes in child sexual abuse cases. *University of Miami Law Review, 40,* 135–166.

MacFarlane. K., & Krebs. S. (1986). Techniques of interviewing and evidence gathering. In K. MacFarlane & J. Waterman (Eds.), *Sexual abuse of young children: Evaluation and treatment* (pp. 67–100). New York: Guilford.

Matter of the Welfare of S. J., 367 N.W. 2d 651 (1985).

Melton, G. B., Petrila, J., Poythress, N. G., Jr., & Slobogin, C. (1987). *Psychological evaluations for the court: A handbook for mental health professionals and lawyers.* New York: Guilford.

Myers, J. E. B. (1986). Hearsay statements by the child abuse victim. *Baylor Law Review, 38,* 775–916

People v. Herring, 515 N.Y.S. 2d 954 (1987).

People v. Rich, 520 N.Y.S. 2d 911 (1987).

People v. Spencer, 457 N.E. 2d 473 (1983).

Quinn, K. M., White, S., & Santilli G. (1989). Influences of an interviewer's behaviors in child sexual abuse investigations. *Bulletin of the American Academy of Psychiatry and the Law, 17,* 45–52.

Rinesmith v. Williams, 376 N.W. 2d 139 (1985).

Sgroi, S. M., Porter, F. S., & Blick, L. C. (1982). Validation of child sexual abuse. In S. M. Sgroi (Ed.), *Handbook of clinical intervention in child sexual abuse* (pp. 3940). Lexington, MA, Heath

Sivan, A., Schor, D., Koeppl, G. K., & Noble, L. D. (1988). Interactions of normal children with anatomically correct dolls. *Child Abuse and Neglect, 12,* 295–304.

State v. Brown, 400 N.W. 2d 74 (1986).

State v. DeLeonardo, 340 S.E. 2d 350 (1986).

State v. Eggert, 358 N.W. 2d 156 (1984).

Weithorn, L. (1987). Psychological consultation in divorce custody litigation: Ethical considerations. In L. Weithorn. (Ed.), *Psychological and child custody determinations: Knowledge, roles and expertise* (pp. 182–209). Lincoln: University of Nebraska Press.

White. S. (1988). Should investigatory use of anatomical dolls be defined by the courts. *Journal of Interpersonal Violence, 3,* 471–475.

White, S., & Quinn, K. M. (1988). Investigatory independence in child sexual abuse evaluations: Conceptual considerations. *Bulletin of the American Academy of Psychiatry and the Law, 16,* 269–278.

White, S., & Santilli, G. (1988). A review of clinical practices and research data on anatomical dolls. *Journal of Interpersonal Violence, 3,* 430–442

White, S., Santilli. G., & Quinn, K. M. (1988). Child evaluator's roles in child sexual abuse assessments. In E. B. Nicholson & J. Bulkley (Eds.), *Sexual abuse allegations in custody and visitation cases* (pp. 94–105 Washington, DO American Bar Association

White, S., Strom, G., Santilli, G., & Halpin, B. (1986). Interviewing young children with anatomically correct dolls. *Child Abuse and Neglect, 10,* 519–529.

White, S., Strom, G., Santilli, G., & Quinn, K. M. (1987*). Clinical guidelines for interviewing young children with anatomically correct dolls.* Unpublished manuscript, Case Western Reserve University School of Medicine, Cleveland, OH.

Yates, A., & Terr, L. (1988a). Debate forum: Anatomically correct dolls: Should they be used as a basis for expert testimony? *Journal of the American Academy of Child and Adolescent Psychiatry, 27,* 254–257.

Yates, A., & Terr, L. (1988b). Debate forum (Issue continued): Anatomically correct dolls: Should they be used as a basis for expert testimony? *Journal of the American Academy of Child and Adolescent Psychiatry, 27,* 387–388.

Chapter 8

LINKING ASSESSMENT TO INTERVENTION FOR CHILDREN WITH DEVELOPMENTAL DISABILITIES OR AT-RISK FOR DEVELOPMENTAL DELAY: THE DEVELOPMENTAL PLAY ASSESSMENT (DPA) INSTRUMENT

Karin Lifter

OVERVIEW

The Developmental Play Assessment (DPA) Instrument[1] (Lifter, Edwards, Avery, Anderson, & Sulzer-Azaroff, 1988; Lifter, 1996) was developed to assess the play activities of children with developmental delays and disabilities in order to determine what they know and what they are ready to learn. This information is then used for the design and implementation of individualized play intervention programs to facilitate the children's progress in development. Thus, the primary purpose of the DPA is its use for planning educational programs, although it can also be used for screening and diagnostic purposes.

Two premises underlie the DPA. First, for young children who have difficulty learning, assessment and intervention for developments in play are as important as assessment and intervention for developments in language and social interaction. Children talk and interact about what they know, and attention to play in intervention programs affords opportunities for expanding children's knowledge base about objects and events, which contributes to their communicative and social interactions. Second, interventions in play activities are enhanced when assessment takes into account the children's developmental

[1] The author wishes to thank the children, families, and staff of the May Center for Early Education, Arlington, MA, and the May Institute, Inc., South Harwich, MA, for supporting the study of play in children developing more slowly or differently from their peers. The author is also deeply grateful to her students—Sandra Pierce-Jordan, Lisa Senavinin Powell, Cathleen Small, and Stephany Woodward—for their careful reading of earlier versions of this chapter and for their dedication to the issues and studies reviewed here.

levels in play. Assessment that distinguishes among the kinds of activities that a child knows, the kinds of activities that a child is in the process of learning, and the kinds of activities that appear to be developmentally too difficult for a child at a particular time, allow for the identification of developmentally based target activities (i.e., categories of activities the child is in the process of learning) that should facilitate learning.

These premises are supported by a theoretical framework that views play as serving both expressive and interpretive functions in development (Bloom, 1993; Lifter & Bloom, 1998). Through play, children express and make manifest what they know and are thinking about. As such, play as expression forms the foundation for using play for assessment. At the same time, play is also "a way for children to embrace and learn about objects, events, and relations in the world through interpreting the results of their own actions and by revising what they know about the world" (Lifter & Bloom, 1998, p. 161). Consequently, play as interpretation underlies the rationale for interventions in play to facilitate progress in development.

The play actions that are identified and quantified in the DPA are conceptualized from a cognitive/developmental perspective. This perspective allows for inferences about the developments in the structure, organization, and content of knowledge, in combination with developments in the symbolic capacity and in memory, that underlie what children are able to hold in mind and think about for expression and interpretation. Structure and organization have to do with the more general knowledge of objects, such as the knowledge that objects are separate entities that can be acted upon, can be moved from place to place, can be found, and can be related to other objects and people. Content centers on the more specific knowledge of objects that includes the particular physical and conventional properties of individual objects and how those properties can be realized in various relationships with other objects and with people with whom the child interacts. Finally, the ability to hold in mind and think about objects and events that are increasingly discrepant from the immediately perceptible context requires developments in memory and recall that are expressed through play activities (Bloom, 1993).

The categories of play activities that are examined in the DPA are presented in Table 8–1 in terms of a developmental progression. The backbone of this progression was derived from the developmental sequence of play categories identified by Lifter and Bloom (1989) during the transition to language, which was then integrated with sequences reported by other researchers to span the developmental period from late infancy through the preschool years (Belsky & Most, 1981; Fenson, Kagan, Kearsley & Zelazo, 1976; Fenson & Ramsay, 1980; Garvey, 1977; Hill & McCune-Nicolich, 1981; Lowe, 1975; Nicolich, 1977). Actions during this period typically progress from simple actions that are applied to all objects (e.g., mouthing all objects), to activities that differentiate among objects (i.e., rolling a ball; squeezing a soft toy); relate objects to one another in general ways (i.e., taking things in and out of containers); relate objects to one another in specific ways that take into account the physical and conventional properties of objects in relation to one another (i.e., stacking a set of nesting cups; stirring with a spoon in a cup); relate objects to the self and to others (e.g., taking a drink from a cup; extending the cup to a caregiver or a doll for a drink); combine actions into sequences (i.e., feeding doll, then putting it to bed); substitute one object for another (e.g., putting a bowl on head for a hat); attribute animacy to doll figures (i.e., moving play figure to load blocks into a truck); and, finally, engage other children in assuming roles in sociodramatic and fantasy play (e.g., playing house; pretending to be aliens).

Table 8–1. Sequence and definitions of play categories used in the Developmental Play Assessment (DPA)

Level	Categories	Definitions
I	*Indiscriminate Actions*	All objects are treated alike (e.g., all objects are mouthed)
II	*Discriminative Actions on Single Objects*	Differentiates among objects, preserving their physical or conventional characteristics (e.g., rolls round beads, squeezes stuffed animal)
	Takes-Apart Combinations	Separates configurations of objects (e.g., takes all pieces out of puzzle)
III	*Presentation Combinations*	Recreates combinations of objects according to their presentation configuration (e.g., puts puzzle pieces into puzzle; nests the nesting cups)
	General Combinations	Creates combinations of objects that result in simple, nonspecific configurations such as container/contained relations (e.g., puts beads & puzzle pieces in cup)
	Pretend Self	Relates objects to self, indicating a pretend quality to the action (e.g., brings empty cup to mouth to drink)
IV	*Specific Combinations (Physical Attributes)*	Preserves unique physical characteristics of objects in the configuration (e.g., stacks nesting cups; strings beads)
V	*Child-as-Agent*	Extends familiar actions to doll figures, with child as agent of the activity (e.g., extends cup to doll's mouth)
	Specific Combinations (Conventional Attributes)	Preserves unique conventional characteristics of object in the configuration (e.g., places cup on saucer; places string of beads on self)
VI	*Single-Scheme Sequences*	Extends same familiar action to two or more figures (e.g., extends cup to baby doll, to stuffed lamb, to interactant)
	Substitutions	Uses one object to stand in place for another (e.g., puts bowl on head for a hat)
VII	*Doll-as-Agent*	Moves doll figures as if they are capable of action (e.g., moves figure to load blocks into a truck; puts mirror into doll's hand to see itself)
	Multischeme Sequences	Extends different actions to same figure (e.g., feeds doll with spoon, wipes it with cloth, then puts it to bed)
VIII	*Sociodramatic Play*	Adopts various familiar roles in play theme (e.g., plays house, assigning the various roles)
	Thematic Fantasy Play	Adopts roles of fantasy characters (e.g., plays "Superman" or "Wonderwoman," assigning the various roles)

Researchers and practitioners have often grouped the foregoing, finely differentiated categories of play into the more global categories of manipulative and pretend play, which reflect the Piagetian stages of sensorimotor development and symbolic development, respectively (Piaget, 1962). Although useful at a descriptive level, it will be argued here that these global groupings are too general for assessment and intervention purposes since there are many developmentally ordered play categories within each global category. Instead, intervention that has the goal of facilitating learning requires assessment procedures that fine-tune the selection of target activities based on developmental readiness.

For the DPA, a 30-minute sample of a child's naturally occurring, unstructured play activities, observed in the presence of a familiar adult and familiar surroundings, is video-recorded. The child's performance is evaluated independently of the child's language abilities, making it particularly suitable for children whose disabilities include language delays and language disorders. The observation is first analyzed to determine the frequency of different activities. These frequencies are then organized into their respective categories to determine the frequency and variety of activities within each play category in the developmental progression. The DPA assumes that play categories that are represented by a reasonable frequency and variety of examples constitute categories that the child knows. In turn, categories that are represented by activities that occur infrequently, but are categories subsequent to the high-frequency categories in the developmental progression, constitute quantitative criteria for categories of activities the child is in the process of learning. Finally, the categories of play that are not represented by activities in a sample of play are most likely categories that the child has not learned at that point in time. In this way, quantitative criteria are applied to a sample of play activities to determine what the child knows, what the child is in the process of learning, and what is beyond the child's developmental level at a point in time.

The purpose of this chapter is to describe the Developmental Play Assessment (DPA) Instrument (Lifter et al., 1988; Lifter, 1996) as a means for evaluating the structure, organization and content of a child's knowledge of objects and events, and, more particularly, as a tool for linking assessment to intervention. This chapter begins with a rationale for (1) attention to play as a target of assessment, and (2) linking play assessment to intervention, for young children with developmental delays and disabilities. The construction of the DPA is presented next, followed by a description of the procedures, with two case studies as illustrations. Then follows a brief review of the PROJECT PLAY studies that demonstrate links from assessment to intervention. The chapter concludes with some caveats, limitations, and future directions for using the DPA.

RATIONALE FOR ATTENTION TO PLAY AS A TARGET FOR ASSESSMENT AND INTERVENTION

The rationale for attention to play as a target of assessment and intervention is discussed in terms of the importance of play in young children's lives, the limitations in play identified in children with developmental delays and disabilities, and the nature of different intervention efforts in children's play.

Importance of Play

The importance of play in children's lives is supported by its pervasiveness in childhood, the opportunities it provides for learning, and the developmental changes it reveals. Given any opportunity, by themselves or with peers, children will play, and their play takes many forms (Fein, 1979; Garvey, 1977; Rubin, Fein, & Vandenberg, 1983). Play is: mouthing objects; tapping objects together to make a sound; moving beads and blocks from one container to another and back again; feeding and bathing dolls; rolling cars and trucks along a highway; splashing at the water table with peers; engaging in rough-and-tumble play in the playground; and assigning and taking on roles in a game of "house." According to Rubin et al. (1983), the defining features of play have traditionally included several dispositional characteristics. Play is: intrinsically motivated; characterized by attention to means; guided by "what can I do with the objects"; generally referred to as pretense; free from externally imposed rules; and requiring active engagement (pp. 698–699). Through play "children learn societal roles, rules, and values," and they learn to adapt to their environments (Rubin et al., 1983, p. 735).

From the cognitive/developmental perspective, play activities have historically been regarded as a window on what children know or feel (i.e., "a happy display of known actions" Piaget, 1962, p. 93; "the child's natural medium of self-expression." Axline, 1947, p. 9), which supports their expressive function. Play as expression is derived from the Piagetian notion of play as assimilation (Piaget, 1962), in which the child incorporates new information onto existing knowledge structures, and can therefore happily display "known actions," reflecting "the child's level of development" (Rubin et al., 1983, p. 705). Play behaviors reflect a knowledge and experiential base that includes a cognitive organization about objects in general, and how they can be related to other objects and people, and also knowledge about the particular properties of objects and particular relationships that exist between and among objects and people (Bloom, 1993).

Because play is so easily identifiable in children's activities, many researchers have described and organized play into developmental taxonomies (Belsky & Most, 1981; Fenson et al., 1976; Fenson & Ramsay, 1980; Garvey, 1977; Hill & McCune-Nicolich, 1981; Lifter & Bloom, 1989; Lowe, 1975; Nicolich, 1977; Odom, 1981). These taxonomies describe children's play as typically progressing from simple manipulation of objects in infancy, to pretend play schemes for toddlerhood, and finally to sociodramatic and fantasy play during the preschool years (Garvey, 1977; Nicolich, 1977; Piaget, 1954, 1962; Rubin et al., 1983; Smilansky, 1968). Moreover, these changes appear to be "little affected by situational or cultural variations" (Rubin et al., 1983, p. 715).

Many researchers have used these taxonomies to make inferences about developmental changes. For example, several researchers have noted a marked increase in symbolic activities between 15 and 18 months of age (Fenson et al., 1976; Lowe, 1975). Indeed, many of these taxonomies form the basis for a number of play assessment scales (e.g., the Developmental Scale of Infant Play, by Belsky & Most, 1981, presented in Vondra & Belsky, 1991; the Symbolic Play Test by Lowe & Costello, reported in Power & Radcliffe, 1991; the Symbolic Play Scale, by Westby, 1980, reported in Westby, 1991; and the DPA, reported by Lifter et al., 1988).

Researchers have also identified developmental relationships between and among play, language, and social development (Bates, Begnigni, Bretherton, Camaioni, & Volterra, 1979; Beeghly, Weiss-Perry, & Cicchetti, 1990; Bloom, Lifter, & Broughton, 1985; Fein, 1979; Guralnick & Groom, 1987; Lifter, 1982; Lifter & Bloom, 1989; Lowe, 1975; Kennedy, Sheridan, Radlinski, & Beeghly, 1991; McCune-Nicolich, 1981; Parten, 1932; Rubin et al., 1983; Sinclair, 1970; Ungerer & Sigman, 1981; Wing, Gould, Yeates, & Brierly, 1977). For example, McCune (1995) identified relationships between categories of symbolic play and early words, word combinations, and rule-governed combinations in language. Lifter and Bloom (1989) reported that changes in categories of thematic relationships between objects were related to two transitions in language (i.e., First Words and the Vocabulary Spurt). Bloom, Beckwith, Capatides, and Hafitz (1988) provided evidence that these same changes in play were related to shifts in language meanings from presentational and action meanings to evident and anticipated meanings.

Play activities are also related to developments in social interactions. For example, Howes and Matheson (1992) reported that the pattern of play forms and the amount of time spent employing more complex play forms were positively related to indices of social competence, from infancy through the preschool period. Pierce-Jordan and Lifter (1998) identified a covariation between play and social coordination; the most complex levels of play observed in preschoolers' play tended to occur outside of episodes of social coordination.

In sum, play activities are pervasive in children's lives, appear to transcend culture, and reveal developmental changes in children's knowledge about objects and events. Moreover, play, language, and social competence/interaction are related and mutually supportive in development.

Limitations in Play for Children with Developmental Disabilities

Several studies reported that children with developmental disabilities do not appear to develop play activities to the same extent as children developing without disabilities. Along with differences in the frequency and variety of play activities, and a predominance of manipulative activities, pretend play and the typical activities of the preschool-age child are limited and often nonexistent in populations of children with disabilities (Fewell & Kaminski, 1988; Hill & McCune-Nicolich, 1981; Malone, Stoneham, & Langone, 1994; Quinn & Rubin, 1984; Rogers, 1988; Sigman & Mundy, 1987; Ungerer & Sigman, 1981; Wing et al., 1977). These children with developmental delays and disabilities often do not appear to be intrinsically motivated to move forward in their play to developmentally more advanced levels. A further problem is that although the children may be competent at certain play activities and engage in these activities with interest and enthusiasm, the relatively simple quality of their activities may go unnoticed or be confusing to caregivers and teachers. As a result, it is difficult for caregivers and teachers to know how to engage children in play activities beyond highlighting what the children are attending to and appear to be doing.

These children's limitations in play and their difficulties in moving to and sustaining more advanced forms of play may be due to their difficulties in learning in general. As a result, play as a vehicle for learning about objects and events, whether at a concrete or a symbolic level, will most likely be restricted.

Not surprisingly, these children's restrictions in play are often manifested in, and further restricted by their difficulties in language and social interaction (Hill & McCune-Nicolich, 1981; Lahey, 1988). Indeed, because preschoolers with developmental disabilities are often delayed in language and social skills, programming is usually centered on language and social goals (Hart & Risley, 1975; Strain, 1985; Strain & Odom, 1986; Warren & Gazdag, 1990), with play activities often used as the activity base for their implementation (Bricker & Cripe, 1992; Lahey, 1988; McGee, Krantz, & McClannahan, 1985; Rogers, Herbison, Lewis, Pantone, & Reis, 1986; Warren, 1992). Although these approaches are used widely, their success may be compromised, in part, by the children's limited abilities in play. For instance, if these children do not fully know about the particular properties of the play objects being employed, the symbolic qualities of these objects, and the relationships of these objects to other objects and people, the children may not be able to attend to, engage in, or understand the play activities that are being used to enhance their language and social development.

The foregoing factors suggest that goals for preschoolers with developmental disabilities should include attention to play *per se* in addition to language and social goals. First, play is a knowledge base in its own right. Second, because developments in play, language, and social interaction are related in development, attention to play is as important as attention to developments in language and social interaction in planning educational programs for children who have difficulty learning.

Play Intervention Studies

Research centered on teaching children to play has taken two broad directions, known as the play training studies and the play intervention studies. The play training studies centered on helping preschoolers with environmental disadvantages (i.e., poverty) make gains in pretense and sociodramatic play, and were spearheaded by Smilansky (1968). Through group activities in classrooms, children were taught to engage in sociodramatic play, and such training enabled them to make gains in social participation to be more similar to their middle-class peers. Many other studies followed, and some even demonstrated positive changes in the children's language abilities (e.g., Lovinger, 1974; Saltz, Dixon, & Johnson, 1977).

The play intervention studies, in contrast, centered on teaching children with developmental disabilities (i.e., children with mental retardation and children with autism) to engage in the play activities of their nondisabled peers. The goals of these studies were not sociodramatic play or social participation *per se,* but play construed more globally as age-appropriate activities for young children. It is this broad line of investigation represented by the play intervention studies that forms the background of the DPA and its links to intervention.

In the play intervention studies, one or another of three approaches has been taken: teaching play activities to compete with the occurrence of children's maladaptive behaviors; teaching play activities to increase children's prosocial behaviors; or teaching play activities that take into account the developmental relevance of the activities being taught. These approaches were formulated largely within a behavioral perspective, although they differed on how the objectives for intervention were identified. They also differed, most specifically, on whether or not systematic assessment procedures were used to identify play goals, and if so, if assessment included attention to the developmental relevance of the goals. They all provided support for the significance of direct intervention in the play activities of children with developmental disabilities.

In the first approach, specific play activities were taught to children who had high levels of maladaptive behaviors with the expectation that the learned play activities would compete with the occurrence of the problematic behaviors. Such interventions were usually accomplished by selecting a variety of appealing toys and directly teaching the children play activities with these toys (Ballard & Medland, 1986; Eason, White, & Newsom, 1982; Haring, 1985; Moran & Whitman, 1985; Stahmer & Schreibman, 1992; Wehman, 1975). In short, the objectives for intervention were determined based on what could be done with appealing toys, and systematic play assessment procedures were not employed. Despite the difficulties in teaching play skills to these children, the studies demonstrated the value of this approach in terms of enhancing skills (e.g., Rogers, et al., 1986) and diminishing maladaptive behaviors (e.g., Eason et al., 1982; Stahmer & Schreibman, 1992).

In the second approach, intervention studies focused on teaching play activities as a form of prosocial behaviors for children with skill deficits, given that play is a natural activity for young children. These studies included teaching the particular properties of objects to children with developmental delays (Haring, 1985), teaching object play and/or symbolic play to children with different developmental disabilities (Fox & Hanline, 1993; Kim, Lombardino, Rothman, & Vinson, 1989), and teaching symbolic play, sociodramatic play scripts, or sociodramatic play activities to children with autism (Goldstein & Cisar, 1992; Stahmer, 1995; Thorp, Stahmer, & Schreibman, 1995). The objectives for intervention appeared to be determined based on a general knowledge of what children do when they play rather than systematic assessment of play, which resulted in a focus on the broad categories of manipulative and symbolic play activities.

In the third approach, developmental relevance was incorporated directly or indirectly into the identification of target activities. In some of these studies, systematic developmental assessment procedures were used. In terms of an indirect approach to developmental assessment, the success of several of the foregoing studies can be explained, in part, according to the developmental relevance of the play activities that were taught to the participating children. The approach is indirect because it is based on *post hoc* analyses of the qualitative nature of the targeted activities in relation to the stated abilities of the participating children. For example, the children in Haring's (1985) study were reported to have considerable developmental delays and were selected as participants because they displayed low rates of object manipulation as well as minimal use of language (e.g., some words). The activities that Haring (1985) taught to these children centered on the particular properties of objects, such as "flying" an airplane. Because activities that express the particular properties of objects are among the earliest object-related play activities that children learn (Belsky & Most, 1981; Lifter & Bloom, 1989), one could argue that such activities were developmentally relevant for teaching to young children with substantial developmental delays.

Another example of indirect attention to developmental relevance can be found in Stahmer's (1995) study, in which symbolic play activities were taught to children with autism who were reported to have language levels of at least 2.5 years. Because symbolic play activities are among the play repertoires of children who are functioning above the 2.5-year developmental level, one could argue here too that the children were at appropriate levels of readiness for learning the symbolic play activities that were targeted. Similar results can be found in other reports (Kim et al., 1989; Goldstein & Cisar, 1992; Murphy, Calias, & Carr, 1985).

Results in support of the direct incorporation of developmental relevance into the selection of play activities with the use of systematic assessment procedures (i.e., the DPA) to identify those activities were provided in Lifter, Sulzer-Azaroff, Anderson, & Cowdery (1993). They distinguished two categories—*Child-as-Agent* and *Doll-as-Agent* play activities—that would both be regarded as symbolic play activities, but have different cognitive requirements. In Child-as-Agent activities, the child extends an object to a doll figure in a pretend gesture (e.g., child extends an empty cup to doll's mouth to give it a drink). In Doll-as-Agent activities, the child acts as if the doll is animate and can act for itself (e.g., child puts cup in doll's hand for doll to give itself a drink). The preschoolers with autism who participated in the study were selected based on their readiness to learn Child-as-Agent play activities. The prerequisite skills for the contrasting Doll-as-Agent activities were completely absent in the children's play, as this category is significantly more advanced than the Child-as-Agent play category (Watson & Fisher, 1977). The results of the Lifter et al. (1993) study supported faster acquisition and greater generalization for the activities from the Child-as-Agent play category, even though both categories would be considered within the broad category of symbolic play and as age-appropriate activities for preschool children (see Table 8–1). More recent studies in this line of investigation have provided preliminary support for the impact of interventions in play on progress in language. As a result of learning developmentally relevant play activities, children increased their commenting about ongoing events, and, in particular, their comments surrounding their new learning in play (Lifter et al., 1997).

The foregoing intervention studies demonstrated that children with developmental disabilities can acquire and learn play activities as a result of systematic intervention procedures. Moreover, the studies in the third group suggested that the success of several intervention studies could be explained in terms of the developmental relevance of the activities selected for instruction, which represents a starting point for linking developmental assessment to intervention. They also suggest that attention to play in intervention programs should contribute to progress in language and social interaction.

RATIONALE FOR LINKING DEVELOPMENTAL ASSESSMENT TO INTERVENTION

One of the premises underlying the DPA is that developmental relevance does influence the rate and quality of play activities that appear to be acquired. The justification for this premise requires specification of (1) what developmental relevance means, (2) the theoretical rationale and empirical support that link developmental relevance to intervention, and (3) the procedures to operationalize and implement developmentally relevant activities.

Developmentally Relevant Activities

In a global sense, developmentally relevant activities mean activities that the child is ready to learn. This global sense is contained in the definition of Developmentally Appropriate Practice (DAP) recommended for Early Childhood Education (Bredekamp, 1987; Bredekamp & Copple, 1997), and includes age-appropriate as well as developmentally appropriate activities. A more specific sense of developmental relevance, on the other hand, could mean the evaluation of a child's activities in relation to a set of all possible age-appropriate activities in order to differentiate among those activities the child knows, those activities the child is in the process of learning, and those activities that are too difficult for the child at a specific point in time.

The claim here is that a high degree of specificity is needed for the identification of developmentally relevant activities to link assessment to intervention in order to facilitate developmental progress. The results of the Lifter et al. (1993) study, discussed earlier, supported the specificity required to distinguish between Child-as-Agent and Doll-as-Agent as play categories of two different levels of developmental relevance (see Table 8–1), even though both fall within the broad category of symbolic play and are age-appropriate activities for preschool children.

Theoretical Rationale and Empirical Support

The theoretical rationale for linking developmental assessment to intervention in play requires a conceptualization of play as an activity for learning. Much of the earlier descriptive work on children's play was conducted within the cognitive/developmental tradition that regarded play as expression (i.e., "a happy display of known actions," Piaget, 1962, p. 93; "the child's natural medium of self-expression," Axline, 1947, p. 9). Play as expression led to the widely held definition of play, offered by Rubin et al. (1983), and presented earlier, as intrinsically motivated; characterized by attention to means; guided by "what can I do with the objects"; generally referred to as pretense; free from externally imposed rules; and requiring active engagement (pp. 698–699). In this perspective, the notion of work was antithetical to play (e.g., Elkind, 1990).

A less widely held view of play, but essential to intervention efforts in play, is the assumption that play also serves an interpretive function in development. This assumption is related to Montessori's view of play as the work of childhood (eg., "the child's work," Montessori, 1967, p. 180), and Vygotsky's (1978) view of play "as an adaptive mechanism promoting cognitive growth during the preschool years" (Rubin et al., 1983, p. 709). Indeed, Piaget (1954) explained the child's construction of reality in terms of the construction of schemes through actions on objects. More recently, the National Association for the Education of Young Children (NAEYC) has recognized that "play is an important vehicle for children's social, emotional, and cognitive development, as well as a reflection of their development" (Bredekamp & Copple, 1997, p. 14). Play is too pervasive an activity in children's lives to be limited to an expressive function.

Lifter and Bloom (1998) proposed a theoretical perspective that incorporates the "work" function of play as an activity for learning and for acquiring new knowledge. In their view, "actions in play display what the child already knows ... (i.e., play as expression) ... but also display what the child is currently thinking about *in efforts to make sense of ongoing events for advancing knowledge*" (italics added) (p. 164). They emphasized the fundamental function of play for acquiring new knowledge in that play serves as a context for interpreting (i.e., making sense of) new events. They offered the following definition of play:

> Play is the expression of intentional states—the representations in consciousness constructed from what children know about and *are learning from ongoing events*—and consists of spontaneous, naturally occurring activities with objects that *engage attention and interest.* Play may or may not involve caregivers or peers, may or may not involve a display of affect, and may or may not involve pretense italics added]. (p. 164)

The notion that play is an activity for interpretation is supported by the engagement of attention and interest observed in children's play. Indeed, both Lifter and Bloom's (1998) and Rubin et al.'s (1983) definitions include an emphasis on active engagement/attention to the ongoing activities. A difference is that Lifter and Bloom's (1998) definition is not limited to pretense play, but includes the wide expanse of object-related activities in which children engage.

Recent studies of active engagement provide empirical support for the relationship between engagement and learning. For example, it was observed that children pay more attention to activities that are developmentally new than to those activities that are relatively well known (Bloom, Tinker, & Beckwith, 1997; Ruff & Saltarelli, 1993; Wikstrom, 1994). By "new" learning, Bloom et al., (1997), for example, meant activities for which the children had not met the criterion levels in the previous samples but had for the sample under study. In addition, children playing with objects tend not to express emotions at the same time (Phillips & Sellito, 1990), but they are more likely to express emotions immediately after play activities that represent new learning rather than old learning (Bloom, et al., 1997). Such results support children's greater allocation of attention to activities that are relatively new for them in contrast to activities they already know something about. They also support the feasibility of making distinctions between what constitutes new learning compared to old learning in samples of children's activities.

Consequently, developmentally relevant activities are defined here to mean activities that represent new learning. They are activities at the threshold of learning that the child allocates attention to in efforts to interpret and make sense of ongoing events. The claim is that developmentally relevant activities represent child-centered or child-directed activities for the purposes of linking assessment to intervention. They are child-centered/ directed in the sense that these activities, if truly identified at the child's level of interpretation, may enable the child to actively participate in and work to make sense of ongoing events, with appropriate environmental support. The selection of such activities is in accordance with "developmentally appropriate practice." "Developmentally appropriate practices provide a framework for instructional practices based on the assumption that the opportunities needed for learning and development come primarily from children's active engagement and participation in their environment" (DEC, 1994, p. 4; taken from Bredekamp, 1987).

Procedures to Operationalize Developmentally Relevant Activities

The operationalization of developmentally relevant activities requires procedures to distinguish between old and new learning. The procedures used in the DPA are based on quantitative criteria applied to qualitatively different categories of play, similar to the quantitative criteria used in Lifter and Bloom (1989) to identify developmental change. The DPA assumes that play categories that are represented by a reasonable frequency and variety of examples constitute categories that the child knows (i.e., "old" learning). In turn, categories that are represented by activities that occur infrequently, but are categories subsequent to the high-frequency categories in the developmental progression, constitute quantitative criteria for categories of activities the child is in the process of learning (i.e., "new" categories). Finally, the categories of play that are not represented by activities in a sample of play, but are subsequent in the developmental sequence to the categories that are represented, are most likely categories that the child has not learned at that point in time. In this way, quantitative criteria are applied to a sample of play activities to determine what the child knows, what the child is in the process of learning, and what is beyond the child's developmental level at the time of assessment.

Procedures to Implement Developmentally Relevant Activities

The recommended procedures for implementation of developmentally relevant activities in working with children with developmental disabilities are based on two primary factors. First, they build on the standard practice in Early Childhood Education (ECE) of following the child's lead. Second, they incorporate the particular behavioral shaping procedure of least-to-most prompting (Sulzer-Azaroff & Mayer, 1991), given a developmentally relevant play target. For example, if a child is playing with a cup, the child is obviously attending to the cup. The ECE practice of following the child's lead would include commenting on the cup and perhaps making a suggestion as to what the child could do with the cup. However, as can be inferred from the many different categories of play that have been described in this chapter, there are many different play activities that are possible with a cup. The child could put things into the cup, stack the cup onto another cup, pretend to drink from the cup, take a spoon and stir in the cup, and give the doll a drink from the cup, to name a few, and these activities represent play categories of different developmental levels.

For children for whom learning is difficult, comments and suggestions by caregivers about activities that are beyond their levels of understanding may be confusing. However, the children's active attention to objects can be taken advantage of and gently shaped into developmentally relevant target actions that they may likely understand. The least-to-most prompting shaping procedures (Sulzer-Azaroff & Mayer, 1991) specify increasing levels of support and guidance (e.g., verbal and gestural prompting; physical guidance) as needed, and can be employed once the child comes to attention around an object, person, or event. For instance, assuming that the Child-as-Agent play category is the developmentally relevant category for a child, the child's attention to a cup can be shaped to the action of giving a doll figure a drink from the cup. Such procedures not only follow the child's lead, but they also guide the child's attention to interpretable activities (i.e., developmentally relevant activities). Such procedures go beyond merely commenting on what the child is attending to or making a random suggestion of what to do. Instead, they build upon the child's readiness to learn certain kinds of activities, potentially maximizing opportunities for facilitating developmental progress.

They also represent a variant on teacher-directed approaches advocated for Early Childhood Special Education (ECSE). Teacher-directed approaches are regarded as those in which the "teacher" decides what is to be learned (Carta, Schwartz, Atwater, & McConnell, 1991), which are frowned upon in the child-directed emphasis of ECE. However, if the teacher knows which developmentally relevant activities to teach or shape, the teacher may take advantage of opportunities of active engagement to guide the children's attention to interpretable activities (i.e., developmentally relevant target activities), thereby linking developmental assessment to intervention. Developmental assessment provides information regarding what to teach/shape, given children's active engagement in ongoing events.

Because many children with developmental disabilities do not appear intrinsically motivated to play, in particular, and to learn, in general, it becomes important to direct their attention to activities that they can make sense of in the context of ongoing events. It is also important to follow their leads in terms of what they appear to be paying attention to, to facilitate their interpretation of ongoing events and thereby their progress in development. The DPA is based on the claim that opportunities for facilitating development may be missed if the environment is not systematically structured and manipulated to facilitate active engagement in ongoing events.

CONSTRUCTION OF THE INSTRUMENT[2]

The foundation for the developmental sequence of play categories presented in the DPA (Table 8–1) was based on the play categories and order of emergence identified in Lifter and Bloom (1989; see also Bloom, 1993; Bloom, Lifter, & Broughton, 1985; and Lifter, 1982), with the remaining categories and sequence derived from the developmental sequences identified in other descriptive studies of the play of children with and without disabilities (Belsky & Most, 1981; Fein, 1981; Fenson, et al., 1976; Fenson & Ramsay, 1980; Garvey, 1977; Lowe, 1975; Nicolich, 1977 (see also McCune, 1995); Piaget, 1962; Smilansky, 1968; Ungerer & Sigman, 1981; Watson & Fischer, 1977). Various criteria were used to order the play categories in relation to one another, and they included quantitative criteria, namely the emergence and achievement of play forms (Lifter & Bloom, 1989), shifts in the relative proportion of categories over time (Bloom et al., 1985; Lifter, 1982; Lowe, 1975; Watson & Fischer, 1977), scalogram analyses (Belsky & Most, 1981; Lifter & Bloom, 1989), and statistical analyses of ranks (Fenson & Ramsay, 1980; Lifter & Bloom, 1989).

Contributions of Lifter and Bloom (1989): The Original Categories

The descriptive study reported in Lifter and Bloom (1989; see also Bloom, 1993) was developed in the same tradition as the descriptive studies of play that led to the play taxonomies described earlier in this chapter. It is presented in some detail here because (1) it generated the taxonomy of play activities that forms the backbone of the DPA for its assessment purposes, (2) it provided the rationale for the developments in the structure, organization, and content of knowledge that are inferred from a sample of play activities obtained with the DPA, and (3) it provided criteria for the quantification of qualitatively different categories that supported inferences of developmental change.

Lifter and Bloom (1989) observed and videorecorded the play activities of 14 children—7 boys and 7 girls—from a variety of ethnic and socioeconomic backgrounds, playing in the presence of their mothers. The monthly, one-hour observations began when the children were 8 months of age and continued until their second birthdays. The children played with six groups of toys that represented toys supporting a balance of manipulative and enactment (i.e., pretend) play. A snack of juice and cookies was introduced midway through the sample. The children's play activities were analyzed at three developmental periods that were related to transitions in language. The first period was fixed at 10 months and designated the Pre-Speech sample. The other two periods—First Words (defined as the first use of conventional words) and the Vocabulary Spurt (defined as a marked increase in the number of new and different words used)—were variable in age and were based on changes in language. Each developmental period consisted of three successive observations. For example,

[2] A more complete description of the DPA is available from the author at 203 Lake Hall, Northeastern University, Boston, MA, 02115.

if the First Word sample was determined to be at age 14 months for a child, that sample in addition to the 13-month and the 15-month samples for that child were analyzed. The mean age of the First Words sample for the 14 children was determined to be 13.8 months (age range: 10–18 months), and the mean age for the Vocabulary Spurt sample was determined to be 19.4 months (age range: 13–25 months). Thus, there was considerable variation among the children when they reached these transitions in language.

The entry point of analysis into the play activities consisted of actions in which the children *displaced* two or more objects in relation to one another, based on the Piagetian theoretical framework for the construction of object knowledge as a function of reversible action schemes (see Piaget, 1954). Displacements were therefore defined as activities of either *taking apart* configurations of objects (e.g., picking up a peg person by removing it from a seesaw; picking up a cup by taking it out of a set of nesting cups), or *constructing* configurations of objects (e.g., putting a peg person into the seesaw; putting a nesting cup into another nesting cup). Using this procedure, the coding scheme was guided by descriptive information provided by the toys and the children's actions with them and not by *a priori* categories based on manipulative and symbolic play distinctions (Bloom, 1993). Aside from the initial scheme defining displacements, no other coding schemes were used to describe the children's play.

The first result was that displacement activities occurred frequently in the samples of play, ranging from an average of 83 displacements at the PreSpeech sample to an average of 179 displacements at the Vocabulary Spurt (VS) sample. Because of their high frequency in a one-hour sample, these activities were taken to represent a valid behavioral sample for analysis of what young children do with objects. Consequently, developmental change in these displacements was interpreted as evidence of developments in knowledge about objects.

At the earliest observations (i.e., the PreSpeech samples), the children predominantly, if not exclusively, separated objects from one another in their play activities (e.g., took peg people out of the seesaw; took nesting cups apart). Overwhelmingly, the children did not put objects together to construct relationships between them, despite the fact that the mothers provided many modeled actions for the children to see how the objects could be put together.

Eventually, the children did begin to construct configurations between objects (i.e., to form combinations of objects in their play), to the point where the children constructed configurations of objects as often as they took them apart. Accordingly, the children's displacements of objects changed in structure and form, from a predominance of separating objects from one another to a balance between separating and constructing objects in relation to one another. This change was interpreted as "reflect(ing) a fundamental development in knowledge of objects in general that is *prerequisite* to acquiring knowledge about more particular characteristics of objects and the relations between them for the development of object concepts" (Lifter & Bloom, 1989, p. 416).

Subsequent qualitative analyses centered on changes in the content of the displacements (i.e., increasing specificity displayed in the configurations constructed between objects), and the children's take-apart actions were not analyzed further. The earliest constructions were characterized either as reconstructions of the relations in which the objects were originally presented to the children (e.g., child puts one nesting cup into another, given the nested presentation of the nesting cups), or as creating a *new* relation that was *different* from the way the objects were presented to the child (e.g., child puts a bead into a nesting cup).

The earliest constructions the children created that differed from the *Given Combinations* were predominantly *General Combinations,* in which the children made use of global properties of objects that were shared by many different objects. These actions mainly took the form of container/contained relations in which a variety of objects, regardless of their particular properties, could serve as containers (e.g., a nesting cup; the dumper section of a dump truck; a plastic bowl in which the beads were presented), and a variety of different objects, regardless of their particular properties, could serve as things to be contained (e.g., beads; pieces of silverware; the truck drivers). Thus, the first two categories of constructing relations to emerge in the Lifter & Bloom (1989) study were Given Combinations and General Combinations.

With development, change was noted in the kinds of new relations the children constructed, moving from a predominance of General Combinations to a steady increase in Specific Combinations. Over time, the children increasingly took into account more particular properties of objects in the relations they constructed, comprising the category of *Specific Relations.* These actions took the form of either: (1) a particular physical relationship between the objects (e.g., inverting the nesting cups and forming a graded stack; stringing the beads; rolling the car down an inclined plane, described as *Inanimate Specific* relations by Lifter & Bloom (1989); or (2) relations in which the children used a replica of a person or animal and a prop in an enactment (e.g., giving a doll a drink with a nesting cup; extending a spoon to the stuffed lamb), described as *Animate Surrogate* relations by Lifter & Bloom (1989).

In terms of a relative frequency analysis of the different categories of constructing activities across the three time periods (PreSpeech, First Words [FW], and the Vocabulary Spurt [VS]), *Given Combinations* held steady at approximately 50% of all constructing activities; *General Combinations* declined from approximately .35 at PreSpeech, to .26 at FW, to .20 at VS; and *Specific Combinations* as a group increased from approximately .13 at PreSpeech, to .21 at FW, to .34 at VS. Thus, although the category General Combinations was not developmentally progressive, its development was interpreted as prerequisite to acquiring knowledge about the more particular characteristics of objects and the relations between them as revealed in the increase in Specific Combinations.

In order to operationalize developmental change, quantitative analyses were applied to the displacement activities, in general, and to the constructing activities, in particular, as qualitatively different categories of constructing activities appeared in the samples. These analyses consisted of frequency counts, the number of different exemplars of a category in relation to the frequency of the category, and the relative proportions of the different play categories in relation to one another.

Emergence was defined as a minimum frequency of five occurrences of actions in a category with at least two different kinds of actions represented. Achievement required twice the criteria for emergence (i.e., a minimum of 10 occurrences with at least four different actions). Achievement also included an evaluation of 40% relative frequency of a category in relation to the earlier emerging category in the developmental hierarchy presented in Lifter and Bloom (1989). For example, General Combinations were the earliest appearing *new* combinations the children constructed. Eventually in these new combinations, the children began to create Specific Combinations between objects. The empirical criteria used for determining *achievement* of Specific Combinations in relation to General Combinations consisted of: (1) at least four different examples of Specific Combinations (e.g., stringing beads; stacking nesting cups; rolling a car along the highway; feeding a doll with a spoon); (2) a minimum total of 10 actions for the category combined (e.g., 2 stringing actions; 3 stacking actions; 3 rolling actions; and 2 feeding actions); and (3) for General and Specific Combinations taken together, Specific Combinations had to represent a minimum of 40% of the General and Specific actions combined. Eventually the Specific Combinations came to dominate the General Combinations, but it was at the .40 relative frequency mark, in addition to the criteria for frequency and variety of the category, that supported inferences that the child had a reasonable knowledge base of the play category.

The results revealed that the children reached achievement in Given and General relations during the same transition (First Words); they reached achievement in General Combinations before achievement in Specific relations; and they reached achievement in Inanimate Specific relations prior to achievement in Animate Surrogate relations. This developmental sequence was the same across the children, despite the wide variability of their ages at the time of these achievements.

Lifter and Bloom (1989; Bloom, 1993) also identified two language-play clusters in their study, which they attributed to developments in underlying cognition. The first cluster was the association between the transition to First Words and reaching the achievement criteria for constructing activities. Achievement was reached in Given Combinations and General Combinations during the same language transition (FW) for all the children. This result was taken to mean that the children began to construct relations between two objects in their play before they began to say words. The ability to create relations between two objects suggested that children had developed general knowledge about objects that included objects as separate entities, independent of the self, that could be entered into relations with other objects and people. This understanding of objects as independent entities is fundamental to the development of object permanence. Further, such general object knowledge contributed to the children's ability to use words in relation to objects and events.

The second cluster consisted of reaching the achievement criteria in the Inanimate Specific and Animate Surrogate categories as a group of Specific Combinations which co-occurred with the Vocabulary Spurt transition in the children's language. The ability to create specific relations between objects suggested that the children had developed specific knowledge about objects and they could access that knowledge in what they did with the toys and what they said about the toys and their activities with the toys. The development of specific object knowledge required, first, the understanding of objects as independent entities onto which specific properties could be attributed and remembered. The children's use of many different words, as is reflected in the Vocabulary Spurt, complemented the specific knowledge expressed in their play activities, and both developments were related to substantial changes in cognition (see also Bloom, 1993).

In summary, in addition to the *Takes-Apart Combinations,* four categories of constructing relations were empirically identified in Lifter and Bloom (1989) that formed the foundation of the sequence identified in the DPA: *Presentation Combinations* (formerly known as Given Relations); General Combinations; Specific Combinations (Physical Attributes) (formerly known as Inanimate Surrogate relations); and Child-as-Agent (formerly known as Animate Surrogate relations in Lifter & Bloom, 1989) activities. Achievement was reached in Presentation Combinations and General Combinations during the same language transition (FW); achievement in Specific Combinations (Physical Attributes) occurred subsequent to Presentation and General Combinations and prior to Child-as-Agent activities; and achievement in Specific relations (Specific [Physical] and Child-as-Agent combined) co-occurred with the Vocabulary Spurt language transition.

Contributions of Other Descriptive Studies

The remaining categories used in the DPA were derived from several other empirical studies of children's play activities (Belsky & Most, 1981; Fein, 1981; Fenson et al., 1976; Fenson & Ramsay, 1980; Garvey, 1977; Lowe, 1975; Nicolich, 1977; Piaget, 1962; Smilansky, 1968; Ungerer & Sigman, 1981; and Watson & Fischer, 1977). Although there were differences among the studies in terms of how play was categorized, measured, and quantified, the studies reported evidence regarding a sequential ordering of the play categories identified. Lifter and Bloom (1989) concentrated their analyses on children's actions on two or more objects at a time, spanning Takes-Apart Combinations to Child-as-Agent activities. Other studies have examined activities at simpler levels, more complex levels, and overlapping levels.

Categories of activities in the DPA centered on actions on single objects include: *Indiscriminate Actions; Discriminative Actions on Single Objects;* and *Substitutions.* Support for the sequential ordering of Indiscriminate and Discriminative categories in relation to Presentation/General Combinations, derived from Lifter and Bloom (1989), was provided by Belsky and Most (1981). They described Indiscriminate Actions as actions on single objects in which there is no differentiation among the objects; all objects are treated alike in actions such as mouthing. They reported that eventually children manipulate objects in ways suitable for the particular objects involved (e.g., spinning the wheels on a toy vehicle; turning the dial on a toy phone), distinguished in the DPA as Discriminative Actions. The categories Belsky and Most identified as "relational" and "functional-relational" appeared subsequent to Discriminative Actions and correspond, respectively, to the General Combinations and Presentation Combinations categories used in the DPA. Consequently, Indiscriminate Actions were assigned to Level I, Discriminative Actions to Level II, and Presentation/General Combinations to Level III.

Activities of the sort included in the category Discriminative Actions on Single Objects have been identified by a number of researchers, including Nicolich (1977), who, along with Belsky and Most (1981), distinguished these activities as occurring prior to *Pretend Self* activities. Included in Discriminative Actions are activities defined by Nicolich as "presymbolic schemes" in which the child shows understanding of what the object is used for (e.g., child picks up a comb and touches it to his or her head) in contrast to "auto-symbolic schemes" in which the child pretends at self-related activities (e.g., the child eats from an empty spoon). Accordingly, Pretend Self activities were placed in Level III, subsequent to the Discriminative Actions of Level II.

The distinctions and sequential relationships among Pretend Self, Child-as-Agent, and the Doll-as-Agent pretend categories have been addressed in whole or part, directly or indirectly, by Belsky and Most (1981), Fenson and Ramsay (1980), Lowe (1975), Nicolich (1977), and Watson & Fischer (1977). Watson and Fischer (1977) explicitly examined the relationships among "Self-as-Agent," "Use of Object as Passive Agent," "Use of Substitute Object as Passive Agent," and "Use of Object as Active Agent," with the first, second, and fourth categories corresponding to the categories used in the DPA, and found that the four types of agent use were acquired in the aforementioned sequence. They also noted that the children stopped using and remembering the categories in the same sequence, with first the "Self-as-Agent" (i.e., Pretend Self), and then the "Use of Object as Passive Agent" (i.e., Child-as-Agent) decreasing in relative frequency overtime. The "Use of Substitute Object as Passive Agent" and the "Use of Object as Active Agent" (i.e., Doll-as-Agent) showed stable (increasing) change with age. Other studies have reported Pretend Self as emerging before a pretend action extended to a figure (Child-as-Agent) (Belsky & Most, 1981; Lowe, 1975; Nicolich, 1977). Studies have also supported the decrease of Pretend Self over time relative to the extension of pretend actions to other figures (i.e., Child-as-Agent) (Belsky & Most, 1981; Lowe, 1975). Lowe (1975) also reported a subsequent decline in Child-as-Agent actions as Doll-as-Agent actions began to emerge.

The co-occurrence of Specific Combinations (Conventional Attributes) (e.g., stirring with a spoon in a cup; pouring from a pitcher into a cup) and the Child-as-Agent category in Level V is supported by a number of studies (Lowe, 1975; Fenson & Ramsay, 1980). Fenson and Ramsay conceptualized both kinds of actions as "decentered acts," which are actions directed away from the self while the child still remains the agent of the action. They regarded actions equivalent to Specific Combinations (Conventional Attributes) as "object-directed acts," and actions equivalent to Child-as-Agent activities as "other-directed" acts, also identified by Lowe (1975).

As noted earlier, Lifter and Bloom (1989) identified activities of Specific Combinations (Physical Attributes) prior to Child-as-Agent activities. In contrast to the Specific Combinations (Physical Attributes), the Child-as-Agent category requires additional, conventional knowledge of objects that is not afforded by their physical characteristics (e.g., the spoon and the doll). Given this requirement of conventional knowledge for the Child-as-Agent category, together with the foregoing results reported by Fenson and Ramsay (1980) and Lowe (1975), the categories Child-as-Agent and Specific Combinations (Conventional Attributes) were placed together in Level V.

The descriptions of, and support for, the sequential ordering between *Single-Scheme Sequences* and *Multischeme Sequences* were taken from Nicolich (1977) and Fenson and Ramsay (1980). In addition, Belsky and Most (1981) and Fenson and Ramsay (1980) reported that sequences of pretend actions, whether single scheme or multischeme, emerged only after individual actions had been mastered. Consequently, the category Single-Scheme Sequences was placed in the play level subsequent to the Child-as-Agent category (Level VI). Further, because Belsky and Most (1981) reported a close association between Single-Scheme Sequences and Substitutions, these two categories were placed together in Level VI.

Fenson and Ramsay (1980) reported a close association between Multischeme Sequences and "Use of Object as Active Agent" (i.e., Doll-as-Agent) activities. They also observed that these two categories did not correspond to the Specific Combinations (Conventional Attributes) and Child-as-Agent activities, but occurred subsequent to them. Consequently, the categories Doll-as-Agent and Multischeme Sequences were placed together in Level VII, subsequent to the Child-as-Agent and Specific Combinations (Conventional Attributes) categories of Level V, and the Single-Scheme Sequences and Substitutions categories of Level VI.

The final categories *Sociodramatic Play* and *Thematic Fantasy Play* are categories of play activities identified by Smilansky (1968) and Piaget (1962), respectively. These activities are typical activities of the preschool child, moving from enactments of familiar, everyday themes (e.g., playing house), to the increasingly imaginative activities enacted in the roles of fantasy characters (e.g., "Superman" and "Wonderwoman"). Within these activities, there is increasing use of role assignment, planning, and distancing from the here and now. Although these activities are grouped together in the final level of the DPA (Level VIII), other researchers have identified progressively more complex levels within these activities (Westby, 1980, 1991).

PROCEDURES FOR ADMINISTRATION
OF THE DPA WITH CASE STUDIES

The procedures used in the DPA include the collection of a 30-minute sample of unstructured play in which the child plays sequentially with four groups of toys in the presence of a familiar caregiver (e.g., teacher, parent). The child's behaviors are videorecorded, allowing for analysis of play subsequent to the observation session. A detailed sequence is set forth with procedures for determining the existence and frequency of various play activities and the developmental status of the play categories that are identified from the developmental sequence.

Participants and Setting

The assessment has been designed to evaluate the play of preschool-age children with developmental disabilities, but is easily adapted to younger and older children. The adult participants include the "interactant," who is the person administering the assessment, and a second person operating the videocamera, although it is possible to arrange the videocamera on a tripod for the assessment session. The assessment should take place in a familiar setting (e.g., classroom play area; living room). The height of the videocamera should be the same height as the child's face when sitting so that good facial views and actions with the toys can be obtained.

Materials

The assessment materials include the videorecording equipment used to make a permanent record of the child's play activities for scoring and analysis, and four sets of toys for the children to play with. Each toy set was constructed to permit a variety of play actions from very simple manipulative play behaviors up through sequences of pretend play, sociodramatic, and fantasy play activities. For example, the puzzle, beads, and blocks in Toy Group 1 might be regarded as toys that support manipulative play, while the dump truck with figures and the stuffed lamb might be regarded as toys that support symbolic play. However, although the manipulative/symbolic distinction motivated the overall selection of toys for a group, the DPA is based on the finding that children of different developmental levels will play differently with the same set of toys (Lifter & Bloom, 1989). For example, a 12-month-old child might take the drivers from the truck and drop them into the bead bowl with the beads, a 30-month-old child might pretend a red bead is an apple and feed it to a driver, and a 60-month-old child might move the driver as if the driver were able to pick up the bead and then load it into the truck. The goal in the toy selection is to have enough toys to allow the children varied opportunities to express what they know about objects, about the relations between objects, and about the relations between objects and people.

The toys listed serve as examples of the toys one could use for evaluating play activities.

Group 1: Five-piece inset puzzle (e.g., animal puzzle), assembled; beads in bowl with string placed alongside bowl; small dump truck with two driver-figures in place; six unpainted wood blocks (3 cubes, 3 cylinders), alongside the bowl; stuffed lamb.

Group 2: Blocks and sticks ("Creative Blocks") in plastic box with lid; small nested cups, nested and upright; babydoll with clothes on, sitting upright; spoon; blanket, folded in four; comb & mirror.

Group 3: Four farm animals (colt, cow, calf, pig), in plastic box with lid; small boy family figure; three part train, uncoupled and upright on floor; cup, saucer, and pitcher, separated; nuts & bolts ("Bolt 'N Nuts") on dish or in shallow bowl.

Group 4: Mother and father family figures, flat on floor; car; gas pump (with oil can, screwdriver, tire gauge); large nested cups (beakers), nested and upright.

Procedures for Collecting a Sample of Play

The goal of the assessment is to obtain a 30-minute sample of a child's spontaneous activities with the sets of toys. Consequently, the procedure emphasizes presentation of the toys to observe the child's independent actions with the toys, without the interactant modeling, prompting, or testing the limits for any particular actions with the toys.

The first of the four sets of toys should be in place on the floor when the child is brought in. The interactant should bring the child to the free-play area and tell the child that it is time to play with some new toys. The child and interactant should sit on the floor, face to face, and close enough to the toys so that the toys can be reached easily. The interactant should say, "Here, (Child's name), these toys are for you to play with." The interactant should not direct the child to do anything with the toys, nor model any activities, but remain reflective and responsive (i.e., verbally reflecting what the child is doing [e.g., saying "You're giving the boy a ride in the train," after the child has placed the boy family figure in one of the train cars], and being responsive to initiations on the child's part [e.g., accepting something that is given; complying when a request for help is made]).

Ideally, the child should have about 7 to 8 minutes to play with each of the four sets of toys so that the entire assessment is 30 minutes in length. The time period with each set of toys should be shortened or lengthened depending upon the child's behavior with the toys. The time period for a toy set should be shortened if the child shows little or no interest in the toys and has had an opportunity to play with each of the toys in the set. The time period should be lengthened if the child is spinning out an elaborate play theme, or if the child appears particularly interested in certain of the toys and is playing purposefully (i.e., not perseveratively) with them. The remaining toy sets do need to be introduced, but the child can be offered the opportunity to resume play with the other toys afterwards. That is, as long as a child has had a reasonable opportunity to play with each of the toys in each set, the child may be offered the opportunity to play with a set again.

When the time period for a set of toys is finished, the current toy set should be moved to the side, out of easy reach, and the next set presented. The interactant should tell the child, "(Child's name), I have more toys for you to play with" and then get the next toy box and lay out the toys as described. The child may want to relate something from the new set to something from the old set and should have that opportunity. If the child becomes distracted by the earlier set of toys, they should be removed altogether by placing them into the storage boxes and out of reach. Accordingly, there is a reasonable degree of flexibility built into the natural observational setting without compromising the goal of obtaining a 30-minute sample of play activities for analysis.

Under certain conditions the interactant should redirect the child's attention to the toys. If the child appears to lose interest in the toy he or she has been playing with and does not turn his or her attention to other toys in the set, the interactant should draw the child's attention to toys in the set that have not been played with by moving the toys into the child's view, saying "These toys are for you to play with." If the child plays perseveratively with an object for more than a minute (e.g., the child sifts his or her fingers through the bowl of beads over and over again), the child's attention should be redirected to other toys in the set. If the interactant is unable to redirect the child from perseverating with a particular object, the next set of toys should be presented while the object the child perseverated with is quietly removed.

Procedures for Coding the Sample of Play

The play observations are analyzed in a three-step sequence. First, the raw frequencies of discrete play actions are recorded. Then, the individual actions are reorganized into categories of activities observed. Frequencies and types of activities for each category are determined. Finally, the results are summarized according to the Developmental Sequence presented in Table 8–1 and analyzed as to "mastery," "emergence," and "absence" of play categories.

These procedures are illustrated here with case studies of two children—Jack and Jill—who were the same age (i.e., 4 years, 6 months) but who yielded two different play profiles. Jack is a preschooler with pervasive developmental disorder and Jill is a preschooler with developmental delay. Both children attend the same preschool where children with and without disabilities are served.

The first step in analyzing the videorecorded observations is designed to record the frequency of the different kinds of play actions the child does that are appropriate with these toys. Only actions that occur spontaneously are counted, which should be all the child's actions if the interactant does not model or prompt any activities. In addition, Takes-Apart Combinations are counted only if there are less than 10 constructing activities, because Takes-Apart Combinations are developmentally nonprogressive. Only *discrete actions* (or discrete episodes) with the toys are counted. Discrete actions are actions with a beginning and an end, and are defined to mean the child takes hold of an object, performs an action with the object, and then lets go of the object. Further, in discrete actions, there must be some separation in the actions that is defined by losing physical contact with the object or the occurrence of a different event intervening in the successive actions. Some actions by their nature take longer to perform (e.g., combing a doll's hair; pushing a train along the floor). These actions have an episodic quality and it is difficult to define the beginning and end. Therefore, a break in the action is required to determine the endpoint. Sequences of activities are to be noted, with each component of the sequence also counted in the tally of discrete actions, and, therefore, double-coded.

The frequencies for the different kinds of play actions that were observed for Jack and Jill are presented in Table 8–2. For both children, enough actions of displaying the discriminative properties of single objects (i.e., Discriminative Actions) and relating one object to another were observed in the sample to dismiss the recording of actions that would be regarded as Indiscriminative Actions and Takes-Apart Combinations. As can be seen in Table 8–2, many more different actions were observed in Jill's play than Jack's play, although their total number of activities were fairly similar (101 play actions for Jack and 115 play actions for Jill).

The second step in analyzing the play activities is designed to reorganize the raw frequency of activities identified in Step 1 into categories of activities in order to determine the frequency and variety of activities identified within a category. The definitions of the categories are presented in Table 8–1. The organization of Jack's and Jill's play actions into their respective categories is presented in Table 8–3. For example, putting puzzle pieces into the puzzle and putting the beads into the bowl were activities observed for both Jack and Jill when they played with the Group 1 toys. These actions are reconstructions of objects into their presentation configuration, and thereby constitute two different exemplars of the Presentation Combinations category. In contrast, stacking beads and stacking nesting cups as well as stringing beads represent activities in which the unique physical characteristics of the objects are preserved in the configuration constructed, and were coded into the Specific Combinations (Physical Attributes) category. This procedure continues until all the activities are assigned to a category.

In certain cases the activities are double-coded. For example, Jill's activity of using a bowl for a hat was coded in the primary category of Self-Pretend, and also in the category of Substitutions. Similarly, the categories that were included in the Single Scheme Sequences were also individually coded into their respective categories.

Some judgment is also required in this step. It is important to recognize what the child is trying to do in an action and not simply to assign the actions to the categories in an automatic fashion. For example, if the child puts blocks into the truck, it is important to determine whether the child is regarding the truck as a general container in moving random objects from place to place (i.e., General Combinations) or whether the child is regarding the truck as a truck that conveys goods from place to place (i.e., Specific Combinations [Conventional Attributes]).

As a result of this process, many more different categories of play were identified in Jill's sample of play than Jack's sample of play, presented in Table 8–3. Most of Jack's 101 play actions clustered in the categories of Discriminative, Presentation Combinations, Specific Combinations (Physical Attributes). The many different activities that were observed for Jill represent a greater variety of different play categories than were observed for Jack.

The third step consists of summarizing the frequency and variety of categories of play behaviors. Once the activities observed and their frequencies are organized according to play categories, the play sample can be analyzed according to the frequency (i.e., occurrences) of a category and the variety (i.e., types) of exemplars within each category. The goal is to determine which activities the child demonstrates evidence of having learned (i.e.,

Table 8–2.   Step 1: Recording frequency of actions

Jack (age 4, 6)		Jill (age 4, 6)	
Toy set 1		*Toy set 1*	
puts pieces in puzzle	5	puts pieces in puzzle	1
puts beads in bowl	6	puts beads in bowl	12
touches bowl to mouth	1	puts bowl on head, "hat"	4
stacks beads	11	puts string in bowl	3
stacks beads in truck	4	strings beads	4
stacks blocks	1	tries to "string" a block	1
		puts drivers into slots in truck	3
Toy set 2		*Toy set 2*	
puts blocks/sticks back in box	5	puts blocks/sticks back in box	4
nests the nesting cups	28	puts blocks on stick	4
stacks the nesting cups	12	nests the nesting cups	7
touches spoon to mouth	2	puts spoon on nesting cup	1
looks in mirror	1	puts spoon to mouth, to "eat"	1
		extends spoon to doll's mouth	3
		takes spoon, scoops from cup	2
		spreads blanket	3
		sits doll on blanket	1
		puts nesting cup on blanket	1
		puts spoon on blanket	1
		puts mirror, comb on blanket	2
		combs doll's hair	1
		extends "nipple" to own mouth	1
		extends "nipple" to doll's mouth	1
		SEQ: nipple, cup, doll, spoon on blanket]	
		SEQ: spoon to doll, scoops cup, to self, to doll]	
Toy set 3		*Toy set 3*	
puts animal back in box	1	puts boy in train	1
puts lid on box	1	"rocks" boy in train	1
puts saucer on top of cup	1	brings pitcher to mouth to drink	1
puts cup on train	1	puts boy into cup	1
puts lid on train	1	puts boy into pitcher	1
stacks nuts	5	puts nut on boy's head, "hat"	1
		puts boy on dish "peepee"	3
		puts cup into mug	1
Toy set 4		*Toy set 4*	
nests nesting beakers	4	nests nesting beakers	9
stacks the nesting beakers	7	stacks nesting beakers	8
"walks" family figure	1	stirs screwdriver in beaker	1
turns car wheels	1	pushes car along floor	1
pushes car on floor	1	puts mother in car	1
turns crank of gas pump	1	puts father in car	1
		turns crank on gas pump	4
		attaches pump handle to pump	17
		pours oil can into pump	1
		"paints" pump with screwdriver	1

Table 8–3.   Step 2: Organizing actions into play categories

Jack		Jill	
Discriminative Actions		*Discriminative Actions*	
touches bowl to mouth	1	spreads blanket	3
touches spoon to mouth	2	pushes car along floor	1
looks in mirror	1	turns crank on gas pump	4
"walks" family figure	1	attaches pump handle to pump	17
turns car wheels	1		
pushes car on floor	1		
turns crank of gas pump	1		
Presentation Combinations		*Presentation Combination*	
puts pieces in puzzle	5	puts pieces in puzzle	1
puts beads in bowl	6	puts beads in bowl	12
puts blocks/sticks back in box	5	puts drivers into slots in truck	3
nests the nesting cups	28	puts blocks/sticks back in box	4
puts animals in plastic box	1	nests nesting cups	7
puts lid on box	1	nests nesting beakers	9
nests the nesting beakers	4		
General Combinations		*General Combinations*	
puts saucer on cup	1	puts string in bowl	3
puts cup on train	1	puts spoon on nesting cup	1
puts lid on train	1	puts boy into cup, pitcher	2
		puts cup to mug	1
Pretend Self		*Pretend Self*	
(no actions)		puts bowl on head, "hat"	4
		puts spoon to mouth to "eat"	1
		puts "nipple" to mouth to drink	1
		puts pitcher to mouth to drink	1
Specific Physical		*Specific Physical*	
stacks nesting cups	12	strings beads	4
stacks blocks	1	tries to string block	1
stacks beads	11	puts blocks on sticks	4
stacks beads in truck	4	stacks the nesting beakers	8
stacks the nuts	5		
stacks the nesting beakers	7		
Child-as-Agent		*Child-as-Agent*	
(no actions)		extends spoon to doll's mouth	3
		sits doll on blanket	1
		combs doll's hair	1
		extends "nipple" to doll's mouth	1
		puts boy in train for ride	1
		rocks boy in train	1
		puts nut on boy's head, "hat"	1
		puts boy on dish "peepee"	3
		puts family figures in car	2

(continues)

Table 8–3.   *(continued)*

Jack	Jill	
Specific Conventional	*Specific Conventional*	
(no actions)	takes spoon, scoops from cup	3
	puts nesting cup on blanket	1
	puts spoon on blanket	1
	puts comb/mirror on blanket	2
	stirs screwdriver in beaker	1
	pours oil into gas pump	1
	"paints" pump with screwdriver	1
Single/Simple Scheme Sequences	*Single/Simple Scheme Sequences**	
(no actions)	nipple, cup, doll, spoon on blanket;	
	spoon to doll, scoops cup, to self, to doll;	
Substitutions	*Substitutions**	
(no actions)	uses bowl for hat	3
	uses end of mirror as nipple	2
	uses train for cradle	1
	uses nut for hat	1
	uses screwdriver as paint brush	1
Doll-as-Agent	*Doll-as-Agent*	
(no actions)	(no actions)	
Multischeme Sequences	*Multischeme Sequences**	
(no actions)	(no actions)	
Sociodramatic/Fantasy Play	*Sociodramatic/Fantasy Play*	
(no actions)	(no actions)	

* Indicates double-coded actions.

mastered), is learning (i.e., emerging), or apparently knows nothing about (i.e., absent) for identifying play objectives for intervention. Mastery is defined as the occurrence of at least 10 instances of the category, with at least four different types represented, within a 30-minute sample. Emergence is defined as the occurrence of at least four instances of the category, with at least two different types represented. Anything less is defined as absent.

The summary data for Jack and Jill are presented in Table 8–4. Although 101 play actions were recorded for Jack, they clustered in a few categories. The largest number of his play actions were characterized as Presentation Combinations (n = 50). Within this category, seven types of Presentation Combinations were identified, which renders this category as mastered for Jack. The next-largest category was Specific Combinations (Physical Attributes) (n = 40). Although this category was represented by six different types of activities, they were all stacking activities, so the judgment is made here to consider this category as consisting of one type of activity. As a result, the category is regarded as absent in Jack's play. The play categories beyond the Specific Combinations (Physical Attributes) were not represented in his play activities. Consequently, a play program for Jack would include play activities in the Specific Combinations (Physical Attributes) category and the Pretend Self category. The General Combinations category may not be targeted directly

Table 8–4.   Step 3: Determining mastery, emergence, and absence of play categories and identifying play goals

Category	Jack			Jill		
	Type/Token	Status	Target?	Type/Token	Status	Target?
Indiscriminative*	—			—		
Discriminative	7/8	(E)		4/25	(M)	
Takes Apart*	—			—	—	
Presentation Comb.	7/50	M		6/36	M	
General Comb.	3/3	E		4/7	E	
Pretend Self	0	A	←	4/7	E	
Specific Physical	1(6)/40	A	←	4/17	M	
Child as Agent				9/17	M	
Specific Conventional				7/9	E	←
Single Scheme Seq.				2	E	←
Substitutions				5/8	E	←
Doll as Agent						
Multischeme Seq.						
Sociodramatic/Fantasy						

* Indicates actions not counted because they are superseded by developmentally more advanced play actions.

because this category is developmentally nonprogressive, and such a high frequency of activities was represented in the Presentation Combinations categories.

Jill presents a very different play profile, as can be seen in Table 8–4. Many more different categories of play are represented, and the analysis reflects mastery of several of these categories. In contrast to Jack, Jill demonstrated competence in Specific Combinations (Physical Attributes) and in Child-as-Agent activities. The diversity of actions represented in the Specific Combinations (Conventional Attributes) is somewhat deceiving, however, because a number of them consisted of putting items on the blanket for a picnic scenario, and were essentially repetitions (i.e., Single-Scheme Sequence). Thus, the diversity of actions in this category is less than it appears. Nevertheless, target actions for Jill in an intervention program would include activities from the Specific Combinations (Conventional Attributes), Single-Scheme Sequences, and Substitutions. She has surpassed the nonprogressive categories of General Combinations and Pretend Self.

SUMMARY OF RESEARCH PROGRAM[3]

Although play is an integral part of any preschool curriculum, and young children's lives in general, the usefulness of specifying finely tuned, developmentally appropriate play

[3] PROJECT PLAY consists of a series of studies that were supported by a grant from the U.S. Department of Education, Office of Special Education Programs, to Karin Lifter, Northeastern University, and to Stephen R. Anderson, then at the May Center for Early Childhood Education and now at the Language Development Program, Tonawanda, NY. Other principal participants include Susan Campbell, Barbara O'Malley Cannon, Maureen Considine, Ellette DiPietro, James Ellis, Rae Ann Pedi, and Stephany Woodward, also of the May Center, and Sandra Pierce-Jordan of Northeastern University. Copies of these studies are available on request from K. Lifter.

activities for direct instruction and for integration with other developmental domains remains largely uncharted. The PROJECT PLAY research program, consisting of a series of studies summarized below, was designed to address this area. The DPA tool was used to identify developmentally relevant (Dev R) play intervention targets that were regarded as finely tuned to the children's developmental levels. Commonalities across these studies consisted of the following components: the participation of preschool age children with developmental disabilities, and, most often, children with autism; the use of child-directed teaching procedures that included capitalizing on the child's focus of attention (with least-to-most prompting) and the selection of activities that were assumed to be at the child's level of understanding; the videorecording of the play sessions for repeated analysis; the use of an event recording system in which the children's play behaviors were coded as spontaneous, prompted, imitated, or generalized occurrences of activities from the target play categories; and assessment of reliability through item-by-item agreements. The results reported below were based on the children's spontaneous occurrences of the target activities. The use of developmental sequences for identifying objectives for intervention was modeled after Bloom and Lahey (1978; Lahey, 1988) and Dyer, Santarcangelo, and Luce (1987) in their studies of language intervention.

Preliminary support for the incorporation of developmental relevance into the selection of play activities for intervention was provided in Lifter, et al. (1993), and reviewed earlier in this chapter. The children demonstrated more rapid acquisition and greater generalization for the developmentally relevant play activities (i.e., Child-as-Agent) in contrast to age-appropriate play activities (Doll-as-Agent). Since that study, the PROJECT PLAY studies have proceeded along several continua.

The first continuum is the continuum of naturalness of implementation, and this has been examined across several parameters. The parameter of who the teacher is has moved from the researcher as teacher (Lifter, et al., 1993), to classroom teacher as teacher (Lifter et al., 1992, 1997), to home-based therapist as teacher (Lifter, Ellis, Cannon, & Anderson, 1994), to parent as teacher (Ellis, Cannon, Woodward, McCaffrey, & Lifter, 1996).

The parameter of naturalness of the setting of play intervention has progressed from teaching in a pull-out arrangement in a quiet area of the classroom (Lifter et al., 1992; Lifter, et al., 1993) to ongoing activities in the classroom (Lifter et al., 1997) and to ongoing activities in the home (Ellis et al., 1996; Lifter et al., 1994).

A second continuum centered on how many play activities to teach at a time and from how many play categories. The studies have progressed from teaching one activity from one play category at a time (Lifter, et al., 1993) to teaching several activities from the same play category (Lifter et al., 1992; Lifter et al., 1997) and to teaching several activities from different but developmentally adjacent play categories at a time (Ellis et al., 1996; Lifter et al., 1994).

A third continuum focused on whether to teach play activities from the "absent" but "next step" categories, or to begin the interventions at the "emergent" level. The studies began with teaching activities at the next step level (Lifter et al., 1992; Lifter, et al., 1993) and currently begin at the emergent level (e.g., Ellis et al., 1996; Lifter et al., 1997).

The continuum of individual to group implementation progressed from a teacher teaching one child at a time (Lifter et al., 1993; Lifter et al., 1992) to a group implementation where children with and/or without disabilities participated in the groups (Lifter et al., 1995, 1997).

Recent and ongoing studies are examining the integration of individualized language objectives with play objectives in the same activity (Lifter et al., 1997) and integration of physical therapy objectives with play objects to increase the efficiency and the naturalness of educational programming for young children with developmental disabilities and delays.

Finally, new descriptive studies are underway to examine developmental relationships between play and social engagement that should inform future intervention studies for both play and social interaction. Pierce-Jordan and Lifter (1997) are investigating whether there is a systematic relationship between social behaviors and play behaviors, as defined with the DPA, for children with and without developmental disabilities. Preliminary results suggest that children's play activities vary as a function of the social requirements of the situation, which have implications for intervention targeting social goals, play goals, or both.

Obviously, considerably more research is needed to support the usefulness of the DPA for identifying Dev R play objectives for intervention. Initial results do support the claim that "developmentally relevant" play activities are more likely than "age-appropriate" play activities to be acquired quickly, to occur spontaneously, and to generalize to other stimuli and situations. If this is the case, then developmentally relevant activities have considerable potential to support developments in play and related developments in social interaction and language. Such activities are therefore well worth teaching.

CAVEATS, LIMITATIONS, AND FUTURE DIRECTIONS

Nevertheless, as a result of the preliminary nature of the studies summarized above, several caveats are offered at this point with respect to the use of the DPA for identifying objectives for intervention.

Caveats for Using the DPA

First, not all the categories identified in the DPA, based on the results reported in Lifter and Bloom (1989) and other descriptive studies (Belsky & Most, 1981; Lowe, 1975; Watson & Fischer, 1977), are developmentally progressive. Some categories decrease in relative frequency as new categories emerge. For example, Lifter and Bloom (1989) observed a progressive decrease over time in the frequency of "General Relations" relative to a progressive increase in "Specific Relations." Therefore, questions arise as to whether General Combinations should be taught before Specific Combinations, or whether General Combinations should be taught at all.

Second, although the sequence of play categories in the DPA is arranged into eight levels, there is no assumption that these levels represent equal intervals in development. The developmental gap between one adjacent pair of levels may be greater than the gap between another adjacent pair of levels. Finer distinctions between and among levels await future research.

Third, the level of play development at which to begin an intervention is not firmly specified at this point. However, as a result of the ongoing PROJECT PLAY studies, the recommendation is to target activities that are assessed at the emergent level to help the child to learn those activities before proceeding to more advanced levels. Increased specification of these decisions awaits further analyses, especially as they may have an impact on developmental progress.

Finally, best methods for implementing interventions and teaching developmentally relevant play activities are still under investigation. The results to date support teaching implementation formats in which several activities are taught at the same time and include activities from more than one category. In addition, teaching procedures have capitalized on following the child's lead (i.e., the child's focus of attention) and incorporating least-to-most prompting procedures to shape new behaviors (Sulzer-Azaroff & Mayer, 1991). These procedures may need to be adjusted as interventions incorporate more variables such as language and social goals.

Limitations and Future Directions

There are several limitations to the studies to date that inform the future directions for play intervention studies. First, the PROJECT PLAY studies that support the use of the DPA have been conducted on small numbers of children, and these have usually been children with autism. Future studies need to be conducted on larger numbers of children and to include children with varying disabilities. Because the DPA is based on the assumption that developmentally relevant play activities can be identified for individual children regardless of their disabilities, it should be effective with a wide range of populations.

Second, the construction of the DPA was based on descriptive studies of children from fairly restricted cultural backgrounds that were conceptualized from European-American theories of psychology and development. Future studies need to include the role of cultural and linguistic diversity in the development of play as these studies will inform both assessment and intervention activities. In addition, conceptualizations of play need to be broadened by theories of psychology and development that take into account development in varied sociocultural contexts.

Finally, the nature of evidence that is needed to support the facilitation of development as a result of implementing interventions centered on teaching developmentally relevant play activities is in its preliminary stages. The strongest results to date regarding an impact on development have come from the study integrating language objectives with play objectives (Lifter et al., 1997). As a result of learning developmentally relevant play activities, the target children increased in their talk about ongoing events, and in particular, the events surrounding their new learning in play. More of these kinds of results and evidence are needed to support the claim that learning developmentally relevant play activities facilitates progress in development.

In conclusion, the DPA appears to be a useful tool for identifying developmentally relevant play activities that can be linked to interventions in play to facilitate progress in development. The full range of capability of the instrument, the usefulness of directly teaching play activities, and in which combinations with which methods, along with evidence supporting the impact of learning play activities on developments in language and social interaction, await further analyses.

REFERENCES

Axline, V. M. (1947). *Play therapy.* Cambridge, MA: Riverside Press.

Ballard, K. D., & Medland, J. L. (1986). Collateral effects from teaching attention, imitation and toy interaction behaviors to a developmentally delayed handicapped child. *Child & Family Behavior Therapy, 7*(4), 47–50.

Bates, E., Begnigni, I., Bretherton, I., Camaioni, L., & Volterra, V. (1979). *The emergence of symbols.* New York: Academic Press.

Beeghly, M., Weiss-Perry, B., & Cicchetti, D. (1990). Beyond sensorimotor functioning: Early communicative and play development of children with Down syndrome. In Cicchetti & M. Beeghly (Eds.), *Children with Down syndrome: A developmental perspective* (pp. 329–368). Cambridge, England: Cambridge University Press.

Belsky, J., & Most, R. (1981). From exploration to play: A cross-sectional study of infant free play behavior. *Developmental Psychology, 17,* 630–639.

Bloom, L. (1993). *The transition from infancy to language: Acquiring the power of expression.* New York: Cambridge University Press.

Bloom, L., Beckwith, R., Capatides, J., & Hafitz, J. (1988). Expression through affects and words in the transition from infancy to language. In P. Baltes, D. Featherman, & R. Lerner (Eds.), *Lifespan development and behavior* (Vol. 8, pp. 99–127). Hillsdale, NJ: Erlbaum.

Bloom, L., & Lahey, M. (1978). *Language development and language disorders.* New York: Wiley.

Bloom, L., Lifter, K., & Broughton, J. (1985). The convergence of early cognition and language in the second year of life: Problems in conceptualization and measurement. In M. Barrett (Ed.), *Children's single-word speech.* Chichester, England: Wiley.

Bloom, L., Tinker, E., & Beckwith, R. (1997). Developments in expression: Language, emotion, and object play. Manuscript in preparation. Teachers College, Columbia University.

Bredekamp, S. (Ed.). (1987). *Developmentally appropriate practice in early childhood programs serving children birth through age 8.* Washington, D.C.: National Association for the Education of Young Children.

Bredekamp, S. and Copple, C. (Eds.). (1997). *Developmentally appropriate practice in early childhood education programs* (Rev. ed.). Washington, D.C.: National Association for the Education of Young Children.

Bricker, D., & Cripe, J. W. (1992). *An activity-based approach to early intervention.* Palo Alto, CA: Paul Brookes.

Carta, J. J., Schwartz, I. S., Atwater, J. B., & McConnell, S. R. (1991). Developmentally appropriate practice: Appraising its usefulness for young children with disabilities. *Topics in Early Childhood Special Education, 11*(1), 1–20.

Division of Early Childhood (DEC). (1994). Personnel standards for early education and early intervention: Guidelines for licensure in early childhood education. Recommendations of the Division for Early Childhood, Council of Exceptional Children, Reston, VA; National Association for the Education of Young Children, Washington, D.C.; and Association of Teacher Educators.

Dyer, K., Santarcangelo, S., & Luce, S. (1987). Developmental influences in teaching language forms to individuals with developmental disabilities. *Journal of Speech & Hearing Disorders, 52,* 335–347.

Eason, L. J., White, M. J., & Newsom, C. (1982). Generalized reduction of self-stimulatory behavior: An effect of teaching appropriate play to autistic children. *Analysis & Intervention in Developmental Disabilities, 2,* 157–169.

Elkind, D. (1990). Academic pressures—Too much, too soon: The demise of play. In E. Klugman & S. Smilansky (Eds.), *Children's play and learning* New York: Teachers College Press.

Ellis, J., Cannon, B., Woodward, S., McCaffrey, D., & Lifter, K. (1996). Parent as teacher: Play interventions in home-based programming (a pilot intervention). *Poster presented to the 23rd International Early Childhood Conference on Children with Special Needs,* Phoenix, AZ, December 1996.

Fein, G. (1979). Echoes from the nursery: Piaget, Vygotsky, and the relationship between language and play. In E. Winner & H. Gardner (Eds.), *New directions for child development, No. 6: Fact, fiction and fantasy in childhood* (pp. 1–14). San Francisco: Jossey-Bass.

Fein, G. G. (1981). Pretend play in childhood: An integrative review. *Child Development, 52,* 1095–1118.

Fenson, L., Kagan, J., Kearsley, R., & Zelazo, P. (1976). The developmental progression of manipulative play in the first two years. *Child Development, 47,* 232–236.

Fenson, L., & Ramsay, D. (1980). Decentration and integration of the child's play in the second year. *Child Development, 51,* 171–178.

Fewell, R. R., & Kaminski, R. (1988). Play skills development and instruction for young children with handicaps. In S. Odom & M. B. Karnes (Eds.), *Early intervention for infants and children with handicaps: An empirical base* (pp. 145–158). Baltimore: Paul Brookes.

Fox, L., & Hanline, M. F. (1993). A preliminary evaluation of learning within developmentally appropriate early childhood settings. *Topics in Early Childhood Special Education, 13*(3), 308–327.

Garvey, C. (1977). *Play.* Cambridge, MA: Harvard University Press.

Goldstein, H., & Cisar, C. L. (1992). Promoting interaction during sociodramatic play: Teaching scripts to typical preschoolers and classmates with disabilities. *Journal of Applied Behavior Analysis, 25,* 265–280.

Guralnick, M. J., & Groom, J. M. (1987). The peer relations of mildly delayed and nonhandicapped preschool children in mainstreamed play groups. *Child Development, 58,* 1556–1572.

Haring, T. G. (1985). Teaching between-class generalization of toy play behavior to handicapped children. *Journal of Applied Behavior Analysis, 18,* 127–139.

Hart, B., & Risley, T. (1975). Incidental teaching of language in the pre-school. *Journal of Applied Behavior Analysis, 8,* 411–420.

Hill, P. M., & McCune-Nicolich, L. (1981). Pretend play and patterns of cognition in Down's Syndrome children. *Child Development, 52,* 611–617.

Howes, C. and Matheson, C. C. (1992). Sequences in the development of competent play with peers: Social and social pretend play. *Developmental Psychology, 28*(5), 961–974.

Kennedy, M. D., Sheridan, M. K., Radlinski, S. H., & Beeghly, M. (1991). Play-language relationships in young children with developmental delays: Implications for assessment. *Journal of Speech & Hearing Research, 34,* 112–122.

Kim, Y. T., Lombardino, L. J., Rothman, H., & Vinson, B. (1989). Effects of symbolic play intervention with children who have mental retardation. *Mental Retardation, 27*(3), 159–165.

Lahey, M. (1988). *Language disorders and language development.* New York: Macmillan.

Lifter, K. (1982). Development of object related behaviors during the transition from prelinguistic to linguistic communication. University Microfilms No. 8222429.

Lifter, K. (1996). Assessing play skills. In M. McLean, D. B. Bailey, Jr., & M. Wolery (Eds.), *Assessing infants and preschoolers with special needs* (2nd ed., pp. 435–461). Englewood Cliffs, NJ: Merrill.

Lifter, K., Anderson, S. R., Campbell, S., Considine, M., Canellas, E., & Page, M. (1995) Using play to teach about objects, events, and language. *Paper presented to the 21st Annual Convention of the Association for Behavior Analysis,* Washington, DC, May 1995. Part of symposium entitled:. Improving the play, social, and communication skills of children with developmental disabilities.

Lifter, K., & Bloom, L. (1989). Object play and the emergence of language. *Infant Behavior & Development, 12,* 395–423.

Lifter, K., & Bloom, L. (1998). Intentionality and the role of play in the transition to language. In A. M. Wetherby, S. F. Warren, & J. Reichle (Eds.), *Transitions in prelinguistic communication: Preintentional to intentional and presymbolic to symbolic* (pp. 161–198). A book in the Communication and Language Intervention Series: Brookes Publishing Company.

Lifter, K., Burger, J., Anderson, S. R., Sulzer-Azaroff, B., & Campbell, S. (1992). Alternative methods for teaching developmentally appropriate play activities. *Paper presented to the 18th Annual Convention of the Association for Behavior Analysis,* San Francisco, CA, May 1992. Part of symposium entitled: Recent advances in social, play, and communication research for individuals with developmental disabilities and language impairments.

Lifter, K., Edwards, G., Avery, D., Anderson, S. R., & Sulzer-Azaroff, B. (1988). The Developmental Play Assessment (DPA) Instrument. *Miniseminar presented to the Annual Convention of the American-Speech-Language-Hearing Association,* Boston, MA, November 1988. Developmental assessment of young children's play: Implications for intervention. Revised, July 1994.

Lifter, K., Ellis, J., Cannon, B., & Anderson, S. R. (1994). Play interventions in home-based programming. *Workshop presented to the 20th Annual Convention of the Association for Behavior Analysis,* Atlanta, GA, May 1994.

Lifter, K., Pierce-Jordan, S., Pedi, R. A., Foley, C., Windham, J., Small, C., Campbell, S., & Considine, M. (1997). PROJECT PLAY: Integrating Language and Play Objectives to Support Full Inclusion. *Paper presented to the International Early Childhood Conference on Children with Special Needs,* New Orleans, November 22, 1997.

Lifter, K., Sulzer-Azaroff, B., Anderson, & Cowdery, G. (1993). Teaching play activities to preschool children with disabilities: The importance of developmental considerations. *Journal of Early Intervention, 17*(2), 139–159.

Lovinger, S. L. (1974). Sociodramatic play and language development in preschool disadvantaged children. *Psychology in the Schools, 11,* 313–320.

Lowe, M. (1975). Trends in the development of representational play in infants from one to three years—An observational study. *Journal of Child Psychology & Psychiatry, 16,* 33–47.

Malone, D. M., Stoneham, Z., & Langone, J. (1994). Contextual variation of correspondences among measures of play and developmental level of preschool children. *Journal of Early Intervention, 18*(2), 199–215.

McCune, L. (1995). A normative study of representational play at the transition to language. *Developmental Psychology, 31*(2), 198–206.

McCune-Nicolich, L. (1981). Toward symbolic functioning: Structure of early pretend games and potential parallels with language. *Child Development, 52,* 785–797.

McGee, G. G., Krantz, P., & McClannahan, L. (1985). The facilitative effects of incidental teaching on preposition use by autistic children. *Journal of Applied Behavior Analysis, 18,* 17–31.

Montessori, M. (1967). *The absorbent mind.* New York: Holt, Rinehart and Winston.

Moran, D., & Whitman, T. (1985). The multiple effects of a play-oriented parent training program for mothers of developmentally delayed children. *Analysis & Intervention in Developmental Disabilities, 5,* 73–96.

Murphy, G., Calias, M., & Carr, J. (1985). Increasing simple toy play in profoundly mentally handicapped children. I. Training to play. *Journal of Autism and Developmental Disorders, 15*(4), 375–388.

Nicolich, L. (1977). Beyond sensorimotor intelligence: Assessment of symbolic maturity and pretend play. *Merrill-Palmer Quarterly, 23,* 89–99.

Odom, S. (1981). The relationship of play to developmental level in mentally retarded preschool children. *Education and Training of the Mentally Retarded, 16,* 136–141.

Parten, M. (1932). Social participation among preschool children. *Journal of Abnormal and Social Psychology, 27,* 243–269.

Phillips, R., & Sellito, V. (1990). Preliminary evidence on emotions expressed by children during solitary play. *Play and Culture, 3,* 79–90.

Piaget, J. (1954). *The construction of reality in the child.* New York: Basic Books

Piaget, J. (1962). *Play, dreams, and imitation in childhood.* New York: W. W. Norton.

Pierce-Jordan, S., & Lifter, K. (1997). Covariation of play and social interaction in preschool children. *Paper presented to the 23rd Annual Convention of the Association for Behavior Analysis,* Chicago, IL, May 1997. Part of symposium entitled: Promoting social interactions in integrated educational settings.

Pierce-Jordan, S., & Lifter, K. (1998). The interactive relationship between the social and play behaviors of young children with and without disabilities. *Poster presented to the International Early Childhood Conference on Children with Special Needs,* Chicago, December 1998.

Power, T. J., & Radcliffe, J. (1991). Cognitive assessment of preschool play using the Symbolic Play Test. In C. E. Schaefer, K. Gitlin, & A. Sandgrund (Eds.), *Play diagnosis and assessment* (pp. 87–113). New York: Wiley.

Quinn, J., & Rubin, K. H. (1984). The play of handicapped children. In T. D. Yawkey & A. D. Pellegrini (Eds.), *Child's play: Developmental and applied* (pp. 63–80). Hillsdale, NJ: Erlbaum.

Rogers, S. (1988). Cognitive characteristics of handicapped children's play: A review. *Journal of the Division for Early Childhood, 12,* 161–168.

Rogers, S., Herbison, J., Lewis, H., Pantone, J., & Reis, K. (1986). An approach for enhancing the symbolic, communicative, and interpersonal functioning of children with autism or severe emotional handicaps. *Journal of the Division for Early Childhood, 10,* 135–148.

Rubin, K., Fein, G., & Vandenberg, B. (1983). Play. In E. M. Hetherington (Ed.), *Handbook of child psychology (vol. 4): Socialization, personality, social development.* New York: Wiley.

Ruff, H. A., & Saltarelli, L. M. (1993). Exploratory play with objects: Basic cognitive processes and individual differences. In M. H. Bornstein & A. W. O'Reilly (Eds.), *The role of play in the development of thought* (pp. 5–16). San Francisco: Jossey-Bass.

Saltz, E., Dixon, D., & Johnson, J. (1977). Training disadvantaged preschoolers on various fantasy activities: Effects on cognitive functioning and impulse control. *Child Development, 48,* 367–380.

Sigman, M., & Mundy, P. (1987). Symbolic processes in young autistic children. In D. Cicchetti & M. Beeghly (Eds.), *New directions for child development (no. 36): Symbolic development in atypical children* (pp. 31–46). San Francisco: Jossey-Bass.

Sinclair, H. (1970). The transition from sensory-motor behavior to symbolic activity. *Interchange, 1,* 119–125.

Smilansky, S. (1968). *The effects of sociodramatic play on disadvantaged preschool children.* New York: Wiley.

Smilansky, S. (1990). Sociodramatic play: Its relevance to behavior and achievement in school. In E. Klugman & S. Smilansky (Eds.), *Children's play and learning: Perspectives and policy implications* (pp. 18–42). New York: Teachers College Press.

Stahmer, A. C. (1995). Teaching symbolic play skills to children with autism using Pivotal Response Training. *Journal of Autism and Developmental Disorders, 25,* 123–141.

Stahmer, A. C., & Schreibman, L. (1992). Teaching children with autism appropriate play in unsupervised environments using a self-management treatment package. *Journal of Applied Behavior Analysis, 25,* 447–459.

Strain, P. S. (1985). Social and nonsocial determinants of acceptability in handicapped preschool children. *Topics in Early Childhood Special Education, 4*(4), 47–58.

Strain, P. S., & Odom, S. L. (1986). Peer social initiations: Effective intervention for social skills development of exceptional children. *Exceptional Children, 52,* 543–552.

Sulzer-Azaroff, B., & Mayer, G. R. (1991). *Behavior analysis for lasting change.* Fort Worth, TX: Holt, Rinehart & Winston.

Thorp, D. M., Stahmer, A. C., & Schreibman, L. (1995). Effects of sociodramatic play training on children with autism. *Journal of Autism and Developmental Disorders, 25,* 265–282.

Ungerer, J., & Sigman, M. (1981). Symbolic play and language comprehension in autistic children. *Journal of the American Academy of Child Psychiatry, 20,* 318–337.

Vondra, J., & Belsky, J. (1991). Infant play as a window on competence and motivation. In C. E. Schaefer, K. Gitlin, & A. Sandgrund (Eds.), *Play diagnosis and assessment* (pp. 13–38). New York: Wiley.

Vygotsky, L. (1978). *Mind in society: The development of higher psychological processes* (M. Cole, V. John-Steiner, S. Scribner, & E. Souberman, Eds.). Cambridge, MA: Harvard University Press. (Original work published in 1930).

Warren, S. F. (1992). Facilitating basic vocabulary acquisition with milieu teaching procedures. *Journal of Early Intervention, 16*(3), 235–251.

Warren, S. F., & Gazdag, G. (1990). Facilitating early language development with milieu intervention procedures. *Journal of Early Intervention, 14,* 62–86.

Watson, M. W., & Fischer, K. W. (1977). A developmental sequence of agent use in late infancy. *Child Development, 48,* 828–836.

Wehman, P. (1975). Establishing play behaviors in mentally retarded youth. *Rehabilitation Literature, 36,* 238–246.

Westby, C. (1980). Assessment of cognitive and language abilities through play. *Language Speech and Hearing Sciences in the Schools, 11,* 154–158.

Westby, C. (1991). A scale for assessing children's play. In C. E. Schaefer, K. Gitlin, & A. Sandgrund (Eds.), *Play diagnosis and assessment* (pp. 131–161). New York: Wiley.

Wikstrom, P. (1994). *The role of attention in early cognitive development.* New York: Columbia University.

Wing, L., Gould, J., Yeates, S. R., & Brierly, L. M. (1977). Symbolic play in severely mentally retarded and in autistic children. *Journal of Child Psychology & Psychiatry, 18,* 167–178.

Chapter 9

THE PLAY OBSERVATION KIT (POKIT): AN OBSERVATIONAL ASSESSMENT TECHNIQUE FOR YOUNG CHILDREN

Kay Mogford-Bevan

INTRODUCTION

POKIT (pronounced to rhyme with *rocket*) stands for the Play Observation Kit. It is a broadly based developmental assessment procedure for children between 12 and 48 months that uses the observation of spontaneous interactive play with a standard set of toys. POKIT is still in the process of development but, as part of that development, a version is being used in a range of clinical settings. Once the development work has been completed, a manual, a set of observation checklists, a play questionnaire, and an assessment summary will be published by Egghead Publications, England.

POKIT is designed for use by any professional who needs to carry out a comprehensive assessment of children who have already been identified as showing delay in one or more areas of development through screening or other forms of developmental surveillance. It is intended to be used with children for whom more formal assessment procedures are unsuitable.

This chapter describes the POKIT play assessment, starting with a general outline and proceeding to more detailed descriptions of the procedure in subsequent sections. The first section explains what the assessment aims to do as well as when and with whom it is designed to be used, emphasizing its principal features. The second section provides a description of the components of the kit and an indication of their function. The third section explains the origin and design of the current version of the assessment. The fourth section describes the method used to develop the *Checklists* and the developmental norms that they incorporate, which are the main element in the assessment. The fifth section provides an outline of the procedure used to carry out the assessment. This is followed by three case studies to illustrate some ways in which POKIT has been used. The final section reflects critically on the procedure and discusses validity and reliability.

WHAT IS POKIT AND WHO MIGHT USE IT?

The Play Observation Kit provides an approach to the developmental assessment of very young children who are showing delays and developmental deviations that may indicate the presence of disorders or disabilities. For example, it could be used for children who are having difficulty with speech and language or social or cognitive functioning. It is designed for children who are developmentally between the ages of 12–48 months.

In general, the purpose of screening early development is to identify children showing delays in one or more areas of development. Once identified they will need to be referred for further assessment by an appropriate professional. This may be a pediatrician, educational psychologist, speech and language pathologist, occupational therapist, or teacher, for example. If significant delays are confirmed at this further assessment then both the child's parents or other caretakers and the professional will want to try to understand the reason for the delays as well as to diagnose conditions that may further hinder the child's development and education. With this information, appropriate intervention can be provided.

When children are very young, however, the investigation of developmental delays and diagnosis cannot be carried out through extensive behavioral testing alone. Very young children are often unable or unwilling to cooperate in tasks set by strange adults and lack the communication skills needed to understand and respond to "formal" test procedures. When the child "fails" an item it is often not possible to tell whether this reflects a lack of competence or cooperation. This means that tests rarely provide positive evidence of the child's most advanced abilities and are hard to interpret with confidence, leaving a great deal of uncertainty surrounding assessment. This does not help the parents of the child being assessed since it is a time when they are already inevitably very anxious. Parents may expect specialists to give them clear-cut opinions that are reached in a short period of time. It is also essential that the child's parents and the specialist conducting the assessment can reach agreement on both the child's abilities and disabilities. Further, parents need to feel that the diagnosis and decisions about intervention are based on a representative sample of the child's typical behavior and are a true reflection of his or her development.

The method usually chosen to assess children in these circumstances is to observe the child's spontaneous play. Child initiated and directed play behaviors are likely to reveal the child's understanding and competence as well as difficulties that may result from impairments. The numerous advantages of play assessment have been outlined by Schaefer, Gitlin, and Sandgrund in 1991. As far as POKIT is concerned, the voluntary nature of play means that children do not need to understand and follow instructions. For children who lack verbal abilities they can express their understanding through the way they handle and interact with the play materials. Since POKIT uses interactive play with a familiar partner it also allows for the assessment of social interaction in a familiar and relatively unstressful situation.

What the POKIT assessment aims to do is to provide a guided approach to a broadly based observational play assessment, which makes the information derived from this approach more reliable, systematic, and productive. It also involves a child's parent at all stages of the process. This is important because as Newson (1976) points out, "parents are experts on their own children. ... They know more about the child, on a very intimate level, than anyone else does." This includes knowledge of the child's play.

POKIT is not intended to be a mechanical procedure but one that draws on clinical knowledge and strengthens clinical judgment. At the same time, it develops the play observation skills of the professionals involved in the assessment process. By involving a parent throughout the play assessment procedure, the professional is using a valuable resource (Newson, 1976). The parent can set the observation in the context of the child's day-to-day play. By encouraging and supporting the child's play that is observed, the parent can help to produce a richer and more typical sample of play. The procedure is also designed to use and develop the parent's knowledge of the child's development. Involving the parent helps to get a more reliable assessment and one that both professional and parent can be confident is typical of the child. In addition, since intervention is likely to involve a parent in daily play activities with the child, it can provide pointers to those aspects of play to encourage and the level at which this encouragement should begin.

It is important for professionals to be able not only to assess the child's developmental status but also to look at the child's ability to develop and learn through adult-child interaction in play. POKIT aims to help professionals assess the child's learning potential as well as his or her developmental status.

A DESCRIPTION OF POKIT

The POKIT assessment uses a standard set of toys. These are used with every child. The toys in the set are as follows: (1) a set of graded stacking tubs and a simple posting box; (2) the Galt's Pop-up toy; (3) the Escor Two-Horse Roundabout; (4) a set of picture- and storybooks; (5) a pretend set, which includes a doll and cot, a tea set, and a telephone. They are described and illustrated in more detail below.

The Checklists

The kit also provides five observational Checklists, one for each of the sets of toys listed above. The main purpose of the Checklists is to prime and guide professionals in their observation; that is, to help them to attend to those aspects of the child's play that change with age and maturity across a broad range of abilities. As Vondra and Belsky (1991) have pointed out, research into children's play from the mid-seventies to the late eighties increased "The realisation that there is a sequence of increasingly sophisticated play acts exhibited across development that corresponds conceptually and empirically with other cognitive achievements." The Checklists embody this realization.

The play acts included on the Checklists have been determined by observational research using the toys with over 100 children whose ages spread across and beyond the age range of the assessment and who show no signs of delay and impairment. Although the age range of the assessment is 12 to 48 months the Checklists were compiled through observation of children between 7 and 55 months. The play items observed and recorded in the research are influenced by accounts of specific aspects of play development (e.g., Fenson, Kagan, Kearsley, & Zelzazo, 1976; McCune-Nicolich, 1981; Ungerer, Zelzazo, Kearsley, & O'Leary, 1981; Leslie, 1987) as well as accounts of cognitive and social development reported in the literature that may be observed in interactive play, in particular, conversational competence (e.g. Gallagher, 1981; Garvey 1984), and emerging literacy (see Mogford-Bevan & Summersall, 1997 for a more detailed account). There is also some overlap with existing developmental assessments, such as the Symbolic Play Test (Lowe & Costello, 1976); the PIP

Developmental Charts (Jeffree & McConkey, 1976); The Test of Pragmatic Skills, (Shulman, 1985); and the Schedule of Growing Skills (Bellman & Cash, 1987), as test items that appear in these, occur spontaneously in play and are therefore included in the Checklists.

The items listed on each checklist relate to one toy or sets of toys in the kit and consist of *specific, objective, and concrete* descriptions of play acts typically observed with that toy. Extracts from one of the Checklists are included in Tables 9.1 and 9.2. Beside each item on the checklist is a guide to the typical age range in which the play was observed in a study of normally developing children. There is also a section (not shown) on each checklist that encourages the observation of qualities in the child's play that relate to their ability to learn and interact with others. This is called the *Qualitative Summary*. For example, this section encourages an assessment of the child's ability to attend, to persist in the face of difficulty, to learn during the session, or to apply prior knowledge. The child's communication and interactive abilities are also highlighted. A list of sections in the qualitative summary is shown in Table 9–3.

Developmental Status Summary

The items observed and the developmental range indicated for each item are collected together and entered onto a *Developmental Status Summary,* which shows a distribution of items by

Table 9–1   Sub-sections on the checklist for the Stacking Toy and Posting Box listed in order that they appear on the checklists.

STACKING TOY
After demonstration
Dismantles and unpacks tubs
Handles and explores tubs
Container play and 'boxes'*
Stacks tubs
Nests tubs
Corrects graded sequence
Uses hands
Prepares and completes
POSTING BOX
After demonstration
Handles and explores shapes
Handles box and lid
Manipulates shapes and co-ordinates hand and eye
Posts
Strategies used on failing to post*
Prepares and completes
Experiments and breaks rules
SUB-SECTIONS CONTAINING ITEMS COMMON TO
POSTING BOX AND STACKING TOY
Pretends
Uses concepts- color, shape, number, size
Uses of language

The sub-sections marked with * are shown in detail in Table 2 below

Table 9–2.   Details of sub-sections from the POKIT checklist for the Stacking Toy and Posting Box.

STACKING   TOY

Container play and 'boxes'

Drops one tub inside another but not nesting (tub is on its side)---------------------------------- ☐ 13-15m→

Puts one tub upside down inside another to form a box-- ☐ 19-21m→

Unpacks a box formed from 2 tubs--- ☐ 22-24m→

Puts any other item inside a tub -- ☐ 13-15m→

Fingers or manipulates items while inside the tub-- ☐ 13-15m→

Puts several items, one at a time, inside a tub -- ☐ 16-18m→

Shakes/rattles the tub with items inside--- ☐ 16-18m→

Turns/tips item out of a tub --- ☐ 19-21m→

Tips object from tub into another container-- ☐ 25-30m→

Inverts a larger tub over a smaller tub --- ☐ 25-30m→

POSTING   BOX

Strategies attempted on failure

Leaves shape on posting box lid-- ☐ 25-30m↓

Throws /discards shape --- ☐ 25-30m↓

Pushes harder --- ☐ 13-15m→

Rubs piece around over holes--- ☐ 16-18m→

Changes hands -- ☐ 19-21m→

Reorientates piece -- ☐ 19-21m→

Tries another hole --- ☐ 19-21m→

Opens box and posts without going through the hole -- ☐ 19-21m→

Selects another shape -- ☐ 25-30m→

Visually scans lid and/or studies shape-- ☐ 25-30m→

Asks for assistance (verbally or non-verbally)-- ☐ 31-36m→

Successfully posts shape as a result of any strategy after failure--------------------------------- ☐ 19-21m→

An arrow pointing forward (→) indicates a developmental item. This is one which is observed from this age band onwards. An arrow pointing downwards (↓) indicates a transitional item. This is one which is not observed beyond the age level given.

age (see Figure 9–1 for a blank example). This provides a systematic basis for making judgments about the child's developmental status, that is, whether the child is delayed or shows play development in the appropriate developmental range for his or her chronological age.

This summary also provides diagnostic information. It illustrates areas of play that may be better developed than others. For example, the play set contains items that encourage symbolic play and some that do not require play at a symbolic level. It is therefore possible to compare the child's play in symbolic and nonsymbolic abilities. The Developmental Status Summary can also play a part in planning goals for intervention by showing the toys on which play is most advanced and those where play is more delayed.

Table 9–3.   Sections in the Qualitative Summary for all of the checklists

1. INITIAL PLAY LEVEL: *(a) Discovers features*
(b) Already knows features
(c) Level of play achieved through interaction
A list of the different ways in which children can play with the toy is used for (a), (b), and (c). Sections (a) and (b) allow the observer to determine the child's prior knowledge and their ability to apply this to the toy. Section (c) allows the observer to see how much the child's play with the toy is extended through interaction with the participating adult.

2. *MANIPULATION AND HAND–EYE COORDINATION*
This section draws attention to the features of the toy that can be used to assess manipulative skills.

3. *QUALITY OF PLAY AND EXPLORATION*
This section draws attention to the child's methods of sensory exploration and degree of curiosity in exploration.

4. *VARIATION AND FLEXIBILITY IN PLAY*
This section draws attention to the variety of different aspects of a toy exploited by the child and the child's ability to combine toys in play. It helps to identify stereotypic play as well as creativity.

5. *PERSISTENCE*
This draws the observer's attention to items where the child fails in his or her intentions. It assesses the child's willingness to persist and the degree of assistance given by the adult play partner.

6. *LEARNING AND PROBLEM SOLVING*
This section prompts the observer to examine those aspects of involvement with each toy in which learning and problem solving can be observed.

7. *ATTENTION*
This section provides the observer with a means to rate the child's ability to attend to a toy until a completion point is reached, with or without the need of the adult to bring the child's attention back to an activity. Completion points are defined for each toy.

8. *COMMUNICATION*
(a) Expression (i) nonverbal (ii) verbal
(b) Reception
This section provides the observer with a checklist to identify the child's means of expression in communication, both nonverbal and verbal. It also prompts the observer to study the interaction to see what forms of communication the child responds to.

The sections in the Qualitative Summary for the Picture and Storybooks are as follows:

1. BOOK HANDLING—level of sophistication in book handling

2. REPRESENTATION—ability to recognize pictures

3. ATTENTION—length of attention given to books

4. LISTENING—ability to listen to adult when paraphrasing or reading text

5. LITERACY AWARENESS AND STORY INTEGRITY—awareness of print and story conventions

6. COMMUNICATION—verbal and nonverbal skills—receptive and expressive

7. CONVERSATION—level of conversational skill

Figure 9–1.   A blank example of the Developmental Status Summary

DEVELOPMENTAL STATUS SUMMARY

Child's Name: **Chronical Age:**

AGE BANDS in months	07–09	10–12	13–15	16–18	19–21	22–24	25–30	31–36	37–42	43–48	49+
Stacking toy & Posting box											
Pop-up toy											
Roundabout											
Pretend— telephone											
Pretend—tea-set											
Pretend—doll/cot											
Picture and story books											

NOTES

1. Complete the Developmental Status Summary directly from the Checklists.

2. The summary distinguishes the representational toys from those that have fewer representational items. The toys above the double line have fewer representational items than those below the line.

3. First enter all Developmental items (those marked with a forward-pointing arrow) on the Checklists. Then, with a different color or symbol, enter the Transitional items (i.e., those marked with a downward-pointing arrow) on the Checklists.

4. The child's Developmental Status is indicated by the most advanced levels checked on the chart for Developmental items. If there are Developmental items in or above this level then the child's play is age appropriate.

5. If there are no items in and above the child's age band *and* a number of Transitional items *below* the child's chronological age, this indicates a developmental delay. Transitional items in or above the child's age band are not significant.

6. The Developmental Level should not be treated as a test score but as evidence for comparability of the observed play with that of children of the age level indicated.

For an illustration of the form in use see Figure 9–6.

Play Questionnaire

A *Play Questionnaire* is used to introduce the assessment to the parents and to gather information about the child's play preferences, opportunities, and play partners. (Sections 2, 3, and 4 of the Questionnaire are shown in the Appendix). This provides an opportunity to learn from the parents about the child's play at home to compare with the play observed in the clinical setting. Included in this guided-interview schedule are questions that prompt parents to report any difficulties their child may have in play or that they have experienced in playing with their child. These difficulties can then be addressed in intervention. The questionnaire also allows the clinician to ask parents about the child's previous experience with the toys in the standard set before the play is observed. A set of photographs is used to illustrate the toys in the kit so that they can be laid out elsewhere or kept out of sight until everyone is prepared for the play session to begin.

Table 9–4.   Summary of the eight stages in the procedure for the POKIT assessment

1. Introduce and explain the procedure to the parent of the child who is to be assessed.
2. Find out from the child's parent about the child's typical play and play experience using the Play Questionnaire.
3. Sample the child's interactive play with parent or other familiar caretaker using the standard set of toys. Videotape and make notes from direct observation.
4. Find out from the child's parent how typical he or she considers the play sample to be, using the framework on the Play Questionnaire—Section 4.
5. Identify items observed on the Checklists for each toy.
6. Transfer items from the Checklists to the Developmental Status Summary.
7. Complete the Qualitative Summaries on each Checklist.
8. Interpret the summaries and draw up reports as appropriate.

The child's parent (or another familiar caretaker) is asked to play and interact with the child and the standard set of toys while the child is observed. This is a critical feature of the assessment since play with a familiar person is more likely to produce a typical sample of play and to increase the amount of adult-child interaction that can be observed than does play with a stranger. It also means that the clinician is free to observe carefully without the need to participate and encourage the child to play.

The play sample is also recorded on videotape and this can be scanned several times to gain the maximum amount of information possible on different aspects of ability. It is often impossible to pay attention to all the necessary details when observing play directly. Replaying a tape allows a clinician to check details and concentrate on a different aspect of behavior each time, such as speech and communication or hand–eye coordination. Notes are also made during the live play session. As the user becomes more familiar with the assessment, more information is noted during the live observation and there is less reliance on the video recording. However, the recording allows for more objective and systematic observations.

The play sample needed for the assessment is between 15 and 20 minutes in length. At the end of the recording parents are invited to say how typical the play was with each of the toys in the kit. They are asked to say if the child failed to meet their expectations or perhaps exceeded them in some way. If it is felt that the child has not shown a satisfactory sample parents are asked to suggest modifications in the circumstances that they think would lead to a better outcome. The assessment can be repeated following their suggestions. A brief outline of the main stages of the procedure is given in Table 9–4.

The Toys and Checklists in Detail

The Roundabout and the Pop-up Toy

The two commercially available toys, the Roundabout and the Pop-up toy, are illustrated in Figures 9.2 and 9.3. The Roundabout is a wooden construction toy that is painted in a variety of primary colors. The pegmen, horses, and seats are detachable. The top of the Roundabout and the central pole on which it rotates can be removed from the base. The Pop-up toy consists of four wooden pegs that fit into a wooden base. Each of the pegs is a different color (red, green, blue, and yellow) with a pink face and hat painted on one

**Figure 9–2.   The Escor Two-Horse Roundabout. Available from Escor Toys, UK.
Photograph: Derek Hawes, Audio Visual Centre, University of Newcastle upon
Tyne. Copyright University of Newcaste upon Tyne.**

end. There are springs at the bottom of each hole so that the pegmen can be made to
bounce up and down and to jump out of the holes. On one side of the wooden base there
is a colored strip that corresponds to each hole (red, green, blue, and yellow), thus allowing the pegmen to be matched to the colored strips. These two toys proved to be the most
unfamiliar to children in the normative study.

Any version of the three remaining sets of toys can be used in the assessment kit so long
as they have the key features in common with the versions used to develop the assessment,
described above. In the normative study different versions of the toys were used in a random way.

Stacking Tubs and Posting Box

(1) The stacking toy is a set of eight or nine round stacking plastic size-graded tubs. Each
neighboring tub in the size sequence is a different color, although some colors are repeated
in some versions of the toy. (2) The posting-box is a plain-colored wooden box with a lid
on the top with holes of various geometric shapes cut in the lid. There are two or three

Figure 9–3.   Galt's Pop-up toy. Available from GaltToys, UK. Photograph: Derek Hawes, Audio Visual Centre, University of Newcastle upon Tyne. Copyright University of Newcaste upon Tyne.

examples of each solid shape that can be posted through only one hole. These pieces are usually color coded (i.e., every circle is red, each square is green, etc.). Each posting box includes a circle, a square, and a triangle as well as two or three other shapes that vary with the version of the toy used.

The Pretend Set

(1) The doll and cot. A dressed baby doll is used. The doll used should be the appropriate color and have appropriate racial features for the family taking part. The doll can vary in size from 12 to 16 inches. A pillow and a bed cover are included with a cot that should be the appropriate size for the doll. (2) The telephone. Each version is a single primary color. Each has buttons with numbers on them for dialing, a base, and a moveable receiver joined by a cord. The receiver and base design can vary but there should be a rest on the base for the receiver. (3) The tea set. This comprises a teapot, milk jug, sugar bowl, two cups and saucers, and two spoons. Each version is made of colored plastic. The teapot and the sugar bowl should have lids.

Picture and Story Books

The books used in the normative study were likely to be familiar and popular with children as they were purchased from retail book shops with branches in most large towns and cities. There are six books in the set that vary in content, illustrations, and physical properties. The aim is to present a progression from the simplest to the more sophisticated picture books. Different sets were used throughout the normative study although in each set there were books that met the following requirements:

1. A first book with thick vinyl pages and one brightly colored simple picture per page. These should be highly familiar pictures (i.e., items that often occur in a child's first word vocabulary). Each double-page spread should reflect the theme of the book but there is no story. The book should be 8 to 12 pages in length.

2. A thick card book with photographic or simple pictures, no written text, and no story. Each double-page spread should deal with a self-contained topic; pictures should depict domestic routines or familiar neighborhood experiences. The book should be approximately 12 pages in length.

3. A "flap" book which should have one written sentence per page and a simple story with a very repetitive verbal theme leading to a climax at the end. There should be paper flaps that when lifted reveal a picture underneath. Pictures should be simple, with uncluttered backgrounds. The book should be approximately 12 pages in length.

4. A "Ladybird Toddler Book" with full or double-page realistic illustrations with background; a single theme (e.g., vehicles, farm animals, or a toddler's day); several lines of text per page. It should have approximately 20 pages made of paper rather than board or vinyl.

5. and 6. Two story books that should have several lines of text per page, complex pictures clearly illustrating story and characters and a fully developed narrative. At least one story book should portray a popular character that is familiar from TV and video. The books should be approximately 20 to 30 paper pages in length.

Checklists

Each checklist is in two parts: the *Main Section* and the *Qualitative Summary*.

The Main Section

The Main Section of each Checklist is divided into subsections with headings that indicate the different types of play activities possible with the toy. These are listed in the developmental order in which they are typically exploited in play by children in the age range of the assessment. Each Checklist makes use of the same format.

Age Bands   At the end of each item is the age band in which it has been observed in children developing without impairments. The same age bands are used for all the Checklists. The bands go up in 3-month intervals from 7 to 24 months (i.e., 7–9m, 10–12m, 13–15m, 16–18m, 19–21m, 21–24m) and in 6-month intervals from 24 to 48 months (24–30m, 31–36m, 37–42m, 43–48m, 49m+).

The age band is followed by an arrow that indicates the type of item, of which there are two types. *Transitional items* (indicated by a downward arrow) are items that drop out of the child's play as he or she grows older. For example, 19–21m ↓ indicates that the play was observed in children up to the age of 19 to 21 months but not beyond it. The majority of items are *Developmental items* that enter the repertoire at a certain age and are observed subsequently in older children. These are shown by the forward-pointing arrow after the age band. For example, 31–36m → indicates that the behavior was first observed at this age and was also observed in older children across the age range of the assessment. See Table 9–2.

The Qualitative Summary

This section on the checklist is broadly the same for four of the toys but is different for the checklist on picture- and storybooks. This is because the abilities demonstrated in picture-book reading with an adult are different from the abilities revealed when children are playing with other toys in the set. A list of the sections included in the Qualitative Summary is given in Table 9–3. The Qualitative Summary is concerned with what can be gleaned from the assessment about the child's learning capacity, motivation, and exploration. Each checklist asks the observer to indicate which aspects of the toy the child was able to exploit on his or her own and how this was extended with adult support and encouragement. It also invites the observer to look for and describe the child's use of existing knowledge and previous experience. Where exploration occurs, observers are asked to note any unusual uses of the senses that might indicate a sensory impairment. Another section invites close observation of hand use and hand–eye coordination. In a section on attention, observers are asked to indicate the extent of the child's ability to sustain attention in play. They are prompted to note the point at which the child's attention shifts away from an activity and whether the adult needs to bring the child's attention back to the activity in order to sustain or complete a play sequence. Attention is assessed in relation to the concept of completion points (i.e., the points in the stream of activity at which a goal or task is completed). There are several for each toy (e.g., Stacking tubs, all the tubs stacked; Roundabout, all pegmen removed or replaced; Pretend set, the doll tucked up in bed). To indicate persistence, all items on the main section of the Checklist that record a failure in an intended action are starred. Observers are asked to use these items to look at the child's response to failure and their persistence in solving problems. The child's flexibility and creativity are also assessed by looking at how many different aspects of the toys are exploited as well as at the combination of items within the standard set. Each section ends with a summary of observations of the child's means of expressive communication and a summary of the child's responses to his or her play partner's communication. This section can be used to identify children with possible hearing and speech impairments.

The Developmental Status Summary

This is simply a way of displaying the range of items recorded on the main section of each checklist on one chart to show the distribution of items by age. The age band in which the child's chronological age falls is shaded in. Developmental items are marked on the chart for all the toys. Transitional items are then marked, either in a different color or using the symbol "T" (see the example in Figure 9–4 on p. 287.)

For children whose development is age appropriate, there should be a number of items falling in the shaded age band or in age bands above this for all the toys. There will always be Developmental items falling in the age bands below the child's age but these are not significant because Developmental items indicate behaviors that enter a child's play repertoire at a certain age and continue as the child gets older. Transitional items that fall above the child's age are also an indication of age-appropriate play since these items should disappear, to be replaced by more mature play behavior, when the child reaches the relevant age. However, Transitional items that fall *below* the child's chronological age band may suggest a delay since these would normally have been replaced by more mature behavior at a younger age. A number of these, especially if these are associated with few or no developmental items in the shaded age band, indicate a developmental delay on that toy or across the board if found on all of the toys.

For example, in Figure 9–4, Peter has 4 Developmental Items in the shaded age band and one in the age band above his age although this item was prompted by his mother and was not spontaneous. The age-appropriate items occur in the nonrepresentational toys, above the double line. However, he has Developmental items across all of the toys in the age band below his chronological age. This suggests that he is in the lower range for his chronological age. His pretend play, especially with the doll and cot, looks more delayed as he has two Transitional items, that would normally not be observed in a child of his chronological age. These items were not observed in normally developing children after the ages of 12 and 21 months respectively.

WHY AND HOW WAS POKIT DEVELOPED?

The Need for the POKIT Assessment

The need for an assessment of this kind became apparent to the author over twenty years ago when employed on an action research project based in the Nottingham University Toy Library (Newson, Newson, Head, & Mogford, 1975). The aim of the research was to look at the role of play and toys in the remediation of a range of developmental disabilities in early childhood. Children and their parents visited the library to borrow play materials that were developmentally appropriate, attractive, and accessible. They also received encouragement and help in providing play activities at home that would be valuable for each child. The majority of clients were under the age of three years and often their development could not be predicted by their chronological age. In addition, the range of impairments and disabilities of each child produced a complex picture of development.

It was obvious that some standard means was needed to observe the play of all clients as a basis for choosing suitable toys and advising parents on intervention. Research established that none of the available means for assessing play development was entirely suitable for this purpose. A set of four toys were selected and these were then used routinely in clinical sessions. When the child had been observed playing with these toys, it was possible to choose suitable toys from the library for the child to try and then to borrow. The assessment toys were chosen because they were consistently attractive and encouraged children to explore and play, they were appropriate to the developmental level of most clients, and they covered a range of different types of play. The procedure was formalized (Mogford, 1979) and called "The Observational Play Repertoires" (OPRs).

Ten years later the OPRs were used by the author in teaching play observation to students who were training as speech and language therapists at the University of Newcastle, England. The response of the students encouraged the author to develop the OPRs and helped to identify problems limiting their usefulness. A major revision of the procedure was undertaken to deal with these problems and this led to the development of the POKIT assessment.

Critique of Some Approaches to Play Assessment

At this stage, some hard thinking was prompted by the author's own clinical experience and concern in regard to the lack of reliability of play as a means of assessment. Children as young as 18 to 24 months were being seen routinely for assessment in the speech and language clinic attached to the university. Play observation was invariably used in their assessment. Although two observers might agree on what was objectively observed, the developmental status given to these observations could vary considerably. There were often reservations about whether the play observed was representative of the child's typical play. The same child could be assessed on different occasions using different play materials with varying results. In some cases the child was engaged in play by a stranger and in others by a familiar person. All of these factors undermined the confidence of the assessors in their conclusions. The process often had to be extended in time before sufficient confidence in the assessment was gained to make diagnostic hypotheses or to take action on intervention. The information derived from the assessment was limited, which meant that a range of other means were also employed to assess development. Because of the age of the children and their limited cooperation, a successful outcome was not always obtained.

By the late 1980s a greater variety of play assessment materials, checklists, and scales were available for use, but often these were narrow in focus, abstract in formulation, or used a "test" procedure that often failed to elicit play from the child being assessed. For example, Lowe and Costello's Symbolic Play Test (1976) was widely used. Although based on empirical observation of play development (Lowe, 1975), it considers only a rather limited interpretation of symbolic play (i.e., the ability to use and relate miniature objects in various ways). It fails to look at the child's double knowledge or the use of imagined elements. It does not look at thematic sequences in pretend play. This is one of the criticisms made by Power and Radcliffe (1991), who also are critical of the test on psychometric grounds. Additionally, it is limited in usefulness because it is concerned only with symbolic play. For some children, particularly those with disorders of language and communication, concentrating on symbolic play alone masks areas of competence and understanding that are nonsymbolic but can provide valuable insight into a child's reasoning, conceptual development, and learning. Pretend play initially takes place in relatively intimate, familiar, and interactive settings with infants. The Symbolic Play Test situation is unnatural in that the parent is asked not to interact with the child. Although, ostensibly, all the child is required to do is play, the testing situation tends to communicate to the child that a performance is expected. These are exactly the pressures that children with communication difficulties often resist. The test also has some serious flaws in the scoring if the child fails to engage in play with any of the toy sets presented through lack of motivation, which is not infrequent.

The developmental scale of infant play (Belsky & Most, 1981) is another possible aid to play assessment but it has a limited age range. While it does refer to nonsymbolic activities that predate the emergence of symbolic play, it does not continue to deal with stages in development in nonsymbolic play after the emergence of pretend play. It also suffers from drawbacks common to most developmental scales of play. The observer often has to interpret levels that are defined and described in fairly abstract and general terms and relate these to very specific examples of observed play. This undermines reliability and also restricts the use of the assessment to those with a knowledge of principles underlying the scale.

Westby's play scale (1980, 1991) covers a broader age range but has similar shortcomings. The definition of some items is ambiguous and could refer to play of differing levels of complexity. Also, some items indicating a particular developmental level may persist and continue to be observed even though the child has reached more advanced levels of development. Consequently, a child may be recorded as playing at several different levels in one play session. This provides problems for interpreting the developmental status of the child being assessed.

Rationale for Design of the POKIT Assessment

The Play Observation Kit was designed to tackle some of these difficulties and to build on the work undertaken in developing the Observational Play Repertoires. By using a standard set of toys observers can develop a familiarity with the typical play behaviors demonstrated and the developmental sequence in which they emerge on each toy. The Checklists consist of items of play behavior that have been repeatedly observed in the 100 or more normal children that have been observed in the process of their development. A normative study of 55 children provides data on which the age levels on each checklist are based.

As Schaefer et al. (1991) point out, the use of operationally described play acts in play assessment "serves to clarify and increase the reliability." Reliability is also increased because two assessors using the POKIT procedure are more likely to observe a similar sample of play using the same toys and to agree on the developmental significance of the items observed because of the developmental levels given on the Checklists. Any child will produce a large number of items that appear on the Checklists in a 15- to 20-minute sample, from which a trend can be determined when these are displayed on the Developmental Status Summary. This helps to make the observation process less selective and allows the observer to make judgments about developmental status using a large number of items.

The problem of providing opportunities to observe different types of play was tackled by choosing items for the standard set of toys that range from those with few symbolic elements (e.g., the shape posting box and the set of graded stacking tubs) to a set that consists of items designed to elicit pretend play, namely a telephone, a tea-set, and a doll and cot. In order to assess emerging literacy, a set of picture- and storybooks were included. The two remaining toys were chosen because of their appeal and novelty and also because of their long-term endurance as commercially available toys.

Another problem identified with play assessment is clinicians' concern that the child's behavior might be atypical when the child is seen in strange surroundings and approached by a strange person. Though it may not always be possible to avoid strange surroundings it is possible to ensure that the child plays with a familiar partner. This is important because it is evident that children of the age at which this type of play assessment is used are rarely able to play for a sustained period without the attention and support of an adult. This also provides the best situation for observing communication and learning.

There are several reasons why POKIT uses the child's parent or familiar caretaker as a play partner to elicit the sample of play. First, in the clinical context, involving parents in the assessment process has many advantages for the relationship between the parent and the professional as has been discussed above. Second, research in child development over the last 30 years, particularly in parent-child interaction, has emphasized the role of the familiar caretaker in developing the child's play. For example, O'Connell and Bretherton (1984) compared independent and collaborative play with mother and found that collaborative play was more diverse than independent play. Fiese (1990) found that when children between 15 and 24 months played with their mothers, the play was more complex than when they played alone. Longer sequences and more advanced play is likely to occur in circumstances in which the child feels emotionally secure and in the presence of a familiar caretaker (Slade, 1987). For young children this is in close proximity to a person with whom they have an emotional attachment. At the same time, observation of parents and children has demonstrated that in a play setting important interactive routines are built up. Familiar caretakers learn to understand and anticipate the child's needs while the child learns to predict the adult's response (Bruner, 1975). Finally, the involvement of the parent allows the clinician to develop knowledge about the child's typical play experiences at home and to evaluate the quality of the sample of play observed. This is important information that needs to be taken into account when developing a strategy for intervention. These design features increase the confidence of the professional in the information gained from observation and its interpretation. They can also reduce the length of time invested in the assessment process.

The video recording of the play session is another way of increasing the reliability of observation. At first, it can take some time to review the tape fully. However, if carried out thoroughly, it can provide detailed information on a wide range of development and learning skills that might otherwise need to be assessed piecemeal, over several sessions.

In the early stages of the development of POKIT, it was used in parallel with a multidisciplinary assessment in a Child Development Centre. This showed that more communication and expressive language was observed in the POKIT assessment than in more conventional clinical investigations. Additionally, the child's motivation was greater with POKIT. For example, the child might play with items previously rejected. The POKIT assessment proved valuable when children had been through a long assessment session, had experienced painful or trying medical investigations, or if they suffered from a chronic illness. In the latter case, because they often felt unwell, the children showed a low threshold of tolerance or had a limited attention span for tasks used during more conventional assessments. When the POKIT play assessment was completed, in similar clinical circumstances, these difficulties were not so apparent. Parents were usually able to confirm that the children being assessed were better motivated and the sample of play recorded was more representative of their usual or best play.

POKIT 1998

The current version of POKIT has been developed over eight years (1991–1998) using two samples of normally developing children and children with delays and disabilities seen in various clinical settings. As data have been accumulated, the Checklists have been revised several times. Each version has been used in clinical settings in consultation with colleagues and students so that gradually the content and the procedure have been developed and refined. Small-scale research studies have been undertaken to look at particular aspects of the assessment. One study was devoted to collecting items for a pilot version of the Checklist on picture- and storybooks (Browning, 1991). A study is currently being conducted to explore a version developed for use in the British-born Chinese community. There are plans to extend this study to see if it is a valid form of assessment for children growing up in a variety of other minority cultures.

The largest part of the development work has been a study undertaken to provide the developmental norms for the assessment. In this study 55 children without delay and disability were recorded on videotape while playing with their mother or a caretaker using the standard set of toys. From these observations, the final revision of the Checklists will be prepared and the age norms determined.

DEVELOPING THE CHECKLISTS AND THE NORMATIVE STUDY

The earliest versions of the Checklists resulted from a reorganization and simplification of the items on the Observational Play Repertoires (OPRs).

The items on the OPRs had been obtained by observing 30 children, without disability, differing in age across the range of 6 months to 5 years. From a single video recording of each child playing with his or her mother, play on the four assessment toys was described. These toys were a doll, a cot and bed clothing, a wooden constructional Roundabout (Escor), a wooden Pop-up toy (Galt) and a plastic Pop-up-cones toy. The last toy was marketed by several companies before it went out of production. On each toy, starting with the youngest child and then in ascending order of age, every play act observed was listed the first time it occurred. Tallies were made against items that had already been observed in younger children, to give a measure of frequency. As anticipated, as children became older, more advanced items were recorded and earlier items were no longer observed. Finally, items that had only been observed once were eliminated from the lists for each toy. The age at which the items were first observed (i.e., in the youngest child) were then recorded beside each item on each list. The items were sorted into those involving the whole toy and those involving parts only. In the OPRs, it was stressed that these age levels were not intended to be age norms.

In reorganizing the OPRs, a number of changes had to be made. First, the play items on the OPRs were often too complex. For example, one item was "Spins Roundabout using several different methods: can control fast and slow spinning, in clockwise and anticlockwise direction." In practice, a child might demonstrate part of this item only. For POKIT the complexity of items, like the example given, was reduced so that each item refers to a single activity (i.e., items on the Roundabout now deal separately with methods of spinning, the direction of turning, and the speed of turning). Second, the structure of each list was rationalized. Subheadings were used to divide the checklists into sections so that it was easier to locate items (see examples in Table 9–3). These sections were organized to reflect the developmental sequence of play with each toy. In addition, items within each section were listed in developmental sequence.

The third modification was the toy selection. While the Roundabout and Pop-up toy were retained the Pop-up cones toy had to be discarded because it was no longer manufactured. To avoid this problem recurring, the replacement items were chosen to be generally available in child-care settings. Thus, a set of size-graded round stacking tubs and a posting box for shapes replaced the Pop-up cones. No specific commercial version of these toys is required, providing they meet some very general specifications. Like the toy that was replaced, these toys did not involve the need for pretend play. A pilot checklist for this toy combination was constructed from available video recordings of children playing with similar toys, and from clinical observation. The symbolic play set, originally consisting of just the doll and cot, had two items added, a telephone and a tea-set. This was to extend the appeal, provide opportunities to combine toys within the set, and encourage thematic sequences. The Checklist was extended to include items previously observed on these two toys with normally developing children. Finally, a set of picture- and storybooks was included. There was already an extensive body of literature describing adults reading picturebooks to infants. The author had also previously carried out a study of picturebook reading with hearing-impaired children that included a control group of children with normal hearing. The analysis of data from the sample of hearing children provided the items for the first draft of this Checklist (Mogford-Bevan & Summersall, 1997). This was amplified by Browning (1991), who revised the first draft using data from another 11 normally developing children within the age range. This gave five pilot Checklists, one relating to each of the five toys used in the assessment.

A new sample of 18 normally developing children was then recruited to try out the newly constructed assessment and provide more data to develop and revise the Checklists. The data from these children were used in a similar way to that described for the OPRs, resulting in another revision of the pilot checklists. This study established that the age range of the toys was appropriate and that they appealed equally to boys and girls from different social backgrounds. At this stage, it was judged appropriate to begin collecting data to establish norms. The method of data collection employed allowed periodic revision of the Checklists so that they could continue to be trialed in various clinical settings.

The procedures used in the study of normal children parallel the procedure used in a clinical setting. Since the intention was to study children who showed no identifiable delay, this was established by administering the Revised Denver Pre-screening Questionnaire (Frankenburg, 1975/1986). This requires parents to answer *yes* or *no* to a series of items drawn from the full Denver schedule. Items on the questionnaire are given the age level at which 90% of children pass the item. Children were excluded from the study if parents answered *no* to more than one item at or below their chronological age, calculated in months. Three children were excluded on these grounds. Questions regarding tests of hearing and vision were asked but it was clear that for most children, the responses of mothers reflected their own opinions and not the results of objective assessments. Questions were also asked about speech development. Responses could be verified against the speech that was recorded during the play session. No children were excluded on grounds of suspected sensory impairment or speech and language delay.

The normative sample was comprised of volunteers recruited through play groups, mother and toddler groups, health visitors, and nursery schools, and by personal contact between volunteers and through acquaintances. The children were from the northeast of England, in and around the city of Newcastle upon Tyne. They were recruited in eight age groups covering the developmental range of the assessment. There were 5 or 6 children in each age group, an equal number of boys and girls, from a variety of social backgrounds. The eight age groups were 13–15 months; 16–18 months; 19–21 months; 22–24 months; 25–30 months; 31–36 months; 37–42 months, and 43–48 months. Three-month age bands were used at the lower end of the assessment because development is more rapid in the second year of life. Six-month age bands were used from 24 to 48 months. In addition, two further groups of 4 children were included in the 6-month age bands immediately below and above the range of the assessment, making ten age groups in all. The decision to start the assessment at 12 months was based on the general observation that until this age infants tend to treat all toys in a similar way. From 12 months onward there is a gradual adaptation to the nature of the play materials that reflects the child's previous experience, knowledge, and understanding. The ceiling was set at four years as it was felt that when children had reached this level of development they would usually be able to cooperate in more structured forms of assessment.

Recordings were made either in a quiet room at the child's nursery, in the child's home or in a playroom at the university according to the volunteers' preference. The parent was asked to play with the child with the toy set provided so that the child would spend some time on each of the items that were placed together in a circle on the floor. The parent was not asked to introduce the toys in any special order but to encourage the child to explore and play as the child and parent wished. It was established in an interview before the recording was made that this was not an unusual occurrence for parent and child. It was stressed that the parent was not expected to use any particular strategies; he or she should try to play as usual, his or her typical style. The parent was also advised that if a child ignored one of the toys when it was first drawn to his or her attention, it was likely that the child might return to it later in the play session and that no pressure should be exerted. Occasionally, during the recording, parents were asked to draw a child's attention to a toy that had been ignored because time was running out. Filming was finished when all the toys had been sampled or it was clear that the child's interest was declining. Each recording lasted approximately 30 minutes. Only 3 of the 55 children failed to play with all of the toys.

All of the video recordings were transcribed onto paper as an observational narrative account of the child's play and the parent's support. This account was then divided into separate items or acts of play. Each of these was given the number of the appropriate item on the checklist for that toy or listed separately as a "new item," if it was not already on the checklist. A distribution of the frequency of occurrence of each item on each check-list was collected by age group. This showed that around 80% of items occurred often enough to be able to use the distribution of an item by age as a way of deriving age norms. It also confirmed that items varied in the age ranges in which they were observed. There were two types of items; one that is termed "transitional" and the other "developmental." Transitional items are observed in younger age groups of children but are no longer observed in older children beyond a certain age. For example, on the Pop-up toy, up to the age of 21 months some children replace the pegmen, who have faces painted on one end, upside down in the wooden base as if they are unaware of the significance of the face. This is a Transitional item because from 21 months onward, children either correct the orientation without a prompt or replace the pegmen the correct way up, with the face peeping out, on every occasion. Developmental items are not present at all in younger groups of children but occur after a certain age and continue to be observed in older groups of children. For example, with the tea-set, children below the age of 22 to 24 months are observed to pick up items indiscriminately, in any orientation and in any grasp. However, from 22 to 24 months onward children pick up cup, jug, and teapot by the handle in the appropriate orientation. This method of handling tea-set items continues to be observed through all the age groups up to the ceiling of the assessment. Table 9–5 illustrates the distribution of occurrence of some Transitional and Developmental items. Some examples of these two types of items found on the Roundabout and the Pop-up toy are illustrated in Table 9–5.

The checklists were revised again to eliminate items with very low frequencies, to include a few items that occurred frequently as "new items," and to clarify the wording.

For developmental items, the age band selected as the age guide was determined by ignoring the youngest band in which the item occurred, taking the next (older) age band in which an item was observed, or the youngest age band if at least two children in that age group produced this item. This was to ensure that unusually advanced children did not influence the ages unduly. Transitional items indicate the oldest age band in which an item was observed. It was felt that transitional items should reflect the range of normal data to prevent children being falsely regarded as developmentally delayed.

BRIEF OUTLINE OF THE ASSESSMENT PROCEDURE

Below is a brief account of the stages in the assessment procedure. The first four stages can be comfortably completed in 45 minutes. Stages 5 to 8 will take longer but the time taken will be reduced with practice and familiarity.

Stage 1. Introduce and Explain the Assessment Procedure

First, introduce and explain the procedure to the adult who will help with the assessment. Usually this will be one of the child's parents. Where this is not possible, another caretaker who regularly plays with the child could do this. This adult needs to be able to provide information about the child's play and also to act as the play partner when the child's play is observed. *Please note that, for convenience, the adult who provides information about the child and plays with the child during the assessment will be referred to throughout as the parent.*

Stage 2. Find Out About the Child's Play and Play Experience

Using the Play Questionnaire, question the parent to find out about the child's play and play experiences in general: at home, with family, with friends, and in preschool or other group situation. This background information is used later to help evaluate the sample of play that was gathered during the evaluation by looking to see if the information given is consistent with the assessment observations. The play questionnaire also asks parents about any difficulties they experience in playing with the child. This information is useful when it comes to helping parents further develop the child's play.

Stage 3. Sample the Child's Play

Observe a sample of the child's interactive play with the child's parent using the standard set of toys. The assessor should make informal written notes on a note pad during the session for later use. No form is supplied for this although suggestions for recording appropriate information succinctly will be provided in the manual. However, it is strongly advised to make a video recording if at all possible. This will enable the assessor to make more reliable and detailed observations. It is possible to record more items when a recording is available and to check on details not noted in live observation. If videotaping is not available a tape recorder may be used to audio record. This recording will be invaluable for assessing the child's language.

Table 9–5.   Examples of Developmental Items-Frequency of selected items observed at 10 different age levels in normally developing children for two toys in the POKIT set (*n*=50)

Item/Toy	Age intervals in months										
ROUNDABOUT	8/12	13/15	16/18	19/21	22/24	25/30	31/36	37/42	43/48	49+	f
Turns roundabout by knob provided	0	0	0	3	6	5	4	7	5	3	33
Turns roundabout by top with fingers or hand	0	0	1	5	4	4	1	4	4	4	27
Names representations: e.g. horse, lady, man	0	0	0	4	2	5	2	5	3	4	22
Comments on people as characters "They all get on, having a ride"	0	0	0	0	0	1	2	3	1	1	8
POP UP TOY											
Bounces single peg man	0	1	1	2	1	3	2	3	0	2	15
Bounces several or all peg men	0	0	0	2	2	4	2	6	2	3	20
Replaces 2/3 pegs successively: any order, not colour matched	0	0	0	3	5	5	4	1	1	1	20

Examples of Transitional items -
Frequency of selected items observed at 10 different age levels in normally developing children for two toys in the POKIT set. (N=50)

Item/Toy	Age intervals in months										
ROUNDABOUT	8/12	13/15	16/18	19/21	22/24	25/30	31/36	37/42	43/48	49+	f
Has difficulty in removing a man: pulls hard	1	0	0	2	1	1	0	0	0	0	5
Accidentally discovers that the roundabout turns	2	2	1	0	0	0	0	0	0	0	5
POP UP TOY											
Replacing a peg: fails, missing hole	1	2	1	1	4	1	0	0	0	0	10
Succeeds in replacing peg: after at least one unsuccessful attempt	1	2	1	3	5	1	0	0	0	0	13

Stage 4. Find Out How Typical the Play Sample Is

Ask the parent how well he or she thinks that the play sample represents the child's typical play. If the parent is not satisfied with all or part of the sample, a further sample should be observed under conditions that are more conducive to the child's play. Parents can usually suggest what these conditions should be.

Stage 5. Identify Significant Items of Play on the Checklists

Based on the written observations taken during observation, complete the checklists for each toy, placing a tick beside each item observed. These can be added to and double checked by replaying the video recording.

Stage 6. Complete the Developmental Status Summary from the Checklist

Enter items marked on each Checklist on the Developmental Status Summary under the appropriate age bands.

Stage 7. Complete the Qualitative Summaries on Each Checklist

Complete the Qualitative Summary at the end of each Checklist.

Stage 8. Interpret the Observations

Interpret the observations in relation to the information collected on the Play Questionnaire, the Developmental Status Summary and the Qualitative Summaries. Draw up reports that may include recommendations for intervention, a preliminary discussion of diagnosis, and, where appropriate, suggestions for further assessment.

CASE STUDIES

Case 1. James—Fragile X Syndrome—1 Year 10 Months

James was referred to a pediatrician at 14 months because of delay in his motor milestones. The pediatrician diagnosed Fragile X syndrome and referred him to a physiotherapist for help with developing mobility. However, when James was 21 months, the physiotherapist became concerned because his play seemed to be very delayed and was not progressing. As he was a first child his mother had little experience of normally developing children to help her decide what to expect from a child of his developmental level. Yet, she and his father were concerned that James did not play in a purposeful and constructive way. He only seemed to show interest in objects that could be rolled or spun or in throwing things. They wanted to support and encourage his play but did not know what toys were suitable for his stage of development. His parents requested a developmental assessment and guidance in developing his play. The author was asked by the physiotherapist to use the POKIT assessment when he was 22 months old. The play assessment was carried out over two sessions. James was not able to walk without support at this stage. Although he produced copious and fluent vocalization it was not evident that he was using intentional communication.

On the first occasion James had just finished a physiotherapy session and was tired. He showed minimal interest in the toys, being distracted by the soft play equipment in the physiotherapy room and his reflection in a mirror. His parents indicated that his play was not his best. They felt another session at a different time and in a less distracting room would produce a typical sample of his play. His parents also felt that they would like to substitute some of his own playthings at the second session: his favorite book and a teddy bear instead of the doll. Their suggestions were followed. Another session was arranged specifically for the play assessment, which took place in a more suitable room. The second play sample showed that James had some well-rehearsed routines, particularly with the picturebooks. He handled a book appropriately and recognized and named a few pictures. Although James listened and attended to his father in the session, his responses to questions and comments were often delayed and unpredictable. He named and responded to pictures but it was unclear whether he was intentionally initiating interaction. There were no conversational exchanges except those "manufactured" by his father's responses to his vocalizations. There were a few play items in James's chronological age range but more in the 16- to-18-month range. His symbolic play showed that he had some very early functional play at the 13- to-15-month level.

James's spontaneous play on the Pop-up toy, the Stacking toy and Posting Box was at best sensori-motor play at the 13- to-15-month level. However, through demonstration, it was possible to elicit some imitation of behaviors that were much closer to his chronological age. His mother was able to get James interested in dropping an object inside a stacking tub using modeling and exaggerated intonation. His imitation responses were often not immediate but delayed. On every toy his attention was noted as frequently needing to be brought back to a task. James lost interest in toys before a completion point was reached. Nonetheless, he was apparently taking in information from his parent's demonstrations that he could apply when his attention was brought back to the toy.

The Qualitative Summary showed that James's parents, who took turns to be the play partner, were adept at using his attention in an opportunistic way and were able to lift the level of his achievements through interaction. The Qualitative Summary also highlighted the methods James used to explore toys. In the section that draws attention to methods that are used to sense and explore, it was noted that James used his mouth, eyes, and fingers to explore the texture and shape of materials. Some of the methods James used for sensory exploration of the toys were unusual in that they had not been routinely observed in the normal sample of children. For example, he repeatedly scratched textured surfaces on the stacking tubs and listened to the sound this made. He sometimes showed fear at unfamiliar sounds. For example, when the shapes inside the posting-box were shaken, he froze. With the Pop-up toy, he picked up a pegman in each hand and threw them but then became preoccupied with watching the pegmen rolling along the floor. He swiped at them with his hand to repeat the rolling movement and studied them intently. Otherwise, he showed no interest in the toy, especially the bouncing movement and the pegmen jumping out. Usually children at both his chronological and developmental age are amused by these features.

In general, the play assessment showed that at 22 months he was functioning at the 13- to-15-month level though book handling was a little more advanced. Significantly, this was an activity that his parents reported they frequently encouraged at home. They also said that they had encouraged his interest in balls and items that could be rolled or spun because this seemed to be a more purposeful activity than throwing and swiping. James's parents also had observed that rolling and spinning objects seemed to hold his attention more than other activities.

James's parents were keen to see him develop to the stage when he was able to use a posting-box and simple jigsaws and to play imaginatively but had little idea how he might progress to this stage from the level of his present play. The play assessment was used to show that many of his play behaviors were part of the developmental sequence even though they were not all age appropriate. Based on the play assessment, activities were suggested to his parents to increase his interest and attention in container play. Suitable toys were recommended. The developmental connection between container play and more constructional toys was outlined. A broader range of simple functional play was encouraged with the pretend toys and James's parents were discouraged from reinforcing his preoccupation with spinning and rolling objects. James's parents agreed to follow up these suggestions in their daily play sessions with their son.

After a 2-month period James was reassessed. He showed a broader range of functional pretend play but the level of this had not developed significantly. He still retained a fascination with objects that he could roll or spin, but this preoccupied him less than on the previous assessment. His picturebook play showed that he could now name more pictures. His response to simple context-bound commands was more evident because he responded more quickly and looked at the speaker as he complied. He showed spontaneous interest in container play, which was expressed in more sustained attention to play materials. His parents thought that his play was more purposeful and involved a greater range of activities. Further discussion took place, which included suggestions for ways James's parents could provide more variety in their play sessions with James and extend his play with existing toys. He was followed up again after a two-month period during which his parents continued their daily play sessions with him.

Case 2. Peter—Delayed Speech and Language—3 Years 9 Months

Peter was referred to a speech and language therapist at 3.9 years because he had very little expressive speech and language and his "words were not very clear." When first seen in the clinic he seemed to understand little that was said to him, responding inappropriately. He used mainly one- and two-word utterances and a few three-word utterances were heard, but these were often unintelligible. His play with some small cars was repetitive and showed little evidence of imaginative content. Additionally he demonstrated a poor grasp of shape and size concepts. Peter seemed to show a delay in all aspects of development but attempts to confirm this with formal testing procedures failed.

Peter's early developmental records showed that motor milestones were age appropriate and he had passed an earlier developmental screening that was carried out by his health visitor. His parents had been concerned about his hearing because he seemed to be unresponsive to speech. Peter's hearing was tested on three occasions but no hearing loss was found. Therefore, hearing loss was not the cause of his speech and language delay. Further investigation was needed to decide whether Peter was showing a specific difficulty with language acquisition or whether he was more globally delayed. His general level of development, independent of his speech and language, needed to be established. The play assessment was carried out and the resulting play session generally exceeded his mother's expectations. She reported in the play interview that it was difficult to interest Peter in reading books although he would look at them alone sometimes. As a result she had stopped trying to read books with him. He was also reported to have little interest in shape sorters and jigsaws. Apart from solitary play with small cars, Peter was happiest when playing out of doors on his bicycle, or in rough-and-tumble play.

Peter played with his mother for 30 minutes before becoming bored. He showed his best performance on the Roundabout. Here he showed age-appropriate activities and in each section on the checklist played at the more mature levels with the exception of the representational section. However, even though he showed little awareness of the representational nature of the toy, Peter was sensitive to the faces on the pegmen and turned the peg-people so that they all faced the same direction in which the Roundabout turned. He was particularly capable in dismantling and reconstructing the Roundabout and showed insight into the mechanical principles employed in unscrewing and removing the horses and seats as well as replacing them. On other toys he showed a systematic approach, for example, collecting and searching for the stacking tubs in preparation for stacking. Although Peter was unable to grade the tubs by size without error, he was able to complete stacking, with all the tubs in the appropriate orientation. On the Pop-up toy, he showed evidence of color-matching the pegs and investigated the mechanism responsible for allowing the men to bounce in their holes. On the nonsymbolic toys his play appeared age appropriate. In contrast, his play with the pretend toys as well as picture- and storybooks was less well developed.

Although Peter's imaginative play was delayed compared to his ability to manipulate and construct with play materials, he surprised his mother in the interest and attention he gave to the picturebooks. Her previous attempts to interest him in books had failed. Looking at his achievements with books, it was clear from the checklists what the next stage of his development should be. This is because the items are arranged in developmental sequence in each section and the qualitative summary helps to highlight the next stage of development. It was felt that encouraging book reading was an appropriate activity to promote his understanding and use of language.

When all the items were plotted on the Developmental Status Summary (see Fig 9.4) it showed that he had a few items in his chronological age band, although the majority of the most advanced developmental items fell in the age band below his chronological age. This indicated that he was functioning at a level approaching his chronological age, especially with the nonsymbolic aspects of his play. It was decided that his speech and language delay could not be explained by a global developmental delay but that his delay was mainly in the area of speech and language. The validity of this decision was later confirmed by an independent assessment carried out by a pediatrician, another speech and language therapist, and an educational psychologist. Subsequently, he was treated for a variety of specific language difficulties over a $2^1/_2$-year period. At age 6.6 years, as part of another research project, he was given the Colored Progressive Matrices (Raven, 1962) and scored at the 10th centile. This showed that at 6.6 years he was performing in nonverbal abilities toward the lower limits of average ability. This was also suggested by the levels of his play development on POKIT when he was 3 years 9 months. Although a few Developmental Items fell in his chronological age band there were more that fell in the age band below his chronological age, across all of the toys.

Case 3. Robert—Renal Failure—Delayed and Uneven Development— 2 Years 1 Month

Robert developed severe kidney failure a few months after he was born. He was given peritoneal dialysis, which was carried out at home until a kidney transplant was possible. Because of a lack of appetite typically associated with renal failure, he was fed by a nasogastric tube. At 2.1 years he had little speech. He was unable to move around at all, although he could sit unsupported. This delay in motor development was commonly observed in chil-

Figure 9–4.   Developmental Status Summary for Case Study 2

Child's Name: Peter   **Chronical Age:** 45m

AGE BANDS in months	07–09	10–12	13–15	16–18	19–21	22–24	25–30	31–36	37–42	43–48	49+
Stacking toy & Posting box	I	III			III	I	II	III	II	I	
Pup-up	III		I		II	IIII II	II	IIII	IIII II	I	
Roundabout	I	I	II			II	I	IIII	I	III	I (P*)
Pretend— telephone			I					II	II		
Pretend— tea-set						III		III	I		
Pretend— doll/cot		T			T	I			I		
Picture & Story Books			II	IIII I	II	I	I	III	I		

KEY: I = Developmental Items, T = Transititional Items, P = Prompted Items.
Shaded column indicates chronological age band for the child assessed.

NOTES
1. Complete the Developmental Status Summary directly from the Checklists.
2. The summary distinguishes the representational toys from those that have fewer representational items. The toys above the double line have fewer representational items than those below the line.
3. First enter all Developmental items (those marked with a forward-pointing arrow) on the Checklists. Then, with a different color or symbol, enter the Transitional items (i.e., those marked with a downward; pointing arrow) on the Checklists.
4. The child's Developmental Status is indicated by the most advanced levels checked on the chart for Developmental items. If there are Developmental items in or above this level then the child's play is age appropriate.
5. If there are no items in and above the child's age band *and* a number of Transitional items *below* the child's chronological age, this indicates a developmental delay. Transitional items in or above the child's age band are not significant.
6. The Developmental Level should not be treated as a test score but as evidence for comparability of the observed play with that of children of the age level indicated.

dren with kidney failure receiving peritoneal dialysis but the cause of the delay had not yet been established. Robert was often upset and fractious when visiting the hospital. He had a long car journey before he arrived and often came for developmental assessment after having blood tests and other medical investigations. In these circumstances it proved difficult to determine how his cognitive and communication skills were developing.

The play assessment was used to determine his developmental status. As with previous assessments, it could only be done at the end of a long visit to the hospital. Although his mother anticipated that it was unlikely that Robert would engage in any play activities, she rated all his play during the 20-minute session as typical.

The play assessment showed that despite Robert's limitations in gross motor ability and a delay in expressive speech, his understanding and competence in play was age appropriate. His lack of mobility meant that he was sometimes unable to position himself appropriately to manipulate toys effectively. This interfered with his ability to spin the Roundabout and to replace the doll deftly in the cot, for example. However, Robert showed clearly his intention to do both of these things. He also showed some gestural and verbal communication that had not been seen or heard before. This showed up most clearly in his symbolic play and with the picturebooks. On the picturebooks, Robert demonstrated familiarity by handling them appropriately. He turned pages, pointed to pictures, and named the characters that he recognized. Additionally, he responded appropriately to his mother's questions although these were of the simple routine kind that are typical in early picturebook reading. On the Roundabout, Robert showed in nonverbal ways that he was able to play in an age-appropriate way with the representational items. He demonstrated that he had the ability to understand verbal instructions and to copy demonstrations given by his mother. His attention and concentration were promising. Robert was particularly persistent in trying to overcome physical difficulties that he encountered in play because of his limited mobility. He used his limited communication effectively. He showed problem solving and learning on the toys that he had not seen before. He seemed able to apply what he learned to similar problems arising during play.

During the assessment, Robert showed a marked preference for using his left hand. This may have been because most toys were placed on his left side. His right arm hung at his side most of the session, although he once used his right hand to help adjust his grip on a peg before replacing it on the Roundabout. Although he tried several times, he was unable to push the pegs down with an index finger in the Pop-up toy. He seemed to lack power. His aim was accurate when grasping and he had no difficulty with releasing items from his grasp.

It was concluded that at 2 years 1 month, his play and level of language comprehension were probably in the range expected for a child of his chronological age who had experienced prolonged ill-health. He showed good potential for learning. His expressive speech was delayed but he showed signs that this was now beginning to improve and he was motivated to communicate. The main area of delay was in his mobility and in the power of hand and arm movements. Suggestions were made for providing physical support for him during play that would help him to reach and manipulate play materials. Suggestions were also made about positioning toys to encourage greater use of his right hand.

Shortly after Robert was assessed he received a successful kidney transplant from a close relative. When last seen, at 2 years 6 months he was making accelerated developmental progress in those areas in which he had previously shown delay. The pattern of delays observed in the initial play assessment are those that have been reported in the literature on children with early renal failure who receive peritoneal dialysis (McGraw, 1985; Warady, Kriley, Lovell, Farrell, & Hellerstein, 1988).

CRITIQUE OF THE ASSESSMENT

One of the reactions to the assessment by those who have not used it before is the degree of detail required in the observation and the time taken to review a videotape. The question of detail is the most straightforward to justify. Clinical experience and the study of normal children have shown that attention to the detail of play provides insights into a child's abilities that might otherwise be missed. The range of information derived in this way might otherwise be available only through a series of further assessments.

For Robert (Case 3), his age-appropriate abilities were evident through detailed observations of his representational play, which could be indicated only briefly and in a simple way because of his limited speech and vocalization. His physical difficulties reduced the number of actions that otherwise might have revealed his ability. By looking at the detail of his hand-use systematically, there was objective evidence of his neglect of his right hand and the lack of power in his arms.

Peter's (Case 2) manipulative and mechanical understanding might have been missed if the observer's attention had not been drawn to these details by the checklists and if he had not been observed on toys that required this kind of knowledge. Frequently, with children who have difficulties similar to Peter's only symbolic play is assessed and although this may appear to save time it limits the information available for assessment and diagnosis and treatment planning.

One of the principal aims of the POKIT assessment is to make play observation more productive. It is argued here that a detailed and thorough review of evidence from a short assessment session can provide a wealth of information that might otherwise be ignored. This can produce a clear profile of a child's development and can increase the assessor's confidence in the conclusions that they draw from the observation. It is the case, however, that in play assessment the conclusions drawn from the observation of one play session are best regarded as informed hypotheses. These hypotheses should be confirmed by further observation or other approaches to assessment, if thought necessary.

The time taken to complete the assessment depends on the familiarity of the observer with the items that appear on each checklist. The draft manual contains a narrative description of the typical developmental sequence observed on each toy or set of toys in the Play Observation Kit. These accounts are designed to help new users tune into those aspects of the child's play that should be noted and observed as they mature with development. It is recommended that the observer attend fully to the play during the live session and make notes only at times when the play is repetitive or at the end of the session. These notes can be amplified by reviewing the tape. It is unlikely that any single observer will record all of the possible behaviors. Observation should be sufficiently systematic to pick up enough items on each toy to give a representative distribution with emphasis given to the most mature items. The tape may be replayed to complete items on the Qualitative Summary.

It needs to be emphasized that the observation procedure is not intended to override the skills and knowledge of the professional and its use will depend on blending the guidelines with the diagnostic knowledge and experience of the observer. The conclusions from the assessment can be followed up with other assessment procedures of a more formal kind, where appropriate.

Even though each checklist has at least 100 items, everything that a child does in play will not appear on the Checklists. One criticism might be that play is by nature divergent rather than convergent. In other words, in play a child is free to choose how to respond to a toy. This response may be individual and idiosyncratic and not conform to the play behavior observed in the majority of children. It is true that the items chosen for the checklists are those that occurred frequently and over a range of ages in the normative study. In this sense, the observer will attend to the convergent aspects of a child's play. When using the assessment for any child, the items that do not appear on the checklists need not be ignored. They may provide the observer with some insight into the child's individuality, inventiveness, and creativity. On the other hand they may also be of diagnostic significance and indicate developmental deviations or disabilities. It was found during the normative study that the more idiosyncratic items were often repeated by the child or that similar items were observed on different toys with the same child. For example, while playing with his mother, one child was particularly inclined to tease her by making deliberate "mistakes" across all of the toys. Another child was particularly taken with the pegmen on the Roundabout and found a way of incorporating them into his play with most of the other toys. Another boy explained the function and purpose of each toy to his mother. If observers wish, the items that do not appear on the checklists can be listed separately to provide this type of information.

Validity

The main issues in reflecting critically on the assessment have to do with reliability and validity. The issue of validity will be considered first. The three main ways being used to determine the validity of POKIT include: concurrent validity, content validity, and predictive validity. As yet these approaches have not been fully carried out and there are no statistical values to report.

Concurrent Validity

This refers to the ability of an assessment to produce data that are similar to or more effective than data gathered concurrently using existing instruments designed for a similar purpose. The classic way of measuring concurrent validity is to correlate scores on a new assessment with other better-known and frequently used assessments that may be thought to be measuring similar abilities. For diagnostic tests there should be agreement between different methods used to determine a person's current status. In the early stages, some attempt was made to incorporate tests into the studies to produce measures of concurrent validity. For example, Browning (1991) used the Egan Bus Puzzle (Egan & Brown, 1984) alongside the picture and storybooks checklist. The Egan Bus Puzzle Test is a test of early language comprehension and expression that uses a simple jig-saw puzzle. The communication abilities assessed by this test were similar to the abilities demonstrated in picturebook reading with an adult. Unfortunately, with the youngest children and with the clinical cases this attempt often met with failure because the child was unable or unwilling to be tested. It was determined that a more successful strategy was to compare the POKIT assessment with outcomes from different kinds of clinical procedures.

Accordingly, during the development of POKIT, a small-scale study was undertaken in 1997 (Wood, 1997) that investigated the use of the play assessment in making a preliminary diagnosis in which the main question asked was whether a child presented with sufficient features to suggest autism. The study was carried out by a final-year speech and language therapist trainee, Elaine Wood. She argued that although it is not appropriate for speech and language therapists to make the diagnosis of autism, speech and language therapists need to be able to recognize children who should be referred to the appropriate specialist team to consider this diagnosis. With the cooperation of the leader of the child psychiatry team, she was referred five children who were attending a diagnostic play group at the local child psy-

chiatry center. These children were all referred to this center because they had been identified as having developmental difficulties that suggested the autistic spectrum. However, they
did not show the classic picture of the disorder and therefore required careful assessment.

Using the POKIT assessment together with a knowledge of the play and early developmental characteristics of autism, Wood assessed each of the five children while remaining
blind to the team diagnosis. Only after her assessment was complete and diagnostic decisions had been made were her results compared with those of the specialist child psychiatry team. There was agreement on all five children. One child was shown to be developing
normally; the reasons for his atypical behavior at referral were probably explained by difficulties within parent-child relationships. Three children were regarded as showing an
autistic disorder. One of these three children demonstrated an additional global developmental delay. The other two exhibited some age-appropriate development on nonrepresentational toys. The fifth child was found not to have an autistic disorder. Instead this
child showed delayed expressive and receptive language development in the context of
age-appropriate nonverbal skills with the absence of impairment in social interaction in
play. This technique of looking at validity through diagnostic agreements needs to be
applied across a wider range of disabilities and in different clinical contexts to confirm
POKIT's level of concurrent validity.

Content Validity

This refers to the systematic examination of an assessment to see that it covers a representative sample of the behavior being assessed. The content validity of POKIT would
seem to require a demonstration that it provides comprehensive data on a child's developmental status and on a child's ability to learn through interaction with others. One strategy
is to go through the checklist and identify items that appear on other forms of developmental assessment or that refer to abilities that research has demonstrated mature during
this age period. There are a substantial number of these items on the five checklists.

Table 9–6 shows some examples from the Picture and Story Book Checklist, which can
be found on two earlier developmental assessment instruments that assess similar abilities:
the Receptive-Expressive Emergent Language Scale (Bzoch & League, 1971) and Sheridan's (1997) *From Birth to Five Years: Children's Developmental Progress.* Though this
was first produced in 1960, it was not published commercially until 1973. Since then it has
been widely used in developmental surveillance. It was recently revised and updated in presentation though not in substance (Sheridan, Frost, & Sharma, 1997). It should be noted that
the POKIT items are sometimes more tightly specified than in the examples from the instruments quoted. Sometimes items from the tests are represented by more than one item on the
POKIT checklist (e.g., item 2). The slight differences in the age levels between the test
items (e.g., item 4) and the POKIT items may be accounted for by the different circumstances in which the behaviors are elicited. The two assessments used in Table 9–3 were
chosen for illustration here because they refer specifically to many items that are included
on this particular checklist. This table illustrates the nature of the exercise, which could be
undertaken for each of the five checklists to demonstrate their content validity using a much
wider range of published tests and assessment procedures with each of the checklists.

However, not all of the items in the assessment can be validated in this way. Some items
have been observed and recorded as part of research studies on specific areas of development. For example, items of conversational and pragmatic competence, particularly those

Table 9–6.   Examples of ten items that appear on two published developmental assessment guides i.e., The REEL Test (Bzoch-League, 1971) and From Birth to Five Years. Children's Developmental Progress (Sheridan–revised edition 1997) and that also appear on the POKIT Picture and Story Books Checklists.

Ten items from two published assessments and similar items from the POKIT Picture and Story Books Checklist (indicated by *)	Source of item and age level
1. Listens as partner talks re: picture--- *"Will sustain interest for up to a full minute in looking at pictures if they are named ."*	10-12m->* REEL. Test 8-9 m
2. Pats book--- *Visually inspects book, any orientation------------------------------------- *"Looks with interest at coloured pictures in book and pats pictures."*	13-15m->* 10-12m->* Sheridan 15 m
3. Indicates picture by pointing (no name given------------------------------ *"Enjoys simple picture books, often recognising and putting index finger on boldly coloured items on the page."*	10-12m->* Sheridan 18m
4. Answers "Where is X?" or "Show me X!" - by pointing at an appropriate picture-------------------- ------------------ *"Appears to understand simple questions like 'Where's the ball ?'"*	13-15m->* REEL test 10-11 m
5. Turns several pages at once-- *"Turns several pages at a time ."*	13-15m->* Sheridan 18 m
6. Turns pages one at a time --- *"Turns pages singly. "*	13-15m->* Sheridan 2yrs
7. Imitates partner's label for picture -- *"Occasionally tries to imitate new words ."*	16-18m->* REEL test 10-11 m
8. Answers "What does X say?" appropriately---------------------------------- *"Imitates environmental sounds (e.g. motors or animals), during play ."*	1 6-18m->* REEL test 18-20 m
9. Answers "What is it?" or request for a label appropriately -------------- *"Names familiar objects and pictures ."*	19-21m->* Sheridan 2 yrs
10. Listens to a complete story (several lines of text read / discussed)----- *"Listens to long stories ."*	37-42m->* Sheridan 4 yrs

in the Picture and Story Book checklist, rely on items identified in research on "picture-book reading with mother." Additionally, some items that indicate significant developments in social cognition (Leslie, 1987) are included on the Pretend set checklist.

Besides the items that are similar to those in existing developmental assessments and those derived from research papers, the other items emerged as significant during the research from which the assessment was constructed. These items are not reported specifically in the literature or in other developmental assessments as indicators of developmental maturity. It is beyond the scope of this chapter to report these in detail. The argument for the validity of these items must rest with the research methodology, described above. By recording and observing 55 children with normal development playing with the toys used in the POKIT assessment and listing these observations in a developmental sequence, new behavioral items were discovered that showed increasing maturity in play.

The final part of demonstrating content validity is to ensure that the assessment samples a comprehensive range of development and is sensitive to developmental change across the age range. Part of demonstrating the comprehensiveness of the assessment lies with using the standard set of toys chosen to elicit a wide range of abilities. Table 9–7 summarizes the range of abilities that can be sampled.

Gross motor and postural development has been deliberately excluded because the focus of the assessment is on social and intellectual abilities. It was felt that gross motor abilities are relatively straightforward to assess by more conventional means. However, symbolic and nonsymbolic conceptual development are both included in the assessment.

Table 9–7.   This table summarizes the qualities assessed and the information yielded by each of the toys in the POKIT assessment. The Developmental level is evident from the entries on the *Developmental Status Summary* and the qualities from the *Qualitative Summary* on each checklist

Information yielded	TOYS IN THE PLAY OBSERVATION KIT				
	Posting Box & Stacking Toy	Pop-up Toy	Roundabout	Pretend Set	Books
Developmental level	✓	✓	✓	✓	✓
Attention	✓	✓	✓	✓	✓
Listening					✓
Communication	✓	✓	✓	✓	✓
Persistence	✓	✓	✓	✓	
Variation in play	✓	✓	✓	✓	
Representation		✓	✓	✓	✓
Pretend/Thematic				✓	
Sensori-motor exploration	✓	✓	✓	✓	
Hand-eye co-ordination/ Manipulation	✓	✓	✓		
Conceptual development	✓	✓	✓		✓
World knowledge			✓	✓	✓
Problem-solving / Learning	✓				
Literacy awareness / Book handling					✓

One criticism of the assessment (Wood, 1997) that arose from its use with children with autism in its current form is that it has too few items that specifically focus on preverbal interpersonal communication. This will be remedied in the next revision.

Finally, to demonstrate content validity, the age range of items needs to be adjusted so that it contains a similar number of developmental items (i.e., those that emerge as children get older), and transitional items (i.e., those that disappear as children get older) at each age level of the assessment to ensure that it is equally sensitive across the whole developmental range. This will not be possible for every toy or set of toys because they cover different developmental age ranges but should be possible to achieve when all five toy sets are taken into account.

Predictive Validity

Predictive validity refers to the ability of an assessment to predict a future level of performance in an individual. It usually requires that subjects are followed up and assessed at a later stage of development using another similar assessment. The outcomes of the two assessments are compared. If an assessment shows predictive validity there should be a close relationship between the outcome of the first and second assessment. Predictive validity has yet to be fully addressed for POKIT and is more properly assessed when the final version of the assessment is complete. In clinical use there have been some attempts to follow children through the later stages of their development. This was illustrated with Peter (Case 2) and Robert (Case 3). Again, the strategy would be to look at the stability of the diagnostic categories with age as well as to look at later intellectual and developmental progress of children using other means of assessment.

However, the value of predictive validity for an assessment of this type is debatable. Bayley is reported to consider that developmental assessment should be used only to determine a child's current developmental status rather than to predict subsequent ability (Anastasi, 1976). This point is especially important considering that in the early stages of development, progress is susceptible to many variables so that long-term predictions are of little value. Anastasi and Urbina (1997) consider infant tests to be "most useful as aids in the diagnosis of defective development." They indicate that predictive validity is higher for nonnormal than for normal populations for infant tests and tends to increase with age.

The problematic nature of assessing predictive validity is illustrated by Robert (Case 3), the victim of renal failure. The developmental outcome was happily much better than would be predicted from his development at 2 years because of the effects of his kidney transplant. In Peter's case, it would be the stability of the diagnostic category that would be predicted. This was demonstrated with other formal assessments that placed him in the same category of ability as suggested by the play assessment. In James's case (Case 1), it would not be meaningful to demonstrate predictive validity, since his chromosomal disorder already indicates a very high probability of some degree of developmental delay of a global kind. Instead of primarily assessing his developmental status POKIT was used to establish the level at which play intervention should begin as well as to look at the communicative context in which this would take place.

Reliability

Now the issue of reliability will be considered. Reliability refers to the consistency or stability of outcome from an assessment. Will the assessment produce the same result for the same individual when used on different occasions or when used by different assessors? The main purpose of the Play Observation Kit is to increase the reliability of play assessment in comparison with informal clinical procedures currently in use. Its principal features and design aim to improve reliability as has been explained above, in comparison with informal and unsystematic approaches to play assessment. However, the reliability of the POKIT procedure itself has not yet been measured at the interobserver level. There is some evidence on stability of developmental status from a small-scale study that repeated the assessment on the same children on two separate occasions in two different locations (Saunders, 1991). Seven children (five developing normally and two with language delay) were assessed both in a university playroom and in their own homes. The order of location was counterbalanced. The play was compared on a number of measures including developmental level. There was no evidence that the performance of the children differed significantly with location although there was a mild familiarity effect on some measures. The children tended to play in longer sequences on the second occasion of assessment. However, this study is not an adequate measure of the reliability of the assessment. A measure of interobserver reliability will be undertaken before publication of the manual and checklists.

SUMMARY

The Play Observation Kit (POKIT) assessment provides a method for assessing the developmental status, the learning potential, and the social interaction skills of children who are developmentally below the age of four years through the observation of spontaneous play. It is intended to be used after screening assessments have identified a child with a developmental delay or disability. It can be valuable for a range of professionals who would be involved clinically with a child at this stage. POKIT makes use of the spontaneous play of the child with a standard set of toys in the company of a familiar and supportive adult. This increases the likelihood that assessment will reveal the child's developmental achievements. In contrast, tests that might be used often assume a level of language comprehension and a degree of compliance with adult wishes that very young children with disabilities may not possess. The POKIT assessment is distinctive in that it includes toys that allow the assessment of both symbolic and nonsymbolic play. The contrast between these different types of play can often assist professionals in making diagnostic judgments.

Although play assessment has been used for many years to assess young children with developmental delays and disabilities, it can be an unreliable procedure. The POKIT assessment aims to make play assessment more reliable and productive. The reliability is increased by the use of observation checklists, which structure observation so that it is more systematic. It uses objectively described play behaviors that have been repeatedly observed with the standard toy kit on normally developing children. Each of the play behaviors on the checklists has empirically researched age ranges that help the observer to assess the developmental status of the child in an objective way. A structured interview is employed to help the parent provide information that the assessor can use to see the play sample in the context of the child's play experience in nonclinical settings. The procedure also asks the parent to evaluate the sample of play according to how well it typifies the child's play. Both of these measures allow the assessor to judge how representative the sample is of the child's typical play.

The assessment is made more productive because the play sample is recorded on videotape. This means that different aspects of the child's behavior and communication can be assessed from the same sample of behavior. The video recording also allows the observer to check the accuracy of observations.

A key feature of the POKIT assessment is that the procedure encourages the professional to use the knowledge and expertise of the child's parent at all stages of the assessment. This is of crucial importance if professionals are to achieve a sound working relationship with parents as a basis for intervention. The play assessment also provides a framework that can be used to guide parents in providing therapeutic and educational play experience to help offset the consequences of impairment and disability.

REFERENCES

Anastasi, A. (1976). *Psychological testing* (4th ed.). New York: Macmillan.

Anastasi, A., & Urbina, S. (1997). *Psychological testing.* New York: Macmillan.

Bellman, M., & Cash, J. (1987). *The schedule of growing skills.* Windsor, Berks: NFER-Nelson.

Belsky, J., & Most, R. K. (1981). From exploration to play: A cross-sectional study of infant free play behaviour. *Developmental Psychology, 17,* 630–639.

Browning, J. (1991). Prereading skills in preschool children: Development of an observational checklist for assessing a clinical population. Unpublished undergraduate dissertation, Department of Speech, University of Newcastle upon Tyne.

Bruner, J. S. (1975). The ontogenesis of speech acts. *Journal of Child Language, 2,* 1–19.

Bzoch, K. R., & League, R. (1971). *Assessing language skills in infancy. Handbook for the multianalysis of emergent language.* Gainsville, FL: Tree of Life Press.

Egan, D. F., & Brown, R. (1984). *The Egan Bus Puzzle Test Developmental Assessment.* High Wycombe, Bucks: The Test Agency.

Fenson, L., Kagan, J., Kearsley, R. B., & Zelzazo, P. R. (1976). The developmental progression of manipulative play in the first two years. *Child Development, 47,* 232–236.

Fiese, B. H. (1990). Playful relationships: A contextual analysis of mother-infant interaction and symbolic play. *Child Development, 61,* 1648–1656.

Frankenburg, W. (1975/1986). *Revised Denver Prescreening Developmental Questionnaire.* High Wycombe, Bucks: The Test Agency.

Gallagher, T. M. (1981). Contingent query discourses within adult-child discourse. *Journal of Child Language, 8,* 51–63.

Garvey, C. (1984). *Children's talk.* The developing child series. Oxford: Fontana.

Jeffree D. M., & McConkey, R (1976). *P.I.P. developmental charts.* Sevenoaks, Kent: Hodder and Stoughton Educational.

Leslie, A. M. (1987). Pretense and representation: The origins of "Theory of Mind." *Psychological Review, 94,* 412–426.

Lowe, M. (1975). Trends in the development of representational play in infants from one to three years—an observational study. *Journal of Child Psychology and Psychiatry, 16,* 33–47.

Lowe, M., & Costello, A. (1976). *The Symbolic Play Test.* Windsor, Berks: NFER-Nelson.

McCune-Nicolich, L. (1981). Toward symbolic functioning: Structure of early pretend games and potential parallels with language. *Child Development, 52,* 785–797.

McGraw, M. E. (1985). Neurologic-developmental sequelae of chronic renal failure. *Journal of Paediatrics, 106,* 579–583.

Mogford, K. (1979). The Observational Play Repertoires. In J. Newson, and E. Newson (Eds.), *Toys and playthings in development and remediation* (pp. 172–189). London: George Allen and Unwin.

Mogford-Bevan, K., & Summersall, J. (1997). Emerging literacy in children with delayed speech and language development: Assessment and intervention. *Child Language Teaching and Therapy, 13,* 143–159.

Newson, E. (1976). Parents as a resource in diagnosis and assessment. *Early Management of Handicapping Disorders.* IRMMH Review of Research and Practice No 19. London: Associated Scientific Publishers.

Newson, J., Newson, E., Head. J., Mogford, K. (1975). Play in the remediation of handicap. *Occasional Papers of the Division of Educational and Child Psychology of the British Psychological Society, 9,* 117–123.

O'Connell, B., & Bretherton, I. (1984). Toddler's play, alone and with mother: The role of maternal guidance. In I. Bretherton (Ed.), *Symbolic play. The development of social understanding* (pp. 337–368). London: Academic Press.

Powcr, T. J., & Radcliffe, J. (1991). Cognitive assessment of preschool play using the Symbolic Play Test. In C. E. Schaefer, K. Gitlin, & A. Sandgrund (Eds.), *Play diagnosis and assessment* (pp. 87–114). New York: John Wiley & Sons.

Raven, J. C. (1962). *Raven's Coloured Progressive Matrices.* Oxford and Windsor, Berks: NFER-Nelson and Oxford Psychologists' Press.

Saunders, J. (1991). Differences in children's play at home and in the clinic: A study of normally developing and language impaired children. Unpublished undergraduate dissertation. Department of Speech, University of Newcastle upon Tyne.

Schaefer, C., Gitlin, K., & Sandgrund, A. (1991). *Play diagnosis and assessment.* New York: John Wiley & Sons.

Sheridan, M., (1973). *From birth to five years. Children's developmental progress.* Windsor, Berks: NFER-Nelson.

Sheridan, M. Revised and updated by Frost, M., & Sharma, A. (1997). *From birth to five years. Children's developmental progress.* London and New York: Routledge.

Shulman, B. R. (1985). *Test of pragmatic skills.* Tucson, AZ: Communication Skill Builders, The Psychological Corporation.

Slade, A. (1987). A longitudinal study of maternal involvement and symbolic play during toddler pretend. *Child Development, 5,* 367–375.

Ungerer, J. A., Zelzazo, P. R., Kcarslcy, R. B., & O'Leary, K. (1981). Developmental changes in the representation of objects in symbolic play from 18 to 34 months of age. *Child Development, 52,* 186–195.

Vondra, J., & Belsky, J. (1991). Infant play as a window on competence and motivation. In C. E. Schaefer, K. Gitlin, & A. Sandgrund (Eds.), *Play diagnosis and assessment* (pp. 13–39). New York: John Wiley & Sons.

Warady, B. A., Kriley, M., Lovell, H., Farrell, S. E., & Hellerstein, S. (1988). Growth and development of infants with end-stage renal disease recieving long-term peritoneal dialysis. *Journal of Paediatrics, 112,* 714–719.

Westby, C. E. (1980). Assessment of cognitive and language abilities through play. *Language, Speech and Hearing Services in Schools, 11,* 154–168.

Westby, C. E. (1991). A scale for assessing children's pretend play. In C.E. Schaefer, K. Gitlin, & A. Sandgrund (Eds.), *Play diagnosis and assessment* (pp. 131–162). New York: John Wiley & Sons.

Wood, E. (1997). Identifying autistic spectrum disorders using play assessment: Can it be done using POKIT? Unpublished undergraduate dissertaion. Department of Speech, University of Newcastle upon Tyne.

Appendix

SECTION 2 PLAY PREFERENCES [For N use child's name]

• What would you say was N's favourite toy, game or activity at home ....

....

• When N has to amuse her/himself what does she/he usually do? ....

....

• What kinds of toys and play does N most enjoy? [Prompt from list below and include relevant comments.]

Developmentally young child only

Mobiles ....

Rattles ....

Activity centres ....

Other ....

Developmentally young and all other children

Push/pull toys ....

Ball games ....

Rough and tumble ....

Running and chasing ....

Climbing...

Swings/slides ....

Bicycle/tricycle ....

Singing/ Nursery/action rhymes ....

Musical/sound toys ....

Pretend play ....

Dressing -up ....

Cars/trains ....

Doll's house/farm layouts, soldiers etc. ....

Dolls/soft toys ....

TV/video ....

Tapes/stories/books ....

Making pictures or patterns ....

Drawing/scribbling/painting ....

Water/sand ....

Jigsaws/shape sorters ....

Stacking/building ....

Board and card games ....

Any other ....

SECTION 3 OPPORTUNITIES FOR SOCIAL PLAY

• Do you have time or opportunity to play with N?   [circle]   daily / most days / sometimes / rarely / never

• Does N have any brothers and sisters at home? [Note names, gender and ages.]...

....•

Do brothers and sisters play with N at home?

....

• What sort of things do they play together? ....

....

Is there anyone else who plays with N at home? (e.g. Mother, Father, Siblings, Grandparents, Friends,

Neighbours)..

....

....[If so, circle frequency] daily / most days / sometimes / rarely / never

• Are there any problems that make it difficult for N to play? ....

....

....

• Does N attend a play group or nursery? [If yes, note details and comments on this experience.] ....

....

....

SECTION 4 FAMILIARITY WITH THE TOYS

• Show the informant the toys in play kit and prompt: "Has N played with this before?"

	Pop-up-men	Roundabout	Posting box & Stacking toy
Owns toy			
Has played at least once with one			
Has experience of similar toy			
Unsure			
Probably not			

	Telephone	Tea set	Doll/cot
Owns toy			
Has played at least once with one			
Has experience of similar toy			
Unsure			
Probably not			

Child's experience with books [where appropriate circle an answer]

• Has N read these or similar books before?..Yes   No   Same   Similar

• Does N like to look at books? ....Often   Sometimes   Rarely   Never

• Will N do this with another person or does N prefer to do this alone?..................With other person   Alone   Both

• If N 'often' or 'sometimes' likes to look at books does N have a favourite book or story? [If 'yes' give details.]

....

....

PART III

PARENT-CHILD INTERACTION PLAY ASSESSMENTS

Historically, clinicians have identified the understanding of parent-child interactions as basic to the assessment of problematic children. Indeed, the literature is replete with articles attempting to specify the etiology of various emotional disorders through reference to early parent-child interactional difficulties. The recognition that children are active participants in shaping their world has led to continuous and increased study of mother-child dyads and, more recently, of father-child dyads.

By its very nature, the assessment of parent-child interactions requires direct observation, as well as interviews. Because symptoms are often manifested in situations that demand spontaneous as well as interactive behaviors, direct observations are particularly useful when seeking to determine the quality of the problems with which the child is confronted. Observational procedures can be extremely varied in their format as well as settings and may range from standardized laboratory situations to naturalistic home-based or school-based environments; from macro- to microanalysis of behaviors; or from frequency counts to intensity ratings of the behavioral events. In all cases, there is a need for reliably structured and standardized ratings systems in order to create a meaningful database from the broad array of behaviors that potentially can be observed.

Since the early 1980s, there has been increasing interest in the mother-infant dyad, which has been spurred on by research involving the nature of attachment. The revised chapter presented by Lori Roggman, Lisa Boyce, and Lisa Newland includes an overview of the theoretical and practical issues involved in studying mother-infant interactions and in the use of play as a medium for such observations. Additionally, they review a variety of macro- as well as microanalytic formats through which mother-infant play can be observed. The authors offer the reader a comprehensive look at recent research in the field, presenting salient criticisms and suggestions regarding this work. Clinicians and researchers will find much practical value in the information reviewed in this chapter.

David Smith's revised chapter provides the reader with a sound overview of the issues involved in observing and rating parent-child interactions. Additionally, he presents the Parent-Child Interaction Play Assessment (P-CIPA) method. Well designed and researched, the P-CIPA is a developmentally scaled system of rating structured and unstructured interactions. While geared toward observing parent-child interplay, the scale is demonstrated to be of value in the diagnostic assessment of specific problems exhibited by the individual child. Thus, it also provides for the identification of target behaviors needed in developing treatment plans and strategies. Case material incorporated in this chapter clearly shows the strengths of this technique in analyzing parent-child behaviors and in coding the reciprocal nature of such interactions. Further, Smith offers validity and reliability data, making this a scale amenable for use in clinical research.

Sandra Lindaman, Phyllis Booth, and Candace Chambers revisit the Marschak Interaction Method (MIM) with increased attention to this technique as a sensitive measure of parent-child interaction. Since its presentation in the 1991 volume, this technique has gained acceptance in a variety of settings including treatment centers, forensic evaluations, and foster care agencies. The procedure is presented in its entirety, from observations, through data analysis, to report writing. Clinical material accompanying this scale brings life to this valuable technique. While simple to administer and score, the MIM offers a rich source of information about interpersonal dynamics. Many clinicians will find the tasks of the MIM particularly suited to parent training and parent-child interventions as well as assessment.

The Going to the Store measure of parent-child interactions presented by Jean Dumas and Peter LaFreniere is a unique and intriguing format of assessment in this area. Through using an intrinsically interesting model of a common daily mother-child activity, these authors provide a snapshot of the working relationships developed between parents and children. In particular, this scale is shown to be effective in assessing the complexity of parent-child relationships and how that relates to emotional problems. Clinical material within the chapter demonstrates with clarity the usefulness of this technique.

From the sampling of the procedures included in this section, one gains a sense of the diversity inherent in the assessment of parent-child interactions. Starting with Roggman's mother-infant assessment through the Grocery Store Game, a format appropriate for school-aged children and their parents, this section taps a wide range of evaluative methods that can be applied by clinicians and researchers working with diverse childhood populations. It would be of interest in the future to determine whether these techniques will be useful for longitudinal or periodic reassessment of parent-child interactions. Increased focus on the development of different styles of interaction through a child's life, and especially on how these styles are altered during adolescence, might offer valuable information to be used in the treatment of parent-child problems. Thus, studies of the predictive validity of these techniques are encouraged.

Chapter 10

ASSESSING MOTHER-INFANT INTERACTION IN PLAY

Lori A. Roggman, Lisa Boyce, and Lisa Newland

The mother-infant relationship is widely studied as a central part of early social-emotional development. Specific behaviors of mothers and infants toward each other are often observed as expressions of that relationship. The quality and quantity of mother-infant interactions and various aspects of their behaviors in relation to each other may provide indications of how well the relationship is functioning. One way of assessing these interactions and behaviors is through direct observation in natural settings. Often, the interactions of interest involve voluntary pleasant, non-caregiving interactions that we would commonly call "play."

Play behaviors offer valuable opportunities for observing the mother-infant interactions for three reasons. First, play interactions are frequent and pervasive in the everyday lives of infants. Play interactions make up a large part, about a third, of the ongoing interactions that occur daily between mothers and infants (Stern, 1974). They can be observed in a wide variety of settings: homes, research laboratories, clinical settings, child care settings (waiting rooms for any community resources, etc.). In addition, although play interactions sometimes include toys or other objects, very simple objects can be used in play, and often play interactions do not require any additional materials other than the mother and infant themselves.

Second, play interactions directly contribute to the mother-infant relationship. Play interactions are considered a primary force in promoting and maintaining the social interaction system that develops between mothers and infants (Stern, 1974). When mothers and infants enjoy their early play interactions, they are likely to continue to express enjoyment in their later interactions (Crawley et al., 1978).

Third, play interactions promote the infant's general competence in both social and cognitive domains. Specific kinds of mother-infant play, such as the sharing of toys and pretend play between mothers and toddlers, are correlated with secure-attachment relationships (Roggman, Langlois, & Hubbs-Tait, 1987; Slade, 1987), which in turn, is related to later social competence (Booth, Rose-Krasnor, Mckinnon, & Rubin, 1994; Suess, Grossmann, & Sroufe, 1992; Youngblade, Park, & Belsky, 1993). Mother-infant play with toys is related to the developing social competence of the infant and to later cognitive competence (Bakeman & Adamson, 1984; Hunter, McCarthy, MacTurk, & Vietze, 1987).

In general, play behavior has been thought to be so closely related to development that it has been used by many researchers as a "window" on the child's current level of competence. This "window" has typically been used to view cognitive more than social development, however. Following Piaget's theory, researchers identified developmental sequences of object play that reveal increasing levels of cognitive skill (Bornstein, Haynes, O'Reilly, & Painter, 1996; Belsky & Most, 1981; Hrncir, Speller, & West, 1985). A developmental sequence has not been specified as clearly for social play as for object play, but the study of developmental changes in social play may reveal potential indicators of increasing levels of social competence. This chapter presents several methods of observing play as a "window" on mother-infant relationships.

MEASURES OF MOTHER-INFANT PLAY

The rationale for using play as an assessment of mother-infant interaction is primarily based on two kinds of empirical evidence: that supporting the importance of play for the mother-infant relationship and that supporting the relation of play to the infant's developing competence. Evidence of play's importance for the mother-infant relationship is represented by findings that certain types of behavior in play are correlated with positive aspects of the mother-infant relationship such as security of attachment. Evidence of the relevance of play to the infant's development is the documentation of age differences in certain kinds of social play reflecting developmental changes in social and cognitive competence. These two kinds of evidence are often interrelated. The developmental level of mother-infant play depends both on the infant's competence and on the quality of the mother-infant relationship. The usefulness of the measures discussed here for assessing mother-infant interaction is supported by previous research showing evidence of age differences or correlations with the quality of the mother-infant relationship or both. Specific age differences and correlations with the quality of the mother-infant relationship will be discussed as each kind of play measure is presented.

There are several kinds of behavior that can be observed during play sessions. The specific content of mother-infant play, the games they play, is used as a measure of the developmental level of mother-infant play in some studies. In other studies, measures include the frequency or complexity of specific play behaviors, such as visual attention and toy sharing, that may be present regardless of the content of play. An increasing number of studies assess mother's support or "scaffolding" of infant play. And in yet other studies, play situations provide the context for observations of other social behaviors of infants, such as emotional expression or attachment behavior, or social behaviors of mothers, such as vocalizations and touching. Some studies also use mother-infant play to observe the general competence of the infant's exploratory play with objects, even if the mother is not involved. Definitions of exploratory play may or may not include social competence or mother-infant interactions, and these studies will be cited only when they do. The measures reviewed below are appropriate for assessing the social competence of the infant or the quality of the mother-infant relationship.

Reliability and agreement between observers vary across measures and studies but are generally at higher than acceptable levels in the research literature. All play measures discussed have had adequate reliability reported. The specific estimates will not be reported, but are available in the articles cited.

Content of Mother-Infant Play

"Games" or Types of Play

Categories or types of social play are the largest unit of play behavior used to observe mother-infant play. Table 10–1 shows several recognizable types of play that have been defined for observations of mother-infant play in many studies, although researchers may vary in how they define them (Crawley et al., 1978; Crawley & Sherrod, 1984; Field, 1979). The advantage of using clearly defined types of play is that they are easy for observers and parents to understand, but the disadvantage is that novel types of play may go unrecognized or unreported.

The most general way of using types of play as a measure of mother-infant play is to describe the types of social play appropriate for the infant age group and then count the frequency of each. For example, between 4 and 8 months, tactile games decrease in frequency and traditional movement and visual demonstration games increase (Crawley et al., 1978), and between 7 and 18 months, physical games decrease and games that require more active infant involvement increase (Adamson & Bakeman, 1985; Crawley & Sherrod, 1984). Games which a typical 1-year-old plays occur an average of 7 times an hour, with the infant actively involved in most and initiating almost half of the games (Gustafson, Green, & West, 1979). Higher-level games, such as pretending, are initiated at first mostly by the mother with 1-year-olds and then shift to more infant initiation by age 2 (Haight & Miller, 1993).

Perhaps because of these developmental changes, only certain types of play are correlated with the quality of the mother-infant relationship. Security of attachment is related to specific kinds of coordinated toy play and pretending (Roggman et al., 1987; Slade, 1987). Thus if play is measured as an indication of the quality of the mother-infant relationship, it may provide a more useful assessment if the measurement focuses on a specific type of play.

Pretending

One particular type of mother-toddler play used in assessing the quality of mother-infant interactions is social pretending. Pretending, or symbolic play, is easily observed and could potentially be reported by the mother. The infant's earliest pretend acts, around the end of the first year, are centered about or directed toward the self (Belsky & Most, 1981; Fenson & Ramsay, 1980). For example, the toddler pretends to drink from a cup. Later in the second year, the toddlers' pretend play becomes more decentered, and pretend acts are more likely to be directed to another person, real or imaginary (e.g., doll, stuffed animal). Then a toddler may offer his or her mother a pretend drink from the cup or hand her a toy telephone saying, "Talk to Grandma." As pretending becomes even more complex, the mother may become involved with her child in storylike sequences of pretend acts such as making "juice," drinking it from a cup, and then washing the dishes. A developmental sequence of definitions that may be useful for coding pretending in a mother-infant play is shown in Table 10–2.

Because pretending is thought to be significant for the child's developing abilities of symbolic representation, the mother's involvement in pretend play is a valuable part of their play interactions. Often mothers' involvement facilitates higher levels and longer episodes of symbolic play among toddlers (Haight & Miller, 1993). For example, Bornstein et al. (1996) found that infants pretended less when playing in solitary play at 20

Table 10–1.   Types of mother-infant play observed at various ages

Age Group	Play Type	Definition
1–6 months	Tell-me-a-story	Mother tries to elicit infant vocalization or asks infant to tell a story, infant makes vocalizations, mother supplies words.
	Gonna-get-you	Mother looms toward infant with wide-eyed, playfully threatening face and comes very close or actually makes physical contact.
	Walking fingers	Mother's fingers crawl spiderlike up torso of infant.
	So big	Mother "tries to make the infant taller" by extending infant's arms upward and saying "so big."
	Pat-a-cake	Mother clasps infant's hands and repeats "pat-a-cake."
	Peek-a-boo	Mother hides infant's face or parent's face, typically with cover of some sort, and then uncovers the face.
3–8 months	Tactile games	Mother tickles or stimulates part of infant's body.
	Body movement	Mother moves infant's body in space, for example, by lifting overhead.
	Limb movement	Mother moves infant's arms and legs.
	Traditional movement	Mother moves infant's arms in meaningful ways such as, for example, pat-a-cake or peek-a-boo (see above), simple clapping or waving bye-bye.
	Visual game	Mother provides visual stimulation by moving her body to get the infant's attention.
	Demonstration	Mother shows a traditional movement such as pat-a-cake, peek-a-boo, clapping, waving bye-bye.
	Horsie	Mother bounces infant who is sitting on her knees or foot, often saying "ride the horsie."
	Ball	Mother and infant exchange a ball in some way.
7–13 months	Rough physical play	Mother moves infant's trunk through space by lifting, shaking, or swinging.
	Stimulate with object	Mother stimulates infant's body surface with object or plays looming games with an object.
	Independent toy play	Mother or infant plays alone with an object without coordinating or sharing objects.
	Coordinated toy play	Mother and infant touch the same object.
	Give and take	Mother and infant exchange objects.
	Tower	Mother or infant builds tower of blocks and other one knocks down.
	Point and name	Mother or infant points to object and then looks at other expectantly or asks, "what's this?" and other one names.
	Read	Mother and infant look at and/or point to pictures in a book or magazine; mother may read aloud or discuss pictures.
	Role games	Mother and infant play together in a game in which both have an obvious role, such as chasing each other.
	Pretend	Mother or infant acts as if an inanimate object were animate or as if a toy were real.

Note: Categories are taken from several sources and are therefore not mutually exclusive.
Adapted from Bruner & Sherwood, 1976; Crawley et al., 1978; Crawley & Sherrod, 1984; Field, 1979; Gustafson et al., 1979.

Table 10–2.   Pretending behaviors

Code	Definition
Presymbolic toy play	Manipulate or combine objects appropriately or in ways that are unique to the properties of the objects (e.g., roll a ball, dial a toy phone, put a cup on a saucer).
Enactive naming	Display only approximate pretend activity (e.g., holding telephone close to ear but not obviously pretending to talk on the phone).
Self-directed pretend	Direct a symbolic act to self (e.g., pretending to drink from an empty cup).
Other-directed pretend	Direct a symbolic act to another person, real or inanimate (e.g., offering pretend drink to mother or doll, kiss or hug doll, make pretend vehicle noises).
Substitution pretense	Pretend activity involving one or more object substitutes (e.g., pretending a cup or block is a telephone and talking into it).
Sequenced pretend	Combine symbolic acts in sequence (e.g., stir pretend drink in a pitcher, then pour into a cup; or offer drink to mother and then offer it to doll).
Planned sequenced pretend	Make verbal plans or clear indications of planned sequence of pretend acts (e.g., "make dinner" followed by stirring and pouring with toy dishes).

Adapted from Belsky & Most, 1981; Bornstein at al. 1996; Fenson & Ramsay, 1980; Slade, 1987; Tamis-LeMonda, Chen, & Bornstein, 1998, Watson & Jackowitz, 1984.

months than when playing with their mothers. Both the frequency and duration of infant pretend play increased during infant-initiated social play with mother, and the frequency of infant pretend acts was highest during mother-initiated social play. From age 1 to 2, there is a shift from primarily maternal pretend play initiations to about half of pretend play initiations originating from the child (Haight & Miller, 1993). Furthermore, securely attached toddlers, compared to anxiously attached toddlers, spend more time in symbolic play, play longer at higher levels of symbolic play, and are helped more by their mothers' involvement in play (Slade, 1987). The average duration of the longest episodes of 2-year-olds' solitary pretend play was from a half to a full minute for both securely attached and anxiously attached toddlers, but when their mothers were involved, securely attached toddlers' pretend episodes lasted up to 3 minutes or more while anxiously attached toddlers pretended only up to a minute and a half or so.

Maternal responsiveness, a correlate of attachment security, is also associated with infant pretense. In one study, maternal responsiveness was related to the amount of simple and sequential pretense acts at 12 months and to the amount of preplanned pretense acts at 18 months (Spencer & Meadow-Orlans, 1996). Perhaps the behaviors of the play partner, not neccessarily the mothers themselves, is what encourages more pretending. In a close look at the context of infant pretense, Bornstein, Haynes, Legler, O'Reilly, and Painter (1997) found that infant play interactions with a stranger who acted similar to the infant's mother yielded similar levels of infant pretense as when the infant played with his or her mother, suggesting that "the models, stimulants, and opportunities partners provide" are the factors that enhance infant pretense during play (p. 202).

Another way of measuring toddler's understanding of pretend play is to model pretend acts and then count the frequency of modeled pretend acts displayed by the infant. Rusher, Cross, and Ware (1995) assessed play behaviors this way in a structured play session.

Infants observed adults modeling three pretend play sequences, which increased in complexity. From this play session, infant pretend play level was coded by counting the frequency of modeled play behaviors displayed by the child, and then weighting these frequencies according to complexity. The sum of these weighted scores was used as the measure of pretend play ability. Thus, rather than simply counting frequency of pretend acts, this study attempted to address the issue of infant capability of modeling complex pretend behaviors.

Specific Play Behaviors

"Game" Behaviors

Mother-infant play has also been defined in more behavior-specific terms that define a "game" (e.g., "rhythmic repetitions of turn alternations"). Games are classified not only according to type but also according to some sort of reciprocity or complexity dimension, such as the level of activity required by the infant, whether the infant's role is more passive or more active, the proportion of games initiated by the infant, the number of turns or repetitions of the game, and so on (Gustafson et al., 1979). Stern (1977) has described mother-infant play in the early months of infancy as episodes of social interaction that are initiated by mutual gaze, maintained by variations in the intensity and tempo of interactive behaviors, and ended by a breaking of attention. Such play may include recognizable games, but the essential components of mutual attention and sustained repetitions of interaction are the defining characteristics of the mother-infant interactions. The advantage of using these behavior-specific definitions is that a game does not have to be recognizable in order to be counted. In fact, novel games, played by only one mother and infant, may be an indication of a particularly well-functioning dyad.

In the early months, the ability of mother and infant to sustain repeated bouts of play interactions through mutual focus of attention is thought to be an especially important indicator of the quality of their relationship (Baldwin, 1991; Roggman, Hart, Carroll, & Egan, in press; Stern, 1974, 1977). In later months and into the second and third year, mother-infant play continues to require mutual involvement and repetition, but also begins to involve more active involvement of the infants (Rome-Flanders, Cossette, Ricard, & Decarie, 1995), more complex social roles, more infant initiation, more pretending, and more turntaking (Gustafson et al., 1979; Ross & Kay, 1980). Three kinds of role patterns become increasingly evident in mother-infant games: (1) similar or imitative roles (e.g., mother and infant alternate beating on a drum), (2) complementary roles (e.g., mother stacks blocks, then infant knocks them down), and (3) reciprocal or reversed roles (e.g., mother and infant roll a ball back and forth) (Ross & Kay, 1980).

A useful measure of mother-infant games is likely to require indications of both complexity and developmental level. The developmental level of a particular game is related to the age group that typically plays it, to the complexity of component social behaviors, and also to the level of infant initiative involved. As infants get older, they acquire more complex social behaviors, new games emerge (Gustafson et al., 1979), and the same games may become more complex (Bruner & Sherwood, 1976). Table 10–3 shows a developmental sequence taken from descriptions by Ross & Kay (1980) based on infants' acquisition of social play skills. By using the kind of analyses used by Belsky & Most (1981) to develop a toy play scale for assessing cognitive competence (Hrncir et al., 1985), it may

Table 10–3.   Sequence of game skill acquisition

Age	How infants respond in social play with mothers
Before 7 months	Show attention and amusement when their mothers play.
After 7 months	Understand structure of games, anticipate mother's actions, assume active role in about 50% of mother-infant games.
After 12 months	Initiate about 50% of mother-infant games, are active in about 90% of mother-infant games, assume role of agent as well as recipient in games, begin to reverse roles.
After 15 months	Invent new forms of old games, initiate novel games with mothers, assume task of game initiation almost exclusively.

Adapted from Ross & Kay, 1980.

be possible to develop a detailed developmental sequence of social play that can be used for assessing social competence. Such a sequence would include specific indications of infants' active involvement, initiation, turntaking, imitation, role playing, and pretending.

The infant's initiation of play, as well as maternal responsiveness to infant initiations, appear to be especially critical components of social play between mothers and 1-year-olds that reflect the quality of their relationship (Newland, Roggman, Boyce, & Cook, 1997, 1998; Roggman, et al., 1987; Spencer & Meadow-Orlans, 1996). Rome-Flanders et al. (1995) longitudinally studied the differences between infant behaviors during games of peek-a-boo and ball by infants from 6 to 24 months. They found that infants were more actively engaged for longer periods and were more likely to initiate modifications during the ball game as compared to games of peek-a-boo. Mothers' helping behavior also varied depending on the game played, increasing from the first to second year when playing peek-a-boo and decreasing from the first to second year when playing ball. The complexity of the rules of the game and the roles of the players may be factors contributing to differences in timing of infant mastery of mother-infant games (Rome-Flanders et al., 1995).

Infant Visual Attention

One of the most important behavioral components of mother-infant games is the organization of social and nonsocial attention. The frequency, duration, and sequencing of infant looking at toys and mother is an important behavioral component of mother-infant play. From the descriptions of the very earliest mother-infant play it is obvious that mutual gaze between mother and infant is the primary marker of their engagement in play episodes (Stern, 1974). In an observation of parent-infant play with 3-month-olds, infants spent an average of 33% of the time looking at their parents who spent 81% of their time looking at the infants with a resulting 28% of the time spent in mutual gaze (Roggman & Peery, 1989). From 6 to 20 months, infants increased the duration and frequency of looking at their mothers, and by 36 months, they participated in gaze patterns similar to those of adults in conversation (Farran & Kasari, 1990). Stern (1977) has suggested that when there are difficulties in coordinating and sustaining mutual gaze, there may be problems in the mother-infant relationship.

As infants get older, mothers begin to introduce more toys into mother-infant social play, and around the end of the first year, infants begin introducing toys on their own into play with their mothers. Thus with 1-year-olds, the assessment of attention during play would necessarily begin to include measures of infant attention to objects in relation to attention to the mother. Infant ability to maintain attention toward toys at 13 months is related to both infant level of pretend play and frequency of maternal attention directing, indicating that both social and cognitive factors are influencing infant looking behaviors (Tamis-LeMonda & Bornstein, 1990). Ross & Lollis (1987) have interpreted infants' alternations of gaze between an adult and a toy as an expression of their desire for mutual involvement in play.

It may also be useful to assess infant attention to mother as it precedes and follows actions with toys. For example, when playing the familiar "game" of dropping toys from a highchair tray, 10-month-old infants continue their attention to the toys after dropping a toy, but 15-month-old infants turn their attention to the mother (Roggman, 1989). This shift in attention is an indication of a change in the goals and complexity of mother-infant-toy play around the beginning of the second year. Also 15-month-olds are more likely than 10-month-olds to intersperse looks to mothers between looks to a shared toy (Roggman, 1989), another indication of their increasing social skill in organizing their attention toward their mothers and toys. Individual differences in the organization of object-directed and mother-directed attention may be a reflection not only of increasing social skill but also of a well-functioning relationship between the infant and mother. These overlapping sequential measures of visual attention, compared to simple frequency or duration measures, can be difficult to obtain without the aid of video cameras and/or event recorders and also require definitions that clarify whether they are mutually exclusive or overlapping and how long a look away must last to be considered a disruption of the sequence.

Joint Attention to Toys

Another aspect of the organization of attention during mother-infant play is the coordination of attention between mother and infant. Joint attention, when mother and infant look at and/or act on the same object, is especially likely to occur during mother-infant play. Along with other joint actions of mother and infant, joint visual attention is correlated with both language development and cognitive development (Dunham & Dunham, 1992; Hunter et al., 1987; Tamis-LeMonda & Bornstein, 1989; Tomasello, 1990). Joint attention at 6 months is related to productive language skills at 17 and 24 months (Saxon, 1997), however the link between language and joint attention may be stronger later on when infants are more capable of intersubjectivity (Saxon, Frick, & Columbo, 1996). In fact, simple gaze following at 12 months is not associated with language abilities, but coordinated joint attention and engagement in shared communicative gestures are, again suggesting the need for intersubjectivity (Rollins, Marchman, & Mehta, 1998). Between 6 and 18 months, the period when language is emerging, the proportion of play time in coordinated joint attention increases substantially (Bakeman & Adamson, 1984).

There are many ways for joint attention to occur. Mother and infant may be looking at the same object, touching the same object, or one may be watching the other play with an object. The amount of time spent in joint attention depends on the situation: The proportion of time spent in joint attention by 6-month-olds was .19 in a study using a free-play situation and over .42 in another study in which the infant was seated and toys were fixed in position (Landry, 1986). The infant may or may not initiate joint attention or be aware of it. Bakeman & Adamson (1984) have distinguished "passive" joint attention, which involves the simple overlap of attention to an object, from "coordinated" joint attention, which involves infant awareness and initiation of shared attention. (See Table 10–4).

Table 10–4.   Joint attention measures

Code	Definition
Unengaged	Infant appears uninvolved with any specific person, object, or activity, although he or she might be scanning the environment as though looking for something to do.
Onlooking	Infant is observing another's activity; often quite intently, but is not taking part of the activity.
Persons	Infant is engaged just with the other persons, typically face-to-face or person play.
Objects	Infant is involved in playing with objects alone, attending just to the toys at hand.
Passive joint	Both infant and mother are actively involved in the same object, but the baby evidences little awareness of the mother's involvement or presence.
Coordinated joint	Infant is actively involved with and coordinates his or her attention to both mother and the object the mother is involved with.

From Bakeman & Adamson, 1984. Reprinted with permission.

The social context of play appears important for the coordination of joint attention, as it is more likely with mothers than with peers (Bakeman & Adamson, 1984; Adamson & Bakeman, 1985). Coordination of attention during play may also be related to the quality of the relationship between the mother and infant. Joint attention was related to security of attachment for boys in one study: mothers with anxious-avoidant boys spent fewer time intervals watching each other play or playing with the same toys than did other mother-infant dyads (Roggman et al., 1987).

Attention-Directing Strategies

Both maternal and infant attention-directing strategies are related to infant representational competence in language and play. Maternal encouragement of attention toward herself or the environment at 5 months is related to variability in infant social versus didactic exploration (Bornstein & Tamis-LeMonda, 1990). Maternal encouragement of infant attention toward objects in the environment at 13 months is also related to infant pretend play competence (Tamis-LeMonda & Bornstein, 1989, 1990). In addition, maternal attention directing toward the play environment at 5 months is related to infant representational competence at 13 months, indicating that early maternal stimulation in play may have a delayed effect on later cognitive competence (Tamis-LeMonda & Bornstein, 1989). Apparently, mothers are often successful in directing infant attention, because their persistence in bids for initiation of joint attention is associated with the duration of joint attention (Saxon & Reilly, 1998). Maternal encouragement of attention was not stable from 5 to 13 months, indicating that attention-directing strategies may be adjusted to changing infant developmental levels.

Infants themselves also contribute to the attentional focus of joint play. By six months of age, infants are capable of directing mothers' attention in order to reach or manipulate a toy. The frequency with which infants use mothers instrumentally in a play session increases dramatically from 6 to 13 months, indicating an increasing ability to manage joint attention (Mosier & Rogoff, 1994). Infants also use nonverbal cues, such as maternal gaze, to identify objects verbally referenced by the mother (Baldwin, 1991; Yale & Mundy, 1998).

Toy Sharing

One particular kind of mother-toddler joint attention to toys is the sharing or exchanging of objects. Sharing may involve both joint visual attention to a toy and joint action with a toy. The earliest forms of sharing begin with the mother bringing objects into the young infant's limited world, highlighting them, and helping the infant to manipulate them. As with other kinds of mother-infant play, the infant comes to take a more active role toward the end of the first year, initiating more sharing by showing and offering objects to the mother (Rheingold, Hay, & West, 1976). By 11 months, infants are capable of both offering and exchanging toys with their mothers in play situations on an average of about 4 times in 10 minutes. (Newland et al., 1997). The frequency of simple exchanges of objects is easily observed and counted whenever an object changes possession. Sharing can be observed with more precision by recording the initiating behaviors of the "giver" (showing, offering, releasing) and the responsive behaviors of the "receiver" (accepting, responding, returning). Table 10–5 shows definitions of toy-exchange behaviors observed in mothers and 1-year-olds (Roggman et al., 1987). The sequence of these behaviors may result in successful or unsuccessful toy exchanges. Unsuccessful exchanges can be inferred from the coding sequences, for example "ignoring" (not accepting an offered object) and "taking" (taking an object that was not offered). It may be useful to distinguish between showing and offering similarly to Rheingold et al. (1976) and Newland et al. (1997) by defining showing as pointing or holding out an object toward someone out of reach and offering as releasing the object or setting it down in front of the other person.

Table 10–5.   Mother-infant toy-exchange behaviors

Code	Definition
Offers a toy	Hands a toy toward someone within reach by extending the toy toward them and releasing it or setting the toy down in front of them.
Shows a toy	Looks at or gestures toward the other person with toy in hand, or points to a toy or shows how it works after getting the other's attention.
Ignores an offer	Is offered/showed a toy, but does not accept it.
Accepts an offer	Is offered/showed a toy and takes it.
Acknowledges an offer	Smiles or talks about a toy that is shown/offered, but does not accept it.
Responds to accepted toy	Manipulates or talks about an accepted toy (labels, describes, labels actions appropriate to the object, etc.).
Returns a toy	Offers to return a toy after accepting it from the other, but without responding to the toy (May say "Thank you," "Your turn," etc.).
Complex exchange	Offers to return a toy that has been accepted and responded to.
Retracts a toy	Pulls back toy other tries to accept after offer or show.
Takes a toy	Takes a toy from the other that the other has not offered.
Retakes	Takes back an unoffered toy that the other had previously accepted or taken.
Completes an action	Performs an action which completes an action begun by the other with a toy the other has not offered (e.g., adds a block to a stack, catches a ball, closes a box the other opened).

Adapted from Roggman et al., 1987.

The infant-initiated integration of toys into social play with the mother is thought to be a significant part of the development of both social and cognitive development. Mother-infant attachment is related to sharing of toys in specific ways; attachment is not related to simply sharing a toy, but it is related to how sharing is combined with other behaviors, whether the infant intiates sharing, and how the infant reponds to a shared toy. Showing a toy while vocalizing or smiling was displayed by almost all securely attached toddlers at 18 months and two-thirds of them at 24 months compared to less than half of anxiously attached infants at 18 months and a third at 24 months (Waters, Wippman, & Sroufe, 1978). Securely attached 1-year-olds were likely to initiate about half of toy exchanges compared with anxiously attached infants, who initiated only about a quarter of toy exchanges (Roggman et al., 1987). Furthermore, when mothers initiated toy exchanges, most securely attached infants played with the offered toy compared to only about half of the anxiously attached infants (Roggman et al., 1987).

These findings are consistent with other studies of toy-sharing behaviors. The fact that securely attached infants initiate more toy exchanges and play more often with toys offered by the mother is most likely related to maternal responsiveness to previous offers by the infant. In fact, 1-year-olds are more likely to offer and exchange toys if their mother accepts and manipulates the toys which the infant offered. Likewise, infants tend to play with toys offered by the mother more often if the mother plays with toys offered by the infant (Newland et al., 1998). Thus, maternal responsiveness to infant toy offers seems to support infant social play.

Mother-infant toy sharing behaviors are also related to developmental outcomes. Infant-initiated toy exchanges that are successfully completed at 11 months are related to infant language abilities at 14 months. Successful infant-initiated toy exchanges are also related to infant pretend play competence at 11 months. These relations are even stronger when mothers continue the exchange by returning the toy to the infant (Newland et al., 1997, 1998). This delayed association between early mother-infant social interactions during play and later infant symbolic representation has been reported in other studies (Tamis-LeMonda & Bornstein, 1989).

Mothers' Support of Infant Play

General Support

As infants get older, there are several general ways that mothers may support or "scaffold" infant play with toys (Landry, Garner, Swank & Baldwin, 1996). Ross and Kay (1980) have suggested several aspects of mothers' involvement in social play that support their infants' developing social play skills. Mothers can change the games they initiate to include a more active infant, they can become more passive and recipient partners, and they can accept and encourage new games. Others have observed mothers who model and prompt play activities (Tamis-Lemonda & Bornstein, 1994). Mothers' attention-focusing behaviors, especially if they provide specific information about toy use, support infants' exploration of toys (Landry et al., 1996). Then, as infants develop more refined play skills, maternal responsiveness to infant attention-directing supports higher levels of play and increased cognition (Smith et al., 1996; Spencer & Meadow-Orlans, 1996).

Specific Support

Other maternal behaviors that support toy play include talking about toys and actual phys-ical assistance with toys. The extent to which mothers label and describe objects in a play session is related to toddler language. In addition, the extent to which mothers demonstrate and suggest specific kinds of pretend acts is related to the frequency of pretend acts dis-played by the infant. These specific maternal behaviors vary across cultures (Tamis-LeMonda, Bornstein, Cyphers, Toda, & Ogino, 1992). Some mothers may also do things that are not supportive of the infant's play: they may interrupt the infant's play or distract the infant from play by calling the infant's attention away from the toys. Maternal support is likely to promote more options in the infant's play while other maternal behaviors may limit the options in the infant's play (Noll, Harding, Stilson, & Weissman, 1998). Mothers talk about toys more with older toddlers (15 versus 10 months) and make more play sug-gestions and fewer play demonstrations with securely attached than with anxiously attached toddlers (Roggman et al., 1987). Table 10–6 shows definitions for mothers' play support behaviors (Roggman et al., 1987; Roggman, 1989).

Infant Social Behaviors in Mother-Infant Play

Positive Affect

There are several other social behaviors that have been assessed in play situations as indi-cations of the quality of mother-infant play. One especially important set of social behav-iors is affective expressions. For example, infants in a play situation are more likely to smile at responsive than nonresponsive mothers and smile less when mothers redirect rather than maintain play (Eckerman & Rheingold, 1974; Garner & Landry, 1994). Also, in a sample of preterm infants maternal attempts to maintain infant attention were posi-tively associated with increased positive affect (Garner & Landry, 1994). Other studies have indicated that infant affect expressed in play reflects the quality of the mother-infant relationship. Compared with infants assessed as anxiously attached, securely attached infants have been observed to express more smiling (95% vs. 40–42%, Waters et al., 1978) and fewer nonpositive vocalizations toward their mothers during play (3% vs. 6%; Rog-gman et al., 1987).

Table 10–6.   Mother's support of infant play behavior

Code	Definition
Talk about toys	Talk to infant about toys by describing the toy, the behavior with the toys, or results of the infant's behavior with the toys.
Assist play	Move infant's hand to help play with toy, or move toy within reach, or call attention to toy by moving it.
Suggest play	Make specific suggestions to infant for play actions with toy.
Demonstrate play	Show infant an action with a toy while infant is watching or while calling infant's attention to the play action.
Distract infant	Call attention to anything other than the toys.
Interrupt play	Do anything which interrupts the child's ongoing play, such as take toy away or physically pick up infant.

Other Social Behaviors

Other behaviors observed in mother-infant play situations include attachment behaviors, social referencing, and instrumental use of the mother. There are several behaviors used for the assessment of attachment that may occur in a play situation, including proximity seeking and contact maintenance, and also the willingness of the child to leave the mother's side and explore a set of unfamiliar toys (Ainsworth et al., 1978). Social referencing, or the extent to which an infant uses the mother's affective expressions to make decisions in uncertain situations, has also been assessed in situations that begin like any laboratory "free-play" situation and then introduce a potentially anxiety-producing stimulus like a remote controlled toy that mysteriously enters the room on its own. Infants refer to their caregiver's expressions of fear or happiness as they attempt to understand the novel toy (Rosen, Adamson, & Bakeman, 1992). Social referencing may be an indication of the infant's developing social skill and also of the pattern of communication between mother and infant (Bradshaw, Goldsmith, & Campos, 1987; Dickstein, Thompson, Estes, Malkin, & Lamb, 1984). Infants' instrumental use of their mothers in gaining access to or working a toy increases from a third of infants at 6 months to over two-thirds at 9 months (Mosier & Rogoff, 1994). Thus, infants use mothers not only as attachment figures and social referents but also instrumentally to attain goals in play.

Maternal Social Behaviors in Mother-Infant Play

Most of the above measures have focused on infant behavior or on specific kinds of play interactions between mother and infant, but there are other behaviors that mothers may use to offer the infant support for play or opportunities for social interaction. One of the most important is mother's looking behavior to the infant and toys, which was discussed in the section on attention and mutual gaze. Other maternal behaviors that have been described as particularly important in mother-infant play in the early months include vocalizations and touching. Play situations seem to elicit particular kinds of maternal vocalizations and touching (Reissland & Snow, 1996; Stern, 1974). The affective tone of mothers' vocalizations in play may reflect the quality of the relationship. Mothers' infant-directed singing sounds more "loving" than noninfant-directed singing (Trainor, 1996), and mothers of securely attached infants express more positive vocalizations than mothers of anxiously attached infants (Roggman et al., 1987). Mothers' touching of their infants is correlated with mutual gaze and other social behaviors in play (Roggman & Peery, 1988, 1989; Bornstein et al., 1996).

METHODS OF MEASURING MOTHER-INFANT PLAY

Designing the Play Situation

In addition to the variety of measures that can be used for assessing mother-infant social interaction through their play, there are also a variety of play situations that can be used for assessing mother-infant interaction. One common play situation used for measuring mother-infant play behavior is "free play," in which there are few restrictions to either the mother or infant. Free play, like several other play situations, can be observed in the home, in a waiting room, in an office, or in a research laboratory. In general, playrooms should be made to appear as homelike as possible to avoid subject reactivity, particularly anxiety in the infant. Although laboratory settings may elicit some differences in behaviors, researchers have found stability between home and laboratory settings in mother and infant behaviors, including play (Bornstein et al., 1997; Boyce, Benson, Roggman, & Cook, 1997; Spangler, Schieche, Ilg, Maier, & Ackermann, 1994).

Whether the observation is done in the home or not, various restrictions can be imposed that offer additional control of the situation and the potential behaviors that can be expressed. Many studies of mother-infant play refer to "free-play" periods of observation but then mention several restrictions that were imposed by the toys provided, by instructions to the mothers, or by limited space. Sometimes the toys and instructions are so specific that the play session does not offer an opportunity for "free play" but rather offers opportunities for teaching or problem-solving.

Controlling the Toys

In a home setting, the available toys may vary from infant to infant. Mother-infant play may then depend on toys that are available during the observation, and there may be fewer toys available than usual if the mother was concerned about making her home presentable for the observers' visit. Also, if there are few toys available because of economic limitations, for example, mother-infant play may not be an accurate representation of their potential interactions compared to other mother-infant dyads. Other limitations to mother-infant play interactions may also reflect more about the environment than about their relationship or the infant's social competence. The toys themselves may also limit or stimulate types of play, since some toys are gender-specific (Idle, Wood, & Desmarais, 1993; Leaper & Gleason, 1996).

In either a home or laboratory setting, these problems can be avoided by providing a standard set of toys. For example, in the Strange Situation developed for assessing the quality of mother-infant attachment (Ainsworth et al., 1978) the toys available for infant solitary or social play were a large red ball, chime ball, plastic butterfly ball, facing-car pull toy, toy telephone, musical clown, Raggedy Andy doll, plastic shapes and sticks, hammer-shaped rattle, plastic milk bottle containing small objects, silver bangles, foil pie plate, and long red tube.

Other studies using the Strange Situation procedure or other research paradigms have used similar though not usually identical sets of age-appropriate toys (e.g., Bornstein et al., 1996; Cielinski, Vaughn, Seifer, & Contreras, 1995; Tamis-LeMonda & Bornstein, 1994; Thompson & Lamb, 1984). In the NICHD child care study as well as other multisite studies, children are presented with three sets of toys in separate bags or boxes (NICHD Early Child Care Research Network, 1997). The toys are chosen to elicit the play behaviors ranging from exploratory to more sophisticated pretense. Toys selected for the bags vary depending on the age of the infant and the study but often include: toy stove, picturebook, Noah's ark, cash register, toy farm or house. Boller (K. Boller, personal communication, March 14, 1997) suggests that toys should not have small pieces that would be hard to see as the infant plays or be large enough to interfere with viewing the play when videotaped. The parent is instructed that "some time should be spent with each toy" and that otherwise they may do whatever they want (Vandell, 1979, p. 381). In some cases only a single large toy (Waters et al., 1978) or a set of novel toys (Jones, 1985) has been used rather than an array of toys that are likely to be familiar to infants. If one particular kind of social-toy play is of interest, it is often useful to restrict both the number and type of toys available. Studies of the development of pretend play in infancy often provide a set of developmentally appropriate toys to stimulate various levels of pretense in play (Belsky & Most, 1981; Bornstein et al., 1996; Newland et al., 1997; Roggman et al., in press).

The descriptions of types of mother-infant social play that were discussed above usually refer to certain kinds of toys. As infants become more competent at social-toy play, toys that are most likely to be integrated into social play include balls, blocks, books, and pretend toys such as dolls, stuffed animals, dishes, vehicles, and toy telephones. Even with very young infants parents are likely to use particular toys when they play with their infants: soft toys or animals, rattles, plastic rings, teething rings, and music boxes (Sutton-Smith, 1986). Sutton-Smith suggests that, regardless of the actual effect of the toy on the infant, parents' use of these toys reflects their concern about their infant's early learning. Even when no toys are present, parents will sometimes use any available object, as was seen in a laboratory study when a parent pulled out a dollar bill and began showing it to a 3-month-old infant (Roggman & Peery, 1988). Often the container that holds the toys, if left available during the play session, will be incorporated into social-toy play, such as when a box lid is used as a hat and then offered to the mother for her to wear. Toys are sometimes put in and out of the container, mixed in with toy exchanges with the mother, or the child gets into the box as part of pretend play.

One study of adult-infant play with a toy focused on a fairly complex toy that often requires adult involvement, a jack-in-the-box (Rogoff, Malkin, & Gilbride, 1984). In a study of 1-year-olds' initiation of social play, the infants were provided with two nesting cups for toy play (Roggman, 1987). These toys were selected because, first, they encompass the skills of a broad developmental range (Belsky & Most, 1981), and second, they are neither novel nor complex so infants would not be too absorbed in the toys to initiate social play. Finally, if the mother's teaching behavior in a play situation is of interest, the toys selected need to be just beyond the developmental level of the child.

In some studies, toys have been specially designed to elicit particular behaviors, such as problem-solving behavior and help-seeking from the mother (Matas, Arend, & Sroufe, 1978). Infants as young as 6 months have been shown to use their mothers instrumentally to either gain access to toys or to work a toy (Mosier & Rogoff, 1994). Studies of social referencing have used specific toys that were designed or selected to elicit uncertainty in the infant: remote-controlled spiders and robots and mechanical, musical monkeys (Bradshaw et al., 1987; Desrochers, Ricard, Decarie, & Allard, 1994; Gunnar & Stone, 1984). In a study of infant organization of attention while playing with mother and toys, infants were observed playing with two trains that were identical in every way except that one required the involvement of the mother and the other did not (Roggman, 1989). Two battery-operated trains moved on a circular path, each path blocked by two lever-operated gates, one in reach of the infant and the other in reach of the mother. For one train, the mother's gate was propped open slightly and did not require the mother's involvement, so the two trains offered a clear choice of social involvement. Infant preference for each toy was evaluated by comparing the amount of manipulation of each train and the amount of visual attention to each toy. From these data, social versus object goals in infant play could be assessed.

Controlling the Adult

Instructions to mother vary widely from one study to another. Mothers are asked to play, not to play, or to do something else. Mothers may be asked explicitly to play with their infants "as they might if they had a few minutes to devote to a spontaneous play period" (Bakeman & Adamson, 1984). In some cases mothers are asked not to initiate play (Matas et al., 1978) or asked not to move from their seat (Hay, 1979). Sometimes the researchers may emphasize their interest in the infant's spontaneous play by saying, for example, "we are interested in seeing how your child plays with the toys. Feel free to play with your child or not, whatever you would do at home" (Roggman et al., 1987). Mothers may be encouraged to act as naturally as possible without actually telling them to play, for example by asking them to "pretend you and your baby are at home with a few free minutes" (Vandell & Wilson, 1987). In the initial "free-play" episode of the Strange Situation used for assessing attachment, mothers are told, "...go to your chair and pretend to read a magazine. You will respond to the baby quietly if he makes overtures to you ... but you are not to try to attract the baby's attention. ... If, at the end of 2 minutes, he has not begun to play with the toys ... take him over to the toys and try to arouse his interest in them..." (Ainsworth et al., 1978). When mothers are told to "behave as they naturally would" their behaviors are much different than when they are asked not to initiate play: They accept toys, play with toys, and vocalize more often (Rheingold et al., 1976).

Another alternative, especially if infant initiation of play is of interest, is to ask the mother to do another task. When the mother is occupied with another task, the infant may be more likely to try to initiate social-toy play to get the mother's attention, an increasingly important social play skill of infants around the end of the first year. In several recent studies, mothers were asked to complete a questionnaire during the observation period (Roggman et al., in press; Newland et al., 1997; Shaw, Keenan, & Vondra, 1994; Vondra, Shaw, & Kevenides, 1995). The purpose of the questionnaire was to distract the mother's attention from the infant in a way that is familiar in a typical infant's life: Mother is working while baby plays. Mother may be asked to do another task but also to attend to the infant however she thinks is appropriate. This allows observation of maternal responsiveness in relation to infant attention seeking (Shaw et al., 1994).

Mothers may also be given specific cues during the course of the observation. Instructions for the mothers in the Strange Situation tell them that there will be a knock after 2 minutes that will cue them to take the baby over to the toys (Ainsworth et al., 1978). In a study testing infant attention, mothers were cued by a flashing light to return toys the infant had dropped (Roggman, 1987).

Controlling the Infant

It is much more difficult to control the infant than to control the toys or the mother, but restricting the available space for play is sometimes necessary. It is often important to restrict the infant to an area that can be kept in view of an observer or video camera. Many observation rooms are small and it may be difficult for either an observer or a video camera to see into corners. To keep the infant in view, it is helpful to use a plexiglas barrier that keeps the infant out from under a camera or observation window but does not occlude the view.

Another restriction that has been used in observations of adult-infant play is to place the infant in a highchair or other fixed seat facing the mother, either at home or in a laboratory. When the infant is in a highchair and the mother is seated nearby, it is easy to videotape all of their interactions. It is also possible to attach toys to the highchair tray or put them in a fixed position nearby and observe joint attention (Landry, 1986). This situation is common for many infants who sometimes sit in a highchair and play before, during, and after mealtimes. Unfortunately, some infants associate this situation with mealtimes and express some frustration at the lack of food. Nevertheless, complex interactions and play behaviors have been observed in such a situation (Rogoff, Mistry, Radziszewska, & Germond, 1992; Shaw et al., 1994; Vondra et al., 1995).

Sometimes, infants create their own restrictions. They may become tired, hungry, in need of a diaper change, or otherwise distressed, and the observation session must be terminated early. It is sometimes possible to interrupt the observation and continue after other needs are met, but this is not always possible. In some play situations, infants may change the play context by dropping toys from a highchair, for example, and thus changing the availability of toys (Roggman, 1987). When the length of time that infants are observed, or the length of various play contexts, varies from infant to infant, it is usually appropriate to standardize frequency or duration measures by dividing by the total amount of time to get a rate or proportion score (Sackett, 1978).

Observational Methods

Coding Mother-Infant Play Behavior

In general, direct observation is more likely to provide accurate data than questionnaires or interviews of the mother. In any observational study, one of the first tasks will be to define the behaviors in a coding scheme that allows observers to recognize particular kinds of behaviors. It is important that the behaviors of interest are defined with enough precision for accurate observation. The more explicit and clear the definition, the more reliable and useful will be the measures (Hawkins, 1982). The simpler the coding scheme, the greater the likelihood that observations will remain reliable throughout the data collection period (Reid, 1982). When developing a new coding scheme of mother-infant play behaviors it is often useful to define a set of behaviors as specifically as possible, and then test the coding scheme and check reliability. If discrimination between similar behaviors is limiting reliable observation, then behaviors can be combined in meaningful ways and the coding scheme retested (Reid, 1982). Later, if analyses of the data reveal similar relationships of a given variable with similar behaviors, then, again, behaviors can be combined in meaningful ways.

There are many tools for coding the behavioral data. A paper-and-pencil checksheet is inexpensive and can be easily used for coding frequencies of games (general or specific), periodic assessments of affect, or instances of infant vocalizations or pretending, and so on. Certain kinds of mother-infant play behaviors may be easily tallied with pencil and paper, such as the simple frequency of toy exchanges. For other kinds of behaviors, it may be the mother's or infant's response to a certain event that is of interest, for example, their response to a toy that has been given to them, in which case the observer may simply wait for the toy exchange to occur and then take note of the toy receiver's response to the toy, using an event-sampling strategy.

When a wider range of play behaviors are being observed, some sort of time-sampling strategy will be used. Sackett (1978) suggests using a "modified frequency" sampling interval, in which the observer notes which behaviors occur in each time interval (typically

10, 15, or 20 seconds) regardless of how many times any given type of behavior occurs. If the observer is coding behavior during a "live" observation, it is helpful to have audible time cues, a click every 15 seconds, for example, playing through an earphone (Holm, 1978). Videotaped observations make it possible to stop the tape as frequently as every second (Landry, 1986) and code behavior more continuously. The advantages of paper-and-pencil coding are that it is inexpensive, available anywhere, and easily portable. The disadvantage is that if several behaviors are observed, it is necessary to restrict the observation to time-sampling techniques that may make the unit of measurement, which is neither frequency nor duration, difficult to interpret. For low-frequency play behaviors, it is appropriate to discuss a measure in terms of the proportion of time intervals in which the behavior occurred, but for high-frequency behaviors or behaviors that may occur very close together, it is misleading to ignore play interactions simply because they occur in the same time interval with a similar interaction.

Mechanical devices of various kinds improve the ease and accuracy of observations of frequency and duration measures. A stopwatch, for example, is widely available and inexpensive, and can be used for duration measures. Observers can learn quickly to use a stopwatch in each hand to reliably measure duration of play with two kinds of toys (e.g., Langlois, Roggman, & Rieser-Danner, 1990). When behavior of both mother and infant need to be coded simultaneously, as, for example, mutual gaze, it may be possible to time the duration of mutual gaze using only a stopwatch if the observer can see a split-screen video display of both mother and infant. Frequency of behaviors can be counted with the kind of "clicker" counter available at some sporting goods stores (used for golf scoring, etc.). Unfortunately, the number of behaviors that can be observed is limited to the number of devices the observer can hold. Mechanical event recorders that can read input from a set of pushbuttons or keys can be useful for coding multiple behaviors using both frequency and duration measures. Computerized event recorders of various kinds, prepackaged or custom programmed, are increasingly available. Coding observational data directly into a computer allows almost immediate calculation of complex and sequential interactional behaviors. Computers can be used to combine separate strings of behavior codes into a "sequential time-ordered record of interactions" (Roach, Barratt, Miller, & Leavitt, 1998). For example, a simple program can quickly calculate duration and frequency of mutual gaze during play or infant gazing to mother interspersed between looks to toys (Roggman, 1989).

One of the simplest methods of coding behavioral data is to use a global rating scale. The observer watches an entire observational episode and then rates one or more play behaviors on ordinal scales. Research in domains related to play have found that global ratings may provide the same information as microanalytic coding data. Cohn and Elmore's (1995) research demonstrated convergent validity between global rating and microanalytic coding in a laboratory setting assessing mother-infant affect and synchrony. Furthermore, global measures of maternal sensitivity were found to be similar in both home and laboratory settings across a period of a few months (Spangler et al., 1994).

Recording Mother-Infant Play Behavior

Behavior may be recorded on videotape or recorded or described verbally onto an audiotape, or an observer may write a description or directly code the behavior of the mother and infant "live," at the same time as it occurs. The disadvantage of "live" recording is that some important behavior may be missed and there will be no other record of the behavior to review. However, comparisons of coding from live and videotaped situations indicate that very little information is lost (Bench & Wilson, 1976), and observers coding simple behaviors from videotape can reach high levels of agreement with observers coding "live" (Roggman, 1989), so this may not be as much of a problem as it would seem. The advantage of "live" observation is that the data are immediately available, and no videotaping equipment is required. There are situations where a video camera is not available or would be obtrusive. Some behaviors such as the direction of visual attention can often be viewed better live than on videotape. Audiotaping can offer another alternative, but making written transcriptions from audiotape can be extremely time consuming (Holm, 1978). Often a combination of live recording, videotaping, and audiotaping may be used to take advantage of the appropriateness of each method for particular measures.

Even if the measures of interest can be reliably recorded in a live situation, it is advisable to videotape if possible. This is especially true for detailed coding schemes which code several different behaviors or sequences of behaviors. Videotaped observations can be repeatedly viewed for increased accuracy and can be reviewed to see what behaviors preceded a play interaction or who initiated it (e.g., Bakeman & Adamson, 1984; Adamson & Bakeman, 1985). It is possible to stop the tape every few seconds and record a large number of behavioral events from a specific time interval. Also, videotaped observations are useful for reviewing later when a new way of assessing play is reported, when a new research question arises, or when new concerns develop about an individual child. The disadvantages are that video cameras are expensive, obtrusive, sometimes miss what the naked eye can see, and increase the amount of time required for coding the behavior. It is advisable, at the very least, to videotape a proportion of the subjects so that videotaped observations can be used for checking reliability and training additional observers.

Another alternative is to audiotape the observation. If transcriptions of the flow of behavior will provide the necessary data, an observer can describe the ongoing behaviors into a tape recorder and then transfer the audio record to a written transcript later. Observers can usually talk faster than they can write, so it is useful to use a playback device with foot pedal controls (Holm, 1978). The advantage of audio recorders is that they are small, portable, and relatively inexpensive. If the observer can watch a mother and infant playing from a separate room through an observation mirror, then the observer's voice is less likely to be heard by the subjects. Even in home observations of play, this technique has been used with some success when an observer talked quietly into a small tape recorder (Belsky, Garduque, & Hrncir, 1984).

Minimizing Subject Reactivity

Because observational methods can elicit self-conscious unrepresentative behavior from subjects who are aware of being observed, it is important, first, to minimize the obtrusiveness of the observer and, second, to allow time for subjects to adapt to the situation (Kazdin, 1982). This is more important for the mothers being observed than for the infants. Although a mother may react self-consciously to an observation situation, a young infant is not likely to be aware of being observed and is likely to respond in a typical way to mother and perhaps even help her relax and play "naturally." Observers can minimize their obtrusiveness by observing from behind a screen with a peephole or an observation mirror. Other alternatives are regular windows with narrow-slatted blinds or dark gauze or scrim cloth used in stage productions. Recording from a discretely placed video camera is sometimes less obtrusive than direct observation. The observer may then be in another room observing from a television monitor or videotaping for later observation. If it is necessary to be in the same room with the subjects, observers should minimize eye contact or conversation with mother or infant.

In addition, it is helpful to allow a time period of adaptation to the situation before behavioral observation begins (Kazdin, 1982). Many mothers report that they "forget" they are being observed after a few minutes. For that reason, it is advisable to allow 5 minutes or more of "warmup" time when play behaviors are not recorded. Also, it is often helpful to reassure mothers that we are interested in how they "typically" play with their infant, and that there is not necessarily a "right" way to play. Sometimes, the word "play" may be omitted altogether in the information provided to the mother. It may make the situation more "natural" to give the mother another task such as completing a questionnaire or reading instructions. Play interactions such as organized attention to a toy will still occur (Roggman, 1987, 1989).

Maximizing Observer Accuracy

Whether observers are recording "live" or from videotape, in the room or from another room, it is essential that observers have had training and practice so they can avoid some of the potential errors and bias of observational methods. When possible, observers should be "blind" to the inferences that will be made from the measures, whether those inferences are about research hypotheses, or individual differences and their correlates, or potential risk indications, or diagnoses. But observers need not be "blind" to the reasons for the selection of play behaviors to be observed. Indeed, when observers understand the reasons for measuring particular kinds of behavior they are likely to be more motivated and accurate than when they do not (Reid, 1982).

The reliability or agreement between observers should be checked frequently and regularly. Agreement is the extent to which observers report seeing exactly the same behavior at exactly the same time; reliability is the degree to which their observations are proportional (Tinsley & Weiss, 1975). During training, interobserver agreement should be checked immediately after each observation session. To assess the dependability of the data to be analyzed, and to prevent observer "drift," the gradual decline of agreement over time, observer agreement or reliability should be monitored regularly throughout the data collection period (Hartmann, 1982; Reid, 1982). Periodic observer training meetings help maintain adequate levels of reliability and agreement. For observational data, the simple proportion of agreement should be greater than .80, chance-corrected agreement greater than .60, and reliability correlations greater than .60 (Gelfand & Hartmann, 1975).

The relative importance of agreement or reliability estimates depends on the nature of the measurement and the plans for analysis: Agreement is important for categorical and sequential measures; reliability is important for frequency and duration measures. Agreement expressed as a simple proportion of agreements to agreements plus disagreements is likely to be inflated when the behavior has a very low or very high frequency (Appelbaum & McCall, 1984), and types of play are likely to vary quite widely in frequency. Therefore, kappa (Cohen, 1960, 1968; Fleiss, 1971) or a comparable statistic that corrects for chance agreement should be used to evaluate the level of observer agreement. Interobserver reliability is generally assessed by an intraclass correlation, and there are several ways to calculate intraclass correlations according to the number of observers, whether all observations are used for data analysis, and other factors (Hartmann, 1982; Shrout & Fleiss, 1979). In general, observational data are likely to be most reliable when at least two observers record all behavior and the average of their observations is used for the data to be analyzed (Tinsley & Weiss, 1975).

Qualitative Methods

Analyses of observations of mother-infant play may be enriched by qualitative approaches which focus on the context of the interaction. Five components of qualitative research as defined by Bogdan and Biklen (1992) are: research occurs in a natural setting with the researcher acting as the instrument, researchers describe the data with words instead of relying on numbers, the focus of this approach is on processes rather than outcomes, analyses are inductive in nature, and the "meaning" of behavior is a primary focus. Qualitative analysis of observational data include describing the observation, classifying or looking for themes, and then connecting the reoccurring themes together to form patterns (Dey, 1993).

A combination of qualitative and quantitative methods "contributes an understanding of the meaning of behavior in context" with "a precision of measurement that makes generalizations and comparisons possible" (Gaskins, 1994, p. 313). In an ongoing study of mothers playing with their infants, qualitative methods are being used in addition to the quantitative coding of sophistication of play and "scaffolding." In this study a mother is interviewed while watching a videotaped interaction of herself and her infant and asked to describe the interaction. Two themes emerged in a preliminary analysis. The first theme was who directed the choice of play activity. Several mothers indicated that they followed the child's lead. "She really just hands me stuff. She is really independent and wants to get it done." Other mothers were more directive during play and explained why: "I probably just got bored with the game and so I started to play a new game. Sometimes it is harder to pay attention to simple games." The second theme that emerged was recognition of how the child felt during play. "I just let her do it (put the doll on the jack-in-the-box) because she thinks it is funny. She thought it was neat that I let her do it even though it wasn't supposed to be there," and "when he can't do what I've done he gets mad" (Boyce, 1997). These statements create the context for quantified maternal behaviors such as responsiveness and intrusiveness. By combining the qualitative and quantitative methodologies, the researcher is able to code maternal behaviors within the context, allowing for more accurate interpretations.

Nonobservational Methods

Most mother-infant play is measured by observation. Asking mothers to report about their play with their infants is an alternative to direct observation, however, and self-report measures may have some advantages. Questionnaires and interviews require less time and expense than direct observation. Also, they are often less inconvenient for the mother and infant. By interviewing mothers while both interviewer and mother have a questionnaire in hand, it is possible to use standardized questions as a guide while allowing further explanation.

The simplest self-report format is a checklist, a list of the kinds of play that are typical of mothers playing with infants and toddlers. An example of such a checklist is included in the appendix. In the form shown, mothers were asked to rate which kinds of mother-infant play they or their infants enjoy the most. On another version of this form, mothers were asked to report the kinds of mother-infant social play they had engaged in within the last 24 hours. Initial piloting of the checklist in the appendix indicated that mothers were more comfortable recording information about their social play with their infant if they could first indicate the variety of kinds of play their infant was involved in alone when they were nearby. Also, their responses about preferred kinds of play were more consistent over time than their responses about the actual occurrences of various kinds of play. Although the interviewer emphasized that mothers and infants were expected to engage in only a few of these kinds of play, many of the mothers that were interviewed using this checklist seemed concerned about how many kinds of play they shared with their child, and some mothers were likely to report very high levels of both frequency and preference for all of the items. This reflects the primary disadvantage of self-report measures, the perceived social desirability of positive responses. Mothers may respond to the questions by giving the answers they believe are "right" and "good." Combining this approach with direct observation is useful in assessing generalization of reported play behaviors in the home to the laboratory setting. In a study of ninety-eight 10-month-old toddlers, infants' preference for pretend play with their mothers and mothers' initiation of these activities at home were correlated with increased cognitive level of play in a laboratory setting (Boyce, et al., 1997). Reliability of this measure has been estimated by coefficient alpha at .84 for child's overall enjoyment of play and .83 for overall enjoyment of play. Reliability estimates were .73 and .71 for pretending for the child and mother respectively, .70 and .71 for language games, .67 and .68 for sharing things, .55 and .61 for sensory games, and .55 for child's enjoyment of play alone.

It is also possible to design a toy that can record mother-infant play when no observer is present. In one study (Roggman, 1989) two toys were designed that were identical except that they differed in the amount of social involvement required for playing with each of them. Each version of the toy had a built-in counter to record the frequency of manipulations of each toy. There are other possibilities. For example, if toys on a shelf have been rated for their social involvement requirements or previous contact by the mother, then the toys that have been removed from the shelf can be recorded after a free-play session.

Related Variables

Mother-infant play interactions may be affected by a variety of factors other than their relationship with each other. Some of these include the caregiving role of the mother, the age and developmental level of the infant, the sex of the infant, family factors, and cultural influences.

One assumption in many studies of mother-infant play is that the mother is the primary caregiver. If the conceptual framework guiding the assessment involves the construct of attachment, for example, the mother observed playing with the infant is assumed to be the infant's primary caregiver. It is possible to determine the infant's primary caregiver by simply asking parents for an estimate of the proportion of caregiving provided by each parent and by other caregivers.

Another assumption is often that a child's chronological age provides an indication of their developmental status. However, for infants under 2, developmental status may depend on gestational age at birth. For this reason, it is often useful to ask for parents' recollection of what the projected "due date" had been during the pregnancy for that child. A birth date within 2 weeks of the due date is usually acceptable. If a subject has a birth date more than 4 weeks before the due date, expectations regarding appropriate mother-infant play may need to be adjusted (Landry, 1986). Generally, of course, the older the infants the less critical is their gestational age at birth.

Another factor that may influence play behavior is the sex of the infant. For example, several studies have documented sex differences in mother-infant play (Power, 1985; Roggman & Peery, 1988, 1989), infant toy play (Roggman, Murphy, & Shiraki, 1988), independent pretend play (Bornstein et al., 1996), and parents' responses to infants and toddlers in a play situation (Power, 1985). Particularly for measures of social-toy play with 1-year-olds and older toddlers, the selection of toys should include toys that are gender neutral as well as toys that are traditional sex-typed toys such as dolls and trucks. Even seemingly gender-neutral toys such as cups have been shown to be more interesting to girls than to boys (Roggman et al., 1988).

There may also be influences from marital or socioeconomic status (SES) that could affect social play behavior. Most of the research on mother-infant play has focused on infants with mothers who are primary caregivers in intact families of middle socioeconomic status. There are many other factors that could affect mother-infant play, but those mentioned can be easily measured by asking parents direct categorical questions in an interview or questionnaire and then considering those factors when analyzing and interpreting data from measures of mother-infant play.

Mother-infant play interactions are affected by larger cultural norms, such as child rearing behaviors and gender roles (Fernald & O'Neill, 1993; Roopnarine, Hooper, Ahmeduzzaman, & Pollack, 1993). Some interactions, such as peek-a-boo, are thought to be universal across cultures (Bruner & Sherwood, 1976). Peek-a-boo is found in many cultures, although the evidence does not clearly indicate that it is universal. Where it is present, however, the game shares many common components, such as vocalizations (Fernald & O'Neill, 1993).

Other interactions seem to be related to cultural norms. Mothers in India, for example, engage in more object-mediated play with their infants than fathers in India (Roopnarine et al., 1993). In addition, Indian mothers engage in play behaviors while they are involved in other daily routines, such as massaging the infant (Roopnarine, Hossain, Gill, & Brophy, 1994). A comparison of three cultures in a low-SES neighborhood of Miami, FL, indicated that Haitian and Black-American mothers differed in their feeding and face-to-face play interactions in the laboratory. Haitian mothers were more responsive to infant gaze aversion and behaviors, displayed more vocalizations and expressive facial expressions, and engaged in more infantilized behavior and games. In addition, Cuban teenage mothers read more to their infants, played with them a higher percentage of the time, and demonstrated toys more frequently (Field, 1993). Cultural traditions in play are also changing as society changes. For example, Taiwanese children engage in traditional play forms such as kite flying and top games, but increasingly engage in more modern play forms, such as symbolic play, due to a lack of outdoor playgrounds in urban areas (Pan, 1994). Thus, cultural effects are not static, but change as the culture changes.

The extent to which mothers demonstrate and suggest specific kinds of pretend acts and label and describe objects in a play session varies across cultures (Tamis-LeMonda et al., 1992). In addition, culture influences the extent to which mothers direct attention to the environment or toward themselves. American mothers tend to respond to their 5-month-olds extradyadically, while Japanese mothers respond more often by directing attention toward themselves (Bornstein et al., 1992). These interactions may carry over into mother-infant play interactions.

EXAMPLES OF MOTHER-INFANT PLAY INTERACTIONS

The 16- to 18-month-old infants described in the following section were observed as part of research on social development and mother-infant attachment. They were all from middle-class intact families and not in any kind of nonparental care situation. Security of attachment was assessed using the Q-sort method (Waters & Deane, 1985). During the observation period, mothers were asked to complete two questionnaires about background information and play preferences. In the 10-minute highchair observation, mothers were asked to return the cups to the highchair tray whenever the child dropped all 3 of them. The mothers were given no instructions for the 10-minute free-play observation.

"Justin"

Background Information

Low security of attachment score, 18-month-old twin boy, born more than 1 month premature. Mental Development Index from Bayley Scales is 88, but would be 98 if compared to norms for children of equal gestational age. Mother reports very low satisfaction with her role as a homemaker and the amount of time she spends with her children. (No data are available for this child on play preferences.)

Highchair Observation

Mom gives 3 nesting cups to Justin, seated in a highchair. She then begins working on the questionnaires. Justin looks briefly at the cups and immediately drops all 3 cups while looking at Mom. Mom says, "You can't get out of that chair." Mom then picks up the cups, and Justin immediately drops all 3 of them again. Mom responds with, "Now what are you gonna do? Huh?" Justin looks around the room and cries. Mom gets the cups. Justin drops all the cups. "Is that fun?" Mom asks. Justin cries, Mom returns cups. Justin drops all 3 cups, cries. "What's wrong?" Mom asks, picks up the cups, and shows Justin how to nest the cups. Justin cries harder. Mom takes him out of the highchair, holds him on her lap, and shows him the cups; he pushes the cups away and cries.

Free-Play Observation

Mom tells Justin to open the toy box, "You can open that box, can't you?" Justin opens the box, then puts the lid back on and goes to Mom crying and clinging. Mom asks Justin to "give Mama the lid." Justin goes and gets a ball and shows it to Mom. Mom says, "You can throw a ball, can't you?" Justin drops the ball, puts the lid back on the box and goes to Mom, crying and clinging. Mom asks, "What's in the box? What's in there?" She then says, "It's okay, that little noise is in the other room. It's okay." [There is evidently a noise from the other room that is not audible on the videotape.] "It's just a little noise. It's okay. Look, find the ball. What's in there? Is that a cup? Is there a drink?" Justin offers cup to Mom, and Mom pretends to drink. Justin cries, takes out another toy, puts it back, and turns to Mom crying and clinging. Mom lifts Justin to her lap and begins to read a book to him. Justin screams and arches his back.

Comments

The amount of negative affect in these interactions is further indication of the low security of attachment in this mother-child relationship. When Justin cries and pushes the cups away and later when he screams and arches his back when his mother tries to share a book with him, he exhibits the kinds of behaviors that are scored as resistant in Ainsworth et al.'s (1978) classification system. The mother appears inconsistent in her responses to Justin in these observations: Although she does respond to his bids for interaction, she often waits until he is already crying. She makes suggestions for him to play but does not comment on his play. The mother's low satisfaction with her role as well as the presence of two infants in the home may contribute to an ongoing pattern of inconsistent responsiveness that is predictive of an anxious/ambivalent attachment (Ainsworth et al., 1978).

"Jennifer"

Background Information

Low security score, 17-month-old girl with no siblings. Mental Development Index from Bayley Scales is 100. Mother reports very high satisfaction with her role as homemaker and with the amount of time she spends with her child. Mother reports that their favorite play with each other is peek-a-boo.

Highchair Observation

Jennifer picks up each cup, begins nesting them, and vocalizes to Mom. Jennifer drops all 3 cups, vocalizes and looks at Mom, looks around the room. Mom returns the cups. Jennifer immediately drops the cups, looks at Mom and looks away at wall. Mom picks up the cups and nests them as she puts them on the highchair. Jennifer drops the cups. Mom returns them and stacks them. Jennifer unstacks and restacks the cups, vocalizes to Mom, drops 2 cups. Mom does not respond. Jennifer pretends to drink from a cup and says "go?" repeatedly. Then she drops the third cup. Mom puts cups at 3 different locations on tray. Jennifer drops all the cups, looks at Mom, says, "hi?" Mom returns cups and points to a picture on the bottom of a cup, "Look at the picture." Jennifer nests the cups, playing for a few minutes, then drops the cups and looks at Mom. Mom returns the cups.

Free-Play Observation

Mom shows Jennifer several of the toys. Jennifer goes to the corner of the room away from Mom, plays with the wall, the outlet, the chair. Jennifer shows Mom a toy that has a noise-maker/spinner on it. Mom ignores it. Jennifer drops the toy. Mom picks up the dropped toy, says, "That's interesting," puts the toy in the toy box. Jennifer gets the toy and plays with it and puts it in Mom's lap. Mom ignores it, but does not remove it from her lap. Jennifer plays with other toys for a few minutes, then gets the toy from Mom's lap, and continues to play alone with it for several minutes. Jennifer moves to the wall farthest away from Mom, drops cups over the partition, moves back to Mom, reaches for Mom's pen and Mom moves it away. Jennifer holds up a toy to show or offer Mom, Mom ignores it, and Jennifer drops the toy. Jennifer reaches for Mom's pen and Mom moves it away again.

Comments

Unlike the preceding child, Jennifer does not express negative affect, but vocalizes frequently to her mother and attempts several initiations of toy sharing and play interaction, behaviors often seen in children who are rated as securely attached. However, it is only successful initiations of toy sharing, rather than unreciprocated attempts, that have been correlated with security of attachment (Roggman, et al., 1987). Jennifer's frequent looks away and moves away from her mother are similar to the kinds of behavior that are scored as avoidant in Ainsworth et al.'s (1978) classification system, consistent with her low security score by the Q-sort method used here. Her mother's responses also are typical of maternal responses that predict an anxious/avoidant attachment. Her mother remains task-oriented for the entire observation period, ignoring Jennifer's attempts to interact with her, but apparently trying to sustain Jennifer's interest in the cups by setting them up differently every time they are put back on the highchair tray. It is surprising that the mother reports that their favorite social play together is peek-a-boo, a game that entails responsive interaction, but perhaps the ritualized nature of the game is more possible for this mother and child than spontaneous responsive interactions in a free-play setting.

"Melissa"

Background Information

High security of attachment score, 16-month-old girl with a 5-year-old brother. Mental Development Index from Bayley Scales is 137. Mother reports very high satisfaction with her role as homemaker and the amount of time she spends with her children. Mother reports that child's favorite play with mother is tickle games, and mother's favorite play with child is rhymes and songs.

Highchair Observation

Mom and Melissa look at each other and both smile. Melissa holds up a cup. "That's a yellow cup," Mom responds. Melissa then holds up each of the other two cups and mom describes them. Melissa holds up all 3 cups, squeals and laughs. "You can hold all 3 cups," Mom says and laughs. Melissa continues to play with cups while Mom works on questionnaires. Mom looks up and smiles. Melissa laughs, tries to stack cups while Mom watches, vocalizes to Mom, laughs. Melissa tries to nest cups. "Did you get it inside?" Mom asks. There is continuing frequent joint attention to the cups and frequent comments by Mom about Melissa's actions with the cups. Melissa drops 1 cup. Mom says, "Boom. Oh-oh, you dropped it." Mom points to a cup still on the highchair tray, "Anything in that cup?" Melissa drops other 2 cups. Mom picks up cups immediately. Melissa looks at mom. Mom stacks and unstacks cups. Melissa continues playing with cups, and Mom goes back to working on the questionnaires. Melissa squirms in highchair. Mom asks, "Look, can I have a drink?" and pretends to drink from one of the cups. Melissa offers each of the 3 cups, and Mom drinks from each one. Melissa pretends to drink from the cups and then squirms in highchair. Mom points to picture on bottom of one of the cups, "Look, is that a horsie?" Mom watches as Melissa continues to play with the cups.

Free-Play Observation

Mom says, "Oh, look at all these toys. See all the toys in this box?" Mom watches as Melissa gets the toys out. Melissa walks around the observation room, goes back to the toys, vocalizes to Mom. "Look at these toys," Mom says. Mom shows Melissa the telephone, "Want to talk on the telephone?" Melissa picks up the telephone, putting receiver to ear, "bye." "Who is it?" asks Mom. Melissa laughs, puts the phone down, gets the ball and walks around the room again, then puts the toys back in the box and puts the lid on the box, walks around, then goes back to Mom. "Can you throw that ball?" asks Mom. Melissa walks around again, then goes back to the toys. Mom picks up a book, shows it to Melissa and begins reading the book. Melissa laughs. Mom asks, "What's the kitty say?" Melissa responds "Meow" and laughs. Mom sets up cup and saucer, "There." Melissa walks around again. Mom shows Melissa a toy, offers it, and Melissa accepts it and plays with it. Mom watches as Melissa continues to play. Mom picks up the phone and offers it. "Say hello," Mom suggests. Melissa takes the phone and says, "allo." Mom says, "Say bye bye." "Bye," says Melissa, looks at Mom, laughs and vocalizes.

Comments

The frequent positive interactions, smiles and laughter, and shared attention to the toys are all further evidence of the secure attachment between this mother and child. Mom responds quickly and positively to Melissa's bids for attention. Mom also initiates play interactions with the toys, makes suggestions for play, watches Melissa play, and comments on her play with the toys. When Melissa begins to get restless in the highchair, her mother is quick to initiate an interactive pretending game with the cups. Again, toward the end of the observation session when Melissa's play is slowing down, her mother initiates social play with the telephone. Mother's report of "tickle" as the child's favorite game is consistent with the frequent laughter and positive affect between mother and child.

"Margaret"

Background Information

High security score, 18-month-old girl, younger sister of two girls age 10 and 11. The Mental Development Index from the Bayley Scales is 109. Mother reports high satisfaction with her role as homemaker and very high satisfaction with the amount of time she spends with her children. Mother reports that child's favorite play with mother is general exploration together, and mother's favorite play with child is rhymes and songs.

Highchair Observation

Margaret nests the 3 cups, vocalizes to Mom. Mom smiles. Margaret continues to nest and stack the cups intently for about 5 minutes, then she drops 1 cup, looks at Mom, and says, "oh-oh." Then she throws cups 2 and 3 at Mom. Mom laughs and returns the cups. Margaret laughs, drops 1 cup, throws another to the floor, and laughs. Then she plays with the third cup for a minute and then throws it on the floor. Mom smiles and returns the cups. Margaret drops 1 cup, looks at Mom, and plays with cups 2 and 3 for several minutes, rolling, stacking, nesting, and pretending to drink with them. Margaret says "Mama," offers the cups, drops all 3 on the floor. Mom returns the cups. Margaret throws 2 cups, looks at Mom and says, "oh-oh," and throws the third cup directly at Mom. Mom returns cups without looking at Margaret. Margaret drops 2 cups. Mom looks sideways at Margaret with her eyebrows raised.

Free-Play Observation

Mom picks up the ball from the toy box and offers it to Margaret. Margaret accepts the ball, looks at it, and shows it to Mom. Mom looks at the ball, smiles, and goes back to working on a questionnaire. Margaret continues to play with the toys for several minutes without interacting with Mom. Margaret then offers a cup to Mom, and Mom accepts it. Margaret then offers the telephone to Mom, and Mom lets it drop to the floor. Margaret picks up the telephone and continues playing with it. Mom puts the cup back in the toy box.

Comments

There is positive affect evident in the shared laughter and smiles of Margaret and her mother, as would be expected with a securely attached child, though not as much as in the preceding observation. Margaret's mother is initially very positive and responsive to her use of the cups to get attention, but even the most responsive of mothers can get very tired of the "dropping game," and Margaret's mother becomes less positive with each return of the cups to the highchair tray, ending the 10 minutes with a somewhat negative expression. The free-play interactions are also not as responsive as in the preceding dyad. Margaret's mother completely ignores one of her attempts to share a toy and lets the toy simply fall to the floor. However, there is none of the looking away or moving away that was indicative of avoidance in the relationship between Jennifer and her mother. In fact, Margaret and her mother each initiate a successful exchange of toys. Although throwing the cups may be an expression of some anger, there is none of the crying, clinging, and resistance that was evident in the interactions between Justin and his mother.

This last play observation of Margaret and her mother shows that the playful interactions between a securely attached child and mother are not always perfectly harmonious and responsive, but rather may differ in only subtle ways from interactions between anxiously attached children and their mothers. The lack of negative affect and avoidance in an interaction may, in some cases, be more telling than the presence of happy sharing and interactive play. Observers of mother-child play interactions would do well to make repeated observations, in multiple settings, using a variety of play measures and other measures of mother-infant interactions.

CONCLUSION

Many behavioral aspects of mother-infant interactions in play are thought to be related to developmental outcomes. Play researchers have used various methods to identify individual differences in those interactions that might predict specific outcomes. This chapter has reviewed a wide range of measures of mother-infant play and/or mother-infant interaction during play that have been used in the research on early infant and toddler development. The measures of play presented all have been found to be related to developmental competence or secure mother-infant attachment or both. The situations that have been used for assessing mother-infant play range from "free-play" situations in which there are few restrictions to situations in which the toys, the mother's behavior, or the infant's behavior are restricted in some way. Although there are some nonobservational alternatives, most measures of mother-infant play have been made by direct observation, "live" or on video-tape, using various tools for recording the data, from paper-and-pencil to direct computer data acquisition devices.

Multiple measures of mother-infant interactions are recommended, and the kinds of play interactions that are most important to observe will depend on the age of the child. In the first few months, the important aspects of play involve the coordination of social attention in face-to-face play. The most useful measures during that period would assess gazing behavior, the mother's initiation of stimulation games, and the ability of the mother and infant to sustain those games without overstimulating or understimulating the infant. During the middle months of the first year, when mother-infant play begins to include more of the recognizable games of infancy, the most useful measures would assess the infant's active involvement in those games and the mother's predictability in the interactions. Around the end of the first year and into the second year, the most useful measures would assess the infant's initiation of interactions and the mother's response to those initiations, particularly those interactions that involve shared attention to toys, the exchange of toys, and interactive pretending with toys. Finally, during all the age periods of infancy, the amount of positive affect expressed in mother-infant play interactions is one of the most valuable sources of information about the mother-infant relationship.

At this point, there are certainly many questions remaining about the use of mother-infant play as an assessment tool. This is not surprising because the behavior under consideration is a complex interaction between two individuals at widely disparate developmental levels, infant and adult, influenced by multiple factors. It is no wonder that the measures, although rich in information, are often imprecise. Nevertheless, play interactions remain valuable for our assessments of mother-infant social interactions for at least three reasons. First, they are the most purely social interactions of infancy. Second, they are interactions which offer the developing infant multiple opportunities for learning skills and building trust. Finally, they are among the most joyful interactions between mothers and their infants.

REFERENCES

Adamson, L. B., & Bakeman, R. (1985). Affect and attention: Infants observed with mothers and peers. *Child Development, 56,* 582–593.

Ainsworth, M. D. S., Blehar, M., Walters, E., & Wall, S. (1978). *Patterns of attachment.* New York: Wiley.

Appelbaum, M. I., & McCall, R. B. (1984). Design and analysis in developmental psychology. In P. Mussen (Series ed.), W. Kesson (Vol. ed.), *Handbook of child psychology, Vol. 1, History, theory, and methods* (pp. 415–476). New York: Wiley.

Bakeman, R., & Adamson, L. B. (1984). Coordinating attention to people and objects in mother-infant and peer-infant interaction. *Child Development, 55,* 1278–1289.

Baldwin, D. (1991). Infants' contribution to the achievement of joint reference. *Child Development, 62,* 875–890.

Belsky, J., Garduque, & Hrncir, E. (1984). Assessing performance, competence, and executive capacity in infant play: Relations to home environment and security of attachment. *Developmental Psychology, 20,* 405–417.

Belsky, J., & Most, R. K. (1981). From exploration to play: A cross-sectional study of infant free-play behavior. *Developmental Psychology, 17,* 630–639.

Bench, J., & Wilson, I. (1976). A comparison of live and videorecord viewing of infant behavior under sound stimulation. *Developmental Psychobiology, 9,* 297–303.

Bogdan, R. K. & Biklen, S. K. (1992). *Qualitative research for education.* Boston: Allyn and Bacon.

Booth, C., Rose-Krosnor, L., McKinnon, J., & Rubin, K. H. (1994). Predicting social adjustment in middle childhood: The role of preschool attachment security and maternal style [Special Issue: From family to peer group: Relations between relationships]. *Social Development, 3,* 189–204.

Bornstein, M. H., Haynes, O. M., Legler, J. M., O'Reilly, A. W., & Painter, K. M. (1997). Symbolic play in childhood: Interpersonal and environmental context and stability. *Infant Behavior and Development, 20,* 197–207.

Bornstein, M. H., Haynes, O. M., O'Reilly, A. W., & Painter, K. M. (1996). Solitary and collaborative pretense play in early childhood: Sources of individual variation in the development of representational competence. *Child Development, 67,* 2910–2929.

Bornstein, M. H., & Tamis-LeMonda, C. S. (1990). Activities and interactions of mothers and their firstborn infants in the first six months of life: Covariation, stability, continuity, correspondence, and prediction. *Child Development, 61,* 1206–1217.

Bornstein, M. H., Tamis-LeMonda, C. S., Tal, J., Ludemann, S. T., Rahn, C. W., Pêcheux, M., Azuma, H., & Vardi, D. (1992). Maternal responsiveness to infants in three societies: The United States, France and Japan. *Child Development, 63,* 808–821.

Boyce, L. (November, 1997). Interactions and play behaviors of mothers of typically and atypically developing infants: A Vygostskian approach. Head Start Research Scholars Meeting, Washington, D.C.

Boyce, L. K., Benson, B., Roggman, L. A., & Cook, G. (April, 1997). Influence of infant-mother play at home on infant's level of cognitive play in a laboratory setting. The Association for the Study of Play, Washington, D.C.

Bradshaw, D. L., Goldsmith, H. H., & Campos, J. J. (1987). Attachment, temperament, and social referencing: Interrelationships among three domains of infant affective behavior. *Infant Behavior and Development, 10,* 223–232.

Bruner, J. S., & Sherwood, V. (1976). Peekaboo and the learning of rule structures. In J. S. Bruner, A. Jolley, & K. Sylva (Eds.), *Play: Its role in development and evolution* (pp. 277–285). New York: Penguin.

Cielinski, K. L., Vaughn, B. E., Seifer, R., & Contreras, J. (1995). Relations among sustained engagement during play, quality of play, and mother-child interaction in samples of children with Down syndrome and normally developing toddlers. *Infant Behavior and Development, 18,* 163–176.

Cohen, J. (1960). A coefficient of agreement for nominal scales. *Educational and Psychological Measurement, 20,* 37–46.

Cohen, J. (1968). Weighted kappa: Nominal scale agreement with provision for scaled disagreement or partial credit. *American Psychologist, 70,* 213–220.

Cohn, J. F., & Elmore, M. A. (April, 1995). A comparison of microanalytic and rating scale approaches to assessing mother-infant affect and synchrony. Presentation at the meeting of the Society for Research in Child Development, Indianapolis, IN.

Crawley, S. B., Rogers, P. P., Friedman, S., Iacobbo, M., Criticos, A., Richardson, L., & Thompson, M. A. (1978). Developmental changes in the structure of mother-infant play. *Developmental Psychology, 14,* 30–36.

Crawley, S. B., & Sherrod, K. B. (1984). Parent-infant play during the first year of life. *Infant Behavior and Development, 7,* 65–76.

Desrochers, S., Ricard, M., Decarie, T. G., & Allard, L. (1994). Developmental synchrony between social referencing and Piagetian sensorimotor causality. *Infant Behavior and Development, 17,* 303–309.

Dey, I. (1993). *Qualitative data analysis: A user-friendly guide for social scientists.* London: Routledge and Kegan Paul.

Dickstein, S., Thompson, R. A., Estes, D., Malkin, C., & Lamb, M. E. (1984). Social referencing and the security of attachment. *Infant Behavior and Development, 7,* 507–516.

Dunham, P., & Dunham, R. (1992). Lexical development during middle infancy: A mutually driven infant-caregiver process. *Developmental Psychology, 28,* 414–420.

Eckerman, C. O., & Rheingold, H. L. (1974). Infants' exploratory responses to toys and people. *Developmental Psychology, 10,* 255–259.

Farran, D. C. & Kasari, C. (1990). A longitudinal analysis of the development of synchrony in mutual gaze in mother-infant dyads. *Journal of Applied Developmental Psychology, 11,* 419–430.

Fenson, L. & Ramsay, D. S. (1980). Decentration and integration of the child's play in the second year. *Child Development, 51,* 171–178.

Fernald, A. & O'Neill, D. K. (1993). Peekaboo across cultures: How mothers and infants play with voices, faces, and expectations. In K. MacDonald (Ed.), *Parent-child play: Descriptions and implications* (pp. 259–285). Albany, NY: State University of New York Press.

Field, T. (1979). Games people play with normal and high-risk infants. *Child Psychiatry and Human Development, 10,* 41–48.

Field, T. M. (1993). Persistence of play and feeding interaction differences in three Miami cultures. In K. MacDonald (Ed.), *Parent-child play: Descriptions and implications.* Albany, NY: State University of New York Press.

Fleiss, J. L. (1971). Measuring nominal scale agreement among many raters. *Psychological Bulletin, 76,* 378–382.

Garner, P. W., & Landry, S. H. (1994). Effects of maternal attention-directing strategies on preterm infants' affective expressions during joint toy play. *Infant Behavior and Development, 17,* 15–22.

Gaskins, S. (1994). Integrating interpretive and qualitative methods in socialization research. *Merrill-Palmer Quarterly, 40,* 313–333.

Gelfand, D. M., Hartmann, D. P. (1975). *Child behavior analysis and therapy.* New York: Pergamon.

Gunnar, M. R., & Stone, C. (1984). The effects of positive maternal affect on infant response to pleasant, ambiguous, and fear-provoking toys. *Child Development, 55,* 1231–1236.

Gustafson, G. E., Green, J. A., & West, M. J. (1979). The infant's changing role in mother-infant games: The growth of social skills. *Infant Behavior and Development, 2,* 301–308.

Haight, W. L., & Miller, P. J. (1993). *Pretending at home: Early development in a sociocultural context.* Albany: State University of New York Press.

Hartmann, D. P. (1982). Assessing the dependability of observational data. In D. P. Hartmann (Ed.), *Using observers to study behavior: Vol. 14, New directions for methodology of social and behavioral science* (pp. 51–66). San Francisco: Jossey-Bass.

Hawkins, R. P. (1982). Developing a behavior code. In D. P. Hartmann (Ed.), *Using observers to study behavior: Vol. 14, New directions for methodology of social and behavioral science* (pp. 21–36). San Francisco: Jossey-Bass.

Hay, D. F. (1979). Cooperative interactions and sharing between very young children and their parents. *Developmental Psychology, 15,* 647–653.

Holm, R. A. (1978). Techniques of recording observational data. In G. P. Sackett (Ed.), *Observing behavior, Vol. II: Data collection and analysis methods.* Baltimore: University Park.

Hrncir, E. J., Speller, G. M., & West, M. (1985). What are we testing? *Developmental Psychology, 21,* 226–232.

Hunter, F. T., McCarthy, M. E., MacTurk, R. H., & Vietze, P. (1987). Infants' social-constructive interactions with mothers and fathers. *Developmental Psychology, 23,* 249–254.

Idle, T., Wood, E., & Desmarais, S. (1993). Gender role socialization in toy play situations: Mothers and fathers with their sons and daughters. *Sex Roles, 28,* 679–691.

Jones, S. S. (1985). On the motivational bases for attachment behavior. *Developmental Psychology, 21,* 848–857.

Kazdin, A. E. (1982). Observer effects: Reactivity of direct observation. In D. P. Hartmann (Ed.), *Using observers to study behavior: Vol. 14, New directions for methodology of social and behavioral science* (pp. 5–20). San Francisco: Jossey-Bass.

Landry, S. H. (1986). Preterm infants' responses in early joint attention interactions. *Infant Behavior and Development, 9,* 1–14.

Landry, S. H., Garner, P. W., Swank, P. R., & Baldwin, C. D. (1996). Effects of maternal scaffolding during joint toy play with preterm and full-term infants. *Merrill-Palmer Quarterly, 42,* 177–199.

Langlois, J. H., Roggman, L. A., & Rieser-Danner, L. A. (1990). Infant's social responses to attractive and unattractive faces: More evidence for a rudimentary stereotype. *Developmental Psychology, 26,* 153–159.

Leaper, L., & Gleason, J. B. (1996). The relationship of play activity and gender to parent and child sex-typed communication. *International Journal of Behavioral Development, 19,* 689–703.

Matas, L., Arend, R. A., & Sroufe, L. A. (1978). Continuity of adaptation in the second year: The relationship between quality of attachment and later competence. *Child Development, 49,* 547–556.

Mosier, C. E., & Rogoff, B. (1994). Infants' instrumental use of their mothers to achieve their goals. *Child Development, 65,* 70–79.

Newland, L. A., Roggman, L. A., Boyce, L., & Cook, G. (1997, April). *Toy sharing, symbolic play, and language development in infancy.* Presentation at the Conference for the Association for the Study of Play, Washington, D.C.

Newland, L. A., Roggman, L. A., Boyce, L. & Cook, G. (1998, April). *Mother-infant social play related to infant language and play at 11 and 14 months.* Presentation at the International Conference on Infant Studies, Atlanta, GA.

NICHD Early Child Care Research Network. (1997). The effects of infant child care on infant-mother attachment security: Results of the NICHD study of early child care. *Child Development, 68,* 860–879.

Noll, L. M., Harding, C. G., Stilson, S. R., & Weissman, L. (1998). The relationship between choice co-construction and symbolic play in mother-child dyads. Presentation at the International Conference on Infant Studies, Atlanta, GA.

Pan, H. L. (1994). Children's play in Taiwan. In J. L. Roopnarine, J. E. Johnson, & F. H. Hooper (Eds.), *Children's play in diverse cultures* (pp. 31–50). Albany, NY: State University of New York Press.

Power, T. G. (1985). Mother- and father-infant play: A developmental analysis. *Child Development, 56,* 1514–1524.

Reid, J. B. (1982). Observer training in naturalistic research. In D. P. Hartmann (Ed.), *Using observers to study behavior: Vol. 14, New directions for methodology of social and behavioral science* (pp. 37–50). San Francisco: Jossey-Bass.

Reissland, N., & Snow, D. (1996). Maternal pitch height in ordinary and play situations. *Journal of Child Language, 23,* 269–278.

Rheingold, H. L., Hay, D. F., & West, M. J. (1976). Sharing in the second year of life. *Child Development, 47,* 1148–1158.

Roach, M. A., Barratt, M. S., Miller, J. F., & Leavitt, L. A. (1998). The structure of mother-child play: Young children with Down syndrome and typically developing children. *Developmental Psychology, 34,* 77–87.

Roggman, L. A. (1987, April). Changes in infant play behavior. Society for Research in Child Development, Baltimore MD.

Roggman, L. A. (1989, April). Age differences in the goals of toddler play. Society for Research in Child Development, Kansas City, MO.

Roggman, L. A., Hart, A. D., Carroll, K. A., & Egan, M. J. (in press). Security of attachment in relation to infant attention in the context of social play. In B. Vaughn & E. Waters (Eds.). Hillsdale, NJ: Erlbaum.

Roggman, L. A., Langlois, J. H., & Hubbs-Tait, L. (1987). Mothers, infants, and toys: Social play correlates of attachment. *Infant Behavior and Development, 10,* 233–237.

Roggman, L. A., Murphy, S. A., & Shiraki, R. (1988, March). Infant sex differences in toy interest: Dolls, trains, and cups. Southwest Society for Research in Human Development, New Orleans, LA.

Roggman, L. A., & Peery, J. C. (1988). Caregiving, emotional involvement and parent-infant play. *Early Child Development, 34,* 191–199.

Roggman, L. A., & Peery, J. C. (1989). Mother-infant play. Early gender differences. *Child Study Journal, 19,* 65–79.

Rogoff, B., Malkin, C., & Gilbride, K. (1984). Interaction with babies as guidance in development. In B. Rogoff & J. V. Wertsch (Eds.), Children's learning in the zone of proximal development. *New directions for child development, 23* (pp. 31–44). San Francisco: Jossey-Bass.

Rogoff, B., Mistry, J., Radziszewska, B., & Germond, J. (1992). Infants' instrumental social interaction with adults. In S. Feinman et. al. (Ed.), *Social referencing and the social construction of reality in infancy* (pp. 323–348). New York: Plenum Press.

Rollins, P. R., Marchman, V. A., Mehta, J. (1998, April). Infant gaze following, joint attention, and vocabulary development. Presentation at the International Conference on Infant Studies, Atlanta, GA.

Rome-Flanders, T., Cossette, L., Ricard, M., & Decarie, T. G. (1995). Comprehension of rules and structures in mother-infant games: A longitudinal study of the first two years of life. *International Journal of Behavioral Development, 18,* 83–103.

Roopnarine, J. L., Hooper, F. H., Ahmeduzzaman, M., & Pollack, B. (1993). Gentle play partners: Mother-child and father-child play in New Delhi, India. In K. MacDonald (Ed.), *Parent-child play: Descriptions and implications* (pp. 287–304). Albany, NY: State University of New York Press.

Roopnarine, J. L., Hossain, Z., Gill, P., & Brophy, H. (1994). Play in the East Indian context. In J. L. Roopnarine, J. E. Johnson, & F. H. Hooper (Eds.), *Children's play in diverse cultures* (pp. 9–30). Albany, NY: State University of New York Press.

Rosen, W. D., Adamson, L. B., & Bakeman, R. (1992). An experimental investigation of infant social referencing: Mother's messages and gender differences. *Developmental Psychology, 14,* 111–123.

Ross, H. S., & Kay, D. A. (1980). The origins of social games. In K. Rubin (Ed.), *New directions for child development: Children's play, 9* (pp. 17–32). San Francisco: Jossey-Bass.

Ross H. S., & Lollis, S. P. (1987). Communication with infant social games. *Developmental Psychology, 23,* 241–248.

Rusher, A. S., Cross, D. R., & Ware, A. M. (1995). Infant and toddler play: Assessment of exploratory style and developmental level. *Early Childhood Research Quarterly, 10,* 297–315.

Sackett, G. P. (1978). Measurement in observational research. In G. P. Sackett (Ed.), *Observing behavior, Vol. II: Data collection and analysis methods.* Baltimore: University Park.

Saxon, T. F. (1997, April). *The relationship between maternal following or switching verbal references to objects and infant language competence.* Presentation at the Society for Research in Child Development, Washington, D.C.

Saxon, T. F., Frick, J. E., & Columbo, J. (1996, April). *Joint attention at 6 and 8 months and later language competence.* Presentation at the International Conference on Infant Studies, 10th Biennial Meeting, Providence, RI.

Saxon, T. F., & Reilly, J. T. (1998, April). *Joint attention and toddler characteristics: Race, sex and socioeconomic status.* Presentation at the International Conference on Infant Studies, Atlanta, GA.

Shaw, D. S., Keenan, K., & Vondra, J. I. (1994). Developmental precursors of externalizing behavior: Ages 1 to 3. *Developmental Psychology, 30,* 355–364.

Shrout, P. E., & Fleiss, J. L. (1979). Intraclass correlations: Uses in assessing rater reliability. *Psychological Bulletin, 86,* 420–428.

Slade, A. (1987). Quality of attachment and early symbolic play. *Developmental Psychology, 23,* 78–85.

Smith, K. E., Landry, S. H., Swank, P. R., Baldwin, C. D., Denson, S. E., & Wildin, S. (1996). The relation of medical risk and maternal stimulation with preterm infants' development of cognitive, language, and daily living skills. *Journal of Child Psychology and Psychiatry and Allied Disciplines, 37,* 855–864.

Spangler, G., Schieche, M., Ilg, U., Maier, U. & Ackermann, C. (1994). Maternal sensitivity as an external organizer for biobehavioral regulation in infancy. *Developmental Psychobiology, 27,* 425–437.

Spencer, P. E., & Meadow-Orlans, K. P. (1996). Play, language, and maternal responsiveness: A longitudinal study of deaf and hearing infants. *Child Development, 67,* 3176–3191.

Stern, D. (1974). The goal and structure of mother-infant play. *Journal of the American Academy of Child Psychiatry, 13,* 402–421.

Stern, D. (1977). *The first relationship.* Cambridge, MA: Harvard University Press.

Suess, G. J., Grossmann, K. E., & Sroufe, L. A. (1992). Effects of infant attachment to mother and father on quality of adaptation in preschool: From dyadic to individual organization of self. *International Journal of Behavioral Development, 15,* 43–65.

Sutton-Smith, B. (1986). *Toys as culture.* New York: Gardner.

Tamis-LeMonda, C. S., & Bornstein, M. H. (1989). Habituation and maternal encouragement of attention in infancy as predictors of toddler language, play, and representational competence. *Child Development, 60,* 738–751.

Tamis-LeMonda, C. S., & Bornstein, M. H. (1990). Language, play, and attention at one year. *Infant Behavior and Development, 13,* 85–98.

Tamis-LeMonda, C. S., & Bornstein, M. H. (1994). Specificity in mother-toddler language-play relations across the second year. *Developmental Psychology, 30,* 283–292.

Tamis-LeMonda, C. S., Bornstein, M. H., Cyphers, L., Toda, S., & Ogino, M. (1992). Language and play at one year: A comparison of toddlers and mothers in the United States and Japan. *International Journal of Behavioral Development, 15,* 19–42.

Thompson, R. A., & Lamb, M. E. (1984). Assessing qualitative dimensions of emotional responsiveness in infants: Separation reactions in the strange situation. *Infant Behavior and Development, 7,* 423–445.

Tinsley, H. E. A., & Weiss, D. J. (1975). Interrater reliability and agreement of subjective judgments. *Journal of Counseling Psychology, 22,* 358–376.

Tomasello, M. (1990). The role of joint attentional processes in early language development. *Language Sciences, 10,* 68–88.

Trainor, L. J. (1996). Infant preferences for infant-directed versus noninfant-directed playsongs and lullabies. *Infant Behavior and Development, 19,* 83–92.

Vandell, D. L. (1979). Effects of a playgroup experience on mother-son and father-son interaction. *Developmental Psychology, 15,* 379–385.

Vandell, D. L., & Wilson, K. S. (1987). Infants' interactions with mother, sibling, and peer: Contrasts and relations between interaction systems. *Child Development, 58,* 176–186.

Vondra, J. I., Shaw, D. S., & Kevenides, M. C. (1995). Predicting infant attachment classification from multiple, contemporaneous measures of maternal care. *Infant Behavior and Development, 18*(4), 415–425.

Waters, E., & Deane, K. E. (1985). Defining and assessing individual differences in attachment relationships: Q-methodology and the organization of behavior in infancy and early childhood. In I. Bretherton & E. Waters (Eds.), Growing points of attachments theory and research, *Monographs of the Society for Research in Child Development, 50,* 41–65.

Waters, E., & Wippman, J., & Sroufe, L. A. (1978). Attachment, positive affect, and competence in the peer group: Two studies in construct validation. *Child Development, 50,* 821–829.

Watson, M. W., & Jackowitz, E. R. (1984). Agents and recipient objects in the development of early symbolic play. *Child Development, 55,* 1091–1097.

Yale, M. E., & Mundy, P. C. (1998, April). Infant gaze direction during a novel labeling task. Presentation at the International Conference on Infant Studies, Atlanta, GA.

Youngblade, L., Park, K., & Belsky, J. (1993). Measurement of young children's close friendships: A comparison of two independent assessment systems and their associations with attachment security. *International Journal of Behavioral Development, 16,* 563–587.

APPENDIX

PARENT-TODDLER PLAY PREFERENCES

INSTRUCTIONS: The first section is the CHILD'S PLAY ALONE. To rate it, you need to have seen your child playing but not joined the activity. Using the scale listed below, rate how well you think your child likes each of these activities. If you don't see him/her playing this activity please rate the activity with a 0. The next section is labeled PLAY WITH PARENT. Fill this section out the same as the CHILD'S PLAY ALONE section, but also rate how well the parent likes the activities.

0 = doesn't do 1 = doesn't like much 2 = likes only a little 3 = likes 4 = likes a lot

CHILD'S PLAY ALONE	How Much Child Likes
1. small motor toys (balls, blocks)	
2. large motor toys (trikes, wagons)	
3. running, climbing, dancing	
4. art materials (crayons)	
5. pretend toys (dolls, dishes, trucks)	
6. books, tapes	
7. general exploration, taking things apart, etc.	
8. other_____	

PLAY WITH PARENT	How Much Child Likes	How Much Parent Likes
Sensory Games		
9. peek-a-boo		
10. tickle games, "eat you up"		
11. bounce, toss, swing baby		
12. dance		
13. chase, catch you		
14. hide and seek		
15. tumbling, wrestling		
16. cuddly, kissy games		

Language Games	How Much Child Likes	How Much Parent Likes
17. "where's your body part]?"		
18. "what's that?", point and name		
19. action rhymes (pat-a-cake, piggies, etc.)		
20. other rhymes & songs		
21. read books		
Sharing Things		
22. general exploration, inside or outside		
23. give & take game		
24. toss or roll ball back and forth		
25. help with blocks, puzzles, etc.		
26. help with wagon, swing, trike, slide, etc.		
27. help with art materials (crayons, etc.)		
28. help with water, sand, snow		
Pretending Together		
29. eating, cleaning, sleeping		
30. talking on phone		
31. trucks, cars, trains		
32. dolls, puppets, animals as characters		

Chapter 11 ———————————————————————————————————

PARENT-CHILD INTERACTION PLAY ASSESSMENT

David T. Smith

EVOLUTION OF THE PARENT-CHILD INTERACTION PLAY ASSESSMENT (P-CIPA)

The evolution of the parent-child diagnostic play system that is described in this chapter is the result of empirical, theoretical, and practical issues that exist in the field of childhood psychopathology. This system is an attempt to integrate the complex reasons children develop problems with the complexities of psychometric technology, in order to arrive at a means to access information, which can generate quick, accurate, and useful hypotheses. A review of the historical development of parent-child assessments within the field can best show this system's background.

Families typically seek the assistance of mental health professionals for their children because of the children's behavioral problems. Whether the child is *failing* to do what *is* desired (e.g., complying with commands, urinary continence, homework) or *doing* what is *not* desired (e.g., aggressive behaviors, temper tantrums, lying), parents are often eager to have their children's responses modified somehow. Disturbed children and their disturbing behaviors challenge the therapist seeking to diagnose and to provide treatment.

Although there is much disagreement regarding how childhood disorders should be conceptualized, measured, and interpreted, there is much agreement regarding a need for systematic assessment of children (Mash & Terdal, 1981). Human social behavior is sufficiently complex, with myriad variables operating, so that clinicians must be ever attentive to obtain accurate, objective, and heuristic data in the search for solutions. On another level, this need for the development of effective assessment strategies becomes a prerequisite for evaluating and improving services for children (Achenbach & Edelbrock, 1978).

Utilizing empirically supported treatments has increasingly been valued in the mental health field (Seligman, 1995; Clarke, 1995), and the need to provide ways to document measurable change with each client has been raised for those working with children and adolescents (Hoagwood, Hibbs, Brent, & Jenson, 1995). An empirical approach to treatment has been highly encouraged within psychological training programs (Beidel, 1997), so that each clinician has a clear set of outcomes that are recorded directly by the client or clinician. Similarly, in the current age of managed care domination over third-party reimbursements, clinicians need to have ways to document the effectiveness of their treatment and ways to communicate justification for additional sessions (Miller, 1996). Thus, measurement of the problem behaviors and the related variables has become even more important for those helping children and their families.

The investigation of the child's behavioral problems traditionally employs various objective, projective, and subjective approaches. They generally seek to identify the role of the child and/or parent in the problem. Regardless of the therapeutic orientation, the interview continues to be the most universally used clinical assessment procedure (Sevan & MacDonald, 1978). Interviews can provide information from the children, parents, teachers, and others involved in observing the children and their contexts. The accuracy and meaning assigned to this data will, naturally, vary.

Standardized assessments of cognition and other areas of functioning can provide information about potential deficits that may explain the possibly misperceived child's behaviors. Such assessments permit behaviors to be judged relative to norms for the child's abilities. This allows more plausible reasons for behaviors to be developed because of an increased awareness of the child's abilities.

Behavioral checklists and rating scales also exist to provide normative data, both for categorical judgments about personality functioning (Wirt, Lachar, Klinedist, & Seat, 1977) or frequency information and types of behavior problems (Achenbach & Edelbrock, 1983; Conners, 1979). Parent and child self-rating scales are also available to determine whether factors such as personality styles (Hathaway & McKinley, 1948), marital adjustment (Locke & Wallace, 1959), or depression (Beck, 1967) might be operating in the child's disturbance. Direct observations of the behavior, whether in the assessment room or in a school or home environment, are also utilized to gather results that can help to plan an intervention.

These traditional approaches carry their various strengths and limitations for the diagnostician/therapist. The results are subject to missing information, questionable accuracy, and unclear validity, which may hinder the ability to generate useful hypotheses. Without specifically reviewing these faults (see Ciminero & Drabman, 1977), the critical issue becomes recognizing that childhood behavior is embedded within normal developmental sequences and occurs within a context of social and situational influences, perceptions, and expectations from significant adults in society (Bronfenbrenner, 1977). The multidimensional perspective of child behavior analysis lends credence to the need for evaluating how the child interacts with the environment and persons within it as part of the diagnostic battery. An approach that elicits dynamic and interactional information may serve to integrate the other data in the multidimensional task.

Various techniques exist to indirectly assess the context of the child's problems, ranging from methods that evaluate parental attitudes as they relate to the child's behavior (Gibson, 1968), to assessments of parental knowledge (O'Dell, Tarler, & Flynn, 1979). The implicit assumption of these approaches is that evaluating, and then changing, the knowledge and belief deficit of the parents would subsequently improve their ability to manage the child with behavior problems. Yet, mere knowledge does not necessarily produce a correct behavioral display of appropriate parental responses when interacting with the child, as Bloom (1956) suggests in describing the hierarchy of cognitive skills. For example, the typical person's expressive language skills may be very limited, in contrast to her or his receptive/comprehension abilities; similarly, the author has often found that a parent's understanding of the child management literature can be greater than their ability to behaviorally express their knowledge.

Direct assessments of parent-child interactions have been relatively recent endeavors to systematically yield contextual and relational information as they may relate to the child's behavioral problems. These procedures seek to elicit the target behaviors of concern and to gather information about the antecedent-behavior and behavior-consequent chain involved in their perpetuation. They attempt to analyze the intricacies of the child and parent's behaviors in the sense that Bronfenbrenner (1977) discussed when considering the microsystem variables. Many families seeking help can be casually observed to interact inappropriately, and a formal sampling of the parent(s) and child interacting can provide structure and specificity about the aberrant responses.

The underlying reasons for the inappropriate interactions may, however, be varied and may be interpreted in terms of differing clinical orientations. Barkley (1984), for example, discussed the importance of viewing the transactional nature of the parent-child interactions, recognizing the bidirectional and reciprocal influence that parents and children have on each other. Rather than viewing a parent's lack of behavioral skills or a child's overactivity as the cause of the problem, the bidirectional perspective recognizes the interaction of a host of factors that each person and the total environment contribute. Thus, techniques that sample the complexities of parent-child interactions can greatly aid the analysis of the determinants of children's difficulties.

A plethora of parent-child assessment systems exist (Hughes & Haynes, 1978), typically employing a behavioral paradigm. Observations of parent-child interactions in either naturalistic settings or structured laboratory situations have frequently been used, with a central issue becoming where the observation occurs. Naturalistic settings, such as the home, can seem to be more realistic and enhance the external validity (Campbell & Stanley, 1963) of the results. Johnson and Bolstad (1973) discuss the crucial methodological issues competing with these advantages, including observer bias, subject reactivity, demand characteristics, and response sets.

Alternatively, structured laboratory observations have their advantages and disadvantages, and are based on two assumptions: (1) They efficiently elicit the behaviors of interest (i.e., the "problem" behaviors), and (2) the standard stimulus situation enables a clinician or experimenter to make valid within- and between-participant comparisons (Hughes & Haynes, 1978). Most approaches use one parent (typically the mother) and the child in a clinical playroom that is organized in a standard manner and is amenable to nonintrusive observation via one-way mirrors or videotaping.

Both time and behavior sampling have been used, with the data expressed as frequency, rate, and/or percentage of total behaviors for normative comparisons (Hanf, 1969; Kogan & Wimberger, 1966; Zegiob & Forehand, 1975). Some investigators attempt to code the interaction between parent and child, generally sampling and coding every 5 seconds (Barkley, 1984; Eyberg & Johnson, 1974; Mash, Terdal, & Anderson, 1973; Wahler, 1975; Eyberg, Bessmer, Newcomb, Edwards, & Robinson, 1994). Several systems focus on parent-command/child-noncompliance interactions (Barkley, 1987a; Forehand & McMahon, 1981), in an effort to assess the salient feature of the child's defiance for subsequent treatment.

Any structured observational system is a measurement instrument, subject to the same considerations of stability, reliability, sensitivity, validity, and efficiency as other, more traditional psychometric instruments. Precise operational definitions of the observed behaviors are important but unfortunately not always provided in some observational approaches (Wimberger & Kagan, 1974). A lack of appropriate standardization of some procedures also prevents comparisons. Mash et al. (1973) note that reliability data are sometimes lacking, or the statistical procedure is not reported when analyzing the repeatability of codes. Additionally, as Hartmann (1982) notes, agreement statistics may tell how observers agree on scores but do not necessarily refer to how consistent the scores are (i.e., by having low error, random, and systematic bias differences).

The parent-child interaction system also must contend with validity issues so that the instrument elicits results that are of clinical significance and reflect relationships with other behaviors/measures as one might predict (Cone, 1982). Reactivity to being observed can affect the behavior and the inferences drawn (Kazdin, 1982), creating serious questions as to whether the observers are measuring what they had intended to sample.

Added to these drawbacks have been more pragmatic issues, such as the training time required to use a complex system (Patterson, 1982). Even less-complex schemes (Mash et. al., 1973) require two or more coders, although some relatively simple systems (Barkley, 1987a; Forehand & McMahon, 1981) have evolved to address these clinical utility drawbacks.

On balance, it would seem that the various parent-child assessment paradigms are mainly different rather than comparatively superior-inferior, each having strengths in various categories of importance. The parent-child assessment procedure discussed in this chapter was developed from a perceived need to create a system that maximized the factors of parsimony, reliability, objectivity, and validity when collecting information on parents' interactions with their children.

DESCRIPTIONS OF THE PARENT-CHILD INTERACTION PLAY ASSESSMENT (P-CIPA)

The P-CIPA is closely related to the response-class matrix (Mash et. al., 1973; Mash & Terdal, 1991) and distantly related to a model developed by Hanf (1969). Response classes (e.g., compliance, negative behavior, command) were developed for the Mash et al. (1973; Mash & Terdal, 1991) system instead of measuring discrete behaviors (e.g., throwing toys). Various behavioral indexes are derived in Mash et al.'s (1973) system (a matrix) from the pattern of response classes that are recorded by two coders during a play session, allowing normative comparisons (Mash & Terdal, 1991). The P-CIPA system was adapted from the response-class matrix on mainly pragmatic grounds. A system that requires only one observer seemed more expedient for most treatment settings. Additional categories of data were also desired in order to appeal to an eclectic group of diagnosticians.

Periodic use of the Infant Behavior Record (Bayley, 1969) serendipitously showed that several classes of behavior (e.g., attention span, social orientation) could be recorded accurately (Darby, 1980) by using a *semantic differential scaling approach* (i.e., continuum of categories with varying numerical values). The scale derived is intended to record and quantify aspects of the parent and child interactions during two laboratory play situations. The P-CIPA assessment should be used as one facet of a comprehensive assessment, which might include interviews, parent-teacher-child behavior and personality scales, cognitive measures, and projective techniques. The parent-child assessment should usually be conducted near the end of an assessment sequence, with one, or both, or multiple parent figures individually observed interacting with the child. By that time, the evaluator would have been able to establish greater client trust, which would potentially reduce the influence of reactivity factors (Kazdin, 1982). Also, the child will likely be less reserved in comparison to reactions in the initially unfamiliar surroundings, and the parents may have less of a need to prove their adequacy.

Setting and Materials

The assessment should be conducted in a quiet room that has at least a 7- by 10-foot floor space. A one-way mirror, allowing the observer to be in another room, is ideal. A stationary video camera would also be acceptable, but the sole use of an audio recorder would not. If necessary, the observer could be seated in a corner of the playroom, providing there were no eye contact or other responses to the parent or child.

The materials in the room vary somewhat according to the age and development of the child. Table 11–1 shows the toys needed, depending on the child's developmental level. A prior assessment of the child's mental age, or a parental estimate, should be used, with a chronological age being the last resort for determining which category of toys to choose. The toys should be conveniently stored in a large box, which will be useful for the second assessment stage when the child is directed to pick up the toys. The room can also have a table, several chairs, and a sink. Any additional objects only further compromise the standards of the procedure and should be avoided.

Directions

For the Examiner

The examiner should randomly disperse the toys throughout the room before the parent and child enter. The storage box can be placed in the corner of the room. A tablet of lined paper will be needed for anecdotal recording (see Table 11–2), with each page divided vertically for a column of parent and child behaviors to be recorded. An anecdotal record of the actions and words of the parent and child will be made, with the lines allowing a visual presentation of the sequences of the behaviors displayed.

Table 11–1.   The toys needed for the P-CIPA

Developmental Age	Toys Needed
0–2 Years	Ball, large crayons, paper, blocks, push toys, busy box (board with bells, buttons and activity centers), cars and trucks, musical toy, stackable plastic rings, stuffed animals/doll.
2–5 Years	Ball, two telephones, crayons and paper, play dough, cars and trucks, train, puzzles (both inset and six- to eight-piece interlocking puzzles), tool bench, doll house, figurines, locks, musical toy, preschooler storybook.
5 Years and above	Ball, basketball hoop, puzzles (10-piece and above interlocking type), crayons, paper, puppets, doll house and furniture, figurines, play dough, checkers and other board games, playing cards, water colors, brush, shoe brush, and cleanser.

Table 11–2.   Example of examiner's anecdotal record for 1-minute of a parent-child interaction

PARENT	CHILD
"Here, let's play with this (puzzle)."	(Goes to crayon, opens box)
	(Ignores, plays with crayons)
"What color is that?"	"Bwue"
"No, it's red."	
"Don't, make it look nice. Here, let's make a house."	(Scribbles on paper)
(Making a house)	(Dumps out all crayons, walks over to telephone, dials phone)
	"Hewo"
"Who are you calling? Daddy?"	(No response) (Brings phone to mother)
	"You"
"Nah, I've got my phone."	(Screams loudly)
"Okay, Okay." (dials) "Here's daddy."	

Two 15-minute periods of observations will occur, followed by a brief interview of the parent concerning how representative the interactions and behaviors seemed. The first 15-minute sessions, called the "unstructured situation" (terminology adapted from Leland & Smith, 1965), involves no specific demands for the child or the parent. The structured situation directs the parent to issue three commands, which are challenging and often resisted by children.

The parent should be given the following instructions out of the hearing range of the child, and the parent and child can then be directed to the playroom to begin.

For the Parent

"I would like to have the chance to observe you and (child's name) interacting as you might at home, in order to see what you have raised as concern. There will be some toys in a playroom you and (child's name) will be in, while I watch (or video record). For the next 15 minutes, pretend that you and (child's name) are at home, your work is done, and you have some uninterrupted free time. Spend the time as you might at home in this situation. I will give you some additional instructions after a while. Are there any questions or concerns?"

After 15 minutes of observation in the unstructured situation, the examiner should interrupt the play and give these instructions to the parent for the structured situation, out of the hearing of the child: "Now, I would like to have you direct (child's name) to do three things":

Task	*If 0–2 years old*
Clean up	Put toys away
Performance	Stack the rings
Self-help	Take off shoes and socks

Task	*If 2–5 years old*
Clean up	Put toys away in the box
Performance	Assemble an 8-piece interlocking puzzle
Self-help	Take off shoes and socks and put them back on

Task	If 5 years and above
Clean up	Put toys away in the box
Performance	Assemble a 15-piece interlocking puzzle
Self-help	Take off shoes, clean them, and put them back on feet

"Do you have any questions?"

After the child has completed the third task or 15 minutes has transpired, whichever occurs first, the structured situation is complete. The following questions should be given to the parent as a validity appraisal: "How typical were the interactions and behaviors during the first situation (unstructured) compared to those occurring at home? Would you say that all, most, half, some, or none of what occurred was typical?" (The rating scale from the validity checks section of Appendix A can be shown to the parent, and the parent's comments can be added next to their rating.)

"How typical were the interactions and behaviors during the situation in which you directed (child's name) to perform the three commands in comparison to those occurring at home? Would you say that all, most, half, some, or none of what occurred was typical?" (The rating scale from Appendix A may, again, be shown.)

"Thank you for your cooperation. I know you may have felt somewhat uncomfortable. I (or someone) will be reviewing the results with you soon."

P-CIPA Recording Form

In an attempt to quantify aspects of the interaction expediently and accurately, the P-CIPA recording sheet was developed (see Appendix A). This sheet should be completed (i.e., circling a numeral for each category) shortly after the observation occurred, referring to the anecdotal notes for specifics and reminders. The 9-point continuum represents a low-to-high progression of behaviors, and it serves as the operational definition for the behavioral categories. Intermediate scoring can be made (e.g., circling 4, as a score between 3 and 5) when the actual behavior is felt to come somewhere between the straddled anchor descriptors. Comments and examples should accompany each scoring in order to add qualitative information to the quantitative data. The scorings can be transferred to the profile sheet (see Appendix B), which provides a graph of the results.

Thirteen categories of behavior compose the scoring for the unstructured play situation and eight for the structured portion of the assessment. Two additional questions exist on the structured scale, asking for a list of inappropriate behaviors observed and differences observed in the child when interacting with the examiner. Two continua exist as a validity measure, according to the parent's judgment. The examiner may also wish to personally assess the interaction's validity.

These categories of behavior were chosen with the intent to prompt the examiner to focus on crucial areas that may theoretically become useful for intervention. A cognitive-behavioral orientation influenced the choice of areas. The overriding goal of subsequent treatment would be for the parent to learn how to interact with more sensitivity to his or her child's processing of information, thus prompting higher levels of appropriate child behaviors. Half of the unstructured categories are ratings on the parent's behaviors, the other half being ratings of the child's behaviors; a remaining category assesses how much interaction generally existed between them. Five of the structured categories focus on parental behaviors, while the remaining three assess the child's responses.

Interpretation

The scale cannot necessarily capture the intricate and reciprocal nature of each person's influence on the other, and the evaluator is encouraged to avoid simply a linear view of analyzing the causal relationship between the parent's and child's behaviors. For example, a parent displaying a low degree of affect during the assessment could be viewed in three ways: (1) as reacting to the child's persistent pattern of negative or difficult behaviors, or (2) as causing the difficult behaviors, or (3) a combination of the above two. Yet, the intervention phase will wish to modify the potentially influencing parental behavior, without identifying blame.

A developmental perspective is incorporated into each continuum, each of which uses a category approach (versus an interval or ratio or nominal scaling approach). While the gradations (i.e., from low to high levels) are neither continuous nor equal, they do reflect increasing degrees toward what is to be believed a highest level of appropriate response. These high scores (i.e., 9 points) provide the descriptors of the therapist's objectives for treatment. The scale becomes a clear means to communicate to the client (i.e., whether the client is a parent, court personnel, or protective agency worker) the strengths and weaknesses of the interactions, and the needs for change. The pretest and posttest plotting on the profile sheet (see Appendix B) can visually demonstrate any changes.

The actual strategy to accomplish the progress can vary. For example, children who show very little ability to attend to activities (i.e., score is 3 on Phase I—unstructured play, Item I—child's attention to activities) before treatment might complete treatment with a high score (i.e., closer to 9) as a result of improved parental responsivity, administration of psychostimulant medication, individual therapy (with a host of approaches), and/or family therapy.

A cautionary note must be considered in that not all items show optimal progress from low to high ratings. The intervening variable of the child's developmental age exists. Further establishment of norms for different ages will help show the typical levels (i.e., scores of 1–9) one might optimally expect. The clinical findings currently suggest that some children have shown little pretest to posttest change on some items simply because of developmental level, not because of limits to the intervention or parenting behaviors. In relation to Phase I, unstructured play, Items H, I, and J would be good examples of this artifact, where a child perhaps functioning at the 18-month cognitive level would probably never produce a high rating. Thus, interpretation of the pre- and posttest results must recognize this phenomenon as hypotheses are being generated.

Hanf's (1969) model of intervention prompted the choice of many of the categories, and Forehand and McMahon (1981), Barkley (1987a), and Eyberg et al. (1994) had reported variations of the intervention. The Phase I categories of parent's intrusiveness (I-B), praise (I-C), attending (I-D), developmental sensitivity (I-E), responsiveness to the child's prompting (I-F), and general interaction with the child (I-G) are crucial aspects of the treatment goal for parents to more effectively attend to appropriate child behavior in a reinforcing manner.

In particular, parent's intrusiveness (I-B) derives from studies and clinical observations that parents of children with behavioral problems often show a high frequency of directiveness in their verbal interactions (Cunningham & Barkley, 1979; Marshall, Hegrenes, & Goldstein, 1973). Aspects of Axline's (1969) nondirective approach to play with children, where the adult describes and interacts nonintrusively, have been incorporated into the choice of these dimensions. Whether the child's poor self-control naturally elicits a high degree of commands and questions, or the opposite, is not directly evident from the data. Yet, again, the parents' high rate of intrusiveness could be interpreted as potentially aversive and not reinforcing, as would be alternative responses. Wahler and Meginnis (1997) found that a positive parenting approach in the form of mirroring or praise contributed to higher percentages of child compliance.

The unstructured categories assessing the child's behaviors (i.e., I-H through I-M) attempt to quantify key areas involved in diagnostic investigations. Assessing the child's social responsivity, response to parental leads or questions, attending skills, and aggressiveness can allow a means to determine how much the parental concerns reflect problematic perceptions versus actual behavioral problems. Relatively positive child behaviors, with high validity ratings, might raise doubts about any intrinsic childhood psychopathology existing. Conversely, a child's nonresponsive and inattentive behaviors, particularly in the midst of relatively positive parental responses would help highlight potentially aberrant behaviors intrinsic to the child.

For example, the author worked with a $3^1/_2$-year-old child and his parents, who all received low scores on their respective domains on the pretreatment assessment. An assessment 1 year after behavioral treatment showed the ratings for the parent's categories to be quite high, while the child's remained constant. This child's suspected pervasive developmental disorder–autistic type was more confidently diagnosed in conjunction with other observations of the child interacting with peers, teachers, and the examiner.

The categories composing the structured play situation (Phase II on the recording sheet—see Appendix A) attempt to assess information related to (a) how a parent directs the child, (b) how a child responds to the command, and (c) what consequences each is using. The categories assessing whether parents are giving direct demands versus indirect question commands (i.e., Phase II, Items A and B) that are developmentally sensitive operate under the cognitive-behavioral notion that children's optimal processing of the directive is important for determining the distinction between willful noncompliance and merely confused noncompliance. Barkley (1987b) reported that a 30% increase in the child's compliance rate occurred solely after the parent learned to give direct commands instead of question-commands (e.g., "Pick up the toys." versus "Would you pick up the toys?").

The structured play situation focuses on the processes involved in the child's noncompliance. Patterson (1982) has shown that disruptive aggressive behaviors usually occur in "bursts" rather than continuously or randomly throughout the day. These episodes are likely to be correlated with parent commands or requests, and there have been many assessments where the aggressive and nonresponsive behaviors were not manifested until this structured play situation was implemented.

Most of the children with behavior problems do not comply with the first commands (Roberts, 1982), and their parents quite frequently respond with repeated commands (i.e., earn low ratings on Phase II, Item A: II-A). Parental frustration may often escalate in the assessment, with a wide range of responses following. Some parents begin cajoling their child, others become overly punitive (i.e., low ratings on II-E), and a not-uncommon parental response is to do the commanded behavior for the child (e.g., pick up the toys while the child continues to play or just watches). Parents rarely earn a rating of 9 in the praise category (i.e., II-D) on pretreatment assessments, and an important element of the intervention becomes instructing parents to reinforce compliance (e.g., "Thanks for doing *what I told you*").

The structured play category ratings of the child's behaviors provide good diagnostic data as well as a useful pretest measure. A child's level of compliance (i.e., category II-F) should be judged relative to each command the parent issues. A child who complies with all three tasks after 15 parental requests is still earning a moderate rating (e.g., 5) at best. Additionally, the distinction between a child's noncompliance and willfulness (i.e., II-F, II-G) may at times be meaningless, yet it can provide useful insight into the child's temperament. Some children may comply with the requests, earning fairly high scores on II-F, while displaying great negativism in the tradition of the strong-willed child.

The section of the recording sheet asking for a description of inappropriate behaviors allows a recording of discrete problem behaviors. These can assist in deciding what target behaviors one might choose for modification if a treatment plan is developed. These inappropriate behaviors might also yield diagnostic information, particularly when they are atypical reactions (e.g., toe-walking, head-banging, or other stereotypic behaviors). Phase II, Item J requests the listing of differences between the child's behavior when interacting with the examiner in contrast to the parent, which may raise several hypotheses. The examiner may possess more appropriate skills for shaping positive behaviors. Children sometimes react more favorably with a stranger in comparison to their behaviors when interacting with their more predictable parent. The finding of few differences would also suggest the presence of more ingrained behaviors that occur across situations, or possibly behavioral traits.

Interpretation of the results obtained by using this system is not confined to the preceding discussion. The data derived can be interpreted from various theoretical perspectives, which is intended in light of the author's eclectic openness (i.e., despite cognitive-behavioral leanings). The same pattern of responses could mean various possible problems, be they underlying marital discord, dysfunctional family dynamics, or severe emotional disturbance of the parent or the child (i.e., versus a skill deficit per se). The assessment system was planned to flexibly accommodate various interpretations, yet reliably and validly measure change subsequent to one's treatment of choice.

Psychometric Aspects of the Procedure

The use of observational procedures has a long history (Darwin, 1872; Piaget, 1962), yet their popularity in recent years seems to have increased. The traditional measurements, with all their psychometric rigor, appear to have been lacking in the ability to obtain information about the nuances and complexities of human behavior. Yet, observational procedures must be subject to the same psychometric considerations, as would any measurement instrument.

The P-CIPA recording sheet is a content-referenced (also called criterion-referenced) instrument, with the potential for becoming norm referenced. The behavioral categories (e.g., parent's affect) lay out varying degrees of one's response relative to the content that theoretically composes the behavior. Thus, one can compare a client's scores from one time to the next, rather than comparing the scores at any time with a norm group. This offers a prescriptive capability, whereby specific objectives can be derived by using the behavior descriptors for the numbers that are above the measured levels. Content-referenced scales have earned wide use in special education realms because of their ease at communicating strengths and weaknesses, rather than how abnormal one is, and the P-CIPA can likewise clearly communicate needs to the therapist and/or client. Easy interpretation of the score in reference to the continuum can aid the learning process if the client is a parent-guardian or the decision process when the client is the court or a protective agency. The objective measures can particularly monitor pre- and posttreatment changes.

The P-CIPA employs a semantic differential scaling approach, in the tradition of the Infant Behavior Record from the original Bayley Scales of Infant Development (Bayley, 1969). The items are not bipolar opposites; rather, they were developed as progressing from a negative (i.e., developmentally inferior) to a positive point. The items, thus, employ a category-scaling approach. The order of behavioral descriptors is believed to be critical, differentiating it from a nominal scale. Yet, no pretense of equality between the intervals exists (e.g., the numerical distance between a 1 and a 2 is not necessarily equivalent to that between a 5 and a 6), as in the interval and ratio scales. These characteristics limit any statistical manipulation one might consider (Nunnally, 1967).

Reliability

Assessing the dependability of an observational code is a complex issue (Hartmann, 1982); nonetheless, there must be some guarantee of the scores' stability. Interrater (or interobserver) reliability data were collected on the P-CIPA using three raters, two of whom did not have prior experience with the scale. The raters were asked to read over the P-CIPA record sheet, observe a parent and child interacting in the unstructured and structured situations, and then score their judgments. Pearson product-moment correlation coefficients between the pairs of scores were .75, .89, .84 (mean $r = .83$). When judging the adequacy of interrater reliability measures, Jones, Reid, and Patterson (1973) suggested .70 agreement as an acceptable level when complex coding schemes are used, while Gelfand and Hartmann (1975) recommended .60 for correlational statistics. Hartmann (1982) noted how interrater reliability levels are raised when specific training about the scale occurs. Periodic checks of observers' agreement levels would be necessary to maintain each rater's accuracy in scoring. There are no data yet on test-retest reliability measures on the P-CIPA, leaving to speculation whether the scores are stable on separate measurements occurring close together in time.

Validity

Content validity is concerned with the degree to which elements of a measurement instrument sample the elements of the construct being measured. Assurances of the P-CIPA's content validity cannot be made beyond the reminder that the items are adapted from other scales and the clinical utility that the scale has shown. Parents and clinicians have indicated the meaningfulness of the data in manifesting critical aspects of problems in the interaction of the parent and child.

Reactivity factors become a perennial problem in observational assessments (Kazdin, 1982). One must always question whether the sample of behaviors obtained validly represents what actually occurs between the interacting pair, or merely how they behave in reaction to being watched under the imposed circumstances. The validity checks at the end of the P-CIPA are designed to somewhat monitor these factors, at least from the parent's vantage. Beyond this, one must merely be cognizant of the methods that reduce the likelihood of these effects: (1) be as nonobtrusive as possible, (2) allow clients to become adapted to the situation, and (3) use the procedure after good rapport has been established. However, rapport may give little assurance, depending on the parents' needs. A parent who wants to "look good or bad" may elicit the intended effect from his or her children, much like Johnson and Lobitz (1974) demonstrated when parents were instructed to positively or negatively influence their child's behavior.

A criterion-related validity check was conducted, using the aggressive and hyperactive scales from the behavior (BP) section of the Revised Child Behavior Profile (Achenbach & Edelbrock, 1983) and the P-CIPA's domains of I-I (attentiveness), I-K (aggressiveness) in unstructured situations, and II-H (aggressiveness) in structured situations. A sample of 5 children whose mothers had completed the BP and had been assessed with the P-CIPA had the following covariations computed: the percentage of agreement divided by the total agreements + disagreements were computed between the BP scales' hyperactivity domain (i.e., t score over 70 equals hyperactive) and the P-CIPA's attentiveness item (i.e., raw score of less than or equal to 4 equals hyperactive). The 75% agreement suggests a modest relationship between the scales. The agreement between the BP and P-CIPA aggressive domains was .83, using a t score above 70 on the BP and a raw score of 7 or less on the P-CIPA aggressive behavior items. The reasons for some degree of disagreement could include the following: (1) the scales are measuring different constructs; (2) one scale is from parental report, while the other involves observational data; and (3) the P-CIPA does not always sample the behavior problem.

Further reliability and validity studies are needed. Foremost would be concurrent validity studies, comparing the P-CIPA with other parent-child assessment systems with similar structure and purpose.

CASE STUDY ILLUSTRATIONS

Case 1

The first illustrative case involves a $4^1/_2$-year-old boy and his parents, who sought treatment following an interdisciplinary evaluation at the University Affiliated Cincinnati Center for Developmental Disorders at the Cincinnati Children's Hospital Medical Center. He was found to show a moderate attention deficit hyperactivity disorder (ADHD: DSM-III-R, American Psychiatric Association, 1987), normal intelligence (IQ score equal to 96 on the Stanford-Binet Intelligence Scale, Form L-M), and frequent noncompliance and aggressive behaviors. He came from a middle-class, intact family with a 1-year-younger brother. The parents were highly motivated to learn how best to manage their son's maladaptive and oppositional behaviors and they showed no other signs of disturbance.

Each parent was evaluated using the P-CIPA, and Figures 11.1 and 11.2 show the profile of ratings they received on the recording sheets. Pretreatment results suggested

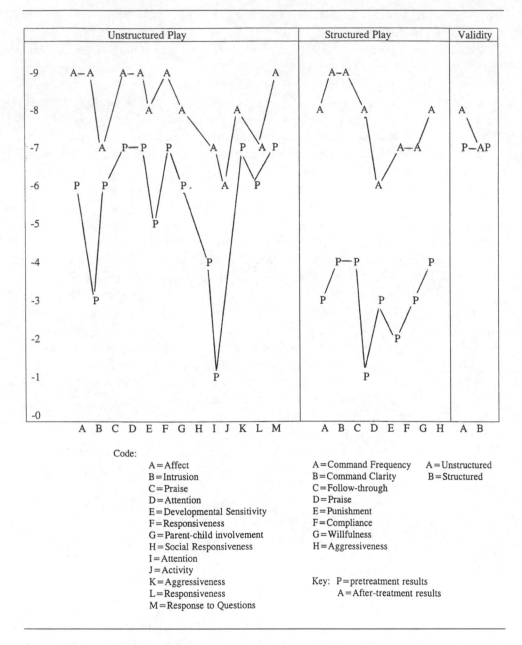

Figure 11–1. P-CIPA profile of mother's pre- and posttreatment results for Case 1

that both parents had midlevel affect, high degrees of intrusiveness (i.e., always trying to question or control their son), excessive commands when directing him, and no praise for compliance. The mother was somewhat better at showing developmentally sensitive interactions and commands, although the father elicited more social responsiveness and less aggression from his son. The son was generally inattentive, overly active, noncompliant, and willful at the pretreatment assessments.

The parents and their son became involved in a series of weekly, 50-minute sessions that lasted 17 weeks. The typical number of sessions across a study of 15 clients was

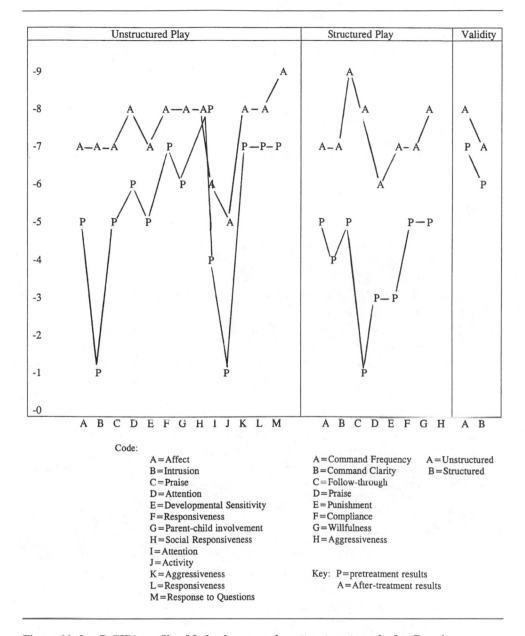

Figure 11–2.   P-CIPA profile of father's pre- and posttreatment results for Case 1

14.06 (Smith, 1997) for this form of treatment. The playroom and adjoining observation room became the learning environment in which the foundations of appropriate interactions were taught by discussions, modeling, role playing, and positive practice (i.e., using a remote microphone and receiver for the examiner to issue immediate feedback). Baumrind's (1967, 1971) notion of *authoritative parenting* (i.e., high in nurturance, communication, control, and maturity demands) provided an overall mission for treatment. The goals were for the parents to broadly learn interactional strategies that would (1) increase the child's display of positive behaviors, (2) give appropriate commands so that 80% of commands were obeyed, and (3) decrease negative behaviors targeted. The parents are essentially shaped by the therapist to shape their child's more desired behaviors within the playroom, with the intent to generalize the new interactional approaches in everyday circumstances. Parents are guided to acquire the competencies that enable them to "tailgate" appropriate behaviors, elicit clear and direct commands, and implement a punishment approach that decreases the targeted behavior. Barkley's (1987a) and Eyberg et al. (1994) model most closely resembles the author's adaptation of Hanf's (1969) program. Information about ADHD and opportunities for the parents to express their feelings were also incorporated into the sessions.

Treatment was discontinued when the therapist and parents mutually felt the goals had been met. The posttreatment results (see Figures 11.1 and 11.2) substantiated this impression, with significant gains being measured. The mother's higher profile was consistent with her generally showing a more-responsive, communicative, and developmentally sensitive style of interacting with her son. She quite successfully became able to effectively use her attention in a manner that did not increase her son's inappropriate behaviors, but motivated him to seek it through positive means. The father emerged with good gains, yet the likelihood of his own ADHD characteristics seemed to limit his ideal expression of the targeted skills.

Their son's behavior showed modest gains in his weakest areas (e.g., activity level and attention span) and a significant increase in his compliance. His aggressiveness with his younger brother was essentially eliminated by his parents' successful implementation of a time-out procedure. Reports of improved peer interactions at his preschool were given. He was by no means "cured," which had never been the goal, but he was entirely more manageable. The parents' initial anger at his responses changed to empathy and tolerance, perhaps because of their better ability to cope with his behaviors. Long-term follow-up contacts noted that his oppositional behaviors remained at a comfortable level for his parents, although his inattentiveness was successfully treated with methylphenidate once formal academic training started.

Case 2

The second case is of an 8-year-old boy, originally referred by a neurologist, whose single parent and school personnel were questioning whether some stimulant medication was needed for his inattention and poor school performance. The neurologist felt that an interdisciplinary evaluation was needed, and the results did not support the original suspicions of ADHD. The boy was found to show signs of moderate depression, which seemed to partly underlie his acting-out behaviors and his inattention. His poor social environment was also felt to be a factor, whereby he would not fall asleep until late at night because his bed was in the kitchen. His intellectual performance measured in the low-average range, with a verbal IQ score of 77, performance IQ Score of 82, and full scale score of 78 attained on the Wechsler Intelligence Scale for Children–Revised. His mother also showed signs of depression and struggled to maintain financial solvency as she cared for her five children.

The pretreatment assessment (see Figure 11–3) revealed much aberrance in the parent-child's behaviors and interactions. The mother showed largely an irritated affect in her contacts with her son, and she generally was not very involved or responsive to her

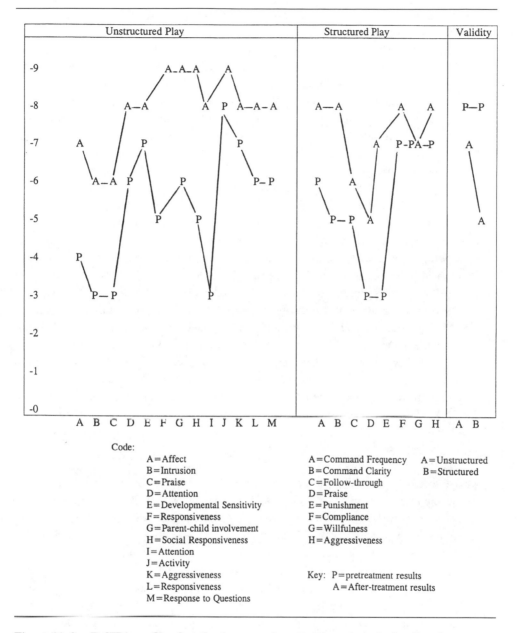

Figure 11–3.   P-CIPA profile of mother's pre- and posttreatment results for Case 2

son's activities. He wandered from one activity to another after a brief exploration, and he seemed rather anxiously aware of his mother's presence. He did not show signs of aggressive behaviors and was moderately responsive to his mother's questions. He was not overly noncompliant during the structured session, which prompted the lowered validity rating because of his more typical noncompliance at home. Older children seem to more frequently show reactivity to the strange situation.

The treatment sessions were similar to those described in Case 1, except for some additional goals, which focused on making some environmental changes and discussions about the role of depression in children's behaviors. The diagnosis of depression for her son was a surprise and a motivating factor for her involvement. Behavioral therapy had been recommended on several occasions, as early as when her son was 3 years old, but was not pursued. One could argue that the mother had never really become attached to her son. The empathy and skills developed in treatment helped her to become more of a positive influence in prompting positive behaviors. The earlier sessions, where she learned to follow and become nonintrusive, created a mutual enjoyment for the interactions and a generally more nurturing maternal attitude.

This new or renewed relationship seemed to have a major impact on the boy. Reports from his school and the home substantiated the gains shown in his posttreatment assessment. Sustained attention to tasks aided his school performance, and he would exert much effort to elicit the praise, which his mother could now give. Curiously, though his compliance level increased during the structured posttreatment assessment, his willfulness and argumentativeness did not particularly change. Perhaps this shows his underlying temperament, which his mother earlier found so difficult to tolerate. Her ability to ignore verbal resistance and to focus her attention on his actual behavior helped him to obey, even if he was not always so inclined.

The posttreatment results for the mother revealed improved, yet not perfect, progress. The high number of "8" and "9" ratings for the boy and their interactions led to the decision that the treatment could be terminated. His advancement to the next grade, and conduct awards from his school, further evidenced probable effects of improved parent-child interactions. Her own depression, curiously, seemed also to subside considerably. One could speculate that such favorable results would not have occurred had the treatment focused only on her depression instead of her interactional skills with her son.

Case 3

This case involved a 6-year-old boy and his parents who were originally referred for an interdisciplinary assessment because of the son's suspected autism. His school personnel had raised concerns about obsessive tendencies, poor peer relations, lack of eye contact, frequent humming out loud, and a shrill scream if he would make a mistake in his kindergarten class. The assessment found him to function intellectually in the normal range, with a composite standard score of 101 on the fourth edition of the Stanford-Binet Intelligence Scale. He did show evidence of language problems, with low average scores in contrast to some visual reasoning scores in the high average range (Abstract/Visual Reasoning standard score of 121). No signs of aloofness or needs for sameness were noted during individual assessments, and his parents' reporting on the Child Behavior Checklist yielded only an elevation for the BP category of Anxious/Depressed behaviors (T score of 70, an average T = 50). Thus, in addition to some school modifications he was referred for therapy so that the therapist could address his social immaturity, maladaptive anxiety reactions, and poor adherence to adult instructions or commands. Another therapist concurrently provided marital therapy and the mother had an individual therapist for personal issues she was negotiating.

Both parents were involved in a series of 11 sessions that utilized the parent-child behavioral paradigm described earlier to shape more appropriate behaviors. Although the boy's mother gained from the sessions, the father made the most significant progress and may have been more of a variable in the emergence of the original problem behaviors. Figure 11–4 shows the father's pre- and posttreatment results using the P-CIPA.

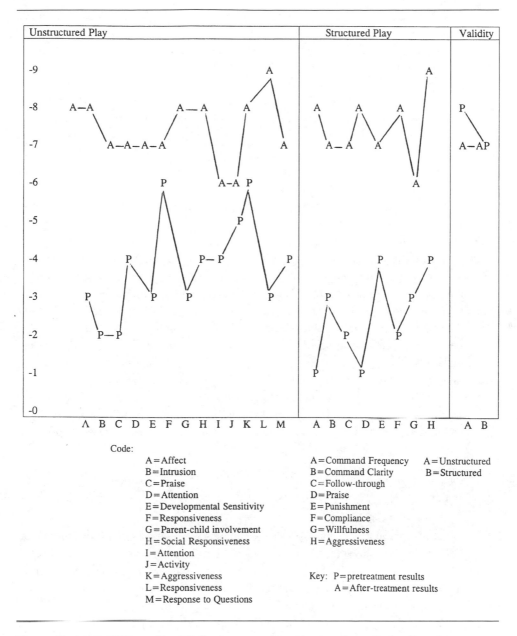

Figure 11–4.   P-CIPA profile of father's pre- and posttreatment results for Case 3

In the present treatment, the parents were instructed to learn how to "tailgate" more adaptive responses to tasks. They were to use the cognitive-behavioral interaction strategies mentioned earlier, so that they could have relaxed interactions with him while shaping responses that elicit more rewarding social exchanges for him in general. They were carefully helped to determine what are appropriate behaviors from their son. Thus, they learned to model and focus on persistence to tasks, optimism, and healthy perceptions during his play. Similarly, they learned to ignore his moodiness, pessimism, and statements of negative misperceptions. Their interactional pattern was similar to the style seen in families who have a child with overanxious tendencies (Vasey, Crnic, & Carter, 1994). The attention and empathy of the parents for their child was encouraging his avoidant style to tasks and poor self-regulation of his emotions. The parents were inconsistent in their approach to maturity demands. His mother tended to make fewer demands as she overly identified with his distress and his father found himself becoming harsh in an attempt to overcompensate for his wife's permissive attitude. Similar to the family who is trying to help their child do well during a painful medical procedure, this family had to shift the power of their attention to more adaptive coping styles in their son instead of his reflexive approach to conveying his emotional pain.

The posttreatment results in Figure 11–4 are in concert with reports from his school of a dramatically different boy in his first grade setting. His father was significantly more playful and positive in his play interactions, and commented that he greatly enjoyed his new relationship with his son. He had been devoid of an appropriate model of a healthy father-son alliance from his own upbringing. His son interacted far more during play with his father and would readily respond to the few questions that he might pose. Few power struggles occurred, and the boy complied with his father's developmentally appropriate and direct commands. The boy found the time-outs for his noncompliance, during the course of treatment, far less aversive than the previous yelling and berating that his father had used. He also learned to comply as a result of the tangible consequence that he would receive, which lessened his father's irritation. Undoubtedly the school administrator's match of his assessment needs with a positive and authoritative teacher also contributed to his year of great academic success (i.e., placed on the honor roll) and numerous behavioral awards. He accepted correction far more readily and was willing to take risks in academic and social situations. His parents were particularly delighted by his new and sustained friendship developed with a classmate.

SUMMARY AND CONCLUSIONS

This chapter presents one of the many parent-child play assessment systems existing in the field of childhood psychopathology. While this system does not propose to be a panacea any more than other parent-child interaction systems contend, the P-CIPA strives to pragmatically help the clinician look at the intricacies of the parent-child relationship. The cutting edge in the diagnosis of childhood disorders appears to involve an analysis of the reciprocal and transactional nature of parent-child interactions. A parent-child assessment procedure, like the P-CIPA, can yield valuable hypotheses that should be integrated with the other data available. The limitations of these procedures are important considerations when interpreting the data, instead of a cause for choosing not to use a structured means to understand how parents and children interact.

The P-CIPA currently yields only within-subject differences, serving as a content-referenced assessment procedure that can measure pre- and posttreatment changes. Nevertheless, such a system can be an invaluable tool in the current climate of managed care for mental health services. The need for documenting a need for services and progress becomes crucial for justifying the need for additional services, and clinicians may not be far from the requirement to provide outcome data for groups of clients who have been served. The eventual development of norms will allow between-participant comparisons, which can assist in the determination of problematic behaviors in comparison with the child's age group. Norms could also be developed for other variables, such as specific handicapping conditions or parental characteristics. Potentially, this system could also be adapted to allow assessments of other interactional pairs, such as teacher-child or residential staff–child dyads. Further development and research of this scale is certainly needed. It is hoped that the P-CIPA can provide utility for the creative clinician and researcher in better understanding the children and their parents within the context of play.

REFERENCES

Achenbach, T. M., & Edelbrock, C. S. (1978). The classification of child psychopathology: A review and analysis of empirical efforts. *Psychological Bulletin, 85,* 1275–1301.

Achenbach, T. M., & Edlebrock, C. S. (1983). *Manual for the Child Behavior Checklist and Revised Child Behavior Profile.* Burlington, VT: Queen City Printers.

American Psychiatric Association. (1987). *Diagnostic and statistical manual of mental disorders* (3rd ed., rev.). Washington, D.C.

Axline, V. M. (1969). *Play therapy* (Rev. ed.). New York: Ballantine Books.

Barkley, R. A. (1984). *Hyperactive children: Handbook for diagnosis and treatment.* New York: Guilford Press.

Barkley, R. A. (1987a). *Defiant children: A clinical manual for parent training.* New York: Guilford Press.

Barklcy, R. A. (1987b). *Treating defiant children.* Workshop presented at the December meeting of the Cincinnati Society of Child Clinical Psychologists, Cincinnati, OH.

Baumrind, D. (1967). Child care practices anteceding three patterns of preschool behavior. *Genetic Psychology Monographs, 75,* 43–88.

Baumrind, D. (1971). Current patterns of parental authority. *Developmental Psychology Monograph, 4,* 1–103.

Bayley, N. (1969). *Bayley Scales of infant development.* New York: Psychological Corporation.

Beck, A. T. (1967). *Depression: Courses and treatment.* Philadelphia: University of Pennsylvania Press.

Beidel, D. (1997). Training and employment issues in psychology. *APPIC Newsletter,* 1–2.

Bloom, B. (1956). *Taxonomy of educational objectives: The classification of educational goals: Handbook I. Cognitive domain.* New York: David McKay.

Bronfenbrenner, U. (1977). Toward an experimental ecology of human development. *American Psychologist, 7*(32), 513–531.

Campbell, D., & Stanley, J. (1963). *Experimental and quasi-experimental designs for research.* Chicago: Rand McNally College Publishing Company.

Ciminero, A. R., & Drabman, R. S. (1977). Current developments in the behavioral assessment of children. In B. B. Lahey & A. E. Kazdin (Eds.) *Advances in clinical child psychology* (Vol. 1, pp. 28–47). New York: Plenum.

Clarke, G. N. (1995). Improving the transition from basic efficacy research to effectiveness studies: Methodological issues and procedures. *Journal of Consulting and Clinical Psychology, 63*(5), 718–725.

Cone, J. D. (1982). Validity of direct observation assessment procedures. In D. Hartmann (Ed.), *Using observers to study behavior* (pp. 67–79). San Francisco: Jossey-Bass.

Conners, C. K. (1979). *Conners parent and teacher rating scales.* North Chicago: Abbott Laboratories.

Cunningham, C. E., & Barkley, R. A. (1979). The interactions of normal and hyperactive children with their mothers in free play and structured tasks. *Child Development, 50,* 217–224.

Darby, B. (1980). *The Bayley scales of infant development.* Workshop presented at the May meeting of the Oregon Health Science University's Child Development and Rehabilitation Center, Portland, OR.

Darwin, C. (1872). *Expressions of the emotions in man and animals.* London: Murray.

Eyberg, S. M., Bessmer, J., Newcomb, K., Edwards, D., & Robinson, E. (1994). Manual for the dyadic Parent-Child Interaction Coding System-II. *Social and Behavioral Sciences Documents* (Ms. no. 2897). (Available from Select Press, P.O. Box 9838, San Rafael, CA 94912.)

Eyberg, S. M., & Johnson, S. M. (1974). Multiple assessment of behavior modification with families. Effects of contingency contracting and order of treated problems. *Journal of Counseling and Clinical Psychology, 41,* 165–174.

Forehand, R., & McMahon, R. (1981). *Helping the noncompliant child: A clinician's guide to parent training.* New York: Guilford Press.

Gelfand, D. M., & Hartmann, D. P. (1975). *Child behavior analysis and therapy.* New York: Pergamon.

Gibson, H. B. (1968). The measurement of parental attitudes and their relation to boy's behavior. *British Journal of Educational Psychology, 38*(3), 233–239.

Hanf, C. (1969). *A two-stage program for modifying maternal controlling during mother-child interaction.* Paper presented at the October meeting of Western Psychological Association, Vancouver, BC.

Hartmann, D. P. (1982). Assessing the dependability of observational data. In D. Hartmann (Ed.), *Using observers to study behavior.* San Francisco: Jossey-Bass.

Hathaway, S. R., & McKinley, J. C. (1948). *Manual for the Minnesota Multiphasic Personality Inventory.* New York: Psychological Corporation.

Hoagwood, K., Hibbs, E., Brent, D., Jenson, P. (1995). Introduction to the special section: Efficacy and effectiveness in studies of child and adolescent psychotherapy. *Journal of Consulting and Clinical Psychology, 63*(5), 683–687.

Hughes, H. M., & Haynes, S. N. (1978). Structured laboratory observation in the behavioral assessment of parent-child interactions: A methodological critique. *Behavior Therapy, 9,* 428–447.

Johnson, S. M. & Bolstad, O. D. (1973). Methodological issues in naturalistic observation: Some problems and solutions for field research. In L. A. Hamerlynck, L. C. Handy, & E. J. Mash (Eds.), *Behavior change: Methodology, concepts, and practice* (pp. 7–67). Champaign, IL: Research Press.

Johnson, S., & Lobitz, G. (1974). Parental manipulation of child behaviors in home observations. *Journal of Applied Behavior Analysis, 7,* 23–31.

Jones. R., Reid, J., & Patterson, G. (1973). Naturalistic observations in clinical assessment. In P. McReynolds (Ed.), *Advances in psychological assessment* (Vol. 3). San Francisco: Jossey-Bass.

Kazdin, A. (1982). Observer effects: Reactivity of direct observation. In D. Hartmann (Ed.), *Using observers to study behavior* (pp. 5–19). San Francisco: Jossey-Bass.

Kogan, D. L. & Wimberger, R. C. (1966). An approach to defining mother-child interactional styles. *Perceptual and Motor Skills, 23,* 1171–1177.

Leland, H., & Smith, D. (1965). *Play therapy with mentally subnormal children.* New York: Grune & Stratton.

Locke, H., & Wallace, K. (1959). Short marital adjustment and prediction tests: Their reliability and validity. *Marriage and Family Living, 21,* 251–255.

Marshall, N. R., Hegrenes, J. R., & Goldstein, S. (1973). Verbal interactions: Mothers and their retarded children vs. mothers and their nonretarded children. *American Journal of Mental Deficiency, 77*(4), 415–419.

Mash, E., & Terdal, L. (1981). *Behavioral assessment of childhood disorders.* New York: Guilford Press.

Mash, E., & Terdal, L. (1991). *Play assessment of noncompliant children with the response-class matrix.* New York: Wiley

Mash, E., Terdal, L., & Anderson (1973). The response-class matrix: A procedure for recording parent-child interactions. *Journal of Consulting and Clinical Psychology, 40,* 163–164.

Miller, I. J. (1996). Managed care is harmful to outpatient mental health services: A call for accountability. *Professional Psychology: Research and Practice, 27*(4), 349–363.

Nunnally, J. C. (1967). *Psychometric theory.* New York: McGraw-Hill.

Odell, S. L., Tarler, B., & Flynn, J. (1979). An instrument to measure knowledge of behavioral principles as applies to children. *Journal of Behavior Therapy & Experimental Psychiatry, 10*(1), 29–34.

Patterson, G. R. (1982). *Coercive family process.* Eugene, OR: Castalia.

Piaget, J. (1962). *Play, dreams and imitation in childhood.* New York: Norton.

Roberts, M. W. (1982). Resistance to time-out: Some normative data. *Behavioral Assessment, 4,* 237–246.

Seligman, M. E. P. (1995). The effectiveness of psychotherapy: The *Consumer Reports* study. *American Psychologist, 50*(12), 965–974.

Sevan, G. E., & MacDonald, M. L. (1978). Behavioral therapy in practice: A national survey of behavioral therapists. *Behavior Therapy, 9,* 799–807.

Smith, D. T. (1997, March). *Utilizing electron technologies for efficacious short-term therapy with young children with developmental disabilities.* Presentation given at the 18th annual international conference on MR/DD for the National Institute for People with Disabilities, New York, NY.

Vasey, M. W., Crnic, K. A. & Carter, W. G. (1994). Worry in childhood: A developmental perspective. *Cognitive Therapy & Research, 18*(6), 529–549.

Wahler, R. (1975). Some structural aspects of deviant child behavior. *Journal of Applied Behavioral Analysis, 8,* 27–42.

Wahler, R. G., & Meginnis, K. L. (1977). Strengthening child compliance through positive parenting practices: What works? *Journal of Clinical Child Psychology, 26*(4), 433–440.

Wimberger, H., & Kagan, J. (1974). A direct approach to altering mother-child interaction in disturbed children. *Archives of General Psychiatry, 30,* 636–639.

Wirt, R. D., Lachar, D., Klinedist, J. K., & Seat, P. D. (1977). *Multidimensional description of child personality: A manual for the Personality Inventory of Children.* Los Angeles: Western Psychological Services.

Zegiob, L., & Forehand, R. (1975). Maternal interactive behavior as a function of race, socioeconomic status, and sex of the child. *Child Development 46,* 564–568.

APPENDIX A

RECORDING SHEET FOR THE PARENT-CHILD INTERACTION PLAY ASSESSMENT (P-CIPA)

Comments

I. Unstructured Play

A. Parent's Affect (Circle one)
1. No affect observed from parent
2. Between 1 & 3
3. Affect typically negative in interaction with child
4. Between 3 & 5
5. Some degree of enjoyment shown in play with child
6. Between 5 & 7
7. Moderate degree of enjoyment shown in play with child
8. Between 7 & 9
9. Free range of affect observed; parent openly showed pleasure in play with child

B. Parent's Intrusiveness
1. Parent continually structured child's play by leading play, asking questions, and giving commands
2. Between 1 & 3
3. Parent fairly intrusive, gave commands led play, and asked questions half the time
4. Between 3 & 5
5. Parent was intrusive by asking questions, but also allowed child to lead play
6. Between 5 & 7
7. Parent did not intrude into child's play
8. Between 7 & 9
9. Parent was not intrusive and was able to follow and nondirectively facilitate child's play (e.g., models activity)

C. Parent's Praise
1. No praise, mostly negative statements
2. Between 1 & 3
3. No praise observed
4. Between 3 & 5
5. Some praise observed, only in response to tasks completed
6. Between 5 & 7
7. Moderate praise observed, in response to completed tasks and attempts to complete
8. Between 7 & 9
9. Good amount of praise, both contingent on completed behaviors and on attempts or effort

Comments

D. Parent Attention
 1. Parent ignored all of child's behaviors
 2. Between 1 & 3
 3. Parent ignored about 50% of child's behaviors
 4. Between 3 & 5
 5. Parent paid attention to all of child's behaviors (if no
    negative behaviors occurred by child, circle 5)
 6. Between 5 & 7
 7. Parent paid attention to all of child's positive behaviors
    and about 50% of negative behaviors
 8. Between 7 & 9
 9. Parent paid attention to all of child's desirable behaviors,
    ignored all negative ones

E. Parent's Developmental Sensitivity
 1. About 100% of this parent's interactions over-and/or
    underestimated child's development
 2. Between 1 & 3
 3. About 75% of this parent's interactions over-and/or
    underestimated child's development
 4. Between 3 & 5
 5. About 50% of this parent's interactions over-and/or
    underestimated child's development
 6. Between 5 & 7
 7. About 25% of this parent's interactions over-and/or
    underestimated child's development
 8. Between 7 & 9
 9. All of the parent's interactions were appropriate to the
    child's developmental level

F. Parent Responsiveness to Child's Interactions
 1. Parent did not respond to any of the child's questions or
    attempts to engage him/her in an activity
 2. Between 1 & 3
 3. Parent responded to about 25% of the child's questions
    or attempts to engage him/her in an activity
 4. Between 3 & 5
 5. Parent responded to about $1/2$ or the child's questions or
    attempts to engage him/her in an activity
 6. Between 5 & 7
 7. Parent responded to about 75% of child's interactions
 8. Between 7 & 9
 9. Parent responded to all of the child's interactions

Comments

G. Parent-Child Involvement
   1. No interaction between parent and child occurred
   2. Between 1 & 3
   3. Parent watched child's play and verbal interaction occurred occasionally
   4. Between 3 & 5
   5. Parent verbally interacted with child; not physically
   6. Between 5 & 7
   7. Parent and child interacted verbally & physically
   8. Between 7 & 9
   9. Parent and child interacted verbally & physically during most of the play; parent described child's play when it was appropriate

H. Child's Social Responsivity
   1. The child's behavior was completely withdrawn/aloof from the toys and parent
   2. Between 1 & 3
   3. The child's behavior toward the toys and parent was the same
   4. Between 3 & 5
   5. The child responded to half the social approaches of the parent and when not approached did not attend
   6. Between 5 & 7
   7. The child responded to most social approaches and occasionally made spontaneous social approaches to parent
   8. Between 7 & 9
   9. The child responded in a friendly, social, and inviting manner with the parent during most of the observation

I. Child's Attention to Activities
   1. Child typically stayed at each activity for ≤ 1 minutes
   2. Between 1 & 3
   3. Child usually stayed with an activity for 1–2 minutes
   4. Between 3 & 5
   5. Child could typically engage in some tasks about 5 minutes after initial exploring
   6. Between 5 & 7
   7. Child could typically engage in most tasks for 5 minutes
   8. Between 7 & 9
   9. Child showed a sustained and absorbed interest in most activities

Comments

J. Child's Activity Level
   1. The child was overly active; excessive body movement occurred most of the time
   2. Between 1 & 3
   3. The child was overly active during a significant period of the evaluation but had periods of calm (e.g., initially active, quieter at end)
   4. Between 3 & 5
   5. The child was overly active for about 50% of the period
   6. Between 5 & 7
   7. The child was overly active for certain situations but usually had no excessive body movement outside of the tasks demanded
   8. Between 7 & 9
   9. The child's activity level was appropriate to the tasks; no excessive movements were observed

K. Child's Aggressiveness
   1. Child was argumentative, destructive, whiney, disobedient, and/or aggressive all of the time
   2. Between 1 & 3
   3. Child was argumentative, destructive, whiney, disobedient, and/or aggressive 75% of the time
   4. Between 3 & 5
   5. Child was argumentative, destructive, whiney, disobedient, and/or aggressive 50% of the time
   6. Between 5 & 7
   7. Child was argumentative, destructive, whiney, disobedient, and/or aggressive 25% of the time
   8. Between 7 & 9
   9. Child was never argumentative, destructive, whiney, disobedient, and/or aggressive

L. Child's Responsiveness to Parent's Interaction
   1. The child did not respond to any of the parent's attempts to engage him/her in an activity
   2. Between 1 & 3
   3. The child responded about 25% of the time to the parent's attempts to engage him/her in an activity
   4. Between 3 & 5
   5. The child responded about 50% of the time to the parent's attempts to engage him/her in an activity
   6. Between 5 & 7
   7. The child responded about 75% of the time to the parent's attempts to engage him/her in an activity
   8. Between 7 & 9
   9. The child responded almost all the time to the parent's attempts to engage him/her in an activity

Comments

M. Child's Responsiveness to Questions
   1. The child-did not respond to any of the parent's questions
   2. Between 1 & 3
   3. The child responded to about 25% of the parent's questions
   4. Between 3 & 5
   5. The child responded to half of the parent's questions
   6. Between 5 & 7
   7. The child responded to about 75% of the parent's questions
   8. Between 7 & 9
   9. The child responded to all of the parent's questions

II. Structured Play
   A. Frequency of Parental Commands
      1. Fifteen or more commands were given for each directed activity
      2. Between 1 & 3
      3. Ten commands were given for each directed activity
      4. Between 3 & 5
      5. Five commands were given for each directed activity
      6. Between 5 & 7
      7. Three commands were given for each directed activity
      8. Between 7 & 9
      9. Only 1 command was given for each directed activity

   B. Clarity of Commands
      1. Commands usually lacked sensitivity to child's developmental level and were stated as question rather than as direct imperatives
      2. Between 1 & 3
      3. Commands at times were insensitive to child's developmental level and were in question form
      4. Between 3 & 5
      5. Commands were at times given in question form (e.g., "Will you pick up the toys?") but were sensitive to the child's understanding level
      6. Between 5 & 7
      7. Commands were usually clear to child and were direct
      8. Between 7 & 9
      9. Commands were always stated clearly and directly (regardless of child's compliance)

Comments

C. Parent's follow-through with Commands (Write "Not
    Applicable" if child always complies)
    1. Overly harsh methods used to facilitate compliance
    2. Between 1 & 3
    3. No effort made to facilitate child's compliance
    4. Between 3 & 5
    5. Only repetition of commands or pleading was used
    6. Between 5 & 7
    7. Physical and verbal prompts used to facilitate compliance
    8. Between 7 & 9
    9. Modeling and/or other positive means used initially,
        though firmness was displayed when necessary

D. Parental Praise
    1. No praise observed
    2. Between 1 & 3
    3. Some praise used but probably not serving to
        increase child's behavior; was not meaningful in
        affect or comprehension to child
    4. Between 3 & 5
    5. Some praise used but was only of a general nature
        (e.g., "good," "fine")
    6. Between 5 & 7
    7. Moderate praise observed, at times was behaviorally
        specific to what is praised
    8. Between 7 & 9
    9. Verbal and physical expressions of approval typically
        given, both in response to completed tasks and to
        attempts to complete tasks

E. Punishment Level
    1. Physical punishment used as first approach
    2. Between 1 & 3
    3. Verbal punishment frequently used, including threats
        (e.g., "You are not going to be able to have your candy
        now..." "Bad boy...") and yelling
    4. Between 3 & 5
    5. Time out was used
    6. Between 5 & 7
    7. Withdrawal of attention usually used for child's
        noncompliance
    8. Between 7 & 9
    9. No punishment used, or only a clear warning of a
        consequence was needed

F. Child's Compliance
 1. Child never complied to a task
 2. Between 1 & 3
 3. Child was usually inappropriate (e.g., had tantrums)
     but eventually complied
 4. Between 3 & 5
 5. Child required a great deal of prompting to comply
 6. Between 5 & 7
 7. Child usually complied to tasks (i.e., more than half
     of the time without prompts)
 8. Between 7 & 9
 9. Child always complied to tasks without additional
     prompts after a warning

G. Child's Willfulness
 1. Child responded negatively, and child openly refused all
     of the parent's commands
 2. Between 1 & 3
 3. Child responded negatively, and child openly refused
     to follow about 75% of the commands given
 4. Between 3 & 5
 5. Child responded negatively, and child openly refused to
     follow about 50% of the commands given
 6. Between 5 & 7
 7. Child responded negatively to about 25% of commands
 8. Between 7 & 9
 9. Child complied with all directives without negativism or
     challenge

H. Child's Aggressiveness
 1. Child was argumentative, destructive, whiney, disobedient,
     and/or aggressive all of the time
 2. Between 1 & 3
 3. Child was argumentative, destructive, whiney, disobedient,
     and/or aggressive 75% of the time
 4. Between 3 & 5
 5. Child was argumentative, destructive, whiney, disobedient,
     and/or aggressive 50% of the time
 6. Between 5 & 7
 7. Child was argumentative, destructive, whiney, disobedient,
     and/or aggressive 25% of the time
 8. Between 7 & 9
 9. Child was never argumentative, destructive, whiney,
     disobedient, and/or aggressive

I. Describe child's inappropriate or unusual behaviors during the observation:

_____

_____

J. List differences noted in child's behavior when with parents(s) versus when with examiner during another assessment:

_____

_____

III. Validity Checks
   A. Parent's Rating on External Validity of Unstructured situation
      1. None of what occurred was an accurate or typical
         reflection of day-to-day interactions/behaviors
      2. 20% of what occurred was typical
      3. 30% of what occurred was typical
      4. 40% of what occurred was typical
      5. 50% of what occurred was typical
      6. 60% of what occurred was typical
      7. 70% of what occurred was typical
      8. 80% of what occurred was typical
      9. 90% of what occurred was typical

   B. Parent's Rating on External Validity of Structured situation
      1. None of what occurred was an accurate or typical
         reflection of day-to-day interactions/behaviors
      2. 20% of what occurred was typical
      3. 30% of what occurred was typical
      4. 40% of what occurred was typical
      5. 50% of what occurred was typical
      6. 60% of what occurred was typical
      7. 70% of what occurred was typical
      8. 80% of what occurred was typical
      9. 90% of what occurred was typical

APPENDIX B: PROFILE OF PARENT-CHILD PLAY INTERACTIONS

	Unstructured Play	Structured Play	Validity
-9			
-8			
-7			
-6			
-5			
-4			
-3			
-2			
-1			
-0			
	A B C D E F G H I J K L M	A B C D E F G H	A B

Code:

A = Affect	A = Command Frequency	A = Unstructured
B = Intrusion	B = Command Clarity	B = Structured
C = Praise	C = Follow-through	
D = Attention	D = Praise	
E = Developmental Sensitivity	E = Punishment	
F = Responsiveness	F = Compliance	
G = Parent-child involvement	G = Willfulness	
H = Social Responsiveness	H = Aggressiveness	
I = Attention		
J = Activity		
K = Aggressiveness	Key: P = pretreatment results	
L = Responsiveness	A = After-treatment results	
M = Response to Questions		

Chapter 12 ——————————————————

ASSESSING PARENT-CHILD INTERACTIONS WITH THE MARSCHAK INTERACTION METHOD (MIM)

Sandra L. Lindaman, Phyllis B. Booth, and Candace L. Chambers

INTRODUCTION

Ms. B., a single parent, requested treatment for herself and her 5-year-old daughter Sara because she is concerned about Sara's angry defiance and controlling manner. Ms. B. and Sara sit side by side at a table. In front of them are ten printed instruction cards. Beyond the cards is a stack of numbered envelopes containing two toy animals, bottles of lotion, a box of raisins, two sets of blocks, and other materials. The clinician has instructed the mother to read each card aloud and then to do the activity for as long as they wish. Sara leans across her mother's lap to take the first card.

Mother: Watches Sara strain to reach card. "Okay, we're going to do them in order though, okay?"

Sara: Grunting in exertion to reach the card, looks at it, sounds out "Adult."

Mother: "Adult, that's right."

Sara: "...and child."

Mother: "That's right, very good Sara."

Sara: "E ... E . ." In a babyish voice, hand to mouth, "I don't know what this says."

Mother: Takes card. "Okay, it says: 'Adult and child each take one squeaky animal. Make the two animals play together'.... So, let's see what we've got." Takes animals out of envelope, hands pig to Sara.

Sara: "Ooooh, are these for me to take home?"

Mother: Smiles to self, shakes head, "No."

Mother and Sara sit close together, turn to each other, and look at each other; their pigs face each other and squeak. They use high-pitched voices in the pig play.

Mother: Looking at Sara. "Hello Mrs. Piggy."

Sara: Looking at pigs. "Hello, Mr. Piggy."

Mother: Looking at Sara. "How are you today?"

Sara: Looking at pigs. "Good."

Mother: You're full of squeals today, aren't you?"

Sara: "Yeah, you too. Let's hear a big squeal." Looks at camera.

Mother: Squeaks pig. "Look at my feet today, it's hard for me to stand up."

Sara: "Me too." Attempts to stand pig on her own leg but pig falls over.

Mother: Her pig playfully bats Sara's pig and knocks it out of Sara's hands.

Sara: Laughs, picks up pig. "Let's trade" and switches pigs with her mother.

Mother: "Oh, I can't stand up either."

Sara: Suddenly takes both pigs in her hands, tosses them across mother to the floor, smiles and laughs excitedly as she watches them fall. Turns her body to the wall, says, in a dismissing tone, "Let's get to the cards."

Mother: "Okay." Looks resigned and disappointed, picks up pigs and puts them back in the envelope.

The Marschak Interaction Method (MIM) is a structured technique for observing and assessing aspects of the relationship between two individuals, for example, biological parent and child, foster or adoptive parent and child, group home worker and child. It consists of a series of simple tasks designed to elicit a range of behaviors in four dimensions. The MIM evaluates the parent's capacity: to set limits and to provide an appropriately ordered environment (Structure), to engage the child in interaction while being attuned to the child's state and reactions (Engagement), to meet the child's needs for attention, soothing and care (Nurture), and to support and encourage the child's efforts to achieve at a developmentally appropriate level (Challenge). At the same time the MIM assesses the child's ability to respond to the parent's efforts within the four dimensions. In addition to allowing a close look at problem areas in the relationship, the MIM provides a unique opportunity for observing the strengths of both adult and child and of their relationship. It is, therefore, a valuable tool in planning for treatment and in determining how to help families strengthen their relationships. Marschak Interaction Method materials are copyrighted and are published by the Theraplay Institute in Wilmette, Illinois.

This chapter describes the nature of the MIM, how to administer and analyze it, and how it is used with different populations. The rich information that the MIM provides will be illustrated through case examples, including an extensive case discussion of a 5-year-old child and her mother.

HISTORY OF THE MIM

The Beginnings of the MIM

The MIM was developed by Marianne Marschak (Marschak, 1960a). First named the Controlled Interaction Schedule (CIS), Marschak conceived the CIS as a method for differentiating imitation from participation as components of the child's identification process. With the CIS, she studied immigrant fathers of Polish and Italian descent as they interacted with their preschool-aged sons (Marschak, 1959, 1960b), rural families in Japan (Marschak,

1967a), Head Start children and their mothers (1967b), schizophrenic and autistic children in interaction with their parents (Marschak & Call, 1965; Marschak, 1967c), and kibbutz-reared and home-reared children in Israel (1975). She also used the MIM as a teaching device for medical students (Marschak & Call, 1964, 1966). Ann Jernberg and others at the Theraplay Institute in Chicago (Jernberg, et al., 1982, 1983, 1985; Jernberg & Booth, 1997) expanded the use of the MIM, applying the method as a clinical tool for evaluation and treatment to older and younger age groups and to married couples.

Some Current Uses of the MIM

The MIM is used as the primary assessment of parent-child interaction prior to initiating Theraplay treatment by the staff and affiliates of the Theraplay Institute and its trainees around the world (Jernberg, 1979; Jernberg & Booth, 1999; Booth & Koller, 1998; Koller & Booth, 1997; Munns, 1997; Rantala, 1998; Ritterfeld, 1993). Published accounts describe the use of the MIM with a range of populations in a variety of public and private settings, including treatment programs for chemically dependent mothers (Jernberg, 1992a), infants with failure to thrive (Bernt, 1990, 1992), Head Start centers (Talen & Warfield, 1997), community mental health centers (Crume, 1996), and hospital settings (Allen & Nissen-Tjarks, 1998). The MIM also has been used to assist court-ordered placement decisions (Safarjan, 1992; Witten, 1994). McKay, Pickens, and Stewart (1996) compared the MIM with the Parenting Stress Index (Abidin, 1995). Additional comparisons of the MIM and aspects of parenting style and the MIM and temperament currently are in process (Stewart, personal communication, 1998).

The Revised Dimensions of the MIM

The original scheme for analyzing the MIM included four dimensions:

1. Promotes Attachment
2. Alerts to Environment
3. Guides Purposive Behavior
4. Assists in Overcoming Tension (Stress Reduction)

In addition to these four dimensions, the tasks were divided according to whether they:

1. *Were to be done together or by each person alone.* These tasks allowed an assessment of issues having to do with appropriate boundary maintenance (variously described as autonomy/separateness vs. intimacy/togetherness, or separation/individuation vs. symbiosis).
2. *Invited regressive or striving behaviors.* These tasks allowed an assessment of the degree of comfort with younger versus more grown-up behaviors.

Over the years the focus of observations of the MIM has shifted as new concepts and issues have become increasingly important. Because the MIM is used primarily for treatment planning, the dimensions have been revised to those used in Theraplay treatment: Structure, Engagement, Nurture, and Challenge. For each dimension both sides of the dyad are examined.

The MIM assesses how well the parents can

- Structure the environment and set clear, appropriate expectations and limits.
- Engage the child in interaction while being attuned to the child's state and reactions.
- Respond in a nurturing way to the child's needs.
- Provide appropriate challenge.

The MIM assesses how well the child can

- Accept structure from the adult—as opposed to insisting on calling all the shots.
- Engage with the adult—as opposed to being withdrawn, avoidant, or superindependent.
- Accept nurturing care from the adult—as opposed to looking only to herself for comfort.
- Respond to appropriate challenge—as opposed to being helpless and clinging, or being competitive, and making too high demands on herself.

THE NATURE OF THE MIM

The MIM and the Assessment of Attachment

The MIM assesses the nature and quality of the relationship between an adult and a child. It is often used to help determine (1) the parent's capacity to protect and care for the child, (2) the child's capacity for forming relationships, (3) the quality of the relationship between a child and a foster or preadoptive parent, or (4) the quality of the relationship between a child and his or her biological parents for decisions about reunification. The MIM is also used to help determine differential attachment between a child and two or more caregivers, for example, biological parent and foster parent.

Often these assessments have been called Bonding and Attachment Assessments. This terminology, however, is not an accurate description of what is being assessed in the MIM. The MIM focuses on the overall nature and quality of the relationship between adult and child rather than on the more narrowly defined concept of secure attachment (which focuses entirely on the child's behavior in response to her parent's absence and return). The assessment of security of attachment (or attachment category) is a well-defined skill based on analysis of toddlers' (12–18 month olds) responses to the Ainsworth Strange Situation (Ainsworth, Blehar, Waters & Wall, 1978). Since the MIM uses a very different set of tasks and is applied to children of all ages, the MIM is not used to determine the attachment category into which the child's behavior falls.

Using the MIM dimensions, each of which is an important element in the development of secure attachment, it is possible to assess how well the parent and child are negotiating the various aspects of parent-child interaction and to make recommendations for treatment, reunification, or placement. While the MIM provides extremely rich information, it should not be the sole basis for making such important decisions. Other valuable sources of information include: the psychosocial history, case worker reports, visits in the home, parent interviews, child interviews and observations of structured and free play, projective tests, and standardized checklists of child behaviors and parenting skills. The use of the MIM in placement decisions will be discussed later in this chapter.

Advantages of Using a Structured Observation Technique

Observing the parent and child as they interact has a number of advantages over using purely interview techniques. The participants' active involvement in concrete tasks allows typical patterns of interaction to emerge. Many patterns of interaction are outside the awareness of either partner and hence direct questioning is of little use. Seeing problem behaviors emerge in the interaction gives added insight into how they occur and how they can be changed. The participants' strengths and coping skills are clearly demonstrated. Adding the element of structure as opposed to observing unstructured play between parent and child allows one to select tasks to spotlight specific problem areas, to address specific research questions, to facilitate comparison between groups, and to compare the interaction before and after treatment.

Normative Information

The MIM is not a standardized test with statistically validated norms. However, it is possible to define particular aspects of the interaction and to establish interrater reliability. For example, two studies using the original dimensions of the MIM achieved satisfactory inter- rater reliability. Koller (1980), in a study of the relationship between infant temperament and parent-infant interaction, developed a system for coding the behavior of 4- to 8-month-old infants in interaction with their parents. Raters in this study obtained a reliability of between .74 and .98. McKay, Pickens, and Stewart (1996) developed a standardized behavior rating system in order to quantify parent-child interaction behavior observed during the MIM. They then used this system in a study of the relationship between reported parenting stress and the quality of parent-child interactions observed during the MIM. Interrater reliability ranged from .46 to .89 on the 16 scale items; 9 of the items were .70 or above. They found that parents reporting more stress on the Parenting Stress Index (PSI) were rated as displaying significantly lower quality parent-child interactions on the MIM. Parents' SES accounted for 65% of the variance and parental stress accounted for an additional 9% of the variance in MIM behavior ratings. There was a significant difference in the total quality of interaction scores between the high and normal stress groups, even with the effects of SES removed.

Because the interpretation of the MIM is based on clinical insight and a thorough knowledge of child development and parent-child interaction, it is necessary that practitioners who use the MIM have extensive clinical experience. Training and supervision in the use of the MIM is available through the Theraplay Institute. The Theraplay Institute regularly holds introductory and intermediate-level training in the use of the MIM in Chicago and in other locations on request. Additional supervision in the use of the MIM is available from Institute staff.

This chapter offers the following aids for developing normative guidelines for the interpretation of the MIM: descriptions of the norm for each dimension based on an understanding of what fosters healthy development in the parent-child relationship; a sample of MIM tasks designed to elicit interactions in the particular dimension; behaviors that indicate that the dyad needs help; and questions designed to help the clinician specify the parent's and the child's ability to negotiate each dimension.

STEPS IN THE ADMINISTRATION OF THE MIM

Typically, information is gathered about the child and family in an intake interview with the parents. Next the child and each parent complete the MIM interaction. Each MIM session usually takes 30 to 45 minutes, although some have been as short as 10 minutes and others as long as 90 minutes. The mother-child and father-child sessions usually are scheduled on different days. If required by the urgency of the assessment or by travel demands, both MIMs can be completed on the same day with a short break in between as long as the child does not become too fatigued. The MIMs are videotaped (if possible) in order to allow careful analysis of the interaction and later viewing by the parents and therapist. A feedback session follows in which the therapist and parents meet to discuss the assessment, to view portions of the videotaped interactions, and to make a treatment plan if appropriate. A written report of the interaction also may be prepared if requested.

Preparation

Task Selection and Task Order

Many MIM tasks are designed to elicit a particular dimension of behavior. The task in which the adult builds a simple structure with one set of blocks and asks the child to "build one just like mine" calls for the parent to structure the activity. It, therefore, assures that one will be able to observe the parent's style of structuring and the child's response to it. More than one dimension of behavior, however, can be displayed in carrying out an activity. For example, a parent can provide a great deal of structure and challenge ("Make my initials in lotion") for the relatively unstructured nurturing task, "Rub lotion on each other's hands." Tasks are selected for a particular MIM based on information from the intake interview. Thus, for a family where adequate structure appears to be a problem, the clinician should choose tasks that ask the parent to give directions that the child should follow. For a child who rejects nurturing, the clinician should include a number of regressive, caregiving activities. It is thus possible, choosing from the large number of tasks available, to design each MIM to elicit information specific to the family being assessed.

   To provide a model that can be followed in designing MIMs, a standard set of tasks that is useful for a basic analysis is listed below. It is recommended that this list be closely followed by clinicians new to the method so that they can become aware of typical responses to the basic tasks.

Recommended Tasks and Sequence for Ages Three and Over

This is the list of tasks that can be used for most preschool and school-age children. (The dimension of each task is indicated here, but does not appear on the administration card.)

Adult and child each take one squeaky animal. Make the two animals play together. (Engagement)

Adult teaches child something the child doesn't know. (Challenge)

Adult and child each take one bottle. Apply lotion to each other.

Or

Adult combs child's hair and asks child to comb adult's hair. (Nurture)

Play a game which is familiar to both of you. (Engagement)

Adult tells child about when child was a baby, beginning, "When you were a little baby…"

Or for children who are adopted or in foster care:

Adult tells child about when child joined the family, beginning, "When you first came to live with us…" (Nurture)

Adult leaves room for one minute without child. (Nurture, Stress Reduction)

Adult and child put hats on each other. (Engagement)

Adult and child each take paper and pencil. Adult draws a quick picture, encourages child to copy.

Or

Adult takes one set of blocks. Hands other set of blocks to child. Adult builds a block structure with own blocks. Then says to child, "Build one just like mine with your blocks." (Structure and Challenge)

Adult and child feed each other. (Nurture)

In order for the procedure to remain novel and interesting to the child on the second administration of the MIM, one should avoid giving exactly the same tasks to the mother and father. When two tasks are listed for the same number in the list above (for example, lotion and comb hair), one should be given to the mother, the other to the father. Other tasks, such as, "Play a game that is familiar to both of you," or "Adult teaches child something the child doesn't know," can be given to both parents because they allow each parent to come up with his or her own activity. It is best to begin with an engaging, playful task, such as "Have the two squeaky animals play together," since it gives the pair something concrete to do and helps them overcome their uneasiness in the unaccustomed situation. One should then vary the demands for performance, the amount of structure inherent in the task, and the amount of nurture or regressive activity so that difficult, stressful, or demanding tasks are not back to back. Feeding is usually placed at the end because it is the most rewarding task.

Site Preparation and Materials

Depending on the developmental stage of the child, the MIM can be administered in one of two ways:

1. The adult and infant/young child can sit on a mat, blanket, or towel on the floor. It is best to provide a back support for the adult.
2. The adult and child sit side by side at a table. A strip of masking tape is placed down the center of the table to delineate each partner's field.

Safarjan (1992), who uses the MIM for forensic purposes, allows the participants to assume a comfortable position relative to each other and to move around the room at will. She feels that this modification reduces stress, makes the participants more comfortable, and gives the opportunity for maximum flexibility in behavior.

The cards with the selected tasks and the corresponding materials in numbered envelopes are placed near the adult. Although it is best to conduct the MIM in a room without other toys and distractions and in a place where the pair will not be interrupted, it is possible to conduct MIMs in busy living rooms, hospital rooms, and in play therapy rooms. The clinician can withdraw to an inconspicuous corner to take notes, or sit behind a one-way mirror, if one is available.

If a parent has difficulty reading, the task cards can be read aloud by the clinician when the parent indicates she is ready. They can also be audiotaped and set up so that the parent can start the tape when she is ready to hear the instructions for the next task. The cards may be translated into another written language or translated aloud. The clinician must insure that the wording or intent of the task is not changed in the process. To date, the MIM is published in English and German (Ritterfeld & Franke, 1994).

Because it is difficult to keep track of more complicated interactions, it is recommended that clinicians new to the use of the MIM assess one parent and child pair at a time, rather than both parents and child or additional family members. However, more experienced clinicians have both parents do a few tasks with the child, or have a sibling enter for a task after the two parent-child MIMs are completed. Safarjan (1992) often administers the MIM to an entire family, with adults taking turns on tasks or participating together; she finds that the richness of information about family dynamics and sibling relationships is worth the increased difficulty in observation and analysis.

Videotaping the MIM

Videotaping the MIM is invaluable to the process of assessment as it allows for repeated reviewing to help in observing, analyzing, and understanding the parent-child interactions. In order to help parents understand the importance of videotaping, the clinician can explain that the tape provides a full record of the process, thus ensuring that nothing will be missed. Parents should be informed that they will have an opportunity to view parts of the tape with the clinician during the feedback session in order to share important observations that will help in the development of a treatment plan. Although some people are more anxious than others about being taped, most participants relax as they begin to interact with each other. Many report at the end that they forgot about the camera and, therefore, their interactions were not influenced by it. The process of watching the interaction in the feedback session is very powerful and effective. It usually convinces even those who were very self-conscious that the taping was valuable.

The use of videotaping in assessment and treatment has become more common and more accepted in the past decade (McDonough, 1993). As noted in the American Academy of Child and Adolescent Psychiatry current Assessment Practice Parameters, "Videotape provides the family and the clinician together an opportunity to identify interactional strengths and concerns" (1997, p. 26S). The tape also is very useful if there is disagreement about the observations or findings of the assessment. Restrictions regarding videotaping of wards of the state vary from place to place and may prohibit the use of this valuable technology in placement decisions. A second observer can be useful in these situations.

Administration

Instructions

Prior to attending the assessment session, parents are instructed to tell their child that they will be playing some games together and that a videotape will be made. The following instructions are given in the actual MIM session after the two are seated at the table with its cards and materials visible: "These cards describe some things we'd like you to do together." (To the parent) "Pick up the top card, read it aloud, and do the activity. It's up to you to decide when to go on to the next activity. There is no right or wrong way to do the activities. When you are finished, I will come back to ask you a few questions." If the clinician remains in the room during the MIM, she should avoid making eye contact or engaging with the pair.

Follow-up Questions

When the pair has completed the tasks, return to the room and ask the following questions:

> Was this a good picture of how things go between the two of you at home?
> If not, what did we miss?
> Were there any surprises?
> What was your favorite activity? Why?
> What was your least favorite activity? Why?
> What do you think your child liked best? Why?
> What do you think your child liked least? Why?

If the child is old enough, she may be asked to guess her parent's likes and dislikes and then to check with her parent to see if her guess corresponds with her parent's preferences. Responses to these questions provide insight into the meaning of the activities to the parent and child.

Analysis

It is recommended that the clinician develop a system that records and keeps observed interactions separate from hypotheses, thoughts, and questions about these interactions. One way to do this is to use a recording sheet that has a heavy center line demarcating the "fields" of the two participants (see Table 12–1).

Each half of the sheet is a mirror image of the other. Going from far left to far right, the eight columns are titled as follows: (1) feedback, (2) hypotheses, (3) verbalizations, (4) nonverbal behavior, (5) nonverbal behavior, (6) verbalizations, (7) hypotheses, (8) feedback. As the clinician observes the live MIM, or, ideally, as the clinician watches the videotape of the MIM a number of times, notes are made about these different types of observations and analyses.

Observations of Nonverbal and Verbal Behaviors

The nonverbal behaviors of the interaction such as eye contact, facial expression, movement toward and away from each other and body contact are recorded in the center

Table 12–1. Sample recording of one task: Squeaky animals

	PARENT				CHILD			
	(1)	(2)	(3)	(4)	(5)	(6)	(7)	(8)
	Feedback	Hypotheses	Verbal	Nonverbal	Nonverbal	Verbal	Hypotheses	Feedback
	Feel?			Watches S reach for ard	Leans across Mom's lap to reach card	Grunts in exertion	Taking over?	
		Asking S's permission to follow the directions	Okay, we're going to do them in order, okay?	Leans toward S to see card	Looking at card	Sounds out, "Adult."		
			Adult, that's right!	Looking at S	Looking at card	And child.		
		Pleased that S reads so well	That's right, very good Sara!		Hand to mouth, shakes foot	Babyish tone, I don't know what this says.	Asserts self, cannot do whole task, regresses	
				Takes card from S				
			Okay, it says … (reads aloud)					
				Hands pig to S	Smiles, looks at pig	Ooooh, are these for me to take home?		
			No… Hello Mrs. Piggy. High pitched voice	Smiles, shakes head Sits closer, turns to S, makes pig face S's pig	Sits closer, turns to M, makes pig face M's pig			
	Point out that mom takes the lead, S accepts					Hello Mr. Piggy. High pitched voice		

	How are you today?					
Point out series of engaged interactions	You're full of squeals, aren't you?	Looks at S	Looks at pigs	Good.	Demanding	
			Looks at camera	Yeah, you too. Let's hear a big squeal.	Waiting to see what M will suggest next—disappointed about weak pigs?	Noticed S looking at camera, trying to reengage?
	Look at my feet, it's hard for me to stand up.	Squeaks pig	Squeaks pig, looks at M's pig			
			Attempts to stand pig but it falls over	Me too.		
		Bats S's pig out of her hand	Picks up pig	Laughs. Let's trade.	Overstimulated by hit?	Ask: Why the hit? Running out of ideas?
		Switch pigs	Switch pigs			
	Oh, look, it's hard for me to stand up too—what's the deal here?		Watches M's pig	Silent	Uncomfortable following M's lead for this long?	Does M's question lead to S's decision to end the activity?
			Takes both pigs, tosses them to floor	Smiles and excited laugh	Responding to M's indecision about what to do next/question by taking charge and ending task.	
			Turns her body to wall	Let's get to the cards. (Dismissing tone)		
Feel?	Okay.	Smile fades. Puts pigs in envelope.	Watches mom			

columns (4 and 5). The line of tape down the center of the table assists the clinician in determining the movement of one partner into the other's space. It is useful to watch the videotape without sound to focus on the nonverbal interactions.

Verbalizations including words, sounds, laughter, and vocal tone are recorded in the next two columns (3 and 6). It is useful to develop some sort of shorthand for recording verbalizations. The nonverbal and verbal data collected in this manner allow one to track the sequence of interaction in detail.

Clinical Hypotheses

Columns 2 and 7, hypotheses, are for the clinician's speculations based on the observed behaviors. For example, in the episode that opens this chapter, one hypothesis is that Sara can tolerate only so much engagement that is initiated by her mother. In order to confirm or disconfirm this hypothesis further evidence should be sought in other tasks. It would also be important to discuss with the mother in the feedback session what she thinks about this hypothesis and to gather other evidence for or against it in Sara's life. If the hypothesis appears to be correct, it then becomes a factor in the treatment plan.

Feedback

In order to prepare for the feedback session, it is useful to make notes during the analysis about specific interactions that the clinician wants to discuss with the parents. One may want to find out more about their perceptions, to demonstrate a particular aspect of the child's behavior, or to highlight a particularly effective move that the parent made. Examples of such reminders and the shorthand in which they may be noted follow:

Support	Give support here.
Avoidance	Point out how the child avoids the parent's efforts.
Active?	Ask, "Is the child always this active?"
Feel?	Ask, "How did that feel to you when she did that?"
Needs?	Ask, "What do you think he's needing right here?"
Self-talk?	Ask, "What do you think he's saying to himself right here?"

Columns 1 and 8, feedback, remind the clinician to articulate these points in the feedback session.

The Feedback Session

The feedback session is the final stage of the MIM process. The session should be scheduled, if possible, within one week of the last MIM to reduce the waiting time and the parents' anxiety concerning their "performance." This session is usually 60 to 90 minutes in length. Parents are asked what their thoughts have been about the interaction, and for any pertinent new information about what has occurred in the meantime. The clinician shares observations and interpretations of what went on in the MIM sessions, explains what interactions led to those interpretations, and illustrates these ideas with selected portions of videotape or the reading of notes on specific sequences of interaction. The feedback session should be a dialogue; the parents are asked for their thoughts and reactions as different interactions are discussed (see questions noted in the feedback section). The focus is on the positive aspects of the interaction, looking for strengths and creative solutions to problems. The discussion is used to develop a therapeutic alliance with the family. The entire MIM videotape is not usually shown. Looking at some of the difficult interactions can be instructive, but it is easy for parents to become discouraged or feel that the whole interaction was problematic if the entire tape is viewed at one sitting. In fact, time usually does not permit the showing of the entire tape along with the necessary discussion. If a parent wants to see a particular task that the clinician had not planned to show, it is best to show it, if possible. In addition to the discussion described above, the silent observation of a significant positive or negative sequence of interaction can be very meaningful and insight producing for the parent.

Written Reports

The writer of the MIM report, as with any assessment, must keep in mind the audience of the report and the basic question or purpose of the evaluation. Because the MIM is not known to all professionals, a brief description of the nature of the MIM should be included. For example, "Ms. P. and her 5-year-old daughter Sara completed the Marschak Interaction Method, a structured observation of the interaction between the two. They participated in ten preselected tasks: (1) Adult and child each take one squeaky animal. Make the two animals play together. (2) Play a game with the child that is familiar to both of you. (3) Adult teaches child something he/she doesn't know…"

The interaction then should be described task by task, first for one parent and then for the other parent. The description does not need to be extensive, but should give a picture of the interaction so that someone reading the report can understand the rationale for the conclusions and recommendations. The summary and recommendation section is the final part of the report. It is helpful to organize this section by dimension, that is, to summarize how the parent and child are negotiating issues in the realms of structure, engagement, nurture, and challenge.

HOW THE MIM IS USED

The recording methods described thus far are a way of organizing the raw data of the observed interaction. The following guidelines were developed to analyze that data through the framework of the MIM dimensions of Structure, Engagement, Nurture, and Challenge. The definition of each of the four dimensions and a description of the norm for that dimension are discussed below. A sample of MIM tasks designed to elicit interactions in the particular dimension is provided. Next, there is a list of behaviors indicating that a dyad needs help. Finally, a list of questions is provided to help specify the parent's and the child's ability to negotiate each dimension. The reader should note that in the clinical example that follows, one task illustrates each dimension; however, in an entire MIM, there are several ways to assess behavior in each dimension. For example, there may be several structuring, engaging, nurturing or challenging tasks; a task meant to elicit one type of behavior may reveal other types of behavior too; and observations are made on between-task behavior as well.

Structure

Structure is the element of good parenting that forms the foundation for all the other dimensions. "Good-enough parents" are trustworthy and predictable, and they help define and clarify the child's experience. The parent sets boundaries to ensure the child's safety and helps the child to understand the world in which she lives. Appropriate structure conveys the message "You are safe with me because I will take good care of you." As a consequence of the caregiver's structuring of the child's environment, the child enjoys physical and emotional security and is able to understand and learn about her environment.

Definition

Tasks in this dimension are designed to assess the parent's ability to take charge, to set limits, provide a safe, orderly, understandable environment for the child, as well as to assess the child's willingness to accept that structure.

Sample Tasks

Build a block structure just like mine

Make a drawing just like mine

Adult asks child to "draw a circle," "draw a square," "draw a face," then "draw something you like."

Adult tells child to listen and follow the instructions. Then adult tells child to put the box onto the chair, put the bracelet inside the box, remove the shoe from adult's foot.

The parent and child negotiate the dimension of structure throughout the MIM, as it is particularly elicited by the procedures of a "structured" technique. So, in addition to specific task performance, one may also look at who handles the materials and cards, who begins and ends activities, who decides what to do, and how these decisions are made.

The Norm

Parent in adult role providing clear structure appropriate to child's developmental level.

Child accepts adult structure.

Signs that the Dyad Needs Help

Parent in peer or child role.

Parent unable to set limits.

Parent turns authority over to child.

Parent in teacher role (pedantic, rigid, focused only on task at hand).

Interaction disorganized or chaotic.

Child defiant, insisting on doing things his own way.

Questions to be Asked

1. Who is in charge? parent? child?
2. What role does the parent take? appropriate parent role? peer? pal? teacher? child in parental role?

3. How consistent and effective are parent's efforts to structure?
4. How well does the child accept parent's structure?

An Example of Structure

The eighth of the ten MIM tasks, which Sara and her mother did together, was "Adult takes one set of 5 blocks. Hands other set of 5 blocks to child. Adult builds a structure with own blocks. Then says to child, 'build one just like it with your blocks.'" This task also taps the dimension of challenge as the parent can choose to build a too-easy, an age-appropriate, or a too-difficult structure, and can give varying levels of assistance.

Mother: "It says I've got to make a block structure and you've got to copy mine, okay?"

Sara: "No, I don't."

Mother: "Yes, you do."

Sara: "No mom, you've got to copy mine."

Mother: "I've got to copy yours? I don't think that's what the card says. Spill them (the blocks) all out."

Sara: "No." Spills the blocks out of the envelope, builds own structure. "I'm done!"

Mother: Copies Sara's structure, sits back to watch her.

Sara: Moves forward quickly, knocks over Mom's structure, gets up and moves away from table.

Mother: "Hey, come here." Begins to build. Sara watches.

Sara: Takes blocks off Mom's building to make her own taller.

Mother: "What are you doing?" Laughs to self in exasperated way, rubs face, looks fatigued.

Sara: Knocks over her own tower. "You clean it up." Flips envelope to Mother.

Discussion

Sara appears to be "in charge" of this interaction; she squabbles, changes the rules so that she is the initiator, and appears to compete with her mother. Although mother invokes the authority of the task card and attempts to be in charge, Sara treats her more like a peer. When Mother clearly tells Sara what to do, she complies. However, when she asks questions or permission, Sara's usual response is "No." Mother appears to have had a useful strategy when she copied Sara's structure, then had Sara make a copy the second time. But Sara's one-upmanship derails Mother's plan. When Mother retreats to watch Sara midway through the task and at the end, Sara moves in and messes things up. At these times Sara is dismissive and disrespectful and her mother appears fatigued. Thus we see that the dimension of structure is difficult for this pair. It requires a sustained effort on the part of the mother to remain in charge because Sara competes for control; if Mother doesn't have the necessary energy, Sara takes over. However, Sara isn't comfortable being in charge nor is she comfortable with her mother's reaction.

Engagement

Parents of young children provide excitement, surprise, and stimulation in order to maintain a maximal level of alertness and engagement. They also soothe and calm the child when necessary so that the child is again available for engagement. These efforts to engage the child must be attuned to the child's emotional state, developmental level, and needs. Appropriate efforts to engage the child communicate the message, "You can interact in appropriate ways with others. You can be close to others. You have feelings that I can appreciate and share. Others have feelings as well. You are fun to be with."

Definition

Tasks in this dimension are designed to assess the parent's ability to encourage interactive engagement appropriate to the child's developmental level and emotional state. In the case of autistic or obsessive-compulsive behavior, the clinician wants to assess the parent's ability to draw the child out of his rigid isolation and into interaction. While playfulness can be part of any interaction, it is clearly an important factor in engaging the child in joyful shared interactions.

Sample Tasks

Engaging activities:

>   Play patty-cake
>   Play peek-a-boo
>   Tickle each other's feet

Attuned, synchronous activities:

>   Make up a tune together
>   Take a three-legged walk
>   Choose the design you like best (shows child's identification with parent's choices)
>   Play a familiar game
>   Have squeaky animals play together (reveals synchronized movements, ability to give and take)

Empathy, awareness of feelings:

>   Mood pictures (gives opportunity to observe parents and child's willingness and ability to discuss feelings, etc.)

The Norm

>   Parent is able to engage the child and work together when appropriate.
>   Parent and child are able to be playful while still accomplishing the tasks.
>   Parent shows empathic awareness and responsiveness to child's emotional state.
>   Parent and child are in sync, are emotionally in tune (cf. Stern's affect attunement, Stern, 1985).

Signs that the Dyad Needs Help

>   Parent remains aloof, allows too much distance or fails to engage the child.
>   Parent can't leave the child alone, takes over tasks the child could accomplish on his own.
>   Child won't let parent get close.
>   Child ignores or rejects parent.

Parent unresponsive to child, unaware of child's feelings, unable to calm child.

Parent projecting his or her own feelings onto child.

Parent unaware of child's feelings.

Parent so serious and task oriented that there is no room for pleasure and light-heartedness.

Parent teases at child's expense.

Parent's joking and playfulness take priority over accomplishing the task.

Child is silly and unable to attend.

Child is too serious.

Questions to Be Asked

1. Can parent engage the child? (Behavioral signs of engagement include making eye contact, moving in synchrony, making physical contact, etc.)
2. Does child respond to parent's efforts to engage him?
3. Is parent able to be empathic?
4. Are parent and child physically and affectively in tune with each other?
5. Does parent match level of stimulation to child's ability to tolerate it?
6. Do these two have fun together?

An Example of Engagement

The "Make the animals play together" task described at the beginning of this chapter is an example of an engaging task.

Discussion

Despite an initial scuffle for control over the cards and materials, Mother takes the initiative in the pig play; Sara responds positively and we see several sequences of attuned engagement in the imitation of movements and dialogue. Mother is empathic in her pleasure at Sara's reading of difficult words and her rescue when Sara cannot read anymore. In this, the first MIM task, Mother may have felt fresh and ready to engage Sara. Toward the end of the task, Sara may be overstimulated when her mother bats her pig away, or may be bothered by the suggestion that the pigs cannot stand up. Ultimately, Sara appears to have tolerated as much of her mother's initiation of engagement as she can, and she abruptly ends the task. Mother is rather easily disappointed and she never takes this much playful initiative again. Thus mother can initiate engagement and Sara can respond positively, but the engagement is rather fragile, and easily falls apart.

Nurture

Healthy parents are warm, tender, soothing, calming, and comforting. In the repeated experience of responsive caregiving, the child learns about himself, about relationships, and about the world and forms a secure attachment to his parents. The comforting presence of the adult helps the child, as he matures, to develop the capacity to take over these functions for himself. The message of nurturing care is: "You are loveable and worthy of care. You can count on me to respond to your needs for care, affection, and praise."

Definition

Tasks in this dimension are designed to assess the parent's ability to respond appropriately to the child's developmentally and situationally appropriate needs, as well as to assess the parent's ability to recognize tension and stress in the child and to help him deal with it. They also allow an assessment of the child's ability to accept the parent's nurturing care and to turn to the adult for comfort. In addition, one can observe the child's capacity for appropriate self-soothing or self-regulation.

Sample Tasks

Feed each other

Adult powders child's back

Put lotion on each other

Put Band-Aid on child

Comb each other's hair

Tell baby memories

While some activities deliberately set up a stressful situation, there are opportunities throughout the MIM to observe how the adult helps the child deal with stress; for example, at the beginning of the session when the child is anxious because of being observed, parents can help reduce stress in a variety of ways.

Specific stress-reduction tasks include:

Unattainable candy

Hampered movement (infant)

Difficult puzzle

Parent leaves the room

Teach (if parent sets task too high)

The Norm

Parent is responsive, empathically attuned to child's needs.

Parent is comfortable with physical touch, with holding, cuddling, and feeding.

Parent is aware of child's need for calming and soothing.

Parent recognizes child's rising tension and has a variety of appropriate ways to soothe and calm the child.

Parent neither jumps in too soon to "bail" the child out, nor waits so long that the child is in despair or out of control.

Parent prepares child for separation (perhaps even providing a transitional object).

Child accepts parent's nurture.

Child shows age-appropriate concern about parent's leaving but can be comforted upon parent's return.

Older child shows pleasure in parent's return and is able to reconnect with the parent.

Signs that the Dyad Needs Help

Parent infantilizes child.

Parent withholds gratifying experiences.

Parent turns nurturing tasks into teaching tasks.

Parent asks child to nurture/take care of him or her.

Parent does not recognize or acknowledge child's tension or distress.

Parent's response to child only escalates child's discomfort.

Parent does not prepare child for separation.

Child is aloof, acts as if it did not matter that parent leaves.

Child is clingy and unable to let parent leave.

Child is timid, helpless, and fearful.

Child has problems accepting care and nurture.

Questions to Be Asked

1. Is parent able to provide nurturing touch, physical contact, and caregiving?
2. Is child able to accept nurturing touch, physical contact, and caregiving?
3. Does parent ask child to take care of him or her?
4. Can parent recognize and act upon child's need for help in calming/having stress reduced?
5. Can child accept parental help for calming and stress reduction?
6. Can child calm or soothe self?
7. Does parent prepare child for separation?

An Example of Nurture

Mother: "You know what the last thing is…?" Pulls bag of crackers out of envelope. "We get to feed each other."

Sara: Sits down, grabs bag and tries to open, hands to mother. "Open this for me." Plunges hand into bag and feeds self crackers with both hands.

Mother: Laughing. "You're supposed to feed me." Holds bag away from Sara. "I'll give you some when you give me some."

Sara: Whines. Puts her mouth on mother's outstretched hand to eat crackers.

Mother: "Okay, now give me some, please."

Sara: Takes crackers in hand and tosses toward mother's mouth, misses.

Mother: Takes a few crackers out of bag. "You give them to me, okay?"

Sara: Out of seat, looking in mirror, watching self chew, dancing around room.

Discussion

The mother is ready to nurture Sara and to receive something in return (as suggested by the task card). Sara finds it hard to delay gratification and appears needy. Her need to make a game out of feeding and her disorganization and increasing excitability show a lack of comfort in giving and receiving nurture. Her mother is not able to help her calm down. Parents usually are disappointed when their children refuse to feed them in the MIM and Sara's mother is no exception. She tries several times to make this a success. She may be too disappointed to recognize Sara's discomfort with nurture as Sara appears energetic and preoccupied with herself. The mother is ready to nurture Sara, but Sara's difficulty giving and receiving nurture aggravates the mother's vulnerability to feelings of failure.

Challenge

Healthy parents encourage their children to move ahead, to strive a bit, and to become more independent. This dimension includes the activities through which parents stimulate development, encourage progress, set appropriate expectations, and take pleasure in the child's achievement. Experience with appropriate challenges gives the child a sense of mastery and develops realistic self-expectations. The message is, "You are capable of growing and of making a positive impact on the world."

Definition

Tasks in this dimension are designed to assess the adult's ability to stimulate the child's development, to set developmentally appropriate expectations, and to take pleasure in the child's achievement. The child's ability to respond to challenge is also assessed.

Sample Tasks

Teach child something he or she doesn't know.

Build a block structure. Ask child to build one just like yours.

Adult asks child to tell about when child is a grownup.

Difficult puzzle.

Adult asks child to close her eyes and describe everything in the room.

The Norm

Parent is aware of the child's developmental level, and sets tasks that the child, with some effort, can master.

Parent gives positive response to child's efforts.

Parent and child share pleasure in the achievement.

Signs that the Dyad Needs Help

Parent's expectations are too high (or too low).

Parent avoids challenging the child.

Parent is too competitive.

Child avoids challenge.

Child expects too much of himself.

Parent or child shows no pleasure in achievement.

Parent does not acknowledge the child's efforts.

Questions to Be Asked

1. Does parent choose tasks that are developmentally appropriate?
2. Does child respond to the task?
3. Does parent make mastery appealing?
4. Is child able to focus and concentrate?
5. Is child able to handle frustration?
6. Can parent help child handle frustration?

An Example of Challenge

Mother: Reads card: "Adult teaches child something the child doesn't know.... What don't you know Sara?"

Sara: Leaning on Mom's legs, staring off into space. Gets up and moves over to materials. "I think it's in here."

Mother: "No, no, no, no, we've got to wait to get to all that stuff, okay?" Sitting still, appears to be thinking of what to teach.

Sara: "But why did we do the piggies?"

Mother: "Because it was on the card."

Sara: "Well, I don't want to…"

Mother: "We're almost done." (Actually this is task 3 of 10.)

Sara: "I don't care."

Mother: "Should I…"

Sara: "Should I…"

Mother: "What should I teach you?"

Sara: "What should I teach you?" Looking at mother's face, smiling, mocking tone.

Mother: "What don't you know … you know everything."

Sara: Twisting and chewing on hair. "I don't want to do it."

Mother: Hasn't moved from position during this whole interchange. Puts card aside. "Okay."

Discussion

This MIM task is the one most likely to be skipped by parents when they are unable to decide what to teach. It is not uncommon for parents to ask children for suggestions of what they "don't know," or to indicate that the child knows "everything," especially children who call the shots in their families. Sara's mother appeared very immobilized by this task, literally not moving while thinking. Sara's response is first to go on the attack, mocking her mother's indecision, and then regressing to hair twisting and chewing and refusal to do anything. Her mother ends the task by deciding to move to the next card. Since nothing was taught, it is difficult to assess how these two negotiate challenge. The mother may be unsure of Sara's fund of knowledge, unaware of age-appropriate activities, concerned about coming up with a bad idea, or wary of Sara's reaction to being taught anything. The feedback session will be the place to discuss these hypotheses and find out what the mother was thinking.

General Questions

Once she has considered the questions relating to each dimension, the clinician should ask herself three general questions in order to gain understanding and empathy for both parent and child:

> What would it be like to live twenty-four hours a day with this child?
> What would it be like to live twenty-four hours a day with this parent?
> Would living with this parent/child make you feel good about yourself?

Discussion

The answers to these questions for Sara and her mother are based on interview information and performance on six additional MIM tasks beyond those described in this chapter. Sara would be a difficult child to live with, but it was clear that she is hungry for more direction and engagement from her mother and could respond positively if they were offered. From Sara's point of view, living with a mother who sometimes observes rather than takes action also would be difficult. Sara's style of moving in, mocking, and messing up when her mother is unsure of what to do makes her mother feel disliked and put down as well as ineffective. These patterns of interaction do not give either of them enough positive engagement to create good feelings about themselves or the relationship.

Treatment Planning

Using the framework of Theraplay treatment, an adult-directed play therapy involving both parent and child, Sara's mother was helped to become comfortable taking the lead in initiating engaging, playful, and nurturing activities and Sara was helped to become comfortable being the recipient of this kind of engagement. The MIM also is used by clinicians to design treatment programs using other forms of play therapy, family therapy, psychotherapy, and parent guidance.

FORMS OF THE MIM

There are MIM administration manuals and sets of task cards for three age groups: prenatal–post-birth, infant, and preschool–school age. Tasks and procedures for adolescents and adult couples are currently in draft form.

The Prenatal/Post-birth MIM

The Prenatal MIM (Jernberg, Thomas, & Wickersham, 1985) is a method for observing the attitudes and behaviors of mothers toward their unborn infants. When indicated, it can be used as an intervention. "It allows mothers first to develop wholesome attitudes toward their fetuses, their pregnancies and themselves as future mothers and second to 'practice' behaviors which will later benefit the mother-child relationship" (Jernberg, 1988, p. 256). A pregnant woman may be referred by her physician or mental health worker if there is a concern about the quality of her attachment to her unborn child or if risk factors exist that may affect the attachment. The prenatal MIM has been used in residential teen maternity programs and in substance abuse programs for pregnant women. Some clients have referred themselves in order to enhance the developing relationship with their child.

Prenatal tasks include: Draw a picture of you and your baby; Talk and play with your baby; Teach your baby something; Tell your baby about his or her other parent. There are special tasks for mothers who are considering placing their babies for adoption. A father-fetus prenatal MIM can be conducted as well; in this procedure the mother holds a newspaper or magazine in front of her face, so that the father is free to interact with the fetus as much as possible. Parents have reported that their participation in the MIM assessment has changed their perceptions of themselves, their babies, and their view of themselves as parents-to-be. The use of the prenatal MIM as an intervention is discussed at the end of this chapter. The tasks of the Prenatal MIM can be repeated (with small changes) in the post-birth period as a form of checking on the attachment process, intervening as necessary, and celebrating the new relationship.

The Infant MIM

The infant MIM (Jernberg, Allert, Koller & Booth, 1983) extends from birth to 18 to 24 months. A family may be referred for an assessment during this period because of concerns about the child's emotional, behavioral, relational, or developmental difficulties; about the parents' capacities and skills, or about risk factors affecting both the parent and child. The MIM's focus on the interaction between parent and child is consistent with current child practice parameters that "infants and toddlers must be understood, evaluated, and treated within the context of the family or primary caregiving unit" (AACAP, 1997, p. 21S).

The Preschool/School Age/Adolescent MIM

The preschool/school age MIM (Jernberg, Booth, Koller, & Allert, 1982) is described extensively in this chapter. It covers the greatest age range and is the most widely used. There is no separate manual for the adolescent age group; however, the procedures and many of the tasks from the school-age group are applicable to adolescents (Koller, 1994; Jernberg & Booth, 1999).

The Marital MIM

The Marital MIM manual is available in draft form (Jernberg & Booth, 1997). A marriage counselor may refer a couple for a Marital MIM to help determine the couple's strengths and weaknesses, characteristic ways of coping, or motivation. Many of the tasks are the same as those of the original MIM and others were modified to tap similar dimensions of behavior at an adult level. Participation in the MIM interaction reveals characteristics including competition, cooperation, empathy, respect, connectedness, view of self, trust, stress, risk-taking, playfulness, and nurture. Jernberg and Booth note, "The MMIM is at its most effective when each of the two partners has the motivation, the time and the luxury to examine in depth the various components that make up the relationship" (1997, p. 19).

THE MIM AND PLACEMENT DECISIONS

The MIM has been used in conjunction with a variety of other measures to assess the quality of interaction between parent and child in court-ordered placement decisions. One of the authors of this chapter (CC) has administered over 600 MIMs in her specialized practice of consultation to various social service/child welfare organizations and AIDS-related service organizations in the Chicago area. Over 250 of these evaluations have been ordered by the Circuit Court of Cook County, Illinois, the largest circuit court system in the United States, for assessment of parental capacity and best interests of the child. Other experienced clinicians use the MIM as a part of their placement battery as well. Safarjan observed, "The fact that specific behavioral dimensions are targeted and expected on each MIM task has numerous advantages over free play or in-vivo home observation for court work.... The evaluator, rather than the parent, controls task selection and thus the behavioral dimensions to be observed" (1992, p. 3). Witten noted, "By reviewing the [MIM] interactions between a child and various caretakers, the observer can determine characteristics of the child's attachment-enhancing behaviors, deviant or paradoxical actions, and overall ability to respond effectively to any specific adult. ... Both the child's working model of interaction and the parent's assumptions about his or her own role as well as expectations about the child can be elicited using this method" (1994, p. 38).

Assessing Parental Capacity and the Best Interests of the Child

As noted above, the MIM assesses the essence of healthy parenting—the capacity to structure, engage, nurture, and challenge. The MIM provides the basic framework that can then be supplemented and clarified by other clinical procedures to produce a well-rounded picture of parental capacity. The instruments included in a comprehensive assessment vary according to the nature of the referral question, the ages of the children, and the availability of all caregivers involved in the child's life. The battery may include:

Clinical interview

Child Developmental Inventory (Ireton, 1992)

Denver Developmental Screening Test-R (Frankenburg, Dodds, Fandal, Kazuk & Cohrs, 1975)

Bayley Scales of Infant Development II (Bayley, 1993)

Marschak Interaction Method

Assessment of Parental Capacity Questionnaire (University of Chicago, 1989)

Parent-child Observation Guide (University of Chicago, 1989)

Parent Awareness of Skills Survey (Bricklin, 1995)

Parenting Stress Index (Abidin, 1995)

Kinetic Family Drawings (Burns, 1982)

Kinetic-House-Tree-Person Drawings (Burns, 1987)

Observation of Structured Play

Observation of Doll House Play

Strange Situation (Ainsworth, et al., 1978)

This suggested battery is not relevant to all forensic, parental capacity/best interest situations. However, the above recommended measures offer the practitioner significant data to incorporate with their own clinical observations and judgment.

The first step in the comprehensive assessment is to conduct a clinical interview in order to develop rapport and a personal relationship with the adults and children involved in the evaluation. The clinical interview also is helpful in understanding the problems presented and the problem as the parent/caregiver understands it. Information from the clinical interview is used eventually to construct a plan for future placement or treatment. The next step is to collect information about the child's developmental level. The Child Developmental

Inventory (CDI) is a useful tool to determine whether those adults involved in the assessment are aware of the child's current developmental level. If the CDI reveals developmental delays, or if information is provided that indicates that the child experienced drug exposure in utero, a Denver Developmental Screening Test-R or the Bayley Scales of Infant Development II is administered to identify suspected delays.

The next measure in the assessment battery is the MIM. It is administered early in the battery as it most directly addresses the issues of parental capacity and attachment. Once information has been obtained from the MIM about the parent's capacity to structure, engage, nurture, and challenge, various questionnaires are administered to the caregiver. The Assessment of Parental Capacity Questionnaire assesses by self-report and specific questions the parent-child attachment, parent self-concept, and the parent's affect and empathy regarding the child. The Parenting Stress Index looks at the magnitude of stress in the parent-child system. These questionnaires provide additional information on the parents' perceptions of themselves, their child, and their life circumstances. The Parental Awareness of Skills asks "what-if" questions about typical and not-so-typical child care situations. This offers information about how the parent thinks about parent-child interactions. Projective techniques such as the Kinetic Family Drawings and the Kinetic-House-Tree-Person Drawings are administered to the caregiver and to the child if age appropriate; these measures allow a nonverbal expression of feelings and attitudes and give further information about nurturance, empathy, connectedness, and sense of self. Next, Structured Play, Free Play or Doll House Play and the Strange Situation are completed, if age appropriate. These measure how the caregiver participates with the child and how the child responds. A typical assessment takes a minimum of six hours to complete; a complicated assessment lasts six to twelve hours and is spread over a number of sessions.

Foster and Adoptive Placements

The MIM also serves as an excellent screening device for determining appropriate foster or preadoptive placements. The MIM records the child's reaction to the parents and can help determine the kinds of services that may be required. Jernberg (1990) recommended using the MIM not only for initial "matchmaking" but also for assessing postadoptive adjustment. Jernberg described the feedback session to the adoptive parents as a place to discuss and illustrate (1) the child's younger-than-chronological level of emotional development and (2) the characteristic patterns of parent-child interaction. The MIM is particularly useful in capturing some adopted children's wariness or rejection of their parents' overtures; viewing the child's reactions can support and inform the parent.

OTHER USES AND POPULATIONS

Prevention/Early Intervention in High-Risk Situations

The MIM has been used as an assessment of parent-child interaction for children with failure to thrive (Bernt, 1990, 1992), for abused and neglected preschoolers (Bostrom, 1995), and for preschoolers with relationship disturbances (Clark, 1997). Talen and Warfield (1997) used the MIM as a part of a Family Wellness Project in several Head Start centers, asserting that children's health is significantly related to the quality of caregiver-child relationships. Their assessment consisted of the Early Screening profile (Harrison et al., 1990), a preschool child development instrument, a clinical interview with the primary caregiver concerning the child's early developmental history and family relationships, the Child Behavior Checklist (Achenbach & Edelbrock, 1983) completed by the primary caregiver, and six tasks of the MIM (Squeaky animals, Teach child, Rub lotion on each other, Parent leaves the room, Build a block structure, and Feed each other). A feedback session was scheduled to discuss each child's development and to review the videotaped interaction. Talen and Warfield found the MIM particularly helpful for giving parents "support and reinforcement for positive parenting, information about how to understand their child's needs and normal child behaviors, and suggestions for enhancing their parenting skills" (Talen & Warfield, 1997, p. 316). A follow-up survey of the small sample indicated a positive response to the project.

The MIM as a Clinical Intervention

From the beginning of the use of the MIM as a research tool, some parents have reported that simply participating in the tasks of the MIM assessment has a positive effect on the parent-child relationship (Jernberg & Des Lauriers, 1962). Parents continue to report this today, mentioning as reasons for this change the exclusive time spent with one child; the focus on engagement and simple activities rather than sports, board games, or passive shared activities; and the insights that they gain on their own as they interact in ways that require structure, engagement, nurture, and challenge. The MIM can be used as an intervention when the interactions are coached or discussed, as is sometimes done with the prenatal and marital MIMs.

If there are significant concerns about attachment disturbance following the prenatal assessment and feedback, the MIM also can be used as a form of intervention. In this procedure the clinician sits with the prospective mother as she repeats the tasks and gives support and encouragement. Jernberg describes, "Each time she does so she is coached to involve herself more and more with her baby—to look at him, value him, touch him, look at him directly, etc.—and to do all this with energy, imagination, emotion, and intensity" (1988, p. 262). Clinicians who have used the MIM at centers for chemically dependent women report that the mothers' participation in the MIM tasks facilitated breaking through denial and strengthening attachment. When the Prenatal MIM was used as a form of intervention for this group, the following changes were noted: the "pre-intervention MIM drawings depicted babies outside of the mother's bodies, babies' appearing to be 2 or 3 years old, or mother and child stick figures on opposite sides of the paper, the post-intervention MIM showed the fetus inside the mother, and having articulated details such as fingers" (Jernberg, 1992a, p. 5).

In Marital MIM intervention, the clinician meets with the couple on several occasions to review the MIM task by task. The couple is encouraged to discuss each segment of the interaction, sometimes reversing roles, or repeating the interaction in a way that feels better to both of them (Jernberg, 1992b).

The MIM has been useful as an assessment and intervention tool for parents whose children have chronic or terminal illnesses such as cancer, arthritis, sickle cell, or diabetes. These parents usually are overwhelmed with a recent diagnosis and seek assistance for dealing with the question of "How do I live with this child and this diagnosis?" The MIM tasks seem to break down the adult's perception of the wall of untouchability or fragility that a seriously ill child presents. The process of doing and reviewing the MIM demonstrates to parents that the child is able to withstand their touch and still requires their predictability and reliability. The tasks also give parents permission to be playfully nurturing, reducing feelings of pity for the child and for themselves.

The MIM has been especially useful for the evaluation of HIV-infected mothers and their newborns. Prior to the relatively new medical protocol that has reduced the transmission of HIV from mother to child, mothers frequently found it difficult to bond with their newborns who also were HIV positive. Some mothers were unable to interact with their babies on the MIM tasks. When shown the videotapes of the interaction, they generally were receptive to a suggested treatment plan with the goal of enhancing the quality of interaction with their infants for as long as the babies or the mothers survived. For example, Angela was a 30-year-old HIV-positive woman whose newborn son went unnamed for nearly a month in the hospital's neonatal unit. Angela visited the baby only when the social worker contacted her. When the baby went home, the family was referred for an evaluation by a visiting nurse who was alarmed by the lack of interaction between Angela and baby Marcos. In the clinical interview, Angela revealed that she felt very guilty about infecting him and also that she was afraid of catching a cold or illness from him because he was so sick. She did not want to hold him and she was not allowed to breastfeed him, so she felt of little use to him. Finally, she said that she believed the baby was going to die, and she did not want to get close to him. She reluctantly agreed to participate in the MIM and as she interacted with Marcos, he smiled and arched his back as if he wanted to be picked up. This small action was caught on the videotape and had a great deal of meaning for the mother. She viewed the tape several times and was fascinated at how Marcos looked at her, followed her voice, and appeared to move toward her. The taking of the MIM created a context in which the mother could see her impact on her child.

The MIM was especially helpful to an HIV-positive mother who had recently regained custody of her 6-year-old and 11-year-old daughters. The younger child developed an extremely severe case of chicken pox and was hospitalized. When the mother reported her own HIV status to the hospital personnel, they tested the child and found that she had a full-blown case of AIDS. The mother was shocked and ceased any kind of meaningful interaction with the daughter. The mother proceeded to give all of her attention to the older child, stating that this child was going to live and needed her. The hospital social worker referred the mother and the 6-year-old for assistance with their relationship. A variety of tasks from the MIM were chosen, especially those which would tap the mother's capacity to engage and nurture her very ill daughter. There were other tasks administered to the mother to determine her general capacity to parent her daughter, but it was the review of the videotaped interactions of the MIM that had a dramatic impact on this mother. She was shocked to see how she visibly pulled back from any kind of touch or reaching out that her daughter made in her direction. The mother averted her eyes and appeared extremely uncomfortable under the gaze of her daughter. As the review of the videotape neared completion, the mother realized that she avoided the child because she saw in her their mutual illness, need for care, and eventual death. A treatment plan was constructed that provided the means for the mother and child to become more comfortable with each other. It was several years before this mother and child died from complications related to AIDS. Three separate MIMs documented the improvement in the mother's ability to engage, structure, nurture, and appropriately challenge her dying daughter. After the last MIM, additional time was spent having the mother and daughter together address special topics on the videotape to the older, uninfected daughter. The videotapes later were given to the older daughter when she was placed with a family member.

SUMMARY

The Marschak Interaction Method (MIM) is a structured technique for observing and assessing aspects of the relationship between two individuals. The observations are categorized into four dimensions: Structure, Engagement, Nurture, and Challenge. At the completion of the MIM, it is possible to describe the parents' efforts within these dimensions and the child's response. In addition to allowing a close look at problem areas in the relationship, the MIM provides a unique opportunity for observing the strengths of both adult and child and of their relationship. It is, therefore, a valuable tool in planning for treatment and in determining how to help families strengthen their relationships. This chapter describes the revised dimensions of the MIM, MIM administration and analysis, forms of the MIM for different age levels, and the use of the MIM as a clinical intervention.

REFERENCES

Abidin, R. R. (1995). *Parenting Stress Index Manual.* Odessa, FL: Psychological Assessment Resources.

Achenbach, T., & Edelbrock, C. (1983). *Manual for the child behavior checklist and revised child behavior profile.* Burlington, VT: University Associates in Psychiatry.

Ainsworth, M. D. S., Blehar, M. C., Waters, W., & Wall, S. (1978). *Patterns of attachment.* Hillsdale, NJ: Erlbaum.

Allen, M., & Nissen-Tjarks, K. (Summer 1998). Theraplay in a health care setting. *Theraplay Institute Newsletter, 10,* 5–7.

American Academy of Child and Adolescent Psychiatry (1997). Practice parameters for the psychiatric assessment of infants and toddlers (0–36 months). *Journal of the American Academy of Child and Adolescent Psychiatry, 36:* 10 Supplement, 21S–36S.

Assessment of Parental Capacity. (1989). University of Chicago, Department of Psychiatry.

Bayley, N. (1993). *Bayley Scales of Infant Development II.* San Antonio: Psychological Corporation.

Bernt, C. (1990). Theraplay as an intervention for failure-to-thrive infants and their parents. Unpublished doctoral dissertation, The Chicago School of Professional Psychology.

Bernt, C. (Fall 1992). Theraplay with failure-to-thrive children and their mothers. *Theraplay Institute Newsletter,* 1–3.

Booth, P. B., & Koller, T. J. (1998). Training parents of failure-to-attach children. In J. M. Briesmeister and C. E. Schaefer (Eds.), *Handbook of parent training: Parents as co-therapists for children's behavior problems,* 2nd ed. (pp. 308–342). New York: Wiley.

Bostrom, J. (Fall 1995). A preschool curriculum based on Theraplay. *Theraplay Institute Newsletter,* 3–4.

Bricklin, B. (1995). *Parent Awareness Skills Survey Manual.* Furlong, PA: Village Publishing.

Burns, R. C. (1982). *Kinetic Family Drawing Test.* New York: Brunner/Mazel.

Burns, R. C. (1987). *Kinetic House-Tree-Person Drawings: An Interpretive Manual.* New York: Brunner/Mazel

Clark, P. A. (1997). The Theraplay preschool assessment and treatment manual: Preparing mental health professionals to use structured play to remediate experience-derived relationship disturbances in three- to five-year-old children and their caregivers. Unpublished doctoral dissertation, Adler School of Professional Psychology.

Crume, J. (Fall 1996). Theraplay: Skills for the timid adoptive parent to deal with her very active three-year-old. *Theraplay Institute Newsletter,* 2–4.

Frankenburg, W. K., Dodds, J. B., Fandal, A. W., Kazuk, E., & Cohrs, M. (1975). *Denver Developmental Screening Test (DDST): Reference manual, revised.* Denver, Colorado: University of Colorado Medical Center.

Harrison, P. L., Kaufman, A. S., Kaufman, M. L., Bruiniks, R. H., Rynders, J., Ilmener, S., Sparrow, S., Cicchetti, D., & McCloskey, G (1990). *Early pre-school profiles.* Minneapolis, MN: American Guidance Service.

Ireton, H. (1992). *Child Development Inventory.* Minneapolis, Minnesota: Behavior Science Systems.

Jernberg, A. M. (1979). *Theraplay: A new treatment using structured play for problem children and their families.* San Francisco: Jossey-Bass.

Jernberg, A. M. (1988). Promoting prenatal and perinatal mother-child bonding: A psychotherapeutic assessment of parental attitudes. In P. G. Fedor-Freybergh, and M. L. V. Vogel (Eds.), *Prenatal and perinatal psychology and medicine* (pp. 253–266). Park Ridge, NJ: Parthenon Publishing Group.

Jernberg, A. M. (1990). Attachment enhancing for adopted children. In P. V. Grabe (Ed.), *Adoption resources for mental health professionals* (pp. 271–279). New Brunswick: Transaction Publishers.

Jernberg, A. M. (Winter 1992a). The Prenatal Marschak Interaction Method (PMIM): A tool for bonding. *Theraplay Institute Newsletter,* 4–5.

Jernberg, A. M. (Winter 1992b). The Marital Marschak Interaction Method (MMIM): A technique for structured observation and clinical intervention in helping troubled marriages. *Theraplay Institute Newsletter,* 1–2.

Jernberg, A. M., Allert, A., Koller, T. J., & Booth, P. B. (1983). *Reciprocity in parent-infant relationships.* Chicago, IL: Theraplay Institute.

Jernberg, A. M., & Booth, P. B. (1997). *Marital Marschak Interaction Method Manual* (Draft). Wilmette, IL: Theraplay Institute.

Jernberg, A. M., & Booth, P. B. (1999). *Theraplay: Helping parents and children build better relationships through attachment-based play,* 2nd ed. San Francisco: Jossey-Bass.

Jernberg, A. M., Booth, P. B., Koller, T. J., & Allert, A. (1982). *Preschoolers and school age children in interaction with their parents: Manual for using the Marschak Interaction Method (MIM).* Chicago, IL: Theraplay Institute.

Jernberg, A. M., & Des Lauriers, A. (1962). Some contributions of three preschool children to behavior changes in their mothers. Paper presented to the research seminar. Psychosomatic and Psychiatric Institute, Michael Reese Hospital, Chicago, IL.

Jernberg, A. M., Thomas, E., & Wickersham, M. (1985). *Mother's behaviors and attitudes toward their unborn infants.* Chicago, IL: Theraplay Institute.

Koller, T. J. (1980). The relationship of infant temperament to mother-infant and father-infant interaction. Unpublished doctoral dissertation, Illinois Institute of Technology, Chicago.

Koller, T. J. (1994). Adolescent Theraplay. In K. J. O'Connor and C. E. Schaefer (Eds.), *The handbook of play therapy, Vol. 2: Advances and innovations* (pp. 159–187). New York: Wiley.

Koller, T. J., & Booth, P. (1997). Fostering attachment through family Theraplay. In K. J. O'Connor and L. M. Braverman (Eds.), *Play therapy: Theory and practice* (pp. 204–233). New York: Wiley.

McDonough, C. (1993). Interaction guidance: Understanding and treating early infant-caregiver relationship disturbances. In C. Zeanah (Ed.), *Handbook of infant mental health* (pp. 414–426). New York: Guilford.

McKay, J. M., Pickens, J., & Stewart, A. (1996). Inventoried and observed stress in parent-child interactions. *Current Psychology: Developmental, Learning, Personality, Social, 15*(3), 223–234.

Marschak, M. (1959). A Comparison of father-son interactions in Polish vs. Italian worker's families. Pittsburgh: Western Psychiatric Institute/Arsenal Nursery School.

Marschak, M. (1960a). A method for evaluating child-parent interactions under controlled conditions. *Journal of Genetic Psychology, 97,* 3–22.

Marschak, M. (1960b). A comparison of Polish and Italian fathers in interaction with their pre-school sons. New Haven: Yale Child Study Center.

Marschak, M. (Summer/Fall 1967a). Child-parent tie in present day Japan. *Child and Family, 6,* 72–79, 80–88.

Marschak, M. (1967b). *Nursery school child/mother interaction.* Film. Available from New York University Film Library, 26 Washington Place, New York City 10003.

Marschak, M. (1967c). Imitation and participation in normal and disturbed young boys in interaction with their parents. *Journal of Clinical Psychology, 23*(4), 421–27.

Marschak, M. (1975). *Two climates of Israel.* Film. Available from New York University Film Library, 26 Washington Place, New York City 10003.

Marschak, M., & Call, J. D. (1964). Exposure to child-parent interaction as a teaching device. *Journal of Medical Education, 39,* 879–880.

Marschak, M., & Call, J. D. (1965). A comparison of normal and disturbed three-year-old boys in interaction with their parents. *American Journal of Orthopsychiatry, 35,* 247–249.

Marschak, M., & Call, J. D. (1966). Observing the disturbed child and his parents: Class demonstrations for medical students. *Journal of the American Academy of Child Psychiatry, 5,* 686–92.

Munns, E. (1997). Theraplay. In B. Bedard-Bidwell & M. Sippel (Eds.), *Hand in hand* (pp. 45–58). London, Ontario: Thames River Publishing. *Parent-Child Observation Guide/Parent-Infant Guide.* (1989). University of Chicago, Department of Psychiatry.

Rantala, K. (1998). Terapeuttin leikka sairaan lapsen hoitona—kokemuksia Theraplay-Työskentely-tavasta Therapeutic play as treatment for a sick child: Using the Theraplay method]. In E. Saarinen (Ed.), Sairaan ja vammaisen lapsen hyvä elämä The good life of the sick and disabled child] (pp. 134–143). Helsinki: Oy Edita Ab.

Ritterfeld, U. (1993). Das Rätsel Paul. Möglichkeiten einer systematischen beobachtung der eltern-kind interaktion Paul, the problem: Possibilities of a systematic observation of parent-child interaction]. *L.O.G.O.S. interdisziplinar, 1*(1), 18–25.

Ritterfeld, U., & Franke, U. (1994). Die Heidelberger Marschak-Interaktionsmethode The Heidelberg Marschak Interaction Method]. Stuttgart: G. Fischer.

Safarjan, P. T. (Winter 1992). Use of the Marschak Interaction Method (MIM) in forensic evaluation. *Theraplay Institute Newsletter, 3.*

Stern, D. N. (1985). *The interpersonal world of the infant: A view from psychoanalysis and developmental psychology.* New York: Basic Books.

Talen, M. R., & Warfield, J. R. (1997). Guidelines for family wellness checkups in primary health care services. In L. VandeCreek, S. Knapp, and T. L. Jackson, (Eds.), *Innovations in clinical practice: A source book* (Vol. 15, pp. 311–322). Sarasota, FL: Professional Resource Exchange.

Witten Whitten (*sic*)], M. R. (1994). Assessment of attachment in traumatized children. In B. James (Ed.), *Handbook for treatment of attachment-trauma problems in children* (pp. 28–49). New York: Lexington Books.

Chapter 13

"GOING TO THE STORE": AN OBSERVATIONAL MEASURE OF PARENT-CHILD INTERACTIONS FOR PRESCHOOLERS

Jean E. Dumas and Peter J. LaFreniere

The Grocery Store Game (GSG) is an informal play technique designed to evaluate the quality of parent-child interactions through direct observation. The GSG takes less than 30 minutes to administer. The technique is based on a laboratory task developed by Gauvain and Rogoff (1989) to assess various aspects of a child's functioning, such as the nature and development of collaborative and planning skills. We have adapted this task for use with preschoolers and relied on it in several studies to compare and contrast mother-child relationships in functional and dysfunctional dyads (Dumas & LaFreniere, 1993; Dumas, LaFreniere, Beaudin, & Verlaan, 1992; Dumas, LaFreniere, & Serketich, 1995; LaFreniere & Dumas, 1992). In these studies, children had been independently rated prior to their participation in the GSG as socially competent, average, anxious-withdrawn, or angry-aggressive by their preschool teachers on the basis of the Social Competence and Behavior Evaluation (SCBE; LaFreniere & Dumas, 1995). We have also used the GSG to assess the impact of intervention with dysfunctional children (LaFreniere & Capuano, 1997). This chapter describes the GSG and its administration, and summarizes the data obtained in group studies of functional and dysfunctional dyads. These studies show how the technique can be used to obtain both molecular and molar data relevant to a comprehensive understanding of the strengths and vulnerabilities of a child's early relationships. The chapter closes with the presentation of two brief case studies—one of a socially competent, the other of an anxious child—that illustrate the usefulness of the GSG in diagnostic and intervention work with young children.

Research described in this chapter was supported by grants from the Social Sciences and Humanities Research Council of Canada to Jean E. Dumas and Peter J. LaFreniere and from the Medical Research Council of Canada to Jean E. Dumas. The authors wish to thank Pierrette Verlaan, Louise Beaudin, Catherine Gosselin, and France Capuano for their major contributions to data collection.

THE GAME

The GSG consists of planning an efficient route through a miniature grocery store. The store, built initially by the authors for research purposes, is laid out as a three-dimensional board game on a 71 × 61-cm table, which a 3- to 4-year-old can reach easily while standing. Fifty-six miniature items of general use are arranged on six shelves on each side of three rows and on four shelves along the inside of the store's outer walls. Items, which are commercially sold plastic toys or actual items of daily use, are grouped in categories: vegetables (5 items), baked goods (7), candy (4), pasta and sauce (3), meat and fish products (6), fruit (6), cereals and dried goods (6), toiletries (10), and dairy products (9) (see Figure 13–1).

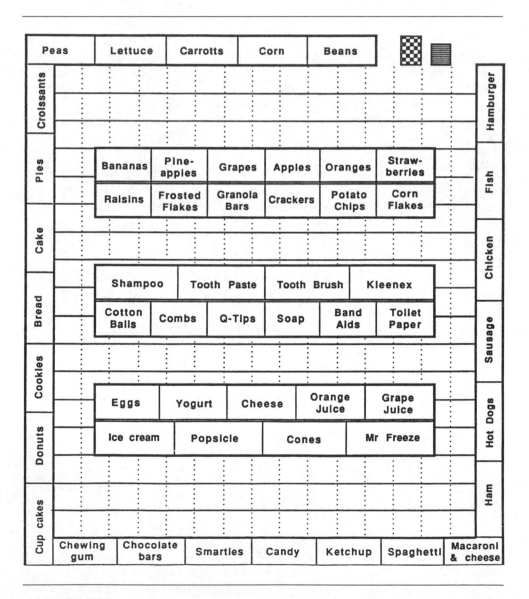

Figure 13–1.   Grocery Store Game.

A trained assistant introduces child and parent to the game through instructions and modeling. Instructions are kept brief and always addressed to the child directly. The child is informed that he or she has been invited to go shopping in the assistant's special store and that the purpose of the game is to find all the items that appear on shopping lists he or she will receive. The child is immediately given a small toy shopper (which matches his or her gender) and a practice shopping list consisting of three 8×12-cm cards with easily identifiable pictures of items available in the store. We have found that most children aged 3 and older understand these instructions readily. In practice, actually, the challenge can be to insure that the child listens to all the instructions before beginning, as most children find the game very attractive and want to play immediately. After receiving the toy shopper and the practice list, the child is asked to move the shopper through the store to "buy" each item on the list, while abiding by three rules: (1) make the shopper take the shortest path to the item; (2) do not allow the shopper to fly over the store to reach an item; and (3) do not allow the shopper to buy items not on the shopping list. Following this practice, the assistant clarifies instructions or provides additional information if needed. The assistant then gives the child different lists of five items each for up to five separate trials, but makes no further intervention except to verify that the child recognizes all five items on the list before each new shopping trip. After each list is completed, the child checks out the groceries using a toy register. Parents are instructed to assist the child as needed for the first three shopping trips, but not to complete the task for the child. After completion of three trips, or after 18 minutes if three trips have not been completed, the assistant asks the parent to complete a different task at an adjacent table (e.g., fill out a questionnaire). The child is asked to continue the grocery task alone, with the understanding that at any time the parent may assist the child, or the child may ask the parent for help. Children then complete two shopping trips alone or work on the task for six minutes, whichever comes first.

COMPARISON OF FUNCTIONAL AND DYSFUNCTIONAL DYADS USING THE GROCERY STORE GAME

The nature of the data collected with the GSG reflects the clinician or researcher's purpose. Depending on the extent to which data collection is structured, the game can be used to collect qualitative descriptions of parent-child interactions, to complete behavior-rating scales, or to quantify detailed aspects of the parent-child relationship. In most of our studies, we have relied on videotapes of the GSG to obtain either molecular or molar measures of mother-child interactions. We summarize the results of these studies here, focusing first on the molecular measures that can be obtained using the GSG.

Our molecular measures are based on the INTERACT coding and software systems (for details see Dumas, 1987; Dumas & LaFreniere, 1993). These measures summarize comparable clusters of mother and child behaviors: (a) positiveness consists of laughter, helping, approving, and affectionate behaviors; (b) positive affect consists of expressions of positive emotions (e.g., words of endearment, affectionate gestures) that accompany any coded behavior; (c) aversiveness consists of critical, punishing, disapproving, or aggressive behaviors, and of intrusive/coercive commands; (d) aversive affect consists of expressions of aversive emotions (e.g., loud or sarcastic tone of voice) that accompany any coded behavior; (e) command consists of clearly stated requests or instructions with which the person can immediately comply or refuse to comply; (f) compliance consists of compliance within 10 seconds with a preceding command; and (g) noncompliance consists of active refusal to comply within 10 seconds with a preceding command.

The INTERACT measures can be used to compute *overall proportions* or *base rates* of occurrence of each behavior cluster. Overall proportions are percentages that address questions such as: Of all behaviors mother directed at child, how many were positive in nature? These measures can be used also to calculate *conditional probabilities* of occurrence of specific behavior cluster combinations to assess the extent to which mothers and children responded contingently to each other's immediately preceding (i.e., within 15 seconds) behaviors and matched each other's affect. Conditional probabilities provide measures of the extent to which specific criterion acts were sufficient to facilitate or inhibit specific target acts. For example, given that "child complies to mother" is the criterion act and that "mother positive to child" is the target act, a high conditional probability indicates that instances of child compliance tend to be followed by maternal positiveness (i.e., that mother tends to be positively responsive to child compliance). Similarly, a low probability indicates that instances of child compliance are rarely followed by maternal positiveness (i.e., that mother tends to be unresponsive to compliance). Details of these measures can be found in Dumas and LaFreniere (1993).

As stated above, we have used the GSG to evaluate mother-child interactions in socially competent, average, anxious-withdrawn, and angry-aggressive dyads. In all our studies, these dyads were formed on the basis of independent teacher ratings of the children's functioning in a preschool setting. With parental permission, teachers completed the *Social Competence and Behavior Evaluation* (SCBE, LaFreniere & Dumas, 1995) on children in their class. This 80-item rating scale provides measures of social competence and emotional and behavioral dysfunction via scores on three factors: Social Competence, Internalizing Problems (or Anxiety-Withdrawal), and Externalizing Problems (or Anger-Aggression) (see Table 13–1). The first factor summarizes a broad range of items that assess the posi-

Table 13–1. SCBE-preschool edition: An overview of basic and summary scales

Basic Scales		Content Domain
Negative Pole	**Positive Pole**	
Depressive	Joyful	Overall Emotional Adjustment (Items 1–30)
Anxious	Secure	
Angry	Tolerant	
Isolated	Integrated	Social Interactions with Peers (Items 31–60)
Aggressive	Calm	
Egotistical	Prosocial	
Oppositional	Cooperational	Social Interactions with Adults (Items 61–80)
Dependent	Autonomous	

Summary Scales	
Social Competence	Summarizes items of all eight positive poles
Internalizing Problems	Summarizes items of four negative poles (i.e., Depressive, Anxious, Isolated, and Dependent)
Externalizing Problems	Summarizes items of the remaining four negative poles (i.e., Angry, Aggressive, Egotistical, and Oppositional)
General Adaptation	Summarizes all 80 items

tive qualities of a child's adaptation, rather than specific behavioral competencies. The second factor summarizes anxious, depressed, isolated, and withdrawn behaviors, while the third factor summarizes angry, aggressive, selfish, and oppositional behaviors. Each factor contains items tapping affective (e.g., sad, worries, doesn't smile or laugh) and social (e.g., remains apart, inactive, watches others play, defiant when reprimanded) characteristics involving peers or adults. Children are described as socially competent, average, anxious-withdrawn, or angry-aggressive as a function of their combined scores on these three factors (see Dumas & LaFreniere, 1993; LaFreniere & Dumas, 1995).

A comprehensive psychometric study (LaFreniere et al., 1992) showed that interreliability of the three SCBE factors was uniformly high (.86, .85, .83), as were internal consistency (Cronbach's alpha .92, .90, .85) and two-week test-retest reliability (.86, .82, .78). Concurrent and discriminant validity of the SCBE was established by direct comparisons with the extensively validated Child Behavior Checklist-Teacher Report Form (Achenbach & Edelbrock, 1981) and by the demonstrated ability of all three factors to differentiate a clinical from a normative sample.

Table 13–2 presents selected base rates and conditional probabilities of maternal responding to child behavior and of child responding to maternal behavior for four groups of socially competent (SC), average (AV), anxious-withdrawn (AW), and angry-aggressive (AA) dyads (N = 120; n = 30 in each group; for complete report see Dumas & LaFreniere, 1993). As this table illustrates, the GSG yields data that reflect meaningful group differences. Mothers in the competent and average groups responded to their children in a coherent fashion, matching their behavior to the immediately preceding child behavior, as they responded with positive behavior or affect to child positive behavior, positive affect, or compliance. High levels of maternal reciprocity were particularly evident in the interactions of competent dyads. Mothers of competent children matched their children's behaviors and affective expressions, praised compliance, and disapproved of noncompliance. In contrast, mothers of aggressive children tended to be indiscriminate in their responses to their children, failing to reliably reinforce positiveness or disapprove of noncompliance, and responding both positively and aversively to aversiveness and compliance. Mothers of anxious children displayed a pattern of negative reciprocity, responding to their children's conduct in exclusively aversive ways. They ignored child positiveness and positive affect but matched child aversiveness and aversive affect and punished or disapproved of both compliance and noncompliance.

Like their mothers, competent and average children generally responded in a coherent fashion, matching their behavior to the immediately preceding maternal behavior. They responded positively to maternal positive behavior or affect, and aversively to maternal aversive behavior or affect. There were two exceptions to this pattern: competent children were positive in response to their own mothers' aversiveness, and average children were aversive in response to their own mothers' positiveness. Aggressive and anxious children generally behaved like their counterparts. They responded positively to their mothers' positive behavior or affect, and aversively to their mothers' aversive behavior or affect. However, anxious children exhibited higher base rates and conditional probabilities of aversive behavior and affect than all other children.

The study just described provided strong evidence that the data collected with the GSG are transactional in nature, reflecting the long-standing nature of the mother-child relationship rather than a narrow snapshot of their immediate interactions. Specifically, in the same

Table 13–2. Molecular analyses: Base rates and conditional probabilities of mother and child responsiveness in four groups of dyads

	Mother Behavior Toward Child $p(A)^1$ $p(A/B)$			Child Behavior Toward Mother $p(A)$ $p(A/B)$		
Positiveness/positiveness						
SC	.093	.153	1.79*	.024	.110	10.08***
AV	.089	.170	2.10*	.018	.081	7.73***
AA	.092	.146	1.32	.016	.056	5.12***
AW	.087	.132	1.18	.019	.105	8.52***
Positive affect/positive affect						
SC	.224	.430	6.05***	.060	.142	8.09***
AV	.193	.330	3.64***	.046	.118	6.73***
AA	.217	.461	5.35***	.036	.096	7.19***
AW	.236	.297	.87	.022	.075	6.33***
Positiveness/compliance (reported for mothers only)						
SC	.099	.144	2.66**			
AV	.081	.107	1.94*			
AA	.082	.142	4.99***			
AW	.063	.054	−.84			
Positiveness/aversiveness						
SC	.094	.105	.34	.024	.062	2.26*
AV	.090	.092	.05	.020	.006	−1.22
AA	.076	.144	2.68**	.018	.023	.50
AW	.056	.065	.52	.019	.022	.39
Aversiveness/aversiveness						
SC	.039	.081	2.03*	.039	.137	4.54***
AV	.067	.184	4.45***	.036	.110	4.98***
AA	.065	.154	3.73***	.039	.131	6.35***
AW	.161	.351	7.11***	.067	.175	8.25***
Aversive affect/aversive affect						
SC	.031	.087	2.62**	.033	.127	3.71***
AV	.077	.172	2.84**	.034	.098	3.83***
AA	.049	.176	4.16***	.012	.063	3.49***
AW	.179	.313	3.32***	.046	.151	9.28***
Aversiveness/compliance (reported for mothers only)						
SC	.027	.038	1.09			
AV	.051	.080	2.62**			
AA	.058	.112	5.23***			
AW	.128	.165	2.29*			
Aversiveness/noncompliance (reported for mothers only)						
SC	.050	.312	4.74***			
AV	.075	.222	3.75***			
AA	.064	.029	−.82			
AW	.165	.383	6.04***			

Note: SC = socially competent, AV = average, AA = angry-aggressive, and AW = anxious-withdrawn.
[1] p(A) corresponds to the base rate of A (e.g., maternal positiveness), and p(A/B) corresponds to the conditional probability of A given that B occurred in the immediately preceding 15 seconds (e.g., maternal positiveness given child compliance).
*p <.05; **p < .01; ***p < .001.

study, we compared the interactions of the four groups of children not only with their own mother but also with a mother they had never met before. Summarizing briefly, this comparison showed that competent and average dyads generally acted with reciprocity, whether mother or child were playing the GSG with a familiar or unfamiliar partner. This was not true of anxious and aggressive dyads, however. In interactions with their own but not with unfamiliar children, mothers of aggressive children were characterized by patterns of indiscriminate responsiveness, and mothers of anxious children by patterns of aversive responsiveness. Aggressive and anxious children behaved most often like their competent and average peers in interactions with their own mothers, but generally ignored, rejected, or were ambivalent toward unfamiliar mothers. These findings have important conceptual and methodological implications. Conceptually, they are consistent with a transactional perspective which assumes that, regardless of individual mother or child characteristics, the relationship with the primary caregiver may serve as an essential source of support or stress in social development and adaptation in the preschool years. Methodologically, they show that the GSG provides a useful tool to assess the complexity of this relationship.

CLINICAL OUTCOME ASSESSMENTS
USING THE GROCERY STORE GAME

After using the GSG and INTERACT successfully to differentiate functional and dysfunctional groups of mother-child dyads, we used the GSG to develop a very different observational rating scheme (for complete report see LaFreniere & Capuano, 1997). Unlike a molecular approach based on the analysis of base rate and conditional probabilities, this new scheme relied on behavioral rating scales designed to capture similar qualities of mother-child interaction at a molar level. This corresponds to a shift in level of analysis from interaction to relationship, reflecting our general hypothesis that many emotional problems of young children are best conceptualized as relationship disturbances (Dumas & LaFreniere, 1995; Emde, 1989; Sroufe, 1989, Sroufe & Fleeson, 1986). In this view, a child's affective and behavioral symptoms are assumed to be strongly influenced by ongoing difficulties of the caregiver (in particular, the mother) that alter the quality of the mother-child relationship. If this is true, it follows that by effectively addressing those maternal difficulties one may alleviate the symptoms observed in the child.

This hypothesis was tested and the behavioral rating scales developed within the framework of an intervention study that incorporated an experimental design in order to address issues of causality and direction of effects. This study focused on the alleviation of anxious-withdrawn symptoms in preschool children. Specifically, we (1) targeted a group of mothers, not on the basis of their symptomatology (e.g., depressed mothers), but on the basis of the emotional and behavioral problems displayed by their children outside the home (i.e., in a preschool setting); (2) conducted a multifaceted intervention specifically for these mothers, but without directly intervening with the children; and (3) evaluated outcome by assessing the children's adjustment in the preschool classroom. The six-month experimental intervention incorporated treatment components from attachment, attributional, and social learning perspectives. It was designed to (1) increase the mother's understanding of the developmental needs of her preschool child; (2) promote parenting competence in terms of sensitivity to these needs; (3) alleviate parenting stress; and (4) provide social support. We hypothesized that the level of maternal involvement in the therapeutic process would be positively related to adaptive maternal functioning at outcome, assessed by pre-post behavioral measures of mother-child interaction in the GSG. Most importantly, we predicted also that intervention would result in an increase in the child's social competence and in a reduction of emotional and behavioral problems in the preschool. As the preschool teachers were blind to the children's group membership (experimental vs. control group) and there was no direct intervention in the preschool classroom, we view this type of design as capable of generating strong scientific evidence for the potency of transactional processes in early affective disorders and for the possibility of bringing about change by focusing on the child's primary relationships.

Children who participated with their mothers were recruited in the course of a comprehensive evaluation of the socioemotional adjustment of children attending preschool on a regular basis. Relying on SCBE teacher ratings, a sample of 43 anxious-withdrawn children (23 girls, 20 boys) were selected from a large sample of French-Canadian preschoolers recruited from 74 different preschool classrooms in the Montreal Metropolitan area. Children ranged in age from 31 to 70 months, with a mean age of 53.4 months. Subjects were divided into two equivalent groups matched on child age and gender, maternal age, education, and marital status, family income, and child's SCBE evaluation. Only children whose scores were 1.0 s.d. or higher above the mean on the anxious-withdrawn scale of the SCBE were recruited. From a total of 137 children evaluated as anxious-withdrawn, 43 (31.4%) of the mothers consented to participate in the study and 42 completed the intervention.

Experimental and control groups were assessed on a battery of measures at six-month intervals. The experimental group received an intensive six-month intervention, while the control group did not. All subjects were assessed via direct observational ratings of maternal warmth and discipline and child motivation/cooperation during the GSG, and teacher ratings of competence and anxious-withdrawn behavior in preschool using the SCBE.

Behavioral Rating Scales

Three seven-point scales were developed to assess the mother-child dyad during their interactions in the GSG. The development of these scales and of their scoring procedures was based in part on rating scales developed earlier by Matas, Arend, and Sroufe (1978) to score mother-toddler interactions in a problem-solving situation expressly designed to surpass the child's independent problem-solving ability. The first two scales assessed maternal behavior involving (1) emotional support, and (2) appropriate control or direction of the child during the task, while the third scale assessed the child's level of motivation and participation in the task. Mother and child had to meet two criteria to obtain a high score on these measures. For the mother to receive a high score on emotional support, the two major criteria were (a) expressing positive affect and approval in a responsive, contingent manner, and (b) providing appropriate, well-timed support and encouragement. Low scores reflected apathetic, indifferent, irritable, sarcastic, or denigrating behavior toward the child. A high score on appropriate control involved (a) proactive control, such as issuing coherent demands and requests, and appropriately structuring the task for the child, and (b) reactive control, such as effectively redirecting the child's attention or deescalating minor conflicts or frustrations. Low scores reflected either ineffectual, under-control involving the absence of limit setting when needed, or harsh, punitive overcontrol, involving rigid, excessive demands leading to conflict escalation. The child's level of motivation reflected (a) enthusiasm for the task, including interacting with the mother as expressed in rapid engagement, and expressions of positive affect and pleasure, and (b) interest, including exploration of the materials, questions and comments, persistence of on-task behavior, and spontaneous reinvolvement following difficulties or distractions.

A team of three experienced observers (two advanced graduate students and a faculty researcher) trained for two months to systematize the scoring of the videotapes. All observers were blind to the status of the mother-child dyads. Interrater agreement was based on the entire data set, as two different observers working independently at different times scored each videotaped session. Percentage agreement ranged from 71% to 85% across the three scales with an average agreement of 75% (for more detailed information see LaFreniere & Capuano, 1997).

Treatment Program

A detailed description of the treatment program can be found in LaFreniere and Capuano (1997). Briefly stated, the program was a 20-session, home-based intervention involving reading, discussion, role-playing, and supervision at regular intervals. Trained home visitors delivered the intervention. It proceeded in four phases:

Phase 1: Assessment of maternal and family characteristics, and of mother-child interactions (1 lab visit, 2 home visits). This phase, which included the GSG, resulted in a comprehensive assessment of each family.

Phase 2: Caregiver-focused education on child developmental needs (3 home visits). This educational phase was structured by a set of readings dealing with basic developmental and parenting issues. These readings were based on five booklets published in French and English by Health and Welfare Canada (1991) and addressed to parents. These booklets, which were provided to all families on a complimentary basis, provided the basis for regular, one-hour discussions.

Phase 3: Determination of family-specific objectives (2 home visits). Working with the mother, the home-visitor elaborated a list of specific intervention objectives, including personal and parenting concerns, and situations that the mother targeted as particularly challenging with her child. Each mother could ask for assistance in any particular area of her relationship with her child. However, the home-visitors relied on a core set of activities and objectives with all mothers in the program, such as child-directed play sessions (Speltz, 1990), parenting skills training (Blechman, 1985), and the use of the GSG videotape of the mother's interaction with her child during the laboratory visit for illustration and discussion of effective and ineffective parenting.

Phase 4: Realization of the intervention plan. Beginning with the ninth visit (and lasting to the 19th) each visit was divided into 3 half-hour periods dealing with the following general concerns: (1) principles of child-directed interaction during mother-child play; (2) problem behavior modification and parenting skills training; and (3) building a more effective network of social support.

Results of this comprehensive, six-month home intervention were generally positive. The most important findings indicate that anxious-withdrawn preschool children whose mothers participated in the home-intervention showed significant improvements over the control children as assessed through teacher ratings of their adaptation in the preschool (see Table 13–3). As teachers were blind to each child's group membership and there was no direct intervention in the preschool classroom, we view this finding as strong evidence of the potency of transactional processes underlying early affective disorders, and of the possibilities of change stemming from a focus on the child's primary relationships.

Further evidence concerning the processes underlying these treatment effects comes from the use of our behavioral rating scales by observers who were also blind to each dyad's group membership (see Table 13–3). It is unclear from these data to what extent characteristic patterns of maternal warmth were modified by our intervention. However, it is clear that the mother's degree of controlling and intrusive parenting behaviors was responsive to a combination of: (1) providing information about developmental issues in early childhood, (2) insight on attributional processes affecting a parent's emotional response to child unresponsiveness, and (3) training in child-centered interactions for parents who are prone to be intrusive and overcontrolling in interaction with their preschooler.

As Table 13–3 shows, the intervention was probably also responsible for changes in the child's behavior assessed with the GSG, even though intervention was explicitly not directed at the child. Specifically, results show a positive change in the child's level of motivation toward sustaining positive and cooperative interchanges with the parent during the game. This result is consistent with our previous research using conditional probability analyses of child responsiveness summarized above. In general, anxious-withdrawn children exhibited a high degree of reciprocity with their caregiver in positive behavior and affective expression (and in aversive behavior and affective expression), matching their mother's immediately preceding behavior or affect. It follows that any successful modification of the mother's behavior is likely to produce comparable changes in her child's behavior and, at a molar level, to be reflected by a positive change in the child's level of motivation.

Taken together, the results summarized above show that, whether one focuses on molecular or molar analyses, the GSG provides a useful tool to assess the quality of the mother-child relationship in preschool children, and to evaluate changes in this relation-

Table 13–3. Molar analyses: Treatment and control group scores on assessment measures at outcome

	Treatment (n=21)		Control (n=21)		
	X	SD	X	SD	t
Teacher ratings					
Social competence	113.1	28.5	91.7	30.7	1.99*
Anxiety	73.9	12.2	61.7	11.4	1.60
Behavioral ratings					
Maternal emotional support	4.17	1.6	3.62	0.9	1.35
Maternal appropriate control	4.57	1.4	3.30	1.2	3.10**
Child motivation	4.98	1.3	4.12	1.3	1.99*

*$p < .05$; **$p < .01$.

ship as a function of intervention. We turn now to two case studies, which contrast the interactions of a socially competent and of an anxious child with their mothers during the GSG. These studies provide a narrative description of the task and illustrate in a more qualitative manner the richness of the data the game can yield.

CASE STUDIES

Hannah, a Socially Competent Child

Hannah is a 4-year, 9-month-old child who attends a private day-care program. She is the younger of two children. According to her mother, Hannah has always been a healthy, outgoing "happy-go-lucky" little girl, who is well adjusted at home and school. Hannah's father is an electrical engineer for a local telephone company. Her mother is a part-time nurse.

Results of the SCBE completed by Hannah's teacher confirm the mother's positive evaluation of her daughter. Briefly stated, her SCBE profile, presented in Figure 13–2, shows that Hannah is well adjusted in the preschool setting, where she displays a level of social and emotional competence that is significantly higher than what would be expected of most children her age. She is a warm, affectionate child, whose cheerful disposition is greatly appreciated by adults and peers alike. She is a positive leader in the class, where she often organizes games with other children and models appropriate conduct in group activities.

Hannah completed the GSG with her mother. She walked into the testing room holding to her mother's hand and immediately noticed the game. "Mom, look! Can I play?" Mother acknowledged her child's enthusiasm and redirected her to wait patiently for the instructions. Hannah listened to the assistant carefully, but always with an eye of anticipation on the store and, as soon as she was allowed to play, declared loudly: "We're going to have fun!" She gave the practice list to her mother, instructing her to fan the cards out like playing cards and set out with determination to shop for each item one by one. Her mother watched attentively, but allowed Hannah to play alone, praising her once and reminding her another time that the toy shopper was not allowed to fly. "You're right. I forgot! I was in a rush."

The child completed the next three lists in the same, efficient manner, but rapidly turned the task into a very active game. First, she asked her mother to play the role of the cashier and pretended to pay for her purchases with imaginary money while commenting on each item. Mother complied readily, addressing her daughter as if she were a customer and asking her questions about her family. At the third list, the child changed roles, asking her mother to do the shopping as she wanted to be the cashier. Her mother again complied, but started to test Hannah by attempting to buy things that were not on the list or by pretending that she was a whining child who wanted ice-cream. This gave rise to considerable joy and laughter, as the child taught her mother how to play the game properly, but only after she had told her firmly, fists on her hips and looking at her directly: "Now please don't whine! You know you can't have the ice-cream, it's not on the list. So don't whine!"

Hannah completed the last two shopping trips without any difficulty. Pretending that the toy shopper was now her playmate, she continued the game she had started with her mother, talking aloud as she used different voices for herself and the toy.

SCBE Profile Peter J. LaFreniere, Ph.D., and Jean E. Dumas, Ph.D. **GIRLS**

Published by
WPS WESTERN PSYCHOLOGICAL SERVICES
Publishers and Distributors
12031 Wilshire Boulevard
Los Angeles, California 90025-1251

Child's Name Hannah

ID XX

Date of Evaluation 6/9

BASIC SCALES

Raw Scores	%	≤2			5				10					20			30			40		
	T	≤30	31	32	33	34	35	36	37	38	39	40	41	42	43	44	45	46	47	48	49
49	Depressive	0–21	22	23	24	25	26	27	28	29	30	31	32	33	34		35	36		37	38
46	Anxious	0–21	22	23	24	25	26	27		28	29	30	31		32	33	34	35		36	37
45	Angry	0–14	15	16	17–18	19	20–21	22–23	24	25	26	27	28	29	30–31	32	33	34	35		36
49	Isolated	0–17	18	19–20	21	22	23	24	25	26	27	28	29	30	31	32	33	34		35	36
49	Aggressive	0–17	18	19–20	21	22	23–24	25	26–27	28	29		30	31	32	33	34		35	36	
46	Egotistical	0–14	15	16	17	18	19–20	21	22	23–24	25	26	27	28	29	30	31	32	33		34
49	Oppositional	0–19	20–21	22	23	24	25–26	27–28	29–30	31	32	33	34		35	36	37	38	39	40	41
47	Dependent	0–16	17–18	19	20	21–22	23	24	25	26	27	28–29	30		31	32	33	34	35		36
	T	≤30	31	32	33	34	35	36	37	38	39	40	41	42	43	44	45	46	47	48	49

%	50		60				70		80					90							≥98	%
T	50	51	52	53	54	55	56	57	58	59	60	61	62	63	64	65	66	67	68	69	≥70	T
Depressive	39		40	41	42		43	44		45	46		47			48		49			50	Joyful
Anxious	38		39	40	41	42	43		44		45		46		47		48			49	50	Secure
Angry	37	38	39	40		41	42		43		44	45			46	47			48		49–50	Tolerant
Isolated	37	38	39		40	41	42		43	44		45	46		47		48			49	50	Integrated
Aggressive	37	38		39		40	41		42	43			44		45		46			47	48–50	Calm
Egotistical	35		36	37	38		39	40	41		42		43	44		45		46		47	48–50	Prosocial
Oppositional		42	43		44		45	46		47		48		49					50			Cooperative
Dependent	37	38	39		40	41	42	43		44		45		46		47			48		49–50	Autonomous
T	50	51	52	53	54	55	56	57	58	59	60	61	62	63	64	65	66	67	68	69	≥70	T

SUMMARY SCALES

Raw Scores	%	≤2			5				10					20			30			40		
	T	≤30	31	32	33	34	35	36	37	38	39	40	41	42	43	44	45	46	47	48	49
189	Difficulty with Social Competence	0–65	66	67–69	70–71	72–73	74–76	77–81	82–85	86–88	89–92	93–96	97–99	100–103	104–108	109–112	113–115	116–118	119–122	123–126	127–130
96	Excessive Internalizing Problems	0–47	48–50	51–53	54–55	56–58	59–60	61	62–63	64–65	66–68	69–70	71	72–73	74–75	76	77	78–79	80	81	82
95	Excessive Externalizing Problems	0–37	38–40	41–44	45–47	48–54	55–58	59–61	62–65	66–67	68–70	71	72–73	74–76	77	78–79	80–81	82	83–84	85	86
380	Difficulty with General Adaptation	0–184	185–188	189–195	196–200	201–206	207–209	210–215	216–220	221–231	232–238	239–242	243–251	252–258	259–263	264–269	270–276	277–281	282–286	287–291	292–297
	T	≤30	31	32	33	34	35	36	37	38	39	40	41	42	43	44	45	46	47	48	49

%	50		60				70		80					90							≥98	%
T	50	51	52	53	54	55	56	57	58	59	60	61	62	63	64	65	66	67	68	69	≥70	T
Difficulty with Social Competence	131–133	134–136	137–139	140–142	143–146	147–149	150–153	154–156	157–159	160–161	162–163	164–167	168–170	171–173	174–175	176–178	179–180	181–183	184	185	186–200	Success with Social Competence
Excessive Internalizing Problems	83–84	85	86	87	88	89	90		91–92		93	94	95	96		97		98			99–100	No Excessive Internalizing Problems
Excessive Externalizing Problems	87–88	89	90	91	92		93	94	95		96		97		98			99			100	No Excessive Externalizing Problems
Difficulty with General Adaptation	298–302	303–309	310–312	313–317	318–322	323–327	328–330	331–335	336–338	339–341	342–344	345–348	349–353	354–357	358–361	362–363	364–366	367–369	370–371	372–375	376–400	Success with General Adaptation
T	50	51	52	53	54	55	56	57	58	59	60	61	62	63	64	65	66	67	68	69	≥70	T

Figure 13–2. Hannah's SCBE profile.

Mark, an Anxious Child

Mark is a 5-year-old boy who attends a church-run kindergarten. His teacher completed the SCBE, on which she described him as anxious and oppositional (see Figure 13–3 for Mark's SCBE profile). She confirmed this assessment in an informal discussion, explaining that Mark was usually a somber child who smiled little and appeared tense, but who was prone to unexplained outbursts of anger and temper tantrums. He was not aggressive toward other children then, but was very challenging to staff, refusing to follow instructions or to participate in group activities, and regularly disrupting the class by his noisy outbursts. He was very difficult to calm or console when upset, and would "hold grudges for a very long time," making himself and others "miserable" in the process, according to his teacher.

Mark lives with his mother and stepfather, and has a younger sister. His mother works as a postal clerk. His stepfather is disabled and cannot work. Mark has no contact with his father.

Although described as anxious and oppositional at school, Mark presented a predominantly anxious picture during the GSG. He followed his mother into the testing room, looking attentively around him but showing no obvious sign of anxiety. He walked to the game table slowly and sat on a small chair, which he moved to a corner. He did not smile, but listened carefully to the instructions, looking back and forth at his mother and the assistant. "That's easy," he said, as the assistant handed him the practice cards. His mother interrupted immediately. "Not so fast, young man!" She took the cards from him and arranged them in a row on a nearby chair, explaining to the assistant: "I'd better take care of them or he'll mess up."

Mark completed the practice list from memory, carefully checking that each item corresponded to the pictures on the cards once he had all of them. He placed the items he had collected on the toy register and told the assistant he had paid for them and was ready for another list. He completed the next three lists in the same, efficient manner, but going through the motions of the task rather than enjoying it. He talked little, only asking his mother from time to time if the items he was collecting were on the list. His mother sat a few feet away from the table, watching her son but looking bored. She interacted with him only to answer his questions, to remind him of the rules (e.g., when he made the shopper fly), or to arrange each new shopping list on the chair beside her.

Mark completed the last two shopping lists in silence, as his mother answered a questionnaire at a nearby table. He worked more slowly than before, at times almost in slow motion, taking care to place each item he had collected beside its corresponding card, before informing the assistant, "I'm done," and returning to sit on the chair in which he had sat at the beginning of the game. He was very cooperative throughout the task but, unlike so many children we have observed in the GCG, showed little interest and took no obvious pleasure in the game.

CONCLUSION

The GSG is an informal play technique that has several characteristics that should be of interest to clinicians and researchers alike: (1) It is an easy task that takes little time to

SCBE Profile Peter J. LaFreniere, Ph.D., and Jean E. Dumas, Ph.D. **BOYS**

Published by
wps WESTERN PSYCHOLOGICAL SERVICES
Publishers and Distributors
12031 Wilshire Boulevard
Los Angeles, California 90025-1251

Child's Name Mark

ID XX Date of Evaluation 10/26

BASIC SCALES

Raw Scores		≤30	31	32	33	34	35	36	37	38	39	40	41	42	43	44	45	46
	%	≤2			5				10				20			30		
	T	≤30	31	32	33	34	35	36	37	38	39	40	41	42	43	44	45	46
22	Depressive	0-20	21	22	23	24	25	26	27		28	29	30	31	32	33	34	
12	Anxious	0-20	21	22	23	24	25		26	27	28		29	30	31	32	33	34
22	Angry	0-10	11	12	13-14	15-16	17	18	19	20	21-22	23	24-25	26	27	28-29	30	31
37	Isolated	0-15	17	18	19	20	21	22	23	24	25	26	27	28	29	30	31	32
27	Aggressive	0-12	13	14	15	16-17	18	19	20	21	22-23	24	25-26	27	28	29	30	31
25	Egotistical	0-12	13	14	15-16	17		18	19	20-21	22	23	24	25	26	27	28	
19	Oppositional	0-14	15-16	17	18	19-20	21-22	23	24-25	26	27	28-29	30	31	32	33	34	35
24	Dependent	0-18	19	20	21		22	23	24-25	26	27		28	29	30	31	32	33
	T	≤30	31	32	33	34	35	36	37	38	39	40	41	42	43	44	45	46

Raw Scores	47	48	49	50	51	52	53	54	55	56	57	58	59	60	61	62	63	64	65	66	67	68	69	≥70	
%	40			50		60			70			80					90							≥98	%
T	47	48	49	50	51	52	53	54	55	56	57	58	59	60	61	62	63	64	65	66	67	68	69	≥70	T
22 Depressive	35	36		37	38	39	40		41	42		43	44	45			46		47		48			49-50	Joyful
12 Anxious		35	36	37	38		39	40	41	42	43		44	45		46		47		48		49		50	Secure
22 Angry		32-33	34	35	36	37	38	39		40	41		42		43		44	45	46		47		48	49-50	Tolerant
37 Isolated	33	34	35	36	37	38		39	40		41	42	43	44	45		46		47		48			49-50	Integrated
27 Aggressive	32	33	34	35	36		37	38		39	40		41	42		43	44		45		46			47-50	Calm
25 Egotistical	29	30	31	32	33	34	35		36	37	38		39	40		41	42		43			44		45-50	Prosocial
19 Oppositional	36	37	38	39	40	41		42	43	44	45		46		47			48		49				50	Cooperative
24 Dependent	34		35	36	37	38		39	40	41		42	43		44	45		46		47		48		49	Autonomous
T	47	48	49	50	51	52	53	54	55	56	57	58	59	60	61	62	63	64	65	66	67	68	69	≥70	T

SUMMARY SCALES

Raw Scores		≤30	31	32	33	34	35	36	37	38	39	40	41	42	43	44	45	46
	%	≤2			5				10				20			30		
	T	≤30	31	32	33	34	35	36	37	38	39	40	41	42	43	44	45	46
73	Difficulty with **Social Competence**	0-56	57-58	59-60	61-64	65-66	67-68	69-71	72-74	75-77	78-81	82-84	85-88	89-92	93-97	98-101	102-105	106-109
48	Excessive **Internalizing Problems**	0-52	53-54	55	56	57-58	59-60	61-62	63	64-65	66-67	68	69	70	71-72	73	74-75	76-77
67	Excessive **Externalizing Problems**	0-33	34	35-36	37-39	40-43	44-47	48-49	50-52	53-55	56-58	59-62	63-66	67-69	70-71	72-73	74-75	76-77
188	Difficulty with **General Adaptation**	0-169	170-173	174-177	178-181	182-187	188-194	195-199	200-206	207-211	212-220	221-225	226-232	233-238	239-245	246-251	252-257	258-262
	T	≤30	31	32	33	34	35	36	37	38	39	40	41	42	43	44	45	46

Raw Scores	47	48	49	50	51	52	53	54	55	56	57	58	59	60	61	62	63	64	65	66	67	68	69	≥70	
%	40			50		60			70			80					90							≥98	%
T	47	48	49	50	51	52	53	54	55	56	57	58	59	60	61	62	63	64	65	66	67	68	69	≥70	T
73 Social Competence	110-112	113-115	116-119	120-123	124-126	127-131	132-133	134-137	138-141	142-144	145-148	149	150-153	154-158	159-161	162-164	165-167	168-171	172-174	175-178	179-180	181	182-184	185-200	Success with **Social Competence**
48 Internalizing Problems	78	79	80	81	82-83	84	85	86-87	88	89	90	91	92	93	94	95		96	97		98		99	100	No Excessive **Internalizing Problems**
67 Externalizing Problems	78	79-80	81-82	83-84	85	86-87	88	89	90	91	92		93	94	95		96		97			98		99-100	No Excessive **Externalizing Problems**
188 General Adaptation	263-269	270-273	274-278	279-284	285-291	292-295	296-302	303-307	308-313	314-318	319-323	324-327	328-333	334-337	338-342	343-346	347-353	354-355	356-358	359-360	361-364	365-368	369-370	371-400	Success with **General Adaptation**
T	47	48	49	50	51	52	53	54	55	56	57	58	59	60	61	62	63	64	65	66	67	68	69	≥70	T

Figure 13–3. Mark's SCBE profile.

administer. (2) It is a nonthreatening task that most young children and their mothers find engaging and pleasurable. (3) It can be used to collect different types of data. (4) It can yield data that differentiate clearly and meaningfully between functional and dysfunctional mother-child dyads. Most importantly for our overall purpose, we have found the GSG to be an effective tool for recreating the relationship dynamics that are characteristic of mothers and their children during the preschool years. Whether one chooses to focus on molecular or molar analyses, the GSG provides an effective and convenient means of assessing the quality of the mother-child relationship, and yields data that predict the child's adjustment across settings. The choice of whether to use a discrete behavioral analysis tool, such as the INTERACT system, or more integrative clinical rating scales obviously depends on the purpose of the study and on the resources and inclinations of the users. Either observational scheme is relatively labor intensive, compared to the demands of scoring a single questionnaire or of taking qualitative, summary notes of the mother's and child's behavior during the game. An important advantage of a molecular approach is that relatively high interobserver agreement can be attained by using narrow-band categories of discrete behaviors. Such categories enable users to quantify the precise behavioral contingencies operating within a dyad and offer a powerful means of documenting differences between groups of dyads, as our research has demonstrated. However, because of their relatively narrow focus, molecular analyses may not offer the most valid means of assessing differences between dyads, or changes within dyads over time as a function of intervention or development. A molar approach, because of its broader focus, may be more useful for understanding how dyads change from one assessment period to another. However, the cost of relying on integrative ratings of behavior is typically a reduction in the level of interobserver agreement on such ratings when compared to molecular categories of behavior. But this cost may be offset by an increase in the predictive validity of the data obtained. In general, specific, low-inference observations tend to have high interobserver agreement, but may lack predictive validity (Sroufe, 1989)). In light of this principle, we are presently working on the development of integrative analyses of relationship quality (e.g., lack of positive reciprocity in behavior or affect) that attempt to combine the advantages of both molecular and molar approaches. And we intend to continue using the GSG in this work.

REFERENCES

Achenbach, T. M., & Edelbrock, C. S. (1981). Behavioral problems and competencies reported by parents of normal and disturbed children aged four through sixteen. *Monographs of the Society for Research in Child Development, 46*(1).

Blechman, E. A. (1985). *Solving behavior problems at home and at school.* Champaign, IL: Research Press.

Dumas, J. E. (1987). INTERACT—A computer-based coding and data management system to assess family interactions. In R. J. Prinz (Ed.), *Advances in behavioral assessment of children and families* (Vol. 3, pp. 177–202). New York: JAI Press.

Dumas, J. E., & LaFrenière, P. J. (1993). Mother-child relationships as sources of support or stress: A comparison of competent, normative, aggressive, and anxious dyads. *Child Development, 64,* 1732–1754.

Dumas, J. E., & LaFrenière, P. J. (1995). Relationships as context: Supportive and coercive interactions in competent, aggressive, and anxious mother-child dyads. In J. McCord (Ed.), *Coercion and punishment in long-term perspectives* (pp. 9–33). New York: Cambridge University Press.

Dumas, J. E., LaFreniere, P. J., Beaudin, L., & Verlaan, P. (1992). Mother-child interactions in competent and aggressive dyads: Implications of relationship stress for behavior therapy with families. *New Zealand Journal of Psychology, 21,* 3–13.

Dumas, J. E., LaFrenière, P. J., & Serketich, W. J. (1995). "Balance of power": A transactional analysis of control in mother-child dyads involving socially competent, aggressive, and anxious children. *Journal of Abnormal Psychology, 104,* 104–113.

Emde, R. N. (1989). The infant's relationship experience: Developmental and affective aspects. In R. N. Emde, & A. J. Sameroff (Eds.), *Relationship disturbances in early childhood* (pp. 33–51). New York: Basic Books.

Gauvain, M., & Rogoff, B. (1989). Collaborative problem solving and children's planning skills. *Development Psychology, 25,* 139–151.

LaFreniere, P. J., & Capuano, F. (1997). Preventive intervention as a means of clarifying direction of effects in socialization: Anxious-withdrawn preschoolers. *Development and Psychopathology, 9,* 551–564.

LaFreniere, P. J., & Dumas, J. E. (1992). A transactional analysis of early childhood anxiety and social withdrawal. *Development and Psychopathology, 4,* 385–402.

LaFreniere, P. J., & Dumas, J. E. (1995). *Social Competence and Behavioral Evaluation (SCBE).* Preschool edition. Los Angeles, CA: Western Psychological Services.

LaFreniere, P. J., Dumas, J. E., Capuano, F., & Dubeau, D. (1992). The development and validation of the Preschool Socioaffective Profile, *Psychological Assessment: A Journal of Consulting and Clinical Psychology, 4,* 442–450.

Matas, L., Arend, R., & Sroufe, L. A. (1978). Continuity of adaptation in the second year. The relationship between quality of attachment and later competence. *Child Development, 49,* 547–556.

Speltz, M. L. (1990). The treatment of preschool conduct problems: An integration of behavioral and attachments concepts. In M. T. Greenberg, D. Cicchetti, & E. M. Cummings (Eds.), *Attachment in preschool years* (pp. 399–426). Chicago, IL: University of Chicago Press.

Sroufe, L. A. (1989). Relationships, self and individual adaptation. In R. N. Emde, & A. J. Sameroff (Eds.), *Relationship disturbances in early childhood* (pp. 70–94). New York: Basic Books.

Sroufe, L. A., & Fleeson, J. (1986). Attachment and the construction of relationships. In W. Hartup, & Z. Rubin (Eds.), *Relationships and development* (pp. 51–71). Hillsdale, N.J.: Erlbaum.

PART IV

FAMILY PLAY ASSESSMENTS

Increasingly, clinical work with children has spread to include the family, both diagnostically and in treatment. It seems only natural that family therapists have begun to acknowledge the need for evaluative procedures that include all family members with particular interest in systems and dynamic interchanges. Family therapy has provided a fertile basis for the development of new techniques. Recognizing the attractiveness and comprehensive applicability of play, family clinicians have utilized this milieu in developing a fascinating range of methods to be used in the assessment process.

This section provides a sampling of techniques including some very structured and standardized approaches as well as others that are more informal. In this way, they offer the clinician many choices that will be able to meet the needs and fit the opportunities available in most assessment situations.

Thomas Gehring and Julie Page offer the strongly researched and standardized technique known as the Family Systems Test (FAST). This fascinating measure provides a concrete picture of how each member perceives the family from a typical, ideal, and conflictual perspective. Providing a clear description of the technique and the accompanying rating scales, this chapter enables the reader to easily appreciate the depth of material that becomes available. The strong statistical properties of the FAST add to its attractiveness for researchers, clinicians, and forensic evaluators.

Gavin Smith's chapter, reprinted from the 1991 edition, thoroughly describes the Collaborative Drawing Technique (CDT), a creative tool for family assessment. Noting the need for family-oriented methods of evaluation, especially those that "encourage the participation of children," Smith presents this diagnostic instrument as a graphic way of viewing the functioning of the family. Because this task involves a sequential and collective effort with each member contributing to a single drawing, it highlights both the emotional and the interactive factors in the family dynamics. Clinical material provides the reader with some idea of the significant information that can be gleaned from this technique as well as its easy adaptability to most mental health settings.

Steve Harvey offers an extensive examination of several formal and informal family play assessment tasks that can be used to identify critical issues such as a family's emotional resourcefulness. Using a combination of active game, dramatic, and drawing tasks, Harvey demonstrates how, in a clinical setting, a family's interactions reveal practical material that can lead to a clear formulation of their problems as well as to recommendations for treatment interventions. These techniques, easily introduced to the family group, add to the clinician's understanding of interaction styles, relationship variables, and emotional strengths of the family. Simple to administer and relatively nonthreatening to the family members, this procedure should prove to be a ready addition to any clinician's assessment repertoire.

Drawing on a broad theoretical base, Gary Stollak, Anat Barlev, and Ioanna Kalogiros present an overview of family interactions and their relevance to child behavior. In particular, they review salient material on attachment theory, parenting styles, family structure and dynamics, and the concept of boundaries as a basis for evaluating family interactions. Offering a number of structured and unstructured approaches to family observation and recognizing the significance of different family constellations, these authors present a variety of tasks appropriate for families with younger (preverbal), as well as older children. Finally, they describe a structured rating scheme for assessing family as well as individual behaviors. This system, the Clinical Rating Scales (CRS), enables the observer to move from behavioral observation into the evaluation of such constructs as family cohesion, adaptability, and communications. A promising technique for family play evaluations, this instrument is particularly attractive in that it can be applied to a variety of situations. This, therefore, enables the clinician to obtain samples across a wide range of behaviors that occur in different settings. It is rare to find such flexibility backed up by a clear and useful rating procedure. This should be very appealing to clinicians favoring a family therapy model as well as to those investigating questions of problematic family interactions such as abuse or separation-attachment disorders.

Assessment of the family system, while similar to the evaluation of parent-child interactions, must also provide a range of experiences that encompasses more than just dyadic interaction. In both formal and informal ways, these techniques need to recognize the structural as well as systemic aspects of family organization and dynamics that contribute to and act upon children's cognitive, social, and emotional adjustment. Evaluating children within the family context can clearly provide family therapists with substantial clinical material that easily translates into therapeutic goals and that assists in the consideration of different treatment options. It is anticipated that future work on the techniques included in this section will follow the lead of the FAST by increasing the strength of their statistical characteristics.

FAMILY SYSTEM TEST (FAST): A SYSTEMIC APPROACH FOR FAMILY EVALUATION IN CLINICAL PRACTICE AND RESEARCH

Thomas M. Gehring and Julie Page

The family is an important unit with regard to its members' physical and mental health. It is well recognized that the development of family members and the organization of their relational structures are intertwined, and that both individual and environmental aspects should thus be taken into account (L'Abate, 1994; Lebow & Gurman, 1995). Therefore, family evaluation deserves the attention and involvement of professionals who work with individuals and families, either therapeutically or to prevent health problems. In particular, psychotherapists could benefit by a systematic use of family assessment methods, which should be a prerequisite for the development of a comprehensive treatment plan (Beutler & Clarkin, 1990; Kaslow, 1996). Evaluation of family functioning in clinical practice requires user-friendly and economical diagnostic tools that allow descriptions of the family from the perspective of parents and children as derived from individual and interactive interview settings (Wilkinson, 1998).

DESCRIBING FAMILY STRUCTURES

Families can be described as open and dynamic systems consisting of members with reciprocal relationships. The latter are characterized by features such as intimacy, generational differentiation, and continuity. Family structures are involved in internal and environmental changes that occur in relation to time and, thus, have a past, a present, and a future. Therefore, an important parameter for understanding family systems is the flexibility of interpersonal patterns (Rigazio-DiGilio, 1993). This can be defined as the ability to adapt relational structures to situationally and developmentally determined demands (Melito, 1985).

The FAST can be ordered from Hogrefe & Huber Publishers, P.O. Box 2487, Kirkland, WA 98083-2487, USA; phone (800) 228-3749, fax (425) 823-8324, e-mail hh@hhpub.com.

Basic Dimensions

Clinicians and researchers from various fields agree that cohesion and hierarchy are two key dimensions that describe family structures (Minuchin & Fishman, 1981; Olson, 1986). Despite divergent approaches to defining and operationalizing cohesion and hierarchy (Forman & Hagan, 1983; Combrinck-Graham, 1990), there is a basic consensus concerning the importance of these dimensions for the assessment of family and its subsystems across the life cycle (Fisher, 1976; Fisher, Giblin, & Regas, 1983; McGoldrick & Gerson, 1985).

Cohesion is generally defined as emotional bonding or attachment between family members (Bowen 1960; Stierlin, 1974; Bying-Hall & Campell, 1981; Kelsey-Smith & Beavers, 1981). The structural patterning of cohesion involves the allocation of priorities and privileges over family territories and pathways to the various subsystems (e.g., parent or parent-child subsystems). It includes the regulation of closeness and remoteness between family members and their respect of personal privacy (Broderick, 1993). In reference to family systems, the term cohesion is used to describe the extent to which family members see themselves as a coherent whole.

Hierarchy covers several fundamental theoretical assumptions and cannot be attached to a single definition (Kranichfeld, 1987; Fish, 1990). It can refer, for example, to authority, dominance, decision-making power, or the amount of influence exercised by one family member over another (Moos & Moos, 1974; Madanes, 1981; Williamson, 1981; Oliveri & Reiss, 1984; Bloom, 1985). The concept of hierarchy has also been used to study changes in the structure of roles and rules within the family (Olson, 1986; Dickerson & Coyne, 1987).

One of the major issues for the evaluation of family structures is the concept of boundaries. The construct of boundary is used to describe relations between families and their social environment as well as relations between various subsystems within the family. Family boundaries can be defined by the rules that determine who belongs to a given system or subsystem and in what way they belong to them (Liddell, Henzi, & Drew, 1987; Minuchin, 1974; Rabinowitz & Eldan, 1984). External family boundaries manifest themselves by the way that family members behave differently toward each other than they do toward outsiders. Internal family boundaries are marked by differences in the behavior among members of the different subsystems. Generational boundaries refer to the structural differences in cohesion and hierarchy between subsystems consisting of members of the same generation as well as those consisting of members of different generations such as parents and children.

Distressed and Nondistressed Families

Numerous studies have shown that distressed and nondistressed families display distinct interpersonal patterns (Lebow & Gurman, 1995). It has been demonstrated that members of healthy families are emotionally close to one another and that relations between the generations are balanced in terms of hierarchy, that is, neither egalitarian nor very hierarchical (Beavers & Voeller, 1983; Olson, Russell, & Sprenkle, 1983; Wood, 1985). In these families, parental dyads generally display a higher degree of cohesion than parent-child subsystems. There are also clear generational boundaries regarding hierarchy, in that parents have a relatively large voice in decision-making because of their experience, responsibility, and material resources (Beavers, 1985; Leigh, 1986; Wood, 1985). Furthermore, the structure of such family relations is flexible in response to developmental demands (Minuchin, 1985; Youniss & Smollar, 1985; Noller & Callan, 1986; Olson, 1986). It is also recognized that family members, in accordance with their ages, are able to express their different needs and perceptions coherently, and work toward a consensus based on common goals (Oliveri & Reiss, 1982).

Relational structures in distressed families are often characterized as either extremely centripetal (i.e., few interests outside of the family) or extremely centrifugal (i.e., little interest in the family). In terms of cohesion, clinicians distinguish between relations or ties that are either enmeshed, with few mutual boundaries, or disengaged, with few reciprocal relationships and an atmosphere of remoteness which may even lead to the expulsion of a family member (Minuchin & Fishman, 1981; Beavers & Voeller, 1983). Troubled families often display unclear generational boundaries (Haley, 1973; Madanes, 1981; Gehring, 1985). This becomes manifest in cross-generational coalitions where cohesion between a parent and a child is stronger than between the parents. There are also hierarchical reversals where the power of a child exceeds that of the parents. Moreover, the interpersonal structures are often characterized by rigid or chaotic organization (Green, Kolevzon, & Vosler, 1985; Olson, 1986). Such patterns are reflected in the difficulties that family members experience in coherently expressing their needs (Selvini-Palazzoli, 1986).

Recent years have seen a great number of studies including clinical and nonclinical samples to determine types of family functioning based on cohesion and hierarchy structures (Anderson & Gavazzi, 1990; Green, Harris, Forte, & Robinson, 1991a, b; Gehring & Marti, 1993a). In general, research has shown that psychologically distressed families have a greater tendency to show extreme values on both dimensions. While cohesion is described as low in such families, the dimension of hierarchy tends to be either high or low (Friedman, Utada, & Morrissey, 1987; Preli & Protinsky, 1988; Gehring, Marti, & Sidler, 1994). Thus, it can be assumed that while there is a linear relationship between cohesion and healthy psychosocial development, there is no such relationship with hierarchy. Accordingly, there is no empirical evidence for the hypothesis frequently heard among clinicians that "problem families" are often marked by enmeshed or very cohesive relations (Wood, Watkins, Boyle, Nogueira, Zimand, & Carroll, 1989; Green & Werner, 1996).

FAMILY ASSESSMENT DEVICES

Comprehensive family assessment calls for a particular set of clinical foci and techniques that allow the integration of developmental and phenomenological aspects into a systemic perspective as based on the hypothesized networks of family structures. However, there is still a paucity of psychometrically validated instruments that meet the requirements of clinical practice (Touliatos, Perlmutter, & Straus, 1990). According to Jameson & Alexander (1994), family measures should consider normative aspects and, at the same time, be appropriate for each case in its particular circumstances. In addition, for the planning of clinical interventions, they should be able to anticipate future family developments.

The two most commonly used methods of analyzing family relations focus on either the individual(s) or observations of family member interactions. Both approaches attempt to illuminate different aspects of the family. Neither provides a complete picture of the family dynamics. Interaction tasks that are rated according to specific observation criteria provide objective data from an outside perspective. However, because systematic analyses of interactions are time-consuming and involve a great deal of commitment of staff, these observation methods are not standard in clinical practice. For economical reasons, questionnaires that provide subjective information from a family insider perspective are more frequently used in clinical practice as well as in research. In general, these questionnaires focus either solely on the family as a whole or on selected dyads such as mother-child relations (Barnes & Olson, 1985; Olson, Portner, & Lavee, 1985) and, therefore, yield limited information on family structures. In addition, such questionnaires cannot be used with preschool children because they require independent reading skills.

It should be mentioned that any test reduces "reality" to a small number of parameters, a simplification required by working models. Furthermore, the structure of a family system cannot be fully derived from the reports of its individual members just as it is not possible to determine, in any detail, the characteristics of the family members solely by analyzing their interactions. A suitable family evaluation, therefore, ideally requires standardized test procedures that allow a quantitative and qualitative evaluation of the family constructs of parents and children as well as of their interactions in various settings (Cromwell & Peterson, 1983; Gurman, 1983; Moon, Dillon & Sprenkle, 1990; L'Abate, 1994).

Figure Placement Techniques

Figure placement techniques, providing spatial representations of family relations, allow the combined analysis of family structures based on the perceptions of parents and children, while at the same time providing standardized observations of their interactions (for a review, see Gehring & Marti, 1993b). The use of figure placement techniques in clinical practice and research has many advantages. They are simple to administer and the representations are easy to analyze both qualitatively (e.g., follow-up interview) and quantitatively (e.g., types of family structure). The family can be portrayed under various conditions (e.g., parental conflict, ideal relationships), and family members unavailable for the study (e.g., grandparents) can also be included in the portrayals. The minimum age of respondents being able to grasp the procedure is as low as 6 years (Rusch & Kuethe, 1979; Buchsbaum & Emde, 1990). An individual representation of the family takes only 5 minutes, and between 10 and 30 minutes when carried out in a group setting. This method elicits the family members' perceptions of structural patterns within the family including all of its subsystems. When used as a group task, figure placement techniques provide information derived from observation about how family members negotiate when attempting to reach a consensus (i.e., joint representation). Yet, despite their versatility and their three-decade history, figure placement techniques have only recently gained recognition as clinical and research instruments. Reasons for this delayed acceptance include imprecise test procedures and modest reliability and validity studies (Gehring & Marti, 1993b; Rigazio-DiGilio, 1993).

FAMILY SYSTEM TEST (FAST)

The FAST (Gehring, 1998) is a clinical and research tool designed to gather data from persons age 6 and older on individual and joint perceptions of the structures governing family relations in various situations. The goal of the FAST is to assess psychosocial issues in family-oriented terms and to facilitate the planning, execution, and evaluation of thera-peutic interventions. Based on structural family systems theory, the test attempts to create an instrument that is both economic and flexible in its application.

In the following sections the FAST procedure is described, including administration, scoring, and interpretation of family representations. Table 14–1 contains an outline of the fundamental concept of the FAST.

Table 14–1.   Fundamental concept of the FAST

Application	As an individual test (with respondents age 6 and over) and as a group test in research and in clinical practice
	Analysis of family structures (perception and interaction)
	Diagnosis of biopsychosocial problems
	Planning and evaluation of preventive and therapeutic interventions
Theoretical basis	Structural family systems theory
	Developmental family psychology
Underlying assumptions	Nonclinical families display balanced structures (cohesive and moderately hierarchical), and have clear generational boundaries and a flexible organization.
Test dimensions	Cohesion and hierarchy in the family and its subsystems
	Quality of generational boundaries
	Flexibility of family structures
Test material	Board (45 cm × 45 cm) with 81 squares (5 cm × 5 cm)
	Schematic male and female figures (8 cm)
	Cylindrical blocks of 3 different heights (1.5 cm, 3 cm, 4.5 cm)
Length of test	Individual test: 5–10 min.; group test: 10–30 min
Quantitative evaluation	
Cohesion	Calculation based on distances between figures on the board. Figures positioned on directly adjacent squares score maximum cohesion while larger distances reflect less cohesive relations.
Cross-generational coalition	A parent-child dyad is more cohesive than the parental dyad.
Hierarchy	Calculation based on number and height of blocks used to elevate the figures. Same height of figures indicates egalitarian power structure. The greater the difference in height, the more hierarchical the relationship.
Hierarchy reversal	The elevation of a child figure surpasses that of a parent figure.
Types of relational structures	Classification of family structures is based on a combination of cohesion and hierarchy. Both dimensions are scored as either high, medium, or low. A balanced structure refers to relations with medium or high cohesion and medium hierarchy. The other family configurations (i.e., problematic relational structures) are called either labile-balanced or unbalanced.
Levels of analysis	
Perception of the family	The structure of typical relations and the changes from typical to ideal or conflict representations (flexibility)
Differences in perception	Comparison of individual representations of different family members
	Comparison of individual representations with the group representation

(continued)

Table 14–1.   (continued)

Qualitative evaluation	
Test behavior	Order in which figures are positioned
	Changes made in the positions of the figures
	Spontaneous remarks uttered while setting up representations
	Representation of persons outside the family or omission of family members
Interaction	Observation of the family during group test (*Systemic Performance Roles in Interaction, SPRINT*)
Follow-up interview	Exploration of subjective meaning of representations (e.g., family configuration)
	Hypothetical questions about ideal family constructs
	Evaluation of conflict and/or problem-solving patterns

Before carrying out the FAST, the evaluator familiarizes the respondents with the test procedure and presents the test materials. He or she emphasizes that the portrayal of family cohesion and hierarchy reflects purely subjective perceptions and that there are no "right" or "wrong" answers. The assessor can add that family representations are similar to snapshots of a changing "reality," and that members of the same family are likely to judge their relations differently.

Test Material

The test material for the respondents includes: (1) a monochromatic square board (45 cm × 45 cm) divided into 81 squares (5 cm × 5 cm), with each square assigned to a coordinate (1/1 to 9/9); (2) 6 male and 6 female figures (8 cm); (3) 18 cylindric blocks of three different heights (1.5 cm, 3 cm, and 4.5 cm). Figure 14–1 shows a FAST representation of a five-member family.

The test material for the evaluator consists of a four-part test form[1] to document (1) anamnestic data; (2) family representations (i.e., typical, ideal, and conflict configurations); (3) the corresponding follow-up interviews, and (4) types of represented family structures.

Test Procedure[2]

To explain to the family members how cohesion is portrayed in the FAST, the assessor first places some figures close to one another and then places them farther apart while explain-

---

[1] The FAST test form for administering and scoring the typical, ideal, and conflict representations and the use of abbreviations are shown in the appendix. The cover page of the test form is used to document information on the client family including anamnestic data. The section "Family Representations" is used to enter data of (a) persons to be included in the representations; (b) family members' behavior during the test; (c) positions of figures on the board including direction in which they are facing and heights of figures, and (d) characteristics of the represented situations as derived from the follow-up interview. Categorical evaluation of relational structures in the FAST is recorded in the section "Evaluation of Relational Structures." It includes (a) type of relational structures in the representations (e.g., balanced); (b) differences between individual representations of different family members and between individual and group representations; (c) flexibility of family structures (e.g., changes from typical to conflict representations), and (d) the quality of generational boundaries.

[2] A detailed description of the FAST test instructions and the follow-up interviews to the typical, ideal, and conflict representations are provided in the appendix.

Figure 14–1.   FAST representation of a five-member family.

ing that these patterns represent different degrees of cohesion among family members. Respondents are told that they are free to use any square on the board. The evaluator then elevates the figures with blocks of various sizes and explains that the differences in the vertical position corresponds to levels of hierarchy within the family. Respondents are informed that they can use any number of blocks in any combination, or, for that matter, none at all.

To start with, respondents are asked to represent their current family relations (i.e., typical representations), in order to elicit their perception of cohesion and hierarchy in their family. When they have completed the typical representation (there are no time limits), the evaluator ascertains which family members are represented by the figures and then records the location and height of each figure in the FAST protocol. The portrayed family relations are explored with a semistructured follow-up interview. The assessor then places the figures next to the board and puts the blocks away. The respondents are asked to picture their desired family structures by placing the figures and the blocks on the board (i.e., ideal representation). After the evaluator has recorded the family configuration and completed the follow-up interview she or he proceeds to clear the board. The assessor then asks the respondents to portray the family in an important conflict (i.e., conflict representation). Following the recording of the conflict representation, the evaluator asks questions concerning the nature of the depicted situation.

The FAST can be used either with one or several family members individually, as a family task, or in any combination thereof. Supplementary test protocols can be used according to the number of family members to be tested.

Scoring the FAST

Cohesion scores are derived from distances between figures and hierarchy scores from differences between the elevation of figures. Cohesion and hierarchy scores can be calculated for the family as a unit as well as for its subsystems. There are two ways to score these two FAST dimensions, namely based on either an arithmetic or a categorical analysis of the family configuration.

Arithmetic Evaluation

In order to distinguish the distance between figures on adjacent squares and the one between diagonally opposed squares, the Pythagorean formula is used. Thus, the distance between figures on adjacent squares is scored 1 and on diagonally adjacent squares 1.4. The maximum dyadic distance score possible on the board is 11.3 (i.e., the diagonal corner squares). In order to generate cohesion scores (as opposed to distance scores) each of the distance scores is subtracted from 12. Cohesion scores thus range from 0.7 to 11. The higher scores indicate increased cohesiveness in the perceived family relations.

Hierarchy scores are derived from the number and size of the blocks used to elevate the figures with growing differences indicating increasingly marked hierarchies. A height difference of zero between two figures means that the relationship is perceived as egalitarian. For cross-generational dyads the height of the child figures is subtracted from the height of each parent figure. Positive scores thus mean that the parents are more powerful than the children.

Categorical Evaluation

Cohesion and hierarchy in the family are classified according to the three categories low, medium, or high. Family cohesion is scored high if all figures are placed in adjacent squares, and medium if they are located within a 3×3 square area. Family cohesion is scored low if one or more figures are placed outside a 3×3 square area. A "cross-generational coalition" is indicated if the parent relationship is less cohesive than any one of the parent-child dyads.

Evaluation of family hierarchy is based on the height difference between the less-elevated parent figure and the most-elevated child figure. It is scored low if the difference is less than a small block, medium if it is a small or middle-sized block, and high if it is a large block or more. The constellation of a child figure being higher than a parent figure is called "reverse hierarchy."

Patterns of cohesion and hierarchy scores are grouped into three types of family structures. "Balanced" indicates a family structure that is medium or highly cohesive and medium hierarchical. A structure with medium-level cohesion and low or high-level hierarchy, or with low cohesion and medium hierarchy is considered "labile-balanced." A family structure is called "unbalanced" if both dimensions show extreme values.

Interpretation

When setting up the representations, respondents are actively involved in a process of reflection and awareness. This is manifested in verbal and nonverbal behavior, and observing this process is useful for generating clinical hypotheses. For the interpretation of the test behavior, it is also interesting to note the order in which the figures are positioned and any subsequent changes thereof. This can provide clues as to which family members are considered central by the respondents or how clearly the positions in the family are defined. For example, omission of family members (e.g., father) or inclusion of persons outside the family (e.g., friends or acquaintances) often occur among divorced families.

A comprehensive interpretation of family representations should always consider quantitative-structural and qualitative-subjective aspects. The former allow economical comparisons of the different perspectives of the various family members or of a single family member at different points in time according to general structural criteria. The latter are necessary to determine specific family structures and their significance for the respondents. When interpreting test results, it is important to integrate information from the representations with the spontaneous remarks and answers provided by the respondent in the follow-up interviews. In other words, a consensus-oriented exchange of information between respondents and evaluator can provide significant data for the systemic interpretation of family constructs.

PSYCHOMETRIC PROPERTIES OF FAST

In order to establish psychometric properties of the FAST, individual and joint representations were studied (Gehring & Feldman, 1988; Feldman, Wentzel & Gehring, 1989). Analysis of individual representations included four criteria: (1) independence of cohesion and hierarchy dimensions, (2) relationships between family and subsystem representations, (3) test-retest reliability, and (4) convergent and discriminant validity as assessed by the Family Cohesion and Adaptability Scale (FACES III; Olson, Portner, & Lavee, 1985) and the Family Environment Scale (FES; Moos & Moos, 1974) as external criteria. Analysis of FAST representations of multiple members of the same family included comparisons of (a) individual representations of different family members, (b) individual and group representations and (c) patterns of family interaction and portrayed relationships.

Table 14–2 provides an overview of the psychometric properties of the FAST in individual and family settings. The data are based on representations of typical family relations by nonclinical respondents from the San Francisco Bay Area. Because no significant differences were found between representations of male and female respondents the results are not broken down according to gender. The same applies to family size and ethnic background.

Results indicate that the FAST has adequate psychometric properties. For example, test-retest stability of FAST scores was similar to that of two commonly used family functioning measures (i.e., FACES and FES). Furthermore, cohesion and hierarchy scores from the FAST representations were correlated with comparable dimensions of the FACES and FES. Evidence for convergent validity could also be demonstrated by the fact that the representation of cohesion and hierarchy with the FAST correlated with observed family functioning. The finding that there were no significant correlations between the representations of members from the same family indicates that one cannot a priori assume that information from one family member is similar to or can serve as a proxy for information from another family member.

Clinical Discriminant Validity

This section presents the main findings on differences between FAST representations of nonclinical respondents and members of families attending a child psychiatric outpatient clinic (Gehring & Marti, 1993a; Gehring, Candrian, Marti, & Real del Sarte, 1996).

Table 14–2.   Psychometric properties of the FAST[a,b,c]

Criteria	Description		
Sample			
Parents, children, and adolescents (11–21 years)	29% parents, 41% children, 30% adolescents of middle-class families from the San Francisco Bay Area ($N = 598$)		
Family status	66% intact families, 34% single-parent or blended families		
Ethnic composition	70% Caucasians, 14% Asians, 10% Hispanics, 6% African-Americans		
Independence of test dimensions			
Cohesion and hierarchy		Family level	Dyad level
Parents ($N = 168$)		$r = .08$	r's = .00 – .06
Children and adolescents ($N = 430$)		$r = .16$	r's = .11 – .17
Reliability			
Test-retest stability (1 week)		Family level	Dyad level
Children in 6th grade ($N = 137$)	Cohesion	$r = .63$	$r = .47$
	Hierarchy	$r = .63$	$r = .65$
Adolescents from 9th to 12th grades ($N = 28$)	Cohesion	$r = .87$	$r = .73$
	Hierarchy	$r = .83$	$r = .75$
Validity			
Convergent validity: FACES III and FES as external validation criteria ($N = 267$)[d]	FAST (family level)		
		Cohesion	Hierarchy
FACES III "Cohesion"/"Adaptability"		$r = .47$	$r = .21$
FES "Cohesion"/"Control"		$r = .49$	$r = .27$
Discriminant validity: FACES III and FES as external validation criteria ($N = 267$)[d]	*For adolescents.* (Children's representations show significant correlation coefficients between conceptually different dimensions.)		
Convergent validity: Family interaction as external validation criteria ($N = 55$)	Group representations of cohesion correlate with family functioning as rated by independent clinicians ($r = .30$)		
Within-family comparisons			
Relationship between representations of different dyads ($N = 598$)		Cohesion r's = .18 – .35	Hierarchy r's = .28 – .57
Relationship between representations of dyads and entire family ($N = 598$)		Cohesion r's = .47 – .95	Hierarchy r's = .04 – .85
Relationship between individual representations of different family members ($N = 165$)	Representation of cohesion and hierarchy by fathers, mothers, and their children do *not* correlate significantly		
Relationship between individual representations ($N = 165$) and group representations ($N = 55$)	Representation of cohesion and hierarchy by parents correlate more strongly and consistently with the group representation than those of their children (r's = .01 – .45)		

[a] Data for typical FAST representations.
[b] Scoring of FAST is based on arithmetic calculations; family cohesion and hierarchy scores are averages of all dyad scores.
[c] Spearman rank correlations (r's describe minimum and maximum correlation coefficients).
[d] Children and adolescents.

Results are based on individual representations of typical, ideal, and conflict situations by parents and children of the two groups. Scoring of the representations focused on the family level and included arithmetic and categorical procedures. Table 14–3 shows that the FAST demonstrated significant clinical discriminant validity for typical representations by parents and children. In eight out of nine comparisons, the clinical and nonclinical samples differed in their family perceptions, with the only exception of mothers with healthy children and with psychiatric patients who were all likely to show relatively low cohesion. In other words, convergent with predictions from structural family theory, clinical respondents were more likely than nonclinical ones to report their family structures as unbalanced. As one might expect, members of clinical families also significantly more often indicated unclear generational boundaries (i.e., cross-generational coalitions and reverse hierarchies) than their counterparts. The ideal family representations yielded only one significant difference between the clinical and nonclinical group. Fewer child psychiatric patients portrayed their desired family relations as cohesive than did their healthy counterparts. The conflict representations of both groups were characterized by unbalanced family structures with unclear generational boundaries.

Analysis of representations from members of the same family (i.e., intrafamily comparisons) revealed that members of clinical families, contrary to nonclinical respondents, agreed on their perceptions of the structure of current relationships. Finally, the type of children's mental disorder as assessed by ICD-10 (WHO, 1989) was unrelated to the portrayal of family structures.

CHANGING FAMILY CONSTRUCTS ACROSS TREATMENT

The following sections focus on the application of the FAST for therapy evaluation. Changes in family constructs of parents and children during the course of child psychiatric therapy in two different settings are presented.

Residential Child Therapy

Gehring, Brägger, Steinebach, and Wössmer (1995) studied how family constructs of school-aged psychiatric patients change in the context of hospitalization. The residential

Table 14–3. **Differences between FAST family scores of nonclinical respondents and members of families attending a child psychiatric outpatient clinic[a,b]**

Respondent	Typical Representation			Ideal Representation			Conflict Representation		
	Cohesion	Hierarchy	TFS[c]	Cohesion	Hierarchy	TFS[c]	Cohesion	Hierarchy	TFS[c]
Father	**	**	**	ns	ns	ns	ns	ns	ns
Mother	ns	**	**	ns	ns	ns	ns	ns	ns
Children[d]	**	**	**	**	ns	ns	ns	ns	ns

[a] ** = significant difference between clinical and nonclinical samples.
[b] ns = no difference between clinical and nonclinical samples.
[c] TFS = Type of family structures (i.e., combination of cohesion and hierarchy dimensions).
[d] The results also hold good for siblings of patients.

treatment of the patients—who all had multiple severe disorders as measured by ICD-10 (WHO, 1989)—also included family therapy.

Using FAST, the children were asked at the onset of the inpatient therapy to represent their family structures as they perceived them currently and how they were prior to entering the clinic. Three months after the patients had left the clinic they were again asked to represent the family as they perceived them prior to entering the clinic and at the beginning of their hospitalization as well as how they currently perceived them. Results showed that the family structures were characterized somewhat more often as unbalanced prior to entering the clinic than at the onset of the hospitalization at the first point of assessment. The follow-up investigation revealed that the patients judged their current family relations predominantly as balanced and therefore as improved. This finding also correlated with the evaluation of the therapeutic outcome by the clinicians and the parents. However, the children's representations of the family before and at the onset of their hospitalization at the follow-up indicated less often unbalanced patterns than at the first point of assessment. This could indicate that the retrospective representations of family structures by the patients were influenced by their "positive" family evaluation after treatment.

Parent Therapy

This research investigated family perceptions of parents who were treated because of psychiatric problems of their offspring (Gehring et al., 1996). Families were from the middle class and had two parents with traditional role allocation. All referred children had one disorder on axis 1 to 4 and two or more problematic conditions on axis 5 as measured by ICD-10 (WHO, 1989).

The problem-solving treatment process was based on a systemic-structural model for the conceptualization of interventions with parents. The employed approach was resource oriented and aimed at improving the parenting competence of both fathers and mothers. On the basis of an analysis of their constructs based on the presenting problem and family relations, the ten-session treatment began with a discussion with the parents about their attempted changes. The therapy plan was jointly worked out, and its implementation was continuously assessed and, if necessary, modified. After completion of therapy, parents and therapists determined the utility of the employed approach and the quality of the collaboration.

In order to establish the therapeutic baseline and to evaluate the effects of the therapy on the perceived family functioning, the parents were asked to individually and jointly portray their current and ideal family relations with the FAST. The assessment included three points in time, namely at the onset of therapy, immediately after, and six months after completion of therapy. A follow-up interview was used to explore the subjective meaning of the representations for the parents. The changes that the parents aimed at were examined in light of the divergence of the typical from the ideal family representations.

Results showed that at the onset of therapy, parents individually and together considered their family structure to be mostly unbalanced and with unclear generational boundaries (i.e., cross-generational coalitions and reverse hierarchies). As predicted, after completion of the problem-solving process, reassessment indicated that the relationships were predominantly perceived as being balanced. Moreover, the parental relation was represented as cohesive and with clear generational boundaries. These changes corresponded also with the patient outcome as evaluated by the parents and clinicians (e.g., remission of target symptoms). In the follow-up, fathers more often showed balanced structures than mothers and were more likely to influence the joint portrayal, a pattern also found in non-clinical families. Analysis of ideal representations did not show significant changes over the three points of assessment. In other words, the greatest differences between current and ideal representations of the parents occurred at the onset of therapy.

SUMMARY AND CONCLUSIONS

There is a continual need for further differentiation in relational diagnosis as it applies to the prevention and therapy of biopsychosocial problems. The diagnostic consideration of the family is a useful addition to the well-recognized notions of individual risk factors and pathology. The FAST is a figure placement technique designed for clinicians and researchers who are interested in a systemic approach to individual and family development. This instrument has demonstrated good psychometric properties and construct validity for samples consisting of healthy and troubled families.

Administration and scoring of the FAST are very economical compared with other instruments that yield similar information. A significant advantage of the FAST lies in its versatility as well as its ability to trigger a process of reflection on family relations among respondents, thus facilitating diagnosis and therapy. A first evaluation of the family structure is possible right after completion of the representations. For example, it is possible to determine structural characteristics such as clarity of generational boundaries without any prior calculations. A review of the follow-up interviews and the spontaneous comments of the respondents permits the formulation of ad hoc individual- and family-oriented systemic hypotheses.

The FAST can easily be used with respondents as young as 6 years because no reading or writing skills are required. The fact that children of this age tend to be egocentric in their views must be considered when evaluating their family portrayals. Recently, it has been demonstrated that the FAST can even be used with 3- to 4-year-olds to explore specific situations and events (Morley-Williams & Cowie, in press). It is noteworthy that preschool children are generally flexible in handling the figures and focus their efforts on persons or dyads that are important to them. However, the representations help them describe a given situation in a playful and narrative manner.

A large number of different social situations can be studied with the FAST. For example, the test procedure can be modified to include different phases of current conflicts as well as past and anticipated events. In principle, the figures need not be limited to the members of the respondents' community. Sometimes respondents spontaneously include persons outside the family or even deceased family members in their set of important figures. If children of divorced or separating families are allowed a free selection of figures, they can provide interesting information regarding their identification with absent family members. In fact, these children often fail to represent the absent parent when the relationship is stressful despite regular contact with this parent.

Depending on the issues at hand, the FAST can be used either with one or several family members individually, as a group test, or in any combination thereof. The use of this tool in individual and group settings allows a comparison of the respondents' individual and shared family constructs as well as of the interactive patterns while they are working on their joint representation. Because members of nonclinical families have distinct perceptions of their interpersonal structures, an exclusive use of the FAST with a single member can only yield limited information on overall family functioning. Thus, in order to obtain a comprehensive insight into the complex dynamics of untroubled families, a combined application of the FAST with several members in individual as well as interactive settings is recommended.

It is noteworthy that clinical studies revealed that in families with an offspring who suffers from mental disorders all members agree that their current interpersonal structures are unbalanced. Moreover, it has been shown that their reports of family patterns do change across therapy. In accordance with structural family theory, after completion of individual or family treatment, parents as well as child psychiatric patients are likely to represent their relations as balanced. These findings suggest that clinicians can already obtain useful preliminary information on overall family functioning on the basis of FAST portrayals of a single family member.

Although numerous studies indicated that the structural features of the representations provide valid information about individual and family problems and resources, there are two limitations. First, neither the FAST nor other family tests have been able to establish specific relations between family patterns and categories of psychiatric disorders (Gehring & Marti, 1994; Jenkins, 1990). This suggests that medical diagnoses (i.e., standardized evaluation by experts) and patients' perceptions of family structures (i.e., subjective evaluation by family members) provide different sources of information, both of which are relevant for the planning and evaluation of clinical interventions. Second, relational structures that are suboptimal according to the criteria of structural family theory (e.g., unbalanced structures) are not necessarily related to individual or family disorders. On the other hand, respondents may present a picture of well-functioning family relations (i.e., balanced structures with clear generational boundaries) to clinicians despite serious problems in the family. Therefore, diagnosis as well as therapeutic interventions should not be solely based on the representations, but should also consider internal and external stresses on various system levels (e.g., individual, family, and extrafamilial context). However, a detailed follow-up interview can determine to what extent the representations are influenced by factors such as social desirability, or whether the problems concerned may be linked directly to the represented family structure.

The ideal representations are particularly useful for therapy planning. Clients' constructs about their ideal family relations help explore the desired changes and improve the chances of attaining such goals. Investigating the differences between typical and ideal family representations also contributes to the evaluation of the efficacy of problem-solving treatment processes. To assess therapeutic outcome, it is recommended that a series of typical and ideal representations be performed at different times during the course of therapy and after completion of the treatment.

The FAST can also be applied by clinicians to explain to the clients their own perception of the family structure as well as potential options for change. Such a procedure promotes participative-discursive planning and evaluation of therapeutic interventions. Based on these principles, the FAST can also be applied to therapist training and in supervision. Furthermore, it has proved useful to include all involved in the problem-solving treatment process in the FAST representations (i.e., family members as well as therapists). This allows a closer examination of expert-client relationships, which are important when evaluating the correspondence between the therapeutic alliance and clinical outcomes (Langewitz, Wössmer, Iseli, & Berger, 1997).

Further research on single-parent, divorced, and blended families with various ethnical backgrounds as well as the study of therapist-client relationships in distinct clinical settings will broaden our perspective on individual and interpersonal problems and help to create comprehensive models of family functioning. The versatility of the FAST might contribute toward a rapprochement between science and practice and, in consequence, promote our understanding of individual and family development.

REFERENCES

Anderson, S. A., & Gavazzi, S. M. (1990). A test of the Olson circumplex model: Examining its curvilinear assumption and the presence of extreme types. *Family Process, 29,* 309–324.

Barnes, H. L., & Olson, D. H. (1985). Parent-adolescent communication and the circumplex model. *Child Development, 56,* 438–447.

Beavers, R. W. (1985). *Successful marriage.* New York: Norton.

Beavers, R. W., & Voeller, M. N. (1983). Family models: Comparing and contrasting the Olson circumplex model with the Beavers systems model. *Family Process, 22,* 85–98.

Beutler, L. E., & Clarkin, J. F. (1990). *Systematic treatment selection.* New York: Brunner/Mazel.

Bloom, B. L. (1985). A factor analysis of self-report measures of family functioning. *Family Process, 24,* 225–239.

Bowen, M. (1960). The family as the unit of study and treatment. *American Journal of Orthopsychiatry, 31,* 40–60.

Broderick, C. B. (1993). *Understanding family process. Basics of family systems theory.* London: Sage Publications.

Buchsbaum, H. K., & Emde, R. N. (1990). Play narratives in 36-month-old children. Early moral development and family relationships. *Psychoanalytic Study of the Child, 45,* 129–155.

Bying-Hall, J., & Campell, D. (1981). Resolving conflicts in family distance regulation: An integrative approach. *Journal of Marital and Family Therapy, 7,* 321–330.

Combrinck-Graham, L. (1990). A developmental model for family systems. *Family Process, 24,* 139–150.

Cromwell, R. E., & Peterson, G. W. (1983). Multisystem-multimethod family assessment in clinical context. *Family Process, 22,* 147–163.

Dickerson, V. C., & Coyne, J. C. (1987). Family cohesion and control: A multitrait-multimethod study. *Journal of Marital and Family Therapy, 13,* 275–285.

Feldman, S. S., Wentzel, K. R., & Gehring, T. M. (1989). A comparison of the views of mothers, fathers and preadolescents about family cohesion and power. *Journal of Family Psychology, 3,* 39–60.

Fish, V. (1990). Introducing causality and power into family therapy theory: A correction to the systemic paradigm. *Journal of Marital and Family Therapy, 16,* 21–37.

Fisher, L. (1976). Dimensions of family assessment: A critical review. *Journal of Marriage and Family Counseling, 13,* 367–382.

Fisher, L., Giblin, P. R., & Regas, S. J. (1983). Healthy family functioning/goals of family therapy II: An assessment of what therapists say and do. *The American Journal of Family Therapy, 11,* 41–54.

Forman, B., & Hagan, B. J. (1983). A comparative review of total family functioning measures. *American Journal of Family Therapy, 11,* 25–40.

Friedman, A. S., Utada, A., & Morrissey, M. R. (1987). Families of adolescent drug abusers are "rigid": Are these families either "disengaged" or "enmeshed," or both? *Family Process, 26,* 131–148.

Gehring, T. M. (1985). Socio-psychosomatic dysfunctions: A case study. *Child Psychiatry and Human Development, 15,* 269–280.

Gehring, T. M. (1998). *The Family System Test.* Seattle: Hogrefe & Huber Publishers.

Gehring, T. M., Brägger, F., Steinebach, C., & Wössmer, B. (1995). Family System Test (FAST): A systemic approach to the analysis of social relationships in the clinical context. In B. Boothe, R. Hirsig, A. Helminger, B. Meier, & R. Volkart (Eds.), *Perception–Evaluation–Interpretation* (pp. 87–92). Seattle: Hogrefe & Huber.

Gehring, T. M., Candrian, M., Marti, D., & Real del Sarte, O. (1996). Family System Test (FAST): The relevance of parental family constructs for clinical intervention. *Child Psychiatry and Human Development, 27,* 55–65.

Gehring, T. M., & Feldman, S. S. (1988). Adolescents' perceptions of family cohesion and power: A methodological study of the Family System Test. *Journal of Adolescent Research, 3,* 33–52.

Gehring, T. M., & Marti, D. (1993a). The Family System Test: Differences in perception of family structures between nonclinical and clinical children. *Journal of Child Psychology and Psychiatry and Allied Disciplines, 34,* 363–377.

Gehring, T. M., & Marti, D. (1993b). The architecture of family structures: Toward a spatial concept for measuring cohesion and hierarchy. *Family Process, 32,* 135–139.

Gehring, T. M., & Marti, D. (1994). Debate and argument: Children's family constructs and classification of mental disorders: Different measurement approaches may yield different results. *Journal of Child Psychology and Psychiatry and Allied Disciplines, 35,* 551–553.

Gehring, T. M., Marti, D., & Sidler, A. (1994). Family System Test (FAST): Are parents' and children's family constructs either different or similar, or both? *Child Psychiatry and Human Development, 25,* 125–138.

Green, R. J., Harris, R. N., Forte, J. A., & Robinson, M. (1991a). Evaluating FACES III and the circumplex model: 2440 families. *Family Process, 30,* 55–73.

Green, R. J., Harris, R. N., Forte, J. A., & Robinson, M. (1991b). The wives data and FACES IV: Making things appear simple. *Family Process, 30,* 79–83.

Green, R. J., Kolevzon, M. S., & Vosler, N. R. (1985). The Beavers-Timberlawn Model of family competence and the Circumplex Model of family adaptability and cohesion: Separate, but equal? *Family Process, 24,* 385–398.

Green, R. J., & Werner, P. D. (1996). Intrusiveness and closeness-caregiving: Rethinking the concept of family "enmeshment." *Family Process, 35,* 115–136.

Gurman, A. S. (1983). Family therapy research and the "new epistomology." *Journal of Marital and Family Therapy, 9,* 227–234.

Haley, J. (1973). Strategic therapy when a child is presented as the problem. *Journal of the American Academy of Child and Adolescent Psychiatry, 12,* 641–659.

Jameson, P. B., & Alexander, J. F. (1994). Implications of a developmental family systems model for clinical practice. In L. L'Abate (Ed.), *Handbook of Developmental Psychology and Psychopathology* (pp. 392–411). New York: Wiley.

Jenkins, H. (1990). Annotation: Family therapy—developments in thinking and practice. *Journal of Child Psychology and Psychiatry and Allied Disciplines, 31,* 1015–1026.

Kaslow, F. W. (Ed.) (1996). *Handbook of relational diagnosis and dysfunctional family patterns.* New York: Wiley.

Kelsey-Smith, M., & Beavers, R. W. (1981). Family assessment: Centripetal and centrifugal family systems. *The American Journal of Family Therapy, 9,* 3–12.

Kranichfeld, M. L. (1987). Rethinking family power. *Journal of Family Issues, 8,* 42–56.

L'Abate, L. (1994). *Family evaluation.* London: Sage.

Langewitz, W., Wössmer, B., Iseli, J., & Berger, W. (1997). Psychological and metabolic improvement after an outpatient teaching program for functional intensified insulin therapy (FIT). *Diabetes Research and Clinical Practice, 37,* 157–164.

Lebow, J. L., & Gurman, A. S. (1995). Research assessing couple and family therapy. *Annual Review of Psychology, 46,* 27–57.

Leigh, G. K. (1986). Adolescent involvement in family systems. In G. K. Leigh & G. W. Peterson (Eds.), *Adolescents in families* (pp. 38–72). Cincinnati: South-Western.

Liddell, C., Henzi, S. P., & Drew, M. (1987). Mothers, fathers and children in an urban park playground: A comparison of dyads and triads. *Development Psychology, 23,* 262–266.

Madanes, C. (1981). *Strategic family therapy.* San Francisco: Jossey-Bass.

McGoldrick, M., & Gerson, R. (1985). *Genograms in family assessment.* New York: Norton.

Melito, R. (1985). Adaptation in family systems: A developmental perspective. *Family Process, 24,* 89–100.

Minuchin, P. (1985). Families and individual development: Provocations from the field of family therapy. *Child Development, 56,* 289–302.

Minuchin, S. (1974). *Families and family therapy.* Cambridge: Harvard University Press.

Minuchin, S., & Fishman, H. C. (1981). *Family therapy techniques.* Cambridge: Harvard University Press.

Moon, S. M., Dillon, D. R., & Sprenkle, D. H. (1990). Family therapy and qualitative research. *Journal of Marital and Family Therapy, 16,* 357–373.

Moos, R., & Moos, B. S. (1974). *Family Environment Scale (FES).* Palo Alto: Consulting Psychologists Press.

Morley-Williams, C., & Cowie, H. (in press). Methodological considerations of using the FAST with three to four year olds. In T. M. Gehring, M. Debry, & P. K. Smith (Eds.), *The Family System Test: Clinical and research applications.* London: Routledge.

Noller, P., & Callan, J. (1986). Adolescent and parent perceptions of family cohesion and adaptability. *Journal of Adolescence, 9,* 97–106.

Oliveri, M. E., & Reiss, D. (1982). Families' schemata of social relationships. *Family Process, 21,* 295–311.

Oliveri, M. E., & Reiss, D. (1984). Family concepts and their measurement: Things are seldom what they seem. *Family Process, 23,* 33–48.

Olson, D. H. (1986). Circumplex Model VII: Validation studies and FACES III. *Family Process, 25,* 337–351.

Olson, D. H., Portner, J., & Lavee, Y. (1985). FACES III. In D. H. Olson, H. I. McCubbin, H. Barnes, A. Larsen, M. Muxen, & M. Wilson (Eds.), *Family Inventories* (pp. 7–42). St. Paul: Family Social Science, University of Minnesota.

Olson, D. H., Russell, C. S., & Sprenkle, D. H. (1983). Circumplex Model of marital and family systems: I. Cohesion and adaptability dimensions, family types and clinical application. *Family Process, 18,* 3–28.

Preli, R., & Protinsky, H. (1988). Aspects of family structures in alcoholic, recovered, and nonalcoholic families. *Journal of Marital and Family Therapy, 14,* 311–314.

Rabinowitz, A., & Eldan, Z. (1984). Social schemata of Israeli children on measures of distance and height in dyad and family placements. *The Psychological Record, 34,* 343–351.

Rigazio-DiGilio, S. A. (1993). The Family System Test (FAST): A spatial representation of family structure and flexibility. *American Journal of Family Therapy, 21,* 369–375.

Rusch, R. R., & Kuethe, J. L. (1979). Measuring the social schemata of preschool children. *Psychological Report, 44,* 265–266.

Selvini-Palazzoli, M. (1986). Toward a general model of psychotic family games. *Journal of Marital and Family Therapy, 12,* 339–349.

Stierlin, H. (1974). *Separating parents and adolescents.* New York: Quadrangle.

Touliatos, J., Perlmutter, B. F., & Straus, M. A. (1990). *Handbook of family measurement techniques.* London: Sage.

Wilkinson, I. (1998). *Child and family assessment. Clinical guidelines for practitioners.* London: Routledge.

Williamson, D. S. (1981). Personal authority via termination of the intergenerational hierarchical boundary: A "new" stage in the family life cycle. *Journal of Marital and Family Therapy, 7,* 441–452.

Wood, B. (1985). Proximity and hierarchy: Orthogonal dimensions of family interconnectedness. *Family Process, 24,* 497–507.

Wood, B., Watkins, J. B., Boyle, J. T., Nogueira, J., Zimand E., & Carroll, L. (1989). The "psychosomatic family" model: An empirical and theoretical analysis. *Family Process, 28,* 399–417.

World Health Organization (WHO), Division of Mental Health (1989). *Mental and Behavioural Disorders, ICD-10.* Geneva.

Youniss, J., & Smollar, S. (1985). *Adolescents' relations with mothers, fathers and friends.* Chicago: University of Chicago Press.

Appendix

FAST Test Instructions

The evaluator (E) demonstrates the test materials and introduces the FAST to the family members taking the test, with the following remarks:

"I would now like to explain a procedure we use for representing family relations. With this board and these figures and blocks (E shows the test material) you can show how close the members of your family are to one another and how much power or influence each member has in the family. Members of the same family usually evaluate their relations differently."

E now explains the representation of *cohesion:*

"Here are male and female figures representing the members of your family. By arranging the figures on the board, you can show how close the members of your family are to each other. You can use any of the spaces on the board."

E then places a pair of figures side-by-side on two adjacent squares on the board (minimum distance) and says:

"This means that these two members of the family have a very close relationship."

E now places the same two figures on two diagonally adjacent squares (closest distance) and then moves them apart to two diagonally opposed corners of the board (maximum distance), and says:

"The further apart you place two figures, the more emotionally distant they are to each other. Placing the figures on diagonally opposite corners of the board means that you think the relationship between these two family members is not at all close."

E now explains the way *hierarchy* is represented using the two figures already positioned on the board:

"Here are blocks of three different sizes that you can use to elevate the figures. You can use these blocks to represent the power or influence that each member has in the family. The higher a figure is placed, the more power or influence that person has in the family. You can use any number of different blocks to elevate the figures."

E demonstrates this by elevating one of the figures with the smallest block (minimum increase, smallest difference in height) and says:

"This means that both family members have relatively little power or influence, although this one has slightly more than the other (points to the respective figures). In other words there is little difference in hierarchy between the two."

E demonstrates varying differences in height between the two figures by using the different-sized blocks, and says:

"The greater the difference in height between the two figures, the more hierarchical their relation is."

E raises both figures to equal height with two of the same-sized blocks and says:

"If you place two figures at the same height, it means that their power or influence is balanced or equal."

E can now answer any questions the family members might have about the FAST.

FOLLOW-UP INTERVIEW TO FAST REPRESENTATIONS

The exploration of the *typical representation* includes the following four questions:

1. Does this representation show a specific situation? If so, which one?
2. How long have the relations been the way that you have shown them here?
3. How are the relations here different from the way they used to be?
4. What is the reason that the relations have become the way you show them here?

The exploration of the *ideal representation* includes the following five questions:

1. Does this representation show a situation that has occurred at some point? If yes, what was the situation? *(If the answer is no, omit Questions 2 and 3)*
2. How often does this situation occur and how long does it last when it does occur?
3. When did this situation first occur and when was the last time it happened?
4. What would have to happen (outside event, change in behavior, etc.) to make typical relations correspond to how you wish they were ideally?
5. How important would this be for you and the other family members?

The exploration of the *conflict representation* includes the following six questions:

1. Who is involved in this conflict?
2. What is this conflict about?
3. How often does this conflict occur and how long does it last each time it does occur?
4. When did this situation first occur and when was the last time it happened?
5. How important is this conflict for you and the other family members?
6. What roles do the different family members have in solving this conflict?

ABBREVIATIONS

B	Balanced
BO	Behavioral observation
C(1,2,3)	Child figure, child or sibling (number indicates birth order in family or household)
Co	Color of figure
CR	Conflict representation
DP	Difference in perception
Fa(T,I,C)	Family level (T=typical, I=ideal, C=conflict)
FLEX	Flexibility
FM	Family member
FM(HH)	Member(s) of the patient's or respondent's household
FM(NHH)	Family member(s) of the patient or respondent not living in the same household
GB	Generational boundary
H	Height of figure
HH	Household
InteR	Interactive representation (consensus representation of two or more family members)
IR	Ideal representation
L	Labile-balanced
M	Mother figure, mother, maternal
N(M,P)	Adult living in the same household as the patient or respondent, but who is not related to any of the family members (M=assumes function of mother, P= assumes function of father)
P	Father figure, father, paternal
Pa(T,I,C)	Parent level (T=typical, I=ideal, C=conflict)
Pat	(Index) Patient
R	Respondent
RPat	Relation to patient
Si(T,I,C)	Sibling level (T=typical, I=ideal, C=conflict)
SPRINT	Systemic performance roles in interaction (patterns of interaction during group test)
TR	Typical representation
TRS	Type of relational structure
U	Unbalanced

FAST Family System Test

Institution/Experimenter _____

Family _____

Patient/Position in family_____

Reason for consultation _____

Consultations to date: Number _____   Persons present _____

Type of sessions _____

		P	M	C1	C2	C3	
R Individual test							
R Group test							

Anamnestic data on persons living in patient's household (FM/HH)

FM	Date of birth	School/Profession	Specific illnesses	Additional information

Family members not living in patient's household (FM/NHH)

FM	Date of birth	School/Profession	Specific illnesses	Additional information

Psychological problems treated at other institutions

FM	Date	Institution	Diagnosis	Therapy

Interpretation of test results

Order # 01 262 03

Evaluation of Relational Structures

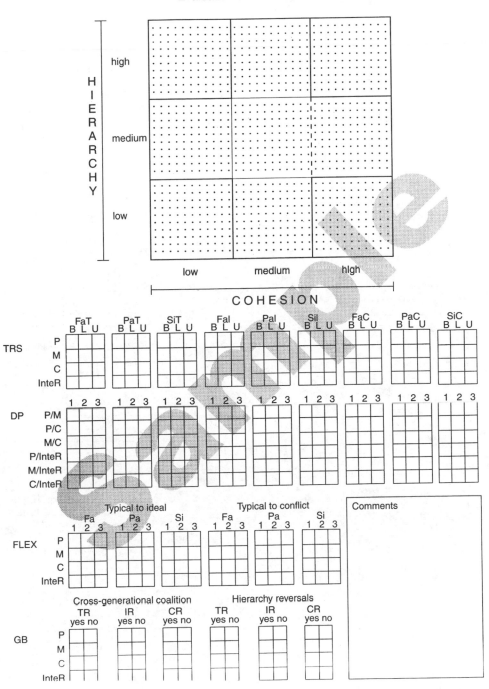

Family Representations

Name _____

Date _____

	P	M	C₁	C₂	C₃			
Figures								
RPat								
Age								
Gender								
R								

H								
Co								

Stability ☐ low ☐ high

Differences ☐ small ☐ large

Typical representation (TR)

BO/SPRINT _____
_____
_____
_____
_____

Ideal representation (IR)

H								
Co								

Situation ☐ routine ☐ special

Frequency ☐ often ☐ seldom

BO/SPRINT _____
_____
_____
_____
_____

Conflict representation (CR)

H								
Co								

Type of conflict ☐ parent ☐ parent-child
☐ sibling ☐ other

Situation ☐ routine ☐ special

Frequency ☐ often ☐ seldom

BO/SPRINT _____
_____

Comments

Follow-up Interview to Typical Representation (TR)

1. Does this representation show a specific situation? If so, which one? _____
_____
_____

2. How long have the relations been the way that you have shown them here *(stability)*? _____
_____

3. How are the relations here different from the way they used to be *(differences)*? _____
_____
_____

4. What is the reason that the relations have become the way you show them here? _____
_____
_____

5. What does the eye contact between the figures or the direction in which they are facing
mean?
_____
_____

6. Why did you replace the figure(s) you did with a colored figure(s)? _____
_____
_____

7. What personal characteristics are being represented by the color(s) you chose?
_____
_____

8. To what extent do these characteristics influence family relations? _____
_____
_____

Comments

Follow-up Interview to Ideal Representation (IR)

1. Does this representation describe a situation that has occurred at some point? If yes, what was the situation *(situation)*? _____
   _____
   _____

2. How often does this situation occur (frequency) and how long does it last when it does occur? _____
   _____
   _____

3. When did this situation first occur and when was the last time it happened? _____
   _____

4. What would have to happen to make typical relations correspond to how you wish they were ideally? _____
   _____
   _____

5. How important would this be for you and the other family members? _____
   _____
   _____

6. What does the eye contact between the figures or the direction in which they are facing mean? _____
   _____
   _____

7. Why did you replace the figure(s) you did with a colored figure(s)? _____
   _____
   _____

8. What personal characteristics are being represented by the color(s) you chose? _____
   _____
   _____

9. To what extent do these characteristics influence family relations? _____
   _____
   _____

Comments

Follow-up Interview to Conflict Representation (CR)

1. Who is involved in this conflict *(type of conflict)*? _____
   _____
   _____

2. What is this conflict about *(situation)*? _____
   _____

3. How often does this conflict occur *(frequency)* and how long does it last each time it does
   occur? _____
   _____
   _____

4. When did this situation first occur and when was the last time it happened? _____
   _____
   _____

5. How important is this conflict for you and the other family members?_____
   _____
   _____

6. What roles do the different family members have in solving this conflict?_____
   _____
   _____

7. What does the eye contact between the figures or the direction in which they are facing
   mean? _____
   _____
   _____

8. Why did you replace the figure(s) you did with a colored figure(s)? _____
   _____
   _____

9. What personal characteristics are being represented by the color(s) you chose?_____
   _____
   _____

10. To what extent do these characteristics influence family relations?_____
    _____
    _____

Comments

Chapter 15

ASSESSING FAMILY INTERACTION BY THE COLLABORATIVE DRAWING TECHNIQUE

Gavin Smith

INTRODUCTION

The collaborative drawing technique (CDT; Smith, 1985) was developed in the early 1980s in a response to a felt need to expand the scope of psychological testing. Since the beginning of the family therapy movement, circa 1952, there has been a growing awareness of the necessity for exploring the effects of both immediate and distant external factors on the functioning and development of the individual. In the earliest days of family therapy, recognition of the effect of immediate family members on the identified patient began dawning on practitioners in a variety of settings and locations. The early history of the family therapy movement is confusing and fragmented by all accounts. One effort to trace the progress of this movement suggests that "it began in a dozen places at once among independent-minded therapists and researchers in many parts of the country" (Broderick & Schrader, 1981, p. 18).

In any event, with the emergence of the family therapy movement, a new focus also developed in the area of psychological testing. Traditional individual psychological testing was intended to provide an intensive analysis of an individual's cognitive, perceptual, and emotional functioning. Such an analysis could then be used to create intervention strategies and treatment plans to address the needs of that individual. This approach was based primarily on a view of the individual as the unit of treatment. With the family therapy movement challenging this focus and asserting the importance of the family and family interaction as the unit of treatment, an alteration in the nature of psychological testing also seemed in order.

It was with this historical perspective in mind that the CDT was devised. The actual technique of the CDT is seen as a logical extension of the lengthy history of projective drawing. From Machover's pioneering work in the analysis of human figure drawings (Machover, 1949) to Hulse's original family drawing technique (Hulse, 1951), to the kinetic family drawing (KFD) work of Burns and Kaufman (1970), the development of projective drawing techniques and methodology has paralleled developments in therapy and treatment modalities.

It was the KFD (Burns & Kaufman, 1970) that most directly presaged the development of the CDT. The KFD allowed an individual to graphically portray his or her own family in action, providing significant insight into that individual's perception of family status and functioning. However, while the KFD did provide some focus on the family interaction, it remained a static and individual measure, in that it provided only the viewpoint of the individual who had completed the drawing. The intent of the CDT was to provide an interactive experience that would be simple to create and reproduce, but that would be capable of providing a wealth of complex and valuable information concerning interaction among family members.

Over the past few years, the CDT has been used by the author and several of his associates in a variety of settings and applications. The most common usage of the CDT thus far has been as an early diagnostic tool with whole families. It has typically been used during the first or second session with the family, and used as a part of the overall diagnostic process. Interestingly, in many cases, this diagnostic procedure appeared to have significant therapeutic effects; that is, on occasion, some families reportedly experienced improvements in their functioning, which they attributed to their session with the CDT.

One of the most valuable features of the CDT has been the nature in which it allows and encourages the expressive participation of children, especially younger children. It is patently obvious that adults generally have the advantage over children when verbal expression is the only avenue of communication. The use of drawings puts children in a much more equitable position in this regard; in fact, in many cases, it has seemed that children are much more adept at expressing themselves pictorially. As Klepsch and Logie observed (1982), children's drawings are particularly useful in assessing their feelings and attitudes because children are able to express thoughts and feelings in their drawings, which are beyond their capacities to communicate in speech or writing.

DiLeo (1983, p.5) has also commented on the value of children's drawings in terms of communicating feelings, stating that "Better than speech, drawings may express a subtlety of intellect and affect that is beyond the power or freedom of verbal expression." However, while it appears that children are frequently at a disadvantage in the adult world of words, adults are frequently less facile in the children's world of crayon drawing. Thus, the CDT seems to reduce the advantage that the verbally accomplished adults have over the less articulate youngsters. Still, it must always be borne in mind that while children have no adult experience on which to call, every adult has the advantage of having once been a child. In this sense, the CDT can be seen as a "communication equalizer."

THE PROCEDURE

In essence, the CDT is a structured nonverbal interactive task assigned to a family or couple and observed by a therapist. A few simple materials are necessary for the task: a selection of crayons in various colors, a sheet of 12″ by 18″ drawing paper, a stopwatch, and a chair placed in front of a table or desk on which the drawing paper can be placed. Once the materials have been assembled, the following instructions are given to the proposed participants:

> Each of you is to select one crayon with which you will be drawing. ... Now that each of you has a crayon, you will need to decide in what order you will go; so, who will go first? Second? ... (and so on, for families). Now from this moment on, there should be no talking and

no effort to communicate with each other. When I say "Start," the first person will sit in the drawing chair and begin to draw whatever they like. When I say "Next," the person drawing will stop immediately, and whoever is next will sit in the chair and begin drawing. We'll continue, in order, until I tell you to stop.

Usually, there will be questions from the participants after the instructions are given, but the therapist should politely rephrase the instructions without giving any further clarification. As quickly as possible, the task should be begun, with the first participant beginning to draw while the therapist begins timing. There is no discussion of the task until it is completed. During the first round of drawing, each person is given 30 seconds in which to work. This length of time seems to provide the individual with the opportunity to begin to draw whatever concept comes to mind but usually does not allow time to complete a drawing, thus enhancing the interactive potential of the exercise by presenting other participants with the opportunity to react to the drawings of others.

During each subsequent round of drawing, the time limit is progressively reduced: 30, 25, 20, 15, 10, 5, and finally 3 seconds. At that point, the task is finished. The continual reduction of drawing time is intended to heighten the intensity of the exercise, enhance the gamelike atmosphere, and depotentiate any possible cognitive processing inhibition. The time needed for the explanation and administration of the technique rarely exceeds 15 minutes, although the discussion that follows may frequently continue for more than an hour.

While the foregoing instructions have proven to be quite clear, it must be emphasized that the CDT is not intended to be a rigidly controlled exercise, and a great deal of flexibility is both permitted and encouraged in its administration, particularly in this early stage of development. Case B, cited later in this chapter, illustrates the adaptability of the exercise to special situations. Other unforeseen outcomes have included participants who have been unable to think of anything to draw during their allotted time: While this produces less of a formal drawing to evaluate, such behavior certainly adds additional information in the process analysis of the exercise. Occasionally, the participating family has had great difficulty in negotiating the decision of choice of crayon or drawing order: in all cases thus far, the examiner has simply remained silent, and within a few moments, the family has worked it out, after seeing that no additional direction was forthcoming.

While the exercise is being completed, the therapist should be observing closely the behavior of all the participants. If at all possible, the use of a second therapist as an observer is highly recommended. Additionally, the videotaping of the entire CDT procedure can be extraordinarily valuable, if circumstances permit. Other resources aside, however, the CDT can be quite capably administered by a single therapist who is a careful observer.

Once the CDT is completed by the family, the therapist initiates a discussion with the participants. This discussion tends to be informal and driven in large part by the responses of the participants. Typically, the therapist begins the discussion by simply soliciting reactions in a very vague fashion. The general question that should be asked at this stage should be something like, "Well, what did you think of it?" directed at no one in particular. After someone has responded, the therapist should ask for reactions from the other participants, taking care to eventually include everyone.

Once this somewhat informal stage of reaction is completed, the therapist should proceed with a series of other questions designed to help the participants process the exercise.

The following questions are typically used in a processing session with a family; however, this list is not meant to be seen as either mandatory or all-inclusive. Any particular session may prompt a different direction—an experience that has been shared by the author and several of his associates—producing vastly different processing sessions, a few examples of which are cited herein later. In any event, the following questions have proven to be ordinarily quite revealing when put to the participants:

1. Who cheated? That is, who broke any of the rules (i.e., no communication during the drawing, quit immediately when the command "Next!" was given)?
2. Who decided on the order in which you drew?
3. Who decided on which color crayon everyone would use?
4. Who used the most space on the paper?
5. Who used the least space on the paper?
6. What do you think of the final product?
7. Can anybody here see a place in this drawing where two or more people worked together cooperatively?
8. Can anybody here see a place in the drawing where two or more people interfered with each other's efforts?
9. What would you have drawn if you had gone first? (Note: asked of all but the person who actually did go first.)
10. Is there anything about this drawing or the whole exercise that reminds anyone of how things work in the family in general?

As mentioned, these questions are merely suggested prompts to aid the family in getting fully involved in the exercise. Frequently, the family members will make spontaneous connections and observations on their own, rendering Question 10 redundant. Frequently, issues of power and rivalry surface and lead to discussions about the family that leave the family drawing behind, with the CDT having served as a springboard into sensitive areas that might otherwise not have been broached. In any event, it is emphasized that the CDT is not a static, standardized instrument, nor is it intended to be. Rather, it is best seen as a projective device used with families in an effort to produce hypotheses that are deserving of further exploration and that may lead to a better understanding of family functioning.

RESEARCH FINDINGS

Because the CDT is relatively new, and because it has been used primarily in a clinical as opposed to a research setting, little formal research has been completed. It is felt that general interpretation of the CDT should be based on the basic principles that apply to all projective techniques, but with a special emphasis on the unique features of this test. Therefore, CDT interpretation is based on a two-dimensional but not mutually exclusive focus on the process and the product. Recently, analysis was begun of the first 100 completed drawings, focusing on the product aspects of the CDT. The process aspects are addressed in the next section.

Product Analysis

It must be emphasized that there was no effort made to select the participants who were the creators of these first 100 drawings in any fashion. If a clinician felt that the CDT would be useful with a particular family, it was used. There was no effort made to separate families according to presenting complaints or initial diagnostic categorizations. As more and more data become available, it will be feasible to do further research that could categorize and compare participants along these and other dimensions (e.g., intact versus broken families, minority versus other ethnic groups). At present, it was felt that some measure of frequency of occurrence of various items would be a good start in beginning to systematically evaluate these drawings, allowing for analysis in much the same way that Rorschach responses can be classified as "Popular" or "Original." The chart in Table 15–1 represents such an effort.

It must be emphasized that these are preliminary data, reported in a naturalistic state, due to the newness of this procedure. Again, there were no controlled selection factors applied to the client population that produced the following data, except that each of the families that participated in the CDT was seeking treatment for problems through the author and his associates. It is worth noting that all families were seen on an outpatient basis, and that most of the families were seen for relatively brief periods (i.e., 8–12 sessions) in family therapy with a strong strategic orientation.

Table 15–1 was created simply by perusing the first 100 collaborative drawings that have been produced. Only those items that occurred with relative frequency were included in the table. One of the interesting patterns revealed in this simple table is the high frequency with which a family will include human figures of one kind or another in a drawing in which the inclusion of a human figure is not specifically instructed. Ninety-four of the first 100 families drew human figures of one kind or another spontaneously, giving weight to the importance of human figure drawings in the general field of projective drawing analysis.

In fact, Table 15–1 reveals that the most frequently drawn figures, in order of frequency, were human figures (94%), houses (86%), and trees and animals (71%). These results certainly call to mind Buck's seminal work in drawing analysis with his House–Tree–Person Technique (1948). As is the case with all projective techniques, the more common a response is, the less it speaks to the individuality of its author. Hence, the frequency of

Table 15–1.   Frequency of item's appearance in the first 100 CDTs

Item	Frequency
House	86
Tree	71
Human figure	94
Self	68
Family members (other than self)	78
Sun	61
Clouds	52
Flowers	51
Animals	71
Geometric shapes	36

human figures, houses, trees, and animals make them indicators of normalcy, to a certain extent, in much the way that popular responses on the Rorschach indicate a well-socialized individual. Hence, an analysis of the drawings themselves, and most particularly their idiosyncratic features, is necessary to gain a deeper insight into the individuals who produced them. Here again, the field is wide open for further research. Extensive work has been done over the years on the significance of particular features in individual drawings of various kinds. For example, an extensive catalog of possible interpretations of various indicators in drawings of houses, trees, and persons is available (Jolles, 1971). However, it is not at all clear what relevance this extensive literature has for CDT interpretation.

It must be kept in mind that by its very nature, the CDT is fundamentally different from other projective drawing techniques. That is, while most drawing techniques involve the production of a single individual, working independently, the CDT involves several people working jointly. Consequently, individuals contributing to a CDT do not have unlimited freedom in their efforts but rather must in some way accommodate their fellow participants. The CDT is intended to study interaction among the participants, a fundamentally different focus than that of the individual drawing analysis.

In terms of product analysis, the techniques developed by Burns and Kaufman to analyze the KFD appear to show great promise for applying to the CDT (Burns & Kaufman, 1972). Both the KFD grid and the KFD analysis sheet, which focus on the style, symbols, and actions of figures seem to lend themselves to CDT analysis. However, again it must be emphasized that the KFD is the product of a single individual working independently, while the CDT is a collaborative effort. Therefore, the data gathered concerning each of these techniques are qualitatively different and cannot be directly compared. However, the techniques themselves seem quite well-suited to product analysis of the CDT, and this area is currently being explored.

Process Analysis

As mentioned previously, the CDT is intended to reveal aspects of interaction. Consequently, analysis of the product of the exercise (i.e., the drawing) is only one part of a thorough analysis of the CDT. Process aspects are actually seen as being of equal or greater importance in CDT analysis. The 10 questions given as discussion prompts in the description of the administration procedure are largely focused on the process aspects of the CDT. Originally, process analysis was based on three main areas: (1) adherence to instructions, (2) sequence, and (3) involvement (Smith, 1985).

Adherence to instructions basically refers to how the family in general and specific family members in particular dealt with the imposed structure of the CDT. *Sequence analysis* focuses on how the family chose and maintained their own sequence of participation, with an emphasis on what is revealed about the family's power distribution and leadership style. *Involvement analysis* refers to the interaction among the family members, in terms of cooperation versus competition. Essentially, these three areas are addressed within the foregoing 10 questions.

As experience with the CDT has increased, new patterns of response interest have begun to emerge. For example, there are those families for whom the task remains a confused jumble of events, even after processing. These families have great difficulty addressing the 10 questions, and they have great difficulty in reaching agreement on such simple issues of fact as "Who decided on the order in which we drew?" Even within this subcategory of families, there seem to be two separate groups. In one set of families, the members remain bewildered and confused, and simply cannot track the family's decision-making procedure, try though they might in a good-natured fashion. In the other group, the members of the family engage in heated discussion, vehemently disagreeing over the facts as they see them.

CASE ILLUSTRATIONS

Case A

The identified patient was a 10-year-old boy, adopted by his parents from a Colombian orphanage at age 3 years. The current family consisted of the father, a 56-year-old computer programmer, the mother, a 47-year-old nursery school teacher, a 14-year-old daughter, and the already described 10-year-old boy. The mother called to arrange for an appointment, and described the problem as "our 10-year-old son is having problems." The boy was attending a local public school, was making limited academic progress despite having been identified and placed in a special educational program as a learning disabled youngster, and was exhibiting mild behavioral difficulties in school as well as at home. Additionally, his relationship with his sister was described as "terrible—they fight like cats and dogs!" The sister was an exceptionally fine student, and in fact was participating in a program for "mentally gifted" children.

When the family arrived for their first session, the mother completely dominated the initial interview. She answered all questions, whether they were addressed to her or not. Direct questions put to the father were slowly and briefly answered by him, and then he would be quickly interrupted by mother, who would elaborate on his answers or contradict him. The same process recurred when the examiner addressed the children. The identified patient barely spoke 10 words during the interview, and he clearly felt it was pointless to make any effort to explain himself.

After the initial interview was completed, the CDT was administered. From the very beginning, the atmosphere in the session changed completely. The young boy immediately took the first crayon, choosing the color blue. He also assigned the other crayons to the other family members, and he established the order in which they would go: "Mom will be first, then sister, then me, and Dad, you can be last!" The mother agreed to go first, and began to draw a girl, which she did not have time to complete. Sister then began, drawing the name of a heavy metal rock group. The boy then spent his turn scribbling heavily over the drawings of his mother and sister with a gleeful smile on his face. The father then began his turn by drawing a geometric figure in the lower left corner of the paper.

As the drawing progressed, the examiner noticed the mother whispering disapprovingly to the boy, who ignored her, smiled at the examiner, and continued his destructive efforts. When the drawing was completed, the boy sat back smiling, obviously pleased with himself, while his mother and sister chided him for "ruining this just like you ruin everything!"

Looking at this case in terms of the process variables, it became obvious that the youngster who was the identified patient was full of anger and resentment about his perceived place in the family. His domination of the exercise and his deliberate defacing of the drawings of his mother and his sister testified to the strength of this young man. It was fascinating to see the mother "break the rules" by whispering admonishments to the boy, while the son gleefully took advantage of this controlled situation to express his displeasure within the rules of the exercise. This passive–aggressive display led to speculation about the amount of effort that the child was exerting in his school setting. It was not considered surprising when individual psychoeducational testing later completed suggested that this youngster's academic failings were more due to emotional factors than to any specific learning disability.

Continuing discussion of this case, the father sat quietly listening to the discussion without contributing. However, as the processing of the exercise continued in earnest under the examiner's prompting, Question 5 focused the entire family's attention on the father: It was absolutely clear that he had used the least space, both to him and to all of the family. Looking at the drawing, he spontaneously commented; "It looks like I'm not even a part of this family!" From that moment on, father took a more active role in the session, and in future sessions as well. He also began to take on more of a parenting role with the children, and the family began to function much more satisfactorily.

Finally, as mentioned previously, an individual psychoeducational evaluation was administered to the young man. Results of the CDT were incorporated into the overall assessment as part of the projective section of the assessment, addressing his emotional development not only on an individual basis but also as a member of a functioning family. As a result of this comprehensive evaluation, a decreased emphasis was placed on the child's "learning disability," and a greater emphasis was placed on motivational factors. To date, this change in focus has produced an improvement in academic success, as well as in overall family functioning. This case is an excellent example of the contribution that the CDT can make to traditional individual psychological testing.

Case B

The identified patient was a 12-year-old boy who was having difficulty with his peers and family members. The family consisted of a 38-year-old doctor; his 37-year-old wife, who served as office manager for his practice; and two younger siblings, a boy age 8 and a girl age 6 years. The family was referred by the principal of the boy's school.

The family entered the office somewhat upset. The identified patient had resisted coming to the appointment, and in fact refused to shake the examiner's hand. After some initial data gathering, the examiner introduced the CDT to the family. All were cooperative except the identified patient, who stated adamantly, "I'm not drawing!" The father began to order his son to participate, but the examiner interrupted quickly, saying, "You don't want to draw—that's great, then you come with me!"

As mentioned, the CDT is not a standardized, static instrument, and occasionally a great deal of flexibility is needed if it is to be useful. In this particular instance, with a hostile and resistant adolescent client, joining him in his resistance was deemed appropriate. The examiner took the boy into another office, briefly explained the CDT to him, and asked if he would help observe how his family handled this task. Further, the boy was asked to make predictions about what would happen, what would be drawn, who would "run" the session, and so forth. He responded very positively to this approach, obviously relishing being in a position of power.

After the drawing was completed, the session of processing developed nicely. The family had created, primarily under the dad's inspiration, a drawing of a tennis match. The theme of competition was obvious, and the expectations of "winning" in all ways were made graphically clear as well. It was also clear that the identified patient had lost all hope of "winning." His absence from the drawing seemed to be a manifest representation of his alienation from the family. Again, while this case is not a good illustration of a "typical" CDT session, it is a fine example of the power of the technique to uncover feelings that might otherwise not surface.

Case C

The identified patient was a 7-year-old girl, an only child who was seen as anxious and fearful, who was experiencing nightmares and stomachaches, and who incessantly bit her nails. She was an excellent student in school, and she was identified as a mentally gifted youngster. Her parents were both researchers in the field of medicine, and each held a doctoral degree in the medical field.

During the initial brief interview, the child was particularly quiet. She answered only direct questions, and then in a monosyllabic fashion. Her parents entreated her to "talk to the doctor, honey!" but to no avail. The family was presented with the CDT, and the session proceeded in much the same fashion. The little girl waited and took the last crayon, went last in the order of drawing, and did the least in terms of drawing. She actually merely elaborated on her parents drawing efforts, never initiating any art on her own.

More specifically, the mother drew first, starting a figure of a girl. The father began a drawing of a boy next to the girl, and then their daughter added shoes on the mother's girl figure. Going next, the mother "straightened out" the shoes, making them look more graceful. As the drawing continued, the little girl continued to make additions to her parents' drawings, which the mother frequently corrected. The tone of the session seemed quite serious, and it did not seem as though the family had any fun at all. As the postdrawing session progressed and the 10 questions were addressed, it became very clear that this family seldom had any fun, in or out of sessions. Interestingly, this same child produced a KFD that was totally compartmentalized, with the father reading in the living room, the mother reading in the kitchen, and the little girl playing alone in her room with her Barbie dolls.

Case D

The identified patient was a 17-year-old girl who had recently been arrested for shoplifting. There were suggestions of possible alcohol and other drug abuse, but the family minimized these issues in the referral. The father made the initial call for an appointment at the urging of his family attorney, as a court date was approaching. The father was a stockbroker and the mother was a part-time nurse. There were two older siblings, boys ages 19 and 21 years old, both away at college and unavailable for the scheduled initial session.

The family presented themselves as being annoyed by having to participate in a therapy situation, with the parents seeming to feel that the situation was just a natural "phase" of no great consequence. The daughter seemed sullen and resentful, but it was not clear whether she resented having to come to the session or whether she resented her parents' attitude toward her situation.

In any event, the CDT was introduced, and the daughter became both excited and interested. She took charge, assigned the crayons to her parents, settled the order, and began the drawing with real enthusiasm. She began with a drawing of a house, put her own address on it, and continued to work on her own drawing as her turn came around. Her mother worked on putting a garden in the side yard of the house. The father worked on a back yard, with a swimming pool and tennis court. In a fascinating fashion, they each worked diligently on their own area, and never so much as touched each others' area.

As time was running out, the father quickly sketched himself and the boys on the tennis court. In her last two drawing segments (i.e., 5 seconds and 3 seconds, respectively), the daughter crossed out the boys and drew herself and her mother on the other side of the net from the father on the same tennis court.

During the postdrawing session, the family seemed to have difficulty discussing any issues or any implications of the CDT. Approximately 2 months later, the father told the wife that he was in love with another woman and left the home.

This case seems to exemplify the situation where the drawing itself, the product of the CDT, may have been more informative than the process aspects. This family seemed to be unable or unwilling to verbalize their feelings, but their graphic productions seemed to be very revealing. Looking at this family's finished drawing, the almost total separation of the colors used, except for the girl's quick effort to "eliminate" her older brothers, spoke eloquently of the isolation of these family members from each other. Their failure to really interact or respond to each other effectively on the blank page seemed to echo the general family functioning. The interpersonal distance that they maintained even on paper seemed to foreshadow the father's later actual total departure from the family.

This case also seemed to typify the notion of the identified patient serving as a "white knight" in bringing the family into therapy, a concept often discussed in family therapy literature. The youngster's shoplifting could easily be seen as an unconscious effort to call for help for the entire family.

SUMMARY AND CONCLUSIONS

Over the past several years, the CDT has proven to be a valuable adjunct to traditional interviewing techniques, as well as a significant addition to traditional psychological testing. With its emphasis on family interaction, it is particularly appropriate for use in settings in which family functioning is a matter of major emphasis. It is difficult to convey the power or flavor of this technique via the written word, but it is hoped that the preceding case examples give some sense of the possible contribution that the CDT can make in both a diagnostic and a therapeutic fashion.

It was mentioned that at times, this basically diagnostic assessment procedure has apparently had a powerful therapeutic effect. In Case A, the father later called the CDT "a real eye-opener. ... I never realized how much I had taken myself out of the picture until I saw that I was barely on the page in that damned drawing." It was clearly the turning point in therapy for that particular family. This most serendipitous effect has proven to be more common than might be imagined. It may simply be that in the CDT, the voices of those who are normally silent can sometimes be heard, and in this new communication, there is a power of healing.

Clearly, the CDT remains in an early stage of development. Further research is certainly indicated, and the possibilities are multiple and fascinating. As mentioned, the techniques developed for KFD analysis (Burns & Kaufman, 1972) show great promise for adaptation and application to CDT analysis. The ideal analysis of the CDT continues to be seen as videotaping of the entire process, from the entry of the participants, through the administration of the technique itself, and finally through the full processing (via the 10 questions) session.

In conclusion, the author and his associates have found the CDT to be a worthwhile procedure with multiple applications and benefits. It is usually fun, generally exciting, and almost always informative. At the best of times, it dramatically improves the understanding of the family, both on the part of the therapist and on the part of the family themselves. As research continues and further information becomes available, it is hoped that the CDT will become even more valuable.

REFERENCES

Broderick, C. B., & Schrader, S. S. (1981). The history of professional marriage and family therapy. In A. S. Gurman & D. O. Kniskern (Eds.), *Handbook of Family Therapy* (pp. 17–25). New York: Brunner/ Mazel.

Buck, J. N., (1948). The H–T–P Technique: A qualitative and quantitative scoring manual. *Journal of Clinical Psychology, 4,* 317–396.

Burns, R. C., & Kaufman, S. H. (1970). Kinetic family drawings (K–F–D). New York: Brunner/Mazel.

Burns, R. C., & Kaufman, S. H. (1972). *Actions, styles and symbols in kinetic family drawings (K–F–D): An interpretive manual.* New York: Brunner/Mazel.

DiLeo, J. H. (1983). *Interpreting children's drawings.* New York: Brunner/Mazel.

Hulse, W. C. (1951). The emotionally disturbed child draws his family. *Quarterly Journal of Child Behavior, 3,* 152–174.

Jolles, I. (1971). *A catalog for the qualitative interpretation of the House–Tree–Person (H–T–P).* Los Angeles: Western Psychological Services.

Klepsch, M., & Logie, L. (1982). *Children draw and tell.* New York: Brunner/Mazel.

Machover, K. (1949). *Personality projection in the drawings of a human figure.* Springfield, IL: Charles C. Thomas.

Smith, G. M. (1985).The collaborative drawing technique. *Journal of Personality Assessment, 49,* 582–585.

Chapter 16

DYNAMIC PLAY APPROACHES IN THE OBSERVATION OF FAMILY RELATIONSHIPS

Steve Harvey

INTRODUCTION

Spontaneously improvised expressive play interaction involving art, drama, and movement games can be very useful in gaining an understanding of families, especially those with young children. Typically, the play of more troubled families is disorganized, lacks creativity, and in general, generates alienation between parents and children while play among families who are more successful is characterized by effective problem solving and mutual activity, and produces positive, intrinsically playful experiences which tend to unite the players. Both the process of how families generate play activities and the resultant content of their drawings, dramas, and games reflect the core emotional atmosphere, the quality of relationships, the primary problem-solving style, and the general sense of social creativity. Such attributes relate to the quality of basic attachments between family members.

In well-functioning families, play occurs spontaneously during daily interactions and can be readily observed on the playground as easily as in the home setting. The essential element of such interactive play is the ease and naturalness by which it emerges from family interactions. Typical examples include a mother's sensitive smiling while her 6-month-old turns away and toward her in a hide-and-seek fashion with responding laughter; a toddler's games of chase with his sibling; a father's improvised game of kicking a soccer ball with his preschooler while walking down the driveway; a dramatic role taking and role reversal as an elementary-aged child describes a playground interaction at the family dinner table; or a pleasurable experience an adolescent and her parent have while they joke with each other's more argumentative comments following a disagreement. An important function of such playful episodes is to provide a way in which a tension-filled family relationship which has become stalled in conflict over daily living can be restarted in a positive way. Such play can be very reassuring and comforting to all parties following the anger or isolation of an argument or disciplinary activity, or the emotional mismatches which occur on a regular basis in typical family life. Additional benefits of improvised play include its potential for a creative working through of the issues at hand, the development of social problem-solving skills, and the achievement of some natural catharsis for the players.

An example of such seemingly effortless play as offering an opportunity for emotional rejoining and as a corrective event occurred after a father of a 3-year-old boy told his son that they could not rent a small boat one afternoon while they were picnicking by a lake due to the dangerousness of not having a life preserver to use. The 3-year-old was instantly extremely disappointed and protested quite loudly. The father initially ignored the protest but then needed to take his son to the car to calm down. About 20 minutes later after the father and 3-year-old rejoined the mother and older sister on a blanket in the grass for lunch, the 3-year-old began a game in which he would jump from the blanket into the "water" (the grass) and ask for his parents to jump in to "rescue" him by carrying him back, first in their arms and later by using a towel as a pretend rope. All this activity was carried out as a spontaneous improvised drama. Not only did the tension from the earlier limit-setting episode between father and son dissipate, but, both in the content and the playful process, the family's positive emotional experience with each other and specifically the father and son attachment was easily repaired.

Clinical observations show that these natural play experiences are negatively influenced by family difficulties such as poor attachments, histories of child abuse, a child or parental history of psychological trauma, divorce, and other significant family distress. At times troubled families cannot play at all. In other cases, their play is distorted and offers little comfort for the players, usually serving only to promote emotional isolation and poor interpersonal problem solving. Without play as a resource, a problematic emotional atmosphere can continue and even build with each interaction within the family.

This chapter will discuss how both directive and more nondirective family play experiences can assist in coming to better understand a family's emotional resourcefulness by observing the style and quality of their play interactions. Such observations usually occur as part of a larger comprehensive evaluation including verbal clinical interviews. They are meant to provide immediate concrete examples of interactive problems. This immediacy is particularly useful in engaging young children with limited verbal skills who usually feel left out and overpowered by their more verbal parents and older siblings in more traditional mental health assessments. By using play activities in which even young children can fully participate, not only do the mental health observers gain a wider view of the presenting problems and potentials for change, but the observations can be presented to even very young children in a relevant way. A preschooler who spends his time running away from his frustrated mother while the two are attempting to play "Follow the Leader" can be told that one goal of treatment might be to help him teach his mother how to play catch and chase with him so that they might both have fun together. Video replays of such activities can also serve to provide very real and concrete examples for parents or families exhibiting troublesome interactive patterns. Alternative options can then be mutually discussed.

Dynamic Play observations are a very flexible method of relationship evaluation. Activities can be set so that whole families may observed together as well as in various subgroups. Usually the most important dyads to observe are the parents individually with their children. Using a series of such observations, the therapist is able to begin to gain some understanding of the quality of the emotional relationships in the family as a whole and between individual members. General family attachments, as well as the attachment between each parent and child, problem-solving styles, and basic creativity resources which may be utilized in the process of change are easily identified. Such insights into the family's functioning can later be discussed with them directly in a participatory way using the specific examples from the initial play experiences. To gain a more complete sense of the family's needs, the clinical impressions may be combined with the results of other individual child or family assessment procedures. This information may then be used to set up therapy goals for a family-oriented play intervention. Because of the action orientation of this treatment approach, such play goals have the potential to be effectively used within brief therapy modalities.

DYNAMIC PLAY

Several approaches have utilized the idea of family members playing together as a way to actively involve children with their parents in the process of identifying and changing their problematic mutual behavior (Griff, 1983; Ariel, 1994). Schaefer and Carey (1994) present an overview of several of the various family-oriented play modalities currently being utilized. Central to these approaches is the beneficial effect for both adults and children from observing and changing their interactions through the use of various types of imaginative play action with each other.

Dynamic Play (Harvey, 1990, 1991, 1994a, b) is a particular style of such family-oriented activity in which parents and children play together using art, movement, drama, and video expression. This play often takes a game-like format. A central premise of this play style is that creativity is a naturally occurring ability that greatly influences the quality, form, and meaning of interpersonal interactions, especially among family members. Both the process and content of family relationships are viewed as being constantly created in an ongoing and effortless fashion by family members. This is especially seen in their non-verbal communications. Much of this creative process is unconscious. Using Dynamic Play observations, family interactive patterns, themes, and metaphors are identified.

Observations of spontaneous play are particularly useful in assessing the quality, security, and organizational level of the attachment styles within family interactions. Play expression and relationship development go hand in hand in a natural way as parents and children establish their initial, all-important emotional ties. For parents and children who are secure in their attachment to each other, their play generates and builds positive connectedness. Even when problems are encountered with play episodes, secure families are able to self-correct their activities to naturally and creatively involve all members in some new task. However, when emotional insecurity or disorganization is present in families, relational play breaks down rather quickly and loses its "funness."

It is useful to think of the expressive/emotional aspects of the relationship between parents and children as an improvisational dance or drama. In healthy relationships, the natural creativity within a parent and child keeps their "dance" moving from gesture to gesture, facial expression to facial expression, dramatic image to dramatic image. One partner's expression stimulates and moves the other, in an intrinsically unique, pleasurable, and problem-solving flow that generates good feeling. The natural creativity can be thought of as the magical "it," or resourcefulness of a relationship, in which parents and children fill out and continue their emotionally expressive experience with each other. Importantly, both parents and children are complementary if not equal participants in this flow and both are aware of shared meaning and feeling states. When a 3-year-old is pulling his father in a "tug-of-war" style back into the home as the father is leaving for work, both adult and child are busily creating a shared good-bye while simultaneously participating in a special feeling state between them which emotionally holds them together during a moment of separation. Importantly, the child as well as the more verbal adult are full participants. If, however, the family containing the father and young boy had been experiencing continued emotional stress from parental conflict, for example, this same leaving for work scene would likely look very different. Rather than entering a shared play state, the boy might well begin to protest his father's going with tantrum-like behavior while the father walked quickly out the door, his attempts at redirection ending in frustration.

From this perspective, children and parents with problems in their attachments might be thought of as experiencing breaks in this ongoing creativity. As the gaps occurring in their mismatched expressions become great enough, their mutual creativity stops, mutual problem solving becomes difficult, and isolation develops. These stops are immediately transparent in their play. Observations, then, of such play activity can help identify underlying emotional conflict in a very useful medium.

TECHNIQUES FOR OBSERVATION

Using these ideas, strategies for organizing observations of specific family play activities have been devised. Certain simple structured movement, drama, and art tasks have proven to be quite useful due to their wide applicability and ease of family completion. Episodes of family free play are also useful in viewing how a family tends to organize themselves in a relatively ambiguous situation which invites their open creative expression. Difficulties with developing organized involved play given no or varying kinds and amounts of structure provides indications of problems in the home setting. While no formal rating system has been developed for clinical application, certain principles guide observations of such activities into very workable units which can be interwoven with the verbal understanding of the presenting child or family problem.

The Playroom

The most advantageous playroom for Dynamic Play is one in which a variety of expressive and imaginative activities are encouraged. It is best if such play is conducted in a relatively large open space where family members can use whole body movements in an open way. There should be potential for activity such as chase games, tug-of-wars, and large-scale dramatic expressions. Stuffed animals of varying sizes help suggest imagined dramatic play scenarios with families. Large, soft pillows can be used to make physical play safe as well as incorporated in making houses or imagined walls. Colorful scarves and elastic ropes are easily employed in simple physical play and as props for large dramatic activity. Large-sized newsprint paper along with varying types of markers, crayons, pencils, and clay should also be available. In general, the play materials are relatively nonspecific and designed to help the family members use their physical, dramatic, and artistic imagination to turn these materials into what their play demands in the moment and then to easily transform them into something else a few moments later. A large pillow might be used by a mother and preschooler as a safe place to fall into together at the ending of a chase game, only to be used as a wall for an imaginary house filled with stuffed animals signifying both parents and children a few minutes later.

Observational Activities

Observations should be carried out with somewhat structured activities involving movement games, art, and drama to view interactions across a variety of expressive modalities. Free play in which families generate expressions of their own choosing when given access to all the play materials also provides useful information as to how activity is improvised and structured and what media are preferred. General interactive themes which are repeated in the various forms of expression are significant. Some families show particular strengths with one medium while being unable to generate useful play in the other areas. To accomplish this multimodal evaluation, observations of activities focus on three types of expression: (1) primarily physical—tasks in which full bodily expression is central, such as tug-of-war, chase, or an improvised soccer match; (2) primarily dramatic—tasks involving mutual role taking, storytelling, and the use of verbal imagination such as becoming an animal; and/or (3) primarily artistic—tasks which involve mutual drawing such as mural making. Free play is accomplished by having the family come into the playroom with no preset directions except to invite them to play as they wish.

Movement Games

1. *Follow the Leader.* In this activity the family is given the instruction to "play a game of 'Follow the Leader' in which everyone gets a chance to be the leader." Some simple concrete examples may be provided, such as "Try leading your children through the room," if a parent has a hard time beginning. If difficulty in starting continues, it is likely related to family difficulties rather than a true lack of understanding of things to do. This activity is applicable with families composed of all-aged children. It helps focus on and demonstrate a family's use of power and power sharing.

    Usually, in healthy families, all members get a turn to be leader and the followers are willing to play along. Roles are exchanged easily and activities take everyone's needs into account in some way. Often the basic game involving simple turn taking is creatively transformed with all members adding ideas simultaneously as the family gets caught up in their shared creativity. Generally this process of transformation of the basic rules of the game is a sign of positive family resources and security. The end result functions to emotionally join the players as they are active in a process of shared problem solving. Such "super" leading and following is also a sign of creative power sharing.

    Problematic families, on the other hand, typically show great difficulty in completing the basic leading and following necessary for mutual enjoyment. Resulting game enactments lose their spontaneity, structure, and appeal. One member may attempt to dominate the others with a leadership style which does not encourage open participation while the other members quickly lose their willingness to accept and contribute to such initiations. Open discussion as well as verbal or nonverbal negotiation stop and opposition or withdrawal easily follows. Small disagreements quickly widen and detract from the emotional atmosphere and mutual focus necessary to successfully complete the game.

2. *Swing Child into Pillows and Calm Down.* In this activity, the parent is told to make a place with the pillows into which a child can safely land and then swing the child into it. After several swings or when the family stops, the parent is asked to calm the child down. This activity is best done with younger children (2–6 years). It provides a view of the level of parent/child attunement as well as the basic emotional and behavioral regulation between them.

In healthy families, the parent(s) is able to swing the child easily and can creatively extend the activity using several improvised ways and rhythms of swinging to match the child's body and excitement. The child usually wants to continue and finds this activity very enjoyable. The most common verbalization is "more." The parent is then asked to calm the child down. The most common and successful strategy involves sitting down next to or close to the child, occasionally using touch with some quiet verbalizations related to the physical aspects of transitioning to a calm energy state such as "Let's take some deep breaths." As in the Follow the Leader game, there are many possible ways to accomplish the actual swinging and calming physical tasks. The basic resource observed in this activity is the parent/child process and motivation to enjoy the shared rise and fall of excitement together.

Problematic families usually have difficulties with the basic physicality of this task. Either parents and/or children can become so tense that all parts of the swinging activity become very awkward to accomplish. Little face-to-face contact occurs, swinging rhythms between the parent(s) and children don't appear to match, and no simple bodily adjustments are made to help smooth out the process. Both the swing and the landings may become so uncomfortable physically that they detract from the enjoyment. The transition to calm can also become hard to accomplish with children refusing to stop and the parents becoming quite frustrated in their attempts to bring the activity to a close by decreasing the level of physical energy being emitted.

Dramatic Activities

1. *Make a Family Story.* In this activity the family is asked to construct a house as well as to make up and show a story about a family of animals, using the props available in the playroom. This activity is useful for families with children of any age and assists in viewing important emotional events through metaphors. Observations of how story themes function in helping families to create closeness or alienation make the specific dramatic images more understandable. After the evaluation a discussion of these metaphors aids the clinician in building the family's understanding of the emotional atmosphere surrounding the problem.

Healthy families are able to make up stories around very literal family events such as bed or meal time. Some families create more imaginative plots and characters. Play episodes which contain conflict and disturbing traumatic or aggressive themes usually resolve themselves. Parents and children show cooperative efforts in using the play materials to construct the props for their imagined scenes as well as contributing to the character and thematic development of their ideas.

Some troubled families have difficulty even starting to make a story of any kind. Others produce stories which are highly disorganized, contain repeated dramatic or conflictual events which have no resolution, and/or have characters who are not able to form positive relationships with each other. When such troubling play develops, these families are not able to change their play through cooperative negotiations.

2. *Free Play with Parents and Children and with Children Only.* In this task, families are asked to play together freely with all of the play props. This episode continues until the players can develop some theme. This usually takes about 20 minutes. The parents are then asked to leave and the child/children are asked to continue their own play. As with the first episode the child/children are allowed to develop a theme by themselves. This episode also usually lasts for about 20 minutes. The children's play period is shortened if they become distressed or if they cannot generate play by themselves. Children under 5 are seen for approximately 5 minutes in order to accommodate their possible developmental difficulties with separation. The parents are then asked back into the playroom to engage the family in play again. Such play continues until some theme develops. This usually takes less time than the initial play episode. Five to 10 minutes are usually sufficient for this play episode.

In larger families, various combinations of parent-child dyads may be added to observe each of the relationships more specifically. Comparison of the quality and the content of each play episode offers an understanding of the possible interactional dynamics and creative resourcefulness within the subgroups of the family. This activity draws on a family's communication and attachment style. In a "normal" situation, parents and children are rather easily able to spontaneously generate play activities and story themes in an improvised way. Children are able to continue elaborating on these conjoint themes when they are alone. Parents are easily incorporated into the activity upon their return. A continuum of play themes occurs. While families may use a preferred play mode (physical, dramatic, or artistic), such expression has a pleasurable, creative quality throughout each of the separate conditions.

Troubled families generate play which is significantly discontinuous and different in each of the parent/child and child-only conditions. Parental separation and reunion are particularly problematic. Occasionally, children will introduce traumatic imagery during their solo play which is not only unresolved but is also not reintroduced upon their parent's return. At other times, children are able to generate very disrupted play by themselves. Such play behaviors suggest problems in the parent/child affective relationships.

Drawing Activities

1. *House and Story Drawings.* In this activity the complete family is asked to gather around a large piece of paper. Each member is instructed to draw a house in front of them and then while taking separate turns they are asked to construct a system of roads connecting the houses together. The families, especially those with older children, may also be asked to elaborate on the drawing by adding towns, restau-

rants, and so on, once the roads are completed to make a neighborhood. The family is then asked to continue in a turn-taking manner, drawing themselves coming out of their house and doing something within the previously created environment. The family members are directed to take another turn and to continue developing the newly created drawing. Several rounds of turns are allowed until the end of a theme is reached. This ending point is determined either by asking the family if they are finished or by the judgment of the evaluator. This drawing activity usually takes about 20 minutes. Some very expressive families may continue for an entire hour, developing a seemingly endless flow of ideas and elaboration.

Healthy families build on each other's ideas and easily transform the original offerings in elaborate ways. Members visit each other and develop imaginative interactions which spring from each other's images. A child may draw herself going to her mother's home only to have her mother draw them both going to a park to swing together at which time the father might draw a restaurant and invite them both to join him for dinner.

More troubled families have difficulty joining with each other and often run out of ideas rather quickly. Sometimes individual members return to their homes or introduce separate destinations and activities which have no visual or imaginative connection between them.

This same activity can be completed with children under 6 by leaving out the roads portion of the task and simply having the families draw individual houses followed by turn-taking rounds of adding imaginative drawings of coming out of the houses to "do something." This task can be accomplished with preschool children by asking the family members to take turns using any form of mark making to indicate their activity while verbalizing their intentions.

2. *Scribble Wars.* This activity is usually best conducted within a family dyad. It creates a competitive, conflictual situation for them to resolve. Each member is asked to pick a different-color crayon with which to scribble on the same large piece of paper with the other member. One is instructed to start the activity by saying "go" and the other is instructed to stop the activity by saying "stop." The two are told that this is a contest to see who can scribble the most of their color onto the paper using the rules or commands of stop and go. They proceed until the page is filled. The final product is held up for them to decide who "won."

The next phase can be completed by most children who are 5 or older. In this part, family members are asked to create images by looking imaginatively at the original scribbles from the contest as starting points. Using any colors they wish to complete their new ideas, they are instructed to draw directly on the "war" by elaborating, adding, and so on. If they have difficulty seeing an image freely, the players are provided suggestions to make animals or fish or to use some other limited category to help focus their imagination.

In healthy families this activity usually turns out to be a delightful experience with both members contributing freely and gaining some enjoyment even in a momentary conflict. This is especially true when members are asked to produce images together. Often such images are extended, and the family members contribute things through short imagined conversations that their graphic images inspire.

Families with difficulties are often unable to draw on the same page with each other, to produce imagery beyond the initial scribble, and may express significant distress in the imagery that is produced. Such family members are usually not able to use the play activity to get out of their immediate feeling of overwhelming conflict with each other. The paper itself may become ripped and members may even draw on each other.

Observational Strategies

Qualitative assessments of activity performance can be organized through a series of more focused categories. Such categories are purposefully general to help the observer gain a view of the whole family atmosphere no matter how many individuals are involved. Using these observational strategies, an overall impression can be generated for a mother-child dyad as well as for a larger family of two parents and five children. The purpose of the categories is to aid in developing a better understanding of the mechanics of the family's play behaviors. The family's play behaviors may contribute in a variety of ways: (1) to encourage a positive emotional atmosphere, (2) to engage in an intrinsic motivation to connect with each other, (3) to produce a sense of alienation and withdrawal from intimacy, or (4) to decrease the desire to solve problems in a mutual way.

Attuned Play

Attunement in play refers to activity in which two or more players (usually parent and child) join together in the same event with a similar intent. Usually in attuned play the participants are using similar physical expressive rhythms within a close time and place proximity. For example, as a child begins a rapid circular walking movement during a Follow the Leader game, his parent matches his quickness and approximate path in attuned play. The parent slows and stops when the child does. Importantly, both family members exhibit similar affective states. Play interactions may have (1) no attuned events, (2) islands of attuned events separated by time and isolated, or (3) long periods of highly matched and attuned play in which the players co-create their play expressions together.

Expressive Momentum

Expressive momentum is generated as parents and children share enough spontaneous attunement with each other so that their play activity becomes more elaborated and includes new ideas, more shared movement, more imaginative metaphors, and more creative engagement over time. It is what is used to unite separate play events and players. Often as players share expressive momentum with each other the resultant play goes off in unexpected directions. Such directions in play can offer solutions to previous interactive difficulties. During this process, parents and children become intimate, flexible, and are open to each other. A great deal of pleasure is generated and experienced by all the family members.

Flow/Break

This is the major observational tool in Dynamic Play. The observer watches when the players use expressive momentum and attuned play in which one event leads easily to the next over time and when such flow is broken or interrupted. This tool is meant to help the observer focus on the play process rather than on the actual content of what is being played out. Here it is more important to identify how, by whom, and when the mutual play is continued or stopped. Flow is the activity which occurs when the players are jointly playing together. Breaks are those events which function to stop that flow. Examples of breaks include: one partner changing the rules of an activity while another continues, strong shifts in emotional states, small injuries, very unexpected and surprising play expressions, harsh verbalizations, and so forth.

Form and Energy Balance

A functional balance between form and energy needs to occur for an improvised flow of family play to proceed. In this context, form is the ability to establish boundaries, definition, and focus for expressive activity. Energy refers to the more improvised and freely generated expressions. Form is usually accomplished through the use of rules and verbalizations as well as the planning and redirecting of activities. Energy is generated by impulsive expression which is quite often physical and has intrinsic or internal motivation. When play has too much form, alienation can occur. When it has too much energy, expression can be random and scattered, and lose a shared focus.

Play Metaphors and Imagery

It is important to make note of dramatic and/or verbal images which are (1) repeated throughout the assessment, (2) suggestive of strong emotional themes such as nurturance, aggression, and victimization, (3) expressed while in isolated play, and (4) not addressed or resolved in family expression. Usually this imagery contains themes which are relevant to the family's functioning and difficulties. It is important to understand how such imagery functions within the context of the created play episode. To accomplish this, the imagery is placed within the categories of attuned play, expressive momentum, or flow/break to help develop a contextual understanding of its importance.

If a child introduces play breaks by physically distancing himself from his parents when nurturant themes are introduced in dramatic play, for example, the evaluator might well raise the question of how nurturance is experienced by the parents and child. Similarly, if a parent and child are able to generate expressive momentum when they introduce themes of leading and following, a possible positive aspect of power sharing might be present in the parent/child relationship.

Parent/Child Roles

Dynamic play can be a very flexible, expressive experience. However, parents are mostly in a role of facilitator/player while the children are mostly in the role of player. While styles can vary widely, parents who have secure relationships with their children usually move a little slower, use more levels, produce less images, and respond to, elaborate with, and organize their children's more spontaneous play impulses. Parents certainly can and do introduce and initiate spontaneous ideas of their own but it is usually accomplished with the flexibility to return to a supportive role when needed. The main model of parent play is to respond to the child's initiation and then to help elaborate and extend these child impulses into a more organized whole. Observation of parent/child functioning in the family play can help the therapist better understand what may be happening between them in a more general way.

Observational Procedures

A clinical interview is first completed with the family prior to conducting the observation of play activities. In this interview, information is gathered from the parents and from the children who are 5 or older. The presenting problem and what all members have done to change the situation are discussed in detail. Additional information is gathered from the parents alone, especially concerning current and past discipline practices, daily routines involving eating and sleeping, history of past psychological trauma or abuse, major separations, history of developmental achievements, description of past and current peer and family relationships, how parents remember the manner in which they were parented, and their current views of themselves as parents. In the presence of all family members, this information is used to develop a revised description of the problem within the family context.

The family is seen on another occasion in which they are observed completing a series of play activities from the above list. All or part of the activities may be employed. When possible, video is used so that the play can be reviewed at another time. The observer records the events while they are happening, noting when attuned play, expressive momentum, flow/break, and imagery occur. This information is used to understand the process of how the family creates form and energy and the role of parents and children within the various stages of play. Following the end of the last play activity, the family is asked if the original problem occurred during the observations as well as what they enjoyed and found difficult about playing together.

The family is seen on a third occasion. The major themes from the observations as well as the verbal interview are discussed. The family is helped to gain an understanding of how their play and the verbal descriptions of the family life fit together. Using specifically relevant examples, which are chosen prior to the session, concrete examples of strengths and problem areas are presented and discussed to help the family broaden their understanding of the situation. Therapy goals are established with the family by discussing how the problematic episodes might turn out more successfully. This is particularly helpful in developing very concrete goals for the treatment of children. The vast majority of family members recognize their issues as they are expressed in the play behaviors. The clinical task for those few families for whom their play and their verbal description is significantly different, is to develop a plan of how to use their play to help in the process of problem solving. Such goal setting can be used to develop a Dynamic Play Therapy intervention (Harvey, 1997) or can be used with other child/family therapy methods. In this way, a family's successful completion of specified creative/expressive play episodes performed either in the office or at home can become a marker for success in treatment.

Case Example

The A family referred themselves for treatment to address their 7-year-old son's increasing behavioral problems. Jimmy was described by his stepmother as becoming increasingly oppositional, withdrawn, and moody. Recently he had been playing with matches and set fire to a large field. Fortunately, no significant damage resulted. However, the police had insisted on mental health involvement after their investigation.

This boy's past included several traumatic incidents which had not yet been addressed. When he was 3, Jimmy had been involved in an episode in which his younger, one-year-old brother had been shot and killed while the two boys were left alone with an unattended weapon when their mother was visiting some adult friends in the same apartment complex. Jimmy's parents were divorced shortly after this event. Jimmy lived primarily with his mother, initially. However, she began to physically abuse him during his preschool years. Mr. A gained custody and moved away from the area. Jimmy's mother eventually stopped all contact with him except for a few phone calls during holiday times.

Mr. A remarried when Jimmy was 5. Jimmy's stepmother gave birth shortly after. Initially, Jimmy was quite well mannered and was eager to please his parents; however, this easy-going behavior changed soon after his halfbrother's first birthday. Jimmy's parents described his presenting problems as "not listening," and refusing to follow their requests, rules, or house expectations. He also had recently started playing with matches, refusing to come home when he was told, and showing extreme anger or sadness. It had become impossible for his parents to know when he was telling the truth. The parents reported that they were unsuccessful in changing Jimmy's behavior despite trying several kinds of consequences or discipline techniques.

When asked about their family experiences, Mr. A reported that he and his brothers had experienced physical abuse while growing up, and he had learned not to call attention to himself in order not to be punished. He currently described himself as not very involved in his family as his profession demanded a great deal of travel. Mrs. A reported that her parents had divorced when she was in elementary school and she became distant from her family during her adolescence. The A's said that they were happy with their current marriage and were committed to helping their son with his current problems. No previous mental health intervention had been attempted prior to the current contact.

Following an initial clinical interview in which much of the family's present concerns and previous history were discussed, the A's were observed completing a series of three play activities over two one-hour sessions. The selected play enactments were (1) Follow the Leader—to view how decision making and power sharing occurred in the family, (2) family free play, in which Jimmy and his parents played together, Jimmy played alone, and the parents rejoined Jimmy—to view how the family attachments were being expressed metaphorically, and (3) drawing/story game of houses and roads—to view similar emotional family themes in more graphic and story form. These sessions were videoed to be later reviewed with the parents and Jimmy. Ideas concerning the resourcefulness, creativity, problem-solving, as well as problematic patterns within the family were then discussed to better focus the future treatment. This conversation included comments from Jimmy on the play enactments and on how such play might be improved.

First Session

After Jimmy and his parents arrived, the therapist led the family into the playroom and instructed them to play a game of Follow the Leader with everyone getting a chance to be a leader. If they were to have problems coming up with ideas, the therapist told them he could furnish a few ideas to help them get started. Mrs. A immediately asked Jimmy to be the first leader, saying that she would enjoy following him. Mr. A agreed.

Jimmy looked around the room and told his parents that he didn't have any good ideas of how to begin. His stepmother led him over to the parachute and brought it out for everyone to get under. Her nonverbal communication indicated that she had become the first leader. Her activity was to have everyone get under the parachute, throw it in the air, and then run to get under it again. Mr. A followed his wife's lead, adding encouraging comments such as "Hey, let's go," and so forth. Jimmy, however, became disinterested and stopped running to get underneath after two turns. After the third throw, Jimmy was clearly outside of the parachute while his parents were underneath. Mrs. A saw this exclusion and stated that it would be a good time for Jimmy to lead. Jimmy again said that he didn't know what to do. Mrs. A told him to begin a game of chase. Jimmy did take up this idea and ran away from the adults. After a few passes around the room, he hid in some pillows and said he didn't want to play. Mr. A stated that it was his turn and he was going to try to find his son. He began looking under all the props in the room. His wife immediately joined him. When Jimmy was eventually found a short time later, he stated that he wanted the game to end and looked up to the therapist. Mr. and Mrs. A also turned to the therapist stating that "I guess it is over." The game was finished in less than five minutes.

The family was told to sit around a large sheet of paper and use markers to each draw a separate house in front of them. Mr. and Mrs. A drew houses of similar sizes and styles with windows, curtains, doors, colorful walls, a yard with flowers and trees, and a chimney. Each house had a pathway to enter and a clear boundary around it, leaving plenty of space on the rest of the page. Jimmy produced a much smaller house with no clear way in or out. The windows and doors were closed and solid dark colors covered the walls. The family was asked to take turns adding a system of roads to connect their neighborhood and then to add any other items such as parks, playgrounds, and so on that they might like. One at a time, the family drew their roads. Jimmy's lines, however, never quite connected to any of those produced by his parents. His stepmother finally drew a "frontage road" directly to Jimmy's house.

The family was asked to take several turns drawing themselves coming out of their houses one at a time and doing something in their newly created "neighborhood." Again the parents took many turns showing themselves trying to contact Jimmy in several imaginative ways by coming over to his house and knocking on his door, telephoning him, and so on. Jimmy, meanwhile, took his first turns not drawing, announcing that he was still inside his house and didn't want anyone to come in. He finally drew himself "running away" to a far and open side of the paper. His parents took turns chasing him. His father drew a park and invited his son to come and play baseball. Jimmy eagerly accepted the invitation. The drawing/story ended with Jimmy and his father in the park playing catch with Mrs. A going to her house to "cook dinner" for them. This activity took almost the rest of the hour to complete and produced more involved imaginative contributions, especially from Jimmy. The family finished by cleaning up the playroom. The next play session was set for the following week.

Second Session

At the beginning of this session, the family was brought into the playroom and told that they could play any way they wished. They were told that such play together would continue for about 15 minutes, Jimmy would then play by himself, and then the adults would return. Mr. and Mrs. A began by making a house and selecting the large bears as the mother and father. Jimmy chose two much smaller animals and took them to a corner of the room and placed them under a small pillow in their house. Jimmy did join his parents in their house when they asked him and played having a dinner prepared by the mother bear. He never did use the animals to establish a character for himself. He would occasionally go over to check on his other animals in the corner. Such leavings did not appear to interrupt the dinner activity. However, Jimmy did not appear to be very involved in the eating. The parents were then asked to leave.

Jimmy had no ideas of how to continue when his parents first left. However, with some encouraging comments from the therapist, Jimmy did start looking around the room. He then saw the animals he had originally chosen and began to cover them with blankets to help them sleep. He also began care-taking activities with them such as assisting them when they were cold and talking with them quietly. He was quite involved in this play. When his parents rejoined the play, Jimmy left his activity and used his stepmother's suggestion of returning to the house with them. The family continued their play having their animals talk with each other. The family cleaned up the playroom in an efficient manner. Jimmy participated.

Play Review

The videotapes were reviewed a short time later using the categories of attuned play, expressive momentum, flow/break, form/energy, dramatic images, and parent/child role. Themes which were repeated throughout the play as well as expressive modalities that appeared stronger or less developed were identified.

The least-attuned play and expressive momentum and most-significant break of flow occurred in the Follow the Leader game. Despite Mrs. A's efforts, and to a lesser degree Mr. A's, the family could not generate enough expressive momentum to continue the game for more than a brief amount of time. However, the family was able to generate far more expressive momentum in the house-drawing activity even though Jimmy again introduced a theme of distancing himself from the parents. The play solution spontaneously generated by Jimmy and his father of playing baseball together while Mrs. A made dinner was very encouraging. This act did offer the new family dynamic of Mr. A finding a way to attune to his son more effectively to help in developing more emotional security.

Another break of flow and lack of attunement occurred in the family story. During this activity, Jimmy introduced characters who were never incorporated into the joint play with the parents. His involvement in the play with his parents further lacked the same expressiveness, imagination, and personal creativity noted in his individual play. Thus, while accepting his stepmother's ideas to organize his interactions with his parents, his personal contributions were not functional in generating emotional closeness or providing the kind of expressive momentum necessary to work through his past traumatic events.

Parent/child role was important throughout the play. Mrs. A did attempt to follow Jimmy's leads and when he would not or could not produce play in which she could join, she did offer several very imaginative ways to include his responses. Her persistence in pursuing Jimmy, despite his tendency to hide, withdraw, or otherwise exclude himself, attested to her efforts to structure her relationship with him. However, without Jimmy's participation in attuned play on his part, the stepmother/son relationship lacked a communicative balance. Mr. A's inability to join his son's play through consistent attunement may well have contributed to this stepmother/son problem. Clearly, when the father was able to attune to his son, Jimmy did respond quite dramatically and with a healthy parent/child role. This father/son interaction did appear to lead to the expressiveness more common in securely attached relationships.

The lack of general attuned play and expressive momentum, and the break within the family story affected the form/energy balance in the play improvisation. Throughout most of the events, the family appeared to be using more form to guide their play rather than encouraging their mutual creative generation of ideas. This was particularly true in both the Follow the Leader game as well as in the free play. During both of these episodes, the family relied on preset ideas to the exclusion of their spontaneity when encountering difficulties. Unfortunately, this style contributed to the decrease in their creative resourcefulness and intrinsic motivation to generate problem-solving activity which generally accompanies more engaged "fun" play.

The dramatic images and general themes of the play gave further indication of some content of the family's difficulties. Jimmy's avoidance reoccurred in the three activities. Such a repeated interaction suggested that this boy experienced elements of insecurity even though his parents and his stepmother in particular were attempting to be sensitive to him. This fearfulness, given his past traumatic experience and subsequent maltreatment at the hands of his birth mother, is not surprising. The dramatic imagery of Jimmy's selecting and nurturing the "smaller" or perhaps "baby" animals suggests that he may well have ongoing concerns about himself and his dead (and his current living and similar-aged) younger brother which he was unable to integrate into his current daily family life. Likewise, his parents may also have been unable to notice or attune to Jimmy's emotional signs, thereby contributing to a familywide avoidance of these core aspects.

Taken together with the family interview, these observations suggested that: (1) Jimmy's presenting problems of fire setting, lying, and opposition were related to both family interactions as well as Jimmy's unresolved emotional conflicts, and (2) his stepmother's attempts to include him may have been contributing to his withdrawal while his father's use of attuned interaction was quite helpful. Clearly the family was more able to use graphic and verbal expression than physical interaction. The following scenes from the videoed play were chosen for the family's review to help illustrate and further discuss these points: (1) a portion of the parents attempting to play Follow the Leader with Jimmy while he moved away and hid (the last scene showing the three members together asking for help was especially clear in showing their collective lack of expressive momentum), (2) Jimmy's positive use of his father's addition of a park and the play that developed between them after they joined with each other, and (3) Jimmy's play with the smaller animals who needed his help while his parents were making a house and failing to notice him as well as his solo play.

The Viewing Session   During the next session the therapist presented these above points along with a review of the scenes on video. Mrs. A said it was important to see how her efforts at trying to include Jimmy were actually being resisted by him. This left her feeling helpless to influence his behavior or affect his withdrawal in any way. After seeing her images in the play, especially how she looked after the Follow the Leader game, she was able to identify how such feelings were similar to her experience with her parents, and they were something that she stated she wanted to change. In watching how Jimmy's mood lightened while they were drawing together, Mr. A expressed surprise at the importance of his efforts to engage Jimmy. He had considered himself as an outsider to his family for so long. Though Jimmy was pleased at the effectiveness of his efforts to keep away from his parents during the houses game, he also genuinely expressed pleasure at watching the games he and his father had created as well.

In discussions of their play, the family members all stated that the Follow the Leader game was how they experienced much of their interactions together especially when limit setting was involved. This was the play episode they also most wanted to change. The parents saw Jimmy's play with the "baby" animals as representing his need to be taken care of following his very difficult early years and they said it gave them some understanding of Jimmy's inner self. They were also able to see how little they actually were addressing this need in their own play by asking Jimmy to leave his animals to follow their more concrete ideas of playing out daily events. Mr. A put the two scenes together and stated that it looked like it was time for him to really begin to do whatever it took to listen to Jimmy. He asked the therapist for help in accomplishing this goal. When they were then asked what scene most expressed the kind of interactions they wished they had, the family all agreed that the end of the houses game in which Mr. A and Jimmy were playing while Mrs. A was inside her house preparing dinner was the way in which they would like it to be.

The therapist suggested that since the drawing activities were the most successful, that father and son could begin drawing and talking together, particularly about the past, until they were able to imagine drawing a new way to play Follow the Leader in which everyone would feel free to participate. Jimmy was told that some sessions of the therapy would be spent on helping his parents play with the younger play figures he had tried to take care of.

The upcoming course of therapy was focused on having the family, and Jimmy in particular, imagine (1) a successful Follow the Leader game to help Jimmy in following his parents' home rules as well as help them better see and encourage his spontaneous ideas, (2) father/son using drawing to begin playing together and using such drawings to build their relationship, and (3) a family drama in which younger members were nurtured. The play would need to include Jimmy showing such needs to his parents so that they could respond. Jimmy was asked if he could imagine a way to show a pretend fire and being lost and found in play with his parents. Jimmy said he could if he was allowed to use all the props in the playroom to do it. He was assured that this was possible. The family left with more focus as to where they would start in their upcoming sessions, including Jimmy.

SUMMARY

Play activities can be very useful in gaining a view of family interaction, especially those exchanges which relate to attachments and other important emotional concerns. Some families naturally can use playful interactions to generate positive feelings for each other, bridge the emotional connection with each other following times of conflict, and create episodes in which important emotional events can be worked through in a natural flow of their everyday life. This play can be thought of as "conversations" which promote intimacy, closeness, and joint "fun" between parents and their children. This is especially true with younger children. Families with more problems, however, have difficulty in generating such play together. Difficulties occur in the process of how family members construct their play together event by event as well as in the content of their resulting play themes.

Dynamic Play (Harvey, 1990, 1991, 1994a,b) offers observation and intervention methods which help identify and focus family play as a way to plan treatment. Family activities are drawn from several different play modalities which involve drama, art, and physical parent/child interactions. Resulting play episodes are viewed using the following concepts: attuned play, expressive momentum, flow/break, form/energy balance, play metaphors and imagery, and parent/child role to gain an understanding of the play style and themes which predominate. Such descriptions are then put together with information collected in a clinical interview related to current and historical family events and interactions to help develop a common understanding with family members as to how their emotional life together is expressed in their play. Goals for change can then be developed which incorporate new and more productive play together.

REFERENCES

Ariel, S. (1994). *Strategic family play therapy* (2nd ed.). Chichester: Wiley.

Griff, M. D. (1983). Family play therapy. In C. Schaefer and K. O'Connor (Eds.), *Handbook of play therapy*. New York: Wiley.

Harvey, S. A. (1990). Dynamic play therapy: An integrated expressive arts approach to the family therapy of young children. *The Arts in Psychotherapy, 17*(3), 239–246.

Harvey, S. A. (1991). Creating a family: An integrated expressive arts approach to adoption. *The Arts in Psychotherapy, 18*(3), 213–222.

Harvey, S. A. (1994a). Dynamic play therapy: Expressive play intervention with families. In K. O'Connor and C. Schaefer (Eds.), *Handbook of play therapy: Vol. 2, Advances and Innovations*. New York: Wiley.

Harvey, S. A. (1994b). Dynamic play therapy: Creating attachments. In B. James, (Ed.), *Handbook for treatment of attachment-trauma problems in children*. New York: Lexington Books.

Harvey, S. A. (1997). A Dynamic play therapy response to divorce. In K. O'Connor and L. Braverman (Eds.), *Play therapy theory and practice: A comparative presentation*. New York: Wiley.

Schaefer, C., & Carey, L. (1994). *Family play therapy*. Northvale, NJ: Jason Aronson.

ASSESSMENT OF THE CHILD AND FAMILY IN PLAY CONTEXTS

Gary E. Stollak, Anat Barlev, and Ioanna D. Kalogiros

INTRODUCTION

The observation and study of family interactions and transactions have been relatively ignored until only recently. Traditionally, mental health professionals have focused on the individual, including the young child, and his or her perceptions of the world in which he or she lives. Within the past thirty years, however, many of us have become aware of ecological and family systems perspectives, focusing on the direct study of the individual and the larger social systems in which he or she is embedded. These perspectives can make significant contributions to our understanding of the variables involved in the etiology, maintenance, and change of personal and larger system malfunctioning. The search for understanding must include the observation of whole families and their subsystems, and not only the perceptions and actions of one or more individuals. Therefore, a comprehensive assessment should include direct study of the relationships between the people within the family system in which the "identified patient" is a member and how those relationships impede or promote growth and development. Such a perspective has only very recently begun to pervade clinical practice and research.

The family system approach guides this presentation of play assessment. After a discussion of its purposes and goals, three major theoretical domains crucial to understanding family functioning are summarized. Practical tasks are presented by which these domains can be evaluated. Finally, two case studies illustrate this assessment process.

PURPOSES OF A PLAY ASSESSMENT

Historically, play (especially play in a well-equipped playroom) has been identified as an ideal activity and therapeutic setting for children because traditional therapeutic strategies

---

Portions of this manuscript were first published as Stollak, G. E., Crandell, L., & Pirsch, L. (1991). Assessment of the family in the playroom. In C. E. Schaefer, K. Gitlin, & A. Sandgrund (Eds.), *Play diagnosis and assessment* (pp. 527–548). New York: Wiley.

The second and third authors are doctoral students, made equal contributions, and are listed alphabetically.

based on verbal exchange and complex cognitive abilities are largely unsuitable, especially with those in the first three years of their lives. Play therapy emerged from the recognition that although adults express themselves most accurately and most comfortably with words, many children are less able to do so, but can express important thoughts, feelings, wishes, desires, and fantasies through action or play. Their flexibility and naturalistic setting also make the playroom and play activities an appropriate context for family assessment, allowing comprehensive and detailed analysis of moment-by-moment verbal and nonverbal interactions (e.g., parent→child, mother→father) and transactions (e.g., parent→child→ parent→child, mother→father→child) among family members. Especially with young children, it can be a useful setting to identify maladaptive or coercive child or parent behavior and characteristics of family enmeshment or disengagement. Knoff and Prout's (1985) discussion of the uses of drawing tasks is also applicable to the multiple uses of family activities in play contexts. They can: (1) facilitate family-assessor rapport and increase a family's comfort, trust, and motivation to participate further in a comprehensive assessment; (2) be most helpful as an adjunct to other assessment strategies, such as questionnaire instruments, structured interviews, or observation in school or home settings; (3) elicit samples of behavior which reflect a family's reactions to structured and unstructured situations; and (4) provide information about relationships in the family that can be tapped as resources and facilitate therapeutic interventions.

Some considerations of this type of family assessment include age of the target child and other children, constellation of the family, and resources available to the assessor. Although a broad overview is provided suggesting some useful tasks in evaluating a family's strengths and weaknesses, obviously each assessment must be tailored to the particular skills and capacities of the child. Young infants cannot and most toddlers may not be able to follow many kinds of instructions. Furthermore, some families consist of only a mother and a child, while others consist of several adults and several children. Alternate family constellations merit special consideration: stepparents, stepsiblings, foster parents, and other significant family members should be included in a play assessment in varying combinations. Finally, to satisfy the interests of children of varying ages and to address a variety of referral questions, the assessor needs access to a large room well-stocked with a variety of imaginative and interactive toys. For younger children, common toys include small human and animal figures, hand puppets, clay or similar material, paints, a sand tray, chalk, crayons, and so forth. For older children, board games, sports equipment, and other toys suitable for this age can be made available in addition to those provided for younger children. Ideally, this room will be equipped with a one-way mirror, observation room, and videotaping equipment. If not available, a video camera with a wide-angle lens can be placed in the room, or the examiner can remain in the room unobtrusively noting family behavior. Family members may be instructed about the need to videotape the family being together. They may also be informed that they may view the videotape at the end of the assessment for the purpose of discussion.

THEORETICAL BACKGROUND

This theoretical review is guided by the empirical research that has the most relevance and utility for the practicing professional in his or her attempts to use a play context to understand the family as the unit of analysis. Three major theoretical domains through which family functioning can be understood are described. These domains include attachment theory, parenting styles, and family structure and dynamics. Additionally, these theoretical dimensions can be conceptualized within the overarching framework of boundary conditions, and a brief integrative model is presented.

Attachment Theory

The attachment relationship between infant and care giver is increasingly being recognized as the cornerstone of infant emotional adjustment and developing social competence Bowlby (1969/1982, 1973, 1980) proposed that diverse behaviors such as smiling, clinging, vocalizing, following, and crying serve to promote proximity with the mother and thereby represent an "attachment behavioral system." Bowlby also maintained that through the continual transactions between the infant and care giver, the infant constructs "internal working models" or expectations concerning self and other. Gradually, these "models" crystallize and form a schema, over time, that the developing child uses to organize his or her affective experiences. Consequently, the patterning of the early attachment relationship lays the groundwork for later social-emotional development and therefore has consequences beyond the parent-infant dyad.

Ainsworth, Blehar, Waters, and Wall (1978) describe an empirical approach to exploring the attachment relationships by observing interactions between 1-year-old infants and their mothers in a standard playroom situation. Each mother-infant dyad was exposed to a novel play situation to assess how readily the infant would explore the environment, and respond to the presence of a stranger and to a sequence of maternal separations and reunions. Infants who were securely attached ("Group B") may or may not have shown distress when their mothers departed, but they all noticed her departure and sought proximity and contact upon reunion. The stranger, at times, was able to provide some comfort to these infants but clearly not to the degree of their mothers. Infants who were insecurely attached were of two types. "Group A" infants often did not notice their mothers' departure or they displayed few to no protesting behaviors. The most conspicuous feature of this group was that during the reunion episodes, these infants actively avoided and/or physically pushed their mothers away. Additionally, when these infants were distressed, simply having the stranger present alleviated their distress as if the stress was in response to being left alone rather than a response to their mother's absence. "Group C" infants displayed marked clinging behaviors prior to the separation episodes and extreme protesting behaviors in response to the separations. The hallmark feature of this group was their ambivalence during the reunion episodes where they would demonstrate simultaneous proximity-seeking and contact-resisting behaviors. These infants were typically either more angry or passive than the other infants in response to both their mothers and the stranger. In terms of play exploration, all infants were more likely to explore when alone with their mothers than with the stranger present. However, there were differences between the groups with respect to their play behavior. Group B infants actively explored the toys and room, engaging their mothers in their discoveries. Group A infants typically explored in a superficial and cursory manner, with virtually no interaction with their mothers. Group C infants generally clung to their mothers and initiated very little exploration.

Subsequent studies indicate that infants who were securely attached to their mothers during infancy were, later in childhood, more ego-resilient and moderate in ego-control

(Arend, Grove, & Sroufe, 1979); more persistent, enthusiastic, and imaginative, exhibited more positive affect, and engaged in more symbolic play (Matas, Arend, & Sroufe, 1978); more compliant and cooperative, (Londerville and Main, 1981); more self-aware (Cassidy, 1988; Schneider-Rosen & Cicchetti, 1984); and more sociable, friendly, and cooperative (Pastor, 1981). In general, they were more socially competent in preschool years than infants who were insecurely attached to their mothers. Conversely, insecurely attached infants were characterized by low self-esteem, dependency, negative affect (angry, aggressive, whiny), noncompliance, less empathy, and less popularity with peers (Sroufe, 1983). They were also found to be "emotionally dependent" (Sroufe, Fox, & Pancake, 1983; Clarke-Stewart and Hevey, 1981) as preschool children.

Supplementing these research efforts are two longitudinal studies which directly investigated the relationship between attachment and subsequent behavioral problems. Lewis, Feiring, McGuffog, and Jaskir (1984) found that 40% of the insecurely attached infants scored above the 90th percentile on the Achenbach Child Behavior Profile (Achenbach & Edelbrock, 1981; 1983) at 6 years of age. Erickson, Sroufe, and Egeland (1985) report that children who were insecurely attached at both 12 and 18 months were more likely to act out, be socially withdrawn, or demonstrate attention difficulties at school age than children who were securely attached. Finally, dysfunctional attachment is considered to be a primary consequence and determinant of child abuse (Main & George, 1985; Main & Weston 1982, 1984).

In summary, this convergent body of literature provides substantial theoretical and empirical support for the idea that the quality of early attachment relationships is consistently related to subsequent social emotional functioning that is clinically significant, and is implicated as a major factor in abusive parent-child relationships. Therefore, evaluating the attachment relationship is a critical aspect of family assessment.

Parenting Styles

Baumrind (1967, 1971, 1989) has reported on the relationship between parental maturity demands, control, nurturance, and the clarity of communication between parents and their 3- to 4-year-olds, and these children's self-control, affiliation, subjective mood, and self-reliance. In her 1967 monograph, Baumrind focused on the effects of parental child-rearing practices on the competence of 3- to 4-year-old children. Because children learn patterns of relating to other people through their parents, Baumrind evaluated different styles of child rearing and the implications such different styles have on the personal and interpersonal development of youngsters. She identified three groups of children who demonstrated clear-cut, stable patterns of social behavior: one group was characterized as self-controlled, explorative, and content; one group was characterized as discontent, withdrawn, and distrustful; and finally a group of children was described as having little self-control or self-reliance and who retreated from new situations.

Baumrind's work identified salient patterns that identified parents' behavior and predicted their children's development. When parents exerted firm control over their children, were nonmanipulative about the distribution of power in the family, were highly nurturant, and communicated clearly, their children tended to be socialized, independent, self-controlled, assertive, and explorative. Parents described as less nurturant, firmly controlling, and using fear as a discipline technique had children who were more insecure, apprehensive, less affiliative, and more likely to be hostile or regressive under stress. Finally, parents who were warm, noncontrolling, and lax about discipline had children who were lacking in self-control and self-reliance. These prototypes have been popularly identified as authoritative, authoritarian, and permissive (we prefer the word submissive) caregiving, respectively.

Significant relationships were also found between these parents' demandingness and responsiveness, and their children's social assertiveness and social responsibility when they were 9 years of age (Baumrind, 1989). Furthermore, the tasks Baumrind used to assess both parents' and children's characteristics are well-suited to encounters in play contexts. The conceptualization of parents and their children as presented by Baumrind is useful in understanding parent-child systems and how each member impacts the other. Consequently, assessors are encouraged to become familiar with her work.

Another component of the parenting relationship is the parenting alliance. As Cohen and Weisman (1984) state, "The parenting alliance encompasses interactions that pertain to child rearing ... and consists of the capacity of a spouse to acknowledge, respect, and value the parenting roles and tasks of the partner (p. 35)." A positive parenting alliance provides a resource on which a parent can depend for assistance, affirmation, and feedback; it enables parents to better satisfy their child's needs and meet the challenge of parenting more successfully. As such, a positive parenting alliance is a primary source of family support and nurturance. Conversely, a negative parenting alliance indicates denigration of one's spouse, poor problem-solving skills, a lack of shared responsibilities, and at least one partner's dissatisfaction with the parenting relationship. Note that parental involvement and the parenting alliance, although related, are not necessarily the same construct. A positive alliance indicates that both partners have complementary, mutually satisfactory roles, regardless of the amount of involvement maintained by each.

Family Structure and Dynamics

The transactional model of development by Sameroff and Friese (1990) for infant and child-parent assessment regards parents as the most direct influence on children's development (with the reverse also being true more often than not!). The model also highlights the impact of social, familial, and psychological factors on parent-child relationships. The model takes into consideration the notion that parent-child relationships can be affected by the economic, social, and familial supports available to the parents.

Such a model focuses on the family system as a whole. For example, Minuchin, Baker, Rosman, Liebman, Milman, and Todd (1975) noted patterns of transactions common to dysfunctional family systems. The following characteristics of family organization and functioning typify these family structures: enmeshment; overprotectiveness; rigidity; lack of conflict resolution; and deflection of parental conflict onto the children.

Enmeshment refers to a relative lack of boundaries between members. This includes interdependence of relationships, intrusions on personal boundaries, poorly differentiated perception of self and others, and excessively fluid family subsystems. In the absence of a clearly defined and effective parental system, executive hierarchies are typically confused and children often assume inappropriate power positions.

Overprotectiveness describes a tendency for family members to be overly concerned for each other's welfare and an unwillingness to allow each other to experience appropriate levels of discomfort. Nurturing and protective responses are so pervasive and extreme that the development of autonomy and competence is curtailed.

Rigidity refers to an inflexible commitment to maintain the status quo. Issues that threaten change are not allowed to surface and developmental attempts for individuality and autonomy are thwarted.

Lack of conflict resolution refers to the family's inability to confront differences. Hence, disagreements are not negotiated and problems are left unresolved. This tendency may be manifested in several forms. Avoidance, denial, and detouring of conflicts are common. Some families may bicker continuously but constant interruptions and subject changing preclude any particular conflict from gaining salience.

Finally, the parental conflict is typically deflected onto a child by three mechanisms. In the first mechanism, triangulation, and the second, parent-child coalitions, the parental dyad is split and the child is forced to ally with one parent against the other. In the third mechanism, detouring, the parental dyad is ostensibly united. One child is identified as the sole source of difficulty in the family and the spousal conflicts are manifested by a preoccupation with protecting or blaming this child.

Olson and his colleagues (e.g., Olson, 1985, 1986, 1988; Olson, Russell, & Sprenkle, 1979, 1983; Thomas & Olson, 1993) conceptualize family cohesion, family adaptability, and family communication as the major dimensions of behavior in family systems (the Circumplex Model). They define family cohesion as the emotional bonding that family members have toward one another. The specific concepts or variables they describe to measure the family cohesion dimensions are: emotional bonding, boundaries, coalitions, time, space, friends, decision-making, interests, and recreation. They list four levels of cohesion, ranging from disengaged (very low) to separated (low to moderate) to connected (moderate to high) to enmeshed (very high). They propose that very high levels of cohesion (an enmeshed system) inhibits the development of autonomy and individuation of each family member. Alternately, disengaged systems encourage individuation while minimizing attachment among family members. Between these two extremes lie balanced family systems, whose members can be characterized as independent from yet securely connected to each other. This construct of family cohesion appears to parallel Minuchin's family structural model.

Olson et al. (1983) define family adaptability as "the ability of a marital or family system to change its power structure, role relationships, and relationship rules in response to situation and developmental stress" (p. 70). The four levels of adaptability range from rigid (very low) to structured (low to moderate) to flexible (moderate to high) to chaotic (very high). They hypothesize that "central levels of adaptability (structured and flexible) are more conducive to marital and family functioning with the extremes (rigid and chaotic) being the most problematic for families as they move through the life cycle" (p. 70). This construct relates to family dynamics in response to the capacity, need, and demands for change. They further propose that characteristics of communication within the family can facilitate or inhibit optimal levels of cohesion and adaptability.

The similarities between Minuchin's family structural model and Olson et al.'s Circumplex Model are evident. Yet, Minuchin's structural approach is more theoretical while Olson's model is designed more for measurement and empirical research. Combined, they provide a useful way to conceptualize and assess family functioning.

Boundaries in Personal and Interpersonal Systems

The concept of boundaries, their characteristics and measurement, pervades and underlies theory and research in the study of person-environment, family, and larger social system transactions, and has significant meaning for the practicing mental health professional. Lewin (e.g., 1951), in his theorizing about the dynamics of personality, described motivation in terms of a system of needs separated from one another by boundaries. Permeability-impermeability refers to the capacity of that boundary to contain or control needs and tensions within the system. Speaking most generally, boundaries could be relatively permeable, such that tensions would spill into other systems and mutually influence each other (e.g., id and ego; or the cell wall of an ovum which, absolutely necessary for reproduction, eventually becomes permeable after repeated "attacks" by a multitude of sperm; or, equally important for life, the cell wall of a leaf becoming permeable to light so that photosynthesis can take place), or they could be relatively impermeable, limiting the spillage, isolating, or compartmentalizing subsystems with a resulting lack of communication across systems (e.g., a rigid, uncompromising superego).

The Blocks and their colleagues (e.g., Block & Block, 1980a, b; Gjerde, Block, & Block, 1986) have made systematic efforts to examine this boundary condition within the person, naming it ego control. The underlying continuum at one end identifies overcontrol, resulting in the containment of impulse, delay of gratification, inhibition of action and affect, and insulation from environmental distractors. The opposite end of the continuum identifies undercontrol: insufficient modulation of impulse, the inability to delay gratification, immediate and direct expression of motivations and affects, and vulnerability to environmental distractors (Block & Block, 1980b, p. 43).

A second property of a boundary, according to Lewin, is its elasticity or resiliency. At one end of this continuum a person is resourceful, is able to change the direction and intensity of involvements, the roles she or he plays, and role rules, in response to situational and developmental stresses. At the other end, the person, or ego, is rigid, brittle, and rule-bound. The person often overreacts to minor frustrations, is often immobilized by stress, plays few roles in life, and is either excessively controlling or excessively submissive in stressful situations (Block & Block, 1980b; p. 48).

The research of the Blocks has entailed a very comprehensive assessment of the personality of children and adults, across many contexts, and over many years, including over 100 families who have been participating in a longitudinal study of personal development initiated in 1968 (Harrington, Block, & Block, 1987). They have found, for example, that egocentrism, measured by performance on a perspective-taking task, was consistently related negatively to ego resiliency in the same boys from age 3 to age 14.

The construct of boundaries also provides an alternate way of conceptualizing the theoretical domains of attachment, parenting styles, and family structure and dynamics. For example, concepts within each of these domains also describe characteristics of the boundaries among family members. Secure attachment, authoritative caregiving, and optimal levels of cohesion and adaptability may imply optimally permeable and resilient boundaries. Insecure and anxious attachment between parent and infant/toddler, excessively permissive/submissive caregiving, and rigidly enmeshed relationships may imply chronically and excessively permeable and/or brittle boundaries among family members. However, no description of optimal boundary characteristics, and family members' satisfaction with them, is possible without an awareness that such characteristics can, and might need to, significantly vary over the family's life span. This is affected by normal individual and family developmental stages and issues, as well as in response to immediate stress and crises.

Assessing the personal and interpersonal domains described above provides information on child and family functioning relevant to intervention goals. In fact, family therapy techniques often include strategies to promote attachment between parents and children, to modify parenting styles, to enhance the parenting alliance, and to alter boundaries' conditions (B. G. Guerney, 1964; L. F. Guerney, 1982; Minuchin, 1974; Stollak, 1981).

PRACTICAL APPLICATIONS

The assessor must be aware that many different variables including family type, individual and family problems, and family traditions and culture may influence the choice of tasks a family is asked to complete. The presence or absence of a child's verbal skills is the single most relevant factor influencing the choice of play activities. Therefore, the review below is divided into assessment of children with few verbal skills (first infants and then 1- to 3-year-olds) and those with sufficient verbal skills to engage in dialogue (typically those 3 years of age and older). Although generally children comprehend language before their expressive vocabulary is functional, most 2- to 3-year-olds are actively and rapidly learning grammar, syntax, and vocabulary and refining their verbal skills through repetition and correction from adults. Typically the family modifies its styles of communication to encourage the acquisition of this developmental skill, and family members expect their 4-year-old child to possess extensive receptive and expressive verbal abilities. The assessment tasks described below are tailored to families with infants and children unable to engage in complex dialogue, and those with children capable of complex exchanges.

Usually some combination of structured and unstructured tasks effectively captures the strengths and difficulties characteristic of a family and provides the assessor with useful data on which to base an evaluation and recommendations for interventions. The combination depends, again, on the age of the child, the family constellation, and the referral questions. Similarly, the interpretation of the data collected via these tasks must reflect an awareness of developmental and cultural norms for both individual members as well as the family system.

Infants and Their Caregivers

General Principles and Issues

Fraiberg (1980) described four fundamental principles of infant mental health assessment, which are relevant for assessment of older children and their caregivers as well. First, the assessment process needs to be a collaborative enterprise between the assessor and the infant's parents or caregivers. Parents need to feel confident about the assessor, and become part of the process. If the caregivers feel good about the assessor, the information gathered from them will likely be more valid and reliable, and more relevant. Also, all child-caregivers need to understand the unique characteristics of the infant (e.g., temperament, physical problems). A good relationship with the assessor would also maximize the chance that the caregivers would agree with, and also implement, recommendations stemming from the assessment. It is important for the assessor to establish a good working alliance with all the child's caregivers. Second, the infant's emotional functioning most often takes place in the context of relationships. It is necessary to assess the infant in the context of relationships with parents and other family members, as well as other childcare providers. Third, infants are influenced by the kind of settings that they are in. It is most important to observe the infant, at least once, in a natural setting, such as the home and childcare settings. Fourth, assessment needs to extend over a period of time. The recommended timeline is between 4 and 8 weeks. During this time, the assessor should be able to thoroughly understand all the emotional themes, range of functioning of the infant and the caregivers, variations in the quality of primary relationships, and the influence of situational factors.

Observations need to be as naturalistic as possible. Mahoney, Spiker, and Boyce (1996) recommend that specific observations should not last for too long. Under normal circumstances and except for feeding, parents do not often sustain interactions with their infants for longer than 5 consecutive minutes.

Mental health programs that are geared toward infants may differ in the methods they use to gather assessment information. Programs that are more clinically and service oriented often do not require, nor engage in, structured and empirical assessments. However, empirically based assessment procedures are essential for evaluation of such programs.

It is also important to have individual sessions with the parents, especially if they feel that the infant's presence would be too distracting. Attention must be paid to when in the transaction there is the emergence of strong emotional expressions between the infant and the parents, and similarities and differences in transactions between the infant when present, older siblings, and one or both of the parents. Even without more formal administration of infant measures, such an observation helps us to assess how the infant is functioning in various areas: sensorimotor, cognitive, social, and emotional domains. The amount of information gathered here allows the assessor to develop a picture of the functioning of the whole family and its various subsystems (Fraiberg, 1980).

One example of such a comprehensive program is the Infant-Parent Program (Liberman, Van Horn, Grandison, & Pekarsky, 1997), a mental health program for infants under 3 years of age and their families who are at risk for abuse, neglect, and/or attachment disorders. The program is based on the premise that disorders of attachment occur, in part, from parents reenacting unresolved conflicts from their own childhood in their encounters with their own children. Infant-parent therapy is often the recommended treatment for problematic relationships between parents and infants. The infant-parent therapist would try to correct attachment relationships by accepting the parent and introducing positive change in the parent's internal working model of the self. Parents would feel better about themselves, and that would improve the relationship between parents and infants. Parents would be better able to modulate the infant's positive and negative feelings.

This program also evaluates the effectiveness of a family intervention for preschoolers who have witnessed domestic violence. Witnessing domestic violence can affect a child in many domains. One of the domains includes security of attachment. The therapy is driven by the play of the child. The goal is for the mother to be able to enter into the world of the child, also to provide both mother and child with a safe place to reenact their conflicts, and to find ways to resolve them (Liberman et al., 1997).

The program reports using the following assessment procedure: a 15-minute assessor-infant play session during which the mother joins them. With children over 3, stories from the MacArthur Story Stem Battery are used (Bretherton, Ridgeway, & Cassidy, 1990). The assessor narrates and acts out the beginning of six separate stories using props and a family of doll figures. The child is to show and tell how the story ends. The stories include various themes including fear, aggression, and separation. Although this family-oriented program involves assessment of infant-mother relationships, the guidelines and instruments they used can also be used with fathers and male caregivers in other clinical contexts.

Whatever the procedure and process, during the feedback session it is very important to maintain an alliance with the parents. This will maximize parent willingness to carry out all the recommendations made. Information given to the parents has to be useful. It is important to convince each parent that the assessor understands that child-caregiving is difficult, and when possible, points out the strengths in their adult-adult relationship, and in their individual transactions with the infant.

The failure of the communication system can place infants at risk for poor developmental outcomes. The success of the system depends on the ability of the infant to communicate the right information, and the ability of the primary and other caregivers to provide appropriate responses. This means that caregivers need to understand the variety and differences in the infant's communications, including, for example, the meaning of different kinds of crying. Lester (1992) found that preterm infants were unable to communicate to their caregivers that they were socially distressed. It is important to know that excitable babies would appear difficult and hard to handle, and depressed babies would appear more quiet and easy to handle. Excitable and impulsive babies are more likely to be abused, and those babies who are less emotional, active, and sociable are more likely to be neglected. Lester recommends that interventions be multilevel, including a focus on the specific needs and unique characteristics of the infant, the interaction between mother and father, the family organization and functioning, and also the kind of resources that the community can offer. It is reasonable to assume that similar relations among patterns of caregiving behavior, attachment strategies, and child outcome measures apply to children who have been diagnosed with a chronic developmental disability (Marvin & Pianta, 1996).

The Strange Situation

As noted earlier, Ainsworth et al. (1978) provide a detailed account of the room configuration, procedures, behaviors to be coded, and subsequent attachment classifications. While it may be a valid procedure for assessing attachment, there have been several problems in the use of the Strange Situation. First, it requires in-depth training for the coding system, which can be illuminating but also cumbersome and time-consuming (see, e.g., Isabella, Belsky, & von Eye, 1989). Second, in the traditional form, the Strange Situation has neglected, until most recently, the father-child relationship (Lamb, 1997). The empirical evidence suggests that when fathers play an active role in child rearing, they form attachments to their infants comparable in magnitude to the mother-child bond (Lamb, 1997; Clarke-Stewart, 1978). Because the role of the father in the socialization of the child is being increasingly recognized (Lamb, 1997; Pedersen, 1980), we have presented, above, a gender-neutral version. Third, the Strange Situation ignores the triadic (and larger family group) interaction between both parents and child(ren). Numerous studies have documented that the presence of the father leads to a decrease in the frequency of interactions between mother and child (Clarke-Stewart, 1978). In light of these considerations, several researchers have modified the Strange Situation to accommodate observations of both parent-child dyads and the parent-child triads. Lamb (1976) details the following procedure:

a nine-minute free-play episode involving the parent-child triad; two nine-minute free-play episodes, alternating one parent being alone with the child; and a final nine-minute episode with the parent-child triad and the introduction of a stranger. Inclusion of older siblings in the Strange Situation may provide additional useful information.

In conclusion, free play and the Strange Situation (or its modifications) yield clinically significant information in three primary areas: the very young child's orientation to exploration; the quality of parent-child and family relationships; and a probable course (absent significant changes in the environment) of emotional and behavioral development of the child. However, as infants and toddlers approach 2 to 3 years of age, many attachment behaviors decline. Thus, this assessment strategy is most salient for children 12 to 18 months and gradually becomes a less potent index as children approach 3 years of age.

We do not know if the Strange Situation creates the same conditions for caregivers and infants in different cultures. Sagi, Van Ijzendoorn, and Koren-Karie (1991) found that infants from Germany, Holland, and Japan reacted in similar ways as American infants in the Strange Situation, but that infants from Sweden and those who reside in Israeli kibbutzim were much more distressed by the separation.

Nakagawa, Lamb, and Miyaki (1992) examined whether the patterns of Strange Situation behavior have the same meaning for Japanese and North American infant-mother dyads, as for American infants. The procedure included a 4-month home observation; mother-infant dyads were videotaped for a total of 90 minutes before and after a nap. They were videotaped for 30 minutes during the 8-month home visit. During the 8-month observation, they were also videotaped in the laboratory for 10 minutes. On all of the occasions, mothers were instructed to behave as naturally as possible. At 12 months, all of the dyads were observed in the Strange Situation. The results suggested that the Strange Situation was not a valid measure of the security of infant-mother attachment in Japan. Ratings of the quality of maternal behavior at home and in the laboratory were not associated with later attachment classifications. In the United States, however, the association between maternal behavior and patterns of behavior in the Strange Situation are the basis for claiming that the Strange Situation provides a valid index of the security of infant-mother attachment. In this study, the conditions of the Strange Situation were more stressful for Japanese babies than for American babies. These Japanese babies may not have been separated as frequently and/or enduringly from their primary caregivers as those in the American sample.

Caution is always needed in interpreting information from the use of the Strange Situation (and any other procedure) when families are from different cultures. Any information collected must be seen in the reflection of the unique cultures in which the family and the observers are embedded.

Other assessment tasks and materials include those used by Harrison and Magill-Evans (1996), who observed parents teaching their infant a standardized task. In comparison to mothers, fathers were found to be less talkative in interactions, use different language forms, and be less able to adjust the content of their speech to the infant's abilities. Bridges, Connell, & Belsky (1988) found that an infant's behavior toward the father systematically predicted subsequent infant-stranger interaction, whereas the infant's behavior with the mother did not.

Usually infant-parent observations are made during feeding, diapering, other caregiving activities, and social play. An important component of attachment and the process through which infant and caregiver build their relationship is distress management, specifically parental responsiveness to the distress cues of the infant in the first 3 months (Carmen, Pedersen, Huffman, & Bryan, 1993). Therefore, we recommend paying particular attention during observation to the caregiver and infant behavior during distressing times.

Another type of semistructured situation for families with 1- to 2-year-old children has been used by Nuttall, Stollak, Fitzgerald, and Messé (1985). They instructed a mother with a 15-month-old infant to play a game of peek-a-boo and "I'm going to get you." After these two three-minute games, the mother was asked to help the child build a tower of six blocks; finally she was asked to teach the child to place the forms of a circle, square, and triangle in the correct places of a puzzle board. Salient interactions include: quality of affect, the parent's demonstration of appropriate developmental expectations for their child, and parental empathy toward the child. These tasks can also be completed by the family triad.

Other recommended assessment procedures (Crowel & Feldman, 1988), modified by Zeanah, et al. (1997), include:

Free play—Caregivers are instructed to play with the child the way they would play at home. A standard set of toys is provided in a container, the length is about 10 minutes, and no other instructions are given.

Cleanup—The caregiver at the end of the session asks the infant to return the toys to the container, helps if the infant needs help, and sets the container with the toys outside the playroom.

Bubbles—The parent blows bubbles and instructs the infant to pop the bubbles. This activity lasts for about 3 minutes and attempts to elicit positive emotions for both parent and infant.

Separation—The parent is instructed to leave the playroom while leaving the cabinet of toys open. The separation will usually last 3 minutes.

Reunion—During the reunion, attachment behavior can be observed, especially how the caregiver and infant reestablish contact following the brief separation.

Walters and Diane (1985) devised a Q-sort that can be used to examine behavior at home over a period of several hours. There are 90 items describing behaviors relevant to secure-base behavior. The degree of similarity of a particular child's sort to a prototype of a secure child's yields a continuous measure of security of the child's attachment, that focuses on various behaviors at home.

Finally, Munson and Odom (1996) have recently provided information about 17 rating scales developed to assess the behavior in families with children from birth to 3 years. Rating scales are generally easy to use and quick to administer, but sometimes are considered more subjective because more judgment by raters is required.

The quality of mother-infant interaction can be affected by the parent's personality, infant temperament, and by social support factors (Fish, Stifter, & Belsky, 1993). If a mother was in a supportive intimate relationship, mother-infant relationships were found to be more reciprocal and synchronous. Broom (1994) reported that mothers with higher marital satisfaction had more responsive interactions with their infants. We believe that it is also true for fathers. Fathers in supportive intimate relationships may have more positive transactions with their infants (Lamb, 1997). Further, Goldsmith and Alansky (1987) have stressed that we need to pay attention to similarities and differences in caregiver and infant temperament, and their effects on attachment.

Other Family Tasks

Free-play time is a good assessment ice-breaker. It allows the family (which may include three or more members) to orient themselves to a playroom and familiarize themselves with its contents, group themselves as they wish, interact with and/or avoid whomever they choose, and address any topic they want, all without the direction of the assessor. Directions can be given as follows:

> First we would like you to spend the first half-hour of our time together in this playroom. You may use the time however you wish. It is up to you to decide what you do here for the next 15 minutes. I will be out of the room, observing and videotaping through the one-way mirror. I'll be back when the 15 minutes are up, and then I'll ask you to do several other things.

The assessor should be alert for conflicts and their resolution, family rules, discipline and limit setting, positive affect, sibling relationships, and the family's ability to enjoy play together.

After 15 minutes of free play, the parents could receive instructions to cease free play and to begin other tasks. For example, they could be asked to tell their child(ren) a story about whatever they wish. This shift in tasks should be presented to the child(ren) by the parents, and not by the assessor. The storytelling usually could last 10 minutes. The assessor should be alert to physical proximity of parents and child(ren), the parents' ability to engage their child(ren)'s interest, the negotiation of conflicts generated by the presence of other toys, and the themes present in the story itself.

Finally, a cleanup task provides a good conclusion to a play session. Although in this instance the assessor assigns the family a task, it is largely unstructured because how they choose to tackle and complete it will be determined by their personal interaction styles. An alert assessor can observe the family's response to a goal-oriented task that requires cooperation and negotiation. Additionally, an evident power hierarchy and any conflicts over leadership status give the assessor more useful and interesting data. Asking a family to clean up the playroom provides an opportunity for the parents to demonstrate their ability to work together, motivate their children, set limits on misbehavior, encourage positive behavior, and wield instrumental and expressive influence. An assessor might consider giving the family a specific time limit for the completion of this task (for example, 10 minutes) because some families are unable to successfully negotiate this task within a reasonable amount of time and this in itself may be clinically significant.

A somewhat more structured situation than the above was designed by Baumrind and used in her research with preschool children (1967). Parents were instructed to teach their child a task that involves understanding the concepts of colors, numerical reasoning including adding, subtracting, and counting, and categorization by size. Directions were given as follows:

> We are interested to see how children learn when their parents are teaching them. Here is a set of elementary number rods. They can be used to give a child of this age some idea of differ-

ences in color and length and the relation between color and length: e.g., the white is the smallest, etc. Also we can, by calling this white rod "1", teach the child to count with the rods from 1 to 10. This is usually taught by ordering the rods from the longest to the shortest to make a staircase. From here we can, of course, point out to the child that another staircase can be built the opposite way, from 10 to 1. When those two are put together the child can read off the number bonds of 10: for example, 9 plus 1 equals 10, 8 plus 2 equals 10, etc. I would like to see if you can teach the child any of these concepts. There will be about 15 minutes to work with your child, and I shall be out of the room behind the one-way mirror. (p. 19)

Baumrind acknowledges that this task evaluates the performance of the parent and the child. Given the stressful conditions of this task, parents are evaluated on enforcement of rules, directiveness in teaching, the ability to motivate the child, the use of praise and disapproval to secure compliance, methods of dealing with the child's anxiety, overall degree of involvement, intellectual expectations of the child, and amount of nurturance provided.

A similar teaching task for families with 3- to 4-year-olds is one in which both parents are instructed to teach their child the rules to a game, and to play that game with their child for 10 minutes. The Treasure Hunt Game (Laub & Frank, 1988) is a board game in which parents and child roll dice, move pieces according to directions on each space, and attempt to reach the center of the board to win the treasure. The game format provides a problem-solving situation for the parents and child, and it represents an interactional medium which is common in most households. Thus, the observed behaviors may be taken as representative of a normal sample of behavior. The game requires greater participation from the parents, and cooperation between parents in negotiating what roles each will take in teaching and helping the child play the game. In addition, it is more difficult for the child to win than the parents. This allows for the observation of the child's response to a frustrating situation, and in turn, the parents' reactions to the child's response.

The Treasure Hunt Game assesses the child's ability to follow directions, play by the rules, stay on task, manipulate game pieces, and take turns. Although no coding system has been developed to date for the interactions generated by this game, it allows a global assessment of the triadic family system, including the parenting partnership and the competence of the individual child.

Children With Verbal Skills

Unstructured Tasks

As with families with less than verbally skilled children, a free-play session and cleanup period could be useful in a family assessment with verbally skilled children. The reader is referred to the previous section for the rationale and instructions for these tasks. Note that instructions can be modified for families with older children so that free play lasts 30 minutes or more, and that a variety of age-appropriate toys are provided.

Families can be asked to engage in other relatively unstructured activities, such as a family drawing task (Bing, 1970; Shearn & Russell, 1969). Bing (1970) recommends placing a large roll of white paper in the middle of the table and handing each member a felt pen of a different color which she or he is told not to exchange for any other color pen. This allows for later analysis of each member's contribution to the drawing. She recommends the following instructions:

I'd like for you, as a family, to draw a picture as you see yourselves now. Tear off as much paper as you need. You can work on the table, the floor, or tape it to the wall. You can draw the picture any way you want to, but I'd like to encourage you to be as creative as you can representing yourselves as a unique family. You can draw the persons any size and place them in any position on the paper. They can be touching each other, or be separate. You can draw yourselves or each other, whichever way you think best describes your family. (p. 176)

She recommends that questions are answered by repeating the appropriate part of the instructions, or replying "You may do it whatever way you think is best." These instructions might be especially useful with families with older children.

We have chosen to provide simpler and somewhat more ambiguous instructions, applicable to families with verbally skilled children as young as 3 and 4 years. A very large sheet of blank paper (at least two feet by two feet) is placed on a table the family is asked to sit around. A closed box of crayons (or sufficient pencils for each family member) is placed on the center of the paper. The assessor then states, while looking at each family member briefly, making sure not to focus instructions on a particular person:

Please draw a picture of your family doing something. Try to draw whole people, not cartoon or stick people. Remember, make a picture of your family doing something—some kind of action.

These instructions for a family drawing of a family are similar to Burns & Kaufman's (1972) instructions to a child in his or her production of a kinetic family drawing (KFD). Useful information might be obtained by comparing a child's KFD with the family drawing of their family doing something (F-KFD).

Family members can also be asked to make individual drawings representing the problem that has brought the family for treatment and how each would like to see it resolved (Oster & Gould, 1987). The nonthreatening manner of individual drawings may facilitate family members' expression of their thoughts and feelings without the fear of criticism they may experience during other conjoint family tasks. Directions for these drawing tasks may also be translated and used cross-culturally, thereby minimizing language difficulties that frequent other assessment techniques (e.g., questionnaires, extensive interviews). While considering each family's cultural context(s), the assessor not only is provided with an insider's view of each member's perception of family roles, but also becomes privy to individual ideas for change which can be used to maximize the implementation of culturally sensitive interventions.

A conjoint family drawing can be examined in terms of the process of creating the drawing, as well as the content of the final product. The freedom of the instructions allows for a variety of responses in structure and performance. The assessor can observe decision making, problem-solving strategies and negotiating skills, family power hierarchies, and involvement and/or intrusiveness of any family members. The content of the drawing itself can be evaluated in terms of the relative size of the persons represented, isolated characters versus characters surrounded by others, and the specific content and unusual themes present in the drawing.

Another relatively unstructured activity involves the family sharing food. Mealtime provides an excellent opportunity to observe family interaction, and if home observation is not practical, we recommend the observation of mealtime dynamics in the playroom. After completion of the F-KFD the family can be offered food, and asked to spend 15 minutes eating together before proceeding with the assessment. Or, refreshments can simply be left on a table in the playroom before the family enters and no further instructions given. In either case, cookies equal in number to the number to be in the playroom plus one, and enough drinks (e.g., juice or punch) to be divided among the family members can be left or brought to the playroom, along with a stack of paper cups, plates, and napkins. We do not recommend the assessor serving the family refreshments, but rather the assessor should observe how the family reacts to the food and the conflicts it may generate. For example, who controls the serving and distribution of the food, who is concerned about cleanup, what do they do with the extra cookie, and how is this decided?

Structured Tasks

Wampler, Halverson, Moore, and Walters (1989) asked families with a 4- to 5-year-old child to spend 7 to 8 minutes building a house of Lincoln Logs or plastic construction blocks to match a model house and another 7 to 8 minutes building a house of any design they wished. During the first task only the child was to be allowed to place small pieces needed between each of the larger pieces. During the second task there were no rules about who could use what pieces.

Other structured tasks may demand greater verbal skills. For example, most clinicians are familiar with projective techniques such as the Thematic Apperception Test (Murray, 1936) or the Roberts Apperception Test for Children (Roberts, 1982). Although these instruments were designed for assessment of the individual, projective cards can be useful tools in family assessment (see, e.g., Winter, Ferreira, & Olson, 1965). The assessor can select cards that she or he believes are most likely to elicit perceptions of family relationships, and instruct the family group:

> Working as a family, please make up a story about the characters on these cards. Include such things as what happened just before the moment depicted on the card; what is happening right now to the characters; how these characters feel about what is going on; and what is going to happen in the future to these characters.

The overall family interaction can be evaluated in terms of such factors as equality of participation, patterns of conflict and dominance, rejection, the process of decision-making, the formation of coalitions, communication among family members, and the content of the story itself. The stories volunteered by any family member as well as the actual story put forth as the conjoint version can be considered reflections of the storyteller's fantasies, wishes, convictions about him- or herself and his or her perceptions of the external world.

Another structured task is the Talking, Feeling, and Doing Game (Gardner, 1983, 1986). Briefly, in a game context, players draw cards that ask them to: (1) comment about intellectual or cognitive issues, (2) explain their feelings about given affective issues, or (3) act out physical directives. Gardner notes that the questions cover a wide range of human experiences, and are designed to direct attention to basic life conflicts. For example, cards ask for opinions and feelings about one's personal strengths, weaknesses, daydreams, sexuality, assertiveness, guilt, fantasies, ideas about death, loneliness, humor, and profanity. As an assessment tool, family members can be instructed that there are no right or wrong answers to any card, and that any answer given by a family member is legitimate. At the discretion of the assessor, the deck of cards can be stacked to guarantee that the cards selected will be relevant to the family situation. Although not designed as an assessment instrument, the Talking, Feeling, and Doing Game can provide information about specific life areas; the family's receptivity to each other's ideas; how they handle competition; what cards produce uneasiness, and so forth.

Family members can be asked to identify what they believe to be the most important three problems for their family from among a list of common areas of conflict (bedtime, homework, television, chores, allowances, sibling or peer fighting, drinking, school, etc.). From these lists, the assessor chooses the highest-ranking area of conflict that all members identify as a problem for their family. The group is asked to discuss this problem for 10 minutes and attempt to come to a solution. Although this can be evaluated as purely a problem-solving task, the discussion process could reveal far more than problem-solving skills.

Other structured tasks involving figure placement techniques (FPT) can be used with family members to assess family cohesion and hierarchy among members. In the Family System Test (FAST) designed by Gehring (1984), figures representing one's family members are arranged on a board in different contexts (i.e., typical, ideal, and conflict situations). Cohesion is evaluated by the distance between figures using the Pythagorean formula while hierarchy is measured by the differences in heights between figures in relation to one another (i.e., blocks are used to elevate figures and indicate hierarchy). The FAST has demonstrated good psychometric properties when based on a sample of adolescents (Gehring & Feldman, 1988), and in comparison with other FPTs (e.g., the Family Hierarchy Test, and the Kvebaek Family Sculpture Technique; Gehring & Marti, 1993b). Discussion of variations in arrangements across contexts with each respective family member may obtain an accurate picture of perceived family structures. This is especially important when assessing family structures of various cultural groups whose normative structures may differ from conventional structural definitions of cohesion and hierarchy, and/or whose members may be at different levels of acculturation. In addition, the novelty and physical manipulation of figures in the FAST may increase its utility with children by sustaining their interest and subsequent engagement.

Another structured assessment procedure involving observed family interactions includes using the Structural Family Systems Rating Scale (SFSR; e.g., Szapocznik, Herris, Kurtines, & Faraci, 1991; Szapocznik & Kurtines, 1989). The SFSR is rooted in the structural family systems tradition of Minuchin (Minuchin, 1974) and uses three family tasks which were modified from the Wiltwick Family Tasks (Minuchin, Rosman, & Baker, 1978) and later standardized. The family tasks of the SFSR, much like family interaction tasks (FIT) used by Thomas and Olson (1993), eliminate the presence of the assessor during the task and the instructions are given via cassette player. The tasks are videotaped with a sound track and take approximately 20 minutes to complete (administration time included). General directions prior to administration of the first task include:

> Let us now move to the family evaluation. There are three tasks that you will perform as a family. The directions will be given to you via the cassette player, so please listen carefully. You have about 5 minutes to complete each task.

The first task is called "Planning the menu." The family members are told:

> Suppose all of you had to work out a menu for dinner tonight and would like to have your favorite foods for dinner, but you can only have one meat, two vegetables, one drink, and one

dessert. Discuss this together; however, you must decide on one meal you would all enjoy that consists of one meat, two vegetables, one drink, and one dessert. Remember, you must end up agreeing on just one meal that everyone would enjoy. Go ahead.

The name of the second task is "Things others do in the family that please or displease you." Instructions include:

Each of you tell about the things everyone does in the family that please you the most and make you feel good, and also the things each one does that make you unhappy or mad. Everyone try to give his or her own ideas about this. Go ahead.

The last task is called "A family argument." Directions are given as follows:

In every family things happen that create a fuss now and then. Together, discuss an argument you have had, a fight or argument at home that you remember. Discuss what started it, who was part of it, what happened, and how it ended. See if you can remember what it was all about. Go ahead.

Each family's interactional patterns are evaluated by trained raters along six structural dimensions of family functioning: Structure, Flexibility, Resonance, Developmental Stage, Identified Patienthood, and Conflict Resolution. Scores from each dimension in addition to a total score of overall family pathology and family functioning are obtained. The SFSR has been found to have good interrater and internal consistency reliability, and be useful for purposes of both assessment as well as treatment evaluation (Szapocznik & Kurtines, 1989).

Before their participating in a playroom assessment the adolescent and adult members of a family may individually and independently complete, and the child(ren) individually be administered, the 20-item FACES-III questionnaire. This instrument was developed by Olson, Portner, & Lavee (1985) to assess individual perceptions of family cohesion, family adaptability, and family communication. While in the playroom and seated around a table, a blank copy of the FACES-III may be placed in front of the family and they are asked to come up with one family answer to each of the items. Along with comparing individual and family responses to the items, this task, like the others described above, allows the assessor to observe family power hierarchies, the parenting alliance, parenting styles, expressive versus instrumental roles, leadership status, coalitions, alliances, and family rigidity or flexibility. Caution should be exercised in using the FACES-III with various ethnic groups or with single-parent families of any group since no information is available yet with these populations.

The above tasks, like the drawing task, can be completed in rooms other than a playroom. When administered in a playroom, how the family members respond to the temptations of the toys and other objects there may be observed. Finally, at the end of the playroom activities, the family may be asked to clean up the playroom.

RATING FAMILY INTERACTION AND CHILD BEHAVIOR

Videotapes of individuals and families in a playroom allow comprehensive and detailed analysis of moment-by-moment displays of verbal and nonverbal behavior and interactions and transactions among family members, including the study of synchronous and asynchronous interdependencies of family interaction. Extensive training of highly reliable coders who observe the videotapes allows more leisurely (and later) scoring of parent-child behavior into categories. Rating scales include those developed by Ainsworth et al. (1978), Hetherington, Hagan, and Eisenberg, (1992), Isabella et al. (1989), and Nuttall et al. (1985). Stollak, Messé, Michaels, Buldain, Catlin, and Paritee (1982) scored for task- or socially/emotionally oriented behaviors indicating moving toward, away, or against, from a dominant, egalitarian, or submissive position. The Interaction Behavior Code (Fagot, 1984; Kavanagh, Youngblade, Reid, & Fagot, 1988) consists of five subcodes: context code, interactive code, recipient code, reactor code, and reaction code.

Whole family transactions can be rated into categories described by Beavers and his colleagues including the Beavers Interactional Scales I and II (Beavers, Hulgus, & Hampson, 1988; Kelsey-Smith & Beavers, 1981; Lewis, Beavers, Gossett, & Phillips, 1976) for the assessment of family competence and style, respectively.

Coding of behavior is even more difficult when videotaping or audiotaping is not possible. When the latter occurs, the assessor may need to be the person who also makes notes and codes behavior into categories that she or he considers clinically meaningful and heuristic, as well as reliable. Information obtained from the observation of the family might also need to be summarized quickly so that decisions concerning interventions could be made. The typical assessor of children and families has been trained to score objective and projective material in the relative peace and quiet of his or her office and has not been trained to score/rate/code behavior as it occurs. The typical assessor has not been trained to summarize behavior via rating scales at the conclusion of a specific assessment procedure or at the conclusion of an entire assessment battery/process. Graduate and professional contexts could provide greater training in the use of these rating scales.

There are many clinically meaningful rating scales to code parental behavior, child behavior, and family interactions/transactions. As noted above, most have been developed to help us understand relationships between, for example, parent actions and infant and child characteristics. In the Isabella et al. study (1989), synchronous and asynchronous interaction, in such behavioral exchanges as infant looking/vocalizing/crying and mother attending/vocalizing/soothing during the first nine months of the infant's life, was found to predict variations in the attachment relationship in the Strange Situation when the infant was 12 months of age. Along with noting and scoring for categories and issues noted above, rating the family interaction, across tasks and, if possible (e.g., if the family was observed in their home), across settings was recommended. Rating schema that: (1) are theoretically based, (2) are consistent with the current research in the attachment process, parenting styles, and family structure and dynamics, (3) can lend themselves to the analysis of videotapes as well as to the assessor's observations of the family in the playroom, and (4) examine familial boundaries are recommended. There are too few standardized and well-researched rating systems that satisfy these criteria or address all these areas, and those that do exist are often cumbersome and too unwieldy for practical use (Wampler, Halverson, Moore, & Walters, 1989).

Rating the Family and Its Subsystems

The Clinical Rating Scale (CRS) developed by Olson and Killorin (1985) provides an efficient and useful global summary of the family relevant to the evaluation of family cohesion, family adaptability, and family communication for the Circumplex Model of Marital and Family Systems (see Tables 17.1, 17.2, and 17.3).

Table 17–1. Family cohesion

Couple/Family Score	Disengaged (Very Low) 1 2	Separated (Low to Moderate) 3 4	Connected (Moderate to High) 5 6	Enmeshed (Very High) 7 8
Emotional bonding	Extreme emotional separateness. Lack of family loyalty.	Emotional separateness. Occasional family loyalty.	Emotional closeness. Loyalty to family expected.	Extreme emotional closeness. Loyalty to family is demanded.
Family involvement	Very low involvement or interaction among members.	Involvement acceptable, but personal distance preferred.	Involvement emphasized, but personal distance allowed.	Very high symbiotic involvement; members very dependent on each other.
Marital relationship	Infrequent affective responsiveness among members.	Some affective responsiveness is demonstrated.	Affective interactions encouraged and preferred.	Affective dependence is demonstrated.
Parent–child coalitions	Extreme emotional separateness. Lack of parent–child closeness.	Emotional separateness. Clear subsystem boundaries: some parent–child closeness.	Emotional closeness. Clear subsystem boundaries with parent–child closeness.	Extreme emotional reactivity. Parent–child coalition; lack of generational boundaries.
Internal boundaries	Personal separateness predominant.	Some personal separateness encouraged.	Need for separateness respected but less valued.	Lack of personal separateness.
Time (physical & emotional)	Time apart from family maximized: rarely time together.	Time alone important; some time together.	Time together important; time alone permitted.	Time together maximized: little time alone permitted.
Space (physical & emotional)	Separate space needed and preferred.	Separate space preferred; sharing of family space.	Sharing family space; private space respected.	Little private space permitted.
Decision making	Independent decision making.	Individual decision making but joint possible.	Joint decisions preferred but not necessary.	Decisions subject to wishes of entire group.

(continued)

Table 17–1. (continued)

Couple/Family Score	Disengaged (Very Low) 1 2	Separated (Low to Moderate) 3 4	Connected (Moderate to High) 5 6	Enmeshed (Very High) 7 8
External boundaries	Mainly focused outside the family.	More focused outside than inside family.	More focused inside than outside family.	Mainly focused inside the family.
Friends	Individual friends seen alone.	Individual friendships seldom shared with family.	Individual friendships shared with family.	Family friends preferred with limited individual friends.
Interests	Disparate interests.	Separate interests.	Joint interests preferred.	Joint interests mandated.
Recreation	Mainly separate recreation.	More separate than shared recreation.	More shared than individual recreation.	Joint recreation mandated.
Global cohesion rating (1–8)				

Note: From Olson & Killorin (1985). Reprinted by permission of the authors.

Table 17-2. Family change (adaptability)

Couple/Family Score	Rigid (Very Low)		Structured (Low to Moderate)		Flexible (Moderate to High)		Chaotic (Very High)	
	1	2	3	4	5	6	7	8
Leadership (control)	Authoritarian leadership; parent(s) highly controlling.		Primarily authoritarian but some equalitarian leadership.		Equalitarian leadership with fluid changes.		Limited and/or erratic leadership: parental control unsuccessful, rebuffed.	
Discipline (for families only)	Autocratic, "law and order." Strict, rigid consequences, not lenient.		Somewhat democratic. Predictable consequences. Seldom lenient.		Usually democratic. Negotiated consequences. Somewhat lenient.		Laissez-faire and ineffective. Inconsistent consequences. Very lenient.	
Negotiation	Limited negotiations. Decisions imposed by parents.		Structured negotiations. Decisions mainly made by parents.		Flexible negotiations. Agreed-upon decisions.		Endless negotiations. Impulsive decisions.	
Roles	Limited repertoire; strictly defined roles.		Roles stable, but may be shared.		Role sharing and making; fluid changes of roles.		Lack of role clarity; role shifts; and role reversals.	
Rules	Unchanging rules. Rules strictly enforced.		Few rule changes. Rules firmly enforced.		Some rule changes. Rules flexibly enforced.		Frequent rule changes. Rules inconsistently enforced.	
Global adaptability rating (1–8)								

Note: From Olson & Killorin (1985). Reprinted by permission of the authors.

Table 17–3. Family communication

	Low		Facilitating		High	
Couple/ Family Score	1	2	3	4	5	6
Continuity tracking	Little continuity of content.		Some continuity but not consistent across time or across all members.		Members consistently tracking.	
	Irrelevant/distracting nonverbals and asides frequently occur.		Some irrelevant/distracting non-verbals and asides.		Few irrelevant/distracting nonverbals and asides; facilitative nonverbals.	
	Frequent/inappropriate topic changes.		Topic changes not consistently appropriate.		Appropriate topic changes.	
Respect and regard	Lack of respect for feelings or message of other(s); possibly overtly disrespectful or belittling attitude.		Somewhat respectful of others but not consistent across time or across all members.		Consistently appears respectful of others' feelings and message.	
Clarity	Inconsistent and/or unclear verbal message.		Some degree of clarity; but not consistent across time or across all members.		Verbal messages very clear.	
	Frequent incongruencies between verbal and nonverbal messages.		Some incongruent messages.		Generally congruent messages.	
Freedom of expression	Infrequent discussion of self, feelings, and relationships.		Some discussion of self, feelings, and relationships.		Open discussion of self, feelings, and relationships.	
Communication skill						
Listeners' skills						
Empathy	Seldom evident.		Sometimes evident.		Often evident.	
Attentive listening	Seldom evident.		Sometimes evident.		Often evident.	
Speakers' skills						
Speaking for self	Seldom evident.		Sometimes evident.		Often evident.	
Speaking for others	Often evident.		Sometimes evident.		Seldom evident.	
Intrusions, interruptions, premature closure	Often evident.		Sometimes evident.		Seldom evident.	
Global family communication rating (1–6)						

Note: From Olson & Killorin (1985). Reprinted by permission of authors.

These scales enable an assessor to translate observations made during clinical interviews and other tasks into family strengths and weaknesses relevant to possible treatment recommendations. Seven family interaction tasks (FIT) have been used with the CRS (Olson, 1988, Thomas & Olson, 1993). The tasks include two action-oriented tasks (solving a puzzle, and arranging family members on a chess board according to closeness and distance) and five discussion tasks (spending $100 as a family, describing a typical evening, spending too much or too little time as a family, discussing what happens when the mother is absent for a month, evaluating family and couple strengths). The tasks themselves are videotaped and completed within 30 minutes. Instructions for the tasks are given by audiotape, eliminating contact between the family and the researchers during and in between tasks.

Olson and Killorin (1985) recommend the following:

> After the interview has been completed, the assessor should carefully read the descriptions for each concept and select the value on the eight-point scale that is most relevant for that couple or family as a unit. Although some individuals or dyadic units might be classified in different ways, it is important to remember that the final classification should be based on how the couple or family functions as a group. However, if one or two persons function differently from the rest of the family, a separate description of that person can be made. For example, it is possible to have a Rigidly Enmeshed family with a Chaotically Disengaged husband. A global rating should be made for each dimension (cohesion, adaptability and communication). Then it becomes possible to classify the couple or family into one of the four categories of cohesion (disengaged, separated, connected or enmeshed), one of the four categories of family adaptability (rigid, structured, flexible, chaotic), and one of the three categories of family communication (poor, good, very good).

Completion of these scales is recommended, following Olson and Killorin's directions for the family as a whole, for each family subsystem, and when relevant, each family member. For example, with a family consisting of a mother, father, and two children, subsystems assessed would be: mother and child A; father and child A; father and mother; mother and child B; father and child B; child A and child B; both parents with child A; both parents with child B; mother and both children; father and both children. In practice, when rating families with three or more members the assessor might only rate those family subsystems that clinically demonstrate significant material such as triangulation and intense conflict, or particularly positive interactions that might be useful in proposed interventions.

To complement the above global rating of family process, Wampler et al. (1989) developed the Georgia Family Q-sort, which contains 43 items pertaining to the dimensions described by Olson and his colleagues (see Table 17–4 for items and clusters). After observing a family the assessor distributes the cards, each containing one item, into 9 piles: the 3 items least like and least descriptive of the family, the 4 items not much at all like the family, the 5 items not like the family, the 6 items a little not like the family, the 7 items most neutral or not salient for the family, the 6 items a little like the family, the 5 items like the family, the 4 items very much like the family, and 3 items most like and most descriptive of the family. They report relationships with the FACES and other self-report questionnaires as well as other rating and microcoding scales. The Q-sort methodology, discussed comprehensively by the Blocks (e.g., Block, 1961), is particularly useful in providing a quick, reliable, and valid summary of the family. Assessors may wish to become familiar with its potential and use.

Table 17–4.   The Georgia Family Q-sort

Cohesion clusters

Cluster 1: Positive affect

    Enjoy being together

    Warm, affectionate with each other

    Relaxed, comfortable with each other

    Seem to understand each other

Cluster 3: Tense

    Intrusive, overinvolved

    Child is not given autonomy

    Concerned about getting task completed correctly

    Tense about accomplishing task

Cluster 2: Reserved

    Lively, spirited(–)

    Laugh, use humor(–)

    Not involved with each other

    Reserved with each other

Cluster 4: Negative affect

    Expression of negative affect

    Conflicts or disagreements

    Critical of each other

    Don't get along with each other

    Parents seem to fight for control

Adaptability clusters

Cluster 5: Organized

    Distinct division of labor

    Not involved with tasks (–)

    Parents work together to accomplish task

    All cooperate in completing task

Cluster 6: Chaotic

    Disorganized

    Confused about how to approach or proceed

    Efficient in completing task

    Can't agree on how to accomplish task

Communication clusters

Cluster 7: Negotiation

    Flexible, willing to try more than one solution

    Use give and take in accomplishing task

    Do not acknowledge other's opinion or feeling (–)

    Listen to each other

    Able to express feelings and thoughts clearly

    Able to negotiate when disagreement occurs

    Seem to hold back opinions or feelings (–)

Cluster 8: Verbal

    Parents adopt a teaching role

    Parents ignore child(–)

    Parents encourage child's participation

    Clarification provided

    Verbally state positives to each other

    Family does not talk much(–)

Leadership items

    Father in charge

    Mother in charge

    Child controls the situations

    Child is more involved with one parent than the other

Note: Adapted from Wampler, Halverson, Moore, & Walters (1989).

Rating a Child's Personal Cohesion and Personal Adaptability

The CRS has been revised to rate an individual child's behavior in play and other contexts. An examination of the multitude of concepts developed by developmental, psychodynamic, and client-centered theorists to describe child (and adult) behavior at different ages and developmental levels suggests that child play, fantasy, and affective behavior, like family behavior, can be subsumed under the dimensions of cohesion and adaptability.

Personal Cohesion

Borrowing especially from Carl Rogers (1959b) and Erik Erikson (1950), at one end the person with the least personal cohesion would, theoretically, have an internal sense of chaos, personal disorganization, and construct defensive instrumental relationships with the physical and social world that narrowly control the nature of experience. Individuals with central ratings and adaptive levels would have a flexible, firm, and resilient but not rigid self, and be able to hold, remain in contact with, and reflect and deliberate upon the experience, dilemma, or emotion aroused and then decide upon necessary action. The person would remain in contact with many of those aspects of the physical and social world with which she or he is engaged, and be "securely attached" to self, accurately perceiving and accurately valuing experiencing. Those with an enmeshed personal cohesion would be expected to be frightened by and made helpless when confronting certain experiences, develop coping strategies which include intense mistrust, shame, doubt, guilt, and inferiority dominating experiences, and become intensely ambivalent in experiencing and enmeshed and dependent in relationships with the physical and social world.

Table 17–5 includes a description of a Personal Cohesion Scale for possible use in the study of child behavior in play contexts. The categories are derived from the theory and research of Rogers (1959a, b), Landisburg and Snyder (1946), Moustakas, Siegel and Schalock (1956), Pulaski (1973), Hudson (1960), Freyberg (1973), Gould (1972), and Gondor (1964) and include the categories of affects, fantasy, conversation, play, experiencing, and relationship to problems.

Personal Adaptability

Personal adaptability is the ability of the person to change the direction and intensity of involvements, the roles played, and role rules in response to situational and developmental stresses. The central (moderate) levels of adaptability, again, are conducive of mature and adaptive functioning. The extreme ends, again, are likely to be related to problematic functioning. Table 17–6 contains a Personal Adaptability Scale. The changes from Table 17–2 are minor. Although these scales have been used in psychological assessments, sufficient data for statistical analyses have not yet been collected.

Additional assessment of the family at home, individual assessment of the child including, for example, his or her completion of a KD, description of parent actions on the Parent Perception Inventory (Hazzard, Christensen, & Margolin, 1983) and a description of a typical day in his or her life, as well as behavioral interviewing of the parents regarding their perceptions of child behavior and their child-caregiving actions in nonstressed, conflict, and coercive situations, will allow more comprehensive (and more reliable and valid) evaluation of family and family subsystem interaction.

There is an absence of cross-referencing by those studying individual and family system boundary conditions. Does the absence of cross-referencing suggest that such concepts are only superficially related, with definition, conceptualization, and measurement distinctive to the specific system described, or are there important similarities across systems? For example, in what ways are self-regulation strategies similar to family regulation strategies when each system is stressed by, for example, having to solve a problem while interacting in a playroom?

Table 17–5. Personal Cohesion Scale

	Disengaged		Seperate		Connected		Enmeshed	
Score	1	2	3	4	5	6	7	8
Affects	No interest or pleasure expressed across tasks, play and activities. Minimal feelings expressed.		Some positive feelings but more instances of negative feelings expressed.		Many expressions of intense positive feelings toward objects/self/situation/others. Blance of positive and negative feelings expressed. Feelings owned, freely expressed.		Extreme hostility. Threats of attack. Extreme ambivalence. Exaggerated denial of feelings	
Fantasy	Minimum or noninteractive fantasy.		Identification with aggressor roles dominates fantasy. Some identification with provider/protector roles. Mainly object/animal use in fantasy play.		Identification with provider/protector roles in fantasy. Mainly humans in fantasy play.		Much identification with victim roles as well as aggressor roles. Fluctuating certainty.	
Conversation	No or minimal conversation.		Some hesitancy to engage in conversation. Questions about toys and activities dominate conversation.		Orients other. Direct conversation about feelings/problems/opinions/attitudes. Confronts and questions.		Talks constantly. Alternates seeking approval and being critics in conversation.	

Play	Minimal play activity. Shallow and brief involvement with toys/activities. Much looking around.	Much of the play is rule bound, structured and unimaginative. Some creativity.	Play is creative and transcendent, of much scope. Divergent thinking. Much concentration and intense absorption.	Much ambivalence in task, play, and activities; begins to be involved and then stops suddenly, moves on and repeats cycle.
Experiencing	Distant from experiencing. Ignores discrepancy between experiencing and behavior.	Reacts to internal and external experiencing as though they were past experience or only shortly after the inner experiencing event. Attitudes experienced as existing at different levels in different aspects of personality.	Immediacy of experiencing, even of feelings previously denied. Openness and trust in present. Differentiation between different experienced referents is sharp and basic. Accurate symbolizing of experience. Congruence.	Actively denies discrepancy between experiencing and behavior.
Relationship to Problems	No problems are recognized. No desire to change.	Recognition of problems but mainly perceived as external of self externally caused and maintained.	Recognizes own contribution to, and own responsibility for problems. Recognizes that problems can exist inside self as well as be externally caused.	Extreme ambivalence: the same problem is sometimes totally owned and sometimes perceived as totally caused by others.
Total Cohesion				

Table 17–6.   Personal Adaptability Scale

	Rigid		Structured		Flexible		Chaotic	
Score	1	2	3	4	5	6	7	8
Assertiveness	Predominantly passive or aggressive styles of interaction.		Generally assertive with some aggression.		Appropriately assertive in fantasy, conversation, play, and discussion of problems.		Alternates extreme dependency passivity with extreme rejection hostile demands.	
Control (Leadership)	Either excessively controlling of activities or excessively submissive.		Generally either somewhat controlling or somewhat submissive. Control of activities and others is kindly imposed.		Equalitarian leadership with fluid changes.		Alternates being excessively *and* excessively controlling *and* excessively submissive in activities.	
Negotiation		Poor problem solving. Refusal or limited negotiations. Solutions wished to be imposed.	Good problem solving. Structured negotiations. Reasonable solutions proposed.		Good problem solving. Flexible negotiations. "Just" compromise reached after negotiations.		Poor problem solving. Endless negotiations. Impulsive solutions that are often "unjust."	
Roles	Few roles displayed in task expressed play activities or fantasy.		Some nonstereotyped roles displayed in task, play activities or fantasy.		Fluid and smooth changes of roles displayed either in task, play activities or fantasy.		Dramatic and sudden role shifts in task, play activities, or fantasy.	
Rules	Rigid rules in conversation, play activities and fantasy. Many explicit and implicit rules. Attempts to rigidly enforce rules.		Few rule changes during conversation, task, play activities and fantasy. Many explicit and some implicit and unclearly communicated rules. Attempts to firmly enforce rules.		Some rule changes. Some explicit rules. Few implicit rules. Rules fairly enforced.		Dramatic rule changes. Many explicit rules. Few implicit rules. Rules unfairly enforced.	

Total Adaptability

From: Olson, Russell, and Sprenkle (1983).

THE GOALS OF INTERVENTION

The goal of most interventions may be best described as the reduction of complaints about, and/or the increase of praiseworthy, cognitive, affective, somatic, and social behaviors of children, adults, and families in specified social contexts. These changes may be likely only with changes in boundary characteristics and conditions. For example:

1. The goals of individual psychotherapy, behavior modification, and psychoeducation may include directly affecting characteristics of ego control and/or ego resiliency within the person.

2. Changes in ego control and/or ego resiliency may be the necessary and sufficient goals of interventions or changes in ego control and/or ego resiliency may be necessary for the facilitation of the necessary and sufficient new learning.

3. The goals of family and community therapies, parent training, and parent and community education programs may include directly affecting characteristics of cohesion and/or adaptability between the persons and/or components of the relevant social systems.

4. Changes in system cohesion and/or adaptability may be the necessary and sufficient goals of interventions or changes in system cohesion and/or adaptability may be necessary for the facilitation of the necessary and sufficient new learning.

5. Interventions that are found to produce positive and significant changes in ego control and/or ego resiliency within the person may also produce positive and significant changes in cohesion and/or adaptability in the primary social systems within which the person is embedded. For example, successful psychotherapy of individual family members, such as the child, may also produce positive and significant changes in family cohesion and family adaptability (a position advanced by Montalvo & Haley, 1973).

6. Interventions that produce positive and significant changes in family cohesion and/or family adaptability may also produce positive and significant changes in ego control and/or ego resiliency within each family member. For example, successful family therapies, or family-centered laws and governmental policies (e.g., responsive domestic relations laws, responsive laws eliminating sexual harassment in work settings, policies involving poor and homeless families) or business practices (e.g., responsive child care, parental leave policies) may also produce positive and significant changes in ego control and/or ego resiliency in the individual family members.

The goal of assessment in clinical practice is to determine whose behavior needs to be changed in which social context. The play context is an appropriate one in which to study individual and family interactions and transactions and, especially with young children, it could also be a useful setting to alter not only child, but also parent and family behavior and boundary conditions (Eyberg & Robinson, 1982; Guerney, 1964; Stollak, 1981).

CASE STUDIES

Case Study 1

We were asked to contribute to an investigation of suspected sexual abuse. The parents, both teenagers, were never married, and their 2-year-old daughter lived with the mother and maternal grandmother. The child was originally placed for adoption at birth. The father, whose parental rights had been terminated, petitioned for custody. The mother resumed custody when the child was 3 months of age. Considerable legal wrangling occurred. The father, who lived with his parent, was granted overnight and weekend visitations. Within two months of these visitations the mother and maternal grandmother became convinced that sexual abuse had taken place and had brought the child to a physician and psychologist. The physician could not confirm the possibility of abuse. However, the psychologist who had observed the child playing with dolls and interviewed the mother concluded that some type of sexual abuse had taken place, and recommended suspension of visitation. The court asked us for an assessment. Our assessment included observation of each parent and child in the playroom as well as a comprehensive individual psychological assessment of each parent.

At the time of the playroom assessment, the father had not seen the child for approximately three months. We used a modification of the Strange Situation and began with the mother and maternal grandmother in the playroom with the child. Although the mother carried the child into the playroom, the child, when put down, went to her grandmother and clung closely. The child did not leave her lap at any time. After approximately five minutes a male assessor entered the room and sat approximately ten feet away. The child hid her eyes in her grandmother's lap. The grandmother stated that the child was afraid of men. The assessor stated that he would come over and pick up the child from the grandmother and that although he was aware this would probably greatly agitate the child the grandmother must allow the child to be picked up, and at his instructions both the mother and grandmother must leave and go to the waiting room for approximately three minutes. The child resisted being picked up and became even more agitated when the women, both in tears, left the room.

After approximately three minutes, the women were led back into the room, the child was put down, the male assessor left and a female assessor entered and the procedure repeated. For the last phase, the father entered the room and followed the same procedure. For all three persons, the child ran to her grandmother when put down and responded to each stranger and her father by making her body rigid and escalating crying when picked up. She avoided eye contact with all three assessors and was not able to be soothed at any time with any of them. There were no indications of responding to her father differently than to the male and female assessors.

These playroom activities, from the mother's and grandmother's perspective, did not "facilitate family-assessor rapport" nor did it lead to their "comfort, trust, and motivation to participate further." The next day the grandmother complained to court personnel that our procedures led to the child having nightmares and demanded that any further contact between the child and father, as well as with us, be terminated. One week later, under court order, the child was brought again to the playroom for a one-half-hour unstructured play encounter, alone first with the father and then alone with the mother.

After great agitation and attempts to leave the playroom with the father kneeling next to her attempting to soothe her, approximately 10 minutes after entering the playroom the child was picked up by the father. With her sitting on his lap, he picked up and described toys that were on a table. She began to play with toys offered. She did not engage in much eye contact but crying decreased in intensity and stopped after approximately 5 minutes. Although there was little pleasure in her playing and the father was near tears, himself, much of the time, the child's intense fear diminished over the half-hour. She was much more comfortable with her mother; she quickly left her lap to play with dolls and a baby carriage. However, there was not much vocalization from the child nor were there many attempts by the mother to talk to or engage the child in conversation. The mother mainly observed the child who, in turn, ignored her.

The child rarely spoke during the two play sessions, and we found it difficult to interpret as words any spontaneous sounds she made even when she was not crying. She was capable of repeating words said to her, especially those of her grandmother. The grandmother seemed confident in her interpretations of the child's sounds. It was the grandmother, who, when responding to the child's cry during an evening's sleep, three months earlier, had concluded that the child's words and body movements in her sleep were indications of sexual abuse. She had initiated the contacts with physician and psychologist.

Our assessment was not able to rule out the possibility of prior sexual abuse. However, the actions of the mother, grandmother, and child in the playroom assessment indicate a significantly enmeshed family triad and a grandmother attempting to exclude anyone else, including the father, from being with the child. The child was insecurely attached to the grandmother and disengaged and avoidant of both mother and father. The father, of course, had had little contact with the child. We believed that the mother did not provide significant amounts of care; in effect, she was the older sister of this child.

Given an absence of any evidence indicating that the father was likely to be dangerous or incompetent as a caregiver we recommended that there should be three months of supervised and monitored overnight father-child visitation and a follow-up after this period of time. Without indicating opposition to this recommendation, but because of the possibility of abuse, the court decided to obtain another assessment.

Case Study 2

The family consisted of a 33-year-old mother, a 35-year-old stepfather, and three daughters, 10, 8, and 7. The 8-year-old was hearing impaired. The 7-year-old was referred for assessment for a possible learning disability. The family was informed that along with cognitive, achievement, and neurological assessments of the referred child, our policy is also to obtain information from and about each family member, as well as marital and family life interactions. We wish to obtain a comprehensive picture of the family.

During the initial approximately 15 minutes of free play, the general pattern for the stepfather was to walk around the playroom with his hands in his pockets observing the other family members in whatever activities they were engaging in separately or together. He did not initiate or join in any activity. He did not speak much to anyone. On several occasions, while the two youngest daughters were engaged in an activity, and had their backs to him, he struck the children softly on their buttocks with a plastic bat he had picked up.

The family next was asked to complete an F-KFD; for the next 15 minutes significant conflict and tension quickly emerged. The 10-year-old, looking at the assessor, pointed first to her mother: "She don't know how to draw." Pointing to the 7-year-old sitting on mother's lap, she said. "Neither can she." She then grabbed the paper and crayon and said: "I want to draw." The 7-year-old attempted to grab the paper but the 10-year-old grabbed it back.

Mother: "Stop fighting."

Stepfather: "You guys are going to pay for this later."

The 10-year-old said: "I know what I want to draw. I am going to draw us on the train in Canada." She angrily said: "Let's go." Looking at the family members, she said. "Can I draw the train? You can draw the people." She proceeded to draw while the others watched.

The 7-year-old said: "You draw sloppy."

The 8-year-old moved away from the table and sat several feet away for a moment and then came back and watched for a minute and then retreated. The 8-year-old said, angrily: "She always has to do her idea. I hate her. I am going to run away from you guys. I will. You wait until I am twelve."

The stepfather laughed: "Twelve, huh? Why are you waiting until twelve?"

The 8-year-old said: "Because I'll be old. She always has to have her idea," and began to loudly sing "aaah, aaah, aaah." The stepfather said: "You're trying to upset people, aren't you? I said quit it."

She stopped.

The 7-year-old: "I hate it when she does that."

The Stepfather turned to the 10-year-old who continued to draw and asked "Are those the tracks?"

The 10-year-old, defensively: "Yeh, what's wrong with them?"

He, defensively: "I don't know, I'm just asking."

She, defensively: "I'm just making a picture."

He, irritably: "Let's go."

Mom, to the 10-year-old: "You have to let someone else have a turn." The 8-year-old said she wanted to draw people waiting in line. After several moments, the 8-year-old, still sitting several feet away, said (referring to the 10-year-old): "You think she's always right."

Mother: "She forces us to listen."

Mother told the 10-year-old to let her 8-year-old sister draw. As she drew, mother said: "You make sure you make me skinny, not fat."

The 10-year-old: "She's taking too long. I did that in 10 seconds. She's taking too long." Criticizing the drawing: "Her feet's too big. Her feet ain't round. Hurry-up! No erasing. I'm not staying here until ten o'clock tonight."

Mother and daughters watched the 8-year-old draw with all three continuously criticizing her efforts.

Stepfather sat back uninvolved.

After about two minutes, mother said to the girls: "Maybe we should let him draw and we'll tell him what to draw."

No response from anyone.

Criticism of the 8-year-old's efforts continued, including the 10-year-old who said: "You're making the people too big." Then, mother to the 10-year-old: "She not in an artistic class. I couldn't do much better than that." Criticism from the 10-year-old continued.

The 8-year-old, angrily: "Fine. I'm going to draw on this side," and began to turn the paper over. Mother grabbed the paper from the 8-year-old, moved it away from the 10-year-old toward the stepfather, and said: "Come over here and draw. There is a time limit here." After about a minute she grabbed the paper and said: "It is (the 7-year-old's) turn."

The 7-year-old began drawing but the 10-year-old continued drawing, too. The 8-year-old retreated and watched as the 10-year-old dominated the drawing again.

Suddenly, the 8-year-old jumped up, looked at the one-way mirror, pointed to the table, and screamed: "Look at her!"

Stepfather: "Are you all right?"

The 8-year-old: "No."

Everyone laughed.

The 8-year-old, pointing to the 10-year-old: "She's showing off. I feel like leaving."

The 7-year-old: "Go ahead."

The 8-year-old: "She gets to do everything her own way." She went to the door and opened it.

Stepfather: "Get in here!"

The 8-year-old slammed the door closed, stood with hands on hips: "Tell her she can't do everything her own way."

He: "Sit down."

She: "No."

He: "Sit down, right now."

She sat on the chair next to the door, away from the table.

He pointed to the table and chairs around it: "No. Over here. I said over here." She got up and sat in another chair away from the family.

During this entire interchange neither the mother nor sisters looked at or commented on stepfather-daughter interaction. The 8-year-old, after several minutes of sitting while the 10-year-old drew, left her seat, picked up a crayon and began drawing. The 10-year-old continued criticizing and demeaning her sister's efforts. Frustrated, the 8-year-old says: "Let's go. Let her draw."

Stepfather: "I have a hunch if this bickering keeps up I know a couple of kids who won't be going anyplace this weekend." No response from the girls. He, to the 8-year-old: "Did you hear that? You are not going to what's-her-name's house if you don't start settling down. You are more than four years old. Stop acting it."

For most of this drawing time, mother had her elbow on the table with her head in her hand. At approximately the 14th minute, mother took the paper away from the 8-year-old and the 7-year-old began drawing. The assessor returned while the 7-year-old was drawing; the 7-year-old was still on her mother's lap.

This family also completed the FACES-III. There was more conflict, teasing, and disagreement during the completion of this task. Again, the mother and stepfather did not speak to each other and left the initiation and control of the activity to the 10-year-old.

Briefly, neither parent offered much structure or leadership during their family playroom interaction. Their efforts were often ignored, challenged, or rebuffed, although after a time were accepted. Conflicts between the sisters were seen as intense and destructive with no effort on the part of the adults to do anything but attempt to moderate them.

The predominant adult activity was an attempt to control the bickering by shouting or ordering compliance, which was often successful for only brief periods of time. The mother and 7-year-old were physically close most of the time together. However, there was little positive verbal interaction between them or between the mother and the other two sisters. The stepfather was a distant and only critical figure. There was little joy demonstrated in participating in these activities. There was little evidence of warmth or caring for each other. We rated their interaction to be that of a chaotically disengaged family, with excessively permeable boundaries between sisters. The 10-year-old's control and domination of the family interaction was striking.

Both parents had to overcome their fear of confronting and firmly controlling the 10-year-old. These latter issues became the focus of the family therapy, which also included filial therapy sessions between the stepfather and the two youngest daughters.

SUMMARY

Assessments conducted via play activities provide unique and useful data, and represent a viable supplement to traditional assessment strategies. In this chapter, several theoretical dimensions of family functioning were discussed, including attachment relationships, parenting styles, and family structure and dynamics. Structured and unstructured tasks designed to evaluate those constructs within play contexts were presented. A variety of referral questions, family constellations, and resources available to the family as well as the assessor must be recognized. The recommended tasks are broad-based and adaptable to the individual characteristics of the families involved. Finally, the case studies presented are two examples of how this information can be integrated into an evaluation of the family's strengths and weaknesses and how these can be translated into treatment goals.

REFERENCES

Achenbach, T. M., & Edelbrock, C. S. (1981). Behavioral problems and competencies reported by parents of normal and disturbed children aged four through sixteen. *Monographs of the Society for Research in Child Development, 46.*

Achenbach, T. M., & Edelbrock, C. S. (1983). *Manual for the Child Behavior Checklist and Revised Child Behavior Profile.* Burlington: University of Vermont, Department of Psychiatry.

Ainsworth, M. D. S., Blehar, M., Waters, E., & Wall, S. (1978). *Patterns of attachment.* Hillsdale, NJ: Erlbaum.

Arend, R., Grove, F. L., & Sroufe, L. A. (1979). Continuity of individual adaptation from infancy to kindergarten: A predictive study of ego-resiliency and curiosity in preschoolers. *Child Development, 50,* 950–959.

Baumrind, D. (1967). Child care practices anteceding three patterns of preschool behavior. *Genetic Psychology Monographs, 75,* 43–88.

Baumrind, D. (1971). Current patterns of parental authority. *Developmental Psychology Monographs, 4*(1), part 2.

Baumrind, D. (1989). Rearing competent children. In W. Damon (Ed.), *Child development: Today and tomorrow* (p. 349–378). San Francisco: Jossey-Bass.

Beavers, W. R., Hulgus, Y. F., & Hampson, R. B. (1988). *Beavers systems model of family functioning: Family competence and family style evaluation manual.* Unpublished manual. Dallas: Southwest Family Institute.

Beavers, W. R., & Voeller, M. N. (1983). Family models: Comparing and contrasting the Olson Circumplex Model with the Beavers System Model. *Family Process, 22,* 85–98.

Belsky, J., & Isabella, R. A. (1988). Maternal, infant, and social-contextual determinants of attachment security. In J. Belsky & T. Nezworski (Eds.), *Clinical implications of attachment.* Hillsdale, NJ: Erlbaum.

Bing, E. (1970). The conjoint family drawing. *Family Process, 9,* 173–194.

Block, J. (1961). *The Q-sort method in personality assessment and psychiatric research.* Springfield, IL: Thomas.

Block, J. (1962). *The California Q-set.* Palo Alto, CA: Consulting Psychologists Press.

Block, J. (1971). *Lives through time.* Berkeley, CA: Bancroft.

Block, J. H., & Block, J. (1980a). *The California Adult Q-sort.* Palo Alto, CA: Consulting Psychologists Press.

Block, J. H., & Block, J. (1980b). The role of ego-control and ego-resiliency in the organization of behavior. In W. A. Collins (Ed.), *Minnesota symposia on child psychology* (Vol. 13, pp. 39–101). Hillsdale, NJ: Erlbaum.

Bowlby, J. (1973). *Attachment and loss: Vol. 2. Separation.* New York: Basic Books.

Bowlby, J. (1980). *Attachment and loss: Vol. 3. Loss, sadness and depression.* New York: Basic Books.

Bowlby, J. (1982). *Attachment and loss: Vol 1. Attachment.* New York: Basic Books. (Original work published 1969).

Bretherton, I., Ridgeway D, & Cassidy, J. (1990). Assessing internal working models of the attachment relationship: An attachment story completion task for 3-year-olds. In M. T. Greenberg, D. Cicchetti, & E. M. Cummings (Eds.), *Attachment in the preschool years: Theory, research and intervention* (pp. 273–308). Chicago: University of Chicago Press.

Bridges, L. J., Connell, J. P., & Belsky, J. (1988). Similarities and differences in infant-mother and infant-father interaction in the strange situation: A component process analysis. *Developmental Psychology, 24,* 92–100.

Broom, B. L. (1994). Impact of marital quality and psychological well-being on parental sensitivity. *Nursing Research, 43,* 138–143.

Burns, R. C., & Kaufman, S. F. (1972). *Actions, styles, and symbols in Kinetic Family Drawings: An interpretive manual.* New York: Brunner/Mazel.

Carmen, R. D., Pedersen, F. A., Huffman, L. C., & Bryan, Y. E. (1993). Dyadic distress management predicts subsequent security of attachment. *Infant Behavior and Development, 16* 131–147.

Cassidy, J. (1988). Child-mother attachment and the self in six-year-olds. *Child Development, 59,* 121–134.

Clarke-Stewart, K. A. (1978). And daddy makes three: The father's impact on mother and young child. *Child Development, 49,* 466–478.

Clarke-Stewart, K. A., & Hevey, C. M. (1981). Longitudinal relations in repeated observations of mother-child interaction from 1 to $2^1/_2$ years. *Developmental Psychology, 17,* 127–145.

Cohen, R. S., & Weisman, S. H. (1984). The parenting alliance. In R. S. Cohen, B. J. Cohler, & S. H. Weisman (Eds.), *Parenthood: A psychodynamic perspective.* New York: Guilford.

Crowell, J., & Feldman, S. (1988). The effects of mothers internal working models of relationships and children's behavioral and developmental status on mother child interaction. *Child Development, 59,* 1273–1285.

Erikson, E. (1950). *Childhood and society.* New York: Norton.

Erickson, M. F., Sroufe, L. A., & Egeland, B. (1985). The relationship between quality of attachment and behavior problems in preschool in a high-risk sample. In I. Bretherton & E. Waters (Eds.), Growing points of attachment theory and research. *Monographs of the Society for Research in Child Development, 50,* 147–165.

Eyberg, S. M., & Robinson, E. A. (1982). Parent-child interaction training: Effects on family functioning. *Journal of Clinical Child Psychology, 11,* 130–137.

Fagot, B. I. (1984). *A training manual for the Fagot (1984) Interactive Behavior Code.* 107 East Fifth Avenue, Eugene, Oregon, 97401.

Fish, M., Stifter, C. A., & Belsky, J. (1993). Early patterns of mother-infant dyadic interaction: Infant, mother, and family demographic antecedents. *Infant Behavior and Development, 16,* 1–18.

Fraiberg, S. (Ed.). (1980). *Clinical studies in infant mental health: The first year of life.* New York: Basic Books.

Freyberg, J. T. (1973). Increasing the imaginative play of urban disadvantaged kindergarten children through systematic training. In J. L. Singer (Ed.), *The child's world of make-believe* (pp. 215–233). New York: Academic Press.

Gardner, R. A. (1983). The Talking, Feeling, and Doing Game. In C. E. Schaefer & K. J. O'Conner (Eds.), *Handbook of play therapy* (pp. 259–273). New York: Wiley.

Gardner, R. A. (1986). *The psychotherapeutic techniques of Richard A. Gardner.* Cresskill, NJ: Creative Therapeutics.

Gehring, T. M., & Feldman, S. S. (1988). Adolescents' perceptions of family cohesion and power: A methodological study of the Family System Test. *Journal of Adolescent Research, 3,* 33–52.

Gehring, T. M., & Marti, D. (1993a). The architecture of family structures: Toward a spatial concept of measuring cohesion and hierarchy. *Family Process, 32,* 135–139.

Gehring, T. M., & Marti, D. (1993b). The Family System Test: Differences in perception of family structures between nonclinical and clinical children. *Journal of Child Psychology and Psychiatry and Allied Disciplines, 34,* 363–377.

Gjerde, P. F., Block, J., & Block, J. H. (1986). Egocentrism and ego resiliency: Personality characteristics associated with perspective-taking from early childhood to adolescence. *Journal of Personality and Social Psychology, 51,* 423–434.

Goldsmith, H. H., & Alansky, J. A. (1987). Maternal and infant temperamental predictors of attachment: A meta-analytic review. *Journal of Consulting and Clinical Psychology, 55,* 805–816.

Gondor, L. H. (1964). Use of fantasy communication in child psychotherapy. In M. R. Haworth (Ed.), *Child psychotherapy.* New York: Basic Books.

Gould, R. (1972). *Child studies through fantasy.* New York: Quadrangle Books.

Green, R. G., Kolevzon, M. S., & Vosler, N. R. (1985). The Beavers-Timberlawn Model of family competence and the Circumplex Model of family adaptability and cohesion: Separate, but equal? *Family Process, 24,* 385–398.

Guerney, B. G., Jr. (1964). Filial therapy: Description and rationale. *Journal of Consulting Psychology, 28,* 303–310.

Guerney, L. F. (1982). Client-centered play therapy. In C. Schaefer & K. O'Connor (Eds.), *Handbook of play therapy* (pp. 21–64). New York: Wiley.

Hampson, R. B., Beavers, W. R., & Hulgus, Y. F. (1988). Commentary: Comparing the Beavers and Circumplex Models of family functioning. *Family Process, 27,* 85–92.

Hampson, R. B., Hulgus, Y. F., Beavers, W. R., & Beavers, J. S. (1988). The assessment of competence in families with a retarded child. *Journal of Family Psychology, 2,* 32–53.

Harrington, D. M., Block, J. H., & Block, J. (1987). Testing aspects of Carl Rogers' theory of creative environments: Child-rearing antecedents of creative potential in young adolescents. *Journal of Personality and Social Psychology, 52,* 851–856.

Harrison, M. J., & Magill-Evans, J. (1996). Mother and father interactions over the first year with term and preterm infants. *Research in Nursing & Health, 19,* 451–459.

Hazzard, A., Christensen, A., & Margolin, G. (1983). Children's perceptions of parental behaviors. *Journal of Abnormal Child Psychology, 11,* 49–60.

Hetherington, E. M., Hagan, M. S., & Eisenberg, M. M. (1992). *Family interaction global coding system.* Manual, University of Virginia.

Hudson, L. (1960). *Contrary imaginations.* New York: Schocken.

Isabella, R. A., Belsky, J., & von Eye, A. (1989). Origins of infant-mother attachment: An examination of interactional synchrony during the infant's first year. *Developmental Psychology, 25,* 12–21.

Kavanagh, K. A., Youngblade, L., Reid, J. B., & Fagot, B. I. (1988). Interactions between children and abusive versus control parents. *Journal of Clinical Child Psychology, 17,* 137–142.

Kelsey-Smith, M., & Beavers, W. R. (1981). Family assessment: Centripetal and centrifugal family systems. *American Journal of Family Therapy, 9,* 3–12.

Knoff, H. M., & Prout, H. T. (1985). *Kinetic drawing system for family and school: A handbook.* Los Angeles: Western Psychological Services.

Lamb, M. E. (1976). Twelve-month-olds and their parent: Interaction in a laboratory playroom. *Developmental Psychology, 12,* 237–244.

Lamb, M. E. (1977a). Father-infant and mother-infant interaction in the first year of life. *Child Development, 48,* 167–181.

Lamb, M. E. (1977b). The development of mother-infant and father-infant attachments in the second year of life. *Developmental Psychology, 13,* 637–648.

Lamb, M. E. (1997). The development of father-infant relationships. In M. Lamb (Ed.), *The role of the father in child development* (3rd ed., pp. 104–120). New York: Wiley.

Landisburg, S., & Snyder, W. U. (1946). Nondirective play therapy. *Journal of Clinical Psychology, 2,* 203–214.

Laub, C. C., & Frank, S. J. (1988). *The Treasure Hunt Game.* Unpublished manuscript. Department of Psychology, Michigan State University, E. Lansing, MI 48824–9904.

Lester, B. M. (1992). Infants and their families at risk: Assessment and intervention. *Infant Mental Health Journal, 13,* 54–66.

Lewin, K. (1951). *Field theory in social science.* New York: Harper & Row.

Lewis, J. M., Beavers, W. R., Gossett, J., & Phillips, V. A., (1976). *No single thread:* Psychological health in family systems. New York: Brunner/Mazel.

Lewis, M., Feiring, C., McGuffog, C., & Jaskir, J. (1984). Predicting psychopathology in six-year-olds from early social relations. *Child Development, 55,* 123–136.

Liberman, A. F., Van Horn, P., Grandison, C. M., & Pekarsky, J. H. (1997). Mental health assessment of infants, toddlers, and preschoolers in a service program and a treatment outcome research program. *Infant Mental Health Journal, 18,* 158–170.

Londerville, S., & Main, M. (1981). Security of attachment, compliance and maternal training methods in the second year of life. *Developmental Psychology, 21,* 289–299.

Mahoney, G., Spiker, D., & Boyce, G. (1996). Clinical assessment of parent-child interaction: Are professionals ready to implement this practice? *Topics in Early Childhood Special Education, 16,* 26–50.

Main, M., & George, C. (1985). Responses of abused and disadvantaged toddlers to distress in age-mates: A study in the day care setting. *Developmental Psychology, 21,* 407–412.

Main, M., Kaplan, N., & Cassidy, J. (1985). Security in infancy, childhood and adulthood: A move to the level of representation. In I. Bretherton & E. Waters (Eds.), Growing points of attachment theory and research, *Monographs of the Society for Research in Child Development, 50,* 66–106.

Main M., & Weston, R. (1982). Avoidance of the attachment figure in infancy: Description and interpretations. In C. M. Parkes & J. Stevenson-Hinde (Eds.), *The place of attachment in human behavior* (pp. 176–198). New York: Basic Books.

Main, M., & Weston, R. (1984). Predicting rejection of her infant from mother's representation of her own experience: Implications for the abuse-abusing intergenerational cycle. *Child Development, 8,* 203–217.

Marvin, R. S., & Pianta, R. C. (1996). Mothers reactions to their child's diagnosis: Relations with security of attachment. *Journal of Clinical Child Psychology, 4,* 436–445.

Matas, L., Arend, R. A., & Sroufe, L. A. (1978). Continuity of adaptation in the second year: The relationship between quality of attachment and later competence. *Child Development, 49,* 547–556.

Miller, I. W., Kabacoff, R. I., Epstein, N. B., Bishop, D. S., Keitner, G. I., Baldwin, L. M., & van der Spuy, H. I. J. (1994). The development of a clinical rating scale for the McMaster model of family functioning. *Family Process, 33,* 53–69.

Minuchin, S. (1974). *Families and family therapy.* Cambridge, MA: Harvard University Press.

Minuchin S., Baker, L., Rosman, B. L., Liebman, R., Milman, L., & Todd, C. (1975). A conceptual model of psychosomatic illness in children. *Archives of General Psychiatry, 32,* 1031–1038.

Minuchin, S., Rosman, B. L., & Baker, L. (1978). *Psychosomatic families: Anorexia in context.* Cambridge, MA: Harvard University Press.

Montalvo, B., & Haley, J. (1973). In defense of child therapy. *Family Process, 12,* 227–244.

Moustakas, C. E., Sigel, I. E., & Schalock, H. D. (1956). An objective method for the measurement and analysis of child-adult interaction. *Child Development, 27,* 109–134.

Munson, L. J., & Odom, S. L. (1996). Review of rating scales that measure parent-infant interaction. *Topics in Early Childhood Special Education, 16,* 1–25.

Murray, H. (1936). *Thematic Apperception Test.* New York: Psychological Corporation.

Nakagawa, M., Lamb, M, E., & Miyaki, K. (1992). Antecedents and correlates of the strange situation behavior of Japanese infants. *Journal of Cross-Cultural Psychology, 23,* 300–310.

Nuttall, J. R., Stollak, G. E., Fitzgerald, H. E., & Messé, L. A. (1985). Maternal perceptual style and mother-infant play behavior. *Infant Mental Health Journal, 6,* 195–203.

Olson, D. H. (1985). Commentary: Struggling with congruence across theoretical models and methods. *Family Process, 24,* 203–207.

Olson, D. H. (1986). Circumplex Model VII: Validation studies and FACES III. *Family Process, 25,* 337–351.

Olson, D. H. (1988). *Clinical Rating Scale for the Circumplex Model of Marital and Family Systems* (revised). Family Social Science, University of Minnesota, 290 McNeal Hall, St. Paul, MN. 55108.

Olson, D. H., Portner, J., & Lavee, Y. (1985). *FACES III.* Family Social Science, University of Minnesota, 290 McNeal Hall, St. Paul, MN. 55108.

Olson, D. H., Russell, C. S., & Sprenkle, D. H. (1979). Circumplex model of marital and family systems II: Empirical studies and clinical intervention. In J. Vincent (Ed.), *Advances in family intervention, assessment and theory.* Greenwich, CT: JAI Press.

Olson, D. H., Russell, C. S., & Sprenkle, D. H. (1983). Circumplex Model VI: Theoretical update. *Family Process, 22,* 69–83.

Olson, D. H., Sprenkle, D. H., & Russell, C. S. (1979). Circumplex model of marital and family systems I: Cohesion and adaptability dimensions, family types, and clinical applications. *Family Process, 18,* 3–28.

Oster, G,. & Gould, P. (1987). *Using drawings in assessment and therapy. A guide for mental health professionals.* New York: Brunner/Mazel Publishers.

Pastor, D. L. (1981). The quality of mother-infant attachment and its relationship to toddlers' initial sociability with peers. *Developmental Psychology, 17,* 326–335.

Pedersen, F. A. (1980). *The father-infant relationship.* New York: Praeger.

Pulaski, M. A. (1973). Toys and imagination. In J. L. Singer (Ed.), *The child's world of make-believe* (pp. 269–288). New York: Academic Press.

Roberts, G. E. (1982). *Roberts Apperception Test for Children.* Los Angeles: Western Psychological Services.

Rogers, C. R. (1959a). A theory of therapy, personality, and interpersonal relationships, as developed in the client-centered framework. In S. Koch (Ed.), *Psychology: A study of a science* (Vol. 3, pp. 184–256). New York: McGraw-Hill.

Rogers, C. R. (1959b). A tentative scale for the measurement of process in psychotherapy. In E. A. Rubinstein & M. B. Parloff (Eds.), *Research in psychotherapy* (pp. 96–107). Washington, D.C.: American Psychological Association.

Sagi, A., Van Ijzendoorn, M. H., & Koren-Karie, N. (1991). Primary appraisal of the strange situation: A cross-cultural analysis of preseparation episodes. *Developmental Psychology, 27,* 587–596.

Sameroff, A. J., & Friese, B. H. (1990). Transactional regulation and early intervention. In S. J. Meisels & J. P. Shonkoff (Eds.), *Handbook of early intervention.* Cambridge: Cambridge University Press.

Schneider-Rosen, K., & Cicchetti, D. (1984). The relationship between affect and cognition in mal-treated infants: Quality of attachment and the development of visual self-recognition. *Child Development, 55,* 648–658.

Shearn, C., & Russell, K. (1969). Use of the family drawing as a technique for studying parent-child interaction. *Journal of Projective Techniques, 33,* 35–44.

Sroufe, L. A. (1983). Infant-care giver attachment and patterns of adaptation in preschool: The roots of maladaptation and competence. In M. Perlmutter (Ed.), *Minnesota Symposium in Child Psychology* (Vol. 16, pp. 78–94). Hillsdale, NJ: Erlbaum.

Sroufe, L. A., Fox, N. E., & Pancake, V. R. (1983). Attachment and dependency in developmental perspective. *Child Development, 54,* 1615–1627.

Stollak, G. E. (1981). Variations and extensions of filial therapy. *Family Process, 20,* 305–309.

Stollak, G. E., Messé, L. A., Michaels, G. Y., Buldain, R., Catlin, T., & Paritee, F. (1982). Parental interpersonal perceptual style, child adjustment and parent-child interactions. *Journal of Abnormal Child Psychology, 10,* 61–76.

Szapocznik, J., Hervis, O., Kurtines, W., & Faraci, A. M. (1991). Assessing change in family functioning as a result of treatment: The structural family systems rating scale (SFSR). *Journal of Marital and Family Therapy, 17,* 295–310.

Szapocznik, J., & Kurtines, W. (1989). *Breakthroughs in family treatment of drug abusing youths.* New York: Springer.

Szapocznik, J., & Kurtines, W., Santisteban, D. A., & Rio, A. T. (1990). Interplay of advances between theory, research, and application in treatment interventions aimed at behavior problem children and adolescents. *Journal of Consulting and Clinical Psychology, 58,* 696–703.

Thomas, V., & Olson, D. H. (1993). Problem families and the Circumplex model: Observational assessment using the clinical rating scale (CRS). *Journal of Marital and Family Therapy, 19,* 159–175.

Walters, E., & Diane, K. (1985). The home behavior Q-sort. In I. Bretherton & E. Waters (Eds.), *New directions in attachment research. Monographs of the Society for Research in Child Development, 50,* 41–65.

Wampler, K. S., Halverson, C. F. Jr., Moore, J. J., & Walters, L. H. (1989). The Georgia Family Q-sort: An observational measure of family functioning. *Family Process, 28,* 223–238.

Winter, W. D., Ferreira, A. J., & Olson, J. L. (1965). Story sequence analysis of family TATs. *Journal of Personality Assessment, 29,* 392–397.

Zeanah, C. H., Boris, N. W., Heller, S. S., Hinshaw-Fuselier, S., Larrieu, J. A., Lewis, M., Palomino, R., Rovaris, M., & Valliere, J. (1997). Relationship assessment in infant mental health. *Infant Mental Health Journal, 18,* 182–197.

PART V

PEER INTERACTION PLAY ASSESSMENTS

Starting in toddlerhood, children spend increasing amounts of time engaging in peer interactions. As they get older, the influence of peers in learning, both socially and cognitively, becomes progressively more important. Observations of children interacting with their peers, therefore, lends invaluable information to the diagnostic process. For many children, difficulty in interpersonal interactions may be one of the first signs of the presence of an emotional disorder. Limitations in related personality characteristics such as social awareness, empathy, and altruism have often been identified as significant diagnostic indicators of various childhood disorders, running the gamut from the most severe (i.e., autistic-spectrum disorders, childhood psychosis) to less pervasive problems such as hyperactivity and attention deficit disorder.

Janet Welsh, Karen Bierman, and Alice Pope's discussion of play assessment and peer interaction is a comprehensive and informative review of the field. Their chapter offers a sense of how qualitative and quantitative peer interaction observations can be used as an additional component to the diagnostic process. It contains specific information on observational techniques, as well as on questionnaires that can be used in the rating of peer interactions. The provision of an additional wealth of clinical data makes this chapter valuable, especially for those who are interested in adapting peer observation techniques to various clinical and educational settings.

In their reprinted chapter, Marilyn Segal, Jeanne Montie, and Timothy Iverson describe the development and validation of the Behavior Observation Record (BOR). The discussion focuses on sequences of behaviors relating to social competence. Used both in research and in clinical settings, the BOR effectively identifies and differentiates social behaviors of children with different interpersonal styles. The authors' delineation of "leader" and "follower" interaction styles through the use of a medieval metaphor of lords, bishops, vassals, and serfs is both engaging and enlightening. Furthermore, the focus of the instrument on behavior sequences allows teachers and clinicians to envision children as initiators of as well as respondents to social events.

Robert Coplan's comprehensive and well-researched article on nonsocial play presents a means of looking at children in natural settings. His scale defines play behaviors in such a way that one looks at nonsocial activities with a more specific and critical eye. With particular attention to the variable of context, Coplan demonstrates how observational recording can differentiate temporary from more long-lasting and characteristic play patterns in children. This scale is strongly researched and is shown to have predictive value in assessing children's vulnerabilities to future behavioral problems.

Developed to assess peer play interactions of children living in disadvantaged urban areas, the Penn Interactive Peer Play Scale (PIPPS), presented by John Fantuzzo and Virginia Hampton, offers a solution to the need for congruent assessment measures for parents and teachers. Used as a screening and assessment tool in Head Start programs, this scale provides an effective and consistent way of assessing and evaluating children despite a diversity of information sources. The authors stress the need for a partnership between parents and teachers in order to encourage the sharing and understanding of information that will lead to a comprehensive and reliable perception of the children under scrutiny. In addition to being an assessment instrument, this tool can be used to develop a social skills training curriculum for the classroom.

The chapters included in this section are consistently geared to the observation of young children and their interactions. They present a number of scales that can be applied to the naturalistic observations of children and their peers. Missing, unfortunately, is a measurement of the development of social skills in order to determine the various historical factors that have resulted in the problems currently being exhibited. Also absent are assessment protocols for older children. When considering the increased importance of this area to the treatment of children, the limitations of the currently available assessment tools for the clinical setting raise many significant concerns. It is hoped that the future will bring increased efforts to the development of additional assessment procedures that will focus on social skills functioning and peer relationships.

Chapter 18 ——————————————————————————

PLAY ASSESSMENT OF PEER INTERACTION IN CHILDREN

Janet A. Welsh, Karen L. Bierman, and Alice W. Pope

INTRODUCTION AND RATIONALE

The past 25 years have seen a proliferation of clinical and developmental research highlighting the importance of peer relations for children's social, emotional, and cognitive development. Within the context of peer relations, children learn perspective taking, self-regulation, cooperation, and negotiation (Parker, Rubin, Price, & DeRosier, 1995). Peers are also instrumental in the socialization of aggression and gender-role behavior (Hartup, 1983). Within the realm of peer relations are friendships, which are special relationships that develop when children establish a mutual emotional bond (Asher, Parker, & Walker, 1993). Increasingly as children grow older, they turn to friends as sources of companionship and social support, and friendships provide important buffers against stressful events across the lifespan (Asher et al., 1993).

By contrast, poor peer relations are correlated with a number of long-term negative outcomes. Retrospective studies of adults with serious psychiatric disorders have revealed childhood histories of social problems (Parker et al., 1995), and the Diagnostic and Statistical Manual of Mental Disorders, fourth edition (DSM-IV; American Psychiatric Association, 1994) lists impaired peer relations as a primary diagnostic criterion of many disorders, including Conduct Disorder, Attention Deficit/Hyperactivity Disorder, Oppositional Defiant Disorder, and Antisocial Personality Disorder in adulthood. In addition, research using prospective methodology has revealed that poor peer relations in childhood are a good predictor of school dropout, poor academic achievement, emotional difficulties, and antisocial behavior later in life (Parker & Asher, 1987; Parker et al., 1995).

Clearly, positive peer relations in childhood can facilitate healthy social and emotional development, while chronic difficulties with peers predict both concurrent and future adjustment and behavioral problems. It is therefore important for clinicians, teachers, and others working with children to consider peer relations when assessing children's social-emotional functioning. The methods used to assess peer relations and friendship vary with the age and developmental status of the child, but often include information obtained from peers through sociometric evaluation and behavioral nominations. In addition, assessment frequently involves both direct observation of social play in naturalistic and structured situations and information about the child's play skills and social behavior collected from parents and teachers in the form of checklists, interviews, or rating scales. Comprehensive assessment may also include information provided from children themselves regarding their thoughts, feelings, and perceptions of both their own social behavior and motivations and those of their peer playmates. Assessing peer play skills and social behaviors is a critical part of a comprehensive assessment of a child's peer problems and social-emotional adjustment. In addition, information about peer play contexts, particularly characteristics of the home, neighborhood, or peer network, often helps to identify factors that impact peer relations. Ideally, assessment of a child's peer play and peer relations should include information from multiple sources and a variety of methods, because each particular method has its own strengths and weaknesses. The goal of this chapter is to list and describe various methods for evaluating children's peer play skills and identifying factors that may mediate peer problems. The chapter begins with an overview of normal developmental processes in peer play, along with a general definition of social competence as it relates to peer interaction at various phases of development. The next section describes general assessment techniques used to identify children with disturbed peer relations, and the problematic play behaviors that characterize peer-rejected children.

SOCIAL COMPETENCE AND DEVELOPMENTAL TRENDS IN PEER PLAY

While there is no generally accepted definition of social competence, developmental research on children's peer relations has identified many behaviors and characteristics related to social success. In general, socially competent children are those who get along well with others and avoid negativity and conflict in relationships (Dodge & Murphy, 1984). They exhibit both positive play behaviors and the social-cognitive skills needed to accurately attend to and interpret social information. A friendly and positive disposition, the capacity to regulate emotions, and good social problem-solving skills are related to successful peer interactions for almost all children. However, children's play with peers and the significance of particular play behaviors vary substantially according to age, development, gender, and culture. Therefore, it is always important to take these factors into consideration when assessing peer play.

Peer Interactions of Preschoolers

For preschool children, most peer interaction involves shared play activities, especially fantasy play. Socially successful children are those who attend well to the activity, demonstrate positive affect toward others, communicate clearly, and negotiate well with their play partners. They are generally able to regulate their emotions even during high-arousal games. Not surprisingly, the play of preschoolers is not as well coordinated as the play of older children, and is marked by frequent squabbles. In addition, the friendships of young children are less stable than those of grade-schoolers and adolescents. Negative behaviors such as aggression are correlated with peer rejection for preschoolers, but not as strongly as in later years (Coie, Dodge, & Kupersmidt, 1990; Hartup, 1983).

Peer Interactions in Middle Childhood

During middle childhood, fantasy play declines and children's play interactions more often involve sports, computer games, board games, and other structured activities with specific rules. The ability to understand and comply with these rules becomes a critical component of social competence. In addition, children who are positive, friendly, helpful, and supportive tend to be popular with others (Coie et al., 1990; Hymel & Rubin, 1985). Aggressive behavior becomes much less common and much less acceptable, and children who continue to be aggressive, impulsive, and disruptive are increasingly likely to be rejected by peers. Children also begin to form "best" friendships during middle childhood. These relationships are more stable over time and involve more than just playing together. Grade-school children expect their friends to be loyal, trustworthy, helpful, and dependable as well as playmates (Bukowski & Hoza, 1989; Furman & Bierman, 1984).

Peer Interactions in Adolescence

During adolescence, play between peers diminishes, and is replaced by "hanging out" together and communicating with each other by phone or by note. The sharing of secrets and intimate thoughts and feelings becomes a critical component of friendship, especially for girls, and friends begin to rival parents as primary sources of intimacy and social support (Furman & Buhrmester, 1992). Relationship problems for adolescents frequently involve loyalty issues such as gossiping or violating a confidence (Hartup & Laursen, 1989). In addition to their individual relationships, adolescents face a socially complicated world of peer groups including cliques, crowds, and gangs. Social behavior is often heavily influenced by the norms of the particular group with which a young person identifies. Group affiliation may require certain styles of dress, modes of speech, and recreational choices. Sometimes these influences are positive and facilitate social adjustment and identity development. At other times, however, peer group norms may support and reinforce deviant behavior that leads to negative outcomes such as delinquency and school dropout (Dishion & Skinner, 1989).

Gender Differences in Peer Relations

Gender differences in peer play are apparent beginning in early childhood and continue across the lifespan. From the preschool years onward, both boys and girls typically prefer to interact with same-gender peers and avoid mixed-sex interactions (Hartup, 1983). Girls often play in intimate groups of two or three, and typically engage in dramatic play and fine motor activities such as coloring and crafts. By contrast, boys often interact in larger groups and tend to play more active, competitive games (Eder & Hallinan, 1978). Given these patterns, it is not surprising that boys tend to have more friends than girls, while girls tend to have more emotionally supportive relationships than boys (Bukowski, Hoza, & Boivin, 1994; Parker & Asher, 1993).

Cultural Influences on Peer Interactions

Finally, the significance of specific play behaviors is influenced by culture. Different cultural groups vary widely in their acceptance and exhibition of aggression, affection, and reticence. When aggressive or withdrawn behaviors are more normative within a particular group, they tend to be more accepted by group members; nonnormative behaviors, by contrast, can lead to peer censure (Wright, Giammarino, & Parad, 1986). For example, in classrooms that contain a number of aggressive children, aggressive behavior is not predictive of peer rejection. In classrooms where aggressive behavior is atypical, aggression is highly predictive of peer rejection. Similarly, withdrawn behaviors elicit rejection when they are atypical in a classroom context (Stormshak et al., in press). Hence, the acceptability of social behaviors often depends upon the context. Children who are able to "fit in" with the behavioral expectations of particular contexts are most likely to be socially successful.

IDENTIFYING CHILDREN WITH PROBLEMATIC PEER RELATIONS

There are typically two steps in assessing a child's peer relations and play skills. First, "screening" assessments are used to determine whether the child has a significant problem in the area of peer relations. If evidence of serious peer problems emerges in this screening, then a more in-depth assessment of the child's play behaviors and play skills can be undertaken to identify child factors that may be contributing to the peer difficulties and to guide intervention efforts. This section of the chapter describes the use of peer sociometric ratings as screening devices to identify children with significant peer problems, and reviews the social behaviors and play problems typically associated with peer rejection.

Prior to qualitative assessments of child peer play, sociometric screening methods can be used to determine the degree to which the child's peer relations are problematic and to determine whether deficits in social competence are evident. Socially competent children are those who are able to initiate and maintain mutually rewarding relationships with peers and who are able to elicit positive and avoid negative peer responses (Dodge, 1989). Hence, one of the most valuable sources of information about children's social competence comes from the peers with whom the child interacts on a regular basis (typically defined as others in the child's class at school). Peers can accurately identify which children are accepted by the group and which are not. In addition, peer assessments correspond well with actual social behavior (Coie, Dodge, & Copotelli, 1982). One widely used technique for identifying children experiencing peer difficulties is the sociometric method. With this assessment approach, peers are asked to provide information about the degree to which they like or dislike other children, and often rate peers on a number of behavioral characteristics. Sociometric data can be obtained in written form from older children or through an individual interview, as is necessary with children too young to read. Some sociometric questions are designed to determine the extent to which children are accepted or rejected by peers. One method of assessment involves the use of "like most" and "like least" nominations. Children are often asked first "Who are the kids in your class who you like the most, they're friends of yours?"; "Sometimes there are kids in our class who we don't like as well as other kids. Who in your class do you not like as much as the others?"

These nominations can then be combined to identify groups of children who represent different patterns of acceptance and rejection by peers. Those who receive many positive and few negative nominations are classified as popular, while those who receive many negative and few positive are labeled rejected. Neglected children are those who receive few positive or negative nominations. Children who receive average numbers of positive and negative nominations are classified as average, and a final group, called controversial, is comprised of children who receive large numbers of both positive and negative nominations.

Play Ratings

Another method of assessing peer acceptance involves asking peers to rate their play preferences. To attain play ratings, children are presented with a list of children in their class, and for each one they are asked "How much do you like to play with (name)?" They respond using a five-point scale, anchored at the ends with "1 = not at all" to "5 = a lot, all the time." When this scale is used with preschool children, pictures are usually provided along with the name of each child in the group and ratings are made on a 3-point scale.

In some cases, in order to avoid the use of "like least" nominations, play ratings are combined with "like most" nominations to assess sociometric status. That is, both "like most" and play ratings are administered. The number of "like most" nominations is used to index peer acceptance, and play ratings of 1 are considered equivalent to "like least" nominations of peer rejection. These two scores are then combined to determine each child's sociometric classification—popular, rejected, neglected, average, or controversial.

Behavioral Nominations

Liking/disliking and play ratings provide information about peer acceptance/rejection, but do not describe the behavioral basis for peer choices. Hence, these questions are often supplemented with behavioral nominations that clarify the reasons for peer liking or disliking. These nominations include questions such as: "Some kids start fights, say mean things, or hit others. Who in your classroom does that?"; "Some kids are shy around other kids. They play alone and work alone most of the time. They seem to be afraid to be around other kids. Who in your classroom does that?"; "Some kids are really good to have in your class because they cooperate, help others, and share. Who in your classroom does that?" In order to obtain a score for each child rated, the nominations of each type are summed and divided by the number of raters, yielding a proportion which can be compared to others in the same class (Coie & Dodge, 1983).

Sociometric Status and Social Behavior

Consistently, sociometric status has been found to be closely related to social behavior. For example, popular children are typically cooperative, friendly, and conforming to group norms and expectations (Hymel & Rubin, 1985). In addition, other children describe them as smart, attractive, good at games, helpful, and understanding (Coie et al., 1982). Neglected children often show low levels of social involvement, and may appear shy and nervous around other children, but typically do not exhibit socially offensive behavior. By contrast, rejected children tend to be noncompliant, disruptive, and both verbally and physically aggressive (Bierman, 1986). Although peer neglect is often a temporary condition, not associated with long-term adjustment problems (Parker & Asher, 1987), peer rejection is of particular clinical concern because it is quite stable and consistently correlated with concurrent and future social problems including school difficulty, emotional disorders, and juvenile delinquency (Coie et al., 1990).

Characteristics of Rejected Children

Rejected children are actively disliked by the majority of their peers, suggesting that their social experiences are largely negative. Although a majority of rejected children show aggressive and disruptive behavior problems (Coie & Kupersmidt, 1983; Foster & Ritchey, 1985), not all of them behave aggressively. Rejected children represent a heterogeneous group with many different characteristics. For example, the insensitive and intrusive behaviors shown by many children with learning disabilities or attention deficits often lead to rejection by peers, even when they are not accompanied by disruptive or aggressive behaviors (Pope & Bierman, 1999). Some children are rejected by peers because of physical and cognitive handicaps, odd appearance, or conditions such as obesity (Bierman, Smoot, & Aumiller, 1993). In these situations, rejection may have more to do with the attitudes of a particular peer group than with the social behavior of the rejected child. Other nonaggressive rejected children, however, have behavioral problems that alienate them from their peers. These can include immature, obnoxious behavior such as whining, cheating, tattling, or excessive demands for attention (Bierman et al., 1993; Bierman & Wargo, 1995). Similarly, children may be rejected if they engage in behavior regarded as "weird" (e.g., stuffing food down their shirts at lunch time) or gender-inappropriate (e.g., boys playing with dolls).

Peer Rejection and Social Withdrawal

Recent developmental research has helped to clarify the significance of withdrawal from peers for social adjustment. Although withdrawal is often associated with neglected sociometric status and has been regarded as nonproblematic by many clinicians and researchers, studies suggest that in some cases withdrawal is correlated with rejection and is indicative of more serious and chronic social difficulty (Rubin & Stewart, 1996; Stewart & Rubin, 1995). Some young children demonstrate high rates of solitary play with toys and show little interest in peers (Coplan, Rubin, Fox, Calkins, & Stewart, 1994), while others spend much time observing the play of peers without participating (Rubin, 1993). Recent studies suggest that the former pattern of noninvolvement with peers is not related to later difficulties with social adjustment, while the latter, termed "reticence," is related to social anxiety and may be stable over time (Asendorpf, 1993; Calkins, Fox, Rubin, Coplan, & Stewart, 1994; Rubin, 1993). Although reticent behavior seems to be tolerated by peers in early childhood, this behavior pattern becomes increasingly nonnormative with age. Those children who remain reticent into adolescence are more at risk for peer rejection, loneliness, and depression (Asendorpf, 1993; Rubin & Krasnor, 1986). This is particularly true for boys. Studies have suggested that social inhibition is more stable for boys than girls and is associated with negative outcomes that may persist into adulthood, such as low self-esteem and marital and vocational instability (Caspi, Elder, & Bem, 1988; Engfer, 1993; Morrison & Masten, 1991).

Aggressive Children

As mentioned earlier, aggression is strongly correlated with peer rejection throughout childhood and adolescence, yet some aggressive children are not rejected. Aggressive boys who are accepted by their peers are more likely than aggressive-rejected boys to use aggression in an instrumental manner (e.g., to defend their turf or authority, to obtain something), and are less likely than aggressive-rejected children to exhibit other negative behaviors such as tantrums, cheating, or verbal insults (Bierman et al., 1993; Dodge &

Coie, 1987). It appears that the combination of aggressive behavior and peer rejection puts children at particular risk for serious, chronic adjustment difficulties. Studies have shown that the sociometric status of aggressive-rejected boys is more stable than the status of other groups, and more predictive of later aggressive behavior (Bierman & Wargo, 1995; Coie, Terry, Lenox, Lochman, & Hyman, 1996; Dodge, 1993).

Qualitative Information from Peers

In addition to sociometric ratings, which are largely quantitative, peers can provide qualitative information about the social behavior of target children. Two measures in which peers provide input regarding children's behavioral characteristics are the Pupil Evaluation Inventory (PEI; Pekarik, Prinz, Liebert, Weintraub, & Neale, 1976) and the Revised Class Play (Masten, Morrison, & Pelligrini, 1985). With these instruments, children are presented with a list of social traits and behaviors (e.g., "Starts fight," "Especially nice," "Doesn't like to play") and are asked to identify classmates who meet these descriptions. These pencil-and-paper measures are appropriate for use with older grade school children and provide standardized scores on aggressive/disruptive, withdrawn, and prosocial/leadership dimensions of peer functioning.

In a less structured approach, Bierman et al. (1993) used an open-ended, individual interview with peers in which they responded to questions regarding the child's general attributes ("Tell me about ___"); specific positive and negative traits/behaviors ("Why would someone like/dislike ___?"); and friendship potential ("Why would someone want/not want to be friends with ___?"). This individualized approach often provides specific information about child play habits and social characteristics that are contributing to "misfit" status in the peer social setting.

Strengths and Weaknesses of Peer Assessment

Input from peers is a valuable source of information regarding a child's social problems. Using sociometrics, it is possible to accurately identify which children are rejected and why in a way that is often not possible with other sources. Parents and teachers are often unaware of the social dynamics of the classroom. Similarly, children's self-reports may be biased or dishonest. In addition, peers have knowledge of low-frequency, covert behavior (such as threats or fighting) that may be unknown to adult raters and difficult to observe directly (Coie & Dodge, 1983). That said, however, there are a number of practical barriers to peer assessment as well as potential ethical issues that must be considered. It is usually necessary to obtain parental permission from all peers who provide information, and schools often have policies that make access to the peer network difficult or time-consuming. In addition, although research has failed to find evidence of any negative impact, parents and school personnel may have concerns about the negative nomination procedures, which they may perceive as drawing undue attention to disliked children and sanctioning negativity toward them (Asher & Hymel, 1981; Bell-Dolan, Foster, & Sikora, 1989). It is sometimes possible to have school guidance personnel collect and compile sociometric data and to elicit only positive nominations. In the "positive only" approach, children are asked to repeatedly identify two peers with whom they like to play, until everyone in the class has been ranked. This method is comparable to the standard technique for identifying rejected children (Bell-Dolan, Foster, & Tishelman, 1989). Despite these modifications, however, there may be times when it is not possible to conduct a sociometric assessment. In this case, it may be necessary to rely on observational methods, parent and teacher ratings, and child self-report for information on children's peer difficulties.

In addition, peer assessment is most appropriate for grade-school children. Although preschoolers can provide accurate information regarding peer status, their behavioral descriptions are less differentiated than those of older children and their sociometric status is less stable (Ladd & Mars, 1986; Younger, Schwartzman, & Ledingham, 1986). With young children, teacher and parent ratings may prove more useful than peer ratings (Connelly & Doyle, 1981). By contrast, middle and high school–aged youth can provide highly accurate descriptions of peers' behavior, but practical barriers to sociometric assessment arise in the large, diffuse peer milieu of the high school, where students change classes frequently and may have little knowledge of a particular classmate. In this case, it may be more useful to use "peer informant" methods, in which peers are asked "who hangs around with whom" and identified informants provide descriptive information about their peers (see Pope & Bierman, in press).

OBSERVING PEER PLAY

Moving Beyond Peer Assessments

Once it has been determined that a child is rejected by the peer group, it is necessary to explore in detail the strengths and weaknesses in his or her social interaction style and play behavior so that appropriate interventions can be planned. First, it is important to evaluate the child's typical patterns of interacting in everyday peer play situations, because it is on this basis that peers develop their feelings of disaffection or rejection. Second, it is necessary to identify the skills and deficits present in specific components of the interaction process so that existing skills can be strengthened and deficits can be targeted for intervention. Techniques for observing and evaluating a child's typical play interactions are described in the next section, followed by a consideration of strategies for assessing specific social skill deficits.

Naturalistic Observation

There are a number of observational approaches to the assessment of peer play. Naturalistic observation involves simply observing social behavior as it occurs in everyday contexts. Although this can include a variety of settings, school is typically the most desirable, as this is often where children experience the most difficulty with peers (Bierman & McCauley, 1987). Naturalistic observation may be particularly useful in preschools, daycare centers, or kindergarten classrooms where there is usually ample unstructured play time during which children are encouraged to interact. In addition, young children are less likely than older children to be aware of or to object to being observed. For grade-school children, playtime is more limited, and it may be most beneficial to observe behavior during relatively unstructured periods such as recess, lunch, and transitions to and from the classroom. In these settings, behaviors that flag peer difficulties include aggressive acts such as hitting, pushing, verbal taunts and threats, and obscene gestures; intrusive, impulsive behaviors such as "butting in" to or otherwise disrupting the ongoing activity of others; immature behavior such as whining or tantruming; solitary or unoccupied behavior; or "weird" behavior such as hand flapping or silly voices/actions that appear out of sync with peer activities (Bierman, Smoot, & Aumiller, 1993). During classroom activities when the teacher is present, disruptive and off-task behavior may be the most salient cues of social difficulties (Foster & Ritchey, 1985). Naturalistic observations may be particularly helpful for identifying contextual factors that contribute to children's social difficulties. For example, peer assessment may identify a child as aggressive, but observations might reveal that the child reacts aggressively only after being provoked by others, or only in the context of gym class, and so on.

When conducting naturalistic assessments, it is necessary to have a method for identifying and recording key behaviors or behavioral sequences. *Narrative* recordings are highly descriptive and involve a "running record" of whatever the observer considers significant. Narrative observations typically yield a diary-type record of events that occurred during a particular time period. More quantitative approaches are *interval sampling, event sampling,* and *duration sampling.* Interval sampling refers to recording targeted behaviors as they occur during prespecified intervals of time (e.g., such as recording the number of intervals during which the child was engaged in positive interaction with a peer). Event sampling involves counting instances of a behavior as it occurs throughout the observational period (e.g., such as counting the number of aggressive acts a child engaged in during the observational period). Both of these methods are desirable when the behaviors of interest are discrete and frequently occurring (Sattler, 1988). By contrast, duration sampling involves recording the length of time that a particular behavior persists, and is most useful for long-lasting behaviors such as crying or being off-task (see Sattler, 1988, for an in-depth description of naturalistic observational methodology).

An example of a time-sampling approach to naturalistic observation of peer play was developed by Bierman et al. (1993). This system codes child behavior into six different categories: physical aggression, verbal aggression, rough-and-tumble play (e.g., playful wrestling, tackling, chasing, etc.), prosocial/agreeable behavior (e.g., helping, sharing, following the suggestions of others, etc.), neutral interaction (e.g., talking or play behaviors that do not fit into any of the above categories), and solitary/unoccupied (e.g., observing others' play, wandering around, etc.). Observers noted the context for each observation and recorded the behaviors peers directed toward target children as well as the social behaviors initiated by target children. Children were observed during lunch and recess for 16 minutes, using a 6-second observation, 6-second recording interval. Using these ratings, it was possible to describe the play behavior and social interactions that characterized children previously identified by peers and teachers as peer-rejected, with good reliability (average kappa of .75, ranging from .66 for prosocial to .86 for physical aggression) (Bierman et al., 1993). In addition to the frequency of the various social behaviors, observers can also collect information about the peer settings that are causing particular difficulties for children, including a sense of the peers with whom conflict occurs and potentially positive, alternative peer partners. Information about the kinds of play activities peers prefer in various groups can assist with intervention planning, so that skill-training efforts are tailored to enhance the target child's ability to fit into his or her naturalistic peer context.

Structured Observations

One drawback to naturalistic observations in the school setting is that behaviors problematic to peer relations may not emerge during the observational period. In addition, it may be difficult to observe key behaviors in naturalistic environments without making children aware that they are being observed. In these cases, structured observations, in which the observer can manipulate the social tasks and demands, may be more successful at eliciting particular social behaviors and revealing underlying deficits. Typically, a structured play group observation involves bringing the target child together with a small group of 4 to 8 children from his or her peer group and introducing a particular play activity (Bierman & Furman, 1984; Bierman, Miller, & Stabb, 1987). Ideally, the group will be comprised of children from the same classroom or other peer group, as research shows that children may not behave typically in the presence of unfamiliar peers. The play task can be arranged to elicit particular social behaviors. For example, if the clinician is interested in the child's ability to self-regulate in an arousing situation, observations can be conducted while children play with exciting gross motor toys or action figures. Similarly, if the clinician suspects that the child has difficulty with communication, cooperation, negotiation, or turn taking, the child and one or more peers can be charged with the task of building something out of Legos, making a poster together, playing a board game, or some other activity that requires these social skills.

Some research using observations with arranged groups has focused on the importance of entry behavior, or the way in which a child tries to integrate him- or herself into the ongoing activities of others. Studies have shown that rejected children often demonstrate unskilled, intrusive entry behavior, while well-accepted children approach unobtrusively, observe, and comment on others' play before asking to be included (Dodge, Schlundt, Schocken, & Delugach, 1983; Putallaz, 1983). A structured observation that introduces the target child into an activity where other children are already playing may yield some important information about entry behavior. For example, neglected children may hover for long periods without ever approaching the group, and end up being ignored. Rejected children, by contrast, may display overly assertive behavior and may engage in irrelevant or self-focused conversation that irritates other children (Putallaz, 1983; Dodge et al., 1983).

In all cases when structured play groups are used, it is ideal to utilize a room with an observation window, so that the observer can withdraw completely. If this is not possible, the observer typically retreats to a corner of the room to become as unobtrusive as possible, while carefully coding the behavioral sequences involving the target child/children.

Strengths and Weaknesses of Observational Assessment

Both structured and naturalistic observations provide opportunities to assess children's social behavior as it actually occurs, and can provide valuable insights into the contextual factors that may influence problematic peer behavior. However, observational methods do have their limitations. First, it may be difficult for the observer to determine whether or not behavior witnessed at a particular time is typical for that child. Therefore, if observational assessment is employed, it is preferable to make multiple observations on several different days. Even with multiple observations, however, low-frequency, covert behaviors (e.g., stealing) may not be seen.

Second, although observations typically occur in schools or clinics, these may not be the contexts in which problematic behaviors arise. For example, a child may have problems with fighting at home or in the neighborhood, where it is usually not practical to observe in an inconspicuous manner. Because children may alter their behavior if they realize that they are being observed, many contexts for problematic peer relations may be impossible to assess using observation. However, even when observations fail to elicit the child's "typical" peer behavior, they can be useful in identifying the child's maximal skill level. That is, even if children are aware of the observer and are attempting to inhibit inappropriate behavior, the observer is able to assess the degree to which the child is able to display positive social behaviors, maintain conversation, and support a positive peer interaction sequence. Information about skill level obtained via observation can then be combined with information about problem behaviors obtained from other sources (e.g., teacher or peer ratings) to provide a comprehensive assessment of the child's social difficulties.

SUPPLEMENTAL RATINGS OF PEER PLAY SKILLS

Parent and/or teacher ratings can be used to supplement naturalistic observations and provide additional information about child play skills in home and school settings.

Parents, particularly those of grade-schoolers and adolescents, often have relatively few opportunities to observe their children interacting with peers and hence may be less able than teachers or peers to accurately describe peer relations. However, parents can often offer insights about child behavior at home that may impact relationships with peers. Parents may also provide information about children's social behavior in the neighborhood and the characteristics of the social network, which may be difficult to access in other ways. The Child Behavior Checklist (CBCL; Achenbach, 1991), the Walker Problem Behavior Identification Checklist (WPBIC; Walker, 1983), and the TROSS-C (Clark, Gresham, & Elliott, 1985) have both a parent and a teacher form. Each of these measures contains items that allow parents to describe the degree to which they have observed various positive and negative social behaviors in their children. In addition, open-ended, descriptive information about child social engagement is collected as part of the CBCL, and can be explored in interviews with parents. In the assessment of child peer relations, it is particularly important to elicit information from parents about the opportunities for peer involvement available to the child. This includes information about potential playmates, opportunities for supervised, unstructured playtime, and opportunities for structured peer involvement (e.g., in sports, scouts, music lessons, etc.).

Even more than information from parents, ratings obtained from teachers can supplement naturalistic observations of child play skills and social behaviors. Many standardized checklists and rating scales have been developed for teachers to assess children's social behavior. Teachers may be aware of problematic classroom behavior that contributes to peer problems, and sensitive teachers may be able to identify cliques and other group dynamics existing in the classroom. Even when teachers are relatively unaware of peer group dynamics, they can often identify target behaviors, academic or cognitive difficulties, or other factors contributing to peer problems. When selecting a teacher checklist or rating scale, there are a number of factors to consider. First, measures should be selected which have good psychometric properties. They should be reliable, valid, and current, and should be used only to evaluate children who are comparable to the norm sample. For example, a measure developed using a white, middle-class, normally developing sample might not be appropriate for children from other ethnic groups or for those with physical or mental impairments. Similarly, the measure should be used with the age group for which it was developed.

Second, the measure should capture the desired information in the most efficient manner possible. This means that the checklist or rating scale should be as brief as possible, easy to understand and complete, and contain items relevant to the problem under evaluation. A checklist with many items measuring internalizing and social withdrawal, for example, might not be particularly helpful if the evaluator is interested primarily in aggressive or undercontrolled behavior. On the other hand, if only one measure is to be completed by the teacher, it is often beneficial to select one that assesses both problem behaviors and social competencies.

One example of a teacher-rating instrument that includes an assessment of both problem behaviors and social competencies is the Walker Problem Behavior Identification Checklist (WPBIC; Walker, 1983). This scale includes 50 items which reflect five subscales: (1) acting out, (2) distractibility, (3) disturbed peer relations, (4) withdrawal, and (5) immaturity. This scale has both a teacher- and a parent-report form, and has documented reliability and validity (Strain, Steele, Ellis, & Timm, 1982). A second example of a valid and reliable comprehensive teacher rating scale is the Teacher-Child Rating Scale (T-CRS; Hightower, Work, Cowen, Lotyczewski, Spinell, Guare, & Rohrbeck, 1986). This scale has 36 items reflecting six subscales: (1) acting out, (2) shy-anxious, (3) learning problems, (4) frustration tolerance, (5) assertive social skills, and (6) task orientation.

In addition to these scales, which were designed to provide comprehensive evaluations of both problem behaviors and social adjustment, some teacher rating measures have been developed to focus specifically on the assessment of children's social competencies and provide a more detailed assessment of specific social skill strengths and social skill deficits. For example, the Teacher Rating of Social Skills—Children (TROSS-C; Clark, Gresham, & Elliott, 1985; Gresham, Elliott, & Black, 1987) includes 52 items, designed to assess four specific domains of social skill: (1) social initiation, (2) cooperation skills, (3) peer reinforcement, and (4) academic performance. Parallel forms of the measure are available to elicit teacher, parent, and self-reports of these skills. Research has established the reliability of the measure, and has documented clear, inverse relations between teacher ratings of social skills on this measure and validity indices including learning difficulties and conduct problems in the school setting (Gresham et al., 1987). A second measure of child social skills developed for use with grade-school children is the Walker-McConnell Scale of social competence and school adjustment (Walker & McConnell, 1988). The 43 items on this scale assess specific social skills that are teacher-preferred, peer-preferred, and that foster school adjustment. Test-retest and internal reliability has been documented for the Walker-McConnell Scale. Designed to assess the social competencies of younger children as well as developmentally delayed older children and adolescents is the Matson Evaluation of Social Skills with Youngsters (MESSY; Matson, Rotatori, & Helsel, 1983). This 64-item scale provides scores on both inappropriate assertiveness/impulsiveness and on appropriate social skills.

ASSESSING THOUGHTS AND FEELINGS AFFECTING PEER PLAY

Careful observations of a child's play in naturalistic peer interactions or in arranged group settings along with supplemental descriptions of problematic play behaviors elicited from peers or familiar adults will usually provide a clear picture of a child's social functioning.

That is, these techniques will illuminate the quality of a child's peer interactions as they occur in typical play settings. However, it is also important to assess key factors that may be contributing to the child's play behavior. The clinician should determine the degree to which inappropriate peer play behaviors reflect social skill deficits (e.g., the child does not have the competencies required to play more appropriately), motivational deficits or asocial goals (e.g., the child does not care about social acceptance), or distress and social anxiety (e.g., the child is highly anxious or demoralized and feels unable to succeed with peers). This section of the chapter will discuss ways to assess these social-cognitive factors that may be contributing to peer play difficulties.

Research on children with peer problems has revealed that these youngsters, in addition to their problematic behavior, also often make errors in thinking and judgment that influence their behavior in negative ways. These mistakes in social cognition, or the ways in which children perceive and process social information, can occur at numerous levels. Children may misread the social cues of others, perceiving hostility and malice where none in fact exists; they may have inappropriate social goals (e.g., to attain domination or revenge rather than make friends); or they may have difficulty generating responses to social situations and making good decisions about how to act. Similarly, children may act impulsively, without first processing all the relevant social information (Crick & Dodge, 1994). Because all of these errors in social information processing can potentially influence play behavior with peers, it is often worthwhile to assess these processes. This is often done through the use of hypothetical situations, in which a written or videotaped story describing a particular social scenario is presented, and children are asked to interpret or respond to the situation. Dodge and his colleagues (Dodge, Murphy, & Buschbaum, 1984; Dodge & Coie, 1987) used 30-second videotaped vignettes to assess children's attributional biases and response tendencies. The vignettes included social situations in which a child had some type of conflictual interaction with a peer (e.g., took a toy, stepped on a foot while standing in the lunch line). The offending child in the vignette alternately displayed openly hostile, openly positive, or ambiguous behavior. Children viewing the tapes were asked what the offender had meant to accomplish with his or her actions, and how they would have responded had they been the victims of these incidents.

A number of published measures use written vignettes to assess attributional style and social cognition. Among these are the Alternative Solutions Test (Caplan, Weissberg, Bersoff, Ezekowitz, & Wells, 1986), the Taxonomy of Problem Situations (Dodge, McClaskey, & Feldman, 1985), and the Social Knowledge Interview (Geraci & Asher, 1980). All of these present youngsters with problematic situations and require them to interpret the problem and generate solutions. Both the number and quality of responses are assessed.

Sometimes it is helpful to use several measures which assess different aspects of the child's social cognitive processes. For example, in the Fast Track Program, a prevention program for high-risk elementary-age students (Conduct Problems Prevention Research Group, 1982), measures are used to assess emotional understanding and emotion recognition, social problem-solving skills, and attributional biases. The *Emotion Recognition Questionnaire* (Ribordy, Camras, Stefani, & Spaccarelli, 1988) assesses the child's ability to identify emotions that are likely to be elicited in various contexts. Sixteen different events are described to children (e.g., "It is Susie's birthday, and she is given a party with lots of cake and fun games to play"), and they are asked to point to one of four pictures to indicate the feeling state of characters in the vignette (e.g., happy, mad, sad, or worried).

Of interest is the overall accuracy of the child's responses, and also whether the child has a tendency to overgeneralize certain emotions, for example, labeling "sad," "worried," and "mad" events as eliciting anger. The *Interview of Emotional Experience* (Greenberg & Kusche, 1990) assesses children's ability to discuss various emotional states. Children are asked to describe the kinds of things that make them feel a certain way (e.g., happy, sad, mad, worried), what they do when they feel that way, and how they respond to others who are showing that feeling. The purpose is to assess children's understanding of and ability to discuss and respond to various emotional states. The *Social Problem Solving* measure (Dodge, Bates, & Pettit, 1990) assesses children's ability to generate appropriate responses to situations involving peer entry or peer conflict. Children are shown pictures of eight scenarios involving peer entry or peer conflict problems, and asked to provide at least three different solutions. Of interest is the child's ability to generate multiple alternative solutions, and to generate solutions that are competent and neither overly aggressive nor avoidant/passive. Finally, the battery of measures also includes the *Home Inventory with Child* (Dodge et al., 1990), which assesses hostile attributional biases. Children are shown pictures of eight situations involving ambiguous provocations with peers (e.g., "You are playing a game of softball. Suddenly, you feel a ball hit you right in the back. It hurts.") Children are asked why they thought the event occurred, and what they would do in the situation. Of interest is the degree to which children view ambiguous events in terms of hostile peer motivations (e.g., "He hurt me on purpose"), and the degree to which they generate appropriate versus revenge-oriented responses. (More detail on these measures is available at the Fast Track Web site, at http://www.fasttrack.vanderbilt.edu.)

Strengths and Weaknesses of Assessment of Social Cognition

Assessment of social cognition is often a worthwhile component of play assessment because it may provide insights into why children have difficulty with peers. Identifying which steps in the information processing sequence are problematic for a child can help to guide intervention. However, children's responses to hypothetical situations are not necessarily representative of how they themselves actually behave in interactions with peers, and should not be considered a substitute for peer assessment or behavioral observation.

Assessing Children's Perceptions of Their Peer Relations

In addition to assessing the way children think about their peer relations, it is important to assess how children feel about these relationships, as both thoughts and feelings affect play with peers. There are a number of self-report measures available to assess children's perceptions of their friendships and peer relationships. The Friendship Questionnaire (Bierman & McCauley, 1987) asks questions relevant to both group acceptance and friendship. Children are asked to name and describe their friends. They are then asked to describe the frequency of a list of different positive and negative interactions that may occur with peers in home and school settings (for example, "Is there someone who saves you a seat at lunch? How often?"; "Is there someone who invites you to play at their house? How often?"; "Is there someone who teases you and makes fun of you? How often?"). The ratings children give on this measure about the frequency of positive and negative interactions with peers are of interest. In the original study, this measure had high internal consistency

(Cronbach's alpha for the three scales were .80 for positive interactions, .82 for negative interactions, and .72 for extensiveness of peer network), and successfully discriminated a clinic sample from a nonclinic sample, and rejected from nonrejected children in a normative sample. In addition to the scores children receive, the items often elicit additional information from children, as they describe various interactions they have had with peers. As such, the questionnaire can be used as a set of prompts in an interview designed to elicit the child's viewpoint on current strengths and problems in his or her peer relations.

A number of written measures have also been developed that assess qualitative aspects of friendships. Generally, these are appropriate for older elementary children and adolescents, for whom other methods of assessment may be impractical. On the *Friendship Qualities Scale* (Bukowski, Hoza, & Boivin, 1994), young people rate a specific relationship on items assessing security and closeness. Similarly, the *Intimate Friendship Scale* (Sharabany, 1994) focuses on a specific friendship, which is rated on 8 dimensions: attachment, frankness/spontaneity, sensitivity/knowing, exclusiveness, giving/sharing, imposition, common activities, and trust/loyalty. The *Network of Relationships Inventory* (Furman & Buhrmester, 1992) uses a semistructured interview format to assess qualitative aspects of intimate relationships with both peers and family members. *My Family and Friends* (Reid, Landesman, Treder, & Jacard, 1989) has children list which relationships fulfill various social roles, including companionship, intimacy, and instrumental support. Both of the latter instruments can be used with both adolescents and elementary school students. Although not designed as a measure of friendship per se, the *Loneliness Scale* (Asher, Hymel, & Renshaw, 1984) assesses feelings of social isolation and distress using a series of yes/no questions (e.g., "It's hard for me to make friends"; "I'm lonely"; I have no friends at school"; "I don't have anyone to play with").

Strengths and Weaknesses of Self-Report Measures

Often, self-report measures of friendship and social adjustment can provide valuable insights into young people's thoughts and feelings about their peer relations. As previously mentioned, they may be one of the most practical methods for assessing the peer problems of adolescents, who do not "play" in the manner of younger children and for whom play observations, sociometrics, and other types of information are sometimes unavailable. As with all self-report data, however, they may be biased and inconsistent with more objective assessments. For example, while many rejected children report feeling lonely and distressed about their peer problems, others deny having any difficulties (Hughes, Cavell, & Grossman, 1997). Whenever possible, self-reports should be used as a supplement to a broader assessment of peer relations and peer play, which includes input from other sources. Observations of children's typical peer play behavior in naturalistic settings or arranged groups may be followed by a more focused examination of specific social skill competencies, using observations of structured social analogue situations and children's responses to hypothetical situations. Some children will demonstrate competencies in the social-skill assessment situations which were not evident in their play interactions with other children. When this occurs, the clinician must consider why these competencies were suppressed in naturalistic peer interactions. A number of possibilities exist, including the interfering effects of strong emotion (such as anger, anxiety, or excitement), contextual effects (e.g., the child may have skills for interacting in dyads or small groups but may have difficulty with the social complexity of large-group interactions), or the influence of peer group expectations for unskilled behavior (e.g., in a child who has a negative reputation). The influence of context deserves particular attention in an assessment of a rejected child's peer play because contextual influences can play a critical role in the maintenance of some children's negative play behavior, or alternatively in the promotion of positive play skills.

CONTEXTUAL INFLUENCES ON PEER PLAY

There are a number of contextual factors that may influence children's peer interactions; among these are family, neighborhood, and peer network characteristics. Assessment of these factors may enhance understanding of children's social difficulties and guide interventions when necessary. For young children in particular, family interaction patterns and parenting style may have a significant impact on behavior with peers. Research has revealed that when family members engage in high levels of conflictual, coercive interactions with one another and when parents use harsh, punitive discipline, children show lower levels of social competence and may generalize these negative interpersonal styles to their peer interactions (Putallaz & Heflin, 1990). In addition, families vary in the degree to which they value and encourage aggressive or submissive behavior. Some cultures, for example, encourage young children to be reticent, especially outside the family, while other groups encourage children to be competitive and to "stand up and fight for themselves." Identification of these familial influences is potentially important, as interventions for peer problems may involve some attempt at modifying the family's values and interaction patterns.

Young children's peer relations are also influenced by the degree to which their parents organize and monitor their peer experiences. Parents promote social competence when they provide opportunities for their children to play with peers and when they provide appropriate monitoring, supervision, and feedback around peer interactions (Parke & Ladd, 1992). Often, whether or not parents actually do this is related to socioeconomic characteristics of their neighborhoods. In safe, middle-class neighborhoods, parents are more likely to encourage their children to play with peers, while parents in lower-income, high-crime neighborhoods are often wary of their neighbors' children and may not encourage peer contacts or monitor them when they do occur.

For older children and adolescents, assessment of the peer network may be most helpful to understanding peer-related difficulties. As mentioned earlier, in adolescence subgroups of peers tend to emerge, and the social behavior of a particular youth may be significantly influenced by the group with which he or she identifies. For example, many children who are rejected by peers form friendships with other unpopular children. These are often low-quality relationships that offer little in the way of stability or emotional support. Instead, they are often conflictual and reinforcing of deviant behavior such as delinquency, truancy, and drug use (Dishion & Skinner, 1989). Even more mainstream groups such as athletic teams or hobby clubs may have attitudes or values that are maladaptive; for example, a high school football team may value and promote sexual conquest, a rock band may encourage experimentation with drugs, and so on. In many cases, assessment of the peer network will guide intervention by identifying which peers have a positive influence on a young person's adjustment and, conversely, which peer contacts should be avoided.

SUMMARY: ASSESSMENT-TO-TREATMENT CONNECTIONS

When there is any suspicion that a child is having difficulties with peer relationships, the first step is to determine the seriousness of the problem. A child who is reserved and shy, but has some playmates, is probably not at risk for future poor outcome and probably should not be treated for this unless he or she is experiencing subjective discomfort with the situation. On the other hand, a child who is actively disliked by many classmates and has few friends (perhaps only younger children) may be considered at significant risk and probably should receive treatment. In order to develop the most effective intervention plan, further assessment should be directed toward learning about the child's typical patterns of interaction in order to develop hypotheses about reasons for other children's negative reactions to him or her. These hypotheses can be compared to information gained from evaluating the child's specific strengths and weaknesses in social skillfulness. An integrated picture of the child's social functioning should be created, with a clear understanding of skill deficits and the influence of situational factors. This understanding will lead to a sensible treatment plan for helping the child to improve his or her peer relations.

Assessment provides information that is needed in order to plan effective interventions. A number of interventions have been developed to promote child social skills and facilitate positive peer relations (see reviews by Bierman, 1989; Coie & Koeppl, 1990; Dodge, 1989). Case assessment can provide guidance for determining the particular intervention components that a child requires and for selecting the best targets and contexts for intervention. Sociometric nominations, when available, facilitate the identification of rejected children who have significant problems with peer relations. Behavioral assessments, including behavior ratings by peers and teachers, as well as direct observations, indicate the child behavior problems and skills deficits that require attention in intervention. This information provides a basis for targeting specific social skills for coaching, and indicates potential behavioral targets for behavioral management and cognitive-behavioral intervention. Assessments of peer play interactions and friendships can provide problematic peer reputations or dynamics that require attention in intervention. In addition to improving social behavior and remediating skills deficits, interventions may be more successful when they focus on building social alliances and creating social niches for children (Bierman & Furman, 1984; Parker et al., 1995). Children who have significant peer difficulties are a heterogeneous group. A careful assessment of their social skills, behaviors, and peer context opportunities and challenges is therefore important in order to inform the design of effective interventions tailored to address their specific needs. In the next section, case examples are provided to illustrate the ways in which careful assessment can enhance understanding and facilitate intervention planning for two children with significant peer problems. Each of the cases illustrates how the various assessment strategies described in this chapter can contribute to a comprehensive picture of a child's problematic peer play behavior and how this picture, in turn, can facilitate treatment planning. The cases illustrate how sociometric ratings and observational assessments of peer play are combined with teacher and parent reports of social problems to provide a working analysis of peer difficulties and how this analysis subsequently guides intervention planning.

Case Illustrations

Eddie

Eddie M., age 7, was brought to the clinic by his mother after his school threatened to rescind Eddie's bus-riding privileges if he did not cease his disruptive conduct and bullying behavior during the unsupervised bus rides. During an initial interview, Ms. M. reported that she was a single mother who worked full-time to support herself, Eddie, and his 16-year-old sister; they had no contact with Eddie's father. Ms. M. was surprised and upset about Eddie's trouble at school. She reported having little trouble with him at home. However, she added that she was not able to spend much time with Eddie on a daily basis and did not expect (or want) him to help with chores that occupied most of her free time at home.

Ms. M. delivered Eddie to a child care center at 7:30 A.M. on her way to work and picked him up at 5:30 P.M. on her way home. From the center, he was bused to and from school. During the early morning and evening time at home, Eddie typically watched TV while his mother prepared food and cleaned up. When asked about Eddie's interaction with peers, Ms. M. replied that due to her hectic schedule, she did not allow Eddie to invite friends over to the house. She knew that Eddie was teased by some of the boys his age in the neighborhood and that he rarely played with them. However, during the weekend, Eddie seemed content to watch TV inside or to "hang out" with some older boys at the nearby convenience store, so Ms. M. did not think he was unduly lonely. Ms. M. expressed both dismay and anger that school officials expected her to correct Eddie's behavior, as she did not know exactly what Eddie was doing wrong and already felt overburdened by her other work and family responsibilities.

An interview with Eddie's teacher provided a more detailed description of Eddie's behavioral and social difficulties. She reported that, although Eddie was a fairly bright student, he had a short attention span and was easily distracted from his work. He often found excuses to get up from his seat during class, and he would disrupt other students by talking to them or touching them as he moved around the room. Although she did not believe that other students actively disliked Eddie, sociometric measures (gathered during an ongoing research project and released to the clinic by Ms. M.) revealed that a full 85% of the boys in Eddie's classroom selected him as someone they "least liked." In their ratings, classmates described Eddie as someone who: "starts fights," "gets other children into trouble," "acts like a baby," "doesn't like to play," and "has few friends." Eddie's teacher also had copies of the bus driver's reports in which he stated that Eddie would not stay in his seat on the bus, frequently pushed and shoved other children, and sometimes stole other children's belongings while teasing and taunting them during the bus rides to and from the daycare center.

Staff at the daycare center did not report having similar difficulties with Eddie. However, it was their policy to isolate children after the first incidence of squabbling. Hence, they usually asked Eddie to play by himself or watch TV. Only rarely did he engage in play with other children at the daycare center, and then only in a situation structured and supervised by staff.

Eddie's play behavior with peers was observed in two settings. First, Eddie was observed during a recess and lunch period at his school. At the start of the recess period, Eddie joined in a kickball game with about 10 other boys in his class. He was an active player, yelling his support for his team and running skillfully to retrieve balls in the out-field. When it was his turn to be up, however, he was called "out" at second base and began to argue with another boy about it. When several classmates agreed that Eddie was "out," Eddie began shouting and pushing until an adult removed him from the game. Muttering his discontent loudly, Eddie sulked next to the school building for the rest of the recess period. Even after the adult and one of his classmates invited him to return to the game, Eddie refused to play with all the "cheaters."

During the lunch period observed later that day, two classmates stated that they would not sit next to Eddie because of his behavior during the kickball game. Eddie said that he didn't care and sat at the end of the table. From where he sat, however, Eddie began to throw peas off his plate toward the offenders. Although some of his classmates laughed at this behavior, others yelled for Eddie to stop, and the lunch monitor repri-manded him. As he was leaving the lunchroom, Eddie took the hat of another classmate and threw it across the room.

During an interview at the clinic, Eddie was asked about his perceptions of his class-mates. Eddie replied that he really liked the boys in his class and that they liked him too. He knew they liked him because they chose him to play kickball, they laughed at his jokes, and they liked to play chase with him. When asked about the reports of his calling names or pushing on the bus, Eddie steadfastly denied them, remarking that he could not recall anything like that ever happening to him. Eddie also reported that he did not like to play with the boys his age in his neighborhood because they were "babies" but that he had two "real good buddies"—two adolescents he had met at the convenience store. Although Eddie would not discuss these teenage friends initially, it later became evident that they had encouraged Eddie to smoke cigarettes with them and had given him beer to drink, finding his reactions amusing.

In addition to working with Eddie's mother and teacher to construct a behavior man-agement program to reduce conduct problems at school and on the bus, Eddie was referred to a boy's playgroup for social skills training. His initial behavior in the novel group setting provided additional information about his play behavior and skill deficits. During the first two sessions, Eddie appeared very fidgety and somewhat anxious. He was very talkative, telling the other boys in the group about his family, his school, and his teenage friends. He initiated very high rates of prosocial behavior, offering to move the game pieces for everyone, get everyone a drink, help everyone finish coloring their parts of the poster, and so on. By the second session, however, the other boys in the group started resisting some of Eddie's offers to help and began to tire of his incessant talking. By the third session, some group members began to complain that Eddie was always bragging. They also began to actively resist his attempts to "help" them, stating that they did not want him to touch their stuff. By the fourth session, Eddie's reaction to the unresponsiveness of other group members was reminiscent of his playground behavior—he became angry, made verbal accusations of their wrongdoing, refused to play anymore, and made a show of his hurt feelings and resentment.

Eddie's social difficulties, as they became evident through these play observations, were similar to the difficulties displayed by many aggressive and rejected children. Although he seemed to have ample motivation to make new friends initially, he was not at all skilled at adopting the frame of reference of the peer group, nor was he able to monitor and respond to his peers' reactions to him. The strategies Eddie used to initiate friendships were active and "high profile."

Although many of his initial behaviors were positive in nature (e.g., his self-disclosures and offers to help), his display of these behaviors was insensitive. He failed to notice when his timing was poor and he was interrupting others, and he did not attend to whether others really wanted or needed the help he was offering. These deficits in self-monitoring and interpersonal perception skills, which became apparent during the group play observations, were not too surprising given the fact that Eddie had revealed in his clinic interview a lack of awareness of his peers' negative feelings toward him and that he tended to deny his own misbehaviors (rather than engage in preventive problem-solving).

In addition to his interpersonal insensitivity, Eddie's social difficulties were heightened by his maladaptive responses to conflict. When upset, Eddie escalated quickly to high-level coercive interpersonal behaviors—verbal accusations and threats, insults, physical aggression, and negativistic sulking. Eddie appeared deficient in the skills necessary for reciprocal interpersonal negotiation and successful conflict resolution.

Finally, Eddie's short attention span, which caused him some difficulties in the classroom situation, seemed also to affect his social interactions. He preferred interpersonal experiences that were active, energetic, and involved. Eddie enjoyed physically active games such as kickball, and when physical activity was constrained (as at lunch or craft and table-game activities), Eddie often "livened things up" by initiating physical contact (e.g., by touching others or their belongings). Eddie often initiated these behaviors in the name of fun, but the recipients often perceived them to be provocative and intrusive. In general, aggressive-rejected boys like Eddie prefer active, rough-and-tumble play. However, this type of play lends itself much more than other types of play to the misperception of hostile intentions by the participants and the subsequent escalation into aggressive conflict.

Based on these reports and observations of Eddie's social behavior with peers, a multifaceted treatment plan was formulated. General goals included increasing Eddie's social skills for peer interactions, providing him with increased opportunities for positive peer interactions, and reducing his exposure to negative peer contacts. A number of complementary intervention strategies were planned, including strategic environmental modifications, parent and teacher-mediated behavioral management programs, and direct social skills training with Eddie.

Environmentally, changes were proposed to increase Eddie's opportunities for and exposure to positive interaction experiences and to decrease his exposure to negative influences. First, it was deemed important to reduce the amount of time outside of school that Eddie spent alone and watching TV. While these times were not labeled as problematic by the teacher or parent, they were targeted as nonproductive times that could be used to facilitate Eddie's social development. Discussions with Eddie's daycare providers were planned to determine whether they could structure daily opportunities for supervised peer interaction; if untenable, alternative after-school placements that could provide Eddie with better social support would be explored.

Additionally, the treatment plan involved referring Eddie to the Big Brother program and enrolling him in a university-sponsored program that provided peer activities for at-risk children on alternate Saturdays. Given Eddie's social skill deficits, proposed opportunities were carefully chosen to ensure that the degree and type of adult supervision available would be sufficient to support positive and to control negative interactions.

Additionally, during the initial contact and referral phase, Eddie's clinician planned to indicate her willingness to serve as an advisor should serious peer-interaction problems arise in these field settings.

Consultation, with Eddie's mother and teacher were planned to institute behavioral management programs at home and at school. Although Eddie's mother was not complaining of behavioral problems at home, the treatment plan identified several changes in her behavior that could foster Eddie's adaptation. First, she could facilitate Eddie's socialization by increasing her positive interactions with him. Second, she could provide backup reinforcement for the behavioral management programs instituted in school settings. Third, she could protect Eddie from damaging peer contacts by increasing the extent to which she monitored and controlled his neighborhood activities (for example, by preventing him from associating with the adolescents at the convenience store). Finally, she could increase his opportunities for positive peer contacts by arranging and supporting such contacts in the community.

Consultation with Eddie's teacher was also planned to design behavioral management procedures that could facilitate control of Eddie's negative behaviors in school settings. Because most of the aversive behaviors that seemed most detrimental to Eddie's peer status occurred in relatively unsupervised settings (e.g., the playground, lunchroom, and bus) and were elicited and consequated by peer responses, it was expected that the control of these behaviors would require some innovation and flexibility on the part of school personnel. Discussions with Eddie's teacher were therefore planned first to devise a system whereby Eddie's aversive behaviors could be accurately monitored, and then to enable the modifications of the antecedents and consequences of these behaviors.

In addition to these environmental and consultative intervention strategies, the treatment plan included Eddie's continued involvement in a small social skills training group. Observations of Eddie's initial interactions in this group indicated core deficits in his social-perception skills, poor responsivity to interpersonal cues, and inadequate self-monitoring, as well as a tendency to respond to conflict with escalating aversive behaviors such as verbal abusiveness and negativism. It was anticipated that instruction and modeling in prosocial behaviors and conflict-resolution skills along with the behavioral management of negative peer-interaction behavior during these skills training groups would foster improvements in Eddie's social behavior. Additionally, the direct cueing and feedback provided by adult group leaders, combined with the prompted discussion of videotaped portions of group interaction, were expected to foster Eddie's self-awareness.

Jonathan

Jonathan was an 8-year-old boy who came to the clinician in an unusual way, having been identified as a peer-rejected child in the course of a research project at his elementary school. Jonathan received no positive nominations at all from his second-grade classmates, and nearly everyone identified him as someone they would rather not play with. This information was shared with his parents, and they agreed to an evaluation at the clinic.

When asked for their perspective, Jonathan's parents (who were college-educated and upper-middle class) expressed surprise at the idea that he had no friends, saying that classmates who lived in their neighborhood often came over to play with Jonathan. They did suggest, however, that Jonathan could be somewhat self-centered in his interactions, which they attributed to the fact that his only sibling was 10 years older than he. They explained that they often played games with him and that they always allowed him to make the rules, or to change them if he was losing. The parents said that Jonathan played happily with one boy at a time (although he was sometimes bossy), but that interactions with two or three boys always ended in arguments.

Jonathan's teacher emphatically denied the possibility that he could have any real friends in his classroom, because she had observed the other children avoiding him. She said that the only reason some of the boys visited Jonathan's house was to play with the very appealing toys his parents bought for him; she said that they tended to lose interest in Jonathan when he did not have a new toy. Further, although Jonathan displayed little overt aggression on a day-to-day basis, his teacher felt that two incidents, in which he was exceptionally mean and spiteful to another child, had adversely affected his peer status. One incident involved an argument on the playground and resulted in Jonathan knocking the other boy up against the wall hard enough to cut his scalp, which, although the injury was not serious, bled profusely. In another incident, Jonathan surreptitiously tore up the carefully constructed and prize-winning art project of a classmate and secretly placed the pieces in the classmate's lunch box. Although there were only a few such incidents during the entire school year, they were highly salient to both teachers and students, who would talk about Jonathan's actions with outrage months after the event.

Jonathan was observed on the playground during a game of football. Although he was not overtly excluded, he remained on the outskirts of the group and clearly was peripheral to the activity. The ball was never thrown to him, nor did anyone appear to notice or acknowledge him in any way. Nevertheless, he ran back and forth with the others and appeared to enjoy himself. Because Jonathan's parents said that they frequently played with him, the family was observed playing a game together. Both parents were attentive and warm, and always did what Jonathan told them to do. Jonathan, on the other hand, insisted on playing according to the rules he made up and protested when his parents made any suggestions.

Later, during an interview, Jonathan stated that playing with other kids was the most important and enjoyable thing to him—in fact, he resented the loss of play time that occurred as a result of his clinic visits. He denied having any problems with friends at all. When asked about what he would do in common social situations, Jonathan seemed to have a good command of social conventions and suggested strategies that were appropriate for boys his age.

A small play group was formed, consisting of two other boys being seen at the clinic (both having been identified as having problems with peers) and the brother of one of those boys (the brother was not a client), all of whom were within a year of Jonathan's age. The four boys were observed interacting in a free-play situation during several different hour-long sessions. Jonathan was initially shy with the other boys, but he demonstrated good skills by asking them questions about what kind of bicycles they owned.

Jonathan always began a session appearing eager to play, and the boys usually agreed quickly on an activity. As time passed, however, Jonathan seemed to tire of the activity, and would suggest another. If the boys did not agree, he would go off by himself and sit in the corner daydreaming. This infuriated the others, particularly when continuation of the game depended on having even teams, but Jonathan did not respond to their entreaties to return to the game. This pattern was repeated several times during the play sessions, each time resulting in utter exasperation and frustration on the part of the other boys, and absolutely no apparent concern or interest in Jonathan.

Another situation that was problematic for Jonathan was conflict resolution. When the group had a disagreement about something that was important to Jonathan, he appeared to have no skills in negotiation. Instead, he became very angry and yelled at the others. Usually, it was necessary for an adult to intervene so that the disagreement could be worked out and play could continue. Sometimes, the disagreement developed from unfair behavior on Jonathan's part. For example, the boys often brought a few of their own toys to the session, but Jonathan was the only one who refused to share his, insisting that they might be broken if someone else played with them.

On the basis of this assessment, it was concluded that Jonathan's social problems lay in two areas: insensitive social goals and poor conflict-resolution skills. Jonathan seemed interested in playing with others only when it was immediately gratifying for himself. He seemed to have little awareness of the negative impact of his behavior on others. When disagreements arose, he was unable to see the perspective of others and became angry when they would not give in to him. The treatment goals that were developed were (a) to help Jonathan become more sensitive to others' viewpoints and feelings, (b) to encourage Jonathan to adopt the perspective that it is more fun to play when everyone is having a good time (i.e., to shift his social goals in a more prosocial direction), and (c) to develop some new skills in resolving disagreements. These treatment goals were pursued using a social-skills training group (comprised of the same boys who were involved in the assessment group). Direct coaching of specific skills was used, along with a free-play portion of each session designed to improve generalization of newly acquired skills to more naturalistic play interactions. Jonathan's parents were enlisted to support his changing behavior in his interactions with peers and themselves at home. The group met weekly for Jonathan's entire third-grade school year, and by the end of the year his acceptance by peers was much improved, as documented by the sociometrics gathered for the research project that had initially identified him. Observations of the group and reports from parents confirmed that Jonathan had become more willing to cooperate with others in order to have more frequent and more enjoyable play interactions.

REFERENCES

Achenbach, T. (1991). *Manual for the Child Behavior Checklist and 1991 profile.* Burlington: University of Vermont, Department of Psychiatry.

American Psychiatric Association. (1994). *Diagnostic and statistical manual of mental disorders* (4th ed.). Washington, D.C.

Asendorpf, J. B. (1993). Beyond temperament: A two-factorial coping model of the development of inhibition during childhood. In K. H. Rubin & J. B. Asendorpf (Eds.), *Social withdrawal, inhibition and shyness in childhood* (pp. 265–289). Hillsdale, NJ: Erlbaum.

Asher, S. R., & Hymel, S. (1981). Children's social competence in peer relations: Sociometric and behavioral assessment. In J. D. Wine & M. D. Smye (Eds.), *Social competence* (pp. 122–157). New York: Guilford Press.

Asher, S. R., Hymel, S., & Renshaw, P. D. (1984). Loneliness in children. *Child Development, 55,* 1456–1464.

Asher, S. R., Parker, J. G., & Walker, D. L. (1993). Distinguishing friendship from acceptance: Implications for intervention and assessment. In W. M. Bukowski, A. F. Newcomb, & W. W. Hartup (Eds.), *The company they keep: Friendship during childhood and adolescence.* New York: Cambridge University Press.

Bell-Dolan, D. J., Foster, S. L., & Sikora, D. M. (1989). Effects of sociometric testing on children's behavior and loneliness in school. *Developmental Psychology, 25,* 306–311.

Bell-Dolan, D. J., Foster, S. L., & Tishelman, A. (1989). An alternative to negative nomination sociometric measures. *Journal of Clinical Child Psychology, 18*(2), 153–157.

Bierman, K. L. (1986). The relationship between social aggression and peer rejection in middle childhood. In R. Prinz (Ed.), *Advances in behavioral assessment of children and families* (Vol. 2, pp. 151–178). Greenwich, CT: JAI Press.

Bierman, K. L. (1989) Improving the peer relationships of rejected children. I. B. Laheys, A. Kazdin (Eds), *Advances in Clinical Child Psychology* (Vol. 6, pp. 53–84). New York: Plenum Press.

Bierman, K. L., & Furman, W. (1984). The effects of social skills training and peer involvement on the social adjustment of preadolescents. *Child Development, 55,* 151–162.

Bierman, K. L., & McCauley, E. (1987). Children's descriptions of their peer interactions: Useful information for clinical child assessment. *Journal of Clinical Child Psychology, 16,* 9–18.

Bierman, K. L., Miller, C. L., & Stabb, S. D. (1987). Improving the social behavior and peer acceptance of rejected boys: Effects of social skill training with instructions and prohibitions. *Journal of Consulting and Clinical Psychology, 55,* 194–200.

Bierman, K. L., Smoot, D. L., & Aumiller, K. (1993). Characteristics of aggressive-rejected, aggressive (nonrejected), and rejected (nonaggressive) boys. *Child Development, 64,* 139–151.

Bierman, K. L., & Wargo, J. (1995). Predicting the longitudinal course associated with aggressive-rejected, aggressive (nonrejected), and rejected (nonaggressive) status. *Development and Psychopathology, 7,* 669–682.

Bukowski, W., & Hoza, B. (1989). Popularity and friendship: Issues in theory, measurement and outcome. In T. J. Berndt & G. W. Ladd (Eds.), *Peer relationships in child development* (pp. 15–45). New York: Wiley.

Bukowski, W., Hoza, B., & Boivin, M. (1994). Measuring friendship quality during pre- and early adolescence: The development and psychometric properties of the Friendship Qualities Scale. *Journal of Social and Personal Relationships, 11,* 471–484.

Calkins, S. D., Fox, N. A., Rubin, K. H., Coplan, R. J., & Stewart, S. (1994). *Longitudinal outcomes of behavioral inhibition: Implications for behavior in a peer setting.* Unpublished manuscript. University of Maryland, 347–356.

Caplan, M., Weissberg, R. P., Bersoff, D. M., Ezekowitz, W., & Wells, M. L. (1986), *The middle school Alternative Solutions Test (AST) scoring manual.* Unpublished manuscript.

Caspi, A., Elder, G. H., & Bem, D. J. (1988). Moving away from the world: The life course patterns of shy children. *Developmental Psychology, 24,* 824–831.

Clark, L., Gresham, F. M., & Elliott, S. N. (1985). Development and validation of a social skills assessment measure: The TROSS-C. *Journal of Psychoeducational Assessment, 3,* 347–356.

Coie, J. D., & Dodge, K. A. (1983). Continuities and changes in children's social status: A five-year longitudinal study. *Merrill-Palmer Quarterly, 29,* 261–282.

Coie, J. D., Dodge, K. A., & Copotelli, H. (1982). Dimensions and types of status: A cross-age perspective. *Developmental Psychology, 18,* 557–570.

Coie, J. D., Dodge, K. A., & Kupersmidt, J. B. (1990). Peer group behavioral and social group status. In S. R. Asher & J. D. Coie (Eds.), *Peer rejection in childhood* (pp. 17–59). Cambridge, England: Cambridge University Press.

Coie, J. D., & Koeppl, G. K. (1990). Adapting intervention to the problems of aggressive and disruptive children. In S. R. Asher & J. D. Coie (Eds.), *Peer rejection in childhood* (pp. 275–308). Cambridge, England: Cambridge University Press.

Coie, J. D., & Kupersmidt, J. B. (1983). A behavioral analysis of emerging social status in boys' groups. *Child Development, 54,* 1400–1416.

Coie, J. D., Terry, R., Lenox, K., Lochman, J., & Hyman, C. (1996). Childhood peer rejection and aggression as predictors of stable patterns of adolescent disorder. *Development and Psychopathology, 7,* 697–713.

Conduct Problems Prevention Research Group (1992). A developmental and clinical model for the prevention of conduct disorders: The Fast Track Program. *Development and Psychopathology, 4,* 509–527.

Connelly, J., & Doyle, A. (1981). Assessment of social competence in preschoolers: Teachers versus peers. *Developmental Psychology, 17,* 454–462.

Coplan, R. J., Rubin, K. H., Fox, N. A., Calkins, S. D., & Stewart, S. L. (1994). Being alone, playing alone, and acting alone: Distinguishing among reticence and passive solitude in young children. *Child Development, 65,* 129–137.

Crick, N. R., & Dodge, K. A. (1994). A review and reformulation of social information processing mechanisms in children's social development. *Psychological Bulletin, 115,* 74–101.

Dishion, T. J., & Skinner, M. (1989, April). *A process measure for the role of peer relations in adolescent social adjustment.* Paper presented at the biennial meeting of the Society for Research in Child Development, Kansas City, MO.

Dodge, K. A. (1989). Problems in social relationships. In E. J. Mash & R. A. Barkley (Eds.), *Treatment of childhood disorders* (pp. 222–246). New York: Guilford.

Dodge, K. A. (1993, March). *Social information processing and peer rejection factors in the development of behavior problems in children.* Paper presented at the biennial meeting of the Society for Research in Child Development, New Orleans.

Dodge, K. A., Bates, J. E., & Pettit, G. S. (1990). Mechanisms in the cycle of violence. *Science, 250,* 1678–1683.

Dodge, K. A., & Coie, J. D. (1987). Social information processing factors in reactive and proactive aggression in children's playgroups. *Journal of Personality and Social Psychology, 53,* 1146–1158.

Dodge, K. A., McClaskey, C. L., & Feldman, E. (1985). A situational approach to assessment of social competence in children. *Journal of Consulting and Clinical Psychology, 53,* 344–353.

Dodge, K. A., & Murphy, R. R. (1984). The assessment of social competence in adolescents. *Advances in Child Behavior Analysis and Therapy, 3,* 61–96.

Dodge, K. A., Murphy, R. R., & Buschbaum, K. (1984). The assessment of intention-cue detection skills in children: Implications for developmental psychopathology. *Child Development, 55,* 163–173.

Dodge, K. A., Schlundt, D., Schocken, I., & Delugach, J. (1983). Social competence and children's sociometric status: The role of peer group entry strategies. *Merrill-Palmer Quarterly, 29,* 309–336.

Eder, D., & Hallinan, M. T. (1978). Sex differences in children's friendships. *American Sociological Review, 43,* 237–250.

Engfer, A. A. (1993). Antecedents and consequences of shyness in boys and girls: A six year longitudinal study. In K. H. Rubin & J. Asendorpf (Eds.), *Social withdrawal, inhibition and shyness in childhood* (pp. 49–80). Hillsdale, NJ: Erlbaum.

Foster, S. L., & Ritchey, W. L. (1985). Behavioral correlates of sociometric status of fourth, fifth and sixth grade children in two classroom situations. *Behavioral Assessment, 7,* 79–93.

Furman, W., & Bierman, K. L. (1984). Perceived determinants of friendship: A multidimensional study of developmental changes. *Developmental Psychology, 20,* 925–931.

Furman, W., & Buhrmester, D. (1992). Age and sex differences in perceptions of networks of personal relationships. *Child Development, 63,* 103–115.

Geraci, R. L., & Asher, S. R. (1980). *Social knowledge interview materials for elementary school children.* Champaign: Bureau of Educational Research, University of Illinois.

Greenberg, M. T., & Kusche, C. A. (1990). *Inventory of emotional experience: Technical report.* Seattle, WA: University of Washington.

Gresham, F. M., Elliot, S. N., & Black, F. L. (1987). Factor structure replication and bias in the investigation of the teacher rating of social skills. *Journal of School Psychology, 25,* 81–92.

Hartup, W. W. (1983). The peer system. In E. M. Hetherington (Vol. Ed.), *Handbook of child psychology* (4th ed.): *Vol. 4: Socialization, personality and development* (pp. 103–196). New York: Wiley.

Hartup, W. W., & Laursen, B. (1989, March). *Contextual constraints and children's friendship relations.* Paper presented at the biennial meeting of the Society for Research in Child Development, Kansas City, MO.

Hightower, A. D., Work, W. C., Cowen, E. L., Lotyczewski, B. S., Spinell, A. P., Guare, J. C., & Rohrbeck, C. A. (1986). The Teacher-Child Rating Scale: A brief objective measure of elementary school children's school problem behaviors and competencies. *School Psychology Review, 15,* 393–409.

Hughes, J. N., Cavell, T. A., & Grossman, P. B. (1997). A positive view of self: Risk or protection for aggressive children? *Development and Psychopathology, 9,* 75–94.

Hymel, S., & Rubin, K. H. (1985). Children with peer relationship and social skills problems: Conceptual, methodological and developmental issues. In G. J. Whitehurst (Ed.), *Annals of child development* (Vol. 2, pp. 251–297). Greenwich, CT: JAI Press.

Ladd, G. W., & Mars, K. T. (1986). Reliability and validity of preschoolers' perceptions of peer behavior. *Journal of Clinical Psychology, 15,* 16–25.

Masten, A. S., Morrison, P., & Pelligrini, D. (1985). A Revised Class Play method of peer assessment. *Developmental Psychology, 21,* 523–533.

Matson, J. L., Rotatori, A. F., & Helsel, W. J. (1983). Development of a rating scale to measure social skills in children: The Matson Evaluation of Social Skills with Youngsters (MESSY). *Behavior Research and Therapy, 21,* 335–340.

Morrison, P., & Masten, A. S. (1991). Peer reputation in middle childhood as a predictor of adaptation in adolescence: A seven-year follow-up. *Child Development, 62,* 991–1007.

Parke, R. D., & Ladd, G. W. (1992). *Family-peer relationships: Modes of linkage.* Hillsdale, NJ: Erlbaum.

Parker, J. G., & Asher, S. R. (1987). Peer acceptance and later personal adjustment: Are low-accepted children at risk? *Psychological Bulletin, 102,* 357–389.

Parker, J. G., & Asher, S. R. (1993). Beyond group acceptance: Friendship adjustment and friendship quality as distinct dimensions of children's peer adjustment. In D. Perlman & W. H. Jones (Eds.), *Advances in personal relationships* (Vol. 4, pp. 261–294). London: Kingsley.

Parker, J. G., Rubin, K. H., Price, J. M., & DeRosier, M. E. (1995). Peer relationships, child development, and adjustment: A developmental psychopathology perspective. In D. Cicchetti & D. Cohen (Eds.), *Developmental psychopathology: Vol 2, Risk, disorder and adaptation* (pp. 96–161). New York: Wiley.

Pekarik, E. G., Prinz, R. J., Liebert, D. E., Weintraub, S., & Neale, J. M. (1976). The Pupil Evaluation Inventory: A sociometric technique for assessing children's social behavior. *Journal of Abnormal Child Psychology, 14,* 83–97.

Pope, A. W., & Bierman, K. L. (1999). Predicting adolescent peer problems and antisocial activities: The relative roles of aggression and dysregulation. *Developmental Psychology, 55,* 335–347.

Putallaz, M. (1983). Predicting children's sociometric status from their behavior. *Child Development, 54,* 1417–1426.

Putallaz, M., & Heflin, A. H. (1990). Parent-child interactions. In S. R. Asher & J. D. Coie (Eds.), *Peer rejection in childhood* (pp. 189–216). Cambridge, England: Cambridge University Press.

Reid, M., Landesman, S., Treder, R., & Jacard, J. (1989). "My family and friends": Six to twelve-year-old children's perceptions of social support. *Child Development, 60,* 896–910.

Ribordy, S. C., Camras, L. A., Stefani, R., & Spaccarelli, S. (1988). Vignettes for emotion recognition research and affective therapy with children. *Journal of Clinical Child Psychology, 17,* 322–325.

Rubin, K. H. (1993). The Waterloo Longitudinal Project: Correlates and consequences of social withdrawal from childhood to adolescence. In K. H. Rubin & J. Asendorpf (Eds.), *Social withdrawal, inhibition and shyness in childhood* (pp. 291–314). Hillsdale, NJ: Erlbaum.

Rubin, K. H., & Krasnor, L. R. (1986). Social cognitive and social behavioral perspectives on problem solving. In M. Perlmutter (Ed.), *Minnesota symposium on child psychopathology* (Vol. 18, pp. 1–68). Hillsdale, NJ: Erlbaum.

Rubin, K. H., & Stewart, S. L. (1996). Social withdrawal. In E. J. Mash & R. A. Barkley (Eds.), *Child psychopathology* (pp. 277–310). New York: Guilford Press.

Sattler, J. M. (1988). *Assessment of children* (3rd ed.). San Diego, CA: Sattler.

Sharabany, R. (1994). Intimate Friendship Scale: Conceptual underpinnings, psychometric properties and construct validity. *Journal of Social and Personal Relationships, 11,* 449–469.

Stormshak, E. A., Bierman, K. L., Bruschi, C. J., Dodge, K. A., Coie, J. D. and the Conduct Problems Prevention Research Group (in press). The relation between behavior problems and peer preference in different classroom contexts. *Child Development.*

Stewart, S. L., & Rubin, K. H. (1995). The social problem solving of anxious-withdrawn children. *Development and Psychopathology, 7,* 323–336.

Stormshak, E. A., Bellanti, C. J., Bierman, K. L., & The Conduct Problems Prevention Research Group (1996). The quality of sibling relationships and the development of social competence and behavioral control in aggressive children. *Developmental Psychology, 32,* 1–11.

Strain, P. S., Steele, P., Ellis, R., & Timm, M. A. (1982). Long term effects of oppositional child treatment with mothers as therapists and therapist trainers. *Journal of Applied Behavior Analysis, 16,* 243–249.

Walker, H. M. (1983). *Walker Problem Behavior Identification Checklist: Test and manual* (2nd ed.). Los Angeles: Western Psychological Services.

Walker, H. M., & McConnell, S. (1988). *Scale of social competence and school adjustment.* Austin, TX: Pro-Ed.

Wright, J. C., Giammarino, M., & Parad, H. W. (1986). Social status in small groups: Individual-group similarity and the social misfit. *Journal of Personality and Social Psychology, 50,* 523–536.

Younger, A. J., Schwartzman, A. E., & Ledingham, J. E. (1986). Age-related differences in children's perceptions of social deviance: Changes in behavior or perspective? *Developmental Psychopathology, 22,* 531–542.

Chapter 19 ————————————————————————

OBSERVING FOR INDIVIDUAL DIFFERENCES IN THE SOCIAL INTERACTION STYLES OF PRESCHOOL CHILDREN

Marilyn Segal, Jeanne Montie, and Timothy J. Iverson

Can I play? I'll be your best friend!
No! We don't got no room and you don't got white sneakers.

Watching a preschool class at play can be difficult for an adult. Children can be cruel to one another. Bigger children beat up on smaller children. Children are excluded from a play group for reasons that make little apparent sense. Yet, despite the seeming lack of manners exhibited by 3-and 4-year-olds when they are playing in a group, preschool children prefer playing with friends to any other activity. Furthermore, children who are successful in making friends and gaining acceptance in the peer group are likely to make a good adjustment in grade school and beyond (Howes, 1988; Rogers & Ross, 1986).

Although no one would dispute the fact that early social competence is associated with later adjustment, important issues related to the definition and measurement of social competence are still unresolved. A typical way of defining early social competence is to equate competence with popularity and to describe other traits, skills, or behaviors that popular children exhibit. The limitation of this approach is that popularity is not a stable or adequate measure of social competence. Shy children may initially avoid group play and later emerge as leaders, while socially assertive children who are sought after as playmates may have social skill deficiencies (Honig, 1987). A more fruitful approach to defining competence is to begin with a theoretical construct that describes the repertoire of interactive behaviors that a competent child acquires and then validate this repertoire with empirical studies. This second approach rejects the assumption that popularity and social competence are necessarily coupled, and it allows for the investigation of individual differences in social styles associated with competent behavior.

In this chapter, we describe the development and validation of the Behavior Observation Record (BOR), an observation instrument designed to record behavioral sequences theoretically related to social competence in accordance with a social discourse model. The first section of this chapter describes the construction of the BOR and provides the rationale for the selection of observation categories. The second section describes three different research projects that have used the BOR to measure social styles and behaviors. The third section focuses on the use of the BOR as a clinical instrument and describes three case studies where the BOR provides clinically relevant data. In a final section, the implications of the research and case studies are discussed, and suggestions are made for further research and additional applications.

THE BEHAVIOR OBSERVATION RECORD (BOR)

In the recent literature on social competence, two major facets of social competence have been identificd; the ability to make friends and the ability to gain acceptance into the peer group. While there is a general consensus that both friend-making and group acceptance are dependent on the acquisition of communicative skills, questions related to how these skills are acquired or developed are still being investigated (Howes, 1987).

In a carefully researched monograph, *How Children Become Friends,* Gottman (1983) provides a detailed description of how newly introduced preschool children proceed from acquaintanceship to friendship. Gottman performed two studies, in which he recorded naturalistic conversations between same-sex peers in a home situation. In the first study, children were paired once with their best friend and once with a same-age peer whom they had not known. Taped conversations of friends were compared with taped conversations with new acquaintances. In a second study, Gottman paired 18 unacquainted dyads and recorded three 90-minute sessions over a 2-week period in which children played together. In both studies, Gottman's purpose was to identify inductively the sequence of events that take place in the process of forming a friendship. Gottman's major findings in these two studies were that

1. The conversations of children who were likely to become friends included more successful information exchange than the conversation of children who were not "hitting it off."
2. Following the successful exchange of information, children who were forming a friendship were more likely than children who were not becoming friends to progress to an agreed-upon play activity or to amity or positive affective exchange.

In contrast to Gottman, whose focus is on friend-making, Hazen and Black (1989) investigated social behaviors that are associated with peer status. The primary purpose of their study, "Preschool Peer Communication Skills: The Role of Social Status and Interaction Context" is to investigate individual differences in preschoolers' discourse skills in relation to their social status with peers. Hazen and Black videotaped triadic play interactions of 48 acquainted preschool children in which one child entered the play of two same-age peers. Using peer nominations to classify children as liked, rejected, or low impact, Hazen and Black identified differences related to social status in a set of skills associated with coherent discourse. Liked children were more apt than unliked children to direct communications to others clearly and to address both, rather than just one, interaction partners. They were also more likely to respond contingently to their peers, and more likely to give information rather than express feeling when attempting to gain entry into a new group.

Hazen and Black conclude that intervention programs to help socially rejected preschool children "should include skills for helping children initiate and maintain coherent discourse and skills for adapting discourse to the demands of the particular social situation" (p. 875).

While the Gottman study and the Hazen and Black study focus on different aspects of social competence, both studies have identified differences between more and less socially competent children in terms of their mastery of subtle discourse skills that govern preschool social interactions. Of particular importance, according to these researchers, are discourse skills that allow children to maintain social interaction or coherent discourse after the initial greeting of a peer or entry into a group. These findings suggest that practitioners who are interested in enhancing social competence in young children need to pay close attention to the way children act, react, respond, and are responded to during the whole course of spontaneous play interactions.

While the research studies on early discourse skills inform our understanding of social competence and provide a starting point for identifying behavioral categories, the measures developed in the laboratory studies of social competence cannot be used to record social competence in a naturalistic setting. A first factor that differentiates laboratory and naturalistic studies of preschool play is the nature of the interactions. The social competencies that are required for initiating and maintaining peer interactions in a laboratory study where peer groups are preselected are not the same as the competencies required for carrying out social exchanges in a preschool. The social scene in a preschool is complex, confusing, and always in a state of flux. Small groups are continually forming and breaking up, sometimes dissolving completely and sometimes just changing players. In order to capture the flavor of the complex preschool social scene, the instrument used to record the behaviors of a target child must also allow for the recording of simultaneously occurring events.

A second factor that differentiates laboratory and naturalistic studies is the data collection process. Electronic data collection techniques that are appropriate for a laboratory study, where peer interactions take place in a confined space, cannot be used in a naturalistic study. In a preschool situation, children race around the playground out of sight of a camera and out of reach of a microphone. The BOR described in this chapter is designed for use by a trained observer who can record preschoolers' interactions wherever they take place.

Characteristics of the BOR Instrument

The BOR is designed for the observation and recording of spontaneous play behaviors and social exchanges in a preschool setting. The BOR is constructed on the premise that social competence depends on the ability of children to engage in successful and sustained discourse exchanges with one or more members of the peer group. It provides for the observation of a sample of spontaneous play behavior and the simultaneous recording of both the behaviors a target child is engaging in and the responses of other children to these behaviors. It is a time-sampling instrument that can be used by a trained observer during a free-play period in a preschool classroom or playground.

The BOR was, in part, derived from the time-sample unit coding sheet developed by Field and Vega-Lahr (e.g., Segal, Peck, Vega-Lahr, & Field, 1987). It was later reconstructed and modified by Iverson and Segal (1986) to include qualitative aspects of social behaviors, in addition to the presence or absence of the behaviors. The current version of the form for the

BOR (see Figure 19–1) is divided into four mutually exclusive categories: (1) child alone, (2) child approaching others, (3) child being approached by others, and (4) child interacting with others. Within each of the four categories, different types of behavior are listed. A child alone, for instance, may be coded in 1 or more of 14 subcategories (e.g., on task, off task—disruptive or not disruptive), wandering, observing, pretending to be, and so forth.

In addition to recording the type of behavior that a child is engaged in, the BOR provides for the recording of qualitative aspects of interaction. In the categories of child alone and child interacting with others, behaviors are recorded as +, –, or 0, to indicate the quality of affect that accompanies the behavior. A child playing alone is coded with a "+" code mark if his or her affect is clearly positive (e.g., smiling, laughing, or singing). If the child is showing neutral affect, a "0" is used as a code mark. If a child is crying or otherwise displaying negative affect, a "–" is used as a code mark.

In the remaining categories of approaching others and being approached, the ratings of +, –, 0 reflect the response the approach elicits. For example, if the target child asks a question, the "asks question" category must be scored. If the peer answers the question, the category is scored with a "+", indicating the child's approach was responded to in a positive way. If the peer responds in a maladaptive manner, such as by pushing, criticizing, or otherwise rebuffing the target child, the category is scored a "–". If the target child is ignored or the question is not heard, a "0" is coded to reflect this. In this manner, both the approach behavior and the elicited response is captured, reflecting the specific behavioral interaction patterns comprising the social situation.

Finally, the bottom line in each category except the child alone category is reserved for recording the individual with whom the child is interacting. Typically, a "C" for child, "T" for teacher, or "P" for parent is indicated, but additional codes can be used as the observation environment requires.

Scoring of the BOR

BOR frequency scores can be summarized in four different ways in accordance with the objectives of the observation. First, frequency scores can be summed within the four major categories to determine the proportion of time a child spends playing alone, approaching others, being approached, or playing with other children. Second, the +(plus), –(minus), and 0 (zero) scores can be summed across categories to determine prevailing affect, effectiveness of the target child's approach behaviors, or the nature of the target child's reaction when approached by others. Third, time spent in different types of play can be summed to determine play style or preference. Finally, incidents of aggressive actions can be summed to yield an aggression score.

In addition to determining summary scores from the BOR, the BOR profile of an individual child can be analyzed to answer more specific questions relating to social behaviors. For example, if a child spends the majority of her or his time playing alone, one can determine, from the approaching others or the being approached categories, the reasons for this apparent isolation. The child may have been rejected (several approaches scored 0 or –) when attempting to play with others, or the child simply may have made no effort to join or interact with the other children (few or no approach behaviors scored). Reliability studies on the BOR are currently in progress, and it appears that satisfactory interobserver agreement can be obtained after training and 1–2 hours of practice observation.

Name_____ DOB_____ Date Observed_____ Age____ Sex____ Race____

Setting_____ Time Intervals____(on), ____(off) Total time_____

CHILD ALONE (code by affect: + positive/ − negative/ 0 neutral or unclear)	1			4			7			10				TOTALS + − 0			COMMENTS
1. ON TASK														1			
2. OFF TASK (not disruptive)														2			
3. OFF TASK (disruptive)														3			
4. To self (wanders, sits)														4			
5. Talks to self														5			
6. Self-stimulation														6			
7. Self-abuse														7			
8. Observes														8			
9. Explores														9			
10. Destructive														10			
(PLAY): 11. Pretending to be														11			
12. Pretending things are														12			
13. Manipulative/constructive														13			
14. Physical (run, climb, swing)														14			

APPROACHING OTHERS (code by response of others: + functional/ − dysfunctional/ 0 no response)	1			4			7			10							
1. Makes statement/comment														1			
2. Gives directives (do)														2			
3. Tells limits (don't)														3			
4. Asks questions														4			
5. Invites														5			
6. Verbal aggression/interruption														6			
7. Nonverbal (gesture, eye contact)														7			
8. Touches														8			
9. Joins/imitates														9			
10. Physical aggression/interruption														10		′	
APPROACHED (C, T, P, or 0):																	

CHILD BEING APPROACHED (code by child's response: + functional/ − dysfunctional/ 0 no response)	1			4			7			10							
1. Makes statement/comment														1			
2. Given directives (do)														2			
3. Told limits (don't)														3			
4. Asked a question														4			
5. Invited							·							5			
6. Verbally aggressed/criticized														6			
7. Nonverbal (gestured toward)														7			
8. Touched														8			
9. Joined/imitated														9			
10. Physically aggressed														10			
APPROACHED BY (C, T, P, or 0):																	

INTERACTING WITH OTHERS (code by affect: + positive/ − negative/ 0 neutral or unclear)	1			4			7			10							
1. ON TASK														1			
2. OFF TASK (not disruptive)														2			
3. OFF TASK (disruptive)														3			
4. Verbal Interaction														4			
5. Physical interaction														5			
6. Parallel Play														6			
(PLAY): 7. Pretending to be														7			
8. Pretending things are														8			
9. Manipulative/constructive														9			
10. Physical play/games														10			
INTERACTED WITH (C, T, P, or 0):																	

Observed by: Nova University Family Center

Figure 19–1.   Blank form for the Behavior Observation Record (BOR)

RESEARCH STUDIES

In this section, we describe three initial research studies that are based on the BOR. In the first study, the BOR is used to validate a social styles system that focused on different types of leader-follower styles. In the second study, the BOR is used to differentiate the social interactions of children who are abused, children who are neglected, and a matched comparison group. In the third study, the BOR is used to identify social interaction sequences associated with social status. All three studies are conducted in naturalistic preschool settings.

Although the BOR is a new instrument, requiring further reliability and standardization studies, these three studies provide evidence of the versatility of the BOR and demonstrate the kinds of information it is able to provide.

Study I: Medieval Kingdom Study

The first research study, using the Time Sample Unit Coding Sheet (see Table 19–1) from which the BOR was derived, was conducted by Segal et al. (1987) in a hospital-based preschool setting with 3- and 4-year-old children. Field and Vega-Lahr were interested in looking at individual differences in the social interaction styles of preschool children. The specific purpose of the study was to validate a social styles classification described by Adcock and Segal (1983) in an ecological study of preschool children.

Based on repeated observations of free-play interactions in seven preschool settings, Adcock and Segal had identified three significant dimensions of differences in the play behavior of children; first, the degree to which they initiated, managed, and organized the play, which Adcock described as "leadership"; second, preferred group size for play; and third, type of affect shown by children engaged in play. Using the first two dimensions as descriptors, Adcock and Segal identified four social styles that were found in all seven preschools. Segal and Adcock used a medieval metaphor to label these four social styles. The first type of leader was a "lord." The lord, who could be either male or female, enjoyed imaginative play with a select retinue of faithful followers. The second type of leader was a "bishop." In contrast to lords, bishops enjoyed intimate conversational play with just one or two other children. Followers were likely to be either "vassals" or "serfs." Vassals attached themselves fervently to a lord and were jealous of other children who tried to

Table 19–1.   Time sample unit coding sheet (items from Segal et al., 1987)

A. Organization–maintenance of play behaviors
   1. Proposes play theme ideas
   2. Assigns role to self–other
   3. Structures the environment
   4. Gives orders–commands
   5. Teaches–models behaviors
   6. Calls or looks for another child
   7. Excludes others from play
B. Nondirective play behaviors
   1. Imitates others' behaviors
   2. Follows suggestions–commands
C. Peripheral behaviors
   1. Observes others at play
   2. Wanders about aimlessly
D. Other behaviors
   1. Requests participation for self
   2. Shares toys and/or includes others
   3. Interacts with teacher
   4. Verbal and physical aggression
   5. Attention-getting behavior

invade their territory. Serfs were more free-floating, sometimes attaching themselves to lords and at other times to bishops.

In order to test the validity of the social style categories described by Adcock & Segal, Segal, Field, and Vega-Lahr conducted a study with 24 preschool children in an all-day nursery (Segal et al., 1987). In the first step of the study, two observers were given global descriptions of the aforementioned four social styles and asked to observe each of the children and label his or her social style in accordance with the global descriptions. The second step was the development of the time sample coding sheet (Table 19–1) on which 16 discrete behaviors were listed in one of categories: Organization/maintenance of play behaviors, nondirective play behaviors, peripheral play behaviors, and other behaviors. In addition, all play was coded as fantasy, constructive, or rough-and-tumble, as well as solitary, dyadic, or group. The observers were trained to an interobserver reliability of .80; an interobserver reliability at 1-month intervals averaged .84 ($r = .75–.95$), as determined by Cohen's *kappa* (Cohen, 1960).

Data analysis using a social role classification as the between-subject factor revealed significant differences in play behaviors in the dimensions of leadership and group size (see Table 19–2). Lords and bishops, as hypothesized, engaged in more leadership behaviors (e.g., maintenance and organization of play) than vassals and serfs. Bishops and vassals, as hypothesized, engaged in more dyadic play, while lords were more likely to engage in small-group interaction. Serfs, in accordance with expectations, spent more time than lords, bishops, and even vassals in follower type activities, including nondirective and peripheral play.

Although the match between the Adcock/Segal global descriptions of role behavior and the observed role behaviors was not perfect, a significant number of children demonstrated behaviors consistent with their role assignment. With the exception of some of the serfs, children demonstrated role-consistent behaviors across several observations. This suggests that the leader–follower styles identified by Adcock and Segal in the ecological study are consistent across other preschool settings. It also demonstrates the usefulness of the BOR for quantifying behaviors that are associated with social style.

Study II: Abused and Neglected Children

The purpose of the second research study was to identify differences in social interactions between children identified as abused or as neglected, and a control group of nonabused peers (Iverson, Tanner, & Segal, 1987). Thirty-four children between 3 and 5 years of age were included in this study, with 7 children categorized as physically abused, 9 children categorized as neglected, and 18 children categorized as nonmaltreated. The maltreated children had been identified as abused or neglected by the State Department of Health and Rehabilitative Services. The maltreated children were enrolled in one of the two Title XX–funded child care centers that offered specialized therapeutic services for maltreated and at-risk children. The non-maltreated children were from the same child care centers as the maltreated children and did not differ significantly from the maltreated children on age, race, gender, socioeconomic status (SES), or intelligence. Using the BOR, all children were observed on the playground during morning free-play sessions. Each child was observed for 10-second intervals, with 5-seconds between observations for recording. Total observation time was 15 minutes. Interrater reliability (percentage of agreement) averaged .92 for the 4 general categories, ranging from .71 for approaching others to .95 for the child interacting

Table 19–2.   Study I: Mean proportion of observation time behaviors coded for lords, bishops, vassals, and serfs—direction of effects

	Groups				Direction of Effects					
	Lords	Bishops	Vassals	Serfs	L/B	L/V	L/S	B/V	B/S	V/S
Age (months)	43.4	42.0	38.1	33.4		L>V**	L>S***		B>S***	V>S***
Behaviors										
Organization/maintenance of play	37.4	20.1	16.0	7.9	L>B**	L>V**	L>S***		B>S**	V>S***
Proposes play theme or idea (.76)	5.3	1.9	2.0	1.4	L>B***	L>V***	L>S***		B>S**	
Assigns role to self or others (.80)	3.4	1.4	.9	.9	L>B**	L>V***	L>S***			
Structures environment (.79)	8.3	5.1	5.4	2.8			L>S***		B>S**	
Gives orders and commands (.81)	12.4	7.1	4.6	1.1		L>V***	L>S***		B>S***	V>S***
Teaches/models behavior (.82)	2.4	1.0	1.2	.5	L>B**	L>V*	L>S***			V>S*
Calls/looks for others (.78)	2.6	2.5	.9	.7		L>V**	L>S***	B>V*	B>S**	
Excludes others (.81)	3.0	1.1	1.1	.6	L>B*	L>V***	L>S***			V>S*
Peripheral behavior	10.7	11.9	14.5	22.1			S>L***		S>B***	S>V***
Wanders aimlessly (.71)	3.9	4.1	5.3	7.1			S>L*			
Observes others (.88)	6.9	7.8	9.3	15.1		V>L***	S>L***		S>B***	S>V***
Nondirective play	3.1	5.3	7.1	6.3		V>L***	S>L**			
Imitates others (.78)	1.4	3.1	3.4	3.6	B>L*	V>L***	S>L**			
Follows suggestions (.91)	1.7	2.1	3.7	2.7		V>L***				
Fantasy play (.87)	55.3	49.1	38.2	38.6		L>V**	L>S**			
Solitary (.95)	33.0	32.5	26.9	52.4			S>L**			S>V***
Dyadic (.95)	34.7	44.8	39.1	23.1					B>S**	V>S**
Group (.88)	28.7	16.8	22.1	10.0	L>B*		L>S***			V>S**
Constructive play (.88)	12.0	24.5	23.9	28.2	B>L**	V>L**	S>L***			
Rough-and-tumble play (.84)	15.9	9.5	16.5	8.9						
Total interaction	56.1	49.4	50.8	31.9			L>S***		B>S*	V>S***
Duration average interaction	10.4	13.4	11.9	6.9			L>S*		B>S*	V>S***
Duration longest interaction	15.6	17.9	18.1	9.5			L>S**		B>S**	V>S***

Note. L > B is Lord > Bishop. Interobserver reliability coefficients are in parentheses following behaviors.
* p = <.10
** p = <.05
*** p = <.01
Reprinted with permission of Ablex Publishing Corporation.

with others category. Reliability for specific behavioral categories ranged from a low of .50 (asks questions) to a high of 1.0 (physical play/games). All the categories except asks questions (.5), makes a statement (.5), and joined/initiated (.67) were between .85 and 1.00.

Two data analyses were conducted utilizing summary scores from the BOR. The purpose of the first analysis was to compare maltreated and nonmaltreated children in terms of the amount of time spent in social interactions. The purpose of the second analysis was to compare maltreated and nonmaltreated children in terms of type and outcome of approach behaviors.

In the first data analysis, all +, −, and 0 observations were pooled to compare the overall frequency of responding in the four general categories of behavior measured by the BOR: child alone, child approaching others, child being approached by others, and child interacting with others. The pooled scores were entered as dependent measures in a multivariate analysis of variance (MANOVA) with abuse status as the independent measure. The MANOVA was significant, (multivariate $F(8, 58) = 2.15$, $p < .05$), and subsequent univariate analysis indicated that the child alone and child interacting with others categories were significant. Neglected children spent more time alone than either physically abused children or control children.

In the second analysis, + (plus) responses were compared to −(minus) and 0(zero) responses for the categories of approaching others and child being approached. The MANOVA was significant (multivariate $F(4, 62) = 3.75$, $p < .01$), with a significant group difference in the approaching others category. A subsequent 2×3 (response $\times$ group) analysis of variance (ANOVA) with frequency of response as the dependent measure produced a significant interaction ($F(2, 53) = 6.02$, $p < .01$), with neglected children eliciting significantly fewer positive responses, and physically abused children eliciting significantly more negative responses than control children.

In general, these results suggest that neglected children played alone more and were more likely to be ignored or rejected when they approached other children than either the comparison or the physically abused group. Physically abused children, on the other hand, spent as much time as the comparison group in social interaction, but they were less likely than the comparison children to elicit positive responses from the other children. In other words, the physically abused children were socially involved in the sense that they sought out and interacted with others, but their interactions were less positive and adaptive than the interactions of nonmaltreated children.

The differences between the abused and the neglected children in this study have significance for clinical intervention. Neglected children need to learn assertive approach techniques that will enable them either to make a close friend or to gain entry into a group. Abused children, on the other hand, need to modify their aggressive or inappropriate approach techniques in order to avoid being rejected. With each group of maltreated children, the goal of a therapeutic program could be to help each child learn effective techniques to achieve his or her own social goals.

Study III: An Investigation of Preschool Social Status

The purpose of the third study was to identify differences in social discourse skills between children who are liked, children who are neglected, and children who are rejected by their peers. The study was conducted in a university preschool setting with middle-SES 4- and

5-year old children. In this study, two different measures of social competence were collected: the BOR and a sociometric measure. The Peabody Picture Vocabulary Test (PPVT) was also administered to measure the receptive language of children. The study looks at the relationships between the two measures of social competence and identifies the unique contributions of the BOR in understanding social acceptance in preschool children.

Method

Forty middle- to upper-middle-SES students (19 boys and 21 girls) attending two prekindergarten classes served as subjects. The preschoolers ranged in age from 4 years, 7 months to 5 years, 9 months; 39 children were Caucasian, 1 child was African-American. All children had been attending the preschool class for 8 months and knew each other well.

The sociometric measure, administered to determine social status, was based on positive and negative peer nominations. Each child was taken individually into a separate room and presented with photographs of all of his or her classmates. The child was then asked, "Show me the person you like to play with most." After the child selected a picture, that picture was removed. The procedure was repeated twice more for a total of three positive nominations. A similar procedure was followed to determine negative nominations.

Based on the number of positive and negative nominations received, each child received an acceptance and rejection score following the general method outlined by Coie, Dodge, and Coppotelli (1982). In order to compute the scores, the nominations were weighted: 8 points for a first-choice positive or negative nomination, 6 points for a second choice, and 4 points for a third choice. Each child then received an acceptance score and a rejection score, based on the sum of his or her positive and negative nominations, respectively. For example, a child chosen as a first-choice friend by one classmate and a second-choice friend by one classmate receives an acceptance score of 12. If this same child is chosen as a first-choice least preferred playmate by three classmates, a second-choice least-preferred playmate by one classmate, and a third-choice least-preferred playmate by three classmates, she or he receives a rejection score of 42. Over the entire group, the mean acceptance score and the mean rejection score equal 18. When scores are standardized with a mean of 0 and standard deviation of 1, our hypothetical child receives an acceptance score less than 0 and a rejection score greater than 0, placing him or her in the rejected group.

The children were divided into four sociometric groups on the basis of the scores: accepted (acceptance score greater than 0 and rejection score less than or equal to 0), rejected (acceptance score less than or equal to 0 and rejection score greater than or equal to 0), ignored (acceptance score less than or equal to 0 and rejection score less than or equal to 0), and controversial (acceptance score greater than 0 and rejection score greater than 0). The resulting groups consisted of 17 accepted children (5 boys, 12 girls), 11 rejected children (8 boys, 3 girls), 11 neglected children (5 boys, 6 girls), and 1 controversial child (boy).

The Peabody Picture Vocabulary Test—Revised (PPVT—Revised) was administered by an experienced tester, and a standard score was obtained for each child. The PPVT—Revised scores ranged from 64 to 130, with a mean of 109.4 (SD = 12.8).

Behavioral observations, using the BOR, were carried out by naive observers. Interrater reliability (percentage of agreement for 3 independent observers) was established at .76, using the four general categories as the basis for scoring. Each child was observed for 10 minutes during an outdoor free-play period. Eight summary scores were derived from the BOR by summarizing frequency scores in the following categories:

1. Time spent alone
2. Time spent with others
3. Number of approaches
4. Number of times approached by others
5. Number of times rebuffed (negative reactions by others to an approach)
6. Number of rebuffs (negative responses to an approaching child)
7. Number of times the child aggressed
8. Number of times the child was aggressed upon

The first four categories represent the categories typically used on the BOR (e.g., Iverson et al., 1987). Categories 5 through 8 were included because it was anticipated that they would add important information for intervention purposes with the sample in this study.

Observations were obtained for a total of 38 children; 2 were unavailable. The focus of the initial analysis was to examine the relationships among the two measures of social functioning and the PPVT—Revised. For that purpose, an intercorrelation matrix was computed, including the 8 variables derived from the BOR, peer status derived from the sociometric data, and the PPVT-Revised scores.

Conclusions

Contrary to expectations, PPVT—Revised scores were not significantly related to peer status (r = .06). It is possible that correlations with the PPVT—Revised were attenuated due to the somewhat restricted range of the PPVT—Revised scores. Most children scored in the average to above-average range on the PPVT—Revised. Correlations between the 8 BOR variables, PPVT—Revised scores, and social status are presented in Table 19–3.

Two of the BOR variables (number of times a child was approached, and number of times a child was aggressed upon) were modestly related to PPVT—Revised scores. The direction of the correlations indicated that children with higher PPVT—Revised scores tended to be approached and aggressed upon less than those with lower PPVT—Revised scores. One possible explanation is that children with higher PPVT—Revised scores may

Table 19–3. Correlations between BOR variables, PPT—revised scores, and peer status as measured by sociometric

	PPVT—Revised	Peer Status
Time alone	.02	.11
Time with others	.06	.01
Number of approaches	−.17	−.22
Number of times approached	−.32*	.14
Number of times rebuffed	−.16	.06
Number of rebuffs	.05	.38**
Number of aggressions	−.22	.26
Number of times aggressed upon	−.32*	.05

* p <.05.
** p <.01.

be playing in established groups and therefore be less open to approach. It is also possible that children with higher verbal scores are more able to defend themselves verbally and therefore less likely to be aggressed upon.

The one variable on the BOR that was significantly correlated with social status was number of rebuffs or negative responses to approach. A closer inspection of the nature of the relationship revealed that it was the ignored children who had significantly more instances of negative reaction to approach than the accepted children. In fact, it is noteworthy that within the accepted group, there were no observed instances of a negative reaction to approach from another child. This suggests that children who are in some way rejecting when other children approach them are unlikely to be selected as being desirable playmates.

Based on the positive relationship between the negative responses to approach and social status, the authors suggest a new direction for intervention efforts. In most intervention programs for ignored or rejected children, the emphasis is placed on teaching children effective ways of gaining entry into established groups. It may be even more important to focus remediation efforts on helping children respond in a positive way when they are approached by others.

Summary of Research Studies Using the BOR

The three research studies described in this chapter differ in the research question that is being asked and in the kind of information that is abstracted from the BOR. The first study explored differences among preschool children in play preference, verbal exchanges, and peer-group selection that correspond to differences in leadership or follower roles. In the second study, the categories of social interaction described in the BOR (plays alone, approaches others, is approached by others, and plays with others) are used to differentiate among children who are neglected, or abused, and a matched control group. In the third study, BOR is used with a university preschool population to identify types of behavioral sequences that are associated with peer status.

Although these three studies differ in format, as well as in the research question that is being asked, each of the studies supports a social-information-processing model of social skill development. According to this model, the social competencies that children acquire depend on their selection of social goals and the degree of mastery the children gain in carrying on the social exchanges required for the achievement of that goal. The medieval kingdom study (Study I) supports the position that children differ in their goals, with some children interested in forming intimate friendships, while others are interested in entering and interacting in groups. The maltreatment study (Study II) identifies deficits in group entry skills associated with maltreatment status. The third peer-status study supports the position that children who are neglected by their peers have not learned, or do not practice, the pragmatic or discourse skill required to gain group acceptance.

CLINICAL APPLICATIONS OF BOR

While the BOR has been used primarily as a research tool to identify group characteristics or variables associated with social competence, the BOR can also be used by clinicians interested in identifying the socially significant behaviors of individual children. In the three case studies that follow, the BOR provides useful information related to social skills that was not picked up by either the parents or the teachers. Although in each case, the BOR was administered as a part of a research study and not for clinical purposes, the information yielded by the BOR had clinical significance.

Case Study I

C.K., at 5 years 8 months, was one of the oldest children in the prekindergarten class. She was tall, awkward in her movement, and not especially attractive. She had been retained in the pre-K class an extra year because she lacked the readiness skills necessary for Kindergarten. Furthermore, her PPVT—Revised score of 64 indicated the possibility of mild retardation. On a teacher's rating scale, C.K. was described as a child who was never a leader, seldom sought out by other children, and sometimes rejected. C.K.'s score on the sociogram corroborated her teacher's impressions. Her total score placed her in the rejected group; she was chosen only once as a desired playmate and was rejected seven times. Behavioral observations using the BOR indicated that C.K. (a) spent most of her time playing alone, with no show of either positive or negative affect, (b) made occasional approaches, and (c) with the exception of one instance, received no positive responses. C.K. was approached twice by other children, and on both occasions she responded positively. In sum, although she spent the majority of her free-play time playing by herself, she displayed no signs of distress and had the skills to approach others and to respond positively when approached.

Case Study II

In contrast to C.K., P.A., at exactly 5 years old, was a very attractive girl with a pretty face, long dark hair, and fashionable clothes. Her PPVT—Revised score of 108 was in the average range, and her teachers described her as sometimes a leader, having many friends, frequently sought out, and seldom rejected. The sociometric scores, however, told a different story. P.A. was never selected as a friend and was rejected three times. Her total score placed her in the neglected group. Behavioral observations of P.A. provided important clues in terms of her social competence. Like C.K., she spend most of her time playing alone, and her affect was neither positive nor negative. When other children approached her, however, she behaved very differently from C.K. P.A. was approached five times during 20 minutes of being observed. On each approach, she either ignored the approacher completely, or else told the approacher to go away.

With both C.K. and P.A., the BOR provided information about their social competence that could not be gleaned through teacher report. C.K., despite the teacher's concerns, and despite her academic problems, had adaptive social skills. C.K. preferred playing alone or with one special friend and was on the road to developing a reciprocal friendship. Although she did not seek out group play, she was able to respond to the overtures of her peers with a positive response. Despite the fact that the teachers described her as being unpopular, and the sociogram corroborated the teacher's classification, C.K. was developing appropriate discourse skills and cannot be considered socially maladjusted. In fact, within the month following the observation, C.K. was successful in finding a best friend.

In contrast to C.K., P.A. was described by her teachers as being a well-liked, socially competent youngster. The BOR observations, conducted as part of the research study, unfortunately belied this optimistic outlook. P.A. lacked the ability to approach other children and elicit a positive response. She also lacked the ability or disposition to respond to peers with a positive response when overtures were made to her. In light of her inability to maintain social exchanges, it is not surprising that selections in the sociogram placed P.A. in the neglected group. While C.K. was demonstrating skills that lead to friendship making, P.A. was turning children away who were attempting to be friendly.

Case Study III

The third case study illustrates how the BOR has been used in treatment planning for a child with deficits in initiating peer interactions and maintaining play interactions once they begin. T. is a 3-year-old child of average height and weight who had a history of physical abuse. He was enrolled in a child care center that offered therapeutic programming for abused and/or neglected children. T. was exhibiting aggressive behavior and an inability to make friends. T.'s PPVT—Revised of 90 was in the average range, and he exhibited no apparent deficits in language, cognition, or motor skills.

T. was observed on the playground during regular morning playtime. A sample of his BOR (condensed to 2 pages) is shown in Figure 19–2. It should be noted that scoring the BOR for research purposes typically involves tallying the +, –, and 0 codings in each of the four general categories. For the purposes of prescriptive treatment planning, however, sequences of social interactions are explored. While the reliability of such single-subject applications has not been empirically tested; clinical experience suggests that behavioral treatment planning based on the BOR, leads to positive outcomes in social functioning (Iverson et al., 1987). Based on this protocol, several hypotheses regarding treatment planning were generated.

First, T.'s BOR gives the impression that he wants to play with other children but has difficulty becoming involved in play interactions. The majority of T.'s time is spent alone, often in peripheral activities, such as observing or wandering. His high incidence of approach behaviors suggests that he wants to join the play or get attention from others, while the relatively low proportion of time spent actually interacting indicates that his efforts for involvement are relatively ineffective.

By examining the approaching others category more closely, it becomes evident that T. relies heavily on comments and statements as a means to gain group entry. For example, he was observed to approach another child getting ready to ride a tricycle and say "I'm gonna ride," to which the other child responded "No you can't." (Statement/comment scored "–"). Of the 4 statements made by T. during efforts to join, 2 received "–" responses, and 2 were scored for "0" responses. One also notes, however, that when T. joined and/or initiated without a verbal remark, he was responded to positively and proceeded to interact with the group. Unfortunately, as indicated in Columns 9–11, these positive interactions were shortlived and minutes later, T.'s interaction was coded with a "–" indicating physical aggression. Finally, during the entire observation period, there was only one instance of T. being approached by others. Apparently, T. spent all his playtime attempting to join in group play and was therefore not accessible to other children seeking out a play partner.

BEHAVIOR OBSERVATION RECORD

Name_____ DOB_____ Date Observed_____ Age____ Sex____ Race____

Setting_____ Time Intervals____(on), ____(off) Total time_____

CHILD ALONE (code by affect: + positive/ − negative/ 0 neutral or unclear)

	1			4			7			10				TOTAL +	−	0	COMMENTS
1. ON TASK													1			
2. OFF TASK (not disruptive)													2			
3. OFF TASK (disruptive)													3			
4. To self (wanders, sits)										0			4			
5. Talks to self													5			
6. Self-stimulation													6			
7. Self-abuse													7			
8. Observes	0	0					0						8			
9. Explores													9			
10. Destructive													10			
(PLAY): 11. Pretending to be													11			
12. Pretending things are													12			
13. Manipulative/constructive													13			
14. Physical (run, climb, swing)							0	0					14			

APPROACHING OTHERS (code by response of others: + functional/ − dysfunctional/ 0 no response)

	1			4			7			10						
1. Makes statement/comment							0						1			
2. Gives directives (do)													2			
3. Tells limits (don't)													3			
4. Asks questions													4			
5. Invites													5			
6. Verbal aggression/interruption													6			
7. Nonverbal (gesture, eye contact)				0									7			
8. Touches													8			
9. Joins/imitates							+						9			
10. Physical aggression/interruption				+									10			
APPROACHED (C, T, P, or 0):			C	C			C	C								

CHILD BEING APPROACHED (code by child's response: + functional/ − dysfunctional/ 0 no response)

	1			4			7			10						
1. Makes statement/comment													1			
2. Given directives (do)													2			
3. Told limits (don't)													3			
4. Asked a question													4			
5. Invited													5			
6. Verbally aggressed/criticized													6			
7. Nonverbal (gestured toward)													7			
8. Touched													8			
9. Joined/imitated													9			
10. Physically aggressed													10			
APPROACHED BY (C, T, P, or 0):																

INTERACTING WITH OTHERS (code by affect: + positive/ − negative/ 0 neutral or unclear)

	1			4			7			10						
1. ON TASK													1			
2. OFF TASK (not disruptive)													2			
3. OFF TASK (disruptive)													3			
4. Verbal Interaction													4			
5. Physical interaction													5			
6. Parallel Play													6			
(PLAY): 7. Pretending to be													7			
8. Pretending things are													8			
9. Manipulative/constructive													9			
10. Physical play/games										0	0		10			
INTERACTED WITH (C, T, P, or 0):										C	C					

Observed by: Nova University Family Center

Figure 19–2. Completed and condensed BOR: T.K.

Based on these observations, a treatment plan was generated for T., which involved, first, prompting and reinforcing efforts to gain group entry by nonverbally joining or imitating (the manner with which T. appeared to have the most success). Second, T. was taught verbal problem-solving strategies to replace aggressive play activities. T. was also taught that if approaches did not work ("sometimes other kids don't want to play") that he should find an activity he could enjoy alone for a while rather than try to force group entry.

BEHAVIOR OBSERVATION RECORD

Name_____ DOB_____ Date Observed_____ Age____ Sex____ Race____

Setting_____ Time Intervals____(on),____(off) Total time_____

CHILD ALONE (code by affect: + positive/ – negative/ 0 neutral or unclear)															TOTALS			COMMENTS
	1			4			7			10						+	–	0	
1. ON TASK													1					
2. OFF TASK (not disruptive)													2					
3. OFF TASK (disruptive)													3					
4. To self (wanders, sits)	0			0									4					
5. Talks to self													5					
6. Self-stimulation													6					
7. Self-abuse													7					
8. Observes						0			0				8					
9. Explores													9					
10. Destructive													10					
(PLAY): 11. Pretending to be													11					
12. Pretending things are													12					
13. Manipulative/constructive													13					
14. Physical (run, climb, swing)										0			14					

APPROACHING OTHERS (code by response of others: + functional/ – dysfunctional/ 0 no response)																	
	1			4			7			10							
1. Makes statement/comment	0	–					–						1				
2. Gives directives (do)													2				
3. Tells limits (don't)													3				
4. Asks questions													4				
5. Invites													5				
6. Verbal aggression/interruption													6				
7. Nonverbal (gesture, eye contact)													7				
8. Touches													8				
9. Joins/imitates										+			9				
10. Physical aggression/interruption													10				
APPROACHED (C, T, P, or 0):	C	C				C			C								

CHILD BEING APPROACHED (code by child's response: + functional/ – dysfunctional/ 0 no response)																	
	1			4			7			10							
1. Makes statement/comment					0								1				
2. Given directives (do)													2				
3. Told limits (don't)													3				
4. Asked a question													4				
5. Invited													5				
6. Verbally aggressed/criticized													6				
7. Nonverbal (gestured toward)													7				
8. Touched													8				
9. Joined/imitated													9				
10. Physically aggressed													10				
APPROACHED BY (C, T, P, or 0):					C												

INTERACTING WITH OTHERS (code by affect: + positive/ – negative/ 0 neutral or unclear)																	
	1			4			7			10							
1. ON TASK													1				
2. OFF TASK (not disruptive)													2				
3. OFF TASK (disruptive)													3				
4. Verbal Interaction													4				
5. Physical interaction													5				
6. Parallel Play													6				
(PLAY): 7. Pretending to be													7				
8. Pretending things are													8				
9. Manipulative/constructive													9				
10. Physical play/games										0	0		10				
INTERACTED WITH (C, T, P, or 0):										C	C						

Observed by: Nova University Family Center

Figure 19–2. *(Continued)*

T. responded well to these fairly simple interventions, and follow-up observation indicated he was making fewer approaches, but most of them were successful and resulted in extended periods of playing with friends. In addition, the time T. spent alone was primarily spent in solitary play, and he was occasionally even accepting other children who joined him at these times. T. still had episodes of aggression, but they were much less disruptive in regard to his overall social functioning.

SUMMARY AND CONCLUSIONS

In this chapter, we have described the BOR, a time-sampling observation record designed to record social interactions in a preschool setting during a free-play period. We have presented a series of empirical studies that demonstrate different ways in which the BOR can be used. We have also described findings related to social competence in preschool children yielded by the studies that have used the BOR. In this section, we discuss the implications and limitations of these studies and describe possible directions for future investigations.

Utility of the BOR as an Observation Instrument

The research studies and case studies presented in this chapter demonstrate some of the ways in which the BOR can be used. In the first study, which was based on a preliminary version of the BOR, the authors used the observation scale to describe the typology of a preschool social system. The authors began with the premise that preschool children who had the opportunity to engage in free play were likely to develop a consistent social style, either as a leader or as a follower. The authors identified social behaviors representative of different leadership and follower roles and used the BOR to validate the classification system.

In the second study, the BOR was used to discriminate among three groups of preschool children on the basis of maltreatment status. Abused and neglected children differed from each other in terms of time spent interacting in a group, with neglected children spending more time alone and abused children tending to elicit a greater number of negative or rejecting responses from others. These differences served as the basis of an intervention program. At the end of the treatment program, the BOR will be used on a posttest basis to test the efficacy of the intervention.

In the third study, the BOR was used to identify the relationship between discourse skills and peer status. The authors were interested in finding out whether the social strategies of children who were accepted by their peers differed in any systematic way from the strategies used by children who were either neglected or rejected. According to this study, the significant difference between the children who are accepted and the children who are either neglected or rejected is their response to being approached. Accepted children are likely to respond in a positive way when other children approach them. Neglected and rejected children are more likely to either ignore or reject a child who approaches them. Like the maltreatment study, the findings yielded by this study have implications for remediation.

In contrast to the research studies, where the focus was on group differences, the case studies presented in this chapter demonstrate the utility of the BOR as a clinical instrument. In contrast to the typical observation record that describes and/or codes the behavior of the target child, the BOR forces the observer to describe the context in which a behavior occurs and to describe the responses evoked by each social behavior. An analysis of the BOR allows the teacher or clinician to identify the types of behaviors a child engages in that elicit a negative peer response. It also allows the teacher or clinician to identify patterns of responding by either peers or teachers that may be maintaining positive or negative behaviors.

In addition to allowing the teacher or clinician to identify patterns of behavior that may interfere with a child's social success, the BOR can also be used to identify individual strengths or socially adaptive behaviors that may not be identified by a teacher rating scale or by a measure of peer acceptance. In accordance with the findings from the medieval kingdom study, there are different ways of being a successful preschool leader or a successful preschool follower. There are also individual differences in terms of social objectives. While some children may be interested in joining a group and gaining group status, other children may prefer to spend some of their time alone and some of their time playing quietly with one or two preferred playmates. Because the BOR records the affect associated with a behavior, the clinician can differentiate between the children who are content with playing alone or with a friend and children who are unhappy when they are not in a group. C.K. (Case study I) is an example of a child who was labeled by teacher report and by a sociogram as not being popular. While not being popular may be a problem for some children, C.K. showed no signs of unhappiness. A real strength of the BOR is that it allows both for the identification of socially competent behavior in shy or neglected children and for the identification of skill deficits in children described as popular.

Limitations and Suggestions for Future Research

While the BOR has potential both as a research and a clinical tool, additional studies must be done to validate its psychometric properties. These studies should include an item analysis to eliminate redundant items or items that may be ambiguous and a measure of test-retest reliability. While there is some evidence that the underlying traits measured by the BOR are stable over time (Segal et al., 1987), more research is needed in order to determine how much variability is due to situational factors, child-related factors, or factors related to measurement. Consideration should also be given to a standardized scoring system and a norming population if the BOR is used for group assessment.

Once its psychometric properties have been established, the BOR could be used as the basis of long-term studies, both of individuals and of groups. The BOR has the potential of shedding light on unanswered questions in terms of the development and attainment of social competence.

REFERENCES

Adcock, D., & Segal, M. (1983). *Making friends.* Englewood Cliffs, NJ: Prentice-Hall.

Cohen, J. (1960). A coefficient of agreement for nominal scales. *Educational and Psychological Measurement, 20,* 37–46.

Coie, J. D., Dodge, K. A., & Coppotelli, H. (1982). Dimensions and types of social status: A cross-age perspective. *Developmental Psychology, 18,* 557–571.

Gottman, J. (1983). How children become friends. *Monographs of the Society for Research in Child Development, 48*(3, Serial No. 201).

Hazen, N., & Black, B. (1989). Preschool peer communication skills: The role of social status and interaction context. *Child Development, 60,* 867–876.

Honig, A. S. (1987). The shy child. *Young Children, 42,* 54–64.

Howes, C. (1988). Peer interaction of young children. *Monographs of the Society for Research in Child Development, 53*(1, Serial No. 217).

Iverson, T. J., & Segal, M. (1986). *Manual for the Behavior Observation Record.* Unpublished manuscript, Nova University, Ft. Lauderdale, FL.

Iverson, T. J., Tanner, S., & Segal, M. (1987). *Assessing maltreated children's social interactions with the Behavior Observation Record.* Unpublished manuscript, Nova University, Ft. Lauderdale, FL.

Rogers, D. L., & Ross, D. D. (1986). Encouraging positive social interaction among young children. *Young Children, 41,* 12–17.

Segal, M., Peck, J., Vega-Lahr, N., & Field, T. (1987). A medieval kingdom: Leader–follower styles of preschool play. *Journal of Applied Developmental Psychology, 8,* 79–95.

Chapter 20

ASSESSING NONSOCIAL PLAY IN EARLY CHILDHOOD: CONCEPTUAL AND METHODOLOGICAL APPROACHES

Robert J. Coplan

It is Monday morning in the preschool classroom. Following a brief "circle" session, a large and somewhat boisterous group of 4- and 5-year-old children are escorted into a large playroom and told that it is time for free play. The playroom is filled with a wide range of age-appropriate toys, including puzzles, games, crayons, balls, hoops, dress-up clothes, dolls, and blocks. After a few minutes of hustling, bustling, and getting settled in, distinct patterns of interaction among the children become evident. In the far corner of the room, Stan, Kenny, Eric, and Wendy are playing "house." Each has taken on an imaginary role (i.e., mother, father, sibling), and at the moment, Wendy is asking Stan to call the baby-sitter so that the two of them can go out for dinner.

Nearby, Simon stands motionless, hovering a few feet from the playing children. He watches them intently for a while, but makes no attempt to join in. After a while, he wanders off aimlessly. A few feet to the left, oriented away from the play group, Vanessa sits, hunched over a pad of paper with some colored markers. She is engrossed in her drawing, and pays little attention to the activities transpiring around her. Finally, over on the other side of the room, Paul is off by himself, banging two wooden blocks together repeatedly, occasionally throwing one of them up in the air and giggling as it hits the ground.

Each of the children described in the above scenario is engaging in qualitatively different forms of social and nonsocial free play activities. A casual observer of the scene, however, might conclude that the children playing together (Stan, Kenny, Eric, and Wendy) are more "sociable" or "outgoing," while the rest of the children described (Simon, Vanessa, and Paul) seem to be more "shy" or "withdrawn" because they are not playing with others. This conclusion would be in keeping with the prevailing zeitgeist of the psychological community, by and large, for the last 50 years.

More recently, it has become evident that *nonsocial* play in early childhood is a complex and multifaceted construct (Asendorpf, 1991; Coplan, Rubin, Fox, Calkins, & Stewart, 1994; Coplan & Rubin, 1998a; Harrist, Zaia, Bates, Dodge, & Petit, 1997; Hinde, Tamplin, & Barrett, 1993). To begin with, nonsocial play may have different meanings as a function of the *context* where it is displayed. For example, in the vignette described above, our perceptions of the "meanings" behind the children's play behaviors would likely alter if we were told that this was the first day of preschool and that the children were previously unacquainted. In addition, a more detailed analysis of the behavioral *content* of nonsocial play provides evidence in support of its heterogeneous nature. In this regard, we might suspect that the different forms of solitary play activities described above might involve quite different "underlying psychological mechanisms." In short, children may play alone for many different reasons. A better understanding of the intricate nature of nonsocial play is critical in terms of identifying "at-risk" children as well as in designing and implementing ameliorative clinical intervention programs.

This chapter begins with an exploration of the various conceptual approaches to the understanding of nonsocial play in early childhood. This includes a discussion of the issues surrounding the context and content of these nonsocial behaviors. The second major section pertains to a review of the various methodologies that are available for the assessment of nonsocial play in young children. Included therein is a detailed description of both an observational taxonomy and a new teacher rating scale that can be used in the assessment of young children's nonsocial play. In the final component of the chapter, the results of a pilot study are presented where these methodological tools were employed to trace conceptual pathways from various forms of nonsocial play to psychosocial adjustment in the preschool classroom.

NONSOCIAL PLAY: CONCEPTUAL AND THEORETICAL ISSUES

Defining Nonsocial Play

For the purposes of this chapter, *nonsocial play* is defined as the display of solitary activities and behaviors in the presence of other potential play partners. An important component of this definition involves the presence of other people, which implies the *opportunity* to engage in social interaction and group-oriented play. Thus, from this perspective, a child who is playing quietly alone in his or her room at home would not be engaging in nonsocial play, per se, as there are no play partners in the immediate vicinity.

It has generally been believed that the consistent and frequent display of nonsocial play behaviors in childhood is indicative of psychological maladaptation of some form. Thus, although the display of nonsocial play in early childhood is quite common (Rubin, 1982), a high frequency of nonsocial play has been used as a generic marker variable for shyness/withdrawal and social maladjustment (e.g., Cowen, Pederson, Bibigian, Izzo, & Trost, 1973; Walker, Greenwood, Hops, & Todd, 1979). Although it will be argued herein that not all forms of nonsocial play are necessarily indicative of behavioral maladaptation, from a clinical perspective there is reason to be concerned about children who are consistently experiencing a paucity of social interaction with peers. There is now a large body of research evidence to suggest that children who experience a poor quality of peer relationships are at risk for a host of later emotional and psychosocial difficulties (see Rubin, Bukowski, & Parker, 1998, for a recent review).

Importance of Social Interaction in Childhood

Historically, the behavioral manifestations of social withdrawal (i.e., nonsocial play activities) have generally been considered to have limited developmental significance. Thus, many researchers have not viewed children who were socially withdrawn as being at risk for psychological maladjustment during adolescence and adulthood (Ensminger, Kellam, & Rubin, 1983; Kohlberg, LaCrosse, & Ricks, 1972).

This is somewhat surprising, given that researchers have stressed the importance of peer interaction since the turn of the century. For example, Cooley (1902) maintained that children's peers (which he referred to as their primary groups) were important socialization agents. Piaget (e.g., 1926, 1932) suggested that peer interaction provided a critical context for social learning. According to Piaget, the experiences of peer interaction—in particular, exposures to instances of conflict and opportunities for social negotiation—aid children in the acquisition and development of sensitive perspective-taking skills in interpersonal relationships.

Mead (1934) stressed the importance of peer interaction in the development of the self-system. He argued that exchanges among peers, in the contexts of cooperation, competition, conflict, and friendly discussion, allowed the child to gain an understanding of the self as both subject and object. In the fifties, Sullivan (1953) proposed that the experience of peer relationships was essential for the child's development of the concepts of mutual respect, equality, and reciprocity. Sullivan emphasized the importance of "chumships," or special relationships, for the emergence of these concepts. Thus, equality, mutuality, and reciprocity were acquired between special friends, and then these concepts were thought to be extended to other relationships.

At present, it is widely accepted that children who consistently experience a low quality of peer interaction during the early and middle childhood years may be at risk for later problems in adolescence and adulthood. These problems include academic difficulties (i.e., poor school performance, school dropout), delinquency and aggression, and other forms of psychological maladjustment such as depression, low self-esteem, and loneliness (see Kupersmidt, Coie, & Dodge, 1990; Rubin, Coplan, Nelson, Cheah, & Lagace-Seguin, in press; Rubin et al., 1998, for reviews).

Researchers have not sought to explore the specific outcomes associated with the continued and frequent display of nonsocial play in early childhood. Instead, nonsocial play has generally been utilized as one component of the operational definition for the broader construct of *social withdrawal*. In this regard, there are longitudinal data that provide empirical support for the connection between social withdrawal and later maladjustment. Rubin and colleagues (e.g., Rubin, 1993; Rubin, Chen, McDougall, Bowker, & McKinnon, 1995; Rubin & Mills, 1988) have examined the stability and predictive outcomes of social withdrawal in early childhood.

Their results indicated that social withdrawal is relatively stable from preschool through to adolescence (e.g., Rubin, 1993; Rubin & Both, 1989). Moreover, a high frequency of nonsocial activities in kindergarten predicted feelings of depression and low self-worth, as well as teacher-rated anxiety in the fifth grade (age 11 years) (Hymel, Rubin, Rowden, & LeMare, 1990; Rubin & Mills, 1988). In turn, social withdrawal in mid-childhood predicted negative self-regard, loneliness, and felt insecurity among peers and family in the ninth grade (age 15 years) (Rubin, 1993; Rubin, Chen, McDougall, Bowker, & McKinnon, 1995).

There is ample empirical evidence to suggest that the frequent display of nonsocial play behaviors in early childhood is a potential risk factor for the later development of psychological maladaptation, particularly in the form of *internalizing* problems. This would support the general clinical contention that young children who do not interact with their peers (i.e., engage in mostly nonsocial play) are at risk, and should therefore be the target of ameliorative intervention programs. However, things are not quite as straightforward as they would first appear. Upon closer examination of the recent extant literature, there appear to be several additional factors that warrant consideration in the understanding and assessment of nonsocial play behaviors.

The "Context" of Nonsocial Play

There are many different contexts within which children may display nonsocial play behaviors. For example, Hinde (1987) has discussed the importance of considering the level of social complexity (i.e., individual, interactions, relationships) when considering children's experiences with peers. When displayed within various contexts, the same behaviors may be reflective of different psychological underpinnings. Two factors that have a profound influence on the contexts for nonsocial play are the nature of available *play partners,* and the *novelty* of the play setting.

Characteristics of Play Partners

The necessity of available play partners for social play introduces a host of potentially influential variables. To begin with, the *characteristics* of play partners may alter the demands of the play setting, and influence children's play behaviors. For example, from an early age, children vary their social overtures as a function of the age and gender of their playmates (Brownell, 1990; Howes, 1988). Moreover, children as young as $3^1/_2$ years direct more social overtures and engage in more social interactions with friends than with nonfriends (Doyle, 1982). The presence of an adult may also influence children's social and play behaviors. For example, if an adult attachment figure is in the playroom, they may provide a secure base that fosters the child's active exploration of the social environment (e.g., Sroufe, 1983). In turn, increased social exploration often results in peer play (Rubin, Fein, & Vandenberg, 1983).

In the classroom, some children may prefer play and interaction with a teacher as opposed to peers. A child who consistently plays with a teacher may not be engaging in nonsocial play in the strictest sense; however, they are still refraining from social interaction with peers. It has long been argued that children's relationships with peers could be clearly distinguished, in form and function, from their relationships with adults (e.g., Piaget, 1932). Children's peer relationships are characterized by a more balanced and egalitarian nature, and fall along a more-or-less horizontal plane of power assertion and dominance. There is some reason to believe that a preference to engage in activities with adults may be reflective of social difficulties. In support of this contention, several researchers have reported an association between teacher-oriented behaviors in the early childhood classroom and indices of social maladjustment (e.g., Factor & Frankie, 1980; Ladd & Mars, 1986; Marturano, 1980; Roper & Hinde, 1978).

These factors need to be taken into consideration when making attributions about the nature of nonsocial play. The contextual setting of the displayed behaviors may be of prime importance. For example, a child who engages in a high frequency of adult-oriented interaction when in the presence of *only* other adults (i.e., when no peers are present) might be quite sociable and outgoing, seeking to interact with their available social partners. However, a child who seeks adult interaction and displays ostensibly the same behaviors, but in a setting where other children are also available as playmates, may be socially anxious, insecure, and maladjusted.

Novel versus Familiar Settings

Another important contextual distinction in the understanding of nonsocial play concerns the *novelty* of the play partners and setting. When faced with a novel setting (i.e., a new environment, unfamiliar peers and/or adults), some children are consistently quiet, vigilant, and restrained. These children have been referred to as *inhibited* (Kagan, 1989, 1997; Kagan, Reznick, & Gibbons, 1989; Kagan, Reznick & Snidman, 1988). At two years of age, extremely inhibited children demonstrate characteristically wary behaviors during interactions in an unfamiliar setting. These behaviors include withdrawal from, or long latencies to interact with, unfamiliar objects or adults, cessation of play and vocalization following the introduction of a novel event, and prolonged proximity to a parent in an unfamiliar setting. In contrast, *uninhibited* children react with spontaneity, and quickly seek to initiate social interaction, as if they do not distinguish between novel and familiar situations.

There is growing evidence to suggest that inhibition has a strong biological component. For example, inhibited children, as compared to their uninhibited counterparts, have higher and more stable heart rates, larger pupillary dilation, and higher levels of morning salivary cortisol as well as urinary norepinephrine (Fox, 1989; Kagan et al., 1988; Reznick et al., 1986; Schmidt et al., in press). Kagan and colleagues (1989) have argued that the differences between inhibited and uninhibited children imply variability in the threshold of arousal in the limbic-hypothalamic axis. Phrased differently, they maintain that inhibited children have a genetically predispositioned low threshold for arousal in the face of novelty.

From a related perspective, nonsocial play in the presence of unfamiliar peers has been considered a behavioral marker for *shyness*. Shyness can be conceptualized as a specific type of inhibition, namely, inhibition in response to novel *social* situations. There is growing evidence to suggest that shyness has an important genetic component (Buss, 1986; Plomin & Daniels, 1986). Implicit in the definition of shyness is the notion that the child's characteristically wary behavioral response pattern will wane as the setting becomes more familiar. This is consistent with the notion of the "slow-to-warm-up" child, first posited by Thomas and Chess (1977; Thomas, Chess, & Birch, 1968). In fact, nonsocial behaviors in novel settings are not strongly predictive of children's social behaviors in more familiar environments (Asendorpf, 1990; Paquette & LaFreniere, 1994). Asendorpf (1994) has argued that the relation between children's behaviors in novel and familiar settings is mediated by peer interactions and the establishment of social relationships.

Notwithstanding, some children continue to engage in a high frequency of nonsocial play behaviors even in familiar social settings. Nonsocial play in this setting has been considered an indicator of *social withdrawal*. Rubin and colleagues (Rubin, 1993; Rubin et al., 1989; Rubin et al., 1990; Rubin et al., in press; Rubin, Stewart, & Coplan, 1995) have explored the *interplay* between physiological and environmental factors. They have speculated that social withdrawal develops as a result of the interaction between intraindividual factors (e.g., a biological predisposition for arousal in the face of novel stimuli); interindividual factors (e.g., parental overcontrol, insecure-anxious attachment relationships, poor peer relationships); and macrosystemic forces (socioeconomic status, availability of social support, cultural factors).

To summarize, the context in which nonsocial play is displayed can have a profound impact upon the interpretation of its meaning and intent. The same behaviors can have very different meanings as a function of their *context*. As such, some researchers have argued that nonsocial behaviors in response to novel stimuli are indicative of *behavioral inhibition*. Others have considered nonsocial behaviors in the face of novel social situations to be a marker variable for *shyness*. Finally, still others have utilized nonsocial play in familiar settings as an indication of *social withdrawal*. As such, it seems clear that interpretation and understanding of nonsocial behaviors must be considered within the parameters of the surrounding environment. Having understood that the same play forms may have different meanings as a function of their context, another important clarification is warranted. In recent years it has also become evident that all structural forms of nonsocial play are not equal. In the following section, the importance of the content of nonsocial play is explored.

The "Content" of Nonsocial Play

As mentioned previously, until recently, it was generally believed that the frequent and continued display of nonsocial play in social contexts was a sufficient criterion for characterizing young children as socially withdrawn, and therefore at risk for contemporaneous and future social, social-cognitive, and emotional difficulties. Over the last few years, researchers have begun to more closely examine the content of nonsocial play, and have identified clusters of nonsocial behaviors that appear to be conceptually and empirically distinct from one another. As illustrated in the vignette described at the opening of this chapter, it seems clear that behavioral solitude is *not* a homogeneous construct. There are indeed various "subtypes" of nonsocial behaviors, each with, apparently, its own underlying psychological meaning. These clusters of nonsocial behaviors include reticent, solitary-passive, and solitary-active behaviors.

Reticent Behaviors

"Nearby, Simon stands motionless, hovering a few feet from the playing children. He watches them intently for a while, but makes no attempt to join in. After a while, he wanders off aimlessly."

The child described in this portion of the vignette is displaying a form of nonsocial play that has been labeled *reticent* behavior. Reticent behavior is identified by the frequent production of onlooking behaviors (prolonged watching of other children without accompanying play) or being unoccupied (wandering aimlessly, staring off into space) (Asendorpf, 1991; Coplan et al., 1994). This form of nonsocial play seems to reflect social fear and anxiety in a social context. From a motivational perspective, reticent behavior has been conceptualized as a manifestation of an approach-avoidance *conflict* (Asendorpf, 1990). Thus, reticent children may be desirous of peer entry (high social *approach* motivation), but this motivation is simultaneously inhibited by social fear and anxiety (high social *avoidance* motivation).

In early childhood, reticent behaviors have been associated empirically with overt demonstrations of anxiety (automanipulatives—digit sucking, hair pulling, and crying), hovering near others during free play, temperamental shyness, and internalizing problems (Coplan & Rubin, 1998a; Coplan et al., 1994). Additionally, Fox and colleagues (Fox et al., 1995) reported that reticent behavior was associated with characteristic patterns of

EEG responses to a variety of stimuli. Preschoolers who displayed a high frequency of reticent behavior (and other socially wary responses) exhibited right-frontal EEG asymmetries (a measure of emotional dysregulation), as compared to their more sociable and outgoing agemates, who were more likely to display left-frontal EEG asymmetries under similar conditions. As well, there is recent evidence to suggest that this form of nonsocial play is associated with peer rejection (more so than other types of solitary behaviors) in early childhood (Hart et al., 1998). Thus, reticent behavior appears to be a behavioral marker for prototypical "shyness/anxious". However, other forms of nonsocial play do not appear to be representative of this stereotype.

Solitary-Passive Behavior

"A few feet to the left, oriented away from the play group, Vanessa sits, hunched over a pad of paper with some colored markers. She is engrossed in her drawing, and pays little attention to the activities transpiring around her."

This child is described as displaying *solitary-passive* behavior. This form of nonsocial play includes the quiescent exploration of objects and/or constructive activity while playing alone (Rubin, 1982). Children who frequently display solitary-passive play (e.g., doing puzzles or artwork) seem to be object-oriented (Jennings, 1975) rather than people-oriented. In this regard, these children have been observed to excel at object-oriented tasks (e.g., ticket-sorting, toy cleanup), and are more task persistent and have higher attention spans (Coplan & Rubin, 1998a; Coplan et al., 1994).

From a motivational perspective, solitary-passive play appears to reflect a *disinterest* in social engagement, indicative of both low approach and low avoidance motivations (Asendorpf, 1990; Rubin & Asendorpf, 1993). A child with such a motivational system might be content to play alone without initiating social contacts, but might also be willing to engage in more socially oriented activities if provided with an attractive social invitation. In this same vein, solitary-passive behaviors seem to be the preferred play modality of nonsociable but emotionally well-regulated preschoolers (Rubin, Coplan, Fox, & Calkins, 1995).

Generally, solitary-passive play among preschoolers has not been associated with concurrent indices of maladaptation (Coplan & Rubin, 1998a; Coplan et al., 1994). Moreover, it has been argued that such behavior is positively reinforced by teachers, parents, and peers, and its display is associated with competent problem solving as well as peer acceptance (Rubin, 1982). Thus, despite being a form of nonsocial play, solitary-passive behavior does not appear to be a risk factor for concurrent maladaptation. However, the continued and consistent display of any form of nonsocial play throughout the early childhood years would deprive children of opportunities for peer group interaction, an important and unique source for the acquisition of myriad social and cognitive skills. Moreover, with age, the frequent display of solitary behaviors becomes increasingly viewed by the child's community of peers as deviant from social behavioral norms (Younger & Daniels, 1992). In this regard, it has been argued that solitary-passive behavior may become increasingly maladaptive in middle and later childhood (Rubin et al., 1989; Rubin & Mills, 1988).

Solitary-Active Behavior

"Finally, over on the other side of the room, Paul is off by himself, banging two wooden blocks together repeatedly, occasionally throwing one of them up in the air and giggling as it hits the ground."

The third subtype of nonsocial play described here is *solitary-active* behavior. Solitary-active play is characterized by repeated sensorimotor actions with or without objects (functional activities) and/or by solitary dramatizing (Coplan et al., 1994; Rubin, 1982). A child engaged in this form of nonsocial play might bang a pair of wood blocks together repeatedly, or "drive" a toy car around in circles while vocalizing the sounds of the engine. It is important to distinguish solitary-dramatic play *in the presence of peers* from dramatic play *when the child is alone,* as well as from *sociodramatic* play in the presence of peers. The former is quite normal for young children, and the latter is actually a marker of social competence (e.g., Howes, 1992).

Solitary-active play is observed to occur quite infrequently during free play (about 3% of the time during free play), and is thus somewhat difficult to study (Coplan et al., 1994). However, this highly salient form of solitary activity is thought to be representative of social immaturity and poor impulse control, particularly in early childhood. During this age period, solitary-active behaviors have been associated with indices of impulsivity, the display of rough play and externalizing problems (in particular, aggressiveness), and peer rejection (Coplan & Rubin, 1998a; Coplan et al., 1994; Hart et al., 1998; Rubin, 1982; Rubin & Mills, 1988). Thus, solitary-active behavior, although nonsocial in nature, appears to be associated with *externalizing,* as opposed to internalizing problems, in childhood.

Rubin, LeMare, and Lollis (1990) have suggested that although some children may voluntarily withdraw *from* peer interaction, others may, in fact, be actively isolated *by* the peer group. In this regard, it can be hypothesized that children who are observed to engage in a high frequency of solitary-active behaviors may be engaging in nonsocial play behaviors not by choice. Instead, lacking in the abilities to competently initiate and maintain social interactions, these children may retreat to solitary-active play in response to social rebuffs from peers.

In summary, it seems clear from the extant literature that different forms of nonsocial play have different psychological "meanings." Moreover, individual differences in these various forms of nonsocial play behaviors are fairly stable, and predict widely variant maladaptive as well as adaptive outcomes. Given the recent findings concerning the complex and multidimensional structure of nonsocial play behaviors, it follows that new measurement tools are required which are designed to be consistent with these theoretical conceptualizations.

METHODOLOGIES FOR THE ASSESSMENT OF NONSOCIAL PLAY

There have been few measures specifically developed to assess the display of children's nonsocial play activities in early childhood. Typically, nonsocial play has been assessed somewhat incidentally, as one component of a broader construct (i.e., social withdrawal). From this perspective, a number of methodological tools are available. As such, a brief review of the extant literature in this area is provided. However, the primary focus of this section concerns a more detailed description of an observational taxonomy and a newly developed teacher rating scale that have been employed to assess the specific structural forms of nonsocial play outlined above.

One way that methodological tools can be characterized is with respect to the source of information concerning children's behavior. For example, in the employment of *direct* observational techniques, the source of information is the researcher, who actually watches and records various aspects of children's behaviors. In the use of *indirect* techniques (i.e., questionnaires, nominations, and ratings scales), the information is provided by an "outside" source, typically, a teacher, parent, or peer, or by self-reports from the children themselves.

Direct Observations

Direct observations involve the systematic observation of children's behaviors. This may be done live (e.g., from behind a one-way mirror or as an unobtrusive observer in the playroom) or with the assistance of videotape recordings. There currently exist several observational coding schemes which can be used to assess social and nonsocial play and related constructs (e.g., Eiferman, 1971; Hart, DeWolf, Wozniak, & Burts, 1992; Ladd & Price, 1993; see Bergen, 1988; Coplan & Rubin, 1998b, for reviews). These coding schemes have been employed to observe social play and other behaviors in the classroom (e.g., Rubin, 1982), on the playground (e.g., Hart et al., 1992), and in the home with adults (e.g., Pettit & Bates, 1990).

There are definite advantages to using direct observational techniques. To begin with, coders can be trained to observe and record very specific and detailed behaviors. As discussed previously, "fine-grained" behavioral distinctions may be particularly important in the observation of nonsocial play. In addition, the use of "blind" observers may reduce biases in the coding process. Moreover, there is clearly face validity in observing real-occurring behaviors in a naturalistic setting. From these observations, age and sex norms can be established for the production of particular forms of nonsocial behaviors. From these norms, procedures may be developed to identify children who deviate from their agemates or from children of the same gender.

The major disadvantage of direct observation techniques is that they are often quite time consuming and thus very expensive. Observational procedures can take weeks or months to complete. This often makes them impractical or impossible to employ. Observations may also be somewhat reactive; for example, children who are aware that they are being observed may behave in an atypical manner as a function of social desirability. Finally, coders are often limited in the contexts, settings, and time frames in which they can observe behaviors. Thus, the limited amount of behavior coded for any given child may not necessarily be indicative of the child's everyday or average behavior. However, methodological advances in "behavior-sampling" techniques have increased the generalizability of direct observational techniques.

For example, in *time-sampling* methodologies (e.g., Frost & Sunderlin, 1985; Hart et al., 1992; Ladd & Price, 1993; Rubin, 1989), individual children are observed, in turn, for a series of short time segments (i.e., 15 seconds). When employing a time-sampling coding scheme, the researcher typically codes each interval for the child's predominant play behavior. The behaviors are selected from a previously derived, mutually exclusive and exhaustive taxonomy. Over an extended period of time, the data from many coding intervals which have been collected can be considered a "random sample" of free-play activities which are representative of the child's everyday behaviors.

Although *event-sampling* coding schemes (e.g., Eiferman, 1971; Mueller & Brenner, 1977; Harrist et al., 1997) also involve a taxonomy of behaviors, it is the behavioral "event" that serves as the unit of analysis instead of time. When coding with an event-sampling scheme, the researcher observes a child, or scans between a group of children, until a specific behavior is noted. When this behavior is observed, coding commences and continues until the behavior event has run its course.

Event-sampling is particularly useful for the coding of low-frequency behaviors. For example, a researcher who is particularly interested in solitary-active play may observe a group of children for an extended time period before any instances of solitary-active behavior are evident. If the researcher was employing a time-sampling methodology, the focus of observation may be on a child who is engaging in an unrelated behavior instead of on a rare instance of solitary-active behavior that is being exhibited by another child. This important information would not be overlooked when using an event-sampling approach. In this case, the researcher is able to scan the classroom until an instance of solitary-active play is observed from any of the children. This event would then become the focus of the coder's continued attention until its completion.

The Play Observation Scale

A particularly diverse observational protocol that can be employed for the assessment of various forms of children's social and nonsocial free-play behaviors is the *Play Observation Scale* (POS; Rubin, 1989). The POS was originally developed as a reliable general taxonomy of play behaviors in early and middle childhood. It utilizes a norm-based time-sampling procedure in which various types of behavior in a play group context are evaluated. Various play forms are examined *within* different social participation categories.

Thus, the POS can be used to simultaneously evaluate the social participatory and the structural components of children's free-play behaviors. Researchers investigating children's social participation are more concerned with the question "With whom is the child playing?" The study of the structural components of children's play behaviors asks the general question "How is the child playing?", or "What is the child doing?"

Social Participation

Most of the earliest work on the social participatory aspects of children's free-play behaviors were biographical studies that included observations of social behavior incidental to other "psychic" (i.e., psychological) behavior (e.g., Baldwin & Stecher, 1925; Cooley, 1902; Hogan, 1898; Shinn, 1893; Tracy, 1910). In the 1920s, several attempts were made to develop taxonomies for describing children's social and nonsocial interactions with peers. For example, Verry (1923) observed spontaneous preschool play groups and distinguished five types of social "attitudes," namely: (1) treating playmates as objects; (2) assuming an adult attitude; (3) seeking attention; (4) doing as others do; and (5) cooperating with the group. Bott (1928) developed a direct observational coding scheme that included a category of "occupied with other children," containing the subcategories of talking, watching, interference, imitation, and cooperation. Finally, Lehman and colleagues (Lehman, 1926; Lehman & Anderson, 1928), attempted to characterize the differences between solitary and social play as they related to measures of sociability and other character traits.

However, the social participatory component of the POS was drawn from the work of Mildred Parten. Parten (1932) examined the social and nonsocial interactions of preschool children who were observed in a nursery school setting over a nine-month period. Observations were collected in a group free-play context both indoors and outdoors. From her extensive observations, Parten derived several categories of social participation. These categories were adapted to provide the basis for the five social participation codes in the POS: unoccupied, onlooker, solitary, parallel, and group. The categories are described as follows (see Rubin, 1989, for more details).

Unoccupied behavior is characterized by a marked absence of focus or intent. The unoccupied child is not playing, but instead may blankly stare into space, or wander around aimlessly (with no specific purpose). When engaged in *onlooking* behavior, the child watches the activities of others but does not attempt to enter in. This differs from unoccupied behavior in that onlooking specifically involves the observation of another child or group of children.

Solitary play is coded when the child plays apart from the other children at a distance greater than three feet. The child is playing alone and independently with toys that are different from those used by the children within speaking distance. Moreover, the child is centered on his or her own activity and pays little or no attention to any of the children in the area. Playing independently next to but not with other children is characteristic of *parallel* play. The activity often, but not necessarily, brings the child within three feet of other children. While engaging in his or her own activities, the child is aware of the other children and may occasionally make reference to their play. In contrast, during *group* play, the child plays directly with other children. There is a common goal or purpose to the activity, with a marked sense of belonging to the group; the efforts of one child are supplemented by those of another (i.e., division of labor).

These social participation categories already provide some distinction between the various forms of nonsocial play. Unoccupied and onlooking behaviors are differentiated from solitary play, which is in turn distinguished from parallel and group activities. However, as previously discussed, there is reason to divide solitary play into further subtypes. The POS allows for this possibility because nested *within* the social participation categories of solitary, parallel, and group play are various levels of the structural quality of play.

Structural Components of "Play"

The second theoretical approach to the observation of children's play behaviors has focused on the structure or content of play activities. The historical roots of this conceptualization can be traced back to Spenser (1873), who was among the first researchers to describe several different structural forms of children's play. These included the superfluous activity of the sensory-motor apparatus; artistic-aesthetic play; games; and mimicry. Stern (1924) attempted to divide children's play into several categories, theorized to represent increasing complexity: (1) mastery of the body (motor games, with the body being used as an instrument); (2) mastery of things (destructive and constructive games); and (3) impersonation (transformation of people and things). In a similar vein, Buhler (1928) proposed a classification of children's play that included functional (or sensory-motor) games, games of make-believe or illusion, passive games (e.g., looking at pictures, listening to stories) and games of construction.

The structural categories of the POS can be traced most directly to the work of Piaget (1962), who outlined a structural classification system for the development of children's games. Piaget distinguished between three main types of structure which characterized children's games, namely, practice games, symbolic games, and games-with-rules. These categories were elaborated upon by Smilansky (1968) and were adapted to provide the basis for the structural codes in the POS. These categories, described below, include functional, exploratory, constructive, and dramatic play (again, see Rubin, 1989, for more details).

Functional play involves activities that are done simply for the enjoyment of the physical sensation they create. These typically involve simple and repetitive motor activities (e.g., banging two blocks together repeatedly). In contrast, *exploratory* activity is defined as focused examination of an object for the purposes of obtaining information about its specific physical properties. A child engaging in exploratory behaviors may be examining an object in his or her hand, looking at something (but not someone) across the room, or listening to a noise. A child engaged in *constructive* play is manipulating objects for the purpose of constructing or creating something. This may include activities like drawing pictures, painting, or building with blocks. Finally, *dramatic* play is coded when there is an element of pretense evident. This may include the child taking on the role of someone else, engaging in a pretend activity, or attributing life to inanimate objects.

It is important to note that the structural quality of play does not depend strictly upon the play material selected. Consider the case of wooden blocks. A child first examining the contents of a wooden block pile would be engaging in exploratory behaviors; if the child then repeatedly banged two blocks together, this would be considered functional play; the activity of building a block tower would be coded as constructive play; and if the child pretended that the block was a car and began "driving" it around on the floor, dramatic play would be evident.

The POS as a Research Tool

The POS was developed as a marriage between the theoretical and descriptive approaches of Parten and Piaget. With the nesting of structural components of play within the various social participation categories, a more complete description of play activities is permitted. Thus, children's free-play activities can be coded as solitary-exploratory or solitary-functional, and group-dramatic or group-constructive.

The POS has been used by researchers to study both individual differences in children's play, and general age-related and context-specific trends. For example, the POS has been employed to study the play behaviors of developmentally delayed children (Guralnick & Groom, 1987), hearing impaired children (Higgenbotham & Baker, 1981), and children learning English as a second language (Wall & Pickert, 1982). Other studies using the POS have examined the temporal and cross-situational stability of children's play behaviors (Enslein & Fein, 1981), as well as the effects of environmental and cognitive factors on social play (Vandenberg, 1981).

Using the POS to Code Nonsocial Play

More recently, the POS has been adapted for use in the study of the various forms of young children's nonsocial behaviors (e.g., Coplan & Rubin, 1998a; Coplan et al., 1994; Rubin, 1982; Rubin, Coplan Fox, & Calkins, 1995). A researcher or clinician with a particular interest in the multiple forms of nonsocial play might choose to employ a somewhat simplified version of the POS. With this in mind, a brief overview of how to adapt the coding procedure is outlined below. However, the reader is encouraged to consult the POS manual (Rubin, 1989) for a more complete description.

Let's assume there is an interest in observing the nonsocial play behaviors of a small sample of children during free play at preschool. Over some predetermined period of time, a few minutes of observational data might be collected each day for each child in the sample. During each coding period, the researcher would observe each child (in random order) for a series of 10-second intervals, until several minutes of observations are completed for each child. This protocol would be repeated for each coding session over a period of several days and/or weeks. If a single child is observed, several minutes of observational data can be collected in a single session. However, it is still recommended that observations take place over a period of several days, so as to better reflect the child's everyday free-play behaviors.

One behavioral code is assigned to each 10-second interval. This code may have both a social participation and a structural component to it. When more than one type of play behavior is demonstrated within a 10-second segment, the *predominant* behavior is coded (i.e., the behavior engaged in for the majority of the time interval). To illustrate, the researcher would watch the target child for a full 10-second coding interval. The coder must then make two decisions. The first decision concerns the social participation component of the observed behavior. The behavior must be coded as either unoccupied, onlooker, solitary, parallel, or group. If the predominant code is unoccupied or onlooker, no additional coding decisions are necessary. If the predominant code is parallel or group, researchers with particular interests in *nonsocial* play may not wish to code any further (in the interest of saving time, and achieving fast interrater reliability). However, if *solitary* play is coded, an additional distinction between solitary-exploratory, solitary-functional, solitary-constructive, and solitary-dramatic must be made. The researcher would then repeat this procedure for each subsequent coding interval.

At the completion of data collection, the observational codes can be summed and proportionalized (dividing by the total number of coding intervals). In this way, the proportion of time that each child was observed to engage in the various forms of nonsocial play can be derived. Although clinical norms have not been specifically established for these play behaviors, a comparison of individual children's scores with reported means for various samples might prove insightful (Enslein, & Fein, 1981; Coplan et al., 1994; Rubin, 1982; Rubin, Maioni, & Hornung, 1976; Rubin, Watson, & Jambor, 1978).

Despite its many advantages, the Play Observation Scale remains a very time-consuming and costly method for collecting observational data about preschoolers' nonsocial play behaviors. As such, limited budgetary resources may not always allow for its use, particularly with larger samples. In this regard, an indirect observational methodology that would allow for the assessment of specific aspects of nonsocial behaviors in young children would be warranted.

Indirect Observations

Indirect observations involve procedures where an outside source is employed to provide an assessment of children's behaviors. With regard to the study of nonsocial play in preschool and classroom settings, these potential "expert" informants include peers and teachers, and to a lesser extent parents, as well as child self-reports. There do not exist many rating scale measures designed to directly assess nonsocial play. Some components of nonsocial play are circuitously assessed by measures that examine children's social competence, personality, temperament, and classroom behaviors. These include peer rating scales and nomination techniques (e.g., the *Revised Class Play,* Masten, Morison, &

Pellegrini, 1985), parent rating scales (e.g., the *Colorado Child Temperament Inventory,* Rowe & Plomin, 1977), and teacher rating scales (e.g., the *Preschool Socio-Affective Profile,* LaFrenière, Dumas, Capuano, & Dubeau, 1992).

There are several advantages to using these paper-and-pencil rating scales. To begin with, outside source assessment is comparatively quick and inexpensive. As well, classmates and teachers have the potential to observe children in many different circumstances and for long periods of time; thus, they can make inferences about specific children's everyday behaviors. The disadvantage of outside source observation methods centers on the use of untrained observers for the purpose of data collection. Because they are untrained, they may not be able to identify specific and detailed aspects of behaviors. There may also be some bias in their recall of the children's characteristic social behavior patterns. In the following section, the rationale for selecting *teachers* as a valid source of information regarding young children's nonsocial free-play behaviors is provided.

Teachers as Informants

It is argued herein that teachers are the best informants of young children's free-play behaviors in the preschool classroom. Acting *in loco parentis,* teachers often get to know the children in their class very well. Teachers spend a large amount of time with the children, and are therefore also likely to be privy to critical but low-frequency social events.

Teacher ratings have been found to correlate more highly with observational ratings than peer ratings (Connolly & Doyle, 1981; Greenwood, Walker, & Hopps, 1977). Although young children can give reliable and valid ratings of their classmates' aggressive behaviors (e.g., Ladd & Mars, 1986; Younger, Schwartzman, & Ledingham, 1985), young children have much more difficulty in accurately and reliably assessing socially withdrawn behaviors (Younger, Gentile, & Burgess, 1993). Unlike aggression, socially withdrawn behaviors are *not* negatively salient to the preschool peer group. Thus, although preschoolers may have a well-developed schema for aggression, allowing them to better encode and remember aggressive behaviors (Bukowski, 1990; Younger & Boyko, 1987; Younger & Piccinin, 1989), it appears as though children do not possess a well-developed schema for social withdrawal until the mid-childhood years (Younger & Boyko, 1987; Younger et al., 1993).

Clearly, it does not seem as if young children would be very successful in assessing the frequency of their peers' engagement in various forms of nonsocial activities (e.g., onlooking, solitary-constructive, solitary-functional, etc.). Teachers are a more reliable source of identifying child problems concerning anxiety and social withdrawal (Ollendick, Oswald, & Francis, 1989; Younger, Schwartzman, & Ledingham, 1985).

Teacher Rating Scales

Given the relative advantages of teachers as informants, it is not surprising that there currently exists a plethora of teacher rating scales and questionnaires designed to assess various aspects of preschool children's social behaviors. These include the *Conners Teacher Rating Scale* (CTRS; Conners, 1969, 1973), the *Social Competence Scale and Symptom Checklist* (SCSSC; Kohn & Rosman, 1972), the *Preschool Behavior Questionnaire* (PBQ; Behar & Springfield, 1974), the *Revised Behavior Problems Checklist* (RBPC; Quay, 1983; Quay & Peterson, 1987), the *Preschool Socioaffective Profile* (PSP; LaFreniere, Dumas, Capuano, & Dubeau, 1992), and recently the *Child Behavior Scale* (CBS; Ladd & Profilet, 1996).

Most of these measures were designed to assess global constructs associated with social and emotional functioning in the classroom. For example, almost all of the above-described scales have an externalizing-aggression-conduct disorder factor and an internalizing-anxious-fearful factor. The assessment of these constructs presumably requires the teacher to assess a child's emotional state (e.g., PSP—"sad, unhappy, or depressed," "worries"; PBQ—"tends to be fearful or afraid of new things or new situations") and social motivation (CBS—"likes to be alone," "keeps peers at a distance").

These scales were *not* designed to specifically assess preschoolers free-play behaviors. Moreover, they do not allow for the assessment of the detailed components of young children's nonsocial play behaviors. Although a few of the specific items in the above-mentioned measures address more global aspects of children's social participatory behaviors (e.g., PSP—"inactive, watches the other children play," "cooperates with other children in group activities"; PBQ—"stares into space," "solitary"), there is no information provided as to the structural quality of children's play (e.g., constructive versus functional versus dramatic play) or the *interaction* between social participation and the structural quality of play. As such, these measures confound the subtypes of nonsocial play behaviors.

With this in mind, the *Preschool Play Behavior Scale* (PPBS, Coplan & Rubin, 1998a) was recently created as an indirect observational measure of children's social and nonsocial play behaviors. The PPBS was designed to provide a teacher rating scale companion or alternative to the time-consuming task of behavioral observations. In the section that follows, a description of the PPBS is provided, along with the details of its psychometric properties.

The Preschool Play Behavior Scale

The PPBS is an 18-item questionnaire designed to assess a number of specific free-play behaviors. Teachers rate items on a 5-point Likert scale, denoting frequency of occurrence (i.e., 1 = never, 2 = hardly ever, 3 = sometimes, 4 = often, 5 = very often). PPBS items were created based on the coding manual descriptions of various behaviors assessed by the Play Observation Scale (POS; Rubin, 1989). Optimally, the PPBS should be administered after preschool teachers have had a reasonable period of time (i.e., several weeks) to get to know the children in their class.

The items from the PPBS are displayed in Table 20–1. The complete scale can be found in the appendix. The first three subscales were designed to assess the three distinct forms of nonsocial play behavior. These include *reticent* behavior, *solitary-passive* behavior, and *solitary-active* behavior. As well, in order for teachers to have a wider and more diverse range of play behaviors to assess, additional items were included to assess *social* play and *rough* play. To score the PPBS, the appropriate items for each of the subscales are summed.

Psychometric Properties

Coplan and Rubin (1998a) reported on the psychometric properties of the PPBS. In a sample of 337 preschoolers, the factor structure of the PPBS was established. Item factor loadings for all subscales were above .63, with no items "cross-loading" on any other factors. An identical pattern of results was observed when the factor analysis was repeated separately for males and females. Measures of internal consistency for the five subscales were quite high, ranging from $\alpha = .76$ to $\alpha = .96$.

Table 20–1.   PPBS items and subscales

Reticent behavior:
• takes on the role of onlooker or spectator
• wanders around aimlessly
• watches or listens to other children without trying to join in
• remains alone and unoccupied, perhaps staring off into space

Solitary-passive behavior:
• plays by himself/herself, examining a toy or object
• plays alone, building things with blocks and/or other toys
• plays by himself/herself, drawing, painting pictures, or doing puzzles
• plays alone, exploring toys or objects, trying to figure out how they work

Solitary-active behavior:
• engages in pretend play by himself/herself
• plays "make-believe," but not with other children

Social play:
• talks to other children during play
• plays "make-believe" with other children
• engages in group play
• plays in groups *with* (not just beside) other children
• engages in active conversations with other children during play
• engages in pretend play with other children

Rough-play:
• plays "rough-and-tumble" with other children
• engages in playful/mock fighting with other children

Together, these results indicated that subscales on the PPBS hung together in a predictable way. For example, children who were rated highly on one of the items pertaining to the reticent behavior subscale (e.g., "wanders around aimlessly") also tended to be rated highly on the other items for that same subscale (e.g., "takes on the role of onlooker or spectator"). In addition, these results also suggested that children who were rated highly on the solitary-passive subscale, for example, did not necessarily also receive high scores in terms of the solitary-active or reticent subscales.

Coplan and Rubin (1998a) also computed interrater reliability coefficients between five pairs of teachers who rated the same samples of children. Moderate-to-high interteacher reliability correlations were observed for the reticent, solitary-passive, social play, and rough play subscales, with coefficients ranging from .61 to .89. Thus, teachers tended to agree in terms of their ratings of the children's behaviors. The solitary-active behavior subscale demonstrated somewhat lower reliability, with a wider range of coefficients from .10 to .83. It appeared as though some teachers had difficulty agreeing upon the frequency with which they observed this form of nonsocial play, most likely due to its low frequency of occurrence during free play.

The *stability* of ratings over a six-month period was also examined. Six-month test-retest reliability correlation coefficients for all subscales were also moderate to high, ranging from .39 to .66. This indicated a fair degree of stability in terms of the teacher ratings over this time period.

The next set of analyses explored the *construct* validity of the PPBS. Construct validity concerns whether a measure assesses what it is supposed to assess. In the first part of this process, subscale scores for the PPBS were correlated with a number of theoretically relevant variables, as assessed by more well-established measures. Among the results, teacher-rated reticent behavior was significantly and positively associated with parent-rated temperamental shyness and emotionality and strongly related to child internalizing problems (teacher-rated). Solitary-active behavior was positively associated with temperamental activity level and negatively associated with shyness. Solitary-passive behavior was not significantly associated with any of the parent-rated child temperament characteristics or teacher-rated behavior problems. Social play was positively correlated with temperamental sociability. Finally, rough play was positively related to activity level and externalizing problems, and negatively associated with attention-span. Thus, each of the subscale scores was associated with assessments of other conceptually related constructs in a predictable and theoretically consistent manner.

In the final stage of establishing the construct validity of the PPBS, data were collected for a second sample of 39 preschool children. The children were observed at regular intervals over a three-month period and their free-play behaviors were recorded and coded using a modified version of the Play Observation Scale (POS; Rubin, 1989). Preschool teachers then completed the PPBS. Results indicated that teacher ratings of nonsocial behaviors (i.e., reticent, solitary-passive, solitary-active), social play, and rough play were generally significantly associated with observed indices of the same behaviors. Thus, for example, for three separate teachers, ratings of children's reticent behavior were significantly correlated with researchers' observations of the same behavior ($r = .50$, $r = .46$, and $r = .54$, all p's $< .05$).

Moreover, there was an overall lack of significant intercorrelations among teacher-rated and observed *noncorresponding* forms of nonsocial behaviors. In other words, teacher ratings of reticent behavior were not associated with observations of solitary-passive or solitary-active play. This provided a measure of *discriminant* validity for the PPBS, indicating that teacher ratings of reticent behavior, for example, were associated with the observed display of reticent behavior only, and not with all forms of nonsocial play.

Thus, these initial findings suggested that the PPBS can provide a reliable and valid outside source assessment measure of nonsocial play in early childhood. A multimethod approach to the study of behaviors is typically beneficial — different informants can contribute different types of information that may help to better define a behavioral construct (e.g., Achenbach, McConaughy, & Howell, 1987). As such, the PPBS can provide an additional informant source in the study of behavioral solitude.

The evaluation and validation of this scale are ongoing. For example, clinical norms for age and gender have not yet been widely established for the PPBS. However, the PPBS has immediate research applications, as illustrated in the final section of this chapter.

NONSOCIAL PLAY AND SOCIOEMOTIONAL MALADJUSTMENT IN THE PRESCHOOL: A PILOT STUDY

In the first part of this chapter, theoretical issues in the definition and conceptualization of nonsocial play behaviors in early childhood were explored. In the second section, an observational taxonomy and a teacher rating scale that can be employed in the assessment of nonsocial play behaviors were described. In the final portion of this chapter, results from a pilot study are presented where these conceptual issues and methodological tools are applied to the pragmatic issue of the prediction of young children's social and emotional adjustment to a new preschool setting.

Social Adjustment in the Preschool

For increasing numbers of children below the age of 5 years, the first formal exposure to a large and diverse peer group occurs when they attend a preschool or childcare program. Recent statistics from the United States indicate that in 1996, 37% of 3-year-olds, 58% of 4-year-olds, and an astounding 90% of 5-year-olds were enrolled in preprimary education programs (Snyder & Wirt, 1998). The introduction to this new group venue represents an important transition period in early childhood. During the preschool years, social play becomes more prominent, there is a substantial increase in the frequency of social contacts, and social interaction episodes become longer, more elaborated, and more varied (e.g., Blurton-Jones, 1972; Rubin, Watson, & Jambor, 1978). In this regard, the preschool classroom is an important and unique context for young children to acquire and implement newly emerging social skills.

For most children, the start of preschool provides the setting for the experience of positive and rewarding social interactions. However, for some children, adjustment to preschool is fraught with anxiety, confusion, anger, or frustration. Preschool behavioral dysfunction beyond the initial adaptation period is quite common (e.g., McGuire & Richman, 1986). Forty to 50% of children experiencing behavioral problems in preschool continue to exhibit some form of dysfunction over the next two to five years (Campbell, Ewing, Breaux, & Szumowski, 1986; Garrisson & Earls, 1985). Moreover, it has been reported that preschoolers exhibiting significant behavioral dysfunctions are at least two times as likely as their well-adjusted counterparts to develop specific adult psychiatric disorders (Lerner et al., 1982).

Children's social functioning in a preschool setting has been explored and investigated in relation to many diverse factors, including child temperament (e.g., Kyrios & Prior, 1990; Jewsuwan, Luster, & Kostelnik, 1993), parent-child attachment (e.g., Melson & Kim, 1990; Suess, Grossman, & Sroufe, 1992), children's communicative competence (e.g., Skarpness & Carson, 1987), and parenting behaviors, marital stress, and marital companionship (e.g., Hart et al., 1992; Roopnarine, Church, & Levy, 1990). To date, however, the role of young children's nonsocial play behaviors in the process of preschool adjustment has not been extensively explored.

Thus, the central goal of this pilot study was to trace conceptual pathways toward socioemotional adjustment and maladjustment over the course of the preschool year. It was hypothesized that the various forms of young children's nonsocial play behaviors (i.e., reticent, solitary-passive, and solitary-active behaviors) would be associated with differing adjustment outcomes. In appreciation of the influential contributory role of context, nonsocial play behaviors were assessed in both novel (i.e., during preschool entry) and familiar (i.e., after six weeks of school) social settings.

Child Temperament and Preschool Adjustment

The conceptualization of the pathways toward social and emotional adjustment explored in this study was derived from a theoretical model proposed by Rubin and colleagues

(Rubin, 1993; Rubin et al., 1990; Rubin et al., in press; Rubin, Stewart, & Coplan, 1995). From this perspective, conceptual pathways toward social competence and various forms of socioemotional maladjustment begin with certain child temperament characteristics.

In fact, child temperament is among the strongest and most consistent predictors of preschool adjustment. Temperament is considered to be an important contributor to children's personality development and social relationships (see Rothbart & Bates 1998, for a recent review). There is growing empirical support for the link between child temperament and preschool adjustment/functioning (e.g., Kyrios & Prior, 1990; Mobley & Pullis, 1991; Zajdeman & Minnes, 1991). Generally, it has been reported that high ratings of approach-withdrawal/shyness and activity level, as well as low ratings of attention span/persistence are concurrently associated with adjustment difficulties in the school context. Moreover, researchers have reported that temperament uniquely predicts adjustment in preschool *over and above* other variables, including marital adjustment, parental psychological functioning and child rearing practices, mother-child attachment, social status, child motor coordination, and stress and life events (Kyrios & Prior, 1990; Zajdeman & Minnes, 1991).

Nonsocial Play and Preschool Adjustment

There is some preliminary evidence to suggest that the analysis of the various forms of children's nonsocial behaviors may also be beneficial in terms of predicting preschool adjustment. For example, Rubin (1982) reported that observed instances of solitary-functional and -dramatic activities were negatively associated with indices of social-cognitive ability and sociometric popularity, while solitary-constructive activity was not generally associated with social or social-cognitive maladaptation. Levy-Shiff and Hoffman (1989) found that observed periods of unoccupied and onlooker behaviors during the first four weeks of preschool predicted later social and emotional adjustment problems (i.e., lack of emotional balance, moodiness, scapegoat role, lack of independence). In comparison, observed instances of solitary play (defined similarly to solitary-passive play) during the same period did not predict any form of preschool maladjustment.

As discussed previously, *context* is an important factor in understanding the meaning of nonsocial play. For the most part, researchers interested in the detailed study of young children's nonsocial play behaviors have explored these phenomena in the novel setting of the laboratory playroom, with unfamiliar peers (e.g., Asendorpf, 1991; Coplan et al., 1994, Rubin, Coplan, Fox, & Calkins, 1995). Less is known about the constructs of reticent, solitary-passive, and solitary-active behaviors in clearly *familiar* settings. This contextual distinction may be important: children's social behaviors in novel situations may not be similar to those in familiar settings (Asendorpf, 1990), and children who are shy in novel settings are not necessarily socially withdrawn in familiar settings (Paquette & LaFreniere, 1994). Moreover, Asendorpf (1994) has argued that the relation between children's behaviors in novel and familiar settings is mediated by peer interactions and the establishment of relationships.

Thus, in order to address these issues, and to trace the *process* of preschool adjustment over time, this pilot study included assessments of (1) child temperament (i.e., shyness, activity level, attention-span) two weeks before the start of preschool; (2) children's nonsocial behaviors during the first day of preschool entry (a novel setting); (3) children's nonsocial behaviors after six weeks of preschool (a familiar setting); and (4) adjustment outcome difficulties (i.e., internalizing and externalizing problems) at four months into the school year.

Hypotheses

The nature of the data collected for this study allowed for the investigation of a series of conceptually derived pathways toward preschool adjustment. In this regard, the direct and indirect relations between child temperament, nonsocial play (in both novel and familiar settings), and the display of classroom behavior problems were explored. From a review of the extant literature (e.g., Asendorpf, 1990, 1991; Coplan & Rubin, 1998a; Coplan et al., 1994; Rubin, 1982; Rubin, Coplan, Fox, & Calkins, 1995) several hypotheses were proposed.

Based on its status as a marker variable for social anxiety in both novel and familiar settings, it was hypothesized that the display of reticent behavior in the preschool would be associated with temperamental shyness, and predictive of the display of internalizing problems at four months. In contrast, solitary-passive behavior was not expected to be associated with any form of adjustment difficulties. As a form of "well-regulated solitude," the object-focused nature of solitary-passive behavior was expected to be evidenced in terms of a relation with temperamental attention-span. Finally, as a potential indicator of impulsivity and social immaturity, solitary-active behavior was predicted to be related to temperamental activity level, and associated with the later display of externalizing problems.

Method

Subjects

The participants in this study were 49 preschool children between the ages (as of the start of data collection) of 36 and 56 months ($M = 45.55$, $SD = 6.74$). There were 25 female and 24 male participants. The children were primarily of middle-class background, living with their families in a mid-sized Ontario community, and about to start an educationally based early childhood education program. The sample was primarily but not exclusively Caucasian.

Facilities

Children engaged in free-play activities for approximately 50 minutes in both the morning and afternoon sessions. The facility included a large and a small playroom, an art room, and a "gross motor" room. Each of these rooms was equipped with one-way mirrors and microphones. At the beginning of September, children entered the center in staggered small groups during the first week of classes. A group of about 10 children came to the preschool on Monday morning, another 10 on Monday afternoon, another 10 on Tuesday morning, and so on throughout the week, for all the children. Six children, for various reasons, did not attend the first day of school.

Procedure

Data were collected at four points during the course of the study: (1) a week before the start of preschool classes; (2) on the first day of preschool for each small group of children; (3) after approximately six weeks of preschool; and (4) after approximately 4 months of preschool.

Maternal Ratings

One week before the start of preschool, mothers completed a short demographic questionnaire and the *Colorado Child Temperament Inventory* (CCTI: Buss & Plomin, 1984; Rowe & Plomin, 1977). The CCTI assesses various temperamental characteristics, including shyness (e.g., "child tends to be shy"), activity level (e.g., "child is always on the go"), and attention-span (e.g., "child goes from toy to toy quickly").

Observational Measures

During the 50-minute free-play session on the first day of preschool, four researchers observed the children's free-play behaviors. Each observer was assigned to two or three children, coding a series of two-minute intervals for each child in random order. Between 10 and 12 minutes of observational data were collected for each child.

Children's free-play behaviors were coded using an adapted version of Rubin's (1989) Play Observation Scale. Ten-second intervals were coded for both social participation (onlooker, unoccupied, solitary, parallel, group) and the structural quality of play (functional, dramatic, exploratory, constructive). This resulted in between 60 and 72 coding intervals per child. Resulting raw frequencies were proportionalized by dividing by the total number of coding intervals per child. Following the procedures outlined in Coplan et al. (1994), the following aggregate variables were created: (1) *reticent* behavior (computed by summing the proportion of coding intervals spent in unoccupied and onlooking behaviors); (2) *solitary-passive* behavior (solitary-exploratory and constructive behaviors); and (3) *solitary-active* behavior (solitary-functional and dramatic behaviors).

Because observational data were collected on the first day of preschool, interobserver reliability data were obtained by having pairs of observers code from a previously collected videotape data pool. The tapes allowed observation of quartets of same-sex preschool-aged children engaging in free play in a room filled with age-appropriate toys (Coplan et. al., 1994). Approximately 90 minutes (540 coding intervals) of reliability data (from these tapes) were collected between pairs of observers. For a complete variable matrix, Cohen's kappa between observer pairs ranged from $K = .77$ to $K = .86$. These results indicated an acceptable degree of interrater agreement among observers.

Teacher Ratings

After approximately six weeks of preschool, teachers completed the Preschool Play Behavior Scale (PPBS, Coplan & Rubin, 1998a) for all the children in the sample. As previously described (see Table 20–1), the PPBS assesses various forms of social and nonsocial free-play activities in the preschool, including reticent behavior, solitary-passive behavior, solitary-active behavior, social play, and rough play.

Approximately four months into the school year, teachers completed the Preschool Behavior Questionnaire (PBQ; Behar & Springfield, 1974). Consistent with the results from several recent studies (e.g., Coplan & Rubin, 1998a; Moller & Rubin, 1988; Tremblay, Desmarais-Gervais, Gagnon, & Charlebois, 1987), the broader two-factor solution of "internalizing" and "externalizing" problems was employed in the present study.

Results

Preliminary Analyses

Means and standard deviations for the behavioral observation variables coded during school entry are presented in Table 20–2. In order to test for potential sex differences, a series of independent group *t*-tests were performed comparing males ($n = 24$) and females ($n = 25$) in terms of (1) parental ratings of child temperament; (2) behavioral observations of entry

Table 20–2.   Means and standard deviations for behavioral observations of children's free-play behaviors during preschool entry (N = 43)

Variable	Mean	SD
Reticent	.14	.12
Solitary-passive	.45	.16
Solitary-active	.02	.03

behaviors; (3) teacher ratings of free-play behaviors at six weeks; and (4) teacher ratings of behavior problems at four months. Results indicated no significant sex differences, with the exception of teacher-rated rough play: males were rated as engaging in significantly more rough play ($M = 4.50$, $SD = 2.00$) than females ($M = 2.64$, $SD = 1.18$, $t = 3.98$, $p < .001$).

Partial correlations (controlling for child age) were computed between child temperament, preschool entry, behavior after six weeks, and four-month adjustment outcome variables. These results are displayed in Tables 20.3 and 20.4.

From these results, patterns of associations were evident among various child temperament characteristics, school entry behaviors, free-play behaviors at six weeks, and four-month adjustment outcomes. For example, shy temperament was associated with the display of reticent behavior, which in turn strongly predicted internalizing problems at four months. In order to better elucidate these associations, a series of regression analyses were computed.

Regression Path Analyses

The primary goal of this study was to describe predictive pathways to preschool maladjustment four months into the school year, from child temperament characteristics, preschool

Table 20–3   Partial correlations, controlling for child age, between child temperament and preschool entry behaviors, free-play behaviors at six weeks, and behavior problems at four months

	Child Temperament		
	Shyness	Activity	Attention
School entry: (n = 43)			
Reticent	.21	−.16	.06
Solitary-passive	.32*	.09	.25
Solitary-active	−.27	.29	.12
Six weeks: (n = 49)			
Reticent	.45***	−.02	−.03
Solitary-passive	.14	.02	.13
Solitary-active	.07	.21	.04
Rough play	−.29*	.03	−.03
Four months: (n = 49)			
Internalizing	.17	−.06	.14
Externalizing	−.42**	.06	.02

* $p<.05$.
** $p<.01$.
*** $p<.001$.

Table 20–4.   Partial correlations, controlling for child age, between preschool entry behaviors, free-play behaviors at six weeks, and behavior problems at four months

	School Entry (n = 43)		
	Reticent-wary	Solitary-passive	Solitary-active
Six weeks:			
Reticent	.31*	.22	−.07
Solitary-passive	.07	.35*	.21
Solitary-active	.05	.20	.12
Rough play	−.18	−.17	.36*
Four months:			
Internalizing	.31*	.16	−.02
Externalizing	−.15	−.16	.03

	Four Months (n = 49):	
	Internalizing	Externalizing
Six weeks:		
Reticent	.61***	−.33*
Solitary-passive	.18	−.17
Solitary-active	.15	.01
Rough play	−.22	.28

* $p<.05$
** $p<.01$
*** $p<.001$

entry behaviors, and behaviors six weeks into the school year. In order to accomplish this goal, path coefficients were calculated by performing a series of multiple regression analyses following the predictive model procedures outlined in Pedhazur (1982). This technique allowed for an examination of the direct and indirect paths between conceptually related variables. Child age was controlled for statistically by entering it first into the regression equation. As an additional check for potential sex differences, all regression analyses were first computed with sex entered as a dummy-coded variable. Since the pattern of the results was identical either way, results without controlling for sex are presented.

A trimmed path diagram (with only significant paths indicated) summarizing the regression analyses is displayed in Figure 20–1. Standardized Beta weights are reported, which indicate the unique contribution of the predictor variable to the dependent variable, above and beyond all other variables previously entered into the regression equation. A summary of findings for pathways leading through each of the three forms of nonsocial play (i.e., reticent, solitary-passive, solitary-active) is presented. In addition, short case examples are provided to further illustrate these associations.

Reticent Behavior.   As presented in Figure 20–1, results indicated that temperamental shyness directly predicted reticent behaviors both during the school entry period and at six weeks. Reticent behavior during school entry was significantly predictive of teacher-rated reticent behavior at six weeks (but not solitary-passive behavior at six weeks). In turn, reticent behavior at six weeks was significantly predictive of internalizing problems at four months.

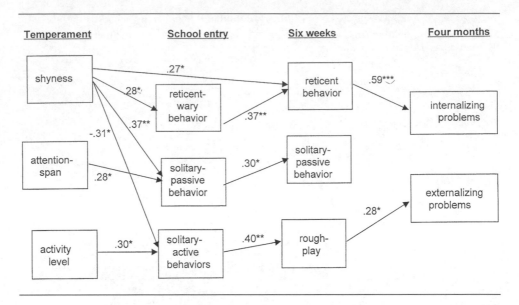

Figure 20–1.   Trimmed path diagram linking child temperament, nonsocial play, and preschool adjustment

Case example: Simon was 4¹/₂ years old at the start of the preschool year. His mother had rated him as quite shy, almost one standard deviation above the sample mean on the shyness subscale of the temperament questionnaire. On the first day of preschool, Simon spent almost 40% of his free-play time engaged in reticent behaviors, either watching others play, or standing motionless and unoccupied. By comparison, his classmates spent, on average, 14% of the time engaged in these types of activities. After six weeks of class, Simon continued to display reticent behaviors more frequently than his peers, as evidenced by his teacher's ratings of his play behaviors. Moreover, after four months of preschool, teacher ratings of Simon's internalizing problems placed him more than 2.5 standard deviations above the class mean. These ratings are cause for clinical concern, and are likely indicative of a young boy who is fraught with social fear and anxiety. If this behavioral pattern were to continue, Simon would be at increased risk for more serious internalizing problems in later childhood and adolescence, including loneliness, low self-esteem, and depression.

Solitary-Passive Behavior.   Solitary-passive entry behavior was predicted by both temperamental shyness and attention span. However, neither of these temperamental characteristics directly predicted teacher-rated solitary-passive play at six weeks. Solitary-Passive behavior during school entry was significantly predictive of solitary-passive behavior at six weeks (but not reticent behavior at six weeks). However, solitary-passive behaviors at six weeks were *not* significantly predictive of any adjustment problems at four months.

Case example: Vanessa had just turned 4 years old when she started the preschool year. Although maternal rating had indicated that Vanessa was above the mean in terms of temperamental shyness, she was also rated quite high in terms of the attention subscale. On the first day of preschool, Vanessa spent almost all of her free-play time (over 80%) in solitary-passive play, drawing pictures and playing in the sand box. This was almost double the average time her classmates spent engaged in these types of activities. Interestingly, despite being rated as somewhat shy by her mother, and spending the vast majority of her time *not* interacting with her peers, Vanessa was not observed to engage in any reticent behaviors during play time on the first day of school. After six weeks of class, Vanessa continued to spend more time than her peers engaged in solitary-passive play. However, after four months of preschool, Vanessa was essentially indistinguishable from her more socially-interactive peers in terms of teacher ratings of behavior problems (both internalizing and externalizing). As such, there does not appear to be any immediate concern in terms of her social adjustment in the preschool settings.

Solitary-Active Behavior.   Solitary-active behavior during school entry was uniquely associated with both temperamental activity level (*positive* relation) and shyness (*negative* relation). Solitary-active behavior during school entry predicted rough play at six weeks. In turn, rough play at six weeks significantly predicted externalizing problems at four months. The relation between solitary-active behavior during school entry and solitary-active behavior at six weeks did not reach significance. In addition, solitary-active behavior at six weeks was nonsignificantly associated with behavior problems at four months.

Case example: Paul was just over 4 years old when he entered preschool. He was not rated as being particularly shy, but was considered to be quite an active young boy, receiving the highest possible maternal rating on the temperamental activity subscale. On the first day of preschool, Paul engaged in a variety of free activities, both social and solitary in nature. Just over 10% of the time during free play, Paul was observed to engage in solitary-active play, which mostly involved lively displays of solitary-make-believe play with action figures. This form of solitary-dramatic activity was rarely observed in the classroom (less than 2% of the time) during free play. After six weeks of class, Paul was rated by his teacher as displaying a high frequency of rough and inappropriate play with peers. This antisocial behavior continued, and, after four months of preschool, teacher ratings of Paul's externalizing problems placed him more than 2 standard deviations above the class mean. Without clinical intervention, it is not difficult to imagine this child having problems with aggression and antisocial behavior in the years to come.

Discussion

The goal of this study was to examine the relation between child temperament characteristics, preschool free-play behaviors, and short-term socioemotional adjustment. Specifically, a series of conceptually derived pathways were examined, exploring outcomes associated with various forms of children's nonsocial free-play behaviors in the preschool. Results indicated that child temperament, in concert with observed school entry behavior and teacher-rated nonsocial free-play behaviors over the course of the first six weeks of preschool, predicted preschool adjustment and various forms of maladjustment four months into the school year. Moreover, the display of different forms of nonsocial play during preschool entry and throughout the school year was associated with decidedly different adjustment outcomes.

Reticent Behavior

Results from the present study provided additional support for the conceptualization of behavioral reticence as a marker variable for social fear, anxiety, and internalizing problems in both novel (e.g., Coplan et al., 1994) and familiar settings (Coplan & Rubin, 1998a). Dispositionally shy or inhibited children demonstrate a low threshold for arousal in the face of novel social stimuli (e.g., Kagan et al., 1988, 1989). When faced with the anxiety-provoking setting of the first day of preschool (a novel setting, with unfamiliar children), these children may become overwhelmed with social fear and anxiety. Thus, although shy children might be desirous of peer interaction, they will most likely engage in the watching of others or else remain unoccupied.

Over the course of the first six weeks of school, some shy children seem to overcome their fears and anxieties as the setting becomes more familiar. These children likely drop out of the pathway toward internalizing problems. However, other shy children apparently continue to display behaviorally wary behaviors, even when the setting becomes more familiar. The child who continues to display reticent behavior six weeks into the school year would seem to be at increased risk for internalizing problems at four months. In this regard, results from the present study indicated that neither temperamental shyness, nor reticent behavior, during school entry directly predicted internalizing problems at four months; rather, these relations were moderated by reticent behavior at six weeks. These findings support Asendorpfs (1994) assertion that the relation between children's behaviors in novel and familiar settings is mediated by peer interactions and the establishment of relationships.

Solitary-Passive Behavior

Consistent with past findings (i.e., Coplan et al., 1994; Rubin, 1982), solitary-passive behavior among preschoolers was not associated with indices of social maladaptation. These findings, along with the observed significant relation between temperamental attention-span and solitary-passive behavior during school entry, were in keeping with the notion that solitary-passive behaviors reflect an object-orientation as opposed to person-orientation (e.g., Jennings, 1975).

It was interesting to note a relation between temperamental shyness and solitary-passive behavior in a novel (during school entry) but not in a familiar setting (after six weeks of school). Along with the results concerning reticent behavior, these findings raise some interesting questions about prototypical temperamentally shy children. Solitary-passive play has been characterized as the preferred nonsocial play behavior of socially-noninteractive children who are also emotionally well-regulated. These children may initially retreat to solitary-passive play as a relatively safe play modality.

There was no evidence from this study to suggest that the frequent display of solitary-passive play behavior in early childhood is associated with social maladjustment in any form. However, it is worth noting that this may not remain the case in later years. As previously mentioned, solitary play, in all its forms, does become increasingly associated with maladaptive outcomes in middle and later childhood (Rubin et al., 1989; Rubin & Mills, 1988).

Solitary-Active Behavior

The results concerning solitary-active behavior provide increasing support for the notion that solitary-active behavior is indicative of social immaturity and impulsivity and may be a risk variable for externalizing problems (Coplan & Rubin, 1998a; Coplan et al., 1994;

Rubin, 1982). This was evidenced by the link between temperamental activity level, solitary-active behavior during school entry, rough play at six weeks, and externalizing problems at four months of preschool.

The pathway linking solitary-active behaviors to externalizing problems might begin with a temperamentally active child entering the preschool setting. The child moves quickly from one activity to another, often engaged in solitary activities, but his or her behaviors are noisy and boisterous. For example, the child engages in solitary-dramatic play with aggressive themes and loud sound effects; or the child repeatedly throws a block against the wall. These activities are salient and viewed as deviant by the child's community of peers. Over the course of the preschool year, the solitary-active child continues to make inappropriate attempts at social interactions. The aggressive themes that may be present in the child's solitary activities become apparent in the child's social interactions. This leads to the display of rough play, which quickly deteriorates into aggressive exchanges and other manifestations of externalizing problems in the preschool. Solitary-active behavior is associated with peer rejection in preschool (Rubin, 1982). Thus, it is not difficult to imagine the solitary-active child responding to this rejection with aggression.

The relation between observed solitary-active behaviors during school entry and teacher-rated solitary-active behaviors at six weeks did not reach significance. This finding merits further discussion. Although there is no theoretical reason to believe that solitary-active play in a novel setting is representative of a different underlying psychological meaning than the same behavior in a familiar setting, it is possible that this change of context may have an impact upon the display of solitary-active play in some yet-undetermined fashion. However, it seems more likely that the lack of observed stability in this construct is a reflection of the extremely low frequency of occurrence of observed solitary-active behaviors during school entry ($M = .02$). Perhaps longer periods of observations will be required to more reliably assess this rarely occurring but salient form of nonsocial play.

Caveats

Some potential shortcomings associated with the current pilot study bear mentioning. To begin with, the sample size in this study was somewhat small for the multiple regression/path analysis that was performed on the data. Small sample size can lead to unreliable Betas that are prone to larger error rates and fluctuations in value. As well, although no sex differences were evident in the current data set, a larger sample would allow for more extensive exploration in this regard. A larger sample would also allow for the use of an "extreme groups" approach. An extreme groups approach would be useful in explaining the logical *discontinuities* that appeared to exist in the present study. For example, not all shy children during school entry became socially withdrawn at six weeks, and not all socially withdrawn children at six weeks displayed internalizing problems at four months. Clearly, the factors that may influence these logical discontinuities (i.e., parenting, peer experiences, emotional regulation) merit future research attention. For example, it might be expected that extremely shy children who were emotionally dysregulated might be expected to be at risk for social fear, anxiety, and other internalizing outcomes in the preschool. In contrast, shy children who were well-regulated might not be at risk for negative outcomes, instead expected to display a high frequency of solitary-passive behaviors.

It should also be noted that the outcomes from this longitudinal study are short term in nature. As such, caution must be observed when speculating as to the longer-term outcomes that may be associated with the display of reticent, solitary-passive, and solitary-active behaviors in the preschool. Moreover, this is not a clinical sample. As such, most of the children who participated in this study did not display behavior problems in the clinical range. However, children who form positive peer relationships during the first few months of school tend to adjust better to the school context than their rejected peers (e.g., Ladd, 1990). As such, an understanding of the temperamental and behavioral constructs that underlie children's initial nonsocial free-play behaviors can provide insight into the process of social and emotional adjustment in the preschool.

Conclusion: Implications for Clinicians

The major goal of this chapter was to elucidate the complex and multidimensional nature of young children's nonsocial play behaviors. In the past, the display of a high frequency of behavioral solitude in the presence of peers was considered a sufficient criterion for characterizing a child as "socially withdrawn," and thus at risk for later socioemotional maladaptation (particularly in terms of internalizing problems). As such, these children might be targeted for ameliorative intervention programs.

It now seems clear that the conceptualization and assessment of nonsocial play must take into account both the context and the content of these behaviors. The meaning of nonsocial play may vary as a function of whether these behaviors are displayed in novel or familiar settings, and with adult or peer play partners. Moreover, the various structural forms of nonsocial play appear to reflect different underlying psychological mechanisms, and are associated with decidedly different outcomes. In short, children appear to play alone for many different reasons. A greater understanding of these differences, and how they are behaviorally manifested, has the potential to greatly improve clinical interventions.

For example, a child who engages in predominantly reticent behaviors in the preschool classroom might be a target for interventions designed to assist in the reduction of social anxiety, improvement of emotional regulation skills, and the building of perceived-competence for interaction with peers. On the other hand, a child who engages in a high frequency of solitary-active behaviors might benefit from an intervention more specifically designed to teach social skills and impulse control. Finally, there is some question as to whether a child who spends most of his or her time in solitary-passive play even warrants a clinical intervention at this time.

To conclude, it seems clear that nonsocial play is a complex and multifaceted construct. Different subtypes of solitary-behaviors evidence very different underlying psychological mechanisms. Moreover, these meanings may vary in different social contexts. The assessment of nonsocial play behaviors can provide a window into children's social and emotional well-being. A continued exploration of this multidimensional construct serves to inform both researchers and clinicians with regard to an understanding of important aspects of young children's development.

REFERENCES

Achenbach, T.M., McConaughy, S. H., & Howell, C. T. (1987). Child/adolescent behavioral and emotional problems: Implications of cross-informant correlations for situational specificity. *Psychological-Bulletin, 101,* 213–232.

Asendorpf, J. (1990). Development of inhibition during childhood: Evidence for situation specificity and a two-factor model. *Developmental Psychology, 26,* 721–730.

Asendorpf, J. (1991). Development of inhibited children's coping with unfamiliarity. *Child Development, 62,* 1460–1474.

Asendorpf, J. (1994). The malleability of behavior inhibition: A study of individual developmental functions. *Developmental Psychology, 30,* 912–919.

Baldwin, J. N., & Stecher, L. (1925). *The psychology of the pre-school child.* New York: Appleton.

Behar, L., & Springfield, S. (1974). A behavior rating scale for the preschool child. *Developmental Psychology, 10,* 601–610.

Bergen, D. (1988). Methods of studying play. In D. Bergen (Ed.), *Play as a medium for learning and development.* Portsmouth, NH: Heinemann.

Blurtin-Jones, N. (1972). Categories of child-child interaction. In N. Blurton-Jones (Ed.), *Ethnological studies of child behavior* (pp. 97–127). Cambridge, England: Cambridge University Press.

Bott, H. (1928). Observation of play activities of three-year-old children. *Genetic Psychology Monographs, 4(1),* 44–88.

Brownell, C. (1990). Peer social skills in toddlers: Competencies and constraints illustrated by same-age and mixed-age interaction. *Child Development, 61,* 838–848.

Buhler, C. (1928). *Kindheit und jugend.* Leipzig: Hirzel Verlag.

Bukowski, W. M. (1990). Age differences in children's memory of information about aggressive, socially withdrawn, and prosociable boys and girls. *Child Development, 61,* 1326–1334.

Buss, A. H. (1986). A theory of shyness. In W. H. Jones, J. M. Cheek, & S. R. Briggs (Eds.), *Shyness: Perspectives on research and treatment* (pp. 39–46). New York: Plenum.

Buss, A. H., & Plomin, R. (1984). *Temperament: Early developing personality traits.* Hillsdale, NJ: Erlbaum.

Campbell, S. B., Ewing, L. J., Breaux, A. M., & Szumowski, A. M. (1986). Parent-referred problem three-year-olds: Follow-up at school entry. *Journal of Child Psychology & Psychiatry, 27,* 473–488.

Conners, C. K. (1969). A teacher rating scale for use in drug studies with children. *American Journal of Psychiatry, 126,* 884–888.

Conners, C. K. (1973). Rating scales for use in drug studies with children. *Psychopharmacology Bulletin* (Special Issue—Pharmacotherapy with Children), 24–84.

Connolly, J., & Doyle, A. (1981). Assessment of social competence in preschoolers: Teachers versus peers. *Developmental Psychology, 17,* 454–462.

Cooley, C. H. (1902). *Human nature and the social order.* New York: Scribner's Sons.

Coplan, R. J., & Rubin, K. H. (1998a). Exploring and assessing non-social play in the preschool: The development and validation of the Preschool Play Behavior Scale. *Social Development, 7,* 72–91.

Coplan, R. J., & Rubin, K. H. (1998b). Social play. In D. P. Fromberg & D. Bergen (Eds.), *Play from birth to twelve: Contexts, perspectives, and meanings* (pp. 368–377). New York: Garland.

Coplan, R. J., Rubin, K. H., Fox, N. A., Calkins, S. D., & Stewart, S. L. (1994). Being alone, playing alone, and acting alone: Distinguishing among reticence, and passive- and active-solitude in young children. *Child Development, 65,* 129–138.

Cowen, E. L., Pederson, A., Bibigian, H., Izzo, L. D., & Trost, M. A. (1973). Long-term follow-up of early detected vulnerable children. *Journal of Consulting and Clinical Psychology, 41,* 438–446.

Doyle, A. (1982). Friends, acquaintances, and strangers: The influence of familiarity and ethnolinguistic background on social interaction. In K. H. Rubin & H. S. Ross (Eds.), *Peer relations and social skills in childhood* (pp. 229–252). New York: Springer-Verlag.

Eiferman, R. R. (1971). Social play in childhood. In R. E. Herron & B. Sutton-Smith (Eds.), *Child's play* (pp. 270–297). New York: Wiley.

Ensminger, M. C., Kellam, S. G., & Rubin, B. R. (1983). School and family origins of delinquency: Comparisons by sex. In K. T. Van Dusen & S. A. Mednick (Eds.), *Prospective studies of crime and delinquency* (pp. 73–97). Hingham, MA: Klumer-Nijhoff.

Enslein, J., & Fein, G. G. (1981). Temporal and cross-situational stability of children's social and play behavior. *Developmental Psychology, 17,* 760–761.

Factor, D. C., & Frankie, G. H. (1980). Free-play behaviors in socially maladjusted and normal preschool children: A naturalistic study. *Canadian Journal of Behavioural Science, 12,* 272–277.

Fox, N. A. (1989). Psychophysical correlates of emotional reactivity during the first year of life. *Developmental Psychology, 25,* 364–372.

Fox, N. A., Rubin, K. H., Calkins, S. D., Marshall, T. R., Coplan, R. J., Porges, S. W., & Long, J. (1995). Frontal activation asymmetry and social competence at four years of age: Left frontal hyper and hypo activation as correlates of social behavior in preschool children. *Child Development, 66,* 1770–1784.

Frost, J. L., & Sunderlin, S. (1985). *When children play.* Wheaton, MD: Association for Childhood Education International.

Garrisson, W., & Earls, F. (1985). Change and continuity in behavior problems from the preschool period through school entry: An analysis of mothers' reports. In J. E. Stevenson (Ed), *Recent research in developmental psychopathology* (pp. 51–65). New York: Pergamon Press.

Greenwood, C. R., Walker, H. M., & Hopps, H. (1977). Issues in social interaction/withdrawal assessment. *Exceptional Children, 443,* 490–499.

Guralnick, M. J., & Groom, J. M. (1987). The peer relations of mildly delayed and nonhandicapped preschool children in preschool groups. *Child Development, 58,* 1556–1572.

Harrist, A. W., Zaia, A. F., Bates, J. E., Dodge, K. A., & Petit, G. S. (1997). Subtypes of social withdrawal in early childhood: Sociometric status and social-cognitive differences across four years. *Child Development, 68,* 278–294.

Hart, C. H., DeWolf, D. M., Wozniak, P., & Burts, D. C. (1992). Maternal and paternal disciplinary styles: Relations with preschoolers' playground behavioral orientations and peer status. *Child Development, 63,* 879–892.

Hart, C. H., Yang, C., Nelson, L., Jin, S., Olsen, J., Nelson, D., Wu, P., Robinson, C., & Porter, C. (1998, July). *Peer acceptance in early childhood and subtypes of socially withdrawn behavior in China, Russia, and the United States.* Paper presented at the Biennial Meetings of the International Society for the Study of Behavioral Development, Switzerland.

Higgenbotham, J., & Baker, B. M. (1981). Social participation and cognitive play differences in hearing impaired and normally hearing preschoolers. *Volta Review, 82,* 135–149.

Hinde, R. A. (1987). *Individuals, relationships, and culture.* Cambridge England: Cambridge University Press.

Hinde, R. A., Tamplin, A., & Barrett, J. (1993). Social isolation in 4-year-olds. *British Journal of Developmental Psychology, 11,* 211–236.

Hogan, L. E. (1898). *A study of a child.* New York: Harper.

Howes, C. (1988). Peer interaction in young children. *Monographs for the Society for Research in Child Development, 53* (217).

Howes, C. (1992). *The collaborative construction of pretend.* New York: State University of New York Press.

Hymel, S., & Rubin, K. H. (1985). Children with peer relationship and social skills problems: Conceptual, methodological, and developmental issues. In G. J. Whitehurst (Ed.), *Annals of child development* (Vol 2, pp. 254–297). Greenwich, Connecticut: JAI Press.

Hymel, S., Rubin, K. H., Rowden, L., & LeMare, L. (1990). A longitudinal study of sociometric status in middle and late childhood. *Child Development, 61,* 2004–2121.

Jennings, K. D. (1975). People versus object orientation, social behavior, and intellectual abilities in children. *Developmental Psychology, 11,* 511–519.

Jewsuwan, R., Luster, T., & Kostelnik, M. (1993). The relations between parents' perceptions of temperament and children's adjustment to preschool. *Early Childhood Research Quarterly, 8,* 33–51.

Kagan, J. (1989). Temperamental contributions to social behavior. *American Psychologist, 44*(4), 668–674.

Kagan, J. (1997). Temperament and the reactions to the unfamiliarity. *Child Development, 68,* 139–143.

Kagan J., Reznick, J. S., & Gibbons, J. (1989). Inhibited and uninhibited types of children. *Child Development, 60,* 838–845.

Kagan J., Reznick, J. S., & Snidman, N. (1988). Biological basis of childhood shyness. *Science, 240,* 167–171.

Kohlberg, L., LaCrosse, J., & Ricks, D. (1972). The predictability of adult mental health from childhood behavior. In B. B. Wolman (Ed), *Manual of child psychopathology* (pp. 1217–1284). New York: McGraw-Hill.

Kohn, M., & Rosman, B. L. (1972). A social competence scale and symptom checklist for the preschool child: Factor dimensions, their cross-instrument generality, and longitudinal persistence. *Developmental Psychology, 6,* 430–444.

Kupersmidt, J. B., Coie, J. D., & Dodge, K. A. (1990). The role of poor peer relationships in the development of disorder. In S. R. Asher & J. D. Coie (Eds.), *Peer rejection in childhood* (pp. 274–308). New York: Cambridge University Press.

Kyrios, M., & Prior, M. (1990). Temperament, stress and family factors in behavioral adjustment of 3–5-year-old children. *International Journal of Behavioral Development, 13,* 67–93.

Ladd, G. W. (1990). Having friends, keeping friends, making friends, and being liked by peers in the classroom: Predictors of children's early school adjustment? *Child Development, 61,* 312–331.

Ladd, G. W., & Mars, K. T. (1986). Reliability and validity of preschoolers' perceptions of peer behavior. *Journal of Clinical Child Psychology, 15,* 16–25.

Ladd, G. W., & Price, J. M. (1993). Play styles of peer-accepted and peer-rejected children on the playground. In C. H. Hart (Ed.), *Children on playgrounds: Research perspectives and applications* (pp. 130–161). New York: State University of New York Press.

Ladd, G. W., & Profilet, S. M. (1996). The Child Behavior Scale: A teacher-report measure of young children's aggressive, withdrawn, and prosocial behaviors. *Developmental Psychology, 32,* 1008–1024.

LaFreniere, Dumas, J. E., Capuano, F., & Dubeau, D. (1992). Development and validation of the preschool socioaffective profile. *Psychological Assessment, 4,* 442–450.

Lehman, H. C. (1926). The play activities of persons of different ages, and growth stages in play behavior. *Pedagogical Seminary* (Vol. 33, pp. 250–272).

Lehman, H. C., & Anderson, T. H. (1928). Social participation vs. solitariness in play. *Pedagogical Seminary* (Vol. 34, pp. 279–289).

Lerner, R. M., Palermo, M., Spiro, A., & Nesselrode, J. R. (1982). Assessing the dimensions of temperamental individuality across the life span: The Dimensions of Temperament Survey (DOTS). *Child Development, 53,* 149–159.

Levy-Shiff, R., & Hoffman, M. A. (1989). Social behavior as a predictor of adjustment among three-year-olds. *Journal of Clinical Child Psychology, 18,* 65–71.

Marturano, E. M. (1980). Behavior characteristics of children during the first year of kindergarten attendance. *Child Psychiatry and Human Development, 10,* 232–245.

Masten, A. S., Morison, P., & Pellegrini, D. S. (1985). A Revised Class Play method of peer assessment. *Developmental Psychology, 3,* 523–533.

McGuire, J., & Richman, M. (1986). The prevalence of behaviour problems in three types of preschool. *Journal of Child Psychology & Psychiatry, 27,* 455–472.

Mead, G. H. (1934). *Mind, self, and society.* Chicago: University of Chicago Press.

Melson, G. F., & Kim, J. (1990). Separations and reunions of preschoolers and their parents at nursery school. *Early Childhood Research Quarterly, 5,* 117–134.

Mobley, C. E., & Pullis M. E. (1991). Temperament and behavioral adjustment in preschool children. *Early Childhood Research Quarterly, 6,* 577–586.

Moller, L. C., & Rubin, K. H. (1988). A psychometric assessment of a two-factor solution for the Preschool Behavior Questionnaire in mid-childhood. *Journal of Applied Developmental Psychology, 9,* 167–180.

Mueller, E. C., & Brenner, J. (1977). The origin of social skills and interactions among playgroup toddlers. *Child Development, 48,* 854–861.

Ollendick, T. H., Oswald, D. P., & Francis, G. (1989). The validity of teacher nominations in identifying aggressive, withdrawn, and popular children. *Journal of Clinical Child Psychology, 18,* 221–229.

Paquette, D., & LaFreniere, P. J. (1994). Are anxious-withdrawn children inhibited in a new social context? *Canadian Journal of Behavioral Science, 26,* 534–550.

Parten, M. B. (1932). Social participation among preschool children. *Journal of Abnormal Psychology, 27,* 243–269.

Pedhazur, E.J. (1982). *Multiple regression in behavioral research.* New York: Holt.

Pettit, G. S., & Bates, J. E. (1990). Describing family interaction patterns and children's behavior problems from infancy to 4 years. *Development Psychology, 25,* 413–420.

Piaget, J. (1926). *The language and thought of the child.* London: Routledge & Kegan Paul.

Piaget, J. (1932). *The moral judgment of the child.* Glencoe: Free Press.

Piaget, J. (1962). *Play dreams and imitation in childhood.* New York: Norton.

Plomin, R., & Daniels, D. (1986). Genetics and shyness. In W. H. Jones, J. M. Cheek, & S. R. Briggs (Eds.), *Shyness: Perspectives on research and treatment* (pp. 63–80). New York: Plenum.

Quay, H. C. (1983). A dimensional approach to behavior disorder: The Revised Behavior Problem Checklist. *School Psychology Review, 12,* 244–249.

Quay, H. C., & Peterson, D. R. (1987). *Manual for the Revised Behavior Problem Checklist.* Coral Gables, FL: Author.

Reznick, J. S., Gibbons, J., Johnson, M., & McDonough, P. (1989). Behavioral inhibition in a normative sample. In J. S. Reznick (Ed.), *Perspective on behavioral inhibition* (pp. 25–49). Chicago: University of Chicago Press.

Reznick, J. S., Kagan, J., Snidman, N., Gersten, M., Baak, K., & Rosenberg, A. (1986). Inhibited and uninhibited children: A follow-up study. *Child Development, 57,* 660–680.

Roopnarine, J. L., Church, C. C., & Levy, G. D. (1990). Day care children's play behaviors: Relationship to their mothers' and fathers' assessments of their parenting behaviors, marital stress, and marital companionship. *Early Childhood Research Quarterly, 5,* 335–346.

Roper, R., & Hinde, R. A. (1978). Social behavior in a play group: Consistency and complexity. *Child Development, 49,* 570–579.

Rothbart, M. K., & Bates, J. E. (1998). Temperament. In W. Damon (Ed.) and N. Eisenberg (Vol. Ed.), *Handbook of child psychology (Vol. 3, 5th ed.): Social, emotional, and personality development* (pp. 105–177). New York: Wiley.

Rowe, D. C., & Plomin, R. (1977). Temperament in early childhood. *Journal of Personality Assessment, 41,* 150–156.

Rubin, K. H. (1982). Non-social play in preschoolers: Necessary evil? *Child Development, 53,* 651–657.

Rubin, K. H. (1989). The Play Observation Scale (POS). University of Waterloo, Waterloo, Ontario, Canada.

Rubin, K. H. (1993). The Waterloo Longitudinal Project: Correlates and consequences of social withdrawal from childhood to adolescence. In K. Rubin & J. Asendorpf (Eds.), *Social withdrawal, inhibition, and shyness in childhood* (pp. 291–314). Hillsdale, NJ: Erlbaum.

Rubin, K. H., & Asendorpf, J. (1993). *Social withdrawal, inhibition, and shyness in childhood.* Hillsdale, NJ: Erlbaum.

Rubin, K. H., & Both, L. (1989). Iris pigmentation and sociability in childhood: A re-examination. *Development Psychology, 22,* 717–726.

Rubin, K. H., Bukowski, W., & Parker, J. (1998). Peer interactions, relationships, and groups. In W. Damon (Ed.) and N. Eisenberg (Vol. Ed.), *Handbook of child psychology (Vol. 3, 5th ed.): Social, Emotional, and Personality Development* (pp. 619–700). New York: Wiley.

Rubin, K. H., Chen, X, McDougall, P., Bowker, A., & McKinnon, J. (1995). The Waterloo Longitudinal Project: Predicting internalizing and externalizing problems in adolescence. *Development and Psychopathology, 7,* 751–764.

Rubin, K. H., Coplan, R. J., Fox, N. A., & Calkins, S. D. (1995). Emotionality, emotion regulation, and preschoolers' social adptation. *Development and Psychopathology, 7,* 49–62.

Rubin, K. H., Coplan, R. J., Nelson, L., Cheah, C., & Lagace-Seguin, D. (in press). Peer relationships in childhood. To appear in M. Bornstein & M. Lamb (Eds.), *Developmental psychology: An advanced textbook* (4th ed.) Hillsdale, NJ: Erlbaum.

Rubin, K. H., Fein, G., & Vandenberg, B. (1983). Play. In E. M. Hetherington (Ed.), *Handbook of child psychology: Vol 4. Socialization, personality, and social development* (pp. 693–774). New York: Wiley.

Rubin, K. H., Hymel, S., & Mills, R. S. L. (1989). Sociability and social withdrawal in childhood: Stability and outcomes. *Journal of Personality, 57,* 238–255.

Rubin, K. H., LeMare L. J., & Lollis, S. (1990). Social withdrawal in childhood: Developmental pathways to rejection. In S. R. Asher & J. D. Coie (Eds.), *Peer Rejection in Childhood* (pp. 217–249). New York: Cambridge University Press.

Rubin, K. H., Maioni, T. L., & Hornung, M. (1976). Free play behaviors in middle and lower class preschoolers: Parten and Piaget revisited. *Child Development, 47,* 414–419.

Rubin, K. H., & Mills, R. S. L. (1988). The many faces of social isolation in childhood. *Journal of Consulting and Clinical Psychology, 6,* 916–924.

Rubin, K. H., Stewart, S., & Coplan, R. J. (1995). Social withdrawal in Childhood: Conceptual and empirical perspectives. In T. H. Ollendick & R. Prinz (Eds.), *Advances in clinical child psychology* (Vol. 17, pp. 157–196). New York: Plenum.

Rubin, K. H., Watson, K. S., & Jambor, T. W. (1978). Free-play behaviors in preschool and kindergarten children. *Child Development, 49,* 534–536.

Schmidt, L. A., Fox, N. A., Rubin, K. H., Sternberg, E. M., Gold, P. W., Smith, C. C., & Schulkin, J. (in press). Behavioral and neuroendocrine responses in shy children. *Developmental Psychobiology.* 367–376.

Shinn, M. W. (1893). *Note of the development of a child.* Berkeley, CA: University of California Studies.

Skarpness, L. R., & Carson, D. K. (1987). Correlates of kindergarten adjustment: Temperament and communicative competence. *Early Childhood Research Quarterly, 2,*

Smilansky, S. (1968). *The effects of sociodramatic play on disadvantaged preschool children.* New York: Wiley.

Snyder, T., & Wirt, J. (1998). *The condition of education.* National Center for Education Statistics, NCES 98013.

Spenser, H. (1873). *Principles of psychology* (Vol. 2, 2nd ed). New York: Appleton.

Sroufe, L. A. (1983). Infant-caregiver attachment and patterns of adaptation in preschool: The roots of maladaptation and competence. In M. Perlmutter (Ed.), *Minnesota Symposium in Child Psychology, 16,* (pp. 41–83). Hillsdale, NJ: Erlbaum.

Stern, L. W. (1924). *The psychology of early childhood.* New York: Henry Holt.

Suess, G. J., Grossman, K. E., & Sroufe, L. A. (1992). Effects of infant attachment to mother and father on quality of adaptation to preschool: From dyadic to individual organization of self. *International Journal of Behavioral Development, 15*(1), 43–65.

Sullivan, H. S. (1953). *The interpersonal theory of psychiatry.* New York: Norton.

Thomas, A., & Chess, S. (1977). *Temperament and development.* New York: Brunner/Mazel.

Thomas, A., Chess, S., & Birch, H. G. (1968). *Temperament and behavior disorders in children.* New York: New York University Press.

Tracy, F. (1910). *The psychology of childhood.* Boston: D.C. Heath.

Tremblay, R. E., Desmarais-Gervais, L., Gagnon, C., & Charlebois, P. (1987). The Preschool Behaviour Questionnaire: Stability of its factor structure between cultures, sexes, ages, and socioeconomic classes. *International Journal of Behavioral Development, 10.* 467–484.

Vandenberg, B. (1981). Environmental and cognitive factors in social play. *Journal of Experimental Psychology, 31,* 169–175.

Verry, E. E. (1923). A study of mental and social attitudes in the free play of preschool children. Thesis for M.A. degree, State University of Iowa.

Walker, H. M., Greenwood, C. R., Hops, H., & Todd, N. M. (1979). Differential effects of reinforcing topographic components of social interaction. *Behavior Modification, 3,* 291–321.

Wall, S. M., & Pickert, S. M. (1982). Language and play of preschool children learning English as a second language and native English speakers. *Psychological Reports, 50,* 119–124.

Younger, A. J., & Boyko, K. A. (1987). Aggression and withdrawal as social schemas underlying children's peer perceptions. *Child Development, 58,* 1094–1100.

Younger, A. J., & Daniels, T. M. (1992). Children's reasons for nominating their peers as passive withdrawn: Passive withdrawal versus active isolation? *Developmental Psychology, 28,* 955–960.

Younger, A. J., Gentile, C., & Burgess, K. (1993). Children's perceptions of social withdrawal: Changes across age. In K. Rubin & J. Asendorpf (Eds.), *Social withdrawal, inhibition, and shyness in childhood* (pp. 215–236). Hillsdale, NJ: Erlbaum.

Younger, A. J., & Piccinin, A. M. (1989). Children's recall of aggressive and withdrawn behaviors: Recognition memory and likeability judgements. *Child Development, 60,* 580–590.

Younger, A. J., Schwartzman. A. E., & Ledingham, J. E. (1985). Age-related changes in children's perceptions of aggression and withdrawal in their peers. *Developmental Psychology, 21,* 70–75.

Zajdeman, H. S., & Minnes, P. M. (1991). Predictors of children's adjustment to daycare. *Early Child Development and Care, 74,* 11–28.

Appendix

The Preschool Play Behavior Scale

The following scale examines various behaviors that children may engage in during *indoor free play.* Please rate the child on each item and *compare him or her to other children of the same age in the class.* Although it is true that children's behaviors may be quite variable, please try to make a general evaluation of the child's "everyday" behaviors.

1. Talks to other children during play.

1	2	3	4	5
never	hardly ever	sometimes	often	very often

2. Plays by himself/herself, examining an object or toy.

1	2	3	4	5
never	hardly ever	sometimes	often	very often

3. Plays "rough-and-tumble" with other children.

1	2	3	4	5
never	hardly ever	sometimes	often	very often

4. Takes on the role of onlooker or spectator.

1	2	3	4	5
never	hardly ever	sometimes	often	very often

5. Plays "make-believe" with other children.

1	2	3	4	5
never	hardly ever	sometimes	often	very often

6. Engages in group play.

1	2	3	4	5
never	hardly ever	sometimes	often	very often

7. Engages in pretend play by himself/herself.

1	2	3	4	5
never	hardly ever	sometimes	often	very often

8. Plays alone, building things with blocks and/or other toys.

1	2	3	4	5
never	hardly ever	sometimes	often	very often

9. Wanders around aimlessly.

1	2	3	4	5
never	hardly ever	sometimes	often	very often

10. Plays in groups *with* (not just beside) other children.

1	2	3	4	5
never	hardly ever	sometimes	often	very often

11. Plays "make-believe," but not with other children.

1	2	3	4	5
never	hardly ever	sometimes	often	very often

12. Watches or listens to other children without trying to join in.

1	2	3	4	5
never	hardly ever	sometimes	often	very often

13. Engages in playful/mock fighting with other children.

1	2	3	4	5
never	hardly ever	sometimes	often	very often

14. Plays by himself/herself, drawing, painting pictures, or doing puzzles.

1	2	3	4	5
never	hardly ever	sometimes	often	very often

15. Engages in active conversations with other children during play.

1	2	3	4	5
never	hardly ever	sometimes	often	very often

16. Engages in pretend play with other children.

1	2	3	4	5
never	hardly ever	sometimes	often	very often

17. Plays alone, exploring toys or objects, trying to figure out how they work.

1	2	3	4	5
never	hardly ever	sometimes	often	very often

18. Remains alone and unoccupied, perhaps staring off into space.

1	2	3	4	5
never	hardly ever	sometimes	often	very often

Chapter 21

PENN INTERACTIVE PEER PLAY SCALE: A PARENT AND TEACHER RATING SYSTEM FOR YOUNG CHILDREN

John W. Fantuzzo and Virginia R. Hampton

Ensuring that young children are ready to succeed in school is a national priority. Numerous problems with the current state of the country's educational system indicate the urgency of meeting this objective. Concerns about the failure of the nation's educational system have led to the establishment of the National Education Goals to improve opportunities for learning. The first of these goals focuses on the importance of early educational experience, and states that by the year 2000 all children will enter school ready to learn (U.S. Department of Education, 1992a). This "readiness" goal and its accompanying objectives highlight the need for quality early childhood programs and emphasize the importance of parent involvement in helping children achieve educational success. Attaining this goal is particularly important for children living in disadvantaged urban areas. Poverty, unemployment, violence, crime, and other stressors threaten the development and academic achievement of these children. Young children and ethnic minority children are most likely to experience the negative consequences associated with urban areas. Recent statistics indicate that 24% of all children under the age of 6 are living in poverty, and ethnic minorities are disproportionately represented among these children (Children's Defense Fund, 1997). Moreover, nearly half of all poor children live in central city areas, and ethnic minority children again comprise a disproportionate number of these children (U.S. General Accounting Office, 1993).

In response to the risks faced by vulnerable young children, community-based early intervention programs are a promising means of meeting the objectives of the first National Education Goal. These programs promote multiple aspects of children's development during early childhood to enhance the social and academic competence of children living in poverty. By addressing the social, physical, and educational needs of young children, early intervention programs strive to help low-income children enter school prepared for success. The most notable example of a community-based program is Head Start, the largest federally funded early childhood program. Head Start has constituted the nation's leading response to childhood poverty by providing comprehensive services for low-income children and families. These services include education, mental health, nutrition, social services, health screenings and referral, and parent involvement (Zigler & Styfco, 1994). Improvements in children's socioemotional functioning, school adjustment, academic achievement, and health attest to the success of Head Start in promoting children's development (Zigler, Styfco, & Gilman, 1993).

To maximize the effectiveness of early childhood programs such as Head Start, three objectives of school readiness must inform the curriculum. These objectives include an emphasis on the nurturance of fundamental emergent competencies, the cultivation of parent involvement in children's education, and an understanding of children's cultural contexts. As programs strive to meet school readiness objectives, they should provide opportunities for play, which can support the implementation of these objectives. During early childhood, play is the primary context for the development of social competence. Professional organizations such as the National Association for the Education of Young Children (NAEYC; Bredekamp & Copple, 1997) and the Association for Childhood Education International (ACEI; Isenberg & Quisenberry, 1988) emphasize the importance of play for children's development and advocate including play as a core component of the curriculum (Bredekamp & Copple, 1997; Van Hoorn, Nourot, Scales, & Alward, 1993). Play also provides opportunities for parents and teachers to establish partnerships to enhance children's development. Not only can parents foster children's peer play experiences, but they also can provide valuable information about their children's competencies and needs. Parents and teachers observe children in different contexts and have unique perspectives about children's peer interactions that can contribute to a more complete understanding of children's relationships with peers. By including parent reports, teachers obtain information about children's behavior at home and in the community that is otherwise unavailable to them (Ruffalo & Elliott, 1997; Diamond & Squires, 1993). The information gained from parents can also provide an understanding of play in different cultural contexts, to help programs meet the needs of diverse groups of children.

To assist early childhood programs with enhancing children's play, tools are needed that can facilitate communication about children's play interactions. Behavior rating scales are useful and practical means of sharing information across multiple informants (Martin, 1986). To promote parent and teacher communication, assessment systems must have psychometrically sound parent and teacher versions. These versions should be empirically examined to ensure that informants are reporting on the same constructs (Manz, Fantuzzo, & McDermott, in press). Unfortunately, the current state of assessment technology has limitations in its ability to obtain information about children's peer play interactions in different contexts. An assessment system that includes these components would advance early childhood assessment and practice.

This chapter presents the Penn Interactive Peer Play Scale (PIPPS), an assessment system that responds to the evaluation needs in early childhood. First, the theoretical and empirical literature that provide the basis for the development of this assessment system are reviewed. Next, the capacities needed by such an assessment system are examined. Subsequently, a discussion of the PIPPS is provided, and includes information about the development and validation of this instrument. Finally, ways that the PIPPS assessment system can be used are explored.

THEORY AND RESEARCH INFORMING PLAY ASSESSMENT

Based on the objective to enhance children's social competence, the conceptual framework and supporting studies that attest to the value of play for establishing effective peer relationships will first be discussed. Subsequently, the literature that reflects the parent involvement objective will be reviewed by describing the importance of maintaining connections in children's experiences. Parents have a primary role in establishing these connections. In addition, this literature highlights the ways that connections can help children enter school "ready to learn," in keeping with the "readiness" goal. Finally, in response to the call for understanding children's culture, the ways that cultural contexts can affect play will be explored.

The Value of Play for Peer Relations

During early childhood, an essential emergent competency is establishing effective peer relationships. The degree to which children attain this competency affects children throughout their lives, since rejection by peers can lead to numerous academic and behavioral problems such as poor school performance, retention, truancy, criminal behavior, and emotional maladjustment (Hartup & Moore, 1990; Kupersmidt, Coie, & Dodge, 1990; Ladd & Coleman, 1993; Parker & Asher, 1987). Not only does peer rejection affect children's current functioning, but the effects can occur throughout childhood and adulthood (Kupersmidt & Coie, 1990; Ladd, 1990; Parker & Asher, 1987). To prevent these negative consequences, opportunities to foster positive interactions with peers are needed during early childhood.

Play is the primary context for fostering positive interactions with peers for young children. Through play, children develop the social, emotional, cognitive, and language skills that contribute to the ability to establish effective relationships with peers (Bredekamp & Copple, 1997). Developmental theories emphasize the importance of play for children's development. Two major frameworks for understanding the contribution of play to development are the theories of Piaget and Vygotsky. According to Piaget (1962), children gain knowledge about the world through play, and incorporate that information into extant cognitive structures (Nicolopoulou, 1993; Saracho & Spodek, 1998). Piaget proposes a progression from "practice play," consisting of individual sensorimotor activities, to "symbolic play," in which children acquire the use of symbols and experience make-believe, and finally, to "play with rules," to regulate social interactions (Nicolopoulou, 1993). As children engage in these activities, they strengthen their existing cognitive schemes (Smolucha & Smolucha, 1998). Piaget also indicates that peer interactions during play provide children with opportunities to develop cognitive skills. Children develop perspective-taking abilities, for example, when they argue or express different viewpoints. Thus, for Piaget, cognitive development occurs not through play itself, but through the enhancement of specific skills during peer interactions in play (Creasey, Jarvis, & Berk, 1998).

Although the Piagetian perspective has been influential for several decades, recent criticisms indicate that this framework does not provide adequate attention to social and cultural issues in development (Corsaro & Schwarz, 1991; Nicolopoulou, 1993). Vygotsky's theory of development (1978) has received increasing support because of its emphasis on social and cultural aspects of play. Vygotsky proposes that children's competencies are affected by the cultural practices and values conveyed through social interactions and communication (Nicolopoulou, 1993; Rogoff, 1993). According to Vygotsky (1978), play creates a "zone of proximal development" which comprises the abilities children have to accomplish tasks on their own, as well as their capabilities for achievement when challenged by peers. Through interactions with more knowledgeable adults and peers, children learn cultural norms, acquire higher mental functions such as logical thinking, and develop symbolic play. Furthermore, Vygotsky indicates that play consists of imaginary situations and rules for behavior. When engaging in pretend play, children must work together to develop rules to govern the activity (Goncu, 1993). In Vygotsky's theory, pretend play provides children with opportunities to learn the implicit rules of social behavior. Vygotsky views play as the "source of development" during early childhood (Vygotsky, 1967) because it enables children to internalize social rules, acquire cognitive processes, and advance their competencies through the zone of proximal development.

Research supports the role of play in facilitating children's development. The results of a meta-analysis of 46 studies of play attests to the value of play. Specifically, the study concluded that sociodramatic play improves children's cognitive abilities, language skills, and socioemotional functioning (Fisher, 1992). Through pretend play, complex cognitive skills such as literacy emerge, as children acquire reading, writing, storytelling, and memory abilities (Berk, 1994; Pellegrini & Galda, 1991). Young children also develop problem-solving skills as they play with peers, and increase their perspective-taking when engaging in role-plays (Frost, 1992; Jacobs, 1994). Linguistic skills also develop during peer interactions. As children negotiate, argue, and discuss plans during play, they learn language from their peers, and practice words and phrases they have heard elsewhere (Ervin-Tripp, 1991). In addition, when engaging in sociodramatic play, children learn how to cooperate, take turns, compromise, and resolve conflicts (Johnson, Christie, & Yawkey, 1987). Furthermore, play provides children with the opportunity to express their ideas and feelings, thereby helping children learn how to handle their emotions and reducing anxiety and stress (Bredekamp & Copple, 1997; Stone, 1995).

The emergence of competencies in cognitive, linguistic, and socioemotional domains also contributes to successful peer interactions. To establish effective play with peers, children need to obtain such skills as recruiting playmates, entering the peer group, gauging other children's responses, and negotiating play activities (Creasey et al., 1998). These complex skills arise from the attainment of specific cognitive, language, and emotional abilities. With the development of cognitive skills such as problem-solving and reasoning, children are better able to resolve disputes and to cooperate during play. In addition, advances in linguistic skills enable children to improve their communication with peers. Furthermore, perspective-taking ability is helpful for engaging in collaborative activity, solving interpersonal problems, and developing empathy (Creasey et al., 1998; Frost, 1992; Goncu, 1993). Positive peer relationships are also enhanced by children's ability to regulate their emotions, a skill that helps children maintain cooperation when experiencing interpersonal conflicts.

The Importance of Continuity

The knowledge gained from research examining the importance of play for children's development must inform the early childhood curriculum. In keeping with the first National Education Goal, as efforts are made to help children obtain opportunities for educational success, the early childhood curriculum must be guided by appropriate strategies for promoting children's play. One such approach is to recognize the necessity of maintaining connections in children's experiences, both between home and school and between school settings. As children make transitions in their lives, discontinuity can have negative consequences on their adjustment. The early years of school have long-term effects on children's cognitive and affective development, and therefore, the transition to full-time schooling is considered a "critical period" for children's future functioning (Entwisle and Alexander, 1993). Evidence for the importance of this transition comes from studies indicating that children who experience social and academic problems by first or second grade are likely to have later difficulties with school and social functioning (Reynolds, Weissberg, & Kasprow, 1992; Parker & Asher, 1987).

Many low-income children, who are less likely to have had preschool experience, have difficulty adjusting to elementary school (U.S. Department of Education, 1992b). Ethnic minority children are particularly vulnerable to adjustment difficulties because they are more likely to experience discontinuities between the cultures of the home and school (Entwisle & Alexander, 1993; Harrison, Wilson, Pine, Chan, & Buriel, 1990). However, sociocultural congruence between the home and school helps children to attain more success at school (Delgato-Gaitan, 1994). A strategy for creating continuity between school settings is to implement a curriculum with an emphasis on play. Children in classrooms with appropriate developmental activities, including opportunities for peer play interactions, experience a better adjustment to kindergarten (Maxwell & Eller, 1994). To assist children with the adjustment from home to school, parents can become involved in their children's education, which is associated with academic and social competence (Epstein, 1994; Reynolds et al., 1992; Stevens, Hough, & Nurss, 1993). In addition, by facilitating children's play at home and in the neighborhood, parents also help children experience a better school adjustment (Ladd & Price, 1987).

Play and Culture

Recognizing the influence of culture on children's play is another important consideration for informing the early childhood curriculum. Although research indicates that interactions with peers enhance children's development, a lack of attention to culture has limited the ability to apply these findings to diverse groups of children (Coll et al., 1996; Ogbu, 1988; Roopnarine & Johnson, 1994; Roopnarine, Lasker, Sacks, & Stores, 1998). Researchers frequently study white, middle-income children, and overlook ethnic minority or low-income populations (Farver, Kim, & Lee, 1995; Ogbu, 1988; Roopnarine et al., 1998). When diverse groups of children are included, the play behavior is often evaluated according to the play of white, middle-income children. These comparisons detract from gaining an understanding of important cultural influences on children's behavior (Pellegrini & Boyd, 1993; Slaughter & Dombrowski, 1989). The toys and materials in a classroom may be unfamiliar to children from different backgrounds, causing children to spend more time exploring the materials than engaging in pretend play (McLoyd, 1982; Pellegrini & Boyd, 1993; Swadener & Johnson, 1989). Moreover, different cultural values, beliefs, and expectations for behavior can influence children's play (Farver et al., 1995; Rubin & Coplan, 1998). These variations in play highlight the importance of understanding the cultural contexts for children's play interactions.

FOUNDATIONS FOR THE DEVELOPMENT OF ASSESSMENT MEASURES

After determining the need for an instrument to assess peer play interactions, certain standards must guide the development process. The development of assessment measures must be informed by two types of standards for assessment: "what we measure" and "how well we measure." The first type of standard refers to what assessment should accomplish. For young children, standards for what is measured emerge from the objectives to promote children's development and educational success, found in the National Education Goals (U.S. Department of Education, 1992a), Head Start Performance Standards (U.S. Department of Health and Human Services, 1997), and the position statements of the NAEYC and National Association of Early Childhood Specialists in State Departments of Education (Bredekamp, 1997; NAEYC & NAECS/SDE, 1991). These objectives focus on the need to nurture the emergence of competencies and to facilitate connections between both parents and schools and prekindergarten and kindergarten. An assessment measure of children's peer play interactions must reflect these objectives by providing the capabilities to assess children's competencies, to link the home and school, and to link school settings.

The second type of assessment standard indicates how to provide appropriate assessment techniques based on sound scientific methods. A primary source for these standards is the Standards for Educational and Psychological Testing (American Educational Research Association, American Psychological Association, & National Council on Measurement in Education [AERA, APA, & NCME], 1985). These standards require that assessment instruments are appropriate for the population being evaluated by demonstrating sensitivity to cultural backgrounds and experiences (Standard 3.5, AERA et al., 1985). Instruments should also demonstrate adequate psychometric properties, particularly reliability and validity. Reliability is necessary to ensure that the measures yield accurate, consistent scores (Standard 2.1, AERA et al., 1985), and validity establishes that the instruments measure what they intended to measure (Standard 1.1., AERA, et al., 1985).

Emphasize Children's Competencies

To respond to the mandate for promoting children's competencies, assessment measures should indicate strengths as well as needs (Achenbach, 1995; Bredekamp & Copple, 1997). The goal of assessment is not only to understand children's areas of difficulty, but also to determine their competencies and progress (NAEYC & NAECS/SDE, 1991). Knowledge of strengths can assist with intervention planning by recognizing areas that need improvement and by building on children's existing competencies to enhance overall functioning (Achenbach, 1995). Furthermore, an awareness of multiple aspects of functioning contributes to a more comprehensive understanding of a child's development, and can help to ensure that services are provided to meet all of a child's needs. Unfortunately, once children are assigned a diagnostic label based on one area of difficulty, other areas of need may be overlooked (Mallory & Kerns, 1988).

The efforts by early childhood programs to promote competence further attest to the importance of including assessments of children's strengths. Methods of evaluating the emergence of these competencies can assist with enhancing children's development and school readiness. Because establishing effective peer relationships in play is a primary competency of early childhood, assessment measures must address both the attainment of this competency and the ways in which this capability has not been mastered.

Establish Cultural Validity

Knowledge of children's culture must also guide the development of assessment measures to ensure that the instruments are appropriate for the children who will be evaluated.

Unfortunately, children's development is often assessed and interpreted without considering the cultural context (Ogbu, 1988). The development of culturally valid measures must include gaining an understanding of the competencies of members of the children's culture to determine which skills are considered culturally appropriate (Gaskins, 1994; Ogbu, 1988). To do so, Gaskins (1994) proposes several steps. The first step involves learning about children's development within that culture, and establishing partnerships with adult members of the culture to determine their perceptions of development. The next step is generating categories based on an understanding of the culture. Subsequently, measures are developed that reflect the cultural norms and expectations. Once the information is collected with these measures, the final step is interpretation. Gaskins (1994) cautions that interpretations can be made only after gaining a thorough understanding of the culture.

Partnerships with parents and teachers are needed when creating assessment measures to evaluate peer play interactions. Through these collaborations, parents and teachers can contribute to an understanding of culturally appropriate peer play behavior. This knowledge can assist with determining which peer play interactions are considered appropriate and which ones are viewed as inappropriate within the culture. The partnerships with parents and teachers would enhance the ability of the assessment measures to evaluate peer play interactions, by recognizing the values and expectations for these behaviors within the children's culture.

Develop Cross-Informant Capacity to Link Home and School

Another important capacity of assessment instruments is to establish a link between the home and school. Cross-informant evaluations of peer play interactions in relevant contexts can provide this linkage. For young children, play primarily occurs at home and at school. The home setting includes play in the home and neighborhood, whereas the school context comprises play in the classroom and at recess. Each context is influenced by culture, situation-specific demands, and the expectations and values of peers and adults. For example, the available materials may reflect cultural influences that may differ among teachers and parents. In addition, play at school is typically limited to certain periods of the day, whereas play at home may not have as many time constraints. The amount of available time can affect the quality of play, with more complex play able to occur when children have extended play periods (Tegano & Burdette, 1991). As a result, the opportunities for play, and experiences within play, can vary across settings. These differences can contribute to variations in play (Meisels, 1994).

A child may demonstrate play strengths in one setting, but experience difficulties in another environment (Achenbach, 1995; Merrell & Popinga, 1994). An assessment of children's peer play interactions must therefore include both the home and school settings, to provide a comprehensive evaluation. Parents and teachers, the primary adults who observe children in these contexts, must contribute information based on their observations of the children's behavior over time. Behavior rating scales are a useful means of sharing information across informants, because raters can observe children in different contexts (Naglieri & Flanagan, 1992). These measures should have parallel parent and teacher versions that assess the same constructs, to provide a means of identifying children's play strengths and needs within relevant contexts. By providing congruent rating scales, assessment can assist with establishing communication between parents and schools, and thereby help maintain connections between the two settings.

Establish Continuity through School Linkages

Assessment instruments should also have the capability to evaluate children across the transition from prekindergarten to kindergarten. This transition is a critical period in children's lives, and continuity between the school settings can enhance the school adjustment. Assessment measures can contribute to maintaining connections between prekindergarten and kindergarten by establishing communication between parents and teachers across the school settings. Providing parents and teachers with information about children's strengths and needs in preschool can facilitate a smooth transition to kindergarten. Furthermore, assessments in the two school settings allow families and schools to follow children's progress. An understanding of children's functioning enables parents and teachers to plan appropriate activities and interventions to facilitate the development of competencies. By working together across school settings, families and schools can enhance children's learning and development.

Given the importance of maintaining connections between school settings, assessment measures for children's peer play interactions must incorporate information from parents and teachers in preschool and kindergarten. To maximize the usefulness of this information, the rating scales should include parallel versions for prekindergarten and kindergarten. By measuring the same constructs, assessment instruments can facilitate communications between families and schools regarding children's areas of strength and difficulty.

THE PENN INTERACTIVE PEER PLAY SCALE

Unfortunately, the available assessment measures for early childhood have limitations and do not meet all of these guidelines. Despite the usefulness of behavior rating scales for assessing young children, recent reviews indicate that many instruments for evaluating social competence have poor psychometric properties (Bracken, Keith, & Walker, 1994; Demaray et al., 1995; Naglieri & Flanagan, 1992). Other problems associated with these measures include a lack of congruence between parent and teacher versions (Manz, Fantuzzo, & McDermott, in press), an inattention to context, and the assessment of global social skills rather than specific aspects comprising social competence such as play skills. The capability for evaluating children across the school transition is also limited. Moreover, many instruments do not include low-income or culturally diverse populations in the development of the scales (Fantuzzo, McDermott, Manz, Hampton, & Burdick, 1996). Therefore, quality measures are needed that can assess the play of diverse groups of children within the home and school across the school transition during early childhood.

The Penn Interactive Peer Play Scale (PIPPS) is a promising approach to meeting the need for congruent assessment measures for parents and teachers across school settings during early childhood. The PIPPS was developed to assess the peer play interactions of children living in disadvantaged urban areas who risk experiencing discontinuity between home and school. This assessment system consists of parallel versions of parent and teacher rating scales, as well as parallel versions for use in preschool and kindergarten. The parent version assesses play in the home and neighborhood, whereas the teacher version examines play in the classroom and at school. Each version consists of 32 four-point Likert-scale items, which indicate how often the parent or teacher has observed the behavior during free play (i.e., "never," "seldom," "often," or "always") during the past two months. The items assess competencies within play to identify children who demonstrate successful relationships with peers and those who have peer difficulties.

The development of the PIPPS occurred in partnership with parents and teachers in a large, urban school district. Children's free play was observed and coded to identify behaviors in successful peer play interactions and unsuccessful peer play. These behaviors became the basis for the PIPPS items. Descriptions of positive and negative play interactions were included, to identify children's strengths and weaknesses. By including parents and teachers in the development of this assessment system, the researchers sought to enhance sensitivity to cultural expressions within play and to assess play in the children's primary contexts of the home and school.

To obtain empirical support for the PIPPS, a series of studies examined the capabilities of this system for addressing four primary aspects of assessment. First, the construct validity of the preschool teacher scale was evaluated to determine whether the behavioral descriptions produced psychologically meaningful categories of interactive peer play behavior for minority children living in low-income, urban areas. Second, the concurrent validity of this instrument was investigated by assessing whether the PIPPS correlates with established measures of school readiness administered at the same time. Third, the ability of the PIPPS to provide cross-informant information about the peer play constructs was studied by examining the congruence of the parent and teacher ratings. Finally, the congruence of the constructs obtained in the preschool and kindergarten versions was examined to explore the capability of this system for assessing children across the school transition.

Does the PIPPS Measure Meaningful Play Constructs?

Analyses of the construct validity of the preschool teacher PIPPS consistently yielded a three-factor solution across multiple cohorts of urban, African-American Head Start children (Coolahan, Fantuzzo, McDermott, & Mendez, 1998; Fantuzzo, Coolahan, Mendez, McDermott, & Sutton-Smith, in press; Fantuzzo, Sutton-Smith, Coolahan, Manz, Canning, & Debnam, 1995). These analyses produced the constructs of Play Interaction, Play Disruption, and Play Disconnection. Play Interaction indicates children's competencies in play, and describes cooperative, helpful, and creative behavior. Play Disruption includes items relating to aggressive, antisocial play behavior that hinders ongoing peer interactions. The Play Disconnection factor refers to nonparticipation in play, such as being withdrawn, hovering outside the play group, and rejecting invitations to play. Table 21–1 presents the item content for the three factors. Each construct demonstrated high reliability, with Cronbach alphas of .90, .91, and .87 for the Play Interaction, Play Disruption, and Play Disconnection factors, respectively.

Do Other Assessment Measures of Social Competence and School Readiness Validate the PIPPS?

After determining that the PIPPS produces three reliable constructs, analyses explored whether these constructs were valid for urban, low-income ethnic minority children in preschool. Multiple methods of evaluating peer interactions and school readiness constructs related to classroom peer interactions were employed. The first study examined whether teacher reports of interactive peer play at school overlap with multiple methods of

Table 21–1.   Items distributed by PIPPS factor

Factor 1: Play Disruption (alpha = .91)	Factor 2: Play Disconnection (alpha = .87)	Factor 3: Play Interaction (alpha = .90)
Starts fights and arguments	Hovers outside play group	Helps other children
Does not take turns	Withdraws	Helps settle peer conflicts
Demands to be in charge	Wanders aimlessly	Directs others' action completely
Rejects the play ideas of others	Is ignored by others	Encourages others to join play
Tattles	Refuses to play when invited	Comforts others who are hurt or sad
Destroys others' things	Needs help to start playing	Verbalizes stories during play
Disagrees without fighting	Confused in play	Shows positive emotions during play (e.g., smiles, laughs)
Verbally assaults others	Needs teacher's direction	Shows creativity in making up play stories and activities
Cries, whines, shows temper	Seems unhappy	
Grabs others' things	Is rejected by others	
Disrupts the play of others	Shares toys with other children	
Is physically aggressive		
Disrupts class during transitions from one activity to another		
Is rejected by others		
Shares toys with other children		

assessing children's social functioning. These methods include teacher reports of children's general social skills on the Social Skills Rating System (SSRS; Gresham & Elliott, 1990), peer sociometric ratings, and nominations to assess children's acceptance or rejection, and direct observations of play. Children who demonstrated high levels of interactive play behavior on the PIPPS obtained high teacher ratings for their social skills. Moreover, these children were well-liked by their peers and were observed to engage in collaborative play, the most interactive level of play. In addition, children who were rated on the PIPPS as disruptive in play were reported to have poor self-control, were not well-accepted by peers, and played alone. Finally, those children who received high ratings on the PIPPS Play Disconnection factor were least likely to be recognized by peers and were observed to play alone.

Although establishing positive relationships with peers is one aspect of school readiness, children also need positive approaches toward learning and the ability to adapt behavior to the demands of the classroom to facilitate educational success. Therefore, the second study explored how the constructs of the PIPPS relate to children's orientations toward learning and to their classroom behavior. Teacher reports were obtained on both the Preschool Learning Behaviors Scale (PLBS; McDermott, 1996), to assess children's competence motivation, attention/persistence, and attitude, and the Conners' Teacher Rating Scales-28 (CTRS-28; Conners, 1990), to evaluate children's hyperactivity, conduct problems, and inattentive-passive behavior. Children who received high ratings of interactive play were engaged in classroom learning activities, cooperated with the teacher, and accepted help from the teacher. The children rated as disruptive in play resisted classroom assistance and tended to have an aggressive attitude toward the teacher. In addition, teachers reported that children who received high ratings for disconnected peer play were also inattentive and passive. Furthermore, these children displayed low levels of activity in the classroom and did not engage in classroom learning activities.

The results of both studies indicate meaningful relationships between the PIPPS and other measures of children's social functioning and school adaptation. These associations help us to understand how interactive peer play relates to other aspects of classroom functioning. In addition, the PIPPS continued to identify positive peer play interactions, confirming the emphasis on competency that guided the development of this measure.

Does the PIPPS Have the Capacity to Assess Children Across Informants?

To enhance the utility of this assessment system, the capability of the PIPPS to provide cross-informant ratings of the same peer play constructs was evaluated. First, analyses explored the construct validity of the parent version. The analyses yielded the same three constructs found in the teacher version: Play Interaction, Play Disruption, and Play Disconnection (Fantuzzo, Mendez, & Tighe, 1988b). Each construct again demonstrated reliability, with Cronbach alphas of .84, .81, and .74 for the respective Play Interaction, Play Disruption and Play Disconnection factors (Fantuzzo et al., 1988b). Subsequently, analyses explored the congruence among the constructs of the parent and teacher versions by using Wrigley-Neuhaus coefficients to assess the degree of similarity of hypothesized like constructs (Fantuzzo et al., 1988b). The results showed high levels of similarity (coefficients ≤ .88) for like factors, indicating that both versions assess the same categories of interactive peer play.

In addition, canonical variance analyses explored the relationships between the parent and teacher versions. Within these analyses, three significant relationships were found. The three constructs of the teacher version corresponded with the same constructs in the parent version, providing additional evidence of the congruence between the parent and teacher versions. Play Interaction had the strongest agreement between the two versions, indicating the ability of the PIPPS to assess play competencies. The parent preschool PIPPS assesses the same constructs as the teacher preschool version, and further attests to the validity of this instrument. Thus, this assessment system obtains information from parents and teachers about the same constructs of interactive peer play across the home and school settings.

Does the PIPPS Have the Capability to Assess Children Across the School Transition?

A series of studies explored the capacity of the PIPPS rating system to assess children across the transition from preschool to kindergarten. The studies began with an investigation of the construct validity of the kindergarten teacher and parent versions. Once again, analyses yielded the three-factor structure found in the preschool PIPPS, and the constructs were reliable. The Play Interaction, Play Disruption, and Play Disconnection factors for the teacher version demonstrated Cronbach alphas of .94, .90, and .91, respectively. For the parent version, the respective factors yielded Cronbach alphas of .82, .76, and .75. The results support the use of the kindergarten PIPPS with urban, low-income, ethnic minority children. Further analyses evaluated the factorial congruence among the constructs of the parent and teacher versions, and found that the parent and teacher constructs demonstrated high congruence (coefficients ≥ = .96) for like factors. These results indicate that the PIPPS reliably measures the same three constructs of interactive peer play behavior in both the parent and teacher versions for kindergarten.

Subsequently, analyses examined the capacity of the PIPPS to assess the interactive peer play behavior of children during the transition from preschool to kindergarten. Factor-matching techniques indicated that the preschool parent and kindergarten parent versions had high levels of congruence (coefficients ≥ .75) for like factors, as did the preschool teacher and kindergarten teacher scales (coefficients ≥ .87). In addition, these analyses found high congruence of like factors for the preschool parent and kindergarten teacher scales (coefficients ≥ .80), and for the preschool teacher and kindergarten parent versions (coefficients ≥ .87). These findings demonstrate that the PIPPS measures the same constructs in preschool and kindergarten.

In summary, the results of these studies provide support for the constructs of Play Interaction, Play Disruption, and Play Disconnection in the parent and teacher versions of both the preschool and kindergarten measures. Furthermore, investigations of the concurrent validity of the PIPPS with established measures of social competence and school readiness indicate that this assessment system identifies children's strengths and needs regarding peer interactions and school adjustment. In addition, this assessment system can assist with establishing continuity between the home and school by providing cross-informant ratings of children's peer play interactions in the primary contexts for these behaviors. Finally, the PIPPS can help with maintaining continuity across the school transition by measuring the same construct in preschool and kindergarten and thereby enabling teachers to continue assessment of the same dimensions of peer play interactions throughout early childhood.

WAYS IN WHICH THE PIPPS CAN BE USED

The capability of the PIPPS to address important aspects of assessment indicates that it is a valuable addition to the early childhood assessment technology. The benefits of this rating system suggest several ways that this instrument can promote children's readiness for school success. This section presents examples of ways that the PIPPS rating system can respond to the objectives of early childhood education.

A Screening and Assessment Tool

Head Start and early childhood organizations emphasize the need to have procedures for screenings and assessments of children's social functioning to identify children's strengths and needs. The Head Start Performance Standards call for screenings of children's social skills within 45 days of entering the program (U.S. Department of Health and Human Services, 1997). These standards indicate that the screening should occur in collaboration with families to obtain multiple perspectives on children's behavior and development, and should be conducted with sensitivity to the children's cultural background. In addition, the standards require ongoing assessments of children's progress to identify any areas of need that may arise. Both parents and staff should contribute information to the assessments, based on their observations of the children's functioning over time. Similarly, the NAEYC and NAECS/SDE (1991) position statement also emphasizes the importance of social skills assessment upon entry into the program and throughout the year. These guidelines indicate that assessments should include observations by parents and teachers in naturally occurring contexts.

To meet these guidelines and standards, early childhood programs need appropriate assessment instruments. The PIPPS fulfills this need in several ways. The rating system provides a tool to assess peer play interactions, a primary social skill for young children. The PIPPS also enables teachers and parents to contribute their perspectives to the assessment. In addition, parents and teachers can follow children's progress by assessing children with a reliable, valid instrument throughout the year. Furthermore, because the observations are based on free play at home and school, the PIPPS allows the assessments to occur in natural play contexts. The ability of the PIPPS to satisfy these needs of early childhood programs attests to its utility as a screening and assessment tool.

Informing the Curriculum

The guidelines and standards of Head Start and professional early childhood organizations indicate that the screenings and assessments should inform the development of a curriculum that is both individually appropriate and age appropriate (NAEYC & NAECS/SDE, 1991; U.S. Department of Health and Human Services, 1997). A curriculum is defined as a written plan that describes the goals for children's learning and development, the experiences necessary to attain these goals, the assistance that parents and staff should provide to achieve these goals, and the contexts in which teaching and learning should occur (NAEYC & NAECS/SDE, 1991; U.S. Department of Health and Human Services, 1997). An individually appropriate curriculum uses the information obtained from the screenings and assessments to determine how the program can best meet individual children's needs, whereas a curriculum that is age appropriate responds to the developmental and learning needs of early childhood (NAEYC & NAECS/SDE, 1991).

To ensure an appropriate curriculum for individual children, the Head Start Performance Standards specify that screenings, ongoing observations, and information from parents must contribute to the decisions regarding the best curriculum for each child. According to these standards, the curriculum must provide the services necessary to meet children's particular strengths and needs as identified through the assessments. NAEYC and NAECS/SDE (1991) also emphasize the importance of having curricula that accommodate children's individual differences in experience, maturation, learning styles, needs, interests, and culture. The PIPPS can contribute to developing curricula that enhance children's social skills by providing information about individual children's areas of competence and difficulty in peer play interactions. Because the PIPPS has empirically validated constructs of peer play interactions, teachers can use this instrument to determine particular areas of play to address in a child's individualized curriculum. Moreover, because the PIPPS is appropriate for urban, low-income, ethnic minority children, it can assist teachers with developing a curriculum that responds to children's cultural differences.

The PIPPS assesses three constructs of play: Play Disruption, Play Disconnection, and Play Interaction. The scores for the items of each construct are summed, then converted to T scores. After each construct receives a T score, interpretations can be made about children's play strengths and needs. T scores are based on a mean of 50 and a standard deviation of 10. Therefore, a score of 50 represents an average score, and scores that are greater than one standard deviation above or below the mean indicate children's strengths and needs regarding each construct. The norms were based on a Head Start population in a large, urban area. To use the PIPPS with other populations, the test user must establish norms.[1]

To illustrate how the PIPPS can facilitate planning an appropriate curriculum for individual children, PIPPS profiles for three children are presented in Figure 21–1. Amber displays a Play Disruption profile. While playing with other children, she fights with them, takes toys away from them, refuses to share toys, and demands control over the play activities. In contrast, Kayla presents a Play Disconnection profile. She watches play groups from a distance, is uncertain how to initiate play interactions, and refuses requests to join the play activities of her peers. Diana, however, demonstrates a profile for Play Interaction. She invites children to join her play activities, is responsive to children playing with her, and develops stories about play themes. The strengths and needs of these children vary considerably, and the teacher had to account for these differences when planning the curriculum.

For Amber, the teacher needed to decrease the amount of disruptive play and increase her positive play interactions. Amber's teacher developed a plan that helped Amber to observe models of appropriate play behavior, and encouraged Amber to engage in play with these models. To facilitate positive play interactions, the teacher planned opportunities for Amber to play individually with Diana, who could model and encourage positive play behaviors for Amber, and to play in small groups with other children demonstrating

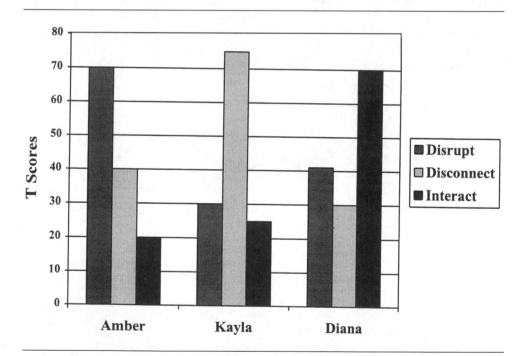

Figure 21–1. PIPPS profile for three children.

[1] To obtain a copy of the PIPPS, write to the first author at University of Pennsylvania, Graduate School of Education, Psychology in Education Division, 3700 Walnut Street, Philadelphia, PA 19104-6216.

positive peer play. The teacher also utilized the teaching assistant and parent volunteers to help redirect Amber's play when she became disruptive.

To help Kayla reduce the level of disconnection, the teacher also wanted to increase Kayla's peer interactions. Her teacher helped Kayla to find activities she enjoyed, and provided opportunities for Diana to play with Kayla in a contained, supportive environment. The teacher, teaching assistant, and parent volunteers encouraged Kayla for her interactions with Diana, as well as for any attempts at interactions with the other children. The interactions with Amber and Kayla helped Diana to capitalize on her strengths and to further develop these abilities. Although Diana demonstrated positive behaviors in peer interactions, the opportunity to play with children who display disruptive or disconnected play can encourage further growth. By pairing this child with children who need assistance with play, the teacher utilized Diana's strengths to present her with additional learning opportunities. Her play skills developed further as she learned how to play in more challenging situations.

The development of an age-appropriate curriculum involves recognizing realistic and attainable goals for children within their age range to provide optimum learning experiences for all of the children (NAEYC & NAECS/SDE, 1991). For early childhood, the curriculum should promote social interactions to enhance social development and to facilitate learning in other domains (NAEYC & NAECS/SDE, 1991; U.S. Department of Health and Human Services, 1997). Decisions about the best ways to facilitate this competency should be made at the classroom level, based on the needs of the children in the class (Bredekamp & Rosegrant, 1992). The PIPPS can assist with establishing an appropriate curriculum by providing a tool for assessing children's social interactions. The knowledge gained from assessments of all children allows the teacher to plan ways that the curriculum can promote this competency at the classroom level.

A Communication Tool for Parents and Teachers

Establishing collaborations between parents and teachers is an important component of early childhood education. Head Start, NAEYC, and NAECS/SDE promote the development of these partnerships to provide comprehensive assessments and to inform the curriculum (NAEYC & NAECS/SDE, 1991; U.S. Department of Health and Human Services, 1997). However, to arrive at a shared understanding of a child's competencies and needs, parents and teachers need effective ways to communicate about a child's functioning. Assistance must be provided for parents to communicate with teachers, to help parents to participate in decision making (U.S. Department of Health and Human Services, 1997). The PIPPS provides a means of establishing this communication. Because the parent and teacher versions measure the same constructs, parents and teachers can use the same terms (i.e., disruptive, disconnected, interactive) when discussing a child's peer play interactions. The ability to communicate with the same words that have shared meaning helps parents and teachers to understand the child's functioning in other contexts. This knowledge can strengthen the effectiveness of the partnership, as parents and teachers can work together toward enhancing children's peer play interactions.

The PIPPS can also facilitate communication between parents and teachers about children's culture. Discussions about children's play experiences at home and in the neighborhood create an opportunity for teachers to learn about cultural customs. Parents can provide information about children's play that enhances the teacher's understanding of the children's culture. This information can include the specific games and activities that children engage in, who teaches the children how to play these games, and the meaning of these games and activities within the culture. Knowledge about these aspects of children's play at home can help teachers in planning curricula and interventions that best meet children's needs.

The capacity of the PIPPS to facilitate communications is not limited to collaborations between parents and teachers. The importance of the transition from prekindergarten to kindergarten necessitates that teachers in the two school settings establish effective communications. Head Start stipulates that programs establish procedures to support the school transition. Meetings between parents and the teachers from both school settings are an important component of this transition (U.S. Department of Health and Human Services, 1997). The PIPPS again provides a means for communications between the teachers, and between the parents and teachers.

Although a primary objective of establishing effective communications between parents and teachers is to facilitate assessment and curriculum planning, another benefit of these communications is the opportunity to educate parents about the importance of play. As parents gain an understanding of the value of play for children's development, and of the relationships of play to children's learning behavior, they can foster opportunities for peer play interactions at home. The PIPPS can also contribute to this process by specifying three particular play constructs that represent positive and problematic peer interactions, and providing descriptions of behavior that exemplify these play categories. This information helps parents to know which play behaviors to support and which behaviors to discourage. Furthermore, an understanding of the correlations of the PIPPS with measures of school adaptation can provide parents with an awareness of the effects of play on children's school success.

Development and Evaluation of Classroom-Based Interventions

The PIPPS can also provide a way to guide the development of interventions and to evaluate treatment outcomes. As early childhood programs strive to enhance children's peer play interactions, interventions must be developed for children with peer difficulties. The development of these interventions must be guided by empirically validated methods of identifying those children. Moreover, to evaluate the effectiveness of the treatment, psychometrically sound instruments are needed.

An example of the way in which the PIPPS can guide the development of an intervention and can evaluate intervention outcomes is through its use in the Play Buddy Intervention (PBI; Fantuzzo & Sutton-Smith, 1994). This intervention was designed to promote positive peer interactions for Head Start children with poor play skills. The PIPPS enabled the research team to examine the peer social competence of Head Start children at home and at school. Children identified as having poor peer play skills had the lowest levels of Play Interaction and the highest levels of Play Disruption and/or Play Disconnection, as indicated by the PIPPS. The children considered resilient were those who demonstrated high levels of Play Interaction and low levels of Play Disruption and Play Disconnection on the PIPPS. The intervention sought to use peer play with resilient children as a context for enhancing the play competencies of children with poor play skills.

The development of the intervention consisted of three tasks: (a) selecting the resilient peers, called Play Buddies, and the children with poor peer play skills, called Play Partners; (b) establishing collaborations with teachers to set up classroom Play Corners for play interactions between the Play Buddy and Play Partner; and (c) identifying and training parent volunteers, called Play Supporters, to support the positive play interactions of the children in the Play Corner. The PIPPS assisted with the identification of Play Buddies and Play Partners by determining the resilient children and the less socially effective children. These children were subsequently observed to determine whether the resilient children demonstrated play tactics that were effective in promoting play interactions with the disruptive or disconnected children.

The PBI classroom session included the following steps. First, the Play Supporter entered the classroom and set up the Play Corner. Next, the Play Supporter spoke individually with the Play Buddy to prepare for the 20-minute play session with the Play Partner. The Play Supporter concretely identified the play activities that the Play Buddy had previously engaged in with the Play Partner that led to positive play interactions. During the play sessions, the Play Supporter observed the play interactions from outside the Play Corner. At the end of the play session, the Play Supporter gave supportive feedback to the children about their play. The intervention consisted of an average of 20 play sessions during an eight-week period. Two studies evaluated the effectiveness of the PBI for socially isolated, African-American children in Head Start (Fantuzzo, Coolahan, & Weiss, 1997). The children were randomly assigned to either the PBI or Control condition. Observations of play, and teacher ratings of children's competencies using the PIPPS and other measures, were collected before and after the intervention. Results from both studies indicate the effectiveness of the intervention.

To illustrate the usefulness of the PIPPS with this intervention, the case study of Tanya is presented. Tanya was a 4-year-old African-American child enrolled in Head Start who displayed a PIPPS profile similar to Kayla in Figure 21–1, with a very high score for Play Disconnection, and very low scores for Play Interaction and Play Disruption. She was withdrawn, wandered aimlessly in the classroom, was ignored by the other children, and appeared unhappy. The teacher and research team learned that prior to entering Head Start, Tanya experienced a traumatic event at 3 years of age. She was walking down the street with her father when he was killed in a drive-by shooting. Subsequently, Tanya did not speak or interact with others. The concerns about Tanya's high level of disconnection led to her participation in the Play Buddy Intervention as a Play Partner.

Tanya's Play Buddy, Brittany, was another 4-year-old African-American girl enrolled in Head Start. Brittany was selected as a Play Buddy based on her high score for Play Interaction, and low scores for Play Disruption and Play Disconnection. Over an eight-week period, Tanya and Brittany spent time in the Play Corner, with the support of Miss Barbara, the Play Supporter. Brittany initially engaged Tanya in play that did not require face-to-face interactions, but instead, utilized verbal encounters. These activities included games of hide-and-seek and turn-taking. Examples of their interactions include hiding behind boxes, talking to each other on two telephones, and Brittany rocking Tanya on a rocking chair. Gradually, Tanya engaged in more direct interactions with Brittany in the Play Corner. In addition, Tanya interacted with Brittany and the other children within the classroom. She was even observed to initiate the same rocking chair activity with a younger boy while laughing and displaying pleasure. At the end of the intervention, Tanya demonstrated a significant reduction in her score for Play Disconnection on the PIPPS, and a significant increase in her score for Play Interaction. She interacted with peers, displayed positive affect, helped other children, verbalized stories, and demonstrated creativity.

The PIPPS was an integral component of the development and evaluation of this intervention. First, this instrument provided the means to determine which children needed assistance in improving interactions with peers, like Tanya. Second, the PIPPS allowed the research team to identify the resilient children, such as Brittany, who facilitated the intervention. Finally, this rating system was used to determine the treatment effectiveness, by assessing the peer play interactions of children before and after the intervention. The changes in the PIPPS profiles for Tanya demonstrate how to assess the effectiveness of the intervention. Each of these functions illustrates important ways in which the PIPPS can be used in interventions for enhancing children's play.

The purpose of this chapter was to present a promising instrument to assess peer play interactions in early childhood for urban, low-income, ethnic minority children. The above applications of the PIPPS represent important ways that this instrument can contribute to children's readiness for school success. These uses for the PIPPS involve partnerships between families and schools to meet the objectives of the readiness goal. As early childhood programs increasingly respond to the national priority for *all* children to enter school ready to learn, the PIPPS can help vulnerable children to attain this important goal.

REFERENCES

Achenbach, T. M. (1995). Diagnosis, assessment, and comorbidity in psychosocial treatment research. *Journal of Abnormal Child Psychology, 23,* 45–65.

American Educational Research Association, American Psychological Association, & National Council on Measurement in Education (1985). *Standards for educational and psychological testing.* Washington, D.C.: American Psychological Association.

Berk, L. E. (1994). Vygotsky's theory: The importance of make-believe play. *Young Children, 50,* 30–39.

Bracken, B. A., Keith, L. K., & Walker, K. C. (1994). Assessment of preschool behavior and social-emotional functioning: A review of thirteen third-party instruments. *Assessment in Rehabilitation and Exceptionality 1,* 331–346.

Bredekamp, S. (1997). NAEYC issues revised position statement on developmentally appropriate practice in early childhood programs. *Young Children, 52,* 34–40.

Bredekamp, S., & Copple, C. (Eds.). (1997). *Developmentally appropriate practice in early childhood programs.* Washington, D.C.: National Association for the Education of Young Children.

Bredekamp, S., & Rosegrant, T. (1992). Reaching potentials through appropriate curriculum: Conceptual frameworks for applying the guidelines. In S. Bredekamp & T. Rosegrant (Eds.), *Reaching potentials: Appropriate curriculum and assessment for young children, Vol. 1,* Washington, D.C.: National Association for the Education of Young Children.

Children's Defense Fund. (1997). *The state of America's children: Yearbook 1997.* Washington, D.C.

Coll, C. G., Lamberty, G., Jenkins, R., McAdoo, H. P., Crnic, K., Waski, B. H., & Garcia, H. V. (1996). An integrative model for the study of developmental competencies in minority children. *Child Development, 67,* 1891–1914.

Conners, K. (1990). *Conners' rating scales manual.* Toronto: Multi-Health Systems.

Coolahan, K. C., Fantuzzo, J., McDermott, P., & Mendez, J. L. (1998). Interactive peer play and school readiness: The relationship between play competencies and learning behaviors and classroom conduct. Manuscript submitted for publication.

Corsaro, W. A., & Schwarz, K. (1991). Peer play and socialization in two cultures. In B. Scales, M. Almy, A. Nicolopoulou, & S. Ervin-Tripp (Eds.), *Play and the social context of development in early care and education* (pp. 234–254). New York: Teachers College Press.

Creasey, G. L., Jarvis, P. A., & Berk, L. A. (1998). Play and social competence. In S. N. Saracho & B. Spodek (Eds.), *Multiple perspectives on play in early childhood education* (pp. 116–143). Albany, NY: State University of New York Press.

Delgato-Gaitan, C. (1994). Spanish-speaking families' involvement in schools. In C. L. Fagnano, & B. Z. Werber (Eds.), *School, family and community interaction: A view from the firing lines.* Boulder, CO: Westview Press.

Demaray, M. K., Ruffalo, S. L., Carlson, J., Busse, R. T., Olson, A. E., McManus, S. M., & Leventhal, A. (1995). Social skills assessment: A comparative evaluation of six published rating scales. *School Psychology Review, 24,* 648–671.

Diamond, K. E., & Squires, J. (1993). The role of parental report in the screening and assessment of young children. *Journal of Early Intervention, 17,* 107–115.

Entwisle, D. R., & Alexander, K. L. (1993). Entry into school: The beginning school transition and educational stratification in the United States. *Annual Review of Sociology, 19,* 401–423.

Epstein, J. L. (1994). Theory to practice: School and family partnerships lead to school improvement and student success. In C. L. Fagnano, & B. Z. Werber (Eds.), *School family and community interaction: A view from the firing lines* (pp. 39–52). Boulder, CO: Westview Press.

Ervin-Tripp, S. (1991). Play in language development. In B. Scales, M. Almy, A. Nicolopoulou, & S. Ervin-Tripp (Eds.), *Play and the Social Context of Development in Early Care and Education* (pp. 84–97). New York: Teachers College Press.

Fantuzzo, J. W., Coolahan, K., Mendez, J., McDermott, P., & Sutton-Smith, B. (1998a). Contextually relevant validation of peer play constructs with African-American Head Start children: Penn Interactive Peer Play Scale. *Early Childhood Research Ouarterly, 13,* 411–431.

Fantuzzo, J., Coolahan, K., & Weiss, A. (1997). Resiliency partnership-directed intervention: Enhancing the social competencies of preschool victims of physical abuse by developing peer resources and community strengths. In D. Cicchetti and S. L. Toth (Eds.), *Rochester Symposium on Developmental Psychopathology, Vols. 8 & 9: The effects of Trauma on the Developmental Process* (pp. 463–490). Rochester, NY: University of Rochester Press.

Fantuzzo, J. W., McDermott, P., Manz, P. H., Hampton, V. R., & Burdick, N. A. (1996). The Pictorial Scale of Perceived Competence for Young Children: Does it work with low-income urban children? *Child Development, 67,* 1071–1084.

Fantuzzo, J., Mendez, J., & Tighe, E. (1998b). Parental assessment of peer play: Development and validation of the parent version of the Penn Interactive Peer Play Scale. *Early Childhood Research Quarterly, 13,* 659–676.

Fantuzzo, J. W., & Sutton-Smith, B. (1994). *Play Buddy project: A preschool-based intervention to improve the social effectiveness of disadvantaged, high-risk children.* Washington, D.C.: U.S. Department of Health and Human Services.

Fantuzzo, J., Sutton-Smith, B., Coolahan, K. C., Manz, P. H., Canning, S., & Debnam, D. (1995). Assessment of preschool play interaction behaviors in young low-income children: Penn Interactive Peer Play Scale. *Early Childhood Research Quarterly, 10,* 105–120.

Farver, J. M., Kim, Y. K., & Lee, Y. (1995). Cultural differences in Korean- and Anglo-American preschoolers' social interaction and play behaviors. *Child Development, 66,* 1088–1099.

Fisher, E. P. (1992). The impact of play on development: A meta-analysis. *Play and Culture, 5,* 159–181.

Frost, J. L. (1992). *Play and playscapes.* Albany, NY: Delmar.

Gaskins, S. (1994). Integrating interpretive and quantitative methods in socialization research. *Merrill-Palmer Quarterly, 40,* 313–333.

Goncu, A. (1993). Development of intersubjectivity in the dyadic play of preschoolers. *Early Childhood Research Quarterly, 8,* 99–116.

Gresham, F. M., & Elliott, S. N. (1990). *Social skills rating system manual.* Circle Pines, MN: American Guidance Service.

Harrison, A. O., Wilson, M. N., Pine, C. J., Chan, S. Q., & Buriel, R. (1990). Family ecologies of ethnic minority children. *Child Development, 61,* 347–362.

Hartup, W. W., & Moore, S. G. (1990). Early peer relations: Developmental significance and prognostic implications. *Early Childhood Research Quarterly, 5,* 1–17.

Isenberg, J., & Quisenberry, N. L. (1988). Play: A necessity for all children. *Childhood Education, 64,* 138–145.

Jacobs, E. V. (1994). Introduction. In H. Goelman & E. V. Jacobs (Eds.), *Children's play in child care settings.* Albany, NY: State University of New York Press.

Johnson, J. E., Christie, J. F., & Yawkey, T. D. (1987). *Play and early development.* Glenview, IL: Scott Foresman.

Kupersmidt, J. B., & Coie, J. D. (1990). Preadolescent peer status, aggression, and school adjustment as predictors of externalizing problems in adolescence. *Child Development, 61,* 1350–1362.

Kupersmidt, J. B., Coie, J. D., & Dodge, K. A. (1990). The role of poor peer relationships in the development of disorder. In S. R. Asher & J. D. Coie (Eds.), *Peer rejection in childhood* (pp. 274–305). Cambridge: Cambridge University Press.

Ladd, G. W. (1990). Having friends, keeping friends, making friends, and being liked by peers in the classroom: Predictors of children's early school adjustment? *Child Development, 61,* 1081–1100.

Ladd, G. W., & Coleman, C. C. (1993). Young children's peer relationships: Forms, features and functions. In B. Spodek (Ed.), *Handbook of research on education of young children* (pp. 57–76). New York: Macmillan.

Ladd, G. W., & Price, J. M. (1987). Predicting children's social and school adjustment following the transition from preschool to kindergarten. *Child Development, 58,* 1168–1189.

Mallory, B. L., & Kerns, G. M. (1988). Consequences of categorical labeling of preschool children. *Topics in Early Childhood Special Education, 8,* 39–50.

Manz, P. H., Fantuzzo, J. W., & McDermott, P. H. (in press). The parent version of the preschool Social Skills Rating Scale: An analysis of its use with low-income, African-American children. *School Psychology Review.*

Martin, R. P. (1986). Assessment of the social and emotional functioning of preschool children. *School Psychology Review, 15,* 216–232.

Maxwell, K. L., & Eller, S. K. (1994). Children's transition to kindergarten. *Young Children, 49,* 56–63.

McDermott, P. A. (1996). *Preschool Learning Behaviors Scale.* Philadelphia: Edumetric and Clinical Science.

McLoyd, V. (1982). Social class differences in sociodramatic play: A critical review. *Developmental Review, 2,* 1–30.

Meisels, S. J. (1994). Designing meaningful measurements for early childhood. In B. L. Mallory & R. S. New (Eds.), *Diversity and developmentally appropriate practices: Challenges for early childhood education* (pp. 202–222). New York: Teachers College Press.

Merrell, K. W., & Popinga, M. R. (1994). Parent-teacher concordance and gender differences in behavioral ratings of social skills and social-emotional problems of primary-age children with disabilities. *Diagnostique, 19,* 1–14.

Naglieri, J. A., & Flanagan, D. P. (1992). A psychometric review of behavior-rating scales. *Comprehensive Mental Health Care, 2,* 225–239.

National Association for the Education of Young Children and the National Association of Early Childhood Specialists in State Departments of Education (1991). Guidelines for appropriate curriculum content and assessment in programs serving children ages 3 through 8. *Young Children, 46,* 21–38.

Nicolopoulou, A. (1993). Play, cognitive development, and the social world: Piaget, Vygotsky, and beyond. *Human Development, 36,* 1–23.

Ogbu, J. U. (1988). Cultural diversity and human development. In D. T. Slaughter (Ed.), *Black children and poverty: A developmental perspective* (pp. 11–28). San Francisco: Jossey-Bass.

Parker, J. G., & Asher, S. R. (1987). Peer relations and personal adjustment: Are low-accepted children at risk? *Psychological Bulletin, 102,* 357–389.

Pellegrini, A. D., & Boyd, B. (1993). The role of play in early childhood development and education: Issues in definition and function. In B. Spodek (Ed.), *Handbook of research on the education of young children* (pp. 105–121). New York: Macmillan.

Pellegrini, A. D., & Galda, L. (1991). Longitudinal relations among preschoolers' symbolic play, metalinguistic verbs, and emergent literacy. In J. F. Christie (Ed.), *Play and early literacy development* (pp. 47–67). Albany: State University of New York Press.

Piaget, J. (1962). *Play, dreams, and imitation in childhood.* New York: Norton.

Reynolds, A. J., Weissberg, R. P., & Kasprow, W. J. (1992). Prediction of early social and academic adjustment of children from the inner city. *American Journal of Community Psychology, 20,* 599–624.

Rogoff, B. (1993). Children's guided participation and participatory appropriation in sociocultural activity. In R. H. Wozniak & K. W. Fischer (Eds), *Development in context: Acting and thinking in specific environments.* Hillsdale, NJ: Erlbaum.

Roopnarine, J. L., & Johnson, J. E. (1994). The need to look at play in diverse cultural settings. In J. L. Roopnarine, J. E. Johnson, & Hooper, F. H. (Eds.), *Children's play in diverse cultures* (pp. 1–8). Albany, NY: State University of New York Press.

Roopnarine, J. L., Lasker, J., Sacks, M., & Stores, M. (1998). The cultural contexts of children's play. In S. N. Saracho & B. Spodek (Eds.), *Multiple Perspectives on Play in Early Childhood Education* (pp. 194–219). Albany, NY: State University of New York Press.

Rubin, K. H., & Coplan, R. J. (1998). Social and nonsocial play in childhood: An individual differences perspective. In S. N. Saracho & B. Spodek (Eds.), *Multiple Perspectives on Play in Early Childhood Education* (pp. 144–170). Albany, NY: State University of New York Press.

Ruffalo, S. L., & Elliott, S. N. (1997). Teachers' and parents' ratings of children's social skills: A closer look at cross-informant agreements through an item analysis protocol. *School Psychology Review, 26*(3), 489–501.

Saracho, O. N., & Spodek, B. (1998). A historical overview of theories of play. In S. N. Saracho & B. Spodek (Eds.), *Multiple perspectives on play in early childhood education* (pp. 1–10). Albany, NY: State University of New York Press.

Slaughter, D. T., & Dombrowski, J. (1989). Cultural continuities and discontinuities: Impact on social and pretend play. In Bloch, M. N., & Pellegrini, A. D. (Eds.), *The ecological context of children's play* (pp. 282–310). Norwood, NJ: Ablex.

Smolucha, L., & Smolucha, F. (1998). The social origins of mind: Post-Piagetian perspectives on pretend play. In S. N. Saracho & B. Spodek (Eds.), *Multiple perspectives on play in early childhood education* (pp. 34–58). Albany, NY: State University of New York Press.

Stevens, J. H., Jr., Hough, R. A., & Nurss, J. R. (1993). The influence of parents on children's development and education. In B. Spodek (Ed.), *Handbook of research on education of young children* (pp. 337–351). New York: Macmillan.

Stone, S. J. (1995). Wanted: Advocates for play in the primary grades. *Young Children, 50,* 45–54.

Swadener, E. B., & Johnson, J. E. (1989). Play in diverse social contexts: Parent and teacher roles. In M. N. Bloch & A. D. Pellegrini (Eds.), *The ecological context of children's play* (pp. 214–244). Norwood, NJ: Ablex Publishing.

Tegano, D. W., & Burdette, M. P. (1991). Length of activity periods and play behaviors of preschool children. *Journal of Research in Childhood Education, 5,* 93–99.

U.S. Department of Education (1992a). *Starting school ready to learn. Questions and answers on reaching national education goal 1: By the year 2000, all children in America will start school ready to learn* (Resource Document). Washington, D.C.: Author. (ERIC Document Reproduction Service No. ED 355 013.)

U.S. Department of Education (1992b). *Transitions to kindergarten in American Schools: Final report of the National Transition Study.* Washington, D.C.

U.S. Department of Health and Human Services, Administration on Children, Youth, and Families (1997). Final rule—*Head Start program performance standards* 45 CFR Part 1304, Federal Register, 61, 57186-57227. Washington, D.C.: U.S. Government Printing Office.

U.S. General Accounting Office (1993). *Poor preschool-aged children: Numbers increase but most not in preschool.* (GAO Publication No. HRD-93-111BR.) Washington, D.C.

Van Hoorn, J., Nourot, P. M., Scales, B., & Alward, K. R. (1993). *Play at the center of the curriculum.* New York: MacMillan.

Vygotsky, L. S. (1967). Play and its role in the mental development of the child. *Soviet Psychology, 12,* 6–18. (A stenographic record of a lecture given in 1933; included in J. S. Bruner, A. Jolly, & K. Sylva, Eds., 1976; partly reproduced in Vygotsky, 1978.)

Vygotsky, L. S. (1978). *Mind in society: The development of higher psychological processes.* Cambridge, MA: Harvard University Press.

Zigler, E., & Styfco, S. J. (1994). Is the Perry Preschool better than Head Start?: Yes and no. *Early Childhood Research Quarterly, 9,* 269–287.

Zigler, E., Styfco, S. J., & Gilman, E. (1993). The national Head Start program for disadvantaged preschoolers. In E. Zigler & S. J. Styfco (Eds.), *Head Start and beyond: A national plan for extended childhood intervention* (pp. 1–41). New Haven, CT: Yale University Press.

PART VI

PROJECTIVE PLAY ASSESSMENTS

By its very nature, play assessment reflects both the strengths and the weaknesses of most projective evaluative procedures. Because play allows for the natural expression of children's thoughts, feelings, perceptions, and beliefs, it lends itself to interpretation on multiple levels. Play permits children to portray rich fantasy themes that they might not have the capacity to verbally express. As can be seen in the chapters that follow, certain toys and activities specifically lend themselves to the projective process. However, similar to the more traditional projective techniques, acceptable levels of reliability and validity have been difficult to obtain. It is with this knowledge in mind that some of the more promising assessment tools have been selected for inclusion in this section.

Using concepts similar to those that underlie the Thematic Apperception Test (TAT), a traditional projective storytelling procedure developed for adults, Ned Mueller set out to develop two similar techniques for use with a child population. The content for both tests is analyzed informally as well as through a standardized coding system. Mueller creatively integrates a case study into the discussion of each instrument, helping to make the administration, scoring, and interpretation procedures more realistic for the reader. Geared toward school-aged children, the MUG (Mueller-Ginsburg Story Technique) includes 12 stimulus picture cards depicting a main character in a variety of familiar settings. Children are asked to create a story for each of the cards. In an effort to adapt this type of assessment process for younger children, Mueller developed the Teddy Bears' Picnic (TBP) story stem technique that, in effect, is a 3-D modified version of the MUG. A teddy bear family and props are presented with a series of story stems in which the bears face various problems and situations. The children are asked to complete the story. Developed very recently, the TBP has not been available long enough to reach its full potential. However, it is a very appealing procedure that should capture the interest of many clinicians. Enjoyable to administer, the information gleaned from the TBP is insightful and valuable.

Puppet play has long been recognized as a staple in the play therapy scene and is reaching a similar status in the area of play assessment. In her reprinted chapter on a family puppet technique, Patricia Ross brings the puppet out of the playroom and into the family therapy office. This technique allows young children, often unheard family members, to more clearly express their views and feelings. Using puppets, Ross provides family members with a format for expression that is natural and more suited to less mature developmental skills than the verbal methods most frequently used in clinical settings. Ross points out that this procedure is often surprisingly revealing in what it encourages adults to express as well. The instructions for this clinical procedure are clear and are structured so that the reader gains a full understanding of how to implement it.

Eleanor Irwin gives us a simple semistructured puppet interview to be used in a play setting with individual clients. The process, materials, and puppet story environment are described in detail and are accompanied by fascinating clinical case examples that have been updated for this volume. Irwin couches her technique in the language of classic analytically oriented play therapy. Her discussion of the theoretical approach to puppet play is intriguing and thought provoking. This chapter should prove to be stimulating for all involved in clinical work with children. Whether the particular technique presented by Irwin or some variant thereof is adopted, Irwin's material is invaluable as an introduction to puppet play and its use diagnostically.

One of the most frequently employed projective techniques in traditional assessments is the sentence-completion task, which is available in a variety of forms. Typically used with adults and adolescents because of the prerequisite need for adequate reading and writing skills, Susan Knell and Kelly Beck describe a unique modification of this task in order to make it available to a younger population. Utilizing puppets as an integral part of the procedure, Knell and Beck have converted a typically independently completed task into an interactive play sequence. They further enrich the use of a basic set of standardized sentence stems by adding optional stems in order to individualize the activity as well as to make it more informative. Clinicians will be impressed with the ease of administration of this relatively simple, developmentally sensitive procedure that results in a tremendous amount of information regarding the emotional functioning of young children. Researchers will also be interested in this practical instrument.

Finally, Sandra Russ, Larissa Niec, and Astrida Seja offer the Affect in Play Scale (APS), a standardized measure of affective expression in the pretend play of children who are between the ages of 6 and 10. In their comprehensive chapter, these authors present the background work and theory that led to the development of this clever and useful scale. A clear description of the technique and the scale that is accompanied by interesting clinical material makes it easily understood. The authors support their work with a considerable discussion of research related to its usefulness. Furthermore, recognizing the need for an extension of this technique to the preschool population, they supply an age-appropriate adaptation. Clinicians and researchers will find their presentation most stimulating and comfortably adaptable to the assessment environment.

The techniques presented in this section provide a bridge that moves from assessment to treatment. In considering projective themes, it is natural to enter into the therapeutic territory of exploration and understanding of dynamic issues that is the meat of classic play therapy. What remains is for an increasing focus to be on the issues of standardization, reliability, and validity, which will bolster these techniques in their application to research as well as clinical settings.

Chapter 22 ───────────────────

THE MUG AND THE TEDDY BEARS' PICNIC: STORYTELLING TECHNIQUES FOR THE ASSESSMENT OF CHILDREN'S EMOTIONAL AND BEHAVIORAL PROBLEMS

Ned Mueller

THE MUG

Background

In 1984, when work on creating the MUG began, a standard storytelling test in child clinical training was the Thematic Apperception Test (TAT: Murray, 1943). The TAT was, and is, valuable in helping formulate clinical hypotheses about how older children and adolescents understand themselves and others. Yet in use, it was clear that the TAT had been developed originally primarily as a test for adults. Some of the cards did not seem wholly appropriate for use with elementary school-aged children. The Children's Apperception Test (CAT: Bellak & Bellak, 1974) had been developed for young children but there seemed to be a gap in middle childhood, ages 7 through 12, where no truly age-appropriate storytelling pictures were available.

One aim of creating the MUG pictures was to show school-aged children in their main adaptation settings. This included the classroom as well as kitchen, and depicted the child on the beach and in the playground, while not forgetting the continuing centrality of the parents in the child's life. Shakong Wang was the artist who drew the MUG cards (see Figure 22–1). He had special ability to translate psychology concepts into pictures whose quality seemed to come closer to art than to "psychology stimuli." The intention was to design ambiguous pictures that could lead to many different stories, depending on what the child brought to the picture (Figure 22–1).

From the outset, the focus was on devising a storytelling method to understand the problem child, regardless of whether the problems chiefly expressed themselves academically (Ginsburg, 1989) or emotionally and behaviorally (Mueller, 1996a). If to "diagnose" means to try to understand the nature of a child's problems, then the aim was to create a technique helpful in diagnosis—clinical diagnosis as well as academic diagnosis.

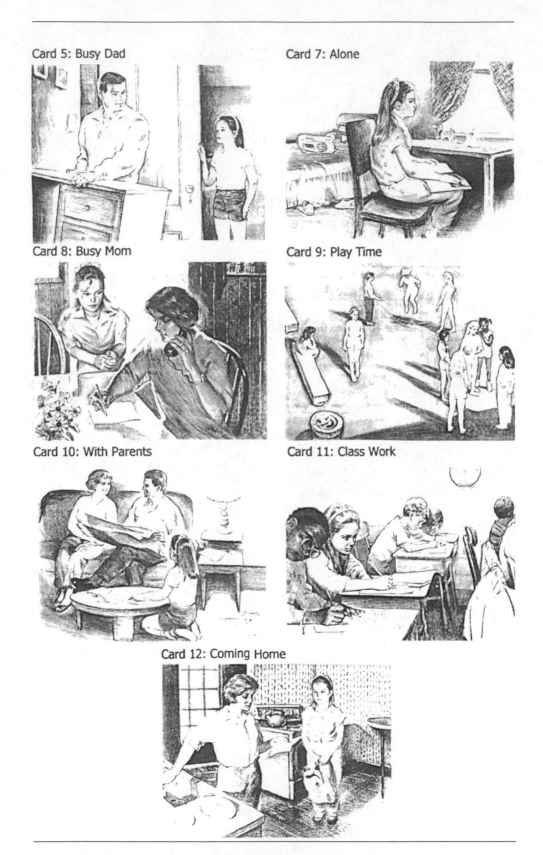

Figure 22–1 Depiction of 7 of 12 MUG cards —Cheryl's story.

The technique was developed so that it would support sensitive clinical interpretation from a variety of tester theoretical orientations. TAT and CAT pictures often depict strong conflict or drive wishes, derived from Freud's conflict and drive theories of personality (see Greenberg & Mitchell, 1983). While the importance of social attachments and relationships was emphasized in the MUG, the pictures did not show aggression, sex, or interpersonal conflict nearly as much as did the earlier projective tests. The pictures were completed in 1989. The technique was called the "MUG," short for "Mueller-Ginsburg Story Technique." (Mueller & Ginsburg, in press)

Is the MUG a projective test? The answer depends on what one means by the term "projection." In Freudian theory (Freud, 1936) one thinks of the projective process as largely defensively driven. Thus one might believe that children will only tell valuable stories when they use the MUG as a projective screen for feelings and impulses they cannot tolerate in themselves. Of course this happens at times, but the MUG is based on a more global theory: everyone, regardless of age, molds their story characters after their own experience and system of beliefs. Both children and adults have a quite basic tendency to become absorbed in fictional worlds even when the story told is not their own (Harris, in press). In short, to make up a story, the creator has to identify more or less with the position of the child in the pictures. In this vague sense of having to project oneself into the picture to tell a story, then of course the MUG is a projective technique.

Unlike most formal tests, the MUG technique relies on a shared story play frame being created by the child with active support from the empathic assessor. The theoretical preferences of the examiner will influence how the stories are interpreted—perhaps as relatively fixed core features of the self-concept, perhaps as more malleable personal constructs, or perhaps as explicit child motivations and needs.

Description of the MUG

The MUG itself comprises 12 cards, each of which shows a main character figure (the same across all cards) in a variety of situations. Figure 22–1 shows seven of the MUG cards. There are sets of MUG pictures showing both boy and girl main characters. Perhaps unique among techniques of its kind, the MUG cards are available for three ethnic groups: white, black, and Hispanic. Also unique may be the MUG's use of a nonscored warmup story. It offers the tester a chance to achieve a playful frame of reference with the child, and to actually help the child with what is expected as part of a complete story with feelings.

Standard Directions for Administering the MUG

The MUG should be given by those trained in its use and by those familiar with similar techniques like the TAT. A common problem is tester anxiety about "doing it right." How can children enter into play mode to invent stories when the testers are themselves anxious? For this reason training involving practicing the MUG with normal adults or children several times, taperecording the stories, and getting first-hand supervision on the results before using the test with clients seems the most sensible way to proceed, even for those with experience in projective methods

The directions for administration include both general rules and specific instructions for what to say. Examples of general rules are to avoid leading questions, and to hold back questions about emotion until the end of the story. The specific wording which introduces the technique follows:

> This is a story telling game, a pretending game. It has nothing to do with school, and there are no "right" or "wrong" stories, so you can make up whatever stories you'd like to. They can be happy stories or sad stories; good or bad things can happen in them. In your stories just try to say how people are feeling and how it turns out in the end.

The complete directions are fairly lengthy. For further information about administering the technique, please contact the author using the information given in Mueller & Ginsburg (in press).

Purposes of the MUG

The MUG technique is very general and, therefore, may be used for a variety of purposes. Table 22–1 summarizes the primary categories of information which can be obtained from the MUG. These are discussed in further detail below.

Social Cognition

In the stories that the child creates, the child constructs models of the social world and of his or her place in it (Kelly, 1955). Such constructions influence the manner in which the child copes with the events she or he encounters. The MUG is one good way for revealing a child's personal constructs.

Quality of Perceived Attachments and Interpersonal Coping

Bowlby (see Bretherton, 1987) stressed that across the early years of life everyone constructs an "internal working model of self and other." This model includes the extent to which the child sees others as devaluing or vulnerable, and also adaptive or unhealthy methods for dealing with various needs and problems. In problem children one expects excessive forms of self-indulgence, devaluing, and defying others. The MUG contributes to an understanding of this model in any school-aged child, well-functioning or problem filled.

Motivation for Achievement and Perceived Competence

The child's success at school is affected not only by basic ability, but also by conceptions of the self as a learner and attitudes toward learning, including feelings about achievement and competence. Developmental research shows that it is also important to consider the type of motivation underlying the child's achievement (Dweck, 1981). For example, does the child see school and learning as worthwhile? Does the child see himself or herself as capable of doing well? The MUG helps one understand both implicit and self-attributed motives (McClelland, Koestner, & Weinberger, 1989).

General Self-Esteem

Watanabe (1991) examined the interrelations of negative themes in MUG stories with the Piers-Harris Self-Concept Scale (Piers & Harris, 1984) and the Positive Self-Concept Task of the *Tasks of Emotional Development* (Cohen & Weil, 1975). Children telling stories on the MUG high in themes of main character loneliness, sadness, or helplessness and stories where other characters were vulnerable were significantly lower in self-esteem on both external mea-

Table 22–1.   A comparison of codes appearing on the MUG and the Teddy Bears' Picnic with interrater reliability

Valuing and Devaluing	MUG Code	TBP Code	Inter-Rater Reliability*(r)**
Valuing Others	V+	V+	.89
Devaluing Others (peers, siblings)	DVP–	DV–	.92
Devaluing Adults (parents, authority figures)	DVA–	DV–	.98
Valuing from Others (parents, authority figures)	VF+	VF+	.91
Others Devalue MC	DF–	DF–	.91
MC defies Authority Figures	D–	DV–	.87
Drives			
Suicide/Death wishes by MC	SD–		No Data
Sexual/Oral Expression/Indulgences	SO–	SO–	.85
Aggression	A–	A–	.93
Physical Punishment	PP–	PP–	.87
Vulnerability			
MC expresses Helplessness/Vulnerability	H–	H–	.88
Vulnerability in Others/Valued possessions	U–	U–	.86
MC Shows Motivation for achievement	SM+		.60
MC Unmotivated towards achievement	SM–		.86
MC Succeeds in school	SA+		.68
MC Fails in schoolwork	SF–		.68
MC Resourceful	R+	R+	.65
MC Unsuccessful/Cannot Do	R–		.66
Resourcefulness in Others	RO+	RO+	.90
Self			
MC Idealized/Perfect/Narcissistic	I–		.89
Idealized Others/Idealized story endings	IO–		.80
Affect or Emotion			
MC expresses Spontaneous Positive Affect/Emotion	PA+	PA+	.76
Spontaneous Positive Affect/Emotion in Others	N/A	PAO+	N/A
MC expresses Unhappy or Sad Emotion	NU–	NA–	.93
Negative Affect in Others	N/A	NAO–	N/A
MC expresses Spontaneous Anger in Story	NA–		.84
MC expresses Boredom or Frustration	BF–		.86
Loneliness/Sad Story Ending	LON–	E–	.80
Happy Story Ending	HAP+		.80
Summary Scores			
Disorientated/Incoherent/Disjointed/Odd story	DIS–	DIS–	.93
Immature Story/Gesticulation instead of words	IMM–	IMM–	No Data
Fantasy Failure/Inaccessible Imagination	FF–		.99
Child Distracted/Impulsive	N/A	DI–	N/A

* These reliabilities refer to the MUG code only. For reliability data on the TBP, consult Mueller (1996a)
** Pearson R. Based on a sample of ten full MUG protocols. For the summary scales, the inter-rater reliability was as follows: MAS1 = .91; MAS2 = .83; MAS3 = .97; MAS4 = .97. (Data from Dimopoulou, 1998)

sures. Put differently, children high in self-esteem did not use these negative themes in their stories as often. This is the only quantitative evidence available to date about the MUG as a measure of self-esteem. Watanabe also found that both traditional self-esteem measures, but not the relevant MUG scores, were somewhat confounded by social desirability in the child's response, which could suggest that the MUG offers a measure of self-esteem relatively unaffected by the child's attempting to give socially desirable material to the interviewer.

Diagnosis of Social-Emotional Problems

The MUG permits systematic assessment of child problems through material that is obtained directly from the child. This is important, because much child diagnosis in mental health clinics remains indirect or second-hand. It relies on parental and teacher report, either in interviews or checklists (Breen & Fiedler, 1996). While valuable, these kinds of data are prone to the inevitable distortions inherent in asking somebody what is wrong with somebody else. While many parents are quite objective about their own children, others err in either of two directions. Some "need" their children to be more troubled than they in fact are (Kelly & Loader, 1997), while others deny that their children have any problems at all, despite overwhelming evidence to the contrary. Using the MUG in conjunction with indirect methods insures a more balanced assessment approach. MUG testing is efficient (the MUG takes 20 to 40 minutes to give) and the child finds the MUG experience compelling, because children like to play.

Preparation for Narrative Therapy

White's (1995) valuable new approach to both individual child therapy and family therapy derives from identical traditions in philosophy as does the MUG. Both approaches share a belief that subjectively significant events that are remembered, and subsequently reconstructed into narrative form, play a central role in the construction of the self. For children, the MUG allows the therapist to concentrate the search for such guiding narratives that have steered lives in unhappy and troubled pathways. Narrative therapy depends on the early identification of the problem story; the MUG is an efficient aid in this process. Narrative therapy then proceeds to locate exceptional instances where the person managed to function in a preferred manner, incompatible with the problem story, and suggestive of an alternative narrative of self. It would be worthwhile studying MUG stories from this point of view, inquiring as to whether besides revealing the problem story in considerable depth, the MUG could also be of use in the search for exceptions that support a preferred way of being. This is not a simple matter, because some children appear over-idealizing on the MUG, as if it were possible for children to err in the direction of belief in a perfect self in a perfect world. In a sense such children have no problem story, yet still find adaptation to the real world very problematic.

A Case Example: Selected MUG Stories from an 11-Year-Old

With this background, a set of MUG stories is presented so the kinds of stories children invent will become clear and so that the MUG code can be explained in more detail. Perhaps it is best to read one's first MUG like a naturalistic inquirer, open to a child's own personal constructs, however different in content or coherence they may at first appear.

    Cheryl (not her real name) was an articulate 11-year-old who was tested as a practice exercise by a student who was learning to give the MUG. The interpretation of her stories will be based purely on the test, because nothing else is known about her. This is good general practice for anyone who is first becoming familiar with the procedure. The MUG should not be viewed as a test for disclosing the child's actual relationships with actual others. Instead, it reveals something deeper: the child's overall conception of whole classes of persons—mothers, fathers, teachers, and peers or siblings.

Only a selected set of stories is included. This was for reasons of length. However, the stories included were the most important ones in arriving at an interpretation. In the first reading, one should ignore the coding shown to the right and immerse oneself in the stories. That way one can form an interpretation of what Cheryl was conveying before being influenced by the interpretation given here. It would be advisable to write down this interpretation after finishing her stories and see how it compares with the one given after the protocol. In the protocol, "Q" identifies the female tester and "G" designates the girl's stories.

Cheryl's MUG Protocol   **Coding Category**

Card: 5

Q. Number five.

G. Here the father, like, he's a carpenter and he likes making things
   and so now *he just finished making this desk for his daughter* and   VF+f
   she's watching him while he's making the last things on that and
   he's taking it into her room. She's ... and she wanted the desk for
   a long time but nobody ever had time to do it ... buy her one, and
   so her father finally decided to make her one. Then when he
   makes her one it *isn't that good,* so when she's using it one day   U–
   the drawer falls apart and then she goes back to the father, and   Repeat
   then he says: *"I can't do any better."* And so then she doesn't have   Repeat
   her desk again. She finally, in the end, *her father buys her one.*   Repeat

Q. I guess I'd like a little more of her feelings about that.

G. Well, *she doesn't think her father's very good* because her older   DV–f
   sister has a desk and hers is really good and it has everything, and
   it has ... um ... everything and so when she doesn't have one, and
   so when her father makes her one, and it isn't good, she *feels*   NA–
   really bad and so, when in the end her father buys her one, she
   becomes happy.

Card: 7

Q. Number seven.

G. The girl has homework to do and ... and ... she ... O.K., *she*   H–
   broke her leg and she ... she doesn't ... and she looks out of her
   window and she sees all the people playing outside and she can't
   play because of her leg is broken and all she has is her book, and
   so she's reading her book but she doesn't want to because she
   wants to play like all the other kids are playing but *she can't.*
   Then later ... later on her leg gets better and she, and while her
   leg was broken *she read a lot of books* 'cause there was nothing   Repeat
   else for her to do and so she got like a little prize for doing it. And   R+
   then afterwards *she got to play with the other kids* and so figured   V+o
   it was O.K. because then ... then: "It's O.K. if I don't play with
   the kids just for a little time, I still got ... I got ... I still got extra
   credit and I got a prize and now I can get to play with them."

Card: 8

Q. Here's number eight.

G. O.K., the girl got in trouble at school and she got in big trouble and she ... and she didn't tell her mother and so ... and so her mother, and so the teacher calls her mother to tell her, and so the mother was writing down what it was and the teacher wanted to see her and have an appointment with her. Then the *girl started crying* 'cause she didn't want the mother to know what she did at school, so she's like trying to figure out something to say so that the teacher wouldn't, so her mother wouldn't get her, um ... get her in trouble, or anything like that, and so when her mother stops talking on the phone she says that she didn't mean to do it and her mother says: "You didn't mean to do what?" and 'cause it wasn't ... she thought it was the teacher on the phone but it wasn't. So then ... so then, when she tells her mother that she did get into trouble 'cause her mother forces her to tell her what she had done at school and *she had hurt another girl* and so she got in trouble, but she wouldn't have got into trouble if she hadn't said anything.

    NA–

    A–

Q. She hurt another girl?

G. Uh-huh. *She got in a fight with the other girl.*

    Repeat

Q. Uh-huh, so let me have a few more of her feelings, one about getting in a fight and two about this whole business with her mother, getting caught.

G. O.K., she didn't ... she didn't mean to, she didn't ... she didn't think this person ... *the other girl started it* like she knew that she shouldn't have done anything back, she should have just told on her, but she thought if she tells on her then everyone will think she's a tattle-tale and the other girl wanted ... said: *"Are you chicken?"* and so she started a fight with her. And what else?

    DF-o

    Repeat

Q. I also wanted to know, um, she kind of slipped and so she got caught, and how she felt about that.

G. Well she, her mother, when her mother heard what happened *she went and talked to the other girl ... the other girl's mother,* but she still grounded this girl because she thought that even if a person starts a fight with you, you shouldn't finish it, so *she got grounded for a week.*

    VF+m

    Repeat

Q. O.K., O.K. fine.

Card: 9

Q. Here's number nine.

G. O.K., um, this girl ... this girl ... this girl is alone and she doesn't have anybody to play with because *nobody likes her* after school because if she's ... *she's smarter than anyone else* and she always, like *she always has the answers* for everything and *nobody likes her because she's smart.* And so she, at first *she wanted to ask these girls if she could play with them* and they said

    DF-o,
    I-,
    Repeat

    V+o

only three people can play, and so they didn't let her play with
them. Then she was walking over to here and they were talking
about her and *they said: "Yeah, you can play" but they wanted to*   Repeat
do something to her. So when they started playing, *they* threw the   Repeat
ball really hard to her and *they made her fall* and so she got up   H-
again and she said: "It's O.K., *I know you didn't mean to do it."*   Repeat
But they did mean to do it, and so *they did it again to her* and *this*   Repeat
time she got hurt and so then they took her to the office and they
said: "We didn't mean to do it" and *she thought it was true,* but   Repeat
they had meant to do it. And so then she went home and her
mother said: "Who did that to you?" and she said the girls did it
to her, and then *the mother went talking to the girl's mother* and   VF+m
the mothers said … the mothers said: "Well, my girl wouldn't do
anything like that." But her girl was … so the girl who did it
didn't get into trouble. The girl got really hurt and…

Q. Is this the girl who did it, the one who's holding the ball in the
part we can see here?
G. Yeah.

Q. O.K., and so she didn't get in trouble.
G. Uh-huh, because her and her mother are really like … um …
they're kind of like show-offs, like the mother always buys her
things and she goes to school and shows off with them and she…

Q. So her daughter can do no wrong, then.
G. Right.

Q. Is that the end of the story? She's just left feeling awful, I guess,
then?
G. And then she's … and then this boy here –

Q. The one sitting down on the bench?
G. Yeah, later, the next few weeks, this is later, she sees him sitting
there and she, like, she has a brother and she doesn't like her
brother but, like, he's the only boy here and he doesn't have any
friends, and I don't have any friends either, so even if he is a boy
I can still be friends with him, and so *they become friends after,*   VF+o
like, the girl's leg becomes better.

Q. After what becomes better?
G. The girl's—because when they made her fall, her leg got a little…

Q. Oh, after her leg gets better. Oh, I see. O.K., fine.

Card: 10

Q. O.K., here's number ten.
G. Um … O.K, it's a Sunday afternoon and the girl just came back
… they just came back from church and they, and she had some
church homework to do. And *so she did it* and her father was read-   R+

ing the newspaper and *her father had an article in the newspaper* RO+
and he read it to his wife and they started talking about it, and the
girl started listening and she forgot about doing her homework.
And so she started listening and she didn't do her homework.
Later, she didn't do her homework later in the week, she didn't
have time to do it. So when next week came to give it, she could-
n't give it to the lady, to the ... um ... to her Sunday school
teacher. And so *she got in trouble* and she told that to her father H-
and her father said that he didn't need to ... he didn't ... *he didn't*
mean to get her messed up and so then ... so then ... um ... I VF+f
don't know what happens next.

Q. Ha, ha, ha, ha, this is the first time. You certainly, you almost
always know right away. Take your time.

G. The next several ... next ... her Sunday school teacher gives her
the homework again and she gives her more homework again and
she goes into her room to do it so nobody can bother her, but her
pet comes and she rips all her papers and so she goes to her Sunday school teacher the next week and she says: "My pet ripped all
my papers" and *the teacher doesn't believe her,* like, because, DF-o
like, last week she had another reason and she always has reasons.
And so she writes home and told her mother and father that. And
her father said: "Well, you didn't do it, the cat did it" and so *her* Repeat
father went and talked to the Sunday school teacher, and she said)
it was O.K. and *so she did her homework. She locked the door of*)Repeat
her room and she locked the cat out of her room, and she did all)
of her homework and nobody bothered her.

Q. O.K.

Card: 11

Q. Here's number eleven.

G. O.K., they have a test and everybody is doing a test but the girl is
thinking about something, because the day before *her dog got run* U-
over and *he died* and she didn't want to do her math because she LON-
was thinking of the dog, and *she was really sad* and she didn't NA-
want to think of anything and she didn't want to do her math and
she didn't want to do anything. She was just gazing and thinking
of her dog. Then the teacher ... then the teacher, like, when everybody was done with the test, she was still thinking and she was
gazing straight ahead and when the teacher started talking, the
teacher asked her a question and *she just kept on looking and she* DIS-
didn't listen, and then the teacher asked her again and she looked
up like she was kind of startled and the teacher said: "What happened?" And the girl didn't say anything and so then, right then
the bell rang and so everybody left, and *she told the girl to stay.* VF+o
And the teacher said: "What happened?" And the girl told her

what happened and the teacher said that she had a dog and the dog just had pups and so *the teacher said that she could have one of the dogs but still she had to finish her homework and that when ... she had to study for the test, the next test that they had.*

)
)Repeat
)

Q. She could have one of the dogs?

G. Yeah, one of the dogs that the teacher's dog had.

Q. I see.

G. And that made her feel better.

Card: 12

Q. Here's number twelve. This is the last one.

G. O.K., the girl just got home and she had her report card and she tried to slip up the stairs to her room.

Q. I'm, sorry, she tried to slip...

G. O.K., *she had a bad report card.*   SF−

Q. Oh.

G. And she tried to slip up to her room but her mother heard her footsteps because the ... um ... the stairway, um ... creaked. And so she came down to the kitchen and her mother said: "What ... why did you go?" and so the girl hid her report card in her back-pack and her cat came, and he came into her back-pack and he took it...

Q. The cat?

G. No, no, not the cat—the baby, her baby.

Q. Her little baby brother or sister.

G. And he came and he started playing with the things in her back-pack and he took out the report card, and he started waving it all around, and then the mother saw it and she was cooking but she had to go and get something, and she saw it and she took it, and then she put the little baby outside, and *she started talking*   VF+m
to the girl, and she said: "Why didn't you tell me about it?"
And she said: "Because *I knew you wouldn't help me, because*
you never help me when I have homework." And so, like, *the*   DF−m
mother got, like, really sad, and so she said that she would help   DF−m
her with her homework from now on, so she wouldn't get a bad grade.

Q. Oh, good. And how did the daughter feel about that?

G. And then *the girl felt good* that her brother had done it, and she   PA+
ran out and *she got her brother a little present* because she was   V+o
really happy because of him her mother was gonna help her, and   I−
she would never get a bad grade again, and then she came home   I−
and gave it to him. And *he was happy and she was happy.*

Clinical Interpretation

At this point, many will have reached an interpretation. The author's interpretation follows.

If one had to write a clinical report about Cheryl, one might interpret these stories in much the same way as the main character (MC) in Story 9. She is portrayed as someone nobody likes because she is cleverer than her peers. Indeed these clever and well-composed stories suggest a child with exceptional symbolic-narrative ability. Other children may find her "too grown-up" for them, and keep their distance. Exactly to point, at the end of Story 9, Cheryl breaks the story frame momentarily to say that she `has no friends' herself. In Story 9 she also portrays the MC as someone who is vulnerable and easily made the fool of by other children's pranks. Surprisingly, her MC does not want to recognize that others are out to get her, and her parent's efforts to help are "morally correct" (see Stories 8 and 10 also) but seem to lack much direct contact with the main character. Whatever her parents' actual investment in their child, parental figures are perceived as ineffectual. But is this so unusual in a girl perhaps near the start of adolescence? Surely this issue would need to be investigated further in therapy before a decision is reached.

Is Cheryl depressed? The most direct expression of the theme of "loss," a traditional component of depression (Bemporad & Wilson, 1978), is given in Story 11. The MC's dog gets run over and it dies. Here Cheryl may be displacing her own core sadness and emotional vulnerability onto a dog. In many other places the MC expresses helplessness herself. Clinically, her sadness, helplessness, and loneliness are at the heart of this interpretation. Cheryl's stories suggest a sad young person who is low in self-esteem. The clinician might consider cognitive-behavioral therapies known to help adolescents on the depressive spectrum.

All clinical interpretation involves selection and emphasis of some material and ignoring other material. Why, for example, was the material in Stories 9 and 11 emphasized over the fighting with another girl in Story 8? For one thing the fighting in Story 8 is rationalized; it was the other girl that started it. If Cheryl has aggressive wishes (and who does not), she keeps them under wraps. A second reason is that, having read all 12 stories, the author knows that this is the only time that direct aggression was mentioned in the entire protocol! Were therapy to be offered to Cheryl, the therapist would be advised to remember that there is deep anger behind most depressions that would need to be addressed in the work.

MUG interpretation allows one to continue to try to understand Cheryl's *perception* of the psychosocial *origins* of her feelings. Clearly, her immediate concern is that her peers do not like her; she has no friends. While this must be addressed in therapy, object relations theory (Greenberg & Mitchell, 1983) has a great influence here: the child enters peer relations with earlier "internal working models" of others. These models were developed at home in relation to primary attachment figures and they influence the child's later success or failure in peer relations. Thus, in listening to MUG stories, one pays particular attention to the child's perception of parental figures.

In Story 12 the MC accuses the mother of never helping the daughter when she has homework. The mother responds with sadness and a promise to be more helpful from now on. Her maternal figure seems to accept that there may be some truth in what was asserted about her lack of availability. Story 5 is also relevant here: the girl wanted a desk but "nobody ever had time to do it." Here the culprit is her father, so it may not be reading too much into the story to suggest that Cheryl *may be* raising a central emotional concern here about parental availability or she may be just reaching adolescence a little early.

Remember that the MUG is about *perceptions* rather than about *factual family reality*. In reality her parents may have been available to all their children and never favored one over the other. Yet MUG interpretation is based on the belief that perceptions affect child mental health. Specifically, her perception of her parents' availability and preferences contributes to her sadness, her belief that her sister has more help in homework and a better desk than she does. In reality there may be no sister at all! Whatever the reality, the MUG has done its job because it is a technique for forming clinical hypotheses about a child's perceptions and beliefs. The therapist is alerted to the area of perceived parental emotional availability as a possible cause of Cheryl's unhappiness and her perception that she is not as worthy as others to receive things and that others are unfairly treating her.

Characterological Problems and the MUG Code

It is important for the reader to understand that while the MUG pictures are very neutral and open to many interpretive possibilities, *the MUG positive and negative codes were developed by the author in an effort to help locate serious childhood problems,* when these are conceptualized as "disorders of the self." With the more objective scoring, there is a gain in specificity but a loss of theoretical neutrality. *The MUG codes derive from Sullivan, Kohut, and Fairbairn, all followers of the psychoanalytic tradition.* Kohut's (1977) theory of the bipolar self was important. In this theory a healthy self can develop from either the narcissistic or idealizing expectations of the attachment figures. Equally important was Sullivan's (1953) concepts of the good and bad self and Winnicott's (1958) concept of the false self. For Sullivan, the key to mothering was the presence or absence of maternal anxiety. The mother's anxious states were experienced as "bad mother" and the mother's nonanxious states as "good mother." He proposed that both aspects of mothering become incorporated into beliefs about the self as "good me" versus "bad me." It was the ratio of "good me" to "bad me" that gave a person their positive, negative, mixed character. Winnicott proposed that poor parenting, marked by poor timing of responsiveness, resulted in a fragmentation of the self into a "true self" (which becomes detached and atrophied) and a "false self" (which provides the illusion of a personal existence). By interrelating these various psychoanalytic concepts of the self, Mueller (1996a) constructed a model of the emerging core self as a simple two-dimensional diamond, a little crystal that represents the child's core self. In this model, there are four possible "false selves" that emerge in early development, and a fifth type called the disoriented self. Each is thought to relate to serious dysfunction in interpersonal functioning and each character type is thought to be indexed by different MUG codes. Temperamental or genetic factors are thought to play a large role in the narcissistic-idealizing dimension of the self, whereas experiential factors are thought to play a large role in the good-bad dimension of the self. Thus, only through both biological and experiential knowledge can the emerging self be adequately understood. The timing of trauma from abuse or other causes is also thought to be crucial in the nature of the emerging self. Severe abuse and neglect prior to the second birthday with no formation of an adequate primary attachment, is thought to generate the disoriented self; whereas the breakdown of an originally adequate attachment relationship between 2 and 6 years is seen as central in formation of the four personality disorders, each with a dominant false self. Table 22–2 introduces each of these distortions of the self, which have life-long consequences for the child if not redressed before the crystallization

Table 22–2.   Character problems in the child's emerging core self

Name of Early Malformations of the Core Self	Region of the False Self	Psychiatric or Psychoanalytic Equivalent Name	MUG Codes Indexing (see Table 22–1)
Disoriented Self	Fragmented Self	Schizoid Disorders of Childhood	DIS–, SO–, SO–
Worthless Self	Bad Self	Childhood Depression	H–, U–, LON–, NU–
Worthless Other	Bad Other	"Acting Out"/Conduct Disorder	D–, DU–, A–, NA–
Striving Self	Perfect Self	Narcissistic Personality	I–, VF+
Idealized Other	Perfect Others	Dependent Personality	IO–, V+

of the self concept or character of the person is complete in later childhood. Table 22–2 also shows which MUG codes were developed to index each core self type. Located early enough in life, the crystal of the self remains malleable, and easier to change through good parenting and corrective therapy.

Quantitative Scoring: The MUG Negative and Positive Codes

Most therapists will probably limit their interpretation of the MUG to narrative summaries for reports and therapy, such as that described for Cheryl above. On the other hand, this level of interpretation will vary with the therapist's training and beliefs. The reader's interpretation of Cheryl's central problems may well have differed from the one presented here. For this reason, and with an eye toward validating the MUG as a measure of childhood problems, a set of scoring categories were developed, attempting to capture the forms of serious childhood disorders of the self.

For example, it was hypothesized that depressed children would tell more stories with sad story endings, expressions of loneliness, and suicidal ideation than other children. For Cheryl one can observe how her stories were actually coded as shown by the brief code symbols to the right of the text. All the symbols are followed by a + or – sign. Negative codes relate to things that characterize the stories of troubled children. The specific meaning of the positive codes is still not fully understood. Normal children tend to use more positive codes in their stories, but sometimes very high positive codes may index overidealization of the other or the self.

Each theme is recorded only once during a given story, and thus the score for each code can range from 0 to 12 because there are 12 cards on the MUG. To understand the kind of material indexed by each code, please consult the list of *MUG positive and negative codes* in Table 22–1 and the full code itself in the appendix

Table 22–1 shows that most individual and summary MUG codes show satisfactory "interrater reliability." This means that if one rater finds instances of, for example, "valuing others" in five stories, then a second independent rater should find about 5 instances also.

Cheryl's score on each of the MUG codes is shown in column 8 of Table 22–3. The first instance of each code in a story is underlined in the transcript text. Later instances of each code are shown in italics. Her most common theme, in 10 of the 12 stories, was the positive theme of mother, father, or others valuing the MC. To understand how Cheryl's scores compare with other children, look at columns 5 and 6 in Table 22–3. They show the mean

Table 22–3. MUG construct and criterion validity and a scored case of a child (Cheryl) with MAS 2 problems

1 MUG Additive Score (MAS)	2 Sum the following primary codes	3 Also note the following secondary codes	4 Average loading of this code on MAS, 4 samples, combined N= 621.	5 Troubled children from dysfunctional families	6 Children functioning well in school without known problems	7 Signif. T test comparison	8 Cheryl's scores, summing 12 stories
MAS 1: Story Disorientation and Drive Expression							
DIS–	Story disoriented, incoherent		.74	5.9	1.0	.0001	1
SO–	Sexual oral expression or indulgence		.74	3.9	0.3	.0001	0
SD–	Suicide/Death expressions		.69	0.8	0.1	.03	0
Sum				**10.6**	**1.4**	**.0001**	**1**
H–		MC helpless, vulnerable	.46	—	—	—	3
U–		Vulnerability in others	.44	—	—	—	3
MAS 2: Story Loneliness, Loss and Sad Ending							
LON–	MC lonely, loss in story, sad story ending		.67	1.4	1.1	n.s.	3
U–	Vulnerability in others, possessions		.55	2.5	1.6	.04	3
H–	MC helpless, vulnerable, afraid		.51	6.3	2.8	.0001	3
Sum				**10.2**	**5.5**	**.01**	**9**
DF–		Devaluing from others	.33	—	—	—	8
NU–*		MC feels sad or bad or unhappy—	.34	—	—	—	4
MAS 3: Story Defiance and Devaluing							
D–	MC defies, acts bad, intentionally naughty		.63	7.3	0.7	.001	0
DV–	MC devalues those in authority		.58	1.2	0.9	n.s	1
DF–	Devaluing from others in authority		.55	4.5	1.4	.0001	8
NA–*	MC feels angry or mad		.55	3.4	2.0	.003	0

(continued)

Table 22–3 (Continued)

1 MUG Additive Score (MAS)	2 Sum the following primary codes	3 Also note the following secondary codes	4 Average loading of this code on MAS, 4 samples, combined N=621.	5 Troubled children from dysfunctional families	6 Children functioning well in school without known problems	7 Signif. T test comparison	8 Cheryl's scores, summing 12 stories
MAS 3: Story Defiance and Devaluing							
Sum				**16.4**	**5.0**	**.0001**	**9**
SM–		MC not motivated for school	.44	0.7	0.7	n.s	1
SF–		School failure	.22	0.8	0.8	n.s	3
[A–]		Aggression in Story	New code-split from SO–; no data	No data	No data	—	1
[PP–]		MC is punished using physical means (smacking)	New code-split from DF–; no data	No data	No data	—	0
MAS 4: Positive Story Features							
V+	MC values Mother, Father or Others		.69	1.6	1.4	n.s	8
VF+	Mother, Father or Others value MC		.77	2.9	3.3	n.s	10
SM+	MC motivated for school, learning		.59	1.4	0.9	.05	0
SA+	School achievement or success		.76	1.0	1.3	n.s	1
PA+	MC feels happy or good etc.		.50	1.3	3.4	.001	1
Sum				**8.2**	**10.3**	**.001**	**20**
R+	MC resourceful			No data	No data	—	3
RO+	Resourcefulness in others			No data	No data	—	1

* The code about negative emotion has recently been split into two: NA– for angry or mad feelings and NU– for unhappy or sad feelings, hoping they will divide between MAS 2 and 3. Regrettably these data were from before the split and so represent a mix of the two emotional expressions

scores for troubled children from dysfunctional families and healthy comparison children (data from D'Alessio, M., Schimmenti, V., Cherubini, A. & Mueller, E., 1996). Looking at the numbers, you can see that Cheryl was particularly high on only one negative code called "Others devalue MC." She saw herself as devalued by her agemates in 6 stories, and by her parents in only the two instances discussed earlier. The numbers suggest we must be careful in not overemphasizing parental devaluing in her personal constructs. This appears to be her central emotional problem, a finding seemingly in agreement with her statement on Card 9 that "I don't have any friends either."

MUG Validity

The data comparing troubled and normal children on the specific MUG codes (columns 5 and 6 in Table 22–3) have an importance beyond that of understanding individual children such as Cheryl. For the MUG codes to be valid, they should discriminate between troubled and normal children. The validity data in columns 5 to 7 come from the most recent validity sample gathered in Italy using the MUG (D'Alessio et al., 1996, p. 221). It included 39 troubled children and 51 normal controls. It is clear from the table that, as expected, on average troubled children score higher on most MUG negative codes than do normal children. The seventh column of Table 22–3 shows exactly which codes significantly separated the groups. Careful study of this table shows that the negative codes separated the two groups more reliably than did the positive codes. In other words, the negative codes showed better "criterion validity" where the criterion was that troubled and normal children should score differently on all MUG codes.

Dimopoulou (1998) has compared scores on the MUG negative code with scores on the Child Behavior Checklist (CBCL) (Achenbach, 1991). The latter is a well-validated parent checklist concerning childhood problems. The two measures agreed about child status in 71% (46/65) of the cases studied. Dimopoulou went on to examine the instances of disagreement between the two measures. She found that 8 of the 10 children who were high on the MUG but low on the CBCL were scored as showing story disorientation in at least one story. As this code often signals childhood thought problems, the low CBCL score could indicate that parents do not recognize, or deny this type of problem in their children. None of these children had elevated scores on the "thought problem" subscale of the CBCL.

For a psychological test to be acceptable, it must demonstrate "construct" as well as criterion validity. This means that the test can identify important underlying constructs, in this case constructs relevant to understanding childhood problems or disorders. Perhaps a child whose main character is frequently vulnerable (H–) will also tell stories whose characters are sad (NU–) and lonely (LON–). If many children show the same pattern, the statistical technique called factor analysis should uncover that pattern. D'Alessio et al (1996) and Mueller and Ginsburg (in press) have gathered MUG stories from a total of 621 children from Italy and the United States. Consistently and in both countries, using factor analysis, it was found that the codes grouped themselves together in the same way in sample after sample. When one understands the factor-based constructs underlying the MUG, it becomes possible to summarize Cheryl's problems more succinctly and reliably.

Table 22–3 organizes the codes according to the constructs from factor analysis. Each is called a *MUG Additive Scale* (MAS). One simply adds together a child's score on each of the codes that measure an underlying factor (or dimension) in the data. These underlying factors represent the *empirically valid* categories of childhood troubles, when the starting point is the MUG individual codes from Table 22–1 and the appendix. In other words, while Table 22–2 hypothesized five kinds of important disturbances in childhood, factor analysis of the MUG only located three kinds of disturbances (MAS 1 to 3). The type of factor analysis procedure used here (called "Varimax rotation") also ensures that the kinds of problems located were independent and separate, one from the other. In other words, the presence of one of these problems gives one no information about the other problems being either present or absent. Each problem type is an empirically separate entity in itself, and each entity is comprised of no less than three separate codes. In advance, it was not understood that these particular codes would go together with such consistency across samples emanating from different societies.

The fourth column in Table 22–3 shows the factor "loadings", in other words, how much each specific code contributed to its underlying factor. Factor loadings are like correlations; the closer to 1.0, the closer is a given code to precisely indexing the underlying factor. We used a loading of .50 or greater to decide which codes to include in each MAS. In the third column, Table 22–3 lists other codes that may also be important in a factor because their average loading, while below .50, was still statistically significantly related to the factor in several samples. For example, the third column shows that the vulnerability codes were somewhat related to MAS 1 themes, as well as being the central codes indexing MAS 2. In other words, just knowing that a child is expressing vulnerability in his or her story does not tell one whether the child is merely sad and unhappy like Cheryl or may suffer from the central fragmentation of the self of MAS 1. Both kinds of syndromes are associated with expressions of helplessness.

There may be no single, mutually exclusive word in natural language that corresponds to each factor construct from factor analysis. The closest one can come is to look at the codes that contribute to it, and try to give a summary label to the category. The four MUG Additive Scales appear to index the following:

- **MAS 1. Fragmenting self-problems**
  - Story disorientation and incoherence
  - Sexual/oral indulgence–drive fixation
  - Wish to kill self

The term "fragmenting self" is used because reality seems to be coming "unstuck" in the content of these stories. They are incoherent, make no sense, or are blatantly strange or bizarre. Children who are high on this scale may be giving up hope of positive attachment relationships and are identifying instead with immediate pleasure seeking and substitute gratification (Fairbairn, 1952).

From an attachment perspective such children are likely to be described as "avoidant." They reject positive relationships as bogus and are likely to use disdain or contempt in their portrayal of their parents. It is these children who talk about their main character wanting to die.

Without help, these children may be at risk of withdrawal, psychosis, and possibly suicide. However at this time, this is merely conjecture: there have been no long-term follow-up studies of children taking the MUG.

- **MAS 2. Depressive problems**
  - MC vulnerable
  - Vulnerability in others
  - Stories with expressions of loneliness, loss, and/or sad endings. If one had to summarize these stories using a few words they would be "anxious and depressed."

From an attachment perspective, these may be children where attachment relations were adequate all across the period of core self-formation, ending at around the sixth birthday. However, on achieving the age range of the MUG test (7–12) something went wrong. Perhaps a key attachment was lost through divorce. Perhaps a previously available attachment figure became distracted through work or the birth of other children. Perhaps an idealized other did or said something that called into question the core of idealization. Perhaps a previously strong parent, through no fault of his or her own, became chronically ill and vulnerable. Any of these changes could result in the changed story expression captured by MAS 2.

- **MAS 3. Externalizing problems**
  - MC defies authority through misbehavior
  - MC devalues others
  - MC is devalued by others

From an object relations perspective children high on this score are those having a "worthless other disorder." (Mueller, 1996a). They presumably start as children with externalizing personalities, being very socially oriented and not too introspective. But then they experience too much rejection in the form of physical hitting and too little attention in families with many children. Additionally their idealized others collapse around them when, for example, a seemingly tough father's alcohol addiction becomes more and more obvious. Under these conditions, the bad other is transferred onto teachers or the police to protect some semblance of the idealized parental images from early childhood. But additionally, the "bad other" has really been there all the time and is internalized as "bad self"; but this part of the self is completely repressed and out of awareness, however much it is also consonant with the bad actions against others.

In research terms, these children are the best-understood in clinical child psychology. There is evidence to show that they are at risk of conduct disorder and juvenile offenses. (Loeber, 1990).

These three negative summary factor scores have emerged in four independent samples, two in Italy and two in America. They indicate that the MUG codes have acceptable construct validity for these empirical constructs. However, it should also be noted that only three of the five types of major childhood character problems proposed in theory were empirically validated. Either "striving self" and "idealized other" malformations of the core self do not exist or the code is not yet sensitive in locating them.

- **MAS 4. Positive Core Self.** All five positive codes formed a single MAS. Valuing others, feeling valued by others, expressing happy emotions in stories, valuing school, and making positive statements about learning achievements all factored together (D'Alessio et al., 1996, Table 2, p. 207). More research is needed about the positive codes because they do not discriminate between the troubled and normal children as well as one might have hoped. Healthy children did use happy emotional expressions in their stories more frequently than did the troubled children.

The most unexpected result of this work on construct validity was that two kinds of internalizing problems were located in children as separate and independent entities (MAS 1 and 2). The most exhaustive checklist-based research on childhood problems appears to equate the concept of "internalizing problems" with MAS 2 depressive problems (Achenbach, 1991). His "withdrawal" and "anxiety-depression" scales were found in parent-reported data about child problems. The present results suggest that the children who have turned the most harshly against the self are the MAS 1 children whose drive spillover and internal turmoil may not be as evident in parent-reported checklists. The active expression of suicidal ideation in the stories, often associated with depressive problems, is here associated with themes of story disorientation and drive expression (MAS 1). This finding could be of importance in understanding a group of troubled children particularly at risk of self-harm and adaptive functioning problems. It must be nearly impossible to form adequate peer relations when one's very thought is disoriented and impulse-driven.

Seemingly there are two kinds of attacks on the self as expressed in MAS 1 and 2. Why do some children show one and some the other? The answer may lie not in the genes (which merely points the child in the direction of internalization), but rather in developmental trauma. Early attack on the coherence of the self—say through abuse or neglect in the preschool years—may provide the road to MAS 1. The self-structures have not yet crystallized and "the diamond of the self" (Mueller, 1996a) is still vulnerable to fragmentation with consequent turning to pleasure seeking. Later assaults on the character after the age of 5 or so do not have the destructive power of earlier assaults because the self is better formed, more crystallized. Instead loneliness, hopelessness, and depression are the outcome in children with healthier core selves from their early years. The positive core self resists fragmentation of the self because early love and valuing made it strong in self-belief and provided basic trust in others. This gives the child the will to fight on, hoping that one day things will be as wonderful as when he or she was little.

And so, in describing depressive problems, the discussion has come full circle, and back to Cheryl. MUG scoring identifies her as someone with MAS 2 problems. Table 22–3, column 8, shows that only one MAS 1 theme occurs; clearly MAS 1 is not her form of problem expression, despite the presence of vulnerability expressions in her stories. In contrast, her MAS 2 score of 9 is like that of troubled children and could be considered much higher if one includes the "devaluing from others" code here as well. The MAS 3 score also looks high at first glance. Her 9 score is higher than the 5 score found as average for normal children. But observe that 8 of these 9 themes were from her frequent use of the theme "being devalued by others." There is little or none of the defiance (D–) and devaluing of others (DV–) expected in an angry externalizing child.

From Table 22–3, one can observe that factor analysis found that DF- (devaluing from others) contributed to both externalizing (MAS 3) and depressive (MAS 2) problems. In Cheryl's data, if we "interpret" the DF– results as being part of MAS2, then the quantitative interpretation clearly attributes her troubles to MAS 2 problems. Notice, however, that even when using summary scores, some considered interpretation of their meaning was needed! The caution is to look not only at sum scores, but instead, to examine where the totals come from in the pattern of individual code scores.

Cheryl's most deviant score was on the positive codes (MAS 4). Why should Cheryl mention valuing others and being valued back by others almost twice as often as the average healthy child? Is she somehow "hyperhealthy"? If you look back at the stories, you will see that much of the time her mother is rushing about trying to be supportive (VF+) by talking with the parents of hostile agemates. Cheryl's main story character is doing something similar with her peers, trying to be accepted by repeatedly asking to join with other children (V+). All these actions contribute to the exceptionally high MAS 4 score. But things never work out—the other children reject her overtures (thus all the DF–) and in the last story the main character gives her mother the message, "You never help me."

Why is Cheryl's positive sum score so high? Rather than just indexing a positive self-concept, it also may index a "wish fulfillment" quality to the stories. It reflects her social neediness and her constant reaching out to others whom she *believes* just don't much care about her. Should this be called a "defense mechanism" or a "striving" from her early healthy core self, trying to reestablish what has been lost, namely, a perception of caring attention from "self-objects"? (Kohut, 1977). Kohut defines self-objects as those whose continued caring and love is necessary for preservation of the healthy self.

To summarize, Cheryl is properly diagnosed as having depressive problems best indexed by the story material contributing to MAS 2 codes, expressions of loss, loneliness, vulnerability, and vulnerability in others. The fact that her positive score was too high may help in our understanding of why the positive codes do not separate healthy and troubled children as clearly as the negative codes. They may commonly represent a kind of wish fulfillment story for a reality that the child has lost (like Cheryl) or for one that she has never had.

In terms of therapy, Cheryl could be offered either cognitive behavioral therapy (CBT) working at an individual level or solution-focused family interventions. Concerning the latter, one could investigate Cheryl's perceptions of the family further in the family meeting, and especially how she is perceived by others in the family. Depending on the outcome, one could consider strategic moves attempting to shift individual social perceptions.

Conclusions About MAS 2 as an Index of Significant Child Problems

For some years there has been doubt about the status of MAS 2. In one North American sample (unpublished) it did not separate troubled from normal children at all! However, the recent Italian data, summarized in Table 22–3 (see columns 5–7), where it did discriminate—together with evidence from past studies and from Cheryl's protocol itself—indicate that MAS 2 is a valid indicator of childhood problems. In this regard, consider the following four points:

1. It is an accepted type of child problem as identified in parent-based behavior checklists, for example, the *Child Behavior Checklist* (Achenbach, 1991).
2. In research MAS 2 scores were significantly higher in children with lower self-esteem according to traditional and accepted measures of self-esteem (Watanabe, 1991).
3. Children who are unhappy, lonely, and depressed often may carry on and be less likely to be referred to mental health centers. For this reason, they are found more

often in "healthy control groups" than children who are totally falling apart emotionally (MAS 1) or causing problems for other people (MAS 3).

4. Cheryl more or less admitted that she has a problem in her statement "I have no friends." There is good research to show that children without friends are at risk for later mental health problems, and this finding is specific to children who have reached the age of 11 (Sundby & Kreyberg, 1968).

Some Problems with the MUG and Need for Further Research

One of the most noticeable difficulties in administering the MUG is that some children tire before reaching the last story. Therefore ways need to be explored for shortening the test for some children while maintaining the test's level of reliability and validity.

Another concern is that little is known about the differences between the home and school pictures. More specifically, the question remains as to whether they contribute similar or different information to total scores and diagnostic groupings. After this research has been conducted, it may be possible to advise on how to give only some of the cards and still proceed with valid scoring. Even now, those not using the MUG codes could give a shortened version based on their own clinical selection of the cards. The TAT has been used in this way for many years.

In the appendix, one of the last summary codes is called "Fantasy Failure" (FF–). This is really a "noncooperation" or "emotional blocking" code. When children score high here, they were unwilling, unable, or afraid to invent MUG stories. Therefore, when FF– is high, the validity of the scoring of the rest of the code is doubtful. However, clinical experience suggests that high FF– is a worrying sign in itself and suggests that the child may be too afraid to allow himself or herself access to what is inside. Additional assessments such as the Rorschach or Family Relations Test should be given to children scoring high in FF–. The Rorschach merely asks the client to describe an ink blot. Clients who become defensive about self-revelation on the MUG may unintentionally reveal important trends in emotion and thought from their Rorschach responses.

Summary

Through the use of a detailed example, the MUG has been shown to offer an efficient method for understanding children's "internal worlds"—their problems and strengths, their fears and aspirations. Furthermore, the MUG code for the more precise diagnosis of childhood problems has been shown to have satisfactory construct and criterion validity. Used in conjunction with checklists, it offers a powerful method for the clinical understanding of what is wrong with any child. The MUG should be of interest to those who believe that play offers a crucial way of understanding children's troubled minds (Irwin, 1991).

THE TEDDY BEARS' PICNIC (TBP)

Background

The *Teddy Bears' Picnic* is the younger sibling of the MUG. It was designed for younger children and was created more recently (Mueller, 1996b). But the family resemblance is unmistakable. Like the MUG, its purpose is to understand the child's internal and personal constructs; and like the MUG it relies on a storytelling task to understand the child. Finally, it stems from the same family tree with ancestry in Kelly (1955), Sullivan (1953), Winnicott (1958), and Fairbairn (1952). As these theoretical roots of the MUG have been mentioned earlier in this chapter, the reader is asked to refer to the earlier part of this chapter because the roots of the TBP are identical.

Description of the TBP

The TBP was developed for children aged 4 to 6 years and utilizes a family of four toy teddy bears about 8 cm tall and dressed for the open air. Toy bears such as the well-known *Sylvanian Family Bears* are suitable. There is a mother, a father, and two children—both of whom are clearly dressed as a boy and a girl. The test also uses a variety of other props, including a tree, a wagon, and a picnic blanket (see Figure 22–2)

Initially, only the child bear of the same sex as the child tested is introduced, along with a tree, at the top of which hangs a honey-pot. The child is told that bears really like honey, and that "your special bear" really wants the honey. What happens next? As in the MUG, this is a practice story to help the child ease gently into a storytelling, fantasy modality.

After the "honey-pot" story, the child meets the other three bears in the family and is told that they are all going on a picnic. Nine further story stems (Table 22–4) follow, in which the main character (MC) bear faces various problems and situations. The child knows when it is his or her turn to finish each story because the tester always says "What happens next?" or "What does your bear do?"

Figure 22–2. The Teddy Bears' picnic.

Table 22–4.   Story stems for the Teddy Bears' Picnic*

Honey-Pot

We're going to make up some stories about this bear. He/she is your special bear. One day your bear is playing by this tree. She/he likes to run around trees. Can you make him/her run around the tree? She/he likes to do roly-polys/somersaults. Can you make him/her do somersaults? Suddenly, your bear looks up in the tree and sees a big pot full of delicious honey. Bears love honey! She/he really wants the honey? What does your bear do?

Now we're going to tell a big story … and along the way I'm going to ask you "What happens next?" just as I did before. When I do, it's your turn to show me "What happens next and how is everyone feeling?" or "What does your bear do or say?"

1. Sibling

One day, the bear family went for a picnic. Mummy and daddy bear are over here busy setting up the picnic. Your bear is over here playing with the wagon. Just then, he/she hears a noise and runs over here to see what it is; it was just a little squirrel. But when he/she gets back, look what has happened; brother/sister bear has taken the wagon! What does your bear do or say?

2. Wagon

Brother/sister bear finishes playing and goes back to the picnic, but your bear is still playing with the wagon. Suddenly the wheel falls off; whoops! Daddy bear comes over and says "What is going on here?" [NB: Daddy's voice should be serious but not angry.] What happens next?

3. Busy Mom

Mummy bear is over here picking blackberries from the bush and she is *very* busy. But your bear comes over and wants to play football with her. What happens next?

4. Soup Bowl

Now it's time for the teddy bears to have their picnic. So they all gather around the picnic blanket for their soup. But your bear is so hungry that she/he knocks over the bowl, and all the soup spills right on the picnic blanket. What happens next?

5. Rock

Your bear and brother/sister bear go for a long walk in the woods, way, way over here [as far as possible from the parent bears]. Suddenly, brother/sister bear trips over a rock and hurts his/her leg, and can't get up. What does your bear do? [Do not accept magical appearance of the parents—say they are far away and do not know what has happened.]

6. School

The next day is the first day of school. Mummy bear takes your bear to school and she says "Goodbye, little bear." What does your bear do? [Be sure to inquire about the maternal departure, if unclear.]

7. Chalkboard

Now it's your bear's turn to come to the chalkboard and write the answer [to the problem]. What happens next?

8. Cave

After school, your bear goes home to the cave where he/she finds sister/brother bear and both parents. Mummy bear says "There is no more food in our cave, so daddy bear and I will have to go catch some fish. But the fishing stream is far, far away, so you children should stay in the cave or play in the sandbox until we come back." [Parent bears say "goodbye" and bears put in coder's pocket so that the child bears cannot get them]. What happens next?

9. Coming Home

Just when it starts to get dark, your bear looks out of the cave and sees one parent bear coming back. [As if holding a bear in it, coder moves empty hand as if it were a bear gradually coming up an invisible hill toward the cave]. Who is it, mummy or daddy, and what happens next? [Always ask about whether or not the second parent bear returns.]

---

* This listing is not intended to provide an adequate basis for giving the test. Please request full directions from the author (http://www.mugtbp.force9.co.uk or ned@mugtbp.force9.co.uk).

Administering the TBP

Learning to give the TBP well requires more practice than giving the MUG. The story stems must be learned by heart, so that the child feels one's interest is in them, not in reading something from a card. It takes practice to get all the props in the right places at the right times. But it can be readily learned by students as well as established professionals. Training videotapes are under preparation but are not yet available.

It is best to practice the test several times before giving it to one's first client. Even then it is advisable to receive some supervision by videotaping or taperecording early attempts. The whole matter of querying the child about his or her stories, tone of voice, and intonation during testing, playful attitude, and so on are all best learned through proper supervision with an experienced tester. The best testing gives the child the feeling that the tester is there with them in a co-constructive process. The skill required is learning how to create this feeling in the child without actually guiding or leading the story in any particular direction. Even 4-year-olds with language delay or elective mutism are often able to create TBP stories.

Specific directions for administering the TBP can be obtained from the author (see Web and e-mail address in the reference section under Mueller & Ginsburg, in press). The scoring categories for the TBP are similar to or the same as those for the MUG. In fact, the TBP code is shorter, because some categories such as reference to suicide do not occur at the younger ages and because there is no need to distinguish problems essentially related to the school context. The main differences in the codes can be understood from Table 22–1. Copies of the full TBP code can be obtained by contacting the author.

A Case Example: Selected TBP Stories from a 6-Year-Old Sexually Abused Girl

In the first part of this chapter, Cheryl's MUG stories were presented. While she satisfied the criteria for a depressive problem, she was clearly a high-functioning child with exceptional abilities and appeared to have come from a reasonably secure background. In the present example, consider another girl, this time from a dysfunctional family, and who has suffered from a history of known trauma.

The health visitor described what Lucy (not her real name) was like just prior to her disclosure. She was a very demanding child with frequent bed-wetting and sore bottoms. She would not go to bed until her mother did. She was not happy to go upstairs alone in her house.

Just short of her fifth birthday, Lucy said that her daddy did "rude things" to her. She was interviewed by social services and said that Daddy touched and poked her in the genital area. On physical examination, the pediatrician concluded that there were physical signs of repeated penetrative sexual abuse. The mother was convinced that the father was the perpetrator and he was asked to leave the family home and a divorce was sought.

Sexual abuse has a social context and this family was no exception. For example, the mother's sister was alleged to have been abused by her uncle, and another sister claimed that the father had abused her. One member of the mother's family attended a special school for children with brain and learning problems. These kinds of problems appear to be more common in children with traumatic early histories. Lucy's own younger sister was slow in developing speech and language and was receiving special programs for early stimulation.

Lucy's father defended his innocence and received permission from the Court for supervised contact with Lucy's sister, aged 3 years. While the contacts appeared to go smoothly, both sisters experienced several nights of bed-wetting around the time of each contact session, and the mother continued to petition the court for the contacts to stop. The current situation is that the judge ordered six contacts per year for the younger sister with the father. However, he cancelled the two most recent visits. The mother worries that the judge will move to unsupervised contact in the future for the younger sister.

In presenting much of Cheryl's MUG protocol the purpose was to give an overall feel for storytelling protocols, and to illustrate the many coding categories used with it. Here the purpose is much narrower so fewer stories will be presented. Lucy was chosen because her stories were high in, "story disorientation" (DIS– code). As was shown above, this is an important code because it contributes to the MUG and TBP scales indexing fragmentation and disintegration of the core self and it requires intensive therapeutic support. But it is also among the more difficult codes to learn. This may be because adults will excuse almost any nonsense from a child as just being "childish," and not realize that it could have clinical significance. Coding DIS– requires the coder to treat each utterance from the child in context. For a story to make sense each utterance must bear a semantic relation to the prior actions and utterances (Mueller, 1972).

Please read Lucy's two stories with the warning that it may be distressing. Try to understand both her intense vulnerability and its expression in ways that look confused and disoriented.

LUCY'S TEDDY BEARS' PICNIC   CODING

Story 5: Story Where Brother Trips Over a Rock

Q. Right, in the next story, the mummy bear's still over at the picnic, but your bear's going far, far away in the woods. But brother bear's not looking where he's going and he trips and falls over a rock and hurts his leg, and says "Sister, help, I've hurt my leg and I can't get up!"

G. *Then mummy come along and dad come along.* So they go in their car and…   VF+p

Q. Mum and dad don't know yet—they're a long way away [moving the figures back to their original places].

G. *She carries him* [MC bear] and *he's bleeding* and so she takes him   R+, U–,
… *"Oh, we can't find mum!* Oh no! We better go find dad. Are you   U– (Repeat)
walking?"

Q. He's walking now.

G. *She fell over* and *he tripped over a stone again.* Then *they both trip*   H–, U- (Repeat)
over. Then "You gotta mind where you going. If you don't, you gotta
go get some glasses." [Boy bear says] *"I've lost my mum!"*   U- (Repeat)

Q. Are they hitting each other?

G. "Stop it!" *[The boy and MC bear are fighting.]* "You whacked me   A-
on the nose!" "We better go find mum, I go and get some help.   (also DIS- as

Mum, mum! Dad, dad! My brother fell over a stone and I don't know where he is." [Mother bear says] "We'll go and find him. Quick, quick, we gonna carry him to hospital. And if he die we get some animals!"

Q. Some what?

G. Animals. [MC bear] "I hope he'll be all right." [Mother bear] "He will."

Q. So where is brother now? Is he at hospital?

G. He died.

Q. So how is your bear feeling now?

G. He [MC/girl bear] is sad 'cause he want his brother. They go home and have a lie down [mother, father, MC bear]. Then they come to see him [mother and MC bear; father bear still lying down at home]. Then doctor says he [boy bear] feeling all right, but he's not dead. He's coming home."

Q. So how is the brother feeling now?

G. He's got a heart missing. He's sad. [Boy bear starts jumping on father bear] ... "Dad, get up! Get up!" So his dad slapped him and mum [hitting both boy bear and mother bear] said "Get up to bed!"

Q. Why did dad slap him?

G. 'Cause he has been naughty, and he had got something that was wicked.

Q. What did he do?

G. [Referring to boy bear] He got a tomato and he eat it. He slap him and mum and he throw this stone.

Q. So that's why he's naughty?

G. That's the end.

Q. So how does your bear feel now?

G. He's feeling well. [Father bear lies down saying] "Mum, I've got a sickness."

Q. What's the matter with dad?

G. He got a bad cough, mum got a sickness, and bear got a hurt neck.

Q. But your bear's OK?

G. Right.

Side annotations:

aggression enters the story 'out of the blue' V+p, U- (Repeat), RO+

V+o

U- (repeat)

(not scored because elicited affect)

H– (repeat), DIS– (repeat), PP– DF–f

(rationale)

DIS– (repeat, confusing)

DIS– (repeat, makes no sense)

U– (Repeat)

Story 6: Leaving MC Bear at School

Q. Right, now, in the next story, let's make it easier. The bears are on their way to school. There is their school. Mum takes her [MC bear] to school and she says "Bye-bye, little bear." What does your bear do?

G. She goes through the door. *Then mum come in. "Can I take my child to the doctor's, please?"*   DIS–

Q. Why is she going to the doctor's?

G. *'Cause him [MC bear] has been sick at school* and she's [mother bear] *not feeling well.* [Mother bear says] "You had better go get in the car and find dad." [They drive off but the car jumps suddenly] *"Oh no, we've crashed!"* So the teacher comes … run, run, run … "Oh, Mrs. Pooley. I'm all right."
She [MC bear] *knocks him down* [MC knocks teacher over]. "I'm all right," I said [referring to MC bear]. … I climbed up the wall, and she comes into the woods. She says, "Oh no, *I've got to get over there to school.* [Pause while child thinks of a way to get into the school; she takes the tree and MC bear climbs up it and drops into the school.] "Then she climbs up."

H–, U– U–, repeat (the car is considered a 'valued possession')
A– (also DIS–, Repeat, hitting comes from nowhere)
DIS– (Repeat, unclear why)

Q. So she's going to school?

G. Then *mum call the Police.* "Police, do you know what? This child is naughty."

DIS– (Repeat, Why call police?)

Q. What has happened to mum?

G. Mum's all right … *but the teacher isn't.*   DIS– (Repeat)

Q. What has happened to the teacher?

G. *The teacher feels sick* 'cause dadda … her [teacher bear's] husband not here. He says "Turn round. We're going decide and we're getting the blackboard and we're going to leave our school and we're going to lay down on the chair, stand up and watch." [Girl has moved the contents of the school into the position of being inside the family's house again and has brought the tree in and placed it on the carpet.]

(rationale added to explain the emotionally driven perception)

Q. Where is she going now?

G. Her got a lot of football and him gotta stay here to do work and brother got to stay with dad.

Q. What is teacher doing?

G. *Teacher putting decorations and stuff* [teacher standing alone in classroom looking at the tree]. Then mum come in and said … she made her jump. She went "Ooh!" *She jumped.* [Teacher jumping and falling over seemingly because MC bear has just entered the room.] [*MC bear then knocks the tree down, then the teacher, and jumps onto the blackboard.*] *Have a nice kip.* Then at last they have a dream. *He [MC bear] had spots over his face.* [*Bears enter the room one by one*]. … *Their dad was a ghost … and the brother was a monster … and mum was a … [long pause] … wolf! Mum got a poison apple, dad got a poison apple and they got a poison apple and the other bear got a poison apple. Then dad got a sharp knife and then* [*father bear jumps onto the teacher and they both lie together on the floor, teacher bear having been stabbed by father bear*].

DIS–(Repeat)
DIS–(Repeat)
A-Repeat
DIS-(Repeat)

It was only a dream.	A-Repeat
They lay down and have a nice, nice kip. The bears [father and	(Is this a
brother bear] were watching television.	rationale?)
That's the end.	

Q. And how did your bear feel?
G. He was happy. *But one was crying...*   NA-

Q. Who was crying?
G. The teacher. 'Cause this one [MC bear] *slapped her in the face*   A- (Repeat)
    'cause *she hates that teacher* [MC bear slaps teacher and mother and   DV-o
    father bear].

Q. Why?
G. 'Cause she didn't like her and she didn't want her to come round her
    house. And *mum invite her over to dinner* but he didn't want to come
    to tea. The teacher didn't wanna come round and this one has   DIS- (Repeat)
    slapped her. He [MC/girl bear] had a temper.

When the story is disoriented, semantic continuity breaks down. In Lucy's response to Story 6 (School), continuity has broken down. Reading Story 6 words like "incongruous," "odd," "inappropriate," "confusing," or "inconsonant" should come to mind. At a more emotional level, the story may be experienced as "weird" or even "bizarre." In recent psychiatric parlance, the term "dissociative" is gaining favor in describing the overall mental state of adults functioning in this manner (Ross, 1997).

In the case of a child, what may be happening is that disturbing memories have not yet been split off into largely separate personality states as in a true dissociative disorder. Nor have they been repressed. Rather, the underlying emotional state of being constantly in danger (H– code), with the vulnerability being projected onto significant others as well (U– code), takes over self-expression. It is for this reason that Lucy has brother bear die in Story 5 and teacher get sick in Story 6. It is the most natural thing in the world for the child to believe that others are like her, and clearly *she* feels in great danger. The abuser, whoever it was, is still free to show up again. Still worse, from Lucy's point of view, he has even been given access to her sister, who now is being put in great danger also.

Thus, another sexually abused person might see the stories as having a deeper truth— fear and retreat from conventional reality—that characterizes the world of the abused child. To most testers, however, the stories just look odd. They try to use everyday logic to make sense of the chaotic internal world revealed. This is the case with the present tester, and Lucy tries to "play along," adding "rationales" to help the tester make sense of them. A few of these rationales have been flagged in the margin for easy recognition. However, Lucy's rationales give only a semblance of clarity to her stories. In reality they introduce extraneous, emotionally driven content that further confuses most readers.

Not only did Lucy invent a complex story, she also included a dream in it. In the dream people act in terrible ways toward each other, using poison apples and knives. But it is impossible to tell the good guys from the bad guys. Lucy seems to be saying that in her internal world, no one is trustworthy; anyone might do something terrible at any moment. With such a perception she indicates a lack of safe attachments. Therefore, the first aim of therapy is becoming able to trust someone again. Initially the therapist must work through a sort of pseudo-trust that poorly attached children show as they reach out for a safety net.

TBP Construct and Criterion Validity

As with the MUG, many users of the TBP will limit their interpretations of TBP to narrative methods in clinical reports. However, also like the MUG the TBP aspires to offer reliable quantitative methods of identifying problems in childhood. To do this, a simplified version of the MUG code was developed for use with younger children. Table 22–1 shows these codes and the MUG codes from which they were derived. There are also a few new codes such as "child impulsivity" which were not in the MUG.

Three studies relevant to TBP validity have been conducted. Mueller and Tingley (1990) rated the quality of mother-child interaction during structured play sessions when the child was aged 20 months. Four dimensions of interaction were examined: maternal sensitivity, sharing of control, child affect, and maternal affect. Maternal initiation of activity during a pause by the child or maternal elaboration of child actions was rated high on maternal sensitivity. Behavior such as maternal persistence with an activity in the face of clear opposition by the child was rated low.

Then all children received the TBP after the fourth birthday. It was found that both maternal sensitivity and maternal affect were related to TBP story features several years later. The higher the rating of maternal sensitivity, the lower the number of devaluing remarks in the child's stories. And conversely, the lower the rating of maternal sensitivity, the higher the number of devaluing remarks toward others by the main character in the story. In addition, for boys only, mothers who used more negative emotion in their interaction at 20 months had boys who were more likely to devalue self and others in their presence at four years. The results suggest that parent-child interaction at age 2 could be playing a role in the construction of the child's beliefs about self and other, when assessed over two years later.

Mueller (1996b) had preschool teachers rate how concerned they were about the children in their group. They also completed a behavior checklist about the children's problems and all children were tested with the TBP. It was found that both the checklist and the negative code of the TBP were quite sensitive at locating the children about whom the teachers were worried. The study was interpreted to show that in their storytelling, children do give important information about their emotional health and well being.

Loader, Kelly, and Mueller (1998) administered the TBP to three groups of children: chronically constipated children scoring in the normal range on the CBCL, and nonconstipated control children recruited from a local school, the third group being a control group. First, considering all constipated children together, it was found that 69% had problems by using both the CBCL and TBP as either/or measures of difficulty. This finding was important because traditionally chronic constipation was seen as a purely physical problem, but it appears to be more correctly seen as having a strong mental health component. As in Mueller (1996b), the TBP was locating children with problems that were being missed on the CBCL and vice versa. This again points to the importance of using both kinds of measures in the assessment process.

Recall that about half the constipated children scored in the normal range on the CBCL. In other words, their mothers did not rate them as having behavioral or emotional problems.

Nevertheless, the same children were found to score significantly higher on the TBP negative code total than did the nonconstipated controls. This means that regardless of the maternal view of the child's level of problem, most constipated children showed psychological problems. Looking at the specific TBP codes contributing to the total, most of the difference was due to the stories being immature, or to there being elevated rates of unhappiness and devaluing the parental figures in the thematic material. The direction of causation could not be inferred from these results, but there was some suggestion that chronic constipation itself might have a direct negative impact on the child's psychological functioning.

None of these studies involved the simple comparison of large numbers of clinic-referred and normal children that is part of validating most tests. Only recently have TBPs from 100 children been available to run such a comparison, and these findings are being presented next for the first time. The children were from East Kent in England, a region of considerable cultural homogeneity. Half were coping well in school and were considered normal. The other half had been referred for problems to a family center where both psychology and social services support was available in an integrated manner.

The Sample

One hundred children were seen of whom 50 were referred to a multi-agency clinic for help with emotional or behavioral problems, and 50 were normal controls of similar cultural background attending a school in the same locality in England. Such samples are seldom pure. Some of the normal children doubtless had problems, and about 20% of the referred sample did *not* score in the clinical range on the total score of the CBCL, suggesting they may have been functioning adequately. The two samples were matched for age (mean age: 66 months) and gender (predominance of boys). However, the groups could not be matched for socioeconomic status (SES), the referred children being significantly lower in income and occupational status of their parents. For this reason, all group comparisons reported here included a control for the effect of SES. This means that any effect of SES has been removed statistically from the reported group differences.

Construct Validity

First, the TBP codes were subjected to factor analysis, searching for underlying constructs in the children's problem expressions. Three factors emerged and are identified as Negative 1,2, and 3 in Table 22–5. The codes contributing to these factors are shown in the second column of Table 22–5 and reveal that the TBP has the same underlying constructs as did the MUG (compare MAS 1–3 in Table 22–3). This result justifies viewing the MUG and TBP as "sibling" tests, measuring similar constructs for two different age groups. In other words, the two tests may be said to be cross-validating each other. It would appear that the constellations of childhood problems, as expressed using storytelling, are well discriminated from each other in children as young as 4 to 6 years. If the codes chosen for study in fact represent the essential features by which children express their problems, these results could represent a step forward in the empirically based diagnosis of early childhood problems.

"Story immaturity" and "child impulsivity" were more frequent problems for the younger children than for those studied using the MUG, and therefore both these areas were formally rated as part of the TBP code. It was expected that these problem areas would factor independently from the main problem factors, but in fact, both features fac-

Table 22–5.   Mean scores for "referred" and matched "normal" controls on TBP negative and positive codes (N = 50 + 50)

Factor	Codes	Mean		F-Test (SES as Covariate)		MUG Result
		'Normals'	'Referred'	f	p	
Negative 1	Story disoriented	1.0	1.4	1.4	–	MAS 1
	Sexual-oral expression	0.3	0.6	2.0	–	MAS 1
	Child impulsive	0.9	1.2	0.6	–	Not Coded
	Content immature	0.9	1.6	3.1	0.08	Not Coded
	SUM	3.1	4.8	3.4	.07	
Negative 2	MC devalues others	0.7	1.9	7.6	0.007	MAS 3
	Aggression in story	0.9	2.5	19.6	0.0001	(MAS 3)
	Others devalue MC	0.5	1.8	9.5	0.0003	MAS 3
	SUM	2.1	6.2	24.8	.0001	
Negative 3	Helplessness/Vulnerability	1.9	1.7	0.1	–	MAS 2
	Sad story ending	0.4	0.4	0.1	–	MAS 2
	Vulnerability in others	1.6	2.3	5.2	0.024	MAS 2
	SUM	3.9	4.4	1.0	=	
Singleton	Physical punishment	0.3	0.6	2.8	–	No Data Yet
Factors	Negative affect in others	0.5	0.5	0.2	–	Not Coded
Positive 1	Others value MC	3.9	3.6	0.4	–	MAS 4
	MC values others	3.7	3.0	3.1	0.08	MAS 4
Positive 2	MC resourceful	1.9	1.5	1.8	–	No Data
	Positive affect in others	0.4	0.4	0.1	–	No Data
Positive 3	Resourcefulness in others	2.1	1.4	0.2	–	No Data
	SUM	12.0	9.9	5.8	.02	

tored with "story disorientation" and "sexual-oral drive expression" in the Negative 1 factor (see Table 22–5). Such a result suggests that, rather than being separate problems, child impulsivity and the inability to tell age-appropriate stories (immaturity) could relate to emotional problems of the most serious kind. Rather than being isolated phenomena, cognitive delay and impulsivity may well be the result of serious emotional problems. In any case, such a hypothesis should be pursued in further study of the TBP and elsewhere.

Concurrent Discriminant Validity

While the factor-analytic results were remarkably similar to those for the MUG, the power of the TBP negative codes to discriminate normal and troubled children was not as good as that reported in Table 22–3 for the MUG. Table 22–5 shows that only Negative 2 (equivalent to MAS 3, "defiance and devaluing" on the MUG) was more frequent in the stories of referred children. The Positive code sum did separate the groups but most individual positive codes showed no significant group differences.

These results suggest that only angry, conduct problems could be discriminated reliably between "troubled" and "healthy" groups in this fairly small sample. In a larger sample, fragmenting-self problems (Negative 1) may also be shown to discriminate groups as its sum score approached significance in this sample. While depressive problems were not found to discriminate the two groups, perhaps they do not cause sufficient concern at this age to lead to differential rates of referral for help. It is equally possible that they are expressed in different ways and are harder to detect.

Need for Further Study

A careful reading of this chapter will show the need for further intercoordination of the MUG and TBP codes. By historical accident, one code symbol (NA-) has a different meaning in the two tests! Beyond these simple needs for change, larger validity samples are needed (such as were used with the MUG) to more adequately test the discriminant validity of the TBP codes. However, it must be added that they already appear to be promising. Eventually, large norm-referred samples should be gathered to allow one to develop cutoff scores for both total and factor scores. Toward this end, in both England and Italy, children are being assessed regularly using the TBP.

Summary

The TBP has been developed as a clinical instrument for understanding 4- to 6-year-olds' personal constructs and beliefs. It is based on the belief that more valid information can be derived indirectly from children through play techniques than through direct interview. Children are not seen to be particularly good informants about their own problems. Like its sibling test, "The MUG", the TBP provides quantitative information about the extent to which clinically referred children have problems in any of three separate and independent dimensions. These are: (1) problems of disorientation and drive expression; (2) problems of aggression and devaluing others; and (3) problems of helplessness and vulnerability. Both tests are united in the finding that story disorientation and drive expression are particularly worrying features in child narratives.

The TBP may be unique in offering both a rich interpretative understanding of each referred 4- to 6-year-old along with quantitative estimates of the types of problems present. As the TBP requires only 20 to 30 minutes to administer, it should be considered for use in programs aimed at the early detection and resolution of childhood problems before school entry. As a play procedure, children often enjoy participating in this assessment which can tell us so very much about them.

REFERENCES

Achenbach, T. M. (1991). *Manual for the Child Behavior Checklist 4–18 and 1991 profile.* University Associates in Psychiatry, Burlington, VT 05401-3456.

Bellak, L., & Bellak, S. S. (1974). *Children's Apperception Test,* 6th and rev. eds. Larchmont, NY: C.P.S.

Bemporad, J. R., & Wilson, A. (1978). A developmental approach to depression in childhood and adolescence. *Journal of the American Academy of Psychoanalysis, 6,* 325–352.

Breen, M. J., & Fiedler, C. R. (Eds.) (1996). *Behavioral approach to assessment of youth with emotional/behavioral disorders.* Austin, TX: Pro-Ed.

Bretherton, I. (1987). New perspectives on attachment relations: Security, communication and internal working models. In J. Osofsky (Ed.), *Handbook of infant development,* 2nd ed. (pp. 192–215). New York: Wiley.

Cohen H., & Weil, G. R. (1975). *Tasks of Emotional Development Test manual.* Boston: T. E. D. Associates.

D'Alessio, M., Schimmenti, V., Cherubini, A., & Mueller, E. (1996). *Valutazione del rischio in eta scolare: relazione con adulti e pari.* Napoli: Guido Gnocchi.

Dimopoulou, E. (1998). Locating childhood problems: Disagreement between checklist and self-disclosure through story-telling technique. Unpublished undergraduate thesis, University of Kent at Canterbury, UK.

Dweck, C. S. (1981). Social-cognitive processes in children's friendships. In S. R. Asher and J. M. Gottman (Eds.), *The development of children's friendships* (pp. 132–149). New York: Cambridge University Press.

Fairbairn, W. R. D. (1952). *Psychoanalytic studies of the personality.* London: Tavistock.

Freud, Anna. (1936). *The ego and the mechanisms of defense (Rev. ed.), Vol. 2 of The writings of Anna Freud.* New York: International Universities Press, 1968.

Ginsburg, H. P. (1989). The role of the personal in intellectual development. *Quarterly Newsletter of the Laboratory of Comparative Human Cognition, 11,* 8–15.

Greenberg J. R., & Mitchell, S. A. (1983). *Object relations in psychoanalytic theory.* London: Harvard University Press.

Harris, P. L. (in press). Fictional absorption: Emotional responses to make-believe. To appear in S. Braten (Ed.), *Intersubjective communication and emotion in early ontogeny.* Cambridge: Cambridge University Press.

Irwin, E. C. (1991). The use of a puppet interview to understand children. In C. E. Schaefer, K. Gitlin, & A. Sandgrund (Eds.), *Play Diagnosis and Assessment* (pp. 617–635). New York: John Wiley & Sons.

Kelly, C., & Loader, P. (1997). Factitious disorder by proxy: The role of the child mental health professionals. *Child Psychology and Psychiatry Review, 2,* 116–124.

Kelly, G. A. (1955). *The psychology of personal constructs, Vols. 1 and 2.* New York: Norton.

Kohut, H. (1977). *The restoration of the self.* Madison, CT: International Universities Press.

Loader, P. Kelly, C., & Mueller, N. (1998). The relation of early childhood constipation to psychiatric status, internal psychology and family functioning. Manuscript submitted for publication.

Loeber, R. (1990). Development and risk factors of juvenile antisocial behaviour and delinquency. *Clinical Psychology Review, 10,* 1–41.

McClelland, D. C., Koestner, R., & Weinberger, J. (1989). How do self-attributed and implicit motives differ? *Psychological Review, 96,* 690–704.

Mueller, E. (1972). The maintenance of verbal exchanges between young children. *Child Development, 49,* 930–938.

Mueller, E. (1996a). Origini del MUG e teoria del "Marker Code." In M. D'Alessio, V. Schimmenti, A. Cherubini, & E. Mueller *Valutazione del rischio in eta scolare: Relazione con adulti e pari* (pp. 1–26). Napoli: Guido Gnocchi. This chapter about the theory of the MUG and Teddy Bears' Picnic is available for downloading in English at: http://www.mugtbp.force9.co.uk.]

Mueller, E., & Tingley, E. (1990). The Bears' Picnic: Children's representations of themselves and their families. In I. Bretherton & M. W. Watson (Eds.), *Children's perspectives on the family, new directions for child development, No. 48* (pp. 48–65). San Francisco: Jossey-Bass.

Mueller, N. (1996b). The Teddy Bears' Picnic: Four-year-old children's personal constructs in relation to behavioural problems and to teacher global concern. *Journal of Child Psychology and Psychiatry, 37,* 381–389.

Mueller, N., & Ginsburg, H. G. (in press). *The MUG technique: Clinical assessment of the school-aged child.* Austin TX: Pro. Ed. Help with the use of both the MUG and TBP can be obtained at the MUG/TBP Web site: http://*www.mugtbp.force9.co.uk.* If you have difficulty reaching this site, or have no access to Web, contact us by e-mail instead: *ned@mugtbp.force9.co.uk* or Ned-Mueller@email.msn.com.]

Murray, H. A. (1943). *Thematic Apperception Test.* Cambridge MA: Harvard University Press.

Piers, E. V., & Harris, D. B. (1984). *Piers-Harris Children's Self-Concept Scale* (Rev. Ed.). Los Angeles: Western Psychological Services.

Ross, C. A. (1997). *Dissociative identity disorder* (2nd ed.). New York: Wiley.

Sullivan, H. S. (1953). *The interpersonal theory of psychiatry.* New York: Norton.

Sundby, H. S., & Kreyberg, P. C. (1968). *Prognosis in child psychiatry.* Baltimore: Williams and Wilkins.

Watanabe, S. T. (1991). Children's self-esteem and the MUG: Issues of assessment and validation. Ph.D. dissertation. Boston University, Graduate School.

White, M. (1995). *Re-authoring lives.* Adelaide: Dulwich Centre Publications.

Winnicott, D. W. (1958). *Through paediatrics to psycho-analysis.* London: Hogarth Press.

Appendix

The MUG Positive and Negative Codes: Definitions and Examples

ID	Code	Definition	Explanation	Examples	Rule Out
Valuing, Devaluing, and Defiance (Acting Out)					
V+*	MC Values • Mother • Father • Parents • Other (all categories of potential importance)	Valuing others is any prosocial initiation by the MC. MC seeks affiliation with others. MC respects others boundaries.	The valuing of others is seeking affiliation or positive interaction with them (playing, sharing, doing) or telling them you care for them (love, worrying about them when they are late, missing them when they are absent); voluntarily doing things for others (such as making valentines when they are not required in school assignment), offering help; acting to join significant others (calling up a friend to play, or confiding in other about problems). Includes compliance (complying with a fair punishment or rule).	*Prosocial examples:* 1/Would you take me in your boat, daddy? 2/Would you come to play with me? 3/Kissing mum or waving to mum. 3/'She gets lots of new friends' 5/Can I help you with the desk?; • Note that statements of reciprocal play, normally between friends, are scored twice as V+ and VF+ (e.g. 4/'Let's all make an elephant' / 'She and her friends were making a big flower'. *Compliance Examples:* Child complies with instruction to go to his room for not eating dinner or because he fought with young brother.	4/ 'She makes a picture with the others' [but are they interacting or is it parallel play? therefore NCA] 8/ 'The girl is gonna have to go to her dad' is not valuing him. • Implicitly discounting the other by saying, "I had nothing better to do so I called my friend" is not valuing. • Saying "good bye" or "hello" to mother is merely "child role" and is not scored. Police helping children to cross the street is not scored as is his job. • When MC values teacher it is scored as SM+. • The mere mention of friends is not valuing. Thus 'He went into school with all his other friends' is not scored because it is unclear that they are really actively involved with each other. The friends must do some activity together, or be newly acquired.

658

	Devalues peers	Talks or feels about others in negative ways; talks back, being angry at without just cause; disliking; avoiding. This score involves 'put downs', nasty jokes, and pranks.	• Captures disliking or putting others down. . All anti-social defiant behaviour when directed against peers is scored here. • Focuses on devaluing behaviour such as lying, exhibiting anger without just cause, being mean towards peers or harms their property, and being selfish. • Desire to be separate from or apart from based on dislike of others. • The emphasis of this code is on devaluing or giving others "a hard time" but it's more in the form of pranks or talking behind their back, or expressing negative attitudes toward.	• Without apparent justification MC calls his brother stupid.	6/ The teacher asked her to do the problem [teacher role] 6/ The teacher gave her the chalk to go and do the problem [teacher role]. • This code is not for school or schoolwork. Talking too loud in class is SM– whereas devaluing the teacher Is always D– • Hitting others is A– • Defiant behavior against all adults (which may break the law or diminish parental authority)—delinquent 'acting out' is D–
DVP–* MC	• peers siblings, or things (physical possessions)				
DVA–* MC	devalues adults, parents, or others in authority	captures putting down a person in authority *behind their back or to a third party.*	All defiance toward peers counts as devaluing them DVP–. However, towards parents, and other adults, defiance is treated separately under D–. This code is limited to negative expressions toward adults that occur outside the context of direct negative acts towards that person. Perhaps some forms of joking against adults that seems not really very defiart also belong here.	• The girl didn't want to make a Valentine for her aunts [with whom she lived after she lost her parents] because he/she told the teacher she didn't like them (indirect dislike). 4/[In school] "It looks like he's foolin' around" (This is also SM–, but that is not a core code). I don't like you; I hate you (directly to the person concerned). 5/She doesn't think her father is very good to her.	All defiance and putting down parents and others in roles of authority is D–. 7/ Asked to clean up her room, the girl responds 'I don't want to clean up my room'. [nca]=not coded anywhere Children may express their dislike of persons to third parties, without it being coded anywhere. • 8/ Boy is bothering his mother' [child role permits bothering parents sometimes; all children do it]

(continued)

The MUG Positive and Negative Codes: Definitions and Examples (Continued)

ID	Code	Definition	Explanation	Examples	Rule Out
VF+*	Perceived Others Value MC • from mother or parents • from father • from others	Valuing from others is any prosocial initiation made by the significant others.	• Valuing from others includes most prosocial behavior towards MC. Also, helping; caring for; nurturing; praising or concern about MC • Appropriate limit setting; boundary setting; "time out" and the like; • Lending assistance or support verbally or physically • A spontaneous desire to be with MC even if not realised. • Valuing from parents goes beyond the performance of basic parental duties, e.g.,: feeding or physical protection. However, valuing includes things such as kissing or waving to the child when saying goodbye as this is not a necessary part of parent role. • Positive parent emotional expressions may be coded here, if they are expressing pleasure about MC qualities or actions or achievements. • Individual attention from the teacher is coded here, when it exceeds routine teacher instructions or commands.	1/Dad wants to talk to child about family issues. 5/Father asking child to help him with furniture. 6/Teacher to child: 'You can solve it yourself.' 6/The child got the problem right (SA+) and the teacher said that it was very good 6/"The other kids raised their hands too, but the teacher choose this girl' 8/Mum asks child to wait because she is dealing with an important call. • 1/Father is giving advice and comfort. • 10/Expression of positive feedback about MC's achievements. • 6/Teacher is happy about child's grades. • Birthday parties and presents. • Mum granting permission to MC to go to a friend's house. • He and his friend decided to make a giant mural together (also coded as V+ at the same time)	Routine 'role performance' by parents and teachers is not coded: • 3/Taking child to school or just saying 'goodbye'. • 8/Mum complying with basic child requests, e.g.: taking the milk out from the fridge. • 12/Mum cooking dinner for child [parent role] • parents or teacher etc. just saying "hello" [parent role] • Just mentioning 'having friends' is not coded here. The friendship must be demonstrated by what they do together for coding here. • Watching TV together isn't doing something together—there must be some reciprocal exchange in the activity for it to count here.

DF_1*	Perceived Others Devalue MC • from mother or parents together • from fathers • from others	Defined as behaviours thoughts etc. that unnecessarily devalue the MC.	Focuses on devaluing behaviour towards the MC, such as lying, cheating on, being mean toward or selfish with regard to; also exhibiting anger at without just cause. • Actions that fail to nurture the emotional wellbeing of the MC such as ignoring, rejecting, and humiliating the MC are also scored here. • Non-physical punishment inappropriate to the misbehaviour is also scored here. • MC is called as "bad" or "naughty" for doing something, which punishment can be taken by the child as a general condemnation or "put-down" in the absence of specific censure. If, however, the parent uses the term "naughty" in conjunction with an appropriate punishment or limit-setting (e.g.: "don't do that again"), then the whole parental act is scored as VF+ (a form of valuing through limit-setting).	• MC is sent to his room for a week for a minor accident • Denying a request without a valid reason • Being hit excessively or yelled at unnecessarily. • 1/Child asks to buy an ice cream, dad says no, and fails to give a reason for it, i.e.: not enough money. • 2/9/Rejection of play initiations without just cause. • 9/Other kids in school will never allow MC to play • 'The teacher gets really mad [at MC]'.	• Boundary setting, e.g.: sending MC to "time-out" for misbehaviour and all other appropriate punishments are scored DF+ or PP–. . • Mum's talking on the phone is not scored as long as she meets her child's needs reasonably soon. • MC being smacked appropriately for misbehaviour is scored PP– (however, if the punishment is excessive, it is scored here). • Mother was unhappy at her daughter's poor report from school [parents have the right to be unhappy, and it is not coded anywhere]. *(continued)*

661

The MUG Positive and Negative Codes: Definitions and Examples (*Continued*)

ID	Code	Definition	Explanation	Examples	Rule Out
D–*	MC defies authority, 'acts out' strong emotions, against authority; misbehaves, gets in trouble acts 'bad' • mothers • fathers • parents • teachers or other adults	MC defies adults as individuals—including parents and teachers or other adults in authority (e.g., policeman). This includes all talking back or playing mean tricks, making fun of adults.	Focus is on talking back or defiant actions against authority figures or the destruction of their property. • Here the anger is "acted out" verbally or physically, and is directed toward those in authority, for example parents, police, and shopkeepers. [However, all actions against peers, except direct aggression, go in DV–]	Includes running away from home, stealing. 6/'It's school time and she was kind of bad' 7/Without justification the MC runs away to America. • MC tells a lie to mother to avoid being told off. • MC wants to go somewhere else because mum will not be there. • Child refuses parent request to learn to ride their bike. • Talks back directly to teacher (or father) as a response of being asked to do their work • MC is rude to the teacher. • Stealing the teacher's book (because it is not to have the book, but to act against the school/teacher)	• Defiance towards peer and friends goes under DV–. • Calling mum stupid behind her back is considered DVA–, because there is no direct defiance. • 8/'boy is bothering his mother' [child role permits bothering parents sometimes; all children do it]

Drive expression

ID	Code	Definition	Explanation	Examples	Rule Out
SD–*	Suicide/ Death wishes by MC	Expressions of wishing to end one's life or die.	MC wants, dreams about or enacts death/suicide. This may include the wish to go to heaven.	7/Child is writing about life being worthless and expressing feelings of the desire to die.	• Feelings of wanting to be far from anybody or disappear could be H–. • Expressions of feeling worthless and uselessness based on failure to achieve is R–.

Code	Category	Definition	Description	Examples	Scoring notes
SO–*	Sexual/Oral Expressions Indulgences	Expression of sexuality, excessive orality, fire-setting or prolonged and driven self-indulgences of any kind by any character.	Focuses on repeated actions where the child or other characters seem more interested in drive gratification than ego functions. Refers to self indulgence, greediness and repeated eating during the story; the behaviour often has an obsessive feel. Includes all sexual expressions of any kind.	10/Mum and dad kiss and hug excessively. 10/'He watches TV all day.' 10/'She watches TV to forget it all.' • Eating constantly, or when eating is unrelated to the story context. E.g.: child asking dad to buy an ice cream, dad says no, someone else in story will buy her an ice cream	Just watching TV in itself is not coded. There must be 'excess' or an explicit statement of 'escape from adaptive tasks' or 'avoidance'.
A–	Aggression	Action intending to physically harm someone else.	This score is for hitting and hurting people outside the context of punishment. At times aggression is displaced onto physical objects, but the aim remains harming others indirectly.	• Biting, thumping, hitting, throwing things. • 9/When child is not allowed to play with group, snatches skipping rope from other children.	• Threatening to hurt is devaluing • Smacking and hitting when used as a punishment is PP– • Aggression by monsters is scored as vulnerability (H–). • Aggression used as a punishment is DF–.
PP–	Physical Punishment	Hitting or smacking in response to misbehaviour as method of punishment.	Score all physical punishments here; if the punishment is excessive, score it twice; once here and once in DF–.		Excessive smacking or hitting when used as a punishment is scored as DF– as well as here.

(continued)

The MUG Positive and Negative Codes: Definitions and Examples *(Continued)*

ID	Code	Definition	Explanation	Examples	Rule Out
Vulnerability					
H–*	MC expresses helplessness or vulnerability	MC's expressions of helplessness, worry, vulnerability, or insecurity. Includes general expressions of low self-esteem.	Direct expressions of feeling vulnerable or tired: includes uncertainty, fear, paranoia, worry. Also not knowing what to do or how to behave in interpersonal situations. • Somatising: being hurt; cut; injured; experiencing physical pain. • World is problem-filled or dangerous. • Vulnerability expresses itself.. •• *Directly:* When children do not want to leave their mothers. When they express a fear that bad things will happen to them. •• *Indirectly:* Displacing their fear: 1) *Outward:* in the belief that others may harm them or not like them (paranoia and social fears) 2) *Inward:* in fears of being physically ill or symptomatic.	Direct expressions: Getting kidnapped or taken away by stranger. Indirect expressions: Child misses his grandmother although he had run away from her earlier. 2/MC does not want to go outside to play because he is worried he will be hurt 4/'She had to go to the toilet, but she didn't know where it was.' 11/"If she does well, she will love herself more" • 'She doesn't know who she is.' • 'She couldn't get her attention.'	8/Mother is on the telephone and the girl doesn't know what she is writing [not coded anywhere]. 8/'She finds her room is very unusual because it doesn't have a desk.' • Not every time a child falls over are they hurt. • All school failure and sense of incompetence related to school learning or homework is scored SM–. • Failure in sports or other achievement is scored R–.
U–*	Vulnerability in Others/possessions	MC perceives vulnerability in significant others or in objects, often valued possessions.	Use the same categories of vulnerability as in H-Anyone mentioned in the story in enough detail to detect their "vulnerability" is considered "significant". Similarly any possession mentioned in a story is considered "valued". Separations, divorces and losses mentioned in the current story are also scored.	Reach/Child gets just wants he wants for his birthday but it breaks the first time he plays with it. 3/"The girl doesn't have any money so she can't call her [the mother] herself" • Somebody else gets injured, e.g.: Mom has a car accident on her way home.	• Past divorces or losses used in setting story context are not scored here.

Motivation and Mastery/Achievement

SM+*	MC is motivated for school.	MC likes, is motivated, and values school, teachers, learning ('Achievement motivation')	Likes, cares about school and/or shows an interest in learning or getting one's work done. This focuses on all aspects of academic motivation. It is like a valuing code for school and homework.	• Says he likes school. • Wants to go to school • She went to her room and started her homework . .	• General valuing, not related to teachers, school or learning is scored V+. If a teacher is valued outside the school setting, it is V+. • General motivation to achieve unrelated to the school context is coded R+ • Being good at sports is scored R+ because athletics are treated as non-academic . .
SM–	MC is not interested in, unmotivated for school and school-related learning and mastery.	MC dislikes, is unmotivated for school or devalues academic learning or mastery at school or in homework.	This score is used when MC expresses a lack of academic motivation or disinterest with school, or conveys a sense that studying is a waste of time. Here the opposition is to the school system as an institution. The naughty behaviour, if present, is acted out using peers or classroom equipment. For example, the child throws his pencil, or talks too loud with agemates.	6/Mother says to child 'Sit down and do your work,' and mum leaves. The child shuts the door and listens to her radio instead of doing her work. 11/Child, not wanting to do class work, knocks the table down. 11/'Did not study'. • Cheating on tests • I'm bored by school work—[could be at desk at home or at school] (all other boredom goes in BF–) • 'Doesn't want to go to school'	4/'The table got to be such a mess' [not possession, and tables do become messed up without implying vulnerability to the object] • Poor marks are scored as SA–. • Talking back to or defying teacher requests or class rules (e.g., leaving the room without permission) are all D–. • Any devaluation of others not related to learning roles (e.g., toward peers at school) is scored as DVP–.
SA+*	succeeds in teacher assigned work or in homework	• MC says she is smart (in school related story)	This score also includes general statement of ability or capable self-concept related to school and learning.	• The teacher said she did her homework well • Does homework without being asked	4/'They're all making Valentines' is not coded because there is no statement of completion, achievement or success.

(continued)

The MUG Positive and Negative Codes: Definitions and Examples *(Continued)*

ID	Code	Definition	Explanation	Examples	Rule Out
SF–	fails or can't do school work well enough	MC gets poor marks; can't do the test or the homework	This code is for school failure only.	• Her report card was mostly C's.	General statements of stupidity or inability unrelated to school tasks are R–.
R+	MC resourceful or successful; achieves.	MC succeeds, masters, competent or resourceful. Shows effectance behavior.	This code is meant for positive expressions of competence outside school and outside school related tasks like homework. Succeeds, masters. Displays competence by completing something or displays resourcefulness by attempting something.	• Learning to ride a bike. • Doing well in a sport, even if in school • Completing something • MC states that he is good at playing the piano. • MC is good at math • MC is smart	Success in school subjects and homework is SA+.
R–	MC unsuccessful.	MC fails, is unable, can't do (Achievement Helplessness), forgetfulness; general statements of low self-esteem.	MC fails (inability to accomplish things). May be exhibited through a sense of "don't know how", "cannot do". This score includes explicit comments depicting the MC as incompetent, low in ability, or in self-belief as a person who can do things successfully.	5/'She forgets to give him [the dentist] his money.' 11/She wasn't studying; she forgot to.' • Includes failure in sports or physical activities; she couldn't skip because she wasn't good at it. • 'She's kind of stupid'	8/'The girl doesn't know what mum is writing' • Failure in joining with parents or peers is scored as an attachment helplessness, H–.

666

RO+	Resourcefulness in others	Others act with confidence and resolve	This is special kind of valuing that is scored separately. Others are capable of devising ways and means to solve problems of interest to the MC.	• 4/The teacher finds enough scissors for the whole class. • 5/The boy's desk wobbled and daddy fixed it in the workshop. • 8/Boy leaves his school bag in the bus and mum calls the bus company.	• General valuing from others not related to problem solving.

Self

I–	MC narcissistic; perfect; idealised self	The child never does anything wrong; has exaggerated skills or abilities; must be perfect to be liked.	Characterised by one or more of the following: • MC depicted as invincible or as having no weaknesses. • The MC is somehow perfect; nothing ever goes wrong.	8/'Hi, I'm the Star you're waiting for.' • 'I was the only one to pass the test'. • 'They like me because I scored six goals'.	
IO–	Idealised others and over-idealised story endings	Story content associated with an impossibly good or fairytale like representation of others [or the belief that one is unimportant compared to valued others or the belief that it is one's own fault if others don't care enough].	Characterised by one or more of the following: • The use of fairytale language ('They lived happily ever after'). • MC's wishes are fulfilled out of the blue and with no justification or explanation. • Other depicted as indestructible or as having no weaknesses (often, over-idealised parents).. • Denial of negative feelings experienced by MC in the presence of negative events from others. • Unjustified happy story endings which appear 'out of the blue' or happy endings to otherwise sad stories, where no plausible basis for the happiness is given	• Although my dad had re-married, and not bothered to contact me in a year, I felt he was the best daddy in the world. • 'They got married and had lots of kids'. • If she does well [in school] her mother will love her.	• Rescuing or altruistic behaviour by others towards the MC is scored RO+. • Situations in which a valid explanation is given for wish fulfilment. For example, the boy wanted to be king and gives a long story about how he rose through the ranks of Duke and Prince first. 1/He took a long walk and ended up in another land • Explained and justified happy story endings are scored HAP+.

(continued)

The MUG Positive and Negative Codes: Definitions and Examples (*Continued*)

ID	Code	Definition	Explanation	Examples	Rule Out
Affect or Emotion					
PA+*	MC spontaneous positive emotion	MC expresses happiness or other positive emotion.	Spontaneous expressions of happiness or other positive emotion. The affect must have been elicited by the explicit 'how was he/she feeling' question.	• Having fun, feeling great. • Expressions of satisfactory emotional states such as "all right", "fine".	• 'I love you mum' is valuing. • Just 'feeling better' is not scored. • Rule out happiness in response to asking how MC feels. Elicited emotion is not scored. • When MC is laughing when highly destructive or disturbing things are happening, the disorientation score (DIS–) should be used.
NU–	Spontaneous negative affect or unhappy self	MC expresses unhappy, upset, or sad emotion. (All direct expression of unhappy feelings)	Intended to capture only spontaneous unhappiness. Do not use this code, when the emotion is expressed in answer to the examiner asking 'how he/she felt'	• She felt bad when her mother had to punish her. [Examiner should clarify whether bad means sad or angry.] • MC sad • MC cries • Sadness because he is leaving the holiday resort.	• Rule out unhappiness in response to asking how MC feels. Elicited emotion is not scored. • Stories with sad or unresolved endings are treated separately as LON–. • Loneliness and loss of loved ones is coded LON–. • Being worried, scared or afraid is H– • Feeling 'spaced out' is DIS–.
NA–	Spontaneous anger in story	MC expresses anger or 'mad at' feelings	This emotion code is only for direct spontaneous expressions of anger and hatred.	She hated those girls, for not letting her play.	• To shout at someone is devaluing. • To say MC dislikes someone is DV–. • 'Mad' in the sense of crazy or 'spaced out' is coded DIS–.

BF–	Expresses boredom or frustration	The child states that they are bored or frustrated	Children hate to be bored. Yet is the experience of boredom and frustration not different from the more definite negative emotions of anger and sadness captured as NA–? Perhaps this code will be associated with emotional health?	He was bored watching TV.	Using the word 'bored' as a way of demeaning or devaluing something like school or someone should be coded DV– or D–.
LON–*	Sad story ending and expressions of loneliness or loss by the MC anywhere in the story	The story finishes with the MC sad or includes clear depressive material (loneliness or loss of a loved person or animal).	This special kind of vulnerability scored separately. MC expresses loneliness, loss, or sad story ending. Here the story must depict more than just fear of loss (scored as vulnerability U–). Here the sadness is related to an actual story event involving loss or loneliness or story-ending sadness. The sadness must be the last feelings expressed in the story; it may be spontaneous or elicited.	• The MC's dog dies during the story. • The MC is left feeling sad at the stories ending or the story just fades away	• Most expressions of negative affect before the story end are scored NA–. • MC fear of having an accident is scored H–. • When MC is worried that mother will die, it is scored as both H– and U–.
HAP +	Happy story ending	The story ends with expressed happiness and this is justified by the events of the story.	Spontaneous and explained happy ending to story. It must be the last feeling expressed by the child in the story; it may be spontaneous or elicited.	4f"And they played ball, and they had lots of fun, and the teacher let them play the whole time." 7f"And it was really fun, 'cause she loves telling about rabbits."	• Happiness before the stories end is scored PA+. • It is not enough for the story merely to have a positive or satisfactory outcome.

(continued)

The MUG Positive and Negative Codes: Definitions and Examples *(Continued)*

ID	Code	Definition	Explanation	Examples	Rule Out
Summary scores[2]					
DIS –	Disorientation	Story disjointed, odd, incoherent, or contains inappropriate material. DIS– can characterise only a few lines in a complete story. The content is likely to feel uncomfortable to the normal scorer, because it comes from strong internal feelings about unresolved past trauma.	• A story is disoriented if parts of the story do not make sense in the context of the overall story. • The story wanders and rambles; there seems to be no way for the child to end it; such stories are usually long. • The story contains some material that is blatantly inappropriate or bizarre. • The story contains incongruent emotions (see example). • The story contains a statement that MC is 'spaced out' or in a 'dream world' or 'off the planet'.	• 8/The boy and mother decided to open a brothel. • 10/Mother kills father and MC just laughs. • 12/The boy held the book-bag up because he had on no pants (also scored SO→)	• Stories containing magic.
IMM –	Immature story	Child must rely on gestures, seemingly because of limited language	• Use of magical solution in story. • Repeating themes from prior stories. • The child becomes an actor in the stories themselves.	• To Card 1 the child continues to talk about the thing he wanted most in world • The child uses words like 'I' in the story, unable to assume the perspective of the story characters.	Rule out fantasy failure. When you use this code, you suspect that child may be delayed in the development of language/cognitive skills. A child may use run-on stories, which continue former story without it being immature.

FF –	Fantasy Failure	Only describes picture, story marked by at least two 'ifs' or 'maybes' or cannot 'tell story at all. Even if there is a minimal story, there is no plot development, leaving a story cf only 3–4 lines.	This score is checked when a child does not comply with the fantasy task for reasons seemingly unrelated to language development. There is minimal plot development, or plot is largely a response to tester probes. Here we think the child is using defensive blocking of fantasy, defiance toward the tester that can normally be distinguished from the quality of the material elicited. The skills are there but the child can or will not use them due to blocking or defiance.	A child with no known mental deficiency protests against the story-telling task saying 'It is too hard'.	• Rule out immaturity. When you use this code, you believe the child is at about age level in their capacity to use language. • Rule out indecision between unimportant details: 'making a picture for Christmas or Halloween or something'.

[1] When is a punishment 'appropriate' (VF+) and when is it devaluing (DF–)? There is no absolute answer to this for all cultures and times. The scorer must decide whether or not a given punishment is *culturally acceptable or not* given the level of seriousness of the child's offense. It is not acceptable to send the child to bed for a week for spilling his soup.

[2] Are often based on whole paragraphs of a story, rather than just parts of sentences; allows scorer to code some content more than once.

* 'Core MUG Code' —if a single unit of story content can be coded in two different codes, give preference to the core code

Chapter 23 ──

THE FAMILY PUPPET TECHNIQUE FOR ASSESSING PARENT–CHILD AND FAMILY INTERACTION PATTERNS

Patricia Ross

As all who have ever worked with young children know, it is no easy task to elicit information from a child of three, four or five that is relevant to the problem areas in the child's life in a diagnostic interview. And those who work with families with young children know equally well that it is no easier, for the most part, to elicit from the parents, or the mother alone (for this kind of work quite often involves a mother and young child as a two-person family), any kind of near-realistic picture of what the relational patterns are that manifest themselves daily in their home life.

No matter how warm and approachable the therapist, no matter how talented at engaging children, he or she will almost invariably meet a wall of silence in any attempts to find out what sorts of difficulties the child has with parents, or with mother. In turn, mother or parents will respond to assessment interviews with almost every "answer" but the all-important truth about what the patterns of interaction between parent and child are indeed really like.

All who have attempted such interviews are familiar with the ease with which one can expect to be given detailed reports on what the teacher, or "the school," or the baby sitter, or the next door neighbors, or grandmother, has to say about what Johnny or Susie does that is "bad," or disturbing, or upsetting. It is not impossible to gain a goodly assortment of detailed behaviors seen by mother or father as things the child "needs help with." Johnny wets the bed; Susie sulks; Susie is fresh; Johnny won't mind; Susie just never does anything I tell her; she throws temper tantrums; he throws blocks at his little sister; she kicked grandma yesterday for no reason; he talks back. The list is endless and we know it by heart. And we know that no matter how many such examples mother or father produce, we have not really learned much at all of what we really need to know in order to begin to make a diagnostic assessment of what sorts of things are "wrong" in Johnny's or Susie's life.

Family-oriented clinicians have long appreciated that the kind of information needed for their work is largely outside the family's awareness, and direct questioning in order to elicit this information would in many cases be as ineffectual as asking an anxiety neurotic why he is anxious and expecting more than a rationalization or a cliché as an answer. In one sense, this is even more true where small children are concerned than when the individuals involved are older. Even where the parent may be aware of some of his or her unfortunate interactional patterns, most parents experience considerable reluctance at admitting even to speaking harshly to a small child; certainly this is very often so in the diagnostic interview situation.

Basically, we have two alternatives available in assessing family patternings.

One, of course, is that we can interview the family over a very long period in the hope that eventually the relevant patterns will present themselves fully. Experience has shown that, for the most part, eventually they will do so. The problem lies in the word eventually. Few, if any, therapists would prefer to invest many weeks or months in learning the patterns underlying the child's, and the family's, difficulties. But even if the therapist is very patient, clearly getting as early as possible to what it is that is really hurting for the child, and for the parents, must have a high priority.

Thus, anything that can be done in the assessment process to reduce interview time, and thus, one hopes, overall therapy time, would seem a decided advantage. Rather than wait for such situations to occur spontaneously, it is possible to create them deliberately, and some family-oriented therapists have opted for methods of so structuring family interviews as to elicit the relevant family interactional patternings in a much shorter time.

My own experience has been that most of the suggestions in the family literature for this kind of structuring of assessment interviews can be valuable, but that they are suited primarily for families where the children are older than those in the preschool and early grade-school range this chapter is geared toward. Indeed, a remarkably large percentage of all the writings on family-oriented clinical work is directed toward, centered on, and applicable to, work with families where the children are at or near adolescence and beyond. Papers dealing with families with small children are difficult to find.

This chapter presents a report of a technique for facilitating the assessment of that communication network, and of the process of repetitive interactions inherent in a family's typical ways of interacting, where quite young children are concerned.

The diagnostic technique for parent–child patterns presented here—the Ross Family Puppet Technique—utilizes the familiar, garden-variety hand puppet, a mainstay of play therapy in most facilities where small children are seen. Any of the relatively realistic representations of a "mother" puppet, a "father" puppet, a little girl, a little boy, a baby, and assorted other adult "family members"—of the type readily available from toy suppliers— would serve the diagnostic purpose. Additionally, I serendipitously learned that it is worthwhile to include in one's puppet assortment a few "real" and "fantasy" animal puppets, when one five-year-old boy, sorting through the proffered puppet collection to choose the puppet that represented himself in his interactions with his mother, tossed aside the little boy puppet (as well as the baby puppet chosen by some youngsters) in favor of a red "dragon–monster" puppet that happened to be part of the collection.

The technique would appear, for the most part, to be best suited for use in cases involving very young children, four and five years old, but is adaptable slightly above and below these ages and can sometimes prove to be useful even with older children.

The usefulness of this technique diagnostically is in its ability to elicit with remarkable facility some of the critical parent (or parents) and child interaction relationship.

DESCRIPTION OF THE TECHNIQUE

After an appropriate degree of acquaintance has been achieved—through whatever means the therapist customarily employs (during which the parent[s] will most often have focused on the "problems" as residing in the child), the therapist introduces the family puppet technique by informing the parent(s) and the child of his or her awareness of the great difficulty parents most often have in describing exactly what sort of "problems" arise between themselves as parents and their small child.

This is a helpful way to begin because the message here is that it is not something *inadequate* about these *particular parents,* or this particular mother, that is keeping them, or her, from easily being able to be "honest" and open in telling the therapist what actually goes on in their home life with the child; but rather, that this is a *universal* phenomenon.

Clearly, it is very reassuring to parents in the intimidating situation of having had to come with the child to a therapist to learn that it is not just they, but all parents, who experience the difficulty they are experiencing.

The therapist goes on to explain that it is even more difficult for a small child to say anything much at all about what's troubling him or her in front of a stranger.

At this point it has worked well for the therapist to say something like this: "One way we have found that often makes that very much easier for parent and child alike, and that makes it possible for me to better understand the ways in which I can be helpful to Susie and the family, is by having the two (or three) of you help me get a clear picture of the kinds of difficulties you have, by using these puppets." (Even if there are three persons, i.e., both parents and the child, present, the technique *begins* with just one parent and child at a time.)

The therapist then holds up the box of puppets, puts it on her[1] lap and takes out two appropriate puppets (mother and child or father and child), actually putting them on her two hands and "working" them, as much in the direction of the child as the parent(s). This has proven an immediately effective way of bringing the perhaps up-to-now recalcitrant, or bored, or anxious child into the therapy situation.

The therapist then explains that in this puppet play, family members, two at a time, take a puppet and simply reenact a recent situation when the mother, say, "had trouble" with Johnny or Susie; adding that this can be "anything at all, perhaps something that happened yesterday, or last night at supper, or bedtime, or just anytime." Having explained this much, the therapist then asks the family if they would be interested in trying this puppet technique, which, it seems good to again remind them, will enable them to help the therapist better understand the family's difficulties.

In my experience, asking for the parent's permission here makes it possible for the parents to see this perhaps potentially embarrassing experience as something they have chosen to do in order to contribute to the resolving of the child's or the family's difficulties, rather than as something that is being done "to" them; and it introduces the reassuring notion that the therapist sees the parents as worthy people whose assistance will be valued in the therapy situation.

Then, putting the puppets back into the box, the therapist walks over to the child and the parent(s), holding out the puppet box. If two parents are present, an interaction will have been generated around which of them will "go first" and why. Often the child will already have run over to the box and begun sorting through it to see which puppet he or she wants to "be." Or one or another of the parents will initiate an interaction with the child (e.g., instructing the child, pleading with him, asking his permission, etc.).

---

[1] To avoid confusing nomenclature, nonspecific references to a therapist will arbitrarily use the pronoun "she," and nonspecific references to a child will use the pronoun "he."

Even if the child spontaneously responds, relational patterns often will begin to evidence themselves as soon as the child makes that move (e.g., one mother of a 5-year-old boy, who throughout an earlier intake interview had spoken only "politely" and "lovingly" to the child, suddenly raised her voice to a high pitch, snapping harshly at the child, "Johnny! How many times do I have to tell you not to grab!", even though the child simply had been contentedly exploring the box of puppets).

In any case, the pair are proffered the box of puppets and permitted to pick the one that in their opinion represents the one they want to "be" in relation to one another. In my experience, most often a child will look through the box and settle on the puppet that does indeed most closely approximate himself or herself (to which the therapist has of course given a "clue" by momentarily holding up and putting on the appropriate puppet). Obviously, the therapist will have additional grist for her assessment mill if, as mentioned above, a child picks up and discards the small-child puppets and instead selects a sharp-toothed dragon with which he begins to growl and viciously attacks the "mommy" puppet his mother has put on her hand.

But we'll return to a more usual use of this technique. As soon as mother[2] and child have donned their respective puppets, the therapist continues with the instructions, telling them both to "try to use the same words, and the same tone of voice, etc., so that you can help me get as real a picture of just what happened as you can." Usually the mother is momentarily surprised, and perhaps a little hesitant, at the introduction of the puppets, but in the use of this technique, both mothers and children have almost immediately set about settling on what recent scene of disturbed interaction they will enact.

One of the real advantages of this technique is that even before the actual reenactment has begun, there are repeated opportunities to observe the interactional patterns between parent and child—useful diagnostic material can come from the interaction surrounding the choice of which scene to reenact. Almost invariably, the matter of making this choice will lead to a discussion between parent and child which will include commentary about perhaps several possibilities of "scenes" they have recently had. If the mother hesitates, as if unable to think of a recent occasion on which she and the child had difficulties, quite often the child may take advantage of this opportunity to make a helpful contribution to the diagnostic process (which more than likely would not have been forthcoming under other interview conditions) by reminding mother of "what happened last night when I was going to bed," or by saying, "Let's do last night when I didn't want to eat my supper."

Here again, of course, one has in very short order been given an opportunity to learn just how agreeable the mother is to bringing out into the open a situation she may not have volunteered, or felt comfortable volunteering, and how she responds to the child in a stressful situation. The therapist newly experimenting with this technique may be tempted at this point, if the mother quickly demurs and hastily offers another situation, to intervene and suggest that the one suggested by the child would seem a relevant selection. My own experience has been that it is probably more effective in the long run for the therapist to sit back and simply observe, once the mother and child have been given the instructions. Valuable interactional material will almost invariably come forth regardless of which scene is chosen for reenactment, and the extent to which the mother needs to control the child's

---

[2] Nonspecific examples of technique will, from here on, use the term mother and child, with the understanding that all of what is said applies equally to father–child pairs.

choices is important to know, and so too of course the ways which the child reacts to the mother's reactions.

However, it is also of great importance to let the mother feel that she is not being directed by the therapist in how she handles this entire situation. If the therapist intervenes at this point, the two will quite possibly begin to direct their comments to the therapist instead of realizing that the whole matter is to be between them and that they are to resolve any and all parts of it on their own.

For this reason it has been useful for the therapist to be quite insistent that she, or he, is an observer only. To this end, I take a pad and move my chair back, as if watching a play, and visibly take notes on the interaction. This seems to help make clear that the scene is to be enacted between the principal actors only, and that the therapist's role is to learn all that she or he can from it. If the father is present, he too is given an "audience" role during the time that mother and child are the actors.

Once the pair has begun to reenact their scene, it is remarkable how "real" they both quickly begin to make it, complete with raised voices, angry tones, etc. In some cases, parent and child manage to reenact the entire scene. In others, their inability to do so can provide just as much diagnostic aid, e.g., mother may stop the puppet play by angrily chastising the child with "You're not doing it right! That's not what you did then!"; or the child will react to whatever the parent is doing with the same kind of comment.

A not uncommon type of comment that this technique has elicited has been one where the mother, in the process of reenacting a scene (after enacting a behavior or comment to the child), suddenly has stopped and looked at the therapist, saying something like "I know I shouldn't talk to Johnny that way, but I just can't help it!" Here the therapist, continuing to hold fast to the posture of outside observer, might nod acceptingly and say simply, "I understand. That's what a later part of the puppet play will deal with." Thus far, the suggestion that there will be an opportunity to "make up" for "unacceptable" behavior toward the child later, has often been enough to permit mother and child to resume playing out their roles. At other times, the mother has stopped at this point and poured forth to the therapist a wealth of interview material at a far more open and frank level about her interactions with the child than had been possible before the puppet play began.

The therapist waits until it is clear that they have either completed the scene or gone as far as they can in that particular situation. If the scene is not completed, it is often because either mother or child has gotten frustrated with the other for being less than factual in his or her representation. In either case, the therapist then instructs them to reverse roles: "Johnny, now you be the mommy, and Mrs. Jones, you be Johnny, and you can play the same scene over again."

The participants seem to enjoy this part perhaps even more than the first, for here each gets an opportunity to demonstrate his or her perception of the other's attitude, behavior, tone of voice, etc. toward the other. Of course, much can be learned from hearing the child imitate the mother's tone and stance, and from hearing which of her words or actions she had knowingly or unknowingly omitted from her own portrayal of the role, and of course from her response to the child's perception of her.

Then, in part three, the scene is enacted once more, this time with instructions to each to play the role as each would wish he or she had acted or spoken. Most often, for both mother and child, this has generated a moving scene. Often the mother has behaved toward, spoken, and responded to the child in a way quite unlike the belligerent, or hostile tone she actually used and uses. The child has often responded in a very loving or affectionate way to the mother's changed mode of behaving, thus eliciting considerable emotion from her.

The mother will therefore very often be enabled to end the assessment session with the feeling that the child—and the therapist—does see her potential "goodness" despite the untoward handling of their interactions in troublesome situations. She will also have been given an opportunity to demonstrate to the child that she does have a desire to change in a positive direction, which is perhaps particularly reassuring to the child who has just listened, at the beginning of the interview, to a long list of the ways in which he is perceived by others as "a rotten kid," to borrow a phrase from one mother of a five-year-old.

Here, too, the mother has had the opportunity to provide a glimpse (often to her surprise) to her child and herself of how differently they are capable of responding to one another. Needless to say, these phenomena hold potential for therapeutic benefit above and beyond their diagnostic implications. They also serve in a very concrete way to help a small child get some inkling of what this whole notion of "coming for therapy" is about, which helps offset the often total bewilderment the child has been experiencing based on what he has been told (or not told) by his parent(s).

Beyond all that it has been possible to elucidate in a remarkably short time (one interview) about the interactional patterns between parent and child, there is an awareness that it is not "just the child" who is having problems. At least some, and often many, of the problem areas can now be seen (often for the first time, parents have said) to exist in the *interaction between* the pair of persons in a reciprocal framework.

Very often, too, this technique has served as a means for the mother to begin to speak to the therapist, spontaneously, forthrightly and openly about her own "personal" difficulties, not only in her relation to the child but often in her relationships with other significant persons in her life.

In some instances however, the mother remains unaware of her contribution even under these revealing circumstances. For example, one mother concluded the puppet play with a sharp, "Now you see what a terrible time he gives me!" The therapist must, of course, refrain from didactically pointing out the mother's contributions.

This sort of statement by the parent is accepted simply as part of the assessment. However, in my experience, two relevant things have transpired. One is that the mother has reflected on the puppet play interactions, or perhaps on the real-life interactions they represent, and has come into the next session saying, "You know I got to thinking about that stuff we did with the puppets and I'm not sure it's all Johnny's fault..." Another has been that in sessions after the puppet assessment, it has proved helpful to be able to refer back to certain specific situations. For instance, when a mother has begun to complain about Johnny having acted in an "awful" way again, the therapist can ask whether it was anything like the situation she and Johnny enacted with the puppets, or perhaps whether this occurrence "ended in the same way," because the therapist now knows "first hand" just how such situations do sometimes end in that family. This seems to help the parent get back on the track of thinking about his or her contributions to the reciprocal interchanges between parent and child. Although this technique has been used thus far primarily with a mother and child (because the families were single-parent families), in families where the father is present the technique is adapted to include his participation as well. In this situation, relational patternings between the parents themselves will also be generated through use of the family puppet technique, as was briefly touched upon earlier, as well as among the three family members.

As one example, in a situation involving two young parents and a four-year-old girl, the father had readily volunteered information during the initial interview that the child (who had been referred by her nursery school teacher as having serious emotional problems) did indeed exhibit a long list of disturbed behaviors in the home as well. However, he made it very explicit that she did so only when she was being cared for by her mother. When the mother was at work and he was caring for the little girl and her younger brother, the children's behavior was described as "absolutely perfect." In a most disarming manner he described in detail the happy, playful relationship he had with the children, and what a remarkably warm and caring parent he was.

He had gone on in that interview to exhibit sincere concern about the mother's serious ineffectiveness in dealing with the children and the unfortunate effect this had on the household. In a not unpleasant way, this sincere young man painted a picture of himself as the parent who knew how to play and to manage comfortably with the children, and of the woman as a person who, despite the many warm and genuinely admired excellent qualities he obviously appreciated in her, was just about "hopeless" when it came to dealing with the children. His wife agreed with this description of both of them. The little girl said nothing, playing quietly throughout.

In the next session, during the puppet assessment, when it was suggested that the mother and the little girl reenact a scene, the first thing that happened was that the father got up and started to walk out, announcing that in order for it to be successful he would have to leave the room while they did it. "When I'm around, they [the children] won't do nothing. If you want to see her act bad with her [the mother], it'll only happen if I'm not here."

The therapist suggested that he first try staying in the room. When he adamantly insisted that the therapist would not be able to get a true picture of the mother and child interactional style if he were there, the therapist suggested he enter into the "pretending," at least at first, by pretending that a far corner of the room was out of the house so that he could assist by being an observer who could later comment on the scene.

The mother and child enjoyed deciding which of several scenes to enact, and quickly decided to enact a scene from the evening before, both agreeing that it was a good example of a time when both the mother and child had been very upset with each other. The scene was enacted with remarkable realism, even though it was clear that the behaviors of both mother and child were very distressing to one another. However, it also became very clear during this reenactment that they had a far more affectionate and trusting relationship than one would have guessed from the preceding interview and the descriptions of the interactions.

Among other things, the mother was readily able to demonstrate, undefensively, the impatient and angry words she had in fact directed at the child in the home situation being enacted. Unlike the case with some other mothers when this technique has been used, the mother did not become angry or impatient with the child in the playing of the scene when the child directed unflattering comments at her. Instead she was easily able to enter into the situation comfortably with the little girl even while seriously portraying an uncomfortable situation. What seemed clearly displayed was that the mother had considerable ego strengths and that the child and her mother very much enjoyed each other, were capable of playing together; and that this did not seem an unfamiliar enjoyment.

In the second part of the technique, where the roles were reversed, the mother was readily able to tolerate the child's imitation of her (the mother's) angry and impatient tone of voice, saying "She's doing me better than I did. That sounds exactly like me when I really get mad at them!" And she said this in a way that made the child feel it was perfectly safe to have displayed accurately the mother's "worst" side. It goes without saying that there are diagnostic implications inherent even in the child's feeling comfortable enough to risk an accurate portrayal of her mother's angry behavior toward her. Some small children are, by contrast, very hesitant about whether it is truly safe to admit to the tone or words the mother uses with them in private (even when the mother "assures" them that it is).

The father, who was participating as an observer in the example cited above, was very vocal in his appraisal of how unbelievably accurately they both had portrayed their respective interactional patterns. "That's really amazing! That's exactly the way they go at each other at home. I can't believe it!" The child said, "That was fun." The mother replied, "That's really a good idea. I could never have explained that to you by telling, but it never would have occurred me to tell you about that anyway."

Before going on to a description of some of the father's participation in that particular family's assessment, by way of contrast, it might be meaningful here to mention another mother of a five-year-old and her response under those circumstances, i.e., when the child took her at her word and attempted to respond to her as he had in fact done in a scene from the previous night. In this instance, the mother was unable to remain consistently in the role-playing. For example, when the child responded with his perception of his role in relation to her, she suddenly snapped sharply at him, "Teddy, it's only a game!" After several abortive attempts, each interrupted by her losing her temper at him for one or another role-playing incident that she didn't like, she turned to the therapist and said, "I give up. See what he does! I can't do anything with him. He just won't do anything right."

Yet here too, when they went on to the third segment in which each had the opportunity to play the scene in the way each wished he or she might have done it, the reparative desire demonstrated by each, and the reciprocal responses evoked by the other's positive response, was experienced by both mother and child as very moving. It permitted them to finish the assessment feeling glad that they had participated in it.

To return to the first family's assessment, when the father's turn came, he was very eager to participate in the technique. However, he insisted instead on doing a scene from the previous day in which he and the little girl had been driving in the car (from nursery school), a scene defined as one of the typical ones in which they, as always, had a good time together. There was no discussion with the child as to the choice of scene; the father simply said he did not have trouble with the child and thus obviously could not reenact such a scene. This man's manner with his wife and with the children, and his abundant openness about many details of the relationship between him and his wife, together with the fact that the wife, in a very believable, earnest manner, had concurred in what he said about his interactions with the children, had put the therapist in the position of assuming that perhaps it was true. And, of course, she would not in any case intervene here by questioning their statements. Thus, although the therapist had not anticipated that a parent would say that there were no distressful scenes that might be reenacted where a troubled child was involved, she kept to the original premise of the technique, retaining the outside observer's stance without regard to which scene was selected or on what basis.

During the enactment of the scene, the father began to utilize the puppet role to interrogate the child about her difficulties at nursery school. When the child suddenly shifted from active participation in the puppet play with him and made no reply, he tried again several times and then put down the father puppet saying that now he was going to "be" the nursery school teacher. Although space does not permit a detailed dialogue of the entire assessment, much of great diagnostic significance regarding the father and child interactional patterns, and the father's self-image, was elucidated by use of this technique. At several points he became very intimidating while playing, yet clearly did not perceive himself in that manner. Eventually, the little girl retreated from the play by suddenly saying, "I don't want to do this any more. I'm tired. I want to go to sleep." She then asked the therapist if she could make herself a bed with the pillows on the floor behind the therapist's chair, which she did, remaining, in silence, for the remainder of the session. It seemed clear that the child did not feel safe in making any of the overt comments with the father that she had with the mother, and that the father was unaware of his contribution.

The family puppet technique enabled both of these families to demonstrate vividly, right from the beginning of therapy, important dimensions of their self-other affective interactions, in a reciprocal way, through joint participation, and about salient parts of their lives together. In both instances, it had not been possible for either of the two families' members to provide the material elicited in verbal interviews, despite cooperative intentions and attitudes. Later weeks and months of therapy corroborated the inferences from the assessment technique that these relational patternings were indeed representative and characteristic, and that clues to the critical underlying issues which the assessment had generated were in fact issues germane to the therapy needs of these families. This reduced the necessary amount of time of therapy by allowing for the immediate construction of a treatment plan based on realistic constructs.

When the family has come with an awareness of their need for family therapy, this technique seems to provide them, on their first or second session, with a great sense of relief that the therapist was able to get to the things that really do happen and that really matter. They seem relieved that the therapist was able to learn of difficulties that they themselves did not know how to relate, or would not have thought to relate.

Perhaps more commonly, when a family has come in as a child referral case (often with no awareness that there is such a concept as "family therapy"), on occasion, following the puppet technique, they have made it known to the therapist that "it looks like maybe we all need help." But even if they do not spontaneously ask (as one family did) to be considered "a *family* in need of help," *instead* of "just a *child* in need of help," the therapist's job of "convincing" the family that resolving the child's difficulties will necessitate working with more of the family than just the child is made much easier. Very often, parents are helped to become almost immediately receptive to child-centered parent therapy after seeing the therapist observing some of their "bad" interactional problems without losing her or his regard for the parents.

In sum, the Family Puppet Technique is a diagnostic technique found to be effective in assessing parent–child, and intrafamily, reciprocal interaction patterns in therapy cases involving a young child.

The technique, developed primarily for use in clinical cases involving children in the preschool and early grade school age range, has been found valuable in eliciting relevant problem areas, and parent–child (and parent–parent) interactional patternings, in much less time than the traditional diagnostic interview alone. This family assessment technique would seem to answer one need for helpful models for family-oriented work where the children are very young, an area in which clinical literature is largely barren.

Chapter 24 ————————————————————

THE USE OF A PUPPET INTERVIEW TO UNDERSTAND CHILDREN

Eleanor C. Irwin

INTRODUCTION

Children's play is an intriguing mixture of fantasies, feelings, and perceptions, of real and not-real reality, glued together with the spirit of pretend. In both education and therapy, play has held an esteemed position, with venerable ancestors all around. On one side of the family tree is Freud, followed by child therapists of many theoretical persuasions; on the other, there is Piaget and a plethora of research psychologists who continue to demonstrate the many ways that play promotes cognitive, social, emotional, and even physical growth.

Although long acknowledged as a valuable medium for promoting emotional development, play suffered academic neglect from the mid-1950s through the 1970s. Eventually noticed by clinical and developmental psychologists, play seemed a bit like Cinderella, finally invited to the ball. While the restoration of play's reputation was welcome, the truth is that play never went out of style in the playroom. There, as though unaware of the lack of official sanction, play continued to serve as scullery maid, doing the bulk of the therapeutic work. Perhaps it was Smilansky's study in 1968 that helped to refocus academic attention on play. Questioning Piaget's assertion that all children engage in dramatic play, Smilansky (1968) suggested that culturally disadvantaged children lack dramatic play skills and fail to develop them, unless helped to do so. Further, she asserted, being a "poor player" has implications for the child's ability to learn to play the "school game" later on (Smilansky, 1968, pp. 11–16).

Challenged by Smilansky's studies, other researchers took a fresh look at play. In the ensuing years, play's image as serious work has been restored. Much has been written about (1) how play begins (Murphy, 1972; Spitz, 1972; Winnicott, 1953); (2) how it is nurtured by parents and other caregivers (Dunn & Wooding, 1977; Henderson, 1984; Mahler, Pine, & Bergman, 1975; Werner & Kaplan, 1963); (3) how it is facilitated by toys and objects (Copple, Cocking, & Matthews, 1984; Pulaski, 1973); (4) how it is influenced by the environment (Curry & Arnaud, 1984); (5) how it develops feelings of "efficacy" which grow into a sense of competence (White, 1959); and (6) how it contributes to a sense of self (Fein, 1979, 1981; Rubin & Pepler, 1980; Stern, 1985).

In recent decades, the research of educational, developmental, and social psychologists has underscored what play therapists have long intuitively known: that to "play it out," as Erikson (1963, p. 222) has said, "is the most natural self-healing measure childhood affords." For the therapist, play—especially fantasy play with role-taking aspects—has historically been seen as a source of rich diagnostic and therapeutic data.

It was just such spontaneous dramatic play that captured Freud's attention. Observing a toddler continually throwing away and retrieving a wooden reel, Freud realized that the child's play, accompanied by alternating states of sadness (about loss) and pleasure (about return), were reenactments of inchoate feelings about his mother's comings and goings. Demonstrating the "impulse to mastery" and "repetition compulsion" (Freud, 1920/1955, p. 17), the child became active rather than passive, and thereby worked to abreact his complicated feelings of loss.

As the therapists who followed Freud looked for ways to work with children, it was natural that they explore the child's innate tendency to "show and tell" via play, especially fantasy play. Reading the case studies of early work by child analysts, such as Bornstein (1945), one is struck by the degree to which dramatic play carried the work of the therapy. Further, what is true for the past is also true for the present; for the clinician who enjoys the vivacity of dramatic play, evoking fantasy material is usually not difficult. Rather, what *is* difficult is to know how to use such rich material: knowing, for example, whether to interpret, and, if so, what, how, and when. Then as now, one needs to have some theoretical base that will help to guide the way.

In some ways, this technique conundrum became the focus of a theoretical battleground for two early workers, each of whom held a unique position in child analysis. Most practitioners are familiar with the works of Melanie Klein (1932) and Anna Freud (1922–1970). Both women were part of Sigmund Freud's inner circle, but their theories and ways of working with children became very different. Klein followed the then-current dictum in psychoanalysis to "make the unconscious conscious." Believing that play was the equivalent of free association, she gave direct interpretations of id content. If, for example, the child crashed two cars together, this was interpreted as parents having intercourse. In spite of disagreement about many aspects of her theory and technique (i.e., the early, direct interpretations of transference and unconscious conflict, the developmental timetable she proposed, with the oedipal conflict beginning in the first year, etc.), there is widespread agreement about the brilliance of many of her contributions. Klein is known today as being one of the originators of object relations theory.

Anna Freud, on the other hand, perhaps because of her earlier training as a teacher, took a very different path from Klein. She stressed the importance of assessing the child's capacity for psychological work, establishing a working alliance, and strengthening the ego. Freud recognized the crucial role of ego defenses, which, because they are *unconscious* and operate outside of awareness, need to be modified to allow safer expression of repressed feelings. Thus, Anna Freud helped to change the focus of psychoanalysis from an id to an ego psychology (Freud, 1922–1970, Hartmann, 1964), changing the dictum to "Where id was, there shall ego be." Since Freud and Klein's early work, the understanding of child therapy has been further enriched by object relations (Kernberg, 1976), self psychology theorists (Kohut, 1971, 1977), and interpersonal psychology (Mitchell, 1988; Spiegel, 1996). This body of knowledge, aided by the insights of child analysts, such as Winnicott (1953) and Mahler and her colleagues (1968, 1975), has provided a developmental perspective that can guide understanding of the clinical process (Pine, 1985).

Realizing that fantasy play presents a kind of X-ray of the child's psyche, therapists have historically used a variety of techniques to elicit such material. An early, instructive account of the value of fantasy obtained via puppets and drawings is given by Madeline Rambert (1949), a French child analyst. As Gould (1972) did some years later, Rambert attempted to combine Piagetian concepts with psychoanalytic ones in understanding fantasy play. Foreshadowing Ekstein (1966) and Sarnoff (1976), Rambert emphasized the importance of repression, which ultimately makes it possible for children to represent perceptions, thoughts, and feelings symbolically, rather than acting them out directly. Woltmann (1940, 1951, 1952, 1960, 1964, 1972) wrote of similar experiences. Woltmann presented marionette shows to hospitalized child audiences, but he also used hand puppets and a variety of art media in individual work. It is likely that Bender's widely known text, *Child Psychiatric Techniques* (1952), further encouraged the use of puppets and other projective techniques in child therapy.

Not surprisingly, puppets have continued to be used in a variety of other clinical and research contexts. This includes individual child therapy (Edington, 1985; Ekstein, 1966; Hawkey, 1976; Howells & Townsend, 1973; Irwin, 1983, 1985; Irwin & Shapiro, 1975; Spiegel, 1996), and group therapy (Jenkins & Beckh, 1942; Lyle & Holly, 1941; Spiegel, 1996). Puppets have been used with specific populations, such as children of divorce (Bunting, 1985; Gendler, 1985), mentally retarded children (Myers, 1971), and hospitalized children (Cassell, 1965; Krause, 1970). In diagnostic and therapeutic work with families, puppets have been found to provide a natural way to address and assess ongoing family dynamics (Irwin & Malloy, 1975; Ross, 1977; Shuttleworth, 1986; Snow & Paternite, 1986).

Rojas-Bermudez (1970) reported using puppets to communicate with adult chronic psychotics. Here, the puppet ("the intermediary object") was hypothesized to be sufficiently innocuous and nonpersecutory so as not to threaten the patient's body integrity. This is similar to Ekstein's (1966) description of work with a psychotic girl, using puppets.

In research contexts, puppets have been used in a program aimed at detecting and preventing child sexual abuse (Borkin & Frank, 1986); assessing the efficacy of certain toys in promoting interaction among preschoolers, including the handicapped (Bechman & Kohl, 1984); and in determining the quality of mother-child attachment and the self in 6-year-olds (Cassidy, 1988). Thus, as can be seen from this selected review of the literature, puppet play can be used in a variety of educational and therapeutic contexts.

This chapter presents a puppet diagnostic technique that can be used in child therapy. As with other techniques, it must be supplemented by other data (e.g., a thorough social and developmental history, other projective interviews) and used in a way that can make sense of symbolic data. A fellow clinician once described how the therapeutic process works. Imagine, he said, that the helping process has the shape of a pyramid. The foundation for therapy is the clinician's personality; this is the sturdy base of the pyramid. The helper must be the sort of person in whom others want to confide, regardless of academic degree or theoretical orientation. Such an individual must possess the unconditional regard, warmth, and integrity of which Carkhuff (1969) spoke. This constitutes what one *is*.

The second layer of the pyramid is the theoretical one. Just as a map or compass serves to orient one on a voyage, in like manner, theory serves to guide the journey toward self-awareness. The theoretical layer constitutes what one *thinks,* the rationale of how one understands and explains how things came to be as they are.

The third and final layer, which, in many ways is the least important, relates to technique. This is what one *does* with another. While this chapter presents a technique, it does so with full appreciation of the importance of the therapist's personality, and the theory that guides understanding.

A DIAGNOSTIC PUPPET INTERVIEW

Age Considerations

The puppet interview described herein is but one of many useful diagnostic-treatment procedures (Schaefer & O'Conner, 1983). Other helpful techniques include Murphy's Miniature Toy Interview (1956), especially with young children; and Art Diagnostic (Rubin, 1978) or Sand World Techniques (Lowenfeld, 1939) with preschool or latency children.

Preschoolers

Young children can benefit from puppetry, but they tend to regress easily, express their wishes directly, and impulsively discharge their feelings in action. The play of preschoolers is usually less verbal, more action oriented, and prone to play disruption. Still, young children respond readily to puppetry, and for the therapist, there is the added bonus of uncensored play. Not yet able to use repression as a reliable defense, the unconscious fantasies of this age group are out in the open, so to speak. Young children often present their conflicts with startling clarity and lack of disguise, thus helping to illuminate the diagnostic picture. In the following example, 4-year-old Beth not only lets the therapist know about her conflicted feelings toward her father, via her fantasy play, she also regresses quickly, unable to tolerate her ambivalent feelings.

Case Study

Beth

Along with her younger brother, Beth had witnessed many physical battles between her now-divorced parents. Beth loved but also feared her father and his raging temper. In Beth's first puppet story, "bad men and animals" threaten to kidnap the princess. Halfway through the story, however, Beth became giggly and anxious. Interrupting her enactment, she ran back and forth from the stage to an area where she had placed the "bad men and animals." While her anxiety may have been partly due to confusion about upcoming custody issues, Beth's behavior and her ways of coping with these worries was not atypical for her age. She regressed, became hyperactive, and moved from "play acting" to "play action" (Ekstein, 1966).

Beth pretended to be a magic horse and galloped around the room with wild abandon, sprinkling sleeping powder (sand) everywhere. In an attempt to help her regain control, I said that the sand had to stay in the sand box. Then, as a pretend character in her story, I encouraged "the horse" to stop and tell me about the sleeping powder. Where did this magic come from and what might it do? When Beth said she thought people *wanted* to go to sleep, this was a clue that she had been scared by something in the story. Still in role, I proposed that we return to the castle (the puppet stage) and find out what was happening to the princess and the king. Maybe they could tell us about the magic sleeping powder.

Beth looked perplexed. She could not make an ending to the story, she said, "'cause I don't know it." But, she insisted, "*You* know it, you say it! 'Cause you have it written down in your book!" she said, referring to my note-taking. To lessen her anxiety and help her to continue her story, I again intervened to wonder if the "magic horse" might sprinkle sleeping powder on the bad men and animals. Maybe then we could see what was going on in the castle. Happily accepting this suggestion, Beth returned to the puppet stage and continued the enactment, which ended with the princess marrying the "good" father/king.

Interventions of this kind, while not ideal because they "contaminate" the child's play, are sometimes needed with young children who become anxious and experience play disruption. In this situation, the history, in conjunction with the diagnostic material, points to Beth's powerfully ambivalent feelings about her father. Part of her loves him very much (the princess, after all, marries the king, and there is no queen in the story to object), but part of her also knows that her father gets very angry and is sometimes aggressive with her mother. Is it safe to love a man who gets so angry? Beth's solution seemed to "split" the father figure into a good king and a "bad man and animals" set of characters.

In subsequent sessions, Beth gradually confronted the "bad man and animals," telling them she "hated" them because they were so loud. In several sequences, she drowned the bad animals in the sand box but later resurrected them, saying they could live if they promised to be good. Over time, it was possible to establish links between the play and scary reality situations with father, whom she sometimes refused to visit. Beth drew "funny" pictures of father with "boogers coming out of his nose," and, when her anger was interpreted, she shifted to role play. There she became the "mean" father, while I was told to be the scared girl. Then, reversing roles, Beth practiced speaking up to her dad, being assertive rather than meek.

Emboldened by this play, Beth began to confront her father about his behavior. At first, he denied her version of events, but ultimately, both communication and interaction improved between them. In this back-and-forth way, from puppets to sand play, to artwork to role play, from fantasy to reality, Beth began to work out some of her dilemmas.

Latency-aged Children

Puppets are familiar items in most playrooms, used frequently with grade-school youngsters who have what Sarnoff (1976) calls a "latency structure." Sarnoff uses this term to refer to a period between the ages of 6 and 12 when children develop a stable set of defenses that enable them to deal with strong feelings, chiefly by channeling them into fantasy. By displacing feelings experienced toward parents and significant others onto symbols, children maintain psychic equilibrium, and are thus enabled to continue to learn and play. The ability to symbolize and the capacity to use repression as a defense contribute to the child's outward appearance of calmness and pliability, while fantasies or fantasy-oriented activities reveal the child's true attitudes and reactions. Thus puppet play, which taps this rich fantasy life, is a natural activity for latency-aged children.

Preschoolers versus Latency-aged Children: Contrasts

Latency-aged children also use a variety of materials and modalities to express their needs of the moment, but, because they are more verbal and better defended, there is generally less play disruption and less diffuse motoric discharge. For them, fantasy is more solidly established and more dependable as a way of expressing and solving conflicts.

> Eight-year-old David was referred for separation anxieties, including intense bedtime fears. In his first session he spied a bird puppet, then quickly chose the cat, witch, snake, shark, and octopus puppets for his story. The mommy bird, he announced, was looking for worms to feed her babies. Flying round and round, the bird was threatened by the cat, witch, and snake, all of whom chased her and tried to catch her for their dinner. Getting covered with dirt and other "yucky stuff," the exhausted bird fell into the ocean, where she was chased by a hungry shark. Suddenly an octopus came by and rescued the bird, carrying her safely to land. Shaking the water and yucky stuff loose, the bird was finally able to fly home, where she was happily greeted by three hungry, crying babies. The poignantly stated moral of the story was: "Don't go too far away from home, or you will lose your mother."

Materials

Number and Diversity of Puppets

If possible, it is helpful to have at least 15 to 20 hand puppets available for the child. This number is enough to stimulate interest and offer real choices within categories. While this selection can initially involve a sizable sum of money, it is a wise (and durable) investment if one continues to work with children over time. Sturdy, attractive puppets can be hand-made by a talented craftsperson, or they can be purchased ready-made.

In addition to offering depth to the clinical picture, an aesthetically pleasing variety of puppets can help to overcome initial inhibitions about play. *Range* and *variety* are important for obvious clinical reasons. The clinician is on firmer ground in noting, for example, that the child chose a fierce-looking wolf puppet, rather than a friendly-looking dog; or that a king was selected instead of a scruffy-looking "bad guy," and so forth.

Categories of Puppets

Choices might include the following categories: racially appropriate, realistic family figures and "royalty" puppets (king, queen, prince, princess, baby). Another useful category are "people" puppets which represent various occupations, such as a police officer, doctor, judge, or even a pirate. Animals—both tame (domestic) and wild (aggressive)—are another necessary category, since animals offer a safe disguise and psychological distance from reality. The witch, devil, ogre, bum, or skeleton are symbolic character types, often chosen to represent "bad" parents or aspects of the self. Puppets like these, chosen with an eye toward aesthetic quality and durability, are vastly appealing to children (and adults) and readily lend themselves to storymaking with all age groups.

Procedure

The Beginning

Initially it is helpful to meet child and family together. In a joint meeting, one can clarify the reasons for the visit, learn what each thinks about coming, and understand how each sees the problem(s). The therapist, the child is told, is someone who knows about kids, and is interested in understanding and helping. Following this discussion, parents wait, while child and therapist spend the rest of the hour together. In the playroom, the child is told that the therapist is interested in what kids think and feel, in order to be of help. One way to understand more is to have the child make up a pretend puppet story, which will be talked about later. Sometimes the metaphor of the puzzle is used, with the notion that it will take the efforts of both to put together all the pieces in a meaningful way.

Selection of Puppets

A basket of puppets can then be spilled out onto the floor. The child is invited to examine the puppet characters, selecting some that seem most interesting. The therapist also sits on the floor (or otherwise at eye level to the child), observing and noting the selection process. This warmup phase is instructive. The youngster's attitude and unique way of coping with this new experience is noted, as are the child's degree of interest or absorption in the task, spontaneous verbalizations, and voluntary and involuntary actions. Some puppets delight and gratify; some stimulate anxiety, frustration, or even hostility. Several examples will illustrate how children displaced certain feelings onto the devil puppet. Carrie became immediately intrigued with the devil, using it to discharge some of her bottled-up aggression. Sammy, on the other hand, made a face and threw the devil puppet away, saying emphatically, "Whoa—get *away!*" Still a third reaction was registered by James:

> Referred for obsessive-compulsive behaviors, 9-year-old James immediately noticed and became preoccupied with the "holes" in the devil's outfit. Half afraid to touch it, he asked if the holes could be repaired. When asked if he wanted to try to do so, he thought of fixing the holes with masking tape. That done, he sighed with relief, carefully put the devil aside, and turned his attention elsewhere. This behavior seemed to reflect his omnipresent concerns about bodily integrity.

The Warmup

Once puppets are selected, the child is invited to go behind a table or a puppet stage to introduce the "characters" for the show. This activity helps to prepare the child, as a kind of "warmup," for the story that is to follow. The therapist adds to the sense of pretend by announcing to a make-believe audience that the child will put on a show. Before the show starts, however, the puppets are introduced to the audience. "And *now* we have our first character in the story. *This* is…" and with this beginning, the therapist "cues" the child to hold up the puppets, one by one, and give them names. Children respond by giving a generic or a specific name to the puppet (i.e., "the king" or "King Know-it-all"). If the child seems shy, the therapist can dialogue briefly with the puppet (not the child), asking open-ended questions or making comments. For example, the therapist might say "King Know-it-all? What an unusual name." or, "Oh, a witch! Well, … what *sort* of a witch are you?" In this way, the child is helped to adopt the spirit of pretend, aiding the "willing suspension of disbelief" that is an inherent in the drama.

The Playing

Once the characters have been introduced, the therapist can announce: "And *now* … the story!" At this point, almost all children are sufficiently involved and can begin on their own. The therapist becomes an appreciative audience, observing, taking notes about plot, characters, action. But if the child indicates that he or she wants help, the therapist complies in a playful way. If the child is stuck, it may be useful to help the child think of the "five w's" of story construction (i.e., who, what, when, where, and why). For example, "Now we know the characters in the story. Let's think. Where might it take place? Let's pretend this is the first scene. The action could start with…" Generally children need only a little structure and some emotional support to get going. The spirit of pretend is contagious; once the child senses that "play is spoken here," and that there are no rights or wrongs, the child's imagination can take over.

The Post-Puppet Interview with the Puppet Characters

Puppet stories are like dreams. Some are long and elaborate; others are short and direct. Often, the plots of the dramas, like dreams, contain primary process elements of symbolization, displacement, and condensation. The more comfortable the therapist is with these ways of communicating, the more the therapist can understand and help the child.

Sometimes, the child gets stuck in a story just as in real life and needs help in articulating the problem or finding a solution. By talking to the puppet characters at the end of the story, the therapist can help clarify plot and theme. "Interviewing" the puppets, speaking directly to them about what happened can help unravel meaning and motivation. This process is also like dream work, wherein the clinician helps the client to associate to the parts of the dream that stand out, or to aspects that are unclear. Focusing on the *puppets*— rather than the *child*—helps extend the sense of make-believe and makes it possible to continue to gather associations to the story. Beginning with general questions, the therapist follows the child's lead to latent material regarding preoccupations and defenses.

The Post-Puppet Interview with the Child

Once the therapist has concluded the post-puppet "interview," the child is invited to talk directly about the experience. The therapist thus has further opportunities to assess the child's defenses, coping styles, and capacity for self-observation. For example, a therapist might ask what brought this particular story to mind. Was this a brand-new, "made-up" fantasy, one not heard before; or did it come from another story or a TV show? As with all fantasy material, puppet stories are stimulated by intrapsychic or interpersonal conflicts, family interactions, and reality events. The therapist listens with the "third ear" to learn more about the conflict and its many meanings. The child can be asked if anything similar ever happened before. What part(s) of the story did the child really like, or not like? And so on.

Gardner (1971), in his *Mutual Storytelling Technique,* suggests asking the child to give a title to the story. He also asks about identification with characters in the story. If possible, whom would the child *like* to be, and *not* like to be, in the story? Gardner asks for a moral or lesson to be learned from the story. These ideas, incorporated into the post-puppet interview, stimulate surprisingly direct and diagnostically helpful responses. Like dreams, puppet creations are influenced by unconscious factors. As with all fantasies, hidden and forbidden impulses are expressed (e.g., the princess can marry the king); and problems can be confronted (e.g., the scared child can encounter the bully who terrorizes her). Whether completed or interrupted, we assume that the puppet fantasy has some significance to the child. Deciphering the story's particular significance is the joint task of the therapist and child. If the therapist can engage the child in looking at the story to see what can be learned, this bodes well for the therapeutic alliance.

With the child's help, the therapist works to clarify theme and plot. Inquiry can be directed to intense or confusing behaviors, or "slips" in the story, as in the following example.

> Timid Brian, engrossed in a fantasy about a town's battle with a powerful witch, enacted a scene wherein a boy killed the witch. A second later, looking scared, Brian amended the plot, saying that the boy had only *"tried* to kill her—he didn't, though." This point was discussed later. "Well," he explained hesitantly, "witches are too powerful to kill. Especially her! She could kill you first—or even your best men—that's how strong she is." His moral: "Don't mess with witches—or you'll get killed!"

Talking with the child about such a story gives the therapist an opportunity to assess the strengths and weaknesses of the child's observing ego. In spite of his anxiety, Brian, for example, was able to hang in there, and talk about people who were as scary as that mean witch. The ability to psychologically step back and rethink the story was a sign of Brian's emotional resilience. Timmy, on the other hand, was emotionally derailed after playing a story about a dog who died in the desert. "He died of too much thirst—not enough to eat." Sighing, unable to go further, Timmy said he had played "Act I"; *maybe* he would do "Act II" next week. For now, he was tired … too tired to play any more. This hurting, deprived child experienced play disruption; he had apparently identified with the starving dog and it was too painful to continue.

EXAMINING THE EMERGENT DATA

Once the interview is concluded, the child's story can be examined for (1) form and content, (2) process, (3) management of anxiety, (4) underlying preoccupations, and (5) defenses and coping style. The interview can also be examined to see the kind of relationship the child begins to establish with the therapist. Was the child cooperative, compliant, combative, collaborative, controlling, seductive? The child's behavior, coupled with the therapist's reactions to it, gives some hint of potential transference and countertransference reactions. Greater understanding of these aspects will help the therapist make appropriate recommendations for treatment, if that is necessary.

Content

An examination of title, setting, characters, plot, and theme—all contribute to an understanding of the child's worries and wishes. The content may be thought of as a series of events that happen to the hero, with whom the child often identifies in some way. The hero:

(a) may represent aspects of the self or others (e.g., self or object representations);

(b) may be *one* character (pirate, alligator, prince, devil, etc.); *or*

(c) may be *many* characters, each representing some aspect of the self.

The child's identification(s) often become clearer in the post-puppet discussion. This is especially the case if the therapist asks which character(s) the child *would* like, and would *not* like to be. Sometimes, characters who are loved and hated represent aspects of the self, parts that may be split off or projected onto someone else. The character(s) with whom the child identifies may be the perception of the self that the child either wishes or fears himself to be. Timid David said he *would* like to be the witch, "'cause I'd like to fly and make everyone afraid. But I *wouldn't* like to be the king, "'cause he's too wimpy!"

During the inquiry, the therapist can ask the child to describe the characters, and perhaps even speculate about how they got to be the way they are. This request gives further information about the child's language skills, intellectual, and emotional development. The youngster who sees characters in a unidimensional way, as in fairy tales, is functioning at a lower emotional and developmental level than one who can see both sides of an issue, and therefore has an understanding of conflict and ambivalence.

Form

As Murphy (1956) has pointed out, the *form* of a story is a better indicator of the child's emotional health than the *content*. While the content is the *what* of the story, the form is the *how* of a story. Length and complexity, intelligibility and coherence, the sequential build to a logical ending—all give clues about the child's emotional development. Some stories are illogical, confused, and confusing; sometimes leading the child to "act out" during the puppet show, as did Beth, described earlier.

Creativity, coherence, and intelligibility are the hallmarks of play that is under the child's control (Portner, 1981). Underlying conflicts (that is, the child's preoccupations and his or her ways of dealing with them) are expressed in a symbolic way through plot and character structure. The child who plays with appropriate control, being neither overcontrolled and rigid, nor undercontrolled and regressed, demonstrates ego strength and a potential for insight-oriented work. A child whose play is chaotic and impulse-ridden, on the other hand, needs a structured, ego-building approach in treatment. Such a youngster needs a "covering" (rather than an "uncovering") approach that would strengthen appropriate defenses and repress/suppress troubling impulses (Sarnoff, 1976; Weil, 1973).

The therapist tries to see the world through the child's eyes. How does the child think and feel? Are the child's stories full of dichotomies, where people are presented in all-or-nothing, good-bad terms? Or does the child demonstrate an awareness of the admixture of good and bad, some neutralization of the love-hate, sexual-aggressive struggles? The latter, of course, reflects greater emotional maturity and development. Sometimes children present their characters in either/or terms (e.g., good guys/bad guys), but in discussion, the child indicates a tolerance for human failings, his or her own included. These self-other views give the therapist a chance to see something of the child's object relations and capacity for self-other differentiation. The following example illustrates the child's identification with her father.

Ten-year-old Eliza, for example, told a story of a princess who was a holy terror. She was bossy, demanding, even abusive to her parents, especially the well-meaning but weak king. When asked in the post-puppet interview what might have stimulated the princess's tirade, Eliza was at first puzzled, then volunteered that the princess became a "brat" when she took a drink. When this association was explored, Eliza said the princess drank when she was mad at her father. "She always thinks she doesn't get enough." A variation of Eliza's story was replayed the next week and led to further understanding of family dynamics, the father's many addictions, and Eliza's recent experimentation with alcohol. The story and ensuing discussion highlighted Eliza's identifications with her father, including narcissistic manipulations of others, with regressions and temper tantrums when frustrated.

Process

In the puppet task, therapists observe and describe the process of play, especially noting transitions, regressions, or disruptions. Although most clinicians try not to intervene in the play, especially in the diagnostic phase (Greenspan, 1981), one may need to do so to facilitate play or to deal with regression, as described earlier with Beth. The overall goal is to observe the ideas and feelings being enacted, and also see how the child deals with these issues. In the enactment, some children demonstrate good ego control; others are under-controlled or overcontrolled. Some rigid, tightly defended youngsters (such as James, described earlier in regard to the devil's outfit, or Cathy, described later) need to maintain tight control. It is as though they constantly prepare to play, but are never really able to do so. Other children are action-oriented. They find one or two puppets and, impulsive and flooded with affect, they begin immediately. For such youngsters, enactments seem to be more a discharge of motoric energy than a representation of symbolic conflict. Even so, such dramatizations vividly "represent" tremendous inner psychological pressure, enabling the therapist to see and feel the child's turmoil.

The therapist looks for congruence or disparity between what the child says and what the child does, between verbal and nonverbal communication, as in the following example.

> Billy giggled as he played out a story rife with scenes of injury and death. A fixed smile seemed to be pasted on his face as he insisted the play was "funny, not scary." The anxious denials continued, even though the words did not fit the music.

Children who are emotionally stable portray conflict through stories that contain character delineation, coherent plots, and logical endings. Thoughtful, psychologically minded children are able to associate to their stories, relating the issues to their own lives.

> Steven, 11 years of age, was referred for night terrors of several years' duration. He played a story of a pirate and his search for the lost treasure. Associations led him to thoughts of his mother ("and her treasures—like her jewelry") as well as of his father, who "always gives me the evil eye."
>
> An artistic child, Steven began to draw a large mural of the pirate's eye and, in doing so, was reminded of an accident he had had when he was four. Running across the street, he was hit by a car. Steven remembered looking up to see a headlight bearing down on him ("like a big eye"), and then he wakened in the hospital. Unable to see for several weeks, he began to have night terrors, which frightened everyone in the family and continued intermittently for several years.
>
> Interestingly, Steven's night terrors stopped after his first puppet session. A year later Steven had several "bad nights" after a brief hospitalization, only to disappear again after a therapeutic session. It is hypothesized that the puppet play allowed access to, and relief from, his troubling unconscious fantasies. Although Steven showed symptomatic improvement immediately after his first session, much work still needed to be done to understand and to work through his many other difficulties.

Management of Anxiety

As can be seen in the above example, puppet play has the power to stimulate ideas and feelings that are usually kept out of conscious awareness. One of the benefits of this kind of dramatization is that the child sees the activity as "just pretend." The usual superego defenses, therefore, may be bypassed, allowing the fantasy to continue. Sometimes, however, conflict emerges as wishes and fears collide. Then, just as with adults, psychological upset can be sensed. How the child manages the resultant anxiety is an important clinical issue.

If *repression,* as a defense mechanism is deficient or absent in the child's development, frightening fantasies may stimulate the child to "act out" unconscious wishes/fears, perhaps expressing them directly. A child who does so has not been able to form a true "psychoanalytic symbol" (Sarnoff, 1976), which can enable him or her to play without undue distress. When anxiety is strong, the therapist will try to determine just what the child is anxious about—what stimulated its emergence? The therapist will also notice how the child copes with anxiety. Is there motoric discharge, play disruption, escalation of fears, regression, or inhibition? The child who becomes upset, but can tolerate the inner tension rather than act it out (like Brian, mentioned earlier), is demonstrating greater psychological strength (structure), along with the potential for insight-oriented therapy. But if anxiety is so great that the child either cannot play, or acts out, then the child may need a structured, supportive, ego-building approach in treatment (Greenspan, 1981, Weil, 1973).

Preoccupation and Defenses

As the child plays, a theme emerges and is elaborated. This theme may be a wish or a fear; it may be welcomed or defended against. The therapist's understanding of the child's preoccupations and his or her way of dealing with them will help chart the path of treatment.

While healthy ego defenses contribute in a positive way to development and emotional stability, primitive or exaggerated defenses can indicate pathology and defensive character traits. Broadly speaking, defenses can be thought of as mental mechanisms that automatically come into being, operating outside of awareness (i.e., unconsciously) when one is anxious or feels distressed. When one begins to become aware of ideas and feelings that heretofore have been repressed, habitual defenses automatically begin to operate. The purpose of such unconscious maneuvering is to relieve tension and/or prevent even greater anxiety. It is an understandable attempt to protect the self against a perceived threat. Sometimes the "protection" works (e.g., the child denies he is angry and feels better); other times, however, the defense is inadequate or fails altogether. If so, then even greater efforts must be made to rid oneself of the unwanted impulses, a process that may result in greater anxiety, or even in symptom formation or pathology over time.

Defenses range along a continuum from primitive to more mature. Some of the more common defenses include splitting, denial, projection, displacement, undoing, repression, reaction formation, externalization, rationalization, intellectualization, altruism, and sublimation. As children approach latency, drives are defended against by a shift in defenses. The primary mechanisms of defense that maintain the latency structure are repression, reaction formation, displacement, symbol formation, and sublimation. Especially important is *repression,* a defense mechanism that serves to hold impulses in check—that is, keep them out of awareness. Projection and displacement are also prominent in latency when impulses and feelings from the inner world are played out in fantasy and daydreams. Stronger defenses in latency represent an achievement that results in a period of calm, which makes learning possible. Stronger defenses also pave the way for symbol formation in fantasy. Reducing tension, fantasy provides a safe outlet for ideas and feelings, thus helping to maintain psychic equilibrium. Emotionally stable children (e.g., "the normal neurotic") can benefit from interpretation of fantasy, provided this is done in an informed and sensitive way. Caution is needed with fragile children, such as borderline or psychotic youngsters, who may need the defense of fantasy (i.e., denial in fantasy) to help them to manage their anxiety (Ekstein, 1966).

Defenses are sometimes vivid and compelling; at other times, they are so much a part of the background that they blend into the landscape. It is important to be able to identify defenses, however, for latency children are often afraid of the strength of their drives, especially their aggression, and one may need to analyze defenses before analyzing underlying (id) impulses.

Ten-year-old John, for example, staged a fight between the "wild dog" and the king. With a flourish, the dog said, "Got him!"—and the king fell over, as though dead. In the discussion that followed, however, John emphatically denied that the king had been killed. "Why would I kill him? Next to the dog and the horse, he's my best guy!" Denial was the way John dealt with many issues, including his adamant refusal to acknowledge any bad feelings toward his often absent, often disappointing father. On the other hand, much anger was felt (displaced?) toward his mother who could do nothing right—a situation, unfortunately, that is not uncommon in divorced families. One could make little progress interpreting John's anger at his father, but helping the child examine his insistent (defensive) need to present his father as a "great guy" was more successful.

CASE EXAMPLES

Issues that Shape Technique

Before presenting case examples to illustrate the varied ways that children use puppets, it might be useful to briefly consider some issues that impact on technique. As the foregoing material suggests, most children respond readily to the opportunity to play with puppets. As all child workers know, however, many youngsters need sensitive and informed therapeutic help before a meaningful encounter can take place.

The reactions of children as they come into the playroom are astonishingly varied. Some troubled children are inhibited and shy away from using puppets because they are afraid of "letting go." On the surface, they seem afraid of the adult, but at a deeper level, they fear their own unconscious fantasies of destruction and rage. Sometimes children, uneasy with intimacy, play hide and seek in their play, dreading/yet wishing that they and their secrets will be found out. Hypercritical and perfectionistic children often project their own negativity onto the therapist, expecting condemnation. Children who have been harshly treated may come in ready for a fight. Angry and hurt, sure that the present will repeat the past, they unconsciously try to provoke the anticipated rejection. Others, disorganized, unfocused, and impulsive, need the adult's "organizing ego" to stay on task. These and countless other situations impact on technique, and call for different responses from the therapist. Since each child is unique, one's technique must be adapted anew each time. No matter what the child brings, however, sensitivity, flexibility, and skill, buttressed by humor and creativity, can help pave the way to a therapeutic alliance.

Having a variety of media and modalities can be helpful in dealing with children who cannot or will not play. Those who are highly resistant can particularly benefit from being given a choice about play materials. The child who declines the use of puppets in an initial interview may feel more comfortable using art materials, or playing in the sand box, or with miniature life toys, depending on his or her interests and psychological state. A session or two later, with a stronger therapeutic bond, the child may be more inclined to respond positively to another modality, as happened in the case examples which follow.

Giving choices not only lessens anxiety, fosters spontaneity, and builds trust, it is also realistic. Most youngsters move back and forth between modalities, exploring issues in one domain in one session, in another the next time. Getting too close to an issue may stimulate resistance, leading a child to (unconsciously) seek emotional distance via another modality (Irwin & Rubin, 1976). The therapist who can follow the child's lead and communicate in the many languages of play has valuable additional tools that can lead to understanding and helping.

The technique one uses is also determined by the diagnostic question and the number of sessions available for assessment and/or treatment. These factors often dictate just how structured the session need be. If one has only one or two sessions with the child, one can limit choices and use a more structured approach. One can turn to the "presenting complaint," and suggest that the problem be explored through puppet play. To George, referred for his aggressive acts, the therapist said, "Since we want to understand more about the fights and how they get started, let's pick an imaginary family and some friends and see what happens. Who could be in the story?" A similar theme was suggested to Louise, who was terrorized by the fantasy that a robber was going to come in her window. With only a thin disguise for cover, the therapist said: "If a make-believe family were getting ready for bed at night, what might happen? Let's pick the family, and see who could be the robber in our story." A more direct approach was used with Robert, who complained that kids at school were always picking on him: "Let's practice what you might do the next time this happens. Pick some puppets to be the kids at school. Let's act this out and find some ways you can protect yourself." In these cases, the therapist took the lead, based on the referral complaint, and invited the child's participation in mutual problem-solving that might lead to greater understanding.

To illustrate some of these common problems, case material will be presented. The first child, Carrie, is an electively mute youngster with marked separation anxiety, who approached puppet work via art and storytelling. Since part of the therapist's stock in trade is words, a youngster who does not talk presents especially vexing problems in treatment. The second child, John, was highly anxious and impulsive, factors that stimulated regression and lack of control. Directness was needed to help lessen his anxiety and dampen down the negative interactions that were threatening to sabotage treatment.

Carrie: Electively Mute and Separation Anxious

Labeled shy, 6-year-old Carrie did not speak to peers or teachers. Since this had been her pattern since preschool, her mother considered this to be a troublesome but not particularly critical problem, particularly since she was talkative and lively at home. In first grade, however, her elective mutism clearly presented an obstacle to learning, and a referral followed.

In the initial therapy session, Carrie smiled broadly but clung tenaciously to her mother, making it clear that separation was impossible. The mother was invited to sit nearby, while Carrie was shown a range of expressive media, including art materials, miniature life toys, the sand box, and puppets. Carrie looked dazed and barely seemed to notice what was happening. Sitting where she could keep an eye on her mother, the child selected the black magic marker and slowly drew an evocative picture of a mother, child, and dog, surrounded by many letters and numbers. She refused to say anything about her drawing, but smiled at the therapist's guesses about the letters and numbers, nodding yes or no. Maintaining a conversational air, the therapist narrated what was happening during the session, occasionally directing a comment to mother. At the end of the session, Carrie insisted on taking the drawing home, although she allowed a copy to be made of her drawing. Once safely out of the playroom, she began to talk excitedly to her mother about the picture, specifically identifying the numbers and letters the therapist had wondered about. In this indirect way, the child communicated with the therapist, albeit through mother.

In the second and third session, Carrie again insisted that mother stay in the room. Again she chose to draw, but this time it seemed she was making a family, using letters and shapes of various sizes. Because some of the figures—especially the number 8—seemed to have facial features, the therapist began, in a playful way, to talk about how "this looks like a Big Daddy 8—this, a Mommy 8—and *here's* a little Baby 8." Carrie promptly drew a "dog 8" and, smiling at this piece of nonsense, made eye contact. She said not a word, but communicated a great deal. In time, the drawings of the 8's became even more differentiated—big ones, small ones, tall ones, fat ones, and so forth. Sensing the approach of an alliance as play signals went flying back and forth (Murphy, 1972), the therapist commented on what looked like cauliflower ears on one figure. Carrie laughed out loud (her first *verbalized* communication) and promply drew elaborate ears, sprouting vegetation. Soon a funny dialogue took place, as the child did the drawing, while the therapist did the talking and the guessing. Each participant influenced the other, even though the therapist tried to follow the child's lead. New themes emerged, all having the flavor of controlled nonsense, as Carrie visibly relaxed and gave herself over to the play process.

In the third session, Carrie's drawing and play became more spontaneous, regressive, intense. By the end of the session, the power of play was too much to resist, and she began to talk. Having been given a drawing book, Carrie drew, and then rhythmically "wrote out" her story, mimicking the therapist's note-taking. The therapist continued to try to narrate what was happening, and eventually a dreamlike story evolved.

Still using only the black magic marker, Carrie developed a drawing/story of a "bad sun." As the action unfolded, the figure 8's (who by now were personified as people) were having a picnic. After drawing happy clouds and cheerful faces on the 8's, Carrie drew a sun with a very sad face. Speaking to the sun in the picture, the therapist said that he looked sad; had something happened to make him feel bad? Responding through her drawing, Carrie began to draw black rays coming out from the sun. These rays came in such abundance that eventually everything in the once-cheerful picture was dense with black lines. When the therapist wondered if the people were "sad and mad" about having their picnic darkened, maybe ruined, Carrie nodded, but just shrugged at questions about why Mr. Sun had spoiled the party with all those dark rays. Then, speaking again to Mr. Sun, the therapist wondered if he might have felt left out—way up there in the sky, not able to picnic with all the 8's. Carrie smiled and nodded, indicating that was so.

Then, with a giggle, Carrie promptly drew a picture of the sun in jail, with a creature (later identified as a spider), sneaking up behind the sun to *bite* him! This piece of revenge was so sudden, the therapist expressed surprise and Carrie, delighted with her solution, laughed out loud. Forgetting her vow of silence, Carrie said the spider was going to bite the sun "because *he's* mad at him, too."

The sun was lonely, she said, because there was no one to play with him. Going to the toy telephone, Carrie suggested that the therapist call Mr. Sun to play, "'cause *we* could be friends." When the therapist did as instructed, however, Carrie repeatedly refused to answer the phone, each refusal becoming more forceful. In this piece of play, she seemed to be acting out her drawing, with each participant being a puppet of sorts. In shifting from art to drama, she laughed out loud, perhaps glad to be active, not passive. Carrie clearly relished playing the role of the aggressor, while the therapist was the "mad and sad" victim.

At the end of the third session, the therapist tried to make some connections between the play and reality. Asked if she was sometimes lonely, just like Mr. Sun, Carrie nodded yes, saying it was her mom she missed the most. The child then immediately went over to her mother and put her head on her lap, fingers in her mouth. The therapist then said, "Carrie, now that you know that it's safe in here, I wonder if you can be *with* me, *without* your mom the next time. In a way, we've been keeping your mom in jail with us—in this room—just like Mr. Sun in the story. Maybe we can let your mom out of jail. What do you say?" Carrie smiled and again laughed out loud when the therapist added that her mom might be lonely, but that her mom would be safe, too; *no spiders* would bite her, as they did to Mr. Sun!

Thereafter, Carrie had no trouble coming into the playroom without her mother. From that beginning, where she used her drawings as projective carriers of her fantasy life, she moved to using puppets in enactment. Emboldened by the earlier play, she became increasingly free to explore her aggression. In her stories, she used the devil to "eat up" all the aggressive animals in the jungle. The theme? Mr. Devil is ANGRY! If she could be anybody in the story, who would she most like to be? *Nobody,* she said with a face, because they all got eaten by the Devil. Who *wouldn't* she like to be? "Mr. Devil, 'cause he is *mean!*" While all characters were either aggressors or victims at this point (Gould, 1972), the core conflict always seemed to center around the theme of loneliness.

From that point on until termination, Carrie continued to talk, expressing and exploring her ambivalent feelings, especially toward her mother. The initial pleasure in attacking the bad animals began to give way and she spoke more about her sadness and loneliness, especially her pain in separating from her mother. In time, the "bad guys," including the devil, became more human, less demonized, as she modified her own tendency toward splitting into good and bad (i.e., negative projective identification, Kernberg, 1976). For the first time Carrie was able to express a range of feelings as she reexperienced the mourning and loss of the "good mother."

In part, what made the reparative work possible was Carrie's recognition of her disappointment and anger at her mother, feelings that mother could understand and accept. The post-puppet dialogue with the puppets was helpful in this regard. In one session, the characters were asked if they knew why Mr. Devil was so mean. The shark answered: "It's 'cause he doesn't have a mom to teach him to be nice!" When the puppets were asked what happened to his mom, the shark responded, "She just went away and never came back." This gave the therapist an opportunity to ask Carrie later if she ever worried that her mom might go to work and not come back, like Mr. Devil's mom. As a single parent, Carrie's mother had to return to work shortly after the birth, something that worried and grieved this sensitive woman. Although Carrie said she knew her mom would *always* come back, this discussion was enough to prompt the child to tell her mom about the puppet story, especially the part about the mom leaving. This gave mother a chance to tell Carrie about her early years, and how hard it was to leave her, crying, in the day care. Another time, when the theme was revisited, Carrie said one of her friends was "mad as heck" about her mom's work. Told that kids could feel that way and still love their moms a lot, Carrie agreed, adding, "even if they're mad as heck."

Carrie began to give up her nonverbal isolation at school shortly after her third session. First she whispered to teachers and a friend, then she talked to them, out loud. In that way, she exchanged her symptom for the uncomfortable awareness of her negative feelings toward her mother. Several conjoint mother-child sessions helped the child to feel confident enough to speak of things that troubled her. And mother, relieved that her child was becoming asymptomatic, began to recognize her part in unconsciously insisting that Carrie be a "good girl" and not speak of negative feelings. Both parties needed the reassurance that anger is a human response to other feelings, like loneliness, sadness, disappointment. Both needed to realize that such feelings could be tolerated, and that there are other ways of dealing with such emotions. Together they decided that they would have a daily talk time; that Carrie would continue to "write" and draw in her feelings book; and, finally, that mother would buy a "really strong" punching bag for Carrie.

John: Echoing his Family's Confusion and Chaos

An especially observant teacher spoke to John's parents, suggesting a referral. Always on the periphery of groups, this 9-year-old seemed depressed at times, overly active and controlling at other times. While John pestered his teachers with a variety of complaints, he also seemed bored and unmotivated, in spite of many intellectual and creative gifts.

At first glance, John seemed anything but depressed. Constantly on the go, he moved like a whirling dervish from one activity to another, giving the impression of a hyperactive, perhaps even ADHD, child. Rejecting the puppets, he made a beeline for the sandbox and alternated between that activity and hastily scribbled pictures. In the sandbox he built and destroyed "mountains," either roughly banging them flat, or drowning them with water until they dissolved into big sandy puddles. When that happened, sand went everywhere. Reminders that "the sand stays in the sandbox" went unheeded.

Spying the toy telephone, John said he would call the therapist. As soon as his call was answered, however, he either slammed the phone down, or answered by saying, "Joe's Pizza Shop," or "Max's Garage, get your car fixed here," or, more frequently, "The hospital—what room do you want?" He clearly enjoyed the therapist's puzzlement and dismay about the repeated wrong numbers, chortling loudly as he banged the phone into the receiver. Like a much younger child, John seemed frenetic and relentless in this play, almost sadistic in his pleasure in frustrating and disappointing the therapist.

By the second session the therapist realized that John's hyperactivity and mess-making, coupled with his lack of control, was eliciting an anxious and depressed countertransference response. Watching him, the therapist became convinced that his behavior had more aspects of ADHD than anxiety, and began to wonder about having the child be tested. At the end of the second session, however, the therapist decided to talk with John about his unrelenting need to "play tricks" on her. Did he have some ideas about why he was always tricking her? John looked blank, and then said, "But you're *supposed* to get mad." Taken aback, the therapist asked why that might be so, a question to which he had no answer. The therapist then suggested that both try to think of other ways that his strong feelings could be expressed, rather than just through playing tricks.

In the third session, when John again began to use the telephone for the tricking game, the therapist suggested instead that he select some puppets to use in playing out that same story. Intrigued by a few fierce-looking puppet animals (the snake, dragon, wolf), John gathered a host of puppets behind the stage. Without much fanfare, John's story began with the animals bumping into each other in the dark. Fights erupted, tempers flared, harsh words were hurtled back and forth, and various animals said they would never be friends again.

After this chaotic beginning scene, John stopped the play. Again, feeling at a loss to understand the powerful feelings in the air, the therapist said that things were very confusing. Could someone in the story help make some sense of this? John then selected some people to be in the play, in addition to the animals. The King appeared and asked several animals why they were fighting. No one knew, but then a wise man appeared. "Oh, your majesty," the wise man said, "it's because the sun refuses to shine." "Why is that?" the King demanded. "The sun says she is too tired. She's sick. She says she works too hard and needs to sleep. The people and animals are mad at her because there's no sunshine."

Angry, the King announced a contest to see who could get the sun out of bed. The wolf made loud noises and ran around in circles to waken her; the gorilla threw stones in her direction; and the cook prepared a feast—all to no avail. The sun refused to get up.

Then John stopped again, saying that it was intermission time. But rather than resume the drama, John bounced from activity to activity, running around in circles, as it were, re-enacting what had just happened in his story. Several times he returned to the telephone play. Grabbing the phone, he yelled: "The hospital! What room do you want?" At that moment, the therapist realized that John was probably referring to his mother, who had been hospitalized many times during his young life. His story of a sleeping sun and resulting chaos seemed to be a symbolic depiction of the confusion in his house. No wonder he was unable to predict an ending, so to speak. With his mother's illness, he was facing a reality he did not understand.

In the initial interviews, John's mother said, briefly, that she had been hospitalized but she made it clear that she did not want to discuss this topic further. Instead, she focused on the details of who took care of the children while she was sick. Watching John pretend to call the hospital, the therapist said, "John, I wonder if you are worried right now, thinking of someone else who is sick and can't get out of bed." John did a double take and then quieted down. He said his mother was sick, and would probably have to go to the hospital again. The child didn't seem to know where his mother was; he was staying with the grandparents "who don't tell me anything." John went on to say that his mom often had to go to the hospital "to get her medicine changed," but he didn't know why. "Couldn't they just tell her on the phone what she should take?" The therapist said that those were good questions that deserved answers. She would talk to his parents or grandparents to find out, and he could do the same.

A phone call to father revealed that mother had just been hospitalized for bipolar disorder, her tenth hospital stay. Her hospitalizations began when John was three months old and continued intermittently over the years. Father explained that they tried "not to bother" John or his brother because they were too young to understand. Also, "John sets her off." Regrettably, John's father said, his wife often yelled that John was making her sick and she would have to go to the hospital. When that happened, the boys went to grandmother's, a helpful distraction, in father's opinion. When the therapist explained how confused John was, father asked for help in explaining the illness to the boys. In the ensuing discussion, John was visibly relieved to be told about mother's illness and her mood swings, especially her debilitating depressions. Relieved, John said, "I thought it was me—running around, making noise." Although still worried and depressed, John became calmer, relieved that some of the confusion had lessened.

SUMMARY

This chapter presents the rationale for the use of puppets in assessment. As projective media, puppets offer the universality and ambiguity of many possible identifications. The fantasy material from the child's puppet story can help to reveal the child's preoccupations and his or her ways of dealing with them. A puppet procedure that can facilitate spontaneous story enactment was outlined, along with suggestions for examining the form and content of the emergent data. Case studies were presented, focusing on common problems one encounters in meeting a child in initial sessions, illustrating the idiosyncratic ways that children respond to this modality, and suggesting some strategies for dealing with these difficulties.

REFERENCES

Bechman, P., & Kohl, F. (1984). The effects of social and isolate toys on the interactions and play of integrated and nonintegrated groups of preschoolers. *Education & Training of the Mentally Retarded, 19* (3), 169–174.

Bender, L. (1952). *Child psychiatric techniques.* Springfield, IL: Thomas.

Borkin, J., & Frank, L. (1986). Sexual abuse prevention for preschoolers: A pilot program. *Child Welfare, 65* (1), 75–82.

Bornstein, B. (1945). Clinical notes on child analysis. *Psychoanalytic Study of the Child, 1,* 151–166.

Brody, S., & Axelrod, S. (1970). *Anxiety and ego formation in infancy.* New York: International Universities Press.

Bunting, K. (1985). The use and effect of puppetry and bibliotherapy in group counseling with children of divorced parents. (Doctoral dissertation, College of William and Mary.) *Dissertation Abstracts International, 45,* 10-A, 3094.

Carkhuff, R. (1969). *Helping and human relationships* (Vols. 1 & 2). New York: Holt, Rinehart and Winston.

Cassell, S. (1965). Effect of brief puppet therapy upon the emotional responses of children undergoing cardiac catherization. *Journal of Consulting Psychology, 29,* 1–8.

Cassidy, J. (1988). Child-mother attachment and the self in six-year olds. *Child Development, 59* (1), 121–134.

Copple, C., Cocking, R., & Matthews, W. (1984). Objects, symbols, and substitutes: The nature of the cognitive activity during symbolic play. In T. Yawkey & A. Pellegrini (Eds.), *Child's play: Developmental and applied.* Hillsdale, NJ: Erlbaum.

Curry, N., & Arnaud, S. (1984). Play in developmental preschool settings. In T. Yawkey & A. Pellegrini (Eds.), *Child's play: Developmental and applied.* Hillsdale, NJ: Erlbaum.

Dunn, J., & Wooding, C. (1977). Play in the home and its implications for learning. In B. Tizard & D. Harvey (Eds.), *Biology of play.* Philadelphia: Lippincott.

Edington. G. (1985). Handpuppets and dolls in psychotherapy with children. *Perceptual-Motor Skills, 61* (3), 691–696.

Ekstein, R. (1966). *Children of time and space, of action and impulse.* New York: Meredith.

Erikson, E. (1963). *Childhood and society.* New York: Norton.

Fein, G. G. (1979). Play with actions and objects. In B. Sutton-Smith (Ed.), *Play and learning.* New York: Gardner Press.

Fein, G. G. (1981). Pretend play in childhood: An integrative review. *Child Development, 52,* 1095–1118.

Freud, A. (1922-1970). *The writings of Anna Freud.* New York: International Universities Press.

Freud, S. (1955). Beyond the pleasure principle. In J. Strachey (Ed. and Trans.), *The standard editions of the complete works of Sigmund Freud* (Vol. 18). London: Hogarth. (Original work published in 1920.)

Gardner, R. (1971). *Therapeutic communications with children: The mutual story-telling technique.* New York: Science House.

Gendler, M. (1985). The wild world of divorce: A thematic, developmental psychological analysis of puppet plays of school age children. (Doctoral dissertation, Boston University.) *Dissertation Abstracts International, 45,* 7-B, 23–31.

Gould, R. (1972). *Child studies through fantasy.* New York: Quadrangle Books.

Greenspan, S. (1981). *The clinical interview of the child.* New York: McGraw-Hill.

Hartmann, H. (1964). *Essays on ego psychology.* New York: International Universities Press.

Hawkey, L. (1976). The use of puppets in child psychotherapy. In C. Schaefer (Ed.), *Therapeutic use of child play* (pp. 359–372). New York: Aronson.

Henderson, B. (1984). Social context of exploratory play. In T. Yawkey & A. Pellegrini (Eds.), *Child's play: Developmental and applied.* Hillsdale, NJ: Erlbaum.

Howells, J., & Townsend, D. (1973). Puppetry as a medium for play diagnoses. *Child Psychiatry Quarterly, 6* (1), 9–14.

Irwin, E. (1983). The diagnostic & therapeutic use of pretend play. In C. Schaefer & K. O'Connor (Eds.), *Handbook of play therapy* (pp. 148–173). New York: Wiley.

Irwin, E. (1985). Puppets in therapy: An assessment procedure. *American Journal of Psychotherapy, 39*(3), 389–400.

Irwin, E., & Malloy, E. (1975). Family puppet interviews, *Family Process, 14,* 179–191.

Irwin, E., & Rubin, J. (1976). Art and drama interviews: Decoding symbolic messages. *Art Psychotherapy, 3,* 169–175.

Irwin, E., & Shapiro, M. (1975). Puppetry as a diagnostic and therapeutic technique. In I. Jakab (Ed.), *Psychiatry and art* (Vol. 4). Basel, Switzerland: Karger.

Jenkins, R., & Beckh. E. (1942). Finger puppets and mask-making as a media for work with children. *American Journal of Psychiatry, 12,* 294–300.

Kernberg, O. (1976). *Object relations theory and clinical psychoanalysis.* New York: Aronson.

Klein, M. (1932). *The psychoanalysis of children.* London: Hogarth.

Kohut, H. (1971). *The analysis of the self.* New York: International Universities Press.

Kohut, H. (1977). *The restoration of the self.* New York: International Universities Press.

Krause. F. (1970). *Jocko goes to the hospital.* Racine, WI: Pace Productions.

Lowenfeld, M. (1939). The world pictures of children: A method of recording and studying them. *British Journal of Medical Psychology, 18,* 65–101.

Lyle, J., & Holly, S. (1941). The therapeutic value of puppets. *Menninger Clinic Bulletin, 5,* 223–226.

Mahler, M. S. (1968). *On human symbiosis and the vicissitudes of individuation.* New York: International University Press.

Mahler, M. S., Pine, F., & Bergman, A. (1975). *The psychological birth of the human infant: Symbiosis and individuation.* New York: Basic Books.

Mitchell, S. (1988). *Relational concepts in psychoanalysis: An integration.* Cambridge, MA: Harvard Universities Press.

Murphy, L. (1956). *Methods for the study of personality in young children* (Vol. 1). New York: Basic Books.

Murphy, L. (1972). Infants' play and cognitive development. In M. Piers (Ed.), *Play and development.* New York: Norton.

Myers, D. (1971). A comparison of the effects of group puppet therapy and group activity with mentally retarded children. (Doctoral dissertation, Lehigh University.) *Dissertation Abstracts International, 31,* 10-A, 5234.

Piaget, J. (1962). *Play, dreams and imitation in childhood.* New York: Norton.

Portner, E. (1981). A normative study of the spontaneous puppet stories of eight-year-old children. Unpublished doctoral dissertation, Department of Higher Education, University of Pittsburgh, Pittsburgh, PA.

Pulaski, M. (1973). Toys and imaginative play. In J. Singer (Ed.), *The child's world of make-believe.* New York: Academic Press.

Rambert, M. (1949). *Children in conflict.* New York: International Universities Press.

Rojas-Bermudez, J. (1970). The intermediary object. *Group Psychotherapy, 22* (3–4), 49–154.

Ross, P. (1977). A diagnostic technique for assessment of parent-child and family interaction patterns. The family puppet technique. *Family Therapy, 4* (2), 129–142.

Rubin, J. (1978). *Child art therapy.* New York: Van Nostrand Reinhold.

Rubin, K. H., & Pepler, D. J. (1980). The relationship of child's play to social-cognitive development. In H. Foot, T. Chapman & J. Smith (Eds.), *Friendship and childhood relationships.* London: Wiley.

Sarnoff, R. (1976). *Latency.* New York: Aronson.

Schaefer, C., & O'Conner, K. (1983). *Handbook of play therapy,* New York: Wiley.

Shuttleworth, R. (1986). Alternative methods of communicating with children in family therapy. *Maladjustment and Therapeutic Education, 4*(2), 129–142.

Smilansky, S. (1968). *The effects of socio-dramatic play on disadvantaged pre-school children.* New York: Wiley.

Snow, J., & Paternite, C. (1986). Individual and family therapy in the treatment of children. *Professional Psychology: Research and Practice, 17* (3), 242–250.

Spiegel, S. (1996). *An Interpersonal approach to child and adolescent psychotherapy.* Northvale: Aronson.

Spitz, R. (1972). Fundamental education. In M. Piers (Ed.), *Play and development.* New York: Norton.

Stern. D. (1985). *The interpersonal world of the infant.* New York: Basic Books.

Weil, A. (1973). Ego strengthening prior to analysis. *Psychoanalytic Study of the Child, 28,* 287–301.

Werner, H., & Kaplan, B. (1963). *Symbol formation.* New York: Wiley.

White, R. W. (1959). Motivation reconsidered: The concept of competence. *Psychological Review, 59*, 297–333.

Winnicott, D. (1953). Transitional objects and transitional phenomena: A study of the first not-me possession. *International Journal of Psychoanalysis, 34*, 89–97.

Woltmann, A. (1940). The use of puppets in understanding children. *Mental Hygiene, 24*, 445–458.

Woltmann, A. (1951). The use of puppetry as a projective method in therapy. In H. H. Anderson & G. L. Anderson (Eds.), *An introduction to projective techniques* (pp. 606–638). New York: Prentice-Hall.

Woltmann, A. (1952). Puppet shows as a psychotherapeutic method. In L. Bender (Ed.), *Child psychiatric techniques.* Springfield, IL: Thomas.

Woltmann, A. (1960). Spontaneous puppetry by children as a projective method. In A. E. Rabin & M. R. Haworth (Eds.), *Projective techniques with children* (pp. 305–312). New York: Grune & Stratton.

Woltmann, A. (1964). Diagnostic and therapeutic consideration of nonverbal projective activities with children. In M. R. Haworth (Ed.), *Child psychotherapy* (pp. 322–329). New York: Basic Books.

Woltmann, A. (1972). Puppetry as a tool in child psychotherapy. *International Journal of Child Psychotherapy, 1* (1), 84–96.

Chapter 25 ————————————————————————————

THE PUPPET SENTENCE COMPLETION TASK

Susan M. Knell and Kelly W. Beck

INTRODUCTION

Projective techniques range from relatively structured to relatively unstructured. Their utility has been well documented in the literature. These techniques are based on the psychoanalytic notion of projection, which is a process where an individual "externalizes" needs, feelings, conflicts, and motivations onto ambiguous stimuli (Rabin, 1960). The sentence completion test or task (SCT) is a projective technique that has been identified as one of the most frequently used psychological assessment tools for adults and adolescents (Lubin, Larsen, & Matarazzo, 1984).

Sentence completion tasks require the subject to complete a sentence stem or fragment related to various contents. The specific content, instructions, and structure of the stem is different for different forms. The content of the stem may be changed to accommodate various clinical and research purposes. The flexibility of the instrument is a likely contributor to its popularity as a projective measure today (Goldberg, 1965).

Assessment and treatment of preschool-age children can be challenging, particularly due to a lack of assessment tools that are developmentally sensitive to the needs of young children. Often the process of play serves as a means of assessment and treatment. Because children so readily express themselves through the process of play it is often the most appropriate means of interaction with young children. One way of providing developmentally sensitive assessment techniques is to integrate puppets into assessment procedures. The use of puppets in both assessment and therapy with young children is both developmentally appropriate and well documented (e.g., Irwin, 1991). The Puppet Sentence Completion Task (PSCT; Knell, 1992) was developed to make the traditional SCT more appropriate for preschool-age children and is presented in this chapter.

HISTORY OF THE SENTENCE COMPLETION TASKS

More than a century ago Ebbinghaus (1897; cited in Hart, 1986) proposed the method of incomplete sentences to assess mental abilities. He hypothesized that the more complex the response to the sentence stem the greater the intellectual potential. Others in the field continued the development of this technique as a means of intellectual assessment until the middle of this century. However, over the course of time, interest in this area weakened due to the difficulties in establishing the psychometric properties that would support the validity and reliability of the technique.

Although the original intent of Ebbinghaus was to assess intellect with sentence completion tasks, Jung began looking at personality assessment using a similar technique (Hart, 1986). In the early 1900s Jung was one of the first to explore the associations between stimulus words and elicited responses, developing the word association technique. However, it was later believed that word association methods constricted the responses given by most individuals to popular responses, which significantly decreased the likelihood of obtaining rich clinical data. Payne (1928) and Tendler (1930) were among the first to abandon the simplistic word association techniques for sentence stems, which they believed produced responses less tainted by cultural stereotypes and more reflective of the subject's individuality. Payne's measure was developed to assist in vocational guidance. There has not been any published material in the psychological literature describing or addressing the psychometric properties of Payne's procedure. Tendler's measure consisted of 20 items, entitled "A Test for Emotional Insight." The majority of sentence stems began with the word "I". Each item was thought to pull for an emotional response. According to Rotter (1951), Tendler "found the test to be of considerable clinical value and felt that informal comparison of the sentence completion with autobiographical sketches was a promising method of validation" (p. 298).

During WWII the sentence completion technique was added to the psychological test battery for the assessment and placement of U.S. soldiers (Hart, 1986). Murray and MacKinnon (1946) developed an instrument that contained 100 items that elicited responses in 12 specific areas of personality, referred to as follows: family, past, goals, drives, inner states, cathexis, optimism, pessimism, energy, reactions to failures and frustrations, reactions to and of others. The purpose of this specific sentence completion test was to provide those assessing soldiers with screening information, which was further explored upon interview. Later, a 40-item sentence completion technique was developed by Rotter and Willerman (1947) for use in military hospitals. The measure was then changed for use with civilian populations and was named the Incomplete Sentences Blank (ISB; Rotter, Rafferty, & Schactitz, 1949). The ISB is still widely used today.

As stated earlier, there has not been a significant attempt to psychometrically validate sentence completion tests. Considering the range of possible responses and even the various forms of the sentence completion test, standardization has been difficult to address scientifically. Yet it has survived for over a century. According to Goldberg (1965), the popular use of this instrument indicates its clinical utility in applied settings. In fact, the implementation of sentence completion tasks as a means of assessing personality and attitudes has evolved into one of the 10 most frequently used psychological tests for adolescents and adults (Lubin, Larsen, & Matarazzo, 1984).

Literature regarding the usefulness of the sentence completion task with children is limited. The majority of publications addressing related research findings and applied uses are focused on adults and adolescents. There have been several issues raised regarding its limitations with the child population. Specifically, Hart (1986) noted initial concerns presented in the literature, such as the child's questionable ability to participate in the projective process, possible difficulty understanding the ambiguity of the task, and difficulty conceptualizing and verbalizing feelings and attitudes. However, when sentence stems are appropriately adapted to the experiences of children it appears that the responses can be helpful in gleaning clinical information.

PROJECTIVE TECHNIQUES WITH CHILDREN

Projective techniques have been classified into various categories based on their purpose, responses elicited, methods of interpretation, and administration. Rabin (1960) presented a method of classification for projective techniques with children. Five separate categories were identified as follows: associative techniques (e.g., Rorschach; Rorschach, 1942), construction techniques (e.g., TAT; Murray, 1938), completion techniques (e.g., SCT; Rotter, Rafferty, & Schactitz, 1949), choice or ordering techniques, such as the Q sort (Stephenson, 1953), and expressive techniques (e.g., free play and puppets; Freud, 1946). Methods were categorized based on the degree of structure versus the degree of ambiguity.

Projective techniques are based on the assumption that individuals project unacknowledged needs, motives, and desires onto ambiguous stimuli. By presenting the individual with test items that have some degree of ambiguity the individual is compelled to create meaning for the stimulus, which is thought to be fabricated by his or her own internal needs, motives, and desires. Some individuals who are highly defended demonstrate a lack of freedom in their responses to stimulus fields (Rabin, 1960). For example, the subject may refuse, or have difficulty completing, a sentence stem related to an area of stress or difficulty in his or her life. Inferentially, then, the clinician may be able to interpret themes of conflict the individual is unwilling or unable to address. However, theorists are uncertain if the same process occurs for the projective responses of children.

According to Rabin (1960), the instability of both the ego and personality structure of a child hamper the understanding of the projective process. Some theorists propose limited use of projective techniques for young children given their restricted verbal and abstract reasoning as well as their limited experiences within the world. According to Obrzut and Bolick (1986), results of projective protocols for preschool-aged children may be more a function of their developmental level rather than personality organization. However, clinicians are probably more limited by the lack of developmentally sensitive projective measures than by the child's development. Many traditional projective assessment tools were not initially developed for children and are, at times, difficult to administer and interpret. In order for children to understand the assessment task and to participate in the procedure, it is necessary for the measures to be developmentally appropriate. Measures that are developmentally inappropriate may lead to conclusions and interpretations that are irrelevant and/or erroneous. In order to design developmentally sensitive measures for children we must explore the abilities of children and methods of interaction that are appropriate.

In assessing and treating young children, the modality that is generally used is play. Rabin (1960) categorized it as an expressive technique whereby the "emphasis is much more on the process than on the product" (p. 9). It is due to the child's limited ability to utilize abstract reasoning and verbally describe experiences and conflicts that clinicians prefer to use the language of play to communicate with the child. Clinicians are better able to interpret the meaning of play because it is a natural form of expression in which the child is comfortable sharing his or her beliefs. By integrating elements of play, such as toys, into assessment procedures, it becomes more developmentally sensitive because the child is provided a familiar means of expression. It is imperative that assessment procedures used with children be developmentally sensitive and presented in a manner that a young child can understand.

When administering projective techniques with children, their age, developmental level, willingness to participate, and ability to understand the task must be taken into consideration (Hart, 1986). In addition, the child's comfort with the examiner and mood are contributing factors that are important in understanding the assessment results. It is essential that the examiner have a clear working knowledge of developmental issues that may affect responses, in order for interpretations to be based in a normative perspective. Interpretations must also be made with collaborative information from various sources. In order to understand the context of responses, it is necessary to have information obtained through clinical interview from both the parent and the child. Additionally, it may be helpful to obtain information from the child's school, if there is parental support for this collateral contact.

In order to maximize the effectiveness and applicability of the assessment, it is imperative that the examiner engage the child in a manner that is likely to increase his or her comfort, promote understanding of the task, and elicit pertinent responses. In so doing it is helpful to utilize the process of play to engage the child in the assessment, if play is appropriate for the procedure. Integrating puppets into the sentence completion task is a means of providing the child with a medium of expression as well as explaining the task through puppet role models without unduly influencing the child's mindset.

THE USE OF PUPPETS IN ASSESSING CHILDREN

Like other objects of play, puppets provide a nonthreatening means of expressing conflicts and feeling "for" the child and not "by" the child. Specifically, from the child's perspective it is the puppet expressing the conflict or feeling and not the child per se. Woltmann (1960) noted that the child actually enters the play due to the hand manipulations required to guide the puppet. The child's hand movements and voice are the carrier of the ideas which, for the child, are expressed by the puppet. Even though these are often difficult to interpret given the distortions frequently seen in play (Irwin, 1985), it still offers one of the best ways of learning about the inner reality of the child. It is children's perceptions of their reality that influence their understanding of the world. By using projective play instruments, such as puppets, children afford us a glimpse of their world.

Puppets have long been used as a medium to reach children vicariously through puppet shows as well as actively by having children create their own stories (Bender & Woltmann, 1936). In 1936 Bender and Woltmann reported the need to reach children who were being treated for severe behavioral problems. They found that providing the children with puppet play allowed the children to project their own problems into the puppet characters. Therefore, the puppet shows were believed to vicariously serve as a means of expression for the children to explore conflicts without producing significant anxiety.

Irwin (1985) reported the use of puppets to assess children in an individual interview. In developing the individual technique, puppets were chosen due to the richness of expressive material produced through the child's spontaneous play. In the individual interview the child is asked to select various hand puppets and to create a pretend television story. At the end, the clinician interviews the characters and the puppeteer in order to follow up on clinical hypotheses and to seek clarity from the child and "characters" in the story. This method has also been developed for use with families (Irwin & Malloy, 1975).

Irwin (1991) presented an extensive review of the use of puppets to aid in diagnosis and treatment for both children and families. In addressing developmental considerations and the use of puppets Irwin stated, "Young children often present their conflicts with startling clarity and lack of disguise, thus helping to illuminate the diagnostic picture" (p. 620). Irwin (1991) also referred to puppet play in the younger age group as less censored and thus more openly full of conflict.

RESEARCH ON THE SENTENCE COMPLETION TEST

As with many projective measures, the SCT lacks standardized scoring procedures and normative data, as well as empirical evidence of reliability and validity. However, these issues have not seemed to hamper its clinical popularity. There are some empirical data suggesting the reliability of specific forms of the SCT (Weiss, Zilberg, & Genevro, 1989), but it is not appropriate to assume generalizability of findings to different populations assessed and various forms used. For example, Loevinger's Washington University SCT of Ego Development (LSCT; Loevinger, Wessler, & Redmore, 1970) was developed based on Loevinger's theorized hierarchical model of ego development, which was characterized by specific level of impulse control, interpersonal styles, and conscious concerns (Beck, 1996). The LSCT was created to assess the subject's level of ego development and psychopathology. It has been empirically assessed for its reliability and different forms of validity (Loevinger, 1979). This particular SCT is thought to be helpful clinically due to the categorical scores obtained based on the subject's responses to the sentence stem. Loevinger's detailed scoring system results in a total protocol rating that falls within one of the nine following categories: impulsive, self-protective, self-protective/conformist, conformist, conscientious/conformist, conscientious, individualistic, autonomous, and integrated. These categories are reflective of the stages of ego development theorized by Loevinger (1966). The LSCT was originally developed and researched based on nonclinical adolescents (Loevinger, Cohn, Bonneville, Redmore, Streich, & Sargent, 1985).

Weiss, Zilberg, and Genevro (1989) attempted to assess the psychometric properties of LSCT in an adult, outpatient population. Results indicated adequate reliability but the issue of validity was not empirically addressed. Developers of other forms of the sentence completion task generally do not address reliability, validity, or scoring criteria but suggest a qualitative analysis of responses. Interpretation of the results of these tasks is primarily a function of the examiner's skill and experience.

In an attempt to develop a standardized scoring procedure specifically for children, Hart developed the Hart Sentence Completion Test for Children (HSCT; Hart, 1986). This instrument focused on four theoretical dimensions: family environment, social environment, school environment, and self-perception. The eight scales that subdivide these dimensions include: perception of family, interaction with family, perception of peers, interaction with peers, perception of school, interaction with school, need orientation, and personal evaluation. The instrument was designed for children ages 6 to 18 and requires 15 to 30 minutes to complete.

Hart created two scoring systems, item-by-item rating and scale rating. In a review of several studies empirically assessing the psychometric properties of the HSCT, Hart, Kehle, and Davies (1983) reported that the two scoring systems did differentiate clinically referred and nonreferred children. However, scores on the HSCT were not able to identify specific areas of needs for the children. In addition, for the younger children responses were often reportedly repetitive (Hart, 1986). It is important to note that this is most likely a function of several different factors. For example, there may be developmental issues that interfere with the ability to respond or a lack of rapport with the examiner.

PUPPET SENTENCE COMPLETION TASK

The use of more traditional sentence completion tasks is typically not appropriate for children under the age of 6 to 7 years. Most children under this age have difficulty comprehending the expectations of the task, and therefore are unable to respond in a coherent manner. Because of the rich clinical material that can be gathered from a sentence completion task, Knell (1992, 1993) proposed the use of a puppet sentence completion task (PSCT). The rationale behind this measure was to present a more developmentally sensitive task to younger children, so that they could understand and respond in an age-appropriate way.

Age Considerations

The PSCT can be used with children from 3 to 7 years old. These ages are approximate boundaries given the individual differences of children in the preschool- and early school-age years. Although there are certainly $2^1/_2$-year-old children who would be able to complete the PSCT, the average child would not have verbal skills sufficient for the task before the age of 3 years. Obviously, the younger the child, the less sophisticated the verbalizations. Despite its limitations for very young children, it still potentially provides important clinical information. Nonetheless, the task tends to elicit more clinical information from older preschool-age children (4–5-year-olds). At the upper age range, older children (6–7-year-olds) may have the verbal abilities to complete the task, but may find that they are uninterested in the puppets. Therefore, children in the 6- to 7-year-old range often are able to move quickly from the puppet task to a more traditional sentence completion task, but may be helped, at first, by the structure of the PSCT.

Population Considerations

With the exception of age considerations, there are no limitations on the use of the PSCT with various populations. Any child, with only a few exceptions, could potentially complete this task. Children with autism or significant speech impairments might not be able to complete the task in the traditional fashion. A hearing-impaired child fluent in sign language could be given the task by a sign-fluent examiner or with the use of a sign interpreter. A child with a mental age below 3 years, regardless of chronological age, would probably be unable to complete the PSCT.

Selection of Sentence Stems

The PSCT was first introduced as a way to utilize a more traditional sentence completion task in a developmentally appropriate way. The stems were derived from standard stems, reflecting areas that might elicit valuable clinical information (e.g., family, self-esteem, feelings, potential traumas). Since no standardized sentence completion test existed, sentence stems were able to be added or deleted as clinical judgment demanded. The PSCT as first described (Knell, 1992, 1993), was designed for use with a general preschool-age population. The goal was to provide a set of common sentence stems that could be used with most children. A number of stems related to possible victimization or maltreatment issues were added at the end of the task. Even for children not known to have been maltreated, these stems were useful in order to rule out the possibility of abuse or trauma. However, they could also be excluded if it was considered clinically inappropriate to include them. Special stems, unique to particular life situations or presenting problems, can be added by the examiner for specific populations (e.g., children of divorced parents, children who have been physically or sexually maltreated). Some commonly used additional stems, related to presenting problems commonly seen in the preschool- and early school-age population, are provided in the optional section of the PSCT (see the appendix).

Ruma (1993) noted that in play therapy with sexually abused children, the therapist may at times introduce themes that are common among maltreated children. She describes efforts to encourage the child without leading. Sentence stems that pull for common sequelae of maltreatment offer such an opportunity. Sentence stems such as "the worst secret is…"; or "when I am in bed I think about…" may provide structure for traumatized or abused children to convey information that would be difficult to reveal in an interview.

For some children, this structure may be too overwhelming. Such children may respond to these sentence stems by their silence or lack of intelligible response. One example was a $4^1/_2$-year-old child, Richard, who had been abused by his babysitter (Ruma, 1993). Although he had disclosed some information about the maltreatment, he had become very reluctant to elaborate on what he had disclosed or discuss any new information. He was able to respond to many sentence stems in the PSCT, but when the stem, "A secret I am not supposed to tell is…," was stated, Richard was unable to give a response. Although Richard did not reveal any new information, his difficulty in responding corroborated that this was a problem area for him.

Selection of Puppets

Many different kinds of puppets can be introduced for use in this task. Because it is important for the child to have choices, but not to be overwhelmed by very large numbers of choices, it is important to keep available a variety of puppets representing different categories (e.g., people vs. animal puppets). The puppets should be either placed in front of the child, or in an accessible place (e.g., bottom shelf of an open toy cabinet). In either case, the puppets should be at the child's eye level. As part of the procedure, the child is told that she or he should choose a puppet. It is helpful to observe the manner of choice, as well as the category of puppet, the child picks. Does he or she quickly make a choice or take a great deal of time? Does the child seem interested in making this choice, and eager to continue with the task, or does the child exhibit and/or express disinterest? It is particularly helpful to note the child's verbalizations during the process. Does the child give any reasons why the particular puppet is chosen? Does the child turn to the examiner and request that he or she make the choice for the child? These types of observations can potentially add a great deal of understanding to the child's level of functioning and needs.

Administration

Establishing rapport is a critical first step in the administration of the PSCT. Given the nature of working with young children, it is often not possible or desirable to administer this task during the first session with a child. Once the child seems comfortable in the playroom with the examiner, the PSCT can be introduced. There is no hard-and-fast rule about when to administer the PSCT. Preferably, it should be given before too many sessions have taken place. For some children, the first session can include the PSCT. For others, it may be preferable to wait until the child is more comfortable and rapport has been established. Because the PSCT is a fairly structured activity, it is harder to introduce it if most of the time with the child has involved unstructured, spontaneous play. Therefore, it is recommended that the task be administered some time within the first 2 to 3 sessions.

The procedure for administration of the PSCT is relatively straightforward. (The PSCT in its entirety is provided in the appendix.) The examiner lets the child choose a puppet, and then the examiner chooses two puppets. The child can be offered the option of picking the puppets for the examiner. The PSCT is broken down into two parts. In Part I, the examiner reads the sentence stems for the first puppet (Puppet A). After the sentence stem is read, the examiner's second puppet (Puppet B) responds. The examiner then turns to Puppet C (the one held by the child), and indicates that the child should respond for the puppet. The manner in which the examiner indicates that it is the child's turn may be through voice inflection, or through hand movement pointing to the child's puppet, or both. There are a total of 5 sentence stems in Part I. However, the examiner moves on to Part II of the PSCT as soon as it is clear that the child understands the tasks. Thus, all 5 sentence stems in Part I are not necessarily given to the child if it is clear that the child understands the task after a few stems are given. This will be clear by the responses that the child gives for Puppet C.

If the child does not understand the task, the examiner can begin with the first sentence stem and have the puppets prompt the child. It is important not to continue to Part II until it is clear that the child understands Part I. Many children catch on quickly and do not seem to like the repetition that is necessary in Part I. In this situation, it is appropriate to move to Part II as quickly as possible.

In Part II, the examiner's first puppet states the sentence stem directly to the child's puppet, and the child responds for his or her puppet. Most children will give only one response, but some will give a response for the puppet and one for themselves. Both responses should be noted. It is not always possible or necessary to give all the sentence stems in Part II. Some children, particularly younger preschoolers, cannot tolerate responding to all of the sentence stems. Others, particularly older children, may be able to do the whole task. When it becomes clear that the PSCT must be shortened, it is recommended that the examiner choose sentence stems that are clinically relevant, or stems that "pull" for certain themes. This often necessitates skipping over some items, in order to get to more relevant sentence stems before the child's interest level drops. Any or all of the optional sentence stems can be used when they are clinically relevant for the child. The order of administration is not critical, and the examiner should be flexible in administering the task, in order to ensure that clinically relevant items are given before the child loses interest.

With the child and parents' permission, it is often helpful to tape the administration of the PSCT. This is particularly helpful with young children whose language articulation skills are not fully developed. This allows the examiner to focus on the child, rather than focusing on asking the child to repeat words that are not readily understood. It also allows the examiner to keep both hands free for puppets, rather than needing one hand for recording the child's responses. Although it is not necessary to have two hands for puppets in Part II, the examiner will need to have puppets on both hands in Part I. Thus, for Part I, written recording of responses is awkward. Of course, using a tape recording necessitates that the examiner have the time to listen and transcribe the tape as soon as possible after the child leaves.

It can be helpful to ask the child for further clarification or information about particular sentence stems. The examiner may want to ask the child to explain his or her response, or may ask a specific question about the response. Because the PSCT is not a standardized, normed measure, the examiner can use clinical judgment in deciding which responses to pursue further, and when to go on to the next sentence stem. Such decisions are based on the examiner's reflection on the child's response, and clinical sense of when it is best to capture material immediately, and when waiting for a later moment is more appropriate.

Further Considerations in the Administration of the PSCT

Adding Clinically Relevant Stems Prior to Administration

Because of the nature of the PSCT, it is possible to individualize the task for each administration. The optional stems do not always meet the needs of all children. Thus, sentence stems can be added to the basic task before administration to make the task relevant to the child and presenting problems. Thus, stems can be added that may pull for information about particular issues unique to the child's environment, family constellation, or life stressors. The limits of sentence stems are endless. The following case example illustrates the use of additional sentence stems to capture clinical information about toileting issues.

Case Example   Seth was a 3-year, 5-month-old boy with presenting problems related to toileting and behavioral concerns. His mother reported that he was often noncompliant and was having a difficult time managing his behavior in his preschool setting. He had been toilet trained for urination, but preferred to withhold his bowel movements, rather than use the toilet. If he withheld his bowel movements for long periods of time, his stools were hard, and thus, his pediatrician had recommended stool softeners.

Due to these toileting concerns, several sentence stems were added to the PSCT. A few examples, including his responses, are listed below:

I love to *play outside.*

I am afraid of *monsters.*

I go poop *flush the toilet.*

I am happiest when *smile, happy, big potty.*

When I go to the bathroom, *I can't.*

I wash my hands when *you go to potty.*

I go to the potty *go wee wee and flush toilet.*

It is important to know and use the child's own words for bodily functions (e.g., "wee wee" for urination; "poop" for bowel movements). These names can usually be gathered in the preliminary interview with parents, which usually takes place before the child is seen.

Seth's responses suggest that he was able to talk about the toileting issues. His quick response of "I can't" to the stem, "When I go to the bathroom" suggests that he is aware of the concerns his parents had about his refusal to use the toilet for a bowel movement. Further, his response of "smile, happy, big potty" may suggest that he would be pleased if he could use the toilet for bowel movements or perhaps that his parents might smile and be happy when he does. Alternatively, they do not smile when he does not use the toilet, and it is his wish that they would! Similarly, when he stated he would "flush the toilet" after he had a bowel movement, this may be a reflection of his fantasy about being able to use and flush the toilet without difficulty, or of the pressures on him to do so.

Adding Clinically Relevant Stems During Administration of the PSCT

At times the examiner may seek further clarification of responses by asking the child to expand upon his or her response. Other times, it can also be helpful to get this clarification through additional sentence stems that are added *spontaneously during the administration* of the task in response to the child's responses. An example of this latter form of clarification is provided by the following case example:

Case Example   Brian was a 5-year, 8-month-old boy who was referred because of behavioral problems in his babysitter's home. According to the parents, Brian was fairly well behaved at home, and did well in structured settings. However, when at his babysitter's home, Brian had a number of instances of pushing, shoving, hitting, and kicking the babysitter's son. A sense of urgency existed on the parent's part because the babysitter had threatened to stop caring for Brian if he continued to be aggressive with her son. Several sentence stems were added to the PSCT in order to gather information regarding Brian's perceptions regarding the situation at the babysitter's. These sentence stems specifically related to the babysitter and her son. In addition, during the administration of the PSCT, it was clear that further clarification of Brian's responses was needed. This was done by adding sentence stems spontaneously based on Brian's responses. (Sentence stems in regular type were added to the protocol *prior* to administration of the PSCT in order to gather specific information about Brian's perceptions of the babysitter's home. Sentence stems in boldface are the ones that were added *spontaneously* by the examiner during the administration of the PSCT.)

Karen (babysitter) is *mean.*

Karen is mean because I *do something wrong and she gets mad at me.*

When she gets mad at me, I *go. I make a picture.*

The picture is *hearts.*

Steven (babysitter's son) is **nice.**

Sometimes Steven is mean when *he's mean I go tell Karen.*
And Karen, she *sometimes puts her kids in time out. She does that to me, too.*
When I'm in time out, I feel *lonely.*
When I'm lonely, I feel *sad.*

In this example, the examiner had planned to use the sentence stems related to the babysitter and her son in order to elicit Brian's feelings about the situation. However, the additional sentence stems were added in order to elicit even more information based on Brian's responses. This example shows how the spontaneous addition of sentence stems can generate much information about the child's feelings. Obviously, these sentence stems could not have been designed in advance.

Using Toys Other than Puppets in the PSCT

Despite the designation of this task as a puppet sentence completion, flexibility is still the mainstay of the assessment process. There are some children, even at the preschool age, who are uninterested in puppets, or who refuse to play with them. Even with such children, it is still possible to proceed with the PSCT. The example that follows illustrates the use of the PSCT with a child who was uninterested in the use of puppets.

Case Example   Mark was a 3-year, 9-month-old child who refused to use the toilet for bowel movements. Mark was toilet trained for urination at approximately 2 $1/2$ years old, and would eagerly use the toilet for urination, but refused to sit on the toilet for bowel movements. Instead, Mark would ask for a diaper (which he no longer wore), and then would use the diaper for his bowel movements. Although the parents continued to comply with this request, his preschool setting refused to allow him to stay in school unless he was "completely toilet trained." They would not permit him to put on a diaper for bowel movements, and therefore he was only allowed to stay in school for a half day. Mark was motivated to stay in school, because he expressed to his parents that he felt that he was missing out on fun activities in the second half of the day. When the parents refused to give Mark a diaper, he would withhold his bowel movements. This option was not appropriate, because of the concerns regarding fecal impaction that might result from his withholding of his stools.

Other presenting problems included Mark's aggressive behavior and noncompliance. At the time of referral he was dealing with feelings regarding the birth of a younger sibling, as well as fears of monsters and witches. Mark's parents also reported that he showed much interest in toy cars, to the point of knowing names and much identifying information about cars. In preparation for the assessment, many sentence stems were added to the standard list in order to gather information regarding Mark's feelings about his toileting issues. Mark, however, refused to use the puppets presented to him. In order to proceed with the task, a set of toy cars were substituted for the puppets. In the following examples, the examiner spoke as if the cars were stating the sentence stems and Mark replied to the stems as if he were speaking for the cars.

My diaper is *My diapers are all gone, so I poop in the toilet.*

They're all gone? *I leave them and throw all in my diaper pail, so I can go poop in the toilet and squeeze my poop out.*

Mr. car (addressing the toy car in Mark's hand), I am afraid of *witches. Know what I'm afraid of? I scared of a creature like a tree. I'm afraid it will come out of my bed.*

I'm sad when *my mommy and daddy leave and I just cry.*

Adding Therapeutic Sentence Stems to the PSCT

With some children, the sentence stems can be designed to be "therapeutically leading." That is, the stems can be created to fit the child's situation, but in a more psychoeducational manner that also helps the child therapeutically. This is typically more appropriate after the examiner feels that there is sufficient assessment information, and such therapeutic stems will not contaminate the information obtained. Examples from a later part of Mark's PSCT follow:

My problem is *I don't know.*

Some kids have potty problems. Do you have a potty problem?

Yes I have. NO. I go poop. I squeeze it out and wipe. I put my poop in the toilet and I flush it down.

Mark's responses suggest that he is well aware of the concerns that his parents have regarding his lack of toilet use for making bowel movements. However, he insists that he does not have a "potty problem," and that he just "squeezed it out, wipes and flushes it." Interestingly, Mark first responded that he did have a potty problem, but quickly changed his response to "no."

Other Case Examples

Case Example   Jason was a 3-year, 10-month-old boy referred for noncompliance, temper tantrums, and aggression. His mother also expressed concern that Jason would not sleep in his own bed, and would insist on falling asleep every night in his parents' bed. His sentence completion responses were fairly nondescript until sentence stems were read that were "near" topics that he did not want to discuss.

My favorite ice cream is *chocolate.*

My favorite toy is *construction.*

My school is *good.*

Little brothers are *babies.*

My bed is *stop saying that froggie.* (The examiner was using a frog puppet.)

Although Jason's responses to the PSCT did not reveal any significant new information, they did suggest that there were topics, such as his sleeping situation, that he did not want to discuss. Rather than actively avoiding the topic, as some children might do, Jason told the puppet to stop discussing it.

Case Example   Marcus was a 6-year, 11-month-old boy referred because of noncompliance, aggressive behavior (including kicking and swearing), and fighting. The parents acknowledged great difficulty in managing his behavior and felt that they needed guidance. Samples of his PSCT responses follow: (Answers in boldface were responded to very quickly.)

At night when I sleep *I scared.*

I am scared of *the dark.*

Mommy is nice when *I get something.*

Mommy is mean when *I get when I don't get my way.*

I am happiest when *I am nice.*

I am saddest when *I am sad because I don't get to play with my friends outside.*

Swearing is **bad.**

My biggest problem is *mad.* (Questioned) *I don't get to watch TV.*

The worst thing about me is *when I don't get. When I need to clean my room.*

When kids kick and fight *they are bad.*

When I am asked to do something **I do it.**

The parents were not aware of Marcus having any particular fears; however, it was clear from the PSCT that he was afraid of the dark and nighttime. It was also suggested that he was well aware of his own ability to control his parents' response to him (i.e., in terms of getting his own way). He was aware of his problems (e.g., "My biggest problem is *mad*").

Although the PSCT is not scored in any way for response time, it is often helpful to note any unusually quick or slow response times. In Marcus's case, he responded extremely quickly to two sentence stems (marked in bold type). This suggests that these are critical items for Marcus. Additionally, the examiner needs to be sensitive to nuances with the use of words. For example, after the stem "at night when I sleep," Marcus states, "I scared." The next sentence stem was, "I am afraid of." Because of Marcus's response to the previous item, the examiner changed the sentence stem from "I am afraid of," to "I am scared of," to be consistent with Marcus's use of words.

SUMMARY

The PSCT is a structured, projective measure designed to facilitate a young child's participation in the sentence completion process. It is more developmentally suited to the preschooler than a traditional sentence completion task for two reasons. First, the task itself is not begun until it is clear that the child understands the directions. The responses to the preliminary section of the task indicate to the examiner whether or not the child understands what is expected. The examiner does not administer the core part of the task until it is clear that the child understands the expectations of the task. Second, the child has the opportunity to complete the stem either by means of the puppet or without the puppet as a prompt. For some children, the use of the puppet provides a tool that makes the task easier because they do not need to directly tell the examiner how they feel. For others, modeling with the puppet explains the task to them, at which point they are comfortable responding freely to the task without the puppets. In either case, the task is introduced with puppets, which are familiar to and enjoyed by most children.

It is important that the data gathered from this task are used in conjunction with all other data gathered, and not in isolation. Often useful are interview information (e.g., parent interview, including developmental history; child play interviews) as well as more objective methods (e.g., Child Behavior Checklist; Achenbach, 1991; Social Competence and Behavior Evaluation—Preschool Edition; LaFreniere & Dumas, 1995). This ideally should involve both verbal and nonverbal information gathered from the child, as well as information from parents and other significant adults, such as teachers, in the child's life. The ultimate goal is to conceptualize a sense of the child's perceptions of his or her situation from all of the information gathered.

There has been recent interest in child assessment and psychotherapy outcome studies, with reviews of play therapy calling for a more systematic program of research (e.g., Russ, 1995; Phillips, 1985). Schaefer, Gitlin, and Sandgrund (1991) noted the need for increased attention in the area of child evaluation, as well. This revised edition of their book reflects the most recent efforts to achieve psychometric reliability and validity in various play assessment procedures. Continued study of the PSCT will be important in order to further understand its psychometric properties.

REFERENCES

Achenbach, T. M. (1991). *Manual for the Child Behavior Checklist 4–18 and 1991 Profile.* Burlington: University of Vermont, Department of Psychiatry.

Beck, K. W. (1996). *Sex-role development in 6th, 7th, and 8th graders.* Unpublished doctoral dissertation, University of Memphis, Memphis, Tennessee.

Bender, L., & Woltmann, A. G. (1936). The use of puppet shows as a psychotherapeutic method for behavior problems in children. *American Journal of Orthopsychiatry, 6,* 341–354.

Freud, A. (1946). *The psychoanalytic treatment of children.* London: Imago.

Goldberg, P. (1965). A review of sentence completion methods in personality assessment. In B. I. Murstein (Ed.), *Handbook of projective techniques* (pp. 777–822). New York: Basic Books.

Hart, D. H. (1986). Sentence completion techniques. In H. M. Knoff (Ed.), *The assessment of child and adolescent personality* (pp. 245–272). New York: Guilford Press.

Hart, D. H., Kehle, T. J., & Davies, M. V. (1983). Effectiveness of sentence completion techniques: A review of the Hart Sentence Completion Test for Children. *School Psychology Review, 12,* 428–434.

Irwin, E. C. (1985). Puppets in therapy: An assessment procedure. *American Journal of Psychotherapy, 39,* 389–400.

Irwin, E. C. (1991). The use of a puppet interview to understand children. In C. Schaefer, K. Gitlin, & A. Sandgrund (Eds.), *Play diagnosis and assessment* (pp. 617–634). New York: Wiley.

Irwin, E., & Malloy, E. (1975). Family puppet interview. *Family Process, 14,* 179–191.

Knell, S. M. (1992). The Puppet Sentence Completion Task. Unpublished manuscript.

Knell, S. M. (1993). *Cognitive-behavioral play therapy.* Hillsdale, NJ: Aronson.

LaFraniere, P. J., & Dumas, J. E. (1995). *Social competence and behavior evaluation: Preschool edition.* Los Angeles: Western Psychological Services.

Loevinger, J. (1966). The meaning and measurement of ego development. *American Psychologist, 21,* 195–206.

Loevinger, J. (1979). Construct validity of the Sentence Completion Test of Ego Development. *Applied Psychological Measurement, 3,* 281–311.

Locvinger, J., Cohn, L. D., Bonneville, L. P., Redmore, C. D., Streich, D. D., & Sargent, M. (1985). Ego development in college. *Journal of Personality and Social Psychology, 48,* 947–962.

Loevinger, J., Wessler, R., & Redmore, C. (1970). *Measuring ego development* (Vol. San Francisco: Jossey-Bass.

Lubin, B., Larsen, R. M., & Matarazzo, J. D. (1984). Patterns of psychological test usage in the United States: 1935–1982. *American Psychologist, 39,* 451–453.

Murray, H. A. (1938). *Manual of Thematic Apperception Test.* Cambridge, MA: Harvard University Press.

Murray, H. A., & MacKinnon, D. W. (1946). Assessment of OSS personnel. *Journal of Consulting Psychology,* 10, 76–80.

Obrzut, J. E., & Bolick, C. A. (1986). Thematic approaches to personality assessment with children and adolescents. In H. M. Knoff (Ed.), *The assessment of child and adolescent personality* (pp. 173–198). New York: Guilford Press.

Payne, A. F. (1928). *Sentence completions.* New York: Guidance Clinic.

Phillips, R. D. (1985). Whistling in the dark: A review of play therapy research. *Psychotherapy, 22,* 752–760.

Rabin, A. I. (1960). Projective methods and projection in children. In A. I. Rabin & M. R. Haworth (Eds.), *Projective techniques with children* (pp. 2–11). New York: Grune & Stratton.

Rorschach, H. (1942). *Psychodiagnostics* (5th ed.). Bern: Hans Huber.

Rotter, J. B. (1951). Word association and sentence completion methods. In H. A. Anderson & G. L. Anderson (Eds.), *An introduction to projective techniques* (pp 279–311). Englewood Cliffs, NJ: Prentice-Hall.

Rotter, J. B., Rafferty, J. E., & Schactitz, E. (1949). Validation of the Rotter Incomplete Sentences Blank for college screening. *Journal of Consulting Psychology, 13,* 348–366.

Rotter, J. B., & Willerman, B. (1947). The incomplete sentences test as a method of studying personality. *Journal of Consulting Psychology, 11,* 43–48.

Ruma, C. R. (1993). Cognitive-Behavioral Play therapy with sexually abused children. In S.M. Knell (Ed.), *Cognitive-Behavioral Play Therapy* (pp. 199–230). Hillsdale, NJ: Aronson.

Russ, S. W. (1995). Play psychotherapy research. In T. H. Ollendick & R. J. Prinz (Eds.), *Advances in clinical child psychology* (Vol. 17, pp. 365–391). New York: Plenum.

Stephenson, W. (1953). *The study of behavior: Q-technique and its methodology.* Chicago: University of Chicago Press.

Tendler, A. D. (1930). A preliminary report on a test for emotional insight. *Journal of Applied Psychology, 14,* 123–136.

Weiss, D. S., Zilberg, N. J., & Genevro, J. L. (1989). Psychometric properties of Loevinger's Sentence Completion Test in an adult psychiatric outpatient sample. *Journal of Personality Assessment, 53,* 478–486.

Woltmann, A. G. (1960). Spontaneous puppetry by children as a projective method. In A. I. Rabin & M. R. Haworth (Eds.), *Projective techniques with children* (pp. 305–338). New York: Grune & Stratton.

APPENDIX

Puppet Sentence Completion Task
Revised—1998

Directions: The examiner should let the child choose a puppet. After the child has chosen a puppet, the examiner chooses two puppets. If the child so wishes, the examiner can let the child pick the puppets for the examiner. The following code is used in the directions:

Puppet A—Examiner's
Puppet B—Examiner's
Puppet C—Child's

PART I

Directions: Puppet A states the sentence stem. Puppet B quickly responds. The examiner then turns to Puppet C (held by the child) for a response. The examiner supplies answers for Puppet B. Move to Part II as soon as it is clear that the child understands the task by providing a response for Puppet C.

Puppet A: My name is _____

[turn to Puppet B:] My name is _____

[turn to Puppet C:] My name is _____

Puppet A: My favorite ice cream is _____

[Puppet B:] <u>Chocolate ice cream.</u>

[Puppet C:] _____

Puppet A: I am: _____

[Puppet B:] <u>4 years old.</u>

[Puppet C:] _____

Puppet A: My favorite toy is: _____

[Puppet B:] <u>my teddy bear.</u>

[Puppet C:] _____

Puppet A: My favorite color is: _____

[Puppet B:] <u>blue.</u>

[Puppet C:] _____

If the child does not understand the task, go back through and have Puppet B prompt the child to help Puppet C give a response. Continue until the task is clearly understood by the child. Do not go on to Part II until it is clear that the child understands the task. If the child does not seem to understand what is expected in Part I, Part II will probably not be understood.

Note: Some children catch on quite quickly and do not seem to like the repetition necessary in Part I. For these children, it is permissible to go directly to Part II. Although it is preferable to write down the child's responses immediately, because the therapist has a puppet on each hand it may be necessary to record responses immediately following the administration of Part I.

PART II

Directions: In Part II, Puppet A states the sentence stem. The sentence is stated directly to Puppet C. The response made by the child (Puppet C) should be written in the blank immediately. Some children will give two responses, one for the puppet and one for themselves. Both responses should be noted.

1. My favorite food is _____
2. I love to _____
3. Outside I play with _____
4. Mommy is _____
5. Daddy is _____
6. My favorite TV show is _____
7. (If applicable) My brother's name is _____
8. (If applicable) My sister's name is _____
9. I like to pretend to be _____
10. If I were bigger I would _____
11. At night when I sleep I _____
12. I am afraid of _____
13. I hate _____
14. The best secret is _____
15. The worst secret is _____
16. Mommy is nice when _____
17. Daddy is nice when _____
18. Daddy is mean when _____
19. Mommy is mean when _____
20. I am happiest when_____
21. I am saddest when _____
22. I get scared when _____
23. My biggest problem is _____
24. The worst thing about me is _____

Optional Sentence Stems:

25. With my hands I like to touch _____
26. With my hands I don't like to touch_____

27. Someone I don't like to touch me is _____

28. Someone I like to touch me is _____

29. My body is _____

30. I don't like to be touched on my _____

31. A secret I am not supposed to tell is _____

32. I am maddest when _____

33. When I heard about my parents' divorce, I felt _____

34. Divorce is _____

35. Visiting my mom/dad is _____

36. When I visit my mom/dad I _____

37. My stepmom/stepdad is _____

38. My potty (toilet) is _____

39. When I go potty (to the bathroom), I _____

40. Diapers are _____

41. When mommy leaves I feel _____

42. Being alone is _____

43. My tummy (stomach) is _____

44. My biggest wish is _____

45. I cry when _____

46. _____

47. _____

48. _____

Chapter 26 —————————————————————————————

PLAY ASSESSMENT OF AFFECT: THE AFFECT IN PLAY SCALE

Sandra W. Russ, Larissa N. Niec, and Astrida S. Kaugars

The need for a reliable and valid scale that measures affective expression in children's fantasy play has been widely recognized (Howe & Silvern, 1981; Rubin, Fein, & Vandenberg, 1983; Stern, et al., 1992). In order for affective processes to be studied in children, we need standardized measures of expression of affect. Play is a natural arena in which to study the expression of emotion.

The Affect in Play Scale (APS) was developed to meet the need for a standardized measure of affective expression in children's pretend play. This chapter reviews the role of pretend play, the APS play task and rating system, reliability and validity studies, extension of the scale to preschoolers, possible clinical use of the scale, and future directions.

THE FUNCTIONS OF PRETEND PLAY

Many cognitive, affective, and personality processes important in child development occur in pretend play. Pretend play involves the use of fantasy and make-believe, and the use of symbolism. Fein (1987) stated that pretend play is a symbolic behavior in which "one thing is playfully treated as if it were something else" (p. 282). Fein also stated that pretense is charged with feelings and emotional intensity. Affect is, thus, intertwined with pretend play.

The study of children's pretend play may inform us about important cognitive-affective interactions (Russ, 1987; Singer & Singer, 1990). Because play is an arena in which both cognitive and affective processes are reflected, it can also teach us about the development of these processes and how they interact. For example, how does the experience of chronic anxiety influence the development of organizational skills? Slade and Wolf (1994) stressed the importance of studying the role of play both in the development of cognitive structure and in the mastering of emotions. Historically, the two domains of cognition and emotion in play have been studied separately, usually from different theoretical and research traditions (Feist, in press). As Morrison (1988) has noted, Piaget did not consider affect to be important in cognitive development, whereas Freud did. As a result, different research traditions evolved. Measures of play processes have reflected this split in research traditions. Rubin, Fein, and Vandenberg (1983) pointed out that most of the measures of children's play have been related to cognitive processes, not affective processes. Thus, they referred to the "cognification" of play. Slade and Wolf (1994) asserted that the cognitive and affective functions of play are intertwined when they stated, "Just as the development of cognitive structures may play an important role in the resolution of emotional conflict, so emotional consolidation may provide an impetus to cognitive advances and integration" (p. xv). They implied that there is a working together of emotional functioning and cognitive structure.

Given that affect and cognition are so intertwined in pretend play and that emotional and cognitive processes work together, it is important to measure both cognitive and affective processes in play to fully capture the phenomena.

Pretend play has been thought to be important in a number of areas in child development. Among these have been creative problem solving (Singer & Singer, 1990), coping ability, (Christiano & Russ, 1996), and mastering of emotional conflicts and traumas (Freedheim & Russ, 1992). Play has frequently been used as a means to assess children's cognitive and language development (Finn & Fewell, 1994; McDonough, Stahmer, Schreibman, & Thompson, 1997; Westby, 1980; 1991). Thus, of the few existing standardized play measures, most were developed for the purpose of differentiating developmental levels.

PLAY ASSESSMENT FOR SCHOOL AGE CHILDREN

Pretend play has been a major tool of child therapists. In play therapy, the child uses play to express feelings, express conflicts, resolve problems, role play, and communicate with the therapist. Two measures appropriate for use with school-age children were developed in the context of assessing therapeutic material: the Play Therapy Observation Instrument and the NOVA Assessment of Psychotherapy (Faust & Burns, 1991; Howe & Silvern, 1981). As clinical instruments, these measures tap both affective and thematic aspects of children's play, rather than solely cognitive aspects of the play.

The Play Therapy Observation Instrument (PTOI), originally developed by Howe and Silvern (1981), and adapted by Perry (Perry & Landreth, 1991), was designed to assist in the assessment of a child's functioning, and in treatment planning, and prognosis. Three areas of functioning are assessed with 13 items: (1) social inadequacy, (2) emotional discomfort, and (3) use of fantasy. The social inadequacy subscale includes items such as incoherent or bizarre content, exclusion of the therapist from activities, body stiffness, and responding to interventions with hostility or withdrawal. The emotional comfort subscale includes assessment of the valence of the child's mood (i.e., positive vs. negative), as well as themes of aggression, conflict, and anxiety. The fantasy subscale includes such items as amount of time spent in fantasy versus reality, the use of characters rather than things in fantasy, number of different fantasy stories, and number of different roles enacted. Brief segments of play therapy interactions are scored from videotape.

The PTOI has been found to discriminate adjusted from maladjusted children most strongly on the emotional discomfort subscale (Perry & Landreth, 1991). Rosen, Faust, and Burns (1994) used the PTOI with children participating in either psychodynamic or client-centered play therapy and found no significant differences between children's play in the two approaches. Differences were found, however, between scores in the first session and a later session, suggesting that the PTOI may be a useful instrument for detecting changes during the treatment process. Two related limitations of the PTOI are the need for developmental norms and a standardized administration (Perry & Landreth, 1991).

The NOVA Assessment of Psychotherapy (NAP) was also designed to assess the play therapy process and outcome by capturing components of the child's and therapist's behavior during play (Faust & Burns, 1991). This scale was intended for use in both clinical and research settings, with both a long and a short version. In the long version, 17 child behaviors and 12 therapist behaviors are coded in 7-second intervals. These behaviors fall into 4 categories: (1) child verbal, (2) child nonverbal, (3) therapist facilitating, and (4) therapist channeling. Some of the relevant aspects of the child's play that are coded include valence of affect expressed (i.e., positive or negative), cooperative behaviors, and aggressive behaviors. The scale can be scored during live interaction or from videotape. Initial single case studies of the validity and reliability of the scale suggest that, similar to the PTOI, the NAP may be useful for assessing affective and behavioral changes during the treatment process (Faust & Burns, 1991).

There is a need for a standardized measure of pretend play that is comprehensive in its assessment of the kinds of affect that occur during fantasy expression. The development of the Affect in Play Scale (APS) was an attempt to meet the need for this type of instrument.

THE APS PLAY TASK

The Affect in Play Scale consists of a standardized play task and a criterion-based rating scale. The APS is appropriate for children from 6 through 10 years of age, which includes children in grades 1 through 3.

The play task consists of two human puppets, one boy and one girl, and three small blocks that are laid out on a table. The puppets have neutral facial expressions. The blocks are brightly colored and of different shapes. The play props and instructions are unstructured enough so that individual differences in play can emerge. The task is administered individually to the child and the play is videotaped. The instructions for the task are:

> I'm here to learn about how children play. I have here two puppets and would like you to play
> with them any way you like for five minutes. For example, you can have the puppets do some-
> thing together. I also have some blocks that you can use. Be sure to have the puppets talk out
> loud. The video camera will be on so that I can remember what you say and do. I'll tell you
> when to stop.

The child is informed when there is 1 minute left. If the child stops playing during the 5-minute period, the prompt "You still have time left, keep going" is given. The task is discontinued if the child cannot play after a 2-minute period.

These instructions are free-play instructions that leave much room for the child to structure the play and present themes and affects that are habitual to him or her. Although the instruction "For example, you could have the puppets do something together" does provide structure, we found that some structure was necessary for many children to be able to carry out the task. These instructions can be altered to elicit different types of affect. For example, to pull for aggression, the instructions would be "Play with them and have the puppets disagree about something," rather than "Play with them any way you like." The play task described here is appropriate for grades 1 through 3. In our experience, many kindergarten children have difficulty with the puppet task. However, the rating criteria could be used in a natural play observation situation for very young children. An adaptation of the APS for young children will be discussed later in this chapter.

THE APS RATING SCALE

The Affect in Play Scale measures the amount and types of affective expression in children's fantasy play. The APS measures affect themes in the play narrative. Both emotion-laden content and expression of emotion in the play are coded. The APS also measures cognitive dimensions of the play, such as quality of fantasy and imagination.

Both Holt's Scoring System for Primary Process on the Rorschach (1977) and Singer's (1973) play scales were used as models for the development of the Affect in Play Scale. In addition, the work of Izard (1977) and Tomkins (1962, 1963) was consulted to ensure that the affect categories were comprehensive and covered all major types of emotion expressed by children in the 4 through 10 age group.

There are three major affect scores for the APS:

1. *Total frequency of units of affective expression:* A unit is defined as one scorable expression by an individual puppet. In a two-puppet dialogue, expressions of each puppet are scored separately. A unit can be the expression of an affect state, an affect theme, or a combination of the two. An example of an affect state would be "This is fun." An example of an affect theme would be "Here is a bomb that is going to explode." The expression can be verbal ("I hate you") or nonverbal (one puppet punching the other). The frequency of affect score is the total number of units of affect expressed in the 5-minute period.

2. *Variety of affect categories:* There are 11 possible affective categories. The categories are: Happiness/Pleasure; Anxiety/Fear; Sadness/Hurt; Frustration/Disappointment; Nurturance/Affection; Aggression; Oral; Oral Aggression; Anal; Sexual; Competition. The variety of affect scores is the number of different categories of affect expressed in the 5-minute period.

   These 11 affect categories can be divided into subsets of positive (happiness, nurturance, oral, sexual, competition) and negative (anxiety, sadness, frustration, aggression, oral aggression, anal) affect. Also, primary process affect themes can be scored (aggression, oral, oral aggression, anal, sexual, competition). Primary process content includes affect-laden oral, aggressive, and libidinal content around which children experience early intense feeling states. It is a subtype of affect in cognition that is based upon psychoanalytic theory (Russ, 1987, 1996).

3. *Mean intensity of affective expression* (1–5 rating): This rating measures the intensity of the feeling state or content theme. Each unit of affect is rated for intensity on a 1–5 scale.

Quality of fantasy and imagination is also scored. Although other scales (Singer, 1973) already tapped this dimension, it was important to include this aspect of pretend play in the scoring system, so that the APS would be comprehensive in its assessment of fantasy play. The fantasy scores are:

Organization (1–5 global rating): This score measures the organization of the play, and considers the quality of the plot.

Elaboration (1–5 global rating): This score measures the amount of embellishment in the play.

Imagination (1–5 global rating): This score measures the novelty and uniqueness of the play.

Quality of fantasy: This score is the mean of the previous three fantasy scores.

In addition, comfort in play is rated on a 1–5 scale. Finally, an affect integration score is obtained by multiplying the quality of fantasy score by the frequency of affect score. The affect integration score is needed because it attempts to measure the construct of cognitive modulation of emotion. It taps how well the affect is integrated and controlled by cognitive processes.

To summarize, the 9 major scores on the APS are total frequency of affect, variety of affect categories, mean intensity of affect, organization of fantasy, elaboration of fantasy, imagination, overall quality of fantasy, comfort, and affect integration. A detailed scoring manual that articulates criteria for all scores is available in Russ (1993).

Practically, the APS is easy to administer and takes only five minutes. The props, human puppets and blocks are simple. The scoring system takes time to learn, but then takes about 15 to 20 minutes per child. A training tape and manual are available. Although the APS has not been used with clinical populations, we do have a number of studies with means for nonclinical populations. Usually, the mean frequency of affect expression is 11–13 units with a mean variety of categories of 3–4. Refinements in the scoring criteria are underway and will be published in Russ (in preparation).

EXAMPLES OF AFFECT IN PLAY SCALE DIALOGUE

In order to give a sense of the play, excerpts from the first 90 seconds (approximately) of play dialogue for three children are presented here. All of these children are girls in the first or second grade. All express some affect in their play, but there are major differences in the amount of affect expressed. The dialogue is always between the puppets. On the videotapes, we can code the nonverbal expressions and affect tone of the verbal expression. The verbal transcripts presented here cannot fully reflect all of the play dimensions, but do give a sense of how these children differ in affective expression. The type of affect scored is given after each unit of expression. These excerpts are from Russ (1993).

Play Transcripts—Puppet Dialogue

Child 1: High Affect/High Quality of Fantasy　　　　　　　　*Type of Affect*

- Let's build a tall building. I'll put this top on.
  (build with blocks)

- No, I want to.   Aggression
- No, I am.   Aggression
- Hey, I said I was—give me those. (tussle)   Aggression
- I want to.   Aggression
- No, I do. (knock it down)   Aggression
- Oh no—we'll have to start all over thanks to you.   Frustration/Disappointment
- It wasn't my fault, it was your fault. (a block fell)   Aggression
- Oh—I better go get that block—it fell down the stairs.   Frustration/Disappointment
- Now you have to put that on top or I'll tell mom.   Aggression
- Ah—what did I do?   Anxiety/Fear
- Be my sister.   Nurturance/Affection
- OK—but we will both build a building—I put 2 on
  and you put on 1 since you get to put on the top.
- Fair enough.
- Uh-oh. (blocks fell)   Frustration/Disappointment
- I'll straighten this out.
- We built a tall building. (with glee)   Happiness/Pleasure
- What should we do now?
- I don't know.
- Let's build a playground.
- The playground is boring. (with feeling)   Frustration/Disappointment
- No—it isn't. There are lots of fun things to do there.   Happiness/Pleasure
- I always hit my hand and get scratches and scrapes.   Sadness/Hurt
- Well maybe if you were more careful, that wouldn't   Aggression
  happen.

Child 2: Moderate Affect/High Quality of Fantasy

- Oh Boo Hoo Boo Hoo. I don't have anyone to play
  with. Boo Hoo. I'll just play with my blocks and
  maybe that will make me feel better. (building)   Sadness/Hurt
- I'll stack this there and this here and stack this
  there—that's about as tall as me.
- Um—that makes me feel better—I'm happy—ha ha ha.   Happiness/Pleasure
- Maybe I'll go to my friend Sally's house. (knock)   Nurturance/Affection
- Who is it?
- It's Rebecca, remember, your friend.   Nurturance/Affection
- Hi Rebecca, come in.
- Hi Sally. I wanted to know if I can play with you.
- OK—you can play with me—anytime you want,
  if I'm home. (laugh) Do you want to go to the
  playground?   Nurturance/Affection

- Oh sure Sally but I don't know how to get there.   Anxiety/Fear
- Oh Rebecca (with feeling) I do, you can just
  follow me. We'll play and jump rope OK?   Nurturance/Affection
- OK Sally.
- Here is the playground—I think or this might be a school.
- Oh what—what day is it—it's Saturday, so we don't
  have school—Here's the playground.
- Oh remember, we were going to play Miss Lucy.
- Yes—ready. (play and sing)

Child 3. Lower Affect/Lower Quality of Fantasy

- Hello little girls—want to play with these blocks?
- OK—let's build something.
- OK. (build)
- Uh oh. (blocks fell over)   Frustration/Disappointment
- We'll build it again. (build)
- There.
- Let's make a picnic table.
- There.
- Now let's play—let's build a tunnel.
- OK.
- Let's go under the tunnel.
- Let's build some monkey bars.
- Let's play house—I'll be the mother. (Much of the
  time was spent building—no verbalization.)

Child 1 had 17 units of affective expression, child 2 had 7, and child 3 had 1 in these 90-second periods. The intensity of each affective expression is also scored and is based on the expression of content themes and actual feeling states. Nonverbal expression (punching, patting) is an important component of the intensity rating as is the amount of emotion in the tone of expression.

EMPIRICAL STUDIES

Once the Affect in Play Scale was constructed, pilot studies were carried out to ensure that the task was appropriate for young children and would result in adequate individual differences among normal school populations (Russ, Grossman-McKee, & Rutkin, 1984). By 1984, the basics of the task and scoring system were in place. Early studies resulted in refinement of the scoring criteria and a shortening of the play period (from 10 minutes to 5 minutes). The next step was to develop reliability and build construct validity for the scale. To date, 11 validity studies have been carried out (see Table 26–1).

Table 26–1.   Validity studies of affect in play scale

Authors	Date	Variables Investigated
Grossman-McKee	1989	Pain complaints
Peterson	1989	Self-esteem
Russ & Grossman-McKee	1990	Divergent thinking; primary process
Russ & Peterson	1990	Divergent thinking; coping in school
D'Angelo	1995	Adjustment; imagination
Niec & Russ	1996	Interpersonal themes in storytelling and interpersonal functioning
Christiano & Russ	1996	Coping and distress in dental visit
Russ, Robins, & Christiano	in press	Longitudinal prediction of creativity, coping, and older version of play task
Niec	1998	Internal representations and empathy
Seja & Russ	1999	Emotional understanding
Seja & Russ	1998	Parents' reports of daily emotional expression
Perry & Russ	1998	Coping and adjustment in homeless children

Reliability

Interrater reliabilities in all of the studies have been consistently good. Because a detailed scoring manual was developed, and raters were carefully trained, interrater reliabilities using a number of different raters have usually been in the .80s and .90s, with some in the .70s. For example, in a study by Russ and Grossman-McKee (1990), based on 15 randomly chosen subjects, Pearson-r correlation coefficients were as follows: total frequency of affect, $r = .90$; variety of categories, $r = .82$; intensity of affect, $r = .53$; mean quality of fantasy, $r = .88$; imagination, $r = .74$; and comfort, $r = .89$. With the exception of intensity of affect, which was therefore not included in the analysis, all of the interrater reliabilities were judged to be good.

In a study by Christiano and Russ (1996), interrater reliabilities for 20 participants were: total frequency of affect, $r = .91$; variety of affect, $r = .90$; quality of fantasy, $r = .85$; and comfort, $r = .90$. In a recent study by Seja and Russ (in press), correlations were: frequency of affect, $r = .83$; quality of fantasy, $r = .80$; organization, $r = .72$; elaboration, $r = 74$; and imagination, $r = .78$.

Two studies have investigated the internal consistency of the APS and found it to be good. The second and fourth minutes were compared with the third and fifth minutes of the play period for frequency of affect. Both studies, using the Spearman-Brown split-half reliability formula, found an internal consistency of $r = .85$ for frequency of affect (Russ & Peterson, 1990; Seja & Russ, 1999).

Test-retest reliability for the APS needs to be determined. In process is the analysis of data on 50 children who were administered the task a second time after a 2 to 4-week interval.

Validity Studies

The development of construct validity for the APS has been carried out by investigating the relationships between the scores on the APS and criteria that should be related to the constructs of fantasy and affect in fantasy (Anastasi, 1988). By finding relationships between a measure and theoretically relevant criteria, conceptual validity is developed (Weiner, 1977). For the APS, validity studies have been carried out with four major types of theoretically relevant criteria: creativity; coping and adjustment; emotional understanding; and interpersonal functioning. (See Table 26–1.) Each area is reviewed below.

APS and Creativity

One of the most robust findings in the literature is the relationship between pretend play and creativity. Russ (1993, in press) postulated that pretend play is important in developing creativity because so many of the cognitive and affective processes involved in creativity occur in play. Russ's (1993) model of affect and creativity identified the major cognitive and affective processes involved in creativity, and the relationships among them, based on the research literature.

Divergent thinking is one major cognitive process important in creativity and was a focus of several validity studies with the APS. As defined by Guilford (1968), divergent thinking is thinking that generates a variety of ideas and associations to a problem. Divergent thinking involves free association, broad scanning ability, and fluidity of thinking. It has been found to be relatively independent of intelligence (Runco, 1991).

Two affective processes important in creativity are access to affect-laden thoughts and the ability to experience affect states (Russ, 1993). Both the ability to think about affect-laden fantasy and the capacity to experience emotion are important in creativity. In play, children express affect in fantasy and experience emotion. For example, Fein (1987) concluded that play facilitated the development of an affective symbol system important in creativity. Waelder (1933) viewed play as a place in which primary process thinking can occur. Morrison (1988) conceptualized play as an arena in which children reconstruct past experiences and rework old metaphors.

Pretend play should facilitate the development of divergent thinking for several reasons. The expression of emotion and affect-laden fantasy in play could help develop a broad repertoire of affect-laden associations (Russ, 1993, 1996). This broad repertoire of associations and use of emotion to access these associations should facilitate divergent thinking because the involvement of emotion broadens the search process for associations (Isen, Daubman, & Nowicki, 1987). Play should also facilitate divergent thinking because in play children practice divergent thinking skills by using toys and objects to represent different things and by role playing different scenarios (Singer & Singer, 1990).

A growing body of research has found a relationship between play and creativity. Most of the research has been correlational in nature and has focused on cognitive processes. A substantial body of studies have found a relationship between play and divergent thinking (Clark, Griffing, & Johnson, 1989; Johnson, 1976; Pepler & Ross, 1981; Singer & Rummo, 1973). In addition, in experimental studies, play has been found to facilitate divergent thinking (Dansky, 1980; Dansky & Silverman, 1973; Feitelson & Ross, 1973; Hughes, 1987) and insight (Vandenberg, 1980). Flexibility in problem solving has also been related to play (Pelligrini, 1992).

A few studies have found a relationship between affective processes in play and creativity. Lieberman (1977) found a relationship between playfulness, which included affective components of spontaneity and joy, and divergent thinking in kindergarten children.

Christie and Johnson (1983) also concluded that there was a relationship between playfulness and creativity. Singer and Singer (1981) found that preschoolers rated as high imagination players showed significantly more themes of danger and power than children with low imagination.

In the first study with the APS, we were particularly interested in the relationship between the affect scores and creativity. Russ and Grossman-McKee (1990) investigated the relationships among the Affect in Play Scale, primary process thinking on the Rorschach, and divergent thinking in first- and second-grade children. Sixty children individually received the Rorschach, Affect in Play Scale, and Alternate Uses Test. A typical item on the Alternate Uses Test is "How many uses for a newspaper can you think of?" Holt's Scoring System was the measure for the Rorschach (1977). Primary process thinking was included in the study because it is affect-laden ideation that has been found to be related to a number of creativity criteria (Russ, 1996; Suler, 1980).

A major finding of this study was that affective expression in play was predictive of divergent thinking (see Table 26–2). The predicted relationships between the play scores and the Alternate Uses test were all significant for that total sample, except for the relationship between frequency of nonprimary process affect and divergent thinking. Divergent thinking was significantly related to frequency of affect [$r(58) = .42, p < .001$], variety of affect categories [$r(58) = .38, p < .001$], comfort [$r(58) = .23, p < .051$], frequency of primary process affect [$r(58) = .41, p < .001$], quality of fantasy [$4(58) = .30, p < .01$], imagination [$4(58) = .35, p < .01$], and integration of affect [$r(58) = .42, p < .001$]. All correlations remained significant when IQ was partialed out, due to the fact that IQ had such low relationships with the play scores (e.g., $r = .09$ with frequency of affect, $r = .01$ with comfort, $r = .08$ with quality, and $r = .12$ with imagination). The fact that intelligence did

Table 26–2.   Pearson product-moment correlations among primary process and affect measures and alternate uses test

	Alternate Uses – # Categories Score		
	Total Sample	Boys	Girls
Rorschach[a]			
Percent Primary Process	.50***	.72***	.27
AR	−.17	−.09	−.27
AR × Number of Primary Process Responses	.10	.34	−.21
Affect in Play Scale[b]			
Frequency of Affect	.42***	.40*	.44**
Number of Categories of Affect	.38**	.56**	.29
Comfort in Play	.23*	.36*	.22
Frequency of Primary Process Affect	.41***	.38*	.48**
Frequency of Nonprimary Process Affect	.20	.20	.22
Quality of Fantasy	.30**	.48**	.32*
Imagination	.35**	.40*	.44**
Integration of Affect	.42**	.45**	.38*

[a] $n = 46$ for total, $n = 22$ for boys, $n = 24$ for girls.
[b] $n = 60$ for total, $n = 30$ for boys, $n = 30$ for girls.
*$p<.05$; **$p<.01$; ***$p<.001$.

not relate to any of the play measures is theoretically consistent with the model for the development of the scale and is similar to the results of Singer (1973). There were no gender differences in the pattern of correlations.

Also, as predicted, amount of primary process thinking on the Rorschach was significantly positively related to the amount of affect in play. Total frequency of primary process on the Rorschach was significantly positively related to the following play measures: frequency of affect [r(44) = .34, p < .01]; variety of affective categories [r(44) = .44, p < .001]; frequency of primary process affect [r(44) = .30, p < .05]; frequency of nonprimary process affect [r(44) = .26, p < .05]; comfort [r(44) = .45, p < .001]; quality of fantasy [r(44) = .48, p < .001]; imagination [r(44) = .47, p < .01]; and the composite integration of affect score [r(44) = .37, p < .01]. Percentage of primary process, which controls for general productivity, was also significantly related to most of the play variables, although the correlations were lower than those with total frequency. Percentage of Primary Process was significantly related to frequency of affect [r(44) = .32, p < .05]; variety of affective categories [r(44) = .28, p < .05]; frequency of primary process [r(44) = .28, p < .05]; frequency of nonprimary process [r(44) = .25, p < .05]; quality of fantasy [r(44) = .27, p < .05]; imagination [r(44) = .30, p < .05]; and integration of affect [r(44) = .32, p < .05].

Primary process thinking on the Rorschach was equally predictive for girls and for boys in the play situation. The relationships between the variables were not affected when intelligence was controlled for. The finding in this study, that primary process expression on the Rorschach was significantly related to affective expression in children's play, is important because it shows that there is some consistency in the construct of affective expression across two different types of situations.

A study by Russ and Peterson (1990) investigated the relationships among the Affect in Play Scale, divergent thinking, and coping in school in first- and second-grade children. The main purpose of this study was to obtain a large enough sample size (121 children) so that a sound factor analysis of the play scale could be carried out for the total sample and separately for boys and girls. A second purpose was to replicate the results of the Russ and Grossman-McKee (1990) study that found a positive relationship between affective expression in play and divergent thinking.

One hundred twenty-one children (64 boys and 57 girls) were individually administered the Affect in Play Scale and a Coping in School scale. In a separate testing session, with a different examiner, they were administered the Alternate Uses Test. The Affect in Play Scale used in this study and subsequent studies was slightly different than the earlier version used in the Russ and Grossman-McKee (1990) study. The play period was 5 minutes instead of 10 minutes. A video camera was used rather than a tape recorder. Also, some of the affect categories were condensed, because of infrequent occurrence. Displeasure and frustration became one category and sadness and hurt became another category. A new category, competition, was added because of its prevalence in children's play and because it is considered to be a derivative of aggressive content in Holt's system. Finally, there were some minor adjustments in the intensity-rating criteria.

The main finding in this study was that the Affect in Play Scale was significantly positively related to divergent thinking. These results replicated the findings of the Russ and Grossman-McKee (1990) study with children of the same age. As in the previous study, there were no gender differences in the pattern of correlations. For the total sample, divergent thinking was significantly related to frequency of total affect [r(115) = .26, p < .01];

variety of affect [$r(115) = .25, p < .01$]; comfort [$r(115) = .37, p < .001$]; quality of fantasy, [$r(115) = .43, p < .001$]; imagination [$r(115) = .42, p < .001$]; primary process [$r(115) = .17, p < .05$]; nonprimary process [$r(115) = .24, p < .01$]; and integration of affect [$r(115) = .30, p < .001$]. These relationships remained significant when IQ was partialed out. Based on this study, we can say with more confidence that affective expression in fantasy relates to divergent thinking, independent of the cognitive processes measured by intelligence tests.

It is important to note that in both the Russ and Grossman-McKee (1990) study and the Russ and Peterson (1990) study, the significant relationship between play and divergent thinking occurred in studies where the play task and the divergent thinking task were administered by different examiners. Given Smith and Whitney's (1987) criticism that previous positive results that linked play and associative fluency were due to experimenter effects, these are important findings.

APS, Coping, and Adjustment

Theoretically, play ability should be related to coping ability and to broader measures of adjustment. This link should occur for several reasons. First, children use play to solve real-life problems and to resolve internal conflicts (Erikson, 1963; Freud, 1965). Children play out their problems in pretend play, express negative emotions in a controllable way, and practice with different behaviors. Second, the creative problem-solving skills developed in play should generalize to problem-solving skills in daily life. Creative problem solvers should be better copers because they bring their problem-solving skills to everyday problems. The ability to generate a variety of associations and alternative solutions should facilitate coping with daily stressors. There is some empirical support for this concept. Russ (1988) found a relationship between divergent thinking and teachers' ratings of coping in fifth grade boys. Similarly, Carson, Bittner, Cameron, Brown, and Meyer (1994) found a significant relationship between figural divergent thinking and teachers' ratings of coping.

Looking specifically at play on the APS and coping ability, Christiano and Russ (1996) found a positive relationship between play and coping and a negative relationship between play and distress in 7- to 9-year-olds. Children who were "good" players on the Affect in Play Scale implemented a greater number and variety of cognitive coping strategies (correlations ranging from .52 to .55) during an invasive dental procedure. In addition, good players reported less distress during the procedure than children who expressed less affect and fantasy in play. Also, the Russ and Peterson study (1990) found a relationship between fantasy in play, self-report coping, and teachers' ratings of coping. Consistent with these findings, a recent study by Perry and Russ (1998) found that fantasy in play on the APS was positively related to frequency and variety of self-reported coping strategies on the Schoolagers Coping Strategies Semistructured Interview (Ryan, 1989) in a group of homeless children. Again, findings were independent of intelligence. This sample of homeless children was primarily African American (77%). Because videotaping was not permitted in the shelter, the play was transcribed as it occurred.

The APS has also been related to more global measures of children's adjustment. Grossman-McKee (1990), using the Affect in Play Scale with first and second-grade boys, found that boys who expressed more affect in play had fewer pain complaints than boys with less affect in play. Good players were also less anxious on the State-Trait Anxiety

Inventory for Children (Spielberger, 1973). The conclusion from this study was that the ability to express affect in play was associated with less anxiety and less psychosomatic complaints.

Peterson (1989), in a one-year follow-up on a subsample of 50 of the original 121 children in the Russ and Peterson study, found that the APS predicted self-esteem on the Self-Perception Profile for Children (Harter, 1985). Also, D'Angelo (1995) found, in a group of inner-city first- and second-grade children, that ego-resilient children had higher APS scores than less resilient children. Also, internalizing children on the Child Behavior Checklist (Edelbrock & Achenbach, 1980) had significantly lower fantasy and affect scores in play than did externalizing and ego-resilient children. Externalizing children had significantly lower fantasy scores (but not affect) than did ego-resilient children.

In the Perry and Russ (1998) study with homeless children, the APS was significantly related to depression in children, but not to anxiety.

APS and Emotional Understanding

Emotional understanding is the process by which people make inferences about their own and others' feelings and behaviors that in turn influence their thoughts and actions (Nannis, 1988). Theoretical and empirical evidence suggest that there may be two reasons for a relationship between children's play and emotional understanding. First, using imagination in play may relate to the cognitive ability to take the perspective of other people. Second, experiencing and expressing different emotions may be central to both fantasy play and emotional understanding.

The relationship between affect and cognitive processes in fantasy play and emotional understanding was examined in children in the first and second grades (Seja & Russ, 1999). In this study, consistent, yet modest, relations were found between dimensions of fantasy play on the APS and emotional understanding as measured by the Kusche Affective Interview—Revised (Kusche, Greenberg, & Beilke, 1988). Cognitive dimensions of fantasy play, but not affect expression, were related to facets of emotional understanding. The children who were able to access and organize their fantasy and emotions in play were more likely to recall and organize memories related to emotional events and had a more sophisticated understanding of others' emotions. These relationships remained significant when verbal ability was partialed out. The relationship between fantasy play and understanding others' emotions supports Harris's (1989) proposition that imaginative understanding may enable children to understand others' mental states and affective experiences. A composite fantasy play score accounted for a significant amount of variance in a composite emotional understanding score (5%) when verbal ability was accounted for.

Contrary to initial hypotheses, frequency of affect expression was not related to emotional understanding of oneself and others. The results of this study have important implications for clinical work and suggest that the mere expression of emotion in play is not related to emotional understanding and may not be as useful as play therapists believe. Instead, the integration of affective and cognitive material may be more important in facilitating the development of emotional understanding.

Seja and Russ (1998) examined the relationships among parents' reports of children's daily behavior, children's affect and fantasy in play, and children's emotional understanding among first-grade children in the previous sample. Parents' ratings of children's daily emotional intensity was expected to relate to children's affect expression in play. Results were that children who demonstrated more positive emotion in their daily behavior were more likely to express more emotion overall and more negative emotion in their play than children who expressed less daily positive emotion. Furthermore, children who demonstrated more negative emotion in their daily behavior displayed fewer different types of emotion, less positive emotion, and less emotion overall in their play than children who expressed less daily negative emotion.

It was also hypothesized that parents' ratings of children's daily emotional intensity would relate to children's emotional understanding. It was found that children who expressed more intense positive emotion in their daily behavior had a better understanding of their own emotions and described more emotional experiences than children with less intense daily positive emotion. Contrary to initial hypotheses, children with more intense negative emotion in daily behavior did not have lower levels of emotional understanding. The results of this study suggest that parents' reports of children's daily behavior may provide important information to clinicians about children's play, emotional development, and adjustment. However, because the sample was small (n = 23), the study should be replicated with another sample of children.

APS and Interpersonal Functioning

Theories of development acknowledge that affect is linked to interpersonal functioning in multiple ways (Emde, 1989; Russ & Niec, 1993; Sroufe, 1989; Strayer, 1987). For example, affective sharing has been related to better quality of infant-parent attachment (Pederson & Moran, 1996; Waters, Wippman, Sroufe, 1979); regulation of affect has been related to better peer relations and fewer behavior problems (Cole, Zahn-Waxler, Fox, Usher, & Welsh, 1996; Rubin, Coplan, Fox, & Calkins, 1995); openness to affect has been described as providing meaning to interpersonal experience (Sandler & Sandler, 1978), and has also been conceptualized as a key component of empathy (Feshbach, 1987). Given these associations between dimensions of affect and interpersonal functioning, two studies were conducted to investigate the relationship of the Affect in Play Scale with children's interpersonal functioning.

Niec and Russ (1996) investigated relationships among affect and fantasy in play, expression of interpersonal themes in projective stories, and peer and teacher ratings of interpersonal functioning in 49 first through third-graders. Access to affect in play was predicted to be positively associated with children's expression of interpersonal themes in stories and interpersonal functioning based on the proposition from object relations theory that a "defense against affect is a defense against objects" and leads to an inability to relate with others on anything but a superficial level (Modell, 1980, p. 266). Children with poor access to affect in play were thus expected to be more likely to have poor peer relationships, while children with good access to affect were expected to have good-quality peer relationships.

Children were administered the APS, the Children's Apperceptive Story Telling Test (CAST), and a brief IQ measure (Schneider, 1989). Teachers and peers rated subjects on their likability, disruptiveness, and withdrawal using the Pupil Evaluation Inventory (PEI; Pekarik, Prinz, Liebert, Weintraub, & Neale, 1976). Results found no relationship between the APS and interpersonal functioning. However, relationships were found between the APS and frequency of interpersonal themes on the CAST. Children who were better players in that they expressed a wide variety of affective categories, frequent positive affect, comfort in their play, and high-quality fantasy were more likely to project themes involving people and relationships in their stories.

In a study by Niec (1998) relationships among affect and fantasy in play, internal representations, and capacity for empathy were investigated. Eighty-six children in third and fourth grades completed the APS, the TAT, and the Bryant Index of Empathy for Children (Bryant, 1982; Murray, 1971). Teachers completed ratings of children's empathy and helpfulness for each child. TAT stories were scored using Westen's (1995) Social Cognition and Object Relations Scale (SCORS-Q).

As predicted, quality of fantasy on the APS was related to self-reported empathy. The finding supported the importance of imaginative ability in children's empathic responding and is consistent with the previously discussed Seja and Russ finding (1999). Children who were able to "put reality aside and imagine the feelings of someone else in a different (make-believe) situation" were likely to be self-described as more empathic to others (Harris, 1994, p. 19).

Access to affect in play did not relate to empathy, perhaps because the APS measures expression of affect-laden themes rather than the experience of emotion so important in empathic understanding.

Neither access to affect nor fantasy in play related to children's representations of relationships on the TAT. This finding helped to answer the question posed by Niec (1994) as to whether access to affect in play would be related to interpersonal representations when content rather than frequency is assessed. While in the Niec and Russ (1996) study, affect and fantasy in play were positively related to frequency of interpersonal themes in projective stories, Niec's (1998) finding suggests that access to affect may not be related to the qualitative aspects of those representations. It may be that access to affect relates to access to interpersonal representations (i.e., frequency) regardless of the content of those representations (i.e., quality).

The two studies have refined the understanding of the constructs of affect and fantasy as measured by the APS. As expected, access to affect has related to access to interpersonal representations (Niec & Russ, 1996); however, it has not related to peer, teacher, or self-reported measures of interpersonal functioning including such dimensions as empathy, helpfulness, likability, disruptiveness, and withdrawal (Niec, 1998; Niec & Russ, 1996). Quality of fantasy on the APS has been related to both access to interpersonal representations (Niec & Russ, 1996) and to self-reported capacity for empathy (Niec, 1998). These findings and those of previous validity studies suggest that the APS may tap affective dimensions important in mental flexibility (e.g., creativity, role taking, problem solving), rather than the affective constructs of communication, and emotional expression. This understanding is consistent with the theoretical conceptualization of the scale. Further studies that investigate both convergent and discriminant validity of the APS based on this conceptualization will enhance the usefulness of the scale.

Longitudinal Prediction

A study by Russ, Robins, and Christiano (in press) followed up the first- and second-graders in the Russ and Peterson (1990) study, which investigated the APS, divergent-thinking and coping. The children were now in the fifth and sixth grades. Thirty-one of the original 121 children participated. This was a longitudinal study that explored the ability of the APS to predict creativity and coping over a four-year period. The Alternate Uses Test was the measure of divergent thinking and a self-report School Coping Scale was the measure of coping. In addition, a version of the APS for older children was administered. The same basic task was administered, but the children were instructed to put on a play. In essence, the puppet play task became a storytelling task in the form of a play. The stories were scored with the same criteria as for the APS.

As predicted, quality of fantasy and imagination in early play predicted divergent thinking over time, independent of IQ (see Table 26–3). Variety of affect categories and comfort showed low positive correlations with divergent thinking, but did not reach significance. The APS also significantly predicted coping over time. The fantasy scores predicted the number of different responses generated on the coping measures.

In addition, the APS was predictive of the version of the scale for older children. Most of the APS scores were significantly related to the comparable score on the modified play task (see Table 26–4). The magnitude of the correlations is quite good for longitudinal data. The strongest correlations were for the affect scores: $r = .51$, $p < .01$ for positive affect; $r = .38$, $p < .05$ for variety of affect; and $r = .33$, $p < .05$ for total frequency of affect expressed. These findings suggest that the cognitive and affective processes measured by the APS are stable over time and are important processes in divergent thinking. Although the APS also predicted coping over time, this finding should be interpreted with caution because the coping measure is a new measure and has not been related to other measures of coping behavior.

Factor Analysis of the APS

An important theoretical question is whether affect in fantasy and the cognitive components in fantasy are separate processes or are one process. The theoretical assumption underlying the play scale was that at least two separate processes are involved—one cognitive and one affective. On the other hand, it is possible that affect and fantasy are so intertwined in play that they cannot be measured separately. In the development of the scale,

Table 26–3.   Longitudinal Pearson correlations of play scale variables at first and second grade with divergent thinking and coping measures at fifth and sixth grade

	Divergent Thinking		Coping	
Affect in Play Scale	Fluency	Spontaneous Flexibility	Frequency	Quality
Frequency of Affect	.13	.11	.02	−.03
Variety of Affect	.25	.20	.26	.23
Comfort	.24	.17	.20	.22
Mean Quality	.34*	.25	.34*	.33*
Organization	.27	.16	.34*	.28
Imagination	.42**	>35*	.42**	.45**

Note: $N = 30$.
*$p < .05$; **$p < .01$.

Table 26–4.   Longitudinal Pearson correlations of affect in play scale variables at first and second grade with similar variables of the modified affect in fantasy task at sixth and seventh grade

	Affect in Fantasy Task (6th & 7th Grade)
Affect in Play Scale (1st & 2nd Grade)	r
Frequency of Affect	.33*
Positive Affect	.51**
Negative Affect	.21
Variety of Affect	.38*
Comfort	.29
Mean Quality of Fantasy	.27
Organization	.31*
Elaboration	.32*
Imagination	.08
Repetition	.08
Affective Integration	.40*

Note: $N = 30$.
*$p < .05$; **$p < .01$.

care was taken to make the scoring criteria of the affect scores separate from the cognitive dimensions. For example, the intensity rating of an aggressive expression should not be influenced by the amount of imagination in the play; the scoring of affective expressions themselves should be independent of the quality of the fantasy. Also, the scoring of imagination should not be influenced by the amount of affect in the response. Thus, if only one underlying dimension were identified in a factor analysis, it would probably not be due to an artifact of the scoring system.

Factor analyses have been carried out with three separate samples of the APS. All three studies had a large enough sample for a solid factor analysis to be carried out. In all three studies, two separate factors were found to be the best model. These two factors appear to be a cognitive factor and an affect factor.

Looking first at the Russ and Peterson (1990) data set of 121 children, a factor analysis of the total sample was carried out using the principal component analysis with oblique rotation (see Table 26–5). Seven major scores for the Affect in Play Scale were included in the factor analysis. (Scores that involved statistical combinations of scores were not included in this particular factor analysis.) An oblique solution, using the method default (Cattell & Jaspers, 1967) yielded two separate factors as the best solution. The first and dominant factor appears to be a cognitive factor. Imagination, organization, quality of fantasy, and comfort in play significantly loaded on this first factor. The second factor appears to be an affective factor. Frequency of affective expression, variety of affect categories, and intensity of affect loaded on this second factor. Although separate factors, there is a significant amount of shared variance ($r = .76$), suggesting that the factors also overlap.

When factor analyses were carried out separately for girls and boys, similar factor structures emerged. For boys, the factor structure replicated that of the total sample. For girls, the only difference from the total sample was that intensity of affect loaded on the cognitive factor.

Table 26–5.   Oblique factor structure of the affect in play scale for total sample

Play Scores	Cognitive	Affective
Frequency of Affect	−.27	.79
Variety of Affect	−.00	.60
Mean Intensity	.12	.40
Comfort	.55	.06
Quality of Fantasy	.62	.04
Organization	.69	−.09
Imagination	.65	−.08

Note: $N = 121$.

The important finding here is that affective expression and cognitive expression in fantasy play, though related, also have significant amounts of unique variance, which suggest that there are separate processes involved.

Similar two-factor structures were found for the D'Angelo (1995) study with 95 children and the Niec (1998) study with 86 children.

In summary, the validity studies suggest that the affective and cognitive processes measured by the APS are predictive of theoretically relevant criteria. The affective processes are related to criteria of creativity, coping, and adjustment. They are not related to measures of emotional understanding, empathy, or interpersonal functioning. The cognitive fantasy processes are related to all criteria. Both cognitive and affective processes are stable over a five-year period. A very important point is that, in this age group, the APS is independent of IQ. Thus, these processes are resources for children that are independent of intelligence. Finally, the factor analyses results suggest that the APS measures two processes, one cognitive and one affective. Thus, future studies should continue to use both sets of scores.

PRESCHOOL AFFECT IN PLAY SCALE

Preschool represents a period of time when children's cognitive and emotional advances intersect and foster the development of fantasy play. Specifically, by 4 and 5 years of age, children are actively engaged in imaginative play that demonstrates the integration of their cognitive skills and emotional expression and understanding.

Advances in children's cognitive development are characterized by the capacity for pretend or symbolic play. Piaget (1962) claimed that symbolic play emerged at 2 years of age, increased the next three or four years, and then declined around 6 years of age. While Piaget believed that these changes were accompanied by a decrease in less mature forms of thought during a young age and an increase in more mature forms in later age, empirical data do not support this assumption (Singer & Singer, 1990). Pretend play in young children has been defined by the following five criteria: (1) familiar activities may be performed in the absence of necessary material or a social context; (2) activities may not be carried out to their logical outcome; (3) a child may treat an inanimate object as animate; (4) one object or gesture may be substituted for another; and (5) a child may carry out an activity usually performed by someone else (Fein, 1981; Singer & Singer, 1990). Pretend play is evident as children arrange stuffed animals around a box, place blocks and pieces of flattened clay in front of each of them, and announce that they are having a tea party. Thus, when pretending, children can incorporate unique combinations of both reality and fantasy themes into their play with an understanding of their distinction.

Young children's play is filled with emotion. This can be seen in the language and facial expressions children use as well as in the themes they recreate in their play. At around 2 years of age, children begin using emotion words such as happy, sad, mad, and scared to refer primarily to themselves and eventually to other people. By 3 $^{1}/_{2}$ years of age children are able to accurately recognize situations that elicit emotional reactions such as happiness, sadness, anger, and fear. In the next three years their understanding expands to more complex emotional states such as pride, shame, guilt, surprise, and gratitude. Similarly, at these ages children are learning to identify prototypical expressions of emotions (summary in Thompson, 1989). The themes enacted in play are often elaborated by children's emotional gestures, facial expressions, statements, and voice tones.

Due to the many developmental milestones that are encountered by 4 and 5 years of age, play is often used to assess cognitive and language functioning. For example, play can be used to identify cognitive and developmental disorders with normal and clinical populations (Sigman & Sena, 1993). In addition, various methods of assessing affect and fantasy with preschool-age children have been developed. The following summary represents a sample of several different assessment scales measuring fantasy and/or affect in play that have been used with individual children as young as 4 to 5 years of age. Some of these measures are also appropriate for older children. First, methods of assessing cognitive dimensions of play will be reviewed. Second, measures of fantasy and thematic content will be presented. Finally, techniques for assessing affect alone in play and both affect and fantasy in play will be discussed.

Identifying different types of play is common in many observations of both individual children's play (Barnett, 1984) and children's play in groups (Dansky, 1980; Rubin, Watson, & Jambor, 1978). Young children's play has frequently been separated into four categories: functional (simple, repetitive muscle movements with or without objects), constructive (creating something), dramatic (substitution of imaginary situations to satisfy one's wishes or needs), and games with rules (Smilansky, 1968). Often a category of make-believe play includes role play, object transformation, verbal communication within the context of role play, and nonverbal interaction during role play (Dansky, 1980).

Measures of Preschool Play

Three measures represent methods of assessing cognitive dimensions of play. The Preschool Play Scale (Bledsoe & Shepherd, 1982) has been developed to measure physical, social, and cognitive aspects of children's play from infancy to 6 years of age. One dimension that observers note is whether the child uses imitation, imagination, dramatization, music, and or books in free-play situations. The Westby Symbolic Play Scale (Westby, 1991; Westby, this volume) describes changes in children's presymbolic play, symbolic play, and language from 9 months to 5 years of age. A method for coding developmental trends in pretend play, developed by Fenson (1984), identifies behavioral examples of decentration, decontextualization, and integration. Lyytinen (1995) describes using this coding paradigm when children 2 to 6 years of age were presented with the following toys in an individual play session: Duplo Legos, dolls, bedroom and kitchen equipment, animals, fences, vehicles, and blocks.

Several methods have been developed to assess fantasy and thematic content in play that are relevant to measuring affect in play. Coding of children's fantasy and nonfantasy play speech has been described by Olszewski (1987) and Olszewski and Fuson (1982). In both of these studies, 3- to 5-year-old children were given materials intended to elicit pretend play themes such as a doll family and home, a farm, and a construction site. Children's speech was transcribed, divided into utterances, and classified as either fantasy or nonfantasy speech.

The Child-Psychoanalytic Play Interview (Marans, Mayes, Cicchetti, Dahl, Marans, & Cohen, 1991) is a technique for identifying and tracking specific themes in a child's play during a therapy session with a child analyst. The authors identified 30 thematic categories with descriptors to aid raters in inferring how play behaviors reflect particular themes. Some categories require making inferences about the play content and include topics such as bodily functions, loss of object/abandonment, and fighting and attacking. Other categories describe the preparations children make for play such as listing and labeling characters and assigning characters properties. Marans et al. (1991) describe using the interview with children 4 to 6 years of age.

An experimental study by Milos and Reiss (1982) concentrated on the presence of separation anxiety themes in play among children beginning to attend nursery school, aged 2 to 6. A score for quality of play was given on a 5-point scale based on the extent to which the child's play expressed separation themes and a desire to master the problem.

Three measures have been used to assess children's affect and/or affect themes while playing or telling stories. The Kiddie-Infant Descriptive Instrument for Emotional States (KIDIES) is a scale that measures behavioral manifestations of affect in infants and young children during individual play, social play, and separation paradigms (Stern, et al., 1992). Frequency and intensity of affect displayed for the face, the voice, and the body/gesture system are scored on a 5-point scale for each of fourteen 2- to 3-minute episodes. The affects that are scored include happiness, sadness, anger, fear, disgust, surprise, distress, soberness, interest in things and persons, regression, aggression, and negativism. Children ranging in age from 2 years, 0 months to 4 years, 11 months have participated in studies using this measure (Stern et al., 1992)

Singer (1973) developed a scoring system for observations of 10-minute segments of preschool children's free play and structured play (ages 2 to 5). Imaginativeness, affect, and concentration were rated on a 5-point scale for the entire play session. Eight moods (angry/annoyed, fearful/tense, lively/excited, elated/pleased, sad/downhearted, ashamed/contrite, contemptuous/disgusted, and fatigued/sluggish) were also evaluated on a 5-point scale considering both the intensity and frequency of mood. Aggression, defined as "the intentional delivery of a harmful stimulus to another person or to personal property" (p. 267), was also coded on a 5-point scale for the play episodes.

The MacArthur Story-Stem Battery (Warren, Oppenheim, & Emde, 1996) asks children to complete story stems that are presented to them with the use of dolls, play furniture, and toys. The narratives reflect a variety of childhood events including looking for a lost dog, stealing candy, and witnessing a parental argument. Children's emotional displays during the storytelling are scored on a 4-point scale for emotions such as distress, anger, sadness, and concern. The presence and absence of content themes including aggression, personal injury, and atypical negative responses are noted. Several factors are considered in scoring the manner of storytelling including coherence, elaboration, conflict resolution, and investment in the task.

The Preschool Affect in Play Scale Task

There is no available measure for preschool children that assesses both affective themes in pretend play and fantasy dimensions in a standardized free-play situation. This review suggests that there is a need for a standardized assessment of affect and fantasy play in preschool-age children. Based on our work with the APS with children 6 to 10 years of age, we are adapting the APS to be used with children 4 and 5 years of age. We believe that it is important to develop a scale, the Preschool Affect in Play Scale (PAPS), that will be sensitive to individual differences in children's play at this younger age. Initially we considered what materials and instructions would be appropriate for younger age groups.

Based on the understanding that puppets might be more difficult for young children to manipulate, we selected toys that would be easy to play with and that could elicit symbolic and fantasy play. The chosen items include a hippopotamus, shark, bear, giraffe, lion, zebra, elephant, three plastic cups, a plastic car, and a "hairy" rubber ball. The variety of stuffed and plastic animals are often associated with a range of typically neutral (giraffe) and aggressive (shark) connotations. Similarly, several items were included that could have a variety of uses in children's play including plastic cups and a "hairy" rubber ball. Pilot testing indicated that children enjoyed playing with the toys and could use them in fantasy play. For example, several children had the animals "eat" the "hairy" rubber ball and "take a bath" in the plastic cups.

The same format for APS instructions is used in the preschool adaptation of the APS with some age-appropriate variations. First, a warmup task is used to introduce the toys to each child and establish some rapport with the examiner. The children are asked to name the different toys and some of their characteristics such as the color and number of various items. Second, children are given more explicit directions to "make up a story" with the toys, and they are provided with several examples of what they can have the toys do (i.e., have the toys do something together like play house or go to the store). Finally, the children are not given a one-minute warning near the end of their play time and instead are just told when to start and stop. The instructions that the children are given are as follows:

> That's all the toys in the basket. Now we're going to make up a story using the toys on the table. You can play with the toys any way that you like and have them do something together like play house or go to the store. Be sure to talk out loud so that I can hear you. The video camera will be on so that I can remember what you say and do. You will have five minutes to play with the toys. I'll tell you when to stop. Now remember to play with the toys and make up a story.

Preschool children are given the same prompts used with the APS for instances when children do not play, do not talk, and stop play early. The identical guideline of stopping after two minutes if a child is unable to play is used with younger children.

At the present time, the APS scoring system is being adapted for younger children. A central consideration is the development of preschoolers' language abilities. While the

APS scoring is based on puppets' expressions, our pilot data with the PAPS suggest that utterances may be more difficult to score in young children. Young children's verbal skills may not be as well developed and their words may not be as clearly articulated as those of older children. Therefore it may be more difficult to understand each utterance and provide a rating of affect frequency. Also, because animals are being used, the children's play may consist of many more animal sounds than are present with older children. Work is underway to address these and other concerns in the PAPS scoring criteria. A more global 1–5 rating system for affect expression will probably be used.

Pilot work is currently being done to establish the validity of the PAPS by demonstrating a relationship between young children's play, creativity, daily play behavior, and daily emotional expression. Furthermore, the PAPS will be used in a study examining play behavior, emotional understanding, and emotional regulation in 4-year-old children who were exposed to cocaine prenatally as compared to a control group.

CLINICAL USE OF THE APS

To date, there have been no studies with the APS and clinical populations. An important next step is to investigate the APS with a variety of such groups. In addition, the scale should be used to assess change in child psychotherapy, especially in those therapies that use play.

The APS should be sensitive to changes in a child's affect expression in play during the therapy process and could be used as a measure of therapy outcome. Changes in the amount of emotional expression and the affect themes are frequently noted by child therapists as therapy progresses. Systematic intervention studies with specifically diagnosed child populations could utilize the APS to assess changes in affect and changes in the organization of fantasy life. For constricted, internalizing children affect expression should increase as a result of effective therapy. We know from the D'Angelo (1995) study that internalizing children are more constricted in their affect expression than other groups. On the other hand, children who have problems with organization of their thinking, such as borderline children and some narcissistic children, should have lower quality of fantasy scores than other children. Successful therapy should result in better organization of their play and better integration of their affect.

The APS could also be used to refine play therapy techniques. The general question of what kinds of intervention by the therapist best facilitate play needs to be studied empirically. There are many guidelines in the clinical literature about how to facilitate play, but few are based on empirical work. How do we best encourage affect in play? When is modeling by the therapist more effective than a more reflective approach? How do we best facilitate modulation of affect? Guidelines from studies investigating these questions could be incorporated into treatment manuals, which are needed in the play therapy area.

Finally, for the practicing clinician, the APS could be used for a quick assessment of play skills. Because the use of a video camera may be impractical for many clinicians, we are working on developing validity for the scale when the child's play is rated as it occurs. We did use this approach in the Perry & Russ (1998) study. The APS in this study demonstrated good interrater reliability (based on transcripts) and predicted relevant criteria. More work is needed to refine the scoring system using this approach.

FUTURE DIRECTIONS

Next steps for the development of the APS are:

1. Determine validity with clinical populations.
2. Continue to refine the scoring system. Of special importance is the addition of a regulation of affect score. Although the combination of the affect and fantasy scores attempts to measure integration of affect, a separate measure may be more valid.
3. Use the APS as a measure of change in child therapy intervention studies.
4. Continue longitudinal studies with the APS.
5. Determine the usefulness of the preschool version of the scale.
6. Develop a version of the APS that can be used without a video camera.

The growing body of validity studies to date suggests that the APS measures processes that are important in child development, predict adaptive functioning in children, and are separate from what traditional intelligence tests measure. The use of the APS in a variety of research programs and clinical settings with a variety of child populations will further the development of the measure. Research with the APS will also tell us about this important resource for children—affect expression in fantasy play.

REFERENCES

Anastasi, A. (1988). *Psychological testing* (6th ed.). New York: Macmillan.

Barnett, L. A. (1984). Research note: Young children's resolution of distress through play. *Journal of Child Psychology and Psychiatry, 25*(3), 477–483.

Bledsoe, N. P., & Shepherd, J. T. (1982). A study of reliability and validity of a preschool play scale. *American Journal of Occupational Therapy, 36*(12), 783–788.

Bryant, B. (1982). An index of empathy for children and adolescents. *Child Development, 53,* 413–425.

Cattell, R. B., & Jaspers, J. (1967). A general plasmode for factor analytic exercises and research. *Multivariate Behavior Research Monographs, 67*(3), No. 30-10-5-2.

Carson, D., Bittner, M., Cameron, B., Brown, D., & Meyer, S. (1994). Creative thinking as a predictor of school-aged children's stress responses and coping abilities. *Creativity Research Journal, 7,* 145–158.

Christiano, B., & Russ, S. (1996). Play as a predictor of coping and distress in children during an invasive dental procedure. *Journal of Clinical Child Psychology, 25,* 130–138.

Christie, J., & Johnson, E. (1983). The role of play in social-intellectual development. *Review of Educational Research, 53,* 93–115.

Clark, P., Griffing, P., & Johnson, L. (1989). Symbolic play and ideational fluency as aspects of the evolving divergent cognitive style in young children. *Early Child Development and Care, 51,* 77–88.

Cole, P., Zahn-Waxler, C., Fox, N., Usher, B., & Welsh, J. (1996). Individual differences in emotion regulation and behavior problems in preschool children. *Journal of Abnormal Psychology, 105*(4), 518–529.

D'Angelo, L. (1995). *Child's play: The relationship between the use of play and adjustment styles.* Unpublished dissertation, Case Western Reserve University, Cleveland, OH.

Dansky, J. (1980). Make-believe: A mediator of the relationship between play and associative fluency. *Child Development, 51,* 576–579.

Dansky, J., & Silverman, F. (1973). Effects of play on associative fluency in preschool-aged children. *Developmental Psychology, 9,* 38–43.

Edelbrock, C., & Achenbach, T. M. (1980). A typology of child behavior profile patterns: Distribution and correlates for disturbed children aged 6–16. *Journal of Abnormal Psychology, 8,* 441–470.

Emde, R. (1989). The infant's relationship experience: Developmental and affective aspects. In A. Sameroff & R. Emde (Eds.), *Relationship disturbances in early childhood* (pp. 33–51). New York: Basic Books.

Erikson, E. (1963). *Childhood and society.* New York: Norton.

Faust, J., & Burns, W. (1991). Coding therapist and child interaction: Progress and outcome in play therapy. In C. Schaefer, K. Gitlin, & A. Sandgrund (Eds.), *Play diagnosis and assessment* (pp. 663–690). New York: Wiley.

Fein, G. G. (1981). Pretend play in childhood: An integrative review. *Child Development, 52,* 1095–1118.

Fein, G. (1987). Pretend play: Creativity and consciousness. In P. Gorlitz & J. Wohlwill (Eds.), *Curiosity, imagination, and play* (pp. 281–304). Hillsdale, NJ: Erlbaum.

Feist, G. (in press). Affective states and traits in creativity: Evidence for non-linear relationships. In M.A. Runco (Ed.), *Handbook of creativity research,* Vol. 2. Cresskill, NJ: Hampton Press.

Feitelson, D., & Ross, G. (1973). The neglected factor-play. *Human Development, 16,* 202–223.

Fenson, L. (1984). Developmental trends for action and speech in pretend play. In I. Bretherton (Ed.), *Symbolic play: The development of social understanding* (pp. 249–270). Orlando, FL: Academic Press.

Feshbach, N. D. (1987). Parental empathy and child adjustment/maladjustment. In N. Eisenberg & J. Strayer (Eds.), *Empathy and its development* (pp. 271–291). New York: Cambridge University Press.

Finn, D., & Fewell, R. (1994). The use of play assessment to examine the development of communication skills in children who are deaf-blind. *Journal of Visual Impairment & Blindness, 88*(4), 349–356.

Freedheim, D., & Russ, S. (1992). Psychotherapy with children. In C. Walker & M. Roberts (Eds.), *Handbook of clinical child psychology* (2nd ed., pp. 765–781). New York: Wiley.

Freud, A. (1965). *Normality and pathology in childhood: Assessment of development.* New York: International Universities Press.

Grossman-McKee, A. (1990). The relationship between affective expression in fantasy play and pain complaints in first and second grade children. *Dissertation Abstracts International, 50,* 4219B.

Guilford, J. P. (1968). *Intelligence, creativity and their educational implications.* San Diego: Knapp.

Harris, P. L. (1989). *Children and emotion: The development of psychological understanding.* Cambridge, MA: Blackwell.

Harris, P. (1994). The child's understanding of emotion: Developmental change, and the family environment. *Journal of Child Psychology and Psychiatry, 35*(1), 3–28.

Harter, S. (1985). *Manual for the Self-Perception Profile for Children.* Denver, CO: University of Denver.

Holt, R. R. (1977). A method for assessing primary process manifestations and their control in Rorschach responses. In M. Rickers-Ovsiankina (Ed.), *Rorschach psychology* (pp. 375–420). New York: Kreiger.

Howe, P., & Silvern, L. (1981). Behavioral observation during play therapy: Preliminary development of a research instrument. *Journal of Personality Assessment, 45,* 168–182.

Hughes, M. (1987). The relationship between symbolic and manipulative (object) play. In D. Gorlitz & J. Wohwill (Eds.), *Curiosity, imagination, and play* (pp. 247–257). Hillsdale, NJ: Erlbaum.

Isen, A., Daubman, K., & Nowicki G. (1987). Positive affect facilitates creative problem solving. *Journal of Personality and Social Psychology, 52,* 1122–1131.

Izard, E. (1977). *Human emotions.* New York: Plenum.

Johnson, J. (1976). Relations of divergent thinking and intelligence test scores with social and nonsocial make-believe play of preschool children. *Child Development, 47,* 1200–1203.

Kusche, C. A., Greenberg, M. T., & Beilke, B. (1988). *The Kusche affective interview.* Unpublished manuscript, University of Washington, Seattle, WA.

Lieberman, J. N. (1977). *Playfulness: Its relationship to imagination and creativity.* New York: Academic Press.

Lyytinen, P. (1995). Cross-situational variation on children's pretend play. *Early Child Development and Care, 105,* 33–41.

Marans, S., Mayes, L., Cicchetti, D., Dahl, K., Marans, W., & Cohen, D. J. (1991). The Child-Psychoanalytic Play Interview: A technique for studying thematic content. *Journal of the American Psychoanalytic Association, 39*(4), 1015–1036.

McDonough, L., Stahmer, A., Schreibman, L., & Thompson, S. (1997). Deficits, delays, and distractions: An evaluation of symbolic play and memory in children with autism. *Development & Psychopathology, 9*(1), 17–41.

Milos, M. E., & Reiss, S. (1982). Effects of three play conditions on separation anxiety in young children. *Journal of Consulting and Clinical Psychology, 50*(3), 389–395.

Modell, A. H. (1980). Affects and their non-communication. *International Journal of Psycho-Analysis, 61,* 259–267.

Morrison, D. (1988). The child's first ways of knowing. In D. Morrison (Ed.), *Organizing early experience: Imagination and cognition in childhood* (pp. 3–14). Amityville: Baywood.

Murray, H. A. (1971). *Thematic Apperception Test Manual.* Cambridge, MA: Harvard University Press.

Nannis, E. D. (1988). Cognitive-developmental differences in emotional understanding. In E. D. Nannis and P. A. Cowan (Eds.), *Developmental psychopathology and its treatment. New Directions for Child Development* (No. 39, pp. 31–49). San Francisco: Jossey-Bass.

Niec, L. N. (1994). *Relationships among affect and interpersonal themes in children's fantasy and interpersonal functioning.* Unpublished Master's thesis. Case Western Reserve University; Cleveland, OH.

Niec, L. N. (1998). *Relationships among internal representations, affect in play, and interpersonal functioning.* Unpublished dissertation. Case Western Reserve University; Cleveland, OH.

Niec, L. N., & Russ, S. W. (1996). Relationships among affect in play, interpersonal themes in fantasy, and children's interpersonal behavior. *Journal of Personality Assessment, 66*(3), 645–649.

Olszewski, P. (1987). Individual differences in preschool children's production of verbal fantasy play. *Merrill-Palmer Quarterly, 33* (1), 69–86.

Olszewski, P., & Fuson, K. C. (1982). Verbally expressed fantasy play of preschoolers as a function of toy structure. *Developmental Psychology, 18,* 47–57.

Pederson, D., & Moran, G. (1996). Expressions of the attachment relationship outside of the Strange Situation. *Child Development, 67* (3), 915–927.

Pekarik, E. R., Prinz, R., Liebert, D., Weintraub, S., & Neale, J. (1976). The Pupil Evaluation Inventory: A sociometric technique for assessing children's social behavior. *Journal of Abnormal Child Psychology, 4*(1), 83–97.

Pelligrini, A. (1992). Rough and tumble play and social problem solving flexibility. *Creativity Research Journal, 5,* 13–26.

Pepler, D., & Ross, H. (1981). The effects of play on convergent and divergent problem solving. *Child Development, 52,* 1202–1210.

Perry, D., & Russ, S. (1998). Play, coping, and adjustment in homeless children. Manuscript submitted for publication.

Perry, L., & Landreth, G. (1991). Diagnostic assessment of children's play therapy behavior. In C. Schaefer, K. Gitlin, & A. Sandgrund (Eds.), *Play diagnosis and assessment* (pp. 641–660). New York: Wiley.

Peterson, N. (1989). *The relationship between affective expression in fantasy play and self-esteem in third grade children.* Unpublished master's thesis. Case Western Reserve University, Cleveland, OH.

Piaget, J. (1962). *Play, dreams and imitation in childhood.* New York: Norton.

Rosen, C., Faust, J., & Burns, W. (1994). The evaluation of process and outcome in individual child psychotherapy. *International Journal of Play Therapy, 3*(2), 33–43.

Rubin, K., Coplan, R., Fox, N., & Calkins, S. (1995). Emotionality, emotion regulation, and preschoolers' social adaptation. *Development and Psychopathology, 7*(1), 49–62.

Rubin, K., Fein, G., Vandenberg, B. (1983). Play. In P. Mussen (Ed.), *Handbook of child psychology* (Vol. 4, pp. 693–774). New York: Wiley.

Rubin, K. H., Watson, K. S., & Jambor, T. W. (1978). Free-play behaviors in preschool and kindergarten children. *Child Development, 49,* 534–536.

Runco, M. A. (1991). *Divergent thinking.* Norwood, NJ: Ablex.

Russ, S. (1987). Assessment of cognitive affective interaction in children: Creativity, fantasy, and play research. In J. Butcher & C. Spielberger (Eds.), *Advances in personality assessment* (Vol. 6, pp. 141–155). Hillsdale, NJ: Erlbaum.

Russ, S. (1988). Primary process thinking on the Rorschach, divergent thinking, and coping in children. *Journal of Personality Assessment, 52,* 539–548.

Russ, S. (1993). *Affect and creativity: The role of affect and play in the creative process.* Hillsdale, NJ: Erlbaum.

Russ, S. (1995). Play psychotherapy research: State of the science. In T. Ollendick & R. Prinz (Eds.), *Advances in clinical child psychology, 17,* (pp. 365–391). New York: Plenum.

Russ, S. (1996). Psychoanalytic theory and creativity: Cognition and affect revisited. In J. Masling & R. Borstein (Eds.), *Psychoanalytic perspectives on developmental psychology* (pp. 69–103). Washington D. C.: APA Books.

Russ, S. (in press). Play and creativity. In M. Runco (Ed.), *Creativity research handbook* (Vol. 3). Hampton Press.

Russ, S. Play in child psychotherapy: Integrating research and practice. Hillsdale, NJ: Erlbaum. Manuscript in preparation.

Russ, S., & Grossman-McKee, A. (1990). Affective expression in children's fantasy play, primary process thinking on the Rorschach, and divergent thinking. *Journal of Personality Assessment, 54,* 756–771.

Russ, S., Grossman-McKee, A., & Rutkin, Z. (1984). Affect in Play Scale: Pilot Project]. Unpublished raw data.

Russ, S., & Niec, L. Affective development and object relations. How much do we know? Paper presented at Society for Personality Assessment meeting, March, 1993.

Russ, S., & Peterson, N. (1990). *The Affect in Play Scale: Predicting creativity and coping in children.* Unpublished manuscript.

Russ, S., Robins, D., & Christiano, B. (in press). Pretend play: Longitudinal prediction of creativity and affect in fantasy in children. *Creativity Research Journal.*

Ryan, N. M. (1989). Stress-coping strategies identified from school-aged childrens' perspective. *Research in Nursing and Health, 12,* 111–122.

Sandler, J., & Sandler, A. M. (1978). On the development of object relationships and affects. *International Journal of Psycho-Analysis, 59,* 285–296.

Saracho, O. N. (1984). Construction and validation of the Play Rating Scale. *Early Child Development and Care, 17* (2–3), 199–230.

Schneider, M. (1989). *Children's Apperceptive Story-telling Test Manual.* Austin, TX: Pro-Ed.

Seja, A. L., & Russ, S. W. (1998, May). *Children's fantasy play, emotional understanding, and parents' reports of children's daily behavior.* Poster session presented at the Great Lakes Regional Conference on Child Health Psychology, Louisville, KY.

Seja, A. L., & Russ, S. W. (1999). Children's fantasy play and emotional understanding. *Journal of Clinical Child Psychology, 28,* 269–277.

Sigman, M., & Sena, R. (1993). Pretend play in high-risk and developmentally delayed children. In M. H. Bornstein & A. W. O'Reilly (Eds.), *The role of play in the development of thought: New directions for child development* (pp. 29–42). San Francisco: Jossey-Bass.

Singer, D. L., & Rummo, J. (1973). Ideational creativity and behavioral style in kindergarten age children. *Developmental Psychology, 8,* 154–161.

Singer, D. G., & Singer, J. L. (1990). *The house of make-believe: Children's play and the developing imagination.* Cambridge, MA: Harvard University Press.

Singer, J. L. (1973). *The child's world of make-believe.* New York: Academic Press.

Singer, J. L., & Singer, D. L. (1981). *Television, imagination, and aggression.* Hillsdale, NJ: Erlbaum.

Slade, A., & Wolf, D. (1994). *Children at play.* New York: Oxford University Press.

Smilansky, S. (1968). *The effects of sociodramatic play on disadvantaged preschool children.* New York: Wiley.

Smith, P. K., & Whitney, S. (1987). Play and associative fluency: Experimenter effects may be responsible for positive results. *Developmental Psychology, 23,* 49–53.

Smolucha, F. (1992). A reconstruction of Vygotsky's theory of creativity. *Creativity Research Journal, 5,* 49–67.

Spielberger, C. D. (1973). *State-trait anxiety inventory for children.* Palo Alto, CA: Consulting Psychological Press.

Sroufe, L. (1989). Relationships, self, and individual adaption. In A. Sameroff & R. Emde (Eds.), *Relationship disturbances in early childhood* (pp. 70–96). New York: Basic Books.

Stern, D. N., MacKain, K., Raduns, K., Hopper, P., Kaminsky, C., Evans, S., Shilling, N., Giraldo, L., Kaplan, M., Nachman, P., Trad, P., Polan, J., Barnard, K., & Spieker, S. (1992). The Kiddie-Infant Descriptive Instrument for Emotional States (KIDIES): An instrument for the measurement of affective state in infancy and early childhood. *Infant Mental Health Journal, 13*(2), 107–118.

Strayer, J. (1987). Affective and cognitive perspectives on empathy. In N. Eisenberg & J. Strayer (Eds.), *Empathy and its development* (pp. 218–244). New York: Cambridge University Press.

Suler, J. (1980). Primary process thinking and creativity. *Psychological Bulletin, 88,* 144–165.

Thompson, R. A. (1989). Causal attributions and children's emotional understanding. In C. Saarni & P. L. Harris (Eds.), *Children's understanding of emotion* (pp. 117–150). New York: Cambridge University Press.

Tomkins, S. S. (1962). *Affect, imagery, consciousness, Vol. 1: The positive affects.* New York: Springer.

Tomkins, S. S. (1963). *Affect, imagery, consciousness, Vol. 2: The negative affects.* New York: Springer.

Vandenberg, B. (1980). Play, problem-solving, and creativity. *New Directions for Child Development, 9,* 49–68.

Vosburg, S., & Kaufmann, G. (in press). Mood and creativity research: The view from a conceptual organizing perspective. In S. Russ (Ed.), *Affect, creative experience, and psychological adjustment* Washington, D.C.: Taylor and Francis.

Waelder, R. (1933). Psychoanalytic theory of play. *Psychoanalytic Quarterly, 2,* 208–224.

Warren, S. L., Oppenheim, D., & Emde, R. N. (1996). Can emotions and themes in children's play predict behavior problems? *Journal of the American Academy of Child and Adolescent Psychiatry, 34*(10), 1331–1337.

Waters, E., Wippman, J., & Sroufe, L. (1979). Attachment, positive affect and competence in the peer group: Two studies in construct validation. *Child Development, 50,* 821–829.

Weiner, I. (1977). Approaches to Rorschach validation. In M. Rickers-OvsianKina (Ed.), *Rorschach Psychology* (pp. 575–608). New York: Kreiger.

Westby, C. (1980). Assessment of cognitive and language abilities through play. *Language, Speech, and Hearing Services in Schools, 11,* 154–168.

Westby, C. E. (1991). A scale for assessing children's pretend play. In C. E. Schaeffer, K. Gitlin, & A. Sandgrund (Eds.), *Play diagnosis and assessment* (pp. 131–161). New York: Wiley.

Westen, D. (1995). *Social Cognition and Object Relations Scale: Q-sort for projective stories (SCORS-Q).* Unpublished manual, Cambridge Hospital and Harvard Medical School, Cambridge, MA.

Author Index

Subject Index